# Collins
# School
## Dictionary

Collins

**HarperCollins Publishers**
Westerhill Road
Bishopbriggs
Glasgow
G64 2QT
Great Britain

Third Edition 2006

This edition published 2008
for Index Books Ltd

© HarperCollins Publishers 1999,
2002, 2006

ISBN 978-0-00-782406-9

Collins® and Bank of English®
are registered trademarks of
HarperCollins Publishers Limited

www.collinslanguage.com

A catalogue record for this book is
available from the British Library

Typographical design (1st edition)
by Kerry Aylin

Computing support by
Stewart C. Russell

Typeset by Wordcraft, Glasgow

Printed in India by Gopsons Papers

**Acknowledgements**
We would like to thank those
authors and publishers who kindly
gave permission for copyright
material to be used in the Collins
Word Web. We would also like to
thank Times Newspapers Ltd for
providing valuable data.

# Introduction

Being able to read, understand and write good English are vital and fundamental skills that underpin success in exams and, ultimately, success in the world beyond school. A dictionary is an essential tool for all students who want to do well in exams, because if you know how to use a dictionary effectively you can improve your performance in all subjects, not just English. This is why literacy strategies all over the world set ambitious targets for students to acquire dictionary skills at every stage of their education.

***Collins New School Dictionary*** has been researched with teachers and students to ensure that it includes the information on language that students need to allow them to improve their performance in English and all other school subjects, and to achieve exam success. It provides:

Essential information on what words mean, how they are used, spelling, grammar and punctuation, so that students can use language well, communicate with others and express their ideas more effectively

Comprehensive coverage of core vocabulary and commonly misspelt words from a wide range of curriculum subjects, such as Science, Information Technology, History, Geography and RE, to help with exam success in *all* subjects, not just English

***Collins New School Dictionary*** is exceptionally easy to use. It is relevant to school work in all subjects, accessible and student friendly, and offers essential help on the route to success.

William Collins' dream of knowledge for all began with the publication of his first book in 1819. A self-educated mill worker, he not only enriched millions of lives, but also founded a flourishing publishing house. Today, staying true to this spirit, Collins books are packed with inspiration, innovation, and practical expertise. They place you at the centre of a world of possibility and give you exactly what you need to explore it.

Language is the key to this exploration, and at the heart of Collins Dictionaries is language as it is really used. New words, phrases, and meanings spring up every day, and all of them are captured and analysed by the Collins Word Web. Constantly updated, and with over 2.5 billion entries, this living language resource is unique to our dictionaries.

Words are tools for life. And a Collins Dictionary makes them work for you.

**Collins. Do more.**

# How To Use The Dictionary

*Collins New School Dictionary* is easy to use and understand. Below are some entries showing the dictionary's main features, along with an explanation of what they are.

The entry word

**fiend** fiends
*Said "feend"* NOUN **1** a devil or evil spirit. **2** a very wicked or cruel person. **3** INFORMAL someone who is very keen on a particular thing *E.G. a fitness fiend.*
🏛 from Old English *feond* meaning 'enemy'

How to say the word

Word history 🏛 explains where the word comes from

What the word means

Other words that come from the entry word

The word's part of speech

Advice on when to use the word

An example of the word being used

**fish** fishes fishing fished
NOUN **1** a cold-blooded creature living in water that has a spine, gills, fins, and a scaly skin. **2** Fish is the flesh of fish eaten as food. ► VERB **3** To fish is to try to catch fish for food or sport. **4** If you fish for information, you try to get it in an indirect way.
fishing NOUN   fisherman NOUN
☑ The plural of the noun *fish* can be either *fish* or *fishes*, but *fish* is more common.

Other forms of the word give help with spelling

Definition number

Usage note ☑ gives more information on how the word is used

**full stop** full stops
NOUN the punctuation mark (.) used at the end of a sentence and after an abbreviation or initial.

> ### What does the Full Stop do?
> The **full stop** (.) marks the end of any sentence which is not a question or an exclamation:
> *E.G. The train is leaving.*
> A full stop is also used after an abbreviation or initial:
> *E.G. etc.* ▪ *Dr. Jenkins* ▪ *J.R. Hartley*
> A full stop is also used after an expression that stands by itself but is not a complete sentence:
> *E.G. Good morning.*

Grammar box gives more information on the way English works
See page vi for a full list of grammar boxes in the dictionary

Similar words list ▤ shows other words with the same meaning

**complain** complains complaining complained
VERB **1** If you complain, you say that you are not satisfied with something. **2** If you complain of pain or illness, you say that you have it.
▤ (sense 1) find fault, grumble, moan

v

# Ff

Spelling tips give help with finding words in the dictionary ●

> **TIP** Some words which sound as if they should begin with the letter *f* actually begin with the letters *ph*, for example *pharmacy, pharaoh* and *phrase*. The *ph* combination, pronounced like *f*, comes in the middle of some words too, for example *amphetamine* and *emphasis*.

**compare** compares comparing compared
VERB 1 (EXAM TERM) When you compare things, you look at them together and see in what ways they are different or similar. **2** If you compare one thing to another, you say it is like the other thing *E.G. His voice is often compared to Michael Stipe's.*

Words used in exam questions are highlighted

**comparison** comparisons
NOUN (ENGLISH) When you make a comparison, you consider two things together and see in what ways they are different or similar.

Core vocabulary from all curriculum subjects, listed in the *Framework for teaching English, years 7, 8 and 9* published in the UK in 2001, is highlighted for easy learning

**fabric** fabrics
NOUN (D & T) **1** cloth *E.G. tough fabric for tents.* **2** The fabric of a building is its walls, roof, and other parts. **3** The fabric of a society or system is its structure, laws, and customs *E.G. the democratic fabric of American society.*

(D & T) = Design and technology

(ICT) = Information and communication technology

(PE) = Physical education

(PSHE) = Personal, social and health education

(RE) = Religious education

**-ful**
SUFFIX **1** '-ful' is used to form adjectives with the meaning 'full of' *E.G. careful.* **2** '-ful' is used to form nouns which mean 'the amount needed to fill' *E.G. spoonful.*

Comprehensive coverage of prefixes and suffixes help with learning new words and spelling

**centi-**
PREFIX 'Centi-' is used to form words that have 'hundred' as part of their meaning *E.G. centimetre.*
📖 from Latin *centum* meaning 'hundred'

Spelling notes give help with tricky words ●

SPELLING NOTE ▸ pAL up with the principAL and principAL staff (principal)

# Grammar Boxes

Throughout the dictionary there are grammar boxes at the end of entries. These boxes contain rules and advice on English grammar, as well as helpful examples. In the list below, we have marked grammar boxes for *Word level* and *Sentence level* so teachers in England and Wales can see how this additional material fits in with the *Framework for teaching English, years 7, 8 and 9*.

You will find out more about grammar at the following entries:

**How words are used** (Word level)
   a
   be
   not
   shall
   that
   the
   which
   who
   whom
   whose
   will

**Punctuation** (Sentence level)
   apostrophe
   bracket
   colon
   comma
   dash
   exclamation mark
   full stop
   hyphen
   inverted comma
   punctuation
   question mark
   semicolon

**Parts of speech** (Word level)
   adjective
   adverb
   conjunction
   interjection
   noun
   part of speech
   preposition
   pronoun
   relative pronoun
   verb

**Verbs** (Sentence level)
   active
   future
   passive
   past tense
   present tense
   tense
   verb

**Nouns** (Word level)
   noun
   plural
   possessive

**Adjectives** (Word level)
   adjective
   comparative
   superlative

**Parts of a Sentence** (Sentence level)
   clause
   phrase
   sentence

**Gender** (Word level)
   feminine
   gender
   masculine
   neuter

**Other**
   Command (Sentence level)
   Number (Word level)
   Question (Sentence level)
   Quotation (Sentence level)

# Aa

## a an

ADJECTIVE The indefinite article 'a', or 'an' if the next sound is a vowel, is used when you are talking about one of something E.G. *an apple… There was a car parked behind the hedge.*

### The Indefinite Article

The word *a* is known as the **indefinite article**. You use it before a singular noun to refer to any example of that noun, or to avoid being specific about which example you mean:

E.G. *a school* ■ *a woman*

The word *an* is used instead of *a* when a word begins with a vowel sound:

E.G. *an elephant* ■ *an umpire*

The word *an* is also used instead of *a* when words sound as though they begin with a vowel:

E.G. *an hour* ■ *an honour*

The word *a* is used instead of *an* when words that begin with a vowel sound as though they begin with a consonant:

E.G. *a union* ■ *a European*

Also look at the grammar box at **the**.

## a- an-

PREFIX **1** When 'a-' comes before an adjective it adds the meaning 'without' or 'opposite to' E.G. *amoral.* 'An-' is the form used before a vowel. **2** When 'a-' comes at the beginning of certain words it adds the meaning 'towards' or 'in the state of' E.G. *aback… asleep.*

🔟 sense 1 from Greek *a-* or *an-* meaning 'not' or 'without'

## aardvark aardvarks

NOUN an ant-eating African animal with a long snout.

🔟 from obsolete Afrikaans meaning 'earth pig'

## aback

ADVERB If you are taken aback, you are very surprised.

## abacus abacuses

NOUN a frame with beads that slide along rods, used for counting.

🔟 from Greek *abax* meaning 'board covered with sand for doing sums on'

## abalone abalones

*Said* "ab-a-**lone**-ee" NOUN a shellfish which can be eaten.

## abandon abandons abandoning abandoned

VERB **1** If you abandon someone or something, you leave them or give them up for good. ▶ NOUN **2** If you do something with abandon, you do it in an uncontrolled way E.G. *He began to laugh with abandon.*

**abandoned** ADJECTIVE

**abandonment** NOUN

■ (sense 1) desert, forsake, leave

## abate abates abating abated

VERB If something abates, it becomes less E.G. *His anger abated.*

## abattoir abattoirs

*Said* "ab-a-**twahr**" NOUN a place where animals are killed for meat.

## abbey abbeys

NOUN a church with buildings attached to it in which monks or nuns live.

an ELegant angEL (angel)   SPELLING NOTE

**abbot** abbots
NOUN the monk or priest in charge of all the monks in a monastery.

**abbreviate** abbreviates abbreviating abbreviated
VERB To abbreviate something is to make it shorter.

**abbreviation** abbreviations
NOUN a short form of a word or phrase. An example is 'W', which is short for 'West'.

**abdicate** abdicates abdicating abdicated
VERB If a king or queen abdicates, he or she gives up being a king or queen.
**abdication** NOUN

**abdomen** abdomens
NOUN the front part of your body below your chest, containing your stomach and intestines.
**abdominal** ADJECTIVE

**abduct** abducts abducting abducted
VERB To abduct someone is to take them away by force.
**abduction** NOUN

**aberration** aberrations
NOUN something that is not normal or usual.

**abet** abets abetting abetted
VERB If you abet someone, you help them to do something E.G. You've aided and abetted criminals to evade justice.

**abhor** abhors abhorring abhorred
VERB; FORMAL If you abhor something, you hate it very much.
**abhorrence** NOUN **abhorrent** ADJECTIVE

**abide** abides abiding abided
VERB 1 If you can't abide something, you dislike it very much. 2 If you abide by a decision or law, you act in agreement with it.

**abiding**
ADJECTIVE lasting for ever E.G. an abiding interest in history.

**ability** abilities
NOUN (PSHE) the intelligence or skill needed to do something E.G. the ability to get on with others.
■ capability, proficiency, skill

**abject**
ADJECTIVE very bad E.G. abject failure.
**abjectly** ADVERB

**ablaze**
ADJECTIVE on fire.

**able** abler ablest
ADJECTIVE (PSHE) 1 If you are able to do something, you can do it. 2 Someone who is able is very clever or talented.

**-able**
SUFFIX 1 forming adjectives which have the meaning 'capable of' an action E.G. enjoyable… breakable. 2 forming adjectives with the meaning 'able to' or 'causing' E.G. comfortable… miserable.
▥ from the Latin suffix -ābilis meaning 'able to'
☑ When you are writing, it is easy to confuse the -able suffix with its other form, -ible. It can be helpful to know that the -able spelling is much commoner than -ible, and that you cannot make new words using -ible. Occasionally, it is correct to use either ending.

**ably**
Said "**ay**-blee" ADVERB skilfully and successfully E.G. He is ably supported by the cast.

**abnormal**
ADJECTIVE not normal or usual.
**abnormally** ADVERB

**abnormality** abnormalities

NOUN something that is not normal or usual.

■ irregularity, oddity, peculiarity

**aboard**

PREPOSITION OR ADVERB on a ship or plane.

**abode** abodes

NOUN; *OLD-FASHIONED* Your abode is your home.

**abolish** abolishes abolishing abolished

VERB To abolish something is to do away with it E.G. *the campaign to abolish hunting.*

**abolition** NOUN

■ do away with, eliminate, end

**abominable**

ADJECTIVE very unpleasant or shocking.

**abominably** ADVERB

**Aborigine** Aborigines

*Said* "ab-or-**rij**-in-ee" NOUN someone descended from the people who lived in Australia before Europeans arrived.

**Aboriginal** ADJECTIVE

🏛 borrowed from *aborigines*, the Latin word for the pre-Roman inhabitants of Italy

**abort** aborts aborting aborted

VERB 1 If a plan or activity is aborted, it is stopped before it is finished. 2 If a pregnant woman aborts, the pregnancy ends too soon and the baby dies.

**abortion** abortions

NOUN If a woman has an abortion, the pregnancy is ended deliberately and the baby dies.

**abortive**

ADJECTIVE unsuccessful E.G. *an abortive bank raid.*

**abound** abounds abounding abounded

VERB If things abound, there are very large numbers of them.

**about**

PREPOSITION OR ADVERB 1 of or concerning. 2 approximately and not exactly. ▶ ADVERB 3 in different directions E.G. *There were some bottles scattered about.* ▶ ADJECTIVE 4 present or in a place E.G. *Is Jane about?* ▶ PHRASE 5 If you are **about to** do something, you are just going to do it.

**above**

PREPOSITION OR ADVERB 1 directly over or higher than something E.G. *above the clouds.* 2 greater than a level or amount E.G. *The temperature didn't rise above freezing point.*

**above board**

ADJECTIVE completely open and legal E.G. *They assured me it was above board and properly licensed.*

🏛 an allusion to the difficulty of cheating at cards with your hands above the table

**abrasion** abrasions

NOUN an area where your skin has been broken.

**abrasive**

ADJECTIVE 1 An abrasive substance is rough and can be used to clean hard surfaces. 2 Someone who is abrasive is unpleasant and rude.

**abreast**

ADJECTIVE 1 side by side E.G. *youths riding their motorbikes four abreast.* 2 If you keep abreast of a subject, you know all the most recent facts about it.

**abroad**

ADVERB (GEOGRAPHY) in a foreign country.

**abrupt**

ADJECTIVE 1 sudden and quick E.G. *His*

A Rude Idiot Thought He Might Eat Toffee In Church (<u>arithmetic</u>)  SPELLING NOTE

a
b
c
d
e
f
g
h
i
j
k
l
m
n
o
p
q
r
s
t
u
v
w
x
y
z

*career came to an abrupt end.* **2** not friendly or polite.

**abruptly** ADVERB **abruptness** NOUN

**abscess** abscesses

*Said "ab-sess"* NOUN a painful swelling filled with pus.

**abseiling**

NOUN Abseiling is the sport of going down a cliff or a tall building by sliding down ropes.

**absent**

ADJECTIVE Something that is absent is not present in a place or situation.

**absence** NOUN

**absentee** absentees

NOUN someone who is not present when they should be.

**absent-minded**

ADJECTIVE forgetful.

**absolute**

ADJECTIVE **1** total and complete *E.G. absolute honesty.* **2** having total power *E.G. the absolute ruler.*

**absolutely** ADVERB

**absolve** absolves absolving absolved

VERB To absolve someone of something is to state they are not to blame for it.

**absorb** absorbs absorbing absorbed

VERB (SCIENCE) If something absorbs liquid or gas, it soaks it up.

■ soak up, take in

**absorbent**

ADJECTIVE Absorbent materials soak up liquid easily.

**absorption**

NOUN **1** the soaking up of a liquid. **2** great interest in something *E.G. my father's absorption in his business affairs.*

**abstain** abstains abstaining abstained

VERB **1** If you abstain from something,

you do not do it or have it *E.G. The patients had to abstain from alcohol.* **2** If you abstain in a vote, you do not vote.

**abstention** NOUN

■ (sense 1) forbear, keep from, refrain

**abstinence**

NOUN Abstinence is deliberately not doing something you enjoy.

**abstract**

ADJECTIVE

*Said "ab-strakt"* **1** An abstract idea is based on thoughts and ideas rather than physical objects or events, for example 'bravery'. **2** (ART) Abstract art is a style of art which uses shapes rather than images of people or objects. **3** Abstract nouns refer to qualities or ideas rather than to physical objects, for example 'happiness' or 'a question'. ► VERB *Said "ab-strakt"* **3** If you abstract information from a piece of writing, you summarize the main points

**abstraction** NOUN

▥ from Latin *abstractus* meaning 'removed'

**absurd**

ADJECTIVE ridiculous and stupid.

**absurdly** ADVERB **absurdity** NOUN

■ ludicrous, preposterous, ridiculous

**abundance**

NOUN Something that exists in abundance exists in large numbers *E.G. an abundance of wildlife.*

**abundant** ADJECTIVE **abundantly** ADVERB

■ plenty, profusion

**abuse** abuses

*Said "ab-yoose"* NOUN **1** cruel treatment of someone *E.G. child* *abuse.* **2** rude and unkind remarks directed towards someone. **3** the wrong use of something E.G. *an abuse of power… alcohol abuse.*

■ (sense 1) ill-treatment, injury, maltreatment

**abuse** abuses abusing abused

*Said* "ab-**yooze**" VERB **1** If you abuse someone, you speak insultingly to them. **2** To abuse someone also means to treat them cruelly. **3** If you abuse something, you use it wrongly or for a bad purpose.
**abuser** NOUN

■ (sense 2) ill-treat, maltreat

**abusive**

ADJECTIVE rude and unkind.
**abusively** ADVERB **abusiveness**
NOUN

**abysmal**

*Said* "ab-**biz**-ml" ADJECTIVE very bad indeed E.G. *an abysmal performance.*
**abysmally** ADVERB

**abyss** abysses

NOUN a very deep hole.

🏛 from Greek *abussos* meaning 'bottomless'

**acacia** acacias

*Said* "a-**kay**-sha" NOUN a type of thorny shrub with small yellow or white flowers.

**academic** academics

ADJECTIVE **1** Academic work is work done in a school, college, or university. ▶ NOUN **2** someone who teaches or does research in a college or university.
**academically** ADVERB

**academy** academies

NOUN **1** a school or college, usually one that specializes in one particular subject E.G. *the Royal Academy of Dramatic Art.* **2** an organization of

scientists, artists, writers, or musicians.
🏛 from Greek *akadēmeia*, the name of the grove where Plato taught

**accelerate** accelerates accelerating accelerated

VERB To accelerate is to go faster.

**acceleration**

NOUN the rate at which the speed of something is increasing.

**accelerator** accelerators

NOUN the pedal in a vehicle which you press to make it go faster.

**accent** accents

NOUN **1** a way of pronouncing a language E.G. *She had an Australian accent.* **2** a mark placed above or below a letter in some languages, which affects the way the letter is pronounced. **3** an emphasis on something E.G. *The accent is on action and special effects.*

**accentuate** accentuates accentuating accentuated

VERB To accentuate a feature of something is to make it more noticeable.

**accept** accepts accepting accepted

VERB **1** If you accept something, you say yes to it or take it from someone. **2** If you accept a situation, you realize that it cannot be changed E.G. *He accepts criticism as part of his job.* **3** If you accept a statement or story, you believe it is true E.G. *The board accepted his explanation.* **4** If a group accepts you, they treat you as one of the group.
**acceptance** NOUN **acceptable** ADJECTIVE **acceptably** ADVERB

**access** accesses accessing accessed

NOUN **1** the right or opportunity to

*a b c d e f g h i j k l m n o p q r s t u v w x y z*

enter a place or to use something.
▶ VERB 2 If you access information from a computer, you get it.

**accessible**

ADJECTIVE 1 easily reached or seen E.G. *The village was accessible by foot only.* 2 easily understood or used E.G. *guidebooks which present information in a clear and accessible style.*
accessibility NOUN

**accession**

NOUN A ruler's accession is the time when he or she becomes the ruler of a country.

**accessory** accessories

NOUN 1 an extra part. 2 someone who helps another person commit a crime.

**accident** accidents

NOUN 1 an unexpected event in which people are injured or killed. 2 Something that happens by accident happens by chance.

**accidental**

ADJECTIVE happening by chance.
accidentally ADVERB
■ inadvertent, unintentional, unplanned

**acclaimed**

ADJECTIVE If someone or something is acclaimed, they are praised enthusiastically.

**accolade** accolades

NOUN; FORMAL great praise or an award given to someone.

**accommodate** accommodates accommodating accommodated

VERB 1 If you accommodate someone, you provide them with a place to sleep, live, or work. 2 If a place can accommodate a number of things or people, it has enough room for them.

☑ *Accommodate* has two cs and two ms.

**accommodation**

NOUN a place provided for someone to sleep, live, or work in.

**accompaniment** accompaniments

NOUN 1 The accompaniment to a song is the music played to go with it. 2 An accompaniment to something is another thing that comes with it E.G. *Melon is a good accompaniment to cold meats.*

**accompany** accompanies accompanying accompanied

VERB 1 If you accompany someone, you go with them. 2 If one thing accompanies another, the two things exist at the same time E.G. *severe pain accompanied by fever.* 3 If you accompany a singer or musician, you play an instrument while they sing or play the main tune.

**accomplice** accomplices

NOUN a person who helps someone else to commit a crime.

**accomplish** accomplishes accomplishing accomplished

VERB If you accomplish something, you succeed in doing it.
☑ The *com* part of *accomplish* can sound like *kum* or *kom*.

**accomplished**

ADJECTIVE very talented at something E.G. *an accomplished cook.*

**accomplishment** accomplishments

NOUN Someone's accomplishments are the skills they have gained.

**accord** accords according accorded

VERB 1 If you accord someone or something a particular treatment, you treat them in that way E.G. *He was accorded a proper respect for his status.* ▶ NOUN **2** agreement. ▶ PHRASE **3** If you do something **of your own accord**, you do it willingly and not because you have been forced to do it.

**accordance**
PHRASE If you act **in accordance with** a rule or belief, you act in the way the rule or belief says you should.

**according to**
PREPOSITION **1** If something is true according to a particular person, that person says that it is true. **2** If something is done according to a principle or plan, that principle or plan is used as the basis for it.

**accordion** accordions
NOUN a musical instrument like an expanding box. It is played by squeezing the two sides together while pressing the keys on it.

**accost** accosts accosting accosted
VERB If someone accosts you, especially someone you do not know, they come up and speak to you E.G. *She says she is accosted when she goes shopping.*

**account** accounts accounting accounted
NOUN **1** a written or spoken report of something. **2** If you have a bank account, you can leave money in the bank and take it out when you need it. ▶ PLURAL NOUN **3** Accounts are records of money spent and received by a person or business. ▶ PHRASE **4** If you **take something into account**, you include it in your planning. **5 On account of** means because of. ▶ VERB **6** To account for something is to

explain it E.G. *This might account for her strange behaviour.* **7** If something accounts for a particular amount of something, it is that amount E.G. *The brain accounts for three per cent of body weight.*

**accountable**
ADJECTIVE If you are accountable for something, you are responsible for it and have to explain your actions E.G. *The committee is accountable to Parliament.*
**accountability** NOUN

**accountancy**
NOUN the job of keeping or inspecting financial accounts.

**accountant** accountants
NOUN a person whose job is to keep or inspect financial accounts.

**accounting**
NOUN the keeping and checking of financial accounts.

**accrue** accrues accruing accrued
VERB If money or interest accrues, it increases gradually.

**accumulate** accumulates accumulating accumulated
VERB If you accumulate things or they accumulate, they collect over a period of time.

**accurate**
ADJECTIVE completely correct or precise.
**accurately** ADVERB **accuracy** NOUN
■ correct, exact, precise

**accuse** accuses accusing accused
VERB If you accuse someone of doing something wrong, you say they have done it.
**accusation** NOUN **accuser** NOUN

**accustom** accustoms accustoming accustomed
VERB If you accustom yourself to

you'll brEAK that Electrical Aerial, Kitty (br**eak**)　　SPELLING NOTE something new or different, you get used to it.

**ace** aces
NOUN **1** In a pack of cards, a card with a single symbol on it. ▶ ADJECTIVE **2** INFORMAL good or skilful E.G. *an ace squash player.*

**acerbic**
*Said* "as-**ser**-bik" ADJECTIVE; FORMAL Acerbic remarks are harsh and bitter.

**ache** aches aching ached
VERB **1** If you ache, you feel a continuous dull pain in a part of your body. **2** If you are aching for something, you want it very much. ▶ NOUN **3** a continuous dull pain.

**achieve** achieves achieving achieved
VERB (PSHE) If you achieve something, you successfully do it or cause it to happen.
■ accomplish, attain, fulfil
✔ The *i* comes before the *e* in *achieve.*

**achievement** achievements
NOUN (PSHE) something which you succeed in doing, especially after a lot of effort.

**acid** acids
NOUN (SCIENCE) **1** a chemical liquid with a pH value of less than 7 and which turns litmus paper red. Strong acids can damage skin, cloth, and metal. ▶ ADJECTIVE **2** Acid tastes are sharp or sour.
**acidic** ADJECTIVE  **acidity** NOUN

**acid rain**
NOUN rain polluted by acid in the atmosphere which has come from factories.

**acknowledge** acknowledges acknowledging acknowledged
VERB **1** If you acknowledge a fact or

situation, you agree or admit it is true. **2** If you acknowledge someone, you show that you have seen and recognized them. **3** If you acknowledge a message, you tell the person who sent it that you have received it.

**acknowledgment** or **acknowledgement** NOUN
■ (sense 1) accept, admit, grant
✔ *Acknowledgment* and *acknowledgement* are both correct spellings.

**acne**
*Said* "**ak**-nee" NOUN lumpy spots that cover someone's face.

**acorn** acorns
NOUN the fruit of the oak tree, consisting of a pale oval nut in a cup-shaped base.

**acoustic**
*Said* "a-**koo**-stik" ADJECTIVE **1** relating to sound or hearing. **2** An acoustic guitar is not made louder with an electric amplifier.

**acoustics**
PLURAL NOUN The acoustics of a room are its structural features which are responsible for how clearly you can hear sounds made in it.

**acquaintance** acquaintances
NOUN someone you know slightly but not well

**acquainted**
ADJECTIVE If you are acquainted with someone, you know them slightly but not well
✔ You say that you are *acquainted with* someone.

**acquire** acquires acquiring acquired
VERB If you acquire something, you obtain it.

**acquisition** acquisitions

NOUN something you have obtained.

**acquit** acquits acquitting acquitted

VERB **1** If someone is acquitted of a crime, they have been tried in a court and found not guilty. **2** If you acquit yourself well on a particular occasion, you behave or perform well.

**acquittal** NOUN

**acre** acres

NOUN a unit for measuring areas of land. One acre is equal to 4840 square yards or about 4047 square metres.

📖 from Old English *æcer* meaning 'field'

**acrid**

ADJECTIVE sharp and bitter *E.G. the acrid smell of burning plastic.*

**acrimony**

*Said* "ak-rim-on-ee" NOUN; FORMAL bitterness and anger.

**acrimonious** ADJECTIVE

**acrobat** acrobats

NOUN an entertainer who performs gymnastic tricks.

**acrobatic** ADJECTIVE   **acrobatics** PLURAL NOUN

📖 from Greek *akrobates* meaning 'someone who walks on tiptoe'

**acronym** acronyms

NOUN a word made up of the initial letters of a phrase. An example of an acronym is 'BAFTA', which stands for 'British Academy of Film and Television Arts'.

**across**

PREPOSITION or ADVERB **1** going from one side of something to the other. **2** on the other side of a road or river.

**acrylic**

*Said* "a-kril-lik" NOUN **1** Acrylic is a type

of man-made cloth. **2** ⟨ART⟩ Acrylics, or acrylic paints, are thick artists' paints which can be used like oil paints or thinned down with water.

**act** acts acting acted

VERB **1** If you act, you do something *E.G. It would be irresponsible not to act swiftly.* **2** If you act in a particular way, you behave in that way. **3** If a person or thing acts as something else, it has the function or does the job of that thing *E.G. She was able to act as an interpreter.* **4** If you act in a play or film, you play a part. ▶ NOUN **5** a single thing someone does *E.G. It was an act of disloyalty to the King.* **6** An Act of Parliament is a law passed by the government. **7** In a play, ballet, or opera, an act is one of the main parts it is divided into.

📱 (sense 4) perform, play
📱 (sense 5) action, deed
📱 (sense 6) bill, decree, law

**acting**

NOUN the profession of performing in plays or films.

**action** actions

NOUN **1** something you do for a particular purpose *E.G. He had to take evasive action to avoid being hit.* **2** a physical movement. **3** In law, an action is a legal proceeding *E.G. a libel action.*

**activate** activates activating activated

VERB To activate something is to make it start working.

📱 set in motion, start

**active**

ADJECTIVE **1** ⟨PE⟩ Active people are full of energy and are always busy. **2** If someone is active in an organization, they are involved in it and work hard for it. **3** In grammar, a verb in the active voice is one where the subject does the action, rather than having it done to them. **actively** ADVERB

---

### The Active Voice

The **active** voice and the **passive** voice are two different ways of presenting information in a sentence. When a sentence is written in the **active** voice, the subject of the verb is doing the action. This is the most natural way of presenting information:

> E.G. *Anna is feeding the cat.*
> *The cat chased a mouse.*

Also look at the grammar box at **passive**.

---

**activist** activists
NOUN a person who tries to bring about political and social change.

**activity** activities
NOUN **1** Activity is a situation in which a lot of things are happening at the same time. **2** (PE) something you do for pleasure E.G. *leisure activities*.

**actor** actors
NOUN a man or woman whose profession is acting.

**actress** actresses
NOUN a woman whose profession is acting.

**actual**
ADJECTIVE real, rather than imaginary or guessed at E.G. *That is the official figure: the actual figure is much higher.*
**actually** ADVERB

☑ Don't use *actual* or *actually* when they don't add anything to the meaning of a sentence. Say *it's a fact*

rather than *it's an actual fact*.

**acumen**
NOUN the ability to make good decisions quickly E.G. *business acumen*.

**acupuncture**
NOUN the treatment of illness or pain by sticking small needles into specific places in a person's body.
📖 from Latin *acus* meaning 'needle' added to 'puncture'

**acute**
ADJECTIVE **1** severe or intense E.G. *an acute shortage of accommodation*. **2** very intelligent E.G. *an acute mind*. **3** An acute angle is less than 90°. **4** In French and some other languages, an acute accent is a line sloping upwards from left to right placed over a vowel to indicate a change in pronunciation, as in the word *café*.

**ad** ads
NOUN; INFORMAL an advertisement.

**AD**
You use 'AD' in dates to indicate the number of years after the birth of Jesus Christ.

**ad-**
PREFIX 'Ad-' means 'near' or 'next to' E.G. *adjoining… adverb*.
📖 from Latin *ad-* meaning 'towards'

**adage** adages
*Said* "ad-dij" NOUN a saying expressing a truth about life.

**adamant**
ADJECTIVE If you are adamant, you are determined not to change your mind.
**adamantly** ADVERB

**Adam's apple** Adam's apples
NOUN the larynx, a lump at the front of the neck which is more obvious in men than in women and young boys.
📖 from the story that the forbidden

apple stuck in Adam's throat

**adapt** adapts adapting adapted
VERB **1** If you adapt to a new situation, you change so you can deal with it successfully. **2** If you adapt something, you change it so it is suitable for a new purpose or situation.
**adaptable** ADJECTIVE **adaptation** NOUN

**adaptor** adaptors; also spelt adapter
NOUN a type of electric plug which can be used to connect two or more plugs to one socket.

**add** adds adding added
VERB **1** If you add something to a number of things, you put it with the things. **2** If you add numbers together or add them up, you work out the total.

**adder** adders
NOUN a small poisonous snake.

**addict** addicts
NOUN (PSHE) someone who cannot stop taking harmful drugs.
**addicted** ADJECTIVE **addiction** NOUN

**addictive**
ADJECTIVE If a drug is addictive, the people who take it cannot stop.

**addition** additions
NOUN **1** something that has been added to something else. **2** (MATHS) the process of adding numbers.
■ (sense 1) extra, supplement

**additional**
ADJECTIVE extra or more E.G. *They made the decision to take on additional staff.*
**additionally** ADVERB

**additive** additives
NOUN something added to something else, usually in order to improve it.

**address** addresses addressing addressed
NOUN **1** the number of the house where you live, together with the name of the street and the town or village. **2** a speech given to a group of people. ▶ VERB **3** If a letter is addressed to you, it has your name and address written on it. **4** If you address a problem or task, you start to deal with it.

**adept**
ADJECTIVE very skilful at doing something E.G. *She is adept at motivating others.*

**adequate**
ADJECTIVE enough in amount or good enough for a purpose.
**adequately** ADVERB **adequacy** NOUN
■ enough, satisfactory, sufficient

**adhere** adheres adhering adhered
VERB **1** If one thing adheres to another, it sticks firmly to it. **2** If you adhere to a rule or agreement, you do what it says. **3** If you adhere to an opinion or belief, you firmly hold that opinion or belief.
**adherence** NOUN

**adherent** adherents
NOUN An adherent of a belief is someone who holds that belief.

**adhesive** adhesives
NOUN **1** any substance used to stick two things together, for example glue. ▶ ADJECTIVE **2** Adhesive substances are sticky and able to stick to things.

**adjacent**
*Said "ad-jay-sent"* ADJECTIVE; FORMAL **1** If two things are adjacent, they are next to each other E.G. *a hotel adjacent to the beach.* **2** (MATHS) Adjacent angles share one side and have the same point opposite to their bases.

have a plEce of plE (piece)    SPELLING NOTE

a b c d e f g h i j k l m n o p q r s t u v w x y z

**adjective** adjectives

NOUN a word that adds to the description given by a noun. For example, in 'They live in a large white Georgian house', 'large', 'white', and 'Georgian' are all adjectives.
**adjectival** ADJECTIVE

---

### What is an Adjective?

An adjective is a word that tells you something about a noun. Adjectives are sometimes called "describing words".

Adjectives may indicate how many of a person or thing there are:

E.G. **three** men ■ **some** fish

Adjectives may describe feelings or qualities:

E.G. a **happy** child ■ a **strange** girl

Adjectives may describe size, age, temperature, or measurement:

E.G. a **large** envelope ■ an **old** jacket

Adjectives may indicate colour:

E.G. **red** socks ■ **dark** hair

Adjectives may indicate nationality or origin:

E.G. my **Indian** cousin ■ a **northern** accent

Adjectives may indicate the material from which something is made:

E.G. a **wooden** box ■ **denim** trousers

---

**adjoining**

ADJECTIVE If two rooms are next to each other and are connected, they are adjoining.

**adjourn** adjourns adjourning adjourned

VERB **1** If a meeting or trial is adjourned, it stops for a time E.G. The case was adjourned until September. **2** If people adjourn to another place, they go there together after a meeting E.G. We adjourned to the lounge.
**adjournment** NOUN

**adjust** adjusts adjusting adjusted

VERB **1** If you adjust something, you change its position or alter it in some other way. **2** If you adjust to a new situation, you get used to it.
**adjustment** NOUN **adjustable** ADJECTIVE

**ad-lib** ad-libs ad-libbing ad-libbed

VERB **1** say something that has not been prepared beforehand E.G. I ad-lib on radio but use a script on TV.
▶ NOUN **2** a comment that has not been prepared beforehand.
📖 short for Latin ad libitum meaning 'according to desire'

**administer** administers administering administered

VERB **1** To administer an organization is to be responsible for managing it. **2** To administer the law or administer justice is to put it into practice and apply it. **3** If medicine is administered to someone, it is given to them.

**administration** administrations

NOUN **1** Administration is the work of organizing and supervising an organization. **2** Administration is also the process of administering something E.G. the administration of criminal justice. **3** The administration is the group of people that manages an organization or a country.
**administrative** ADJECTIVE
**administrator** NOUN

**admirable**

ADJECTIVE very good and deserving to be admired.
**admirably** ADVERB

---

**admiral** admirals

NOUN the commander of a navy.
🏛 from Arabic *amir* meaning 'commander'

**admire** admires admiring admired

VERB to respect and approve of someone or something.
admiration NOUN admirer NOUN
admiring ADJECTIVE admiringly ADVERB

**admission** admissions

NOUN 1 If you are allowed admission to a place, you are allowed to go in. 2 If you make an admission of something, you agree, often reluctantly, it is true. *E.G. It was an admission of guilt.*

**admit** admits admitting admitted

VERB 1 to agree, often reluctantly, that something is true. 2 To admit someone or something to a place or organization is to allow them to enter it. 3 If you are admitted to hospital, you are taken there to stay until you are better.

**admittedly**

ADVERB People use 'admittedly' to show that what they are saying contrasts with something they have already said or are about to say, and weakens their argument *E.G. My studies, admittedly only from books, taught me much.*

**adolescent** adolescents

NOUN a young person who is no longer a child but who is not yet an adult.
adolescence NOUN
🏛 from Latin *adolescere* meaning 'to grow up'

**adopt** adopts adopting adopted

VERB 1 If you adopt a child that is not your own, you take him or her into your family as your son or daughter. 2 FORMAL If you adopt a particular attitude, you start to have it.
adoption NOUN

**adorable**

ADJECTIVE sweet and attractive.

**adore** adores adoring adored

VERB If you adore someone, you feel deep love and admiration for them.
adoration NOUN

**adorn** adorns adorning adorned

VERB To adorn something is to decorate it *E.G. The cathedral is adorned with statues.*
adornment NOUN

**adrenalin** or **adrenaline**

*Said* "a-**dren**-al-in" NOUN a substance which is produced by your body when you are angry, scared, or excited and which makes your heart beat faster.

**adrift**

ADJECTIVE OR ADVERB If a boat is adrift or goes adrift, it floats on the water without being controlled.

**adulation**

*Said* "ad-yoo-**lay**-shn" NOUN great admiration and praise for someone.
adulatory ADJECTIVE

**adult** adults

NOUN a mature and fully developed person or animal.

**adultery**

NOUN sexual intercourse between a married person and someone he or she is not married to.
adulterer NOUN adulterous ADJECTIVE

**adulthood**

NOUN the time during someone's life when they are an adult.

**advance** advances advancing advanced

VERB 1 To advance is to move forward. 2 To advance a cause or interest is to

a b c d e f g h i j k l m n o p q r s t u v w x y z

I went to see (C) the doctor's new practiCe (practice)    SPELLING NOTE

help it to be successful. **3** If you advance someone a sum of money, you lend it to them. ▶ NOUN
**4** Advance in something is progress in it *E.G. scientific advance.* **5** a sum of money lent to someone. ▶ ADJECTIVE
**6** happening before an event *E.G. The event received little advance publicity.* ▶ PHRASE **7** If you do something **in advance**, you do it before something else happens *E.G. We booked up the room well in advance.*

■ (sense 4) development, progress

**advantage advantages**

NOUN **1** a benefit or something that puts you in a better position. ▶ PHRASE **2** If you **take advantage of** someone, you treat them unfairly for your own benefit. **3** If you **take advantage of** something, you make use of it.

**advantageous**

ADJECTIVE likely to benefit you in some way *E.G. an advantageous marriage.*

**advent**

NOUN **1** The advent of something is its start or its coming into existence *E.G. The advent of the submarine changed naval warfare.* **2** Advent is the season just before Christmas in the Christian calendar.

**adventure adventures**

NOUN a series of events that are unusual and exciting.

**adventurer adventurers**

NOUN someone who enjoys doing dangerous and exciting things.

**adventurous**

ADJECTIVE willing to take risks and do new and exciting things.

**adventurously** ADVERB

**adverb adverbs**

NOUN a word that adds information about a verb or a following adjective

or other adverb, for example, 'slowly', 'now', and 'here' which say how, when, or where something is done.

**adverbial** ADJECTIVE

---

### What is an Adverb?

An adverb is a word that gives information about a verb. Many adverbs end with the letters -*ly*.

**Adverbs of manner** answer the question "how?":

*E.G. She runs **quickly**.* ■ *She sings **badly**.*

**Adverbs of place** answer the question "where?":

*E.G. We travelled **northwards**.* ■ *I live **here**.*

**Adverbs of time** answer the question "when?":

*E.G. You must stop **immediately**.* *I arrived **yesterday**.*

**Adverbs of degree** answer the question "to what extent?":

*E.G. I **really** hope you will stay.* ■ *I play golf **fairly** often.*

**Adverbs of frequency** answer the question "how often?":

*E.G. We **sometimes** meet for lunch.* *You **never** answer my questions.*

Sometimes adverbs can refer to the whole sentence rather than just the verb:

*E.G. **Fortunately**, she was not badly hurt.*

---

**adversary adversaries**

*Said "**ad**-ver-sar-ee"* NOUN someone who is your enemy or who opposes what you are doing.

**adverse**

ADJECTIVE not helpful to you or opposite to what you want or need

A
B
C
D
E
F
G
H
I
J
K
L
M
N
O
P
Q
R
S
T
U
V
W
X
Y
Z

*E.G. adverse weather conditions.*
**adversely** ADVERB

**adversity adversities**
NOUN a time of danger or difficulty.

**advert adverts**
NOUN; *INFORMAL* an advertisement.

**advertise advertises advertising advertised**
VERB (ENGLISH) **1** to tell people about something in a newspaper or poster, or on TV. **2** to make an announcement in a newspaper or poster, or on TV.
**advertiser** NOUN **advertising** NOUN

**advertisement advertisements**
*Said* "ad-**ver**-tiss-ment" NOUN (ENGLISH) an announcement about something in a newspaper or poster, or on TV.
■ ad, advert, commercial

**advice**
NOUN a suggestion from someone about what you should do.
■ counsel, guidance, suggestion
✔ The noun *advice* is spelt with a 'c' and the verb *advise* is spelt with an 's'.

**advisable**
ADJECTIVE sensible and likely to achieve the result you want *E.G. It is advisable to have a visa.*
**advisably** ADVERB **advisability** NOUN

**advise advises advising advised**
VERB **1** If you advise someone to do something, you tell them you think they should do it. **2** *FORMAL* If you advise someone of something, you inform them of it.
**adviser** NOUN **advisory** ADJECTIVE
■ (sense 1) counsel, recommend, suggest
✔ The verb *advise* is spelt with an 's' and the noun *advice* is spelt with a 'c'.

**advocate advocates advocating advocated**

VERB **1** If you advocate a course of action or plan, you support it publicly. ▶ NOUN **2** An advocate of something is someone who supports it publicly. **3** *FORMAL* a lawyer who represents clients in court.
**advocacy** NOUN

**aerial aerials**
*Said* "**air**-ee-al" ADJECTIVE **1** happening in the air *E.G. aerial combat.* ▶ NOUN **2** a piece of wire for receiving television or radio signals.

**aerial top dressing**
NOUN In Australia and New Zealand, aerial top dressing is the spreading of fertilizer from an aeroplane onto land in remote country areas.

**aero-**
PREFIX 'Aero-' means involving the air, the atmosphere, or aircraft *E.G. aerobatics.*
⌦ from Greek *aēr* meaning 'air'

**aerobics**
NOUN a type of fast physical exercise, which increases the oxygen in your blood and strengthens your heart and lungs.
**aerobic** ADJECTIVE

**aerodynamic**
ADJECTIVE having a streamlined shape that moves easily through the air.

**aeroplane aeroplanes**
NOUN a vehicle with wings and engines that enable it to fly.

**aerosol aerosols**
NOUN a small metal container in which liquid is kept under pressure so that it can be forced out as a spray
✔ *Aerosol* starts with *aer* and not with *air*.

**aerospace**
ADJECTIVE involved in making and

a b c d e f g h i j k l m n o p q r s t u v w x y z

designing aeroplanes and
spacecraft.

**aesthetic** or **esthetic**
*Said "eess-thet-ik"* ADJECTIVE (D & T);
FORMAL relating to the appreciation of
beauty or art.
**aesthetically** ADVERB  **aesthetics**
NOUN

**afar**
NOUN; LITERARY From afar means from a
long way away.

**affable**
ADJECTIVE pleasant and easy to talk to.
**affably** ADVERB  **affability** NOUN

**affair affairs**
NOUN 1 an event or series of events E.G.
*The funeral was a sad affair.* 2 to have
a secret sexual or romantic
relationship, especially when one of
the people is already in a
relationship. ▶ PLURAL NOUN 3 Your
affairs are your private and personal
life E.G. *Why had he meddled in her
affairs?*

**affect affects affecting affected**
VERB 1 If something affects you, it
influences you in some way. 2 FORMAL
If you affect a particular way of
behaving, you behave in that way E.G.
*He affected an Italian accent.*
✓ Do not confuse the spelling of
the verb *affect* with the noun *effect*.
Something that *affects* you has an
*effect* on you.

**affectation affectations**
NOUN An affectation is behaviour that
is not genuine but is put on to
impress people.

**affection affections**
NOUN 1 a feeling of love and fondness
for someone. ▶ PLURAL NOUN 2 Your
affections are feelings of love you
have for someone.

**affectionate**
ADJECTIVE full of fondness for someone
E.G. *an affectionate embrace.*
**affectionately** ADVERB

**affiliate affiliates affiliating
affiliated**
VERB If a group affiliates itself to
another, larger group, it forms a close
association with it E.G. *organizations
affiliated to the ANC.*
**affiliation** NOUN

**affinity affinities**
NOUN a close similarity or
understanding between two things
or people E.G. *There are affinities
between the two poets.*

**affirm affirms affirming affirmed**
VERB If you affirm an idea or belief,
you clearly indicate your support for
it E.G. *We affirm our commitment to
broadcast quality programmes.*
**affirmation** NOUN

**affirmative**
ADJECTIVE An affirmative word or
gesture is one that means yes.

**afflict afflicts afflicting afflicted**
VERB If illness or pain afflicts someone,
they suffer from it E.G. *She was
afflicted by depression.*
**affliction** NOUN

**affluent**
ADJECTIVE having a lot of money and
possessions.
**affluence** NOUN

**afford affords affording
afforded**
VERB 1 If you can afford to do
something, you have enough money
or time to do it. 2 If you cannot
afford something to happen, it
would be harmful or embarrassing
for you if it happened.
**affordable** ADJECTIVE

**affray** affrays
NOUN; *FORMAL* a noisy and violent fight.

**affront** affronts affronting
affronted
VERB **1** If you are affronted by
something, you are insulted and
angered by it. ▶ NOUN **2** something
that is an insult *E.G. Our prisons are an
affront to civilized society.*
☑ Notice that *affront*, the noun, is
followed by *to*.

**afield**
ADVERB Far afield means a long way
away *E.G. competitors from as far
afield as Russia and China.*

**afloat**
ADVERB OR ADJECTIVE **1** floating on water.
**2** successful and making enough
money *E.G. Companies are struggling
hard to stay afloat.*

**afoot**
ADJECTIVE OR ADVERB happening or being
planned, especially secretly *E.G. Plans
are afoot to build a new museum.*

**afraid**
ADJECTIVE **1** If you are afraid, you are
very frightened. **2** If you are afraid
something might happen, you are
worried it might happen.
◼ (sense 1) fearful, frightened,
scared

**afresh**
ADVERB again and in a new way *E.G.
They moved abroad to start life afresh.*

**Africa**
NOUN Africa is the second largest
continent. It is almost surrounded by
sea, with the Atlantic on its west
side, the Mediterranean to the north
and the Indian Ocean and the Red
Sea to the east.

**African** Africans
ADJECTIVE **1** belonging or relating to

Africa. ▶ NOUN **2** someone, especially a
Black person, who comes from Africa.

**African-American** African-
Americans
NOUN an American whose ancestors
came from Africa.

**Afrikaans**
*Said* "af-rik-**ahns**" NOUN a language
spoken in South Africa, similar to
Dutch.

**Afrikaner** Afrikaners
NOUN a white South African with
Dutch ancestors.

**aft**
ADVERB OR ADJECTIVE towards the back of
a ship or boat.

**after**
PREPOSITION OR ADVERB **1** later than a
particular time, date, or event.
**2** behind and following someone or
something *E.G. They ran after her.*
◼ (sense 1) afterwards, following,
later

**afterlife**
NOUN The afterlife is a life some
people believe begins when you die.

**aftermath**
NOUN The aftermath of a disaster is
the situation that comes after it.

**afternoon** afternoons
NOUN the part of the day between
noon and about six o'clock.

**aftershave**
NOUN a pleasant-smelling liquid men
put on their faces after shaving.

**afterthought** afterthoughts
NOUN something you do or say as an
addition to something else you have
already done or said.

**afterwards**
ADVERB after an event or time.

**again**
ADVERB **1** happening one more time

A B C D E F G H I J K L M N O P Q R S T U V W X Y Z

*E.G. He looked forward to becoming a father again.* **2** returning to the same state or place as before *E.G. there and back again.*

■ (sense 1) anew, once more

**against**

PREPOSITION **1** touching and leaning on *E.G. He leaned against the wall.* **2** in opposition to *E.G. the Test match against England.* **3** in order to prevent *E.G. precautions against fire.* **4** in comparison with *E.G. The pound is now at its lowest rate against the dollar.*

**age** ages ageing or aging aged
NOUN **1** The age of something or someone is the number of years they have lived or existed. **2** Age is the quality of being old *E.G. a wine capable of improving with age.* **3** a particular period in history *E.G. the Iron Age.* ▶ PLURAL NOUN **4** INFORMAL Ages means a very long time *E.G. He's been talking for ages.* ▶ VERB **5** To age is to grow old or to appear older
☑ *Ageing* and *aging* are both correct spellings.

**aged**
*Rhymes with "*raged*"* ADJECTIVE having a particular age *E.G. people aged 16 to 24.*

**aged**
*Said "*ay-gid*"* ADJECTIVE very old *E.G. an aged invalid.*
■ elderly, old

**agency** agencies
NOUN an organization or business which provides certain services *E.G. a detective agency.*

**agenda** agendas
NOUN a list of items to be discussed at a meeting.

**agent** agents
NOUN **1** someone who arranges work or business for other people,

especially actors or singers. **2** someone who works for their country's secret service.

**aggravate** aggravates aggravating aggravated
VERB **1** To aggravate a bad situation is to make it worse. **2** INFORMAL If someone or something aggravates you, they make you annoyed.
aggravating ADJECTIVE aggravation NOUN
☑ Some people think that using *aggravate* to mean 'annoy' is wrong.

**aggregate** aggregates
NOUN a total that is made up of several smaller amounts.

**aggression**
NOUN violent and hostile behaviour.

**aggressive**
ADJECTIVE full of hostility and violence.
aggressively ADVERB
aggressiveness NOUN
■ belligerent, hostile

**aggressor** aggressors
NOUN a person or country that starts a fight or a war.

**aggrieved**
ADJECTIVE upset and angry about the way you have been treated.

**aghast**
*Said "*a-gast*"* ADJECTIVE shocked and horrified.

**agile**
ADJECTIVE ( PE ) able to move quickly and easily *E.G. He is as agile as a cat.*
agilely ADVERB agility NOUN

**agitate** agitates agitating agitated
VERB **1** If you agitate for something, you campaign energetically to get it. **2** If something agitates you, it worries you.
agitation NOUN agitator NOUN

**agnostic** agnostics
NOUN or ADJECTIVE Someone who believes we cannot know definitely whether God exists or not.
**agnosticism** NOUN
📖 from Greek *agnōstos* meaning 'unknown'

**ago**
ADVERB in the past E.G. *She bought her flat three years ago.*

**agog**
ADJECTIVE excited and eager to know more about an event or situation E.G. *She was agog to hear his news.*

**agonizing** or **agonising**
ADJECTIVE extremely painful, either physically or mentally E.G. *an agonizing decision.*

**agony**
NOUN very great physical or mental pain.
■ pain, suffering, torment

**agoraphobia**
*Said* "a-gor-a-**foe**-bee-a" NOUN the fear of open spaces.
**agoraphobic** ADJECTIVE
📖 from Greek *agora* meaning 'market place' + *phobia*

**agrarian**
*Said* "ag-**rare**-ee-an" ADJECTIVE; FORMAL relating to farming and agriculture E.G. *agrarian economies.*

**agree** agrees agreeing agreed
VERB 1 If you agree with someone, you have the same opinion as them. 2 If you agree to do something, you say you will do it. 3 If two stories or totals agree, they are the same. 4 Food that doesn't agree with you makes you ill.
■ (sense 1) be of the same opinion, concur
■ (sense 2) comply, consent

**agreeable**
ADJECTIVE 1 pleasant or enjoyable. 2 If you are agreeable to something, you are willing to allow it or to do it E.G. *She was agreeable to the project.*
**agreeably** ADVERB

**agreement** agreements
NOUN 1 a decision that has been reached by two or more people.
2 Two people who are in agreement have the same opinion about something.

**agriculture**
NOUN (HISTORY) Agriculture is farming.
**agricultural** ADJECTIVE

**aground**
ADVERB If a boat runs aground, it becomes stuck in a shallow stretch of water.

**ahead**
ADVERB 1 in front E.G. *He looked ahead.*
2 more advanced than someone or something else E.G. *We are five years ahead of the competition.* 3 in the future E.G. *I haven't had time to think far ahead.*

**aid** aids aiding aided
NOUN 1 Aid is money, equipment, or services provided for people in need E.G. *food and medical aid.* 2 something that makes a task easier E.G. *teaching aids.* ▶ VERB 3 FORMAL If you aid a person or an organization, you help or support them.

**aide** aides
NOUN an assistant to an important person, especially in the government or the army E.G. *the Prime Minister's closest aides.*

**AIDS**
NOUN a disease which destroys the body's natural system of immunity to diseases. AIDS is an abbreviation for 'acquired immune deficiency syndrome'.

a b c d e f g h i j k l m n o p q r s t u v w x y z

Rhythmical Hounds Yap To Heavy Music (<u>rhythm</u>)          SPELLING NOTE

**ailing**
ADJECTIVE **1** sick or ill, and not getting better. **2** getting into difficulties, especially with money *E.G. an ailing company*.

**ailment** ailments
NOUN a minor illness.

**aim** aims aiming aimed
VERB **1** If you aim an object or weapon at someone or something, you point it at them. **2** If you aim to do something, you are planning or hoping to do it. ▶ NOUN **3** Your aim is what you intend to achieve. **4** If you take aim, you point an object or weapon at someone or something.
▇ (sense 1) point
▇ (sense 2) intend, mean, plan
▇ (sense 4) goal, intention, objective

**aimless**
ADJECTIVE having no clear purpose or plan.

**aimlessly** ADVERB **aimlessness** NOUN

**air** airs airing aired
NOUN **1** Air is the mixture of oxygen and other gases which we breathe and which forms the earth's atmosphere. **2** An air someone or something has is the impression they give *E.G. an air of defiance*. **3** 'Air' is used to refer to travel in aircraft *E.G. I have to travel by air a great deal*. ▶ VERB **4** If you air your opinions, you talk about them to other people.

**airborne**
ADJECTIVE in the air and flying.

**air-conditioning**
NOUN a system of providing cool, clean air in buildings.

**air-conditioned** ADJECTIVE

**aircraft**
NOUN any vehicle which can fly.

**airfield** airfields
NOUN an open area of ground with runways where small aircraft take off and land.

**air force** air forces
NOUN the part of a country's armed services that fights using aircraft.

**air gun** air guns
NOUN a gun which uses air pressure to fire pellets.

**air hostess** air hostesses
NOUN a woman whose job is to look after passengers on an aircraft.

**airless**
ADJECTIVE having no wind or fresh air.

**airlift** airlifts
NOUN an operation to move people or goods by air, especially in an emergency.

**airline** airlines
NOUN a company which provides air travel.

**airliner** airliners
NOUN a large passenger plane.

**airmail**
NOUN the system of sending letters and parcels by air.

**airman** airmen
NOUN a man who serves in his country's air force.

**airport** airports
NOUN a place where people go to catch planes.

**air raid** air raids
NOUN an attack by enemy aircraft, in which bombs are dropped.

**airship** airships
NOUN a large, light aircraft, consisting of a rigid balloon filled with gas and powered by an engine, with a passenger compartment underneath.

**airstrip** airstrips
NOUN a stretch of land that has been

cleared for aircraft to take off and land.

**airtight**
ADJECTIVE not letting air in or out.

**airy** airier airiest
ADJECTIVE full of fresh air and light.
**airily** ADVERB

**aisle** aisles
*Rhymes with* "**mile**" NOUN a long narrow gap that people can walk along between rows of seats or shelves.

**ajar**
ADJECTIVE A door or window that is ajar is slightly open.

**akin**
ADJECTIVE; *FORMAL* similar E.G. *The taste is akin to veal.*

**alabaster**
NOUN a type of smooth stone used for making ornaments.
from Latin *alabaster* meaning 'vase for perfume'

**alacrity**
NOUN; *FORMAL* eager willingness E.G. *He seized this offer with alacrity.*

**alarm** alarms alarming alarmed
NOUN 1 a feeling of fear and worry E.G. *The cat sprang back in alarm.* 2 an automatic device used to warn people of something E.G. *a car alarm.*
► VERB 3 If something alarms you, it makes you worried and anxious.
**alarming** ADJECTIVE

**alas**
ADVERB unfortunately or regrettably E.G. *But, alas, it would not be true.*

**Albanian** Albanians
ADJECTIVE 1 belonging or relating to Albania. ► NOUN 2 someone who comes from Albania. 3 Albanian is the main language spoken in Albania.

**albatross** albatrosses
NOUN a large white sea bird.

**albeit**
*Said* "awl-**bee**-it" CONJUNCTION; *FORMAL* although E.G. *He was making progress, albeit slowly.*

**albino** albinos
NOUN a person or animal with very white skin, white hair, and pink eyes.

**album** albums
NOUN 1 a CD, cassette, or record with a number of songs on it. 2 a book in which you keep a collection of things such as photographs or stamps.

**alchemy**
*Said* "al-**kem**-ee" NOUN a medieval science that attempted to change ordinary metals into gold.
**alchemist** NOUN

**alcheringa**
*Said* "al-cher-**ring**-ga" NOUN Alcheringa is the same as Dreamtime.

**alcohol**
NOUN Alcohol is any drink that can make people drunk; also the colourless flammable liquid found in these drinks, produced by fermenting sugar.

**alcoholic** alcoholics
ADJECTIVE 1 An alcoholic drink contains alcohol. ► NOUN 2 someone who is addicted to alcohol.
**alcoholism** NOUN

**alcopop** alcopops
NOUN; *INFORMAL* an alcoholic drink that tastes like a soft drink.

**alcove** alcoves
NOUN an area of a room which is set back slightly from the main part.
from Arabic *al-qubbah* meaning 'arch'

a b c d e f g h i j k l m n o p q r s t u v w x y z

A
B
C
D
E
F
G
H
I
J
K
L
M
N
O
P
Q
R
S
T
U
V
W
X
Y
Z

**ale**
NOUN a type of beer.

**alert** alerts alerting alerted
ADJECTIVE **1** paying full attention to what is happening *E.G. The criminal was spotted by an alert member of the public.* ▶ NOUN **2** a situation in which people prepare themselves for danger *E.G. The troops were on a war alert.* ▶ VERB **3** to warn someone of a problem or danger.
**alertness** NOUN
▦ (sense 1) attentive, vigilant, watchful

**A level** A levels
NOUN an advanced exam taken by students in many British schools and colleges, usually following GCSEs.

**algae**
*Said "al-jee"* PLURAL NOUN plants that grow in water or on damp surfaces.

**algebra**
NOUN a branch of mathematics in which symbols and letters are used instead of numbers to express relationships between quantities.
**algebraic** ADJECTIVE
▦ from Arabic *al-jabr* meaning 'reunion'

**Algerian** Algerians
ADJECTIVE **1** belonging or relating to Algeria. ▶ NOUN **2** someone who comes from Algeria.

**alias** aliases
*Said "ay-lee-ass"* NOUN a false name *E.G. Leonard Nimoy, alias Mr Spock.*

**alibi** alibis
*Said "al-li-bye"* NOUN An alibi is evidence proving you were somewhere else when a crime was committed.

**alien** aliens
*Said "ay-lee-an"* ADJECTIVE **1** not normal to you *E.G. a totally alien culture.* ▶ NOUN **2** someone who is not a citizen of the country in which he or she lives. **3** In science fiction, an alien is a creature from outer space.

**alienate** alienates alienating alienated
VERB If you alienate someone, you do something that makes them stop being sympathetic to you *E.G. The Council's approach alienated many local residents.*
**alienation** NOUN

**alight** alights alighting alighted
ADJECTIVE **1** Something that is alight is burning. ▶ VERB **2** If a bird or insect alights somewhere, it lands there. **3** FORMAL When passengers alight from a vehicle, they get out of it at the end of a journey.

**align** aligns aligning aligned
*Said "a-line"* VERB **1** If you align yourself with a particular group, you support them. **2** If you align things, you place them in a straight line.
**alignment** NOUN

**alike**
ADJECTIVE **1** Things that are alike are similar in some way. ▶ ADVERB **2** If people or things are treated alike, they are treated in a similar way.

**alimony**
*Said "al-li-mon-ee"* NOUN money someone has to pay regularly to their wife or husband after they are divorced.

**alive**
ADJECTIVE **1** living. **2** lively and active.
▦ (sense 1) animate, living

**alkali** alkalis
*Said "al-kal-eye"* NOUN (SCIENCE) a chemical substance that turns litmus

paper blue.

**alkaline** ADJECTIVE    **alkalinity** NOUN

**all**

ADJECTIVE, PRONOUN, or ADVERB **1** used when referring to the whole of something *E.G. Why did he have to say all that?… She managed to finish it all.* ► ADVERB **2** 'All' is also used when saying the two sides in a game or contest have the same score *E.G. The final score was six points all.*

**Allah**

PROPER NOUN the Muslim name for God.

**allay** allays allaying allayed

VERB To allay someone's fears or doubts is to stop them feeling afraid or doubtful.

**allege** alleges alleging alleged

*Said "a-lej"* VERB If you allege that something is true, you say it is true but do not provide any proof *E.G. It is alleged that she died as a result of neglect.*

**allegation** NOUN    **alleged** ADJECTIVE

**allegiance** allegiances

*Said "a-lee-jenss"* NOUN loyal support for a person or organization.

**allegory** allegories

*Said "al-li-gor-ee"* NOUN a piece of writing or art in which the characters and events are symbols for something else. Allegories usually make some moral, religious, or political point. For example, George Orwell's novel 'Animal Farm' is an allegory in that the animals who revolt in the farmyard are symbols of the political leaders in the Russian Revolution.

**allergy** allergies

*Said "al-er-jee"* NOUN a sensitivity someone has to something, so that they become ill when they eat it or touch it *E.G. an allergy to cows' milk.*

**alleviate** alleviates alleviating alleviated

VERB To alleviate pain or a problem is to make it less severe *E.G. measures to alleviate poverty.*

**alleviation** NOUN

**alley** alleys

NOUN a narrow passage between buildings.

**alliance** alliances

NOUN a group of people, organizations, or countries working together for similar aims.

■ association, league, union

**alligator** alligators

NOUN a large animal, similar to a crocodile.

🏛 from Spanish *el lagarto* meaning 'lizard'

**alliteration**

NOUN ( ENGLISH ); *LITERARY* the use of several words together which all begin with the same sound, for example 'around the ragged rock the ragged rascal ran'.

**alliterative** ADJECTIVE

**allocate** allocates allocating allocated

VERB If you allocate something, you decide it should be given to a person or place, or used for a particular purpose *E.G. funds allocated for nursery education.*

**allocation** NOUN

**allot** allots allotting allotted

VERB If something is allotted to you, it is given to you as your share *E.G. Space was allotted for visitors' cars.*

**allotment** allotments

NOUN **1** a piece of land which people can rent to grow vegetables on. **2** a share of something.

a
b
c
d
e
f
g
h
i
j
k
l
m
n
o
p
q
r
s
t
u
v
w
x
y
z

**allow** allows allowing allowed

VERB **1** If you allow something, you say it is all right or let it happen. **2** If you allow a period of time or an amount of something, you set it aside for a particular purpose *E.G. Allow four hours for the paint to dry.*
**allowable** ADJECTIVE

☑ Do not confuse the spellings of the past tense form *allowed* and the adverb *aloud*, which sound the same.

**allowance** allowances

NOUN **1** money given regularly to someone for a particular purpose *E.G. a petrol allowance.* ▶ PHRASE **2** If you **make allowances** for something, you take it into account *E.G. The school made allowances for Muslim cultural customs.*

**alloy** alloys

NOUN a mixture of two or more metals.

**all right** or **alright**

ADJECTIVE **1** If something is all right, it is acceptable. **2** If someone is all right, they are safe and not harmed. **3** You say 'all right' to agree to something.

**allude** alludes alluding alluded

VERB If you allude to something, you refer to it in an indirect way.

☑ You *allude to* something. Do not confuse *allude* with *elude*.

**allure**

NOUN The allure of something is an exciting quality that makes it attractive *E.G. the allure of foreign travel.*
**alluring** ADJECTIVE

**allusion** allusions

NOUN an indirect reference to or comment about something *E.G. English literature is full of classical allusions.*

**ally** allies allying allied

NOUN **1** a person or country that helps and supports another. ▶ VERB **2** If you ally yourself with someone, you agree to help and support each other.
▤ (sense 1) friend, helper, partner
▤ (sense 2) associate, join, unite

**almanac** almanacs

NOUN a book published every year giving information about a particular subject.

**almighty**

ADJECTIVE **1** very great or serious *E.G. I've just had an almighty row with the chairman.* ▶ PROPER NOUN **2** The Almighty is another name for God.

**almond** almonds

NOUN a pale brown oval nut.

**almost**

ADVERB very nearly *E.G. Prices have almost doubled.*
▤ just about, nearly, practically

**alms**

PLURAL NOUN; OLD-FASHIONED Alms are gifts of money, food, or clothing to poor people.

**aloft**

ADVERB up in the air or in a high position *E.G. He held aloft the trophy.*

**alone**

ADJECTIVE or ADVERB not with other people or things *E.G. He just wanted to be alone.*
▤ by oneself, solitary, unaccompanied

**along**

PREPOSITION **1** moving, happening, or existing continuously from one end to the other of something, or at various points beside it *E.G. Put rivets along the top edge.* ▶ ADVERB **2** moving forward *E.G. We marched along,*

*singing as we went.* **3** with someone E.G. *Why could she not take her along?*
▶ PHRASE **4 All along** means from the beginning of a period of time right up to now E.G. *You've known that all along.*

**alongside**
PREPOSITION or ADVERB **1** next to something E.G. *They had a house in the park alongside the river.*
▶ PREPOSITION **2** If you work alongside other people, you are working in the same place and cooperating with them E.G. *He was thrilled to work alongside Robert De Niro.*
☑ Do not use of after *alongside*.

**aloof**
ADJECTIVE distant from someone or something.

**aloud**
ADVERB When you read or speak aloud, you speak loudly enough for other people to hear you
☑ Do not confuse the spellings of *aloud* and *allowed*, the past tense form of *allow*.

**alphabet** alphabets
NOUN (LIBRARY) a set of letters in a fixed order that is used in writing a language.
**alphabetical** ADJECTIVE
**alphabetically** ADVERB

**alpine**
ADJECTIVE existing in or relating to high mountains E.G. *alpine flowers.*
▦ from *the Alps*, a mountain range in central Europe

**already**
ADVERB having happened before the present time or earlier than expected E.G. *She has already gone to bed.*

**alright**
another spelling of **all right**.

☑ Some people think that *all right* is the only correct spelling and that *alright* is wrong.

**Alsatian** Alsatians
*Said* "al-**say**-shn" NOUN a large wolflike dog.

**also**
ADVERB in addition to something that has just been mentioned.

**altar** altars
NOUN a holy table in a church or temple.

**alter** alters altering altered
VERB If something alters or if you alter it, it changes.
**alteration** NOUN
☑ Do not confuse the spellings of *alter* and *altar*.

**altercation** altercations
NOUN; FORMAL a noisy disagreement.

**alternate** alternates alternating alternated
VERB **1** If one thing alternates with another, the two things regularly occur one after the other. ▶ ADJECTIVE **2** If something happens on alternate days, it happens on the first day but not the second, and happens again on the third day but not the fourth, and so on. **3** (MATHS) Alternate angles are two angles on opposite sides of a line that crosses two other lines.
**alternately** ADVERB **alternation** NOUN

**alternating current** alternating currents
NOUN a current that regularly changes its direction, so that the electrons flow first one way and then the other.

**alternative** alternatives
NOUN **1** something you can do or have instead of something else E.G.

a b c d e f g h i j k l m n o p q r s t u v w x y z

alternatives to prison such as community service. ▶ ADJECTIVE

**2** Alternative plans or actions can happen or be done instead of what is already happening or being done.

**alternatively** ADVERB

☑ If there are more than two choices in a situation you should say *there are three choices* rather than *there are three alternatives* because the strict meaning of *alternative* is a choice between two things.

**although**

CONJUNCTION in spite of the fact that *E.G. He wasn't well known in America, although he did make a film there.*

**altitude** altitudes

NOUN The altitude of something is its height above sea level *E.G. The mountain range reaches an altitude of 1330 metres.*

**altogether**

ADVERB **1** entirely *E.G. She wasn't altogether sorry to be leaving.* **2** in total; used of amounts *E.G. I get paid 1000 pounds a month altogether.*

**aluminium**

NOUN a silvery-white lightweight metal.

**always**

ADVERB all the time or for ever *E.G. She's always moaning.*

**am**

the first person singular, present tense of be.

**a.m.**

used to specify times between 12 midnight and 12 noon, eg *I get up at 6 a.m.* It is an abbreviation for the Latin phrase 'ante meridiem', which means 'before noon'.

**amalgamate** amalgamates amalgamating amalgamated

VERB If two organizations amalgamate, they join together to form one new organization.

**amalgamation** NOUN

**amandla**

NOUN In South Africa, amandla is a political slogan which calls for power for Black people.

**amass** amasses amassing amassed

VERB If you amass something such as money or information, you collect large quantities of it *E.G. He amassed a huge fortune.*

**amateur** amateurs

NOUN someone who does something as a hobby rather than as a job.

**amateurish**

ADJECTIVE not skilfully made or done.

**amateurishly** ADVERB

**amaze** amazes amazing amazed

VERB If something amazes you, it surprises you very much.

**amazement** NOUN

**≡** astonish, astound, stun, surprise

**amazing**

ADJECTIVE very surprising or remarkable.

**amazingly** ADVERB

**ambassador** ambassadors

NOUN a person sent to a foreign country as the representative of his or her own government.

**amber**

NOUN **1** a hard, yellowish-brown substance used for making jewellery. ▶ NOUN or ADJECTIVE **2** orange-brown.

**ambi-**

PREFIX 'Ambi-' means 'both'. For example, something which is *ambiguous* can have either of two meanings.

🔲 from Latin *ambo* meaning 'both'

**ambidextrous**

ADJECTIVE Someone who is ambidextrous is able to use both hands equally skilfully.

**ambience**

NOUN; *FORMAL* The ambience of a place is its atmosphere.

**ambient**

ADJECTIVE 1 surrounding *E.G. low ambient temperatures.* 2 creating a relaxing atmosphere *E.G. ambient music.*

**ambiguous**

ADJECTIVE A word or phrase that is ambiguous has more than one meaning.

**ambiguously** ADVERB    **ambiguity** NOUN

**ambition** ambitions

NOUN 1 If you have an ambition to achieve something, you want very much to achieve it *E.G. His ambition is to be an actor.* 2 a great desire for success, power, and wealth *E.G. He's talented and full of ambition.*

**ambitious**

ADJECTIVE 1 Someone who is ambitious has a strong desire for success, power, and wealth. 2 An ambitious plan is a large one and requires a lot of work *E.G. an ambitious rebuilding schedule.*

**ambivalent**

ADJECTIVE having or showing two conflicting attitudes or emotions.

**ambivalence** NOUN

**amble** ambles ambling ambled

VERB If you amble, you walk slowly and in a relaxed manner.

**ambulance** ambulances

NOUN a vehicle for taking sick and injured people to hospital.

**ambush** ambushes ambushing ambushed

VERB 1 To ambush someone is to attack them after hiding and lying in wait for them. ▶ NOUN 2 an attack on someone after hiding and lying in wait for them.

**amen**

INTERJECTION Amen is said at the end of a Christian prayer. It means 'so be it'.

**amenable**

*Said* "am-**mee**-na-bl" ADJECTIVE willing to listen to suggestions, or to cooperate with someone *E.G. Both brothers were amenable to the arrangement.*

**amenably** ADVERB    **amenability** NOUN

**amend** amends amending amended

VERB 1 To amend something that has been written or said is to alter it slightly *E.G. Our constitution had to be amended.* ▶ PLURAL NOUN 2 If you make amends for something bad you have done, you say you are sorry and try to make up for it.

**amendment** NOUN

**amenity** amenities

*Said* "am-**mee**-nit-ee" NOUN (GEOGRAPHY) Amenities are things that are available for the public to use, such as sports facilities or shopping centres.

**America**

NOUN America refers to the United States, or to the whole of North, South, and Central America.

**American** Americans

ADJECTIVE 1 belonging or relating to the United States, or to the whole of North, South, and Central America. ▶ NOUN 2 someone who comes from the United States.

a b c d e f g h i j k l m n o p q r s t u v w x y z

A
B
C
D
E
F
G
H
I
J
K
L
M
N
O
P
Q
R
S
T
U
V
W
X
Y
Z

**amethyst** amethysts
NOUN a type of purple semiprecious stone.
🏛 from Greek *amethustos* meaning 'not drunk'. It was thought to prevent intoxication

**amiable**
ADJECTIVE pleasant and friendly *E.G. The hotel staff were very amiable.*
**amiably** ADVERB **amiability** NOUN

**amicable**
ADJECTIVE fairly friendly *E.G. an amicable divorce.*
**amicably** ADVERB

**amid** or **amidst**
PREPOSITION; *FORMAL* surrounded by *E.G. She enjoys cooking amid her friends.*
☑ The form *amidst* is a bit old-fashioned and *amid* is more often used.

**amiss**
ADJECTIVE If something is amiss, there is something wrong.

**ammonia**
NOUN Ammonia is a colourless, strong-smelling gas or liquid.

**ammunition**
NOUN anything that can be fired from a gun or other weapon, for example bullets and shells.

**amnesia**
NOUN loss of memory.

**amnesty** amnesties
NOUN an official pardon for political or other prisoners.

**amoeba** amoebas or amoebae
*Said* "am-**mee**-ba"; also spelt **ameba**
NOUN the smallest kind of living creature, consisting of one cell. Amoebas reproduce by dividing into two.

**amok**
*Said* "am-**muk**" PHRASE If a person or animal **runs amok**, they behave in a violent and uncontrolled way.
🏛 a Malay word

**among** or **amongst**
PREPOSITION **1** surrounded by *E.G. The bike lay among piles of chains and pedals.* **2** in the company of *E.G. He was among friends.* **3** between more than two *E.G. The money will be divided among seven charities.*
☑ If there are more than two things, you should use *among*. If there are only two things you should use *between*. The form *amongst* is a bit old-fashioned.

**amoral**
ADJECTIVE Someone who is amoral has no moral standards by which to live
☑ Do not confuse *amoral* and *immoral*. You use *amoral* to talk about people with no moral standards, but *immoral* for people who are aware of moral standards but go against them.

**amorous**
ADJECTIVE passionately affectionate *E.G. an amorous relationship.*
**amorously** ADVERB **amorousness** NOUN

**amount** amounts amounting amounted (MATHS)
NOUN **1** An amount of something is how much there is of it. ▶ VERB **2** If something amounts to a particular total, all the parts of it add up to that total *E.G. Her vocabulary amounted to only 50 words.*
▤ (sense 1) extent, number, quantity

**amp** amps
NOUN the same as an ampere.

**ampere** amperes
*Said* "**am**-pair" NOUN a unit which is

used for measuring electric current.

**ampersand** ampersands

NOUN the character &, meaning 'and'.

**amphetamine** amphetamines

NOUN a drug that increases people's energy and makes them excited. It can have dangerous and unpleasant side effects.

**amphibian** amphibians

NOUN (SCIENCE) a creature that lives partly on land and partly in water, for example a frog or a newt.

**amphibious**

ADJECTIVE An amphibious animal, such as a frog, lives partly on land and partly in the water.

📖 from Greek *amphibios* meaning 'having a double life'

**amphitheatre** amphitheatres

NOUN a large, semicircular open area with sloping sides covered with rows of seats.

**ample**

ADJECTIVE If there is an ample amount of something, there is more than enough of it.

amply ADVERB

**amplifier** amplifiers

NOUN a piece of equipment in a radio or stereo system which causes sounds or signals to become louder.

**amplify** amplifies amplifying amplified

VERB If you amplify a sound, you make it louder.

amplification NOUN

**amplitude**

NOUN In physics, the amplitude of a wave is how far its curve moves away from its normal position.

**amputate** amputates amputating amputated

VERB To amputate an arm or a leg is to cut it off as a surgical operation.

amputation NOUN

**Amrit**

NOUN 1 In the Sikh religion, Amrit is a special mixture of sugar and water used in rituals. 2 The Amrit or Amrit ceremony takes place when someone is accepted as a full member of the Sikh community, and drinks Amrit as part of the ceremony.

**amuse** amuses amusing amused

VERB 1 If something amuses you, you think it is funny. 2 If you amuse yourself, you find things to do which stop you from being bored.

amused ADJECTIVE　amusing ADJECTIVE

**amusement** amusements

NOUN 1 Amusement is the state of thinking something is funny. 2 Amusement is also the pleasure you get from being entertained or from doing something interesting. 3 Amusements are ways of passing the time pleasantly.

**an**

ADJECTIVE 'An' is used instead of 'a' in front of words that begin with a vowel sound

☑ You use *an* in front of abbreviations that start with a vowel sound when they are read out loud: *an MA; an OBE*.

**-an**

SUFFIX '-an' comes at the end of nouns and adjectives which show where or what someone or something comes from or belongs to E.G. American… Victorian… Christian.

📖 from Latin *-ānus* meaning 'of or belonging to'

**anachronism** anachronisms

*Said* "an-**ak**-kron-izm" NOUN something that belongs or seems to

a b c d e f g h i j k l m n o p q r s t u v w x y z

belong to another time.

**anachronistic** ADJECTIVE

📖 from Greek *anakhronismos* meaning 'mistake in time'

**anaemia**

*Said* "a-**nee**-mee-a" NOUN a medical condition resulting from too few red cells in a person's blood. People with anaemia look pale and feel tired.

**anaemic**

ADJECTIVE

**anaesthetic** anaesthetics

*Said* "an-niss-**thet**-ik" NOUN a substance that stops you feeling pain. A general anaesthetic stops you from feeling pain in the whole of your body by putting you to sleep, and a local anaesthetic makes just one part of your body go numb.

**anaesthetist** anaesthetists

NOUN a doctor who is specially trained to give anaesthetics.

**anaesthetize** anaesthetizes anaesthetizing anaesthetized; also spelt **anesthetize** or **anaesthetise**

VERB To anaesthetize someone is to give them an anaesthetic to make them unconscious.

**anagram** anagrams

NOUN a word or phrase formed by changing the order of the letters of another word or phrase. For example, 'triangle' is an anagram of 'integral'.

**anal**

*Said* "**ay**-nl" ADJECTIVE relating to the anus.

**analgesic** analgesics

*Said* "an-al-**jee**-sik" NOUN a substance that relieves pain.

**analogy** analogies

*Said* "an-**al**-o-jee" NOUN a comparison showing that two things are similar in some ways.

**analogous** ADJECTIVE

**analyse** analyses analysing analysed

VERB (EXAM TERM) To analyse something is to break it down into parts, or investigate it carefully, so that you can describe its main aspects, or find out what it consists of.

**analysis** analyses

NOUN the process of investigating something in order to understand it or find out what it consists of *E.G. a full analysis of the problem.*

**analyst** analysts

NOUN a person whose job is to analyse things to find out about them.

**analytic** or **analytical**

ADJECTIVE using logical reasoning *E.G. Planning in detail requires an acute analytical mind.*

**analytically** ADVERB

**anarchy**

*Said* "**an**-nar-kee" NOUN a situation where nobody obeys laws or rules.

📖 from Greek *anarkhos* meaning 'without a ruler'

**anatomy** anatomies

NOUN **1** the study of the structure of the human body or of the bodies of animals. **2** An animal's anatomy is the structure of its body.

**anatomical** ADJECTIVE  **anatomically** ADVERB

**ANC**

NOUN one of the main political parties in South Africa. ANC is an abbreviation for 'African National Congress'.

**ancestor** ancestors

NOUN Your ancestors are the members of your family who lived many years ago and from whom you are descended.

**ancestral** ADJECTIVE
■ forebear, forefather

**ancestry** ancestries
NOUN Your ancestry consists of the people from whom you are descended *E.G. a French citizen of Greek ancestry*.

**anchor** anchors anchoring anchored
NOUN **1** a heavy, hooked object at the end of a chain, dropped from a boat into the water to keep the boat in one place. ▶ VERB **2** To anchor a boat or another object is to stop it from moving by dropping an anchor or attaching it to something solid.

**anchorage** anchorages
NOUN a place where a boat can safely anchor.

**anchovy** anchovies
NOUN a type of small edible fish with a very strong salty taste.

**ancient**
*Said "ayn-shent"* ADJECTIVE **1** existing or happening in the distant past *E.G. ancient Greece*. **2** very old or having a very long history *E.G. an ancient monastery*.

**ancillary**
*Said "an-sil-lar-ee"* ADJECTIVE The ancillary workers in an institution are the people such as cooks and cleaners, whose work supports the main work of the institution.
▥ from Latin *ancilla* meaning 'maidservant'

**and**
CONJUNCTION You use 'and' to link two or more words or phrases together.

**androgynous**
*Said "an-droj-in-uss"* ADJECTIVE; *FORMAL* having both male and female characteristics.

**android** androids
NOUN In science fiction, a robot that looks like a human being.

**anecdote** anecdotes
NOUN a short, entertaining story about a person or event.
**anecdotal** ADJECTIVE

**anemone** anemones
*Said "an-em-on-ee"* NOUN a plant with red, purple, or white flowers.

**anew**
ADVERB If you do something anew, you do it again *E.G. They left their life in Britain to start anew in France*.

**angel** angels
NOUN Angels are spiritual beings some people believe live in heaven and act as messengers for God.
**angelic** ADJECTIVE

**anger** angers angering angered
NOUN **1** the strong feeling you get when you feel someone has behaved in an unfair or cruel way.
▶ VERB **2** If something angers you, it makes you feel angry.
■ (sense 1) fury, rage, wrath
■ (sense 2) enrage, infuriate, madden

**angina**
*Said "an-jy-na"* NOUN a brief but very severe heart pain, caused by lack of blood supply to the heart. It is also known as 'angina pectoris'.

**angle** angles
NOUN **1** (MATHS) the distance between two lines at the point where they join together. Angles are measured in degrees. **2** the direction from which you look at something *E.G. He had painted the vase from all angles*. **3** An angle on something is a particular way of considering it *E.G. the same story from a German angle*.

an ELegant angEL (ang**el**)    ▶ SPELLING NOTE

A
B
C
D
E
F
G
H
I
J
K
L
M
N
O
P
Q
R
S
T
U
V
W
X
Y
Z

**angler** anglers
NOUN someone who fishes with a fishing rod as a hobby.
**angling** NOUN
📖 from Old English *angul* meaning 'fish-hook'

**Anglican** Anglicans
NOUN or ADJECTIVE a member of one of the churches belonging to the Anglican Communion, a group of Protestant churches which includes the Church of England.

**Anglo-Saxon** Anglo-Saxons
NOUN **1** The Anglo-Saxons were a race of people who settled in England from the fifth century AD and were the dominant people until the Norman invasion in 1066. They were composed of three West Germanic tribes, the Angles, Saxons, and Jutes. **2** Anglo-Saxon is another name for **Old English**.

**Angolan** Angolans
*Said* "ang-**goh**-ln" ADJECTIVE
**1** belonging or relating to Angola.
▶ NOUN **2** someone who comes from Angola.

**angora**
ADJECTIVE **1** An angora goat or rabbit is a breed with long silky hair. ▶ NOUN **2** Angora is this hair, usually mixed with other fibres to make clothing.
📖 from *Angora*, the former name of Ankara in Turkey

**angry** angrier angriest
ADJECTIVE very cross or annoyed.
**angrily** ADVERB
▤ enraged, furious, infuriated, mad

**angst**
NOUN a feeling of anxiety and worry.

**anguish**
NOUN extreme suffering.
**anguished** ADJECTIVE

**angular**
ADJECTIVE Angular things have straight lines and sharp points *E.G. He has an angular face and pointed chin.*

**animal** animals
NOUN any living being except a plant, or any mammal except a human being.
📖 from Latin *anima* meaning 'life' or 'soul'

**animate** animates animating animated
VERB To animate something is to make it lively and interesting.

**animated**
ADJECTIVE lively and interesting *E.G. an animated conversation.*

**animation**
NOUN **1** a method of film-making in which a series of drawings are photographed. When the film is projected, the characters in the drawings appear to move. **2** Someone who has animation shows liveliness in the way they speak and act *E.G. The crowd showed no sign of animation.*
**animator** NOUN

**animosity** animosities
NOUN a feeling of strong dislike and anger towards someone.

**aniseed**
NOUN a substance made from the seeds of a Mediterranean plant and used as a flavouring in sweets, drinks, and medicine.

**ankle** ankles
NOUN the joint which connects your foot to your leg.

**annex** annexes annexing annexed; also spelt **annexe**
NOUN **1** an extra building which is joined to a larger main building. **2** an

extra part added to a document.

▶ VERB **3** If one country annexes another, it seizes the other country and takes control of it.

**annexation** NOUN

**annihilate** annihilates annihilating annihilated

*Said* "an-**nye**-ill-ate" VERB If something is annihilated, it is completely destroyed.

**annihilation** NOUN

**anniversary** anniversaries

NOUN a date which is remembered because something special happened on that date in a previous year.

**announce** announces announcing announced

VERB If you announce something, you tell people about it publicly or officially *E.G. The team was announced on Friday morning.*

**announcement** NOUN

■ broadcast, make known, proclaim

**announcer** announcers

NOUN someone who introduces programmes on radio and television.

**annoy** annoys annoying annoyed

VERB If someone or something annoys you, they irritate you and make you fairly angry.

**annoyance** NOUN    **annoyed** ADJECTIVE

■ bother, exasperate, irritate, vex

**annual** annuals

ADJECTIVE **1** happening or done once a year *E.G. their annual conference.*
**2** happening or calculated over a period of one year *E.G. the United States' annual budget for defence.*

▶ NOUN **3** a book or magazine published once a year. **4** a plant that grows, flowers, and dies within a year.

**annually** ADVERB

**annuity** annuities

NOUN a fixed sum of money paid to someone every year from an investment or insurance policy.

**annul** annuls annulling annulled

VERB If a marriage or contract is annulled, it is declared invalid, so that legally it is considered never to have existed.

**annulment** NOUN

**anoint** anoints anointing anointed

VERB To anoint someone is to put oil on them as part of a ceremony.

**anointment** NOUN

**anomaly** anomalies

*Said* "an-**nom**-al-ee" NOUN Something is an anomaly if it is unusual or different from normal.

**anomalous** ADJECTIVE

**anon.**

an abbreviation for **anonymous**.

**anonymous**

ADJECTIVE If something is anonymous, nobody knows who is responsible for it *E.G. The police received an anonymous phone call.*

**anonymously** ADVERB    **anonymity** NOUN

**anorak** anoraks

NOUN a warm waterproof jacket, usually with a hood.

🏛 an Inuit word

**anorexia**

NOUN a psychological illness in which the person refuses to eat because they are frightened of becoming fat.

**anorexic** ADJECTIVE

🏛 from Greek *an-* + *orexis* meaning 'no appetite'

**another**

ADJECTIVE *or* PRONOUN Another thing or person is an additional thing or person.

a b c d e f g h i j k l m n o p q r s t u v w x y z

**answer** answers answering answered

VERB **1** If you answer someone, you reply to them using words or actions or in writing. ▶ NOUN **2** the reply you give when you answer someone. **3** a solution to a problem.

■ (sense 1) reply, respond, retort
■ (sense 2) reply, response, retort

**answerable**

ADJECTIVE If you are answerable to someone for something, you are responsible for it *E.G. He must be made answerable for these crimes.*

**answering machine** answering machines

NOUN a machine which records telephone calls while you are out.

**ant** ants

NOUN Ants are small insects that live in large groups.

**-ant**

SUFFIX '-ant' is used to form adjectives *E.G. important.*
🏛

**antagonism**

NOUN hatred or hostility.

**antagonist** antagonists

NOUN an enemy or opponent.

**antagonistic**

ADJECTIVE Someone who is antagonistic towards you shows hate or hostility.
**antagonistically** ADVERB

**antagonize** antagonizes antagonizing antagonized; also spelt **antagonise**

VERB If someone is antagonized, they are made to feel anger and hostility.

**Antarctic**

NOUN The Antarctic is the region south of the Antarctic Circle.

**Antarctic Circle**

NOUN The Antarctic Circle is an imaginary circle around the southern part of the world.

**ante-**

PREFIX 'Ante-' means 'before'. For example, *antenatal* means 'before birth'.
🏛 from Latin *ante*, a preposition or adverb meaning 'before'

**antecedent** antecedents

*Said "an-tis-see-dent"* NOUN **1** An antecedent of a thing or event is something that happened or existed before it and is related to it in some way *E.G. the prehistoric antecedents of the horse.* **2** Your antecedents are your ancestors, the relatives from whom you are descended.

**antelope** antelopes

NOUN an animal which looks like a deer.

**antenatal**

ADJECTIVE concerned with the care of pregnant women and their unborn children *E.G. an antenatal clinic.*

**antenna** antennae or antennas

NOUN **1** The antennae of insects and certain other animals are the two long, thin parts attached to their heads which they use to feel with. The plural is 'antennae'. **2** In Australian, New Zealand, and American English, an antenna is a radio or television aerial. The plural is 'antennas'.

**anthem** anthems

NOUN a hymn written for a special occasion.

**anther** anthers

NOUN in a flower, the part of the stamen that makes pollen grains.
🏛 from Greek *anthos* meaning 'flower'

**anthology** anthologies

NOUN (LIBRARY) a collection of writings by various authors published in one book.

**anthropo-**

PREFIX 'Anthropo-' means involving or to do with human beings E.G. *anthropology*.

📖 from Greek *anthrōpos* meaning 'human being'

**anthropology**

NOUN the study of human beings and their society and culture.
**anthropological** ADJECTIVE
**anthropologist** NOUN

**anti-**

PREFIX 'Anti-' means opposed to or opposite to something E.G. *antiwar marches*.

📖 from Greek *anti-* meaning 'opposite' or 'against'

**antibiotic** antibiotics

NOUN a drug or chemical used in medicine to kill bacteria and cure infections.

**antibody** antibodies

NOUN a substance produced in the blood which can kill the harmful bacteria that cause disease.

**anticipate** anticipates anticipating anticipated

VERB If you anticipate an event, you are expecting it and are prepared for it E.G. *She had anticipated his visit.*
**anticipation** NOUN

**anticlimax** anticlimaxes

NOUN something that disappoints you because it is not as exciting as expected, or because it occurs after something that was very exciting.

**anticlockwise**

ADJECTIVE OR ADVERB moving in the opposite direction to the hands of a clock.

**antics**

PLURAL NOUN funny or silly ways of behaving.

**antidote** antidotes

NOUN a chemical substance that acts against the effect of a poison.

**antihistamine** antihistamines

NOUN a drug used to treat an allergy.

**antipathy**

NOUN a strong feeling of dislike or hostility towards something or someone.

**antiperspirant** antiperspirants

NOUN a substance which stops you sweating when you put it on your skin.

**antipodes**

*Said* "an-**tip**-pod-eez" PLURAL NOUN any two points on the earth's surface that are situated directly opposite each other. In Britain, Australia and New Zealand are sometimes called the Antipodes as they are opposite Britain on the globe.
**antipodean** ADJECTIVE

📖 from Greek *antipous* meaning 'with the feet opposite'

**antiquarian**

ADJECTIVE relating to or involving old and rare objects E.G. *antiquarian books.*

**antiquated**

ADJECTIVE very old-fashioned E.G. *an antiquated method of teaching.*

**antique** antiques

*Said* "an-**teek**" NOUN **1** an object from the past that is collected because of its value or beauty. ▶ ADJECTIVE **2** from or concerning the past E.G. *antique furniture.*

a b c d e f g h i j k l m n o p q r s t u v w x y z

**antiquity** antiquities

NOUN **1** Antiquity is the distant past, especially the time of the ancient Egyptians, Greeks, and Romans. **2** Antiquities are interesting works of art and buildings from the distant past.

**anti-Semitism**

NOUN hatred of Jewish people. **anti-Semitic** ADJECTIVE **anti-Semite** NOUN

**antiseptic**

ADJECTIVE Something that is antiseptic kills germs.

**antisocial**

ADJECTIVE **1** An antisocial person is unwilling to meet and be friendly with other people. **2** Antisocial behaviour is annoying or upsetting to other people E.G. Smoking in public is antisocial.

**antithesis** antitheses

Said "an-**tith**-iss-iss" NOUN; FORMAL The antithesis of something is its exact opposite E.G. Work is the antithesis of leisure.

**antivenene** antivenenes

NOUN a substance which reduces the effect of a venom, especially a snake venom.

**antler** antlers

NOUN A male deer's antlers are the branched horns on its head.

**antonym** antonyms

NOUN a word which means the opposite of another word. For example, 'hot' is the antonym of 'cold'.

**anus** anuses

NOUN the hole between the buttocks.

**anvil** anvils

NOUN a heavy iron block on which hot metal is beaten into shape.

**anxiety** anxieties

NOUN nervousness or worry.

**anxious**

ADJECTIVE **1** If you are anxious, you are nervous or worried. **2** If you are anxious to do something or anxious that something should happen, you very much want to do it or want it to happen E.G. She was anxious to have children.

**anxiously** ADVERB

**any**

ADJECTIVE or PRONOUN **1** one, some, or several E.G. Do you have any paperclips I could borrow? **2** even the smallest amount or even one E.G. He was unable to tolerate any dairy products. **3** whatever or whichever, no matter what or which E.G. Any type of cooking oil will do.

**anybody**

PRONOUN any person.

**anyhow**

ADVERB **1** in any case. **2** in a careless way E.G. They were all shoved in anyhow.

**anyone**

PRONOUN any person.

**anything**

PRONOUN any object, event, situation, or action.

**anyway**

ADVERB in any case.

**anywhere**

ADVERB in, at, or to any place.

**Anzac** Anzacs

NOUN **1** In World War I, an Anzac was a soldier with the Australia and New Zealand Army Corps. **2** an Australian or New Zealand soldier.

**aorta**

Said "ay-**or**-ta" NOUN the main artery in the body, which carries blood away from the heart.

## apart

ADVERB or ADJECTIVE **1** When something is apart from something else, there is a space or a distance between them E.G. *The couple separated and lived apart for four years… The gliders landed about seventy metres apart.*
▶ ADVERB **2** If you take something apart, you separate it into pieces.

## apartheid

*Said* "ap-**par**-tide" NOUN In South Africa apartheid was the government policy and laws which kept people of different races apart. It was abolished in 1994.
🏛 an Afrikaans word

## apartment apartments

NOUN a set of rooms for living in, usually on one floor of a building.

## apathetic

ADJECTIVE not interested in anything.
∎ indifferent, uninterested

## apathy

*Said* "**ap**-path-ee" NOUN a state of mind in which you do not care about anything.

## ape apes aping aped

NOUN **1** Apes are animals with a very short tail or no tail. They are closely related to man. Apes include chimpanzees, gorillas, and gibbons.
▶ VERB **2** If you ape someone's speech or behaviour, you imitate it.

## aphid aphids

NOUN a small insect that feeds by sucking the juices from plants.

## aphrodisiac aphrodisiacs

NOUN a food, drink, or drug which makes people want to have sex.

## apiece

ADVERB If people have a particular number of things apiece, they have that number each.

## aplomb

*Said* "uh-**plom**" NOUN If you do something with aplomb, you do it with great confidence.

## apocalypse

*Said* "uh-**pok**-ka-lips" NOUN The Apocalypse is the end of the world.

**apocalyptic** ADJECTIVE
🏛 from Greek *apokaluptein* meaning 'to reveal'; the way the world will end is considered to be revealed in the last book of the Bible, called 'Apocalypse' or 'Revelation'

## apocryphal

ADJECTIVE A story that is apocryphal is generally believed not to have really happened.

## apolitical

*Said* "ay-poll-**it**-i-kl" ADJECTIVE not interested in politics.

## apologetic

ADJECTIVE showing or saying you are sorry.
**apologetically** ADVERB

## apologize apologizes apologizing apologized; also spelt **apologise**

VERB When you apologize to someone, you say you are sorry for something you have said or done.

## apology apologies

NOUN something you say or write to tell someone you are sorry.

## apostle apostles

NOUN The Apostles are the twelve followers who were chosen by Christ.

## apostrophe apostrophes

*Said* "ap-**poss**-troff-ee" NOUN (ENGLISH) a punctuation mark used to show that one or more letters have been missed out of a word, for example "he's" for "he is". Apostrophes are also

a
b
c
d
e
f
g
h
i
j
k
l
m
n
o
p
q
r
s
t
u
v
w
x
y
z

A
B
C
D
E
F
G
H
I
J
K
L
M
N
O
P
Q
R
S
T
U
V
W
X
Y
Z

used with -s at the end of a noun to show that what follows belongs to or relates to the noun, for example *my brother's books*. If the noun already has an -s at the end, for example because it is plural, you just add the apostrophe, eg *my brothers' books*, referring to more than one brother.

---

### What does the Apostrophe do?

The **apostrophe** (') is used to show possession. It is usually added to the end of a word and followed by an *s*:

*E.G. Matthew's book* ■ *children's programmes*

If a plural word already ends in -s, the apostrophe follows that letter:

*E.G. my parents' generation* ■ *seven years' bad luck*

You should not use an apostrophe to form plurals or possessive pronouns:

*E.G. a pound of tomatoes* [not *tomato's*] ■ *I happen to be a fan of hers* [not *her's*]

You can, however, add an apostrophe to form the plural of a number, letter, or symbol:

*E.G. P's and Q's* ■ *7's* ■ *£'s*

The apostrophe is also used to show that a letter or letters have been omitted:

*E.G. rock'n'roll* ■ *Who's next?*

---

**appal** appals appalling appalled
VERB If something appals you, it shocks you because it is very bad.
**appalling**
ADJECTIVE so bad as to be shocking *E.G. She escaped with appalling injuries.*

**apparatus**
NOUN (SCIENCE) The apparatus for a particular task is the equipment used for it.
**apparent**
ADJECTIVE 1 seeming real rather than actually being real *E.G. an apparent hit and run accident.* 2 obvious *E.G. It was apparent that he had lost interest.*
**apparently** ADVERB
■ (sense 1) ostensible, seeming
**apparition** apparitions
NOUN something you think you see but that is not really there *E.G. a ghostly apparition on the windscreen.*
**appeal** appeals appealing appealed
VERB 1 If you appeal for something, you make an urgent request for it *E.G. The police appealed for witnesses to come forward.* 2 If you appeal to someone in authority against a decision, you formally ask them to change it. 3 If something appeals to you, you find it attractive or interesting. ▶ NOUN 4 a formal or serious request *E.G. an appeal for peace.* 5 The appeal of something is the quality it has which people find attractive or interesting *E.G. the rugged appeal of the Rockies.*
**appealing** ADJECTIVE
**appear** appears appearing appeared
VERB 1 When something which you could not see appears, it moves (or you move) so that you can see it. 2 When something new appears, it begins to exist. 3 When an actor or actress appears in a film or show, they take part in it. 4 If something appears to be a certain way, it seems or looks that way *E.G. He appeared to*

*be searching for something.*
■ (sense 1) come into view, emerge, show up

**appearance appearances**
NOUN 1 The appearance of someone in a place is their arrival there, especially when it is unexpected.
2 The appearance of something new is the time when it begins to exist *E.G. the appearance of computer technology.* 3 Someone's or something's appearance is the way they look to other people *E.G. His gaunt appearance had sparked fears for his health.*

**appease appeases appeasing appeased**
VERB If you try to appease someone, you try to calm them down when they are angry, for example by giving them what they want.
**appeasement** NOUN

**appendage appendages**
NOUN a less important part attached to a main part.

**appendicitis**
*Said "app-end-i-*site*-uss"* NOUN a painful illness in which a person's appendix becomes infected.

**appendix appendices or appendixes**
NOUN 1 a small closed tube forming part of your digestive system. 2 An appendix to a book is extra information placed after the end of the main text.
✔ The plural of the part of the body is *appendixes*. The plural of the extra section in a book is *appendices*.

**appetite appetites**
NOUN 1 Your appetite is your desire to eat. 2 If you have an appetite for something, you have a strong desire

for it and enjoyment of it *E.G. She had lost her appetite for air travel.*

**appetizing** or **appetising**
ADJECTIVE Food that is appetizing looks and smells good, and makes you want to eat it.

**applaud applauds applauding applauded**
VERB 1 When a group of people applaud, they clap their hands in approval or praise. 2 When an action or attitude is applauded, people praise it.

**applause**
NOUN (DRAMA) Applause is clapping by a group of people.

**apple apples**
NOUN a round fruit with smooth skin and firm white flesh.

**appliance appliances**
NOUN any machine in your home you use to do a job like cleaning or cooking *E.G. kitchen appliances.*

**applicable**
ADJECTIVE Something that is applicable to a situation is relevant to it *E.G. The rules are applicable to everyone.*

**applicant applicants**
NOUN someone who is applying for something *E.G. We had problems recruiting applicants for the post.*

**application applications**
NOUN 1 a formal request for something, usually in writing. 2 The application of a rule, system, or skill is the use of it in a particular situation.

**apply applies applying applied**
VERB 1 If you apply for something, you formally ask for it, usually by writing a letter. 2 If you apply a rule or skill, you use it in a situation *E.G. He applied his mind to the problem.* 3 If

a
b
c
d
e
f
g
h
i
j
k
l
m
n
o
p
q
r
s
t
u
v
w
x
y
z

something applies to a person or a situation, it is relevant to that person or situation *E.G. The legislation applies only to people living in England and Wales.* **4** If you apply something to a surface, you put it on *E.G. She applied lipstick to her mouth.*

**appoint** appoints appointing appointed

VERB **1** If you appoint someone to a job or position, you formally choose them for it. **2** If you appoint a time or place for something to happen, you decide when or where it will happen.

**appointed** ADJECTIVE

**appointment** appointments

NOUN **1** an arrangement you have with someone to meet them. **2** The appointment of a person to do a particular job is the choosing of that person to do it. **3** a job or a position of responsibility *E.G. He applied for an appointment in Russia.*

■ (sense 1) date, engagement, meeting

**apposite**

*Said "*app-*o*-zit*"* ADJECTIVE well suited for a particular purpose *E.G. He went before Cameron could think of anything apposite to say.*

**appraise** appraises appraising appraised

VERB If you appraise something, you think about it carefully and form an opinion about it.

**appraisal** NOUN

**appreciable**

*Said "*a-*pree*-shuh-bl*"* ADJECTIVE large enough to be noticed *E.G. an appreciable difference.*

**appreciably** ADVERB

**appreciate** appreciates appreciating appreciated

VERB **1** If you appreciate something, you like it because you recognize its good qualities *E.G. He appreciates fine wines.* **2** If you appreciate a situation or problem, you understand it and know what it involves. **3** If you appreciate something someone has done for you, you are grateful to them for it *E.G. I really appreciate you coming to visit me.* **4** If something appreciates over a period of time, its value increases *E.G. The property appreciated by 50% in two years.*

**appreciation** NOUN

■ (sense 1) prize, rate highly, value

**appreciative**

ADJECTIVE **1** understanding and enthusiastic *E.G. They were a very appreciative audience.* **2** thankful and grateful *E.G. I am particularly appreciative of the help.*

**appreciatively** ADVERB

**apprehend** apprehends apprehending apprehended

VERB; FORMAL **1** When the police apprehend someone, they arrest them and take them into custody. **2** If you apprehend something, you understand it fully *E.G. They were unable to apprehend his hidden meaning.*

**apprehensive**

ADJECTIVE afraid something bad may happen *E.G. I was very apprehensive about the birth.*

**apprehensively** ADVERB

**apprehension** NOUN

**apprentice** apprentices

NOUN a person who works for a period of time with a skilled craftsman in order to learn a skill or trade.

**apprenticeship** NOUN

📖 from Old French *aprendre* meaning 'to learn'

A B C D E F G H I J K L M N O P Q R S T U V W X Y Z

**approach** approaches approaching approached

VERB **1** To approach something is to come near or nearer to it. **2** When a future event approaches, it gradually gets nearer E.G. *As winter approached, tents were set up to accommodate refugees.* **3** If you approach someone about something, you ask them about it. **4** If you approach a situation or problem in a particular way, you think about it or deal with it in that way. ▶ NOUN **5** The approach of something is the process of it coming closer E.G. *the approach of spring.* **6** An approach to a situation or problem is a way of thinking about it or dealing with it. **7** a road or path that leads to a place.
**approaching** ADJECTIVE

**appropriate** appropriates appropriating appropriated

ADJECTIVE **1** suitable or acceptable for a particular situation E.G. *He didn't think jeans were appropriate for a vice-president.* ▶ VERB **2** FORMAL If you appropriate something which does not belong to you, you take it without permission.
**appropriately** ADVERB
**appropriation** NOUN

**approval**

NOUN (PSHE) **1** Approval is agreement given to a plan or request E.G. *The plan will require approval from the local authority.* **2** Approval is also admiration E.G. *She looked at James with approval.*
■ (sense 1) agreement, consent, permission

**approve** approves approving approved

VERB (PSHE) **1** If you approve of something or someone, you think

that thing or person is acceptable or good. **2** If someone in a position of authority approves a plan or idea, they formally agree to it.
**approved** ADJECTIVE    **approving** ADJECTIVE
■ (sense 1) commend, favour, like
■ (sense 2) agree to, authorize, pass, permit

**approximate**

ADJECTIVE almost exact E.G. *What was the approximate distance between the cars?*
**approximately** ADVERB (MATHS)
■ close, near

**apricot** apricots

NOUN a small, soft, yellowish-orange fruit.
📷 from Latin *praecox* meaning 'early ripening'

**April**

NOUN the fourth month of the year. April has 30 days.
📷 from Latin *Aprīlis*

**apron** aprons

NOUN a piece of clothing worn over the front of normal clothing to protect it.

**apse** apses

NOUN a domed recess in the east wall of a church.

**apt**

ADJECTIVE **1** suitable or relevant E.G. *a very apt description.* **2** having a particular tendency E.G. *They are apt to jump to the wrong conclusions.*

**aptitude**

NOUN Someone's aptitude for something is their ability to learn it quickly and to do it well E.G. *I have a natural aptitude for painting.*

**aqua-**

PREFIX 'Aqua-' means 'water'.
📷 from Latin *aqua* meaning 'water'

LEarn the principLEs (principle)    **SPELLING NOTE**

**aquarium** aquaria or aquariums
NOUN a glass tank filled with water in which fish are kept.

**Aquarius**
NOUN Aquarius is the eleventh sign of the zodiac, represented by a person carrying water. People born between January 20th and February 18th are born under this sign.

**aquatic**
ADJECTIVE 1 An aquatic animal or plant lives or grows in water. 2 involving water E.G. *aquatic sports.*

**aqueduct** aqueducts
NOUN a long bridge with many arches carrying a water supply over a valley.

**Arab** Arabs
NOUN a member of a group of people who used to live in Arabia but who now live throughout the Middle East and North Africa.

**Arabic**
NOUN a language spoken by many people in the Middle East and North Africa.

**arable**
ADJECTIVE Arable land is used for growing crops.

**arbiter** arbiters
NOUN the person who decides about something.
🔲 judge, referee, adjudicator

**arbitrary**
ADJECTIVE An arbitrary decision or action is one that is not based on a plan or system.
**arbitrarily** ADVERB

**arbitrate** arbitrates arbitrating arbitrated
VERB When someone arbitrates between two people or groups who are in disagreement, they consider the facts and decide who is right.

**arbitration** NOUN  **arbitrator** NOUN

**arc** arcs
NOUN 1 a smoothly curving line. 2 in geometry, a section of the circumference of a circle.
☑ Do not confuse the spellings of *arc* and *ark*.

**arcade** arcades
NOUN a covered passage with shops or market stalls along one or both sides.

**arcane**
ADJECTIVE mysterious and difficult to understand.

**arch** arches arching arched
NOUN 1 a structure that has a curved top supported on either side by a pillar or wall. 2 the curved part of bone at the top of the foot. ▶ VERB 3 When something arches, it forms a curved line or shape. ▶ ADJECTIVE 4 most important E.G. *my arch enemy.*

**arch-**
PREFIX 'Arch-' means 'most important' or 'chief' E.G. *archangel.*
🏛 from Greek *arkhein* meaning 'to rule'

**archaeology** or **archeology**
*Said* "ar-kee-**o**l-loj-ee" NOUN the study of the past by digging up and examining the remains of buildings, tools, and other things.
**archaeological** ADJECTIVE
**archaeologist** NOUN
🏛 from Greek *arkhaios* meaning 'ancient'

**archaic**
*Said* "ar-**kay**-ik" ADJECTIVE very old or old-fashioned.

**archangel** archangels
*Said* "ark-**ain**-jel" NOUN an angel of the highest rank.

**archbishop** archbishops
NOUN a bishop of the highest rank in

a Christian Church.

**archdeacon** archdeacons
NOUN an Anglican clergyman ranking just below a bishop.

**archeology**
another spelling of **archaeology**.

**archer** archers
NOUN someone who shoots with a bow and arrow.

**archery**
NOUN a sport in which people shoot at a target with a bow and arrow.

**archipelago** archipelagos
*Said* "ar-kip-**pel**-lag-oh" NOUN a group of small islands.
📖 from Italian *arcipelago* meaning 'chief sea'; originally referring to the Aegean Sea

**architect** architects
*Said* "**ar**-kit-tekt" NOUN a person who designs buildings.

**architecture**
NOUN the art or practice of designing buildings.
**architectural** ADJECTIVE

**archive** archives
*Said* "**ar**-kive" NOUN Archives are collections of documents and records about the history of a family or some other group of people.

**arctic**
NOUN 1 The Arctic is the region north of the Arctic Circle. ► ADJECTIVE 2 Arctic means very cold indeed *E.G. arctic conditions.*
📖 from Greek *arktos* meaning 'bear'; originally it referred to the northern constellation of the Great Bear

**Arctic Circle**
NOUN The Arctic Circle is an imaginary circle around the northern part of the world.

**ardent**
ADJECTIVE full of enthusiasm and passion.
**ardently** ADVERB

**ardour**
NOUN a strong and passionate feeling of love or enthusiasm.

**arduous**
*Said* "**ard**-yoo-uss" ADJECTIVE tiring and needing a lot of effort *E.G. the arduous task of rebuilding the country.*

**are**
the plural form of the present tense of **be**.

**area** areas
NOUN 1 a particular part of a place, country, or the world *E.G. a built-up area of the city.* 2 The area of a piece of ground or a surface is the amount of space it covers, measured in square metres or square feet.
📑 (sense 1) district, region, zone

**arena** arenas
NOUN 1 a place where sports and other public events take place. 2 A particular arena is the centre of attention or activity in a particular situation *E.G. the political arena.*
📖 from Latin *harena* meaning 'sand', hence the sandy centre of an amphitheatre where gladiators fought

**Argentinian** Argentinians
*Said* "ar-jen-**tin**-ee-an" ADJECTIVE 1 belonging or relating to Argentina. ► NOUN 2 someone who comes from Argentina.

**arguable**
ADJECTIVE An arguable idea or point is not necessarily true or correct and should be questioned.
**arguably** ADVERB

**argue** argues arguing argued
VERB 1 If you argue with someone

a
b
c
d
e
f
g
h
i
j
k
l
m
n
o
p
q
r
s
t
u
v
w
x
y
z

about something, you disagree with them about it, sometimes in an angry way. **2** If you argue that something is the case, you give reasons which you think it is so *E.G. She argued that her client had been wrongly accused.*

**argument** arguments

NOUN **1** a disagreement between two people which causes a quarrel. **2** a point or a set of reasons you use to try to convince people about something.

**argumentative**

ADJECTIVE An argumentative person is always disagreeing with other people.

**aria** arias

*Said* "**ah-ree-a**" NOUN a song sung by one of the leading singers in an opera.

📖 an Italian word meaning 'tune'

**arid**

ADJECTIVE Arid land is very dry because it has very little rain.

**Aries**

*Said* "**air-reez**" NOUN Aries is the first sign of the zodiac, represented by a ram. People born between March 21st and April 19th are born under this sign.

**arise** arises arising arose arisen

VERB **1** When something such as an opportunity or problem arises, it begins to exist. **2** *FORMAL* To arise also means to stand up from a sitting, kneeling, or lying position.

**aristocracy** aristocracies

NOUN a class of people who have a high social rank and special titles.

**aristocrat** aristocrats

NOUN someone whose family has a high social rank, and who has a title.

**aristocratic** ADJECTIVE

**arithmetic**

NOUN the part of mathematics which is to do with the addition, subtraction, multiplication, and division of numbers.

**arithmetical** ADJECTIVE

**arithmetically** ADVERB

📖 from Greek *arithmos* meaning 'number'

**ark**

NOUN In the Bible, the ark was the boat built by Noah for his family and the animals during the Flood.

✔ Do not confuse the spellings of *arc* and *ark*.

**arm** arms arming armed

NOUN **1** Your arms are the part of your body between your shoulder and your wrist. **2** The arms of a chair are the parts on which you rest your arms. **3** An arm of an organization is a section of it *E.G. the political arm of the armed forces.* ▶ PLURAL NOUN **4** Arms are weapons used in a war. ▶ VERB **5** To arm someone is to provide them with weapons.

**armada** armadas

*Said* "**ar-mah-da**" NOUN a large fleet of warships.

**armadillo** armadillos

NOUN a mammal from South America which is covered with strong bony plates like armour.

📖 a Spanish word meaning 'little armed man'

**Armageddon**

NOUN In Christianity, Armageddon is the final battle between good and evil at the end of the world.

📖 from Hebrew *har megiddon*, the mountain district of Megiddo, the site of many battles

A B C D E F G H I J K L M N O P Q R S T U V W X Y Z

**armament** armaments
NOUN Armaments are the weapons and military equipment that belong to a country.

**armchair** armchairs
NOUN a comfortable chair with a support on each side for your arms.

**armed**
ADJECTIVE A person who is armed is carrying a weapon or weapons.

**armistice** armistices
*Said* "ar-miss-tiss" NOUN an agreement in a war to stop fighting in order to discuss peace.

**armour**
NOUN In the past, armour was metal clothing worn for protection in battle.

**armoured**
ADJECTIVE covered with thick steel for protection from gunfire and other missiles *E.G. an armoured car.*

**armoury** armouries
NOUN a place where weapons are stored.

**armpit** armpits
NOUN the area under your arm where your arm joins your shoulder.

**army** armies
NOUN a large group of soldiers organized into divisions for fighting on land.

**aroma** aromas
NOUN a strong, pleasant smell.

**aromatic** ADJECTIVE
🔲 a Greek word meaning 'spice'

**around**
PREPOSITION **1** placed at various points in a place or area *E.G. There are many seats around the building.* **2** from place to place inside an area *E.G. We walked around the showroom.* **3** at approximately the time or place

mentioned *E.G. The attacks began around noon.* ▶ ADVERB **4** here and there *E.G. His papers were scattered around.*

**arouse** arouses arousing aroused
VERB If something arouses a feeling in you, it causes you to begin to have this feeling *E.G. His death still arouses very painful feelings.*

**arousal** NOUN

**arrange** arranges arranging arranged
VERB **1** If you arrange to do something, you make plans for it. **2** If you arrange something for someone, you make it possible for them to have it or do it *E.G. The bank has arranged a loan for her.* **3** If you arrange objects, you set them out in a particular position *E.G. He started to arrange the books in piles.*

**arrangement** NOUN

**array** arrays
NOUN An array of different things is a large number of them displayed together.

**arrears**
PLURAL NOUN **1** Arrears are amounts of money you owe *E.G. mortgage arrears.* ▶ PHRASE **2** If you are paid **in arrears**, you are paid at the end of the period for which the payment is due.

**arrest** arrests arresting arrested
VERB **1** If the police arrest someone, they take them into custody to decide whether to charge them with an offence. ▶ NOUN **2** An arrest is the act of taking a person into custody.

**arrival** arrivals
NOUN **1** the act or time of arriving *E.G. The arrival of the train was delayed.*

**2** something or someone that has arrived E.G. *The tourist authority reported record arrivals over Christmas.*

**arrive** arrives arriving arrived

VERB **1** When you arrive at a place, you reach it at the end of your journey. **2** When a letter or a piece of news arrives, it is brought to you E.G. *A letter arrived at her lawyer's office.* **3** When you arrive at an idea or decision you reach it. **4** When a moment, event, or new thing arrives, it begins to happen E.G. *The Easter holidays arrived.*

**arrogant**

ADJECTIVE Someone who is arrogant behaves as if they are better than other people.

**arrogantly** ADVERB   **arrogance** NOUN

**arrow** arrows

NOUN a long, thin weapon with a sharp point at one end, shot from a bow.

**arsenal** arsenals

NOUN a place where weapons and ammunition are stored or produced. 📖 from Italian *arsenale* meaning 'dockyard', originally in Venice

**arsenic**

NOUN a very strong poison which can kill people.

**arson**

NOUN the crime of deliberately setting fire to something, especially a building.

**art** arts

NOUN **1** Art is the creation of objects such as paintings and sculptures, which are thought to be beautiful or which express a particular idea; also used to refer to the objects themselves. **2** An activity is called an art when it requires special skill or

ability E.G. *the art of diplomacy.*
▸ PLURAL NOUN **3** The arts are literature, music, painting, and sculpture, considered together.

**artefact** artefacts

*Said* "**ar**-tif-fact" NOUN any object made by people.

**artery** arteries

NOUN **1** Your arteries are the tubes that carry blood from your heart to the rest of your body. **2** a main road or major section of any system of communication or transport.

**artful**

ADJECTIVE clever and skilful, often in a cunning way.

**artfully** ADVERB

**arthritis**

NOUN a condition in which the joints in someone's body become swollen and painful.

**arthritic** ADJECTIVE

**artichoke** artichokes

NOUN **1** the round green partly edible flower head of a thistle-like plant; the flower head is made up of clusters of leaves that have a soft fleshy part that is eaten as a vegetable. **2** A Jerusalem artichoke is a small yellowish-white vegetable that grows underground and looks like a potato. 📖 from Arabic *al-kharshuf*

**article** articles

NOUN **1** (LIBRARY) a piece of writing in a newspaper or magazine. **2** a particular item E.G. *an article of clothing.* **3** In English grammar, 'a' and 'the' are sometimes called articles: 'a' (or 'an') is the indefinite article; 'the' is the definite article.

**articulate** articulates articulating articulated

ADJECTIVE **1** If you are articulate, you are

able to express yourself well in words. ► VERB **2** When you articulate your ideas or feelings, you express in words what you think or feel *E.G. She could not articulate her grief.* **3** When you articulate a sound or word, you speak it clearly.

**articulation** NOUN

**artificial**

ADJECTIVE **1** created by people rather than occurring naturally *E.G. artificial colouring.* **2** pretending to have attitudes and feelings which other people realize are not real *E.G. an artificial smile.*

**artificially** ADVERB

**artillery**

NOUN **1** Artillery consists of large, powerful guns such as cannons. **2** The artillery is the branch of an army which uses large, powerful guns.

**artist** artists

NOUN **1** a person who draws or paints or produces other works of art. **2** a person who is very skilled at a particular activity.

**artiste** artistes

*Said "ar-teest"* NOUN a professional entertainer, for example a singer or a dancer.

**artistic**

ADJECTIVE **1** able to create good paintings, sculpture, or other works of art. **2** concerning or involving art or artists.

**artistically** ADVERB

**artistry**

NOUN Artistry is the creative skill of an artist, writer, actor, or musician *E.G. a supreme demonstration of his artistry as a cellist.*

**arty** artier artiest

ADJECTIVE; *INFORMAL* interested in

painting, sculpture, and other works of art.

**as**

CONJUNCTION **1** at the same time that *E.G. She waved at fans as she arrived for the concert.* **2** in the way that *E.G. They had talked as only the best of friends can.* **3** because *E.G. As I won't be back tonight, don't bother to cook a meal.* **4** You use the structure as ... as when you are comparing things that are similar *E.G. It was as big as four football pitches.* ► PREPOSITION **5** You use 'as' when you are saying what role someone or something has *E.G. She worked as a waitress.* **6** You use **as if** or **as though** when you are giving a possible explanation for something *E.G. He looked at me as if I were mad.*

**asbestos**

NOUN a grey heat-resistant material used in the past to make fireproof articles.

**ASBO**

NOUN an abbreviation for 'antisocial behaviour order': an order from a judge preventing people who have been persistently annoying or upsetting other people from continuing to do so.

**ascend** ascends ascending ascended

*Said "ass-end"* VERB; *FORMAL* To ascend is to move or lead upwards *E.G. We finally ascended to the brow of a steep hill.*

**ascendancy**

NOUN; *FORMAL* If one group has ascendancy over another, it has more power or influence than the other.

a b c d e f g h i j k l m n o p q r s t u v w x y z

A
B
C
D
E
F
G
H
I
J
K
L
M
N
O
P
Q
R
S
T
U
V
W
X
Y
Z

**ascendant**

ADJECTIVE **1** rising or moving upwards.
▶ PHRASE **2** Someone or something **in the ascendant** is increasing in power or popularity.

**ascent** ascents

NOUN an upward journey, for example up a mountain.

**ascertain** ascertains ascertaining ascertained

*Said* "ass-er-**tain**" VERB; *FORMAL* If you ascertain that something is the case, you find out it is the case *E.G. He had ascertained that she had given up smoking.*

**ascribe** ascribes ascribing ascribed

VERB **1** If you ascribe an event or state of affairs to a particular cause, you think that it is the cause of it *E.G. His stomach pains were ascribed to his intake of pork.* **2** If you ascribe a quality to someone, you think they have it.

**ash** ashes

NOUN **1** the grey or black powdery remains of anything that has been burnt. **2** a tree with grey bark and hard tough wood used for timber.

**ashamed**

ADJECTIVE **1** feeling embarrassed or guilty. **2** If you are ashamed of someone, you feel embarrassed to be connected with them.

**ashen**

ADJECTIVE grey or pale *E.G. Her face was ashen with fatigue.*

**ashore**

ADVERB on land or onto the land.

**ashtray** ashtrays

NOUN a small dish for ash from cigarettes and cigars.

**Asia**

NOUN Asia is the largest continent. It has Europe on its western side, with the Arctic to the north, the Pacific to the east, and the Indian Ocean to the south. Asia includes several island groups, including Japan, Indonesia, and the Philippines.

**Asian** Asians

ADJECTIVE **1** belonging or relating to Asia. ▶ NOUN **2** someone who comes from India, Pakistan, Bangladesh, or from some other part of Asia.

**aside** asides

ADVERB **1** If you move something aside, you move it to one side. ▶ NOUN **2** a comment made away from the main conversation or dialogue that all those talking are not meant to hear.

**ask** asks asking asked

VERB **1** If you ask someone a question, you put a question to them for them to answer. **2** If you ask someone to do something, you tell them you want them to do it. **3** If you ask for something, you say you would like to have it. **4** If you ask someone's permission or forgiveness, you try to obtain it. **5** If you ask someone somewhere, you invite them there *E.G. Not everybody had been asked to the wedding.*

**askew**

ADJECTIVE not straight.

**asleep**

ADJECTIVE sleeping.

**AS level** AS levels

NOUN an exam taken by students in many British schools and colleges, more advanced than GCSE but less advanced than A level.

**asparagus**

NOUN a vegetable that has long

shoots which are cooked and eaten.

**aspect** aspects
NOUN 1 An aspect of something is one of its features E.G. *Exam results illustrate only one aspect of a school's success.* 2 The aspect of a building is the direction it faces E.G. *The southern aspect of the cottage faces over fields.*

**asphalt**
NOUN a black substance used to make road surfaces and playgrounds.

**aspiration** aspirations
NOUN Someone's aspirations are their desires and ambitions.

**aspire** aspires aspiring aspired
VERB If you aspire to something, you have an ambition to achieve it E.G. *He aspired to work in music journalism.*
**aspiring** ADJECTIVE

**aspirin** aspirins
NOUN 1 a white drug used to relieve pain, fever, and colds. 2 a tablet of this drug.

**ass** asses
NOUN a donkey.

**assailant** assailants
NOUN someone who attacks another person.

**assassin** assassins
NOUN someone who has murdered a political or religious leader.
from Arabic *hashshashin* meaning 'people who eat hashish'; the name comes from a medieval Muslim sect who ate hashish and went about murdering Crusaders

**assassinate** assassinates assassinating assassinated
VERB To assassinate a political or religious leader is to murder him or her.
**assassination** NOUN

**assault** assaults assaulting assaulted
NOUN 1 a violent attack on someone.
▶ VERB 2 To assault someone is to attack them violently.

**assegai** assegais
*Said "ass-i-guy"; also spelt* **assagai**
NOUN In South African English, a sharp, light spear.

**assemble** assembles assembling assembled
VERB 1 To assemble is to gather together. 2 If you assemble something, you fit the parts of it together.

**assembly** assemblies
NOUN 1 a group of people who have gathered together for a meeting. 2 The assembly of an object is the fitting together of its parts E.G. *DIY assembly of units.*

**assent** assents assenting assented
*Said "as-sent"* NOUN 1 If you give your assent to something, you agree to it.
▶ VERB 2 If you assent to something, you agree to it.

**assert** asserts asserting asserted
VERB 1 If you assert a fact or belief, you state it firmly and forcefully. 2 If you assert yourself, you speak and behave in a confident and direct way, so that people pay attention to you.

**assertive**
ADJECTIVE If you are assertive, you speak and behave in a confident and direct way, so that people pay attention to you.
**assertively** ADVERB **assertiveness** NOUN

**assess** assesses assessing assessed
VERB (EXAM TERM) If you assess something, you consider it carefully

and make a judgment about it.

**assessment** NOUN
◼ appraise, judge, size up

**assessor** assessors
NOUN someone whose job is to assess the value of something.

**asset** assets
NOUN **1** a person or thing considered useful E.G. *He will be a great asset to the club.* ▶ PLURAL NOUN **2** The assets of a person or company are all the things they own that could be sold to raise money.

**assign** assigns assigning assigned
VERB **1** To assign something to someone is to give it to them officially or to make them responsible for it. **2** If someone is assigned to do something, they are officially told to do it.
◼ (sense 1) appoint, choose, select
◼ (sense 2) allocate, allot, give

**assignation** assignations
*Said* "ass-ig-**nay**-shn" NOUN; *LITERARY* a secret meeting with someone, especially a lover.

**assignment** assignments
NOUN a job someone is given to do.

**assimilate** assimilates assimilating assimilated
VERB **1** If you assimilate ideas or experiences, you learn and understand them. **2** When people are assimilated into a group, they become part of it.
**assimilation** NOUN

**assist** assists assisting assisted
VERB To assist someone is to help them do something.
**assistance** NOUN

**assistant** assistants
NOUN someone whose job is to help another person in their work.

**associate** associates associating associated
VERB **1** If you associate one thing with another, you connect the two things in your mind. **2** If you associate with a group of people, you spend a lot of time with them. ▶ NOUN **3** Your associates are the people you work with or spend a lot of time with.
◼ (sense 1) connect, link, relate
◼ (sense 2) consort, mix, socialize

**association** associations
NOUN **1** an organization for people who have similar interests, jobs, or aims. **2** Your association with a person or group is the connection or involvement you have with them. **3** An association between two things is a link you make in your mind between them E.G. *The place contained associations for her.*

**assonance**
NOUN the use of similar vowel or consonant sounds in words near to each other or in the same word, for example 'a long storm'.

**assorted**
ADJECTIVE Assorted things are different in size and colour E.G. *assorted swimsuits.*

**assortment** assortments
NOUN a group of similar things that are different sizes and colours E.G. *an amazing assortment of old toys.*

**assume** assumes assuming assumed
VERB **1** If you assume that something is true, you accept it is true even though you have not thought about it E.G. *I assumed that he would turn up.* **2** To assume responsibility for something is to put yourself in charge of it.

---

**SPELLING NOTE**  King IAn went to ParlIAment in a carrIAge for his marrIAge (-ia-)

■ (sense 1) believe, presume, suppose, take for granted
■ (sense 2) accept, shoulder, take on

**assumption** assumptions
NOUN **1** a belief that something is true, without thinking about it.
**2** Assumption of power or responsibility is the taking of it.

**assurance** assurances
NOUN **1** something said which is intended to make people less worried E.G. *She was emphatic in her assurances that she wanted to stay.*
**2** Assurance is a feeling of confidence E.G. *He handled the car with ease and assurance.* **3** Life assurance is a type of insurance that pays money to your dependants when you die.

**assure** assures assuring assured
VERB If you assure someone that something is true, you tell them it is true.

**asterisk** asterisks
NOUN the symbol (*) used in printing and writing.
🏛 from Greek *asterikos* meaning 'small star'

**astern**
ADVERB or ADJECTIVE; *NAUTICAL* backwards or at the back.

**asteroid** asteroids
NOUN one of the large number of very small planets that move around the sun between the orbits of Jupiter and Mars.

**asthma**
*Said* "**ass**-ma" NOUN a disease of the chest which causes wheezing and difficulty in breathing.
**asthmatic** ADJECTIVE

**astonish** astonishes astonishing astonished
VERB If something astonishes you, it surprises you very much.
**astonished** ADJECTIVE  **astonishing** ADJECTIVE  **astonishingly** ADVERB
**astonishment** NOUN

**astound** astounds astounding astounded
VERB If something astounds you, it shocks and amazes you.
**astounded** ADJECTIVE  **astounding** ADJECTIVE

**astray**
PHRASE **1** To **lead someone astray** is to influence them to do something wrong. **2** If something **goes astray**, it gets lost E.G. *The money had gone astray.*

**astride**
PREPOSITION with one leg on either side of something E.G. *He is pictured astride his new motorbike.*

**astringent** astringents
*Said* "ass-**trin**-jent" NOUN a liquid that makes skin less greasy and stops bleeding.

**astro-**
PREFIX 'Astro-' means involving the stars and planets. For example, *astrology* is predicting the future from the positions and movements of the stars and planets, and *astronomy* is the scientific study of the stars and planets.
🏛 from Greek *astron* meaning a 'star'

**astrology**
NOUN the study of the sun, moon, and stars in order to predict the future.
**astrological** ADJECTIVE  **astrologer** NOUN

**astronaut** astronauts
NOUN a person who operates a

a
b
c
d
e
f
g
h
i
j
k
l
m
n
o
p
q
r
s
t
u
v
w
x
y
z

spacecraft.

from Greek *astron* meaning 'star' and *nautēs* meaning 'sailor'

**astronomical**

ADJECTIVE 1 involved with or relating to astronomy. 2 extremely large in amount *E.G. astronomical legal costs*.
**astronomically** ADVERB

**astronomy**

NOUN the scientific study of stars and planets.
**astronomer** NOUN

**astute**

ADJECTIVE clever and quick at understanding situations and behaviour *E.G. an astute diplomat*.

**asunder**

ADVERB; *LITERARY* If something is torn asunder, it is violently torn apart.

**asylum** asylums

*Said* "ass-**eye**-lum" NOUN 1 *OLD-FASHIONED* a hospital for mental patients. 2 Political asylum is protection given by a government to someone who has fled from their own country for political reasons.

**asymmetrical** or **asymmetric**

*Said* "ay-sim-**met**-ri-kl" ADJECTIVE unbalanced or with one half not exactly the same as the other half.
**asymmetry** NOUN

**at**

PREPOSITION 1 used to say where someone or something is *E.G. Bert met us at the airport*. 2 used to mention the direction something is going in *E.G. He threw his plate at the wall*. 3 used to say when something happens *E.G. The game starts at 3 o'clock*. 4 used to mention the rate or price of something *E.G. The shares were priced at fifty pence*.

**atheist** atheists

*Said* "**ayth**-ee-ist" NOUN someone who believes there is no God.
**atheistic** ADJECTIVE **atheism** NOUN

**athlete** athletes

NOUN ( PE ) someone who is good at sport and takes part in sporting events.

**athletic**

ADJECTIVE ( PE ) 1 strong, healthy, and good at sports. 2 involving athletes or athletics *E.G. I lost two years of my athletic career because of injury*.

**athletics**

NOUN Sporting events such as running, jumping, and throwing are called athletics.

**Atlantic**

NOUN The Atlantic is the ocean separating North and South America from Europe and Africa.

from the *Atlas* mountains in North Africa; the Atlantic lies to the west of these mountains

**atlas** atlases

NOUN ( GEOGRAPHY ) a book of maps.

from the giant *Atlas* in Greek mythology, who supported the sky on his shoulders

**atmosphere** atmospheres

NOUN 1 the air and other gases that surround a planet; also the air in a particular place *E.G. a musty atmosphere*. 2 the general mood of a place *E.G. a relaxed atmosphere*. 3 ( ENGLISH ) the mood created by the writer of a novel or play.
**atmospheric** ADJECTIVE

**atom** atoms

NOUN the smallest part of an element that can take part in a chemical reaction.

**atomic**

ADJECTIVE relating to atoms or to the power released by splitting atoms E.G. *atomic energy*.

**atomic bomb** atomic bombs

NOUN an extremely powerful bomb which explodes because of the energy that comes from splitting atoms.

**atone** atones atoning atoned

VERB; FORMAL If you atone for something wrong you have done, you say you are sorry and try to make up for it.

**atrocious**

ADJECTIVE extremely bad.

**atrocity** atrocities

NOUN an extremely cruel and shocking act.

**attach** attaches attaching attached

VERB If you attach something to something else, you join or fasten the two things together.

**attaché** attachés

Said "at-**tash**-ay" NOUN a member of staff in an embassy E.G. *the Russian Cultural Attaché.*

**attached**

ADJECTIVE If you are attached to someone, you are very fond of them.

**attachment** attachments

NOUN 1 Attachment to someone is a feeling of love and affection for them. 2 Attachment to a cause or ideal is a strong belief in it and support for it. 3 a piece of equipment attached to a tool or machine to do a particular job. 4 an extra document attached to or included with another document. 5 a file that is attached to an e-mail.

**attack** attacks attacking attacked

VERB 1 To attack someone is to use violence against them so as to hurt or kill them. 2 If you attack someone or their ideas, you criticize them strongly E.G. *He attacked the government's economic policies.* 3 If a disease or chemical attacks something, it damages or destroys it E.G. *fungal diseases that attack crops.* 4 In a game such as football or hockey, to attack is to get the ball into a position from which a goal can be scored. ▶ NOUN 5 An attack is violent physical action against someone. 6 An attack on someone or on their ideas is strong criticism of them. 7 An attack of an illness is a short time in which you suffer badly with it.

**attacker** NOUN

▤ (sense 1) assault, set upon
▤ (sense 2) censure, criticize
▤ (sense 5) assault, onslaught

**attain** attains attaining attained

VERB; FORMAL If you attain something, you manage to achieve it E.G. *He eventually attained the rank of major.*
**attainable** ADJECTIVE **attainment** NOUN

**attempt** attempts attempting attempted

VERB 1 If you attempt to do something, you try to do it or achieve it, but may not succeed E.G. *They attempted to escape.* ▶ NOUN 2 an act of trying to do something E.G. *He made no attempt to go for the ball.*

**attend** attends attending attended

VERB 1 If you attend an event, you are present at it. 2 To attend school, church, or hospital is to go there regularly. 3 If you attend to something, you deal with it E.G. *We*

a b c d e f g h i j k l m n o p q r s t u v w x y z

*have business to attend to first.*
**attendance** NOUN

**attendant** attendants
NOUN someone whose job is to serve people in a place such as a garage or cloakroom.

**attention**
NOUN Attention is the thought or care you give to something *E.G. The woman needed medical attention.*

**attentive**
ADJECTIVE paying close attention to something *E.G. an attentive audience.*
**attentively** ADVERB **attentiveness** NOUN

**attest** attests attesting attested
VERB; *FORMAL* To attest something is to show or declare it is true.
**attestation** NOUN

**attic** attics
NOUN a room at the top of a house immediately below the roof.

**attire**
NOUN; *FORMAL* Attire is clothing *E.G. We will be wearing traditional wedding attire.*

**attitude** attitudes
NOUN Your attitude to someone or something is the way you think about them and behave towards them.

**attorney** attorneys
*Said "at-**turn**-ee"* NOUN; *AMERICAN* An attorney is the same as a lawyer.

**attract** attracts attracting attracted
VERB 1 If something attracts people, it interests them and makes them want to go to it *E.G. The trials have attracted many leading riders.* 2 If someone attracts you, you like and admire them *E.G. He was attracted to her outgoing personality.* 3 If

something attracts support or publicity, it gets it.

**attraction** attractions
NOUN 1 Attraction is a feeling of liking someone or something very much. 2 something people visit for interest or pleasure *E.G. The temple is a major tourist attraction.* 3 a quality that attracts someone or something *E.G. the attraction of moving to seaside resorts.*

**attractive**
ADJECTIVE 1 interesting and possibly advantageous *E.G. an attractive proposition.* 2 pleasant to look at or be with *E.G. an attractive woman… an attractive personality.*
**attractively** ADVERB **attractiveness** NOUN
≡ (sense 1) appealing, tempting
≡ (sense 2) charming, lovely, pleasant

**attribute** attributes attributing attributed
VERB 1 If you attribute something to a person or thing, you believe it was caused or created by that person or thing *E.G. Water pollution was attributed to the use of fertilizers… a painting attributed to Raphael.* ▶ NOUN 2 a quality or feature someone or something has.
**attribution** NOUN **attributable** ADJECTIVE

**attrition**
NOUN Attrition is the constant wearing down of an enemy.

**attuned**
ADJECTIVE accustomed or well adjusted to something *E.G. His eyes quickly became attuned to the dark.*

**aubergine** aubergines
*Said "**oh**-ber-jeen"* NOUN a dark purple,

pear-shaped fruit that is eaten as a vegetable. It is also called an **eggplant**.

📖 from Arabic *al-badindjan* meaning 'aubergine'

**auburn**

ADJECTIVE Auburn hair is reddish brown.

**auction** auctions auctioning auctioned

NOUN **1** a public sale in which goods are sold to the person who offers the highest price. ▶ VERB **2** To auction something is to sell it in an auction.

**auctioneer** auctioneers

NOUN the person in charge of an auction.

**audacious**

ADJECTIVE very daring *E.G. an audacious escape from jail.*

**audaciously** ADVERB **audacity** NOUN

**audi-**

PREFIX 'Audi-' means involving hearing or sound *E.G. audible… auditorium.*

📖 from Latin *audire* meaning 'to hear'

**audible**

ADJECTIVE loud enough to be heard *E.G. She spoke in a barely audible whisper.*

**audibly** ADVERB **audibility** NOUN

**audience** audiences

NOUN **1** the group of people who are watching or listening to a performance. **2** a private or formal meeting with an important person *E.G. an audience with the Queen.*

**audio**

ADJECTIVE used in recording and reproducing sound *E.G. audio equipment.*

**audit** audits auditing audited

VERB **1** To audit a set of financial accounts is to examine them

officially to check they are correct.

▶ NOUN **2** an official examination of an organization's accounts.

**auditor** NOUN

**audition** auditions

NOUN a short performance given by an actor or musician, so that a director can decide whether they are suitable for a part in a play or film or for a place in an orchestra.

**auditorium** auditoriums or auditoria

NOUN the part of a theatre where the audience sits.

**augment** augments augmenting augmented

VERB; FORMAL To augment something is to add something to it.

**August**

NOUN the eighth month of the year. August has 31 days.

📖 from the name of the Roman emperor *Augustus*

**aunt** aunts

NOUN Your aunt is the sister of your mother or father, or the wife of your uncle.

**au pair** au pairs

*Said* "oh **pair**" NOUN a young foreign girl who lives with a family to help with the children and housework and sometimes to learn the language.

📖 a French expression meaning 'on equal terms'

**aura** auras

NOUN an atmosphere that surrounds a person or thing *E.G. She has a great aura of calmness.*

**aural**

*Rhymes with* "**floral**" ADJECTIVE relating to or done through the sense of hearing *E.G. an aural comprehension test.*

a b c d e f g h i j k l m n o p q r s t u v w x y z

**auspices**

*Said* "aw-spiss-eez" PLURAL NOUN; FORMAL
If you do something under the
auspices of a person or organization,
you do it with their support *E.G.*
*military intervention under the*
*auspices of the United Nations.*

**auspicious**

ADJECTIVE; FORMAL favourable and
seeming to promise success *E.G. It*
*was an auspicious start to the month.*

**austere**

ADJECTIVE plain and simple, and
without luxury *E.G. an austere grey*
*office block.*
**austerity** NOUN

**Australasia**

*Said* "ost-ral-**lay**-sha" NOUN
Australasia consists of Australia, New
Zealand, and neighbouring islands in
the Pacific.
**Australasian** ADJECTIVE

**Australia**

NOUN Australia is the smallest
continent and the largest island in
the world, situated between the
Indian Ocean and the Pacific.

**Australian** Australians
ADJECTIVE **1** belonging or relating to
Australia. ▶ NOUN **2** someone who
comes from Australia.

**Austrian** Austrians
ADJECTIVE **1** belonging or relating to
Austria. ▶ NOUN **2** someone who
comes from Austria.

**authentic**

ADJECTIVE real and genuine.
**authenticity** NOUN

**author** authors

NOUN (ENGLISH) The author of a book is
the person who wrote it.
☑ Use *author* to talk about both
men and women writers, as

*authoress* is now felt to be insulting.

**authoritarian**

ADJECTIVE believing in strict obedience
*E.G. thirty years of authoritarian*
*government.*
**authoritarianism** NOUN

**authoritative**

ADJECTIVE **1** having authority *E.G. his*
*deep, authoritative voice.* **2** accepted
as being reliable and accurate *E.G. an*
*authoritative biography of the*
*President.*
**authoritatively** ADVERB

**authority** authorities

NOUN **1** Authority is the power to
control people *E.G. the authority of the*
*state.* **2** (GEOGRAPHY) In Britain, an
authority is a local government
department *E.G. local health*
*authorities.* **3** Someone who is an
authority on something knows a lot
about it *E.G. the world's leading*
*authority on fashion.* ▶ PLURAL NOUN
**4** The authorities are the people who
have the power to make decisions.

**authorize** authorizes authorizing
authorized; also spelt **authorise**
VERB To authorize something is to
give official permission for it to
happen.
**authorization** NOUN

**auto-**

PREFIX 'Auto-' means 'self'. For example,
an automatic machine works by
itself without needing to be
operated by hand.
🔒 from Greek *autos* meaning 'self'

**autobiography** autobiographies

NOUN Someone's autobiography is an
account of their life which they have
written themselves.
**autobiographical** ADJECTIVE

**autograph** autographs
NOUN the signature of a famous person.

**automated**
ADJECTIVE If a factory or way of making things is automated, it works using machinery rather than people.
**automation** NOUN

**automatic**
ADJECTIVE 1 An automatic machine is programmed to perform tasks without needing a person to operate it E.G. *The plane was flying on automatic pilot.* 2 Automatic actions or reactions take place without involving conscious thought. 3 A process or punishment that is automatic always happens as a direct result of something E.G. *The penalty for murder is an automatic life sentence.*
**automatically** ADVERB

**automobile** automobiles
NOUN; *AMERICAN or FORMAL* a car.

**autonomous**
*Said* "aw-**ton**-nom-uss" ADJECTIVE An autonomous country governs itself rather than being controlled by anyone else.
**autonomy** NOUN

**autopsy** autopsies
NOUN a medical examination of a dead body to discover the cause of death.

**autumn** autumns
NOUN the season between summer and winter.
**autumnal** ADJECTIVE

**auxiliary** auxiliaries
NOUN 1 a person employed to help other members of staff E.G. *nursing auxiliaries.* ▶ ADJECTIVE 2 Auxiliary equipment is used when necessary in addition to the main equipment E.G. *Auxiliary fuel tanks were stored in the bomb bay.*

**auxiliary verb** auxiliary verbs
NOUN In grammar, an auxiliary verb is a verb which forms tenses of other verbs or questions. For example in 'He has gone', 'has' is the auxiliary verb and in 'Do you understand?', 'do' is the auxiliary verb.

**avail**
PHRASE If something you do is **of no avail** or **to no avail**, it is not successful or helpful.

**available**
ADJECTIVE 1 Something that is available can be obtained E.G. *Artichokes are available in supermarkets.* 2 Someone who is available is ready for work or free for people to talk to E.G. *She will no longer be available at weekends.*
**availability** NOUN
▪ (sense 2) accessible

**avalanche** avalanches
*Said* "**av**-a-lahnsh" NOUN a huge mass of snow and ice that falls down a mountain side.

**avant-garde**
*Said* "av-vong-**gard**" ADJECTIVE extremely modern or experimental, especially in art, literature, or music.

**avarice**
NOUN; *FORMAL* greed for money and possessions.
**avaricious** ADJECTIVE

**avenge** avenges avenging avenged
VERB If you avenge something harmful someone has done to you or your family, you punish or harm the other person in return E.G. *He was prepared to avenge the death of his friend.*
**avenger** NOUN

a b c d e f g h i j k l m n o p q r s t u v w x y z

**avenue** avenues
NOUN a street, especially one with trees along it.

**average** averages averaging averaged
NOUN (MATHS) 1 a result obtained by adding several amounts together and then dividing the total by the number of different amounts *E.G. Six pupils were examined in a total of 39 subjects, an average of 6.5 subjects per pupil.* ▶ ADJECTIVE 2 Average means standard or normal *E.G. the average American teenager.* ▶ VERB 3 To average a number is to produce that number as an average over a period of time *E.G. Monthly sales averaged more than 110,000.* ▶ PHRASE 4 You say **on average** when mentioning what usually happens in a situation *E.G. Men are, on average, taller than women.*
■ (sense 2) normal, ordinary, typical, usual

**averse**
ADJECTIVE unwilling to do something *E.G. He was averse to taking painkillers.*

**aversion** aversions
NOUN If you have an aversion to someone or something, you dislike them very much.

**avert** averts averting averted
VERB 1 If you avert an unpleasant event, you prevent it from happening. 2 If you avert your eyes from something, you turn your eyes away from it.

**aviary** aviaries
NOUN a large cage or group of cages in which birds are kept.

**aviation**
NOUN the science of flying aircraft.

**aviator** aviators
NOUN; *OLD-FASHIONED* a pilot of an aircraft.

**avid**
ADJECTIVE eager and enthusiastic for something.
**avidly** ADVERB

**avocado** avocados
NOUN a pear-shaped fruit, with dark green skin, soft greenish yellow flesh, and a large stone.
📖 from a South American Indian word *ahuacatl* meaning 'testicle', from its shape

**avoid** avoids avoiding avoided
VERB 1 If you avoid doing something, you make a deliberate effort not to do it. 2 If you avoid someone, you keep away from them.
**avoidable** ADJECTIVE **avoidance** NOUN
■ (sense 1) dodge, refrain from, shirk
■ (sense 2) dodge, evade, keep away from

**avowed**
ADJECTIVE 1 *FORMAL* If you are an avowed supporter or opponent of something, you have declared that you support it or oppose it. 2 An avowed belief or aim is one you hold very strongly.

**avuncular**
ADJECTIVE friendly and helpful in manner towards younger people, rather like an uncle.

**await** awaits awaiting awaited
VERB 1 If you await something, you expect it. 2 If something awaits you, it will happen to you in the future.

**awake** awakes awaking awoke awoken
ADJECTIVE 1 Someone who is awake is not sleeping. ▶ VERB 2 When you awake, you wake up. 3 If you are awoken by something, it wakes you up.

**awaken** awakens awakening awakened

VERB If something awakens an emotion or interest in you, you start to feel this emotion or interest.

**award** awards awarding awarded
NOUN **1** a prize or certificate for doing something well. **2** a sum of money an organization gives to students for training or study. ▶ VERB **3** If you award someone something, you give it to them formally or officially.

**aware**
ADJECTIVE If you are aware of something, you know about it or realize it is there.
**awareness** NOUN
■ conscious of, knowing about, mindful of

**awash**
ADJECTIVE or ADVERB covered with water E.G. *After the downpour the road was awash.*

**away**
ADVERB **1** moving from a place E.G. *I saw them walk away.* **2** at a distance from a place E.G. *Our nearest vet is 12 kilometres away.* **3** in its proper place E.G. *He put his chequebook away.* **4** not at home, school, or work E.G. *She had been away from home for years.*

**awe**
NOUN; FORMAL a feeling of great respect mixed with amazement and sometimes slight fear.

**awesome**
ADJECTIVE **1** Something that is awesome is very impressive and frightening. **2** INFORMAL Awesome also means excellent or outstanding.

**awful**
ADJECTIVE **1** very unpleasant or very bad. **2** INFORMAL very great E.G. *It took an awful lot of courage.*
**awfully** ADVERB

■ (sense 1) appalling, dreadful, terrible

**awkward**
ADJECTIVE **1** clumsy and uncomfortable E.G. *an awkward gesture.* **2** embarrassed or nervous E.G. *He was a shy, awkward young man.* **3** difficult to deal with E.G. *My lawyer is in an awkward situation.*
📖 from Old Norse *ofugr* meaning 'turned the wrong way'

**awning** awnings
NOUN a large roof of canvas or plastic attached to a building or vehicle.

**awry**
*Said* "a-rye" ADJECTIVE wrong or not as planned E.G. *Why had their plans gone so badly awry?*

**axe** axes axing axed
NOUN **1** a tool with a handle and a sharp blade, used for chopping wood. ▶ VERB **2** To axe something is to end it.

**axiom** axioms
NOUN a statement or saying that is generally accepted to be true.

**axis** axes
*Said* "ak-siss"
NOUN (MATHS) **1** an imaginary line through the centre of something, around which it moves. **2** one of the two sides of a graph.

**axle** axles
NOUN the long bar that connects a pair of wheels on a vehicle.

**ayatollah** ayatollahs
NOUN an Islamic religious leader in Iran.
📖 from Arabic *ayatullah* meaning 'manifestation of God'

**azure**
*Said* "az-yoor" ADJECTIVE; LITERARY bright blue.

a
b
c
d
e
f
g
h
i
j
k
l
m
n
o
p
q
r
s
t
u
v
w
x
y
z

# Bb

**babble** babbles babbling babbled
VERB When someone babbles, they talk in a confused or excited way.

**baboon** baboons
NOUN an African monkey with a pointed face, large teeth, and a long tail.
🏛 from Old French *baboue* meaning 'grimace'

**baby** babies
NOUN a child in the first year or two of its life.
**babyhood** NOUN **babyish** ADJECTIVE
▣ babe, infant

**baby-sit** baby-sits baby-sitting baby-sat
VERB To baby-sit for someone means to look after their children while that person is out.
**baby-sitter** NOUN **baby-sitting** NOUN

**baccalaureate** baccalaureates
*Said* "back-uh-law-ree-it" NOUN an internationally recognized course of study made up of several different subjects, offered by some schools as an alternative to A levels.

**bach** baches baching bached
*Said* "batch" NOUN 1 In New Zealand, a small holiday cottage. ▶ VERB 2 INFORMAL In Australian and New Zealand English, to bach is to live and keep a house on your own, especially when you are not used to it.

**bachelor** bachelors
NOUN a man who has never been married.

**back** backs backing backed
ADVERB 1 When people or things move back, they move in the opposite direction from the one they are facing. 2 When people or things go back to a place or situation, they return to it *E.G. She went back to sleep.* 3 If you get something back, it is returned to you. 4 If you do something back to someone, you do to them what they have done to you *E.G. I smiled back at them.* 5 Back also means in the past *E.G. It happened back in the early eighties.* ▶ NOUN 6 the rear part of your body. 7 the part of something that is behind the front. ▶ ADJECTIVE 8 The back parts of something are the ones near the rear *E.G. an animal's back legs.* ▶ VERB 9 If a building backs onto something, its back faces in that direction. 10 When a car backs, it moves backwards. 11 To back a person or organization means to support or finance that person or organization.

**back down** VERB If you back down on a demand or claim, you withdraw and give up.

**back out** VERB If you back out of a promise or commitment, you decide not to do what you had promised to do.

**back up** VERB 1 If you back up a claim or story, you produce evidence to show that it is true. 2 If you back someone up, you help and support them.

**backbone** backbones
NOUN 1 the column of linked bones along the middle of a person's or animal's back. 2 strength of character.

**backdate** backdates backdating backdated
VERB If an arrangement is backdated, it is valid from a date earlier than the one on which it is completed or signed.

**backdrop** backdrops
NOUN the background to a situation or event *E.G. The visit occurred against the backdrop of the political crisis.*

**backer** backers
NOUN The backers of a project are the people who give it financial help.

**backfire** backfires backfiring backfired
VERB 1 If a plan backfires, it fails. 2 When a car backfires, there is a small but noisy explosion in its exhaust pipe.

**background** backgrounds
NOUN 1 the circumstances which help to explain an event or caused it to happen. 2 the kind of home you come from and your education and experience *E.G. a rich background.* 3 If sounds are in the background, they are there but no one really pays any attention to them *E.G. She could hear voices in the background.*

**backing**
NOUN support or help *E.G. The project got government backing.*

**backlash**
NOUN a hostile reaction to a new development or a new policy.

**backlog** backlogs
NOUN a number of things which have not yet been done, but which need to be done.

**backpack** backpacks
NOUN a large bag that hikers or campers carry on their backs.

**backside** backsides
NOUN; INFORMAL the part of your body that you sit on.

**backward**
ADJECTIVE 1 Backward means directed behind you *E.G. without a backward glance.* 2 A backward country or society is one that does not have modern industries or technology. 3 A backward child is one who is unable to learn as quickly as other children of the same age.
**backwardness** NOUN

**backwards**
ADVERB 1 Backwards means behind you *E.G. Lucille looked backwards.* 2 If you do something backwards, you do it the opposite of the usual way *E.G. He instructed them to count backwards.*

**bacon**
NOUN meat from the back or sides of a pig, which has been salted or smoked.

**bacteria**
PLURAL NOUN Bacteria are very tiny organisms which can cause disease.
**bacterial** ADJECTIVE
☑ The word *bacteria* is plural. The singular form is *bacterium*.

**bad** worse worst
ADJECTIVE 1 Anything harmful or upsetting can be described as bad *E.G. I have some bad news… Is the pain bad?* 2 insufficient or of poor quality *E.G. bad roads.* 3 evil or immoral in character or behaviour *E.G. a bad person.* 4 lacking skill in something *E.G. I was bad at sports.* 5 Bad language consists of swearwords. 6 If you have a bad temper, you become angry easily.
**badly** ADVERB   **badness** NOUN
▤ (sense 3) evil, sinful, wicked, wrong

**bade**
a form of the past tense of **bid**.

**badge** badges
NOUN a piece of plastic or metal with a design or message on it that you can pin to your clothes.

a b c d e f g h i j k l m n o p q r s t u v w x y z

A
B
C
D
E
F
G
H
I
J
K
L
M
N
O
P
Q
R
S
T
U
V
W
X
Y
Z

**badger** badgers badgering badgered

NOUN **1** a wild animal that has a white head with two black stripes on it. ▸ VERB **2** If you badger someone, you keep asking them questions or pestering them to do something.

**badminton**

NOUN a game in which two or four players use rackets to hit a shuttlecock over a high net

**Bafana bafana**

PLURAL NOUN In South Africa, Bafana bafana is a name for the South African national soccer team.

**baffle** baffles baffling baffled

VERB If something baffles you, you cannot understand or explain it E.G. *The symptoms baffled the doctors.* **baffled** ADJECTIVE **baffling** ADJECTIVE

**bag** bags

NOUN **1** a container for carrying things in. ▸ PLURAL NOUN **2** *INFORMAL* Bags of something is a lot of it E.G. *bags of fun.* 🔲 from Old Norse *baggi* meaning 'bundle'

**baggage**

NOUN the suitcases and bags that you take on a journey.

**baggy** baggier baggiest

ADJECTIVE Baggy clothing hangs loosely.

**bagpipes**

PLURAL NOUN a musical instrument played by squeezing air out of a leather bag through pipes, on which a tune is played.

**bail** bails bailing bailed

NOUN **1** Bail is a sum of money paid to a court to allow an accused person to go free until the time of the trial E.G. *He was released on bail.* ▸ VERB **2** If you bail water from a boat, you scoop it out.

**bailiff** bailiffs

NOUN **1** a law officer who makes sure that the decisions of a court are obeyed. **2** a person employed to look after land or property for the owner.

**Baisakhi**

*Said* "buy-**sah**-kee" NOUN a Sikh festival celebrated every April.

**bait** baits baiting baited

NOUN **1** a small amount of food placed on a hook or in a trap, to attract a fish or wild animal so that it gets caught. ▸ VERB **2** If you bait a hook or trap, you put some food on it to catch a fish or wild animal.

**baize**

NOUN a smooth woollen material, usually green, used for covering snooker tables.

**bake** bakes baking baked

VERB **1** To bake food means to cook it in an oven without using liquid or fat. **2** To bake earth or clay means to heat it until it becomes hard.

**baker** bakers

NOUN a person who makes and sells bread and cakes.

**bakery** bakeries

NOUN a building where bread and cakes are baked and sold

**bakkie** bakkies

*Said* "**buck**-ee" NOUN In South African English, a bakkie is a small truck.

**balaclava** balaclavas

NOUN a close-fitting woollen hood that covers every part of your head except your face.

**balance** balances balancing balanced

VERB **1** When someone or something balances, they remain steady and do not fall over. ▸ NOUN **2** Balance is the state of being upright and steady.

**3** Balance is also a situation in which all the parts involved have a stable relationship with each other *E.G. the chemical balance of the brain*. **4** The balance in someone's bank account is the amount of money in it.

**balcony** balconies

NOUN **1** a platform on the outside of a building with a wall or railing round it. **2** an area of upstairs seats in a theatre or cinema.

**bald** balder baldest

ADJECTIVE **1** A bald person has little or no hair on their head. **2** A bald statement or question is made in the simplest way without any attempt to be polite.
**baldly** ADVERB **baldness** NOUN
🏛 from Middle English *ballede* meaning 'having a white patch'

**bale** bales baling baled

NOUN **1** a large bundle of something, such as paper or hay, tied tightly.
▶ VERB **2** If you bale water from a boat, you remove it using a container; also spelt **bail**.

**balk** balks balking balked; also spelt **baulk**

VERB If you balk at something, you object to it and may refuse to do it *E.G. He balked at the cost*.

**ball** balls

NOUN **1** a round object used in games such as cricket and soccer. **2** The ball of your foot or thumb is the rounded part where your toes join your foot or your thumb joins your hand. **3** a large formal social event at which people dance.
■ (sense 1) globe, orb, sphere

**ballad** ballads

NOUN **1** a long song or poem which tells a story. **2** a slow, romantic pop song.

🏛 from Old French *ballade* meaning 'song for dancing to'

**ballast**

NOUN any heavy material placed in a ship to make it more stable.

**ballerina** ballerinas

NOUN a woman ballet dancer.

**ballet**

*Said "bal-lay"* NOUN Ballet is a type of artistic dancing based on precise steps.

**balloon** balloons

NOUN **1** a small bag made of thin rubber that you blow into until it becomes larger and rounder. **2** a large, strong bag filled with gas or hot air, which travels through the air carrying passengers in a compartment underneath.
🏛 from Italian *ballone* meaning 'large round object'

**ballot** ballots balloting balloted

NOUN **1** a secret vote in which people select a candidate in an election, or express their opinion about something. ▶ VERB **2** When a group of people are balloted, they are asked questions to find out what they think about a particular problem or question.
🏛 from Italian *ballotta* meaning 'little round object'; in medieval Venice votes were cast by dropping black or white pebbles or balls into a box

**ballpoint** ballpoints

NOUN a pen with a small metal ball at the end which transfers the ink onto the paper.

**ballroom** ballrooms

NOUN a very large room used for dancing or formal balls.

**balm**

*Said "bahm"* NOUN; *OLD-FASHIONED* a

a
b
c
d
e
f
g
h
i
j
k
l
m
n
o
p
q
r
s
t
u
v
w
x
y
z

I went to see (C) the doctor's new practiCe (practice)         **SPELLING NOTE**

sweet-smelling soothing ointment.

**balmy** balmier balmiest

ADJECTIVE mild and pleasant E.G. *balmy summer evenings*.

**balsa**

NOUN Balsa is very lightweight wood.

**balustrade** balustrades

NOUN a railing or wall on a balcony or staircase.

**bamboo**

NOUN Bamboo is a tall tropical grass with hard, hollow stems used for making furniture.

**ban** bans banning banned

VERB 1 If something is banned, or if you are banned from doing it or using it, you are not allowed to do it or use it. ▶ NOUN 2 If there is a ban on something, it is not allowed.

■ (sense 1) forbid, outlaw, prohibit

■ (sense 2) disqualification, embargo, prohibition

**banal**

*Said* "ba-**nahl**" ADJECTIVE very ordinary and not at all interesting E.G. *He made some banal remark*.

**banality** NOUN

▥ Old French *banal* referred to military service which all tenants had to do; hence the word came to mean 'common to everyone' or 'ordinary'

**banana** bananas

NOUN a long curved fruit with a yellow skin.

▥ from a West African language, via Portuguese

**band** bands

NOUN 1 a group of musicians who play jazz or pop music together, or a group who play brass instruments together. 2 a group of people who share a common purpose E.G. *a band of rebels*. 3 a narrow strip of

something used to hold things together or worn as a decoration E.G. *an elastic band… a headband*.

**bandage** bandages bandaging bandaged

NOUN 1 a strip of cloth wrapped round a wound to protect it. ▶ VERB 2 If you bandage a wound, you tie a bandage round it.

**bandicoot** bandicoots

NOUN a small Australian marsupial with a long pointed muzzle and a long tail.

**bandit** bandits

NOUN; OLD-FASHIONED a member of an armed gang who rob travellers.

▥ from Italian *bandito* meaning 'man who has been banished or outlawed'

**bandstand** bandstands

NOUN a platform, usually with a roof, where a band can play outdoors.

**bandwagon**

PHRASE To **jump on the bandwagon** means to become involved in something because it is fashionable or likely to be successful.

**bandy** bandies bandying bandied

VERB If a name is bandied about, many people mention it.

▥ from Old French *bander* meaning 'to hit a tennis ball back and forth'

**bane**

NOUN; LITERARY Someone or something that is the bane of a person or organization causes a lot of trouble for them E.G. *the bane of my life*.

▥ from Old English *bana* meaning 'murderer'

**bang** bangs banging banged

VERB 1 If you bang something, you hit it or put it somewhere violently, so that it makes a loud noise E.G. *He banged down the receiver.* **2** If you bang a part of your body against something, you accidentally bump it. ► NOUN **3** a sudden, short, loud noise. **4** a hard or painful bump against something.

**Bangladeshi** Bangladeshis
*Said* "bang-glad-**desh**-ee" ADJECTIVE **1** belonging or relating to Bangladesh. ► NOUN **2** someone who comes from Bangladesh.

**bangle** bangles
NOUN an ornamental band worn round someone's wrist or ankle. 🕮 from Hindi *bangri* meaning 'bracelet'

**banish** banishes banishing banished
VERB **1** To banish someone means to send them into exile. **2** To banish something means to get rid of it *E.G. It will be a long time before cancer is banished.*
**banishment** NOUN
■ (sense 1) exile, expel, outlaw

**banister** banisters; also spelt **bannister**
NOUN a rail supported by posts along the side of a staircase.

**banjo** banjos or banjoes
NOUN a musical instrument, like a small guitar with a round body.

**bank** banks banking banked
NOUN **1** a business that looks after people's money. **2** a bank of something is a store of it kept ready for use *E.G. a blood bank.* **3** the raised ground along the edge of a river or lake. **4** the sloping side of an area of raised ground. ► VERB **5** When you bank money, you pay it into a bank. **6** If you bank on something happening, you expect it and rely on it.

**banker** NOUN **banking** NOUN
**bank holiday** bank holidays
NOUN a public holiday, when banks are officially closed.

**banknote** banknotes
NOUN a piece of paper money.

**bankrupt** bankrupts bankrupting bankrupted
ADJECTIVE **1** People or organizations that go bankrupt do not have enough money to pay their debts. ► NOUN **2** someone who has been declared bankrupt. ► VERB **3** To bankrupt someone means to make them bankrupt *E.G. Restoring the house nearly bankrupted them.*
**bankruptcy** NOUN

**banksia** banksias
NOUN an evergreen Australian tree or shrub with yellow flowers.

**banner** banners
NOUN a long strip of cloth with a message or slogan on it.

**bannister**
another spelling of **banister**.

**banquet** banquets
NOUN a grand formal dinner, often followed by speeches.

**banter**
NOUN Banter is friendly joking and teasing.

**baobab** baobabs
*Said* "**bay**-oh-bab" NOUN a small fruit tree with a very thick trunk which grows in Africa and northern Australia.

**baptism** baptisms
NOUN ⟨RE⟩ a ceremony in which someone is baptized.

**Baptist** Baptists
NOUN or ADJECTIVE a member of a Protestant church who believe that people should be baptized when

a
**b**
c
d
e
f
g
h
i
j
k
l
m
n
o
p
q
r
s
t
u
v
w
x
y
z

they are adults rather than when they are babies.

**baptize baptizes baptizing baptized**; also spelt **baptise**

VERB When someone is baptized water is sprinkled on them, or they are immersed in water, as a sign that they have become a Christian.

📖 from Greek *baptein* meaning 'to dip in water'

**bar bars barring barred**

NOUN **1** a counter or room where alcoholic drinks are served. **2** a long, straight piece of metal. **3** a piece of something made in a rectangular shape *E.G. a bar of soap*. **4** The bars in a piece of music are the many short parts of equal length that the piece is divided into. ▶ VERB **5** If you bar a door, you place something across it to stop it being opened. **6** If you bar someone's way, you stop them going somewhere by standing in front of them.

**barb barbs**

NOUN a sharp curved point on the end of an arrow or fish-hook.

**barbarian barbarians**

NOUN a member of a wild or uncivilized people.

📖 from Greek *barbaros* meaning 'foreigner', originally 'person saying *bar-bar*'

**barbaric**

ADJECTIVE cruel or brutal *E.G. Ban the barbaric sport of fox hunting*.

**barbarity** NOUN

**barbecue barbecues barbecuing barbecued**

NOUN **1** a grill with a charcoal fire on which you cook food, usually outdoors; also an outdoor party where you eat food cooked on a barbecue. ▶ VERB **2** When food is barbecued, it is cooked over a charcoal grill.

📖 from a Caribbean word meaning 'framework'

**barbed**

ADJECTIVE A barbed remark is one that seems straightforward but is really unkind or spiteful.

**barbed wire**

NOUN Barbed wire is strong wire with sharp points sticking out of it, used to make fences.

**barber barbers**

NOUN a man who cuts men's hair.

**barbiturate barbiturates**

NOUN a drug that people take to make them calm or to put them to sleep.

**bar code bar codes**

NOUN a small pattern of numbers and lines on something you buy in a shop, which can be electronically scanned at a checkout to give the price.

**bard bards**

NOUN; *LITERARY* A bard is a poet. Some people call Shakespeare the Bard.

**bare bares baring bared**

ADJECTIVE **1** If a part of your body is bare, it is not covered by any clothing. **2** If something is bare, it has nothing on top of it or inside it *E.G. bare floorboards… a small bare office*. **3** When trees are bare, they have no leaves on them. **4** The bare minimum or bare essentials means the very least that is needed *E.G. They were fed the bare minimum*. ▶ VERB **5** If you bare something, you uncover or show it.

▤ (sense 1) naked, nude, uncovered

▤ (sense 2) plain, stark

**barefoot**
ADJECTIVE or ADVERB not wearing anything on your feet.

**barely**
ADVERB only just E.G. *The girl was barely sixteen.*

☑ Do not use *barely* with negative words like *not*: *she was barely sixteen* rather than *she was not barely sixteen.*

**bargain** bargains bargaining bargained
NOUN **1** an agreement in which two people or groups discuss and agree what each will do, pay, or receive in a matter which involves them both. **2** something which is sold at a low price and which is good value. ▸ VERB **3** When people bargain with each other, they discuss and agree terms about what each will do, pay, or receive in a matter which involves them both.

**barge** barges barging barged
NOUN **1** a boat with a flat bottom used for carrying heavy loads, especially on canals. ▸ VERB **2** INFORMAL If you barge into a place, you push into it in a rough or rude way.

**baritone** baritones
NOUN a man with a fairly deep singing voice.

**bark** barks barking barked
VERB **1** When a dog barks, it makes a short, loud noise, once or several times. ▸ NOUN **2** the short, loud noise that a dog makes. **3** the tough material that covers the outside of a tree.

**barley**
NOUN a cereal that is grown for food and is also used for making beer and whisky.

**bar mitzvah**
NOUN A Jewish boy's bar mitzvah is a ceremony that takes place on his 13th birthday, after which he is regarded as an adult.
📖 a Hebrew phrase meaning 'son of the law'

**barmy** barmier barmiest
ADJECTIVE; INFORMAL mad or very foolish.

**barn** barns
NOUN a large farm building used for storing crops or animal food.

**barnacle** barnacles
NOUN a small shellfish that fixes itself to rocks and to the bottom of boats.

**barometer** barometers
NOUN an instrument that measures air pressure and shows when the weather is changing.

**baron** barons
NOUN a member of the lowest rank of the nobility.
**baronial** ADJECTIVE

**baroness** baronesses
NOUN a woman who has the rank of baron, or who is the wife of a baron.

**baronet** baronets
NOUN a man with an honorary knighthood which has been passed to him from his father.

**barracks**
NOUN a building where soldiers live.
📖 from Spanish *barraca* meaning 'hut'

**barracuda** barracudas
NOUN a large, fierce tropical fish with sharp teeth.

**barrage** barrages
NOUN **1** A barrage of questions or complaints is a lot of them all coming at the same time. **2** A barrage is continuous artillery fire over a wide area, to prevent the enemy from moving.
■ (sense 1) deluge, stream, torrent

a
b
c
d
e
f
g
h
i
j
k
l
m
n
o
p
q
r
s
t
u
v
w
x
y
z

A
B
C
D
E
F
G
H
I
J
K
L
M
N
O
P
Q
R
S
T
U
V
W
X
Y
Z

■ (sense 2) bombardment, fusillade, volley

**barrel** barrels

NOUN **1** a wooden container with rounded sides and flat ends. **2** The barrel of a gun is the long tube through which the bullet is fired.

**barren**

ADJECTIVE **1** Barren land has soil of such poor quality that plants cannot grow on it. **2** A barren woman or female animal is not able to have babies.

■ (sense 1) desert, empty, unproductive

■ (sense 2) infertile, sterile

**barricade** barricades barricading barricaded

NOUN **1** a temporary barrier put up to stop people getting past. ► VERB **2** If you barricade yourself inside a room or building, you put something heavy against the door to stop people getting in.

**barrier** barriers

NOUN a fence or wall that prevents people or animals getting from one area to another.

■ barricade, fence, wall

**barrister** barristers

NOUN a lawyer who is qualified to represent people in the higher courts.

**barrow** barrows

NOUN **1** the same as a wheelbarrow. **2** a large cart from which fruit and other goods are sold in the street.

**barter** barters bartering bartered

VERB **1** If you barter goods, you exchange them for other goods, rather than selling them for money. ► NOUN **2** Barter is the activity of exchanging goods.

**base** bases basing based

NOUN **1** the lowest part of something, which often supports the rest. **2** A place which part of an army, navy, or air force works from. **3** In chemistry, a base is any compound that reacts with an acid to form a salt. ► VERB **4** To base something on something else means to use the second thing as a foundation or starting point of the first *E.G. The opera is based on a work by Pushkin.* **5** If you are based somewhere, you live there or work from there.

■ (sense 1) bottom, foot, stand, support

**baseball**

NOUN Baseball is a team game played with a bat and a ball, similar to rounders.

**basement** basements

NOUN a floor of a building built completely or partly below the ground.

**bases**

NOUN **1** *Said "bay-seez"* the plural of **basis**. **2** *Said "bay-siz"* the plural of **base**.

**bash** bashes bashing bashed

VERB; *INFORMAL* If you bash someone or bash into them, you hit them hard.

**bashful**

ADJECTIVE shy and easily embarrassed.

**basic** basics

ADJECTIVE **1** The basic aspects of something are the most necessary ones *E.G. the basic necessities of life.* **2** Something that is basic has only the necessary features without any extras or luxuries *E.G. The accommodation is pretty basic.* ► PLURAL NOUN **3** The basics of something are the things you need

to know or understand *E.G. the basics
of map-reading.*
**basically** ADVERB
▣ (sense 1) essential, necessary, vital
**basilica** basilicas
NOUN an oblong church with a
rounded end called an apse.
🏛 from Greek *basilikē* meaning 'royal
hall'
**basin** basins
NOUN **1** a round wide container which
is open at the top. **2** The basin of a
river is a bowl of land from which
water runs into the river.
**basis** bases
NOUN **1** The basis of something is the
essential main principle from which
it can be developed *E.G. The same
colour theme is used as the basis for
several patterns.* **2** The basis for a
belief is the facts that support it *E.G.
There is no basis for this assumption.*
▣ (sense 1) base, foundation
▣ (sense 2) foundation, ground,
support
**bask** basks basking basked
VERB If you bask in the sun, you sit or
lie in it, enjoying its warmth.
**basket** baskets
NOUN a container made of thin strips
of cane woven together.
**basketball**
NOUN Basketball is a game in which
two teams try to score goals by
throwing a large ball through one of
two circular nets suspended high up
at each end of the court.
**bass** basses
*Rhymes with "lace"* NOUN **1** a man with
a very deep singing voice. **2** a
musical instrument that provides the
rhythm and lowest part in the
harmonies.

**bass** basses
*Rhymes with "gas"* NOUN a type of
edible sea fish.
**basset hound** basset hounds
NOUN a smooth-haired dog with a
long body and ears, and short legs.
**bassoon** bassoons
NOUN a large woodwind instrument.
**bastard** bastards
NOUN **1** OFFENSIVE People sometimes call
someone a bastard when they
dislike them or are very angry with
them. **2** OLD-FASHIONED A bastard is
someone whose parents were not
married when he or she was born.
**baste** bastes basting basted
VERB When you baste meat that is
roasting, you pour hot fat over it so
that it does not become dry while
cooking.
**bastion** bastions
NOUN; LITERARY something that protects
a system or way of life *E.G. The
country is the last bastion of
communism.*
**bat** bats batting batted
NOUN **1** a specially shaped piece of
wood with a handle, used for hitting
the ball in a game such as cricket or
table tennis. **2** a small flying animal,
active at night, that looks like a
mouse with wings. ▶ VERB **3** In certain
sports, when someone is batting, it is
their turn to try to hit the ball and
score runs.
**batch** batches
NOUN a group of things of the same
kind produced or dealt with together.
**bated**
PHRASE **With bated breath** means
very anxiously.
**bath** baths
NOUN a long container which you fill

a
b
c
d
e
f
g
h
i
j
k
l
m
n
o
p
q
r
s
t
u
v
w
x
y
z

A
**B**
C
D
E
F
G
H
I
J
K
L
M
N
O
P
Q
R
S
T
U
V
W
X
Y
Z

with water and sit in to wash yourself.

**bathe bathes bathing bathed**
VERB 1 When you bathe, you swim or play in open water. 2 When you bathe a wound, you wash it gently. 3 LITERARY If a place is bathed in light, a lot of light reaches it E.G. *The room was bathed in spring sunshine.*
**bather** NOUN **bathing** NOUN

**bathroom bathrooms**
NOUN a room with a bath or shower, a washbasin, and often a toilet in it.

**baths**
NOUN The baths is a public swimming pool.

**baton batons**
NOUN 1 a light, thin stick that a conductor uses to direct an orchestra or choir. 2 In athletics, the baton is a short stick passed from one runner to another in a relay race.

**batsman batsmen**
NOUN In cricket, the batsman is the person who is batting.

**battalion battalions**
NOUN an army unit consisting of three or more companies.

**batten battens battening battened**
NOUN a strip of wood that is fixed to something to strengthen it or hold it firm.
**batten down** VERB If you batten something down, you make it secure by fixing battens across it.

**batter batters battering battered**
VERB 1 To batter someone or something means to hit them many times E.G. *The waves kept battering the life raft.* ▶ NOUN 2 Batter is a mixture of flour, eggs, and milk, used to make

pancakes, or to coat food before frying it.
**battering** NOUN

**battery batteries**
NOUN 1 a device, containing two or more cells, for storing and producing electricity, for example in a torch or a car. 2 a large group of things or people. ▶ ADJECTIVE 3 A battery hen is one of a large number of hens kept in small cages for the mass production of eggs.

**battle battles**
NOUN 1 a fight between armed forces or a struggle between two people or groups with conflicting aims E.G. *the battle between town and country*. 2 A battle for something difficult is a determined attempt to obtain or achieve it E.G. *the battle for equality*.

**battlefield battlefields**
NOUN a place where a battle is or has been fought.

**battlements**
PLURAL NOUN The battlements of a castle consist of a wall built round the top, with gaps through which guns or arrows could be fired.

**battleship battleships**
NOUN a large, heavily armoured warship.

**batty battier battiest**
ADJECTIVE; INFORMAL crazy or eccentric.

**bauble baubles**
NOUN a pretty but cheap ornament or piece of jewellery.

**bawdy bawdier bawdiest**
ADJECTIVE a bawdy joke or song contains humorous references to sex. ▥ from Middle English *baude* meaning 'brothel keeper'

**bawl bawls bawling bawled**
VERB 1 INFORMAL To bawl at someone

means to shout at them loudly and harshly. **2** When a child is bawling, it is crying very loudly and angrily.

**bay bays baying bayed**
NOUN **1** a part of a coastline where the land curves inwards. **2** a space or area used for a particular purpose E.G. *a loading bay.* **3** Bay is a kind of tree similar to the laurel, with leaves used for flavouring in cooking. ▶ PHRASE **4** If you **keep something at bay**, you prevent it from reaching you E.G. *Eating oranges keeps colds at bay.* ▶ VERB **5** When a hound or wolf bays, it makes a deep howling noise.
◾ (sense 1) cove, gulf, inlet

**bayonet bayonets**
NOUN a sharp blade that can be fixed to the end of a rifle and used for stabbing.
▣ named after *Bayonne* in France, where it originated

**bazaar bazaars**
NOUN **1** an area with many small shops and stalls, especially in Eastern countries. **2** a sale to raise money for charity.
▣ from Persian *bazar* meaning 'market'

**BC**
BC means 'before Christ' E.G. *in 49 BC.*

**be am is are; being; was were; been**
AUXILIARY VERB **1** 'Be' is used with a present participle to form the continuous tense E.G. *Crimes of violence are increasing.* **2** 'Be' is also used to say that something will happen E.G. *We are going to America next month.* **3** 'Be' is used to form the passive voice E.G. *The walls were being repaired.* ▶ VERB **4** 'Be' is used to give more information about the subject of a sentence E.G. *Her name is Melanie.*

---

### The Verb Be

The verb **to be** has a lot of unusual forms, and does not follow the usual rules.

The main form is *be*. This is used with an auxiliary verb to make compound tenses, and after the preposition *to*:

> E.G. She will **be** five years old in April.

The verb forms *am, are,* and *is* are used to talk about the present time. *Am* is used for the first person singular; *are* is used for the second person and for all plural forms; *is* is used for the third person singular:

> E.G. I **am** exhausted. ■ You **are** very welcome. ■ Robbie **is** always cheerful. ■ They **are** a pair of rascals.

The present participle is *being*. This form is used with an auxiliary verb to make compound tenses:

> E.G. Matthew **was being** very helpful.

The verb forms *was* and *were* talk about past time. *Was* is used for the first and third person singular; *were* is used for the second person and for all plural forms:

> E.G. I **was** exhausted. ■ You **were** very welcome. ■ Robbie **was** always cheerful. ■ They **were** a pair of rascals.

The past participle is *been*. This form is used with an auxiliary verb to make compound tenses:

> E.G. I **shall have been** here five years in April. ■ Robbie **has been** polite at all times.

**be-**

PREFIX **1** 'Be-' is used to form verbs from nouns and adds the meaning 'treat as'. For example, to *befriend* someone is to make friends with them. **2** 'Be-' is also sometimes used to form verbs from verbs when it is used for emphasis or to mean 'covering completely'. For example, to *besmear* means to smear all over.

**beach** beaches

NOUN an area of sand or pebbles beside the sea.

■ seashore, seaside, shore

**beacon** beacons

NOUN In the past, a beacon was a light or fire on a hill, which acted as a signal or warning.

**bead** beads

NOUN **1** Beads are small pieces of coloured glass or wood with a hole through the middle, strung together to make necklaces. **2** Beads of liquid are drops of it.

**beady**

ADJECTIVE Beady eyes are small and bright like beads.

**beagle** beagles

NOUN a short-haired dog with long ears and short legs.

**beak** beaks

NOUN A bird's beak is the hard part of its mouth that sticks out.

**beaker** beakers

NOUN **1** a cup for drinking out of, usually made of plastic and without a handle. **2** a glass container with a lip which is used in laboratories.

**beam** beams beaming beamed

NOUN **1** a broad smile. **2** A beam of light is a band of light that shines from something such as a torch. **3** a long, thick bar of wood or metal,

especially one that supports a roof. ▶ VERB **4** If you beam, you smile because you are happy.

**bean** beans

NOUN Beans are the seeds or pods of a climbing plant, which are eaten as a vegetable; also used of some other seeds, for example the seeds from which coffee is made.

**bear** bears bearing bore borne

NOUN **1** a large, strong wild animal with thick fur and sharp claws. ▶ VERB **2** FORMAL To bear something means to carry it or support its weight E.G. *The ice wasn't thick enough to bear their weight.* **3** If something bears a mark or typical feature, it has it E.G. *The room bore all the signs of a violent struggle.* **4** If you bear something difficult, you accept it and are able to deal with it E.G. *He bore his last illness with courage.* **5** If you can't bear someone or something, you dislike them very much. **6** FORMAL When a plant or tree bears flowers, fruit, or leaves, it produces them.

**bearable** ADJECTIVE

**beard** beards

NOUN the hair that grows on the lower part of a man's face.

**bearded** ADJECTIVE

**bearer** bearers

NOUN The bearer of something is the person who carries or presents it E.G. *the bearer of bad news.*

**bearing**

NOUN **1** If something has a bearing on a situation, it is relevant to it. **2** the way in which a person moves or stands.

**beast** beasts

NOUN **1** OLD-FASHIONED a large wild animal. **2** INFORMAL If you call someone a beast, you mean that they are cruel or spiteful.

**beastly** beastlier beastliest
ADJECTIVE; *OLD-FASHIONED* cruel or spiteful.

**beat** beats beating beat beaten
VERB **1** To beat someone or something means to hit them hard and repeatedly *E.G. He threatened to beat her*. **2** If you beat someone in a race or game, you defeat them or do better than them. **3** When a bird or insect beats its wings, it moves them up and down. **4** When your heart is beating, it is pumping blood with a regular rhythm. **5** If you beat eggs, cream, or butter, you mix them vigorously using a fork or a whisk.
▶ NOUN **6** The beat of your heart is its regular pumping action. **7** The beat of a piece of music is its main rhythm. **8** A police officer's beat is the area which he or she patrols.
■ (sense 1) batter, hit, strike
■ (sense 2) conquer, defeat, vanquish

**beat up** VERB To beat someone up means to hit or kick them repeatedly.
**beater** NOUN **beating** NOUN

**beaut** beauts
NOUN; *INFORMAL* **1** In Australian and New Zealand English, a beaut is an outstanding person or thing.
▶ ADJECTIVE **2** In Australian and New Zealand English, beaut means good or excellent *E.G. a beaut house*.

**beautiful**
ADJECTIVE very attractive or pleasing *E.G. a beautiful girl… beautiful music*.
**beautifully** ADVERB
■ attractive, gorgeous, lovely

**beauty** beauties
NOUN **1** Beauty is the quality of being beautiful. **2** *OLD-FASHIONED* a very

attractive woman. **3** The beauty of an idea or plan is what makes it attractive or worthwhile *E.G. The beauty of the fund is its simplicity*.

**beaver** beavers
NOUN an animal with a big, flat tail and webbed hind feet.

**because**
CONJUNCTION **1** 'Because' is used with a clause that gives the reason for something *E.G. I went home because I was tired*. ▶ PHRASE **2 Because of** is used with a noun that gives the reason for something *E.G. He quit playing because of a knee injury*.

**beck**
PHRASE If you are at someone's **beck and call**, you are always available to do what they ask.

**beckon** beckons beckoning beckoned
VERB **1** If you beckon to someone, you signal with your hand that you want them to come to you. **2** If you say that something beckons, you mean that you find it very attractive *E.G. A career in journalism beckons*.

**become** becomes becoming became become
VERB To become something means to start feeling or being that thing *E.G. I became very angry… He became an actor*.

**bed** beds
NOUN **1** a piece of furniture that you lie on when you sleep. **2** A bed in a garden is an area of ground in which plants are grown. **3** The bed of a sea or river is the ground at the bottom of it.

**bedclothes**
PLURAL NOUN the sheets and covers that you put over you when you get into bed.

a
b
c
d
e
f
g
h
i
j
k
l
m
n
o
p
q
r
s
t
u
v
w
x
y
z

Beautiful Elephants Are Usually Tiny (<u>beautiful</u>) ▶ SPELLING NOTE

A
B
C
D
E
F
G
H
I
J
K
L
M
N
O
P
Q
R
S
T
U
V
W
X
Y
Z

**bedding**

NOUN Bedding is sheets, blankets, and other covers that are used on beds.

**bedlam**

NOUN You can refer to a noisy and disorderly place or situation as bedlam E.G. *The delay caused bedlam at the station.*

📖 from *Bedlam*, a shortened form of the Hospital of St. Mary of Bethlehem in London, an institution for the insane or mentally ill

**bedpan** bedpans

NOUN a container used as a toilet by people who are too ill to get out of bed.

**bedraggled**

ADJECTIVE A bedraggled person or animal is in a messy or untidy state.

**bedridden**

ADJECTIVE Someone who is bedridden is too ill or disabled to get out of bed.

**bedrock**

NOUN 1 Bedrock is the solid rock under the soil. 2 The bedrock of something is the foundation and principles on which it is based E.G. *His life was built on the bedrock of integrity.*

**bedroom** bedrooms

NOUN a room used for sleeping in.

**bedspread** bedspreads

NOUN a cover put over a bed, on top of the sheets and blankets.

**bedstead** bedsteads

NOUN the metal or wooden frame of an old-fashioned bed.

**bee** bees

NOUN a winged insect that makes honey and lives in large groups.

**beech** beeches

NOUN a tree with a smooth grey trunk and shiny leaves.

**beef**

NOUN Beef is the meat of a cow, bull, or ox.

📖 from Old French *boef* meaning 'ox' or 'bull'

**beefy** beefier beefiest

ADJECTIVE; INFORMAL A beefy person is strong and muscular.

**beehive** beehives

NOUN a container in which bees live and make their honey.

**beeline**

PHRASE; INFORMAL If you **make a beeline** for a place, you go there as quickly and directly as possible.

**been**

the past participle of **be**.

**beer** beers

NOUN an alcoholic drink made from malt and flavoured with hops.

**beet** beets

NOUN a plant with an edible root and leaves, such as sugar beet or beetroot.

**beetle** beetles

NOUN a flying insect with hard wings which cover its body when it is not flying.

**beetroot** beetroots

NOUN the round, dark red root of a type of beet, eaten as a vegetable.

**befall** befalls befalling befell befallen

VERB; OLD-FASHIONED If something befalls you, it happens to you E.G. *A similar fate befell my cousin.*

**before**

ADVERB, PREPOSITION, or CONJUNCTION

1 'Before' is used to refer to a previous time E.G. *Apply the ointment before going to bed.* ► ADVERB 2 If you have done something before, you

SPELLING NOTE    'i' before 'e' except after 'c'

have done it on a previous occasion
*E.G. Never before had he seen such
poverty.* ▶ PREPOSITION **3** *FORMAL* Before
also means in front of *E.G. They
stopped before a large white villa.*
■ (sense 1) earlier than, prior to
■ (sense 2) previously

**beforehand**
ADVERB before *E.G. It had been agreed
beforehand that they would spend the
night there.*

**befriend** befriends befriending
befriended
VERB If you befriend someone, you act
in a kind and helpful way and so
become friends with them.

**beg** begs begging begged
VERB **1** When people beg, they ask for
food or money, because they are
very poor. **2** If you beg someone to
do something, you ask them very
anxiously to do it.
■ (sense 2) beseech, implore,
plead

**beggar** beggars
NOUN someone who lives by asking
people for money or food.

**begin** begins beginning began
begun
VERB If you begin to do something,
you start doing it. When something
begins, it starts.
■ commence, start

**beginner** beginners
NOUN someone who has just started
learning to do something and
cannot do it very well yet.
■ learner, novice

**beginning** beginnings
NOUN The beginning of something is
the first part of it or the time when it
starts *E.G. They had now reached the
beginning of the city.*

☑ Remember that *beginning* has
one *g* and two *n*s.

**begonia** begonias
*Said "be-go-nya"* NOUN a plant with
brightly coloured flowers.

**begrudge** begrudges begrudging
begrudged
VERB If you begrudge someone
something, you are angry or envious
because they have it *e.g. No one
could begrudge him the glory.*

**beguiling**
*rhymes with "smiling"* ADJECTIVE
charming, but often in a deceptive
way.

**behalf**
PHRASE To do something **on behalf of**
someone or something means to do
it for their benefit or as their
representative.

**behave** behaves behaving
behaved
VERB **1** If you behave in a particular
way, you act in that way *E.G. They
were behaving like animals.* **2** To
behave yourself means to act
correctly or properly.

**behaviour**
NOUN Your behaviour is the way in
which you behave.

**behead** beheads beheading
beheaded
VERB To behead someone means to
cut their head off.

**beheld**
the past tense of **behold**.

**behind**
PREPOSITION **1** at the back of *E.G. He was
seated behind the desk.* **2** responsible
for or causing *E.G. He was the driving
force behind the move.* **3** supporting
someone *E.G. The whole country was
behind him.* ▶ ADVERB **4** If you stay

a
b
c
d
e
f
g
h
i
j
k
l
m
n
o
p
q
r
s
t
u
v
w
x
y
z

A
B
C
D
E
F
G
H
I
J
K
L
M
N
O
P
Q
R
S
T
U
V
W
X
Y
Z

behind, you remain after other people have gone. **5** If you leave something behind, you do not take it with you.

**behold**

INTERJECTION; *LITERARY* You say 'behold' when you want someone to look at something.

**beholder** NOUN

**beige**

*Said* "bayj" NOUN or ADJECTIVE pale creamy-brown.

**being** beings

**1** Being is the present participle of **be**. NOUN **2** Being is the state or fact of existing *E.G. The party came into being in 1923.* **3** a living creature, either real or imaginary *E.G. alien beings from a distant galaxy.*

**belated**

ADJECTIVE; *FORMAL* A belated action happens later than it should have done *E.G. a belated birthday present.*

**belatedly** ADVERB

**belch** belches belching belched

VERB **1** If you belch, you make a sudden noise in your throat because air has risen up from your stomach. **2** If something belches smoke or fire, it sends it out in large amounts *E.G. Smoke belched from the steelworks.* ▶ NOUN **3** the noise you make when you belch.

**beleaguered**

ADJECTIVE **1** struggling against difficulties or criticism *E.G. the beleaguered meat industry.* **2** besieged by an enemy *E.G. the beleaguered garrison.*

**belfry** belfries

NOUN the part of a church tower where the bells are.

🔲 from Old French *berfrei* meaning

'tower'; because towers often contained bells this word was later changed to *belfrey*

**Belgian** Belgians

ADJECTIVE **1** belonging or relating to Belgium. ▶ NOUN **2** someone who comes from Belgium.

**belief** beliefs

NOUN **1** a feeling of certainty that something exists or is true. **2** one of the principles of a religion or moral system.

🔲 (sense 2) creed, doctrine, faith

**believe** believes believing believed

VERB **1** If you believe that something is true, you accept that it is true. **2** If you believe someone, you accept that they are telling the truth. **3** If you believe in things such as God and miracles, you accept that they exist or happen. **4** If you believe in something such as a plan or system, you are in favour of it *E.G. They really believe in education.*

**believable** ADJECTIVE **believer** NOUN

**belittle** belittles belittling belittled

VERB If you belittle someone or something, you make them seem unimportant *E.G. He belittled my opinions.*

🔲 deprecate, disparage, scoff at

**bell** bells

NOUN **1** a cup-shaped metal object with a piece inside that swings and hits the sides, producing a ringing sound. **2** an electrical device that rings or buzzes in order to attract attention.

**bellbird** bellbirds

NOUN an Australian or New Zealand bird that makes a sound like a bell.

---

**belligerent**

ADJECTIVE aggressive and keen to start a fight or an argument.

**belligerence** NOUN

**bellow** bellows bellowing bellowed

VERB 1 When an animal such as a bull bellows, it makes a loud, deep roaring noise. 2 If someone bellows, they shout in a loud, deep voice.

▶ PLURAL NOUN 3 Bellows are a piece of equipment used for blowing air into a fire to make it burn more fiercely.

**belly** bellies

NOUN 1 Your belly is your stomach or the front of your body below your chest. 2 An animal's belly is the underneath part of its body.

**belong** belongs belonging belonged

VERB 1 If something belongs to you, it is yours and you own it. 2 To belong to a group means to be a member of it. 3 If something belongs in a particular place, that is where it should be.

**belongings**

PLURAL NOUN Your belongings are the things that you own.

**beloved**

*Said* "bil-**luv**-id" ADJECTIVE A beloved person or thing is one that you feel great affection for.

▣ adored, dear, loved, precious

**below**

PREPOSITION or ADVERB 1 If something is below a line or the surface of something else, it is lower down E.G. *six inches below soil level.* 2 Below also means at or to a lower point, level, or rate E.G. *The temperature fell below the legal minimum.*

**belt** belts belting belted

NOUN 1 a strip of leather or cloth that

you fasten round your waist to hold your trousers or skirt up. 2 In a machine, a belt is a circular strip of rubber that drives moving parts or carries objects along. 3 a specific area of a country E.G. *Poland's industrial belt.* ▶ VERB 4 INFORMAL To belt someone means to hit them very hard.

**bemused**

ADJECTIVE If you are bemused, you are puzzled or confused.

**bench** benches

NOUN 1 a long seat that two or more people can sit on. 2 a long, narrow table for working at, for example in a laboratory.

▣ (sense 1) form, pew, seat

**bend** bends bending bent

VERB 1 When you bend something, you use force to make it curved or angular. 2 When you bend, you move your head and shoulders forwards and downwards. ▶ NOUN 3 a curved part of something.

**bent** ADJECTIVE

▣ (sense 1) arch, bow, curve

▣ (sense 3) arch, bow, curve

**bene-**

PREFIX 'Bene-' means 'good' or 'well'. For example, something *beneficial* makes you well or produces a good result, and a *benevolent* person is kind and good to others.

▥ from Latin *bene* meaning 'well'

**beneath**

PREPOSITION, ADJECTIVE AND ADVERB 1 an old-fashioned word for **underneath**.

▶ PREPOSITION 2 If someone thinks something is beneath them, they think that it is too unimportant for them to bother with it.

**benefactor** benefactors

NOUN a person who helps to support

a person or institution by giving money.

■ patron, sponsor, supporter

**beneficial**

ADJECTIVE Something that is beneficial is good for people *E.G. the beneficial effects of exercise.*
**beneficially** ADVERB

■ advantageous, favourable, helpful

**beneficiary beneficiaries**

NOUN A beneficiary of something is someone who receives money or other benefits from it.

**benefit benefits benefiting benefited**

NOUN 1 The benefits of something are the advantages that it brings to people. 2 Benefit is money given by the government to people who are unemployed or ill. ▶ VERB 3 If you benefit from something, it helps you.

☑ *Benefit* is spelt with two *e*s, not two *i*s.

■ (sense 1) advantage, good, help
■ (sense 3) gain, profit

**benevolent**

ADJECTIVE kind and helpful.
**benevolence** NOUN **benevolently** ADVERB

**benign**

*Said* "be-**nine**" ADJECTIVE 1 Someone who is benign is kind and gentle. 2 A benign tumour is one that will not cause death or serious illness.
**benignly** ADVERB

**bent**

1 Bent is the past participle and past tense of **bend.** ▶ PHRASE 2 If you are **bent on** doing something, you are determined to do it.

**bequeath bequeaths bequeathing bequeathed**

VERB; *FORMAL* If someone bequeaths money or property to you, they give it to you in their will, so that it is yours after they have died.

**bequest bequests**

NOUN; *FORMAL* money or property that has been left to someone in a will.

**berate berates berating berated**

VERB; *FORMAL* If you berate someone, you scold them angrily *E.G. He berated them for getting caught.*

**bereaved**

ADJECTIVE; *FORMAL* You say that someone is bereaved when a close relative of theirs has recently died.
**bereavement** NOUN

**bereft**

ADJECTIVE; *LITERARY* If you are bereft of something, you no longer have it *E.G. The government seems bereft of ideas.*

**beret berets**

*Said* "**ber**-ray" NOUN a circular flat hat with no brim.

**berm berms**

NOUN 1 a narrow path at the edge of a slope, road, or canal. 2 In New Zealand English, a strip of grass between the road and the footpath in areas where people live.

**berry berries**

NOUN Berries are small, round fruits that grow on bushes or trees.

**berserk**

PHRASE If someone **goes berserk**, they lose control of themselves and become very violent.

🔤 from Icelandic *berserkr*, a kind of Viking who wore a shirt (*serkr*) made from the skin of a bear (*björn*). They worked themselves into a frenzy before battle

**berth berths**

NOUN 1 a space in a harbour where a

ship stays when it is being loaded or unloaded. **2** In a boat or caravan, a berth is a bed.

**beseech** beseeches beseeching beseeched or besought

VERB; *LITERARY* If you beseech someone to do something, you ask them very earnestly to do it *E.G. Her eyes beseeched him to show mercy.*
**beseeching** ADJECTIVE

**beset**

ADJECTIVE; *FORMAL* If you are beset by difficulties or doubts, you have a lot of them.

**beside**

PREPOSITION If one thing is beside something else, they are next to each other.
◼ adjacent to, alongside, next to

**besiege** besieges besieging besieged

VERB **1** When soldiers besiege a place, they surround it and wait for the people inside to surrender. **2** If you are besieged by people, many people want something from you and continually bother you.

**besought**

a past tense and past participle of beseech.

**best**

**1** the superlative of **good** and **well**.
▶ ADVERB **2** The thing that you like best is the thing that you prefer to everything else.
◼ (sense 1) finest, supreme, top

**best man**

NOUN The best man at a wedding is the man who acts as the bridegroom's attendant.

**bestow** bestows bestowing bestowed

VERB; *FORMAL* If you bestow something

on someone, you give it to them.

**bet** bets betting bet

VERB **1** If you bet on the result of an event, you will win money if something happens and lose money if it does not. ▶ NOUN **2** the act of betting on something, or the amount of money that you agree to risk. ▶ PHRASE; *INFORMAL* **3** You say **I bet** to indicate that you are sure that something is or will be so *E.G. I bet the answer is no.*
**betting** NOUN

**betray** betrays betraying betrayed

VERB **1** If you betray someone who trusts you, you do something which harms them, such as helping their enemies. **2** If you betray your feelings or thoughts, you show them without intending to.
**betrayal** NOUN   **betrayer** NOUN
◼ (sense 1) be disloyal to, double-cross
◼ (sense 2) give away, reveal

**betrothal** betrothals

NOUN; *OLD-FASHIONED* an engagement to be married.
**betrothed** ADJECTIVE or NOUN

**better**

**1** the comparative of **good** and **well**.
ADVERB **2** If you like one thing better than another, you like it more than the other thing. ▶ ADJECTIVE **3** If you are better after an illness, you are no longer ill.
◼ (sense 1) finer, greater, superior

**between**

PREPOSITION or ADVERB **1** If something is between two other things, it is situated or happens in the space or time that separates them *E.G. flights between Europe and Asia.* **2** A

a
b
c
d
e
f
g
h
i
j
k
l
m
n
o
p
q
r
s
t
u
v
w
x
y
z

A
B
C
D
E
F
G
H
I
J
K
L
M
N
O
P
Q
R
S
T
U
V
W
X
Y
Z

relationship or difference between two people or things involves only those two.

☑ If there are two things you should use *between*. If there are more than two things you should use *among*.

**beverage** beverages
NOUN; *FORMAL* a drink.

**bevy** bevies
NOUN a group of people *E.G. a bevy of lawyers*.

**beware**
VERB If you tell someone to beware of something, you are warning them that it might be dangerous or harmful.

**bewilder** bewilders bewildering bewildered
VERB If something bewilders you, it is too confusing or difficult for you to understand.
**bewildered** ADJECTIVE **bewildering** ADJECTIVE **bewilderment** NOUN

**bewitch** bewitches bewitching bewitched
VERB 1 To bewitch someone means to cast a spell on them. 2 If something bewitches you, you are so delighted by it that you cannot pay attention to anything else.
**bewitched** ADJECTIVE **bewitching** ADJECTIVE

**beyond**
PREPOSITION 1 If something is beyond a certain place, it is on the other side of it *E.G. Beyond the hills was the Sahara*. 2 If something continues beyond a particular point, it continues further than that point *E.G. an education beyond the age of 16*. 3 If someone or something is beyond understanding or help, they cannot be understood or helped.

**bi-**
PREFIX 'Bi-' means 'two' or 'twice'. *E.G. bicycle, bigamy*.
📖 from Latin *bis* meaning 'two'

**bias**
NOUN (HISTORY) Someone who shows bias favours one person or thing unfairly.
☰ favouritism, partiality, prejudice

**biased** or **biassed**
ADJECTIVE favouring one person or thing unfairly *E.G. biased attitudes*.
☰ one-sided, prejudiced

**bib** bibs
NOUN a piece of cloth or plastic which is worn under the chin of very young children when they are eating, to keep their clothes clean.

**Bible** Bibles
NOUN (RE) The Bible is the sacred book of the Christian religion.
**biblical** ADJECTIVE
📖 from Greek *biblia* meaning 'the books'

**bicentenary** bicentenaries
NOUN The bicentenary of an event is its two-hundredth anniversary.

**biceps**
NOUN (PE) Your biceps are the large muscles on your upper arms.

**bicker** bickers bickering bickered
VERB When people bicker, they argue or quarrel about unimportant things.

**bicycle** bicycles
NOUN a two-wheeled vehicle which you ride by pushing two pedals with your feet.

**bid** bids bidding bade bidden bid
NOUN 1 an attempt to obtain or do something *E.G. He made a bid for freedom*. 2 an offer to buy something for a certain sum of money. ▶ VERB 3 If you bid for something, you offer to

pay a certain sum of money for it.
**4** OLD-FASHIONED If you bid someone a greeting or a farewell, you say it to them

☑ When *bid* means 'offer to pay a certain sum of money' (sense 3), the past tense and past participle is *bid*. When *bid* means 'say a greeting or farewell' (sense 4), the past tense is *bade* and the past participle is *bidden*.

**biddy-biddy** biddy-biddies
NOUN a prickly low-growing plant found in New Zealand.

**bide** bides biding bided
PHRASE If you **bide your time**, you wait for a good opportunity before doing something.

**bidet** bidets
*Said "**bee**-day"* NOUN a low basin in a bathroom which is used for washing your bottom in.
🏛 a French word meaning 'small horse'

**big** bigger biggest
ADJECTIVE large or important.
**biggish** ADJECTIVE **bigness** NOUN
🔳 enormous, huge, large

**bigamy**
NOUN Bigamy is the crime of marrying someone when you are already married to someone else.
**bigamist** NOUN

**bigot** bigots
NOUN someone who has strong and unreasonable opinions which they refuse to change.
**bigoted** ADJECTIVE **bigotry** NOUN

**bike** bikes
NOUN; INFORMAL a bicycle or motorcycle.

**bikini** bikinis
NOUN a small two-piece swimming costume worn by women.
🏛 after *Bikini* atoll, from a comparison

between the devastating effect of the atom-bomb test and the effect caused by women wearing bikinis

**bilateral**
ADJECTIVE A bilateral agreement is one made between two groups or countries.

**bile**
NOUN Bile is a bitter yellow liquid produced by the liver which helps the digestion of fat.

**bilge**
NOUN the lowest part of a ship, where dirty water collects.

**bilingual**
ADJECTIVE involving or using two languages E.G. *bilingual street signs*.

**bill** bills
NOUN **1** a written statement of how much is owed for goods or services. **2** a formal statement of a proposed new law that is discussed and then voted on in Parliament. **3** a notice or a poster. **4** A bird's bill is its beak.
🔳 (sense 1) charges, invoice

**billabong** billabongs
NOUN In Australia, a billabong is a lagoon or pool formed from part of a river.

**billboard** billboards
NOUN a large board on which advertisements are displayed.

**billet** billets billeting billeted
VERB When soldiers are billeted in a building, arrangements are made for them to stay there.

**billiards**
NOUN Billiards is a game in which a long cue is used to move balls on a table.

**billion** billions
NOUN a thousand million. Formerly, a billion was a million million.
☑ As the meaning of *billion* has changed from one million million to

a b c d e f g h i j k l m n o p q r s t u v w x y z

A
B
C
D
E
F
G
H
I
J
K
L
M
N
O
P
Q
R
S
T
U
V
W
X
Y
Z

one thousand million, a writer may mean either of these things when using it, depending on when the book or article was written.

**billow billows billowing billowed**
VERB **1** When things made of cloth billow, they swell out and flap slowly in the wind. **2** When smoke or cloud billows, it spreads upwards and outwards. ▶ NOUN **3** a large wave.

**billy** or **billycan billies** or **billycans**
NOUN In Australian and New Zealand English, a metal pot for boiling water over a camp fire.

**bin bins**
NOUN a container, especially one that you put rubbish in.

**binary**
*Said* "by-nar-ee" ADJECTIVE  (ICT) The binary system expresses numbers using only two digits, 0 and 1.

**bind binds binding bound**
VERB **1** If you bind something, you tie rope or string round it so that it is held firmly. **2** If something binds you to a course of action, it makes you act in that way *E.G. He was bound by that decision.*

**bindi-eye bindi-eyes**
NOUN a small Australian plant with prickly fruits.

**binding bindings**
ADJECTIVE **1** If a promise or agreement is binding, it must be obeyed. ▶ NOUN **2** The binding of a book is its cover.

**binge binges**
NOUN; INFORMAL a wild bout of drinking or eating too much.

**bingo**
NOUN Bingo is a game in which players aim to match the numbers that someone calls out with the numbers on the card that they have been given.

**binoculars**
PLURAL NOUN Binoculars are an instrument with lenses for both eyes, which you look through in order to see objects far away.

**bio-**
PREFIX 'Bio-' means 'life' or 'living things'. For example, a *biography* is the story of someone's life and *biology* is the study of living things.
🔲 from Greek *bios* meaning 'life'

**biochemistry**
NOUN Biochemistry is the study of the chemistry of living things.
**biochemical** ADJECTIVE **biochemist** NOUN

**biodegradable**
ADJECTIVE If something is biodegradable, it can be broken down into its natural elements by the action of bacteria *E.G. biodegradable cleaning products.*

**biodiversity**
NOUN the existence of a wide variety of plant and animal species in a particular area.

**biography biographies**
NOUN the history of someone's life, written by someone else.
**biographer** NOUN **biographical** ADJECTIVE

**biology**
NOUN Biology is the study of living things.
**biological** ADJECTIVE **biologically** ADVERB **biologist** NOUN

**biometric**
ADJECTIVE relating to biometrics *E.G. a biometric passport.*

**biometrics**
NOUN the use of mathematical

measurements to analyse physical characteristics, especially to identify people.

**bionic**

ADJECTIVE having a part of the body that works electronically.

**biopsy biopsies**

NOUN an examination under a microscope of tissue from a living body to find out the cause of a disease.

**birch birches**

NOUN a tall deciduous tree with thin branches and thin bark.

**bird birds**

NOUN an animal with two legs, two wings, and feathers.

**birth births**

NOUN 1 The birth of a baby is when it comes out of its mother's womb at the beginning of its life. 2 The birth of something is its beginning E.G. *the birth of modern art*.

**birthday birthdays**

NOUN Your birthday is the anniversary of the date on which you were born.

**birthmark birthmarks**

NOUN a mark on someone's skin that has been there since they were born.

**biscuit biscuits**

NOUN a small flat cake made of baked dough.

📖 from Old French *bes* + *cuit* meaning 'twice-cooked'

**bisect bisects bisecting bisected**

VERB To bisect a line or area means to divide it in half.

**bisexual**

ADJECTIVE sexually attracted to both men and women.

**bishop bishops**

NOUN 1 a high-ranking clergyman in some Christian Churches. 2 In chess, a bishop is a piece that is moved

diagonally across the board.

**bison**

NOUN a large hairy animal related to cattle.

**bistro bistros**

*Said "bee-stroh"* NOUN a small informal restaurant.

**bit bits**

1 Bit is the past tense of **bite**. ► NOUN 2 A bit of something is a small amount of it E.G. *a bit of coal*. ► PHRASE; INFORMAL 3 A bit means slightly or to a small extent E.G. *That's a bit tricky*.

▣ (sense 2) fragment, part, piece

**bitch bitches**

NOUN 1 a female dog. 2 OFFENSIVE If someone refers to a woman as a bitch, it means that they think she behaves in a spiteful way.

**bitchy** ADJECTIVE

**bite bites biting bit bitten**

VERB 1 If you bite something, you use your teeth to cut into it or through it. 2 When an animal or insect bites you, it cuts into your skin with its teeth or mouth. ► NOUN 3 a small amount that you bite off something with your teeth. 4 the injury you get when an animal or insect bites you.

**bitter bitterest**

ADJECTIVE 1 If someone is bitter, they feel angry and resentful. 2 A bitter disappointment or experience makes people feel angry or unhappy for a long time afterwards. 3 In a bitter argument or war, people argue or fight fiercely and angrily E.G. *a bitter power struggle*. 4 A bitter wind is an extremely cold wind. 5 Something that tastes bitter has a sharp, unpleasant taste.

**bitterly** ADVERB    **bitterness** NOUN

a
**b**
c
d
e
f
g
h
i
j
k
l
m
n
o
p
q
r
s
t
u
v
w
x
y
z

A
B
C
D
E
F
G
H
I
J
K
L
M
N
O
P
Q
R
S
T
U
V
W
X
Y
Z

■ (sense 1) acrimonious, resentful, sour

■ (sense 5) acid, sharp, sour

**bivouac** bivouacs
*Said* "**biv**-oo-ak" NOUN a temporary camp in the open air.

**bizarre**
*Said* "biz-**zahr**" ADJECTIVE very strange or eccentric.

**blab** blabs blabbing blabbed
VERB; INFORMAL When someone blabs, they give away secrets by talking carelessly.

**black** blacker blackest; blacks
NOUN OR ADJECTIVE **1** Black is the darkest possible colour, like tar or soot.
**2** Someone who is Black is a member of a dark-skinned race. ▶ ADJECTIVE
**3** Black coffee or tea has no milk or cream added to it. **4** Black humour involves jokes about death or suffering.
**blackness** NOUN
■ (sense 1) dark, jet, pitch-black
✔ When you are writing about a person or people, *Black* should start with a capital letter.

**blackberry** blackberries
NOUN Blackberries are small black fruits that grow on prickly bushes called brambles.

**blackbird** blackbirds
NOUN a common European bird, the male of which has black feathers and a yellow beak.

**blackboard** blackboards
NOUN a dark-coloured board in a classroom, which teachers write on using chalk.

**black box** black boxes
NOUN an electronic device in an aircraft which collects and stores information during flights.

**blackcurrant** blackcurrants
NOUN Blackcurrants are very small dark purple fruits that grow in bunches on bushes.

**blacken** blackens blackening blackened
VERB To blacken something means to make it black E.G. *The smoke from the chimney blackened the roof.*

**blackhead** blackheads
NOUN a very small black spot on the skin caused by a pore being blocked with dirt.

**blacklist** blacklists blacklisting blacklisted
NOUN **1** a list of people or organizations who are thought to be untrustworthy or disloyal. ▶ VERB
**2** When someone is blacklisted, they are put on a blacklist.

**blackmail** blackmails blackmailing blackmailed
VERB **1** If someone blackmails another person, they threaten to reveal an unpleasant secret about them unless that person gives them money or does something for them. ▶ NOUN
**2** Blackmail is the action of blackmailing people.
**blackmailer** NOUN

**black market**
NOUN If something is bought or sold on the black market, it is bought or sold illegally.

**blackout** blackouts
NOUN If you have a blackout, you lose consciousness for a short time.

**blacksmith** blacksmiths
NOUN a person whose job is making things out of iron, such as horseshoes.

**bladder** bladders
NOUN the part of your body where

SPELLING NOTE ▶ I want to see (C) your licenCe (licence)

urine is held until it leaves your body.

**blade** blades

NOUN **1** The blade of a weapon or cutting tool is the sharp part of it. **2** The blades of a propeller are the thin, flat parts that turn round. **3** A blade of grass is a single piece of it.

**blame** blames blaming blamed

VERB **1** If someone blames you for something bad that has happened, they believe you caused it. ▶ NOUN **2** The blame for something bad that happens is the responsibility for letting it happen.

■ (sense 1) accuse, hold responsible

**blameless**

ADJECTIVE Someone who is blameless has not done anything wrong.

**blanch** blanches blanching blanched

VERB If you blanch, you suddenly become very pale.

**bland** blander blandest

ADJECTIVE tasteless, dull or boring E.G. *a bland diet… bland pop music.*

**blandly** ADVERB

**blank** blanker blankest

ADJECTIVE **1** Something that is blank has nothing on it E.G. *a blank sheet of paper.* **2** If you look blank, your face shows no feeling or interest. ▶ NOUN **3** If your mind is a blank, you cannot think of anything or remember anything.

**blanket** blankets

NOUN **1** a large rectangle of thick cloth that is put on a bed to keep people warm. **2** A blanket of something such as snow is a thick covering of it.

**blare** blares blaring blared

VERB To blare means to make a loud, unpleasant noise E.G. *The radio blared pop music.*

**blaspheme** blasphemes blaspheming blasphemed

VERB When people blaspheme, they are disrespectful about God or religion.

🏛 from Greek *blapsis* meaning 'evil' and *phēmein* meaning 'to speak'

**blasphemy** blasphemies

NOUN Blasphemy is speech or behaviour that shows disrespect for God or religion.

**blasphemous** ADJECTIVE

**blast** blasts blasting blasted

VERB **1** When people blast a hole in something they make a hole with an explosion. ▶ NOUN **2** a big explosion, especially one caused by a bomb. **3** a sudden strong rush of wind or air.

**blatant**

ADJECTIVE If you describe something you think is bad as blatant, you mean that rather than hide it, those responsible actually seem to be making it obvious E.G. *a blatant disregard for the law.*

**blaze** blazes blazing blazed

NOUN **1** a large, hot fire. **2** A blaze of light or colour is a great or strong amount of it E.G. *a blaze of red.* **3** A blaze of publicity or attention is a lot of it. ▶ VERB **4** If something blazes it burns or shines brightly.

**blazer** blazers

NOUN a kind of jacket, often in the colours of a school or sports team.

**bleach** bleaches bleaching bleached

VERB **1** To bleach material or hair means to make it white, usually by using a chemical. ▶ NOUN **2** Bleach is a chemical that is used to make material white or to clean thoroughly and kill germs.

a
b
c
d
e
f
g
h
i
j
k
l
m
n
o
p
q
r
s
t
u
v
w
x
y
z

**bleak** bleaker bleakest
ADJECTIVE **1** If a situation is bleak, it is bad and seems unlikely to improve. **2** If a place is bleak, it is cold, bare, and exposed to the wind.

**bleary**
ADJECTIVE If your eyes are bleary, they are red and watery, usually because you are tired.

**bleat** bleats bleating bleated
VERB **1** When sheep or goats bleat, they make a high-pitched cry. ▶ NOUN **2** the high-pitched cry that a sheep or goat makes.

**bleed** bleeds bleeding bled
VERB When you bleed, you lose blood as a result of an injury.

**bleep** bleeps
NOUN a short high-pitched sound made by an electrical device such as an alarm.

**blemish** blemishes
NOUN a mark that spoils the appearance of something.

**blend** blends blending blended
VERB **1** When you blend substances, you mix them together to form a single substance. **2** When colours or sounds blend, they combine in a pleasing way. ▶ NOUN **3** A blend of things is a mixture of them, especially one that is pleasing. **4** a word formed by joining together the beginning and the end of two other words; for example, 'brunch' is a blend of 'breakfast' and 'lunch'.

**blender** blenders
NOUN a machine used for mixing liquids and foods at high speed.

**bless** blesses blessing blessed or blest
VERB When a priest blesses people or things, he or she asks for God's protection for them.
📖 from Old English *blædsian* meaning 'to sprinkle with sacrificial blood'

**blessed**
ADJECTIVE
*Said "blest"* If someone is blessed with a particular quality or skill, they have it *E.G. He was blessed with a sense of humour.*
**blessedly** ADVERB

**blessing** blessings
NOUN **1** something good that you are thankful for *E.G. Good health is the greatest blessing.* ▶ **2** If something is done **with someone's blessing**, they approve of it and support it.

**blew**
the past tense of **blow**.

**blight** blights blighting blighted
NOUN **1** something that damages or spoils other things *E.G. the blight of the recession.* ▶ VERB **2** When something is blighted, it is seriously harmed *E.G. His life had been blighted by sickness.*

**blind** blinds blinding blinded
ADJECTIVE **1** Someone who is blind cannot see. **2** If someone is blind to a particular fact, they do not understand it. ▶ VERB **3** If something blinds you, you become unable to see, either for a short time or permanently. ▶ NOUN **4** a roll of cloth or paper that you pull down over a window to keep out the light.
**blindly** ADVERB **blindness** NOUN

**blindfold** blindfolds blindfolding blindfolded
NOUN **1** a strip of cloth tied over someone's eyes so that they cannot see. ▶ VERB **2** To blindfold someone

means to cover their eyes with a strip of cloth.

**blinding**

ADJECTIVE A blinding light is so bright that it hurts your eyes E.G. *There was a blinding flash*.

**blindingly**

ADVERB; INFORMAL If something is blindingly obvious, it is very obvious indeed.

**blink** blinks blinking blinked

VERB When you blink, you close your eyes quickly for a moment.

**blinkers**

PLURAL NOUN Blinkers are two pieces of leather placed at the side of a horse's eyes so that it can only see straight ahead.

**bliss**

NOUN Bliss is a state of complete happiness.

**blissful** ADJECTIVE    **blissfully** ADVERB

**blister** blisters blistering blistered

NOUN 1 a small bubble on your skin containing watery liquid, caused by a burn or rubbing. ▶ VERB 2 If someone's skin blisters, blisters appear on it as result of burning or rubbing.

**blithe**

ADJECTIVE casual and done without serious thought E.G. *a blithe disregard for their safety*.

**blithely** ADVERB

**blitz** blitzes blitzing blitzed

NOUN 1 a bombing attack by enemy aircraft on a city. ▶ VERB 2 When a city is blitzed, it is bombed by aircraft and is damaged or destroyed.

🏛 from German *Blitzkrieg* meaning 'lightning war'

**blizzard** blizzards

NOUN a heavy snowstorm with strong winds.

**bloated**

ADJECTIVE much larger than normal, often because there is a lot of liquid or gas inside it.

**blob** blobs

NOUN a small amount of a thick or sticky substance is.

**bloc** blocs

NOUN A group of countries or political parties with similar aims acting together is often called a bloc E.G. *the world's largest trading bloc*.

**block** blocks blocking blocked

NOUN 1 A block of flats or offices is a large building containing flats or offices. 2 In a town, a block is an area of land with streets on all its sides E.G. *He lives a few blocks down*. 3 A block of something is a large rectangular piece of it. ▶ VERB 4 To block a road or channel means to put something across it so that nothing can get through. 5 If something blocks your view, it is in the way and prevents you from seeing what you want to see. 6 If someone blocks something, they prevent it from happening E.G. *The council blocked his plans*.

▤ (sense 3) bar, chunk, piece

▤ (senses 4, 5 & 6) obstruct

**blockade** blockades blockading blockaded

NOUN 1 an action that prevents goods from reaching a place. ▶ VERB 2 When a place is blockaded, supplies are prevented from reaching it.

**blockage** blockages

NOUN When there is a blockage in a pipe or tunnel, something is clogging it.

▤ impediment, obstruction, stoppage

a b c d e f g h i j k l m n o p q r s t u v w x y z

**blog** blogs

NOUN; *INFORMAL* short for weblog: a person's online diary that he or she puts on the Internet so that other people can read it.

**blogger** bloggers

NOUN; *INFORMAL* a person who keeps a blog.

**bloke** blokes

NOUN; *INFORMAL* a man.

**blonde** blondes or **blond** blonds

ADJECTIVE 1 Blonde hair is pale yellow in colour. The spelling 'blond' is used when referring to men. ▶ NOUN 2 A blonde, or blond, is a person with light-coloured hair.

**blood**

NOUN 1 Blood is the red liquid that is pumped by the heart round the bodies of human beings and other mammals. ▶ PHRASE 2 If something cruel is done **in cold blood**, it is done deliberately and without showing any emotion.

**bloodhound** bloodhounds

NOUN a large dog with an excellent sense of smell.

**bloodless**

ADJECTIVE 1 If someone's face or skin is bloodless, it is very pale. 2 In a bloodless coup or revolution, nobody is killed.

**blood pressure**

NOUN Your blood pressure is a measure of the force with which your blood is being pumped round your body.

**bloodshed**

NOUN When there is bloodshed, people are killed or wounded.

**bloodshot**

ADJECTIVE If a person's eyes are bloodshot, the white parts have become red.

**blood sport** blood sports

NOUN any sport that involves deliberately killing or injuring animals.

**bloodstained**

ADJECTIVE covered with blood.

**bloodstream**

NOUN the flow of blood through your body.

**bloodthirsty**

ADJECTIVE Someone who is bloodthirsty enjoys using or watching violence.

**blood transfusion** blood transfusions

NOUN a process in which blood is injected into the body of someone who has lost a lot of blood.

**blood vessel** blood vessels

NOUN Blood vessels are the narrow tubes in your body through which your blood flows.

**bloody** bloodier bloodiest

ADJECTIVE OR ADVERB 1 Bloody is a common swearword, used to express anger or annoyance. ▶ ADJECTIVE 2 A bloody event is one in which a lot of people are killed *E.G. a bloody revolution*. 3 Bloody also means covered with blood *E.G. a bloody gash on his head*.

**bloom** blooms blooming bloomed

NOUN 1 a flower on a plant. ▶ VERB 2 When a plant blooms, it produces flowers. 3 When something like a feeling blooms, it grows *E.G. Romance can bloom where you least expect it*.

**blossom** blossoms blossoming blossomed

NOUN 1 Blossom is the growth of flowers that appears on a tree before the fruit. ▶ VERB 2 When a tree blossoms, it produces blossom.

A
B
C
D
E
F
G
H
I
J
K
L
M
N
O
P
Q
R
S
T
U
V
W
X
Y
Z

**blot** blots blotting blotted
NOUN **1** a drop of ink that has been spilled on a surface. **2** A blot on someone's reputation is a mistake or piece of bad behaviour that spoils their reputation.

**blot out** VERB To blot something out means to be in front of it and prevent it from being seen *E.G. The smoke blotted out the sky.*

**blotch** blotches
NOUN a stain or a patch of a different colour.

**blotchy** ADJECTIVE

**blouse** blouses
NOUN a light shirt, worn by a girl or a woman.

**blow** blows blowing blew blown
VERB **1** When the wind blows, the air moves. **2** If something blows or is blown somewhere, the wind moves it there. **3** If you blow a whistle or horn, you make a sound by blowing into it. ▶ NOUN **4** If you receive a blow, someone or something hits you. **5** something that makes you very disappointed or unhappy *E.G. Marc's death was a terrible blow.*

**blow up** VERB **1** To blow something up means to destroy it with an explosion. **2** To blow up a balloon or a tyre is to fill it with air.

**blubber**
NOUN The blubber of animals such as whales and seals is the layer of fat that protects them from the cold.

**bludge** bludges bludging bludged
VERB *INFORMAL* **1** In Australian and New Zealand English, to bludge is to scrounge or cadge. **2** In Australian and New Zealand English, to bludge is also to avoid work or responsibilities.

**bludgeon** bludgeons bludgeoning bludgeoned
VERB to hit several times with a heavy object.

**blue** bluer bluest
ADJECTIVE or NOUN **1** Blue is the colour of the sky on a clear, sunny day. ▶ PHRASE **2** If something happens **out of the blue**, it happens suddenly and unexpectedly. ▶ ADJECTIVE **3** Blue films and jokes are about sex.

**bluish** or **blueish** ADJECTIVE

**bluebell** bluebells
NOUN a woodland plant with blue, bell-shaped flowers.

**bluebottle** bluebottles
NOUN **1** a large fly with a shiny dark-blue body. **2** In Australia and New Zealand, a bluebottle is also a small stinging jellyfish.

**blue-collar**
ADJECTIVE Blue-collar workers do physical work as opposed to office work.

**blueprint** blueprints
NOUN a plan of how something is expected to work *E.G. the blueprint for successful living.*

**blues**
NOUN The blues is a type of music which is similar to jazz, but is always slow and sad.

**bluff** bluffs bluffing bluffed
NOUN **1** an attempt to make someone wrongly believe that you are in a strong position. ▶ VERB **2** If you are bluffing, you are trying to make someone believe that you are in a position of strength.

**blunder** blunders blundering blundered
VERB **1** If you blunder, you make a silly mistake. ▶ NOUN **2** a silly mistake.

a
b
c
d
e
f
g
h
i
j
k
l
m
n
o
p
q
r
s
t
u
v
w
x
y
z

You must practiSe your Ss (practise)  **SPELLING NOTE**

# blunt ≫ bob

**blunt** blunter bluntest
ADJECTIVE **1** A blunt object has a rounded point or edge, rather than a sharp one. **2** If you are blunt, you say exactly what you think, without trying to be polite.
■ (sense 2) forthright, outspoken, straightforward

**blur** blurs blurring blurred
NOUN **1** a shape or area which you cannot see clearly because it has no distinct outline or because it is moving very fast. ▶ VERB **2** To blur the differences between things means to make them no longer clear *E.G. The dreams blurred confusingly with her memories.*
**blurred** ADJECTIVE

**blurt out** blurts out blurting out blurted out
VERB If you blurt something out, you say it suddenly, after trying to keep it a secret.

**blush** blushes blushing blushed
VERB **1** If you blush, your face becomes red, because you are embarrassed or ashamed. ▶ NOUN **2** the red colour on someone's face when they are embarrassed or ashamed.

**bluster** blusters blustering blustered
VERB **1** When someone blusters, they behave aggressively because they are angry or frightened. ▶ NOUN **2** Bluster is aggressive behaviour by someone who is angry or frightened.

**blustery**
ADJECTIVE Blustery weather is rough and windy.

**boa** boas
NOUN **1** A boa, or a boa constrictor, is a large snake that kills its prey by coiling

round it and crushing it. **2** a woman's long thin scarf of feathers or fur.

**boar** boars
NOUN a male wild pig, or a male domestic pig used for breeding.

**board** boards boarding boarded
NOUN **1** a long, flat piece of wood. **2** the group of people who control a company or organization. **3** Board is the meals provided when you stay somewhere *E.G. The price includes full board.* ▶ VERB **4** If you board a ship or aircraft, you get on it or in it. ▶ PHRASE **5** If you are **on board** a ship or aircraft, you are on it or in it.

**boarder** boarders
NOUN a pupil who lives at school during term.

**boarding school** boarding schools
NOUN a school where the pupils live during the term.

**boardroom** boardrooms
NOUN a room where the board of a company meets.

**boast** boasts boasting boasted
VERB **1** If you boast about your possessions or achievements, you talk about them proudly. ▶ NOUN **2** something that you say which shows that you are proud of what you own or have done.
**boastful** ADJECTIVE
■ (sense 1) blow your own trumpet, brag, crow

**boat** boats
NOUN a small vehicle for travelling across water.

**bob** bobs bobbing bobbed
VERB **1** When something bobs, it moves up and down. ▶ NOUN **2** a woman's hair style in which her hair is cut level with her chin.

**bobbin** bobbins
NOUN a small round object on which thread or wool is wound.

**bobby** bobbies
NOUN; OLD-FASHIONED a policeman.

**bode** bodes boding boded
PHRASE; LITERARY If something **bodes ill**, or **bodes well**, it makes you think that something bad, or good, will happen.

**bodice** bodices
NOUN the upper part of a dress.

**bodily**
ADJECTIVE 1 relating to the body E.G. bodily contact. ▶ ADVERB 2 involving the whole of someone's body E.G. He was carried bodily up the steps.

**body** bodies
NOUN 1 Your body is either all your physical parts, or just the main part not including your head, arms, and legs. 2 a person's dead body. 3 the main part of a car or aircraft, not including the engine. 4 A body of people is also an organized group.
■ (sense 1) build, figure, form, physique

**bodyguard** bodyguards
NOUN a person employed to protect someone.

**bodywork**
NOUN the outer part of a motor vehicle

**boer** boers
Said "boh-er" NOUN In South Africa, a boer is a white farmer, especially one who is descended from the Dutch people who went to live in South Africa.

**boerewors**
Said "boo-rih-vorse" NOUN In South Africa, boerewors is a type of meat sausage.

**bog** bogs
NOUN an area of land which is always wet and spongy.
■ from Gaelic bogach meaning 'swamp'

**boggle** boggles boggling boggled
VERB If your mind boggles at something, you find it difficult to imagine or understand.

**bogus**
ADJECTIVE not genuine E.G. a bogus doctor.

**bohemian**
Said "boh-hee-mee-an" ADJECTIVE Someone who is bohemian does not behave in the same way as most other people in society, and is usually involved in the arts.

**boil** boils boiling boiled
VERB 1 When a hot liquid boils, bubbles appear in it and it starts to give off steam. 2 When you boil a kettle, you heat it until the water in it boils. 3 When you boil food, you cook it in boiling water. ▶ NOUN 4 a red swelling on your skin.

**boiler** boilers
NOUN a piece of equipment which burns fuel to provide hot water.

**boiling**
ADJECTIVE; INFORMAL very hot.

**boisterous**
ADJECTIVE Someone who is boisterous is noisy and lively.
■ loud, noisy, rowdy, unruly

**bold** bolder boldest
ADJECTIVE 1 confident and not shy or embarrassed E.G. He was not bold enough to ask them. 2 not afraid of risk or danger. 3 clear and noticeable E.G. bold colours.
**boldly** ADVERB  **boldness** NOUN

**bollard** bollards
NOUN a short, thick post used to keep vehicles out of a road.

a
b
c
d
e
f
g
h
i
j
k
l
m
n
o
p
q
r
s
t
u
v
w
x
y
z

LEarn the principLEs (princip**le**)  **SPELLING NOTE**

**bolster bolsters bolstering bolstered**

VERB To bolster something means to support it or make it stronger E.G. *She relied on others to bolster her self-esteem.*

**bolt bolts bolting bolted**

NOUN 1 a metal bar that you slide across a door or window in order to fasten it. 2 a metal object which screws into a nut and is used to fasten things together. ▶ VERB 3 If you bolt a door or window, you fasten it using a bolt. If you bolt things together, you fasten them together using a bolt. 4 To bolt means to escape or run away. 5 To bolt food means to eat it very quickly.

**bomb bombs bombing bombed**

NOUN 1 a container filled with material that explodes when it hits something or is set off by a timer. ▶ VERB 2 When a place is bombed, it is attacked with bombs.
📖 from Greek *bombos* meaning 'a booming sound'

**bombard bombards bombarding bombarded**

VERB 1 To bombard a place means to attack it with heavy gunfire or bombs. 2 If you are bombarded with something you are made to face a great deal of it E.G. *I was bombarded with criticism.*
**bombardment** NOUN

**bomber bombers**

NOUN an aircraft that drops bombs.

**bombshell bombshells**

NOUN a sudden piece of shocking or upsetting news.

**bona fide**

Said "boh-na **fie**-dee" ADJECTIVE genuine E.G. *We are happy to donate to bona fide charities.*

📖 a Latin expression meaning 'in good faith'

**bond bonds bonding bonded**

NOUN 1 a close relationship between people. 2 LITERARY Bonds are chains or ropes used to tie a prisoner up. 3 a certificate which records that you have lent money to a business and that it will repay you the loan with interest. 4 Bonds are also feelings or obligations that force you to behave in a particular way E.G. *the social bonds of community.* ▶ VERB 5 When two things bond or are bonded, they become closely linked or attached.
**≡** (sense 1) connection, link, tie

**bondage**

NOUN Bondage is the condition of being someone's slave.

**bone bones**

NOUN Bones are the hard parts that form the framework of a person's or animal's body.
**boneless** ADJECTIVE

**bonfire bonfires**

NOUN a large fire made outdoors, often to burn rubbish.
📖 from 'bone' + 'fire'; bones were used as fuel in the Middle Ages

**bonnet bonnets**

NOUN 1 the metal cover over a car's engine. 2 a baby's or woman's hat tied under the chin.

**bonny bonnier bonniest**

ADJECTIVE; SCOTTISH AND NORTHERN ENGLISH nice to look at.

**bonus bonuses**

NOUN 1 an amount of money added to your usual pay. 2 Something that is a bonus is a good thing that you get in addition to something else.

**bony bonier boniest**

ADJECTIVE Bony people or animals are

thin, with very little flesh covering their bones.

**boo** boos booing booed
NOUN **1** a shout of disapproval. ▶ VERB **2** When people boo, they shout 'boo' to show their disapproval.

**boobook** boobooks
NOUN a small brown Australian owl with a spotted back and wings.

**book** books booking booked
NOUN **1** a number of pages held together inside a cover. ▶ VERB **2** When you book something such as a room, you arrange to have it or use it at a particular time.

**bookcase** bookcases
NOUN a piece of furniture with shelves for books.

**bookie** bookies
NOUN; *INFORMAL* a bookmaker.

**booking** bookings
NOUN an arrangement to book something such as a hotel room.

**book-keeping**
NOUN Book-keeping is the keeping of a record of the money spent and received by a business.

**booklet** booklets
NOUN a small book with a paper cover.

**bookmaker** bookmakers
NOUN a person who makes a living by taking people's bets and paying them when they win.

**bookmark** bookmarks
NOUN a piece of card which you put between the pages of a book to mark your place.

**boom** booms booming boomed
NOUN **1** a rapid increase in something *E.G. the baby boom.* **2** a loud deep echoing sound. ▶ VERB **3** When something booms, it increases

rapidly *E.G. Sales are booming.* **4** To boom means to make a loud deep echoing sound.

**boomerang** boomerangs
NOUN a curved wooden missile that can be thrown so that it returns to the thrower, originally used as a weapon by Australian Aborigines.

**boon** boons
NOUN Something that is a boon makes life better or easier *E.G. Credit cards have been a boon to shoppers.*

**boost** boosts boosting boosted
VERB **1** To boost something means to cause it to improve or increase *E.G. The campaign had boosted sales.* ▶ NOUN **2** an improvement or increase *E.G. a boost to the economy.*
**booster** NOUN

**boot** boots booting booted
NOUN **1** Boots are strong shoes that come up over your ankle and sometimes your calf. **2** the covered space at the back, for carrying things in. ▶ VERB **3** *INFORMAL* If you boot something, you kick it.
▶ PHRASE **4 To boot** means also or in addition *E.G. The story was compelling and well written to boot.*

**booth** booths
NOUN **1** a small partly enclosed area *E.G. a telephone booth.* **2** a stall where you can buy goods.

**booty**
NOUN Booty is valuable things taken from a place, especially by soldiers after a battle.

**booze** boozes boozing boozed
*INFORMAL*
NOUN **1** Booze is alcoholic drink. ▶ VERB **2** When people booze, they drink alcohol.
**boozer** NOUN  **boozy** ADJECTIVE

a
b
c
d
e
f
g
h
i
j
k
l
m
n
o
p
q
r
s
t
u
v
w
x
y
z

the QUeen stood on the QUay (quay)  ▶ **SPELLING NOTE**

A
B
C
D
E
F
G
H
I
J
K
L
M
N
O
P
Q
R
S
T
U
V
W
X
Y
Z

from Old Dutch *busen* meaning 'to drink to excess'

**border** borders bordering bordered

NOUN **1** the dividing line between two countries. **2** a strip or band round the edge of something *E.G. plain tiles with a bright border*. **3** a long flower bed in a garden. ▶ VERB **4** To border something means to form a boundary along the side of it *E.G. Tall poplar trees bordered the fields*.

**borderline**

ADJECTIVE only just acceptable as a member of a class or group *E.G. a borderline case*.

**bore** bores boring bored

VERB **1** If something bores you, you find it dull and not at all interesting. **2** If you bore a hole in something, you make it using a tool such as a drill. ▶ NOUN **3** someone or something that bores you.

**bored**

ADJECTIVE If you are bored, you are impatient because you do not find something interesting or because you have nothing to do.

**boredom** NOUN

☑ You can say that you are *bored with* or *bored by* someone or something, but you should not say *bored of*.

**boring**

ADJECTIVE dull and lacking interest.

▦ dull, tedious, uninteresting

**born**

VERB **1** When a baby is born, it comes out of its mother's womb at the beginning of its life. ▶ ADJECTIVE **2** You use 'born' to mean that someone has a particular quality from birth *E.G. He was a born pessimist*.

**borne**

the past participle of **bear**.

**borough** boroughs

*Said "bur-uh"* NOUN a town, or a district within a large town, that has its own council.

**borrow** borrows borrowing borrowed

VERB If you borrow something that belongs to someone else, they let you have it for a period of time.

**borrower** NOUN

☑ You *borrow* something *from* a person, not *off* them. Do not confuse *borrow* and *lend*. If you *borrow* something, you get it from another person for a while; if you *lend* something, someone gets it from you for a while.

**Bosnian** Bosnians

ADJECTIVE **1** belonging to or relating to Bosnia. ▶ NOUN **2** someone who comes from Bosnia.

**bosom** bosoms

NOUN **1** A woman's bosom is her breasts. ▶ ADJECTIVE **2** A bosom friend is a very close friend.

**boss** bosses bossing bossed

NOUN **1** Someone's boss is the person in charge of the place where they work. ▶ VERB **2** If someone bosses you around, they keep telling you what to do.

**bossy** bossier bossiest

ADJECTIVE A bossy person enjoys telling other people what to do.

**bossiness** NOUN

▦ dictatorial, domineering, overbearing

**botany**

NOUN Botany is the scientific study of plants.

**botanic** or **botanical** ADJECTIVE
**botanist** NOUN

**botch** botches botching botched
VERB; *INFORMAL* If you botch something,
you do it badly or clumsily.
■ bungle, mess up

**both**
ADJECTIVE or PRONOUN 'Both' is used
when saying something about two
things or people
☑ You can use *of* after *both*, but it is
not essential. *Both the boys* means
the same as *both of the boys*.

**bother** bothers bothering
bothered
VERB **1** If you do not bother to do
something, you do not do it because
it takes too much effort or it seems
unnecessary. **2** If something bothers
you, you are worried or concerned
about it. If you do not bother about
it, you are not concerned about it *E.G.*
*She is not bothered about money.* **3** If
you bother someone, you interrupt
them when they are busy. ▶ NOUN
**4** Bother is trouble, fuss, or difficulty.
**bothersome** ADJECTIVE

**bottle** bottles bottling bottled
NOUN **1** a glass or plastic container for
keeping liquids in. ▶ VERB **2** To bottle
something means to store it in
bottles.

**bottleneck** bottlenecks
NOUN a narrow section of road where
traffic has to slow down or stop

**bottle store** bottle stores
NOUN In Australian, New Zealand, and
South African English, a bottle store
is a shop that sells sealed alcoholic
drinks which can be drunk
elsewhere.

**bottom** bottoms
NOUN **1** The bottom of something is its
lowest part. **2** Your bottom is your
buttocks. ▶ ADJECTIVE **3** The bottom
thing in a series of things is the
lowest one.

**bottomless** ADJECTIVE

**bough** boughs
*Rhymes with "now"* NOUN a large
branch of a tree.

**bought**
the past tense and past participle of
buy.
☑ Do not confuse *bought* and
*brought*. *Bought* comes from *buy* and
*brought* comes from *bring*.

**boulder** boulders
NOUN a large rounded rock.

**boulevard** boulevards
*Said "boo-le-vard"* NOUN a wide street
in a city, usually with trees along
each side.

**bounce** bounces bouncing
bounced
VERB **1** When an object bounces, it
springs back from something after
hitting it. **2** To bounce also means to
move up and down *E.G. Her long*
*black hair bounced as she walked.* **3** If
a cheque bounces, the bank refuses
to accept it because there is not
enough money in the account.
■ (sense 1) rebound, recoil, ricochet

**bouncy** bouncier bounciest
ADJECTIVE **1** Someone who is bouncy is
lively and enthusiastic. **2** Something
that is bouncy is capable of
bouncing or being bounced on *E.G. a*
*bouncy ball… a bouncy castle.*

**bound** bounds bounding bounded
ADJECTIVE **1** If you say that something is
bound to happen, you mean that it is
certain to happen. **2** If a person or a
vehicle is bound for a place, they are
going there. **3** If someone is bound

a
b
c
d
e
f
g
h
i
j
k
l
m
n
o
p
q
r
s
t
u
v
w
x
y
z

by an agreement or regulation, they must obey it. ► NOUN **4** a large leap. ► PLURAL NOUN **5** Bounds are limits which restrict or control something E.G. *Their enthusiasm knew no bounds.* ► PHRASE **6** If a place is **out of bounds**, you are forbidden to go there. ► VERB **7** When animals or people bound, they move quickly with large leaps E.G. *He bounded up the stairway.* **8** Bound is also the past tense and past participle of **bind**.

**boundary boundaries**
NOUN something that indicates the farthest limit of anything E.G. *the city boundary… the boundaries of taste.*

**boundless**
ADJECTIVE without end or limit E.G. *her boundless energy.*

**bountiful**
ADJECTIVE; LITERARY freely available in large amounts E.G. *a bountiful harvest.*

**bounty**
NOUN **1** LITERARY Bounty is a generous supply E.G. *autumn's bounty of fruits.* **2** Someone's bounty is their generosity in giving a lot of something.

**bouquet bouquets**
*Said "boo-***kay***"* NOUN an attractively arranged bunch of flowers.

**bourgeois**
*Said "boor-***jhwah***"* ADJECTIVE typical of fairly rich middle-class people.

**bourgeoisie**
*Said "boor-jhwah-***zee***"* NOUN the fairly rich middle-class people in a society.

**bout bouts**
NOUN **1** If you have a bout of something such as an illness, you have it for a short time E.G. *a bout of flu.* **2** If you have a bout of doing something, you do it enthusiastically

for a short time. **3** a boxing or wrestling match.

**boutique boutiques**
*Said "boo-***teek***"* NOUN a small shop that sells fashionable clothes.

**bovine**
ADJECTIVE; TECHNICAL relating to cattle.

**bow bows bowing bowed**
*Rhymes with "***now***"* VERB **1** When you bow, you bend your body or lower your head as a sign of respect or greeting. **2** If you bow to something, you give in to it E.G. *He bowed to public pressure.* ► NOUN **3** the movement you make when you bow. **4** the front part of a ship.

**bow bows**
*Rhymes with "***low***"* NOUN **1** a knot with two loops and two loose ends. **2** a long thin piece of wood with horsehair stretched along it, which you use to play a violin. **3** a long flexible piece of wood used for shooting arrows.

**bowel bowels**
*Rhymes with "***towel***"* NOUN Your bowels are the tubes leading from your stomach, through which waste passes before it leaves your body. 🔲 from Latin *botellus* meaning 'little sausage'

**bowerbird bowerbirds**
NOUN a bird found in Australia, the male of which builds a shelter during courtship.

**bowl bowls bowling bowled**
*Rhymes with "***mole***"* NOUN **1** a round container with a wide uncovered top, used for holding liquid or for serving food. **2** the hollow, rounded part of something E.G. *a toilet bowl.* **3** a large heavy ball used in the game of bowls or tenpin bowling. ► VERB

**4** In cricket, to bowl means to throw the ball towards the batsman.
**bowler** NOUN

**bowling**
NOUN Bowling is a game in which you roll a heavy ball down a narrow track towards a group of wooden objects called pins and try to knock them down.

**bowls**
NOUN Bowls is a game in which the players try to roll large wooden balls as near as possible to a small ball.

**bow tie** bow ties
*Rhymes with "low"* NOUN a man's tie in the form of a bow, often worn at formal occasions.

**box** boxes boxing boxed
NOUN **1** a container with a firm base and sides and usually a lid. **2** On a form, a box is a rectangular space which you have to fill in. **3** In a theatre, a box is a small separate area where a few people can watch the performance together. ▶ VERB **4** To box means to fight someone according to the rules of boxing.

**boxer** boxers
NOUN **1** a person who boxes. **2** a type of medium-sized, smooth-haired dog with a flat face.

**boxing**
NOUN Boxing is a sport in which two people fight using their fists, wearing padded gloves.

**box office** box offices
NOUN the place where tickets are sold in a theatre or cinema.

**boy** boys
NOUN a male child.
**boyhood** NOUN    **boyish** ADJECTIVE
■ lad, youngster, youth

**boycott** boycotts boycotting boycotted

VERB **1** If you boycott an organization or event, you refuse to have anything to do with it. ▶ NOUN **2** the boycotting of an organization or event *E.G. a boycott of the elections.*
▥ from the name of Captain C.C. Boycott (1832–1897), an Irish land agent, who offended the tenants, so that they refused to pay their rents
■ (sense 1) ban, black, embargo

**boyfriend** boyfriends
NOUN Someone's boyfriend is the man or boy with whom they are having a romantic relationship.

**bra** bras
NOUN a piece of underwear worn by a woman to support her breasts

**braaivleis** or **braai** braaivleises or braais
*Said "**bry**-flayss"* NOUN In South African English, a braaivleis is a picnic where meat is cooked on an open fire.

**brace** braces bracing braced
VERB **1** When you brace yourself, you stiffen your body to steady yourself *E.G. The ship lurched and he braced himself.* **2** If you brace yourself for something unpleasant, you prepare yourself to deal with it *E.G. The police are braced for violent reprisals.* ▶ NOUN **3** an object fastened to something to straighten or support it *E.G. a neck brace.* ▶ PLURAL NOUN **4** Braces are a pair of straps worn over the shoulders and fastened to the trousers to hold them up.

**bracelet** bracelets
NOUN a chain or band worn around someone's wrist as an ornament.

**bracing**
ADJECTIVE Something that is bracing

a
b
c
d
e
f
g
h
i
j
k
l
m
n
o
p
q
r
s
t
u
v
w
x
y
z

makes you feel fit and full of energy *E.G. the bracing sea air.*

**bracken**

NOUN Bracken is a plant like a large fern that grows on hills and in woods.

**bracket** brackets

NOUN 1 Brackets are a pair of written marks, ( ), [ ], or { }, placed round a word or sentence that is not part of the main text, or to show that the items inside the brackets belong together. 2 a range between two limits, for example of ages or prices *E.G. the four-figure price bracket.* 3 a piece of metal or wood fastened to a wall to support something such as a shelf.

---

### What do Brackets do?

**Brackets** ( ) enclose material that has been added to the text, but could be omitted and still leave a meaningful sentence. In formal writing this sort of material is usually marked off with commas or dashes, and brackets are used for giving references or translations of foreign phrases:

*E.G. Buddhism is discussed in Chapter 7 (see pages 152–197).*
■ *The boat was called "La Ardilla Roja" (The Red Squirrel).*

**Square brackets** [] are used to enclose remarks and explanations which are inserted by an author to make a quotation clearer:

*E.G. The minister said, "I think that five million [pounds] should do it."*

---

**brag** brags bragging bragged

VERB When someone brags, they boast about their achievements *E.G. Both leaders bragged they could win by a landslide.*

**Brahma**

*Said "brah-ma"* PROPER NOUN Brahma is a Hindu god and is one of the Trimurti.

▥ from a Sanskrit word meaning 'praise'

**Brahman**

*Said "brah-men"* NOUN In the Hindu religion Brahman is the ultimate and impersonal divine reality of the universe.

**brahmin** brahmins

*Said "brah-min"* NOUN a member of the highest or priestly caste in Hindu society.

**braid** braids braiding braided

NOUN 1 Braid is a strip of decorated cloth used to decorate clothes or curtains. 2 a length of hair which has been plaited and tied. ▶ VERB 3 To braid hair or thread means to plait it.

**Braille**

NOUN Braille is a system of printing for blind people in which letters are represented by raised dots that can be felt with the fingers.

**brain** brains

NOUN 1 Your brain is the mass of nerve tissue inside your head that controls your body and enables you to think and feel; also used to refer to your mind and the way that you think *E.G. I admired his legal brain.* ▶ PLURAL NOUN 2 If you say that someone has brains, you mean that they are very intelligent.

**brainchild**

NOUN; *INFORMAL* Someone's brainchild is something that they have invented or created.

**brainwash** brainwashes
brainwashing brainwashed
VERB If people are brainwashed into
believing something, they accept it
without question because they are
told it repeatedly.
**brainwashing** NOUN

**brainwave** brainwaves
NOUN; *INFORMAL* a clever idea you think
of suddenly.

**brainy** brainier brainiest
ADJECTIVE; *INFORMAL* clever.

**braise** braises braising braised
VERB To braise food means to fry it for
a short time, then cook it slowly in a
little liquid.

**brake** brakes braking braked
NOUN 1 a device for making a vehicle
stop or slow down. ▶ VERB 2 When a
driver brakes, he or she makes a
vehicle stop or slow down by using
its brakes
✔ Do not confuse the spellings of
*brake* and *break*, or *braking* and
*breaking*.

**bramble** brambles
NOUN a wild, thorny bush that
produces blackberries.

**bran**
NOUN Bran is the ground husks that
are left over after flour has been
made from wheat grains.

**branch** branches branching
branched
NOUN 1 The branches of a tree are the
parts that grow out from its trunk.
2 A branch of an organization is one
of a number of its offices or shops.
3 A branch of a subject is one of its
areas of study or activity *E.G.
specialists in certain branches of
medicine.* ▶ VERB 4 A road that
branches off from another road splits

off from it to lead in a different
direction.

**brand** brands branding branded
NOUN 1 A brand of something is a
particular kind or make of it *E.G. a
popular brand of chocolate.* ▶ VERB
2 When an animal is branded, a mark
is burned on its skin to show who
owns it.

**brandish** brandishes brandishing
brandished
VERB; *LITERARY* If you brandish
something, you wave it vigorously.

**brand-new**
ADJECTIVE completely new.

**brandy**
NOUN a strong alcoholic drink, usually
made from wine.
▥ from Dutch *brandewijn* meaning
'burnt wine'

**brash** brasher brashest
ADJECTIVE If someone is brash, they are
overconfident or rather rude.

**brass**
NOUN *or* ADJECTIVE 1 Brass is a yellow-
coloured metal made from copper
and zinc. 2 In an orchestra, the brass
section consists of brass wind
instruments such as trumpets and
trombones.

**brassière** brassières
NOUN; *FORMAL* a bra.

**brat** brats
NOUN; *INFORMAL* A badly behaved child
may be referred to as a brat.

**bravado**
*Said* "bra-**vah**-doh" NOUN Bravado is a
display of courage intended to
impress other people.

**brave** braver bravest; braves
braving braved
ADJECTIVE 1 A brave person is willing to
do dangerous things and does not

a
b
c
d
e
f
g
h
i
j
k
l
m
n
o
p
q
r
s
t
u
v
w
x
y
z

A
B
C
D
E
F
G
H
I
J
K
L
M
N
O
P
Q
R
S
T
U
V
W
X
Y
Z

show any fear. ▶ VERB 2 If you brave an unpleasant or dangerous situation, you face up to it in order to do something E.G. *His fans braved the rain to hear him sing.*

**bravely** ADVERB **bravery** NOUN

■ (sense 1) courageous, daring, fearless, plucky

**bravo**

INTERJECTION People shout 'Bravo!' to express appreciation when something has been done well.

**brawl brawls brawling brawled**

NOUN 1 a rough fight. ▶ VERB 2 When people brawl, they take part in a rough fight.

**brawn**

NOUN Brawn is physical strength.

**brawny** ADJECTIVE

**bray brays braying brayed**

VERB 1 When a donkey brays, it makes a loud, harsh sound. ▶ NOUN 2 the sound a donkey makes.

**brazen**

ADJECTIVE When someone's behaviour is brazen, they do not care if other people think they are behaving wrongly.

**brazenly** ADVERB

**brazier braziers**

NOUN a metal container in which coal or charcoal is burned to keep people warm out of doors.

**Brazilian Brazilians**

ADJECTIVE 1 belonging or relating to Brazil. ▶ NOUN 2 someone who comes from Brazil.

**breach breaches breaching breached**

VERB 1 FORMAL If you breach an agreement or law, you break it. 2 To breach a barrier means to make a gap in it E.G. *The river breached its*

banks. ▶ NOUN 3 A breach of an agreement or law is an action that breaks it E.G. *a breach of contract.* 4 a gap or break.

■ (sense 3) contravention, infringement, violation

**bread**

NOUN a food made from flour and water, usually raised with yeast, and baked.

**breadth**

NOUN The breadth of something is the distance between its two sides.

**breadwinner breadwinners**

NOUN the person who earns the money in a family.

**break breaks breaking broke broken**

VERB 1 When an object breaks, it is damaged and separates into pieces. 2 If you break a rule or promise you fail to keep it. 3 When a boy's voice breaks, it becomes permanently deeper. 4 When a wave breaks, it falls and becomes foam. ▶ NOUN 5 a short period during which you rest or do something different.

■ (sense 1) crack, fracture, separate, snap

■ (sense 2) breach, contravene, disobey, violate

**break down** VERB 1 When a machine or a vehicle breaks down, it stops working. 2 When a discussion or relationship breaks down, it ends because of problems or disagreements.

**break up** VERB If something breaks up, it ends E.G. *The marriage broke up after a year.*

**breakable** ADJECTIVE

☑ Do not confuse the spellings of *break* and *brake*, or *breaking* and *braking*.

**breakage** breakages
NOUN the act of breaking something or a thing that has been broken.

**breakaway**
ADJECTIVE A breakaway group is one that has separated from a larger group.

**breakdown** breakdowns
NOUN 1 The breakdown of something such as a system is its failure E.G. *a breakdown in communications.* 2 the same as a nervous breakdown. 3 If a driver has a breakdown, their car stops working.

**breaker** breakers
NOUN Breakers are big sea waves.

**breakfast** breakfasts
NOUN the first meal of the day.

**break-in** break-ins
NOUN the illegal entering of a building, especially by a burglar.

**breakneck**
ADJECTIVE; *INFORMAL* Someone or something that is travelling at breakneck speed is travelling dangerously fast.

**breakthrough** breakthroughs
NOUN a sudden important development E.G. *a medical breakthrough.*

**breakwater** breakwaters
NOUN a wall extending into the sea which protects a coast from the force of the waves.

**bream** breams
NOUN an edible fish.

**breast** breasts
NOUN A woman's breasts are the two soft, fleshy parts on her chest, which produce milk after she has had a baby.

**breath** breaths
NOUN 1 Your breath is the air you take into your lungs and let out again when you breathe. ► PHRASE 2 If you are **out of breath**, you are breathing with difficulty after doing something energetic. 3 If you say something **under your breath**, you say it in a very quiet voice.

**breathe** breathes breathing breathed
VERB When you breathe, you take air into your lungs and let it out again.

**breathless**
ADJECTIVE If you are breathless, you are breathing fast or with difficulty.
**breathlessly** ADVERB
**breathlessness** NOUN

**breathtaking**
ADJECTIVE If you say that something is breathtaking, you mean that it is very beautiful or exciting.

**bred**
the past tense and past participle of **breed.**

**breeches**
*Said* "**brit-chiz**" PLURAL NOUN Breeches are trousers reaching to just below the knee, nowadays worn especially for riding.

**breed** breeds breeding bred
NOUN 1 A breed of a species of domestic animal is a particular type of it. ► VERB 2 Someone who breeds animals or plants keeps them in order to produce more animals or plants with particular qualities. 3 When animals breed, they mate and produce offspring.
■ (sense 3) multiply, procreate, reproduce

**breeze** breezes
NOUN a gentle wind.

**brevity**
NOUN; *FORMAL* Brevity means shortness

a
b
c
d
e
f
g
h
i
j
k
l
m
n
o
p
q
r
s
t
u
v
w
x
y
z

A
B
C
D
E
F
G
H
I
J
K
L
M
N
O
P
Q
R
S
T
U
V
W
X
Y
Z

*E.G. the brevity of his report.*

**brew brews brewing brewed**

VERB **1** If you brew tea or coffee, you make it in a pot by pouring hot water over it. **2** To brew beer means to make it, by boiling and fermenting malt. **3** If an unpleasant situation is brewing, it is about to happen *E.G. Another scandal is brewing.*

**brewer** NOUN

**brewery breweries**

NOUN a place where beer is made, or a company that makes it.

**briar briars**

NOUN a wild rose that grows on a dense prickly bush.

**bribe bribes bribing bribed**

NOUN **1** a gift or money given to an official to persuade them to make a favourable decision. ▸ VERB **2** To bribe someone means to give them a bribe.

**bribery** NOUN

**bric-a-brac**

NOUN Bric-a-brac consists of small ornaments or pieces of furniture of no great value.

🔲 from an obsolete French phrase *à bric et à brac* meaning 'at random'

**brick bricks**

NOUN Bricks are rectangular blocks of baked clay used in building.

**bricklayer bricklayers**

NOUN a person whose job is to build with bricks.

**bride brides**

NOUN a woman who is getting married or who has just got married.

**bridal** ADJECTIVE

**bridegroom bridegrooms**

NOUN a man who is getting married or who has just got married.

**bridesmaid bridesmaids**

NOUN a woman who helps and accompanies a bride on her wedding day.

**bridge bridges**

NOUN **1** a structure built over a river, road, or railway so that vehicles and people can cross. **2** the platform from which a ship is steered and controlled. **3** the hard ridge at the top of your nose. **4** Bridge is a card game for four players based on whist.

**bridle bridles**

NOUN a set of straps round a horse's head and mouth, which the rider uses to control the horse.

**brief briefer briefest; briefs briefing briefed**

ADJECTIVE **1** Something that is brief lasts only a short time. ▸ VERB **2** ⬭D & T⬭ When you brief someone on a task, you give them all the necessary instructions and information about it.

**briefly** ADVERB

■ (sense 1) fleeting, momentary, quick, short

**briefcase briefcases**

NOUN a small flat case for carrying papers.

**briefing briefings**

NOUN a meeting at which information and instructions are given.

**brier**

another spelling of **briar**.

**brigade brigades**

NOUN an army unit consisting of three battalions.

🔲 from Italian *brigare* meaning 'to fight'

**brigadier brigadiers**

*Said* "brig-ad-**ear**" NOUN an army

officer of the rank immediately above colonel.

**brigalow** brigalows
NOUN a type of Australian acacia tree that grows in the bush.

**bright** brighter brightest
ADJECTIVE **1** strong and startling E.G. *a bright light*. **2** clever E.G. *my brightest student*. **3** cheerful E.G. *a bright smile*.
**brightly** ADVERB **brightness** NOUN
■ (sense 1) brilliant, dazzling, shining, vivid

**brighten** brightens brightening brightened
VERB **1** If something brightens, it becomes brighter E.G. *The weather had brightened*. **2** If someone brightens, they suddenly look happier.
**brighten up** VERB To brighten something up means to make it more attractive and cheerful.

**brilliant**
ADJECTIVE **1** A brilliant light or colour is extremely bright. **2** A brilliant person is extremely clever. **3** A brilliant career is extremely successful.
**brilliantly** ADVERB **brilliance** NOUN

**brim** brims
NOUN **1** the wide part of a hat is the part that sticks outwards at the bottom. ► PHRASE **2** If a container is filled **to the brim**, it is filled right to the top.

**brine**
NOUN Brine is salt water.

**bring** brings bringing brought
VERB **1** If you bring something or someone with you when you go to a place, you take them with you E.G. *You can bring a friend to the party*. **2** To bring something to a particular state means to cause it to be like

that E.G. *Bring the vegetables to the boil*.

**bring about** VERB To bring something about means to cause it to happen E.G. *We must try to bring about a better world*.

**bring up** VERB **1** To bring up children means to look after them while they grow up. **2** If you bring up a subject, you introduce it into the conversation E.G. *She brought up the subject at dinner*.

**brinjal** brinjals
NOUN In Indian and South African English, an aubergine.

**brink**
NOUN If you are on the brink of something, you are just about to do it or experience it.

**brisk** brisker briskest
ADJECTIVE **1** A brisk action is done quickly and energetically E.G. *A brisk walk restores your energy*. **2** If someone's manner is brisk, it shows that they want to get things done quickly and efficiently.
**briskly** ADVERB **briskness** NOUN

**bristle** bristles bristling bristled
NOUN **1** Bristles are strong animal hairs used to make brushes. ► VERB **2** If the hairs on an animal's body bristle, they rise up, because it is frightened.
**bristly** ADJECTIVE

**British**
ADJECTIVE belonging or relating to the United Kingdom of Great Britain and Northern Ireland.

**Briton** Britons
NOUN someone who comes from the United Kingdom of Great Britain and Northern Ireland.

**brittle**
ADJECTIVE An object that is brittle is

hard but breaks easily.

**broach** broaches broaching broached

VERB When you broach a subject, you introduce it into a discussion.

**broad** broader broadest

ADJECTIVE 1 wide E.G. *a broad smile*. 2 having many different aspects or concerning many different people E.G. *A broad range of issues was discussed*. 3 general rather than detailed E.G. *the broad concerns of the movement*. 4 If someone has a broad accent, the way that they speak makes it very clear where they come from E.G. *She spoke in a broad Irish accent*.

**broadband**

NOUN Broadband is a digital system used on the Internet and in other forms of telecommunication which can process and transfer information input from various sources, such as from telephones, computers or televisions.

**broad bean** broad beans

NOUN Broad beans are light-green beans with thick flat edible seeds.

**broadcast** broadcasts broadcasting broadcast

NOUN 1 a programme or announcement on radio or television. ▶ VERB 2 To broadcast something means to send it out by radio waves, so that it can be seen on television or heard on radio.
**broadcaster** NOUN   **broadcasting** NOUN

**broaden** broadens broadening broadened

VERB 1 When something broadens, it becomes wider E.G. *His smile broadened*. 2 To broaden something

means to cause it to involve more things or concern more people E.G. *We must broaden the scope of this job*.

**broadly**

ADVERB true to a large extent or in most cases E.G. *There are broadly two schools of thought on this*.

**broad-minded**

ADJECTIVE Someone who is broad-minded does not disapprove of behaviour or attitudes that many other people disapprove of.
■ liberal, open-minded, tolerant

**broadsheet** broadsheets

NOUN a newspaper with large pages and long news stories.

**brocade**

NOUN Brocade is a heavy, expensive material, often made of silk, with a raised pattern.
▥ from Spanish *brocado* meaning 'embossed fabric'

**broccoli**

NOUN Broccoli is a green vegetable, similar to cauliflower.

**brochure** brochures

*Said* "**broh-sher**" NOUN a booklet which gives information about a product or service.

**brogue** brogues

*Said* "**broag**" NOUN 1 a strong accent, especially an Irish one. 2 Brogues are thick leather shoes.
▥ from Irish Gaelic *bróg* meaning 'boot' or 'shoe'

**broke**

1 the past tense of **break**. ▶ ADJECTIVE 2 *INFORMAL* If you are broke, you have no money.

**broken**

the past participle of **break**.

**broker** brokers

NOUN a person whose job is to buy

and sell shares for other people.

**brolga** brolgas
NOUN a large grey Australian crane with a red-and-green head.

**brolly** brollies
NOUN; *INFORMAL* an umbrella.

**bronchitis**
NOUN Bronchitis is an illness in which the two tubes which connect your windpipe to your lungs become infected, making you cough.

**brontosaurus** brontosauruses
NOUN a type of very large, plant-eating dinosaur.

**bronze**
NOUN Bronze is a yellowish-brown metal which is a mixture of copper and tin; also the yellowish-brown colour of this metal.

**brooch** brooches
*Rhymes with "coach"* NOUN a piece of jewellery with a pin at the back for attaching to clothes.

**brood** broods brooding brooded
NOUN 1 a family of baby birds. ▶ VERB 2 If you brood about something, you keep thinking about it in a serious or unhappy way.

**brook** brooks
NOUN a stream.

**broom** brooms
NOUN 1 a long-handled brush. 2 Broom is a shrub with yellow flowers.

**broth**
NOUN Broth is soup, usually with vegetables in it.

**brothel** brothels
NOUN a house where men pay to have sex with prostitutes.

**brother** brothers
NOUN Your brother is a boy or man who has the same parents as you.
**brotherly** ADJECTIVE

**brotherhood** brotherhoods
NOUN 1 Brotherhood is the affection and loyalty that brothers or close male friends feel for each other. 2 a group of men with common interests or beliefs.

**brother-in-law** brothers-in-law
NOUN Someone's brother-in-law is the brother of their husband or wife, or their sister's husband.

**brought**
the past tense and past participle of bring.
☑ Do not confuse *brought* and *bought*. *Brought* comes from *bring* and *bought* comes from *buy*.

**brow** brows
NOUN 1 Your brow is your forehead. 2 Your brows are your eyebrows. 3 The brow of a hill is the top of it.

**brown** browner brownest
ADJECTIVE OR NOUN Brown is the colour of earth or wood.

**brownie** brownies
NOUN a junior member of the Guides.

**browse** browses browsing browsed
VERB 1 If you browse through a book, you look through it in a casual way. 2 If you browse in a shop, you look at the things in it for interest rather than because you want to buy something.

**browser** browsers
NOUN a piece of computer software that lets you look at websites on the World Wide Web.

**bruise** bruises bruising bruised
NOUN 1 a purple mark that appears on your skin after something has hit it. ▶ VERB 2 If something bruises you, it hits you so that a bruise appears on your skin.

a b c d e f g h i j k l m n o p q r s t u v w x y z

Betty Eats Cakes And Uses Seven Eggs (<u>because</u>)　　　SPELLING NOTE

A
B
C
D
E
F
G
H
I
J
K
L
M
N
O
P
Q
R
S
T
U
V
W
X
Y
Z

**brumby** brumbies
NOUN In Australia and New Zealand, a wild horse.

**brunette** brunettes
NOUN a girl or woman with dark brown hair.

**brunt**
PHRASE If you **bear the brunt** of something unpleasant, you are the person who suffers most E.G. *Women bear the brunt of crime.*

**brush** brushes brushing brushed
NOUN 1 an object with bristles which you use for cleaning things, painting, or tidying your hair. ▶ VERB 2 If you brush something, you clean it or tidy it with a brush. 3 To brush against something means to touch it while passing it E.G. *Her lips brushed his cheek.*

**brusque**
*Said "broosk"* ADJECTIVE Someone who is brusque deals with people quickly and without considering their feelings. **brusquely** ADVERB

**brussels sprout** brussels sprouts
NOUN Brussels sprouts are vegetables that look like tiny cabbages.

**brutal**
ADJECTIVE Brutal behaviour is cruel and violent E.G. *the victim of a brutal murder.*
**brutally** ADVERB **brutality** NOUN

**brute** brutes
NOUN 1 a rough and insensitive man. ▶ ADJECTIVE 2 Brute force is strength alone, without any skill E.G. *You have to use brute force to open the gates.*
**brutish** ADJECTIVE

**bubble** bubbles bubbling bubbled
NOUN 1 a ball of air in a liquid. 2 a hollow, delicate ball of soapy liquid.

▶ VERB 3 When a liquid bubbles, bubbles form in it. 4 If you are bubbling with something like excitement, you are full of it.
**bubbly** ADJECTIVE

**buck** bucks bucking bucked
NOUN 1 the male of various animals, including the deer and the rabbit. ▶ VERB 2 If a horse bucks, it jumps into the air with its feet off the ground.

**bucket** buckets
NOUN a deep round container with an open top and a handle.

**buckle** buckles buckling buckled
NOUN 1 a fastening on the end of a belt or strap. ▶ VERB 2 If you buckle a belt or strap, you fasten it. 3 If something buckles, it becomes bent because of severe heat or pressure.

**bud** buds budding budded
NOUN 1 a small, tight swelling on a tree or plant, which develops into a flower or a cluster of leaves. ▶ VERB 2 When a tree or plant buds, new buds appear on it.

**Buddha**
PROPER NOUN The Buddha is the title of Gautama Siddhartha, a religious teacher living in the 6th century BC in India and founder of Buddhism. Buddha means 'the enlightened one'

**Buddhism**
NOUN Buddhism is a religion, founded by the Buddha, which teaches that the way to end suffering is by overcoming your desires.
**Buddhist** NOUN OR ADJECTIVE

**budding**
ADJECTIVE just beginning to develop E.G. *a budding artist.*

**budge** budges budging budged
VERB If something will not budge, you cannot move it.

**budgerigar** budgerigars

NOUN a small brightly coloured pet bird.

**budget** budgets budgeting budgeted

NOUN 1 a plan showing how much money will be available and how it will be spent. ► VERB 2 If you budget for something, you plan your money carefully, so that you are able to afford it.

**budgetary** ADJECTIVE

**budgie** budgies

NOUN; *INFORMAL* a budgerigar.

**buff** buffs

ADJECTIVE 1 a pale brown colour. ► NOUN 2 *INFORMAL* someone who knows a lot about a subject *E.G. a film buff.*

**buffalo** buffaloes

NOUN a wild animal like a large cow with long curved horns.

**buffer** buffers

NOUN 1 Buffers on a train or at the end of a railway line are metal discs on springs that reduce shock when they are hit. 2 something that prevents something else from being harmed *E.G. keep savings as a buffer against unexpected cash needs.*

**buffet** buffets

*Said "***boof***-ay"* NOUN 1 a café at a station. 2 a meal at which people serve themselves.

**buffet** buffets buffeting buffeted

*Said "***buff***-it"* VERB If the wind or sea buffets a place or person, it strikes them violently and repeatedly.

**bug** bugs bugging bugged

NOUN 1 an insect, especially one that causes damage. 2 a small error in a computer program which means that the program will not work properly. 3 *INFORMAL* a virus or minor

infection *E.G. a stomach bug.* ► VERB 4 If a place is bugged, tiny microphones are hidden there to pick up what people are saying.

**bugle** bugles

NOUN a brass instrument that looks like a small trumpet.

**bugler** NOUN

**build** builds building built

VERB 1 To build something such as a house means to make it from its parts. 2 To build something such as an organization means to develop it gradually. ► NOUN 3 Your build is the shape and size of your body.

**builder** NOUN

■ (sense 1) assemble, construct, erect

**building** buildings

NOUN a structure with walls and a roof.

**building society** building societies

NOUN a business in which some people invest their money, while others borrow from it to buy a house.

**bulb** bulbs

NOUN 1 the glass part of an electric lamp. 2 an onion-shaped root that grows into a flower or plant.

**Bulgarian** Bulgarians

ADJECTIVE 1 belonging or relating to Bulgaria. ► NOUN 2 someone who comes from Bulgaria. 3 the main language spoken in Bulgaria.

**bulge** bulges bulging bulged

VERB 1 If something bulges, it swells out from a surface. ► NOUN 2 a lump on a normally flat surface.

**bulk** bulks

NOUN 1 a large mass of something *E.G. The book is more impressive for its*

a
b
c
d
e
f
g
h
i
j
k
l
m
n
o
p
q
r
s
t
u
v
w
x
y
z

bulk than its content. **2** The bulk of something is most of it *E.G. the bulk of the world's great poetry.* ▶ PHRASE **3** To buy something **in bulk** means to buy it in large quantities.

**bulky** bulkier bulkiest
ADJECTIVE large and heavy *E.G. a bulky package.*
■ cumbersome, large, unwieldy

**bull** bulls
NOUN the male of some species of animals, including the cow family, elephants and whales.

**bulldog** bulldogs
NOUN a squat dog with a broad head and muscular body.

**bulldozer** bulldozers
NOUN a powerful tractor with a broad blade in front, which is used for moving earth or knocking things down.

**bullet** bullets
NOUN a small piece of metal fired from a gun.

**bulletin** bulletins
NOUN **1** a short news report on radio or television. **2** a leaflet or small newspaper regularly produced by a group or organization.
圙 from Italian *bulletino* meaning 'small Papal edict'

**bullion**
NOUN Bullion is gold or silver in the form of bars.

**bullock** bullocks
NOUN a young castrated bull.

**bullroarer** bullroarers
NOUN a wooden slat attached to a string that is whirled round to make a roaring noise. Bullroarers are used especially by Australian Aborigines in religious ceremonies.

**bully** bullies bullying bullied
NOUN **1** someone who uses their

strength or power to hurt or frighten other people. ▶ VERB **2** If someone bullies you into doing something, they make you do it by using force or threats.
圙 a 16th century word meaning 'fine fellow' or 'hired ruffian'

**bump** bumps bumping bumped
VERB **1** If you bump into something, you knock into it with a jolt. ▶ NOUN **2** a soft or dull noise made by something knocking into something else. **3** a raised, uneven part of a surface.
**bumpy** ADJECTIVE
■ (sense 3) bulge, lump, protuberance

**bumper** bumpers
NOUN **1** Bumpers are bars on the front and back of a vehicle which protect it if there is a collision. ▶ ADJECTIVE **2** A bumper crop or harvest is larger than usual.

**bun** buns
NOUN a small, round cake.

**bunch** bunches bunching bunched
NOUN **1** a group of people or things. **2** A bunch of flowers is a number of them held or tied together. **3** A bunch of bananas or grapes is a group of them growing on the same stem. ▶ VERB **4** When people bunch together or bunch up, they stay very close to each other.

**bundle** bundles bundling bundled
NOUN **1** a number of things tied together or wrapped up in a cloth. ▶ VERB **2** If you bundle someone or something somewhere, you push them there quickly and roughly.

**bung** bungs bunging bunged
NOUN **1** a stopper used to close a hole

in something such as a barrel. ▶ VERB **2** INFORMAL If you bung something somewhere, you put it there quickly and carelessly.

**bungalow** bungalows
NOUN a one-storey house.
🏛 from Hindi *bangla* meaning 'of Bengal'

**bungle** bungles bungling bungled
VERB To bungle something means to fail to do it properly.

**bunion** bunions
NOUN a painful lump on the first joint of a person's big toe.

**bunk** bunks
NOUN a bed fixed to a wall in a ship or caravan.

**bunker** bunkers
NOUN **1** On a golf course, a bunker is a large hole filled with sand. **2** A coal bunker is a storage place for coal. **3** an underground shelter with strong walls to protect it from bombing.

**bunting**
NOUN Bunting is strips of small coloured flags displayed on streets and buildings on special occasions.

**bunyip** bunyips
NOUN a legendary monster said to live in swamps and lakes in Australia.

**buoy** buoys
*Said* "boy" NOUN a floating object anchored to the bottom of the sea, marking a channel or warning of danger.

**buoyant**
ADJECTIVE **1** able to float. **2** lively and cheerful *E.G. She was in a buoyant mood.*
**buoyancy** NOUN

**burble** burbles burbling burbled
VERB To burble means to makes a soft bubbling sound *E.G. The water*

burbled over the gravel.

**burden** burdens
NOUN **1** a heavy load. **2** If something is a burden to you, it causes you a lot of worry or hard work.
**burdensome** ADJECTIVE
🔲 (sense 1) load, weight
🔲 (sense 2) millstone, trouble, worry

**bureau** bureaux
*Said* "**b**yoo-**roh**" NOUN **1** an office that provides a service *E.G. an employment bureau.* **2** a writing desk with shelves and drawers.

**bureaucracy**
NOUN Bureaucracy is the complex system of rules and procedures which operates in government departments.
**bureaucratic** ADJECTIVE

**bureaucrat** bureaucrats
NOUN a person who works in a government department, especially one who follows rules and procedures strictly.

**burgeoning**
ADJECTIVE growing or developing rapidly *E.G. a burgeoning political crisis.*

**burglar** burglars
NOUN a thief who breaks into a building.
**burglary** NOUN

**burgle** burgles burgling burgled
VERB If your house is burgled, someone breaks into it and steals things.

**burial** burials
NOUN ⬭RE a ceremony held when a dead person is buried.

**burly** burlier burliest
ADJECTIVE A burly man has a broad body and strong muscles.
🔲 brawny, well-built

I want to see (C) your licen**C**e (licen**c**e)    SPELLING NOTE

A
**B**
C
D
E
F
G
H
I
J
K
L
M
N
O
P
Q
R
S
T
U
V
W
X
Y
Z

**burn** burns burning burned or burnt

VERB **1** If something is burning, it is on fire. **2** To burn something means to destroy it with fire. **3** If you burn yourself or are burned, you are injured by fire or by something hot. ▶ NOUN **4** an injury caused by fire or by something hot.

■ (sense 1) be on fire, blaze

■ (sense 2) incinerate, set on fire

✔ You can write either *burned* or *burnt* as the past form of *burn*.

**burp** burps burping burped

VERB **1** If you burp, you make a noise because air from your stomach has been forced up through your throat. ▶ NOUN **2** the noise that you make when you burp.

**burrow** burrows burrowing burrowed

NOUN **1** a tunnel or hole in the ground dug by a small animal. ▶ VERB **2** When an animal burrows, it digs a burrow.

**bursary** bursaries

NOUN a sum of money given to someone to help fund their education.

**burst** bursts bursting burst

VERB **1** When something bursts, it splits open because of pressure from inside it. **2** If you burst into a room, you enter it suddenly. **3** To burst means to happen or come suddenly and with force *E.G. The aircraft burst into flames.* **4** INFORMAL If you are bursting with something, you find it difficult to keep it to yourself *E.G. We were bursting with joy.* ▶ NOUN **5** A burst of something is a short period of it *E.G. He had a sudden burst of energy.*

■ (sense 5) outbreak, rush, spate

**bury** buries burying buried

VERB **1** When a dead person is buried, their body is put into a grave and covered with earth. **2** To bury something means to put it in a hole in the ground and cover it up. **3** If something is buried under something, it is covered by it *E.G. My bag was buried under a pile of old newspapers.*

**bus** buses

NOUN a large motor vehicle that carries passengers.

🖽 from Latin *omnibus* meaning 'for all'; buses were originally called omnibuses

**bush** bushes

NOUN **1** a thick plant with many stems branching out from ground level. **2** In Australia and South Africa, an area of land in its natural state outside of city areas is called the bush. **3** In New Zealand, the bush is land covered with rain forest.

**bushman** bushmen

NOUN **1** In Australia and New Zealand, someone who lives or travels in the bush. **2** In New Zealand, a bushman is also someone whose job it is to clear the bush for farming.

**Bushman** Bushmen

NOUN A Bushman is a member of a group of people in southern Africa who live by hunting and gathering food.

**bushranger** bushrangers

NOUN In Australia and New Zealand in the past, an outlaw living in the bush.

**bushy** bushier bushiest

ADJECTIVE Bushy hair or fur grows very thickly *E.G. bushy eyebrows.*

**business** businesses

NOUN **1** Business is work relating to the buying and selling of goods and services. **2** an organization which produces or sells goods or provides a service. **3** You can refer to any event, situation, or activity as a business *E.G. This whole business has upset me.*

**businessman** NOUN

**businesswoman** NOUN

◼ (sense 2) company, establishment, firm, organization

**businesslike**

ADJECTIVE dealing with things in an efficient way.

**busker** buskers

NOUN someone who plays music or sings for money in public places.

**bust** busts busting bust or busted

NOUN **1** a statue of someone's head and shoulders. *a bust of Beethoven.* **2** A woman's bust is her chest and her breasts. ▶ VERB **3** *INFORMAL* If you bust something, you break it.

▶ ADJECTIVE **4** *INFORMAL* If a business goes bust, it becomes bankrupt and closes down.

**bustle** bustles bustling bustled

VERB **1** When people bustle, they move in a busy, hurried way. ▶ NOUN **2** Bustle is busy, noisy activity.

**busy** busier busiest; busies busying busied

ADJECTIVE **1** If you are busy, you are in the middle of doing something. **2** A busy place is full of people doing things or moving about *E.G. a busy seaside resort.* ▶ VERB **3** If you busy yourself with something, you occupy yourself by doing it.

**busily** ADVERB

◼ (sense 1) employed, engaged, occupied

**but**

CONJUNCTION **1** used to introduce an idea that is opposite to what has gone before *E.G. I don't miss teaching but I miss the pupils.* **2** used when apologizing *E.G. I'm sorry, but I can't come tonight.* **3** except *E.G. We can't do anything but wait.*

**butcher** butchers

NOUN a shopkeeper who sells meat.

**butler** butlers

NOUN the chief male servant in a rich household.

🏛 from Old French *bouteillier* meaning 'a dealer in bottles'

**butt** butts butting butted

NOUN **1** The butt of a weapon is the thick end of its handle. **2** If you are the butt of teasing, you are the target of it. ▶ VERB **3** If you butt something, you ram it with your head.

**butt in** VERB If you butt in, you join in a private conversation or activity without being asked to.

**butter** butters buttering buttered

NOUN **1** Butter is a soft fatty food made from cream, which is spread on bread and used in cooking. ▶ VERB **2** To butter bread means to spread butter on it.

**buttercup** buttercups

NOUN a wild plant with bright yellow flowers.

**butterfly** butterflies

NOUN a type of insect with large colourful wings.

**buttocks**

PLURAL NOUN Your buttocks are the part of your body that you sit on.

a
b
c
d
e
f
g
h
i
j
k
l
m
n
o
p
q
r
s
t
u
v
w
x
y
z

**button** buttons buttoning buttoned

NOUN **1** Buttons are small, hard objects sewn on to clothing, and used to fasten two surfaces together. **2** a small object on a piece of equipment that you press to make it work. ▶ VERB **3** If you button a piece of clothing, you fasten it using its buttons.

**buttonhole** buttonholes

NOUN **1** a hole that you push a button through to fasten a piece of clothing. **2** a flower worn in your lapel.

**buxom**

ADJECTIVE A buxom woman is large, healthy, and attractive.

**buy** buys buying bought

VERB If you buy something, you obtain it by paying money for it.
**buyer** NOUN

**buzz** buzzes buzzing buzzed

VERB **1** If something buzzes, it makes a humming sound, like a bee. ▶ NOUN **2** the sound something makes when it buzzes.

**buzzard** buzzards

NOUN a large brown and white bird of prey.

**buzzer** buzzers

NOUN a device that makes a buzzing sound, to attract attention.

**by**

PREPOSITION **1** used to indicate who or what has done something E.G. *The statement was issued by his solicitor.* **2** used to indicate how something is done E.G. *He frightened her by hiding behind the door.* **3** located next to E.G. *I sat by her bed.* **4** before a particular time E.G. *It should be ready by next spring.* ▶ PREPOSITION OR ADVERB **5** going past E.G. *We drove by his house.*

**by-election** by-elections

NOUN an election held to choose a new member of parliament after the previous member has resigned or died.

**bygone**

ADJECTIVE; LITERARY happening or existing a long time ago E.G. *the ceremonies of a bygone era.*

**bypass** bypasses

NOUN a main road which takes traffic round a town rather than through it.

**bystander** bystanders

NOUN someone who is not included or involved in something but is there to see it happen.

**byte** bytes

NOUN ( ICT ) a unit of storage in a computer.

A B C D E F G H I J K L M N O P Q R S T U V W X Y Z

Plaice the fish has a glittering 'EYE' (I) (plaice)

# Cc

a
b
c ,
d
e
f
g
h
i
j
k
l
m
n
o
p
q
r
s
t
u
v
w
x
y
z

**TIP** Some words which sound as if they might begin with *s*, actually begin with *c*, for example *centre* and *cynic*. Some words which sound as if they might begin with *sh* actually begin with *ch*, for example *chute*. Some words which sound as if they might begin with *ch* are spelt with *c* alone, for example *cello*.

**cab** cabs
NOUN **1** a taxi. **2** In a lorry, bus, or train, the cab is where the driver sits.
📖 from French *cabriolet* meaning 'light two-wheeled carriage'. Cabs were originally horse-drawn

**cabaret** cabarets
*Said* "**kab**-bar-ray" NOUN a show consisting of dancing, singing, or comedy acts.
📖 from French *cabaret* meaning 'tavern'

**cabbage** cabbages
NOUN a large green leafy vegetable.
📖 from Norman French *cabache* meaning 'head'

**cabbage tree** cabbage trees
NOUN a palm-like tree found in New Zealand with a tall bare trunk and big bunches of spiky leaves; also a similar tree found in eastern Australia.

**cabin** cabins
NOUN **1** a room in a ship where a passenger sleeps. **2** a small house, usually in the country and often made of wood. **3** the area where the passengers or the crew sit in a plane.

**cabinet** cabinets
NOUN **1** a small cupboard. **2** The cabinet in a government is a group of ministers who advise the leader and decide policies.

**cable** cables
NOUN **1** a strong, thick rope or chain. **2** a bundle of wires with a rubber covering, which carries electricity. **3** (ICT) a message sent abroad by using electricity.

**cable car** cable cars
NOUN a vehicle pulled by a moving cable, for taking people up and down mountains.

**cable television**
NOUN a television service people can receive from underground wires which carry the signals.

**cacao**
*Said* "ka-**kah**-oh" NOUN a type of small tropical evergreen tree, whose berries are used to produce chocolate and cocoa.

**cache** caches
*Said* "kash" NOUN a store of things hidden away *E.G. a cache of guns.*

**cachet**
*Said* "**kash**-shay" NOUN; FORMAL Cachet is the status and respect something has *E.G. the cachet of shopping at Harrods.*

**cackle** cackles cackling cackled
VERB **1** If you cackle, you laugh harshly.
► NOUN **2** a harsh laugh.

**cacophony**
*Said* "kak-**koff**-fon-nee" NOUN; FORMAL a loud, unpleasant noise *E.G. a*

I went to see (C) the doctor's new practiCe (practi<u>c</u>e)   **SPELLING NOTE**

A
B
C
D
E
F
G
H
I
J
K
L
M
N
O
P
Q
R
S
T
U
V
W
X
Y
Z

*cacophony of barking dogs.*
📖 from Greek *kakos + phōnē*
meaning 'bad sound'

**cactus** cacti or cactuses
NOUN a thick, fleshy plant that grows
in deserts and is usually covered in
spikes.

**cad** cads
NOUN; OLD-FASHIONED a man who treats
people unfairly.

**caddie** caddies; also spelt **caddy**
NOUN 1 a person who carries golf
clubs for a golf player. 2 A tea caddy
is a box for keeping tea in.

**cadence** cadences
NOUN The cadence of someone's voice
is the way it goes up and down as
they speak.

**cadet** cadets
NOUN a young person being trained
in the armed forces or police.

**cadge** cadges cadging cadged
VERB If you cadge something off
someone, you get it from them and
don't give them anything in return
E.G. *I cadged a lift ashore.*

**caesarean** caesareans
*Said* "siz-**air**-ee-an"; also spelt
**caesarian** and **cesarean**
NOUN A caesarean or caesarean
section is an operation in which a
baby is lifted out of a woman's
womb through a cut in her
abdomen.

**café** cafés
*Said* "**kaf**-fay" NOUN 1 a place where
you can buy light meals and drinks.
2 In South African English, a café is a
corner shop or grocer's shop.

**cafeteria** cafeterias
*Said* "kaf-fit-**ee**-ree-ya" NOUN a
restaurant where you serve yourself.

**caffeine** or **caffein**
*Said* "**kaf**-feen" NOUN a chemical in
coffee and tea which makes you
more active.

**cage** cages
NOUN a box made of wire or bars in
which birds or animals are kept.
**caged** ADJECTIVE

**cagey** cagier cagiest
*Said* "**kay**-jee" ADJECTIVE; INFORMAL
cautious and not open E.G. *They're
very cagey when they talk to me.*

**cagoule** cagoules
*Said* "ka-**gool**" NOUN a lightweight
waterproof jacket with a hood.

**cahoots**
PHRASE; INFORMAL If you are **in cahoots**
with someone, you are working
closely with them on a secret plan.

**cairn** cairns
NOUN a pile of stones built as a
memorial or a landmark.
📖 from Gaelic *carn* meaning 'heap of
stones' or 'hill'

**cajole** cajoles cajoling cajoled
VERB If you cajole someone into doing
something, you persuade them to do
it by saying nice things to them.

**cake** cakes caking caked
NOUN 1 a sweet food made by baking
flour, eggs, fat, and sugar. 2 a block of
a hard substance such as soap. ▶ VERB
3 If something cakes or is caked, it
forms or becomes covered with a
solid layer E.G. *caked with mud.*
📖 from Old Norse *kaka* meaning
'oatcake'

**calamity** calamities
NOUN an event that causes disaster or
distress.
**calamitous** ADJECTIVE

**calcium**
*Said* "**kal**-see-um" NOUN a soft white

substance found in bones and teeth.

**calculate** calculates calculating calculated

VERB 1 (MATHS) If you calculate something, you work it out, usually by doing some arithmetic. 2 If something is calculated, it is deliberately planned to have a particular effect *E.G. Everything they said to each other was calculated to wound.*

**calculation** NOUN

🔲 from Latin *calculus* meaning 'stone' or 'pebble'. The Romans used pebbles to count with

**calculating**

ADJECTIVE carefully planning situations to get what you want *E.G. Toby was always a calculating type.*

**calculator** calculators

NOUN a small electronic machine used for doing mathematical calculations.

**calculus**

NOUN a branch of mathematics concerned with amounts that can change and rates of change.

**calendar** calendars

NOUN 1 a chart showing the date of each day in a particular year. 2 a system of dividing time into fixed periods of days, months, and years *E.G. the Jewish calendar.*

🔲 from Latin *kalendae* the day of the month on which interest on debts was due

**calf** calves

NOUN 1 a young cow, bull, elephant, whale, or seal. 2 the thick part at the back of your leg below your knee.

**calibre** calibres

*Said* "kal-lib-ber" NOUN 1 the ability or

intelligence someone has *E.G. a player of her calibre.* 2 The calibre of a gun is the width of the inside of the barrel of the gun.

🔲 from Arabic *qalib* meaning 'cobbler's last'

**call** calls calling called

VERB 1 If someone or something is called a particular name, that is their name *E.G. a man called Jeffrey.* 2 If you call people or situations something, you use words to describe your opinion of them *E.G. They called me crazy.* 3 If you call someone, you telephone them. 4 If you call or call out something, you say it loudly *E.G. He called out his daughter's name.* 5 If you call on someone, you pay them a short visit *E.G. Don't hesitate to call on me.* ▶ NOUN 6 If you get a call from someone, they telephone you or pay you a visit. 7 a cry or shout *E.G. a call for help.* 8 a demand for something *E.G. The call for art teachers was small.*

🔳 (sense 1) christen, label, name

**call off** VERB If you call something off, you cancel it.

**call up** VERB If someone is called up, they are ordered to join the army, navy, or air force.

**call box** call boxes

NOUN a telephone box.

**call centre** call centres

NOUN an office in which most staff are employed to answer telephone calls on behalf of a particular company or organization.

**calling**

NOUN 1 a profession or career. 2 If you have a calling to a particular job, you have a strong feeling that you should do it.

a
b
c
d
e
f
g
h
i
j
k
l
m
n
o
p
q
r
s
t
u
v
w
x
y
z

A B C D E F G H I J K L M N O P Q R S T U V W X Y Z

**callous**
ADJECTIVE cruel and not concerned with other people's feelings.
**callously** ADVERB **callousness** NOUN
▪ hardhearted, heartless, unfeeling

**calm calmer calmest; calms calming calmed**
ADJECTIVE 1 Someone who is calm is quiet and does not show any worry or excitement. 2 If the weather or the sea is calm, it is still because there is no strong wind. ▶ NOUN 3 a state of quietness and peacefulness E.G. He liked the calm of the evening. ▶ VERB 4 To calm someone means to make them less upset or excited.
**calmly** ADVERB **calmness** NOUN
▪ (sense 1) composed, cool, self-possessed
▪ (sense 3) peacefulness, quiet
▪ (sense 4) quieten, soothe

**calorie calories**
NOUN a unit of measurement for the energy food gives you E.G. All alcohol is high in calories.

**calves**
the plural of **calf**.

**calypso calypsos**
Said "kal-lip-soh" NOUN a type of song from the West Indies, accompanied by a rhythmic beat, about something happening at the time.

**calyx calyxes** or **calyces**
Said "kay-lix" NOUN; TECHNICAL In a flower, the calyx is the ring of petal-like sepals that protects the developing bud.

**camaraderie**
Said "kam-mer-rah-der-ree" NOUN a feeling of trust and friendship between a group of people.

**camber cambers**
NOUN a slight downwards slope from the centre of a road to each side of it.

**camel camels**
NOUN a large mammal with either one or two humps on its back. Camels live in hot desert areas and are sometimes used for carrying things.
▥ from Hebrew gamal

**cameo cameos**
NOUN 1 a small but important part in a play or film played by a well-known actor or actress. 2 a brooch with a raised stone design on a flat stone of another colour.

**camera cameras**
NOUN a piece of equipment used for taking photographs or for filming.
▥ from Latin camera meaning 'vault'

**camomile**
NOUN a plant with a strong smell and daisy-like flowers which are used to make herbal tea.
▥ from Greek khamaimēlon meaning 'apple on the ground'

**camouflage camouflages camouflaging camouflaged**
Said "kam-mof-flahj" NOUN 1 a way of avoiding being seen by having the same colour or appearance as the surroundings. ▶ VERB 2 To camouflage something is to hide it by giving it the same colour or appearance as its surroundings.

**camp camps camping camped**
NOUN 1 a place where people live in tents or stay in tents on holiday. 2 a collection of buildings for a particular group of people such as soldiers or prisoners. 3 a group of people who support a particular idea or belief E.G. the pro-government camp. ▶ VERB 4 If you camp, you stay in a tent.
**camper** NOUN **camping** NOUN

**campaign** campaigns campaigning campaigned
*Said* "kam-**pane**" NOUN **1** a set of actions aiming to achieve a particular result *E.G. a campaign to educate people.* ▶ VERB **2** To campaign means to carry out a campaign *E.G. He has campaigned against smoking.*
**campaigner** NOUN

**camp-drafting**
NOUN In Australia, camp-drafting is a competition in which men on horseback select cattle or sheep from a herd or flock.

**campus** campuses
NOUN the area of land and the buildings that make up a university or college.

**can** could
VERB **1** If you can do something, it is possible for you to do it or you are allowed to do it *E.G. You can go to the cinema.* **2** If you can do something, you have the ability to do it *E.G. I can speak Italian.*

**can** cans canning canned
NOUN **1** a metal container, often a sealed one with food or drink inside. ▶ VERB **2** To can food or drink is to seal it in cans.

**Canadian** Canadians
ADJECTIVE **1** belonging or relating to Canada. ▶ NOUN **2** someone who comes from Canada.

**canal** canals
NOUN a long, narrow man-made stretch of water.

**canary** canaries
NOUN a small yellow bird.

**can-can** can-cans
NOUN a lively dance in which women kick their legs high in the air to fast music.

**cancel** cancels cancelling cancelled
VERB **1** If you cancel something that has been arranged, you stop it from happening. **2** If you cancel a cheque or an agreement, you make sure that it is no longer valid.
**cancellation** NOUN

**cancer** cancers
NOUN **1** a serious disease in which abnormal cells in a part of the body increase rapidly, causing growths. **2** Cancer is also the fourth sign of the zodiac, represented by a crab. People born between June 21st and July 22nd are born under this sign.
**cancerous** ADJECTIVE
🏛 from Latin *cancer* meaning 'crab'

**candelabra** or **candelabrum** candelabras
NOUN an ornamental holder for a number of candles.

**candid**
ADJECTIVE honest and frank.
**candidly** ADVERB    **candour** NOUN

**candidate** candidates
NOUN **1** a person who is being considered for a job. **2** a person taking an examination.
**candidacy** NOUN
🏛 from Latin *candidatus* meaning 'white-robed'. In Rome, a candidate wore a white toga

**candied**
ADJECTIVE covered or cooked in sugar *E.G. candied fruit.*

**candle** candles
NOUN a stick of hard wax with a wick through the middle. The lighted wick gives a flame that provides light.

**candlestick** candlesticks
NOUN a holder for a candle.

**candy** candies
NOUN; *ESPECIALLY AMERICAN ENGLISH* Candies

a
**c**
d
e
f
g
h
i
j
k
l
m
n
o
p
q
r
s
t
u
v
w
x
y
z

are sweets.

🔲 from Arabic *qand* meaning 'cane sugar'

**cane canes caning caned**
NOUN 1 Cane is the long, hollow stems of a plant such as bamboo. 2 Cane is also strips of cane used for weaving things such as baskets. 3 a long narrow stick, often one used to beat people as a punishment. ▶ VERB 4 To cane someone means to beat them with a cane as a punishment.

**canine**
*Said* "kay-nine" ADJECTIVE relating to dogs.

**canister canisters**
NOUN a container with a lid, used for storing foods such as sugar or tea.

**cannabis**
NOUN Cannabis is a drug made from the hemp plant, which some people smoke.

**canned**
ADJECTIVE 1 Canned food is kept in cans. 2 Canned music or laughter on a television or radio show is recorded beforehand.

**cannibal cannibals**
NOUN a person who eats other human beings; also used of animals that eat animals of their own type.
**cannibalism** NOUN

**cannon cannons or cannon**
NOUN a large gun, usually on wheels, used in battles to fire heavy metal balls.

**cannot**
VERB Cannot is the same as can not *E.G. She cannot come home yet.*

**canny**
ADJECTIVE clever and cautious *E.G. canny business people.*
**cannily** ADVERB

**canoe canoes**
*Said* "ka-noo" NOUN a small, narrow

boat that you row using a paddle.
**canoeing** NOUN

**canon canons**
NOUN 1 a member of the clergy in a cathedral. 2 a basic rule or principle *E.G. the canons of political economy.*

**canopy canopies**
NOUN a cover for something, used for shelter or decoration *E.G. a frilly canopy over the bed.*
🔲 from Greek *kōnōpeion* meaning 'bed with a mosquito net'

**cantankerous**
ADJECTIVE Cantankerous people are bad-tempered and quarrel a lot with other people.

**canteen canteens**
NOUN 1 the part of a workplace where the workers can go to eat. 2 A canteen of cutlery is a set of cutlery in a box.

**canter canters cantering cantered**
VERB When a horse canters, it moves at a speed between a gallop and a trot.

**cantilever cantilevers**
NOUN a long beam or bar fixed at only one end and supporting a bridge or other structure at the other end.

**canton cantons**
NOUN a political and administrative region of a country, especially in Switzerland.

**canvas canvases**
NOUN 1 Canvas is strong, heavy cloth used for making things such as sails and tents. 2 a piece of canvas on which an artist does a painting.

**canvass canvasses canvassing canvassed**
VERB 1 If you canvass people or a place, you go round trying to

persuade people to vote for a particular candidate or party in an election. **2** If you canvass opinion, you find out what people think about a particular subject by asking them.

**canyon** canyons
NOUN a narrow river valley with steep sides.

**cap** caps capping capped
NOUN **1** a soft, flat hat, often with a peak at the front. **2** the top of a bottle. **3** Caps are small explosives used in toy guns. ▸ VERB **4** To cap something is to cover it with something. **5** If you cap a story or a joke that someone has just told, you tell a better one.

**capable**
ADJECTIVE **1** able to do something E.G. *a man capable of extreme violence.* **2** skilful or talented E.G. *She was a very capable woman.*
**capably** ADVERB   **capability** NOUN

**capacity** capacities
*Said* "kap-**pas**-sit-tee" NOUN **1** the maximum amount that something can hold or produce E.G. *a seating capacity of eleven thousand.* **2** A person's power or ability to do something E.G. *his capacity for consuming hamburgers.* **3** Someone's position or role E.G. *in his capacity as councillor.*

**cape** capes
NOUN **1** a short cloak with no sleeves. **2** a large piece of land sticking out into the sea E.G. *the Cape of Good Hope.*

**caper** capers
NOUN **1** Capers are the flower buds of a spiky Mediterranean shrub, which are pickled and used to flavour food. **2** a light-hearted practical joke E.G.

*Jack would have nothing to do with such capers.*

**capillary** capillaries
*Said* "kap-**pill**-lar-ree" NOUN Capillaries are very thin blood vessels.

**capital** capitals
NOUN **1** The capital of a country is the city where the government meets. **2** Capital is the amount of money or property owned or used by a business. **3** Capital is also a sum of money that you save or invest in order to gain interest. **4** A capital or capital letter is a larger letter used at the beginning of a sentence or a name.

**capitalism**
NOUN Capitalism is an economic and political system where businesses and industries are not owned and run by the government, but by individuals who can make a profit from them.
**capitalist** ADJECTIVE OR NOUN

**capitalize** capitalizes capitalizing capitalized; also spelt **capitalise**
VERB If you capitalize on a situation, you use it to get an advantage.

**capital punishment**
NOUN Capital punishment is legally killing someone as a punishment for a crime they have committed.

**capitulate** capitulates capitulating capitulated
VERB To capitulate is to give in and stop fighting or resisting E.G. *The Finns capitulated in March 1940.*
**capitulation** NOUN

**cappuccino** cappuccinos
*Said* "kap-poot-**sheen**-oh" NOUN coffee made with frothy milk.

**capricious**
*Said* "kap-**prish**-uss" ADJECTIVE often

a
b
c
d
e
f
g
h
i
j
k
l
m
n
o
p
q
r
s
t
u
v
w
x
y
z

changing unexpectedly *E.G. the capricious English weather.*

**Capricorn**
NOUN Capricorn is the tenth sign of the zodiac, represented by a goat. People born between December 22nd and January 19th are born under this sign.

📖 from Latin *caper* meaning 'goat' and *cornu* meaning 'horn'

**capsize** capsizes capsizing capsized
VERB If a boat capsizes, it turns upside down.

**capsule** capsules
NOUN 1 a small container with medicine inside which you swallow. 2 the part of a spacecraft in which astronauts travel.

📖 from Latin *capsula* meaning 'little box'

**captain** captains captaining captained
NOUN 1 the officer in charge of a ship or aeroplane. 2 an army officer of the rank immediately above lieutenant. 3 a navy officer of the rank immediately above commander. 4 the leader of a sports team *E.G. captain of the cricket team.* ▶ VERB 5 If you captain a group of people, you are their leader.

**caption** captions
NOUN a title printed underneath a picture or photograph.

**captivate** captivates captivating captivated
VERB To captivate someone is to fascinate or attract them so that they cannot take their attention away *E.G. I was captivated by her.*
**captivating** ADJECTIVE

**captive** captives
NOUN 1 a person who has been captured and kept prisoner. ▶ ADJECTIVE 2 imprisoned or enclosed *E.G. a captive bird.*
**captivity** NOUN

**captor** captors
NOUN someone who has captured a person or animal.

**capture** captures capturing captured
VERB 1 To capture someone is to take them prisoner. 2 To capture a quality or mood means to succeed in representing or describing it *E.G. capturing the mood of the riots.* ▶ NOUN 3 The capture of someone or something is the capturing of them *E.G. the fifth anniversary of his capture.*

**car** cars
NOUN 1 a four-wheeled road vehicle with room for a small number of people. 2 a railway carriage used for a particular purpose *E.G. the buffet car.*

**carafe** carafes
*Said* "kar-**raf**" NOUN a glass bottle for serving water or wine.

📖 from Arabic *gharrafah* meaning 'vessel for liquid'

**caramel** caramels
NOUN 1 a chewy sweet made from sugar, butter, and milk. 2 Caramel is burnt sugar used for colouring or flavouring food.

**carat** carats
NOUN 1 a unit for measuring the weight of diamonds and other precious stones. 2 a unit for measuring the purity of gold.

**caravan** caravans
NOUN 1 a vehicle pulled by a car in which people live or spend their

holidays. **2** a group of people and animals travelling together, usually across a desert.

📖 from Persian *karwan*

**carbohydrate** carbohydrates
NOUN (D&T) Carbohydrate is a substance that gives you energy. It is found in foods like sugar and bread.

**carbon**
NOUN Carbon is a chemical element that is pure in diamonds and also found in coal. All living things contain carbon.

**carbonated**
ADJECTIVE carbonated drinks contain bubbles of carbon dioxide that make them fizzy.

**carbon dioxide**
NOUN a colourless, odourless gas that humans and animals breathe out. Carbon dioxide is used in industry, for example in making fizzy drinks and in fire extinguishers.

**carburettor** carburettors
*Said* "kahr-bur-ret-ter" NOUN the part of the engine in a vehicle in which air and petrol are mixed together.

**carcass** carcasses; also spelt carcase
NOUN the body of a dead animal.

**card** cards
NOUN **1** a piece of stiff paper or plastic with information or a message on it *E.G. a birthday card.* **2** Cards can mean playing cards *E.G. a poor set of cards with which to play.* **3** When you play cards, you play any game using playing cards. **4** Card is strong, stiff paper.

📖 from Greek *khartēs* meaning 'papyrus leaf'

**cardboard**
NOUN Cardboard is thick, stiff paper.

**cardiac**
ADJECTIVE; *MEDICAL* relating to the heart *E.G. cardiac disease.*

**cardigan** cardigans
NOUN a knitted jacket that fastens up the front.

**cardinal** cardinals
NOUN **1** a high-ranking member of the Roman Catholic clergy who chooses and advises the Pope. ▶ ADJECTIVE **2** extremely important *E.G. a cardinal principle of law.*

📖 from Latin *cardo* meaning 'hinge'. When something is important, other things hinge on it

**care** cares caring cared
VERB **1** If you care about something, you are concerned about it and interested in it. **2** If you care about someone, you feel affection towards them. **3** If you care for someone, you look after them. ▶ NOUN **4** Care is concern or worry. **5** Care of someone or something is treatment for them or looking after them *E.G. the care of the elderly.* **6** If you do something with care, you do it with close attention.

**career** careers careering careered
NOUN **1** the series of jobs that someone has in life, usually in the same occupation *E.G. a career in insurance.* ▶ VERB **2** To career somewhere is to move very quickly, often out of control *E.G. His car careered off the road.*

**carefree**
ADJECTIVE having no worries or responsibilities.

**careful**
ADJECTIVE **1** acting sensibly and with care *E.G. Be careful what you say to*

a b **c** d e f g h i j k l m n o p q r s t u v w x y z

A
B
C
D
E
F
G
H
I
J
K
L
M
N
O
P
Q
R
S
T
U
V
W
X
Y
Z

him. **2** complete and well done *E.G. It needs very careful planning.*
**carefully** ADVERB
■ (sense 1) cautious, prudent

**careless**
ADJECTIVE **1** done badly without enough attention *E.G. careless driving.* **2** relaxed and unconcerned *E.G. careless laughter.*
**carelessly** ADVERB **carelessness** NOUN
■ (sense 1) slapdash, sloppy

**caress caresses caressing caressed**
VERB **1** If you caress someone, you stroke them gently and affectionately. ► NOUN **2** a gentle, affectionate stroke.
■ (sense 1) fondle, stroke

**caretaker caretakers**
NOUN **1** a person who looks after a large building such as a school. ► ADJECTIVE **2** having an important position for a short time until a new person is appointed *E.G. O'Leary was named caretaker manager.*

**cargo cargoes**
NOUN the goods carried on a ship or plane.

**Caribbean**
NOUN The Caribbean consists of the Caribbean Sea east of Central America and the islands in it.

**caricature caricatures caricaturing caricatured**
NOUN **1** a drawing or description of someone that exaggerates striking parts of their appearance or personality. ► VERB **2** To caricature someone is to give a caricature of them.

**carjack carjacks carjacking carjacked**
VERB If a car is carjacked, its driver is attacked and robbed, or the car is stolen.

**carnage**
*Said* "**kahr**-nij" NOUN Carnage is the violent killing of large numbers of people.

**carnal**
ADJECTIVE; FORMAL sexual and sensual rather than spiritual *E.G. carnal pleasure.*

**carnation carnations**
NOUN a plant with a long stem and white, pink, or red flowers.

**carnival carnivals**
NOUN a public festival with music, processions, and dancing.

**carnivore carnivores**
NOUN an animal that eats meat.
**carnivorous** ADJECTIVE

**carol carols**
NOUN a religious song sung at Christmas time.

**carousel carousels**
*Said* "kar-ros-**sel**" NOUN a merry-go-round.

**carp carps carping carped**
NOUN **1** a large edible freshwater fish. ► VERB **2** To carp means to complain about unimportant things.

**carpel carpels**
NOUN the seed-bearing female part of a flower.

**carpenter carpenters**
NOUN a person who makes and repairs wooden structures.
**carpentry** NOUN
▥ from Latin *carpentarius* meaning 'wagon-maker'

**carpet carpets carpeting carpeted**
NOUN **1** a thick covering for a floor, usually made of a material like wool.

▶ VERB **2** To carpet a floor means to cover it with a carpet.

**carriage** carriages
NOUN **1** one of the separate sections of a passenger train. **2** an old-fashioned vehicle for carrying passengers, usually pulled by horses. **3** a machine part that moves and supports another part E.G. *a typewriter carriage.* **4** Someone's carriage is the way they hold their head and body when they move.

**carriageway** carriageways
NOUN one of the sides of a road which traffic travels along in one direction only.

**carrier** carriers
NOUN **1** a vehicle that is used for carrying things E.G. *a troop carrier.* **2** A carrier of a germ or disease is a person or animal that can pass it on to others.

**carrier bag** carrier bags
NOUN a bag made of plastic or paper, which is used for carrying shopping.

**carrion**
NOUN Carrion is the decaying flesh of dead animals.

**carrot** carrots
NOUN a long, thin orange root vegetable.

**carry** carries carrying carried
VERB **1** To carry something is to hold it and take it somewhere. **2** When a vehicle carries people, they travel in it. **3** A person or animal that carries a germ can pass it on to other people or animals E.G. *I still carry the disease.* **4** If a sound carries, it can be heard far away E.G. *Jake's voice carried over the cheering.* **5** In a meeting, if a proposal is carried, it is accepted by a majority of the people there.

▤ (sense 2) bear, convey, take

**carry away** VERB If you are carried away, you are so excited by something that you do not behave sensibly.

**carry on** VERB To carry on doing something means to continue doing it.

**carry out** VERB To carry something out means to do it and complete it E.G. *The conversion was carried out by a local builder.*

**cart** carts
NOUN a vehicle with wheels, used to carry goods and often pulled by horses or cattle.

**cartilage**
NOUN Cartilage is a strong, flexible substance found around the joints and in the nose and ears.

**carton** cartons
NOUN a cardboard or plastic container.

**cartoon** cartoons
NOUN **1** a drawing or a series of drawings which are funny or make a point. **2** a film in which the characters and scenes are drawn.
**cartoonist** NOUN
▥ from Italian *cartone* meaning 'sketch on stiff paper'

**cartridge** cartridges
NOUN **1** a tube containing a bullet and an explosive substance, used in guns. **2** a thin plastic tube containing ink that you put in a pen. **3** (ICT) a container for ink that you insert into a printer.

**cartwheel** cartwheels
NOUN an acrobatic movement in which you throw yourself sideways onto one hand and move round in a circle with arms and legs stretched until you land on your feet again.

A
B
C
D
E
F
G
H
I
J
K
L
M
N
O
P
Q
R
S
T
U
V
W
X
Y
Z

**carve** carves carving carved
VERB **1** To carve an object means to cut it out of a substance such as stone or wood. **2** To carve meat means to cut slices from it.

**carving** carvings
NOUN a carved object.

**cascade** cascades cascading cascaded
NOUN **1** a waterfall or group of waterfalls. ➤ VERB **2** To cascade means to flow downwards quickly E.G. *Gallons of water cascaded from the attic.*

**case** cases
NOUN **1** a particular situation, event, or example E.G. *a clear case of mistaken identity.* **2** a container for something, or a suitcase E.G. *a camera case.* **3** Doctors sometimes refer to a patient as a case. **4** Police detectives refer to a crime they are investigating as a case. **5** In an argument, the case for an idea is the reasons used to support it. **6** In law, a case is a trial or other inquiry. **7** In grammar, the case of a noun or pronoun is the form of it which shows its relationship with other words in a sentence E.G. *the accusative case.* ➤ PHRASE **8** You say **in case** to explain something that you do because a particular thing might happen E.G. *I didn't want to shout in case I startled you.* **9** You say **in that case** to show that you are assuming something said before is true E.G. *In that case we won't do it.*
◼ (sense 1) instance, circumstance(s), situation

**casement** casements
NOUN a window that opens on hinges at one side.

**cash** cashes cashing cashed
NOUN **1** Cash is money in notes and coins rather than cheques. ➤ VERB **2** If you cash a cheque, you take it to a bank and exchange it for money.
▥ from Italian *cassa* meaning 'money-box'

**cashew** cashews
*Said* "kash-oo" NOUN a curved, edible nut.

**cash flow**
NOUN Cash flow is the money that a business makes and spends.

**cashier** cashiers
NOUN the person that customers pay in a shop or get money from in a bank.

**cashmere**
NOUN Cashmere is very soft, fine wool from goats.

**cash register** cash registers
NOUN a machine in a shop which records sales, and where the money is kept.

**casing** casings
NOUN a protective covering for something.

**casino** casinos
*Said* "kass-ee-noh" NOUN a place where people go to play gambling games.

**cask** casks
NOUN a wooden barrel.
▥ from Spanish *casco* meaning 'helmet'

**casket** caskets
NOUN a small box for jewellery or other valuables.
▥ from Old French *cassette* meaning 'little box'

**casserole** casseroles
NOUN a dish made by cooking a mixture of meat and vegetables slowly in an oven; also used to refer

---

**SPELLING NOTE** ▸ 'i' before 'e' except after 'c'

to the pot a casserole is cooked in.
🏛 from Old French *casse* meaning
'ladle' or 'dripping pan'

**cassette** cassettes

NOUN a small flat container with
magnetic tape inside, which is used
for recording and playing back sounds.

**cassette recorder** cassette
recorders

NOUN a machine used for recording
and playing cassettes.

**cassock** cassocks

NOUN a long robe that is worn by
some members of the clergy.

**cassowary** cassowaries

NOUN a large bird found in Australia
with black feathers and a brightly
coloured neck. Cassowaries cannot fly.

**cast** casts casting cast

NOUN 1 all the people who act in a
play or film. 2 an object made by
pouring liquid into a mould and
leaving it to harden E.G. *the casts of
classical sculptures.* 3 a stiff plaster
covering put on broken bones to
keep them still so that they heal
properly. ▶ VERB 4 To cast actors is to
choose them for roles in a play or
film. 5 When people cast their votes
in an election, they vote. 6 To cast
something is to throw it. 7 If you cast
your eyes somewhere, you look there
E.G. *I cast my eyes down briefly.* 8 To
cast an object is to make it by
pouring liquid into a mould and
leaving it to harden E.G. *An image of
him has been cast in bronze.*

**cast off** VERB If you cast off, you
untie the rope fastening a boat to a
harbour or shore.

**castanets**

PLURAL NOUN Castanets are a Spanish
musical instrument consisting of two

small round pieces of wood that are
clicked together with the fingers.
🏛 from Spanish *castañetas* meaning
'little chestnuts'

**castaway** castaways

NOUN a person who has been
shipwrecked.

**caste** castes

NOUN 1 one of the four classes into
which Hindu society is divided.
2 Caste is a system of social classes
decided according to family, wealth,
and position.
🏛 from Portuguese *casto* meaning
'pure'

**caster sugar** or **castor sugar**

NOUN Caster sugar is very fine white
sugar used in cooking.

**castigate** castigates castigating
castigated.

VERB; FORMAL To castigate someone is to
criticize them severely.

**cast iron**

NOUN 1 Cast iron is iron which is made
into objects by casting. ▶ ADJECTIVE 2 A
cast-iron excuse or guarantee is
absolutely certain and firm.

**castle** castles

NOUN 1 (HISTORY) a large building with
walls or ditches round it to protect it
from attack. 2 In chess, a castle is the
same as a rook.

**cast-off** cast-offs

NOUN a piece of outgrown or
discarded clothing that has been
passed on to someone else.

**castor** castors; also spelt **caster**

NOUN a small wheel fitted to furniture
so that it can be moved easily.

**castor oil**

NOUN Castor oil is a thick oil that
comes from the seeds of the castor
oil plant. It is used as a laxative.

a
b
**c**
d
e
f
g
h
i
j
k
l
m
n
o
p
q
r
s
t
u
v
w
x
y
z

A B C D E F G H I J K L M N O P Q R S T U V W X Y Z

**castrate** castrates castrating castrated
VERB To castrate a male animal is to remove its testicles so that it can no longer produce sperm.
**castration** NOUN

**casual**
ADJECTIVE **1** happening by chance without planning E.G. *a casual remark.* **2** careless or without interest E.G. *a casual glance over his shoulder.* **3** Casual clothes are suitable for informal occasions. **4** Casual work is not regular or permanent.
**casually** ADVERB **casualness** NOUN
■ (sense 2) careless, nonchalant, offhand

**casualty** casualties
NOUN a person killed or injured in an accident or war E.G. *Many of the casualties were office workers.*

**casuarina** casuarinas
*Said* "kass-you-a-rine-a" NOUN an Australian tree with jointed green branches.

**cat** cats
NOUN **1** a small furry animal with whiskers, a tail and sharp claws, often kept as a pet. **2** any of the family of mammals that includes lions and tigers.
▥ from Latin *cattus*

**catacomb** catacombs
*Said* "kat-a-koom" NOUN Catacombs are underground passages where dead bodies are buried.
▥ from Latin *catacumbas*, an underground cemetery near Rome

**catalogue** catalogues cataloguing catalogued
NOUN **1** a book containing pictures and descriptions of goods that you can buy in a shop or through the post. **2** (LIBRARY) a list of things such as the objects in a museum or the books in a library. ▶ VERB **3** To catalogue a collection of things means to list them in a catalogue.

**catalyst** catalysts
*Said* "kat-a-list" NOUN **1** something that causes a change to happen E.G. *the catalyst which provoked civil war.* **2** a substance that speeds up a chemical reaction without changing itself.

**catamaran** catamarans
NOUN a sailing boat with two hulls connected to each other.
▥ from Tamil *kattumaram* meaning 'tied logs'

**catapult** catapults catapulting catapulted
NOUN **1** a Y-shaped object with a piece of elastic tied between the two top ends used for shooting small stones. ▶ VERB **2** To catapult something is to throw it violently through the air. **3** If someone is catapulted into a situation, they find themselves unexpectedly in that situation E.G. *Tony has been catapulted into the limelight.*

**cataract** cataracts
NOUN **1** an area of the lens of someone's eye that has become white instead of clear, so that they cannot see properly. **2** a large waterfall.

**catarrh**
*Said* "kat-tahr" NOUN Catarrh is a condition in which you get a lot of mucus in your nose and throat.

**catastrophe** catastrophes
*Said* "kat-tass-trif-fee" NOUN a terrible disaster.
**catastrophic** ADJECTIVE

**catch** catches catching caught

VERB **1** If you catch a ball moving in the air, you grasp hold of it when it comes near you. **2** To catch an animal means to trap it E.G. *I caught ten fish.* **3** When the police catch criminals, they find them and arrest them. **4** If you catch someone doing something they should not be doing, you discover them doing it E.G. *He caught me playing the church organ.* **5** If you catch a bus or train, you get on it and travel somewhere. **6** If you catch a cold or a disease, you become infected with it. **7** If something catches on an object, it sticks to it or gets trapped E.G. *The white fibres caught on the mesh.*
▶ NOUN **8** a hook that fastens or locks a door or window. **9** a problem or hidden complication in something.
▦ (sense 2) capture, snare, trap
▦ (sense 3) apprehend, arrest, capture
▦ (sense 6) contract, develop, go down with

**catch on** VERB **1** If you catch on to something, you understand it. **2** If something catches on, it becomes popular E.G. *This drink has never really caught on in New Zealand.*

**catch out** VERB To catch someone out is to trick them or trap them.

**catch up** VERB **1** To catch up with someone in front of you is to reach the place where they are by moving slightly faster than them. **2** To catch up with someone is also to reach the same level or standard as them.

**catching**
ADJECTIVE tending to spread very quickly E.G. *Measles is catching.*

**catchy** catchier catchiest
ADJECTIVE attractive and easily remembered E.G. *a catchy little tune.*

**catechism** catechisms
*Said* "**kat**-ik-kizm" NOUN a set of questions and answers about the main beliefs of a religion.

**categorical**
ADJECTIVE absolutely certain and direct E.G. *a categorical denial.*
**categorically** ADVERB

**categorize** categorizes categorizing categorized; also spelt **categorise**
VERB To categorize things is to arrange them in different categories.

**category** categories
NOUN a set of things with a particular characteristic in common E.G. *Occupations can be divided into four categories.*

**cater** caters catering catered
VERB To cater for people is to provide them with what they need, especially food.

**caterer** caterers
NOUN a person or business that provides food for parties and groups.

**caterpillar** caterpillars
NOUN the larva of a butterfly or moth. It looks like a small coloured worm and feeds on plants.
▥ from Old French *catepelose* meaning 'hairy cat'

**catharsis** catharses
*Said* "kath-**ar**-siss" NOUN; *FORMAL* Catharsis is the release of strong emotions and feelings by expressing them through drama or literature.
▥ from Greek *kathairein* meaning 'to purge' or 'to purify'

**cathedral** cathedrals
NOUN (HISTORY) an important church with a bishop in charge of it.

a
**c**
d
e
f
g
h
i
j
k
l
m
n
o
p
q
r
s
t
u
v
w
x
y
z

LEt's measure the angLE (an**gle**)    **SPELLING NOTE**

A
B
C
D
E
F
G
H
I
J
K
L
M
N
O
P
Q
R
S
T
U
V
W
X
Y
Z

**Catholic** Catholics

NOUN or ADJECTIVE **1** (HISTORY) a Roman Catholic. ▶ ADJECTIVE **2** If a person has catholic interests, they have a wide range of interests.

**Catholicism** NOUN

📖 from Greek *katholikos* meaning 'universal'

✔ When *Catholic* begins with a capital letter, it refers to the religion. When it begins with a small letter, it means 'covering a wide range'.

**cattle**

PLURAL NOUN Cattle are cows and bulls kept by farmers.

**catty** cattier cattiest

ADJECTIVE unpleasant and spiteful.

**cattiness** NOUN

**catwalk** catwalks

NOUN a narrow pathway that people walk along, for example over a stage.

**Caucasian** Caucasians

*Said* "kaw-**kayz**-yn" NOUN a person belonging to the race of people with fair or light-brown skin.

📖 from *Caucasia*, a region in the former USSR

**caught**

the past tense and past participle of **catch**.

**cauldron** cauldrons

NOUN a large, round metal cooking pot, especially one that sits over a fire.

**cauliflower** cauliflowers

NOUN a large, round, white vegetable surrounded by green leaves.

**cause** causes causing caused

NOUN **1** The cause of something is the thing that makes it happen *E.G. the most common cause of back pain.*
**2** an aim or principle which a group of people are working for *E.G.*

*dedication to the cause of peace.* **3** If you have cause for something, you have a reason for it *E.G. They gave us no cause to believe that.* ▶ VERB **4** To cause something is to make it happen *E.G. This can cause delays.*

**causal** ADJECTIVE

**causeway** causeways

NOUN a raised path or road across water or marshland.

📖 from Latin *calciatus* meaning 'paved with limestone'

**caustic**

ADJECTIVE **1** A caustic chemical can destroy substances *E.G. caustic liquids such as acids.* **2** bitter or sarcastic *E.G. your caustic sense of humour.*

**caution** cautions cautioning cautioned

NOUN **1** Caution is great care which you take to avoid danger *E.G. You will need to proceed with caution.* **2** a warning *E.G. Sutton was let off with a caution.* ▶ VERB **3** If someone cautions you, they warn you, usually not to do something again *E.G. A man has been cautioned by police.*

**cautionary** ADJECTIVE

**cautious**

ADJECTIVE acting very carefully to avoid danger *E.G. a cautious approach.*

**cautiously** ADVERB

**cavalcade** cavalcades

NOUN a procession of people on horses or in cars or carriages.

**cavalier**

*Said* "kav-val-**eer**" ADJECTIVE arrogant and behaving without sensitivity *E.G. a cavalier attitude to women.*

**cavalry**

NOUN The cavalry is the part of an army that uses armoured vehicles or horses.

**SPELLING NOTE** A Rude Idiot Thought He Might Eat Toffee In Church (<u>arithmetic</u>)

**cave** caves caving caved
NOUN **1** a large hole in rock, that is underground or in the side of a cliff.
▶ VERB **2** If a roof caves in, it collapses inwards.

**caveman** cavemen
NOUN Cavemen were people who lived in caves in prehistoric times.

**cavern** caverns
NOUN a large cave.

**cavernous**
ADJECTIVE large, deep, and hollow E.G. *a cavernous warehouse.*

**caviar** or **caviare**
*Said* "**kav**-vee-ar" NOUN Caviar is the tiny salted eggs of a fish called the sturgeon.

**cavity** cavities
NOUN a small hole in something solid E.G. *There were dark cavities in his back teeth.*

**cavort** cavorts cavorting cavorted
VERB When people cavort, they jump around excitedly.

**caw** caws cawing cawed
VERB When a crow or rook caws, it makes a harsh sound.

**cc**
an abbreviation for 'cubic centimetres'.

**CD**
an abbreviation for 'compact disc'.

**CD-ROM**
( ICT ) CD-ROM is a method of storing video, sound, or text on a compact disc which can be played on a computer using a laser. CD-ROM is an abbreviation for 'Compact Disc Read-Only Memory'.

**cease** ceases ceasing ceased
VERB **1** If something ceases, it stops happening. **2** If you cease to do

something, or cease doing it, you stop doing it.

**cease-fire** cease-fires
NOUN an agreement between groups that are fighting each other to stop for a period and discuss peace.

**ceaseless**
ADJECTIVE going on without stopping E.G. *the ceaseless movement of the streets.*

**ceaselessly** ADVERB

**cedar** cedars
NOUN a large evergreen tree with wide branches and needle-shaped leaves.

**cede** cedes ceding ceded
*Said* "**seed**" VERB To cede something is to give it up to someone else E.G. *Haiti was ceded to France in 1697.*

**ceiling** ceilings
NOUN the top inside surface of a room.

**celebrate** celebrates celebrating celebrated
VERB **1** If you celebrate or celebrate something, you do something special and enjoyable because of it E.G. *a party to celebrate the end of the exams.* **2** ( RE ) When a priest celebrates Mass, he performs the ceremonies of the Mass.

**celebration** NOUN **celebratory** ADJECTIVE

**celebrated**
ADJECTIVE famous E.G. *the celebrated Italian mountaineer.*

**celebrity** celebrities
NOUN a famous person.

**celery**
NOUN Celery is a vegetable with long pale green stalks.

**celestial**
*Said* "sil-**lest**-yal" ADJECTIVE; FORMAL

a
b
**c**
d
e
f
g
h
i
j
k
l
m
n
o
p
q
r
s
t
u
v
w
x
y
z

A
B
**C**
D
E
F
G
H
I
J
K
L
M
N
O
P
Q
R
S
T
U
V
W
X
Y
Z

concerning the sky or heaven *E.G. The telescope is pointed at a celestial object.*

**celibate**
*Said* "sel-lib-bit" ADJECTIVE Someone who is celibate does not marry or have sex.
**celibacy** NOUN

**cell cells**
NOUN 1 In biology, a cell is the smallest part of an animal or plant that can exist by itself. Each cell contains a nucleus. 2 a small room where a prisoner is kept in a prison or police station. 3 a small group of people set up to work together as part of a larger organization. 4 a device that converts chemical energy to electricity.

**cellar cellars**
NOUN a room underneath a building, often used to store wine.

**cello cellos**
*Said* "chel-loh" NOUN a large musical stringed instrument which you play sitting down, holding the instrument upright with your knees.
**cellist** NOUN

**Cellophane**
NOUN; TRADEMARK Cellophane is thin, transparent plastic material used to wrap food or other things to protect them.

**cellphone cellphones**
NOUN a small portable telephone.

**cellular**
ADJECTIVE Cellular means relating to the cells of animals or plants.

**cellular phone cellular phones**
NOUN the same as **cellphone**.

**celluloid**
*Said* "sel-yul-loyd" NOUN Celluloid is a type of plastic which was once used to make photographic film.

**Celsius**
*Said* "sel-see-yuss" NOUN Celsius is a

scale for measuring temperature in which water freezes at 0 degrees (0°C) and boils at 100 degrees (100°C). Celsius is the same as 'Centigrade'.

**Celtic**
*Said* "kel-tik" ADJECTIVE A Celtic language is one of a group of languages that includes Gaelic and Welsh.

**cement cements cementing cemented**
NOUN 1 Cement is a fine powder made from limestone and clay, which is mixed with sand and water to make concrete. ▶ VERB 2 To cement things is to stick them together with cement or cover them with cement.
3 Something that cements a relationship makes it stronger *E.G. to cement relations between them.*

**cemetery cemeteries**
NOUN an area of land where dead people are buried.

**cenotaph cenotaphs**
*Said* "sen-not-ahf" NOUN a monument built in memory of dead people, especially soldiers buried elsewhere.
🏛 from Greek *kenos* + *taphos* meaning 'empty tomb'

**censor censors censoring censored**
NOUN 1 a person officially appointed to examine books or films and to ban parts that are considered unsuitable. ▶ VERB 2 If someone censors a book or film, they cut or ban parts of it that are considered unsuitable for the public.
**censorship** NOUN

**censure censures censuring censured**
*Said* "sen-sher" NOUN 1 Censure is strong disapproval of something.

▶ VERB **2** To censure someone is to criticize them severely.

**census censuses**

NOUN an official survey of the population of a country.

**cent cents**

NOUN a unit of currency. In the USA, a cent is worth one hundredth of a dollar; in Europe, it is worth one hundredth of a Euro.

**centaur centaurs**

*Said* "**sen**-tawr" NOUN a creature in Greek mythology with the top half of a man and the lower body and legs of a horse.

**centenary centenaries**

*Said* "sen-**teen**-er-ee" NOUN the 100th anniversary of something.

**centi-**

PREFIX 'Centi-' is used to form words that have 'hundred' as part of their meaning E.G. *centimetre*.

🏛 from Latin *centum* meaning 'hundred'

**Centigrade**

Centigrade is another name for Celsius.

☑ Scientists say and write *Celsius* rather than *Centigrade*.

**centilitre centilitres**

NOUN a unit of liquid volume equal to one hundredth of a litre.

**centime centimes**

*Said* "**sonn**-team" NOUN a unit of currency used in Switzerland and some other countries, and formerly used in France and Belgium.

**centimetre centimetres**

NOUN ( MATHS ) a unit of length equal to ten millimetres or one hundredth of a metre.

**centipede centipedes**

NOUN a long, thin insect-like creature with many pairs of legs.

**central**

ADJECTIVE **1** in or near the centre of an object or area E.G. *central ceiling lights*. **2** main or most important E.G. *the central idea of this work*.

**centrally** ADVERB   **centrality** NOUN

**Central America**

NOUN Central America is another name for the Isthmus of Panama, the area of land joining North America to South America.

**central heating**

NOUN Central heating is a system of heating a building in which water or air is heated in a tank and travels through pipes and radiators round the building.

**centralize centralizes centralizing centralized**; also spelt **centralise**

VERB To centralize a system is to bring the organization of it under the control of one central group.

**centralization** NOUN

**centre centres centring centred**

NOUN **1** the middle of an object or area. **2** a building where people go for activities, meetings, or help E.G. *a health centre*. **3** Someone or something that is the centre of attention attracts a lot of attention.

▶ VERB **4** To centre something is to move it so that it is balanced or at the centre of something else. **5** If something centres on or around a particular thing, that thing is the main subject of attention E.G. *The discussion centred on his request*.

▤ (sense 1) heart, middle

**centrifugal**

*Said* "sen-trif-**yoo**-gl" ADJECTIVE In

a
b
c
d
e
f
g
h
i
j
k
l
m
n
o
p
q
r
s
t
u
v
w
x
y
z

physics, centrifugal force is the force that makes rotating objects move outwards.
🔲 from Latin *centrum* + *fugere* meaning 'to flee from the centre'

**centripetal**
*Said* "sen-**trip**-pe-tl" ADJECTIVE In physics, centripetal force is the force that makes rotating objects move inwards.
🔲 from Latin *centrum* + *petere* meaning 'to seek the centre'

**centurion centurions**
NOUN a Roman officer in charge of a hundred soldiers.

**century centuries**
NOUN 1 a period of one hundred years. 2 In cricket, a century is one hundred runs scored by a batsman.

**ceramic ceramics**
*Said* "sir-**ram**-mik" NOUN 1 Ceramic is a hard material made by baking clay to a very high temperature. 2 Ceramics is the art of making objects out of clay.

**cereal cereals**
NOUN 1 a food made from grain, often eaten with milk for breakfast. 2 a plant that produces edible grain, such as wheat or oats.
🔲 from Latin *cerealis* meaning 'concerning the growing of grain'

**cerebral**
*Said* "**ser**-reb-ral" ADJECTIVE; FORMAL relating to the brain E.G. *a cerebral haemorrhage.*

**cerebral palsy**
NOUN Cerebral palsy is an illness caused by damage to a baby's brain, which makes its muscles and limbs very weak.

**ceremonial**
ADJECTIVE relating to a E.G. *ceremonial dress.*
**ceremonially** ADVERB

**ceremony ceremonies**
NOUN 1 (RE) a set of formal actions performed at a special occasion or important public event E.G. *his recent coronation ceremony.* 2 Ceremony is very formal and polite behaviour E.G. *He hung up without ceremony.*

**certain**
ADJECTIVE 1 definite and with no doubt at all E.G. *He is certain to be in Italy.* 2 You use 'certain' to refer to a specific person or thing E.G. *certain aspects of the job.* 3 You use 'certain' to suggest that a quality is noticeable but not obvious E.G. *There's a certain resemblance to Joe.*

**certainly**
ADVERB 1 without doubt E.G. *My boss was certainly interested.* 2 of course E.G. *'Will you be there?' – 'Certainly'.*

**certainty certainties**
NOUN 1 Certainty is the state of being certain. 2 something that is known without doubt E.G. *There are no certainties and no guarantees.*

**certificate certificates**
NOUN a document stating particular facts, for example of someone's birth or death E.G. *a marriage certificate.*

**certify certifies certifying certified**
VERB 1 To certify something means to declare formally that it is true E.G. *certifying the cause of death.* 2 To certify someone means to declare officially that they are insane.

**cervix cervixes or cervices**
NOUN; TECHNICAL the entrance to the womb at the top of the vagina.
**cervical** ADJECTIVE

**cessation**
NOUN; FORMAL The cessation of something is the stopping of it E.G. *a*

*swift cessation of hostilities.*

**cf.**

cf. means 'compare'. It is written after something in a text to mention something else which the reader should compare with what has just been written.

**CFC CFCs**

NOUN CFCs are manufactured chemicals that are used in aerosol sprays. They damage the ozone layer. CFC is an abbreviation for 'chlorofluorocarbon'.

**chaff**

NOUN Chaff is the outer parts of grain separated from the seeds by beating.

**chaffinch chaffinches**

NOUN a small European bird with black and white wings.

**chagrin**

*Said "shag-rin"* NOUN; FORMAL Chagrin is a feeling of annoyance or disappointment.

**chain chains chaining chained**

NOUN 1 a number of metal rings connected together in a line E.G. *a bicycle chain.* 2 a number of things in a series or connected to each other E.G. *a chain of shops.* ▶ VERB 3 If you chain one thing to another, you fasten them together with a chain E.G. *They had chained themselves to railings.*

**chain saw chain saws**

NOUN a large saw with teeth fixed in a chain that is driven round by a motor.

**chain-smoke chain-smokes chain-smoking chain-smoked**

VERB To chain-smoke is to smoke cigarettes continually.

**chair chairs chairing chaired**

NOUN 1 a seat with a back and four legs for one person. 2 the person in charge of a meeting who decides when each person may speak. ▶ VERB 3 The person who chairs a meeting is in charge of it.

**chair lift chair lifts**

NOUN a line of chairs that hang from a moving cable and carry people up and down a mountain.

**chairman chairmen**

NOUN 1 the person in charge of a meeting who decides when each person may speak. 2 the head of a company or committee.

**chairperson** NOUN **chairwoman** NOUN **chairmanship** NOUN

☑ Some people don't like to use *chairman* when talking about a woman. You can use *chair* or *chairperson* to talk about a man or a woman.

**chalet chalets**

*Said "shall-lay"* NOUN a wooden house with a sloping roof, especially in a mountain area or a holiday camp.

**chalice chalices**

*Said "chal-liss"* NOUN a gold or silver cup used in churches to hold the Communion wine.

**chalk chalks chalking chalked**

NOUN 1 Chalk is a soft white rock. Small sticks of chalk are used for writing or drawing on a blackboard. ▶ VERB 2 To chalk up a result is to achieve it E.G. *He chalked up his first win.*

**chalky** ADJECTIVE

**challenge challenges challenging challenged**

NOUN 1 something that is new and exciting but requires a lot of effort E.G. *It's a new challenge at the right time in my career.* 2 a suggestion

a
b
c
d
e
f
g
h
i
j
k
l
m
n
o
p
q
r
s
t
u
v
w
x
y
z

A
B
C
D
E
F
G
H
I
J
K
L
M
N
O
P
Q
R
S
T
U
V
W
X
Y
Z

from someone to compete with them. **3** A challenge to something is a questioning of whether it is correct or true *E.G. a challenge to authority*. ▶ VERB **4** If someone challenges you, they suggest that you compete with them in some way. **5** If you challenge something, you question whether it is correct or true.

**challenger** NOUN **challenging** ADJECTIVE

■ (sense 5) dispute, question

**chamber** chambers
NOUN **1** a large room, especially one used for formal meetings *E.G. the Council Chamber*. **2** a group of people chosen to decide laws or administrative matters. **3** a hollow place or compartment inside something, especially inside an animal's body or inside a gun *E.G. the chambers of the heart*.

**chambermaid** chambermaids
NOUN a woman who cleans and tidies rooms in a hotel.

**chameleon** chameleons
*Said* "kam-**mee**-lee-on" NOUN a lizard which is able to change the colour of its skin to match the colour of its surroundings.

▥ from Greek *khamai* + *leōn* meaning 'ground lion'

**chamois leather** chamois leathers
*Said* "**sham**-mee" NOUN a soft leather cloth used for polishing.

**champagne** champagnes
*Said* "sham-**pain**" NOUN Champagne is a sparkling white wine made in France.

**champion** champions championing championed
NOUN **1** a person who wins a

competition. **2** someone who supports or defends a cause or principle *E.G. a champion of women's causes*. ▶ VERB **3** Someone who champions a cause or principle supports or defends it.

▥ from Latin *campus* meaning 'battlefield'

**championship** championships
NOUN a competition to find the champion of a sport.

**chance** chances chancing chanced
NOUN **1** The chance of something happening is how possible or likely it is *E.G. There's a chance of rain later*. **2** an opportunity to do something *E.G. Your chance to be a TV star!* **3** a possibility that something dangerous or unpleasant may happen *E.G. Don't take chances, he's armed*. **4** Chance is also the way things happen unexpectedly without being planned *E.G. I only found out by chance*. ▶ VERB **5** If you chance something, you try it although you are taking a risk.

■ (sense 4) accident, coincidence, luck

**chancellor** chancellors
NOUN **1** the head of government in some European countries. **2** In Britain, the Chancellor is the Chancellor of the Exchequer. **3** the honorary head of a university.

**Chancellor of the Exchequer**
NOUN In Britain, the minister responsible for finance and taxes.

**chandelier** chandeliers
*Said* "shan-del-**leer**" NOUN an ornamental light fitting which hangs from the ceiling.

## change changes changing changed

NOUN **1** a difference or alteration in something *E.G. Steven soon noticed a change in Penny's attitude.* **2** a replacement of something by something else *E.G. a change of clothes.* **3** Change is money you get back when you have paid more than the actual price of something. ▶ VERB **4** When something changes or when you change it, it becomes different *E.G. It changed my life.* **5** If you change something, you exchange it for something else. **6** When you change, you put on different clothes. **7** To change money means to exchange it for smaller coins of the same total value, or to exchange it for foreign currency.

## changeable

ADJECTIVE likely to change all the time.
≡ erratic, inconstant, variable

## changeover changeovers

NOUN a change from one system or activity to another *E.G. the changeover between day and night.*

## channel channels channelling channelled

NOUN **1** a wavelength used to receive programmes broadcast by a television or radio station; also the station itself *E.G. I was watching the other channel.* **2** a passage along which water flows or along which something is carried. **3** The Channel or the English Channel is the stretch of sea between England and France. **4** a method of achieving something *E.G. We have tried to do things through the right channels.* ▶ VERB **5** To channel something such as money or energy means to direct it in a particular way *E.G. Their efforts are being channelled*

*into worthy causes.*

## chant chants chanting chanted

NOUN **1** a group of words repeated over and over again *E.G. a rousing chant.* **2** a religious song sung on only a few notes. ▶ VERB **3** If people chant a group of words, they repeat them over and over again *E.G. Crowds chanted his name.*

## Chanukah

another spelling of **Hanukkah**.

## chaos

*Said* "**kay-oss**" NOUN Chaos is a state of complete disorder and confusion.
**chaotic** ADJECTIVE

## chap chaps chapping chapped

NOUN **1** INFORMAL a man. ▶ VERB **2** If your skin chaps, it becomes dry and cracked, usually as a result of cold or wind.

## chapel chapels

NOUN **1** a section of a church or cathedral with its own altar. **2** a type of small church.
▥ from Latin *capella* meaning 'small cloak'; originally used of the place where St Martin's cloak was kept as a relic

## chaperone chaperones

*Said* "**shap-per-rone**"; also spelt **chaperon**
NOUN an older woman who accompanies a young single woman on social occasions, or any person who accompanies a group of younger people.

## chaplain chaplains

NOUN a member of the Christian clergy who regularly works in a hospital, school, or prison.
**chaplaincy** NOUN

## chapter chapters

NOUN **1** one of the parts into which a

The government licenSes Schnapps (licenSes) ◀ SPELLING NOTE

book is divided. **2** a particular period in someone's life or in history.

**char chars charring charred**

VERB If something chars, it gets partly burned and goes black.

**charred** ADJECTIVE

**character characters**

NOUN **1** all the qualities which combine to form the personality or atmosphere of a person or place. **2** A person or place that has character has an interesting, attractive, or admirable quality *E.G. an inn of great character and simplicity.* **3** (DRAMA) The characters in a film, play, or book are the people in it. **4** a person *E.G. an odd character.* **5** a letter, number, or other written symbol.

■ (sense 1) nature, personality, quality

**characteristic characteristics**

NOUN **1** (DRAMA) a quality that is typical of a particular person or thing *E.G. Silence is the characteristic of the place.* ▶ ADJECTIVE **2** Characteristic means typical of a particular person or thing *E.G. Two things are very characteristic of his driving.*

**characteristically** ADVERB

**characterize characterizes characterizing characterized**; also spelt **characterise**

VERB A quality that characterizes something is typical of it *E.G. a condition characterized by muscle stiffness.*

**characterless**

ADJECTIVE without atmosphere or any interesting qualities *E.G. a tiny characterless flat.*

**charade charades**

*Said "shar-rahd"* NOUN a ridiculous

and unnecessary activity or pretence.

▥ from Provençal *charrado* meaning 'chat'

**charcoal**

NOUN (ART) Charcoal is a black form of carbon made by burning wood without air, used as a fuel and also for drawing.

**charge charges charging charged**

VERB **1** If someone charges you money, they ask you to pay it for something you have bought or received *E.G. The company charged 150 pounds on each loan.* **2** To charge someone means to accuse them formally of having committed a crime. **3** To charge a battery means to pass an electrical current through it to make it store electricity. **4** To charge somewhere means to rush forward, often to attack someone *E.G. The rhino charged at her.* ▶ NOUN **5** the price that you have to pay for something. **6** a formal accusation that a person is guilty of a crime and has to go to court. **7** To have charge or be in charge of someone or something means to be responsible for them and be in control of them. **8** an explosive put in a gun or other weapon. **9** An electrical charge is the amount of electricity that something carries.

**charger chargers**

NOUN a device for charging or recharging batteries.

**chariot chariots**

NOUN a two-wheeled open vehicle pulled by horses.

**charisma**

*Said "kar-riz-ma"* NOUN Charisma is a

special ability to attract or influence people by your personality.

**charismatic** ADJECTIVE

**charity charities**

NOUN 1 an organization that raises money to help people who are ill, poor, or disabled. 2 Charity is money or other help given to poor, disabled, or ill people *E.G. to help raise money for charity.* 3 Charity is also a kind, sympathetic attitude towards people.

**charitable** ADJECTIVE

**charlatan charlatans**

*Said "shar-lat-tn"* NOUN someone who pretends to have skill or knowledge that they do not really have.

**charm charms charming charmed**

NOUN 1 Charm is an attractive and pleasing quality that some people and things have *E.G. a man of great personal charm.* 2 a small ornament worn on a bracelet. 3 a magical spell or an object that is supposed to bring good luck. ▶ VERB 4 If you charm someone, you use your charm to please them.

**charmer charmers**

NOUN someone who uses their charm to influence people.

**charming**

ADJECTIVE very pleasant and attractive *E.G. a rather charming man.*

**charmingly** ADVERB

**chart charts charting charted**

NOUN 1 a diagram or table showing information *E.G. He noted the score on his chart.* 2 a map of the sea or stars. ▶ VERB 3 If you chart something, you observe and record it carefully.

**charter charters chartering chartered**

NOUN 1 a document stating the rights

or aims of a group or organization, often written by the government *E.G. the new charter for commuters.* ▶ VERB 2 To charter transport such as a plane or boat is to hire it for private use.

**chartered** ADJECTIVE

**chase chases chasing chased**

VERB 1 If you chase someone or something, you run or go after them in order to catch them or drive them away. ▶ NOUN 2 the activity of chasing or hunting someone or something *E.G. a high-speed car chase.*

■ (sense 1) hunt, pursue

**chasm chasms**

*Said "kazm"* NOUN 1 a deep crack in the earth's surface. 2 a very large difference between two ideas or groups of people *E.G. the chasm between rich and poor in America.*

**chassis chassis**

*Said "shas-ee"* NOUN the frame on which a vehicle is built.

☑ The plural of *chassis* is also *chassis*.

**chaste**

*Said "chayst"* ADJECTIVE OLD-FASHIONED not having sex with anyone outside marriage.

**chastity** NOUN

**chastise chastises chastising chastised**

VERB; FORMAL If someone chastises you, they criticize you or punish you for something that you have done.

**chat chats chatting chatted**

NOUN 1 a friendly talk with someone, usually about things that are not very important. ▶ VERB 2 When people chat, they talk to each other in a friendly way.

■ (senses 1 & 2) gossip, natter, talk

**chat up** VERB; INFORMAL If you chat up

a b c d e f g h i j k l m n o p q r s t u v w x y z

A
B
**C**
D
E
F
G
H
I
J
K
L
M
N
O
P
Q
R
S
T
U
V
W
X
Y
Z

someone, you talk to them in a friendly way, because you are attracted to them.

**chateau chateaux**
*Said "shat-toe"* NOUN a large country house or castle in France.

**chatroom chatrooms**
NOUN an Internet site where users have group discussions using e-mail.

**chatter chatters chattering chattered**
VERB 1 When people chatter, they talk very fast. 2 If your teeth are chattering, they are knocking together and making a clicking noise because you are cold. ▶ NOUN 3 Chatter is a lot of fast unimportant talk.

**chatty chattier chattiest**
ADJECTIVE talkative and friendly.

**chauffeur chauffeurs**
*Said "show-fur"* NOUN a person whose job is to drive another person's car.

**chauvinist chauvinists** NOUN 1 a person who thinks their country is always right. 2 A male chauvinist is a man who believes that men are superior to women.
**chauvinistic** ADJECTIVE **chauvinism** NOUN

**cheap cheaper cheapest**
ADJECTIVE 1 Something that is cheap costs very little money, and is sometimes of poor quality. 2 A cheap joke or cheap remark is unfair and unkind.
**cheaply** ADVERB
■ (sense 1) inexpensive, reasonable

**cheat cheats cheating cheated**
VERB 1 If someone cheats, they do wrong or unfair things to win or get something that they want. 2 If you are cheated of or out of something, you do not get what you are entitled

to. ▶ NOUN 3 a person who cheats.
■ (sense 1) con, deceive, swindle

**check checks checking checked**
VERB 1 To check something is to examine it in order to make sure that everything is all right. 2 To check the growth or spread of something is to make it stop *E.G. a policy to check fast population growth.* ▶ NOUN 3 an inspection to make sure that everything is all right. 4 Checks are different coloured squares which form a pattern. ▶ PHRASE 5 If you keep something **in check**, you keep it under control *E.G. She kept her emotions in check.* ▶ ADJECTIVE 6 Check or checked means marked with a pattern of squares *E.G. check design.*

**check out** VERB If you check something out, you inspect it and find out whether everything about it is right.

**checkmate**
NOUN In chess, checkmate is a situation where one player cannot stop their king being captured and so loses the game.
▥ from Arabic *shah mat* meaning 'the King is dead'

**checkout checkouts**
NOUN a counter in a supermarket where the customers pay for their goods.

**checkpoint checkpoints**
NOUN a place where traffic has to stop in order to be checked.

**checkup checkups**
NOUN an examination by a doctor to see if you are healthy.

**cheek cheeks**
NOUN 1 Your cheeks are the sides of your face below your eyes. 2 Cheek is speech or behaviour that is rude or

disrespectful *E.G. an expression of sheer cheek.*

■ (sense 2) impertinence, impudence, insolence

**cheeky** cheekier cheekiest
ADJECTIVE rather rude and disrespectful.

**cheer** cheers cheering cheered
VERB **1** When people cheer, they shout with approval or in order to show support for a person or team. ▸ NOUN **2** a shout of approval or support.
**cheer up** VERB When you cheer up, you feel more cheerful.

**cheerful**
ADJECTIVE **1** happy and in good spirits *E.G. I had never seen her so cheerful.* **2** bright and pleasant-looking *E.G. a cheerful and charming place.*
**cheerfully** ADVERB **cheerfulness** NOUN

**cheerio**
INTERJECTION Cheerio is a friendly way of saying goodbye.

**cheery** cheerier cheeriest
ADJECTIVE happy and cheerful *E.G. He gave me a cheery nod.*

**cheese** cheeses
NOUN a hard or creamy food made from milk.

**cheesecake** cheesecakes
NOUN a dessert made of biscuit covered with cream cheese.

**cheetah** cheetahs
NOUN a wild animal like a large cat with black spots.
📖 from Sanskrit *citra + kaya* meaning 'speckled body'

**chef** chefs
NOUN a head cook in a restaurant or hotel.

**chemical** chemicals
NOUN ( SCIENCE ) **1** Chemicals are substances manufactured by

chemistry. ▸ ADJECTIVE **2** involved in chemistry or using chemicals *E.G. chemical weapons.*
**chemically** ADVERB

**chemist** chemists
NOUN **1** a person who is qualified to make up drugs and medicines prescribed by a doctor. **2** a shop where medicines and cosmetics are sold. **3** a scientist who does research in chemistry.

**chemistry**
NOUN Chemistry is the scientific study of substances and the ways in which they change when they are combined with other substances.

**chemotherapy**
*Said* "keem-oh-**ther**-a-pee" NOUN Chemotherapy is a way of treating diseases such as cancer by using chemicals.

**cheque** cheques
NOUN a printed form on which you write an amount of money that you have to pay. You sign the cheque and your bank pays the money from your account.

**chequered**
*Said* "**chek**-kerd" ADJECTIVE **1** covered with a pattern of squares. **2** A chequered career is a varied career that has both good and bad parts.

**cherish** cherishes cherishing cherished
VERB **1** If you cherish something, you care deeply about it and want to keep it or look after it lovingly. **2** If you cherish a memory or hope, you have it in your mind and care deeply about it *E.G. I cherish the good memories I have of him.*

**cherry** cherries
NOUN **1** a small, juicy fruit with a red or

a b **c** d e f g h i j k l m n o p q r s t u v w x y z

A
B
**C**
D
E
F
G
H
I
J
K
L
M
N
O
P
Q
R
S
T
U
V
W
X
Y
Z

black skin and a hard stone in the centre. **2** a tree that produces cherries.

**cherub** cherubs or cherubim
NOUN an angel, shown in pictures as a plump, naked child with wings.
**cherubic** ADJECTIVE

**chess**
NOUN Chess is a board game for two people in which each player has 16 pieces and tries to move his or her pieces so that the other player's king cannot escape.

**chessboard** chessboards
NOUN A chessboard is a board divided into 64 squares of two alternating colours on which chess is played.

**chest** chests
NOUN **1** the front part of your body between your shoulders and your waist. **2** a large wooden box with a hinged lid.

**chestnut** chestnuts
NOUN **1** Chestnuts are reddish-brown nuts that grow inside a prickly green outer covering. **2** a tree that produces these nuts. ▶ ADJECTIVE **3** Something that is chestnut is reddish-brown.

**chest of drawers** chests of drawers
NOUN a piece of furniture with drawers in it, used for storing clothes.

**chew** chews chewing chewed
VERB When you chew something, you use your teeth to break it up in your mouth before swallowing it.
**chewy** ADJECTIVE

**chewing gum**
NOUN Chewing gum is a kind of sweet that you chew for a long time, but which you do not swallow.

**chic**
*Said* "sheek" ADJECTIVE elegant and fashionable *E.G. a chic restaurant.*

**chick** chicks
NOUN a young bird.

**chicken** chickens chickening chickened
NOUN **1** a bird kept on a farm for its eggs and meat; also the meat of this bird *E.G. roast chicken.* ▶ VERB **2** INFORMAL If you chicken out of something, you do not do it because you are afraid.

**chickenpox**
NOUN Chickenpox is an illness which produces a fever and blister-like spots on the skin.

**chicory**
NOUN Chicory is a plant with bitter leaves that are used in salads.

**chide** chides chiding chided
VERB; OLD-FASHIONED To chide someone is to tell them off.

**chief** chiefs
NOUN **1** the leader of a group or organization. ▶ ADJECTIVE **2** most important *E.G. the chief source of oil.*
**chiefly** ADVERB

**chieftain** chieftains
NOUN the leader of a tribe or clan.

**chiffon**
*Said* "shif-fon" NOUN Chiffon is a very thin lightweight cloth made of silk or nylon.

**chihuahua** chihuahuas
*Said* "chi-wah-wah" NOUN a breed of very small dog with short hair and pointed ears.

**chilblain** chilblains
NOUN a sore, itchy swelling on a finger or toe.

**child** children
NOUN **1** a young person who is not yet an adult. **2** Someone's child is their

son or daughter.

**▤** (sense 1) baby, kid, youngster

**childbirth**

NOUN the act of giving birth to a child E.G. *Many women used to die in childbirth.*

**childhood** childhoods

NOUN Someone's childhood is the time when they are a child.

**childish**

ADJECTIVE immature and foolish E.G. *I don't have time for childish arguments.*

**childishly** ADVERB **childishness** NOUN

**▤** immature, infantile, juvenile

**✔** If you call someone *childish*, you think they are immature or foolish. If you call them *childlike*, you think they are innocent like a young child.

**childless**

ADJECTIVE having no children.

**childlike**

ADJECTIVE like a child in appearance or behaviour E.G. *childlike enthusiasm.*

**childminder** childminders

NOUN a person who is qualified and paid to look after other people's children while they are at work.

**Chilean** Chileans

ADJECTIVE 1 belonging or relating to Chile. ▶ NOUN 2 someone who comes from Chile.

**chill** chills chilling chilled

VERB 1 To chill something is to make it cold E.G. *Chill the cheesecake.* 2 If something chills you, it makes you feel worried or frightened E.G. *The thought chilled her.* ▶ NOUN 3 a feverish cold. 4 a feeling of cold E.G. *the chill of the night air.*

**chilli** chillies

NOUN the red or green seed pod of a

type of pepper which has a very hot, spicy taste.

**chilly** chillier chilliest

ADJECTIVE 1 rather cold E.G. *the chilly November breeze.* 2 unfriendly and without enthusiasm E.G. *a chilly reception.*

**chilly-bin** chilly-bins

NOUN; *INFORMAL* In New Zealand English, a container for keeping food and drink cool that can be carried.

**chime** chimes chiming chimed

VERB When a bell chimes, it makes a clear ringing sound.

**chimney** chimneys

NOUN a vertical pipe or other hollow structure above a fireplace or furnace through which smoke from a fire escapes.

**▥** from Greek *kaminos* meaning 'fireplace' or 'oven'

**chimpanzee** chimpanzees

NOUN a small ape with dark fur that lives in forests in Africa.

**chin** chins

NOUN the part of your face below your mouth

**china** chinas

NOUN 1 China is items like cups, saucers, and plates made from very fine clay. 2 *INFORMAL* In South African English, a china is a friend.

**Chinese**

ADJECTIVE 1 belonging or relating to China. ▶ NOUN 2 someone who comes from China. 3 Chinese refers to any of a group of related languages and dialects spoken by Chinese people.

**chink** chinks

NOUN 1 a small, narrow opening E.G. *a chink in the roof.* 2 a short, light, ringing sound, like one made by glasses touching each other.

a
b
c
d
e
f
g
h
i
j
k
l
m
n
o
p
q
r
s
t
u
v
w
x
y
z

A
B
C
D
E
F
G
H
I
J
K
L
M
N
O
P
Q
R
S
T
U
V
W
X
Y
Z

**chintz**
NOUN Chintz is a type of brightly patterned cotton fabric.
🔳 from Hindi *chint* meaning 'brightly coloured'

**chip chips chipping chipped**
NOUN **1** Chips are thin strips of fried potato. **2** In electronics, a chip is a tiny piece of silicon inside a computer which is used to form electronic circuits. **3** a small piece broken off an object, or the mark made when a piece breaks off. **4** In some gambling games, chips are counters used to represent money. ▸ VERB **5** If you chip an object, you break a small piece off it.

**chipboard**
NOUN Chipboard is a material made from wood scraps pressed together into hard sheets.

**chipmunk chipmunks**
NOUN a small rodent with a striped back.

**chiropodist chiropodists**
*Said* "kir-**rop**-pod-dist" NOUN a person whose job is treating people's feet.
**chiropody** NOUN

**chirp chirps chirping chirped**
VERB When a bird chirps, it makes a short, high-pitched sound.

**chisel chisels chiselling chiselled**
NOUN **1** a tool with a long metal blade and a sharp edge at the end which is used for cutting and shaping wood, stone, or metal. ▸ VERB **2** To chisel wood, stone, or metal is to cut or shape it using a chisel.

**chivalry**
*Said* "**shiv**-val-ree" NOUN Chivalry is polite and helpful behaviour, especially by men towards women.
**chivalrous** ADJECTIVE

🔳 from Latin *caballarius* meaning 'horseman'

**chive chives**
NOUN Chives are grasslike hollow leaves that have a mild onion flavour.

**chlorine**
*Said* "**klaw**-reen" NOUN Chlorine is a poisonous greenish-yellow gas with a strong, unpleasant smell. It is used as a disinfectant for water, and to make bleach.

**chloroform**
*Said* "**klor**-rof-form" NOUN Chloroform is a colourless liquid with a strong, sweet smell used in cleaning products.

**chlorophyll**
*Said* "**klor**-rof-fil" NOUN Chlorophyll is a green substance in plants which enables them to use the energy from sunlight in order to grow.

**chock-a-block** or **chock-full**
ADJECTIVE completely full.

**chocolate chocolates**
NOUN **1** Chocolate is a sweet food made from cacao seeds. **2** a sweet made of chocolate. ▸ ADJECTIVE **3** dark brown.
🔳 from Aztec *xococ* + *atl* meaning 'bitter water'

**choice choices**
NOUN **1** a range of different things that are available to choose from E.G. *a wider choice of treatments.*
**2** something that you choose E.G. *You've made a good choice.* **3** Choice is the power or right to choose E.G. *I had no choice.*
▤ (sense 1) range, selection, variety

**choir choirs**
*Said* "kwire" NOUN (MUSIC) a group of singers, for example in a church.

**choke** chokes choking choked
VERB **1** If you choke, you stop being
able to breathe properly, usually
because something is blocking your
windpipe E.G. *the diner who choked on
a fish bone.* **2** If things choke a place,
they fill it so much that it is blocked
or clogged up E.G. *The canal was
choked with old tyres.*

**choko** chokos
NOUN a fruit that is shaped like a pear
and used as a vegetable in Australia
and New Zealand.

**cholera**
*Said* "kol-ler-ra" NOUN Cholera is a
serious disease causing severe
diarrhoea and vomiting. It is caused
by infected food or water.

**cholesterol**
*Said* "kol-less-ter-rol" NOUN
Cholesterol is a substance found in
all animal fats, tissues, and blood.

**chook** chooks
NOUN; *INFORMAL* In Australian and New
Zealand English, a chicken.

**choose** chooses choosing chose
chosen
VERB To choose something is to
decide to have it or do it E.G. *He chose
to live in Kenya.*
■ opt for, pick, select
✔ The present tense *chooses* and
present participle *choosing* are spelt
with two os. The past tense *chose*
and past participle *chosen* have only
one o.

**choosy** choosier choosiest
ADJECTIVE fussy and difficult to satisfy
E.G. *You can't be too choosy about jobs.*

**chop** chops chopping chopped
VERB **1** To chop something is to cut it
with quick, heavy strokes using an
axe or a knife. ▶ NOUN **2** a small piece

of lamb or pork containing a bone,
usually cut from the ribs.

**chopper** choppers
NOUN; *INFORMAL* a helicopter.

**choppy** choppier choppiest
ADJECTIVE Choppy water has a lot of
waves because it is windy.

**chopstick** chopsticks
NOUN Chopsticks are a pair of thin
sticks used by people in the Far East
for eating food.

**choral**
ADJECTIVE relating to singing by a choir
E.G. *choral music*.

**chord** chords
NOUN (MUSIC) a group of three or
more musical notes played together.

**chore** chores
NOUN a boring job that has to be
done E.G. *the chore of cleaning*.

**choreography**
*Said* "kor-ree-og-raf-fee" NOUN
Choreography is the art of
composing dance steps and
movements.
**choreographer** NOUN

**chortle** chortles chortling
chortled
VERB To chortle is to laugh with
amusement.

**chorus** choruses chorusing
chorused
NOUN **1** a large group of singers; also a
piece of music for a large group of
singers. **2** a part of a song which is
repeated after each verse. **3** (ENGLISH)
the chorus is a group of actors,
singers or dancers that performs
together, either with the main
performers or between solo
performances. ▶ VERB **4** If people
chorus something, they all say or
sing it at the same time.

a
b
c
d
e
f
g
h
i
j
k
l
m
n
o
p
q
r
s
t
u
v
w
x
y
z

the QUeen stood on the QUay (<u>quay</u>)     SPELLING NOTE

from Greek *khoros*, the group of actors who gave the commentary in Classical plays

**Christ**

PROPER NOUN Christ is the name for Jesus. Christians believe that Jesus is the son of God.

**christen** christens christening christened

VERB When a baby is christened, it is named by a member of the clergy in a religious ceremony.

**Christian** Christians

NOUN 1 (RE) a person who believes in Jesus Christ and his teachings.
► ADJECTIVE 2 (RE) relating to Christ and his teachings E.G. *the Christian faith.* 3 good, kind, and considerate.
**Christianity** NOUN

**Christian name** Christian names

NOUN the name given to someone when they were born or christened.

**Christmas** Christmases

NOUN the Christian festival celebrating the birth of Christ, falling on December 25th.

**chromatic**

Said "kro-**ma**-tik" ADJECTIVE (MUSIC) A chromatic scale is one which is based on an octave of 12 semitones.

**chrome**

Said "krome" NOUN Chrome is metal plated with chromium, a hard grey metal.

**chromosome** chromosomes

NOUN In biology, a chromosome is a part of a cell which contains genes that determine the characteristics of an animal or plant.

**chronic**

Said "**kron**-nik" ADJECTIVE lasting a very long time or never stopping E.G. *a*

*chronic illness.*
**chronically** ADVERB

**chronicle** chronicles chronicling chronicled

NOUN 1 a record of a series of events described in the order in which they happened. ► VERB 2 To chronicle a series of events is to record or describe them in the order in which they happened.

**chronological**

Said "kron-nol-**loj**-i-kl" ADJECTIVE (HISTORY) arranged in the order in which things happened E.G. *Tell me the whole story in chronological order.*
**chronologically** ADVERB

**chronology**

Said "kron-**nol**-loj-jee" NOUN (HISTORY) The chronology of events is the order in which they happened.
from Greek *khronos* meaning 'time' and *legein* meaning 'to say'

**chrysalis** chrysalises

Said "**kriss**-sal-liss" NOUN a butterfly or moth when it is developing from being a caterpillar to being a fully grown adult.

**chrysanthemum** chrysanthemums

Said "kriss-**an**-thim-mum" NOUN a plant with large, brightly coloured flowers.

**chubby** chubbier chubbiest

ADJECTIVE plump and round E.G. *his chubby cheeks.*

**chuck** chucks chucking chucked

VERB; INFORMAL To chuck something is to throw it casually.

**chuckle** chuckles chuckling chuckled

VERB When you chuckle, you laugh quietly.

SPELLING NOTE    Rhythmical Hounds Yap To Heavy Music (<u>rhythm</u>)

**chug** chugs chugging chugged
VERB When a machine or engine chugs, it makes a continuous dull thudding sound.

**chum** chums
NOUN; INFORMAL a friend.

**chunk** chunks
NOUN a thick piece of something.
■ hunk, lump, piece

**chunky** chunkier chunkiest
ADJECTIVE Someone who is chunky is broad and heavy but usually short.

**church** churches
NOUN 1 a building where Christians go for religious services and worship.
2 In the Christian religion, a church is one of the groups with their own particular beliefs, customs, and clergy E.G. the Catholic Church.
▥ from Greek kuriakon meaning 'master's house'

**Church of England**
NOUN The Church of England is the Anglican church in England, where it is the state church, with the King or Queen as its head.

**churchyard** churchyards
NOUN an area of land around a church, often used as a graveyard.

**churn** churns
NOUN a container used for making milk or cream into butter.

**chute** chutes
Said "shoot" NOUN a steep slope or channel used to slide things down E.G. a rubbish chute.

**chutney**
NOUN Chutney is a strong-tasting thick sauce made from fruit, vinegar, and spices.

**cider**
NOUN Cider is an alcoholic drink made from apples.

**cigar** cigars
NOUN a roll of dried tobacco leaves which people smoke.
▥ from Mayan sicar meaning 'to smoke'

**cigarette** cigarettes
NOUN a thin roll of tobacco covered in thin paper which people smoke.

**cinder** cinders
NOUN Cinders are small pieces of burnt material left after something such as wood or coal has burned.

**cinema** cinemas
NOUN 1 a place where people go to watch films. 2 Cinema is the business of making films.

**cinnamon**
NOUN Cinnamon is a sweet spice which comes from the bark of an Asian tree.

**cipher** ciphers
Said "sy-fer"; also spelt **cypher**
NOUN a secret code or system of writing used to send secret messages.

**circa**
Said "sir-ka" PREPOSITION; FORMAL about or approximately; used especially before dates E.G. portrait of a lady, circa 1840.

**circle** circles circling circled
NOUN 1 a completely regular round shape. Every point on its edge is the same distance from the centre. 2 a group of people with the same interest or profession E.G. a character well known in yachting circles. 3 an area of seats on an upper floor of a theatre. ▶ VERB 4 To circle is to move round and round as though going round the edge of a circle E.G. A police helicopter circled above.

**circuit** circuits
Said "sir-kit" NOUN 1 any closed line or

a b **c** d e f g h i j k l m n o p q r s t u v w x y z

A
B
C
D
E
F
G
H
I
J
K
L
M
N
O
P
Q
R
S
T
U
V
W
X
Y
Z

path, often circular, for example a racing track; also the distance round this path E.G. *three circuits of the 26-lap race remaining.* **2** An electrical circuit is a complete route around which an electric current can flow.

**circular circulars**

ADJECTIVE **1** in the shape of a circle. **2** A circular argument or theory is not valid because it uses a statement to prove a conclusion and the conclusion to prove the statement. ▶ NOUN **3** a letter or advert sent to a lot of people at the same time. **circularity** NOUN

**circulate circulates circulating circulated**

VERB **1** (SCIENCE) When something circulates or when you circulate it, it moves easily around an area E.G. *an open position where the air can circulate freely.* **2** When you circulate something among people, you pass it round or tell it to all the people E.G. *We circulate a regular newsletter.*

**circulation circulations**

NOUN **1** The circulation of something is the act of circulating it or the action of it circulating E.G. *traffic circulation.* **2** The circulation of a newspaper or magazine is the number of copies that are sold of each issue. **3** (SCIENCE) Your circulation is the movement of blood through your body.

**circum-**

PREFIX 'Circum-' means 'around' or 'surrounding' E.G. *circumference.* 📖 from Latin *circus* meaning 'circle'

**circumcise circumcises circumcising circumcised**

VERB If a boy or man is circumcised, the foreskin at the end of his penis is removed. This is carried out mainly as part of a Muslim or Jewish religious ceremony.

**circumcision** NOUN

**circumference circumferences**

NOUN (MATHS) The circumference of a circle is its outer line or edge; also the length of this line.

**circumstance circumstances**

NOUN **1** The circumstances of a situation or event are the conditions that affect what happens E.G. *He did well in the circumstances.* **2** Someone's circumstances are their position and conditions in life E.G. *Her circumstances had changed.*

**circus circuses**

NOUN a show given by a travelling group of entertainers such as clowns, acrobats, and specially trained animals.

**cistern cisterns**

NOUN a tank in which water is stored, for example one in the roof of a house or above a toilet.

**citadel citadels**

NOUN a fortress in or near a city.

**cite cites citing cited**

VERB **1** FORMAL If you cite something, you quote it or refer to it E.G. *He cited a letter written by Newall.* **2** If someone is cited in a legal action, they are officially called to appear in court.

**citizen citizens**

NOUN (HISTORY) The citizens of a country or city are the people who live in it or belong to it E.G. *American citizens.*

**citizenship**

NOUN the status of being a citizen, with all the rights and duties that go with it E.G. *I'm applying for Australian citizenship.*

**citrus fruit** citrus fruits
NOUN Citrus fruits are juicy, sharp-tasting fruits such as oranges, lemons, and grapefruit.

**city** cities
NOUN a large town where many people live and work.

**civic**
ADJECTIVE relating to a city or citizens E.G. *the Civic Centre.*

**civil**
ADJECTIVE 1 relating to the citizens of a country E.G. *civil rights.* 2 relating to people or things that are not connected with the armed forces E.G. *the history of civil aviation.* 3 polite.
**civilly** ADVERB **civility** NOUN

**civil engineering**
NOUN Civil engineering is the design and construction of roads, bridges, and public buildings.

**civilian** civilians
NOUN a person who is not in the armed forces.

**civilization** civilizations; also spelt **civilisation**
NOUN (HISTORY) 1 a society which has a highly developed organization and culture E.G. *the tale of a lost civilization.* 2 Civilization is an advanced state of social organization and culture.

**civilized**
ADJECTIVE 1 A civilized society is one with a developed social organization and way of life. 2 A civilized person is polite and reasonable.

**civil servant** civil servants
NOUN a person who works in the civil service.

**civil service**
NOUN The civil service is the government departments responsible for the administration of a country.

**civil war** civil wars
NOUN a war between groups of people who live in the same country.

**cl**
an abbreviation for 'centilitres'.

**clad**
ADJECTIVE; *LITERARY* Someone who is clad in particular clothes is wearing them.

**claim** claims claiming claimed
VERB 1 If you claim that something is the case, you say that it is the case E.G. *He claims to have lived in the same house all his life.* 2 If you claim something, you ask for it because it belongs to you or you have a right to it E.G. *Cartier claimed the land for the King of France.* ▶ NOUN 3 a statement that something is the case, or that you have a right to something E.G. *She will make a claim for damages.*
■ (sense 1) allege, assert, maintain

**claimant** claimants
NOUN someone who is making a claim, especially for money.

**clairvoyant** clairvoyants
ADJECTIVE 1 able to know about things that will happen in the future. ▶ NOUN 2 a person who is, or claims to be, clairvoyant.
🏛 from French *clair* + *voyant* meaning 'clear-seeing'

**clam** clams
NOUN a kind of shellfish.

**clamber** clambers clambering clambered
VERB If you clamber somewhere, you climb there with difficulty.

**clammy** clammier clammiest
ADJECTIVE unpleasantly damp and sticky E.G. *clammy hands.*

a
b
c
d
e
f
g
h
i
j
k
l
m
n
o
p
q
r
s
t
u
v
w
x
y
z

**clamour** clamours clamouring clamoured

VERB 1 If people clamour for something, they demand it noisily or angrily E.G. *We clamoured for an explanation.* ► NOUN 2 Clamour is noisy or angry shouts or demands by a lot of people.

**clamp** clamps clamping clamped

NOUN 1 an object with movable parts that are used to hold two things firmly together. ► VERB 2 To clamp things together is to fasten them or hold them firmly with a clamp.

**clamp down on** VERB To clamp down on something is to become stricter in controlling it E.G. *The Queen has clamped down on all expenditure.*

**clan** clans

NOUN a group of families related to each other by being descended from the same ancestor.

**clandestine**

ADJECTIVE secret and hidden E.G. *a clandestine meeting with friends.*

**clang** clangs clanging clanged

VERB When something metal clangs or when you clang it, it makes a loud, deep sound.

**clank** clanks clanking clanked

VERB If something metal clanks, it makes a loud noise.

**clap** claps clapping clapped

VERB 1 When you clap, you hit your hands together loudly to show your appreciation. 2 If you clap someone on the back or shoulder, you hit them in a friendly way. 3 If you clap something somewhere, you put it there quickly and firmly E.G. *I clapped a hand over her mouth.* ► NOUN 4 a sound made by clapping your hands. 5 A clap of thunder is a sudden loud

noise of thunder.

**claret** clarets

NOUN a type of red wine, especially one from the Bordeaux region of France.

**clarify** clarifies clarifying clarified

VERB (EXAM TERM) To clarify something is to make it clear and easier to understand E.G. *Discussion will clarify your thoughts.*

**clarification** NOUN

**clarinet** clarinets

NOUN a woodwind instrument with a straight tube and a single reed in its mouthpiece.

**clarity**

NOUN The clarity of something is its clearness.

**clash** clashes clashing clashed

VERB 1 If people clash with each other, they fight or argue. 2 Ideas or styles that clash are so different that they do not go together. 3 If two events clash, they happen at the same time so you cannot go to both. 4 When metal objects clash, they hit each other with a loud noise. ► NOUN 5 a fight or argument. 6 A clash of ideas, styles, or events is a situation in which they do not go together. 7 a loud noise made by metal objects when they hit each other.

**clasp** clasps clasping clasped

VERB 1 To clasp something means to hold it tightly or fasten it E.G. *He clasped his hands.* ► NOUN 2 a fastening such as a hook or catch.

**class** classes classing classed

NOUN 1 A class of people or things is a group of them of a particular type or quality E.G. *the old class of politicians.* 2 a group of pupils or students

149 classic >> clause

taught together, or a lesson that they have together. **3** Someone who has class is elegant in appearance or behaviour. ▶ VERB **4** To class something means to arrange it in a particular group or to consider it as belonging to a particular group E.G. *They are officially classed as visitors.* ■ (sense 1) category, group, kind, type

**classic classics**
ADJECTIVE **1** typical and therefore a good model or example of something E.G. *a classic case of misuse.* **2** of very high quality E.G. *one of the classic films of all time.* **3** simple in style and form E.G. *the classic dinner suit.* ▶ NOUN **4** something of the highest quality E.G. *one of the great classics of rock music.* **5** Classics is the study of Latin and Greek, and the literature of ancient Greece and Rome.

**classical**
ADJECTIVE **1** traditional in style, form, and content E.G. *classical ballet.* **2** Classical music is serious music considered to be of lasting value. **3** characteristic of the style of ancient Greece and Rome E.G. *Classical friezes decorate the walls.*
**classically** ADVERB

**classified**
ADJECTIVE officially declared secret by the government E.G. *access to classified information.*

**classify classifies classifying classified**
VERB To classify things is to arrange them into groups with similar characteristics E.G. *We can classify the differences into three groups.*
**classification** NOUN (LIBRARY)

**classroom classrooms**
NOUN a room in a school where pupils have lessons.

**classy classier classiest**
ADJECTIVE; *INFORMAL* stylish and elegant.

**clatter clatters clattering clattered**
VERB **1** When things clatter, they hit each other with a loud rattling noise. ▶ NOUN **2** a loud rattling noise made by hard things hitting each other.

**clause clauses**
NOUN **1** a section of a legal document. **2** (ENGLISH) In grammar, a clause is a group of words with a subject and a verb, which may be a complete sentence or one of the parts of a sentence.

---

### What is a Clause?

A **clause** is a group of words which form part of a sentence and express an idea or describe a situation. A clause often gives information about the main idea or situation:

E.G. *Matthew ate a cake **which was covered in chocolate.**
Anna crossed the street **after looking carefully in both directions**.*

**Main Clauses and Subordinate Clauses**
Clauses can be either **main clauses** or **subordinate clauses**.
A **main clause** is the core of a sentence. It would make sense if it stood on its own. Every sentence contains a main clause:

E.G. ***Matthew ate a cake*** *which was covered in chocolate.*

CONTINUED ON NEXT PAGE →

'i' before 'e' except after 'c'    SPELLING NOTE

# claustrophobia ›› clear

150

*After looking carefully in both directions, **Anna crossed the road**.*

A **subordinate clause** is a less important part of a sentence. It would not make sense on its own, but gives information about the main clause:

E.G. ***After looking carefully**, Anna crossed the road.*
*Anna had to cross the road, **which was often very busy**.*

### Relative Clauses

Relative clauses give additional information about a person or thing mentioned in the main clause.

Relative clauses are introduced by a relative pronoun – *who, whom, whose, which* or *that*:

E.G. *Robbie has a cat **who likes fish**.*
*Anna has one sister, **whose name is Rosie**.*

**claustrophobia**
*Said* "klos-trof-**foe**-bee-ya" NOUN Claustrophobia is a fear of being in enclosed spaces.
**claustrophobic** ADJECTIVE

**claw claws clawing clawed**
NOUN **1** An animal's claws are hard, curved nails at the end of its feet. **2** The claws of a crab or lobster are the two jointed parts, used for grasping things. ▶ VERB **3** If an animal claws something, it digs its claws into it.

**clay**
NOUN Clay is a type of earth that is soft and sticky when wet and hard when baked dry. It is used to make pottery and bricks.

**clean cleaner cleanest; cleans cleaning cleaned**
ADJECTIVE **1** free from dirt or other unwanted substances or marks. **2** If humour is clean it is not rude and does not involve bad language. **3** A clean movement is skilful and accurate. **4** Clean also means free from fault or error E.G. *a clean driving licence.* ▶ VERB **5** To clean something is to remove dirt from it.
**cleanly** ADVERB **cleaner** NOUN

**cleanliness**
*Said* "**klen**-lin-ness" NOUN Cleanliness is the practice of keeping yourself and your surroundings clean.

**cleanse cleanses cleansing cleansed**
*Said* "klenz" VERB To cleanse something is to make it completely free from dirt.

**clear clearer clearest; clears clearing cleared**
ADJECTIVE **1** easy to understand, see, or hear E.G. *He made it clear he did not want to talk.* **2** easy to see through E.G. *a clear liquid.* **3** free from obstructions or unwanted things E.G. *clear of snow.* ▶ VERB **4** To clear an area is to remove unwanted things from it. **5** If you clear a fence or other obstacle, you jump over it without touching it. **6** When fog or mist clears, it disappears. **7** If someone is cleared of a crime, they are proved to be not guilty.
**clearly** ADVERB **clearness** NOUN
■ (sense 1) evident, obvious, plain
**clear up** VERB **1** If you clear up, you tidy a place and put things away. **2** When a problem or misunderstanding is cleared up, it is solved or settled.

SPELLING NOTE  King IAn went to ParlIAment in a carrIAge for his marrIAge (-ia-)

**clearance**
NOUN **1** Clearance is the removal of old buildings in an area. **2** If someone is given clearance to do something, they get official permission to do it.

**clearing** clearings
NOUN an area of bare ground in a forest.

**cleavage** cleavages
NOUN the space between a woman's breasts.

**cleaver** cleavers
NOUN a knife with a large square blade, used especially by butchers.

**cleft** clefts
NOUN a narrow opening in a rock.

**clementine** clementines
NOUN a type of small citrus fruit that is a cross between an orange and a tangerine.

**clench** clenches clenching clenched
VERB **1** When you clench your fist, you curl your fingers up tightly. **2** When you clench your teeth, you squeeze them together tightly.

**clergy**
PLURAL NOUN The clergy are the ministers of the Christian Church.

**clergyman** clergymen
NOUN a male member of the clergy.

**clerical**
ADJECTIVE **1** relating to work done in an office E.G. *clerical jobs with the City Council.* **2** relating to the clergy.

**clerk** clerks
*Said* "klahrk" NOUN a person who keeps records or accounts in an office, bank, or law court.

**clever** cleverer cleverest
ADJECTIVE **1** intelligent and quick to understand things. **2** very effective or skilful E.G. *a clever plan.*

**cleverly** ADVERB **cleverness** NOUN
■ (sense 1) bright, intelligent, smart

**clianthus**
*Said* "klee-**an**-thuss" NOUN A clianthus is a plant found in Australia and New Zealand which has clusters of scarlet flowers.

**cliché** clichés
*Said* "klee-shay" NOUN (ENGLISH) an idea or phrase which is no longer effective because it has been used so much.

**click** clicks clicking clicked
VERB **1** When something clicks or when you click it, it makes a short snapping sound. **2** INFORMAL When something clicks, you suddenly understand it. **3** When you click on an area of a computer screen, you point the cursor at it and press one of the buttons on the mouse. ▶ NOUN **3** a sound of something clicking E.G. *I heard the click of a bolt.*

**client** clients
NOUN someone who pays a professional person or company to receive a service.

**clientele**
*Said* "klee-on-**tell**" PLURAL NOUN The clientele of a place are its customers.

**cliff** cliffs
NOUN a steep high rock face by the sea.

**climate** climates
NOUN **1** (GEOGRAPHY) The climate of a place is the typical weather conditions there E.G. *The climate was dry in the summer.* **2** the general attitude and opinion of people at a particular time E.G. *the American political climate.*
**climatic** ADJECTIVE

**climax** climaxes
NOUN The climax of a process, story, or

A
B
C
D
E
F
G
H
I
J
K
L
M
N
O
P
Q
R
S
T
U
V
W
X
Y
Z

piece of music is the most exciting moment in it, usually near the end. 🔲 from Greek *klimax* meaning 'ladder'

**climb** climbs climbing climbed
VERB 1 To climb is to move upwards. 2 If you climb somewhere, you move there with difficulty *E.G. She climbed out of the driving seat.* ▶ NOUN 3 a movement upwards *E.G. this long climb up the slope… the rapid climb in murders.*
**climber** NOUN

**clinch** clinches clinching clinched
VERB If you clinch an agreement or an argument, you settle it in a definite way *E.G. Peter clinched a deal.*

**cling** clings clinging clung
VERB To cling to something is to hold onto it or stay closely attached to it *E.G. still clinging to old-fashioned values.*

**clingfilm**
NOUN; TRADEMARK a clear thin plastic used for wrapping food.

**clinic** clinics
NOUN a building where people go for medical treatment.

**clinical**
ADJECTIVE 1 relating to the medical treatment of patients *E.G. clinical tests.* 2 Clinical behaviour or thought is logical and without emotion *E.G. the cold, clinical attitudes of his colleagues.*
**clinically** ADVERB

**clip** clips clipping clipped
NOUN 1 a small metal or plastic object used for holding things together. 2 a short piece of a film shown by itself. ▶ VERB 3 If you clip things together, you fasten them with clips. 4 If you clip something, you cut bits from it

to shape it *E.G. clipped hedges.*

**clippers**
PLURAL NOUN Clippers are tools used for cutting.

**clipping** clippings
NOUN an article cut from a newspaper or magazine.

**clique** cliques
*Rhymes with "seek"* NOUN a small group of people who stick together and do not mix with other people.

**clitoris** clitorises
*Said "klit-tor-riss"* NOUN a small highly sensitive piece of flesh near the opening of a woman's vagina.

**cloak** cloaks cloaking cloaked
NOUN 1 a wide, loose coat without sleeves. ▶ VERB 2 To cloak something is to cover or hide it *E.G. a land permanently cloaked in mist.*

**cloakroom** cloakrooms
NOUN a room for coats or a room with toilets and washbasins in a public building.

**clock** clocks
NOUN 1 a device that measures and shows the time. ▶ PHRASE 2 If you work **round the clock**, you work all day and night.

**clockwise**
ADJECTIVE or ADVERB in the same direction as the hands on a clock.

**clockwork**
NOUN 1 Toys that work by clockwork move when they are wound up with a key. ▶ PHRASE 2 If something happens **like clockwork**, it happens with no problems or delays.

**clog** clogs clogging clogged
VERB 1 To clog something is to block it *E.G. pavements clogged up with people.* ▶ NOUN 2 Clogs are heavy wooden shoes.

SPELLING NOTE      LEt's measure the angLE (ang**le**)

**cloister** cloisters
NOUN a covered area in a monastery or a cathedral for walking around a square.

**clone** clones cloning cloned
NOUN **1** In biology, a clone is an animal or plant that has been produced artificially from the cells of another animal or plant and is therefore identical to it. ▸ VERB **2** To clone an animal or plant is to produce it as a clone.

**close** closes closing closed; closer closest
VERB **1** To close something is to shut it. **2** To close a road or entrance is to block it so that no-one can go in or out. **3** If a shop closes at a certain time, then it does not do business after that time. ▸ ADJECTIVE OR ADVERB **4** near to something E.G. *a restaurant close to their home.* ▸ ADJECTIVE **5** People who are close to each other are very friendly and know each other well. **6** You say the weather is close when it is uncomfortably warm and there is not enough air.
**closely** ADVERB **closeness** NOUN **closed** ADJECTIVE
▪ (sense 4) near, nearby

**close down** VERB If a business closes down, all work stops there permanently.

**closed shop** closed shops
NOUN a factory or other business whose employees have to be members of a trade union.

**closet** closets closeting closeted
NOUN **1** a cupboard. ▸ VERB **2** If you are closeted somewhere, you shut yourself away alone or in private with another person. ▸ ADJECTIVE

**3** Closet beliefs or habits are kept private and secret E.G. *a closet romantic.*

**close-up** close-ups
NOUN a detailed close view of something, especially a photograph taken close to the subject.

**closure** closures
*Said* "klohz-yur" NOUN **1** The closure of a business is the permanent shutting of it. **2** The closure of a road is the blocking of it so it cannot be used.

**clot** clots clotting clotted
NOUN **1** a lump, especially one that forms when blood thickens. ▸ VERB **2** When a substance such as blood clots, it thickens and forms a lump.

**cloth** cloths
*Rhymes with* "**moth**" NOUN **1** Cloth is fabric made by a process such as weaving. **2** a piece of material used for wiping or protecting things
☑ 'Cloth' and 'clothe' have different spellings and pronunciations.

**clothe** clothes clothing clothed
*Rhymes with* "**both**" PLURAL NOUN **1** Clothes are the things people wear on their bodies. ▸ VERB **2** To clothe someone is to give them clothes to wear.

**clothing**
NOUN Clothing is the clothes people wear.

**cloud** clouds clouding clouded
NOUN **1** a mass of water vapour that forms in the air and is seen as a white or grey patch in the sky. **2** A cloud of smoke or dust is a mass of it floating in the air. ▸ VERB **3** If something clouds or is clouded, it becomes cloudy or difficult to see through E.G. *The sky clouded over.* **4** Something that clouds an issue

a
b
c
d
e
f
g
h
i
j
k
l
m
n
o
p
q
r
s
t
u
v
w
x
y
z

A
B
C
D
E
F
G
H
I
J
K
L
M
N
O
P
Q
R
S
T
U
V
W
X
Y
Z

makes it more confusing.

🔖 from Old English *clud* meaning 'hill'

**cloudy** cloudier cloudiest

ADJECTIVE 1 full of clouds E.G. *the cloudy sky*. 2 difficult to see through E.G. *a glass of cloudy liquid*.

▤ (sense 1) dull, overcast

**clout**

NOUN; *INFORMAL* Someone who has clout has influence.

**clove** cloves

NOUN 1 Cloves are small, strong-smelling dried flower buds from a tropical tree, used as a spice in cooking. 2 A clove of garlic is one of the separate sections of the bulb.

**clover**

NOUN Clover is a small plant with leaves made up of three similar parts.

**clown** clowns clowning clowned

NOUN 1 a circus performer who wears funny clothes and make-up and does silly things to make people laugh. ▶ VERB 2 If you clown, you do silly things to make people laugh.

**cloying**

ADJECTIVE unpleasantly sickly, sweet, or sentimental E.G. *something less cloying than whipped cream*.

**club** clubs clubbing clubbed

NOUN 1 an organization of people with a particular interest, who meet regularly; also the place where they meet. 2 a thick, heavy stick used as a weapon. 3 a stick with a shaped head that a golf player uses to hit the ball. 4 Clubs is one of the four suits in a pack of playing cards. It is marked by a black symbol in the shape of a clover leaf. ▶ VERB 5 To club someone is to hit them hard with a heavy object.

▤ (sense 1) association, group, society

**club together** VERB If people club together, they all join together to give money to buy something.

**cluck** clucks clucking clucked

VERB When a hen clucks, it makes a short, repeated, high-pitched sound.

**clue** clues

NOUN something that helps to solve a problem or mystery.

**clump** clumps clumping clumped

NOUN 1 a small group of things close together. ▶ VERB 2 If you clump about, you walk with heavy footsteps.

**clumsy** clumsier clumsiest

ADJECTIVE 1 moving awkwardly and carelessly. 2 said or done without thought or tact E.G. *his clumsy attempts to catch her out*.

**clumsily** ADVERB **clumsiness** NOUN

▤ (sense 1) awkward, gauche, ungainly

**cluster** clusters clustering clustered

NOUN 1 A cluster of things is a group of them together E.G. *a cluster of huts at the foot of the mountains*. ▶ VERB 2 If people cluster together, they stay together in a close group.

**clutch** clutches clutching clutched

VERB 1 If you clutch something, you hold it tightly or seize it. ▶ PLURAL NOUN 2 If you are in someone's clutches, they have power or control over you.

**clutter** clutters cluttering cluttered

NOUN 1 Clutter is an untidy mess. ▶ VERB 2 Things that clutter a place fill it and make it untidy.

**cm**

an abbreviation for 'centimetres'.

**co-**

PREFIX Co- means together E.G. *Paula is*

*now co-writing a book with Pierre.*

**coach** coaches coaching coached

NOUN **1** a long motor vehicle used for taking passengers on long journeys. **2** a section of a train that carries passengers. **3** a four-wheeled vehicle with a roof pulled by horses, which people used to travel in. **4** a person who coaches a sport or a subject.
▶ VERB **5** If someone coaches you, they teach you and help you to get better at a sport or a subject.
🔲 (sense 4) instructor, trainer
🔲 (sense 5) instruct, train

**coal** coals

NOUN **1** Coal is a hard black rock obtained from under the earth and burned as a fuel. **2** Coals are burning pieces of coal.

**coalition** coalitions

NOUN a temporary alliance, especially between different political parties forming a government.

**coarse** coarser coarsest

ADJECTIVE **1** Something that is coarse is rough in texture, often consisting of large particles *E.G. a coarse blanket.* **2** Someone who is coarse talks or behaves in a rude or rather offensive way.

**coarsely** ADVERB   **coarseness** NOUN
✔ Do not confuse the spellings of *coarse* and *course.*

**coast** coasts coasting coasted

NOUN **1** the edge of the land where it meets the sea. ▶ VERB **2** A vehicle that is coasting is moving without engine power.

**coastal** ADJECTIVE

**coastguard** coastguards

NOUN an official who watches the sea near a coast to get help for

sailors when they need it, and to prevent smuggling.

**coastline** coastlines

NOUN the outline of a coast, especially its appearance as seen from the sea or air.

**coat** coats coating coated

NOUN **1** a piece of clothing with sleeves which you wear outside over your other clothes. **2** An animal's coat is the fur or hair on its body. **3** A coat of paint or varnish is a layer of it.
▶ VERB **4** To coat something means to cover it with a thin layer of a something *E.G. walnuts coated with chocolate.*

**coating** NOUN

**coax** coaxes coaxing coaxed

VERB If you coax someone to do something, you gently persuade them to do it.
🔲 cajole, persuade, talk into, wheedle

**cobalt**

NOUN Cobalt is a hard silvery-white metal which is used for producing a blue dye.

**cobble** cobbles

NOUN Cobbles or cobblestones are stones with a rounded surface that were used in the past for making roads.

**cobbler** cobblers

NOUN a person who makes or mends shoes.

**cobra** cobras

*Said* "koh-bra" NOUN a type of large poisonous snake from Africa and Asia.

**cobweb** cobwebs

NOUN the very thin net that a spider spins for catching insects.

**cocaine**

NOUN Cocaine is an addictive drug.

from Spanish *coca* meaning 'preparation of cocoa leaves'

**cock cocks**
NOUN an adult male chicken; also used of any male bird.

**cockatoo cockatoos**
NOUN a type of parrot with a crest, found in Australia and New Guinea.

**cockerel cockerels**
NOUN a young cock.

**Cockney Cockneys**
NOUN a person born in the East End of London.

**cockpit cockpits**
NOUN The place in a small plane where the pilot sits.

**cockroach cockroaches**
NOUN a large dark-coloured insect often found in dirty rooms.

**cocktail cocktails**
NOUN an alcoholic drink made from several ingredients.

**cocky cockier cockiest; cockies**
INFORMAL
ADJECTIVE **1** cheeky or too self-confident. ▶ NOUN **2** In Australian English, a cockatoo. **3** In Australian and New Zealand English, a farmer, especially one whose farm is small.
**cockiness** NOUN

**cocoa**
NOUN Cocoa is a brown powder made from the seeds of a tropical tree and used for making chocolate; also a hot drink made from this powder.

**coconut coconuts**
NOUN a very large nut with white flesh, milky juice, and a hard hairy shell.

**cocoon cocoons**
NOUN a silky covering over the larvae of moths and some other insects.
from Provençal *coucoun* meaning 'eggshell'

**cod**
NOUN a large edible fish
☑ The plural of *cod* is also *cod*.

**code codes**
NOUN **1** a system of replacing the letters or words in a message with other letters or words, so that nobody can understand the message unless they know the system. **2** a group of numbers and letters which is used to identify something E.G. *the telephone code for Melbourne*.
**coded** ADJECTIVE

**coffee**
NOUN Coffee is a substance made by roasting and grinding the beans of a tropical shrub; also a hot drink made from this substance.
from Arabic *qahwah* meaning 'wine' or 'coffee'

**coffin coffins**
NOUN a box in which a dead body is buried or cremated.

**cog cogs**
NOUN a wheel with teeth which turns another wheel or part of a machine.

**cognac**
*Said* "kon-yak" NOUN Cognac is a kind of brandy.

**coherent**
ADJECTIVE **1** If something such as a theory is coherent, its parts fit together well and do not contradict each other. **2** If someone is coherent, what they are saying makes sense and is not jumbled or confused.
**coherence** NOUN

**cohesive**
ADJECTIVE If something is cohesive, its parts fit together well E.G. *The team must work as a cohesive unit*.
**cohesion** NOUN

**coil** coils coiling coiled
NOUN **1** a length of rope or wire wound into a series of loops; also one of the loops. ▶ VERB **2** If something coils, it turns into a series of loops.

**coin** coins coining coined
NOUN **1** a small metal disc which is used as money. ▶ VERB **2** If you coin a word or a phrase, you invent it.

**coinage**
NOUN The coinage of a country is the coins that are used there.

**coincide** coincides coinciding coincided
VERB **1** If two events coincide, they happen at about the same time. **2** When two people's ideas or opinions coincide, they agree E.G. What she said coincided exactly with his own thinking.

**coincidence** coincidences
NOUN **1** what happens when two similar things occur at the same time by chance E.G. I had moved to London, and by coincidence, Helen had too. **2** the fact that two things are surprisingly the same.
**coincidental** ADJECTIVE
**coincidentally** ADVERB

**coke**
NOUN Coke is a grey fuel produced from coal.

**colander** colanders
Said "kol-an-der" NOUN a bowl-shaped container with holes in it, used for washing or draining food.

**cold** colder coldest; colds
ADJECTIVE **1** Something that is cold has a very low temperature. **2** If it is cold, the air temperature is very low. **3** Someone who is cold does not show much affection. ▶ NOUN **4** You

can refer to cold weather as the cold E.G. She was complaining about the cold. **5** a minor illness in which you sneeze and may have a sore throat.
**coldly** ADVERB **coldness** NOUN

**cold-blooded**
ADJECTIVE **1** Someone who is cold-blooded does not show any pity E.G. two cold-blooded killers. **2** A cold-blooded animal has a body temperature that changes according to the surrounding temperature.

**cold war**
NOUN Cold war is a state of extreme unfriendliness between countries not actually at war.

**coleslaw**
NOUN Coleslaw is a salad of chopped cabbage and other vegetables in mayonnaise.
from Dutch koolsla meaning 'cabbage salad'

**colic**
NOUN Colic is pain in a baby's stomach.

**collaborate** collaborates collaborating collaborated
VERB When people collaborate, they work together to produce something E.G. The two bands have collaborated in the past.
**collaboration** NOUN **collaborator** NOUN

**collage** collages
Said "kol-lahj" NOUN ( ART ) a picture made by sticking pieces of paper or cloth onto a surface.

**collapse** collapses collapsing collapsed
VERB **1** If something such as a building collapses, it falls down suddenly. If a person collapses, they fall down suddenly because they are ill. **2** If

A B **C** D E F G H I J K L M N O P Q R S T U V W X Y Z

something such as a system or a business collapses, it suddenly stops working E.G. *50,000 small firms collapsed last year.* ▶ NOUN **3** The collapse of something is what happens when it stops working E.G. *the collapse of his marriage.*

**collapsible**
ADJECTIVE A collapsible object can be folded flat when it is not in use E.G. *a collapsible ironing board.*

**collar** collars
NOUN **1** The collar of a shirt or coat is the part round the neck which is usually folded over. **2** a leather band round the neck of a dog or cat.

**collateral**
NOUN Collateral is money or property which is used as a guarantee that someone will repay a loan, and which the lender can take if the loan is not repaid.

**colleague** colleagues
NOUN A person's colleagues are the people he or she works with.

**collect** collects collecting collected
VERB **1** To collect things is to gather them together for a special purpose or as a hobby E.G. *collecting money for charity.* **2** If you collect someone or something from a place, you call there and take them away E.G. *We had to collect her from school.* **3** When things collect in a place, they gather there over a period of time E.G. *Food collects in holes in the teeth.*
**collector** NOUN

**collected**
ADJECTIVE calm and self-controlled.

**collection** collections
NOUN **1** ( ART ) a group of things acquired over a period of time E.G. *a*

*collection of paintings.* **2** the collecting of something E.G. *tax collection.* **3** the organized collecting of money, for example for charity, or the sum of money collected.
■ (sense 1) accumulation, compilation, set

**collective** collectives
ADJECTIVE **1** involving every member of a group of people E.G. *The wine growers took a collective decision.*
▶ NOUN **2** a group of people who share the responsibility both for running something and for doing the work.
**collectively** ADVERB

**collective noun** collective nouns
NOUN a noun that refers to a single unit made up of a number of things, for example 'flock' and 'swarm'.

**college** colleges
NOUN **1** a place where students study after they have left school. **2** a name given to some secondary schools. **3** one of the institutions into which some universities are divided. **4** In New Zealand English, a college can also refer to a teacher training college.

**collide** collides colliding collided
VERB If a moving object collides with something, it hits it.

**collie** collies
NOUN a dog that is used for rounding up sheep.

**colliery** collieries
NOUN a coal mine.

**collision** collisions
NOUN A collision occurs when a moving object hits something.
■ crash, impact, smash

**colloquial**
*Said* "kol-**loh**-kwee-al" ADJECTIVE Colloquial words and phrases are

informal and used especially in conversation.

**colloquially** ADVERB   **colloquialism** NOUN

**cologne**

*Said* "kol-**lone**" NOUN Cologne is a kind of weak perfume.

**colon colons**

NOUN **1** the punctuation mark (:). **2** part of your intestine.

---

### What does the Colon do?

The **colon** (:) and the **semicolon** (;) are often confused and used incorrectly.

The **colon** is used to introduce a list:

> *E.G. I bought fruit: pears, apples, grapes and plums.*

The colon can also be used to introduce a quotation:

> *E.G. He received a message which read: "You can't fool all of the people all of the time."*

Another use of the colon is to introduce an explanation of a statement:

> *E.G. They did not enjoy the meal: the food was cold.*

Also look at the grammar box at **semicolon**.

---

**colonel colonels**

*Said* "kur-nl" NOUN an army officer with a fairly high rank.

**colonial**

ADJECTIVE **1** relating to a colony. **2** In Australia, colonial is used to relate to the period of Australian history before the Federation in 1901.

**colonize colonizes colonizing colonized**; also spelt **colonise**

VERB (HISTORY) When people colonize a place, they go to live there and take control of it *E.G. the Europeans who colonized North America.* When a lot of animals colonize a place, they go there and make it their home *E.G. Toads are colonizing the whole place.*

**colonization** NOUN   **colonist** NOUN

**colony colonies**

NOUN (HISTORY) **1** a country controlled by a more powerful country. **2** a group of people who settle in a country controlled by their homeland.

**colossal**

ADJECTIVE very large indeed.

**colour colours colouring coloured**

NOUN **1** (ART) the appearance something has as a result of reflecting light. **2** Someone's colour is the normal colour of their skin. **3** Colour is also a quality that makes something interesting or exciting *E.G. bringing more culture and colour to the city.* ▶ VERB **4** If something colours your opinion, it affects the way you think about something.

**coloured** ADJECTIVE   **colourful** ADJECTIVE   **colourfully** ADVERB   **colourless** ADJECTIVE   **colouring** NOUN

■ (sense 1) hue, shade, tint

**colour blind**

ADJECTIVE Someone who is colour blind cannot distinguish between colours.

**colt colts**

NOUN a young male horse.

**column columns**

NOUN **1** a tall solid upright cylinder,

I want to see (C) your licenCe (licen<u>c</u>e)    SPELLING NOTE especially one supporting a part of a building. **2** a group of people moving in a long line.

**columnist** columnists
NOUN a journalist who writes a regular article in a newspaper or magazine.

**com-** or **con-**
PREFIX 'Com-' or 'con-' means 'together', 'with' or 'jointly' E.G. combine… consult.
🔲 from Latin prefix com- meaning 'with'

**coma** comas
NOUN Someone who is in a coma is in a state of deep unconsciousness.

**comb** combs combing combed
NOUN **1** a flat object with pointed teeth used for tidying your hair.
▶ VERB **2** When you comb your hair, you tidy it with a comb. **3** If you comb a place, you search it thoroughly to try to find someone or something.

**combat** combats combating combated
NOUN **1** Combat is fighting E.G. his first experience of combat. ▶ VERB **2** To combat something means to try to stop it happening or developing E.G. a way to combat crime.

**combination** combinations
NOUN **1** a mixture of things E.G. a combination of charm and skill. **2** a series of letters or numbers used to open a special lock.

**combine** combines combining combined
VERB **1** To combine things is to cause them to exist together E.G. to combine a career with being a mother. **2** To combine things also means to join them together to make a single thing E.G. Combine all the ingredients.

**3** If something combines two qualities or features, it has them both E.G. a film that combines great charm and scintillating performances.

**combustion**
NOUN (SCIENCE) Combustion is the act of burning something or the process of burning.

**come** comes coming came come
VERB **1** To come to a place is to move there or arrive there. **2** To come to a place also means to reach as far as that place E.G. The sea water came up to his waist. **3** 'Come' is used to say that someone or something reaches a particular state E.G. They came to power in 1997… We had come to a decision. **4** When a particular time or event comes, it happens E.G. The peak of his career came early in 1990. **5** If you come from a place, you were born there or it is your home.
▶ PHRASE **6** A time or event **to come** is a future time or event E.G. The public will thank them in years to come.

**come about** VERB The way something comes about is the way it happens E.G. The discussion came about because of the proposed changes.

**come across** VERB If you come across something, you find it by chance.

**come off** VERB If something comes off, it succeeds E.G. His rescue plan had come off.

**come on** VERB If something is coming on, it is making progress E.G. Let's go and see how the grapes are coming on.

**come up** VERB If something comes up in a conversation or meeting, it is mentioned or discussed.

**come up with** VERB If you come up with a plan or idea, you suggest it.

**comeback comebacks**
NOUN To make a comeback means to be popular or successful again.

**comedian comedians**
NOUN an entertainer whose job is to make people laugh.

**comedienne comediennes**
*Said* "kom-mee-dee-*en*" NOUN a female comedian.

**comedy comedies**
NOUN a light-hearted play or film with a happy ending.
from Greek *kōmos* meaning 'village festival' and *aeidein* meaning 'to sing'

**comet comets**
NOUN an object that travels around the sun leaving a bright trail behind it.

**comfort comforts comforting comforted**
NOUN 1 Comfort is the state of being physically relaxed E.G. *He settled back in comfort.* 2 Comfort is also a feeling of relief from worries or unhappiness E.G. *The thought is a great comfort to me.* ▶ PLURAL NOUN 3 Comforts are things which make your life easier and more pleasant E.G. *all the comforts of home.* ▶ VERB 4 To comfort someone is to make them less worried or unhappy.

**comfortable**
ADJECTIVE 1 If you are comfortable, you are physically relaxed. 2 Something that is comfortable makes you feel relaxed E.G. *a comfortable bed.* 3 If you feel comfortable in a particular situation, you are not afraid or embarrassed.
**comfortably** ADVERB

**comic comics**
ADJECTIVE 1 funny E.G. *a comic monologue.* ▶ NOUN 2 someone who tells jokes. 3 a magazine that contains stories told in pictures.

**comical**
ADJECTIVE funny E.G. *a comical sight.*

**comma commas**
NOUN (ENGLISH) the punctuation mark ( , ).

---

### What does the Comma do?

The **comma** ( , ) indicates a short pause between different elements within a sentence. This happens, for example, when a sentence consists of two main clauses joined by a conjunction:

E.G. *Anna likes swimming, but Matthew prefers fishing.*

A comma may also separate an introductory phrase or a subordinate clause from the main clause in a sentence:

E.G. *After a month of sunshine, it rained on Thursday.*

However, a short introductory phrase does not need to be followed by a comma:

E.G. *After lunch the classes continued.*

When words such as *therefore*, *however*, and *moreover* are put into a sentence to show how a train of thought is progressing, they should be marked off by commas:

E.G. *We are confident, however, that the operation will be successful.*

CONTINUED ON NEXT PAGE →

---

have a plEce of plE (pi**e**ce)        SPELLING NOTE

a b **c** d e f g h i j k l m n o p q r s t u v w x y z

A
B
C
D
E
F
G
H
I
J
K
L
M
N
O
P
Q
R
S
T
U
V
W
X
Y
Z

The comma also separates items in a list or series:

*E.G. I made this soup with carrots, leeks, and potatoes.*

Commas separate the name of a person or people being addressed from the rest of the sentence:

*E.G. Thank you, ladies and gentlemen, for your attention.*

The comma also separates words in quotation marks from the rest of the sentence, if there is no question or exclamation mark at the end of the quotation:

*E.G. "This is a terrific picture," she said.*

**command** commands commanding commanded

VERB **1** To command someone to do something is to order them to do it. **2** If you command something such as respect, you receive it because of your personal qualities. **3** An officer who commands part of an army or navy is in charge of it. ➤ NOUN **4** an order to do something. **5** Your command of something is your knowledge of it and your ability to use this knowledge *E.G. a good command of English.*

▣ (sense 1) direct, order

→ SEE BOX OPPOSITE

**commandant** commandants

*Said* "kom-man-dant" NOUN an army officer in charge of a place or group of people.

**commander** commanders

NOUN an officer in charge of a military operation or organization.

**commandment** commandments

NOUN ( RE ) The commandments are

---

### What is a Command?

Commands are used to give orders, instructions, or warnings. Commands are made by putting the verb at the start of the sentence. The verb is used in its **imperative form** which is the basic form without any endings added:

*E.G. **Come** over here.*

Commands do not need a subject, as people who are being told to do something already know who they are. So commands may consist of a single verb:

*E.G. **Stop**!*

The negative form of a command is introduced by *do not* or *don't*:

*E.G. **Don't** put that on the table.*

Commands often end with an exclamation mark rather than a full stop, especially if they express urgency:

*E.G. Run for your life**!***

---

ten rules of behaviour that, according to the Old Testament, people should obey.

**commando** commandos

NOUN Commandos are soldiers who have been specially trained to carry out raids.

**commemorate** commemorates commemorating commemorated

VERB **1** An object that commemorates a person or an event is intended to remind people of that person or event. **2** If you commemorate an event, you do something special to show that you remember it.

**commemorative** ADJECTIVE

**commemoration** NOUN

**commence** commences
commencing commenced
VERB; *FORMAL* To commence is to begin.
**commencement** NOUN

**commend** commends
commending commended
VERB To commend someone or
something is to praise them *E.G. He
has been commended for his work.*
**commendation** NOUN
**commendable** ADJECTIVE

**comment** comments
commenting commented
VERB 1 If you comment on something,
you make a remark about it. ► NOUN
2 a remark about something *E.G. She
received many comments about her
appearance.*
■ (sense 1) observe, remark

**commentary** commentaries
NOUN a description of an event which
is broadcast on radio or television
while the event is happening.

**commentator** commentators
NOUN someone who gives a radio or
television commentary.

**commerce**
NOUN Commerce is the buying and
selling of goods.

**commercial** commercials
ADJECTIVE 1 relating to commerce.
2 Commercial activities involve
producing goods on a large scale in
order to make money *E.G. the
commercial fishing world.* ► NOUN 3 an
advertisement on television or radio.
**commercially** ADVERB

**commission** commissions
commissioning commissioned
VERB 1 If someone commissions a
piece of work, they formally ask
someone to do it *E.G. a study

commissioned by the government.*
► NOUN 2 a piece of work that has
been commissioned. 3 Commission
is money paid to a salesman each
time a sale is made. 4 an official body
appointed to investigate or control
something.

**commit** commits committing
committed
VERB 1 To commit a crime or sin is to
do it. 2 If you commit yourself, you
state an opinion or state that you
will do something. 3 If someone is
committed to hospital or prison,
they are officially sent there.
**committal** NOUN
■ (sense 1) do, perform, perpetrate

**commitment** commitments
NOUN 1 ( RE ) Commitment is a
strong belief in an idea or system.
2 something that regularly takes up
some of your time *E.G. business
commitments.*

**committed**
ADJECTIVE A committed person has
strong beliefs *E.G. a committed
feminist.*

**committee** committees
NOUN a group of people who make
decisions on behalf of a larger group.

**commodity** commodities
NOUN; *FORMAL* Commodities are things
that are sold.

**common** commoner
commonest; commons
ADJECTIVE 1 Something that is common
exists in large numbers or happens
often *E.G. a common complaint.* 2 If
something is common to two or
more people, they all have it or use it
*E.G. I realized we had a common
interest.* 3 'Common' is used to
indicate that something is of the

a
b
c
d
e
f
g
h
i
j
k
l
m
n
o
p
q
r
s
t
u
v
w
x
y
z

A
B
C
D
E
F
G
H
I
J
K
L
M
N
O
P
Q
R
S
T
U
V
W
X
Y
Z

ordinary kind and not special. **4** If you describe someone as common, you mean they do not have good taste or good manners. ▶ NOUN **5** an area of grassy land where everyone can go. ▶ PHRASE **6** If two things or people have something **in common**, they both have it.

**commonly** ADVERB
▣ (sense 1) customary, frequent
▣ (sense 4) coarse, vulgar

**commoner commoners**
NOUN someone who is not a member of the nobility.

**commonplace**
ADJECTIVE Something that is commonplace happens often *E.G. Foreign holidays have become commonplace.*

**common sense**
NOUN Your common sense is your natural ability to behave sensibly and make good judgments.

**Commonwealth**
NOUN **1** The Commonwealth is an association of countries around the world that are or used to be ruled by Britain. **2** a country made up of a number of states *E.G. the Commonwealth of Australia.*

**commotion**
NOUN A commotion is a lot of noise and excitement.

**communal**
ADJECTIVE shared by a group of people *E.G. a communal canteen.*

**commune communes**
*Said* "kom-yoon" NOUN a group of people who live together and share everything.

**communicate communicates communicating communicated**
VERB **1** When people communicate

with each other, they exchange information, usually by talking or writing to each other. **2** If you communicate an idea or a feeling to someone, you make them aware of it.
▣ (sense 2) convey, make known

**communication**
**communications**
NOUN **1** (PSHE) Communication is the process by which people or animals exchange information. ▶ PLURAL NOUN **2** Communications are the systems by which people communicate or broadcast information, especially using electricity or radio waves. ▶ NOUN **3** FORMAL a letter or telephone call.

**communicative**
ADJECTIVE Someone who is communicative is willing to talk to people.

**communion**
NOUN **1** Communion is the sharing of thoughts and feelings. **2** In Christianity, Communion is a religious service in which people share bread and wine in remembrance of the death and resurrection of Jesus Christ.

**communism**
NOUN Communism is the doctrine that the state should the means of production and that there should be no private property.
**communist** ADJECTIVE or NOUN

**community communities**
NOUN all the people living in a particular area; also used to refer to particular groups within a society *E.G. the heart of the local community… the Asian community.*

**commute** commutes commuting commuted

VERB People who commute travel a long distance to work every day.
**commuter** NOUN

**compact**

ADJECTIVE taking up very little space
E.G. *a compact microwave.*

**compact disc** compact discs

NOUN a music or video recording in the form of a plastic disc which is played using a laser on a special machine, and gives good quality sound or pictures. The abbreviation for compact disc is CD.

**companion** companions

NOUN someone you travel or spend time with.
**companionship** NOUN

🔲 from Latin *com-* meaning 'together' and *panis* meaning 'bread'. A companion was originally someone you shared a meal with

**company** companies

NOUN **1** a business that sells goods or provides a service E.G. *the record company.* **2** a group of actors, opera singers, or dancers E.G. *the Royal Shakespeare Company.* **3** If you have company, you have a friend or visitor with you E.G. *I enjoyed her company.*

**comparable**

*Said* "**kom-**pra-bl" ADJECTIVE If two things are comparable, they are similar in size or quality E.G. *The skill is comparable to playing the violin.*
**comparably** ADVERB

◼ equal, equivalent, on a par

**comparative** comparatives

ADJECTIVE **1** You add comparative to indicate that something is true only when compared with what is normal E.G. *eight years of comparative calm.*

▶ NOUN **2** In grammar, the comparative is the form of an adjective which indicates that the person or thing described has more of a particular quality than someone or something else. For example, 'quicker', 'better', and 'easier' are all comparatives.
**comparatively** ADVERB

---

### What is a Comparative?

Many adjectives have three different forms. These are known as the **positive**, the **comparative**, and the **superlative**. The comparative and superlative are used when you make comparisons.

The **positive** form of an adjective is given as the entry in the dictionary. It is used when there is no comparison between different objects:

E.G. *Matthew is **tall**.*

The **comparative** form is usually made by adding the ending -er to the positive form of the adjective. It shows that something possesses a quality to a greater extent than the thing it is being compared with:

E.G. *Matthew is **taller** than Anna.*

You can also make comparisons by using the words *more* or *less* with the positive (not the comparative) form of the adjective:

E.G. *Matthew is **more energetic** than Robbie.*

### Irregular Forms

When the comparative and superlative of an adjective are not formed in the regular way, the irregular forms of the adjective are

CONTINUED ON NEXT PAGE →

a
b
c
d
e
f
g
h
i
j
k
l
m
n
o
p
q
r
s
t
u
v
w
x
y
z

A
B
C
D
E
F
G
H
I
J
K
L
M
N
O
P
Q
R
S
T
U
V
W
X
Y
Z

shown in the dictionary after the main entry.

Many adjectives – especially ones that have more than one syllable and do not end in -y – do not have separate spelling forms for the comparative and superlative. For these adjectives comparisons must be made using *more, less, most,* and *least*:

E.G. *beautiful* ➤ *more beautiful*
  ➤ *most beautiful*
*boring* ➤ *less boring*
  ➤ *least boring*

Look also at the grammar box at **superlative**.

**compare** compares comparing compared

VERB 1 (EXAM TERM) When you compare things, you look at them together and see in what ways they are different or similar. 2 If you compare one thing to another, you say it is like the other thing E.G. *His voice is often compared to Michael Stipe's.*

**comparison** comparisons

NOUN (ENGLISH) When you make a comparison, you consider two things together and see in what ways they are different or similar.

**compartment** compartments

NOUN 1 a section of a railway carriage. 2 one of the separate parts of an object E.G. *a special compartment inside your vehicle.*

**compass** compasses

NOUN 1 an instrument with a magnetic needle for finding directions. ➤ PLURAL NOUN 2 Compasses are a hinged instrument for drawing circles.

☑ The proper name for the drawing instrument is *a pair of compasses.*

**compassion**

NOUN Compassion is pity and sympathy for someone who is suffering.
**compassionate** ADJECTIVE

**compatible**

ADJECTIVE If people or things are compatible, they can live or work together successfully.
**compatibility** NOUN

**compatriot** compatriots

NOUN Your compatriots are people from your own country.

**compel** compels compelling compelled

VERB To compel someone to do something is to force them to do it.

**compelling**

ADJECTIVE 1 If a story or event is compelling, it is extremely interesting E.G. *a compelling novel.* 2 A compelling argument or reason makes you believe that something is true or should be done E.G. *compelling new evidence.*

**compensate** compensates compensating compensated

VERB 1 To compensate someone is to give them money to replace something lost or damaged. 2 If one thing compensates for another, it cancels out its bad effects E.G. *The trip more than compensated for the hardship.*

**compensatory** ADJECTIVE
**compensation** NOUN
▤ (sense 1) recompense, refund
▤ (sense 2) make up for

**compere** comperes compering compered

*Said* "kom-pare" NOUN 1 the person

who introduces the guests or performers in a show. ▶ VERB 2 To compere a show is to introduce the guests or performers.

**compete** competes competing competed

VERB 1 When people or firms compete, each tries to prove that they or their products are the best. 2 If you compete in a contest or game, you take part in it.

**competent**

ADJECTIVE Someone who is competent at something can do it satisfactorily E.G. *a very competent engineer*.
**competently** ADVERB `competence` NOUN

**competition** competitions

NOUN 1 When there is competition between people or groups, they are all trying to get something that not everyone can have E.G. *There's a lot of competition for places*. 2 an event in which people take part to find who is best at something. 3 When there is competition between firms, each firm is trying to get people to buy its own goods.

**competitive**

ADJECTIVE 1 A competitive situation is one in which people or firms are competing with each other E.G. *a crowded and competitive market*. 2 A competitive person is eager to be more successful than others. 3 Goods sold at competitive prices are cheaper than other goods of the same kind.
**competitively** ADVERB

**competitor** competitors

NOUN a person or firm that is competing to become the most successful.

**compilation** compilations

NOUN A compilation is a book, record, or programme consisting of several items that were originally produced separately E.G. *this compilation of his solo work*.

**compile** compiles compiling compiled

VERB When someone compiles a book or report, they make it by putting together several items.

**complacent**

ADJECTIVE If someone is complacent, they are unconcerned about a serious situation and do nothing about it.
**complacency** NOUN

**complain** complains complaining complained

VERB 1 If you complain, you say that you are not satisfied with something. 2 If you complain of pain or illness, you say that you have it.
■ (sense 1) find fault, grumble, moan

**complaint** complaints

NOUN If you make a complaint, you complain about something.

**complement** complements complementing complemented

VERB 1 If one thing complements another, the two things go well together E.G. *The tiled floor complements the pine furniture*.
▶ NOUN 2 If one thing is a complement to another, it goes well with it. 3 In grammar, a complement is a word or phrase that gives information about the subject or object of a sentence. For example, in the sentence 'Rover is a dog', 'is a dog' is a complement.
**complementary** ADJECTIVE

a b **c** d e f g h i j k l m n o p q r s t u v w x y z

**complete completes completing completed**

ADJECTIVE **1** to the greatest degree possible E.G. *a complete mess.* **2** If something is complete, none of it is missing E.G. *a complete set of tools.* **3** When a task is complete, it is finished E.G. *The planning stage is now complete.* ▶ VERB **4** If you complete something, you finish it. **5** If you complete a form, you fill it in.
**completely** ADVERB **completion** NOUN
🔲 (sense 1) absolute, thorough, total
🔲 (sense 2) entire, full, whole

**complex complexes**

ADJECTIVE **1** Something that is complex has many different parts E.G. *a very complex problem.* ▶ NOUN **2** A complex is a group of buildings, roads, or other things connected with each other in some way E.G. *a hotel and restaurant complex.* **3** If someone has a complex, they have an emotional problem because of a past experience E.G. *an inferiority complex.*
**complexity** NOUN
🔲 (sense 1) complicated, intricate, involved

**complexion complexions**

NOUN the quality of the skin on your face E.G. *a healthy glowing complexion.*

**complicate complicates complicating complicated**

VERB To complicate something is to make it more difficult to understand or deal with.

**complicated**

ADJECTIVE Something that is complicated has so many parts or aspects that it is difficult to understand or deal with.

**complication complications**

NOUN something that makes a situation more difficult to deal with E.G. *One possible complication was that it was late in the year.*

**compliment compliments complimenting complimented**

NOUN **1** If you pay someone a compliment, you tell them you admire something about them.
▶ VERB **2** If you compliment someone, you pay them a compliment.
🏛 from Spanish *cumplir* meaning 'to do what is fitting'

**complimentary**

ADJECTIVE **1** If you are complimentary about something, you express admiration for it. **2** A complimentary seat, ticket, or publication is given to you free.

**comply complies complying complied**

VERB If you comply with an order or rule, you obey it.
**compliance** NOUN

**component components**

NOUN (D & T) The components of something are the parts it is made of.

**compose composes composing composed**

VERB **1** If something is composed of particular things or people, it is made up of them. **2** To compose a piece of music, letter, or speech means to write it. **3** If you compose yourself, you become calm after being excited or upset.

**composed**

ADJECTIVE calm and in control of your feelings.

**composer** composers
NOUN someone who writes music.

**composition** compositions
NOUN 1 The composition of something is the things it consists of E.G. *the composition of the ozone layer.* 2 (MUSIC) The composition of a poem or piece of music is the writing of it. 3 (MUSIC) a piece of music or writing.

**compost**
NOUN Compost is a mixture of decaying plants and manure added to soil to help plants grow.

**composure**
NOUN Someone's composure is their ability to stay calm E.G. *Jarvis was able to recover his composure.*

**compound** compounds compounding compounded
NOUN 1 an enclosed area of land with buildings used for a particular purpose E.G. *the prison compound.* 2 In chemistry, a compound is a substance consisting of two or more different substances or chemical elements. ▶ VERB 3 To compound something is to put together different parts to make a whole. 4 To compound a problem is to make it worse by adding to it E.G. *Water shortages were compounded by taps left running.*

**comprehend** comprehends comprehending comprehended
VERB; FORMAL To comprehend something is to understand or appreciate it E.G. *He did not fully comprehend what was puzzling me.*
**comprehension** NOUN

**comprehensible**
ADJECTIVE able to be understood.

**comprehensive** comprehensives
ADJECTIVE 1 Something that is comprehensive includes everything necessary or relevant E.G. *a comprehensive guide.* ▶ NOUN 2 a school where children of all abilities are taught together.
**comprehensively** ADVERB

**compress** compresses compressing compressed
VERB To compress something is to squeeze it or shorten it so that it takes up less space E.G. *compressed air.*
**compression** NOUN

**comprise** comprises comprising comprised
VERB; FORMAL What something comprises is what it consists of E.G. *The district then comprised 66 villages.* ☑ You do not need of after comprise. For example, you say *the library comprises 500,000 books.*

**compromise** compromises compromising compromised
NOUN 1 an agreement in which people accept less than they originally wanted E.G. *In the end they reached a compromise.* ▶ VERB 2 When people compromise, they agree to accept less than they originally wanted.
**compromising** ADJECTIVE

**compulsion** compulsions
NOUN a very strong desire to do something.

**compulsive**
ADJECTIVE 1 You use 'compulsive' to describe someone who cannot stop doing something E.G. *a compulsive letter writer.* 2 If you find something such as a book or television programme compulsive, you cannot stop reading or watching it.

a
**c**
d
e
f
g
h
i
j
k
l
m
n
o
p
q
r
s
t
u
v
w
x
y
z

**compulsory**

ADJECTIVE If something is compulsory, you have to do it E.G. *School attendance is compulsory*.

■ mandatory, obligatory

**computer computers**

NOUN (ICT) an electronic machine that can quickly make calculations or store and find information.

**computer-aided design**

NOUN Computer-aided design is the use of computers and computer graphics to help design things.

**computerize computerizes computerizing computerized**; also spelt **computerise**

VERB When a system or process is computerized, the work is done by computers.

**computing**

NOUN Computing is the use of computers and the writing of programs for them.

**comrade comrades**

NOUN A soldier's comrades are his fellow soldiers, especially in battle.

**comradeship** NOUN

**con cons conning conned** INFORMAL

VERB 1 If someone cons you, they trick you into doing or believing something. ▶ NOUN 2 a trick in which someone deceives you into doing or believing something.

**con-**

PREFIX Con- is another form of com-.

**concave**

ADJECTIVE A concave surface curves inwards, rather than being level or bulging outwards.

**conceal conceals concealing concealed**

VERB To conceal something is to hide it E.G. *He had concealed his gun*.

**concealment** NOUN

**concede concedes conceding conceded**

*Said* "kon-**seed**" VERB 1 If you concede something, you admit that it is true E.G. *I conceded that he was entitled to his views*. 2 When someone concedes defeat, they accept that they have lost something such as a contest or an election.

**conceit**

NOUN Conceit is someone's excessive pride in their appearance or abilities.

■ pride, self-importance

**conceited**

ADJECTIVE Someone who is conceited is too proud of their appearance or abilities.

■ bigheaded, full of oneself, self-important

**conceivable**

ADJECTIVE If something is conceivable, you can believe that it could exist or be true E.G. *It's conceivable that you also met her*.

**conceivably** ADVERB

**conceive conceives conceiving conceived**

VERB 1 If you can conceive of something, you can imagine it or believe it E.G. *Could you conceive of doing such a thing yourself?* 2 If you conceive something such as a plan, you think of it and work out how it could be done. 3 When a woman conceives, she becomes pregnant.

**concentrate concentrates concentrating concentrated**

VERB 1 If you concentrate on something, you give it all your attention. 2 When something is concentrated in one place, it is all there rather than in several places

*E.G. They are mostly concentrated in the urban areas.*
**concentration** NOUN

**concentrated**
ADJECTIVE A concentrated liquid has been made stronger by having water removed from it *E.G. concentrated apple juice.*

**concentration camp**
**concentration camps**
NOUN a prison camp, especially one set up by the Nazis during World War Two.

**concept** concepts
NOUN an abstract or general idea *E.G. the concept of tolerance.*
**conceptual** ADJECTIVE
**conceptually** ADVERB

**conception** conceptions
NOUN **1** Your conception of something is the idea you have of it.
**2** Conception is the process by which a woman becomes pregnant.

**concern** concerns concerning concerned
NOUN **1** Concern is a feeling of worry about something or someone *E.G. public concern about violence.* **2** If something is your concern, it is your responsibility. **3** a business *E.G. a large manufacturing concern.* ▶ VERB **4** If something concerns you or if you are concerned about it, it worries you. **5** You say that something concerns you if it affects or involves you *E.G. It concerns you and me.*
▶ PHRASE **6** If something is **of concern** to you, it is important to you.
**concerned** ADJECTIVE
■ (sense 5) be relevant to, involve, regard

**concerning**
PREPOSITION You use 'concerning' to

show what something is about *E.G. documents concerning arm sales to Iraq.*

**concert** concerts
NOUN a public performance by musicians.

**concerted**
ADJECTIVE A concerted action is done by several people together *E.G. concerted action to cut interest rates.*

**concerto** concertos or concerti
*Said "kon-cher-toe"* NOUN a piece of music for a solo instrument and an orchestra.

**concession** concessions
NOUN If you make a concession, you agree to let someone have or do something *E.G. Her one concession was to let me come into the building.*

**conch** conches
NOUN a shellfish with a large, brightly coloured shell; also the shell itself.

**concise**
ADJECTIVE giving all the necessary information using as few words as necessary *E.G. a concise guide.*
■ brief, short, succinct

**conclude** concludes concluding concluded
VERB **1** If you conclude something, you decide that it is so because of the other things that you know *E.G. An inquiry concluded that this was untrue.* **2** When you conclude something, you finish it *E.G. At that point I intend to conclude the interview.*
**concluding** ADJECTIVE **conclusion** NOUN

**conclusive**
ADJECTIVE Facts that are conclusive show that something is certainly true.
**conclusively** ADVERB

A
B
C
D
E
F
G
H
I
J
K
L
M
N
O
P
Q
R
S
T
U
V
W
X
Y
Z

**concoct** concocts concocting
concocted
VERB **1** If you concoct an excuse or
explanation, you invent one. **2** If you
concoct something, you make it by
mixing several things together.
**concoction** NOUN

**concourse** concourses
NOUN a wide hall in a building where
people walk about or gather
together.

**concrete**
NOUN **1** Concrete is a solid building
material made by mixing cement,
sand, and water. ▶ ADJECTIVE **2** definite,
rather than general or vague E.G. *I
don't really have any concrete plans.*
**3** real and physical, rather than
abstract E.G. *concrete evidence.*

**concubine** concubines
*Said "kong-kyoo-bine"* NOUN; *OLD-
FASHIONED* A man's concubine is his
mistress.

**concur** cóncurs concurring
concurred
VERB; *FORMAL* To concur is to agree E.G.
*She concurred with me.*

**concurrent**
ADJECTIVE If things are concurrent, they
happen at the same time.
**concurrently** ADVERB

**concussed**
ADJECTIVE confused or unconscious
because of a blow to the head.
**concussion** NOUN

**condemn** condemns condemning
condemned
VERB **1** If you condemn something,
you say it is bad and unacceptable
E.G. *Teachers condemned the new
plans.* **2** If someone is condemned to
a punishment, they are given it E.G.
*She was condemned to death.* **3** If

are condemned to something
unpleasant, you must suffer it E.G.
*Many women are condemned to
poverty.* **4** When a building is
condemned, it is going to be pulled
down because it is unsafe.
**condemnation** NOUN
▣ (sense 1) censure, criticize,
disapprove
▣ (sense 2) sentence
▣ (sense 3) doom

**condensation**
NOUN (SCIENCE) Condensation is a
coating of tiny drops formed on a
surface by steam or vapour.

**condense** condenses
condensing condensed
VERB **1** If you condense a piece of
writing or a speech, you shorten it.
**2** When a gas or vapour condenses, it
changes into a liquid.

**condescending**
ADJECTIVE If you are condescending,
you behave in a way that shows you
think you are superior to other
people.
▣ patronizing, superior

**condition** conditions
conditioning conditioned
NOUN **1** the state someone or
something is in. ▶ PLURAL NOUN **2** The
conditions in which something is
done are the location and other
factors likely to affect it E.G. *The very
difficult conditions continued to affect
our performance.* **3** a requirement
that must be met for something else
to be possible E.G. *He had been
banned from drinking alcohol as a
condition of bail.* **4** You can refer to an
illness or other medical problem as a
condition E.G. *a heart condition.*
▶ PHRASE **5** If you are **out of
condition**, you are unfit. ▶ VERB **6** If

someone is conditioned to behave or think in a certain way, they do it as a result of their upbringing or training.

◼ (sense 3) prerequisite, requirement, stipulation

**conditional**

ADJECTIVE If one thing is conditional on another, it can only happen if the other thing happens E.G. *You feel his love is conditional on you pleasing him.*

**condolence** condolences

NOUN Condolence is sympathy expressed for a bereaved person.

**condom** condoms

NOUN a rubber sheath worn by a man on his penis or by a woman inside her vagina as a contraceptive.

**condominium** condominiums

NOUN In Canadian, Australian, and New Zealand English, an apartment block in which each apartment is owned by the person who lives in it.

**condone** condones condoning condoned

VERB If you condone someone's bad behaviour, you accept it and do not try to stop it E.G. *We cannot condone violence.*

**conducive**

*Said* "kon-**joo**-siv" ADJECTIVE If something is conducive to something else, it makes it likely to happen E.G. *a situation that is conducive to relaxation.*

**conduct** conducts conducting conducted

VERB 1 To conduct an activity or task is to carry it out E.G. *He seemed to be conducting a conversation.* 2 FORMAL The way you conduct yourself is the way you behave. 3 When someone

conducts an orchestra or choir, they stand in front of it and direct it. 4 If something conducts heat or electricity, heat or electricity can pass through it. ▶ NOUN 5 If you take part in the conduct of an activity or task, you help to carry it out. 6 Your conduct is your behaviour.

**conductor** conductors

NOUN 1 ( MUSIC ) someone who conducts an orchestra or choir. 2 someone who moves round a bus or train selling tickets. 3 a substance that conducts heat or electricity.

**cone** cones

NOUN 1 a regular three-dimensional shape with a circular base and a point at the top. 2 A fir cone or pine cone is the fruit of a fir or pine tree.

**confectionery**

NOUN Confectionery is sweets.

**confederation** confederations

NOUN an organization formed for business or political purposes.

**confer** confers conferring conferred

VERB When people confer, they discuss something in order to make a decision.

**conference** conferences

NOUN a meeting at which formal discussions take place.

**confess** confesses confessing confessed

VERB If you confess to something, you admit it E.G. *Your son has confessed to his crimes.*

◼ admit, own up

**confession** confessions

NOUN 1 If you make a confession, you admit you have done something wrong. 2 Confession is the act of confessing something, especially a

**A**
**B**
**C**
**D**
**E**
**F**
**G**
**H**
**I**
**J**
**K**
**L**
**M**
**N**
**O**
**P**
**Q**
**R**
**S**
**T**
**U**
**V**
**W**
**X**
**Y**
**Z**

religious act in which people confess their sins to a priest.

■ (sense 1) acknowledgment, admission

**confessional** confessionals

NOUN a small room in some churches where people confess their sins to a priest.

**confetti**

NOUN Confetti is small pieces of coloured paper thrown over the bride and groom at a wedding.

📖 from Italian *confetto* meaning 'a sweet'

**confidant** confidants

*Said* "**kon-fid-dant**" NOUN; *FORMAL* a person you discuss your private problems with

☑ When the person you discuss your private problems with is a girl or a woman, the word is spelt *confidante*.

**confide** confides confiding confided

VERB If you confide in or to someone, you tell them a secret *E.G. Marian confided in me that she was very worried.*

**confidence** confidences

NOUN 1 If you have confidence in someone, you feel you can trust them. 2 Someone who has confidence is sure of their own abilities or qualities. 3 a secret you tell someone.

**confident**

ADJECTIVE 1 If you are confident about something, you are sure it will happen the way you want it to. 2 People who are confident are sure of their own abilities or qualities.

**confidently** ADVERB

■ (sense 1) certain, positive, sure
■ (sense 2) assured, self-assured

**confidential**

ADJECTIVE Confidential information is meant to be kept secret.

**confidentially** ADVERB
**confidentiality** NOUN

**confine** confines confining confined

VERB 1 If something is confined to one place, person, or thing, it exists only in that place or affects only that person or thing. 2 If you confine yourself to doing or saying something, it is the only thing you do or say *E.G. They confined themselves to discussing the weather.* 3 If you are confined to a place, you cannot leave it *E.G. She was confined to bed for two days.* ► PLURAL NOUN 4 The confines of a place are its boundaries *E.G. outside the confines of the prison.*

**confinement** NOUN

**confined**

ADJECTIVE A confined space is small and enclosed by walls.

**confirm** confirms confirming confirmed

VERB 1 To confirm something is to say or show that it is true *E.G. Police confirmed that they had received a call.* 2 If you confirm an arrangement or appointment, you say it is definite. 3 When someone is confirmed, they are formally accepted as a member of a Christian church.

**confirmation** NOUN

■ (sense 1) prove, verify

**confirmed**

ADJECTIVE You use 'confirmed' to describe someone who has a belief or way of life that is unlikely to change *E.G. a confirmed bachelor.*

**confiscate** confiscates confiscating confiscated

VERB To confiscate something is to take it away from someone as a punishment.

**conflict** conflicts conflicting conflicted

NOUN 1 Conflict is disagreement and argument E.G. *conflict between workers and management.* 2 (HISTORY) a war or battle. 3 When there is a conflict of ideas or interests, people have different ideas or interests which cannot all be satisfied. ▶ VERB 4 When ideas or interests conflict, they are different and cannot all be satisfied.

■ (sense 1) disagreement, dissension

■ (sense 2) battle, clash

■ (sense 4) be incompatible, clash, disagree

**conform** conforms conforming conformed

VERB 1 If you conform, you behave the way people expect you to. 2 If something conforms to a law or to someone's wishes, it is what is required or wanted.

**conformist** NOUN or ADJECTIVE

**confront** confronts confronting confronted

VERB 1 If you are confronted with a problem or task, you have to deal with it. 2 If you confront someone, you meet them face to face like an enemy. 3 If you confront someone with evidence or a fact, you present it to them in order to accuse them of something.

**confrontation** confrontations

NOUN a serious dispute or fight E.G. *a confrontation between police and fans.*

**confuse** confuses confusing confused

VERB 1 If you confuse two things, you mix them up and think one of them is the other E.G. *You are confusing facts with opinion.* 2 To confuse someone means to make them uncertain about what is happening or what to do. 3 To confuse a situation means to make it more complicated.

**confused** ADJECTIVE **confusing** ADJECTIVE **confusion** NOUN

■ (sense 2) baffle, bewilder

**congeal** congeals congealing congealed

*Said* "kon-**jeel**" VERB When a liquid congeals, it becomes very thick and sticky.

**congenial**

*Said* "kon-**jeen**-yal" ADJECTIVE If something is congenial, it is pleasant and suits you E.G. *We wanted to talk in congenial surroundings.*

**congenital**

ADJECTIVE; MEDICAL If someone has a congenital disease or handicap, they have had it from birth but did not inherit it.

**congested**

ADJECTIVE 1 When a road is congested, it is so full of traffic that normal movement is impossible. 2 If your nose is congested, it is blocked and you cannot breathe properly.

**congestion** NOUN

**conglomerate** conglomerates

NOUN a large business organization consisting of several companies.

**congratulate** congratulates congratulating congratulated

VERB If you congratulate someone, you express pleasure at something good that has happened to them, or praise them for something they have achieved.

a b c d e f g h i j k l m n o p q r s t u v w x y z

A
B
C
D
E
F
G
H
I
J
K
L
M
N
O
P
Q
R
S
T
U
V
W
X
Y
Z

**congratulation** NOUN
**congratulatory** ADJECTIVE
**congregate** congregates
congregating congregated
VERB When people congregate,
they gather together somewhere.
**congregation** congregations
NOUN the congregation are the
people attending a service in a
church.
**congress** congresses
NOUN a large meeting held to discuss
ideas or policies E.G. *a medical
congress.*
**conical**
ADJECTIVE shaped like a cone.
**conifer** conifers
NOUN any type of evergreen tree that
produces cones.
**coniferous** ADJECTIVE
**conjecture**
NOUN Conjecture is guessing about
something E.G. *There was no evidence,
only conjecture.*
**conjugate** conjugates
conjugating conjugated
*Said* "kon-joo-gate" VERB When you
conjugate a verb, you list the
different forms of it you use with the
pronouns 'I' 'you' (singular) 'he' 'she'
'it' 'you' (plural) and 'they'.
**conjunction** conjunctions
NOUN 1 (ENGLISH) In grammar, a
conjunction is a word that links two
other words or two clauses, for
example 'and', 'but', 'while', and 'that'.
▶ PHRASE 2 If two or more things are
done **in conjunction**, they are done
together.
→ SEE BOX OPPOSITE.
**conjurer** conjurers
NOUN someone who entertains
people by doing magic tricks.

---

### What is a Conjunction?

A conjunction is a word that joins
two words or two parts of a
sentence together. Conjunctions
are sometimes called "joining
words".
**Co-ordinating conjunctions** join
items of equal importance:
  E.G. *I ordered fish **and** chips.*
**Contrasting conjunctions** are a
type of co-ordinating conjunction
which are used to join opposites or
contrasting items:
  E.G. *He was not walking **but**
  running.*
**Correlative conjunctions** are
pairs of conjunctions, such as *either
… or*, or *both … and*, each of which
introduces a separate item in the
sentence:
  E.G. *She speaks **both** French **and**
  German.
  You can drink **either** tea **or**
  coffee.*
**Subordinating conjunctions** join
additional items to the main part
of the sentence:
  E.G. *He was happy **because** he had
  finished his work.
  I will come **if** I have time.*

**conker** conkers
NOUN Conkers are hard brown nuts
from a horse chestnut tree.
**connect** connects connecting
connected
VERB 1 (ICT) To connect two things is
to join them together E.G. *a modem
connecting your PC to the Internet.* 2 If
you connect something with
something else, you think of them as

being linked *E.G. High blood pressure is closely connected to heart disease.*

**connection** connections; also spelt **connexion**

NOUN **1** a link or relationship between things. **2** the point where two wires or pipes are joined together *E.G. a loose connection.* **3** ⟨ ICT ⟩ a link made between two telephones or computers via telephone lines or cables *E.G. a bad connection.* ▶ PLURAL NOUN **4** Someone's connections are the people they know *E.G. He had powerful connections in the army.*

**connective** connectives

NOUN a word or short phrase that connects clauses, phrases or words.

**connoisseur** connoisseurs

*Said* "kon-nis-**sir**" NOUN someone who knows a lot about the arts, or about food or drink *E.G. a great connoisseur of champagne.*

🏛 from Old French *connoistre* meaning 'to know'

**connotation** connotations

NOUN The connotations of a word or name are what it makes you think of *E.G. a grey man for whom grey has no connotation of dullness.*

**conquer** conquers conquering conquered

VERB **1** To conquer people is to take control of their country by force. **2** If you conquer something difficult or dangerous, you succeed in controlling it *E.G. Conquer your fear!*
**conqueror** NOUN

**conquest** conquests

NOUN **1** Conquest is the conquering of a country or group of people. **2** Conquests are lands captured by conquest.

**conscience** consciences

*Said* "**con**-shinz" NOUN the part of your mind that tells you what is right and wrong.

☑ Do not confuse the spellings or pronunciations of *conscience* and *conscious*.

**conscientious**

*Said* "kon-shee-**en**-shus" ADJECTIVE Someone who is conscientious is very careful to do their work properly.

**conscientiously** ADVERB

▤ careful, meticulous, thorough

**conscious**

ADJECTIVE

*Said* "**con**-shus" **1** If you are conscious of something, you are aware of it *E.G. She was not conscious of the time.* **2** A conscious action or effort is done deliberately *E.G. I made a conscious decision not to hide.* **3** Someone who is conscious is awake, rather than asleep or unconscious *E.G. Still conscious, she was taken to hospital.*

**consciously** ADVERB

**consciousness** NOUN

☑ Do not confuse the spellings or pronunciations of *conscious* and *conscience*.

**consecrated**

ADJECTIVE A consecrated building or place is one that has been officially declared to be holy.

**consecutive**

ADJECTIVE Consecutive events or periods of time happen one after the other *E.G. eight consecutive games.*

**consensus**

NOUN general agreement among a group of people *E.G. The consensus was that it could be done.*

☑ There are three s's in *consensus*,

a
b
c
d
e
f
g
h
i
j
k
l
m
n
o
p
q
r
s
t
u
v
w
x
y
z

do not confuse the spelling with *census*. You should not say *consensus of opinion*, as *consensus* already has *of opinion* in its meaning.

**consent** consents consenting consented

NOUN **1** permission to do something E.G. *Thomas reluctantly gave his consent to my writing this book.* **2** agreement between two or more people E.G. *By common consent it was the best game of these championships.* ▶ VERB **3** If you consent to something, you agree to it or allow it.

**consequence** consequences

NOUN **1** The consequences of something are its results or effects E.G. *the dire consequences of major war.* **2** FORMAL If something is of consequence, it is important.

**consequent**

ADJECTIVE Consequent describes something as being the result of something else E.G. *an earthquake in 1980 and its consequent damage.*

**consequently** ADVERB

**conservation**

NOUN the preservation of the environment.

**conservationist** NOUN or ADJECTIVE

**conservative** conservatives

NOUN **1** In Britain, a member or supporter of the Conservative Party, a political party that believes that the government should interfere as little as possible in the running of the economy. ▶ ADJECTIVE **2** In Britain, Conservative views and policies are those of the Conservative Party. **3** Someone who is conservative is not willing to accept changes or new ideas. **4** A conservative estimate or

guess is a cautious or moderate one.

**conservatively** ADVERB

**conservatism** NOUN

**conservatory** conservatories

NOUN a room with glass walls and a glass roof in which plants are kept.

**conserve** conserves conserving conserved

VERB If you conserve a supply of something, you make it last E.G. *the only way to conserve energy.*

**consider** considers considering considered

VERB **1** If you consider something to be the case, you think or judge it to be so E.G. *The manager does not consider him an ideal team member.* **2** To consider something is to think about it carefully E.G. *If an offer were made, we would consider it.* **3** (EXAM TERM) To consider is to think about something carefully and to include your own opinions about it in your answer. **4** If you consider someone's needs or feelings, you take account of them.

▪ (sense 2) contemplate, think about

**considerable**

ADJECTIVE A considerable amount of something is a lot of it E.G. *a considerable sum of money.*

**considerably** ADVERB

**considerate**

ADJECTIVE Someone who is considerate pays attention to other people's needs and feelings.

**consideration** considerations

NOUN **1** careful thought about something E.G. *a decision demanding careful consideration.* **2** If you show consideration for someone, you take account of their needs and feelings.

**3** something that has to be taken into account E.G. *Money was also a consideration.*

■ (sense 1) deliberation, thought

**considered**
ADJECTIVE A considered opinion or judgment is arrived at by careful thought.

**considering**
CONJUNCTION or PREPOSITION You say considering to indicate that you are taking something into account E.G. *I know that must sound callous, considering that I was married to the man for seventeen years.*

**consign** consigns consigning consigned
VERB; FORMAL To consign something to a particular place is to send or put it there.

**consignment** consignments
NOUN a load of goods being delivered somewhere.

**consist** consists consisting consisted
VERB What something consists of is its different parts or members E.G. *The brain consists of millions of nerve cells.*

**consistency** consistencies
NOUN **1** the quality of being consistent. **2** The consistency of a substance is how thick or smooth it is. E.G. *the consistency of single cream.*

**consistent**
ADJECTIVE **1** If you are consistent, you keep doing something the same way E.G. *one of our most consistent performers.* **2** If something such as a statement or argument is consistent, there are no contradictions in it.

**consistently** ADVERB

**console** consoles consoling consoled

VERB *Said "con-sole"* **1** To console someone who is unhappy is to make them more cheerful. ▶ NOUN *Said "con-sole"* **2** a panel with switches or knobs for operating a machine.

**consolation** NOUN

**consolidate** consolidates consolidating consolidated
VERB To consolidate something you have gained or achieved is to make it more secure.

**consolidation** NOUN

**consonant** consonants
NOUN (ENGLISH) a sound such as 'p' or 'm' which you make by stopping the air flowing freely through your mouth.

▥ from Latin *consonare* meaning 'to sound at the same time'

**consort** consorts consorting consorted
VERB *Said "con-sort"* **1** FORMAL If you consort with someone, you spend a lot of time with them. ▶ NOUN *Said "con-sort"* **2** the wife or husband of the king or queen.

**consortium** consortia or consortiums
NOUN a group of businesses working together.

**conspicuous**
ADJECTIVE If something is conspicuous, people can see or notice it very easily.

**conspicuously** ADVERB

**conspiracy** conspiracies
NOUN When there is a conspiracy, a group of people plan something illegal, often for a political purpose.

**conspirator** conspirators
NOUN someone involved in a conspiracy.

a
b
c
d
e
f
g
h
i
j
k
l
m
n
o
p
q
r
s
t
u
v
w
x
y
z

A
B
C
D
E
F
G
H
I
J
K
L
M
N
O
P
Q
R
S
T
U
V
W
X
Y
Z

**conspire** conspires conspiring conspired

VERB **1** When people conspire, they plan together to do something illegal, often for a political purpose. **2** LITERARY When events conspire towards a particular result, they seem to work together to cause it E.G. *Circumstances conspired to doom the business.*

**constable** constables

NOUN a police officer of the lowest rank.

🏛 from Latin *comes stabuli* meaning 'officer of the stable'

**constabulary** constabularies

NOUN a police force.

**constant**

ADJECTIVE **1** Something that is constant happens all the time or is always there E.G. *a city under constant attack.* **2** If an amount or level is constant, it stays the same. **3** People who are constant stay loyal to a person or idea.

**constantly** ADVERB **constancy** NOUN

∎ (sense 2) fixed, steady, unchanging

**constellation** constellations

NOUN a group of stars.

**consternation**

NOUN anxiety or dismay E.G. *There was some consternation when it began raining.*

**constipated**

ADJECTIVE Someone who is constipated is unable to pass solid waste from their bowels.

**constipation** NOUN

**constituency** constituencies

NOUN a town or area represented by an MP.

**constituent** constituents

NOUN **1** An MP's constituents are the voters who live in his or her constituency. **2** The constituents of something are its parts E.G. *the major constituents of bone.*

**constitute** constitutes constituting constituted

VERB If a group of things constitute something, they are what it consists of E.G. *Jewellery constitutes 80 per cent of the stock.*

**constitution** constitutions

NOUN **1** (HISTORY) The constitution of a country is the system of laws which formally states people's rights and duties. **2** Your constitution is your health E.G. *a very strong constitution.*

**constitutional** ADJECTIVE
**constitutionally** ADVERB

**constrained**

ADJECTIVE If a person feels constrained to do something, they feel that they should do that.

**constraint** constraints

NOUN something that limits someone's freedom of action E.G. *constraints on trade union power.*

**constrict** constricts constricting constricted

VERB To constrict something is to squeeze it tightly.

**constriction** NOUN

**construct** constructs constructing constructed

VERB To construct something is to build or make it.

**construction** constructions

NOUN **1** The construction of something is the building or making of it E.G. *the construction of the harbour.* **2** something built or made E.G. *a shoddy modern* *construction built of concrete.*

**constructive**

ADJECTIVE Constructive criticisms and comments are helpful..

**constructively** ADVERB

**consul** consuls

NOUN an official who lives in a foreign city and who looks after people there who are citizens of his or her own country.

**consular** ADJECTIVE

**consulate** consulates

NOUN the place where a consul works.

**consult** consults consulting consulted

VERB 1 If you consult someone, you ask for their opinion or advice. 2 When people consult each other, they exchange ideas and opinions. 3 If you consult a book or map, you look at it for information.

**consultancy** consultancies

NOUN an organization whose members give expert advice on a subject.

**consultant** consultants

NOUN 1 an experienced doctor who specializes in one type of medicine. 2 someone who gives expert advice E.G. *a management consultant.*

**consultation** consultations

NOUN 1 a meeting held to discuss something. 2 Consultation is discussion or the seeking of advice E.G. *There has to be much better consultation with the public.*

**consultative** ADJECTIVE

**consume** consumes consuming consumed

VERB 1 FORMAL If you consume something, you eat or drink it. 2 To consume fuel or energy is to use it up.

**consumer** consumers

NOUN someone who buys things or uses services E.G. *two new magazines for teenage consumers.*

**consumerism**

NOUN Consumerism is the belief that a country will have a strong economy if its people buy a lot of goods and spend a lot of money.

**consuming**

ADJECTIVE A consuming passion or interest is more important to you than anything else.

**consummate** consummates consummating consummated

VERB *Said* "**kons**-yum-mate" 1 To consummate something is to make it complete. 2 FORMAL If two people consummate a marriage or relationship, they make it complete by having sex. ▶ ADJECTIVE 3 *Said* "kon-**sum**-mit" You use 'consummate' to describe someone who is very good at something E.G. *a consummate politician.*

**consummation** NOUN

**consumption**

NOUN The consumption of fuel or food is the using of it, or the amount used.

**contact** contacts contacting contacted

NOUN 1 If you are in contact with someone, you regularly talk to them or write to them. 2 When things are in contact, they are touching each other. 3 someone you know in a place or organization from whom you can get help or information. ▶ VERB 4 If you contact someone, you telephone them or write to them.

▪ (sense 4) get *or* be in touch with, reach

a
**c**
d
e
f
g
h
i
j
k
l
m
n
o
p
q
r
s
t
u
v
w
x
y
z

contemplated his drawings.
**contemplation** NOUN
**contemplative** ADJECTIVE
**contemporary** contemporaries
ADJECTIVE **1** produced or happening
now E.G. contemporary literature.
**2** produced or happening at the time
you are talking about E.G.
contemporary descriptions of Lizzie
Borden. ▶ NOUN **3** Someone's
contemporaries are other people
living or active at the same time as
them E.G. Shakespeare and his
contemporaries.
**contempt**
NOUN If you treat someone or
something with contempt, you show
no respect for them at all.
**contemptible**
ADJECTIVE not worthy of any respect
E.G. this contemptible piece of
nonsense.
**contemptuous**
ADJECTIVE showing contempt.
**contemptuously** ADVERB
**contend** contends contending
contended
VERB **1** To contend with a difficulty is
to deal with it E.G. They had to
contend with injuries. **2** FORMAL If you
contend that something is true, you
say firmly that it is true. **3** When
people contend for something, they
compete for it.
**contender** NOUN
**content** contents contenting
contented
PLURAL NOUN Said "con-tents" **1** The
contents of something are the things
inside it. ▶ NOUN Said "con-tent"
**2** (LIBRARY) The content of an article
or speech is what is expressed in it.
**3** Content is the proportion of

**contact lens** contact lenses
NOUN Contact lenses are small plastic
lenses that you put in your eyes
instead of wearing glasses, to help
you see better.
**contagious**
ADJECTIVE A contagious disease can be
caught by touching people or things
infected with it.
**contain** contains containing
contained
VERB **1** If a substance contains
something, that thing is a part of it
E.G. Alcohol contains sugar. **2** The
things a box or room contains are
the things inside it. **3** FORMAL To
contain something also means to
stop it increasing or spreading E.G.
efforts to contain the disease.
**containment** NOUN
**container** containers
NOUN **1** something such as a box or a
bottle that you keep things in. **2** a
large sealed metal box for
transporting things.
■ (sense 1) holder, receptacle
**contaminate** contaminates
contaminating contaminated
VERB If something is contaminated by
dirt, chemicals, or radiation, it is
made impure and harmful E.G. foods
contaminated with lead.
**contamination** NOUN
**contemplate** contemplates
contemplating contemplated
VERB **1** To contemplate is to think
carefully about something for a long
time. **2** If you contemplate doing
something, you consider doing it E.G.
I never contemplated
marrying Charles. **3** If you
contemplate something, you look
at it for a long time E.G. He

something that a substance contains
E.G. *White bread is inferior in vitamin
content.* ▶ ADJECTIVE *Said "con-***tent***"*
**4** happy and satisfied with your life.
**5** willing to do or have something E.G.
*He would be content to telephone her.*
▶ VERB *Said "con-***tent***"* **6** If you content
yourself with doing something, you
do it and do not try to do anything
else E.G. *He contented himself with an
early morning lecture.*

**contented**
ADJECTIVE happy and satisfied with
your life.
**contentedly** ADVERB    **contentment**
NOUN

**contention contentions**
NOUN; *FORMAL* Someone's contention is
the idea or opinion they are
expressing E.G. *It is our contention that
the 1980s mark a turning point in
planning.*

**contest contests contesting
contested**
NOUN *Said "con-***test***"* **1** a competition
or game E.G. *a boxing contest.* **2** a
struggle for power E.G. *a presidential
contest.* ▶ VERB *Said "con-***test***"* **3** If you
contest a statement or decision, you
object to it formally.
■ (sense 1) competition, game,
match

**contestant contestants**
NOUN someone taking part in a
competition.
■ competitor, player

**context contexts**
NOUN **1** The context of something
consists of matters related to it
which help to explain it E.G. *English
history is treated in a European
context.* **2** The context of a word or
sentence consists of the words or

sentences before and after it.
**continent continents**
NOUN **1** a very large area of land, such
as Africa or Asia. **2** The Continent is
the mainland of Europe.
**continental** ADJECTIVE

**contingency contingencies**
*Said "kon-***tin***-jen-see"* NOUN
something that might happen in the
future E.G. *I need to examine all
possible contingencies.*

**contingent contingents**
NOUN **1** a group of people
representing a country or
organization E.G. *a strong South
African contingent.* **2** a group of
police or soldiers.

**continual**
ADJECTIVE **1** happening all the time
without stopping E.G. *continual
headaches.* **2** happening again and
again E.G. *the continual snide remarks.*
**continually** ADVERB
■ constant, incessant

**continuation continuations**
NOUN **1** The continuation of
something is the continuing of it E.G.
*the continuation of the human race.*
**2** Something that is a continuation of
an event follows it and seems like a
part of it E.G. *a meeting which was a
continuation of a conference.*

**continue continues continuing
continued**
VERB **1** If you continue to do
something, you keep doing it. **2** If
something continues, it does not
stop. **3** You also say something
continues when it starts again after
stopping E.G. *She continued after a
pause.*
■ (senses 2, 3 & 4) carry on, go on,
proceed

a
b
**c**
d
e
f
g
h
i
j
k
l
m
n
o
p
q
r
s
t
u
v
w
x
y
z

**continuous**
ADJECTIVE **1** Continuous means happening or existing without stopping. **2** A continuous line or surface has no gaps or holes in it.
**continuously** ADVERB **continuity** NOUN

**contorted**
ADJECTIVE twisted into an unnatural, unattractive shape.

**contour** contours
NOUN **1** The contours of something are its general shape. **2** (GEOGRAPHY) On a map, a contour is a line joining points of equal height.

**contra-**
PREFIX Contra- means against or opposite to E.G. contraflow… contraindication.

**contraception**
NOUN Contraception is methods of preventing pregnancy.

**contraceptive** contraceptives
NOUN a device or pill for preventing pregnancy.

**contract** contracts contracting contracted
NOUN Said "con-trakt" **1** a written legal agreement about the sale of something or work done for money. ► VERB Said "con-**trakt**" **2** When something contracts, it gets smaller or shorter. **3** FORMAL If you contract an illness, you get it E.G. Her husband contracted a virus.
**contractual** ADJECTIVE **contraction** NOUN

**contractor** contractors
NOUN a person or company who does work for other people or companies E.G. a building contractor.

**contradict** contradicts contradicting contradicted

VERB (HISTORY) If you contradict someone, you say that what they have just said is not true, and that something else is.
**contradiction** NOUN
**contradictory** ADJECTIVE

**contraption** contraptions
NOUN a strange-looking machine or piece of equipment.

**contrary**
ADJECTIVE **1** Contrary ideas or opinions are opposed to each other and cannot be held by the same person. ► PHRASE **2** You say **on the contrary** when you are contradicting what someone has just said.

**contrast** contrasts contrasting contrasted
NOUN Said "**kon**-trast" **1** a great difference between things E.G. the real contrast between the two poems. **2** If one thing is a contrast to another, it is very different from it E.G. I couldn't imagine a greater contrast to Maxwell. ► VERB Said "kon-**trast**" **3** (EXAM TERM) If you contrast things, you describe or emphasize the differences between them. **4** If one thing contrasts with another, it is very different from it E.G. The interview contrasted completely with the one she gave after Tokyo.

**contravene** contravenes contravening contravened
VERB; FORMAL If you contravene a law or rule, you do something that it forbids.

**contribute** contributes contributing contributed
VERB **1** If you contribute to something, you do things to help it succeed E.G. The elderly have much to contribute to the community. **2** If you contribute

money, you give it to help to pay for something. **3** If something contributes to an event or situation, it is one of its causes *E.G. The dry summer has contributed to perfect conditions.*

**contribution** NOUN **contributor** NOUN **contributory** ADJECTIVE
■ (sense 2) donate, give

**contrive** contrives contriving contrived
VERB; *FORMAL* If you contrive to do something difficult, you succeed in doing it *E.G. Anthony contrived to escape with a few companions.*

**contrived**
ADJECTIVE Something that is contrived is unnatural *E.G. a contrived compliment.*

**control** controls controlling controlled
NOUN **1** Control of a country or organization is the power to make the important decisions about how it is run. **2** (PSHE) Your control over something is your ability to make it work the way you want it to. **3** The controls on a machine are knobs or other devices used to work it. ▶ VERB **4** To control a country or organization means to have the power to make decisions about how it is run. **5** To control something such as a machine or system means to make it work the way you want it to. **6** (PSHE) If you control yourself, you make yourself behave calmly when you are angry or upset. ▶ PHRASE **7** If something is **out of control**, nobody has any power over it.

**controller** NOUN
■ (sense 6) hold back, restrain

**controversial**
ADJECTIVE Something that is

controversial causes a lot of discussion and argument, because many people disapprove of it.

**controversy** controversies
*Said* "kon-triv-ver-see" or "kon-**trov**-ver-see" NOUN discussion and argument because many people disapprove of something.
🏛 from Latin *controversus* meaning 'turned in an opposite direction'
☑ Notice that there are two ways to say *controversy*. The first way is older, and the second is becoming more common.

**conundrum** conundrums
NOUN; *FORMAL* a puzzling problem.

**convalesce** convalesces convalescing convalesced
VERB When people convalesce, they rest and regain their health after an illness or operation.

**convection**
NOUN Convection is the process by which heat travels through gases and liquids.

**convene** convenes convening convened
VERB **1** *FORMAL* To convene a meeting is to arrange for it to take place. **2** When people convene, they come together for a meeting.

**convenience** conveniences
NOUN **1** The convenience of something is the fact that it is easy to use or that it makes something easy to do. **2** something useful.

**convenient**
ADJECTIVE If something is convenient, it is easy to use or it makes something easy to do.

**conveniently** ADVERB
■ handy, useful

a
b
c
d
e
f
g
h
i
j
k
l
m
n
o
p
q
r
s
t
u
v
w
x
y
z

**convent** convents
NOUN a building where nuns live, or a school run by nuns.

**convention** conventions
NOUN 1 an accepted way of behaving or doing something. 2 a large meeting of an organization or political group *E.G. the Democratic Convention*.

**conventional**
ADJECTIVE 1 You say that people are conventional when there is nothing unusual about their way of life. 2 Conventional methods are the ones that are usually used.
**conventionally** ADVERB

**converge** converges converging converged
VERB To converge is to meet or join at a particular place.

**conversation** conversations
NOUN If you have a conversation with someone, you spend time talking to them.
**conversational** ADJECTIVE
**conversationalist** NOUN

**converse** converses conversing conversed
VERB *Said "con-verse"* 1 *FORMAL* When people converse, they talk to each other. ▸ NOUN *Said "con-verse"* 2 The converse of something is its opposite *E.G. Don't you think that the converse might also be possible?*
**conversely** ADVERB

**convert** converts converting converted
VERB *Said "con-vert"* 1 To convert one thing into another is to change it so that it becomes the other thing. 2 If someone converts you, they persuade you to change your religious or political beliefs. ▸ NOUN

*Said "con-vert"* 3 someone who has changed their religious or political beliefs.

**conversion** NOUN **convertible** ADJECTIVE

**convex**
ADJECTIVE A convex surface bulges outwards, rather than being level or curving inwards.

**convey** conveys conveying conveyed
VERB 1 To convey information or ideas is to cause them to be known or understood. 2 *FORMAL* To convey someone or something to a place is to transport them there.

**conveyor belt** conveyor belts
NOUN a moving strip used in factories for moving objects along.

**convict** convicts convicting convicted
VERB 1 To convict someone of a crime is to find them guilty. ▸ NOUN 2 someone serving a prison sentence.

**conviction** convictions
NOUN 1 a strong belief or opinion. 2 The conviction of someone is what happens when they are found guilty in a court of law.

**convince** convinces convincing convinced
VERB To convince someone of something is to persuade them that it is true.
■ persuade, sway

**convincing**
ADJECTIVE 'Convincing' is used to describe things or people that can make you believe something is true *E.G. a convincing argument*.
**convincingly** ADVERB
■ credible, persuasive, plausible

**convoluted**
*Said* "kon-vol-**yoo**-tid" ADJECTIVE
Something that is convoluted has
many twists and bends E.G. *the*
*convoluted patterns of these designs.*

**convoy convoys**
NOUN a group of vehicles or ships
travelling together.

**convulsion convulsions**
NOUN If someone has convulsions,
their muscles move violently and
uncontrollably.

**coo coos cooing cooed**
VERB When pigeons and doves coo,
they make a soft flutelike sound.

**cook cooks cooking cooked**
VERB 1 To cook food is to prepare it for
eating by heating it. ▶ NOUN
2 someone who prepares and cooks
food, often as their job.

**cooker cookers**
NOUN a device for cooking food.

**cookery**
NOUN the activity of preparing and
cooking food.

**cookie cookies**
NOUN 1 a sweet biscuit. 2 a small file
placed on a user's computer by a
website, containing information
about the user's preferences that will
be used on any future visits he or
she may make to the site.

**cool cooler coolest; cools**
**cooling cooled**
ADJECTIVE 1 Something cool has a low
temperature but is not cold. 2 If you
are cool in a difficult situation, you
stay calm and do not get upset.
▶ VERB 3 When something cools or
when you cool it, it becomes less warm.
**coolly** ADVERB    **coolness** NOUN

**coolabah coolabahs**; also spelt
**coolibar**

NOUN an Australian eucalypt that
grows along rivers.

**coop coops**
NOUN a cage for chickens or rabbits.

**cooperate cooperates**
**cooperating cooperated**
*Said* "koh-**op**-er-rate" VERB 1 When
people cooperate, they work or act
together. 2 To cooperate also means
to do what someone asks.
**cooperation** NOUN

**cooperative cooperatives**
*Said* "koh-**op**-er-ut-tiv" NOUN 1 a
business or organization run by the
people who work for it, and who
share its benefits or profits. ▶ ADJECTIVE
2 A cooperative activity is done by
people working together. 3 Someone
who is cooperative does what you
ask them to.

**coordinate coordinates**
**coordinating coordinated**
*Said* "koh-**or**-din-ate" VERB 1 To
coordinate an activity is to organize
the people or things involved in it
E.G. *to coordinate the campaign.*
▶ PLURAL NOUN 2 (MATHS) Coordinates
are a pair of numbers or letters
which tell you how far along and up
or down a point is on a grid.
**coordination** NOUN    **coordinator**
NOUN

**cop cops**
NOUN; *INFORMAL* a policeman.

**cope copes coping coped**
VERB If you cope with a problem or
task, you deal with it successfully.

**copious**
ADJECTIVE; *FORMAL* existing or produced
in large quantities E.G. *I wrote copious*
*notes for the solicitor.*

**copper coppers**
NOUN 1 Copper is a soft reddish-

a
b
**c**
d
e
f
g
h
i
j
k
l
m
n
o
p
q
r
s
t
u
v
w
x
y
z

Plaice the fish has a glittering 'EYE' (I) (pla*i*ce)    SPELLING NOTE

is to get them into a place they
cannot escape from.

**cornet** cornets
NOUN a small brass instrument used in
brass and military bands.

**cornflour**
NOUN Cornflour is a fine white flour
made from maize and used in
cooking to thicken sauces.

**cornflower** cornflowers
NOUN a small plant with bright
flowers, usually blue.

**cornice** cornices
NOUN a decorative strip of plaster,
wood, or stone along the top edge
of a wall.

**corny** cornier corniest
ADJECTIVE very obvious or sentimental
and not at all original E.G. corny old
love songs.

**coronary** coronaries
NOUN If someone has a coronary,
blood cannot reach their heart
because of a blood clot.

**coronation** coronations
NOUN the ceremony at which a king
or queen is crowned.

**coroner** coroners
NOUN an official who investigates the
deaths of people who have died in a
violent or unusual way.

**coronet** coronets
NOUN a small crown.

**corporal** corporals
NOUN an officer of low rank in the
army or air force.

**corporal punishment**
NOUN Corporal punishment is the
punishing of people by beating
them.

**corporate**
ADJECTIVE; FORMAL belonging to or done
by all members of a group together

E.G. a corporate decision.

**corporation** corporations
NOUN **1** a large business. **2** a group of
people responsible for running a
city.

**corps**
Rhymes with "more" NOUN **1** a part of
an army with special duties E.G. the
engineering Corps. **2** a small group of
people who do a special job E.G. the
world press corps.
☑ The plural of corps is also corps.

**corpse** corpses
NOUN a dead body.

**corpuscle** corpuscles
Said "kor-pus-sl" NOUN a red or white
blood cell.

**correa** correas
NOUN an Australian shrub with large
green and white flowers.

**correct** corrects correcting
corrected
ADJECTIVE **1** If something is correct,
there are no mistakes in it. **2** The
correct thing in a particular situation
is the right one E.G. Each has the
correct number of coins. **3** Correct
behaviour is considered to be
socially acceptable. ▶ VERB **4** If you
correct something which is wrong,
you make it right.

**correctly** ADVERB  **correction** NOUN
**corrective** ADJECTIVE or NOUN
▤ (sense 4) emend, rectify

**correlate** correlates correlating
correlated
VERB If two things correlate or are
correlated, they are closely
connected or strongly influence
each other E.G. Obesity correlates
with increased risk of stroke and
diabetes.

**correlation** NOUN

a b c d e f g h i j k l m n o p q r s t u v w x y z

**correspond** corresponds corresponded
VERB **1** If one thing corresponds to another, it has a similar purpose, function, or status. **2** (MATHS) If numbers or amounts correspond, they are the same. **3** When people correspond, they write to each other.

**correspondence**
NOUN **1** Correspondence is the writing of letters; also the letters written. **2** If there is a correspondence between two things, they are closely related or very similar.

**correspondent** correspondents
NOUN a newspaper, television, or radio reporter.

**corresponding**
ADJECTIVE **1** You use 'corresponding' to describe a change that results from a change in something else E.G. *the rise in interest rates and corresponding fall in house values*. **2** You also use 'corresponding' to describe something which has a similar purpose, status to something else E.G. *Alfard is the corresponding Western name for the star*. **3** (MATHS) 'Corresponding' is used to describe two amounts, numbers or shapes that are the same.
**correspondingly** ADVERB

**corridor** corridors
NOUN a passage in a building or train.

**corroboree** corroborees
NOUN an Australian Aboriginal gathering or dance that is festive or warlike.

**corrode** corrodes corroding corroded
VERB When metal corrodes, it is gradually destroyed by a chemical or rust.
**corrosion** NOUN **corrosive** ADJECTIVE

**corrugated**
ADJECTIVE Corrugated metal or cardboard is made in parallel folds to make it stronger.
📖 from Latin *corrugare* meaning 'to wrinkle up'

**corrupt** corrupts corrupting corrupted
ADJECTIVE **1** Corrupt people act dishonestly or illegally in return for money or power E.G. *corrupt ministers*.
▶ VERB **2** To corrupt someone means to make them dishonest or immoral.
**corruptible** ADJECTIVE
▦ (sense 1) crooked, dishonest
▦ (sense 2) deprave

**corruption**
NOUN Corruption is dishonesty and illegal behaviour by people in positions of power.
▦ depravity, immorality, vice

**corset** corsets
NOUN Corsets are stiff underwear worn by some women round their hips and waist to make them look slimmer.

**cosmetic** cosmetics
NOUN **1** Cosmetics are substances such as lipstick and face powder which improve a person's appearance. ▶ ADJECTIVE **2** Cosmetic changes improve the appearance of something without changing its basic.

**cosmic**
ADJECTIVE belonging or relating to the universe.

**cosmopolitan**
ADJECTIVE A cosmopolitan place is full of people from many countries.
📖 from Greek *kosmos* meaning 'universe' and *politēs* meaning 'citizen'

**cosmos**

NOUN The cosmos is the universe.

**cosset** cossets cosseting cosseted

VERB If you cosset someone, you spoil them and protect them too much.

**cost** costs costing cost

NOUN 1 The cost of something is the amount of money needed to buy it, do it, or make it. 2 The cost of achieving something is the loss or injury in achieving it E.G. *the total cost in human misery.* ▶ VERB 3 You use 'cost' to talk about the amount of money you have to pay for things E.G. *The air fares were going to cost a lot.* 4 If a mistake costs you something, you lose that thing because of the mistake E.G. *a reckless gamble that could cost him his job.*

**costly** costlier costliest

ADJECTIVE expensive E.G. *the most costly piece of furniture.*

**costume** costumes

NOUN 1 (DRAMA) a set of clothes worn by an actor. 2 Costume is the clothing worn in a particular place or during a particular period E.G. *eighteenth-century costume.*

**cosy** cosier cosiest; cosies

ADJECTIVE 1 warm and comfortable E.G. *her cosy new flat.* 2 Cosy activities are pleasant and friendly E.G. *a cosy chat.* ▶ NOUN 3 a soft cover put over a teapot to keep the tea warm.

**cosily** ADVERB **cosiness** NOUN

**cot** cots

NOUN a small bed for a baby, with bars or panels round it to stop the baby falling out.

🔲 from Hindi *khat* meaning 'bedstead'

**cottage** cottages

NOUN a small house in the country.

**cottage cheese**

NOUN Cottage cheese is a type of soft white lumpy cheese.

**cotton** cottons

NOUN 1 Cotton is cloth made from the soft fibres of the cotton plant. 2 Cotton is also thread used for sewing.

🔲 from Arabic *qutn*

**cotton wool**

NOUN Cotton wool is soft fluffy cotton, often used for dressing wounds.

**couch** couches couching couched

NOUN 1 a long, soft piece of furniture which more than one person can sit on. ▶ VERB 2 If a statement is couched in a particular type of language, it is expressed in that language E.G. *a comment couched in impertinent terms.*

**cough** coughs coughing coughed

*Said* "koff" VERB 1 When you cough, you force air out of your throat with a sudden harsh noise. ▶ NOUN 2 an illness that makes you cough a lot; also the noise you make when you cough.

**could**

VERB 1 You use 'could' to say that you were able or allowed to do something E.G. *He could hear voices… She could come and go as she wanted.* 2 You also use 'could' to say that something might happen or might be the case E.G. *It could rain.* 3 You use 'could' when you are asking for something politely E.G. *Could you tell me the name of that film?*

**coulomb** coulombs

*Said* "koo-lom" NOUN a unit used to measure electric charge.

LEarn the principLEs (principLe)　　SPELLING NOTE

A
B
C
D
E
F
G
H
I
J
K
L
M
N
O
P
Q
R
S
T
U
V
W
X
Y
Z

**council** councils
NOUN **1** a group of people elected to look after the affairs of a town, district, or county. **2** Some other groups have Council as part of their name *E.G. the World Gold Council.*

**councillor** councillors
NOUN an elected member of a local council.

**counsel** counsels counselling counselled
NOUN **1** *FORMAL* To give someone counsel is to give them advice. ▶ VERB **2** To counsel people is to give them advice about their problems.

**counselling** NOUN **counsellor** NOUN

**count** counts counting counted
VERB **1** To count is to say all the numbers in order up to a particular number. **2** If you count all the things in a group, you add them up to see how many there are. **3** What counts in a situation is whatever is most important. **4** To count as something means to be regarded as that thing *E.G. I'm not sure whether this counts as harassment.* **5** If you can count on someone or something, you can rely on them. ▶ NOUN **6** a number reached by counting. **7** *FORMAL* If something is wrong on a particular count, it is wrong in that respect. **8** a European nobleman.

**countdown** countdowns
NOUN the counting aloud of numbers in reverse order before something happens, especially before a spacecraft is launched.

**countenance** countenances
NOUN; *FORMAL* Someone's countenance is their face.

**counter** counters countering countered
NOUN **1** a long, flat surface over which goods are sold in a shop. **2** a small, flat, round object used in board games. ▶ VERB **3** If you counter something that is being done, you take action to make it less effective *E.G. I countered that argument with a reference to our sales report.*

**counter-**
PREFIX **1** 'Counter-' means 'opposite' or 'contrary' *E.G. counterbalance.* **2** 'Counter-' can also mean 'copy' or 'substitute' *E.G. counterfeit.*
📖 from Latin *contrā* meaning 'against' or 'opposite'

**counteract** counteracts counteracting counteracted
VERB To counteract something is to reduce its effect by producing an opposite effect.

**counterfeit** counterfeits counterfeiting counterfeited
*Said* "**kown**-ter-fit" ADJECTIVE **1** Something counterfeit is not genuine but has been made to look genuine to deceive people *E.G. counterfeit money.* ▶ VERB **2** To counterfeit something is to make a counterfeit version of it.

**counterpart** counterparts
NOUN The counterpart of a person or thing is another person or thing with a similar function in a different place *E.G. Unlike his British counterpart, the French mayor is an important personality.*

**countess** countesses
NOUN the wife of a count or earl, or a woman with the same rank as a count or earl.

**counting**
PREPOSITION You say 'counting' when including something in a calculation E.G. *nearly 4000 of us, not counting women and children.*

**countless**
ADJECTIVE too many to count E.G. *There had been countless demonstrations.*
◼ incalculable, innumerable

**country countries**
NOUN (GEOGRAPHY) 1 one of the political areas the world is divided into. 2 The country is land away from towns and cities. 3 'Country' is used to refer to an area with particular features or associations E.G. *the heart of wine country.*
◼ (sense 1) nation, state

**countryman countrymen**
NOUN Your countrymen are people from your own country.

**countryside**
NOUN The countryside is land away from towns and cities.

**county counties**
NOUN (GEOGRAPHY) a region with its own local government.
🏛 from Old French *conté* meaning 'land belonging to a count'

**coup coups**
*Rhymes with* "you" NOUN When there is a coup, a group of people seize power in a country.
🏛 from French *coup* meaning 'a blow'

**couple couples coupling coupled**
NOUN 1 two people who are married or having a sexual or romantic relationship. 2 A couple of things or people means two of them E.G. *a couple of weeks ago.* ▶ VERB 3 If one thing is coupled with another, the two things are done or dealt with

together E.G. *Its stores offer high quality coupled with low prices.*

**couplet couplets**
NOUN two lines of poetry together, especially two that rhyme.

**coupon coupons**
NOUN 1 a piece of printed paper which, when you hand it in, entitles you to pay less than usual for something. 2 a form you fill in to ask for information or to enter a competition.

**courage**
NOUN Courage is the quality shown by people who do things knowing they are dangerous or difficult.
**courageous** ADJECTIVE
**courageously** ADVERB

**courgette courgettes**
*Said* "koor-**jet**" NOUN a type of small marrow with dark green skin. Courgettes are also called **zucchini**.
🏛 from French *courgette* meaning 'little marrow'

**courier couriers**
*Said* "**koo**-ree-er" NOUN 1 someone employed by a travel company to look after people on holiday. 2 someone employed to deliver special letters quickly.

**course courses**
NOUN 1 a series of lessons or lectures. 2 a series of medical treatments E.G. *a course of injections.* 3 one of the parts of a meal. 4 A course or a course of action is one of the things you can do in a situation. 5 a piece of land where a sport such as golf is played. 6 the route a ship or aircraft takes. 7 If something happens in the course of a period of time, it happens during that period E.G. *Ten people died in the course of the day.* ▶ PHRASE

the QUeen stood on the QUay (*quay*)    SPELLING NOTE

**8** If you say **of course**, you are showing that something is totally expected or that you are sure about something *E.G. Of course she wouldn't do that.*

☑ Do not confuse the spellings of *coarse* and *course*.

**court** courts courting courted
NOUN **1** a place where legal matters are decided by a judge and jury or a magistrate. The judge and jury or magistrate can also be referred to as the court. **2** a place where a game such as tennis or badminton is played. **3** the place where a king or queen lives and carries out ceremonial duties. ▶ VERB **4** *OLD-FASHIONED* If a man and woman are courting, they are spending a lot of time together because they intend to get married.

**courteous**
*Said* "kur-*tee*-yuss" ADJECTIVE Courteous behaviour is polite and considerate.
🔲 from Old French *corteis* meaning 'courtly-mannered'

**courtesy**
NOUN Courtesy is polite, considerate behaviour.

**courtier** courtiers
NOUN Courtiers were noblemen and noblewomen at the court of a king or queen.

**court-martial** court-martials court-martialling court-martialled
NOUN **1** a military trial. ▶ VERB **2** If a member of the armed forces is court-martialled, he or she is tried by a court martial.

**courtship**
NOUN; *FORMAL* Courtship is the activity of courting or the period of time during which a man and a woman are courting.

**courtyard** courtyards
NOUN a flat area of ground surrounded by buildings or walls.

**cousin** cousins
NOUN Your cousin is the child of your uncle or aunt.

**cove** coves
NOUN a small bay.

**covenant** covenants
*Said* "kuv-vi-nant" NOUN a formal written agreement or promise.

**cover** covers covered
VERB **1** If you cover something, you put something else over it to protect it or hide it. **2** If something covers something else, it forms a layer over it *E.G. Tears covered his face.* **3** If you cover a particular distance, you travel that distance *E.G. He covered 52 kilometres in 210 laps.* ▶ NOUN **4** something put over an object to protect it or keep it warm. **5** The cover of a book or magazine is its outside. **6** Insurance cover is a guarantee that money will be paid if something is lost or harmed. **7** In the open, cover consists of trees, rocks, or other places where you can shelter or hide.

**cover up** VERB If you cover up something you do not want people to know about, you hide it from them *E.G. He lied to cover up his crime.*
**cover-up** NOUN

**coverage**
NOUN The coverage of something in the news is the reporting of it.

**covering** coverings
NOUN a layer of something which protects or conceals something else

*E.G. A morning blizzard left a covering of snow.*

**covert**
*Said* "kuv-vert" ADJECTIVE; FORMAL Covert activities are secret, rather than open.
**covertly** ADVERB

**covet** covets coveting coveted
*Said* "kuv-vit" VERB; FORMAL If you covet something, you want it very much.

**cow** cows
NOUN a large animal kept on farms for its milk.

**coward** cowards
NOUN someone who is easily frightened and who avoids dangerous or difficult situations.
**cowardly** ADJECTIVE **cowardice** NOUN

**cowboy** cowboys
NOUN a man employed to look after cattle in America.

**cower** cowers cowering cowered
VERB When someone cowers, they crouch or move backwards because they are afraid.
▤ cringe, shrink

**cox** coxes
NOUN a person who steers a boat.

**coy** coyer coyest
ADJECTIVE If someone is coy, they pretend to be shy and modest.
**coyly** ADVERB

**coyote** coyotes
*Said* "koy-**ote**-ee" NOUN a North American animal like a small wolf.

**crab** crabs
NOUN a sea creature with four pairs of legs, two pincers, and a flat, round body covered by a shell.

**crack** cracks cracking cracked
VERB 1 If something cracks, it becomes damaged, with lines appearing on its surface. 2 If you crack a joke, you tell it. 3 If you crack a problem or code, you solve it. ▶ NOUN 4 one of the lines appearing on something when it cracks. 5 a narrow gap. ▶ ADJECTIVE 6 A crack soldier or sportsman is highly trained and skilful.
▤ (sense 5) break, fracture, gap

**cracker** crackers
NOUN 1 a thin, crisp biscuit that is often eaten with cheese. 2 a paper-covered tube that pulls apart with a bang and usually has a toy and paper hat inside.

**crackle** crackles crackling crackled
VERB 1 If something crackles, it makes a rapid series of short, harsh noises. ▶ NOUN 2 a short, harsh noise.

**cradle** cradles cradling cradled
NOUN 1 a box-shaped bed for a baby. ▶ VERB 2 If you cradle something in your arms or hands, you hold it there carefully.

**craft** crafts
NOUN 1 an activity such as weaving, carving, or pottery. 2 a skilful occupation *E.G. the writer's craft.* 3 a boat, plane, or spacecraft.
☑ When *craft* means 'a boat, plane, or spacecraft' (sense 3), the plural is **craft**.

**craftsman** craftsmen
NOUN a man who makes things skilfully with his hands.
**craftsmanship** NOUN
**craftswoman** NOUN

**crafty** craftier craftiest
ADJECTIVE Someone who is crafty gets what they want by tricking people in a clever way.

**crag** crags
NOUN a steep rugged rock or peak.

a
b
c
d
e
f
g
h
i
j
k
l
m
n
o
p
q
r
s
t
u
v
w
x
y
z

A B **C** D E F G H I J K L M N O P Q R S T U V W X Y Z

**craggy** craggier craggiest

ADJECTIVE A craggy mountain or cliff is steep and rocky.

**cram** crams cramming crammed

VERB If you cram people or things into a place, you put more in than there is room for.

■ pack, squeeze, stuff

**cramp** cramps

NOUN Cramp or cramps is a pain caused by a muscle contracting.

**cramped**

ADJECTIVE If a room or building is cramped, it is not big enough for the people or things in it.

**cranberry** cranberries

NOUN Cranberries are sour-tasting red berries, often made into a sauce.

**crane** cranes craning craned

NOUN 1 a machine that moves heavy things by lifting them in the air. 2 a large bird with a long neck and long legs. ▶ VERB 3 If you crane your neck, you extend your head in a particular direction to see or hear something better.

**crank** cranks cranking cranked

NOUN 1 INFORMAL someone with strange ideas who behaves in an odd way. 2 a device you turn to make something move E.G. The adjustment is made by turning the crank. ▶ VERB 3 If you crank something, you make it move by turning a handle.

**cranky** ADJECTIVE

**cranny** crannies

NOUN a very narrow opening in a wall or rock E.G. nooks and crannies.

**crash** crashes crashing crashed

NOUN 1 an accident in which a moving vehicle hits something violently. 2 a sudden loud noise E.G. the crash of the waves on the rocks. 3 the sudden failure of a business or financial institution. ▶ VERB 4 When a vehicle crashes, it hits something and is badly damaged.

**crash helmet** crash helmets

NOUN a helmet worn by motor cyclists for protection when they are riding.

**crate** crates

NOUN a large box used for transporting or storing things.

**crater** craters

NOUN a wide hole in the ground caused by something hitting it or by an explosion.

**cravat** cravats

NOUN a piece of cloth a man can wear round his neck tucked into his shirt collar.

▥ from Serbo-Croat Hrvat meaning 'Croat'. Croat soldiers wore cravats during the Thirty Years' War

**crave** craves craving craved

VERB If you crave something, you want it very much E.G. I crave her approval.

**craving** NOUN

**crawl** crawls crawling crawled

VERB 1 When you crawl, you move forward on your hands and knees. 2 When a vehicle crawls, it moves very slowly. 3 INFORMAL If a place is crawling with people or things, it is full of them E.G. The place is crawling with drunks.

**crawler** NOUN

**crayfish** crayfishes or crayfish

NOUN a small shellfish like a lobster.

▥ from Old French crevice meaning 'crab'

**crayon** crayons

NOUN a coloured pencil or a stick of coloured wax.

**craze** crazes
NOUN something that is very popular for a short time.

**crazy** crazier craziest
ADJECTIVE; *INFORMAL* 1 very strange or foolish *E.G. The guy is crazy… a crazy idea.* 2 If you are crazy about something, you are very keen on it *E.G. I was crazy about dancing.*
**crazily** ADVERB   **craziness** NOUN

**creak** creaks creaking creaked
VERB 1 If something creaks, it makes a harsh sound when it moves or when you stand on it. ▶ NOUN 2 a harsh squeaking noise.
**creaky** ADJECTIVE

**cream** creams
NOUN 1 Cream is a thick, yellowish-white liquid taken from the top of milk. 2 Cream is also a substance people can rub on their skin to make it soft. ▶ ADJECTIVE 3 yellowish-white.
**creamy** ADJECTIVE

**crease** creases creasing creased
NOUN 1 an irregular line that appears on cloth or paper when it is crumpled. 2 a straight line on something that has been pressed or folded neatly. ▶ VERB 3 To crease something is to make lines appear on it.
**creased** ADJECTIVE

**create** creates creating created
VERB 1 To create something is to cause it to happen or exist *E.G. This is absolutely vital but creates a problem.* 2 When someone creates a new product or process, they invent it.
**creator** NOUN

**creation** creations
NOUN 1 Creation is the creating of something or bringing it into

existence. 2 A creation is something original that has been made or invented. 3 ( RE ) The Creation is the time when God is believed to have made the world and everything in it.

**creative**
ADJECTIVE 1 Creative people are able to invent and develop original ideas. 2 Creative activities involve the inventing and developing of original ideas *E.G. creative writing.*
**creatively** ADVERB   **creativity** NOUN

**creature** creatures
NOUN any living thing that moves about.

**crèche** crèches
*Said* "kresh" NOUN a place where small children are looked after while their parents are working.
📖 from Old French *crèche* meaning 'crib' or 'manger'

**credence**
NOUN; *FORMAL* If something gives credence to a theory or story, it makes it easier to believe.

**credentials**
PLURAL NOUN Your credentials are your past achievements or other things in your background that make you qualified for something.

**credible**
ADJECTIVE If someone or something is credible, you can believe or trust them.
**credibility** NOUN

**credit** credits crediting credited
NOUN 1 If you are allowed credit, you can take something and pay for it later *E.G. to buy goods on credit.* 2 If you get the credit for something, people praise you for it. 3 If you say someone is a credit to their family or school, you mean that their family or

a
b
c
d
e
f
g
h
i
j
k
l
m
n
o
p
q
r
s
t
u
v
w
x
y
z

A B C D E F G H I J K L M N O P Q R S T U V W X Y Z

school should be proud of them.
▶ PLURAL NOUN 4 The list of people who helped make a film, record, or television programme is called the credits. ▶ PHRASE 5 If someone or their bank account is **in credit**, their account has money in it. ▶ VERB 6 If you are credited with an achievement, people believe that you were responsible for it.

**creditable**
ADJECTIVE satisfactory or fairly good E.G. *a creditable performance.*

**credit card** credit cards
NOUN a plastic card that allows someone to buy goods on credit.

**creditor** creditors
NOUN Your creditors are the people you owe money to.

**creed** creeds
NOUN 1 a religion. 2 any set of beliefs E.G. *the feminist creed.*

**creek** creeks
NOUN a narrow inlet where the sea comes a long way into the land.
🔲 from Old Norse *kriki* meaning 'nook'

**creep** creeps creeping crept
VERB To creep is to move quietly and slowly.

**creepy** creepier creepiest
ADJECTIVE; INFORMAL strange and frightening E.G. *a creepy feeling.*

**cremate** cremates cremating cremated
VERB When someone is cremated, their dead body is burned during a funeral service.
**cremation** NOUN

**crematorium** crematoriums or crematoria
NOUN a building in which the bodies of dead people are burned.

**crepe**
*Said "krayp"* NOUN 1 a thin ridged material made from cotton, silk, or wool. 2 a type of rubber with a rough surface.

**crescendo** crescendos
*Said "krish-en-doe"* NOUN When there is a crescendo in a piece of music, the music gets louder.

**crescent** crescents
NOUN a curved shape that is wider in its middle than at the ends, which are pointed.

**cress**
NOUN a plant with small, strong-tasting leaves. It is used in salads.

**crest** crests
NOUN 1 The crest of a hill or wave is its highest part. 2 a tuft of feathers on top of a bird's head. 3 a small picture or design that is the emblem of a noble family, a town, or an organization.
**crested** ADJECTIVE

**crevice** crevices
NOUN a narrow crack or gap in rock.

**crew** crews
NOUN 1 The crew of a ship, aeroplane, or spacecraft are the people who operate it. 2 people with special technical skills who work together E.G. *the camera crew.*

**crib** cribs cribbing cribbed
VERB 1 INFORMAL If you crib, you copy what someone else has written and pretend it is your own work. ▶ NOUN 2 OLD-FASHIONED a baby's cot.

**crib-wall** crib-walls
NOUN In New Zealand English, a wooden wall built against a bank of earth to support it.

**crick** cricks
NOUN a pain in your neck or back caused by muscles becoming stiff.

**cricket** crickets

NOUN **1** an outdoor game played by two teams who take turns at scoring runs by hitting a ball with a bat. **2** a small jumping insect that produces sounds by rubbing its wings together.

**cricketer** NOUN

**crime** crimes

NOUN an action for which you can be punished by law E.G. *a serious crime.*

■ misdemeanour, offence

**criminal** criminals

NOUN **1** someone who has committed a crime. ▶ ADJECTIVE **2** involving or related to crime E.G. *criminal activities.*

**criminally** ADVERB

■ (sense 1) crook, lawbreaker, offender

**criminology**

NOUN the scientific study of crime and criminals.

**criminologist** NOUN

**crimson**

NOUN or ADJECTIVE dark purplish-red.

**cringe** cringes cringing cringed

VERB If you cringe, you back away from someone or something because you are afraid or embarrassed.

🔟 from Old English *cringan* meaning 'to yield in battle'

**crinkle** crinkles crinkling crinkled

VERB **1** If something crinkles, it becomes slightly creased or folded. ▶ NOUN **2** Crinkles are small creases or folds.

**cripple** cripples crippling crippled

NOUN **1** someone who cannot move their body properly because it is weak or affected by disease. ▶ VERB

**2** To cripple someone is to injure them severely so that they can never move properly again.

**crippled** ADJECTIVE **crippling** ADJECTIVE

**crisis** crises

*Said "kry-seez in the plural"* NOUN a serious or dangerous situation.

**crisp** crisper crispest; crisps

ADJECTIVE **1** Something that is crisp is pleasantly fresh and firm E.G. *crisp lettuce leaves.* **2** If the air or the weather is crisp, it is pleasantly fresh, cold, and dry E.G. *crisp wintry days.* ▶ NOUN **3** Crisps are thin slices of potato fried until they are hard and crunchy.

**crispy** crispier crispiest

ADJECTIVE Crispy food is pleasantly hard and crunchy E.G. *a crispy salad.*

**criterion** criteria

*Said "kry-teer-ee-on"* NOUN a standard by which you judge or decide something.

☑ *Criteria* is the plural of *criterion*, and needs to be used with a plural verb.

**critic** critics

NOUN **1** someone who writes reviews of books, films, plays, or musical performances. **2** A critic of a person or system is someone who criticizes them publicly E.G. *the government's critics.*

**critical**

ADJECTIVE **1** A critical time is one which is very important in determining what happens in the future E.G. *critical months in the history of the world.* **2** A critical situation is a very serious one E.G. *Rock music is in a critical state.* **3** If an ill or injured person is critical, they are in danger

a
b
c
d
e
f
g
h
i
j
k
l
m
n
o
p
q
r
s
t
u
v
w
x
y
z

A
B
C
D
E
F
G
H
I
J
K
L
M
N
O
P
Q
R
S
T
U
V
W
X
Y
Z

of dying. **4** If you are critical of something or someone, you express severe judgments or opinions about them. **5** If you are critical, you examine and judge something carefully *E.G. a critical look at the way he led his life.*

**critically** ADVERB

**criticism criticisms**
NOUN **1** When there is criticism of someone or something, people express disapproval of them. **2** If you make a criticism, you point out a fault you think someone or something has.

**criticize criticizes criticizing criticized**; also spelt **criticise**
VERB If you criticize someone or something, you say what you think is wrong with them.
◼ disparage, find fault with

**croak croaks croaking croaked**
VERB **1** When animals and birds croak, they make harsh, low sounds. ▶ NOUN **2** a harsh, low sound.
▥ from Old Norse *kraka* meaning 'crow'

**Croatian Croatians**
ADJECTIVE **1** belonging to or relating to Croatia. ▶ NOUN **2** someone who comes from Croatia. **3** Croatian is the form of Serbo-Croat spoken in Croatia.

**crochet**
*Said* "kroh-shay" NOUN a way of making clothes and other things out of thread using a needle with a small hook at the end.

**crockery**
NOUN Crockery is plates, cups, and saucers.

**crocodile crocodiles**
NOUN a large scaly meat-eating reptile

which lives in tropical rivers.
▥ from Greek *krokodeilos* meaning 'lizard'

**crocus crocuses**
NOUN Crocuses are yellow, purple, or white flowers that grow in early spring.

**croft crofts**
NOUN a small piece of land, especially in Scotland, which is farmed by one family.

**crofter** NOUN

**croissant croissants**
*Said* "krwus-son" NOUN a light, crescent-shaped roll eaten at breakfast.
▥ from French *croissant* meaning 'crescent'

**crony cronies**
NOUN; *OLD-FASHIONED* Your cronies are the friends you spend a lot of time with.

**crook crooks**
NOUN **1** *INFORMAL* a criminal. **2** The crook of your arm or leg is the soft inside part where you bend your elbow or knee.

**crooked**
*Said* "kroo-kid" ADJECTIVE **1** bent or twisted. **2** Someone who is crooked is dishonest.

**croon croons crooning crooned**
VERB To croon is to sing or hum quietly and gently *E.G. He crooned a love song.*
▥ from Old Dutch *kronen* meaning 'to groan'

**crop crops cropping cropped**
NOUN **1** Crops are plants such as wheat and potatoes that are grown for food. **2** the plants collected at harvest time *E.G. You should have two crops in the year.* ▶ VERB **3** To crop someone's hair is to cut it very short.

**croquet**
*Said* "kroh-kay" NOUN a game in which the players use long-handled mallets to hit balls through metal arches pushed into a lawn.

**cross** crosses crossing crossed; crosser crossest
VERB **1** If you cross something such as a room or a road, you go to the other side of it. **2** Lines or roads that cross meet and go across each other. **3** If a thought crosses your mind, you think of it. **4** If you cross your arms, legs, or fingers, you put one on top of the other. ▸ NOUN **5** a vertical bar or line crossed by a shorter horizontal bar or line; also used to describe any object shaped like this. **6** The Cross is the cross-shaped structure on which Jesus Christ was crucified. A cross is also any symbol representing Christ's Cross. **7** a written mark shaped like an X *E.G. I drew a small bicycle and put a cross by it.* **8** Something that is a cross between two things is neither one thing nor the other, but a mixture of both. ▸ ADJECTIVE **9** Someone who is cross is rather angry.
**crossly** ADVERB

**crossbow** crossbows
NOUN a weapon consisting of a small bow fixed at the end of a piece of wood.

**cross-country**
NOUN **1** Cross-country is the sport of running across open countryside, rather than on roads or on a track. ▸ ADVERB or ADJECTIVE **2** across country.

**cross-eyed**
ADJECTIVE A cross-eyed person has eyes that seem to look towards each other.

**crossfire**
NOUN gunfire crossing the same place from opposite directions.

**crosshatching**
NOUN (ART) Crosshatching is drawing an area of shade in a picture using two or more sets of parallel lines.

**crossing** crossings
NOUN **1** a place where you can cross a road safely. **2** a journey by ship to a place on the other side of the sea.

**cross-legged**
ADJECTIVE If you are sitting cross-legged, you are sitting on the floor with your knees pointing outwards and your feet tucked under them.

**cross section** cross sections
NOUN A cross section of a group of people is a representative sample of them.

**crossword** crosswords
NOUN a puzzle in which you work out the answers to clues and write them in the white squares of a pattern of black and white squares.

**crotch** crotches
NOUN the part of your body between the tops of your legs.

**crotchet** crotchets
NOUN (MUSIC) a musical note (♩) equal in time value to a quarter of a semibreve. In the United States and Canada, a crotchet is called a quarter note.

**crouch** crouches crouching crouched
VERB If you are crouching, you are leaning forward with your legs bent under you.

**crow** crows crowing crowed
NOUN **1** a large black bird which makes a loud, harsh noise. ▸ VERB **2** When a cock crows, it utters a loud

A
B
C
D
E
F
G
H
I
J
K
L
M
N
O
P
Q
R
S
T
U
V
W
X
Y
Z

squawking sound.

**crowbar** crowbars

NOUN a heavy iron bar used as a lever or for forcing things open.

**crowd** crowds crowding crowded

NOUN 1 a large group of people gathered together. ▶ VERB 2 When people crowd somewhere, they gather there close together or in large numbers.

▤ (sense 1) mass, mob, multitude, throng

**crowded**

ADJECTIVE A crowded place is full of people.

**crown** crowns crowning crowned

NOUN 1 a circular ornament worn on a royal person's head. 2 The crown of something such as your head is the top part of it. ▶ VERB 3 When a king or queen is crowned, a crown is put on their head during their coronation ceremony. 4 When something crowns an event, it is the final part of it E.G. The news crowned a dreadful week.

**crucial**

Said "kroo-shl" ADJECTIVE If something is crucial, it is very important in determining how something else will be in the future.

▥ from Latin crux meaning 'a cross'

▤ critical, decisive, vital

**crucifix** crucifixes

NOUN a cross with a figure representing Jesus Christ being crucified on it.

**crucify** crucifies crucifying crucified

VERB To crucify someone is to tie or nail them to a large wooden cross and leave them there to die.

**crucifixion** NOUN

**crude** cruder crudest

ADJECTIVE 1 rough and simple E.G. a crude weapon… a crude method of entry. 2 A crude person speaks or behaves in a rude and offensive way E.G. You can be quite crude at times.

**crudely** ADVERB **crudity** NOUN

▤ (sense 1) makeshift, primitive

▤ (sense 2) coarse, vulgar

**cruel** crueller cruellest

ADJECTIVE Cruel people deliberately cause pain or distress to other people or to animals.

**cruelly** ADVERB **cruelty** NOUN

▤ brutal, callous, unkind

**cruise** cruises cruising cruised

NOUN 1 a holiday in which you travel on a ship and visit places. ▶ VERB 2 When a vehicle cruises, it moves at a constant moderate speed.

**cruiser** cruisers

NOUN 1 a motor boat with a cabin you can sleep in. 2 a large, fast warship.

**crumb** crumbs

NOUN Crumbs are very small pieces of bread or cake.

**crumble** crumbles crumbling crumbled

VERB When something crumbles, it breaks into small pieces.

**crumbly**

ADJECTIVE Something crumbly easily breaks into small pieces.

**crumpet** crumpets

NOUN a round, flat, breadlike cake which you eat toasted.

**crumple** crumples crumpling crumpled

VERB To crumple paper or cloth is to squash it so that it is full of creases and folds.

**crunch** crunches crunching crunched

VERB If you crunch something, you crush it noisily, for example between your teeth or under your feet.

**crunchy crunchier crunchiest**
ADJECTIVE Crunchy food is hard or crisp and makes a noise when you eat it.

**crusade crusades**
NOUN a long and determined attempt to achieve something E.G. the crusade for human rights.
**crusader** NOUN

**crush crushes crushing crushed**
VERB 1 To crush something is to destroy its shape by squeezing it. 2 To crush a substance is to turn it into liquid or powder by squeezing or grinding it. 3 To crush an army or political organization is to defeat it completely. ▶ NOUN 4 a dense crowd of people.

**crust crusts**
NOUN 1 the hard outside part of a loaf. 2 a hard layer on top of something E.G. The snow had a fine crust on it.

**crusty crustier crustiest**
ADJECTIVE 1 Something that is crusty has a hard outside layer. 2 Crusty people are impatient and irritable.

**crutch crutches**
NOUN a support like a long stick which you lean on to help you walk when you have an injured foot or leg.

**crux**
NOUN the most important or difficult part of a problem or argument.

**cry cries crying cried**
VERB 1 When you cry, tears appear in your eyes. 2 To cry something is to shout it or say it loudly E.G. 'See you soon!' they cried. ▶ NOUN 3 If you have a cry, you cry for a period of time. 4 a shout or other loud sound made with your voice. 5 a loud sound made

by some birds E.G. the cry of a seagull.
■ (sense 1) sob, weep

**crypt crypts**
NOUN an underground room beneath a church, usually used as a burial place.
▥ from Greek kruptein meaning 'to hide'

**cryptic**
ADJECTIVE A cryptic remark or message has a hidden meaning.

**crystal crystals**
NOUN 1 a piece of a mineral that has formed naturally into a regular shape. 2 Crystal is a type of transparent rock, used in jewellery. 3 Crystal is also a kind of very high quality glass.
**crystalline** ADJECTIVE

**crystallize crystallizes crystallizing crystallized**; also spelt **crystallise**
VERB 1 If a substance crystallizes, it turns into crystals. 2 If an idea crystallizes, it becomes clear in your mind.

**cub cubs**
NOUN 1 Some young wild animals are called cubs E.G. a lion cub. 2 The Cubs is an organization for young boys before they join the Scouts.

**Cuban Cubans**
Said "kyoo-ban" ADJECTIVE 1 belonging or relating to Cuba. ▶ NOUN 2 someone who comes from Cuba.

**cube cubes cubing cubed**
NOUN 1 a three-dimensional shape with six equally-sized square surfaces. 2 If you multiply a number by itself twice, you get its cube. ▶ VERB 3 To cube a number is to multiply it by itself twice.

**cubic**
ADJECTIVE used in measurements of

a b c d e f g h i j k l m n o p q r s t u v w x y z

**cubicle** cubicles

NOUN a small enclosed area in a place such as a sports centre, where you can dress and undress.

**cuckoo** cuckoos

NOUN a grey bird with a two-note call that lays its eggs in other birds' nests.

**cucumber** cucumbers

NOUN a long, thin, green-skinned fruit eaten raw in salads.

**cuddle** cuddles cuddling cuddled

VERB 1 If you cuddle someone, you hold them affectionately in your arms. ▶ NOUN 2 If you give someone a cuddle, you hold them affectionately in your arms.

**cuddly** cuddlier cuddliest

ADJECTIVE Cuddly people, animals, or toys are soft or pleasing in some way so that you want to cuddle them.

**cue** cues

NOUN 1 something said or done by a performer that is a signal for another performer to begin E.G. *Chris never misses a cue*. 2 a long stick used to hit the balls in snooker and billiards.

**cuff** cuffs

NOUN the end part of a sleeve.

**cufflink** cufflinks

NOUN Cufflinks are small objects for holding shirt cuffs together.

**cuisine**

*Said* "kwiz-*een*" NOUN The cuisine of a region is the style of cooking that is typical of it.

📖 from French *cuisine* meaning 'kitchen'

**cul-de-sac** cul-de-sacs

*Said* "kul-*des*-*sak*" NOUN a road that does not lead to any other roads because one end is blocked off.

**culinary**

ADJECTIVE; *FORMAL* connected with the kitchen or cooking.

📖 from Latin *culina* meaning 'kitchen'

**cull** culls culling culled

VERB 1 If you cull things, you gather them from different places or sources E.G. *information culled from movies*. ▶ NOUN 2 When there is a cull, weaker animals are killed to reduce the numbers in a group.

**culminate** culminates culminating culminated

VERB To culminate in something is to finally develop into it E.G. *a campaign that culminated in a stunning success*. **culmination** NOUN

**culprit** culprits

NOUN someone who has done something harmful or wrong.

📖 from Anglo-French *culpable* meaning 'guilty' and *prit* meaning 'ready' (i.e. ready for trial)

**cult** cults

NOUN 1 A cult is a religious group with special rituals, usually connected with the worship of a particular person. 2 'Cult' is used to refer to any situation in which someone or something is very popular with a large group of people E.G. *the American sports car cult*.

**cultivate** cultivates cultivating cultivated

VERB 1 To cultivate land is to grow crops on it. 2 If you cultivate a feeling or attitude, you try to develop it in yourself or other people. **cultivation** NOUN

**culture** cultures

NOUN 1 Culture refers to the arts and to people's appreciation of them E.G. *He was a man of culture*. 2 The culture

---

volume E.G. *cubic centimetres*.

of a particular society is its ideas, customs, and art *E.G. Japanese culture.* **3** In science, a culture is a group of bacteria or cells grown in a laboratory.
**cultured** ADJECTIVE **cultural** ADJECTIVE

**cumulative**
ADJECTIVE Something that is cumulative keeps being added to.

**cunjevoi** cunjevois
*Said* "kun-jiv-voi" NOUN a very small Australian sea creature that lives on rocks.

**cunning**
ADJECTIVE **1** Someone who is cunning uses clever and deceitful methods to get what they want. ▶ NOUN
**2** Cunning is the ability to get what you want using clever and deceitful methods.
**cunningly** ADVERB
▥ from Old Norse *kunna* meaning 'to know'
▤ (sense 1) crafty, sly, wily

**cup** cups cupping cupped
NOUN **1** a small, round container with a handle, which you drink out of. **2** a large metal container with two handles, given as a prize. ▶ VERB **3** If you cup your hands, you put them together to make a shape like a cup.

**cupboard** cupboards
NOUN a piece of furniture with doors and shelves.

**curable**
ADJECTIVE If a disease or illness is curable, it can be cured.

**curate** curates
NOUN a clergyman who helps a vicar or a priest.

**curator** curators
NOUN the person in a museum or art gallery in charge of its contents.

**curb** curbs curbing curbed
VERB **1** To curb something is to keep it within limits *E.G. policies designed to curb inflation.* ▶ NOUN **2** If a curb is placed on something, it is kept within limits *E.G. the curb on spending.*

**curdle** curdles curdling curdled
VERB When milk curdles, it turns sour.

**curds**
PLURAL NOUN Curds are the thick white substance formed when milk turns sour.

**cure** cures curing cured
VERB **1** To cure an illness is to end it. **2** To cure a sick or injured person is to make them well. **3** If something cures you of a habit or attitude, it stops you having it. **4** To cure food, tobacco, or animal skin is to treat it in order to preserve it. ▶ NOUN **5** A cure for an illness is something that cures it.
▤ (sense 2) heal, make better

**curfew** curfews
NOUN If there is a curfew, people must stay indoors between particular times at night.

**curiosity** curiosities
NOUN **1** Curiosity is the desire to know about something or about many things. **2** something unusual and interesting.

**curious**
ADJECTIVE **1** Someone who is curious wants to know more about something. **2** Something that is curious is unusual and hard to explain.
**curiously** ADVERB
▤ (sense 1) inquiring, inquisitive, nosy

**curl** curls curling curled
NOUN **1** Curls are lengths of hair shaped in tight curves and circles. **2** a

a
b
**c**
d
e
f
g
h
i
j
k
l
m
n
o
p
q
r
s
t
u
v
w
x
y
z

curved or spiral shape *E.G. the curls of morning fog.* ▶ VERB **3** If something curls, it moves in a curve or spiral.

**curly** ADJECTIVE

**curler curlers**

NOUN Curlers are plastic or metal tubes that women roll their hair round to make it curly.

**curlew curlews**

*Said "kur-lyoo"* NOUN a large brown bird with a long curved beak and a loud cry.

**currant currants**

NOUN **1** Currants are small dried grapes often put in cakes and puddings. **2** Currants are also blackcurrants or redcurrants.

📖 sense 1 is from Middle English *rayson of Coraunte* meaning 'Corinth raisin'

**currawong currawongs**

NOUN an Australian bird like a crow.

**currency currencies**

NOUN **1** A country's currency is its coins and banknotes, or its system of money generally *E.G. foreign currency… a strong economy and a weak currency.* **2** If something such as an idea has currency, it is used a lot at a particular time.

**current currents**

NOUN **1** a strong continuous movement of the water in a river or in the sea. **2** a flowing movement in the air. **3** a flow of electricity through a wire or circuit. ▶ ADJECTIVE **4** (HISTORY) Something that is current is happening, being done, or being used now.

**currently** ADVERB

**current affairs**

PLURAL NOUN Current affairs are political and social events discussed in newspapers and on television and radio.

**curriculum curriculums or curricula**

*Said "kur-rik-yoo-lum"* NOUN the different courses taught at a school or university.

**curriculum vitae curricula vitae**

*Said "vee-tie"* NOUN Someone's curriculum vitae is a written account of their personal details, education, and work experience which they send when they apply for a job.

**curried**

ADJECTIVE Curried food has been flavoured with hot spices *E.G. curried lamb.*

**curry curries currying curried**

NOUN **1** Curry is an Indian dish made with hot spices. ▶ PHRASE **2** To **curry favour** with someone means to try to please them by flattering them or doing things to help them.

📖 sense 1 is from Tamil *kari* meaning 'sauce'; sense 2 is from Old French *correer* meaning 'to make ready'

**curse curses cursing cursed**

VERB **1** To curse is to swear because you are angry. **2** If you curse someone or something, you say angry things about them using rude words. ▶ NOUN **3** what you say when you curse. **4** something supernatural that is supposed to cause unpleasant things to happen to someone. **5** a thing or person that causes a lot of distress *E.G. the curse of recession.*

**cursed** ADJECTIVE

**cursor cursors**

NOUN (ICT) an arrow or box on a computer monitor which indicates where the next letter or symbol is.

**cursory**

ADJECTIVE When you give something a cursory glance or examination, you look at it briefly without paying attention to detail.

**curt curter curtest**

ADJECTIVE If someone is curt, they speak in a brief and rather rude way. **curtly** ADVERB

**curtail curtails curtailing curtailed**

VERB; FORMAL To curtail something is to reduce or restrict it E.G. *Injury curtailed his career.*

**curtain curtains**

NOUN 1 a hanging piece of material which can be pulled across a window for privacy or to keep out the light. 2 (DRAMA) a large piece of material which hangs in front of the stage in a theatre until a performance begins.

📖 from Latin *cortina* meaning 'enclosed space'

**curtsy curtsies curtsying curtsied**; also spelt **curtsey**

VERB 1 When a woman curtsies, she lowers her body briefly, bending her knees, to show respect. ► NOUN 2 the movement a woman makes when she curtsies E.G. *She gave a mock curtsy.*

**curve curves curving curved**

NOUN 1 a smooth, gradually bending line. ► VERB 2 When something curves, it moves in a curve or has the shape of a curve E.G. *The track curved away below him… His mouth curved slightly.* **curved** ADJECTIVE

**cushion cushions cushioning cushioned**

NOUN 1 a soft object put on a seat to make it more comfortable. ► VERB 2 To

cushion something is to reduce its effect E.G. *We might have helped to cushion the shock for her.*

**custard**

NOUN Custard is a sweet yellow sauce made from milk and eggs or milk and a powder.

**custodian custodians**

NOUN the person in charge of a collection in an art gallery or a museum.

**custody**

NOUN 1 To have custody of a child means to have the legal right to keep it and look after it E.G. *She won custody of her younger son.* ► PHRASE 2 Someone who is **in custody** is being kept in prison until they can be tried in a court.
**custodial** ADJECTIVE

**custom customs**

NOUN 1 a traditional activity E.G. *an ancient Chinese custom.* 2 something usually done at a particular time or in particular circumstances by a person or by the people in a society E.G. *It was also my custom to do Christmas shows.* 3 Customs is the place at a border, airport, or harbour where you have to declare any goods you are bringing into a country. 4 FORMAL If a shop or business has your custom, you buy things or go there regularly E.G. *Banks are desperate to get your custom.*
≡ (sense 1) convention, tradition
≡ (sense 2) habit, practice

**customary**

ADJECTIVE usual E.G. *his customary modesty… her customary greeting.*
**customarily** ADVERB

**custom-built** or **custom-made**

ADJECTIVE Something that is custom-built or custom-made is made to someone's special requirements.

**customer customers**

NOUN 1 A shop's or firm's customers are the people who buy its goods. 2 INFORMAL You can use 'customer' to refer to someone when describing what they are like to deal with E.G. *a tough customer*.

■ (sense 1) buyer, client, consumer

**cut cuts cutting cut**

VERB 1 If you cut something, you use a knife, scissors, or some other sharp tool to mark it or remove parts of it. 2 If you cut yourself, you injure yourself on a sharp object. 3 If you cut the amount of something, you reduce it E.G. *Some costs could be cut*. 4 When writing is cut, parts of it are not printed or broadcast. 5 To cut from one scene or shot to another in a film is to go instantly to the other scene or shot. ▶ NOUN 6 a mark made with a knife or other sharp tool. 7 an injury caused by a sharp object. 8 a reduction E.G. *another cut in interest rates*. 9 a part in something written that is not printed or broadcast. 10 a large piece of meat ready for cooking. ▶ ADJECTIVE 11 Well cut clothes have been well designed and made E.G. *this beautifully cut coat*.

**cut back** VERB To cut back or cut back on spending means to reduce it. **cutback** NOUN

**cut down** VERB If you cut down on an activity, you do it less often E.G. *cutting down on smoking*.

**cut off** VERB 1 To cut someone or something off means to separate them from things they are normally connected with E.G. *The President had cut himself off from the people*. 2 If a supply of something is cut off, you

no longer get it E.G. *The water had been cut off*. 3 If your telephone or telephone call is cut off, it is disconnected.

**cut out** VERB 1 If you cut out something you are doing, you stop doing it E.G. *Cut out drinking*. 2 If an engine cuts out, it suddenly stops working.

**cute cuter cutest**

ADJECTIVE pretty or attractive.

**cuticle cuticles**

NOUN Cuticles are the pieces of skin that cover the base of your fingernails and toenails.

**cutlass cutlasses**

NOUN a curved sword that was used by sailors.

**cutlery**

NOUN Cutlery is knives, forks, and spoons.

▥ from Latin *culter* meaning 'knife'

**cutlet cutlets**

NOUN a small piece of meat which you fry or grill.

**cutting cuttings**

NOUN 1 something cut from a newspaper or magazine. 2 a part cut from a plant and used to grow a new plant. ▶ ADJECTIVE 3 A cutting remark is unkind and likely to hurt someone.

**CV**

an abbreviation for **curriculum vitae**.

**cyanide**

*Said* "sigh-an-nide" NOUN Cyanide is an extremely poisonous chemical.

**cyber-**

PREFIX Words that begin with 'cyber-' have something to do with computers in their meaning. For example, a *cybercafé* is a place where computers are provided for customers to use.

🏛 From *cybernetic*, from Greek *kybernētēs* meaning 'a steerman'

**cyberpet** cyberpets

NOUN an electronic toy that imitates the activities of a pet, and needs to be fed and entertained.

**cyberspace**

NOUN all of the data stored in a large computer, seen as a three-dimensional model.

**cycle** cycles cycling cycled

VERB **1** When you cycle, you ride a bicycle. ▶ NOUN **2** a bicycle or a motorcycle. **3** a series of events which is repeated again and again in the same order *E.G. the cycle of births and deaths.* **4** ( SCIENCE ) a single complete series of movements or events in an electrical, electronic, mechanical, or organic process. **5** a series of songs or poems intended to be performed or read together.

🏛 from Greek *kuklos* meaning 'ring' or 'wheel'

**cyclical** or **cyclic**

ADJECTIVE happening over and over again in cycles *E.G. a clear cyclical pattern.*

**cyclist** cyclists

NOUN someone who rides a bicycle.

**cyclone** cyclones

NOUN a violent tropical storm.

**cygnet** cygnets

*Said* "**sig**-net" NOUN a young swan.

🏛 from Latin *cygnus* meaning 'swan'

**cylinder** cylinders

NOUN **1** a regular three-dimensional shape with two equally-sized flat circular ends joined by a curved surface. **2** the part in a motor engine in which the piston moves backwards and forwards.

**cylindrical** ADJECTIVE

**cymbal** cymbals

NOUN a circular brass plate used as a percussion instrument. Cymbals are clashed together or hit with a stick.

**cynic** cynics

*Said* "**sin**-nik" NOUN a cynical person.

🏛 from Greek *kunikos* meaning 'dog-like'

**cynical**

ADJECTIVE believing that people always behave selfishly or dishonestly.

**cynically** ADVERB    **cynicism** NOUN

**cypher**

another spelling of **cipher**.

**cypress** cypresses

NOUN a type of evergreen tree with small dark green leaves and round cones.

**cyst** cysts

*Said* "**sist**" NOUN a growth containing liquid that can form under your skin or inside your body.

**czar**

another spelling of **tsar**.

**czarina**

another spelling of **tsarina**.

**Czech** Czechs

*Said* "**chek**" ADJECTIVE **1** belonging or relating to the Czech Republic. ▶ NOUN **2** someone who comes from the Czech Republic. **3** Czech is the language spoken in the Czech Republic.

**Czechoslovak** Czechoslovaks

*Said* "**chek**-oh-**slow**-vak" ADJECTIVE **1** belonging to or relating to the country that used to be Czechoslovakia. ▶ NOUN **2** someone who came from the country that used to be Czechoslovakia.

a
b
c
d
e
f
g
h
i
j
k
l
m
n
o
p
q
r
s
t
u
v
w
x
y
z

I want to see (C) your licen**C**e (licen**c**e)    SPELLING NOTE

# D d

 **TIP** Words that sound as if they should start with *di* are often spelt with *de* instead, for example *determination* and *dessert*.

**dab** dabs dabbing dabbed
VERB **1** If you dab something, you touch it with quick light strokes *E.G. He dabbed some disinfectant on to the gash.* ▸ NOUN **2** a small amount of something that is put on a surface *E.G. a dab of perfume.*

**dabble** dabbles dabbling dabbled
VERB If you dabble in something, you work or play at it without being seriously involved in it *E.G. All his life he dabbled in poetry.*

**dachshund** dachshunds
*Said* "**dake**-hoond" NOUN a small dog with a long body and very short legs. 🔲 a German word meaning 'badger-dog'

**dad** or **daddy** dads or daddies
NOUN; *INFORMAL* Your dad or your daddy is your father.

**daddy-long-legs**
NOUN a harmless flying insect with very long legs.

**daffodil** daffodils
NOUN a plant with a yellow trumpet-shaped flower.

**daft** dafter daftest
ADJECTIVE stupid and not sensible. 🔲 from Old English *gedæfte* meaning 'gentle'

**dagga**
NOUN; *INFORMAL* In South African English, dagga is cannabis.

**dagger** daggers
NOUN a weapon like a short knife.

**dahlia** dahlias
*Said* "**dale**-ya" NOUN a type of brightly coloured garden flower.

**daily**
ADJECTIVE **1** occurring every day *E.G. our daily visit to the gym.* **2** of or relating to a single day or to one day at a time *E.G. the average daily wage.*

**dainty** daintier daintiest
ADJECTIVE very delicate and pretty.
**daintily** ADVERB

**dairy** dairies
NOUN **1** a shop or company that supplies milk and milk products. **2** In New Zealand, a small shop selling groceries, often outside of usual opening hours. ▸ ADJECTIVE **3** Dairy products are foods made from milk, such as butter, cheese, cream, and yogurt. **4** A dairy farm is one which keeps cattle to produce milk
☑ Do not confuse the order of the vowels in *dairy* and *diary.*

**dais**
*Said* "**day**-is" NOUN a raised platform, normally at one end of a hall and used by a speaker.

**daisy** daisies
NOUN a small wild flower with a yellow centre and small white petals. 🔲 from Old English *dæges eage* meaning 'day's eye', because the daisy opens in the daytime and closes at night

**dale** dales
NOUN a valley.

**dalmatian** dalmatians
NOUN a large dog with short smooth white hair and black or brown spots.

**dam** dams
NOUN a barrier built across a river to hold back water.

A B C **D** E F G H I J K L M N O P Q R S T U V W X Y Z

**damage** damages damaging damaged
VERB **1** To damage something means to harm or spoil it. ▶ NOUN **2** Damage to something is injury or harm done to it. **3** Damages is the money awarded by a court to compensate someone for loss or harm.
**damaging** ADJECTIVE

**dame** dames
NOUN the title given to a woman who has been awarded the OBE or one of the other British orders of chivalry.

**damn** damns damning damned
Said "*dam*" VERB **1** To damn something or someone means to curse or condemn them. ▶ INTERJECTION **2** 'Damn' is a swearword.
**damned** ADJECTIVE

**damnation**
Said "*dam-**nay**-shun*" NOUN Damnation is eternal punishment in Hell after death.

**damp** damper dampest
ADJECTIVE **1** slightly wet. ▶ NOUN **2** Damp is slight wetness, especially in the air or in the walls of a building.
**dampness** NOUN
🔲 from Old German *damp* meaning 'steam'

**dampen** dampens dampening dampened
VERB **1** If you dampen something, you make it slightly wet. **2** To dampen something also means to reduce its liveliness or strength E.G. *The whole episode has rather dampened my enthusiasm.*

**damper**
AN INFORMAL PHRASE To **put a damper on** something means to stop it being enjoyable.

**damson** damsons
NOUN a small blue-black plum; also the tree that the fruit grows on.
🔲 from Latin *prunum Damascenum* meaning 'Damascus plum'

**dance** dances dancing danced
VERB **1** To dance means to move your feet and body rhythmically in time to music. ▶ NOUN **2** a series of rhythmic movements or steps in time to music. **3** a social event where people dance with each other.
**dancer** NOUN **dancing** NOUN

**dandelion** dandelions
NOUN a wild plant with yellow flowers which form a ball of fluffy seeds.

**dandruff**
NOUN Dandruff is small, loose scales of dead skin in someone's hair.

**D and T**
NOUN an abbreviation for 'Design and Technology'.

**dandy** dandies
NOUN; OLD-FASHIONED a man who always dresses in very smart clothes.

**Dane** Danes
NOUN someone who comes from Denmark.

**danger** dangers
NOUN **1** Danger is the possibility that someone may be harmed or killed. **2** something or someone that can hurt or harm you.
▦ (sense 1) hazard, peril, risk

**dangerous**
ADJECTIVE able to or likely to cause hurt or harm.
**dangerously** ADVERB
▦ hazardous, perilous, unsafe

**dangle** dangles dangling dangled
VERB When something dangles or when you dangle it, it swings or hangs loosely.

**Danish**
ADJECTIVE **1** belonging or relating to

a b c d e f g h i j k l m n o p q r s t u v w x y z

Denmark. ► NOUN 2 Danish is the main language spoken in Denmark.

**dank** danker dankest
ADJECTIVE A dank place is damp and chilly.

**dapper**
ADJECTIVE slim and neatly dressed.
📖 from Old Dutch *dapper* meaning 'active' or 'nimble'

**dappled**
ADJECTIVE marked with patches of a different or darker shade.

**dare** dares daring dared
VERB 1 To dare someone means to challenge them to do something in order to prove their courage. 2 To dare to do something means to have the courage to do it. ► NOUN 3 a challenge to do something dangerous.
☑ When *dare* is used in a question or with a negative, it does not add an s: *dare she come?*; *he dare not come*.

**daredevil** daredevils
NOUN a person who enjoys doing dangerous things.

**dark** darker darkest
ADJECTIVE 1 If it is dark, there is not enough light to see properly. 2 Dark colours or surfaces reflect little light and so look deep-coloured or dull. 3 'Dark' is also used to describe thoughts or ideas which are sinister or unpleasant. ► NOUN 4 The dark is the lack of light in a place.

**darkly** ADVERB **darkness** NOUN
🟰 (sense 1) dim, murky

**darken** darkens darkening darkened
VERB If something darkens, or if you darken it, it becomes darker than it was.

**darkroom** darkrooms
NOUN a room from which daylight is shut out so that photographic film can be developed.

**darling** darlings
NOUN 1 Someone who is lovable or a favourite may be called a darling.
► ADJECTIVE 2 much admired or loved
E.G. *his darling daughter*.

**darn** darns darning darned
VERB 1 To darn a hole in a garment means to mend it with crossing stitches. ► NOUN 2 a part of a garment that has been darned.

**dart** darts darting darted
NOUN 1 a small pointed arrow. 2 Darts is a game in which the players throw darts at a round board divided into numbered sections. ► VERB 3 To dart about means to move quickly and suddenly from one place to another.

**dash** dashes dashing dashed
VERB 1 To dash somewhere means to rush there. 2 If something is dashed against something else, it strikes it or is thrown violently against it. 3 If hopes or ambitions are dashed, they are ruined or frustrated. ► NOUN 4 a sudden movement or rush. 5 a small quantity of something. 6 the punctuation mark (–) which shows a change of subject, or which may be used instead of brackets.

---

### What does the Dash do?

The **dash** (–) marks an abrupt change in the flow of a sentence, either showing a sudden change of subject, or marking off extra information. The dash can also show that a speech has been cut off suddenly:

E.G. *I'm not sure – what was the question again?*
*"Go ahead and –" He broke off as Robbie seized his arm.*

**dashboard** dashboards
NOUN the instrument panel in a motor vehicle.

**dashing**
ADJECTIVE A dashing man is stylish and confident E.G. *He was a dashing figure in his younger days.*

**dasyure** dasyures
*Said* "**dass-ee-your**" NOUN a small marsupial that lives in Australia and eats meat.

**data**
NOUN **1** information, usually in the form of facts or statistics. **2** ICT any information put into a computer and which the computer works on or processes.
🏛 from Latin *data* meaning 'things given'
☑ *Data* is really a plural word, but it is usually used as a singular.

**database** databases
NOUN ICT a collection of information stored in a computer.

**date** dates dating dated
NOUN **1** a particular day or year that can be named. **2** If you have a date, you have an appointment to meet someone; also used to refer to the person you are meeting. **3** a small dark-brown sticky fruit with a stone inside, which grows on palm trees. ▶ VERB **4** If you are dating someone, you have a romantic relationship with them. **5** If you date something, you find out the time when it began or was made. **6** If something dates from a particular time, that is when it happened or was made. ▶ PHRASE **7** If something is **out of date**, it is old-fashioned or no longer valid.

**datum**
the singular form of **data**.

**daub** daubs daubing daubed
VERB If you daub something such as mud or paint on a surface, you smear it there.

**daughter** daughters
NOUN Someone's daughter is their female child.

**daughter-in-law** daughters-in-law
NOUN Someone's daughter-in-law is the wife of their son.

**daunt** daunts daunting daunted
VERB If something daunts you, you feel worried about whether you can succeed in doing it E.G. *He was not the type of man to be daunted by adversity.*

**daunting** ADJECTIVE

**dawn** dawns dawning dawned
NOUN **1** the time in the morning when light first appears in the sky. **2** the beginning of something E.G. *the dawn of the radio age.* ▶ VERB **3** If day is dawning, morning light is beginning to appear. **4** If an idea or fact dawns on you, you realize it.

**day** days
NOUN **1** one of the seven 24-hour periods of time in a week, measured from one midnight to the next. **2** Day is the period of light between sunrise and sunset. **3** You can refer to a particular day or days meaning a particular period in history E.G. *in Gladstone's day.*

**daybreak**
NOUN Daybreak is the time in the morning when light first appears in the sky.

**daydream** daydreams daydreaming daydreamed
NOUN **1** a series of pleasant thoughts about things that you would like to

a
b
c
**d**
e
f
g
h
i
j
k
l
m
n
o
p
q
r
s
t
u
v
w
x
y
z

I went to see (C) the doctor's new practiCe (practice)     **SPELLING NOTE**

A
B
C
D
E
F
G
H
I
J
K
L
M
N
O
P
Q
R
S
T
U
V
W
X
Y
Z

happen. ► VERB 2 When you daydream, you drift off into a daydream.

**daylight**

NOUN 1 Daylight is the period during the day when it is light. 2 Daylight is also the light from the sun.

**day-to-day**

ADJECTIVE happening every day as part of ordinary routine life.

**day trip day trips**

NOUN a journey for pleasure to a place and back again on the same day.

**daze**

PHRASE If you are **in a daze**, you are confused and bewildered.

**dazed**

ADJECTIVE If you are dazed, you are stunned and unable to think clearly.

**dazzle dazzles dazzling dazzled**

VERB 1 If someone or something dazzles you, you are very impressed by their brilliance. 2 If a bright light dazzles you, it blinds you for a moment.

**dazzling** ADJECTIVE

**de-**

PREFIX When de- is added to a noun or verb, it changes the meaning to its opposite E.G. de-ice.

**deacon deacons**

NOUN 1 In the Church of England or Roman Catholic Church, a deacon is a member of the clergy below the rank of priest. 2 In some other churches, a deacon is a church official appointed to help the minister.

**deaconess** NOUN

**dead**

ADJECTIVE 1 no longer living or supporting life. 2 no longer used or no longer functioning E.G. a dead

language. 3 If part of your body goes dead, it loses sensation and feels numb. ► NOUN 4 the middle part of night or winter, when it is most quiet and at its darkest or coldest.

**dead end dead ends**

NOUN a street that is closed off at one end.

**deadline deadlines**

NOUN a time or date before which something must be completed.

**deadlock deadlocks**

NOUN a situation in which neither side in a dispute is willing to give in.
■ impasse, stalemate

**deadly deadlier deadliest**

ADJECTIVE 1 likely or able to cause death. ► ADVERB OR ADJECTIVE 2 'Deadly' is used to emphasize how serious or unpleasant a situation is E.G. He is deadly serious about his comeback.

**deadpan**

ADJECTIVE OR ADVERB showing no emotion or expression.

**deaf deafer deafest**

ADJECTIVE 1 partially or totally unable to hear. 2 refusing to listen or pay attention to something E.G. He was deaf to all pleas for financial help.

**deafness** NOUN

**deafening**

ADJECTIVE If a noise is deafening, it is so loud that you cannot hear anything else.

**deal deals dealing dealt**

NOUN 1 an agreement or arrangement, especially in business. ► VERB 2 If you deal with something, you do what is necessary to sort it out E.G. He must learn to deal with stress. 3 If you deal in a particular type of goods, you buy and sell those goods. 4 If you deal someone or something a blow, you hurt or harm them *E.G. Competition from abroad dealt a heavy blow to the industry.*

**dealer** dealers
NOUN a person or firm whose business involves buying or selling things.

**dealings**
PLURAL NOUN Your dealings with people are the relations you have with them or the business you do with them.

**dean** deans
NOUN **1** In a university or college, a dean is a person responsible for administration or for the welfare of students. **2** In the Church of England, a dean is a clergyman who is responsible for administration.
🏛 from Latin *decanus* meaning 'someone in charge of ten people'

**dear** dears; dearer dearest
NOUN **1** 'Dear' is used as a sign of affection *E.G. What's the matter, dear?* ▶ ADJECTIVE **2** much loved *E.G. my dear son.* **3** Something that is dear is very expensive. **4** You use 'dear' at the beginning of a letter before the name of the person you are writing to.
**dearly** ADVERB
▣ (sense 2) beloved, cherished
▣ (sense 3) costly, expensive

**dearth**
*Said "derth"* NOUN a shortage of something.

**death** deaths
NOUN Death is the end of the life of a person or animal.

**debacle** debacles
*Said "day-bah-kl"* NOUN; FORMAL a sudden disastrous failure.

**debase** debases debasing debased
VERB To debase something means to reduce its value or quality.

**debatable**
ADJECTIVE not absolutely certain *E.G. The justness of these wars is debatable.*
▣ doubtful, questionable

**debate** debates debating debated
NOUN **1** Debate is argument or discussion *E.G. There is much debate as to what causes depression.* **2** a formal discussion in which opposing views are expressed. ▶ VERB **3** When people debate something, they discuss it in a fairly formal manner. **4** If you are debating whether or not to do something, you are considering it *E.G. He was debating whether or not he should tell her.*

**debilitating**
ADJECTIVE; FORMAL If something is debilitating, it makes you very weak *E.G. a debilitating illness.*

**debit** debits debiting debited
VERB **1** to take money from a person's bank account. ▶ NOUN **2** a record of the money that has been taken out of a person's bank account.

**debrief** debriefs debriefing debriefed
VERB When someone is debriefed, they are asked to give a report on a task they have just completed.
**debriefing** NOUN

**debris**
*Said "day-bree"* NOUN Debris is fragments or rubble left after something has been destroyed.
🏛 from Old French *débrisier* meaning 'to shatter'

A
B
C
**D**
E
F
G
H
I
J
K
L
M
N
O
P
Q
R
S
T
U
V
W
X
Y
Z

**debt** debts
*Said* "**det**" NOUN **1** a sum of money that is owed to one person by another. **2** Debt is the state of owing money.

**debtor** debtors
NOUN a person who owes money.

**debut** debuts
*Said* "**day**-*byoo*" NOUN a performer's first public appearance.

**debutante** debutantes
*Said* "**deb**-*yoo*-*tant*" NOUN; OLD-FASHIONED a girl from the upper classes who has started going to social events.

**dec-** or **deca-**
PREFIX Words beginning with 'dec-' or 'deca-' have 'ten' in their meaning E.G. *decathlon*.
📖 from Greek *deka* meaning 'ten'

**decade** decades
NOUN a period of ten years.

**decadence**
NOUN Decadence is a decline in standards of morality and behaviour.
**decadent** ADJECTIVE

**decaffeinated**
*Said* "*dee*-**kaf**-*in*-*ate*-*ed*" ADJECTIVE
Decaffeinated coffee or tea has had most of the caffeine removed.

**decanter** decanters
NOUN a glass bottle with a stopper, from which wine and other drinks are served.

**decapitate** decapitates decapitating decapitated
VERB To decapitate someone means to cut off their head.

**decathlon** decathlons
*Said* "*de*-**cath**-*lon*" NOUN a sports contest in which athletes compete in ten different events.
📖 from Greek *deka* meaning 'ten' and *athlon* meaning 'contest'

**decay** decays decaying decayed
VERB **1** When things decay, they rot or go bad. ▶ NOUN **2** Decay is the process of decaying.

**deceased** FORMAL
ADJECTIVE **1** A deceased person is someone who has recently died.
▶ NOUN **2** The deceased is someone who has recently died.

**deceit**
NOUN Deceit is behaviour that is intended to mislead people into believing something that is not true.
**deceitful** ADJECTIVE

**deceive** deceives deceiving deceived
VERB If you deceive someone, you make them believe something that is not true.

**decelerate** decelerates decelerating decelerated
VERB If something decelerates, it slows down.
**deceleration** NOUN

**December**
NOUN December is the twelfth and last month of the year. It has 31 days.
📖 from Latin *December* meaning 'the tenth month'

**decency**
NOUN **1** Decency is behaviour that is respectable and follows accepted moral standards. **2** Decency is also behaviour which shows kindness and respect towards people E.G. *No one had the decency to tell me to my face.*

**decent**
ADJECTIVE **1** of an acceptable standard or quality E.G. *He gets a decent pension.* **2** Decent people are honest and respectable E.G. *a decent man.*
**decently** ADVERB

■ (sense 2) respectable

**decentralize** decentralizes decentralizing decentralized; also spelt **decentralise**

VERB To decentralize an organization means to reorganize it so that power is transferred from one main administrative centre to smaller local units.

**decentralization** NOUN

**deception** deceptions

NOUN **1** something that is intended to trick or deceive someone.
**2** Deception is the act of deceiving someone.

**deceptive**

ADJECTIVE likely to make people believe something that is not true.

**deceptively** ADVERB

■ false, misleading

**decibel** decibels

NOUN a unit of the intensity of sound.

**decide** decides deciding decided

VERB If you decide to do something, you choose to do it.

■ make up one's mind, reach *or* come to a decision

**deciduous**

ADJECTIVE Deciduous trees lose their leaves in the autumn every year.

**decimal** decimals

ADJECTIVE (MATHS) **1** The decimal system expresses numbers using all the digits from 0 to 9. ► NOUN **2** a fraction in which a dot called a decimal point is followed by numbers representing tenths, hundredths, and thousandths. For example, 0.5 represents $^5/_{10}$ (or $^1/_2$); 0.05 represents $^5/_{100}$ (or $^1/_{20}$).

🏛 from Latin *decima* meaning 'a tenth'

**decimate** decimates decimating decimated

VERB To decimate a group of people or animals means to kill or destroy a large number of them.

**decipher** deciphers deciphering deciphered

VERB If you decipher a piece of writing or a message, you work out its meaning.

**decision** decisions

NOUN a choice or judgment that is made about something *E.G. The editor's decision is final.*

■ judgment, resolution

**decisive**

*Said* "dis-**sigh**-siv" ADJECTIVE **1** having great influence on the result of something *E.G. It was the decisive moment of the race.* **2** A decisive person is able to make decisions firmly and quickly.

**decisively** ADVERB **decisiveness** NOUN

**deck** decks

NOUN **1** a floor or platform built into a ship, or one of the two floors on a bus. **2** a pack of cards.

**deck chair** deck chairs

NOUN a light folding chair, made from canvas and wood and used outdoors.

**declaration** declarations

NOUN a firm, forceful statement, often an official announcement *E.G. a declaration of war.*

■ assertion, statement

**declare** declares declaring declared

VERB **1** If you declare something, you say it firmly and forcefully *E.G. He declared early he was going to be famous.* **2** To declare something means to announce it officially or formally *E.G. Catholicism was declared*

a
b
c
**d**
e
f
g
h
i
j
k
l
m
n
o
p
q
r
s
t
u
v
w
x
y
z

A
B
C
**D**
E
F
G
H
I
J
K
L
M
N
O
P
Q
R
S
T
U
V
W
X
Y
Z

the state religion. **3** If you declare goods or earnings, you state what you have bought or earned, in order to pay tax or duty.

■ (sense 1) announce, proclaim, state

**decline** declines declining declined

VERB **1** If something declines, it becomes smaller or weaker. **2** If you decline something, you politely refuse to accept it or do it. ▶ NOUN **3** a gradual weakening or decrease *E.G. a decline in the birth rate.*

**decode** decodes decoding decoded

VERB If you decode a coded message, you convert it into ordinary language.

**decompose** decomposes decomposing decomposed

VERB If something decomposes, it decays through chemical or bacterial action.

**decor**

*Said "day-kor"* NOUN The decor of a room or house is the style in which it is decorated and furnished.

**decorate** decorates decorating decorated

VERB **1** If you decorate something, you make it more attractive by adding some ornament or colour to it. **2** If you decorate a room or building, you paint or wallpaper it.

■ (sense 1) adorn, ornament

**decoration** decorations

NOUN **1** Decorations are features added to something to make it more attractive. **2** The decoration in a building or room is the style of the furniture and wallpaper.

**decorative**

ADJECTIVE intended to look attractive.

**decorator** decorators

NOUN a person whose job is painting and putting up wallpaper in rooms and buildings.

**decorum**

*Said "dik-ore-um"* NOUN; *FORMAL*
Decorum is polite and correct behaviour.

**decoy** decoys

NOUN a person or object that is used to lead someone or something into danger.

**decrease** decreases decreasing decreased

VERB **1** If something decreases or if you decrease it, it becomes less in quantity or size. ▶ NOUN **2** a lessening in the amount of something; also the amount by which something becomes less.

**decreasing** ADJECTIVE

**decree** decrees decreeing decreed

VERB **1** If someone decrees something, they state formally that it will happen. ▶ NOUN **2** an official decision or order, usually by governments or rulers.

**dedicate** dedicates dedicating dedicated

VERB If you dedicate yourself to something, you devote your time and energy to it.

**dedication** NOUN

■ commit, devote

**deduce** deduces deducing deduced

VERB If you deduce something, you work it out from other facts that you know are true.

■ conclude, reason

**deduct** deducts deducting deducted

VERB To deduct an amount from a

total amount means to subtract it from the total.

**deduction** deductions

NOUN **1** an amount which is taken away from a total. **2** a conclusion that you have reached because of other things that you know are true.

**deed** deeds

NOUN **1** something that is done. **2** a legal document, especially concerning the ownership of land or buildings.

**deem** deems deeming deemed

VERB; *FORMAL* If you deem something to be true, you judge or consider it to be true E.G. *His ideas were deemed unacceptable.*

**deep** deeper deepest

ADJECTIVE **1** situated or extending a long way down from the top surface of something, or a long way inwards E.G. *a deep hole.* **2** great or intense E.G. *deep suspicion.* **3** low in pitch E.G. *a deep voice.* **4** strong and fairly dark in colour E.G. *The wine was deep ruby in colour.*

**deeply** ADVERB

**deepen** deepens deepening deepened

VERB If something deepens or is deepened, it becomes deeper or more intense.

**deer**

NOUN a large, hoofed mammal that lives wild in parts of Britain.
🔲 from Old English *deor* meaning 'beast'

**deface** defaces defacing defaced

VERB If you deface a wall or notice, you spoil it by writing or drawing on it E.G. *She spitefully defaced her sister's poster.*

**default** defaults defaulting defaulted

VERB **1** If someone defaults on something they have legally agreed to do, they fail to do it E.G. *He defaulted on repayment of the loan.*
▶ PHRASE **2** If something happens **by default**, it happens because something else which might have prevented it has failed to happen.

**defeat** defeats defeating defeated

VERB **1** If you defeat someone or something, you win a victory over them, or cause them to fail. ▶ NOUN **2** Defeat is the state of being beaten or of failing E.G. *He was gracious in defeat.* **3** an occasion on which someone is beaten or fails to achieve something E.G. *It was a crushing defeat for the government.*

**defecate** defecates defecating defecated

VERB To defecate means to get rid of waste matter from the bowels through the anus.

**defect** defects defecting defected

NOUN **1** a fault or flaw in something.
▶ VERB **2** If someone defects, they leave their own country or organization and join an opposing one.

**defection** NOUN

**defective**

ADJECTIVE imperfect or faulty E.G. *defective eyesight.*

**defence** defences

NOUN **1** Defence is action that is taken to protect someone or something from attack. **2** any arguments used in support of something that has been criticized or questioned. **3** the case

a
b
c
**d**
e
f
g
h
i
j
k
l
m
n
o
p
q
r
s
t
u
v
w
x
y
z

A B C **D** E F G H I J K L M N O P Q R S T U V W X Y Z

presented, in a court of law, by a lawyer for the person on trial; also the person on trial and his or her lawyers. 4 (HISTORY) A country's defences are its military resources, such as its armed forces and weapons.

**defend** defends defending defended
VERB 1 To defend someone or something means to protect them from harm or danger. 2 If you defend a person or their ideas and beliefs, you argue in support of them. 3 To defend someone in court means to represent them and argue their case for them. 4 In a game such as football or hockey, to defend means to try to prevent goals being scored by your opponents.
**defender** NOUN

**defendant** defendants
NOUN a person who has been accused of a crime in a court of law.

**defensible**
ADJECTIVE able to be defended against criticism or attack.

**defensive**
ADJECTIVE 1 intended or designed for protection E.G. defensive weapons.
2 Someone who is defensive feels unsure and threatened by other people's opinions and attitudes E.G. Don't get defensive, I was only joking about your cooking.
**defensively** ADVERB **defensiveness** NOUN

**defer** defers deferring deferred
VERB 1 If you defer something, you delay or postpone it until a future time. 2 If you defer to someone, you agree with them or do what they want because you respect them.

**deference**
Said "def-er-ense" NOUN Deference is polite and respectful behaviour.
**deferential** ADJECTIVE

**defiance**
NOUN Defiance is behaviour which shows that you are not willing to obey or behave in the expected way E.G. a gesture of defiance.
**defiant** ADJECTIVE **defiantly** ADVERB

**deficiency** deficiencies
NOUN a lack of something E.G. vitamin deficiency.
**deficient** ADJECTIVE

**deficit** deficits
Said "def-iss-it" NOUN the amount by which money received by an organization is less than money spent.

**define** defines defining defined
VERB (EXAM TERM) If you define something, you say clearly what it is or what it means E.G. Culture can be defined in hundreds of ways.

**definite**
ADJECTIVE 1 firm and unlikely to be changed E.G. The answer is a definite 'yes'. 2 certain or true rather than guessed or imagined E.G. definite proof.
**definitely** ADVERB

**definition** definitions
NOUN a statement explaining the meaning of a word or idea.

**definitive**
ADJECTIVE 1 final and unable to be questioned or altered E.G. a definitive answer. 2 most complete, or the best of its kind E.G. a definitive history of science fiction.
**definitively** ADVERB

**deflate** deflates deflating deflated
VERB 1 If you deflate something such

as a tyre or balloon, you let out all the air or gas in it. **2** If you deflate someone, you make them seem less important.

**deflect** deflects deflecting deflected
VERB To deflect something means to turn it aside or make it change direction.
**deflection** NOUN

**deforestation**
NOUN Deforestation is the cutting down of all the trees in an area.

**deformed**
ADJECTIVE disfigured or abnormally shaped.

**defraud** defrauds defrauding defrauded
VERB If someone defrauds you, they cheat you out of something that should be yours.

**defrost** defrosts defrosting defrosted
VERB **1** If you defrost a freezer or refrigerator, you remove the ice from it. **2** If you defrost frozen food, you let it thaw out.

**deft** defter deftest
ADJECTIVE Someone who is deft is quick and skilful in their movements.
**deftly** ADVERB

**defunct**
ADJECTIVE no longer existing or functioning.

**defuse** defuses defusing defused
VERB **1** To defuse a dangerous or tense situation means to make it less dangerous or tense. **2** To defuse a bomb means to remove its fuse or detonator so that it cannot explode.

**defy** defies defying defied
VERB **1** If you defy a person or a law,

you openly refuse to obey. **2** FORMAL If you defy someone to do something that you think is impossible, you challenge them to do it.
**≡** (sense 1) disregard, flout, resist

**degenerate** degenerates degenerating degenerated
VERB **1** If something degenerates, it becomes worse E.G. *The election campaign degenerated into farce.*
▸ ADJECTIVE **2** having low standards of morality. ▸ NOUN **3** someone whose standards of morality are so low that people find their behaviour shocking or disgusting.
**degeneration** NOUN

**degradation**
NOUN Degradation is a state of poverty and misery.

**degrade** degrades degrading degraded
VERB If something degrades people, it humiliates them and makes them feel that they are not respected.
**degrading** ADJECTIVE
**≡** debase, demean

**degree** degrees
NOUN **1** an amount of a feeling or quality E.G. *a degree of pain.* **2** a unit of measurement of temperature; often written as ° after a number E.G. *20°C.* **3** (MATHS) a unit of measurement of angles in mathematics, and of latitude and longitude E.G. *The yacht was 20° off course.* **4** a course of study at a university or college; also the qualification awarded after passing the course.

**dehydrated**
ADJECTIVE If someone is dehydrated, they are weak or ill because they have lost too much water from their body.

a
b
c
**d**
e
f
g
h
i
j
k
l
m
n
o
p
q
r
s
t
u
v
w
x
y
z

**deign** deigns deigning deigned
*Said "dane"* VERB; FORMAL If you deign to do something, you do it even though you think you are too important to do such a thing.

**deity** deities
NOUN a god or goddess.

**deja vu**
*Said "day-ja voo"* NOUN Deja vu is the feeling that you have already experienced in the past exactly the same sequence of events as is happening now.
📖 from French *déjà vu* meaning literally 'already seen'

**dejected**
ADJECTIVE miserable and unhappy.
**dejection** NOUN

**delay** delays delaying delayed
VERB 1 If you delay doing something, you put it off until a later time. 2 If something delays you, it hinders you or slows you down. ▶ NOUN 3 Delay is time during which something is delayed.
▣ (sense 1) postpone, put off

**delectable**
ADJECTIVE very pleasing or delightful.

**delegate** delegates delegating delegated
NOUN 1 a person appointed to vote or to make decisions on behalf of a group of people. ▶ VERB 2 If you delegate duties, you give them to someone who can then act on your behalf.

**delegation** delegations
NOUN 1 a group of people chosen to represent a larger group of people. 2 Delegation is the giving of duties, responsibilities, or power to someone who can then act on your behalf.

**delete** deletes deleting deleted
VERB ( ICT ) To delete something means to cross it out or remove it E.G. *He had deleted the computer file by mistake.*
**deletion** NOUN

**deliberate** deliberates deliberating deliberated
ADJECTIVE 1 done on purpose or planned in advance E.G. *It was a deliberate insult.* 2 careful and not hurried in speech and action E.G. *She was very deliberate in her movements.*
▶ VERB 3 If you deliberate about something, you think about it seriously and carefully.
**deliberately** ADVERB
▣ (sense 1) intentional, planned

**deliberation** deliberations
NOUN Deliberation is careful consideration of a subject.

**delicacy** delicacies
NOUN 1 Delicacy is grace and attractiveness. 2 Something said or done with delicacy is said or done tactfully so that nobody is offended. 3 Delicacies are rare or expensive foods that are considered especially nice to eat.

**delicate**
ADJECTIVE 1 fine, graceful, or subtle in character E.G. *a delicate fragrance.* 2 fragile and needing to be handled carefully E.G. *delicate antique lace.* 3 precise or sensitive, and able to notice very small changes E.G. *a delicate instrument.*
**delicately** ADVERB

**delicatessen** delicatessens
NOUN a shop selling unusual or imported foods.
📖 from German *Delikatessen* meaning 'delicacies'

SPELLING NOTE  Eddy Ant thinks mEAt is a grEAt trEAt to EAt (-ea-)

223

## delicious >> demeanour

**delicious**
ADJECTIVE very pleasing, especially to taste.
**deliciously** ADVERB
■ delectable, scrumptious

**delight** delights delighting delighted
NOUN 1 Delight is great pleasure or joy. ▶ VERB 2 If something delights you or if you are delighted by it, it gives you a lot of pleasure.
**delighted** ADJECTIVE

**delightful**
ADJECTIVE very pleasant and attractive.

**delinquent** delinquents
NOUN a young person who commits minor crimes.
**delinquency** NOUN

**delirious**
ADJECTIVE 1 unable to speak or act in a rational way because of illness or fever. 2 wildly excited and happy.
**deliriously** ADVERB

**deliver** delivers delivering delivered
VERB 1 If you deliver something to someone, you take it to them and give them it. 2 To deliver a lecture or speech means to give it.

**delivery** deliveries
NOUN 1 Delivery or a delivery is the bringing of letters or goods to a person or firm. 2 Someone's delivery is the way in which they give a speech.

**dell** dells
NOUN; LITERARY a small wooded valley.

**delta** deltas
NOUN a low, flat area at the mouth of a river where the river has split into several branches to enter the sea.

**delude** deludes deluding deluded
VERB To delude people means to

deceive them into believing something that is not true.

**deluge** deluges deluging deluged
NOUN 1 a sudden, heavy downpour of rain. ▶ VERB 2 To be deluged with things means to be overwhelmed by a great number of them.

**delusion** delusions
NOUN a mistaken or misleading belief or idea.

**de luxe**
Said "de luks" ADJECTIVE rich, luxurious, or of superior quality.
🏛 from French de luxe meaning literally 'of luxury'

**delve** delves delving delved
VERB If you delve into something, you seek out more information about it.

**demand** demands demanding demanded
VERB 1 If you demand something, you ask for it forcefully and urgently. 2 If a job or situation demands a particular quality, it needs it. E.G. This situation demands hard work. ▶ NOUN 3 a forceful request for something. 4 If there is a demand for something, a lot of people want to buy it or have it
☑ The verb demand is either followed by of or from: at least one important decision was demanded of me; he had demanded an explanation from Daphne.

**demean** demeans demeaning demeaned
VERB If you demean yourself, you do something which makes people have less respect for you.
**demeaning** ADJECTIVE

**demeanour**
NOUN Your demeanour is the way you behave and the impression that this creates.

a b c **d** e f g h i j k l m n o p q r s t u v w x y z

Elaine and Emily shout EE when they mEEt to grEEt each other (-ee-)   SPELLING NOTE

**demented**
ADJECTIVE Someone who is demented behaves in a wild or violent way.

**dementia**
*Said "dee-men-sha"* NOUN; MEDICAL Dementia is a serious illness of the mind.

**demi-**
PREFIX Demi- means half.

**demise**
*Said "dee-myz"* NOUN; FORMAL Someone's demise is their death.

**demo** demos
NOUN; INFORMAL a demonstration.

**democracy** democracies
NOUN Democracy is a system of government in which the people choose their leaders by voting for them in elections.

**democrat** democrats
NOUN a person who believes in democracy, personal freedom, and equality.

**democratic**
ADJECTIVE having representatives elected by the people.

**democratically** ADVERB
🔲 from Greek *dēmos* meaning 'the people' and *kratos* meaning 'power'

**demography**
NOUN Demography is the study of the changes in the size and structure of populations.

**demographic** ADJECTIVE

**demolish** demolishes demolishing demolished
VERB To demolish a building means to pull it down or break it up.

**demolition** NOUN

**demon** demons
NOUN 1 an evil spirit or devil. ▶ ADJECTIVE 2 skilful, keen, and energetic E.G. a

*demon squash player.*

**demonic** ADJECTIVE

**demonstrate** demonstrates demonstrating demonstrated
VERB 1 (EXAM TERM) To demonstrate a fact or theory means to prove or show it to be true. 2 If you demonstrate something to somebody, you show and explain it by using or doing the thing itself E.G. *She demonstrated how to apply the make-up.* 3 If people demonstrate, they take part in a march or rally to show their opposition or support for something.

**demonstration** demonstrations
NOUN 1 a talk or explanation to show how to do or use something. 2 Demonstration is proof that something exists or is true. 3 a public march or rally in support of or opposition to something.

**demonstrator** NOUN

**demote** demotes demoting demoted
VERB A person who is demoted is put in a lower rank or position, often as a punishment.

**demotion** NOUN

**demure**
ADJECTIVE Someone who is demure is quiet, shy, and behaves very modestly.

**demurely** ADVERB

**den** dens
NOUN 1 the home of some wild animals such as lions or foxes. 2 a secret place where people meet.

**denial** denials
NOUN 1 A denial of something is a statement that it is untrue E.G. *He published a firm denial of the report.* 2 The denial of a request or

something to which you have a right is the refusal of it *E.G. the denial of human rights.*

**denigrate** denigrates denigrating denigrated

VERB; FORMAL To denigrate someone or something means to criticize them in order to damage their reputation.

**denim** denims

NOUN 1 Denim is strong cotton cloth, used for making clothes. ▶ PLURAL NOUN 2 Denims are jeans made from denim.

🔲 from French *serge de Nîmes*, meaning 'serge (a type of cloth) from Nîmes'

**denomination** denominations

NOUN 1 a particular group which has slightly different religious beliefs from other groups within the same faith. 2 a unit in a system of weights, values, or measures *E.G. a high denomination note.*

**denominator** denominators

NOUN (MATHS) In maths, the denominator is the bottom part of a fraction.

**denote** denotes denoting denoted

VERB If one thing denotes another, it is a sign of it or it represents it *E.G. Formerly, a tan denoted wealth.*

**denounce** denounces denouncing denounced

VERB 1 If you denounce someone or something, you express very strong disapproval of them *E.G. He publicly denounced government nuclear policy.* 2 If you denounce someone, you give information against them *E.G. He was denounced as a dangerous agitator.*

**dense** denser densest

ADJECTIVE 1 thickly crowded or packed together *E.G. the dense crowd.* 2 difficult to see through *E.G. dense black smoke.*

**densely** ADVERB

**density** densities

NOUN the degree to which something is filled or occupied *E.G. a very high population density.*

**dent** dents denting dented

VERB 1 To dent something means to damage it by hitting it and making a hollow in its surface. ▶ NOUN 2 a hollow in the surface of something.

**dental**

ADJECTIVE relating to the teeth.

**dentist** dentists

NOUN a person who is qualified to treat people's teeth.

**dentistry**

NOUN Dentistry is the branch of medicine concerned with disorders of the teeth.

**dentures**

PLURAL NOUN Dentures are false teeth.

**denunciation** denunciations

NOUN A denunciation of someone or something is severe public criticism of them.

**deny** denies denying denied

VERB 1 If you deny something that has been said, you state that it is untrue. 2 If you deny that something is the case, you refuse to believe it *E.G. He denied the existence of God.* 3 If you deny someone something, you refuse to give it to them *E.G. They were denied permission to attend.*

▣ (sense 1) contradict, gainsay

**deodorant** deodorants

NOUN a substance or spray used to hide the smell of perspiration.

A
B
C
**D**
E
F
G
H
I
J
K
L
M
N
O
P
Q
R
S
T
U
V
W
X
Y
Z

**depart** departs departing departed

VERB When you depart, you leave.
**departure** NOUN

**department** departments

NOUN one of the sections into which an organization is divided *E.G. the marketing department.*
**departmental** ADJECTIVE

**depend** depends depending depended

VERB 1 If you depend on someone or something, you trust them and rely on them. 2 If one thing depends on another, it is influenced by it *E.G. Success depends on the quality of the workforce.*

■ (sense 1) count on, rely on, trust

**dependable**

ADJECTIVE reliable and trustworthy.

**dependant** dependants

NOUN (PSHE) someone who relies on another person for financial support.

**dependence**

NOUN Dependence is a constant need that someone has for something or someone in order to survive or operate properly *E.G. He was flattered by her dependence on him.*

**dependency** dependencies

NOUN 1 (PSHE) Dependency is relying on someone or something to give you what you need *E.G. drug dependency.* 2 a country or area controlled by another country.

**dependent**

ADJECTIVE reliant on someone or something.

**depict** depicts depicting depicted

VERB To depict someone or something means to represent them in painting or sculpture.

**deplete** depletes depleting depleted

VERB To deplete something means to reduce greatly the amount of it available.
**depletion** NOUN

**deplorable**

ADJECTIVE shocking or regrettable *E.G. deplorable conditions.*

**deplore** deplores deploring deplored

VERB If you deplore something, you condemn it because you feel it is wrong.

**deploy** deploys deploying deployed

VERB To deploy troops or resources means to organize or position them so that they can be used effectively.
**deployment** NOUN

**deport** deports deporting deported

VERB If a government deports someone, it sends them out of the country because they have committed a crime or because they do not have the right to be there.
**deportation** NOUN

**depose** deposes deposing deposed

VERB If someone is deposed, they are removed from a position of power.

**deposit** deposits depositing deposited

VERB 1 If you deposit something, you put it down or leave it somewhere. 2 If you deposit money or valuables, you put them somewhere for safekeeping. ▶ NOUN 3 a sum of money given in part payment for goods or services.

**depot** depots

*Said "dep-oh"* NOUN a place where

large supplies of materials or equipment may be stored.

**depraved**

ADJECTIVE morally bad.

**depress depresses depressing depressed**

VERB 1 If something depresses you, it makes you feel sad and gloomy. 2 If wages or prices are depressed, their value falls.

**depressive** ADJECTIVE

**depressant depressants**

NOUN a drug which reduces nervous activity and so has a calming effect.

**depressed**

ADJECTIVE 1 unhappy and gloomy. 2 A place that is depressed has little economic activity and therefore low incomes and high unemployment E.G. *depressed industrial areas.*

■ (sense 1) dejected, despondent, low-spirited

**depression depressions**

NOUN 1 a state of mind in which someone feels unhappy and has no energy or enthusiasm. 2 a time of industrial and economic decline.

**deprive deprives depriving deprived**

VERB If you deprive someone of something, you take it away or prevent them from having it.

**deprived** ADJECTIVE **deprivation** NOUN

**depth depths**

NOUN 1 The depth of something is the measurement or distance between its top and bottom, or between its front and back. 2 The depth of something such as emotion is its intensity E.G. *the depth of her hostility.*

**deputation deputations**

NOUN a small group of people sent to speak or act on behalf of others.

**deputy deputies**

NOUN Someone's deputy is a person appointed to act in their place.

**deranged**

ADJECTIVE mad, or behaving in a wild and uncontrolled way.

**derby derbies**

*Said "dar-bee"* NOUN A local derby is a sporting event between two teams from the same area.

**derelict**

ADJECTIVE abandoned and falling into ruins.

**deride derides deriding derided**

VERB To deride someone or something means to mock or jeer at them with contempt.

**derision**

NOUN Derision is an attitude of contempt or scorn towards something or someone.

**derivation derivations**

NOUN The derivation of something is its origin or source.

**derivative derivatives**

NOUN 1 something which has developed from an earlier source.

▶ ADJECTIVE 2 not original, but based on or copied from something else E.G. *The record was not deliberately derivative.*

**derive derives deriving derived**

VERB 1 FORMAL If you derive something from someone or something, you get it from them E.G. *He derived so much joy from music.* 2 If something derives from something else, it develops from it.

**derogatory**

ADJECTIVE critical and scornful E.G. *He*

a
b
c
**d**
e
f
g
h
i
j
k
l
m
n
o
p
q
r
s
t
u
v
w
x
y
z

LEt's measure the angLE (ang<u>le</u>)    SPELLING NOTE

A
B
C
**D**
E
F
G
H
I
J
K
L
M
N
O
P
Q
R
S
T
U
V
W
X
Y
Z

*made derogatory remarks about them.*

**descant** descants

NOUN The descant to a tune is another tune played at the same time and at a higher pitch.

**descend** descends descending descended

VERB 1 To descend means to move downwards. 2 If you descend on people or on a place, you arrive unexpectedly.

**descendant** descendants

NOUN A person's descendants are the people in later generations who are related to them.

**descended**

ADJECTIVE If you are descended from someone who lived in the past, your family originally derived from them.

**descent** descents

NOUN 1 a movement or slope from a higher to a lower position or level. 2 Your descent is your family's origins.

**describe** describes describing described

VERB To describe someone or something means to give an account or a picture of them in words.

**description** descriptions

NOUN an account or picture of something in words.

**descriptive** ADJECTIVE

**desert** deserts

*Said "**dez**-ert"* NOUN (GEOGRAPHY) a region of land with very little plant life, usually because of low rainfall.

**desert** deserts deserting deserted

*Said "**dez**-zert"* VERB To desert a person means to leave or abandon

them *E.G. His clients had deserted him.*

**desertion** NOUN

**deserter** deserters

NOUN someone who leaves the armed forces without permission.

**deserve** deserves deserving deserved

VERB If you deserve something, you are entitled to it or earn it because of your qualities, achievements, or actions *E.G. He deserved a rest.*

■ be worthy of, justify, merit

**deserving**

ADJECTIVE worthy of being helped, rewarded, or praised *E.G. a deserving charity.*

**design** designs designing designed (D & T)

VERB 1 To design something means to plan it, especially by preparing a detailed sketch or drawings from which it can be built or made. ▶ NOUN 2 a drawing or plan from which something can be built or made. 3 The design of something is its shape and style.

**designer** NOUN

**designate** designates designating designated

*Said "**dez**-ig-nate"* VERB 1 To designate someone or something means to formally label or name them *E.G. The room was designated a no smoking area.* 2 If you designate someone to do something, you appoint them to do it *E.G. He designated his son as his successor.*

**designation** designations

NOUN a name or title.

**designing**

ADJECTIVE crafty and cunning.

**desirable**
ADJECTIVE 1 worth having or doing E.G.
*a desirable job.* 2 sexually attractive.
**desirability** NOUN

**desire desires desiring desired**
VERB 1 If you desire something, you
want it very much. ▶ NOUN 2 a strong
feeling of wanting something.
3 Desire for someone is a strong
sexual attraction to them.
▣ (sense 1) long for, want, wish for
▣ (sense 2) longing, want, wish

**desist desists desisting
desisted**
VERB; *FORMAL* To desist from doing
something means to stop doing it.

**desk desks**
NOUN 1 a piece of furniture designed
for working at or writing on. 2 a
counter or table in a public building
behind which a receptionist sits.

**desktop**
ADJECTIVE of a convenient size to be
used on a desk or table E.G. *a desktop
computer.*

**desolate**
ADJECTIVE 1 deserted and bleak E.G. *a
desolate mountainous region.*
2 lonely, very sad, and without hope
E.G. *He was desolate without her.*
**desolation** NOUN

**despair despairs despairing
despaired**
NOUN 1 Despair is a total loss of hope.
▶ VERB 2 If you despair, you lose hope
E.G. *He despaired of finishing it.*
**despairing** ADJECTIVE
▣ (sense 1) desperation,
hopelessness

**despatch**
another spelling of **dispatch**.

**desperate**
ADJECTIVE 1 If you are desperate, you

are so worried or frightened that you
will try anything to improve your
situation E.G. *a desperate attempt to
save their marriage.* 2 A desperate
person is violent and dangerous. 3 A
desperate situation is extremely
dangerous or serious.
**desperately** ADVERB    **desperation**
NOUN

**despicable**
ADJECTIVE deserving contempt.

**despise despises despising
despised**
VERB If you despise someone or
something, you dislike them very
much.

**despite**
PREPOSITION in spite of E.G. *He fell asleep
despite all the coffee he'd drunk.*
▣ in spite of, regardless of

**despondent**
ADJECTIVE dejected and unhappy.
**despondency** NOUN

**dessert desserts**
*Said* "diz-**ert**" NOUN a sweet food
served after the main course of a meal.
▣ from French *desservir* meaning 'to
clear the table after a meal'

**destination destinations**
NOUN a place to which someone or
something is going or is being sent.

**destined**
ADJECTIVE meant or intended to
happen E.G. *I was destined for fame
and fortune.*

**destiny destinies**
NOUN 1 Your destiny is all the things
that happen to you in your life,
especially when they are considered
to be outside human control.
2 Destiny is the force which some
people believe controls everyone's
life.

a
b
c
d
e
f
g
h
i
j
k
l
m
n
o
p
q
r
s
t
u
v
w
x
y
z

Beautiful Elephants Are Usually Tiny (<u>beauti</u>ful)          SPELLING NOTE

**destitute**

ADJECTIVE without money or possessions, and therefore in great need.
**destitution** NOUN

**destroy destroys destroying destroyed**

VERB 1 To destroy something means to damage it so much that it is completely ruined. 2 To destroy something means to put an end to it E.G. *The holiday destroyed their friendship.*

▣ (sense 1) demolish, ruin, wreck

**destruction**

NOUN Destruction is the act of destroying something or the state of being destroyed.

▣ devastation, ruin

**destructive**

ADJECTIVE causing or able to cause great harm, damage, or injury.
**destructiveness** NOUN

**desultory**

*Said "dez-ul-tree".* ADJECTIVE passing from one thing to another in a fitful or random way E.G. *A desultory, embarrassed chatter began again.*

**detach detaches detaching detached**

VERB To detach something means to remove it E.G. *The hood can be detached.*
**detachable** ADJECTIVE

**detached**

ADJECTIVE 1 separate or standing apart E.G. *a detached house.* 2 having no real interest or emotional involvement in something E.G. *He observed me with a detached curiosity.*

**detachment detachments**

NOUN 1 Detachment is the feeling of not being personally involved with something E.G. *A stranger can view your problems with detachment.* 2 a small group of soldiers sent to do a special job.

**detail details**

NOUN 1 an individual fact or feature of something E.G. *We discussed every detail of the performance.* 2 Detail is all the small features that make up the whole of something E.G. *Look at the detail.*
**detailed** ADJECTIVE

**detain detains detaining detained**

VERB 1 To detain someone means to force them to stay E.G. *She was being detained for interrogation.* 2 If you detain someone, you delay them E.G. *I mustn't detain you.*

**detect detects detecting detected**

VERB 1 If you detect something, you notice it E.G. *I detected a glimmer of interest in his eyes.* 2 To detect something means to find it E.G. *Cancer can be detected by X-rays.*
**detectable** ADJECTIVE

**detection**

NOUN 1 Detection is the act of noticing, discovering, or sensing something. 2 Detection is also the work of investigating crime.

**detective detectives**

NOUN a person, usually a police officer, whose job is to investigate crimes.

**detector detectors**

NOUN an instrument which is used to detect the presence of something E.G. *a metal detector.*

**detention**

NOUN The detention of someone is their arrest or imprisonment.

**deter deters deterring deterred**

VERB To deter someone means to

discourage or prevent them from doing something by creating a feeling of fear or doubt E.G. *99 per cent of burglars are deterred by the sight of an alarm box.*

**detergent** detergents
NOUN a chemical substance used for washing or cleaning things.

**deteriorate** deteriorates deteriorating deteriorated
VERB If something deteriorates, it gets worse E.G. *My father's health has deteriorated lately.*
**deterioration** NOUN

**determination**
NOUN Determination is great firmness, after you have made up your mind to do something E.G. *They shared a determination to win the war.*

**determine** determines determining determined
VERB **1** If something determines a situation or result, it causes it or controls it E.G. *The track surface determines his tactics in a race.* **2** To determine something means to decide or settle it firmly E.G. *The date has still to be determined.* **3** To determine something means to find out or calculate the facts about it E.G. *He bit the coin to determine whether it was genuine.*
■ (sense 2) decide, settle
■ (sense 3) ascertain, find out, verify

**determined**
ADJECTIVE firmly decided E.G. *She was determined not to repeat her error.*
**determinedly** ADVERB
■ intent on, resolute

**determiner** determiners
NOUN a word that can go before a noun or noun group to show, for instance, which thing you are

referring to or whether you are referring to one thing or several. For example, in 'my house', 'the windows', 'this red book', and 'each time', 'my', 'the', 'this', and 'each' can be called determiners.

**deterrent** deterrents
NOUN something that prevents you from doing something by making you afraid of what will happen if you do it E.G. *Capital punishment was no deterrent to domestic murders.*
**deterrence** NOUN

**detest** detests detesting detested
VERB If you detest someone or something, you strongly dislike them.

**detonate** detonates detonating detonated
VERB To detonate a bomb or mine means to cause it to explode.
**detonator** NOUN

**detour** detours
NOUN an alternative, less direct route.

**detract** detracts detracting detracted
VERB To detract from something means to make it seem less good or valuable.

**detriment**
NOUN Detriment is disadvantage or harm E.G. *a detriment to their health.*
**detrimental** ADJECTIVE

**deuce** deuces
Said "joos" NOUN In tennis, deuce is the score of forty all.

**devalue** devalues devaluing devalued
VERB To devalue something means to lower its status, importance, or worth.
**devaluation** NOUN

**devastate** devastates devastating devastated

a b c d e f g h i j k l m n o p q r s t u v w x y z

VERB To devastate an area or place means to damage it severely or destroy it.
**devastation** NOUN

**devastated**
ADJECTIVE very shocked or upset E.G. The family are devastated by the news.

**develop** develops developing developed
VERB 1 When something develops or is developed, it grows or becomes more advanced E.G. The sneezing developed into a full blown cold. 2 To develop an area of land means to build on it. 3 To develop an illness or a fault means to become affected by it.

**developer** developers
NOUN a person or company that builds on land.

**development** developments
NOUN 1 Development is gradual growth or progress. 2 The development of land or water is the process of making it more useful or profitable by the expansion of industry or housing E.G. the development of the old docks. 3 a new stage in a series of events E.G. developments in technology.
**developmental** ADJECTIVE

**deviant** deviants
ADJECTIVE 1 Deviant behaviour is unacceptable or different from what people consider as normal. ▶ NOUN 2 someone whose behaviour or beliefs are different from what people consider to be acceptable.

**deviate** deviates deviating deviated
VERB To deviate means to differ or depart from what is usual or acceptable.
**deviation** NOUN

**device** devices
NOUN 1 a machine or tool that is used for a particular purpose E.G. a device to warn you when the batteries need changing. 2 a plan or scheme E.G. a device to pressurise him into selling.

**devil** devils
NOUN 1 In Christianity and Judaism, the Devil is the spirit of evil and enemy of God. 2 an evil spirit.
from Greek diabolos meaning 'slanderer', 'enemy', or 'devil'

**devious**
ADJECTIVE insincere and dishonest.
**deviousness** NOUN

**devise** devises devising devised
VERB To devise something means to work it out E.G. Besides diets, he devised punishing exercise routines.

**devoid**
ADJECTIVE lacking in a particular thing or quality E.G. His glance was devoid of expression.

**devolution**
NOUN Devolution is the transfer of power from a central government or organization to local government departments or smaller organizations.

**devote** devotes devoting devoted
VERB If you devote yourself to something, you give all your time, energy, or money to it E.G. She has devoted herself to women's causes.

**devoted**
ADJECTIVE very loving and loyal.

**devotee** devotees
NOUN a fanatical or enthusiastic follower of it.

**devotion**
NOUN Devotion to someone or something is great love or affection for them.

**devotional** ADJECTIVE

**devour** devours devouring
devoured
VERB If you devour something, you eat
it hungrily or greedily.

**devout**
ADJECTIVE deeply and sincerely
religious E.G. *a devout Buddhist.*
**devoutly** ADVERB

**dew**
NOUN Dew is drops of moisture that
form on the ground and other cool
surfaces at night.

**dexterity**
NOUN Dexterity is skill or agility in
using your hands or mind E.G. *He had
learned to use the crutches with dexterity.*
**dexterous** ADJECTIVE

**dharma**
Said "**dar**-ma" NOUN In the Buddhist
religion, dharma is ideal truth as set
out in the teaching of the Buddha.
🔲 a Sanskrit word

**diabetes**
Said "dy-a-**bee**-tiss" NOUN Diabetes is
a disease in which someone has too
much sugar in their blood, because
they do not produce enough insulin
to absorb it.
**diabetic** NOUN OR ADJECTIVE

**diabolical**
ADJECTIVE 1 *INFORMAL* dreadful and very
annoying E.G. *The pain was diabolical.*
2 extremely wicked and cruel.

**diagnose** diagnoses diagnosing
diagnosed
VERB To diagnose an illness or
problem means to identify exactly
what is wrong.

**diagnosis** diagnoses
NOUN the identification of what is
wrong with someone who is ill.
**diagnostic** ADJECTIVE

**diagonal**
ADJECTIVE in a slanting direction.
**diagonally** ADVERB
🔲 from Greek *diagōnios* meaning
'from angle to angle'

**diagram** diagrams
NOUN a drawing that shows or
explains something.

**dial** dials dialling dialled
NOUN 1 the face of a clock or meter,
with divisions marked on it so that a
time or measurement can be
recorded and read. 2 a part of a
device, such as a radio, used to
control or tune it. ▶ VERB 3 To dial a
telephone number means to press
the number keys to select the
required number.

**dialect** dialects
NOUN a form of a language spoken in
a particular geographical area.

**dialogue** dialogues
NOUN 1 (ENGLISH) In a novel, play, or
film, dialogue is conversation.
2 Dialogue is communication or
discussion between people or
groups of people E.G. *The union
sought dialogue with the council.*

**dialysis**
NOUN Dialysis is a treatment used for
some kidney diseases, in which
blood is filtered by a special machine
to remove waste products.
🔲 from Greek *dialuein* meaning 'to
rip apart'

**diameter** diameters
NOUN (MATHS) The diameter of a circle
is the length of a straight line drawn
across it through its centre.

**diamond** diamonds
NOUN 1 a precious stone made of pure
carbon. 2 a shape with four straight
sides of equal length forming two

a
b
c
d
e
f
g
h
i
j
k
l
m
n
o
p
q
r
s
t
u
v
w
x
y
z

opposite angles less than 90° and two opposite angles greater than 90°. **3** Diamonds is one of the four suits in a pack of playing cards. It is marked by a red diamond-shaped symbol. ► ADJECTIVE **4** A diamond anniversary is the 60th anniversary of an event.

## diaphragm diaphragms
*Said "***dy***-a-fram"* NOUN In mammals, the diaphragm is the muscular wall that separates the lungs from the stomach.

## diarrhoea
*Said "***dy***-a-***ree***-a"* NOUN Diarrhoea is a condition in which the faeces are more liquid and frequent than usual.

## diary diaries
NOUN a book which has a separate space or page for each day of the year on which to keep a record of appointments. **diarist** NOUN

☑ Do not confuse the order of the vowels in *diary* and *dairy*.

## dice dices dicing diced
NOUN **1** a small cube which has each side marked with dots representing the numbers one to six. ► VERB **2** To dice food means to cut it into small cubes.
**diced** ADJECTIVE

## dictate dictates dictating dictated
VERB **1** If you dictate something, you say or read it aloud for someone else to write down. **2** To dictate something means to command or state what must happen *E.G. What we wear is largely dictated by our daily routine.*
**dictation** NOUN

## dictator dictators
NOUN a ruler who has complete

power in a country, especially one who has taken power by force.
**dictatorial** ADJECTIVE

## diction
NOUN Someone's diction is the clarity with which they speak or sing.

## dictionary dictionaries
NOUN (LIBRARY) a book in which words are listed alphabetically and explained, or equivalent words are given in another language.
📖 from Latin *dictio* meaning 'phrase' or 'word'

## didgeridoo didgeridoos
NOUN an Australian musical wind instrument made in the shape of a long wooden tube.

## die dies dying died
VERB **1** When people, animals, or plants die, they stop living. **2** When things die or die out, they cease to exist *E.G. That custom has died out now.* **3** When something dies, dies away, or dies down, it gradually fades away *E.G. The footsteps died away.* **4** INFORMAL If you are dying to do something, you are longing to do it. ► NOUN **5** a dice.
▤ (sense 1) expire, pass away, perish

## diesel
*Said "***dee***-zel"* NOUN **1** a heavy fuel used in trains, buses, and lorries. **2** a vehicle with a diesel engine.

## diet diets
NOUN (D&T) **1** Someone's diet is the usual food that they eat *E.G. a vegetarian diet.* **2** a special restricted selection of foods that someone eats to improve their health or regulate their weight.
**dietary** ADJECTIVE
📖 from Greek *diaita* meaning 'mode of living'

**dietician** dieticians; also spelt
dietitian
NOUN a person trained to advise
people about healthy eating.

**differ** differs differing differed
VERB 1 If two or more things differ,
they are unlike each other. 2 If
people differ, they have opposing
views or disagree about something.

**difference** differences
NOUN 1 The difference between things
is the way in which they are unlike
each other. 2 The difference between
two numbers is the amount by
which one is less than another. 3 A
difference in someone or something
is a significant change in them E.G.
*You wouldn't believe the difference in
her.*
■ (sense 1) disparity, dissimilarity,
distinction

**different**
ADJECTIVE 1 unlike something else.
2 unusual and out of the ordinary.
3 distinct and separate, although of
the same kind E.G. *The lunch supports
a different charity each year.*

**differently** ADVERB
■ (sense 1) dissimilar, unlike
✓ You should say that one thing is
*different from* another thing. Some
people think that *different to* is
incorrect. *Different than* is American.

**differentiate** differentiates
differentiating differentiated
VERB 1 To differentiate between things
means to recognize or show how
one is unlike the other. 2 Something
that differentiates one thing from
another makes it distinct and unlike
the other.

**differentiation** NOUN

**difficult**
ADJECTIVE 1 not easy to do, understand,
or solve E.G. *a very difficult decision to
make.* 2 hard to deal with, especially
because of being unreasonable or
unpredictable E.G. *a difficult child.*
■ (sense 1) demanding, hard,
laborious

**difficulty** difficulties
NOUN 1 a problem E.G. *The central
difficulty is his drinking.* 2 Difficulty
is the fact or quality of being
difficult.

**diffident**
ADJECTIVE timid and lacking in self-
confidence.

**diffidently** ADVERB    **diffidence** NOUN

**diffract** diffracts diffracting
diffracted
VERB When rays of light or sound
waves diffract, they break up after
hitting an obstacle.

**diffraction** NOUN

**diffuse** diffuses diffusing
diffused
VERB 1 Said "dif-*yooz*" If something
diffuses, it spreads out or scatters in
all directions. ► ADJECTIVE 2 Said "dif-
*yoos*" spread out over a wide area.

**diffusion** NOUN

**dig** digs digging dug
VERB 1 If you dig, you break up soil or
sand, especially with a spade or
garden fork. 2 To dig something into
an object means to push, thrust, or
poke it in. ► NOUN 3 a prod or jab,
especially in the ribs. 4 INFORMAL A dig
at someone is a spiteful or
unpleasant remark intended to hurt
or embarrass them. ► PLURAL NOUN
5 Digs are lodgings in someone else's
house.

a b c d e f g h i j k l m n o p q r s t u v w x y z

The government licenSes Schnapps (licenSes)    SPELLING NOTE

A
B
C
**D**
E
F
G
H
I
J
K
L
M
N
O
P
Q
R
S
T
U
V
W
X
Y
Z

**digest** digests digesting digested

VERB (SCIENCE) **1** To digest food means to break it down in the gut so that it can be easily absorbed and used by the body. **2** If you digest information or a fact, you understand it and take it in.

**digestible** ADJECTIVE

**digestion** digestions

NOUN (SCIENCE) **1** Digestion is the process of digesting food. **2** Your digestion is your ability to digest food E.G. *Camomile tea aids poor digestion.*

**digestive** ADJECTIVE

**digger** diggers

NOUN In Australian English, digger is a friendly name to call a man.

**digit** digits

*Said* "dij-it" NOUN FORMAL Your digits are your fingers or toes. **2** (MATHS) a written symbol for any of the numbers from 0 to 9.

**digital**

ADJECTIVE displaying information, especially time, by numbers, rather than by a pointer moving round a dial E.G. *a digital watch.*

**digitally** ADVERB

**dignified**

ADJECTIVE full of dignity.

**dignitary** dignitaries

NOUN a person who holds a high official position.

**dignity**

NOUN Dignity is behaviour which is serious, calm, and controlled E.G. *She conducted herself with dignity.*

**digression** digressions

NOUN A digression in speech or writing is leaving the main subject for a while.

**dilapidated**

ADJECTIVE falling to pieces and generally in a bad condition E.G. *a dilapidated castle.*

**dilate** dilates dilating dilated

VERB To dilate means to become wider and larger E.G. *The pupil of the eye dilates in the dark.*

**dilated** ADJECTIVE    **dilation** NOUN

**dilemma** dilemmas

NOUN a situation in which a choice has to be made between alternatives that are equally difficult or unpleasant.

▥ from Greek *di-* meaning 'two' and *lemma* meaning 'assumption'

✔ A *dilemma* involves a difficult choice between two things. If there are more than two choices you should say *problem* or *difficulty.*

**diligent**

ADJECTIVE hard-working, and showing care and perseverance.

**diligently** ADVERB    **diligence** NOUN

▤ conscientious, hard-working, industrious

**dill**

NOUN Dill is a herb with yellow flowers and a strong sweet smell.

**dilly bag** dilly bags

NOUN In Australian English, a dilly bag is a small bag used to carry food.

**dilute** dilutes diluting diluted

VERB To dilute a liquid means to add water or another liquid to it to make it less concentrated.

**dilution** NOUN

**dim** dimmer dimmest; dims dimming dimmed

ADJECTIVE **1** badly lit and lacking in brightness. **2** very vague and unclear in your mind E.G. *dim recollections.* **3** INFORMAL stupid or mentally dull E.G.

*He is rather dim.* ▶ VERB **4** If lights dim or are dimmed, they become less bright.

**dimly** ADVERB  **dimness** NOUN

**dimension** dimensions

NOUN **1** A dimension of a situation is an aspect or factor that influences the way you understand it *E.G. This process had a domestic and a foreign dimension.* **2** You can talk about the size or extent of something as its dimensions *E.G. It was an explosion of major dimensions.* **3** (ART) The dimensions of something are also its measurements, for example its length, breadth, height, or diameter.

**diminish** diminishes diminishing diminished

VERB If something diminishes or if you diminish it, it becomes reduced in size or importance.

**diminutive**

ADJECTIVE very small.

**dimple** dimples

NOUN a small hollow in someone's cheek or chin.

**din** dins

NOUN a loud and unpleasant noise.

**dinar** dinars

*Said "dee-nar"* NOUN a unit of currency in several countries in Southern Europe, North Africa and the Middle East.

**dine** dines dining dined

VERB; FORMAL To dine means to eat dinner in the evening *E.G. We dined together in the hotel.*

**diner** diners

NOUN **1** a person who is having dinner in a restaurant. **2** a small restaurant or railway restaurant car.

**dinghy** dinghies

*Said "ding-ee"* NOUN a small boat which is rowed, sailed, or powered by outboard motor.

**dingo** dingoes

NOUN an Australian wild dog.

**dingy** dingier dingiest

*Said "din-jee"* ADJECTIVE dusty, dark, and rather depressing *E.G. a dingy bedsit.*

**dinkum**

ADJECTIVE; INFORMAL In Australian and New Zealand English, dinkum means genuine or right *E.G. a fair dinkum offer.*

**dinner** dinners

NOUN **1** the main meal of the day, eaten either in the evening or at lunchtime. **2** a formal social occasion in the evening, at which a meal is served.

**dinosaur** dinosaurs

*Said "dy-no-sor"* NOUN a large reptile which lived in prehistoric times. 🔳 from Greek *deinos + sauros* meaning 'fearful lizard'

**dint**

PHRASE **By dint of** means by means of *E.G. He succeeds by dint of hard work.*

**diocese** dioceses

NOUN a district controlled by a bishop.
**diocesan** ADJECTIVE

**dip** dips dipping dipped

VERB **1** If you dip something into a liquid, you lower it or plunge it quickly into the liquid. **2** If something dips, it slopes downwards or goes below a certain level *E.G. The sun dipped below the horizon.* **3** To dip also means to make a quick, slight downward movement *E.G. She dipped her fingers into the cool water.* ▶ NOUN **4** a rich creamy mixture which you scoop up with biscuits or raw vegetables and eat *E.G. an avocado dip.* **5** INFORMAL a swim.

a
b
c
d
e
f
g
h
i
j
k
l
m
n
o
p
q
r
s
t
u
v
w
x
y
z

**diploma** diplomas

NOUN a certificate awarded to a student who has successfully completed a course of study.

📖 from Greek *diploma* meaning 'folded paper' or 'letter of recommendation'

**diplomacy**

NOUN 1 Diplomacy is the managing of relationships between countries. 2 Diplomacy is also skill in dealing with people without offending or upsetting them.

**diplomatic** ADJECTIVE

**diplomatically** ADVERB

**diplomat** diplomats

NOUN an official who negotiates and deals with another country on behalf of his or her own country.

**dire** direr direst

ADJECTIVE disastrous, urgent, or terrible E.G. *people in dire need.*

**direct** directs directing directed

ADJECTIVE 1 moving or aimed in a straight line or by the shortest route E.G. *the direct route.* 2 straightforward, and without delay or evasion E.G. *his direct manner.* 3 without anyone or anything intervening E.G. *Schools can take direct control of their own funding.* 4 exact E.G. *the direct opposite.* ▶ VERB 5 To direct something means to guide and control it. 6 To direct people or things means to send them, tell them, or show them the way. 7 To direct a film, a play, or a television programme means to organize the way it is made and performed.

▤ (sense 2) frank, open, straightforward

**direct current**

NOUN Direct current is a term used in physics to refer to an electric current that always flows in the same direction.

**direction** directions

NOUN 1 the general line that someone or something is moving or pointing in. 2 Direction is the controlling and guiding of something E.G. *He was chopping vegetables under the chef's direction.* ▶ PLURAL NOUN 3 Directions are instructions that tell you how to do something or how to get somewhere.

**directive** directives

NOUN an instruction that must be obeyed E.G. *a directive banning cigarette advertising.*

**directly**

ADVERB in a straight line or immediately E.G. *He looked directly at Rose.*

**director** directors

NOUN 1 a member of the board of a company or institution. 2 (DRAMA) the person responsible for the making and performance of a programme, play, or film.

**directorial** ADJECTIVE

**directorate** directorates

NOUN a board of directors of a company or organization.

**directory** directories

NOUN 1 a book which gives lists of facts, such as names and addresses, and is usually arranged in alphabetical order. 2 another name for **folder**.

**direct speech**

NOUN the reporting of what someone has said by quoting the exact words.

**dirge** dirges

NOUN a slow, sad piece of music,

sometimes played or sung at funerals.

**dirt**

NOUN **1** Dirt is any unclean substance, such as dust, mud, or stains. **2** Dirt is also earth or soil.

📖 from Old Norse *drit* meaning 'excrement'

▤ (sense 1) filth, grime, muck

**dirty dirtier dirtiest**

ADJECTIVE **1** marked or covered with dirt. **2** unfair or dishonest E.G. *a dirty fight*. **3** about sex in a way that many people find offensive E.G. *dirty jokes*.

▤ (sense 1) filthy, grubby, mucky, unclean

**dis-**

PREFIX Dis- is added to the beginning of a word to form a word that means the opposite E.G. *discontented*.

**disability disabilities**

NOUN a physical or mental condition or illness that restricts someone's way of life.

**disable disables disabling disabled**

VERB If something disables someone, it injures or harms them physically or mentally and severely affects their life.

**disablement** NOUN

**disabled**

ADJECTIVE lacking one or more physical powers, such as the ability to walk or to coordinate one's movements.

**disadvantage disadvantages**

NOUN an unfavourable or harmful circumstance.

**disadvantaged** ADJECTIVE

▤ drawback, handicap

**disaffected**

ADJECTIVE If someone is disaffected with an idea or organization, they no

longer believe in it or support it E.G. *disaffected voters*.

**disagree disagrees disagreeing disagreed**

VERB **1** If you disagree with someone, you have a different view or opinion from theirs. **2** If you disagree with an action or proposal, you disapprove of it and believe it is wrong E.G. *He detested her and disagreed with her policies*. **3** If food or drink disagrees with you, it makes you feel unwell.

**disagreement** NOUN

▤ (sense 1) differ, dispute, dissent

**disagreeable**

ADJECTIVE unpleasant or unhelpful and unfriendly E.G. *a disagreeable odour*.

**disappear disappears disappearing disappeared**

VERB **1** If something or someone disappears, they go out of sight or become lost. **2** To disappear also means to stop existing or happening E.G. *The pain has disappeared*.

**disappearance** NOUN

▤ fade away, vanish

**disappoint disappoints disappointing disappointed**

VERB If someone or something disappoints you, it fails to live up to what you expected of it.

**disappointed** ADJECTIVE

**disappointment** NOUN

**disapprove disapproves disapproving disapproved**

VERB To disapprove of something or someone means to believe they are wrong or bad E.G. *Everyone disapproved of their marrying so young*.

**disapproval** NOUN   **disapproving** ADJECTIVE

have a plEce of plE (pi<u>e</u>ce)        SPELLING NOTE

### disarm disarms disarming disarmed
VERB **1** To disarm means to get rid of weapons. **2** If someone disarms you, they overcome your anger or doubt by charming or soothing you E.G. *Mahoney was almost disarmed by the frankness.*
**disarming** ADJECTIVE

### disarmament
NOUN Disarmament is the reducing or getting rid of military forces and weapons.

### disarray
NOUN Disarray is a state of disorder and confusion E.G. *Our army was in disarray and practically weaponless.*

### disassemble disassembles disassembling disassembled
VERB (D&T) To disassemble a structure or object which has been made up or built from several smaller parts is to separate its parts from one another.

### disaster disasters
NOUN **1** an event or accident that causes great distress or destruction. **2** a complete failure.
**disastrous** ADJECTIVE **disastrously** ADVERB
■ (sense 1) calamity, catastrophe

### disband disbands disbanding disbanded
VERB When a group of people disbands, it officially ceases to exist.

### disc discs; also spelt disk
NOUN **1** a flat round object E.G. *a tax disc, a compact disc.* **2** one of the thin circular pieces of cartilage which separate the bones in your spine. **3** In computing, another spelling of disk.

### discard discards discarding discarded
VERB To discard something means to get rid of it, because you no longer want it or find it useful.
■ dump, get rid of, throw away

### discern discerns discerning discerned
*Said "dis-ern"* VERB; FORMAL To discern something means to notice or understand it clearly E.G. *The film had no plot that I could discern.*

### discernible
ADJECTIVE able to be seen or recognized E.G. *no discernible talent.*

### discerning
ADJECTIVE having good taste and judgment.
**discernment** NOUN

### discharge discharges discharging discharged
VERB **1** If something discharges or is discharged, it is given or sent out E.G. *Oil discharged into the world's oceans.* **2** To discharge someone from hospital means to allow them to leave. **3** If someone is discharged from a job, they are dismissed from it. ▶ NOUN **4** a substance that is released from the inside of something E.G. *a thick nasal discharge.* **5** a dismissal or release from a job or an institution.

### disciple disciples
*Said "dis-sigh-pl"* NOUN (RE) a follower of someone or something, especially one of the twelve men who were followers and helpers of Christ.

### discipline disciplines disciplining disciplined
NOUN **1** (PSHE) Discipline is making people obey rules and punishing

them when they break them.
**2** (PSHE) Discipline is the ability to behave and work in a controlled way. ► VERB (PSHE) **3** If you discipline yourself, you train yourself to behave and work in an ordered way. **4** To discipline someone means to punish them.

**disciplinary** ADJECTIVE **disciplined** ADJECTIVE

**disc jockey** disc jockeys
NOUN someone who introduces and plays pop records on the radio or at a night club.

**disclose** discloses disclosing disclosed
VERB To disclose something means to make it known or allow it to be seen.
**disclosure** NOUN

**disco** discos
NOUN a party or a club where people go to dance to pop records.

**discomfort** discomforts
NOUN **1** Discomfort is distress or slight pain. **2** Discomfort is also a feeling of worry or embarrassment.
**3** Discomforts are things that make you uncomfortable.

**disconcert** disconcerts disconcerting disconcerted
VERB If something disconcerts you, it makes you feel uneasy or embarrassed.
**disconcerting** ADJECTIVE

**disconnect** disconnects disconnecting disconnected
VERB **1** To disconnect something means to detach it from something else. **2** If someone disconnects your fuel supply or telephone, they cut you off.

**discontent**
NOUN Discontent is a feeling of dissatisfaction with conditions or with life in general E.G. *He was aware of the discontent this policy had caused.*

**discontented** ADJECTIVE

**discontinue** discontinues discontinuing discontinued
VERB To discontinue something means to stop doing it.

**discord**
NOUN Discord is unpleasantness or quarrelling between people.

**discount** discounts discounting discounted
NOUN **1** a reduction in the price of something. ► VERB **2** If you discount something, you reject it or ignore it E.G. *I haven't discounted her connection with the kidnapping case.*

**discourage** discourages discouraging discouraged
VERB To discourage someone means to take away their enthusiasm to do something.
**discouraging** ADJECTIVE
**discouragement** NOUN
■ demoralize, dishearten, put off

**discourse** discourses FORMAL
NOUN **1** a formal talk or piece of writing intended to teach or explain something. **2** Discourse is serious conversation between people on a particular subject.

**discover** discovers discovering discovered
VERB When you discover something, you find it or find out about it.
**discovery** NOUN **discoverer** NOUN

**discredit** discredits discrediting discredited
VERB **1** To discredit someone means to damage their reputation. **2** To discredit an idea means to cause it

a b c **d** e f g h i j k l m n o p q r s t u v w x y z

to be doubted or not believed.

**discreet**

ADJECTIVE If you are discreet, you avoid causing embarrassment when dealing with secret or private matters.

**discreetly** ADVERB

**discrepancy** discrepancies

NOUN a difference between two things which ought to be the same E.G. *discrepancies in his police interviews.*

**discrete**

ADJECTIVE; *FORMAL* separate and distinct E.G. *two discrete sets of nerves.*

**discretion**

NOUN 1 Discretion is the quality of behaving with care and tact so as to avoid embarrassment or distress to other people E.G. *You can count on my discretion.* 2 Discretion is also freedom and authority to make decisions and take action according to your own judgment E.G. *Class teachers have very limited discretion in decision-making.*

**discretionary** ADJECTIVE

**discriminate** discriminates discriminating discriminated

VERB 1 To discriminate between things means to recognize and understand the differences between them. 2 To discriminate against a person or group means to treat them unfairly, usually because of their race, colour, or sex. 3 To discriminate in favour of a person or group means to treat them more favourably than others.

**discrimination** NOUN

**discriminatory** ADJECTIVE

**discus** discuses

NOUN a disc-shaped object with a heavy middle, thrown by athletes.

**discuss** discusses discussing discussed

VERB 1 When people discuss something, they talk about it in detail. 2 (EXAM TERM) To discuss a question is to look at the points or arguments of both sides and try to reach your own opinion.

**discussion** discussions

NOUN (PSHE) a conversation or piece of writing in which a subject is considered in detail.

■ conversation, discourse, talk

**disdain**

NOUN Disdain is a feeling of superiority over or contempt for someone or something E.G. *The candidates shared an equal disdain for the press.*

**disdainful** ADJECTIVE

**disease** diseases

NOUN (HISTORY) an unhealthy condition in people, animals, or plants.

**diseased** ADJECTIVE

**disembark** disembarks disembarking disembarked

VERB To disembark means to land or unload from a ship, aircraft, or bus.

**disembodied**

ADJECTIVE 1 separate from or existing without a body E.G. *a disembodied skull.* 2 seeming not to be attached or to come from anyone E.G. *disembodied voices.*

**disenchanted**

ADJECTIVE disappointed with something, and no longer believing that it is good or worthwhile E.G. *She is very disenchanted with the marriage.*

**disenchantment** NOUN

**disfigure** disfigures disfiguring disfigured

VERB To disfigure something means to spoil its appearance E.G. *Graffiti or posters disfigured every wall.*

**disgrace** disgraces disgracing disgraced

NOUN 1 Disgrace is a state in which people disapprove of someone. 2 If something is a disgrace, it is unacceptable E.G. *The overcrowded prisons were a disgrace.* 3 If someone is a disgrace to a group of people, their behaviour makes the group feel ashamed E.G. *You're a disgrace to the school.* ▶ VERB 4 If you disgrace yourself or disgrace someone else, you cause yourself or them to be strongly disapproved of by other people.

■ (sense 1) dishonour, shame
■ (sense 4) discredit, dishonour, shame

**disgraceful**

ADJECTIVE If something is disgraceful, people disapprove of it strongly and think that those who are responsible for it should be ashamed.

**disgracefully** ADVERB
■ scandalous, shameful, shocking

**disgruntled**

ADJECTIVE discontented or in a bad mood.

**disguise** disguises disguising disguised

VERB 1 To disguise something means to change its appearance so that people do not recognize it. 2 To disguise a feeling means to hide it E.G. *I tried to disguise my relief.* ▶ NOUN 3 something you wear or something you do to alter your appearance so that you cannot be recognized by other people.

**disgust** disgusts disgusting disgusted

NOUN 1 Disgust is a strong feeling of dislike or disapproval. ▶ VERB 2 To disgust someone means to make them feel a strong sense of dislike or disapproval.

**disgusted** ADJECTIVE
■ (sense 1) loathing, repugnance, revulsion
■ (sense 2) revolt, sicken

**dish** dishes

NOUN 1 a shallow container for cooking or serving food. 2 food of a particular kind or food cooked in a particular way E.G. *two fish dishes to choose from.*

**disheartened**

ADJECTIVE If you are disheartened, you feel disappointed.

**dishevelled**

*Said* "dish-*ev*-ld" ADJECTIVE If someone looks dishevelled, their clothes or hair look untidy.

**dishonest**

ADJECTIVE not truthful or able to be trusted.

**dishonestly** ADVERB

**dishonesty**

NOUN Dishonesty is behaviour which is meant to deceive people, either by not telling the truth or by cheating.

**disillusioned**

ADJECTIVE If you are disillusioned with something, you are disappointed because it is not as good as you had expected.

**disinfectant** disinfectants

NOUN a chemical substance that kills germs.

**disintegrate** disintegrates disintegrating disintegrated

VERB 1 If something disintegrates, it

a b c d e f g h i j k l m n o p q r s t u v w x y z

A
B
**D**
E
F
G
H
I
J
K
L
M
N
O
P
Q
R
S
T
U
V
W
X
Y
Z

becomes weakened and is not effective *E.G. My confidence disintegrated.* **2** If an object disintegrates, it breaks into many pieces and so is destroyed.

**disintegration** NOUN

**disinterest**

NOUN **1** Disinterest is a lack of interest. **2** Disinterest is also a lack of personal involvement in a situation.

**disinterested**

ADJECTIVE If someone is disinterested, they are not going to gain or lose from the situation they are involved in, and so can act in a way that is fair to both sides *E.G. a disinterested judge.*

✓ Some people use *disinterested* to mean 'not interested', but the word they should use is *uninterested*.

**disjointed**

ADJECTIVE If thought or speech is disjointed, it jumps from subject to subject and so is difficult to follow.

**disk disks**

NOUN **1** ICT In a computer, the disk is the part where information is stored *E.G. The program takes up 2.5 megabytes of disk space.* **2** another spelling of **disc**.

**dislike dislikes disliking disliked**

VERB **1** If you dislike something or someone, you think they are unpleasant and do not like them. ▶ NOUN **2** Dislike is a feeling that you have when you do not like someone or something.

■ (sense 2) aversion, distaste

**dislocate dislocates dislocating dislocated**

VERB To dislocate your bone or joint means to put it out of place.

**dislodge dislodges dislodging dislodged**

VERB To dislodge something means to

move it or force it out of place.

**dismal**

*Said* "**diz**-mal" ADJECTIVE rather gloomy and depressing *E.G. dismal weather.*

**dismally** ADVERB

🏛 from Latin *dies mali* meaning 'evil days'

**dismantle dismantles dismantling dismantled**

VERB To dismantle something means to take it apart.

**dismay dismays dismaying dismayed**

NOUN **1** Dismay is a feeling of fear and worry. ▶ VERB **2** If someone or something dismays you, it fills you with alarm and worry.

**dismember dismembers dismembering dismembered**

VERB; FORMAL To dismember a person or animal means to cut or tear their body into pieces.

**dismiss dismisses dismissing dismissed**

VERB **1** If you dismiss something, you decide to ignore it because it is not important enough for you to think about. **2** To dismiss an employee means to ask that person to leave their job. **3** If someone in authority dismisses you, they tell you to leave.

**dismissal** NOUN

**dismissive**

ADJECTIVE If you are dismissive of something or someone, you show that you think they are of little importance or value *E.G. a dismissive gesture.*

**disobey disobeys disobeying disobeyed**

VERB To disobey a person or an order means to deliberately refuse to do what you are told.

**disorder disorders**

NOUN **1** Disorder is a state of

untidiness. **2** Disorder is also a lack of organization E.G. *The men fled in disorder*. **3** a disease E.G. *a stomach disorder*.

■ (sense 2) chaos, confusion

**disorganized** or **disorganised**
ADJECTIVE If something is disorganized, it is confused and badly prepared or badly arranged.
**disorganization** NOUN

**disown** disowns disowning disowned
VERB To disown someone or something means to refuse to admit any connection with them.

**disparaging**
ADJECTIVE critical and scornful E.G. *disparaging remarks*.

**disparate**
ADJECTIVE; FORMAL Things that are disparate are utterly different from one another.
**disparity** NOUN

**dispatch** dispatches dispatching dispatched; also spelt **despatch**
VERB **1** To dispatch someone or something to a particular place means to send them there for a special reason E.G. *The president dispatched him on a fact-finding visit*.
▶ NOUN **2** an official written message, often sent to an army or government headquarters.

**dispel** dispels dispelling dispelled
VERB To dispel fears or beliefs means to drive them away or to destroy them E.G. *The myths are being dispelled*.

**dispensary** dispensaries
NOUN a place where medicines are prepared and given out.

**dispense** dispenses dispensing dispensed

VERB **1** FORMAL To dispense something means to give it out E.G. *They dispense advice*. **2** To dispense medicines means to prepare them and give them out. **3** To dispense with something means to do without it or do away with it E.G. *We'll dispense with formalities*.

**dispenser** dispensers
NOUN a machine or container from which you can get things E.G. *a cash dispenser*.

**disperse** disperses dispersing dispersed
VERB **1** When something disperses, it scatters over a wide area. **2** When people disperse or when someone disperses them, they move apart and go in different directions.
**dispersion** NOUN

**dispirited**
ADJECTIVE depressed and having no enthusiasm for anything.

**dispiriting**
ADJECTIVE Something dispiriting makes you depressed E.G. *a dispiriting defeat*.

**displace** displaces displacing displaced
VERB **1** If one thing displaces another, it forces the thing out of its usual place and occupies that place itself. **2** If people are displaced, they are forced to leave their home or country.

**displacement**
NOUN Displacement is the removal of something from its usual or correct place or position.

**display** displays displaying displayed
VERB **1** If you display something, you show it or make it visible to people. **2** If you display something such as an

Psychiatrists Seldom Yell Callously Hard (<u>psychiatrist</u>) ▶ SPELLING NOTE emotion, you behave in a way that shows you feel it. ▶ NOUN 3 (ART) an arrangement of things designed to attract people's attention.

**displease** displeases displeasing displeased
VERB If someone or something displeases you, they make you annoyed, dissatisfied, or offended.
**displeasure** NOUN

**disposable**
ADJECTIVE designed to be thrown away after use E.G. *disposable nappies.*

**disposal**
NOUN Disposal is the act of getting rid of something that is no longer wanted or needed.

**dispose** disposes disposing disposed
VERB 1 To dispose of something means to get rid of it. 2 If you are not disposed to do something, you are not willing to do it.

**disprove** disproves disproving disproved
VERB If someone disproves an idea, belief, or theory, they show that it is not true.

**dispute** disputes disputing disputed
NOUN 1 an argument. ▶ VERB 2 To dispute a fact or theory means to question the truth of it.

**disqualify** disqualifies disqualifying disqualified
VERB If someone is disqualified from a competition or activity, they are officially stopped from taking part in it E.G. *He was disqualified from driving for 18 months.*
**disqualification** NOUN

**disquiet**
NOUN Disquiet is worry or anxiety.
**disquieting** ADJECTIVE

**disregard** disregards disregarding disregarded
VERB 1 To disregard something means to pay little or no attention to it.
▶ NOUN 2 Disregard is a lack of attention or respect for something E.G. *He exhibited a flagrant disregard of the law.*

**disrepair**
PHRASE If something is **in disrepair** or **in a state of disrepair**, it is broken or in poor condition.

**disrespect**
NOUN Disrespect is contempt or lack of respect E.G. *his disrespect for authority.*
**disrespectful** ADJECTIVE

**disrupt** disrupts disrupting disrupted
VERB To disrupt something such as an event or system means to break it up or throw it into confusion E.G. *Strikes disrupted air traffic in Italy.*
**disruption** NOUN **disruptive** ADJECTIVE

**dissatisfied**
ADJECTIVE not pleased or not contented.
**dissatisfaction** NOUN

**dissect** dissects dissecting dissected
VERB To dissect a plant or a dead body means to cut it up so that it can be scientifically examined.
**dissection** NOUN

**dissent** dissents dissenting dissented
NOUN 1 Dissent is strong difference of opinion E.G. *political dissent.* ▶ VERB 2 When people dissent, they express

a difference of opinion about something.

**dissenting** ADJECTIVE

**dissertation** dissertations
NOUN a long essay, especially for a university degree.

**disservice**
NOUN To do someone a disservice means to do something that harms them.

**dissident** dissidents
NOUN someone who disagrees with and criticizes the strict and unjust government of their country.

**dissimilar**
ADJECTIVE If things are dissimilar, they are unlike each other.

**dissipate** dissipates dissipating dissipated
VERB 1 FORMAL When something dissipates or is dissipated, it completely disappears E.G. The cloud seemed to dissipate there. 2 If someone dissipates time, money, or effort, they waste it.

**dissipated**
ADJECTIVE Someone who is dissipated shows signs of indulging too much in alcohol or other physical pleasures.

**dissolve** dissolves dissolving dissolved
VERB 1 (SCIENCE) If you dissolve something or if it dissolves in a liquid, it becomes mixed with and absorbed in the liquid. 2 To dissolve an organization or institution means to officially end it.

**dissuade** dissuades dissuading dissuaded
Said "dis-wade" VERB To dissuade someone from doing something or from believing something means to persuade them not to do it or not to believe it.

**distance** distances distancing distanced
NOUN 1 The distance between two points is how far it is between them. 2 Distance is the fact of being far away in space or time. ► VERB 3 If you distance yourself from someone or something or are distanced from them, you become less involved with them.

**distant**
ADJECTIVE 1 far away in space or time. 2 A distant relative is one who is not closely related to you. 3 Someone who is distant is cold and unfriendly.
**distantly** ADVERB
■ (sense 3) aloof, reserved, standoffish

**distaste**
NOUN Distaste is a dislike of something which you find offensive.

**distasteful**
ADJECTIVE If you find something distasteful, you think it is unpleasant or offensive.

**distil** distils distilling distilled
VERB (SCIENCE) When a liquid is distilled, it is heated until it evaporates and then cooled to enable purified liquid to be collected.
**distillation** NOUN

**distillery** distilleries
NOUN a place where whisky or other strong alcoholic drink is made, using a process of distillation.

**distinct**
ADJECTIVE 1 If one thing is distinct from another, it is recognizably different from it E.G. A word may have two quite distinct meanings. 2 If something is distinct, you can hear, smell, or see it clearly and plainly E.G. There was a

a b c d e f g h i j k l m n o p q r s t u v w x y z

Rhythmical Hounds Yap To Heavy Music (<u>rhythm</u>)     ▶ SPELLING NOTE

A
B
C
**D**
E
F
G
H
I
J
K
L
M
N
O
P
Q
R
S
T
U
V
W
X
Y
Z

*distinct buzzing noise.* **3** If something such as a fact, idea, or intention is distinct, it is clear and definite *E.G. She had a distinct feeling someone was watching them.*
**distinctly** ADVERB

**distinction** distinctions
NOUN **1** a difference between two things *E.G. a distinction between the body and the soul.* **2** Distinction is a quality of excellence and superiority *E.G. a man of distinction.* **3** a special honour or claim *E.G. It had the distinction of being the largest square in Europe.*

**distinctive**
ADJECTIVE Something that is distinctive has a special quality which makes it recognizable *E.G. a distinctive voice.*
**distinctively** ADVERB

**distinguish** distinguishes distinguishing distinguished
VERB **1** To distinguish between things means to recognize the difference between them *E.G. I've learned to distinguish business and friendship.* **2** To distinguish something means to make it out by seeing, hearing, or tasting it *E.G. I heard shouting but was unable to distinguish the words.* **3** If you distinguish yourself, you do something that makes people think highly of you.
**distinguishable** ADJECTIVE
**distinguishing** ADJECTIVE

**distort** distorts distorting distorted
VERB **1** If you distort a statement or an argument, you represent it in an untrue or misleading way. **2** If something is distorted, it is changed so that it seems strange or unclear *E.G. His voice was distorted.* **3** If an object is distorted, it is twisted or

pulled out of shape.
**distorted** ADJECTIVE **distortion** NOUN

**distract** distracts distracting distracted
VERB If something distracts you, your attention is taken away from what you are doing.
**distracted** ADJECTIVE **distractedly** ADVERB **distracting** ADJECTIVE
◼ divert, sidetrack

**distraction** distractions
NOUN **1** something that takes people's attention away from something. **2** an activity that is intended to amuse or relax someone.

**distraught**
ADJECTIVE so upset and worried that you cannot think clearly *E.G. He was distraught over the death of his mother.*

**distress** distresses distressing distressed
NOUN **1** Distress is great suffering caused by pain or sorrow. **2** Distress is also the state of needing help because of difficulties or danger.
▶ VERB **3** To distress someone means to make them feel alarmed or unhappy *E.G. Her death had profoundly distressed me.*
◼ (sense 3) trouble, upset

**distressing**
ADJECTIVE very worrying or upsetting.

**distribute** distributes distributing distributed
VERB **1** To distribute something such as leaflets means to hand them out or deliver them *E.G. They publish and distribute brochures.* **2** If things are distributed, they are spread throughout an area or space *E.G. Distribute the cheese evenly on top of*

*the quiche.* **3** To distribute something means to divide it and share it out among a number of people.

◼ (sense 3) dispense, share out

**distribution distributions**
NOUN **1** Distribution is the delivering of something to various people or organizations *E.G. the distribution of vicious leaflets.* **2** Distribution is the sharing of something to various people *E.G. distribution of power.*

**distributor distributors**
NOUN a company that supplies goods to other businesses who then sell them to the public.

**district districts**
NOUN an area of a town or country *E.G. a residential district.*

**district nurse district nurses**
NOUN a nurse who visits and treats people in their own homes.

**distrust distrusts distrusting distrusted**
VERB **1** If you distrust someone, you are suspicious of them because you are not sure whether they are honest. ▸ NOUN **2** Distrust is suspicion.

**distrustful** ADJECTIVE

**disturb disturbs disturbing disturbed**
VERB **1** If you disturb someone, you break their peace or privacy. **2** If something disturbs you, it makes you feel upset or worried. **3** If something is disturbed, it is moved out of position or meddled with.

**disturbing** ADJECTIVE

◼ (sense 2) trouble, upset, worry

**disturbance disturbances**
NOUN **1** Disturbance is the state of being disturbed. **2** a violent or unruly incident in public.

**disuse**
NOUN Something that has fallen into disuse is neglected or no longer used.

**disused** ADJECTIVE

**ditch ditches**
NOUN a channel at the side of a road or field, to drain away excess water.

**dither dithers dithering dithered**
VERB To dither means to be unsure and hesitant.

**ditto**
Ditto means 'the same'. In written lists, ditto is represented by a mark („) to avoid repetition.

🏛 from Italian *detto* meaning 'said'

**ditty ditties**
NOUN; *OLD-FASHIONED* a short simple song or poem.

**diva divas**
NOUN a great or leading female singer, especially in opera.

🏛 from Latin *diva* meaning 'a goddess'

**dive dives diving dived**
VERB **1** To dive means to jump into water with your arms held straight above your head. **2** If you go diving, you go down under the surface of the sea or a lake using special breathing equipment. **3** If an aircraft or bird dives, it flies in a steep downward path, or drops sharply.

**diver** NOUN   **diving** NOUN

**diverge diverges diverging diverged**
VERB **1** If opinions or facts diverge, they differ *E.G. Theory and practice sometimes diverged.* **2** If two things such as roads or paths which have been going in the same direction diverge, they separate and go off in different directions.

**divergence** NOUN   **divergent** ADJECTIVE

a
b
c
d
e
f
g
h
i
j
k
l
m
n
o
p
q
r
s
t
u
v
w
x
y
z

A
B
C
D
E
F
G
H
I
J
K
L
M
N
O
P
Q
R
S
T
U
V
W
X
Y
Z

**diverse**

ADJECTIVE **1** If a group of things is diverse, it is made up of different kinds of things E.G. *a diverse range of goods and services.* **2** People, ideas, or objects that are diverse are very different from each other.

**diversity** NOUN

**diversify** diversifies diversifying diversified

VERB To diversify means to increase the variety of something E.G. *Has the company diversified into new areas?*

**diversification** NOUN

**diversion** diversions

NOUN **1** a special route arranged for traffic when the usual route is closed. **2** something that takes your attention away from what you should be concentrating on E.G. *A break for tea created a welcome diversion.* **3** a pleasant or amusing activity.

**divert** diverts diverting diverted

VERB To divert something means to change the course or direction it is following.

**diverting** ADJECTIVE

**divide** divides dividing divided

VERB **1** When something divides or is divided, it is split up and separated into two or more parts. **2** If something divides two areas, it forms a barrier between them. **3** If people divide over something or if something divides them, it causes strong disagreement between them. **4** (MATHS) In mathematics, when you divide, you calculate how many times one number contains another. ▶ NOUN **5** a separation E.G. *the class divide.*

**dividend** dividends

NOUN a portion of a company's profits that is paid to shareholders.

**divine** divines divining divined

ADJECTIVE **1** having the qualities of a god or goddess. ▶ VERB **2** To divine something means to discover it by guessing.

**divinely** ADVERB

**divinity** divinities

NOUN **1** Divinity is the study of religion. **2** Divinity is the state of being a god. **3** a god or goddess.

**division** divisions

NOUN **1** Division is the separation of something into two or more distinct parts. **2** (MATHS) Division is also the process of dividing one number by another. **3** a difference of opinion that causes separation between ideas or groups of people E.G. *There were divisions in the Party on economic policy.* **4** any one of the parts into which something is split E.G. *the Research Division.*

**divisional** ADJECTIVE

**divisive**

ADJECTIVE causing hostility between people so that they split into different groups E.G. *Inflation is economically and socially divisive.*

**divisor** divisors

NOUN a number by which another number is divided.

**divorce** divorces divorcing divorced

NOUN **1** Divorce is the formal and legal ending of a marriage. ▶ VERB **2** When a married couple divorce, their marriage is legally ended.

**divorced** ADJECTIVE **divorcee** NOUN

**divulge** divulges divulging divulged

VERB To divulge information means to reveal it.

**Diwali**
*Said* "dih-**wah**-lee" NOUN a Hindu religious festival in honour of the goddess of wealth. It is celebrated by feasting, exchanging gifts, and lighting lamps.

**DIY**
NOUN DIY is the activity of making or repairing things yourself. DIY is an abbreviation for 'do-it-yourself'.

**dizzy dizzier dizziest**
ADJECTIVE having or causing a whirling sensation.
**dizziness** NOUN

**DNA**
NOUN DNA is deoxyribonucleic acid, which is found in the cells of all living things. It is responsible for passing on characteristics from parents to their children.

**do does doing did done; dos**
VERB 1 Do is an auxiliary verb, which is used to form questions, negatives, and to give emphasis to the main verb of a sentence. 2 If someone does a task or activity, they perform it and finish it *E.G. He just didn't want to do any work*. 3 If you ask what people do, you want to know what their job is *E.G. What will you do when you leave school?* 4 If you do well at something, you are successful. If you do badly, you are unsuccessful. 5 If something will do, it is adequate but not the most suitable option *E.G. Home-made stock is best, but cubes will do*. ▶ NOUN 6 *INFORMAL* a party or other social event.
■ (sense 2) carry out, execute, perform

**do up** VERB 1 To do something up

means to fasten it. 2 To do up something old means to repair and decorate it.

**docile**
ADJECTIVE quiet, calm, and easily controlled.

**dock docks docking docked**
NOUN 1 an enclosed area in a harbour where ships go to be loaded, unloaded, or repaired. 2 In a court of law, the dock is the place where the accused person stands or sits. ▶ VERB 3 When a ship docks, it is brought into dock at the end of its voyage. 4 To dock someone's wages means to deduct an amount from the sum they would normally receive. 5 To dock an animal's tail means to cut part of it off.
**docker** NOUN

**doctor doctors doctoring doctored**
NOUN 1 a person who is qualified in medicine and treats people who are ill. 2 A doctor of an academic subject is someone who has been awarded the highest academic degree *E.G. She is a doctor of philosophy*. ▶ VERB 3 To doctor something means to alter it in order to deceive people *E.G. Stamps can be doctored*.

**doctorate doctorates**
NOUN the highest university degree.
**doctoral** ADJECTIVE

**doctrine doctrines**
NOUN a set of beliefs or principles held by a group.
**doctrinal** ADJECTIVE

**document documents documenting documented**
NOUN 1 (HISTORY) a piece of paper which provides an official record of

a
b
c
d
e
f
g
h
i
j
k
l
m
n
o
p
q
r
s
t
u
v
w
x
y
z

something. **2** (ICT) a piece of text or graphics stored in a computer as a file that can be amended or altered by document processing software. ▶ VERB **3** (HISTORY) If you document something, you make a detailed record of it.

**documentation** NOUN

**documentary** documentaries
NOUN **1** a radio or television programme, or a film, which gives information on real events. ▶ ADJECTIVE **2** Documentary evidence is made up of written or official records.

**dodge** dodges dodging dodged
VERB **1** If you dodge or dodge something, you move suddenly to avoid being seen, hit, or caught. **2** If you dodge something such as an issue or accusation, you avoid dealing with it.

**dodgy**
ADJECTIVE; *INFORMAL* dangerous, risky, or unreliable *E.G. He has a dodgy heart.*

**dodo** dodos
NOUN a large, flightless bird which is now extinct.

**doe** does
NOUN a female deer, rabbit, or hare.

**does**
the third person singular of the present tense of **do**.

**dog** dogs dogging dogged
NOUN **1** a four-legged, meat-eating animal, kept as a pet, or to guard property or go hunting. ▶ VERB **2** If you dog someone, you follow them very closely and never leave them.

**dog collar** dog collars
NOUN; *INFORMAL* a white collar with no front opening worn by Christian clergy.

**dog-eared**
ADJECTIVE A book that is dog-eared has been used so much that the corners of the pages are turned down or worn.

**dogged**
*Said "**dog**-ged"* ADJECTIVE showing determination to continue with something, even if it is very difficult *E.G. dogged persistence.*

**doggedly** ADVERB

**dogma** dogmas
NOUN a belief or system of beliefs held by a religious or political group.

**dogmatic**
ADJECTIVE Someone who is dogmatic about something is convinced that they are right about it.

**dogmatism** NOUN

**doldrums**
AN INFORMAL PHRASE If you are **in the doldrums**, you are depressed or bored.

**dole** doles doling doled
VERB If you dole something out, you give a certain amount of it to each individual in a group.

**doll** dolls
NOUN a child's toy which looks like a baby or person.

**dollar** dollars
NOUN the main unit of currency in Australia, New Zealand, the USA, Canada, and some other countries. A dollar is worth 100 cents.

**dollop** dollops
NOUN an amount of food, served casually in a lump.

**dolphin** dolphins
NOUN a mammal which lives in the sea and looks like a large fish with a long snout.

A B C D E F G H I J K L M N O P Q R S T U V W X Y Z

**SPELLING NOTE**       'i' before 'e' except after 'c'

**domain** domains

NOUN 1 a particular area of activity or interest E.G. *the domain of science.* 2 an area over which someone has control or influence E.G. *This reservation was the largest of the Apache domains.*

**dome** domes

NOUN a round roof.

**domed** ADJECTIVE

**domestic**

ADJECTIVE 1 happening or existing within one particular country E.G. *domestic and foreign politics.* 2 involving or concerned with the home and family E.G. *routine domestic tasks.*

**domesticated**

ADJECTIVE If a wild animal or plant has been domesticated, it has been controlled or cultivated.

**domesticity**

NOUN; *FORMAL* Domesticity is life at home with your family.

**dominance**

NOUN 1 Dominance is power or control. 2 If something has dominance over other similar things, it is more powerful or important than they are E.G. *the dominance of the United States in the film business.*

**dominant** ADJECTIVE

**dominate** dominates dominating dominated

VERB 1 If something or someone dominates a situation or event, they are the most powerful or important thing in it and have control over it E.G. *The civil service dominated public affairs.* 2 If a person or country dominates other people or places, they have power or control over them. 3 If something dominates an area, it

towers over it E.G. *The valley was dominated by high surrounding cliffs.*

**dominating** ADJECTIVE **domination** NOUN

**domineering**

ADJECTIVE Someone who is domineering tries to control other people E.G. *a domineering mother.*

**dominion**

NOUN Dominion is control or authority that a person or a country has over other people.

**domino** dominoes

NOUN Dominoes are small rectangular blocks marked with two groups of spots on one side, used for playing the game called dominoes.

**don** dons donning donned

NOUN 1 a lecturer at Oxford or Cambridge university. ▶ VERB 2 *LITERARY* If you don clothing, you put it on.

**donate** donates donating donated

VERB To donate something to a charity or organization means to give it as a gift.

**donation** NOUN

**done**

the past participle of **do**.

**donkey** donkeys

NOUN an animal like a horse, but smaller and with longer ears.

**donor** donors

NOUN 1 someone who gives some of their blood while they are alive or an organ after their death to be used to help someone who is ill E.G. *a kidney donor.* 2 someone who gives something such as money to a charity or other organization.

**doodle** doodles doodling doodled

NOUN 1 a drawing done when you are thinking about something else or when you are bored. ▶ VERB 2 To

A
B
C
D
E
F
G
H
I
J
K
L
M
N
O
P
Q
R
S
T
U
V
W
X
Y
Z

doodle means to draw doodles.

**doom**
NOUN Doom is a terrible fate or event in the future which you can do nothing to prevent.

**doomed**
ADJECTIVE If someone or something is doomed to an unpleasant or unhappy experience, they are certain to suffer it E.G. *doomed to failure.*

**doomsday**
NOUN Doomsday is the end of the world.

**door doors**
NOUN a swinging or sliding panel for opening or closing the entrance to something; also the entrance itself.

**doorway doorways**
NOUN an opening in a wall for a door.

**dope dopes doping doped**
NOUN 1 Dope is an illegal drug. ▶ VERB 2 If someone dopes you, they put a drug into your food or drink.
📖 from Dutch *doop* meaning 'sauce'

**dormant**
ADJECTIVE Something that is dormant is not active, growing, or being used E.G. *The buds will remain dormant until spring.*

**dormitory dormitories**
NOUN a large bedroom where several people sleep.

**dormouse dormice**
NOUN an animal, like a large mouse, with a furry tail.

**dosage dosages**
NOUN the amount of a medicine or a drug that should be taken.

**dose doses**
NOUN a measured amount of a medicine or drug.

**dossier dossiers**
*Said* "**doss**-ee-ay" NOUN a collection of

papers with information on a particular subject or person.

**dot dots dotting dotted**
NOUN 1 a very small, round mark. ▶ VERB 2 If things dot an area, they are scattered all over it E.G. *Fishing villages dot the coastline.* ▶ PHRASE 3 If you arrive somewhere **on the dot**, you arrive there at exactly the right time.

**dotcom dotcoms**
NOUN a company that does most of its business on the Internet.

**dote dotes doting doted**
VERB If you dote on someone, you love them very much.

**doting** ADJECTIVE

**double doubles doubling doubled**
ADJECTIVE 1 twice the usual size E.G. *a double whisky.* 2 consisting of two parts E.G. *a double album.* ▶ VERB 3 If something doubles, it becomes twice as large. 4 To double as something means to have a second job or use as well as the main one E.G. *Their home doubles as an office.* ▶ NOUN 5 Your double is someone who looks exactly like you. 6 Doubles is a game of tennis or badminton which two people play against two other people.

**doubly** ADVERB

**double bass double basses**
NOUN a musical instrument like a large violin, which you play standing up.

**double-cross double-crosses double-crossing double-crossed**
VERB If someone double-crosses you, they cheat you by pretending to do what you both planned, when in fact they do the opposite.

**double-decker double-deckers**
ADJECTIVE 1 having two tiers or layers.

▶ NOUN **2** a bus with two floors.

**double glazing**

NOUN Double glazing is a second layer of glass fitted to windows to keep the building quieter or warmer.

**doubt** doubts doubting doubted

NOUN **1** Doubt is a feeling of uncertainty about whether something is true or possible. ▶ VERB **2** If you doubt something, you think that it is probably not true or possible.

■ (sense 1) misgiving, qualm, uncertainty

**doubtful**

ADJECTIVE unlikely or uncertain.

**dough**

*Rhymes with "go"* NOUN **1** Dough is a mixture of flour and water and sometimes other ingredients, used to make bread, pastry, or biscuits. **2** INFORMAL Dough is money.

**doughnut** doughnuts

NOUN a ring of sweet dough cooked in hot fat.

**dour**

*Rhymes with "poor"* ADJECTIVE severe and unfriendly *E.G. a dour portrait of his personality.*

**douse** douses dousing doused; also spelt **dowse**

VERB If you douse a fire, you stop it burning by throwing water over it.

**dove** doves

NOUN a bird like a small pigeon.

**dovetail** dovetails dovetailing dovetailed

VERB If two things dovetail together, they fit together closely or neatly.

**dowager** dowagers

NOUN a woman who has inherited a title from her dead husband *E.G. the Empress Dowager.*

**dowdy** dowdier dowdiest

ADJECTIVE wearing dull and unfashionable clothes.

**down** downs downing downed

PREPOSITION or ADVERB **1** Down means towards the ground, towards a lower level, or in a lower place. **2** If you go down a road or river, you go along it. ▶ ADVERB **3** If you put something down, you place it on a surface. **4** If an amount of something goes down, it decreases. ▶ ADJECTIVE **5** If you feel down, you feel depressed. ▶ VERB **6** If you down a drink, you drink it quickly. ▶ NOUN **7** Down is the small, soft feathers on young birds.

**downcast**

ADJECTIVE **1** feeling sad and dejected. **2** If your eyes are downcast, they are looking towards the ground.

**downfall**

NOUN **1** The downfall of a successful or powerful person or institution is their failure. **2** Something that is someone's downfall is the thing that causes their failure *E.G. His pride may be his downfall.*

**downgrade** downgrades downgrading downgraded

VERB If you downgrade something, you give it less importance or make it less valuable.

**downhill**

ADVERB **1** moving down a slope. **2** becoming worse *E.G. The press has gone downhill in the last 10 years.*

**download** downloads downloading downloaded

VERB **1** If you download data you transfer it from the memory of one computer to that of another, especially over the Internet. ▶ NOUN **2** a piece of data transferred in this way.

a
b
c
d
e
f
g
h
i
j
k
l
m
n
o
p
q
r
s
t
u
v
w
x
y
z

LEt's measure the angLE (ang**le**)    **SPELLING NOTE**

**downpour** downpours
NOUN a heavy fall of rain.

**downright**
ADJECTIVE or ADVERB You use 'downright' to emphasize that something is extremely unpleasant or bad E.G. Staff are often discourteous and sometimes downright rude.

**downstairs**
ADVERB 1 going down a staircase towards the ground floor. ▶ ADJECTIVE or ADVERB 2 on a lower floor or on the ground floor.

**downstream**
ADJECTIVE or ADVERB Something that is downstream or moving downstream is nearer or moving nearer to the mouth of a river from a point further up.

**down-to-earth**
ADJECTIVE sensible and practical E.G. a down-to-earth approach.

**downtrodden**
ADJECTIVE People who are downtrodden are treated badly by those with power and do not have the ability to fight back.

**downturn** downturns
NOUN a decline in the economy or in the success of a company or industry.

**downwards** or **downward**
ADVERB or ADJECTIVE 1 If you move or look downwards, you move or look towards the ground or towards a lower level E.G. His eyes travelled downwards… She slipped on the downward slope. 2 If an amount or rate moves downwards, it decreases.

**downwind**
ADVERB If something moves downwind, it moves in the same direction as the wind E.G. Sparks

drifted downwind.

**dowry** dowries
NOUN A woman's dowry is money or property which her father gives to the man she marries.

**doze** dozes dozing dozed
VERB 1 When you doze, you sleep lightly for a short period. ▶ NOUN 2 a short, light sleep.

**dozen** dozens
NOUN A dozen things are twelve of them.

**Dr**
Said "*dock*-ter" 1 'Dr' is short for 'Doctor' and is used before the name of someone with the highest form of academic degree or who practises medicine. 2 'Dr' is short for 'drive'.

**drab** drabber drabbest
ADJECTIVE dull and unattractive.
**drabness** NOUN
▤ dreary, dull

**draft** drafts drafting drafted
NOUN 1 an early rough version of it of a document or speech. ▶ VERB 2 When you draft a document or speech, you write the first rough version of it. 3 To draft people somewhere means to move them there so that they can do a specific job E.G. Various different presenters were drafted in. 4 In Australian and New Zealand English, to draft cattle or sheep is to select some from a herd or flock.

**drag** drags dragging dragged
VERB 1 If you drag a heavy object somewhere, you pull it slowly and with difficulty. 2 If you drag someone somewhere, you make them go although they may be unwilling. 3 If things drag behind you, they trail along the ground as you move along. 4 If an event or a period of

time drags, it is boring and seems to last a long time. ▶ NOUN **5** Drag is the resistance to the motion of a body passing through air or a fluid.
■ (sense 1) drag, haul, pull

**dragon** dragons
NOUN In stories and legends, a dragon is a fierce animal like a large lizard with wings and claws that breathes fire.
🏛 from Greek *drakōn* meaning 'serpent'

**dragonfly** dragonflies
NOUN a colourful insect which is often found near water.

**dragoon** dragoons dragooning dragooned
NOUN **1** Dragoons are soldiers. Originally, they were mounted infantry soldiers. ▶ VERB **2** If you dragoon someone into something, you force them to do it.

**drain** drains draining drained
VERB **1** If you drain something or if it drains, liquid gradually flows out of it or off it. **2** If you drain a glass, you drink all its contents. **3** If something drains strength or resources, it gradually uses them up E.G. *The prolonged boardroom battle drained him of energy and money.* ▶ NOUN **4** a pipe or channel that carries water or sewage away from a place. **5** a metal grid in a road, through which rainwater flows.

**drainage**
NOUN **1** Drainage is the system of pipes, drains, or ditches used to drain water or other liquid away from a place. **2** Drainage is also the process of draining water away, or the way in which a place drains E.G. *To grow these well, all you need is good drainage.*

**drake** drakes
NOUN a male duck.

**drama** dramas
NOUN **1** a serious play for the theatre, television, or radio. **2** Drama is plays and the theatre in general E.G. *Japanese drama.* **3** You can refer to the exciting events or aspects of a situation as drama E.G. *the drama of real life.*

**dramatic**
ADJECTIVE A dramatic change or event happens suddenly and is very noticeable E.G. *a dramatic departure from tradition.*
**dramatically** ADVERB

**dramatist** dramatists
NOUN (DRAMA) a person who writes plays.

**drape** drapes draping draped
VERB If you drape a piece of cloth, you arrange it so that it hangs down or covers something in loose folds.

**drastic**
ADJECTIVE A drastic course of action is very severe and is usually taken urgently E.G. *It's time for drastic action.*
**drastically** ADVERB
■ extreme, radical

**draught** draughts
*Said* "draft" NOUN **1** a current of cold air. **2** an amount of liquid that you swallow. **3** Draughts is a game for two people played on a chessboard with round pieces. ▶ ADJECTIVE **4** Draught beer is served straight from barrels rather than in bottles.

**draughtsman** draughtsmen
NOUN a person who prepares detailed drawings or plans.

**draughty** draughtier draughtiest
ADJECTIVE A place that is draughty has

a b c **d** e f g h i j k l m n o p q r s t u v w x y z

A
B
C
**D**
E
F
G
H
I
J
K
L
M
N
O
P
Q
R
S
T
U
V
W
X
Y
Z

currents of cold air blowing through it.

**draw** draws drawing drew drawn

VERB 1 When you draw, you use a pen or crayon to make a picture or diagram. 2 To draw near means to move closer. To draw away or draw back means to move away. 3 If you draw something in a particular direction, you pull it there smoothly and gently E.G. *He drew his feet under the chair.* 4 If you draw a deep breath, you breathe in deeply. 5 If you draw the curtains, you pull them so that they cover or uncover the window. 6 If something such as water or energy is drawn from a source, it is taken from it. 7 If you draw a conclusion, you arrive at it from the facts you know. 8 If you draw a distinction or a comparison between two things, you point out that it exists. ▶ NOUN 9 the result of a game or competition in which nobody wins.

**draw up** VERB To draw up a plan, document, or list means to prepare it and write it out.

**drawback** drawbacks
NOUN a problem that makes something less acceptable or desirable E.G. *Shortcuts usually have a drawback.*

**drawbridge** drawbridges
NOUN a bridge that can be pulled up or lowered.

**drawer** drawers
NOUN a sliding box-shaped part of a piece of furniture used for storing things.

**drawing** drawings
NOUN 1 a picture made with a pencil, pen, or crayon. 2 Drawing is the skill or work of making drawings.

**drawing room** drawing rooms
NOUN; *OLD-FASHIONED* a room in a house where people relax or entertain guests.

**drawl** drawls drawling drawled
VERB If someone drawls, they speak slowly with long vowel sounds.

**drawn**
Drawn is the past participle of **draw**.

**dread** dreads dreading dreaded
VERB 1 If you dread something, you feel very worried and frightened about it E.G. *He was dreading the journey.* ▶ NOUN 2 Dread is a feeling of great fear or anxiety.
**dreaded** ADJECTIVE

**dreadful**
ADJECTIVE very bad or unpleasant.
**dreadfully** ADVERB
≡ atrocious, awful, terrible

**dream** dreams dreaming dreamed or dreamt
NOUN 1 a series of events that you experience in your mind while asleep. 2 a situation or event which you often think about because you would very much like it to happen E.G. *his dream of winning the lottery.* ▶ VERB 3 When you dream, you see events in your mind while you are asleep. 4 When you dream about something happening, you often think about it because you would very much like it to happen. 5 If someone dreams up a plan or idea, they invent it. 6 If you say you would not dream of doing something, you are emphasizing that you would not do it E.G. *I wouldn't dream of giving the plot away.* ▶ ADJECTIVE 7 too good to be true E.G. *a dream holiday.*
**dreamer** NOUN

**Dreamtime**

NOUN In Australian Aboriginal legends, Dreamtime is the time when the world was being made and the first people were created.

**dreamy dreamier dreamiest**

ADJECTIVE Someone with a dreamy expression looks as if they are thinking about something very pleasant.

**dreary drearier dreariest**

ADJECTIVE dull or boring.

**dregs**

PLURAL NOUN The dregs of a liquid are the last drops left at the bottom of a container, and any sediment left with it.

**drenched**

ADJECTIVE soaking wet.

**dress dresses dressing dressed**

NOUN 1 a piece of clothing for women or girls made up of a skirt and top attached. 2 Dress is any clothing worn by men or women. ▶ VERB 3 When you dress, you put clothes on. 4 If you dress for a special occasion, you put on formal clothes. 5 To dress a wound means to clean it up and treat it.

**dresser dressers**

NOUN a piece of kitchen or dining room furniture with cupboards or drawers in the lower part and open shelves in the top part.

**dress rehearsal dress rehearsals**

NOUN the last rehearsal of a show or play, using costumes, scenery, and lighting.

**dribble dribbles dribbling dribbled**

VERB 1 When liquid dribbles down a surface, it trickles down it in drops or

a thin stream. 2 If a person or animal dribbles, saliva trickles from their mouth. 3 In sport, to dribble a ball means to move it along by repeatedly tapping it with your foot or a stick. ▶ NOUN 4 a small quantity of liquid flowing in a thin stream or drops.

**drift drifts drifting drifted**

VERB 1 When something drifts, it is carried along by the wind or by water. 2 When people drift, they move aimlessly from one place or activity to another. 3 If you drift off to sleep, you gradually fall asleep. ▶ NOUN 4 A snow drift is a pile of snow heaped up by the wind. 5 The drift of an argument or a speech is its main point.

**drifter** NOUN

**drill drills drilling drilled**

NOUN 1 a tools for making holes E.G. an electric drill. 2 Drill is a routine exercise or routine training E.G. lifeboat drill. ▶ VERB 3 To drill into something means to make a hole in it using a drill. 4 If you drill people, you teach them to do something by repetition.

**drink drinks drinking drank drunk**

VERB 1 When you drink, you take liquid into your mouth and swallow it. 2 To drink also means to drink alcohol E.G. He drinks little and eats carefully. ▶ NOUN 3 an amount of liquid suitable for drinking. 4 an alcoholic drink.

**drinker** NOUN

▤ (sense 1) imbibe, sip, swallow
▤ (sense 2) booze, tipple

**drip drips dripping dripped**

VERB 1 When liquid drips, it falls in small drops. 2 When an object drips,

a b c **d** e f g h i j k l m n o p q r s t u v w x y z

A
B
C
**D**
E
F
G
H
I
J
K
L
M
N
O
P
Q
R
S
T
U
V
W
X
Y
Z

drops of liquid fall from it. ► NOUN **3** a
drop of liquid falling from
something. **4** a device for allowing
liquid food to enter the bloodstream
of a person who cannot eat properly
because they are ill.

**drive** drives driving drove driven
VERB **1** To drive a vehicle means to
operate it and control its
movements. **2** If something or
someone drives you to do
something, they force you to do it E.G.
*The illness of his daughter drove him
to religion.* **3** If you drive a post or nail
into something, you force it in by
hitting it with a hammer. **4** If
something drives a machine, it
supplies the power that makes it
work. ► NOUN **5** a journey in a vehicle.
**6** a private road that leads from a
public road to a person's house.
**7** Drive is energy and determination.
**driver** NOUN **driving** NOUN

**drivel**
NOUN Drivel is nonsense E.G. *He is still
writing mindless drivel.*
📖 from Old English *dreflian* meaning
'to dribble'

**drizzle**
NOUN Drizzle is light rain.

**dromedary** dromedaries
NOUN a camel which has one hump.

**drone** drones droning droned
VERB **1** If something drones, it makes a
low, continuous humming noise. **2** If
someone drones on, they keep
talking or reading aloud in a boring
way. ► NOUN **3** a continuous low dull
sound.

**drool** drools drooling drooled
VERB If someone drools, saliva
dribbles from their mouth without
them being able to stop it.

**droop** droops drooping drooped
VERB If something droops, it hangs or
sags downwards with no strength or
firmness.

**drop** drops dropping dropped
VERB **1** If you drop something, you let
it fall. **2** If something drops, it falls
straight down. **3** If a level or amount
drops, it becomes less. **4** If your voice
drops, or if you drop your voice, you
speak more quietly. **5** If you drop
something that you are doing or
dealing with, you stop doing it or
dealing with it E.G. *She dropped the
subject and never mentioned it again.*
**6** If you drop a hint, you give
someone a hint in a casual way. **7** If
you drop something or someone
somewhere, you deposit or leave
them there. ► NOUN **8** A drop of liquid
is a very small quantity of it that
forms or falls in a round shape. **9** a
decrease E.G. *a huge drop in income.*
**10** the distance between the top and
bottom of something tall, such as a
cliff or building E.G. *It is a sheer drop to
the foot of the cliff.*

**droplet** droplets
NOUN a small drop.

**droppings**
PLURAL NOUN Droppings are the faeces
of birds and small animals.

**drought** droughts
*Rhymes with "shout"* NOUN a long
period during which there is no
rain.

**drove** droves droving droved
**1** Drove is the past tense of **drive**.
VERB **2** To drove cattle or sheep is to
drive them over a long distance.

**drown** drowns drowning
drowned
VERB **1** When someone drowns or is

drowned, they die because they have gone under water and cannot breathe. **2** If a noise drowns a sound, it is louder than the sound and makes it impossible to hear it.

**drowsy** drowsier drowsiest
ADJECTIVE feeling sleepy.

**drudgery**
NOUN Drudgery is hard boring work.

**drug** drugs drugging drugged
NOUN **1** a chemical given to people to treat disease. **2** Drugs are chemical substances that some people smoke, swallow, smell, or inject because of their stimulating effects. ▶ VERB **3** To drug a person or animal means to give them a drug to make them unconscious. **4** To drug food or drink means to add a drug to it in order to make someone unconscious.
**drugged** ADJECTIVE

**druid** druids
*Said* "**droo**-id" NOUN a priest of an ancient religion in Northern Europe.

**drum** drums drumming drummed
NOUN **1** a musical instrument consisting of a skin stretched tightly over a round frame. **2** an object or container shaped like a drum *E.G. an oil drum*. **3** INFORMAL In Australian English, the drum is information or advice *E.G. The manager gave me the drum*. ▶ VERB **4** If something is drumming on a surface, it is hitting it regularly, making a continuous beating sound. **5** If you drum something into someone, you keep saying it to them until they understand it or remember it.
**drummer** NOUN

**drumstick** drumsticks
NOUN **1** a stick used for beating a

drum. **2** A chicken drumstick is the lower part of the leg of a chicken, which is cooked and eaten.

**drunk** drunks
**1** Drunk is the past participle of **drink**. ▶ ADJECTIVE **2** If someone is drunk, they have drunk so much alcohol that they cannot speak clearly or behave sensibly. ▶ NOUN **3** a person who is drunk, or who often gets drunk.
**drunken** ADJECTIVE    **drunkenly** ADVERB    **drunkenness** NOUN
■ (sense 2) inebriated, intoxicated

**dry** drier or dryer driest; dries drying dried
ADJECTIVE **1** Something that is dry contains or uses no water or liquid. **2** Dry bread or toast is eaten without a topping. **3** Dry sherry or wine does not taste sweet. **4** Dry also means plain and sometimes boring *E.G. the dry facts*. **5** Dry humour is subtle and sarcastic. ▶ VERB **6** When you dry something, or when it dries, liquid is removed from it.
■ (sense 1) arid, dehydrated, parched

**dry up** VERB **1** If something dries up, it becomes completely dry. **2** INFORMAL If you dry up, you forget what you were going to say, or find that you have nothing left to say.
**dryness** NOUN    **drily** ADVERB

**dry-clean** dry-cleans dry-cleaning dry-cleaned
VERB When clothes are dry-cleaned, they are cleaned with a liquid chemical rather than with water.

**dryer** dryers; also spelt **drier**
NOUN a device for removing moisture from something by heating or by hot air *E.G. a hair dryer*.

a b c d e f g h i j k l m n o p q r s t u v w x y z

**dual**

ADJECTIVE having two parts, functions, or aspects E.G. *a dual-purpose trimmer*.

**dub dubs dubbing dubbed**

VERB 1 If something is dubbed a particular name, it is given that name E.G. *Smiling has been dubbed 'nature's secret weapon'*. 2 If a film is dubbed, the voices on the soundtrack are not those of the actors, but those of other actors speaking in a different language.

**dubious**

*Said "dyoo-bee-uss"* ADJECTIVE 1 not entirely honest, safe, or reliable E.G. *dubious sales techniques*. 2 doubtful E.G. *I felt dubious about the entire proposition*.

**dubiously** ADVERB

■ (sense 1) questionable, suspect

**duchess duchesses**

NOUN a woman who has the same rank as a duke, or who is a duke's wife or widow.

**duchy duchies**

*Said "dut-shee"* NOUN the land owned and ruled by a duke or duchess.

**duck ducks ducking ducked**

NOUN 1 a bird that lives in water and has webbed feet and a large flat bill. ► VERB 2 If you duck, you move your head quickly downwards in order to avoid being hit by something. 3 If you duck a duty or responsibility, you avoid it. 4 To duck someone means to push them briefly under water.

**duckling ducklings**

NOUN a young duck.

**duct ducts**

NOUN 1 a pipe or channel through

which liquid or gas is sent. 2 a bodily passage through which liquid such as tears can pass.

**dud duds**

NOUN something which does not function properly.

**due dues**

ADJECTIVE 1 expected to happen or arrive E.G. *The baby is due at Christmas*. 2 If you give something due consideration, you give it the consideration it needs. ► PHRASE 3 **Due to** means because of E.G. *Headaches can be due to stress*. ► ADVERB 4 Due means exactly in a particular direction E.G. *About a mile due west lay the ocean*. ► PLURAL NOUN 5 Dues are sums of money that you pay regularly to an organization you belong to.

**duel duels**

NOUN 1 a fight arranged between two people using deadly weapons, to settle a quarrel. 2 Any contest or conflict between two people can be referred to as a duel.

**duet duets**

NOUN a piece of music sung or played by two people.

**dug**

Dug is the past tense and past participle of **dig**.

**dugong dugongs**

NOUN an animal like a whale that lives in warm seas.

**dugout dugouts**

NOUN 1 a canoe made by hollowing out a log. 2 MILITARY a shelter dug in the ground for protection.

**duke dukes**

NOUN a nobleman with a rank just below that of a prince.
🏛 from Latin *dux* meaning 'leader'

**dull** duller dullest; dulls dulling
dulled
ADJECTIVE **1** not at all interesting in any
way. **2** slow to learn or understand.
**3** not bright, sharp, or clear. **4** A dull
day or dull sky is very cloudy. **5** Dull
feelings are weak and not intense E.G.
*He should have been angry but felt
only dull resentment.* ▶ VERB **6** If
something dulls or is dulled, it
becomes less bright, sharp, or clear.
**dully** ADVERB **dullness** NOUN
■ (sense 4) cloudy, overcast

**duly**
ADVERB **1** FORMAL If something is duly
done, it is done in the correct way E.G.
*I wish to record my support for the
duly elected council.* **2** If something
duly happens, it is something that
you expected to happen E.G. *Two
chicks duly emerged from their eggs.*

**dumb** dumber dumbest
ADJECTIVE **1** unable to speak. **2** INFORMAL
slow to understand or stupid.

**dumbfounded**
ADJECTIVE speechless with amazement
E.G. *She was too dumbfounded to
answer.*

**dummy** dummies
NOUN **1** a rubber teat which a baby
sucks or bites on. **2** an imitation or
model of something which is used
for display. ▶ ADJECTIVE **3** imitation or
substitute.

**dump** dumps dumping dumped
VERB **1** When unwanted waste is
dumped, it is left somewhere. **2** If you
dump something, you throw it down
or put it down somewhere in a
careless way. ▶ NOUN **3** a place where
rubbish is left. **4** a storage place,
especially used by the military for
storing supplies. **5** INFORMAL You refer

to a place as a dump when it is
unattractive and unpleasant to live
in.

**dumpling** dumplings
NOUN a small lump of dough that is
cooked and eaten with meat and
vegetables.

**dunce** dunces
NOUN a person who cannot learn what
someone is trying to teach them.

**dune** dunes
NOUN A dune or sand dune is a hill of
sand near the sea or in the desert.

**dung**
NOUN Dung is the faeces from large
animals, sometimes called manure.

**dungarees**
PLURAL NOUN Dungarees are trousers
which have a bib covering the chest
and straps over the shoulders.

**dungeon** dungeons
*Said "dun-jen"* NOUN an underground
prison.

**dunk** dunks dunking dunked
VERB To dunk something means to dip
it briefly into a liquid E.G. *He dunked a
single tea bag into two cups.*

**duo** duos
NOUN **1** a pair of musical performers;
also a piece of music written for two
players. **2** Any two people doing
something together can be referred
to as a duo.

**dupe** dupes duping duped
VERB **1** If someone dupes you, they
trick you. ▶ NOUN **2** someone who has
been tricked.
▣ from Old French *de huppe*
meaning 'of the hoopoe', a bird
thought to be stupid

**duplicate** duplicates duplicating
duplicated
VERB **1** To duplicate something means

A
B
C
D
E
F
G
H
I
J
K
L
M
N
O
P
Q
R
S
T
U
V
W
X
Y
Z

to make an exact copy of it. ► NOUN
**2** something that is identical to
something else. ► ADJECTIVE **3** identical
to or an exact copy of *E.G. a duplicate
key.*

**duplication** NOUN

**durable**

ADJECTIVE strong and lasting for a long
time.

**durability** NOUN

**duration**

NOUN The duration of something is
the length of time during which it
happens or exists.

**duress**

*Said "dyoo-**ress**"* NOUN If you do
something under duress, you are
forced to do it, and you do it very
unwillingly.

**during**

PREPOSITION happening throughout a
particular time or at a particular
point in time *E.G. The mussels will
open naturally during cooking.*

**dusk**

NOUN Dusk is the time just before
nightfall when it is not completely
dark.

🔲 from Old English *dox* meaning
'dark' or 'swarthy'

**dust** dusts dusting dusted

NOUN **1** Dust is dry fine powdery
material such as particles of earth,
dirt, or pollen. ► VERB **2** When you dust
furniture or other objects, you
remove dust from them using a
duster. **3** If you dust a surface with
powder, you cover it lightly with the
powder.

**dustbin** dustbins

NOUN a large container for rubbish.

**duster** dusters

NOUN a cloth used for removing dust

from furniture and other objects.

**dustman** dustmen

NOUN someone whose job is to
collect the rubbish from people's
houses.

**dusty** dustier dustiest

ADJECTIVE covered with dust.

**Dutch**

ADJECTIVE **1** belonging or relating to
Holland. ► NOUN **2** Dutch is the main
language spoken in Holland.

**dutiful**

ADJECTIVE doing everything you are
expected to do.

**dutifully** ADVERB

**duty** duties

NOUN **1** Duties are things you ought to
do or feel you should do, because it
is your responsibility to do them *E.G.
We have a duty as adults to listen to
children.* ► PLURAL NOUN **2** Your duties
are the tasks which you do as part of
your job. ► NOUN **3** Duty is tax paid to
the government on some goods,
especially imports.

🔲 (sense 1) obligation,
responsibility

**duty-free**

ADJECTIVE Duty-free goods are sold at
airports or on planes or ships at a
cheaper price than usual because
they are not taxed *E.G. duty-free vodka.*

**duvet** duvets

*Said "**doo**-vay"* NOUN a cotton quilt
filled with feathers or other material,
used on a bed in place of sheets and
blankets.

**DVD** DVDs

NOUN an abbreviation for 'digital
video *or* digital versatile disc': a type
of compact disc that can store large
amounts of video and sound
information.

**dwarf** dwarfs dwarfing dwarfed
VERB 1 If one thing dwarfs another, it is so much bigger that it makes it look very small. ▶ ADJECTIVE 2 smaller than average. ▶ NOUN 3 a person who is much smaller than average size.

**dwell** dwells dwelling dwelled or dwelt
VERB 1 *LITERARY* To dwell somewhere means to live there. 2 If you dwell on something or dwell upon it, you think or write about it a lot.

**dwelling** dwellings
NOUN; *FORMAL* Someone's dwelling is the house or other place where they live.

**dwindle** dwindles dwindling dwindled
VERB If something dwindles, it becomes smaller or weaker.

**dye** dyes dyeing dyed
VERB 1 To dye something means to change its colour by applying coloured liquid to it. ▶ NOUN 2 a colouring substance which is used to change the colour of something such as cloth or hair.

**dyke** dykes; also spelt **dike**
NOUN a thick wall that prevents water flooding onto land from a river or from the sea.

**dynamic** dynamics
ADJECTIVE 1 A dynamic person is full of energy, ambition, and new ideas. 2 relating to energy or forces which produce motion. ▶ PLURAL NOUN 3 In physics, dynamics is the study of the forces that change or produce the motion of bodies or particles. 4 The dynamics of a society or a situation are the forces that cause it to change. 5 (MUSIC) Dynamics is the various degrees of loudness needed in the performance of a piece of music, or the symbols used to indicate this in written music.

**dynamite**
NOUN Dynamite is a kind of explosive.

**dynamo** dynamos
NOUN a device that converts mechanical energy into electricity.

**dynasty** dynasties
NOUN (HISTORY) a series of rulers of a country all belonging to the same family.

**dysentery**
*Said "diss-en-tree"* NOUN an infection of the bowel which causes fever, stomach pain, and severe diarrhoea.

**dyslexia**
*Said "dis-lek-see-a"* NOUN Dyslexia is difficulty with reading caused by a slight disorder of the brain.

**dyslexic** ADJECTIVE AND NOUN

a b c **d** e f g h i j k l m n o p q r s t u v w x y z

Plaice the fish has a glittering 'EYE' (I) (plaice)    SPELLING NOTE

# Ee

**TIP** The words *aesthetic*, *oesophagus* and *oestrogen* sound as if they should start with letter *e*, but in British English they are spelt with *ae* and *oe*. These two combinations of letters, which both sound like ee, can come in the middle of words too, for example in *anaethestic* and *amoeba*.

**each**

ADJECTIVE OR PRONOUN **1** every one taken separately *E.G. Each time she went out, she would buy a plant.* ▶ PHRASE **2** If people do something to **each other**, each person does it to the other or others *E.G. She and Chris smiled at each other.*

☑ Wherever you use *each other* you could also use *one another*.

**eager**

ADJECTIVE wanting very much to do or have something.

**eagerly** ADVERB **eagerness** NOUN

**eagle eagles**

NOUN a large bird of prey.

**ear ears**

NOUN **1** the parts of your body on either side of your head with which you hear sounds. **2** An ear of corn or wheat is the top part of the stalk which contains seeds.

**eardrum eardrums**

NOUN Your eardrums are thin pieces of tightly stretched skin inside your ears which vibrate so that you can hear sounds.

**earl earls**

NOUN a British nobleman.

🏛 from Old English *eorl* meaning 'chieftain'

**early earlier earliest**

ADJECTIVE OR ADVERB **1** before the arranged or expected time *E.G. He wasn't late for our meeting, I was early.*

**2** near the beginning of a day, evening, or other period of time *E.G. the early 1970s.*

▦ (sense 1) premature, untimely

**earmark earmarks earmarking earmarked**

VERB If you earmark something for a special purpose, you keep it for that purpose.

🏛 from identification marks on the ears of domestic or farm animals

**earn earns earning earned**

VERB **1** If you earn money, you get it in return for work that you do. **2** If you earn something such as praise, you receive it because you deserve it.

**earner** NOUN

**earnest**

ADJECTIVE **1** sincere in what you say or do *E.G. I answered with an earnest smile.* ▶ PHRASE **2** If something begins **in earnest**, it happens to a greater or more serious extent than before *E.G. The battle began in earnest.*

**earnestly** ADVERB

**earnings**

PLURAL NOUN Your earnings are money that you earn.

**earphones**

PLURAL NOUN small speakers which you wear on your ears to listen to a radio or cassette player.

**earring earrings**

NOUN Earrings are pieces of jewellery that you wear on your ear lobes.

**earshot**
PHRASE If you are **within earshot** of something, you can hear it.

**earth** earths
NOUN **1** The earth is the planet on which we live. **2** Earth is the dry land on the surface of the earth, especially the soil in which things grow. **3** a hole in the ground where a fox lives. **4** The earth in a piece of electrical equipment is the wire through which electricity can pass into the ground and so make the equipment safe for use.

**earthenware**
NOUN pottery made of baked clay.

**earthly**
ADJECTIVE concerned with life on earth rather than heaven or life after death.

**earthquake** earthquakes
NOUN a shaking of the ground caused by movement of the earth's crust.

**earthworm** earthworms
NOUN a worm that lives under the ground.

**earthy** earthier earthiest
ADJECTIVE **1** looking or smelling like earth. **2** Someone who is earthy is open and direct, often in a crude way E.G. earthy language.

**earwig** earwigs
NOUN a small, thin, brown insect which has a pair of pincers at the end of its body.
🔲 from Old English earwicga meaning 'ear insect'; it was believed to creep into people's ears

**ease** eases easing eased
NOUN **1** lack of difficulty, worry, or hardship E.G. He had sailed through life with relative ease. ▶ VERB **2** When something eases, or when you ease

it, it becomes less severe or less intense E.G. to ease the pain. **3** If you ease something somewhere, you move it there slowly and carefully E.G. He eased himself into his chair.
🔲 (sense 1) easiness, effortlessness
🔲 (sense 2) alleviate, relieve

**easel** easels
NOUN (ART) an upright frame which supports a picture that someone is painting.
🔲 from Dutch ezel meaning 'ass' or 'donkey'

**easily**
ADVERB **1** without difficulty. **2** without a doubt E.G. The song is easily one of their finest.

**east**
NOUN **1** East is the direction in which you look to see the sun rise. **2** The east of a place is the part which is towards the east when you are in the centre E.G. the east of Africa. **3** The East is the countries in the south and east of Asia. ▶ ADJECTIVE OR ADVERB **4** East means in or towards the east E.G. The entrance faces east. ▶ ADJECTIVE **5** An east wind blows from the east.

**Easter**
NOUN a Christian religious festival celebrating the resurrection of Christ.
🔲 from Old English Eostre, a pre-Christian Germanic goddess whose festival was at the spring equinox

**easterly**
ADJECTIVE **1** Easterly means to or towards the east. **2** An easterly wind blows from the east.

**eastern**
ADJECTIVE in or from the east E.G. a remote eastern corner of the country.

A
B
C
D
**E**
G
G
H
I
J
K
L
M
N
O
P
Q
R
S
T
U
V
W
X
Y
Z

**eastward** or **eastwards**
ADVERB 1 Eastward or eastwards means towards the east *E.G. the eastward expansion of the city*.
▶ ADJECTIVE 2 The eastward part of something is the east part.

**easy easier easiest**
ADJECTIVE 1 able to be done without difficulty *E.G. It's easy to fall*.
2 comfortable and without any worries *E.G. an easy life*.
☑ Although *easy* is an adjective, it can be used as an adverb in fixed phrases like *take it easy*.

**eat eats eating ate eaten**
VERB 1 To eat means to chew and swallow food. 2 When you eat, you have a meal *E.G. We like to eat early*.
**eat away** VERB If something is eaten away, it is slowly destroyed *E.G. The sea had eaten away at the headland*.

**eaves**
PLURAL NOUN The eaves of a roof are the lower edges which jut out over the walls.

**eavesdrop eavesdrops eavesdropping eavesdropped**
VERB If you eavesdrop, you listen secretly to what other people are saying.
📖 from Old English *yfesdrype* meaning 'water dripping down from the eaves'; people were supposed to stand outside in the rain to hear what was being said inside the house

**ebb ebbs ebbing ebbed**
VERB 1 When the sea or the tide ebbs, it flows back. 2 If a person's feeling or strength ebbs, it gets weaker *E.G. The strength ebbed from his body*.

**ebony**
NOUN 1 a hard, dark-coloured wood, used for making furniture. ▶ NOUN or ADJECTIVE 2 very deep black.

**ebullient**
ADJECTIVE; FORMAL lively and full of enthusiasm.
**ebullience** NOUN

**EC**
NOUN The EC is an old name for the European Union. EC is an abbreviation for 'European Community'.

**eccentric eccentrics**
*Said* "ik-**sen**-trik" ADJECTIVE 1 having habits or opinions which other people think are odd or peculiar.
▶ NOUN 2 someone who is eccentric.
**eccentricity** NOUN    **eccentrically** ADVERB
▤ (sense 1) odd, peculiar, strange
▤ (sense 2) crank, oddball, weirdo

**ecclesiastical**
*Said* "ik-**leez**-ee-**ass**-ti-kl" ADJECTIVE of or relating to the Christian church.
📖 from Greek *ekklēsia* meaning 'assembly' or 'church'

**echelon echelons**
*Said* "**esh**-el-on" NOUN a level of power or responsibility in an organization.

**echidna echidnas** or **echidnae**
*Said* "ik-**kid**-na" NOUN a small, spiny mammal that lays eggs and has a long snout and claws, found in Australia.

**echo echoes echoing echoed**
NOUN 1 a sound which is caused by sound waves reflecting off a surface. 2 a repetition, imitation, or reminder of something *E.G. Echoes of the past are everywhere*. ▶ VERB 3 If a sound echoes, it is reflected off a surface so that you can hear it again after the original sound has stopped.

**eclipse eclipses**
NOUN An eclipse occurs when one

planet passes in front of another and hides it from view for a short time.

**eco-**

PREFIX Words beginning with 'eco-' have something to do with ecology or the environment.

📖 from Greek *oikos* meaning 'environment'

**ecology**

NOUN the relationship between living things and their environment; also used of the study of this relationship.
**ecological** ADJECTIVE **ecologically** ADVERB **ecologist** NOUN

**economic**

ADJECTIVE 1 (HISTORY) concerning the management of the money, industry, and trade of a country. 2 concerning making a profit *E.G. economic to produce.*

**economical**

ADJECTIVE 1 (HISTORY) another word for **economic**. 2 Something that is economical is cheap to use or operate. 3 Someone who is economical spends money carefully and sensibly.
**economically** ADVERB

**economics**

NOUN Economics is the study of the production and distribution of goods, services, and wealth in a society and the organization of its money, industry, and trade.

**economist economists**

NOUN a person who studies or writes about economics.

**economy economies**

NOUN 1 (HISTORY) The economy of a country is the system it uses to organize and manage its money, industry, and trade; also used of the wealth that a country gets from

business and industry. 2 Economy is the careful use of things to save money, time, or energy *E.G. Max dished up deftly, with an economy of movement.*

📖 from Greek *oikonomia* meaning 'domestic management'

**ecosystem ecosystems**

NOUN; TECHNICAL the relationship between plants and animals and their environment.

**ecstasy ecstasies**

NOUN 1 Ecstasy is a feeling of extreme happiness. 2 INFORMAL a strong illegal drug that can cause hallucinations.
**ecstatic** ADJECTIVE **ecstatically** ADVERB

**eczema**

*Said* "ek-sim-ma" *or* "ek-**see**-ma" NOUN a skin disease that causes the surface of the skin to become rough and itchy.

📖 from Greek *ekzein* meaning 'to boil over'

**-ed**

SUFFIX '-ed' is used to form the past tense of most English verbs *E.G. jumped… tried.*

📖 from Old English

**eddy eddies**

NOUN a circular movement in water or air.

**edge edges edging edged**

NOUN 1 The edge of something is a border or line where it ends or meets something else. 2 The edge of a blade is its thin, sharp side. 3 If you have the edge over someone, you have an advantage over them. ▶ VERB 4 If you edge something, you make a border for it *E.G. The veil was edged with matching lace.* 5 If you edge somewhere, you move there very

LEarn the principLEs (principl**e**)          SPELLING NOTE

gradually E.G. *The ferry edged its way out into the river.*

■ (sense 1) border, brink, margin

**edgy edgier edgiest**
ADJECTIVE anxious and irritable.

**edible**
ADJECTIVE safe and pleasant to eat.

**edifice edifices**
*Said* "ed-if-iss" NOUN; *FORMAL* a large and impressive building.

**edit edits editing edited**
VERB 1 If you edit a piece of writing, you correct it so that it is fit for publishing. 2 To edit a film or television programme means to select different parts of it and arrange them in a particular order. 3 Someone who edits a newspaper or magazine is in charge of it.

**edition editions**
NOUN 1 An edition of a book or magazine is a particular version of it printed at one time. 2 An edition of a television or radio programme is a single programme that is one of a series.

**editor editors**
NOUN (LIBRARY) 1 a person who is responsible for the content of a newspaper or magazine. 2 a person who checks books and makes corrections to them before they are published. 3 a person who selects different parts of a television programme or a film and arranges them in a particular order.

**editorship** NOUN

**editorial editorials**
ADJECTIVE 1 involved in preparing a newspaper, book, or magazine for publication. 2 involving the contents and the opinions of a newspaper or magazine E.G. *an editorial comment.*

▶ NOUN 3 an article in a newspaper or magazine which gives the opinions of the editor or publisher on a particular topic.

**editorially** ADVERB

**educate educates educating educated**
VERB To educate someone means to teach them so that they gain knowledge about something.

**educated**
ADJECTIVE having a high standard of learning and culture.

**education**
NOUN 1 Education is the process of gaining knowledge and understanding through learning. 2 Education also refers to the system of teaching people at school or university.

**educational** ADJECTIVE
**educationally** ADVERB

**eel eels**
NOUN a long, thin, snakelike fish.

**eerie eerier eeriest**
ADJECTIVE strange and frightening E.G. *an eerie silence.*

**eerily** ADVERB

**effect effects**
NOUN 1 a direct result of someone or something on another person or thing E.G. *the effect of divorce on children.* 2 An effect that someone or something has is the overall impression or result that they have E.G. *The effect of the decor was cosy and antique.* ▶ PHRASE 3 If something **takes effect** at a particular time, it starts to happen or starts to produce results at that time E.G. *The law will take effect next year.*

☑ Remember that effect is a *noun* and *affect* is a verb.

A B C D E F G H I J K L M N O P Q R S T U V W X Y Z

**effective**

ADJECTIVE **1** working well and producing the intended results. **2** coming into operation or beginning officially E.G. *The agreement has become effective immediately.*
**effectively** ADVERB

**effeminate**

ADJECTIVE A man who is effeminate behaves, looks, or sounds like a woman.

**efficient**

ADJECTIVE capable of doing something well without wasting time or energy.
**efficiently** ADVERB   **efficiency** NOUN
■ capable, competent, proficient

**effigy effigies**

*Said* "ef-fij-ee" NOUN a statue or model of a person.

**effluent effluents**

*Said* "ef-loo-ent" NOUN Effluent is liquid waste that comes out of factories or sewage works.

**effluvium effluvia**

*Said* "ef-**floo**-vi-um" Effluvium is an unpleasant smell or gas that is given off by something, especially something that is decaying.

**effort efforts**

NOUN **1** (PSHE) Effort is the physical or mental energy needed to do something. **2** an attempt or struggle to do something E.G. *I went to keep-fit classes in an effort to fight the flab.*
■ (sense 1) exertion, trouble, work

**effortless**

ADJECTIVE done easily.
**effortlessly** ADVERB

**eg** or **e.g.**

eg means 'for example', and is abbreviated from the Latin expression 'exempli gratia'.

**egalitarian**

ADJECTIVE favouring equality for all people E.G. *an egalitarian country.*

**egg eggs**

NOUN **1** an oval or rounded object laid by female birds, reptiles, fishes, and insects. A baby creature develops inside the egg until it is ready to be born. **2** a hen's egg used as food. **3** In a female animal, an egg is a cell produced in its body which can develop into a baby if it is fertilized.

**eggplant eggplants**

NOUN a dark purple pear-shaped fruit eaten as a vegetable. It is also called **aubergine**.

**ego egos**

*Said* "ee-goh" NOUN Your ego is your opinion of what you are worth E.G. *It'll do her good and boost her ego.*
🔲 from Latin *ego* meaning 'I'

**egocentric**

ADJECTIVE only thinking of yourself.

**egoism** or **egotism**

NOUN Egoism is behaviour and attitudes which show that you believe that you are more important than other people.
**egoist** or **egotist** NOUN   **egoistic**,
**egotistic** or **egotistical** ADJECTIVE

**Egyptian Egyptians**

*Said* "ij-**jip**-shn" ADJECTIVE **1** belonging or relating to Egypt. ▶ NOUN **2** An Egyptian is someone who comes from Egypt.

**Eid-ul-Adha**

*Said* "eed-dool-ah-de" NOUN an annual Muslim festival marking the end of the pilgrimage to Mecca known as the hajj. Animals are sacrificed and their meat is shared among the poor.
🔲 from Arabic *id ul adha* festival of sacrifice

a
b
c
d
e
f
g
h
i
j
k
l
m
n
o
p
q
r
s
t
u
v
w
x
y
z

the QUeen stood on the QUay (quay)    SPELLING NOTE

A
B
C
D
E
F
G
H
I
J
K
L
M
N
O
P
Q
R
S
T
U
V
W
X
Y
Z

**eight** eights
the number 8.
**eighth**
**eighteen**
the number 18.
**eighteenth**
**eighty** eighties
the number 80.
**eightieth**
**either**

ADJECTIVE, PRONOUN, or CONJUNCTION **1** one
or the other of two possible
alternatives E.G. *You can spell it either
way… Either of these schemes would
cost billions of pounds… Either take it
or leave it.* ► ADJECTIVE **2** both one and
the other E.G. *on either side of the
head.*

☑ When *either* is followed by a
plural noun, the following verb can
be plural too: *either of these books are
useful.*

**ejaculate** ejaculates ejaculating
ejaculated

VERB **1** When a man ejaculates, he
discharges semen from his penis. **2** If
you ejaculate, you suddenly say
something.
**ejaculation** NOUN
🔲 from Latin *jacere* meaning 'to
throw'

**eject** ejects ejecting ejected

VERB If you eject something or
someone, you forcefully push or
send them out E.G. *He was ejected
from the club.*
**ejection** NOUN
■ expel, throw out

**elaborate** elaborates
elaborating elaborated

ADJECTIVE **1** having many different
parts E.G. *an elaborate system of
drains.* **2** carefully planned, detailed,

and exact E.G. *elaborate plans.*
**3** highly decorated and complicated
E.G. *elaborate designs.* ► VERB **4** If you
elaborate on something, you add
more information or detail about it.
**elaborately** ADVERB  **elaboration**
NOUN
■ (sense 3) complicated, fancy,
ornate

**eland** elands
NOUN a large African antelope with
twisted horns.

**elapse** elapses elapsing elapsed
VERB When time elapses, it passes by
E.G. *Eleven years elapsed before you
got this job.*

**elastic**
ADJECTIVE **1** able to stretch easily.
► NOUN **2** Elastic is rubber material
which stretches and returns to its
original shape.
**elasticity** NOUN
🔲 from Greek *elastikos* meaning
'pushing'

**elation**
NOUN Elation is a feeling of great
happiness.
**elated** ADJECTIVE

**elbow** elbows elbowing elbowed
NOUN **1** Your elbow is the joint
between the upper part of your arm
and your forearm. ► VERB **2** If you
elbow someone aside, you push
them away with your elbow.

**elder** eldest; elders
ADJECTIVE **1** Your elder brother or sister
is older than you. ► NOUN **2** a senior
member of a group who has
influence or authority. **3** a bush or
small tree with dark purple berries.
☑ The adjectives *elder* and *eldest*
can only be used when talking about
the age of people within families.

You can use *older* and *oldest* to talk about the age of other people or things.

**elderly**
ADJECTIVE **1** Elderly is a polite way to describe an old person. ► NOUN **2** The elderly are old people *E.G. Priority is given to services for the elderly.*

**elect** elects electing elected
VERB **1** If you elect someone, you choose them to fill a position, by voting *E.G. He's just been elected president.* **2** FORMAL If you elect to do something, you choose to do it *E.G. I have elected to stay.* ► ADJECTIVE **3** FORMAL voted into a position, but not yet carrying out the duties of the position *E.G. the vice-president elect.*

**election** elections
NOUN the selection of one or more people for an official position by voting.
**electoral** ADJECTIVE

**electorate** electorates
NOUN all the people who have the right to vote in an election.

**electric**
ADJECTIVE **1** powered or produced by electricity. **2** very tense or exciting *E.G. The atmosphere is electric.*
☑ The word *electric* is an adjective and should not be used as a noun.

**electrical**
ADJECTIVE using or producing electricity *E.G. electrical goods.*
**electrically** ADVERB

**electrician** electricians
NOUN a person whose job is to install and repair electrical equipment.

**electricity**
NOUN Electricity is a form of energy used for heating and lighting, and to provide power for machines.
📖 from Greek *ēlektron* meaning

'amber'; in early experiments, scientists rubbed amber in order to get an electrical charge

**electrified**
ADJECTIVE connected to a supply of electricity.

**electrifying**
ADJECTIVE Something that is electrifying makes you feel very excited.

**electro-**
PREFIX 'Electro-' means 'electric' or involving electricity.
📖 from Greek *ēlectron*

**electrocute** electrocutes electrocuting electrocuted
VERB If someone is electrocuted, they are killed by touching something that is connected to electricity.
**electrocution** NOUN

**electrode** electrodes
NOUN a small piece of metal which allows an electric current to pass between a source of power and a piece of equipment.

**electron** electrons
NOUN In physics, an electron is a tiny particle of matter, smaller than an atom.

**electronic**
ADJECTIVE (ICT) having transistors or silicon chips which control an electric current.
**electronically** ADVERB

**electronics**
NOUN Electronics is the technology of electronic devices such as televisions, and computers; also the study of how these devices work.

**elegant**
ADJECTIVE attractive and graceful or stylish *E.G. an elegant and beautiful city.*
**elegantly** ADVERB    **elegance** NOUN

a
b
c
d
e
f
g
h
i
j
k
l
m
n
o
p
q
r
s
t
u
v
w
x
y
z

**elegy elegies**
Said "*el*-lij-ee" NOUN a sad poem or song about someone who has died. 📖 from Greek *elegos* meaning 'lament sung to the flute'

**element elements**
NOUN 1 a part of something which combines with others to make a whole. 2 (SCIENCE) In chemistry, an element is a substance that is made up of only one type of atom. 3 A particular element within a large group of people is a section of it which is similar *E.G. criminal elements.* 4 An element of a quality is a certain amount of it *E.G. Their attack has largely lost the element of surprise.* 5 The elements of a subject are the basic and most important points. 6 The elements are the weather conditions *E.G. Our open boat is exposed to the elements.*

**elemental**
ADJECTIVE; *FORMAL* simple and basic, but powerful *E.G. elemental emotions.*

**elementary**
ADJECTIVE simple, basic, and straightforward *E.G. an elementary course in woodwork.*

**elephant elephants**
NOUN a very large four-legged mammal with a long trunk, large ears, and ivory tusks.

**elevate elevates elevating elevated**
VERB 1 To elevate someone to a higher status or position means to give them greater status or importance *E.G. He was elevated to the rank of major in the army.* 2 To elevate something means to raise it up.

**elevation elevations**
NOUN 1 The elevation of someone or something is the raising of them to a higher level or position. 2 The elevation of a place is its height above sea level or above the ground.

**eleven elevens**
1 Eleven is the number 11. ▶ NOUN 2 a team of cricket or soccer players.

**eleventh**

**elf elves**
NOUN In folklore, an elf is a small mischievous fairy.

**elicit elicits eliciting elicited**
Said "il-*iss*-it" VERB 1 *FORMAL* If you elicit information, you find it out by asking careful questions. 2 If you elicit a response or reaction, you make it happen *E.G. He elicited sympathy from the audience.*

**eligible**
Said "*el*-lij-i-bl" ADJECTIVE suitable or having the right qualifications for something *E.G. You will be eligible for a grant in the future.*

**eligibility** NOUN

**eliminate eliminates eliminating eliminated**
VERB 1 If you eliminate something or someone, you get rid of them *E.G. They eliminated him from their inquiries.* 2 If a team or a person is eliminated from a competition, they can no longer take part.

**elimination** NOUN

**elite elites**
Said "ill-*eet*" NOUN a group of the most powerful, rich, or talented people in a society.

**Elizabethan**
ADJECTIVE Someone or something that is Elizabethan lived or was made during the reign of Elizabeth I.

**elk elks**
NOUN a large kind of deer.

**ellipse ellipses**
NOUN a regular oval shape, like a circle seen from an angle.

**elm elms**
NOUN a tall tree with broad leaves.

**elocution**
NOUN the art or study of speaking clearly or well in public.

**elongated**
ADJECTIVE long and thin.

**elope elopes eloping eloped**
VERB If someone elopes, they run away secretly with their lover to get married.

**eloquent**
ADJECTIVE able to speak or write skilfully and with ease E.G. *an eloquent politician.*
**eloquently** ADVERB **eloquence** NOUN

**else**
ADVERB 1 other than this or more than this E.G. *Can you think of anything else?* ▶ PHRASE 2 You say **or else** to introduce a possibility or an alternative E.G. *You have to go with the flow or else be left behind in the rush.*

**elsewhere**
ADVERB in or to another place E.G. *He would rather be elsewhere.*

**elude eludes eluding eluded**
*Said "ill-ood"* VERB 1 If a fact or idea eludes you, you cannot understand it or remember it. 2 If you elude someone or something, you avoid them or escape from them E.G. *He eluded the authorities.*

**elusive**
ADJECTIVE difficult to find, achieve, describe, or remember E.G. *the elusive million dollar prize.*

**elves**
the plural of **elf**.

**em-**
PREFIX 'Em-' is another form of the prefix en-.
☑ em- is the form which is used before the letters *b, m* and *p.*

**emaciated**
*Said "im-may-see-ate-ed"* ADJECTIVE extremely thin and weak, because of illness or lack of food.

**e-mail** or **email**
NOUN 1 the sending of messages from one computer to another. 2 a message sent in this way. ▶ VERB 3 If you e-mail someone, you send an e-mail to them.

**emancipation**
NOUN The emancipation of a person means the act of freeing them from harmful or unpleasant restrictions.

**embargo embargoes**
NOUN an order made by a government to stop trade with another country.

**embark embarks embarking embarked**
VERB 1 If you embark, you go onto a ship at the start of a journey. 2 If you embark on something, you start it E.G. *He embarked on a huge spending spree.*

**embarrass embarrasses embarrassing embarrassed**
VERB If you embarrass someone, you make them feel ashamed or awkward E.G. *I won't embarrass you by asking for details.*
**embarrassed** ADJECTIVE
**embarrassing** ADJECTIVE
**embarrassment** NOUN

**embassy embassies**
NOUN the building in which an ambassador and his or her staff work; also used of the ambassador and his or her staff.

A
B
C
D
E
F
G
H
I
J
K
L
M
N
O
P
Q
R
S
T
U
V
W
X
Y
Z

**embedded**

ADJECTIVE Something that is embedded is fixed firmly and deeply E.G. *glass decorated with embedded threads.*

**ember embers**

NOUN Embers are glowing pieces of coal or wood from a dying fire.

**embittered**

ADJECTIVE If you are embittered, you are angry and resentful about things that have happened to you.

**emblazoned**

*Said "im-blaze-nd"* ADJECTIVE If something is emblazoned with designs, it is decorated with them E.G. *vases emblazoned with bold and colourful images.*

📖 originally a heraldic term from Old French *blason* meaning 'shield'

**emblem emblems**

NOUN an object or a design representing an organization or an idea E.G. *a flower emblem of Japan.*

**embody embodies embodying embodied**

VERB 1 To embody a quality or idea means to contain it or express it E.G. *A young dancer embodies the spirit of fun.* 2 If a number of things are embodied in one thing, they are contained in it E.G. *the principles embodied in his report.*

**embodiment** NOUN

**embossed**

ADJECTIVE decorated with designs that stand up slightly from the surface E.G. *embossed wallpaper.*

**embrace embraces embracing embraced**

VERB 1 If you embrace someone, you hug them to show affection or as a greeting. 2 If you embrace a belief or

cause you accept it and believe in it.
▶ NOUN 3 a hug.

**embroider embroiders embroidering embroidered**

VERB If you embroider fabric, you sew a decorative design onto it.

**embroidery**

NOUN Embroidery is decorative designs sewn onto fabric; also the art or skill of embroidery.

**embroiled**

ADJECTIVE If someone is embroiled in an argument or conflict they are deeply involved in it and cannot get out of it E.G. *The two companies are now embroiled in the courts.*

**embryo embryos**

*Said "em-bree-oh"* NOUN an animal or human being in the very early stages of development in the womb.

**embryonic** ADJECTIVE

📖 from Greek *embruon* meaning 'new-born animal'

**emerald emeralds**

NOUN 1 a bright green precious stone. ▶ NOUN OR ADJECTIVE 2 bright green.

**emerge emerges emerging emerged**

VERB 1 If someone emerges from a place, they come out of it so that they can be seen. 2 If something emerges, it becomes known or begins to be recognized as existing E.G. *It later emerged that he faced bankruptcy proceedings.*

**emergence** NOUN **emergent** ADJECTIVE

**emergency emergencies**

NOUN an unexpected and serious event which needs immediate action to deal with it.

≡ crisis, extremity

**emigrant** emigrants
NOUN a person who leaves their native country and goes to live permanently in another one.

**emigrate** emigrates emigrating emigrated
VERB If you emigrate, you leave your native country and go to live permanently in another one.

**emigration**
NOUN (HISTORY) Emigration is the process of emigrating, especially by large numbers of people at various periods of history.

**eminence**
NOUN 1 Eminence is the quality of being well-known and respected for what you do E.G. *lawyers of eminence*. 2 'Your Eminence' is a title of respect used to address a Roman Catholic cardinal.

**eminent**
ADJECTIVE well-known and respected for what you do E.G. *an eminent scientist*.

**eminently**
ADVERB; FORMAL very E.G. *eminently reasonable*.

**emir** emirs
Said "em-**eer**" NOUN a Muslim ruler or nobleman.
▥ from Arabic *amir* meaning 'commander'

**emission** emissions
NOUN; FORMAL The emission of something such as gas or radiation is the release of it into the atmosphere.

**emit** emits emitting emitted
VERB To emit something means to give it out or release it E.G. *She emitted a long, low whistle.*
▤ exude, give off, give out

**emoticon** emoticons
NOUN a symbol used in e-mail which represents a particular emotion and is made up of normal keyboard characters that are viewed sideways. For example, the symbol (:+( means 'frightened' or 'scared'.

**emotion** emotions
NOUN (PSHE) a strong feeling, such as love or fear.

**emotional**
ADJECTIVE (PSHE) 1 causing strong feelings E.G. *an emotional appeal for help.* 2 to do with feelings rather than your physical condition E.G. *emotional support.* 3 showing your feelings openly E.G. *The child is in a very emotional state.*
**emotionally** ADVERB

**emotive**
ADJECTIVE concerning emotions, or stirring up strong emotions E.G. *emotive language.*

**empathize** empathizes empathizing empathized; also spelt **empathise**
VERB If you empathize with someone, you understand how they are feeling.
**empathy** NOUN

**emperor** emperors
NOUN a male ruler of an empire.
▥ from Latin *imperator* meaning 'commander-in-chief'

**emphasis** emphases
NOUN Emphasis is special importance or extra stress given to something.

**emphasize** emphasizes emphasizing emphasized; also spelt **emphasise**
VERB If you emphasize something, you make it known that it is very important E.G. *It was emphasized that the matter was of international concern.*

a b c d e f g h i j k l m n o p q r s t u v w x y z

'i' before 'e' except after 'c'     SPELLING NOTE

A
B
C
D
E
F
G
H
I
J
K
L
M
N
O
P
Q
R
S
T
U
V
W
X
Y
Z

**emphatic**

ADJECTIVE expressed strongly and with force to show how important something is E.G. *I answered both questions with an emphatic 'Yes'.*

**emphatically** ADVERB

**empire empires**

NOUN 1 a group of countries controlled by one country. 2 a powerful group of companies controlled by one person.

🏛 from Latin *imperium* meaning 'rule'

**employ employs employing employed**

VERB 1 If you employ someone, you pay them to work for you. 2 If you employ something for a particular purpose, you make use of it E.G. *the techniques employed in turning grapes into wine.*

▣ (sense 1) engage, hire, take on

**employee employees**

NOUN a person who is paid to work for another person or for an organization.

**employer employers**

NOUN Someone's employer is the person or organization that they work for.

**employment**

NOUN (GEOGRAPHY) Employment is the state of having a paid job, or the activity of recruiting people for a job.

**empower empowers empowering empowered**

VERB If you are empowered to do something, you have the authority or power to do it.

**empress empresses**

NOUN a woman who rules an empire, or the wife of an emperor.

**empty emptier emptiest; empties emptying emptied**

ADJECTIVE 1 having nothing or nobody inside. 2 without purpose, value, or meaning E.G. *empty promises.* ▶ VERB 3 If you empty something, or empty its contents, you remove the contents.

**emptiness** NOUN

▣ (sense 1) bare, blank, vacant

▣ (sense 3) clear, evacuate

**emu emus**

*Said* "*ee*-myoo" NOUN a large Australian bird which can run fast but cannot fly.

🏛 from Portuguese *ema* meaning 'ostrich'

**emulate emulates emulating emulated**

VERB If you emulate someone or something, you imitate them because you admire them.

**emulation** NOUN

**emulsion emulsions**

NOUN a water-based paint.

**en-**

PREFIX 1 'En-' means to surround or cover E.G. *enclose, encrusted.* 2 'En-' means to cause to be in a certain state or condition E.G. *enamoured… endanger.*

🏛 from Latin prefix *in-*

**enable enables enabling enabled**

VERB To enable something to happen means to make it possible.

**enact enacts enacting enacted**

VERB 1 If a government enacts a law or bill, it officially passes it so that it becomes law. 2 If you enact a story or play, you act it out.

**enactment** NOUN

**enamel enamels enamelling enamelled**

NOUN 1 a substance like glass, used to decorate or protect metal or china.

**2** The enamel on your teeth is the hard, white substance that forms the outer part. ▶ VERB **3** If you enamel something, you decorate or cover it with enamel.

**enamelled** ADJECTIVE

**enamoured**
*Said* "in-**am**-erd" ADJECTIVE If you are enamoured of someone or something, you like them very much.

**encapsulate** encapsulates encapsulating encapsulated
VERB If something encapsulates facts or ideas, it contains or represents them in a small space.

**encased**
ADJECTIVE Something that is encased is surrounded or covered with a substance E.G. *encased in plaster.*

**-ence**
SUFFIX '-ence' is used to form nouns which mean a state, condition or quality E.G. *residence… patience.*
🗠 from Latin *-ēns*

**enchanted**
ADJECTIVE If you are enchanted by something or someone, you are fascinated or charmed by them.

**enchanting**
ADJECTIVE attractive, delightful, or charming E.G. *an enchanting baby.*

**encircle** encircles encircling encircled
VERB To encircle something or someone means to completely surround them.

**enclave**
NOUN a place that is surrounded by areas that are different from it in some important way, for example because the people there are from a different culture E.G. *a Muslim enclave in Bosnia.*

🗠 from Old French *enclaver* meaning 'to enclose'

**enclose** encloses enclosing enclosed
VERB To enclose an object or area means to surround it with something solid.

**enclosed** ADJECTIVE

**enclosure** enclosures
NOUN an area of land surrounded by a wall or fence and used for a particular purpose.

**encompass** encompasses encompassing encompassed
VERB To encompass a number of things means to include all of those things E.G. *The book encompassed all aspects of maths.*

**encore** encores
*Said* "**ong**-kor" NOUN a short extra performance given by an entertainer because the audience asks for it.
🗠 from French *encore* meaning 'again'

**encounter** encounters encountering encountered
VERB **1** If you encounter someone or something, you meet them or are faced with them E.G. *She was the most gifted child he ever encountered.*
▶ NOUN **2** a meeting, especially when it is difficult or unexpected.

**encourage** encourages encouraging encouraged
VERB (PSHE) **1** If you encourage someone, you give them courage and confidence to do something. **2** If someone or something encourages a particular activity, they support it E.G. *The government will encourage the creation of nursery places.*

**encouraging** ADJECTIVE
**encouragement** NOUN

a
b
c
d
**e**
f
g
h
i
j
k
l
m
n
o
p
q
r
s
t
u
v
w
x
y
z

A
B
C
D
E
F
G
H
I
J
K
L
M
N
O
P
Q
R
S
T
U
V
W
X
Y
Z

■ (sense 1) hearten, inspire

**encroach** encroaches
**encroaching encroached**
VERB If something encroaches on a place or on your time or rights, it gradually takes up or takes away more and more of it.
**encroachment** NOUN

**encrusted**
ADJECTIVE covered with a crust or layer of something E.G. *a necklace encrusted with gold.*

**encyclopedia** encyclopedias
*Said* "en-sigh-klop-**ee**-dee-a"; also spelt **encyclopaedia**
NOUN (LIBRARY) a book or set of books giving information about many different subjects.
⊞ from Greek *enkuklios paideia* meaning 'general education'

**encyclopedic** or **encyclopaedic**
ADJECTIVE knowing or giving information about many different things.

**end** ends ending ended
NOUN 1 The end of a period of time or an event is the last part. 2 The end of something is the farthest point of it E.G. *the room at the end of the passage.* 3 the purpose for which something is done E.G. *the use of taxpayers' money for overt political ends.* ▶ VERB 4 If something ends or if you end it, it comes to a finish.

**endanger** endangers
**endangering endangered**
VERB To endanger something means to cause it to be in a dangerous and harmful situation E.G. *a driver who endangers the safety of others.*
■ jeopardize, put at risk

**endear** endears endearing
**endeared**
VERB If someone's behaviour endears

them to you, it makes you fond of them.
**endearing** ADJECTIVE **endearingly** ADVERB

**endeavour** endeavours
**endeavouring endeavoured**
*Said* "in-**dev**-er" VERB 1 FORMAL If you endeavour to do something, you try very hard to do it. ▶ NOUN 2 an effort to do or achieve something.

**endless**
ADJECTIVE having or seeming to have no end.
**endlessly** ADVERB

**endorse** endorses endorsing
**endorsed**
VERB 1 If you endorse someone or something, you give approval and support to them. 2 If you endorse a document, you write your signature or a comment on it, to show that you approve of it.
**endorsement** NOUN

**endowed**
ADJECTIVE If someone is endowed with a quality or ability, they have it or are given it E.G. *He was endowed with great willpower.*

**endurance**
NOUN Endurance is the ability to put up with a difficult situation for a period of time.

**endure** endures enduring
**endured**
VERB 1 If you endure a difficult situation, you put up with it calmly and patiently. 2 If something endures, it lasts or continues to exist E.G. *The old alliance still endures.*
**enduring** ADJECTIVE

**enema** enemas
NOUN a liquid that is put into a

person's rectum in order to empty their bowels.

**enemy** enemies

NOUN a person or group that is hostile or opposed to another person or group.

■ adversary, foe

**energetic**

ADJECTIVE having or showing energy or enthusiasm.

**energetically** ADVERB

■ active, lively, vigorous

**energy** energies

NOUN 1 the physical strength to do active things. 2 the power which drives machinery.

■ (sense 1) drive, stamina, vigour

**enforce** enforces enforcing enforced

VERB If you enforce a law or a rule, you make sure that it is obeyed.

**enforceable** ADJECTIVE

**enforcement** NOUN

**engage** engages engaging engaged

VERB 1 If you engage in an activity, you take part in it E.G. *Officials have declined to engage in a debate.* 2 To engage someone or their attention means to make or keep someone interested in something E.G. *He engaged the driver in conversation.*

**engaged**

ADJECTIVE 1 When two people are engaged, they have agreed to marry each other. 2 If someone or something is engaged, they are occupied or busy E.G. *Mr Anderson was otherwise engaged… The emergency number was always engaged.*

**engagement** engagements

NOUN 1 an appointment that you have

with someone. 2 an agreement that two people have made with each other to get married.

**engine** engines

NOUN 1 a machine designed to convert heat or other kinds of energy into mechanical movement. 2 a railway locomotive.

🔳 from Latin *ingenium* meaning 'ingenious device'

**engineer** engineers engineering engineered

NOUN 1 a person trained in designing and building machinery and electrical devices, or roads and bridges. 2 a person who repairs mechanical or electrical devices.

▶ VERB 3 If you engineer an event or situation, you arrange it cleverly, usually for your own advantage.

**engineering**

NOUN Engineering is the profession of designing and constructing machinery and electrical devices, or roads and bridges.

**English**

ADJECTIVE 1 belonging or relating to England. ▶ NOUN 2 English is the main language spoken in the United Kingdom, the USA, Canada, Australia, New Zealand, and many other countries.

**Englishman** Englishmen

NOUN a man who comes from England.

**Englishwoman** NOUN

**engrave** engraves engraving engraved

VERB To engrave means to cut letters or designs into a hard surface with a tool.

**engraving** engravings

NOUN a picture or design that has

A Rude Idiot Thought He Might Eat Toffee In Church (<u>arithmetic</u>)    SPELLING NOTE

been cut into a hard surface.
**engraver** NOUN

**engrossed**
ADJECTIVE If you are engrossed in something, it holds all your attention E.G. *He was engrossed in a video game.*

**engulf** engulfs engulfing engulfed
VERB To engulf something means to completely cover or surround it E.G. *Black smoke engulfed him.*

**enhance** enhances enhancing enhanced
VERB To enhance something means to make it more valuable or attractive E.G. *an outfit that really enhances his good looks.*
**enhancement** NOUN

**enigma** enigmas
NOUN anything which is puzzling or difficult to understand.

**enigmatic**
ADJECTIVE mysterious, puzzling, or difficult to understand E.G. *an enigmatic stranger.*
**enigmatically** ADVERB

**enjoy** enjoys enjoying enjoyed
VERB 1 If you enjoy something, you find pleasure and satisfaction in it.
2 If you enjoy something, you are lucky to have it or experience it E.G. *The mother has enjoyed a long life.*

**enjoyable**
ADJECTIVE giving pleasure or satisfaction.

**enjoyment**
NOUN Enjoyment is the feeling of pleasure or satisfaction you get from something you enjoy.

**enlarge** enlarges enlarging enlarged
VERB 1 When you enlarge something, it gets bigger. 2 If you enlarge on a subject, you give details about it.

**enlargement** enlargements
NOUN 1 An enlargement of something is the action of making it bigger.
2 something, especially a photograph, which has been made bigger.

**enlighten** enlightens enlightening enlightened
VERB To enlighten someone means to give them more knowledge or understanding of something.
**enlightening** ADJECTIVE
**enlightenment** NOUN

**enlightened**
ADJECTIVE well-informed and willing to consider different opinions E.G. *an enlightened government.*

**enlist** enlists enlisting enlisted
VERB 1 If someone enlists, they join the army, navy, or air force. 2 If you enlist someone's help, you persuade them to help you in something you are doing.

**enliven** enlivens enlivening enlivened
VERB To enliven something means to make it more lively or more cheerful.

**en masse**
*Said "on mass"* ADVERB If a group of people do something en masse, they do it together and at the same time.

**enormity** enormities
NOUN 1 The enormity of a problem or difficulty is its great size and seriousness. 2 something that is thought to be a terrible crime or offence.

**enormous**
ADJECTIVE very large in size or amount.
**enormously** ADVERB

**enough**
ADJECTIVE or ADVERB 1 as much or as

many as required *E.G. He did not have enough money for a coffee.* ▶ NOUN **2** Enough is the quantity necessary for something *E.G. There's not enough to go round.* ▶ ADVERB **3** very or fairly *E.G. She could manage well enough without me.*

**enquire** enquires enquiring enquired; also spelt **inquire**
VERB If you enquire about something or someone, you ask about them.

**enquiry** enquiries; also spelt **inquiry**
NOUN **1** a question that you ask in order to find something out. **2** an investigation into something that has happened and that needs explaining.

**enrage** enrages enraging enraged
VERB If something enrages you, it makes you very angry.
**enraged** ADJECTIVE

**enrich** enriches enriching enriched
VERB To enrich something means to improve the quality or value of it *E.G. new woods to enrich our countryside.*
**enriched** ADJECTIVE **enrichment** NOUN

**enrol** enrols enrolling enrolled
VERB If you enrol for something such as a course or a college, you register to join or become a member of it.
**enrolment** NOUN

**en route**
*Said "on root"* ADVERB If something happens en route to a place, it happens on the way there.

**ensconced**
ADJECTIVE If you are ensconced in a particular place, you are settled there firmly and comfortably.

**ensemble** ensembles
*Said "on-som-bl"* NOUN **1** a group of things or people considered as a whole rather than separately. **2** a small group of musicians who play or sing together.

**enshrine** enshrines enshrining enshrined
VERB If something such as an idea or a right is enshrined in a society, constitution, or a law, it is protected by it *E.G. Freedom of speech is enshrined in the American Constitution.*

**ensign** ensigns
NOUN a flag flown by a ship to show what country that ship belongs to.

**ensue** ensues ensuing ensued
*Said "en-syoo"* VERB If something ensues, it happens after another event, usually as a result of it *E.G. He entered the house and an argument ensued.*
**ensuing** ADJECTIVE

**ensure** ensures ensuring ensured
VERB To ensure that something happens means to make certain that it happens *E.G. We make every effort to ensure the information given is correct.*

**entangled**
ADJECTIVE If you are entangled in problems or difficulties, you are involved in them.

**enter** enters entering entered
VERB **1** To enter a place means to go into it. **2** If you enter an organization or institution, you join and become a member of it *E.G. He entered Parliament in 1979.* **3** If you enter a competition or examination, you take part in it. **4** If you enter

something in a diary or a list, you write it down.

**enterprise** enterprises
NOUN **1** a business or company. **2** a project or task, especially one that involves risk or difficulty.
🔳 from French *entreprendre* meaning 'to undertake'

**enterprising**
ADJECTIVE ready to start new projects and tasks and full of boldness and initiative E.G. *an enterprising company*.

**entertain** entertains entertaining entertained
VERB **1** If you entertain people, you keep them amused or interested. **2** If you entertain guests, you receive them into your house and give them food and hospitality.

**entertainer** entertainers
NOUN someone whose job is to amuse and please audiences, for example a comedian or singer.

**entertainment** entertainments
NOUN Entertainment is anything that people watch for pleasure, such as shows and films.

**enthral** enthrals enthralling enthralled
*Said* "in-**thrawl**" VERB If you enthral someone, you hold their attention and interest completely.
**enthralling** ADJECTIVE

**enthuse** enthuses enthusing enthused
*Said* "inth-**yooz**" VERB If you enthuse about something, you talk about it with enthusiasm and excitement.

**enthusiasm** enthusiasms
NOUN Enthusiasm is interest, eagerness, or delight in something that you enjoy.
🔳 from Greek *enthousiasmos*

meaning 'possessed or inspired by the gods'
🔳 keenness, passion, zeal

**enthusiastic**
ADJECTIVE showing great excitement, eagerness, or approval for something E.G. *She was enthusiastic about poetry*.
**enthusiastically** ADVERB

**entice** entices enticing enticed
VERB If you entice someone to do something, you tempt them to do it E.G. *We tried to entice the mouse out of the hole*.

**enticing**
ADJECTIVE extremely attractive and tempting.

**entire**
ADJECTIVE all of something E.G. *the entire month of July*.

**entirely**
ADVERB wholly and completely E.G. *He and I were entirely different*.

**entirety**
*Said* "en-**tire**-it-tee" PHRASE If something happens to something **in its entirety**, it happens to all of it E.G. *This message will now be repeated in its entirety*.

**entitle** entitles entitling entitled
VERB If something entitles you to have or do something, it gives you the right to have or do it.
**entitlement** NOUN

**entity** entities
*Said* "en-**tit**-ee" NOUN any complete thing that is not divided and not part of anything else.

**entourage** entourages
*Said* "on-too-**rahj**" NOUN a group of people who follow or travel with a famous or important person.

**entrails**
PLURAL NOUN Entrails are the inner

parts, especially the intestines, of people or animals.

**entrance** entrances
*Said "en-trunss"* NOUN **1** The entrance of a building or area is its doorway or gate. **2** A person's entrance is their arrival in a place, or the way in which they arrive *E.G. Each creation is designed for you to make a dramatic entrance.* **3** (DRAMA) In the theatre, an actor makes his or her entrance when he or she comes on to the stage. **4** Entrance is the right to enter a place *E.G. He had gained entrance to the Hall by pretending to be a heating engineer.*

**entrance** entrances entrancing entranced
*Said "en-trahnss"* VERB If something entrances you, it gives you a feeling of wonder and delight.
**entrancing** ADJECTIVE

**entrant** entrants
NOUN a person who officially enters a competition or an organization.

**entrenched**
ADJECTIVE If a belief, custom, or power is entrenched, it is firmly established.

**entrepreneur** entrepreneurs
*Said "on-tre-pren-ur"* NOUN a person who sets up business deals, especially ones in which risks are involved, in order to make a profit.
**entrepreneurial** ADJECTIVE

**entrust** entrusts entrusting entrusted
VERB If you entrust something to someone, you give them the care and protection of it *E.G. Miss Fry was entrusted with the children's education.*

**entry** entries
NOUN **1** Entry is the act of entering a place. **2** a place through which you

enter somewhere. **3** anything which is entered or recorded *E.G. Send your entry to the address below.*
■ (sense 2) entrance, way in

**envelop** envelops enveloping enveloped
VERB To envelop something means to cover or surround it completely *E.G. A dense fog enveloped the area.*

**envelope** envelopes
NOUN a flat covering of paper with a flap that can be folded over to seal it, which is used to hold a letter.

**enviable**
ADJECTIVE If you describe something as enviable, you mean that you wish you had it yourself.

**envious**
ADJECTIVE full of envy.
**enviously** ADVERB

**environment** environments
NOUN **1** Your environment is the circumstances and conditions in which you live or work *E.G. a good environment to grow up in.* **2** The environment is the natural world around us *E.G. the waste which is dumped in the environment.*
**environmental** ADJECTIVE
**environmentally** ADVERB
☑ There is an *n* before the *m* in *environment.*

**environmentalist** environmentalists
NOUN a person who is concerned with the problems of the natural environment, such as pollution.

**envisage** envisages envisaging envisaged
VERB If you envisage a situation or state of affairs, you can picture it in your mind as being true or likely to happen.

*a b c d **e** f g h i j k l m n o p q r s t u v w x y z*

A
B
C
D
E
F
G
H
I
J
K
L
M
N
O
P
Q
R
S
T
U
V
W
X
Y
Z

**envoy** envoys
NOUN a messenger, sent especially from one government to another.

**envy** envies envying envied
NOUN 1 Envy is a feeling of resentment you have when you wish you could have what someone else has. ▶ VERB 2 If you envy someone, you wish that you had what they have.

**enzyme** enzymes
NOUN a chemical substance, usually a protein, produced by cells in the body.

**ephemeral**
*Said "if-em-er-al"* ADJECTIVE lasting only a short time.

**epic** epics
NOUN 1 a long story of heroic events and actions. ▶ ADJECTIVE 2 very impressive or ambitious *E.G. epic adventures*.

**epidemic** epidemics
NOUN 1 an occurrence of a disease in one area, spreading quickly and affecting many people. 2 a rapid development or spread of something *E.G. the country's crime epidemic*.

**epigram** epigrams
NOUN a short saying which expresses an idea in a clever and amusing way.

**epigraph**
NOUN 1 a quotation at the beginning of a book. 2 an inscription on a monument or building.

**epilepsy**
NOUN Epilepsy is a condition of the brain which causes fits and periods of unconsciousness.
**epileptic** NOUN OR ADJECTIVE

**episode** episodes
NOUN 1 an event or period *E.G. After*
this episode, she found it impossible to trust him. 2 one of several parts of a novel or drama appearing for example on television *E.G. I never miss an episode of Neighbours*.

**epistle** epistles
*Said "ip-piss-sl"* NOUN; FORMAL a letter.

**epitaph** epitaphs
*Said "ep-it-ahf"* NOUN some words on a tomb about the person who has died.

**epithet** epithets
NOUN a word or short phrase used to describe some characteristic of a person.

**epitome**
*Said "ip-pit-om-ee"* NOUN; FORMAL The epitome of something is the most typical example of its sort *E.G. She was the epitome of the successful woman*.
☑ Do not use *epitome* to mean 'the peak of something'. It means 'the most typical example of something'.

**epoch** epochs
*Said "ee-pok"* NOUN a long period of time.

**eponymous**
*Said "ip-on-im-uss"* ADJECTIVE; FORMAL The eponymous hero or heroine of a play or book is the person whose name forms its title *E.G. the eponymous hero of 'Eric the Viking'*. 📖 from Greek *eponumos* meaning 'given as a name'

**equal** equals equalling equalled
ADJECTIVE 1 having the same size, amount, value, or standard. 2 If you are equal to a task, you have the necessary ability to deal with it. ▶ NOUN 3 Your equals are people who have the same ability, status, or rights as you. ▶ VERB 4 If one thing

equals another, it is as good or remarkable as the other *E.G. He equalled the course record of 63.*
**equally** ADVERB **equality** NOUN

**equate equates equating equated**
VERB If you equate a particular thing with something else, you believe that it is similar or equal *E.G. You can't equate lives with money.*

**equation equations**
NOUN (MATHS) a mathematical formula stating that two amounts or values are the same.

**equator**
*Said "ik-way-tor"* NOUN an imaginary line drawn round the middle of the earth, lying halfway between the North and South poles.
**equatorial** ADJECTIVE

**equestrian**
*Said "ik-west-ree-an"* ADJECTIVE relating to or involving horses.

**equilateral**
ADJECTIVE (MATHS) An equilateral triangle has sides that are all the same length.

**equilibrium equilibria**
NOUN a state of balance or stability in a situation.

**equine**
ADJECTIVE relating to horses.
📖 from Latin *equus* meaning 'horse'

**equinox equinoxes**
NOUN one of the two days in the year when the day and night are of equal length, occurring in September and March.
📖 from Latin *aequinoctium* meaning 'equal night'

**equip equips equipping equipped**
VERB If a person or thing is equipped with something, they have it or are provided with it *E.G. The test boat was*

*equipped with a folding propeller.*
📖 provide, supply

**equipment**
NOUN Equipment is all the things that are needed or used for a particular job or activity.
📖 apparatus, gear, tools

**equitable**
ADJECTIVE fair and reasonable.

**equity**
NOUN Equity is the quality of being fair and reasonable *E.G. It is important to distribute income with some sense of equity.*

**equivalent equivalents**
ADJECTIVE 1 equal in use, size, value, or effect. ► NOUN 2 something that has the same use, value, or effect as something else *E.G. One glass of wine is the equivalent of half a pint of beer.*
**equivalence** NOUN
📖 (sense 2) equal, match

**-er**
SUFFIX 1 When '-er' is used to form some nouns it means 'for' or 'belonging to' *E.G. fastener… Highlander.* 2 '-er' is also used to form nouns which mean someone or something that does something *E.G. climber… teacher… baker.* 3 '-er' is used to make adjectives and adverbs that have the meaning 'more' *E.G. lighter… funnier.*
📖 from Old English

**era eras**
*Said "ear-a"* NOUN a period of time distinguished by a particular feature *E.G. a new era of prosperity.*
📖 from Latin *aera* meaning 'copper counters used for counting', hence for counting time

**eradicate eradicates eradicating eradicated**

a
b
c
d
e
f
g
h
i
j
k
l
m
n
o
p
q
r
s
t
u
v
w
x
y
z

**A**
**B**
**C**
**D**
**E**
**F**
**G**
**H**
**I**
**J**
**K**
**L**
**M**
**N**
**O**
**P**
**Q**
**R**
**S**
**T**
**U**
**V**
**W**
**X**
**Y**
**Z**

VERB To eradicate something means to get rid of it or destroy it completely.
**eradication** NOUN

**erase erases erasing erased**
VERB To erase something means to remove it.

**erect erects erecting erected**
VERB 1 To erect something means to put it up or construct it E.G. *The building was erected in 1900.*
▶ ADJECTIVE 2 in a straight and upright position E.G. *She held herself erect and looked directly at him.*
■ (sense 2) straight, upright, vertical

**erection erections**
NOUN 1 the process of erecting something. 2 anything which has been erected. 3 When a man has an erection, his penis is stiff, swollen, and in an upright position.

**ermine**
NOUN Ermine is expensive white fur.

**erode erodes eroding eroded**
VERB If something erodes or is eroded, it is gradually worn or eaten away and destroyed.

**erosion**
NOUN (GEOGRAPHY) the gradual wearing away and destruction of something E.G. *soil erosion.*

**erotic**
ADJECTIVE involving or arousing sexual desire.
**erotically** ADVERB **eroticism** NOUN
🏛 from Greek *erotikos* meaning 'of love'

**err errs erring erred**
VERB If you err, you make a mistake.

**errand errands**
NOUN a short trip you make in order to do a job for someone.

**erratic**
ADJECTIVE not following a regular

pattern or a fixed course E.G. *Police officers noticed his erratic driving.*
**erratically** ADVERB

**erroneous**
*Said "ir-rone-ee-uss"* ADJECTIVE Ideas or methods that are erroneous are incorrect or only partly correct.
**erroneously** ADVERB

**error errors**
NOUN a mistake or something which you have done wrong.

**erudite**
*Said "eh-roo-dite"* ADJECTIVE having great academic knowledge.

**erupt erupts erupting erupted**
VERB 1 When a volcano erupts, it violently throws out a lot of hot lava and ash. 2 When a situation erupts, it starts up suddenly and violently E.G. *A family row erupted.*
**eruption** NOUN

**escalate escalates escalating escalated**
VERB If a situation escalates, it becomes greater in size, seriousness, or intensity.

**escalator escalators**
NOUN a mechanical moving staircase.

**escapade escapades**
NOUN an adventurous or daring incident that causes trouble.

**escape escapes escaping escaped**
VERB 1 To escape means to get free from someone or something. 2 If you escape something unpleasant or difficult, you manage to avoid it E.G. *He escaped the death penalty.* 3 If something escapes you, you cannot remember it E.G. *It was an actor whose name escapes me for the moment.*
▶ NOUN 4 an act of escaping from a particular place or situation E.G. *his*

*escape from North Korea.* **5** a situation or activity which distracts you from something unpleasant *E.G. Television provides an escape.*

**escapee escapees**
*Said* "is-kay-**pee**" NOUN someone who has escaped, especially an escaped prisoner.

**escapism**
NOUN avoiding the real and unpleasant things in life by thinking about pleasant or fantastic things *E.G. Most horror movies are simple escapism.*
**escapist** ADJECTIVE

**eschew eschews eschewing eschewed**
*Said* "is-**chew**" VERB; FORMAL If you eschew something, you deliberately avoid or keep away from it.

**escort escorts escorting escorted**
NOUN **1** a person or vehicle that travels with another in order to protect or guide them. **2** a person who accompanies another person of the opposite sex to a social event. ▶ VERB **3** If you escort someone, you go with them somewhere, especially in order to protect or guide them.

**-ese**
*Said* "-*eez*" SUFFIX '-ese' forms adjectives and nouns which show where a person or thing comes from *E.G. Japanese.*
📖 from Latin suffix *-ensis* meaning 'from'

**Eskimo Eskimos**
NOUN a name that was formerly used for the Inuit people and their language.

**especially**
ADVERB You say especially to show

that something applies more to one thing, person, or situation than to any other *E.G. Regular eye tests are important, especially for the elderly.*

**espionage**
*Said* "**ess**-pee-on-ahj" NOUN Espionage is the act of spying to get secret information, especially to find out military or political secrets.
📖 from French *espionner* meaning 'to spy'

**espouse espouses espousing espoused**
VERB; FORMAL If you espouse a particular policy, cause, or plan, you give your support to it *E.G. They espoused the rights of man.*

**espresso**
NOUN Espresso is strong coffee made by forcing steam through ground coffee.
📖 from Italian *caffè espresso* meaning 'pressed coffee'
✅ The second letter of *espresso* is s and not x.

**-ess**
SUFFIX '-ess' added at the end of a noun indicates a female *E.G. lioness.*
📖 from Late Latin suffix *-issa*
✅ Special words for a woman who does a particular job or activity, such as *actress, poetess* and *authoress*, are now used less often because many women prefer to be referred to simply as an *actor, poet* or *author.*

**essay essays**
NOUN a short piece of writing on a particular subject, for example one done as an exercise by a student.

**essence essences**
NOUN **1** The essence of something is its most basic and most important part, which gives it its identity *E.G. the*

*very essence of being a woman.* 2 a concentrated liquid used for flavouring food *E.G. vanilla essence.*

**essential essentials**

ADJECTIVE 1 vitally important and absolutely necessary *E.G. Good ventilation is essential in the greenhouse.* 2 very basic, important, and typical *E.G. the essential aspects of international banking.* ▶ NOUN 3 something that is very important or necessary *E.G. the bare essentials of furnishing.*

**essentially** ADVERB

**-est**

SUFFIX '-est' is used to form adjectives and adverbs that have the meaning 'most' *E.G. greatest… furthest.*
📖 from Old English

**establish establishes establishing established**

VERB 1 To establish something means to set it up in a permanent way. 2 If you establish yourself or become established as something, you achieve a strong reputation for a particular activity *E.G. He had just established himself as a film star.* 3 If you establish a fact or establish the truth of something, you discover it and can prove it *E.G. Our first priority is to establish the cause of her death.*

**established** ADJECTIVE

⬛ (sense 1) create, found, set up

**establishment establishments**

NOUN 1 The establishment of an organization or system is the act of setting it up. 2 a shop, business, or some other sort of organization or institution. 3 The Establishment is the group of people in a country who have power and influence *E.G. lawyers, businessmen and other pillars of the Establishment.*

**estate estates**

NOUN 1 a large area of privately owned land in the country, together with all the property on it. 2 an area of land, usually in or near a city, which has been developed for housing or industry. 3 LEGAL A person's estate consists of all the possessions they leave behind when they die.

**estate agent estate agents**

NOUN a person who works for a company that sells houses and land.

**esteem**

NOUN admiration and respect that you feel for another person.

**esteemed** ADJECTIVE

**estimate estimates estimating estimated**

VERB 1 (MATHS) If you estimate an amount or quantity, you calculate it approximately. 2 If you estimate something, you make a guess about it based on the evidence you have available *E.G. Often it's possible to estimate a person's age just by knowing their name.* ▶ NOUN 3 an approximate calculation of an amount or quantity. 4 a guess you make about something based on the evidence you have available. 5 a formal statement from a company who may do some work for you, telling you how much it is likely to cost.

**estimation estimations**

NOUN 1 an approximate calculation of something that can be measured. 2 the opinion or impression you form about a person or situation.

**estranged**

ADJECTIVE 1 If someone is estranged from their husband or wife, they no longer live with them. 2 If someone is estranged from their family or friends, they have quarrelled with them and no longer keep in touch with them.

**estrogen**

NOUN a female sex hormone which regulates the reproductive cycle.

**estuary** estuaries

Said "*est*-yoo-ree" NOUN (GEOGRAPHY) the wide part of a river near where it joins the sea and where fresh water mixes with salt water.

**etc.**

a written abbreviation for **et cetera**.

**et cetera**

Said "it *set*-ra" 'Et cetera' is used at the end of a list to indicate that other items of the same type you have mentioned could have been mentioned if there had been time or space.

☑ As *etc.* means 'and the rest', you should not write *and etc.*

**etch** etches etching etched

VERB 1 If you etch a design or pattern on a surface, you cut it into the surface by using acid or a sharp tool. 2 If something is etched on your mind or memory, it has made such a strong impression on you that you feel you will never forget it.

**etched** ADJECTIVE

**etching** etchings

NOUN a picture printed from a metal plate that has had a design cut into it.

**eternal**

ADJECTIVE lasting forever, or seeming to last forever E.G. *eternal life*.

**eternally** ADVERB

▤ endless, everlasting, perpetual

**eternity** eternities

NOUN 1 Eternity is time without end, or a state of existing outside time,

especially the state some people believe they will pass into when they die. 2 a period of time which seems to go on for ever E.G. *We arrived there after an eternity*.

**ether**

Said "*eeth*-er" NOUN a colourless liquid that burns easily. Used in industry as a solvent and in medicine as an anaesthetic.

**ethereal**

Said "ith-*ee*-ree-al" ADJECTIVE light and delicate E.G. *misty ethereal landscapes*.

**ethereally** ADVERB

**ethical**

ADJECTIVE in agreement with accepted principles of behaviour that are thought to be right E.G. *teenagers who become vegetarian for ethical reasons*.

**ethically** ADVERB

**ethics**

PLURAL NOUN Ethics are moral beliefs about right and wrong E.G. *The medical profession has a code of ethics*.

**Ethiopian** Ethiopians

Said "eeth-ee-*oh*-pee-an" ADJECTIVE 1 belonging to or relating to Ethiopia. ▶ NOUN 2 someone who comes from Ethiopia.

**ethnic**

ADJECTIVE 1 involving different racial groups of people E.G. *ethnic minorities*. 2 relating to a particular racial or cultural group, especially when very different from modern western culture E.G. *ethnic food*.

**ethnically** ADVERB

**ethos**

Said "*eeth*-oss" NOUN a set of ideas and attitudes that is associated with a particular group of people E.G. *the ethos of journalism*.

I went to see (C) the doctor's new practiCe (practice)　　SPELLING NOTE

**etiquette**
*Said* "et-ik-ket" NOUN a set of rules for behaviour in a particular social situation.

**-ette**
SUFFIX '-ette' is used to form nouns which have 'small' as part of their meaning *E.G. launderette… cigarette.* 🔲 from French, the feminine form of the French suffix *-et*

**etymology**
*Said* "et-tim-ol-loj-ee" NOUN Etymology is the study of the origin and changes of form in words.

**EU**
NOUN EU is an abbreviation for 'European Union'.

**eucalyptus** or **eucalypt**
**eucalyptuses** or **eucalypts**
NOUN an evergreen tree, grown mostly in Australia; also the wood and oil from this tree.

**Eucharist** Eucharists
*Said* "yoo-kar-rist" NOUN a religious ceremony in which Christians remember and celebrate Christ's last meal with his disciples. 🔲 from Greek *eucharistia* meaning 'thanksgiving'

**eunuch** eunuchs
*Said* "yoo-nuk" NOUN a man who has been castrated.

**euphemism** euphemisms
NOUN a polite word or expression that you can use instead of one that might offend or upset people *E.G. action movies, a euphemism for violence.*
**euphemistic** ADJECTIVE
**euphemistically** ADVERB

**euphoria**
NOUN a feeling of great happiness.
**euphoric** ADJECTIVE

**euro** euros
NOUN the official unit of currency in some countries of the European Union, replacing their old currencies at the beginning of January 2002.

**Europe**
NOUN Europe is the second smallest continent. It has Asia on its eastern side, with the Arctic to the north, the Atlantic to the west, and the Mediterranean and Africa to the south.

**European** Europeans
ADJECTIVE **1** belonging or relating to Europe. ▶ NOUN **2** someone who comes from Europe.

**European Union**
NOUN The group of countries who have joined together under the Treaty of Rome for economic and trade purposes are officially known as the European Union.

**euthanasia**
*Said* "yooth-a-nay-zee-a" NOUN Euthanasia is the act of painlessly killing a dying person in order to stop their suffering. 🔲 from Greek *eu-* meaning 'easy' and *thanatos* meaning 'death'

**evacuate** evacuates evacuating evacuated
VERB If someone is evacuated, they are removed from a place of danger to a place of safety *E.G. A crowd of shoppers had to be evacuated from a store after a bomb scare.*
**evacuation** NOUN **evacuee** NOUN

**evade** evades evading evaded
VERB **1** If you evade something or someone, you keep moving in order to keep out of their way *E.G. For two months he evaded police.* **2** If you evade a problem or question, you

avoid dealing with it.

**evaluate** evaluates evaluating evaluated

VERB (EXAM TERM) If you evaluate something, you assess its strengths and weaknesses.

**evaluation** evaluations

NOUN 1 Evaluation is assessing something strengths and weaknesses. 2 (D&T) To carry out an evaluation of a design, product or system is to do an assessment to find out how well it works or will work.

**evangelical**

Said "ee-van-jel-ik-kl" ADJECTIVE Evangelical beliefs are Christian beliefs that stress the importance of the gospels and a personal belief in Christ.

**evangelist** evangelists

Said "iv-van-jel-ist" NOUN a person who travels from place to place preaching Christianity.

**evangelize** VERB **evangelism** NOUN

📖 from Greek evangelion meaning 'good news'

**evaporate** evaporates evaporating evaporated (SCIENCE)

VERB 1 When a liquid evaporates, it gradually becomes less and less because it has changed from a liquid into a gas. 2 If a substance has been evaporated, all the liquid has been taken out so that it is dry or concentrated.

**evaporation** NOUN

**evasion** evasions

NOUN deliberately avoiding doing something E.G. evasion of arrest.

**evasive**

ADJECTIVE deliberately trying to avoid talking about or doing something

E.G. He was evasive about his past.

**eve** eves

NOUN the evening or day before an event or occasion E.G. on the eve of the battle.

**even** evens evening evened

ADJECTIVE 1 flat and level E.G. an even layer of chocolate. 2 regular and without variation E.G. an even temperature. 3 In maths, numbers that are even can be divided exactly by two E.G. 4 is an even number. 4 Scores that are even are exactly the same. ▶ ADVERB 5 'Even' is used to suggest that something is unexpected or surprising E.G. I haven't even got a bank account. 6 'Even' is also used to say that something is greater in degree than something else E.G. This was an opportunity to obtain even more money. ▶ PHRASE 7 **Even if** or **even though** is used to introduce something that is surprising in relation to the main part of the sentence E.G. She was too kind to say anything, even though she was jealous.

**evenly** ADVERB

▦ (sense 1) flat, level, straight
▦ (sense 4) equal, level

**evening** evenings

NOUN the part of the day between late afternoon and the time you go to bed.

**event** events

NOUN 1 something that happens, especially when it is unusual or important. 2 one of the competitions that are part of an organized occasion, especially in sports. ▶ PHRASE 3 If you say **in any event**, you mean whatever happens E.G. In any event we must get on with our own lives.

a
b
c
e
f
g
h
i
j
k
l
m
n
o
p
q
r
s
t
u
v
w
x
y
z

A
B
C
D
E
F
G
H
I
J
K
L
M
N
O
P
Q
R
S
T
U
V
W
X
Y
Z

■ (sense 1) happening, incident, occurrence

**eventful**
ADJECTIVE full of interesting and important events.

**eventual**
ADJECTIVE happening or being achieved in the end E.G. He remained confident of eventual victory.

**eventuality** eventualities
NOUN a possible future event or result E.G. equipment to cope with most eventualities.

**eventually**
ADVERB in the end E.G. Eventually I got to Berlin.

**ever**
ADVERB 1 at any time E.G. Have you ever seen anything like it? 2 all the time E.G. The President will come under ever more pressure to resign. 3 'Ever' is used to give emphasis to what you are saying E.G. I'm as happy here as ever I was in England. ▶ PHRASE 4 INFORMAL Ever so means very E.G. Thank you ever so much.

**evergreen** evergreens
NOUN a tree or bush which has green leaves all the year round.

**everlasting**
ADJECTIVE never coming to an end.

**every**
ADJECTIVE 1 'Every' is used to refer to all the members of a particular group, separately and one by one E.G. We eat out every night. 2 'Every' is used to mean the greatest or the best possible degree of something E.G. He has every reason to avoid the subject. 3 'Every' is also used to indicate that something happens at regular intervals E.G. renewable every five years.

▶ PHRASE 4 **Every other** means each alternate E.G. I see Lisa at least every other week.

**everybody**
PRONOUN 1 all the people in a group E.G. He obviously thinks everybody in the place knows him. 2 all the people in the world E.G. Everybody has a hobby.
☑ Everybody and everyone mean the same.

**everyday**
ADJECTIVE usual or ordinary E.G. the everyday drudgery of work.

**everyone**
PRONOUN 1 all the people in a group. 2 all the people in the world
☑ Everyone and everybody mean the same.

**everything**
PRONOUN 1 all or the whole of something. 2 the most important thing E.G. When I was 20, friends were everything to me.

**everywhere**
ADVERB in or to all places.

**evict** evicts evicting evicted
VERB To evict someone means to officially force them to leave a place they are occupying.
**eviction** NOUN

**evidence**
NOUN 1 Evidence is anything you see, read, or are told which gives you reason to believe something. 2 Evidence is the information used in court to attempt to prove or disprove something.

**evident**
ADJECTIVE easily noticed or understood E.G. His love of nature is evident in his paintings.
**evidently** ADVERB

**evil** evils
NOUN **1** Evil is a force or power that is believed to cause wicked or bad things to happen. **2** a very unpleasant or harmful situation or activity E.G. *the evils of war.* ► ADJECTIVE **3** Someone or something that is evil is morally wrong or bad E.G. *evil influences.*

**evoke** evokes evoking evoked
VERB To evoke an emotion, memory, or reaction means to cause it E.G. *Enthusiasm was evoked by the appearance of the Prince.*

**evolution**
*Said "ee-vol-oo-shn"* NOUN **1** Evolution is a process of gradual change taking place over many generations during which living things slowly change as they adapt to different environments. **2** Evolution is also any process of gradual change and development over a period of time E.G. *the evolution of the European Union.*
**evolutionary** ADJECTIVE

**evolve** evolves evolving evolved
VERB **1** If something evolves or if you evolve it, it develops gradually over a period of time E.G. *I was given a brief to evolve a system of training.* **2** When living things evolve, they gradually change and develop into different forms over a period of time.

**ewe** ewes
*Said "yoo"* NOUN a female sheep.

**ex-**
PREFIX 'Ex' means 'former' E.G. *her ex-husband.*
🔳 from Greek *ek-* meaning 'out of' or 'away from'

**exacerbate** exacerbates exacerbating exacerbated
*Said "ig-zass-er-bate"* VERB To exacerbate something means to make it worse.

**exact** exacts exacting exacted
ADJECTIVE **1** correct and complete in every detail E.G. *an exact replica of the Santa Maria.* **2** accurate and precise, as opposed to approximate E.G. *Mystery surrounds the exact circumstances of his death.* ► VERB **3** FORMAL If somebody or something exacts something from you, they demand or obtain it from you, especially through force E.G. *The navy was on its way to exact a terrible revenge.*

**exactly**
ADVERB **1** with complete accuracy and precision E.G. *That's exactly what happened.* **2** You can use 'exactly' to emphasize the truth of a statement, or a similarity or close relationship between one thing and another E.G. *It's exactly the same colour.*

**exaggerate** exaggerates exaggerating exaggerated
VERB **1** If you exaggerate, you make the thing you are describing seem better, worse, bigger, or more important than it really is. **2** To exaggerate something means to make it more noticeable than usual E.G. *His Irish accent was exaggerated for the benefit of the joke he was telling.*
**exaggeration** NOUN

**exalted**
ADJECTIVE; FORMAL Someone who is exalted is very important.

**exam** exams
NOUN an official test set to find out your knowledge or skill in a subject.

**examination** examinations
NOUN **1** an exam. **2** If you make an

examination of something, you inspect it very carefully *E.G. I carried out a careful examination of the hull.*
**3** A medical examination is a check by a doctor to find out the state of your health.

**examine** examines examining examined
VERB **1** If you examine something, you inspect it very carefully. **2** (EXAM TERM) To examine a subject is to look closely at the issues involved and form your own opinion. **3** To examine someone means to find out their knowledge or skill in a particular subject by testing them. **4** If a doctor examines you, he or she checks your body to find out the state of your health.

**examiner** examiners
NOUN a person who sets or marks an exam.

**example** examples
NOUN **1** something which represents or is typical of a group or set *E.G. some examples of early Spanish music.* **2** If you say someone or something is an example to people, you mean that people can imitate and learn from them. ▶ PHRASE **3** You use **for example** to give an example of something you are talking about.
■ (sense 1) sample, specimen

**exasperate** exasperates exasperating exasperated
VERB If someone or something exasperates you, they irritate you and make you angry.
**exasperating** ADJECTIVE
**exasperation** NOUN

**excavate** excavates excavating excavated
VERB To excavate means to remove

earth from the ground by digging.
**excavation** NOUN

**exceed** exceeds exceeding exceeded
VERB To exceed something such as a limit means to go beyond it or to become greater than it *E.G. the first aircraft to exceed the speed of sound.*

**exceedingly**
ADVERB extremely or very much.

**excel** excels excelling excelled
VERB If someone excels in something, they are very good at doing it.

**Excellency** Excellencies
NOUN a title used to address an official of very high rank, such as an ambassador or a governor.

**excellent**
ADJECTIVE very good indeed.
**excellence** NOUN
■ first-rate, outstanding, superb

**except**
PREPOSITION Except or except for means other than or apart from *E.G. All my family were musicians except my father.*

**exception** exceptions
NOUN somebody or something that is not included in a general statement or rule *E.G. English, like every language, has exceptions to its rules.*

**exceptional**
ADJECTIVE **1** unusually talented or clever. **2** unusual and likely to happen very rarely.
**exceptionally** ADVERB

**excerpt** excerpts
NOUN a short piece of writing or music which is taken from a larger piece.

**excess** excesses
NOUN **1** Excess is behaviour which goes beyond normally acceptable

limits *E.G. a life of excess.* **2** a larger amount of something than is needed, usual, or healthy *E.G. an excess of energy.* ▶ ADJECTIVE **3** more than is needed, allowed, or healthy *E.G. excess weight.* ▶ PHRASE **4 In excess of** a particular amount means more than that amount *E.G. a fortune in excess of 150 million pounds.* **5** If you do something **to excess**, you do it too much *E.G. She drank to excess.*

**excessive**
ADJECTIVE too great in amount or degree *E.G. using excessive force.*
**excessively** ADVERB

**exchange** exchanges exchanging exchanged
VERB (SCIENCE) **1** To exchange things means to give or receive one thing in return for another *E.G. They exchange small presents on Christmas Eve.* ▶ NOUN **2** the act of giving or receiving something in return for something else *E.G. an exchange of letters… exchanges of gunfire.* **3** a place where people trade and do business *E.G. the stock exchange.*

**exchequer**
*Said "iks-chek-er"* NOUN The exchequer is the department in the government in Britain and other countries which is responsible for money belonging to the state.

**excise**
NOUN Excise is a tax put on goods produced for sale in the country that produces them.

**excitable**
ADJECTIVE easily excited.

**excite** excites exciting excited
VERB **1** If somebody or something excites you, they make you feel very happy and nervous or very

interested and enthusiastic. **2** If something excites a particular feeling, it causes somebody to have that feeling *E.G. This excited my suspicion.*
**excited** ADJECTIVE   **excitedly** ADVERB
**exciting** ADJECTIVE   **excitement** NOUN
■ (sense 1) arouse, thrill

**exclaim** exclaims exclaiming exclaimed
VERB When you exclaim, you cry out suddenly or loudly because you are excited or shocked.

**exclamation** exclamations
NOUN (ENGLISH) a word or phrase spoken suddenly to express a strong feeling.

**exclamation mark** exclamation marks
NOUN a punctuation mark (!) used in writing to express a strong feeling.

---

### What does the Exclamation Mark do?

The **exclamation mark** (!) is used after emphatic expressions and exclamations:
 *E.G. I can't believe it!*
The exclamation mark can lose its effect if used too much. After a sentence expressing mild excitement or humour, it is better to use a full stop:
 *E.G. It is a beautiful day.*

---

**exclude** excludes excluding excluded
VERB **1** If you exclude something, you deliberately do not include it or do not consider it. **2** If you exclude

a b c d e f g h i j k l m n o p q r s t u v w x y z

somebody from a place or an activity, you prevent them from entering the place or taking part in the activity.

**exclusion** NOUN

**exclusive** exclusives

ADJECTIVE **1** available to or for the use of a small group of rich or privileged people *E.G. an exclusive club*.
**2** belonging to a particular person or group only *E.G. exclusive rights to coverage of the Olympic Games*.
▶ NOUN **3** a story or interview which appears in only one newspaper or on only one television programme.

**exclusively** ADVERB

**excrement**

*Said "eks-krim-ment"* NOUN Excrement is the solid waste matter that is passed out of a person's or animal's body through their bowels.

**excrete** excretes excreting excreted

VERB When you excrete waste matter from your body, you get rid of it, for example by going to the lavatory or by sweating.

**excretion** NOUN   **excretory** ADJECTIVE

**excruciating**

*Said "iks-kroo-shee-ate-ing"* ADJECTIVE unbearably painful.

**excruciatingly** ADVERB

📖 from Latin *excruciare* meaning 'to torture'

**excursion** excursions

NOUN a short journey or outing.

**excuse** excuses excusing excused

NOUN **1** a reason which you give to explain why something has been done, has not been done, or will not be done. ▶ VERB **2** If you excuse

yourself or something that you have done, you give reasons defending your actions. **3** If you excuse somebody for something wrong they have done, you forgive them for it. **4** If you excuse somebody from a duty or responsibility, you free them from it *E.G. He was excused from standing trial because of ill health*.
▶ PHRASE **5** You say **excuse me** to try to catch somebody's attention or to apologize for an interruption or for rude behaviour.

**execute** executes executing executed

VERB **1** To execute somebody means to kill them as a punishment for a crime. **2** If you execute something such as a plan or an action, you carry it out or perform it *E.G. The crime had been planned and executed in Montreal*.

**execution** NOUN

**executioner** executioners

NOUN a person whose job is to execute criminals.

**executive** executives

NOUN **1** a person who is employed by a company at a senior level. **2** The executive of an organization is a committee which has the authority to make decisions and ensure that they are carried out. ▶ ADJECTIVE **3** concerned with making important decisions and ensuring that they are carried out *E.G. the commission's executive director*.

**executor** executors

*Said "ig-zek-yoo-tor"* NOUN a person you appoint to carry out the instructions in your will.

**exemplary**

ADJECTIVE **1** being a good example and

worthy of imitation *E.G. an exemplary performance.* **2** serving as a warning *E.G. an exemplary tale.*

**exemplify exemplifies exemplifying exemplified**
VERB **1** To exemplify something means to be a typical example of it *E.G. This aircraft exemplifies the advantages of European technological cooperation.* **2** If you exemplify something, you give an example of it.

**exempt exempts exempting exempted**
ADJECTIVE **1** excused from a rule or duty *E.G. people exempt from prescription charges.* ► VERB **2** To exempt someone from a rule, duty, or obligation means to excuse them from it.
**exemption** NOUN

**exercise exercises exercising exercised**
NOUN **1** ( PE ) Exercise is any activity which you do to get fit or remain healthy. **2** Exercises are also activities which you do to practise and train for a particular skill *E.G. piano exercises… a mathematical exercise.* ► VERB **3** When you exercise, you do activities which help you to get fit and remain healthy. **4** If you exercise your rights or responsibilities, you use them.

**exert exerts exerting exerted**
VERB **1** To exert pressure means to apply it. **2** If you exert yourself, you make a physical or mental effort to do something.
**exertion** NOUN
NOUN Exertion is vigorous physical effort or exercise.

**exhale exhales exhaling exhaled**
VERB When you exhale, you breathe out.

**exhaust exhausts exhausting exhausted**
VERB **1** To exhaust somebody means to make them very tired *E.G. Several lengths of the pool left her exhausted.* **2** If you exhaust a supply of something such as money or food, you use it up completely. **3** If you exhaust a subject, you talk about it so much that there is nothing else to say about it. ► NOUN **4** a pipe which carries the gas or steam out of the engine of a vehicle.
**exhaustion** NOUN
■ (sense 1) fatigue, tire out, wear out

**exhaustive**
ADJECTIVE thorough and complete *E.G. an exhaustive series of tests.*
**exhaustively** ADVERB

**exhibit exhibits exhibiting exhibited**
VERB **1** To exhibit things means to show them in a public place for people to see. **2** If you exhibit your feelings or abilities, you display them so that other people can see them. ► NOUN **3** anything which is put on show for the public to see.

**exhibition exhibitions**
NOUN ( ART ) a public display of works of art, products, or skills.

**exhibitor exhibitors**
NOUN a person whose work is being shown in an exhibition.

**exhilarating**
ADJECTIVE Something that is exhilarating makes you feel very happy and excited.

On WEDNESday Wayne WED NESta (<u>Wednesday</u>)  SPELLING NOTE

A
B
C
D
E
F
G
H
I
J
K
L
M
N
O
P
Q
R
S
T
U
V
W
X
Y
Z

**exile exiles exiling exiled**

NOUN 1 If somebody lives in exile, they live in a foreign country because they cannot live in their own country, usually for political reasons. 2 a person who lives in exile. ▶ VERB 3 If somebody is exiled, they are sent away from their own country and not allowed to return.

**exist exists existing existed**

VERB If something exists, it is present in the world as a real or living thing.

**existence**

NOUN 1 Existence is the state of being or existing. 2 a way of living or being E.G. an idyllic existence.

**exit exits exiting exited**

NOUN 1 a way out of a place. 2 If you make an exit, you leave a place. ▶ VERB 3 To exit means to go out. 4 (DRAMA) An actor exits when he or she leaves the stage.

**exodus**

NOUN An exodus is the departure of a large number of people from a place.

**exotic**

ADJECTIVE 1 attractive or interesting through being unusual E.G. exotic fabrics. 2 coming from a foreign country E.G. exotic plants.

📖 from Greek exotikos meaning 'foreign'

**expand expands expanding expanded**

VERB 1 If something expands or you expand it, it becomes larger in number or size. 2 If you expand on something, you give more details about it E.G. The minister's speech expanded on the aims which he outlined last month.

**expansion** NOUN

**expanse expanses**

NOUN a very large or widespread area E.G. a vast expanse of pine forests.

**expansive**

ADJECTIVE 1 Something that is expansive is very wide or extends over a very large area E.G. the expansive countryside. 2 Someone who is expansive is friendly, open, or talkative.

**expatriate expatriates**

Said "eks-pat-ree-it" NOUN someone who is living in a country which is not their own.

**expect expects expecting expected**

VERB 1 If you expect something to happen, you believe that it will happen E.G. The trial is expected to end today. 2 If you are expecting somebody or something, you believe that they are going to arrive or to happen E.G. The Queen was expecting the chambermaid. 3 If you expect something, you believe that it is your right to get it or have it E.G. He seemed to expect a reply.

■ (sense 1) anticipate, look forward to

**expectancy**

NOUN Expectancy is the feeling that something is about to happen, especially something exciting.

**expectant**

ADJECTIVE 1 If you are expectant, you believe that something is about to happen, especially something exciting. 2 An expectant mother or father is someone whose baby is going to be born soon.

**expectantly** ADVERB

**expectation expectations**

NOUN Expectation or an expectation

is a strong belief or hope that
something will happen.

**expedient** expedients
*Said* "iks-**pee**-dee-ent" NOUN **1** an
action or plan that achieves a
particular purpose but that may not
be morally acceptable *E.G. Many firms
have improved their profitability by
the simple expedient of cutting staff.*
► ADJECTIVE **2** Something that is
expedient is useful or convenient in
a particular situation.
**expediency** NOUN

**expedition** expeditions
NOUN **1** an organized journey made
for a special purpose, such as to
explore; also the party of people
who make such a journey. **2** a short
journey or outing *E.G. shopping
expeditions.*
**expeditionary** ADJECTIVE

**expel** expels expelling expelled
VERB **1** If someone is expelled from a
school or club, they are officially told
to leave because they have behaved
badly. **2** If a gas or liquid is expelled
from a place, it is forced out of it.

**expend** expends expending
expended
VERB To expend energy, time, or money
means to use it up or spend it.

**expendable**
ADJECTIVE no longer useful or
necessary, and therefore able to be
got rid of.

**expenditure**
NOUN Expenditure is the total amount
of money spent on something.

**expense** expenses
NOUN **1** Expense is the money that
something costs *E.G. the expense of
installing a burglar alarm.* ► PLURAL
NOUN **2** Expenses are the money

somebody spends while doing
something connected with their
work, which is paid back to them by
their employer.
■ (sense 1) cost, expenditure, outlay

**expensive**
ADJECTIVE costing a lot of money.
**expensively** ADVERB

**experience** experiences
experiencing experienced
NOUN **1** Experience consists of all the
things that you have done or that
have happened to you. **2** something
that you do or something that
happens to you, especially
something new or unusual. ► VERB **3** If
you experience a situation or feeling,
it happens to you or you are affected
by it.
■ (sense 3) go through, undergo

**experiment** experiments
experimenting experimented
NOUN **1** the testing of something,
either to find out its effect or to
prove something. ► VERB **2** If you
experiment with something, you do
a scientific test on it to prove or
discover something.
**experimentation** NOUN
**experimental** ADJECTIVE
**experimentally** ADVERB

**expert** experts
NOUN **1** a person who is very skilled at
doing something or very
knowledgeable about a particular
subject. ► ADJECTIVE **2** having or
requiring special skill or knowledge
*E.G. expert advice.*
**expertly** ADVERB
■ (sense 1) authority, master,
specialist

**expertise**
*Said* "eks-per-**teez**" NOUN Expertise is

a
b
c
d
e
f
g
h
i
j
k
l
m
n
o
p
q
r
s
t
u
v
w
x
y
z

special skill or knowledge.

**expire** expires expiring expired
VERB When something expires, it reaches the end of the period of time for which it is valid E.G. *My contract expires in the summer.*
**expiry** NOUN

**explain** explains explaining explained
VERB If you explain something, you give details about it or reasons for it so that it can be understood.
**explanation** NOUN **explanatory** ADJECTIVE
■ clarify, elucidate, make clear

**explicit**
ADJECTIVE shown or expressed clearly and openly E.G. *an explicit death threat.*
**explicitly** ADVERB

**explode** explodes exploding exploded
VERB 1 If something such as a bomb explodes, it bursts loudly and with great force, often causing damage. 2 If somebody explodes, they express strong feelings suddenly or violently E.G. *I half expected him to explode in anger.* 3 When something increases suddenly and rapidly, it can be said to explode E.G. *Sales of men's toiletries have exploded.*
▥ from Latin *explodere* meaning 'to clap someone offstage', from *ex* meaning 'out of' + *plodere* meaning 'to clap'

**exploit** exploits exploiting exploited
VERB 1 If somebody exploits a person or a situation, they take advantage of them for their own ends E.G. *Critics claim he exploited black musicians.* 2 If you exploit something, you make the

best use of it, often for profit E.G. *exploiting the power of computers.*
▶ NOUN 3 something daring or interesting that somebody has done E.G. *His courage and exploits were legendary.*
**exploitation** NOUN

**explore** explores exploring explored
VERB 1 If you explore a place, you travel in it to find out what it is like. 2 If you explore an idea, you think about it carefully.
**exploration** NOUN **exploratory** ADJECTIVE **explorer** NOUN

**explosion** explosions
NOUN a sudden violent burst of energy, for example one caused by a bomb.

**explosive** explosives
ADJECTIVE 1 capable of exploding or likely to explode. 2 happening suddenly and making a loud noise. 3 An explosive situation is one which is likely to have serious or dangerous effects. ▶ NOUN 4 a substance or device that can explode.

**exponent** exponents
NOUN 1 An exponent of an idea or plan is someone who puts it forward. 2 FORMAL An exponent of a skill or activity is someone who is good at it.

**export** exports exporting exported
VERB 1 To export goods means to send them to another country and sell them there. ▶ NOUN 2 Exports are goods which are sent to another country and sold.
**exporter** NOUN

**expose** exposes exposing exposed
VERB 1 To expose something means to

uncover it and make it visible. **2** To expose a person to something dangerous means to put them in a situation in which it might harm them *E.G. exposed to tobacco smoke*. **3** To expose a person or situation means to reveal the truth about them.

**exposition** expositions

NOUN a detailed explanation of a particular subject.

**exposure** exposures

NOUN **1** Exposure is the exposing of something. **2** Exposure is the harmful effect on the body caused by very cold weather.

**express** expresses expressing expressed

VERB **1** When you express an idea or feeling, you show what you think or feel by saying or doing something. **2** If you express a quantity in a particular form, you write it down in that form *E.G. The result of the equation is usually expressed as a percentage.* ▶ ADJECTIVE **3** very fast *E.G. express delivery service.* ▶ NOUN **4** a fast train or coach which stops at only a few stations.

**expression** expressions

NOUN **1** Your expression is the look on your face which shows what you are thinking or feeling. **2** ( ENGLISH ) The expression of ideas or feelings is the showing of them through words, actions, or art. **3** a word or phrase used in communicating *E.G. the expression 'nosey parker'.*

**expressive**

ADJECTIVE **1** showing feelings clearly. **2** full of expression.

**expressway** expressways

NOUN a road designed for fast-moving traffic.

**expulsion** expulsions

NOUN The expulsion of someone from a place or institution is the act of officially banning them from that place or institution *E.G. the high number of school expulsions.*

**exquisite**

ADJECTIVE extremely beautiful and pleasing.

**extend** extends extending extended

VERB **1** If something extends for a distance, it continues and stretches into the distance. **2** If something extends from a surface or an object, it sticks out from it. **3** If you extend something, you make it larger or longer *E.G. The table had been extended to seat fifty.*

**extension** extensions

NOUN **1** a room or building which is added to an existing building. **2** an extra period of time for which something continues to exist or be valid *E.G. an extension to his visa.* **3** an additional telephone connected to the same line as another telephone.

**extensive**

ADJECTIVE **1** covering a large area. **2** very great in effect *E.G. extensive repairs.*

**extensively** ADVERB

**extent** extents

NOUN The extent of something is its length, area, or size.

**exterior** exteriors

NOUN **1** The exterior of something is its outside. **2** Your exterior is your outward appearance.

**exterminate** exterminates exterminating exterminated

VERB When animals or people are

A
B
C
D
E
F
G
H
I
J
K
L
M
N
O
P
Q
R
S
T
U
V
W
X
Y
Z

exterminated, they are deliberately killed.

**extermination** NOUN

**external externals**

ADJECTIVE existing or happening on the outside or outer part of something.

**externally** ADVERB

**extinct**

ADJECTIVE 1 An extinct species of animal or plant is no longer in existence. 2 An extinct volcano is no longer likely to erupt.

**extinction** NOUN

**extinguish extinguishes extinguishing extinguished**

VERB To extinguish a light or fire means to put it out.

**extortionate**

ADJECTIVE more expensive than you consider to be fair.

**extra extras**

ADJECTIVE 1 more than is usual, necessary, or expected. ► NOUN 2 anything which is additional. 3 a person who is hired to play a very small and unimportant part in a film. ■ (sense 1) added, additional, further

**extra-**

PREFIX 'Extra' means 'outside' or 'beyond' E.G. extraordinary. 🔛 from Latin exterus meaning 'outward'

**extract extracts extracting extracted**

VERB 1 To extract something from a place means to take it out or get it out, often by force. 2 If you extract information from someone, you get it from them with difficulty. ► NOUN (LIBRARY) 3 a small section taken from a book or piece of music.

**extraction**

NOUN 1 Your extraction is the country or people that your family originally comes from E.G. a Malaysian citizen of Australian extraction. 2 Extraction is the process of taking or getting something out of a place.

**extraordinary**

ADJECTIVE unusual or surprising.

**extraordinarily** ADVERB

■ exceptional, remarkable, unusual

**extravagant**

ADJECTIVE 1 spending or costing more money than is reasonable or affordable. 2 going beyond reasonable limits.

**extravagantly** ADVERB

**extravagance** NOUN

**extravaganza extravaganzas**

NOUN a spectacular and expensive public show.

**extreme extremes**

ADJECTIVE 1 very great in degree or intensity E.G. extreme caution. 2 going beyond what is usual or reasonable E.G. extreme weather conditions. 3 at the furthest point or edge of something E.G. the extreme northern corner of Spain. ► NOUN 4 the highest or furthest degree of something.

**extremely** ADVERB

**extremist extremists**

NOUN a person who uses unreasonable or violent methods to bring about political change.

**extremism** NOUN

**extremity extremities**

NOUN The extremities of something are its furthest ends or edges.

**extricate extricates extricating extricated**

VERB To extricate someone from a place or a situation means to free them from it.

**extrovert** extroverts
NOUN a person who is more interested in other people and the world around them than their own thoughts and feelings.
📖 from Latin *extra* meaning 'outwards' + *vertere* meaning 'to turn'

**exuberant**
ADJECTIVE full of energy and cheerfulness.
**exuberantly** ADVERB **exuberance** NOUN

**exude** exudes exuding exuded
VERB If someone exudes a quality or feeling, they seem to have it to a great degree.

**eye** eyes eyeing or eying eyed
NOUN **1** the organ of sight. **2** the small hole at the end of a needle through which you pass the thread. ▶ VERB **3** To eye something means to look at it carefully or suspiciously.

**eyeball** eyeballs
NOUN the whole of the ball-shaped part of the eye.

**eyebrow** eyebrows
NOUN Your eyebrows are the lines of hair which grow on the ridges of bone above your eyes.

**eyelash** eyelashes
NOUN Your eyelashes are hairs that grow on the edges of your eyelids.

**eyelid** eyelids
NOUN Your eyelids are the folds of skin which cover your eyes when they are closed.

**eyesight**
NOUN Your eyesight is your ability to see.

**eyesore** eyesores
NOUN Something that is an eyesore is extremely ugly.

**eyewitness** eyewitnesses
NOUN a person who has seen an event and can describe what happened.

**eyrie** eyries
*Said "ear-ee"* NOUN the nest of an eagle or other bird of prey.

LEt's measure the angLE (ang*le*) ▶ SPELLING NOTE

# Ff

A B C D E F G H I J K L M N O P Q R S T U V W X Y Z

TIP
Some words which sound as if they should begin with the letter *f* actually begin with the letters *ph*, for example *pharmacy*, *pharaoh* and *phrase*. The *ph* combination, pronounced like *f*, comes in the middle of some words too, for example *amphetamine* and *emphasis*.

**fable fables**
NOUN a story intended to teach a moral lesson.
🔲 from Latin *fabula* meaning 'story'

**fabled**
ADJECTIVE well-known because many stories have been told about it *E.G. the fabled city of Troy.*

**fabric fabrics**
NOUN (D&T) 1 cloth *E.G. tough fabric for tents.* 2 The fabric of a building is its walls, roof, and other parts. 3 The fabric of a society or system is its structure, laws, and customs *E.G. the democratic fabric of American society.*

**fabricate fabricates fabricating fabricated**
VERB 1 If you fabricate a story or an explanation, you invent it in order to deceive people. 2 To fabricate something is to make or manufacture it.
**fabrication** NOUN

**fabulous**
ADJECTIVE 1 wonderful or very impressive *E.G. a fabulous picnic.* 2 not real, but happening in stories and legends *E.G. fabulous creatures.*

**facade facades**
*Said "fas-sahd"* NOUN 1 the front outside wall of a building. 2 a false outward appearance *E.G. the facade of honesty.*

**face faces facing faced**
NOUN 1 the front part of your head

from your chin to your forehead. 2 the expression someone has or is making *E.G. a grim face.* 3 a surface or side of something, especially the most important side *E.G. the north face of Everest.* 4 the main aspect or general appearance of something *E.G. We have changed the face of language study.* ▶ VERB 5 To face something or someone is to be opposite them or to look at them or towards them *E.G. a room that faces on to the street.* 6 If you face something difficult or unpleasant, you have to deal with it *E.G. She faced a terrible dilemma.* ▶ PHRASE 7 **On the face of it** means judging by the appearance of something or your initial reaction to it *E.G. On the face of it the palace looks gigantic.*
▪ (sense 1) countenance, visage

**faceless**
ADJECTIVE without character or individuality *E.G. anonymous shops and faceless coffee-bars.*

**face-lift face-lifts**
NOUN 1 an operation to tighten the skin on someone's face to make them look younger. 2 If you give something a face-lift, you clean it or improve its appearance.

**facet facets**
*Said "fas-it"* NOUN 1 a single part or aspect of something *E.G. the many facets of his talent.* 2 one of the flat,

cut surfaces of a precious stone.
📖 from French *facette* meaning 'little face'

**facetious**
*Said* "fas-**see**-shuss" ADJECTIVE witty or amusing but in a rather silly or inappropriate way E.G. *He didn't appreciate my facetious suggestion.*
📖 from Latin *facetiae* meaning 'witty remarks'

**facial**
*Said* "**fay**-shal" ADJECTIVE appearing on or being part of the face E.G. *facial expressions.*

**facilitate facilitates facilitating facilitated**
VERB To facilitate something is to make it easier for it to happen E.G. *a process that will facilitate individual development.*

**facility facilities**
NOUN 1 a service or piece of equipment which makes it possible to do something E.G. *excellent shopping facilities.* 2 A facility for something is an ability to do it easily or well E.G. *a facility for novel-writing.*

**fact facts**
NOUN 1 a piece of knowledge or information that is true or something that has actually happened. ▶ PHRASES 2 **In fact, as a matter of fact,** and **in point of fact** mean 'actually' or 'really' and are used for emphasis or when making an additional comment E.G. *Very few people, in fact, have this type of skin.*
**factual** ADJECTIVE   **factually** ADVERB

**faction factions**
NOUN a small group of people belonging to a larger group, but differing from the larger group in some aims or ideas E.G. *a conservative faction in the Church.*

**fact of life facts of life**
NOUN 1 The facts of life are details about sexual intercourse and how babies are conceived and born. 2 If you say that something is a fact of life, you mean that it is something that people expect to happen, even though they might find it shocking or unpleasant E.G. *War is a fact of life.*

**factor factors**
NOUN 1 something that helps to cause a result E.G. *House dust mites are a major factor in asthma.* 2 The factors of a number are the whole numbers that will divide exactly into it. For example, 2 and 5 are factors of 10. 3 If something increases by a particular factor, it is multiplied that number of times E.G. *The amount of energy used has increased by a factor of eight.*
🔲 (sense 1) cause, element, part

**factory factories**
NOUN a building or group of buildings where goods are made in large quantities.

**faculty faculties**
NOUN 1 Your faculties are your physical and mental abilities E.G. *My mental faculties are as sharp as ever.* 2 In some universities, a Faculty is a group of related departments E.G. *the Science Faculty.*

**fad fads**
NOUN a temporary fashion or craze E.G. *the latest exercise fad.*

**fade fades fading faded**
VERB If something fades, the intensity of its colour, brightness, or sound is gradually reduced.

**faeces** or **feces**
*Said* "**fee**-seez" PLURAL NOUN the solid

Beautiful Elephants Are Usually Tiny (<u>beautiful</u>)   ◀ SPELLING NOTE

**waste substances** discharged from a person's or animal's body.

🔲 from Latin *faeces* meaning 'dregs'

## fag fags
NOUN *INFORMAL* a cigarette.

## Fahrenheit
*Said* "far-ren-hite" NOUN a scale of temperature in which the freezing point of water is 32° and the boiling point is 212°.

## fail fails failing failed
VERB 1 If someone fails to achieve something, they are not successful. 2 If you fail an exam, your marks are too low and you do not pass. 3 If you fail to do something that you should have done, you do not do it *E.G. They failed to phone her.* 4 If something fails, it becomes less effective or stops working properly *E.G. The power failed… His grandmother's eyesight began to fail.* ▶ NOUN 5 In an exam, a fail is a piece of work that is not good enough to pass. ▶ PHRASE 6 **Without fail** means definitely or regularly *E.G. Every Sunday her mum would ring without fail.*

🔲 (sense 1) be unsuccessful, flop

## failing failings
NOUN 1 a fault in something or someone. ▶ PREPOSITION 2 used to introduce an alternative *E.G. Failing that, get a market stall.*

## failure failures
NOUN 1 lack of success *E.G. Not all conservation programmes ended in failure.* 2 an unsuccessful person, thing, or action *E.G. The venture was a complete failure.* 3 Your failure to do something is not doing something that you were expected to do *E.G. a statement explaining his failure to turn up as a speaker.*

🔲 (sense 2) flop, loser, washout

## faint fainter faintest; faints fainting fainted
ADJECTIVE 1 A sound, colour, or feeling that is faint is not very strong or intense. 2 If you feel faint, you feel weak, dizzy, and unsteady. ▶ VERB 3 If you faint, you lose consciousness for a short time.

**faintly** ADVERB

🔲 (sense 3) black out, pass out, swoon

## fair fairer fairest; fairs
ADJECTIVE 1 reasonable and just *E.G. fair and prompt trials for political prisoners.* 2 quite large *E.G. a fair size envelope.* 3 moderately good or likely to be correct *E.G. He had a fair idea of what to expect.* 4 having light coloured hair or pale skin. 5 with pleasant and dry weather *E.G. Ireland's fair weather months.* ▶ NOUN 6 a form of entertainment that takes place outside, with stalls, sideshows, and machines to ride on. 7 an exhibition of goods produced by a particular industry *E.G. International Wine and Food Fair.*

**fairly** ADVERB **fairness** NOUN

🔲 (sense 1) impartial, just, unbiased

## fairground fairgrounds
NOUN an outdoor area where a fair is set up.

## fairway fairways
NOUN the area of trimmed grass between a tee and a green on a golf course.

## fairy fairies
NOUN In stories, fairies are small, supernatural creatures with magical powers.

## fairy tale fairy tales
NOUN a story of magical events.

**faith** faiths
NOUN **1** Faith is a feeling of confidence, trust or optimism about something. **2** ( RE ) someone's faith is their religion.

**faithful**
ADJECTIVE **1** loyal to someone or something and remaining firm in support of them. **2** accurate and truthful E.G. *a faithful copy of an original*.
**faithfully** ADVERB **faithfulness** NOUN
■ (sense 1) loyal, steadfast, trusty

**fake** fakes faking faked
NOUN **1** an imitation of something made to trick people into thinking that it is genuine. ► ADJECTIVE **2** imitation and not genuine E.G. *fake fur*. ► VERB **3** If you fake a feeling, you pretend that you are experiencing it.
■ (sense 1) copy, imitation, sham
■ (sense 2) artificial, false, phoney
■ (sense 3) feign, pretend, simulate

**falcon** falcons
NOUN a bird of prey that can be trained to hunt other birds or small animals.
🏛 from Latin *falco* meaning 'hawk'

**fall** falls falling fell fallen
VERB **1** If someone or something falls or falls over, they drop towards the ground. **2** If something falls somewhere, it lands there E.G. *The spotlight fell on her.* **3** If something falls in amount or strength, it becomes less E.G. *Steel production fell about 25%.* **4** If a person or group in a position of power falls, they lose their position and someone else takes control. **5** Someone who falls in battle is killed. **6** If, for example, you fall asleep, fall ill, or fall in love, you change quite quickly to that new state. **7** If you fall for someone, you become strongly attracted to them and fall in love. **8** If you fall for a trick or lie, you are deceived by it. **9** Something that falls on a particular date occurs on that date. ► NOUN **10** If you have a fall, you accidentally fall over. **11** A fall of snow, soot, or other substance is a quantity of it that has fallen to the ground. **12** A fall in something is a reduction in its amount or strength. **13** In America, autumn is called the fall.

**fall down** VERB An argument or idea that falls down on a particular point is weak on that point and as a result will be unsuccessful.

**fall out** VERB If people fall out, they disagree and quarrel.

**fall through** VERB If an arrangement or plan falls through, it fails or is abandoned.

**fallacy** fallacies
*Said* "**fal**-lass-ee" NOUN something false that is generally believed to be true.
🏛 from Latin *fallacia* meaning 'deception'

**fallopian tube** fallopian tubes
*Said* "fal-**loh**-pee-an" NOUN one of two tubes in a woman's body along which the eggs pass from the ovaries to the uterus.

**fallout**
NOUN radioactive particles that fall to the earth after a nuclear explosion.

**fallow**
ADJECTIVE Land that is fallow is not being used for crop growing so that it has the chance to rest and improve.

**false**
ADJECTIVE **1** untrue or incorrect E.G. *I*

a b c d e f g h i j k l m n o p q r s t u v w x y z

A B C D E F G H I J K L M N O P Q R S T U V W X Y Z

*think that's a false argument.* **2** not real or genuine but intended to seem real *E.G. false hair.* **3** unfaithful or deceitful.

**falsely** ADVERB  **falsity** NOUN

**falsehood** falsehoods
NOUN **1** the quality or fact of being untrue *E.G. the difference between truth and falsehood.* **2** a lie.

**falsify** falsifies falsifying falsified
VERB If you falsify something, you change it in order to deceive people.
**falsification** NOUN

**falter** falters faltering faltered
VERB If someone or something falters, they hesitate or become unsure or unsteady *E.G. Her voice faltered.*

**fame**
NOUN the state of being very well-known.
 ▪ prominence, renown, repute

**famed**
ADJECTIVE very well-known *E.G. an area famed for its beauty.*

**familiar**
ADJECTIVE **1** well-known or easy to recognize *E.G. familiar faces.*
**2** knowing or understanding something well *E.G. Most children are familiar with stories.*
**familiarity** NOUN  **familiarize** VERB
 ▪ (sense 1) recognizable, well-known

**family** families
NOUN **1** a group consisting of parents and their children; also all the people who are related to each other, including aunts and uncles, cousins, and grandparents. **2** a group of related species of animals or plants.
**familial** ADJECTIVE

**family planning**
NOUN the practice of controlling the

number of children you have, usually by using contraception.

**famine** famines
NOUN a serious shortage of food which may cause many deaths.

**famished**
ADJECTIVE; *INFORMAL* very hungry.

**famous**
ADJECTIVE very well-known.
 ▪ prominent, renowned, well-known

**famously**
ADVERB; *OLD-FASHIONED* If people get on famously, they enjoy each other's company very much.

**fan** fans fanning fanned
NOUN **1** If you are a fan of someone or something, you like them very much and are very enthusiastic about them. **2** a hand-held or mechanical object which creates a draught of cool air when it moves. ▶ VERB **3** To fan someone or something is to create a draught in their direction *E.G. The gentle wind fanned her from all sides.*
 ▪ (sense 1) admirer, enthusiast, supporter

**fan out** VERB If things or people fan out, they move outwards in different directions.

**fanatic** fanatics
NOUN a person who is very extreme in their support for a cause or in their enthusiasm for a particular activity.
**fanaticism** NOUN
 ▥ from Latin *fanaticus* meaning 'possessed by a god'

**fanatical**
ADJECTIVE If you are fanatical about something, you are very extreme in your enthusiasm or support for it.
**fanatically** ADVERB
 ▪ obsessive, overenthusiastic

**fancy** fancies fancying fancied; fancier fanciest

VERB **1** If you fancy something, you want to have it or do it *E.G. She fancied living in Canada.* ▶ ADJECTIVE **2** special and elaborate *E.G. dressed up in some fancy clothes.*

**fanciful** ADJECTIVE

◼ (sense 2) elaborate, ornate

**fancy dress**

NOUN clothing worn for a party at which people dress up to look like a particular character or animal.

**fanfare** fanfares

NOUN a short, loud, musical introduction to a special event, usually played on trumpets.

**fang** fangs

NOUN Fangs are long, pointed teeth.

**fantail** fantails

NOUN **1** a pigeon with a large tail that can be opened like a fan. **2** In Australia and New Zealand, a fantail is also a small, insect-eating bird with a fan-shaped tail.

**fantasize** fantasizes fantasizing fantasized; also spelt **fantasise**

VERB If you fantasize, you imagine pleasant but unlikely events or situations.

**fantastic**

ADJECTIVE **1** wonderful and very pleasing *E.G. a fantastic view of the sea.* **2** extremely large in degree or amount *E.G. fantastic debts.* **3** strange and difficult to believe *E.G. fantastic animals found nowhere else on earth.*

**fantastically** ADVERB

◼ (sense 1) marvellous, wonderful

**fantasy** fantasies

NOUN **1** an imagined story or situation. **2** Fantasy is the activity of imagining things or the things that you

imagine *E.G. She can't distinguish between fantasy and reality.*

**3** (LIBRARY) In books and films, fantasy is the people or situations in books or films which are created in the writer's imagination and do not reflect reality.

▥ from Greek *phantasia* meaning 'imagination'

**far** farther farthest; further furthest

ADVERB **1** If something is far away from other things, it is a long distance away. **2** Far also means very much or to a great extent or degree *E.G. far more important.* ▶ ADJECTIVE **3** Far means very distant *E.G. in the far south of Africa.* **4** Far also describes the more distant of two things rather than the nearer one *E.G. the far corner of the goal.* ▶ PHRASE **5 By far** and **far and away** are used to say that something is the best *E.G. Walking is by far the best way to get around.* **6 So far** means up to the present moment *E.G. So far, it's been good news.* **7 As far as**, **so far as**, and **in so far as** mean to the degree or extent that something is true *E.G. As far as I know he is progressing well.*

◼ (sense 2) considerably, much

◼ (sense 3) distant, remote

☑ When you are talking about a physical distance you can use *farther* and *farthest* or *further* and *furthest*. If you are talking about extra effort or time, use *further* and *furthest: a further delay is likely.*

**farce** farces

NOUN **1** a humorous play in which ridiculous and unlikely situations occur. **2** a disorganized and ridiculous situation.

**farcical** ADJECTIVE

a
b
c
d
e
f
g
h
i
j
k
l
m
n
o
p
q
r
s
t
u
v
w
x
y
z

**fare** fares faring fared

NOUN 1 the amount charged for a journey on a bus, train, or plane. ▶ VERB 2 How someone fares in a particular situation is how they get on *E.G. The team have not fared well in this tournament.*

📖 from Old English *faran* meaning 'to go'

**Far East**

NOUN The Far East consists of the countries of East Asia, including China, Japan, and Malaysia.

**Far Eastern** ADJECTIVE

**farewell**

INTERJECTION 1 Farewell means goodbye. ▶ ADJECTIVE 2 A farewell act is performed by or for someone who is leaving a particular job or career *E.G. a farewell speech.*

**far-fetched**

ADJECTIVE unlikely to be true.

**farm** farms farming farmed

NOUN 1 an area of land together with buildings, used for growing crops and raising animals. ▶ VERB 2 Someone who farms uses land to grow crops and raise animals.

**farmer** NOUN **farming** NOUN

📖 from Old French *ferme* meaning 'rented land'

**farmhouse** farmhouses

NOUN the main house on a farm.

**farmyard** farmyards

NOUN an area surrounded by farm buildings.

**fascinate** fascinates fascinating fascinated

VERB If something fascinates you, it interests you so much that you think about it and nothing else.

**fascinating** ADJECTIVE

■ absorb, enthral, intrigue

**fascism**

*Said* "**fash**-izm" NOUN an extreme right-wing political ideology or system of government with a powerful dictator and state control of most activities. Nationalism is encouraged and political opposition is not allowed.

**fascist** NOUN OR ADJECTIVE

**fashion** fashions fashioning fashioned

NOUN 1 a style of dress or way of behaving that is popular at a particular time. 2 The fashion in which someone does something is the way in which they do it. ▶ VERB 3 If you fashion something, you make or shape it.

■ (sense 1) style, trend, vogue

**fashionable**

ADJECTIVE Something that is fashionable is very popular with a lot of people at the same time.

**fashionably** ADVERB

■ in, in vogue, popular, trendy

**fast** faster fastest; fasts fasting fasted

ADJECTIVE OR ADVERB 1 moving, doing something, or happening quickly or with great speed. 2 If a clock is fast, it shows a time that is later than the real time. ▶ ADVERB 3 Something that is held fast is firmly fixed. ▶ PHRASE 4 If you are **fast asleep**, you are in a deep sleep. ▶ VERB 5 If you fast, you eat no food at all for a period of time, usually for religious reasons. ▶ NOUN 6 a period of time during which someone does not eat food.

■ (sense 1) quick, rapid, speedy, swift

**fasten** fastens fastening fastened

VERB 1 To fasten something is to close

it or attach it firmly to something else. **2** If you fasten your hands or teeth around or onto something, you hold it tightly with them.
**fastener** NOUN **fastening** NOUN
■ (sense 1) fix, secure

**fast food**
NOUN hot food that is prepared and served quickly after you have ordered it.

**fastidious**
ADJECTIVE extremely choosy and concerned about neatness and cleanliness.

**fast-track** **fast-tracks** **fast-tracking** **fast-tracked**
VERB To fast-track something is to make it happen or put it into effect as quickly as possible, usually giving it priority over other things.

**fat** **fatter fattest; fats**
ADJECTIVE **1** Someone who is fat has too much weight on their body.
**2** large or great E.G. *a fat pile of letters.*
▶ NOUN **3** Fat is the greasy, cream-coloured substance that animals and humans have under their skin, which is used to store energy and to help keep them warm. **4** Fat is also the greasy solid or liquid substance obtained from animals and plants and used in cooking.
**fatness** NOUN **fatty** ADJECTIVE
■ (sense 1) overweight, plump, podgy, tubby

**fatal**
ADJECTIVE **1** causing death E.G. *fatal injuries.* **2** very important or significant and likely to have an undesirable effect E.G. *The mistake was fatal to my plans.*
**fatally** ADVERB
■ (sense 1) deadly, lethal, mortal

**fatality fatalities**
NOUN a death caused by accident or violence.

**fate fates**
NOUN **1** Fate is a power that is believed to control events.
**2** Someone's fate is what happens to them E.G. *She was resigned to her fate.*
■ (sense 1) destiny, providence

**fateful**
ADJECTIVE having an important, often disastrous, effect E.G. *fateful political decisions.*

**father fathers fathering fathered**
NOUN **1** A person's father is their male parent. **2** The father of something is the man who invented or started it E.G. *the father of Italian painting.*
**3** 'Father' is used to address a priest in some Christian churches. **4** Father is another name for God. ▶ VERB
**5** LITERARY When a man fathers a child, he makes a woman pregnant.
**fatherly** ADJECTIVE **fatherhood** NOUN

**father-in-law fathers-in-law**
NOUN A person's father-in-law is the father of their husband or wife.

**fathom fathoms fathoming fathomed**
NOUN **1** a unit for measuring the depth of water. It is equal to 6 feet or about 1.83 metres. ▶ VERB **2** If you fathom something, you understand it after careful thought E.G. *Daisy tries to fathom what it means.*

**fatigue fatigues fatiguing fatigued**
*Said* "fat-*eeg*" NOUN **1** Fatigue is extreme tiredness. ▶ VERB **2** If you are fatigued by something, it makes you extremely tired.

a b c d e **f** g h i j k l m n o p q r s t u v w x y z

The government licenSes Schnapps (licenses)   **SPELLING NOTE**

A
B
C
D
E
F
G
H
I
J
K
L
M
N
O
P
Q
R
S
T
U
V
W
X
Y
Z

**fault** faults faulting faulted
NOUN **1** If something bad is your fault, you are to blame for it. **2** a weakness or imperfection in someone or something. **3** a large crack in rock caused by movement of the earth's crust. ▶ PHRASE **4** If you are **at fault**, you are mistaken or are to blame for something E.G. *If you were at fault, you accept it.* ▶ VERB **5** If you cannot fault someone, you cannot criticize them for what they are doing because they are doing it so well.
**faultless** ADJECTIVE **faulty** ADJECTIVE
■ (sense 2) defect, failing, flaw

**favour** favours favouring favoured
NOUN **1** If you regard someone or something with favour, you like or support them. **2** If you do someone a favour, you do something helpful for them. ▶ PHRASE **3** Something that is in **someone's favour** is a help or advantage to them E.G. *The arguments seemed to be in our favour.* **4** If you are **in favour of** something, you agree with it and think it should happen. ▶ VERB **5** If you favour something or someone, you prefer that person or thing.
**favourable** ADJECTIVE **favourably** ADVERB

**favourite** favourites
ADJECTIVE **1** Your favourite person or thing is the one you like best. ▶ NOUN **2** Someone's favourite is the person or thing they like best. **3** the animal or person expected to win in a race or contest.

**favouritism**
NOUN Favouritism is behaviour in which you are unfairly more helpful or more generous to one person than to other people.

**fawn** fawns fawning fawned
NOUN OR ADJECTIVE **1** pale yellowish-brown. ▶ NOUN **2** a very young deer. ▶ VERB **3** To fawn on someone is to seek their approval by flattering them.

**fax** faxes
NOUN an exact copy of a document sent electronically along a telephone line.

**fear** fears fearing feared
NOUN **1** Fear is an unpleasant feeling of danger. **2** a thought that something undesirable or unpleasant might happen E.G. *You have a fear of failure.* ▶ VERB **3** If you fear someone or something, you are frightened of them. **4** If you fear something unpleasant, you are worried that it is likely to happen E.G. *Artists feared that their pictures would be forgotten.*
**fearless** ADJECTIVE **fearlessly** ADVERB
■ (sense 1) dread, fright, terror

**fearful**
ADJECTIVE **1** afraid and full of fear. **2** extremely unpleasant or worrying E.G. *The world's in such a fearful mess.*
**fearfully** ADVERB

**fearsome**
ADJECTIVE terrible or frightening E.G. *a powerful, fearsome weapon.*

**feasible**
ADJECTIVE possible and likely to happen E.G. *The proposal is just not feasible.*
**feasibility** NOUN

**feast** feasts
NOUN a large and special meal for many people.

**feat** feats
NOUN an impressive and difficult achievement E.G. *It was an astonishing feat for Leeds to score six away from home.*

**feather feathers**

NOUN one of the light fluffy things covering a bird's body.

**feathery** ADJECTIVE

**feature features featuring featured**

NOUN 1 an interesting or important part or characteristic of something. 2 Someone's features are the various parts of their face. 3 a special article or programme dealing with a particular subject. 4 the main film in a cinema programme. ▶ VERB 5 To feature something is to include it or emphasize it as an important part or subject.

**featureless** ADJECTIVE

**February**

NOUN February is the second month of the year. It has 28 days, except in a leap year, when it has 29 days. 📖 from *Februa*, a Roman festival of purification

**fed**

the past tense and past participle of feed.

**federal**

ADJECTIVE relating to a system of government in which a group of states is controlled by a central government, but each state has its own local powers E.G. *The United States of America is a federal country*.

**federation federations**

NOUN a group of organizations or states that have joined together for a common purpose.

**fed up**

ADJECTIVE; INFORMAL unhappy or bored.

**fee fees**

NOUN a charge or payment for a job, service, or activity.

**feeble feebler feeblest**

ADJECTIVE weak or lacking in power or

influence E.G. *feeble and stupid arguments*.

**feed feeds feeding fed**

VERB 1 To feed a person or animal is to give them food. 2 When an animal or baby feeds, it eats. 3 To feed something is to supply what is needed for it to operate or exist E.G. *The information was fed into a computer database*. ▶ NOUN 4 Feed is food for animals or babies.

**feedback**

NOUN 1 Feedback is comments and information about the quality or success of something. 2 Feedback is also a condition in which some of the power, sound, or information produced by electronic equipment goes back into it.

**feel feels feeling felt**

VERB 1 If you feel an emotion or sensation, you experience it E.G. *I felt a bit ashamed*. 2 If you feel that something is the case, you believe it to be so E.G. *She feels that she is in control of her life*. 3 If you feel something, you touch it. 4 If something feels warm or cold, for example, you experience its warmth or coldness through the sense of touch E.G. *Real marble feels cold to the touch*. 5 To feel the effect of something is to be affected by it E.G. *The shock waves of this fire will be felt by people from all over the world*. ▶ NOUN 6 The feel of something is how it feels to you when you touch it E.G. *skin with a velvety smooth feel*. ▶ PHRASE 7 If you **feel like** doing something, you want to do it.

📘 (sense 1) be aware of, experience
📘 (sense 2) believe, consider, think

**feeler feelers**

NOUN An insect's feelers are the two

a b c d e f g h i j k l m n o p q r s t u v w x y z

A B C D E F G H I J K L M N O P Q R S T U V W X Y Z

thin antennae on its head with which it senses things around it.

**feeling feelings**
NOUN **1** an emotion or reaction E.G. *feelings of envy.* **2** a physical sensation E.G. *a feeling of pain.* **3** Feeling is the ability to experience the sense of touch in your body E.G. *He had no feeling in his hands.* **4** Your feelings about something are your general attitudes or thoughts about it E.G. *He has strong feelings about our national sport.*

**feet**
the plural of **foot**.

**feign feigns feigning feigned**
*Rhymes with* "rain" VERB If you feign an emotion or reaction, you pretend to experience it E.G. *I feigned a headache.*

**feline**
*Said* "fee-line" ADJECTIVE belonging or relating to the cat family.
🏛 from Latin *feles* meaning 'cat'

**fell fells felling felled**
**1** the past tense of **fall**. ► VERB **2** To fell a tree is to cut it down.

**fellow fellows**
NOUN **1** OLD-FASHIONED a man E.G. *I knew a fellow by that name.* **2** a senior member of a learned society or a university college. **3** Your fellows are the people who share work or an activity with you. ► ADJECTIVE **4** You use 'fellow' to describe people who have something in common with you E.G. *his fellow editors.*
🏛 from Old Norse *felagi* meaning 'partner' or 'associate'

**fellowship fellowships**
NOUN **1** a feeling of friendliness that a group of people have when they are doing things together. **2** a group of people that join together because

they have interests in common E.G. *the Dickens Fellowship.* **3** an academic post at a university which involves research work.

**felt**
**1** the past tense and past participle of **feel**. ► NOUN **2** Felt is a thick cloth made by pressing short threads together.

**female females**
NOUN **1** a person or animal that belongs to the sex that can have babies or young. ► ADJECTIVE **2** concerning or relating to females.

**feminine**
ADJECTIVE **1** relating to women or considered to be typical of women. **2** belonging to a particular class of nouns in some languages, such as French, German, and Latin.
**femininity** NOUN

---

### What is the Feminine?

**Feminine nouns** denote female people and animals:

E.G. *The girl put on her coat.* ► *girl is feminine*

It is customary to refer to countries and vehicles as if they were feminine:

E.G. *The ship came into view, her sails swelling in the breeze.*

**Common nouns** may be either masculine or feminine. Other words in the sentence may tell us if they are male or female:

E.G. *The doctor parked his car.*
*The doctor parked her car.*

Also look at the grammar boxes at **gender**, **masculine** and **neuter**.

---

**feminism**

NOUN Feminism is the belief that women should have the same rights and opportunities as men.
**feminist** NOUN OR ADJECTIVE

**fen fens**

NOUN The fens are an area of low, flat, very wet land in the east of England.

**fence fences fencing fenced**

NOUN 1 a wooden or wire barrier between two areas of land. 2 a barrier or hedge for the horses to jump over in horse racing or show jumping. ▶ VERB 3 To fence an area of land is to surround it with a fence. 4 When two people fence, they use special swords to fight each other as a sport.

**fend fends fending fended**

PHRASE 1 If you have to **fend for yourself**, you have to look after yourself. ▶ VERB 2 If you fend off an attack or unwelcome questions or attention, you defend and protect yourself.

**ferment ferments fermenting fermented**

VERB When wine, beer, or fruit ferments, a chemical change takes place in it, often producing alcohol.
**fermentation** NOUN

**fern ferns**

NOUN a plant with long feathery leaves and no flowers.

**ferocious**

ADJECTIVE violent and fierce E.G. ferocious dogs… ferocious storms.
**ferociously** ADVERB **ferocity** NOUN
📖 from Latin ferox meaning 'like a wild animal'

**ferret ferrets**

NOUN a small, fierce animal related to the weasel and kept for hunting rats

and rabbits.
📖 from Old French furet meaning 'little thief'

**ferry ferries ferrying ferried**

NOUN 1 a boat that carries people and vehicles across short stretches of water. ▶ VERB 2 To ferry people or goods somewhere is to transport them there, usually on a short, regular journey.

**fertile**

ADJECTIVE 1 capable of producing strong, healthy plants E.G. fertile soil. 2 creative E.G. fertile minds. 3 able to have babies or young.
**fertility** NOUN

**fertilize fertilizes fertilizing fertilized**; also spelt **fertilise**

VERB 1 When an egg, plant, or female is fertilized, the process of reproduction begins by sperm joining with the egg, or by pollen coming into contact with the reproductive part of a plant. 2 To fertilize land is to put manure or chemicals onto it to feed the plants.

**fertilizer fertilizers**; also spelt **fertiliser**

NOUN a substance put onto soil to improve plant growth.

**fervent**

ADJECTIVE showing strong, sincere, and enthusiastic feeling E.G. a fervent nationalist.
**fervently** ADVERB

**fervour**

NOUN a very strong feeling for or belief in something E.G. a wave of religious fervour.
📖 from Latin fervor meaning 'heat'

**fester festers festering festered**

VERB If a wound festers it becomes

a
b
c
d
e
f
g
h
i
j
k
l
m
n
o
p
q
r
s
t
u
v
w
x
y
z

infected and produces pus.
🔲 from Latin *fistula* meaning 'ulcer'

**festival festivals**
NOUN 1 an organized series of events and performances *E.G. the Cannes Film Festival.* 2 ⟨RE⟩ a day or period of religious celebration.

**festive**
ADJECTIVE full of happiness and celebration *E.G. a festive time of singing and dancing.*

**festivity festivities**
NOUN celebration and happiness *E.G. the wedding festivities.*

**festooned**
ADJECTIVE If something is festooned with objects, the objects are hanging across it in large numbers.

**fetch fetches fetching fetched**
VERB 1 If you fetch something, you go to where it is and bring it back. 2 If something fetches a particular sum of money, it is sold for that amount *E.G. Portraits fetch the highest prices.*

**fetching**
ADJECTIVE attractive in appearance *E.G. a fetching purple frock.*

**fete fetes feting feted**
*Rhymes with "*date*"* NOUN 1 an outdoor event with competitions, displays, and goods for sale. ▶ VERB 2 Someone who is feted receives a public welcome or entertainment as an honour.

**feud feuds feuding feuded**
*Said "*fyood*"* NOUN 1 a long-term and very bitter quarrel, especially between families. ▶ VERB 2 When people feud, they take part in a feud.

**feudalism**
NOUN Feudalism is a social and political system that was common in the Middle Ages in Europe. Under

this system, ordinary people were given land and protection by a lord, and in return they worked and fought for him.
**feudal** ADJECTIVE

**fever fevers**
NOUN 1 Fever is a condition occurring during illness, in which the patient has a very high body temperature. 2 A fever is extreme excitement or agitation *E.G. a fever of impatience.*

**feverish**
ADJECTIVE 1 in a state of extreme excitement or agitation *E.G. increasingly feverish activity.* 2 suffering from a high body temperature.
**feverishly** ADVERB

**few fewer fewest**
ADJECTIVE or NOUN 1 used to refer to a small number of things *E.G. I saw him a few moments ago… one of only a few.* ▶ PHRASES 2 **Quite a few** or a **good few** means quite a large number of things
☑ You use *fewer* to talk about things that can be counted: *fewer than five visits.* When you are talking about amounts that can't be counted you should use *less.*

**fiancé fiancés**
*Said "*fee-on-say*"* NOUN A woman's fiancé is the man to whom she is engaged.

**fiancée fiancées**
NOUN A man's fiancée is the woman to whom he is engaged.

**fiasco fiascos**
*Said "*fee-ass-koh*"* NOUN an event or attempt that fails completely, especially in a ridiculous or disorganized way *E.G. The game ended in a complete fiasco.*

**fib** fibs fibbing fibbed
NOUN **1** a small, unimportant lie. ▸ VERB
**2** If you fib, you tell a small lie.

**fibre** fibres
NOUN **1** (D&T) a thin thread of a
substance used to make cloth.
**2** Fibre is also a part of plants that
can be eaten but not digested; it
helps food pass quickly through the
body.
**fibrous** ADJECTIVE

**fickle**
ADJECTIVE A fickle person keeps
changing their mind about who or
what they like or want.
📖 from Old English *ficol* meaning
'treacherous' or 'deceitful'

**fiction** fictions
NOUN **1** Fiction is stories about people
and events that have been invented
by the author. **2** something that is
not true.
**fictional** ADJECTIVE **fictitious**
ADJECTIVE

**fiddle** fiddles fiddling fiddled
VERB **1** If you fiddle with something,
you keep moving it or touching it
restlessly. **2** INFORMAL If someone
fiddles something such as an
account, they alter it dishonestly to
get money for themselves. ▸ NOUN
**3** INFORMAL a dishonest action or
scheme to get money. **4** a violin.
**fiddler** NOUN

**fiddly** fiddlier fiddliest
ADJECTIVE small and difficult to do or
use E.G. *fiddly nuts and bolts*.

**fidelity**
NOUN Fidelity is remaining firm in
your beliefs, friendships, or loyalty to
another person.

**fidget** fidgets fidgeting fidgeted
VERB **1** If you fidget, you keep

changing your position because of
nervousness or boredom. ▸ NOUN
**2** someone who fidgets.
**fidgety** ADJECTIVE

**field** fields fielding fielded
NOUN **1** an area of land where crops
are grown or animals are kept.
**2** (PE) an area of land where sports
are played E.G. *a hockey field*. **3** A coal
field, oil field, or gold field is an area
where coal, oil, or gold is found. **4** a
particular subject or area of interest
E.G. *He was doing well in his own field
of advertising*. ▸ ADJECTIVE **5** A field trip
or a field study involves research or
activity in the natural environment
rather than theoretical or laboratory
work. **6** In an athletics competition,
the field events are the events such
as the high jump and the javelin
which do not take place on a
running track. ▸ VERB **7** In cricket,
when you field the ball, you stop it
after the batsman has hit it. **8** To field
questions is to answer or deal with
them skilfully.

**fielder** fielders
NOUN In cricket, the fielders are the
team members who stand at various
parts of the pitch and try to get the
batsmen out or to prevent runs from
being scored.

**field marshal** field marshals
NOUN an army officer of the highest
rank.

**fieldwork**
NOUN Fieldwork is the study of
something in the environment
where it naturally lives or occurs,
rather than in a class or laboratory.

**fiend** fiends
*Said "feend"* NOUN **1** a devil or evil
spirit. **2** a very wicked or cruel

a b c d e f g h i j k l m n o p q r s t u v w x y z

person. **3** *INFORMAL* someone who is very keen on a particular thing *E.G. a fitness fiend.*

📖 from Old English *feond* meaning 'enemy'

**fierce** fiercer fiercest
ADJECTIVE **1** very aggressive or angry. **2** extremely strong or intense *E.G. a sudden fierce pain… a fierce storm.*
**fiercely** ADVERB
■ (sense 1) ferocious, savage, wild

**fiery** fierier fieriest
ADJECTIVE **1** involving fire or seeming like fire *E.G. a huge fiery sun.* **2** showing great anger, energy, or passion *E.G. a fiery debate.*

**fifteen**
the number 15.
**fifteenth**

**fifth** fifths
ADJECTIVE **1** The fifth item in a series is the one counted as number five. ▶ NOUN **2** one of five equal parts.

**fifty** fifties
the number 50.
**fiftieth**

**fifty-fifty**
ADVERB **1** divided equally into two portions. ▶ ADJECTIVE **2** just as likely not to happen as to happen *E.G. You've got a fifty-fifty chance of being right.*

**fig** figs
NOUN a soft, sweet fruit full of tiny seeds. It grows in hot countries and is often eaten dried.

**fight** fights fighting fought
VERB **1** When people fight, they take part in a battle, a war, a boxing match, or in some other attempt to hurt or kill someone. **2** To fight for something is to try in a very determined way to achieve it *E.G. I must fight for respect.* ▶ NOUN **3** a

situation in which people hit or try to hurt each other. **4** a determined attempt to prevent or achieve something *E.G. the fight for independence.*
**fighter** NOUN
■ (sense 1) battle, come to blows, struggle
■ (sense 3) battle, conflict, struggle

**figurative**
ADJECTIVE (ENGLISH) If you use a word or expression in a figurative sense, you use it with a more abstract or imaginative meaning than its ordinary one.
**figuratively** ADVERB

**figure** figures figuring figured
NOUN **1** a written number or the amount a number stands for. **2** a geometrical shape. **3** a diagram or table in a written text. **4** the shape of a person whom you cannot see clearly *E.G. A human figure leaped at him.* **5** Your figure is the shape of your body *E.G. his slim and supple figure.* **6** a person *E.G. He was a major figure in the trial.* ▶ VERB **7** To figure in something is to appear or be included in it *E.G. the many people who have figured in his life.* **8** *INFORMAL* If you figure that something is the case, you guess or conclude this *E.G. We figure the fire broke out around four in the morning.*

**figurehead** figureheads
NOUN the leader of a movement or organization who has no real power.

**figure of speech** figures of speech
NOUN A figure of speech is an expression such as a simile or idiom in which the words are not used in their literal sense.

**file** files filing filed
NOUN **1** a box or folder in which a

group of papers or records is kept; also used of the information kept in the file. **2** In computing, a file is a stored set of related data with its own name. **3** a line of people one behind the other. **4** a long steel tool with a rough surface, used for smoothing and shaping hard materials. ▶ VERB **5** When someone files a document, they put it in its correct place with similar documents. **6** When a group of people file somewhere, they walk one behind the other in a line. **7** If you file something, you smooth or shape it with a file.

**fill** fills filling filled
VERB **1** If you fill something or if it fills up, it becomes full. **2** If something fills a need, it satisfies the need *E.G. Ella had in some small way filled the gap left by Molly's absence.* **3** To fill a job vacancy is to appoint someone to do that job. ▶ NOUN **4** If you have had your fill of something, you do not want any more.

**fill in** VERB **1** If you fill in a form, you write information in the appropriate spaces. **2** If you fill someone in, you give them information to bring them up to date.

**fillet** fillets filleting filleted
NOUN **1** a strip of tender, boneless beef, veal, or pork. **2** a piece of fish with the bones removed. ▶ VERB **3** To fillet meat or fish is to prepare it by cutting out the bones.

**filling** fillings
NOUN **1** the soft food mixture inside a sandwich, cake, or pie. **2** a small amount of metal or plastic put into a hole in a tooth by a dentist.

**filly** fillies
NOUN a female horse or pony under

the age of four.

**film** films filming filmed
NOUN **1** a series of moving pictures projected onto a screen and shown at the cinema or on television. **2** a thin flexible strip of plastic used in a camera to record images when exposed to light. **3** a very thin layer of powder or liquid on a surface. **4** Plastic film is a very thin sheet of plastic used for wrapping things.
▶ VERB **5** If you film someone, you use a video camera to record their movements on film.
🏛 from Old English *filmen* meaning 'membrane'

**filter** filters filtering filtered
NOUN **1** a device that allows some substances, lights, or sounds to pass through it, but not others *E.G. a filter against the harmful rays of the sun.*
▶ VERB **2** To filter a substance is to pass it through a filter. **3** If something filters somewhere, it gets there slowly or faintly *E.G. Traffic filtered into the city.*
**filtration** NOUN

**filth**
NOUN **1** Filth is disgusting dirt and muck. **2** People often use the word filth to refer to very bad language or to sexual material that is thought to be crude and offensive.

**filthy** ADJECTIVE
🏛 from Old English *fylth* meaning 'pus' or 'corruption'
📘 (sense 1) dirt, muck, squalor

**fin** fins
NOUN a thin, flat structure on the body of a fish, used to help guide it through the water.

**final** finals
ADJECTIVE **1** last in a series or

a
b
c
d
e
f
g
h
i
j
k
l
m
n
o
p
q
r
s
t
u
v
w
x
y
z

A
B
C
D
E
F
G
H
I
J
K
L
M
N
O
P
Q
R
S
T
U
V
W
X
Y
Z

happening at the end of something.
**2** A decision that is final cannot be changed or questioned. ► NOUN **3** the last game or contest in a series which decides the overall winner.
► PLURAL NOUN **4** Finals are the last and most important examinations of a university or college course.
■ (sense 1) concluding, last

**finale finales**
*Said* "fin-**nah**-lee" NOUN the last section of a piece of music or show.

**finalist finalists**
NOUN a person taking part in the final of a competition.

**finalize finalizes finalizing finalized**; also spelt **finalise**
VERB If you finalize something, you complete all the arrangements for it.

**finally**
ADVERB If something finally happens, it happens after a long delay.
■ (sense 1) at last, eventually
■ (sense 2) in conclusion, lastly

**finance finances financing financed**
VERB **1** To finance a project or a large purchase is to provide the money for it. ► NOUN **2** Finance for something is the money or loans used to pay for it. **3** Finance is also the management of money, loans, and investments.

**financial**
ADJECTIVE relating to or involving money.
**financially** ADVERB

**financier financiers**
NOUN a person who deals with the finance for large businesses.

**finch finches**
NOUN a small bird with a short strong beak.

**find finds finding found**
VERB **1** If you find someone or

something, you discover them, either as a result of searching or by coming across them unexpectedly. **2** If you find that something is the case, you become aware of it or realize it *E.G. I found my fists were clenched.*
**3** Something that is found in a particular place typically lives or exists there. **4** When a court or jury finds a person guilty or not guilty, they decide that the person is guilty or innocent *E.G. He was found guilty and sentenced to life imprisonment.*
► NOUN **5** If you describe something or someone as a find, you mean that you have recently discovered them and they are valuable or useful.
**finder** NOUN
■ (sense 1) come across, discover

**find out** VERB **1** If you find out something, you learn or discover something that you did not know. **2** If you find someone out, you discover that they have been doing something they should not have been doing.

**findings**
PLURAL NOUN Someone's findings are the conclusions they reach as a result of investigation.

**fine finer finest; fines fining fined**
ADJECTIVE **1** very good or very beautiful *E.G. a fine school… fine clothes.*
**2** satisfactory or suitable *E.G. Pasta dishes are fine if not served with a rich sauce.* **3** very narrow or thin *E.G. fine paper.* **4** A fine net or sieve has very small holes. Fine powder or dust consists of very small particles. **5** A fine detail, adjustment, or distinction is very delicate, exact, or subtle.
**6** When the weather is fine, it is not raining and is bright or sunny. ► NOUN

**7** a sum of money paid as a punishment. ▶ VERB **8** Someone who is fined has to pay a sum of money as a punishment.

**finery**
NOUN Finery is very beautiful clothing and jewellery.

**finesse**
*Said* "fin-**ness**" NOUN If you do something with finesse, you do it with skill and subtlety.

**finger** fingers fingering fingered
NOUN **1** Your fingers are the four long jointed parts of your hands, sometimes including the thumbs.
▶ VERB **2** If you finger something you feel it with your fingers.

**fingernail** fingernails
NOUN Your fingernails are the hard coverings at the ends of your fingers.

**fingerprint** fingerprints
NOUN a mark made showing the pattern on the skin at the tip of a person's finger.

**finish** finishes finishing finished
VERB **1** When you finish something, you reach the end of it and complete it. **2** When something finishes, it ends or stops. ▶ NOUN **3** The finish of something is the end or last part of it. **4** The finish that something has is the texture or appearance of its surface *E.G. a healthy, glossy finish.*
■ (sense 1) complete, conclude, end
■ (sense 3) close, conclusion, end

**finite**
*Said* "**fie**-nite" ADJECTIVE having a particular size or limit which cannot be increased *E.G. There's only finite money to spend.*

**Finn** Finns
NOUN someone who comes from Finland.

**Finnish**
ADJECTIVE **1** belonging or relating to Finland. ▶ NOUN **2** Finnish is the main language spoken in Finland.

**fir** firs
NOUN a tall pointed evergreen tree that has thin needle-like leaves and produces cones.

**fire** fires firing fired
NOUN **1** Fire is the flames produced when something burns. **2** a pile or mass of burning material. **3** a piece of equipment that is used as a heater *E.G. a gas fire.* ▶ VERB **4** If you fire a weapon or fire a bullet, you operate the weapon so that the bullet or missile is released. **5** If you fire questions at someone, you ask them a lot of questions very quickly. **6** *INFORMAL* If an employer fires someone, he or she dismisses that person from their job. ▶ PHRASE **7** If someone **opens fire**, they start shooting.

**firearm** firearms
NOUN a gun.

**fire brigade** fire brigades
NOUN the organization which has the job of putting out fires.

**fire engine** fire engines
NOUN a large vehicle that carries equipment for putting out fires.

**fire escape** fire escapes
NOUN an emergency exit or staircase for use if there is a fire.

**fire extinguisher** fire extinguishers
NOUN a metal cylinder containing water or foam for spraying onto a fire.

**firefighter** firefighters
NOUN a person whose job is to put out fires and rescue trapped people.

a b c d e f g h i j k l m n o p q r s t u v w x y z

A
B
C
D
E

**F**

G
H
I
J
K
L
M
N
O
P
Q
R
S
T
U
V
W
X
Y
Z

**firefly** fireflies
NOUN an insect that glows in the dark.
**fireplace** fireplaces
NOUN the opening beneath a
chimney where a fire can be lit.
**fireproof**
ADJECTIVE resistant to fire.
**fire station** fire stations
NOUN a building where fire engines
are kept and where firefighters wait
to be called out.
**firework** fireworks
NOUN a small container of gunpowder
and other chemicals which explodes
and produces coloured sparks or
smoke when lit.
**firing squad** firing squads
NOUN a group of soldiers ordered to
shoot a person condemned to death.
**firm** firmer firmest; firms
ADJECTIVE 1 Something that is firm
does not move easily when pressed
or pushed, or when weight is put on
it. 2 A firm grasp or push is one with
controlled force or pressure. 3 A firm
decision is definite. 4 Someone who
is firm behaves with authority that
shows they will not change their
mind. ▸ NOUN 5 a business selling or
producing something.
**firmly** ADVERB   **firmness** NOUN
**first**
ADJECTIVE or ADVERB 1 happening,
coming, or done before everything
or everyone else. ▸ ADJECTIVE 2 more
important than anything else E.G. Her
cheese won first prize. ▸ NOUN
3 something that has never
happened or been done before.
**firstly** ADVERB
▣ (sense 2) chief, foremost, principal
**first aid**
NOUN First aid is medical treatment

given to an injured person.
**first class**
ADJECTIVE 1 Something that is first class
is of the highest quality or standard.
2 First-class accommodation on a
train, aircraft, or ship is the best and
most expensive type of
accommodation. 3 First-class
postage is quick but more expensive.
**first-hand**
ADJECTIVE First-hand knowledge or
experience is gained directly rather
than from books or other people.
**First Lady** First Ladies
NOUN The First Lady of a country is
the wife of a president.
**first-rate**
ADJECTIVE excellent.
**fiscal**
ADJECTIVE involving government or
public money, especially taxes.
▥ from Latin *fiscus* meaning 'money-
bag' or 'treasury'
**fish** fishes fishing fished
NOUN 1 a cold-blooded creature living
in water that has a spine, gills, fins,
and a scaly skin. 2 Fish is the flesh of
fish eaten as food. ▸ VERB 3 To fish is to
try to catch fish for food or sport. 4 If
you fish for information, you try to
get it in an indirect way.
**fishing** NOUN   **fisherman** NOUN
☑ The plural of the noun *fish* can be
either *fish* or *fishes*, but *fish* is more
common.
**fishery** fisheries
NOUN an area of the sea where fish
are caught commercially.
**fishmonger** fishmongers
NOUN a shopkeeper who sells fish;
also the shop itself.
**fishy** fishier fishiest
ADJECTIVE 1 smelling of fish. 2 INFORMAL

**SPELLING NOTE**   On WEDNESday Wayne WED NESta (Wednesday) suspicious or doubtful E.G. *He spotted something fishy going on.*

**fission**
*Rhymes with "mission"* NOUN 1 Fission is the splitting of something into parts. 2 Fission is also nuclear fission.

**fissure fissures**
NOUN a deep crack in rock.

**fist fists**
NOUN a hand with the fingers curled tightly towards the palm.

**fit fits fitting fitted; fitter fittest**
VERB 1 Something that fits is the right shape or size for a particular person or position. 2 If you fit something somewhere, you put it there carefully or securely E.G. *Very carefully he fitted the files inside the compartment.* 3 If something fits a particular situation, person, or thing, it is suitable or appropriate E.G. *a sentence that fitted the crime.* ▶ NOUN 4 The fit of something is how it fits E.G. *This bolt must be a good fit.* 5 If someone has a fit, their muscles suddenly start contracting violently and they may lose consciousness. 6 A fit of laughter, coughing, anger, or panic is a sudden uncontrolled outburst. ▶ ADJECTIVE 7 good enough or suitable E.G. *Housing fit for frail elderly people.* 8 Someone who is fit is healthy and has strong muscles as a result of regular exercise.

**fitness** NOUN
▤ (sense 3) match, suit
▤ (sense 5) convulsion, seizure, spasm

**fitful**
ADJECTIVE happening at irregular intervals and not continuous E.G. *a fitful breeze.*

**fitfully** ADVERB

**fitter fitters**
NOUN a person who assembles or installs machinery.

**fitting fittings**
ADJECTIVE 1 right or suitable E.G. *a fitting reward for his efforts.* ▶ NOUN 2 a small part that is fixed to a piece of equipment or furniture. 3 If you have a fitting, you try on a garment that is being made to see if it fits properly.

**five fives**
the number 5.

**fix fixes fixing fixed**
VERB 1 If you fix something somewhere, you attach it or put it there securely. 2 If you fix something broken, you mend it. 3 If you fix your attention on something, you concentrate on it. 4 If you fix something, you make arrangements for it E.G. *The opening party is fixed for the 24th September.* 5 INFORMAL To fix something is to arrange the outcome unfairly or dishonestly. ▶ NOUN 6 INFORMAL something that has been unfairly or dishonestly arranged. 7 INFORMAL If you are in a fix, you are in a difficult situation. 8 an injection of a drug such as heroin.

**fixed** ADJECTIVE **fixedly** ADVERB
▤ (sense 2) mend, repair

**fixation fixations**
NOUN an extreme and obsessive interest in something.

**fixture fixtures**
NOUN 1 a piece of furniture or equipment that is fixed into position in a house. 2 a sports event due to take place on a particular date.

**fizz fizzes fizzing fizzed**
VERB Something that fizzes makes a hissing sound.

Eddy Ant thinks mEAt is a grEAt trEAt to EAt (-ea-)   ▶ SPELLING NOTE

**fizzle** fizzles fizzling fizzled
VERB Something that fizzles makes a weak hissing or spitting sound.

**fizzy** fizzier fizziest
ADJECTIVE Fizzy drinks have carbon dioxide in them to make them bubbly.

**fjord** fjords
Said "fee-ord"; also spelt **fiord**
NOUN a long narrow inlet of the sea between very high cliffs, especially in Norway.
🔲 a Norwegian word

**flab**
NOUN Flab is large amounts of surplus fat on someone's body.

**flabbergasted**
ADJECTIVE extremely surprised.

**flabby** flabbier flabbiest
ADJECTIVE Someone who is flabby is rather fat and unfit, with loose flesh on their body.

**flag** flags flagging flagged
NOUN 1 a rectangular or square cloth which has a particular colour and design, and is used as the symbol of a nation or as a signal. ▶ VERB 2 If you or your spirits flag, you start to lose energy or enthusiasm.

**flagrant**
Said "flay-grant" ADJECTIVE very shocking and bad in an obvious way E.G. a flagrant defiance of the rules.

**flagship** flagships
NOUN 1 a ship carrying the commander of the fleet. 2 the most modern or impressive product or asset of an organization.

**flail** flails flailing flailed
VERB If someone's arms or legs flail about, they move in a wild, uncontrolled way.

**flair**
NOUN Flair is a natural ability to do

something well or stylishly.

**flak**
NOUN 1 Flak is anti-aircraft fire. 2 If you get flak for doing something, you get a lot of severe criticism.
🔲 from the first letters of the parts of German *Fliegerabwehrkanone* meaning 'anti-aircraft gun'

**flake** flakes flaking flaked
NOUN 1 a small thin piece of something. ▶ VERB 2 When something such as paint flakes, small thin pieces of it come off.
**flaky** ADJECTIVE **flaked** ADJECTIVE

**flamboyant**
ADJECTIVE behaving in a very showy and confident.
**flamboyance** NOUN

**flame** flames
NOUN 1 a flickering tongue or blaze of fire. 2 A flame of passion, desire, or anger is a sudden strong feeling.
🔲 from Latin *flamma* meaning 'blazing fire'

**flamenco**
NOUN Flamenco is a type of very lively, fast Spanish dancing, accompanied by guitar music.

**flamingo** flamingos or flamingoes
NOUN a long-legged wading bird with pink feathers and a long neck.

**flammable**
ADJECTIVE likely to catch fire and burn easily
☑ Although *flammable* and *inflammable* both mean 'likely to catch fire', *flammable* is used more often as people sometimes think that *inflammable* means 'not likely to catch fire'.

**flan** flans
NOUN an open sweet or savoury tart

with a pastry or cake base.

**flank** flanks flanking flanked
NOUN 1 the side of an animal between the ribs and the hip. ▶ VERB 2 Someone or something that is flanked by a particular thing or person has them at their side E.G. He was flanked by four bodyguards.

**flannel** flannels
NOUN 1 Flannel is a lightweight woollen fabric. 2 a small square of towelling, used for washing yourself. In Australian English it is called a **washer**.

**flap** flaps flapping flapped
VERB 1 Something that flaps moves up and down or from side to side with a snapping sound. ▶ NOUN 2 a loose piece of something such as paper or skin that is attached at one edge.

**flare** flares flaring flared
NOUN 1 a device that produces a brightly coloured flame, used especially as an emergency signal. ▶ VERB 2 If a fire flares, it suddenly burns much more vigorously. 3 If violence or a conflict flares or flares up, it suddenly starts or becomes more serious.

**flash** flashes flashing flashed
NOUN 1 a sudden short burst of light. ▶ VERB 2 If a light flashes, it shines for a very short period, often repeatedly. 3 Something that flashes past moves or happens so fast that you almost miss it. 4 If you flash something, you show it briefly E.G. Michael Jackson flashed his face at the crowd. ▶ PHRASE 5 Something that happens in a flash happens suddenly and lasts a very short time.

**flashback** flashbacks
NOUN a scene in a film, play, or book that returns to events in the past.

**flashlight** flashlights
NOUN a large, powerful torch.

**flashy** flashier flashiest
ADJECTIVE expensive and fashionable in appearance, in a vulgar way E.G. flashy clothes.

**flask** flasks
NOUN a bottle used for carrying alcoholic or hot drinks around with you.

**flat** flats; flats flatting flatted; flatter flattest
NOUN 1 a self-contained set of rooms, usually on one level, for living in. 2 In music, a flat is a note or key a semitone lower than that described by the same letter. It is represented by the symbol (♭). ▶ VERB 3 In Australian and New Zealand English, to flat is to live in a flat E.G. flatting in London. ▶ ADJECTIVE 4 Something that is flat is level and smooth. 5 A flat object is not very tall or deep E.G. a low flat building. 6 A flat tyre or ball has not got enough air in it. 7 A flat battery has lost its electrical charge. 8 A flat refusal or denial is complete and firm. 9 Something that is flat is without emotion or interest. 10 A flat rate or price is fixed and the same for everyone E.G. The company charges a flat fee for its advice. 11 A musical instrument or note that is flat is slightly too low in pitch. ▶ ADVERB 12 Something that is done in a particular time flat, takes exactly that time E.G. They would find them in two minutes flat.
**flatly** ADVERB **flatness** NOUN
■ (sense 3) even, level

**flatfish**
NOUN a sea fish with a wide flat body,

such as a plaice or sole.

**flathead** flatheads

NOUN a common Australian edible fish.

**flatten** flattens flattening flattened

VERB If you flatten something or if it flattens, it becomes flat or flatter.

**flatter** flatters flattering flattered

VERB 1 If you flatter someone, you praise them in an exaggerated way, either to please them or to persuade them to do something. 2 If you are flattered by something, it makes you feel pleased and important E.G. *He was very flattered because she liked him.* 3 If you flatter yourself that something is the case, you believe, perhaps mistakenly, something good about yourself or your abilities. 4 Something that flatters you makes you appear more attractive.

**flattering** ADJECTIVE

◼ (sense 1) butter up, praise

**flattery**

NOUN Flattery is flattering words or behaviour.

**flatting**

PHRASE In New Zealand English, to **go flatting** is to leave home and live with others in a shared house or flat.

**flatulence**

NOUN Flatulence is the uncomfortable state of having too much gas in your stomach or intestine.

▥ from Latin *flatus* meaning 'gust of wind'

**flaunt** flaunts flaunting flaunted

VERB If you flaunt your possessions or talents, you display them too obviously or proudly

☑ Be careful not to confuse *flaunt*

with *flout*, which means 'disobey'.

**flautist** flautists

NOUN someone who plays the flute.

**flavour** flavours flavouring flavoured

NOUN 1 The flavour of food is its taste. 2 The flavour of something is its distinctive characteristic or quality. ▶ VERB 3 If you flavour food with a spice or herb, you add it to the food to give it a particular taste.

**flavouring** NOUN

**flaw** flaws

NOUN 1 a fault or mark in a piece of fabric or glass, or in a decorative pattern. 2 a weak point or undesirable quality in a theory, plan, or person's character.

**flawed** ADJECTIVE **flawless** ADJECTIVE

◼ (sense 1) blemish, spot

◼ (sense 2) fault, weakness

**flax**

NOUN Flax is a plant used for making rope and cloth.

**flay** flays flaying flayed

VERB 1 To flay a dead animal is to cut off its skin. 2 To flay someone is to criticize them severely.

**flea** fleas

NOUN a small wingless jumping insect which feeds on blood.

**fleck** flecks

NOUN a small coloured mark or particle.

**flecked** ADJECTIVE

**fled**

the past tense and past participle of **flee**.

**fledgling** fledglings

NOUN 1 a young bird that is learning to fly. ▶ ADJECTIVE 2 Fledgling means new, or young and inexperienced E.G. *the fledgling American President.*

**flee** flees fleeing fled
VERB To flee from someone or something is to run away from them.

**fleece** fleeces fleecing fleeced
NOUN 1 A sheep's fleece is its coat of wool. ▶ VERB 2 To fleece someone is to swindle them or charge them too much money.

**fleet** fleets
NOUN a group of ships or vehicles owned by the same organization or travelling together.

**fleeting**
ADJECTIVE lasting for a very short time.

**Flemish**
NOUN Flemish is a language spoken in many parts of Belgium.

**flesh**
NOUN 1 Flesh is the soft part of the body. 2 The flesh of a fruit or vegetable is the soft inner part that you eat.
**fleshy** ADJECTIVE

**flew**
the past tense of **fly**.

**flex** flexes flexing flexed
NOUN 1 a length of wire covered in plastic, which carries electricity to an appliance. ▶ VERB 2 If you flex your muscles, you bend and stretch them.

**flexible**
ADJECTIVE 1 able to be bent easily without breaking. 2 able to adapt to changing circumstances.
**flexibility** NOUN

**flick** flicks flicking flicked
VERB 1 If you flick something, you move it sharply with your finger. 2 If something flicks somewhere, it moves with a short sudden movement E.G. *His foot flicked forward*. ▶ NOUN 3 a sudden quick movement or sharp touch with the

finger E.G. *a sideways flick of the head*.

**flicker** flickers flickering flickered
VERB 1 If a light or a flame flickers, it shines and moves unsteadily. ▶ NOUN 2 a short unsteady light or movement of light E.G. *the flicker of candlelight*. 3 A flicker of a feeling is a very brief experience of it E.G. *a flicker of interest*.

**flight** flights
NOUN 1 a journey made by aeroplane. 2 Flight is the action of flying or the ability to fly. 3 Flight is also the act of running away. 4 A flight of stairs or steps is a set running in a single direction.

**flight attendant** flight attendants
NOUN a person who looks after passengers on an aircraft.

**flightless**
ADJECTIVE Flightless birds, such as penguins and ostriches, are birds that cannot fly.

**flimsy** flimsier flimsiest
ADJECTIVE 1 made of something very thin or weak and not providing much protection. 2 not very convincing E.G. *flimsy evidence*.

**flinch** flinches flinching flinched
VERB If you flinch, you make a sudden small movement in fear or pain.
■ cringe, recoil, wince

**fling** flings flinging flung
VERB 1 If you fling something, you throw it with a lot of force. ▶ NOUN 2 a short period devoted to pleasure and free from any restrictions or rules.

**flint** flints
NOUN Flint is a hard greyish-black form of quartz. It produces a spark

a
b
c
d
e
**f**
g
h
i
j
k
l
m
n
o
p
q
r
s
t
u
v
w
x
y
z

**flip** flips flipping flipped

VERB **1** If you flip something, you turn or move it quickly and sharply E.G. *He flipped over the first page.* **2** If you flip something, you hit it sharply with your finger or thumb.

**flippant**

ADJECTIVE showing an inappropriate lack of seriousness E.G. *a flippant attitude to money.*

**flippancy** NOUN

**flipper** flippers

NOUN **1** one of the broad, flat limbs of sea animals, for example seals or penguins, used for swimming. **2** Flippers are broad, flat pieces of rubber that you can attach to your feet to help you swim.

**flirt** flirts flirting flirted

VERB **1** If you flirt with someone, you behave as if you are sexually attracted to them but without serious intentions. **2** If you flirt with an idea, you consider it without seriously intending to do anything about it. ► NOUN **3** someone who often flirts with people.

**flirtation** NOUN **flirtatious** ADJECTIVE

**flit** flits flitting flitted

VERB To flit somewhere is to fly or move there with quick, light movements.

**float** floats floating floated

VERB **1** Something that floats is supported by water. **2** Something that floats through the air moves along gently, supported by the air. **3** If a company is floated, shares are sold to the public for the first time and the company gains a listing on the stock exchange. ► NOUN **4** a light object that floats and either supports

something or someone or regulates the level of liquid in a tank or cistern. **5** In Australian English, a float is also a vehicle for transporting horses.

**flock** flocks flocking flocked

NOUN **1** a group of birds, sheep, or goats. ► VERB **2** If people flock somewhere, they go there in large numbers.

**flog** flogs flogging flogged

VERB **1** INFORMAL If you flog something, you sell it. **2** To flog someone is to beat them with a whip or stick.

**flogging** NOUN

**flood** floods flooding flooded

NOUN **1** a large amount of water covering an area that is usually dry. **2** A flood of something is a large amount of it suddenly occurring E.G. *a flood of angry language.* ► VERB **3** If liquid floods an area, or if a river floods, the water or liquid overflows, covering the surrounding area. **4** If people or things flood into a place, they come there in large numbers E.G. *Refugees have flooded into Austria in the last few months.*

■ (sense 1) deluge, spate, torrent
■ (sense 2) stream, torrent

**floodgates**

PHRASE To **open the floodgates** is suddenly to give a lot of people the opportunity to do something they could not do before.

**floodlight** floodlights

NOUN a very powerful outdoor lamp used to light up public buildings and sports grounds.

**floodlit** ADJECTIVE

**floor** floors flooring floored

NOUN **1** the part of a room you walk on. **2** one of the levels in a building E.G. *the top floor of a factory.* **3** the ground at the bottom of a valley, forest, or the sea. ▶ VERB **4** If a remark or question floors you, you are completely unable to deal with it or answer it.

**floorboard** floorboards
NOUN one of the long planks of wood from which a floor is made.

**flop** flops flopping flopped
VERB **1** If someone or something flops, they fall loosely and rather heavily. **2** INFORMAL Something that flops fails. ▶ NOUN **3** INFORMAL something that is completely unsuccessful.

**floppy** floppier floppiest
ADJECTIVE tending to hang downwards in a rather loose way E.G. *a floppy, outsize jacket.*
■ droopy, limp

**floppy disk** floppy disks; also spelt **floppy disc**
NOUN a small flexible magnetic disk on which computer data is stored.

**floral**
ADJECTIVE patterned with flowers or made from flowers E.G. *floral cotton dresses.*

**florid**
*Rhymes with "horrid"* ADJECTIVE **1** highly elaborate and extravagant E.G. *florid language.* **2** having a red face.

**florist** florists
NOUN a person or shop selling flowers.

**floss**
NOUN Dental floss is soft silky threads or fibre which you use to clean between your teeth.

**flotation** flotations
NOUN **1** The flotation of a business is the issuing of shares in order to launch it or to raise money. **2** Flotation is the act of floating.

**flotilla** flotillas
*Said "flot-til-la"* NOUN a small fleet or group of small ships.
🏛 from Spanish *flotilla* meaning 'little fleet'

**flotsam**
NOUN Flotsam is rubbish or wreckage floating at sea or washed up on the shore.

**flounce** flounces flouncing flounced
VERB **1** If you flounce somewhere, you walk there with exaggerated movements suggesting that you are feeling angry or impatient about something E.G. *She flounced out of the office.* ▶ NOUN **2** a big frill around the bottom of a dress or skirt.

**flounder** flounders floundering floundered
VERB **1** To flounder is to struggle to move or stay upright, for example in water or mud. **2** If you flounder in a conversation or situation, you find it difficult to decide what to say or do. ▶ NOUN **3** a type of edible flatfish.

**flour**
NOUN (D&T) Flour is a powder made from finely ground grain, usually wheat, and used for baking and cooking.
**floured** ADJECTIVE  **floury** ADJECTIVE

**flourish** flourishes flourishing flourished
VERB **1** Something that flourishes develops or functions successfully or healthily. **2** If you flourish something, you wave or display it so that people notice it. ▶ NOUN **3** a bold sweeping or waving movement.

**flout** flouts flouting flouted
VERB If you flout a convention or law, you deliberately disobey it

a
b
c
d
e
f
g
h
i
j
k
l
m
n
o
p
q
r
s
t
u
v
w
x
y
z

☑ Be careful not to confuse *flout* with *flaunt*, which means 'display obviously'.

**flow flows flowing flowed**
VERB 1 If something flows, it moves or happens in a steady continuous stream. ► NOUN 2 A flow of something is a steady continuous movement of it; also the rate at which it flows E.G. *a steady flow of complaints.*

**flow chart flow charts**
NOUN (D&T) a diagram showing the sequence of steps that lead to various results.

**flower flowers flowering flowered**
NOUN 1 the part of a plant containing the reproductive organs from which the fruit or seeds develop. ► VERB 2 When a plant flowers, it produces flowers.

**flowery**
ADJECTIVE Flowery language is full of elaborate expressions.

**flown**
the past participle of **fly**.

**flu**
NOUN Flu is an illness similar to a very bad cold, which causes headaches, sore throat, weakness, and aching muscles. Flu is short for 'influenza'.

**fluctuate fluctuates fluctuating fluctuated**
VERB Something that fluctuates is irregular and changeable E.G. *fluctuating between feeling well and not so well.*

**flue flues**
NOUN a pipe which takes fumes and smoke away from a stove or boiler.

**fluent**
ADJECTIVE 1 able to speak a foreign language correctly and without

hesitation. 2 able to express yourself clearly and without hesitation.
**fluently** ADVERB

**fluff fluffs fluffing fluffed**
NOUN 1 Fluff is soft, light, woolly threads or fibres bunched together. ► VERB 2 If you fluff something up or out, you brush or shake it to make it seem larger and lighter E.G. *Fluff the rice up with a fork before serving.*
**fluffy** ADJECTIVE

**fluid fluids**
NOUN 1 a liquid. ► ADJECTIVE 2 Fluid movement is smooth and flowing. 3 A fluid arrangement or plan is flexible and without a fixed structure.
**fluidity** NOUN

**fluke flukes**
NOUN an accidental success or piece of good luck.

**flung**
the past tense of **fling**.

**fluorescent**
Said "floo-er-ess-nt" ADJECTIVE 1 having a very bright appearance when light is shone on it, as if it is shining itself E.G. *fluorescent yellow dye.* 2 A fluorescent light is in the form of a tube and shines with a hard bright light.

**fluoride**
NOUN Fluoride is a mixture of chemicals that is meant to prevent tooth decay.

**flurry flurries**
NOUN a short rush of activity or movement.

**flush flushes flushing flushed**
NOUN 1 A flush is a rosy red colour E.G. *The flowers are cream with a pink flush.* 2 In cards, a flush is a hand all of one suit. ► VERB 3 If you flush, your

face goes red. **4** If you flush a toilet or something such as a pipe, you force water through it to clean it.
▶ ADJECTIVE **5** *INFORMAL* Someone who is flush has plenty of money.
**6** Something that is flush with a surface is level with it or flat against it.

**flustered**
ADJECTIVE If you are flustered, you feel confused, nervous, and rushed.

**flute flutes**
NOUN a musical wind instrument consisting of a long metal tube with holes and keys. It is held sideways to the mouth and played by blowing across a hole in its side.

**fluted**
ADJECTIVE decorated with long grooves.

**flutter flutters fluttering fluttered**
VERB **1** If something flutters, it flaps or waves with small, quick movements.
▶ NOUN **2** If you are in a flutter, you are excited and nervous. **3** *INFORMAL* If you have a flutter, you have a small bet.

**flux**
NOUN Flux is a state of constant change *E.G. stability in a world of flux*.

**fly flies flying flew flown**
NOUN **1** an insect with two pairs of wings. **2** The front opening on a pair of trousers is the fly or the flies. **3** The fly or fly sheet of a tent is either a flap at the entrance or an outer layer providing protection from rain. ▶ VERB **4** When a bird, insect, or aircraft flies, it moves through the air. **5** If someone or something flies, they move or go very quickly. **6** If you fly at someone or let fly at them, you attack or criticize them suddenly and

aggressively.
**flying** ADJECTIVE or NOUN　**flyer** NOUN

**fly-fishing**
NOUN Fly-fishing is a method of fishing using imitation flies as bait.

**flying fox flying foxes**
NOUN **1** a large bat that eats fruit, found in Australia and Africa. **2** In Australia and New Zealand, a cable car used to carry people over rivers and gorges.

**flying saucer flying saucers**
NOUN a large disc-shaped spacecraft which some people claim to have seen.

**flyover flyovers**
NOUN a structure carrying one road over another at a junction or intersection.

**foal foals foaling foaled**
NOUN **1** a young horse. ▶ VERB **2** When a female horse foals, she gives birth.

**foam foams foaming foamed**
NOUN **1** Foam is a mass of tiny bubbles. **2** Foam is light spongy material used, for example, in furniture or packaging. ▶ VERB **3** When something foams, it forms a mass of small bubbles.
■ (sense 1) bubbles, froth

**fob off fobs off fobbing off fobbed off**
VERB; *INFORMAL* If you fob someone off, you provide them with something that is not very good or not adequate.

**focus focuses** or **focusses focusing** or **focussing focused** or **focussed; focuses** or **foci**
VERB **1** If you focus your eyes or an instrument on an object, you adjust them so that the image is clear.
▶ NOUN **2** The focus of something is its

a
b
c
d
e
**f**
g
h
i
j
k
l
m
n
o
p
q
r
s
t
u
v
w
x
y
z

A
B
C
D
E
**F**
G
H
I
J
K
L
M
N
O
P
Q
R
S
T
U
V
W
X
Y
Z

centre of attention *E.G. The focus of the conversation had moved around during the meal.*

**focal** ADJECTIVE

☑ When you add the verb endings to *focus*, you can either add them straight to *focus* (*focuses, focusing, focused*), or you can put another s at the end of *focus* before adding the endings (*focusses, focussing, focussed*). Either way is correct, but the first way is much more common. The plural of the noun is either *focuses* or *foci*, but *focuses* is the commoner.

**fodder**

NOUN Fodder is food for farm animals or horses.

**foe foes**

NOUN an enemy.

**foetus foetuses**

*Said "fee-tus"*; also spelt **fetus**
NOUN an unborn child or animal in the womb.

**foetal** ADJECTIVE

**fog fogs fogging fogged**

NOUN 1 Fog is a thick mist of water droplets suspended in the air. ► VERB 2 If glass fogs up, it becomes clouded with steam or condensation.

**foggy** ADJECTIVE

**foil foils foiling foiled**

VERB 1 If you foil someone's attempt at something, you prevent them from succeeding. ► NOUN 2 Foil is thin, paper-like sheets of metal used to wrap food. 3 Something that is a good foil for something else contrasts with it and makes its good qualities more noticeable. 4 a thin, light sword with a button on the tip, used in fencing.

**foist foists foisting foisted**

VERB If you foist something on someone, you force or impose it on them.

**fold folds folding folded**

VERB 1 If you fold something, you bend it so that one part lies over another. 2 INFORMAL If a business folds, it fails and closes down. 3 In cooking, if you fold one ingredient into another, you mix it in gently. ► NOUN 4 a crease or bend in paper or cloth. 5 a small enclosed area for sheep.

≡ (sense 1) bend, crease, double over

**folder folders**

NOUN 1 a thin piece of folded cardboard for keeping loose papers together. 2 In computing, a folder is a named area of computer disk where you can group together files and subdirectories; also called **directory**.

**foliage**

NOUN Foliage is leaves and plants.

**folk folks**

NOUN 1 Folk or folks are people. ► ADJECTIVE 2 Folk music, dance, or art is traditional or representative of the ordinary people of an area.

**folklore**

NOUN Folklore is the traditional stories and beliefs of a community.

**follicle follicles**

NOUN a small sac or cavity in the body *E.G. hair follicles.*

**follow follows following followed**

VERB 1 If you follow someone, you move along behind them. If you follow a path or a sign, you move along in that direction. 2 Something that follows a particular thing happens after it. 3 Something that follows is true or logical as a result of something else being the case *E.G. Just because she is pretty, it doesn't follow that she can sing.* **4** If you follow instructions or advice, you do what you are told. **5** If you follow an explanation or the plot of a story, you understand each stage of it.

**follower followers**
NOUN The followers of a person or belief are the people who support them.
■ adherent, supporter

**folly follies**
NOUN Folly is a foolish act or foolish behaviour.
■ foolishness, stupidity

**fond fonder fondest**
ADJECTIVE **1** If you are fond of someone or something, you like them. **2** A fond hope or belief is thought of with happiness but is unlikely to happen.
**fondly** ADVERB **fondness** NOUN
■ (sense 1) affectionate, loving

**fondle fondles fondling fondled**
VERB To fondle something is to stroke it affectionately.

**font fonts**
NOUN a large stone bowl in a church that holds the water for baptisms.

**food foods**
NOUN Food is any substance consumed by an animal or plant to provide energy.
■ fare, nourishment

**food chain food chains**
NOUN a series of living things which are linked because each one feeds on the next one in the series. For example, a plant may be eaten by a rabbit which may be eaten by a fox.

**foodstuff foodstuffs**
NOUN anything used for food.

**food technology**
NOUN Food technology is the study of foods and what they consist of, and

their effect on the body.

**fool fools fooling fooled**
NOUN **1** someone who behaves in a silly or stupid way. **2** a dessert made from fruit, eggs, cream, and sugar whipped together. ▶ VERB **3** If you fool someone, you deceive or trick them.

**foolhardy**
ADJECTIVE foolish and involving too great a risk.

**foolish**
ADJECTIVE very silly or unwise.
**foolishly** ADVERB **foolishness** NOUN

**foolproof**
ADJECTIVE Something that is foolproof is so well designed or simple to use that it cannot fail.

**foot feet**
NOUN **1** the part of your body at the end of your leg. **2** the bottom, base, or lower end of something *E.G. the foot of the mountain.* **3** a unit of length equal to 12 inches or about 30.5 centimetres. **4** In poetry, a foot is the basic unit of rhythm containing two or three syllables. ▶ ADJECTIVE **5** A foot brake, pedal, or pump is operated by your foot.

**footage**
NOUN Footage is a length of film *E.G. library footage of prison riots.*

**football footballs**
NOUN **1** Football is any game in which the ball can be kicked, such as soccer, Australian Rules, rugby union, and American football. **2** a ball used in any of these games.
**footballer** NOUN

**foothills**
PLURAL NOUN Foothills are hills at the base of mountains.

**foothold footholds**
NOUN **1** a place where you can put

A B C D E **F** G H I J K L M N O P Q R S T U V W X Y Z

your foot when climbing. **2** a position from which further progress can be made.

**footing**
NOUN **1** Footing is a secure grip by or for your feet E.G. *He missed his footing and fell flat.* **2** a footing is the basis or nature of a relationship or situation E.G. *Steps to put the nation on a war footing.*

**footman** footmen
NOUN a male servant in a large house who wears uniform.

**footnote** footnotes
NOUN a note at the bottom of a page or an additional comment giving extra information.

**footpath** footpaths
NOUN a path for people to walk on.

**footprint** footprints
NOUN a mark left by a foot or shoe.

**footstep** footsteps
NOUN the sound or mark made by someone walking.

**for**
PREPOSITION **1** meant to be given to or used by a particular person, or done in order to help or benefit them E.G. *private beaches for their exclusive use.* **2** 'For' is used when explaining the reason, cause, or purpose of something E.G. *This is my excuse for going to Italy.* **3** You use 'for' to express a quantity, time, or distance E.G. *I'll play for ages… the only house for miles around.* **4** If you are for something, you support it or approve of it E.G. *votes for or against independence.*

**forage** forages foraging foraged
VERB When a person or animal forages, they search for food.

**foray** forays

NOUN **1** a brief attempt to do or get something E.G. *her first foray into acting.* **2** an attack or raid by soldiers.

**forbid** forbids forbidding forbade forbidden
VERB If you forbid someone to do something, you order them not to do it.
**forbidden** ADJECTIVE

**force** forces forcing forced
VERB **1** To force someone to do something is to make them do it. **2** To force something is to use violence or great strength to move or open it. ➤ NOUN **3** The use of force is the use of violence or great strength. **4** The force of something is its strength or power E.G. *The force of the explosion shook buildings.* **5** a person or thing that has a lot of influence or effect E.G. *She became the dominant force in tennis.* **6** an organized group of soldiers or police. **7** In physics, force is a pushing or pulling influence that changes a body from a state of rest to one of motion, or changes its rate of motion. ➤ PHRASE **8** A law or rule that is **in force** is currently valid and must be obeyed.
▣ (sense 1) compel, drive, make

**forceful**
ADJECTIVE powerful and convincing E.G. *a forceful, highly political lawyer.*
**forcefully** ADVERB

**forceps**
PLURAL NOUN Forceps are a pair of long tongs or pincers used by a doctor or surgeon.

**forcible**
ADJECTIVE **1** involving physical force or violence. **2** convincing and making a strong impression E.G. *a forcible reminder.*
**forcibly** ADVERB

**SPELLING NOTE** I always visit my FRIend on a FRIday (<u>fri</u>end)

**ford** fords fording forded
NOUN **1** a shallow place in a river where it is possible to cross on foot or in a vehicle. ▶ VERB **2** To ford a river is to cross it on foot or in a vehicle.

**fore**
PHRASE Someone or something that comes **to the fore** becomes important or popular.

**forearm** forearms
NOUN the part of your arm between your elbow and your wrist.

**forebear** forebears
NOUN Your forebears are your ancestors.

**foreboding** forebodings
NOUN a strong feeling of approaching disaster.

**forecast** forecasts forecasting forecast or forecasted
NOUN **1** a prediction of what will happen, especially a statement about what the weather will be like. ▶ VERB **2** To forecast an event is to predict what will happen.

**forecourt** forecourts
NOUN an open area at the front of a petrol station or large building.

**forefather** forefathers
NOUN Your forefathers are your ancestors.

**forefinger** forefingers
NOUN the finger next to your thumb.

**forefront**
NOUN The forefront of something is the most important and progressive part of it.

**forego** foregoes foregoing forewent foregone; also spelt forgo
VERB If you forego something pleasant, you give it up or do not insist on having it.

**foregoing**
A FORMAL PHRASE You can say **the foregoing** when talking about something that has just been said E.G. *The foregoing discussion has highlighted the difficulties.*

**foregone conclusion** foregone conclusions
NOUN A foregone conclusion is a result or conclusion that is bound to happen.

**foreground**
NOUN ⟨ART⟩ In a picture, the foreground is the part that seems nearest to you.

**forehand** forehands
NOUN or ADJECTIVE a stroke in tennis, squash, or badminton made with the palm of your hand facing in the direction that you hit the ball.

**forehead** foreheads
NOUN the area at the front of your head, above your eyebrows and below your hairline.

**foreign**
ADJECTIVE **1** belonging to or involving countries other than your own E.G. *foreign coins… foreign travel.*
**2** unfamiliar or uncharacteristic E.G. *Such daft enthusiasm was foreign to him.* **3** A foreign object has got into something, usually by accident, and should not be there E.G. *a foreign object in my eye.*
**foreigner** NOUN
■ (sense 2) alien, unfamiliar

**foreman** foremen
NOUN **1** a person in charge of a group of workers, for example on a building site. **2** The foreman of a jury is the spokesman.

**foremost**
ADJECTIVE The foremost of a group of

a
b
c
d
e
**f**
g
h
i
j
k
l
m
n
o
p
q
r
s
t
u
v
w
x
y
z

things is the most important or the best.

**forensic**

ADJECTIVE 1 relating to or involving the scientific examination of objects involved in a crime. 2 relating to or involving the legal profession.

**forerunner** forerunners

NOUN The forerunner of something is the person who first introduced or achieved it, or the first example of it.

**foresee** foresees foreseeing foresaw foreseen

VERB If you foresee something, you predict or expect that it will happen. **foreseeable** ADJECTIVE

**foresight**

NOUN Foresight is the ability to know what is going to happen in the future.

**foreskin** foreskins

NOUN A man's foreskin is the fold of skin covering the end of his penis.

**forest** forests

NOUN a large area of trees growing close together.

**forestry**

NOUN Forestry is the study and work of growing and maintaining forests.

**foretaste** foretastes

NOUN a slight taste or experience of something in advance.

**foretell** foretells foretelling foretold

VERB If you foretell something, you predict that it will happen.

**forever**

ADVERB permanently or continually.

**forewarn** forewarns forewarning forewarned

VERB If you forewarn someone, you warn them in advance about something.

**foreword** forewords

NOUN an introduction in a book.

**forfeit** forfeits forfeiting forfeited

VERB 1 If you forfeit something, you have to give it up as a penalty. ▶ NOUN 2 something that you have to give up or do as a penalty.

**forge** forges forging forged

NOUN 1 a place where a blacksmith works making metal goods by hand. ▶ VERB 2 To forge metal is to hammer and bend it into shape while hot. 3 To forge a relationship is to create a strong and lasting relationship. 4 Someone who forges money, documents, or paintings makes illegal copies of them. 5 To forge ahead is to progress quickly.

**forgery** forgeries

NOUN Forgery is the crime of forging money, documents, or paintings; also something that has been forged. **forger** NOUN

**forget** forgets forgetting forgot forgotten

VERB 1 If you forget something, you fail to remember or think about it. 2 If you forget yourself, you behave in an unacceptable, uncontrolled way.

**forgetful** ADJECTIVE

**forget-me-not** forget-me-nots

NOUN a small plant with tiny blue flowers.

**forgive** forgives forgiving forgave forgiven

VERB If you forgive someone for doing something bad, you stop feeling angry and resentful towards them. **forgiveness** NOUN **forgiving** ADJECTIVE

■ absolve, excuse, pardon

**forgo**
another spelling of **forego**.

**fork** forks forking forked
NOUN 1 a pronged instrument used for eating food. 2 a large garden tool with three or four prongs. 3 a Y-shaped junction or division in a road, river, or branch. ▶ VERB 4 To fork something is to move or turn it with a fork.

**fork out** VERB; *INFORMAL* If you fork out for something, you pay for it, often unwillingly.

**forlorn**
ADJECTIVE 1 lonely, unhappy and pitiful. 2 desperate and without any expectation of success E.G. *a forlorn fight for a draw*.
**forlornly** ADVERB

**form** forms forming formed
NOUN 1 A particular form of something is a type or kind of it E.G. *a new form of weapon*. 2 The form of something is the shape or pattern of something E.G. *a brooch in the form of a bright green lizard*. 3 a sheet of paper with questions and spaces for you to fill in the answers. 4 a class in a school. ▶ VERB 5 The things that form something are the things it consists of E.G. *events that were to form the basis of her novel*. 6 When someone forms something or when it forms, it is created, organized, or started.

**formal**
ADJECTIVE 1 correct, serious, and conforming to accepted conventions E.G. *a very formal letter of apology*. 2 official and publicly recognized E.G. *the first formal agreement of its kind*.
**formally** ADVERB

**formaldehyde**
*Said* "for-**mal**-di-hide" NOUN Formaldehyde is a poisonous, strong-smelling gas, used for preserving specimens in biology.

**formality** formalities
NOUN an action or process that is carried out as part of an official procedure.

**format** formats
NOUN the way in which something is arranged or presented.

**formation** formations
NOUN 1 The formation of something is the process of developing and creating it. 2 the pattern or shape of something.

**formative**
ADJECTIVE having an important and lasting influence on character and development E.G. *the formative days of his young manhood*.

**former**
ADJECTIVE 1 happening or existing before now or in the past E.G. *a former tennis champion*. ▶ NOUN 2 You use 'the former' to refer to the first of two things just mentioned E.G. *If I had to choose between happiness and money, I would have the former*.
**formerly** ADVERB

**formidable**
ADJECTIVE very difficult to deal with or overcome, and therefore rather frightening or impressive E.G. *formidable enemies*.
🏛 from Latin *formido* meaning 'terror'
📙 daunting, intimidating

**formula** formulae or formulas
NOUN 1 a group of letters, numbers, and symbols which stand for a mathematical or scientific rule. 2 a list of quantities of substances that

a b c d e f g h i j k l m n o p q r s t u v w x y z

when mixed make another substance, for example in chemistry. **3** a plan or set of rules for dealing with a particular problem *E.G. my secret formula for keeping in trim.*

**formulate** formulates formulating formulated
VERB If you formulate a plan or thought, you create it and express it in a clear and precise way.

**fornication**
NOUN; *FORMAL* Fornication is the sin of having sex with someone when you are not married to them.

**forsake** forsakes forsaking forsook forsaken
VERB To forsake someone or something is to give up or abandon them.

**fort** forts
NOUN **1** a strong building built for defence. ▶ PHRASE **2** If you **hold the fort** for someone, you manage their affairs while they are away.

**forte** fortes
*Said* "for-tay" **1** In music, forte is an instruction to play or sing something loudly.
NOUN **2** If something is your forte, you are particularly good at doing it.
■ (sense 2) speciality, strong point

**forth**
ADVERB **1** out and forward from a starting place *E.G. Christopher Columbus set forth on his epic voyage of discovery.* **2** into view *E.G. he brought forth a slim volume of his newly published verse.*

**forthcoming**
ADJECTIVE **1** planned to happen soon *E.G. their forthcoming holiday.* **2** given or made available *E.G. Medical aid might be forthcoming.* **3** willing to

give information *E.G. He was not too forthcoming about this.*

**forthright**
ADJECTIVE Someone who is forthright is direct and honest about their opinions and feelings.

**fortification** fortifications
NOUN Fortifications are buildings, walls, and ditches used to protect a place.

**fortitude**
NOUN Fortitude is calm and patient courage.

**fortnight** fortnights
NOUN a period of two weeks.
**fortnightly** ADVERB OR ADJECTIVE

**fortress** fortresses
NOUN a castle or well-protected town built for defence.

**fortuitous**
*Said* "for-**tyoo**-it-uss" ADJECTIVE happening by chance or good luck *E.G. a fortuitous winning goal.*

**fortunate**
ADJECTIVE **1** Someone who is fortunate is lucky. **2** Something that is fortunate brings success or advantage.
**fortunately** ADVERB

**fortune** fortunes
NOUN **1** Fortune or good fortune is good luck. **2** A fortune is a large amount of money. ▶ PHRASE **3** If someone **tells your fortune**, they predict your future.

**forty** forties
the number 40.
**fortieth**

**forum** forums
NOUN **1** a place or meeting in which people can exchange ideas and discuss public issues. **2** a square in Roman towns where people met to discuss business and politics.

**forward forwards forwarding forwarded**

ADVERB OR ADJECTIVE **1** Forward or forwards means in the front or towards the front *E.G. A photographer moved forward to capture the moment.* **2** Forward means in or towards a future time *E.G. a positive atmosphere of looking forward and making fresh starts.* **3** Forward or forwards also means developing or progressing *E.G. The new committee would push forward government plans.* ▶ ADVERB **4** If someone or something is put forward, they are suggested as being suitable for something. ▶ VERB **5** If you forward a letter that you have received, you send it on to the person to whom it is addressed at their new address. ▶ NOUN **6** In a game such as football or hockey, a forward is a player in an attacking position.

■ (sense 3) ahead, on

**fossick fossicks fossicking fossicked**

VERB **1** In Australian and New Zealand English, to fossick for gold nuggets or precious stones is to look for them in rivers or old mines. **2** In Australian and New Zealand English, to fossick for something is to search for it.

**fossil fossils**

NOUN the remains or impression of an animal or plant from a previous age, preserved in rock.
**fossilize** VERB

**fossil fuel fossil fuels**

NOUN Fossil fuels are fuels such as coal, oil, and natural gas, which have been formed by rotting animals and plants from millions of years ago.

**foster fosters fostering fostered**

VERB **1** If someone fosters a child, they are paid to look after the child for a period, but do not become its legal parent. **2** If you foster something such as an activity or an idea, you help its development and growth by encouraging people to do or think it *E.G. to foster and maintain this goodwill.*
**foster child** NOUN **foster home** NOUN **foster parent** NOUN

**fought**

the past tense and past participle of **fight.**

**foul fouler foulest; fouls fouling fouled**

ADJECTIVE **1** Something that is foul is very unpleasant, especially because it is dirty, wicked, or obscene. ▶ VERB **2** To foul something is to make it dirty, especially with faeces *E.G. Dogs must not be allowed to foul the pavement.* ▶ NOUN **3** In sport, a foul is an act of breaking the rules.

**found founds founding founded**

**1** Found is the past tense and past participle of **find.** ▶ VERB **2** If someone founds an organization or institution, they start it and set it up.

**foundation foundations**

NOUN **1** The foundation of a belief or way of life is the basic ideas or attitudes on which it is built. **2** a solid layer of concrete or bricks in the ground, on which a building is built to give it a firm base. **3** an organization set up by money left in someone's will for research or charity.

**founder founders foundering foundered**

NOUN **1** The founder of an institution

a b c d e f g h i j k l m n o p q r s t u v w x y z

A B C D E F G H I J K L M N O P Q R S T U V W X Y Z

or organization is the person who sets it up. ▶ VERB **2** If something founders, it fails.

**foundry** foundries
NOUN a factory where metal is melted and cast.

**fountain** fountains
NOUN an ornamental structure consisting of a jet of water forced into the air by a pump.

**fountain pen** fountain pens
NOUN a pen which is supplied with ink from a container inside the pen.

**four** fours **1** the number 4.
PHRASE **2** If you are **on all fours**, you are on your hands and knees.

**four-poster** four-posters
NOUN a bed with a tall post at each corner supporting a canopy and curtains.

**fourteen**
the number 14.
**fourteenth**

**fourth**
The fourth item in a series is the one counted as number four.

**fowl** fowls
NOUN a bird such as chicken or duck that is kept or hunted for its meat or eggs.

**fox** foxes foxing foxed
NOUN **1** a dog-like wild animal with reddish-brown fur, a pointed face and ears, and a thick tail. ▶ VERB **2** If something foxes you, it is too confusing or puzzling for you to understand.

**foxglove** foxgloves
NOUN a plant with a tall spike of purple or white trumpet-shaped flowers.

**foxhound** foxhounds
NOUN a dog trained for hunting foxes.

**foyer** foyers
*Said* "foy-ay" NOUN a large area just

inside the main doors of a cinema, hotel, or public building.

**fracas**
*Said* "frak-ah" NOUN a rough noisy quarrel or fight.

**fraction** fractions
NOUN **1** (MATHS) In arithmetic, a fraction is a part of a whole number. **2** a tiny proportion or amount of something *E.G. an area a fraction of the size of London.*
**fractional** ADJECTIVE **fractionally** ADVERB

**fractious**
ADJECTIVE When small children are fractious, they become upset or angry very easily, often because they are tired.

**fracture** fractures fracturing fractured
NOUN **1** a crack or break in something, especially a bone. ▶ VERB **2** If something fractures, it breaks.

**fragile**
ADJECTIVE easily broken or damaged *E.G. fragile glass… a fragile relationship.*
**fragility** NOUN
■ breakable, delicate, frail

**fragment** fragments fragmenting fragmented
NOUN **1** a small piece or part of something. ▶ VERB **2** If something fragments, it breaks into small pieces or different parts.
**fragmentation** NOUN **fragmented** ADJECTIVE

**fragmentary**
ADJECTIVE made up of small pieces, or parts that are not connected *E.G. fragmentary notes in a journal.*

**fragrance** fragrances
NOUN a sweet or pleasant smell.
■ aroma, perfume, scent

**fragrant**

ADJECTIVE Something that is fragrant smells sweet or pleasant.

**frail** frailer frailest

ADJECTIVE **1** Someone who is frail is not strong or healthy. **2** Something that is frail is easily broken or damaged.
**frailty** NOUN

**frame** frames framing framed

NOUN **1** the structure surrounding a door, window, or picture. **2** an arrangement of connected bars over which something is built. **3** The frames of a pair of glasses are the wire or plastic parts that hold the lenses. **4** Your frame is your body *E.G. his large frame.* **5** one of the many separate photographs of which a cinema film is made up. ▶ VERB **6** To frame a picture is to put it into a frame *E.G. I've framed pictures I've pulled out of magazines.* **7** The language something is framed in is the language used to express it.

**framework** frameworks

NOUN **1** a structure acting as a support or frame. **2** a set of rules, beliefs, or ideas which you use to decide what to do.

**franc** francs

NOUN the main unit of currency in Switzerland, and formerly in France and Belgium. A franc is worth 100 centimes.

**franchise** franchises

NOUN **1** The franchise is the right to vote in an election *E.G. a franchise that gave the vote to about 2% of the population.* **2** the right given by a company to someone to allow them to sell its goods or services.

**frank** franker frankest

ADJECTIVE If you are frank, you say

things in an open and honest way.
**frankly** ADVERB    **frankness** NOUN

■ candid, honest, open

**frantic**

ADJECTIVE If you are frantic, you behave in a wild, desperate way because you are anxious or frightened.
**frantically** ADVERB

▥ from Greek *phrenitikis* meaning 'delirious'

**fraternal**

ADJECTIVE 'Fraternal' is used to describe friendly actions and feelings between groups of people *E.G. an affectionate fraternal greeting.*

**fraternity** fraternities

NOUN **1** Fraternity is friendship between groups of people. **2** a group of people with something in common *E.G. the golfing fraternity.*

**fraud** frauds

NOUN **1** Fraud is the crime of getting money by deceit or trickery. **2** something that deceives people in an illegal or immoral way. **3** Someone who is not what they pretend to be.

**fraudulent**

ADJECTIVE dishonest or deceitful *E.G. fraudulent cheques.*

**fraught**

ADJECTIVE If something is fraught with problems or difficulties, it is full of them *E.G. Modern life was fraught with hazards.*

**fray** frays fraying frayed

VERB **1** If cloth or rope frays, its threads or strands become worn and it is likely to tear or break. ▶ NOUN **2** a fight or argument.

**freak** freaks

NOUN **1** someone whose appearance or behaviour is very unusual.
▶ ADJECTIVE or NOUN **2** A freak event is

a
b
c
d
e
**f**
g
h
i
j
k
l
m
n
o
p
q
r
s
t
u
v
w
x
y
z

A
B
C
D
E
F
G
H
I
J
K
L
M
N
O
P
Q
R
S
T
U
V
W
X
Y
Z

very unusual and unlikely to happen
E.G. *a freak allergy to peanuts*.

**freckle freckles**
NOUN Freckles are small, light brown
spots on someone's skin, especially
their face.
**freckled** ADJECTIVE

**free freer freest; frees freeing
freed**
ADJECTIVE **1** not controlled or limited
E.G. *the free flow of aid … free trade*.
**2** Someone who is free is no longer a
prisoner. **3** To be free of something
unpleasant is not to have it E.G. *She
wanted her aunt's life to be free of
worry*. **4** If someone is free, they are
not busy or occupied. If a place, seat,
or machine is free, it is not occupied
or not being used E.G. *Are you free for
dinner?* **5** If something is free, you can
have it without paying for it. ▶ VERB
**6** If you free something that is
fastened or trapped, you release it
E.G. *a campaign to free captive
animals*. **7** When a prisoner is freed,
he or she is released.
■ (sense 2) at liberty, liberated
■ (sense 5) complimentary, gratis
■ (sense 7) liberate, release

**freedom**
NOUN **1** If you have the freedom to do
something, you have the scope or
are allowed to do it E.G. *We have the
freedom to decide our own futures*.
**2** When prisoners gain their freedom,
they escape or are released. **3** When
there is freedom from something
unpleasant, people are not affected
by it E.G. *freedom from guilt*.
■ (sense 2) liberty, release

**freehold freeholds**
NOUN the right to own a house or
piece of land for life without
conditions.

**freelance**
ADJECTIVE or ADVERB A freelance
journalist or photographer is not
employed by one organization, but
is paid for each job he or she does.

**freely**
ADVERB Freely means without
restriction E.G. *the pleasure of being
able to walk about freely*.

**free-range**
ADJECTIVE Free-range eggs are laid by
hens that can move and feed freely
on an area of open ground.

**freestyle**
NOUN Freestyle refers to sports
competitions, especially swimming,
in which competitors can use any
style or method.

**freeway freeways**
NOUN In Australia, South Africa, and
the United States, a road designed
for fast-moving traffic.

**free will**
PHRASE If you do something **of your
own free will**, you do it by choice
and not because you are forced to.

**freeze freezes freezing froze
frozen**
VERB **1** (SCIENCE) When a liquid freezes,
it becomes solid because it is very
cold. **2** If you freeze, you suddenly
become very still and quiet. **3** (DRAMA)
To freeze the action in a film is to
stop the film at a particular frame.
**4** If you freeze food, you put it in a
freezer to preserve it. **5** When wages
or prices are frozen, they are officially
prevented from rising. ▶ NOUN **6** an
official action taken to prevent
wages or prices from rising. **7** a
period of freezing weather.

**freezer freezers**
NOUN a large refrigerator which freezes

and stores food for a long time.

**freezing**
ADJECTIVE extremely cold.

**freight**
NOUN Freight is goods moved by lorries, ships, or other transport; also the moving of these goods.

**French**
ADJECTIVE 1 belonging or relating to France. ▶ NOUN 2 French is the main language spoken in France, and is also spoken by many people in Belgium, Switzerland, and Canada.

**French bean** French beans
NOUN French beans are green pods eaten as a vegetable, which grow on a climbing plant with white or mauve flowers.

**French horn** French horns
NOUN a brass musical wind instrument consisting of a tube wound in a circle.

**Frenchman** Frenchmen
NOUN a man who comes from France.
**Frenchwoman** NOUN

**french window** french windows
NOUN French windows are glass doors that lead into a garden or onto a balcony.

**frenetic**
ADJECTIVE Frenetic behaviour is wild and excited.

**frenzy** frenzies
NOUN If someone is in a frenzy, their behaviour is wild and uncontrolled.
**frenzied** ADJECTIVE

**frequency** frequencies
NOUN 1 The frequency of an event is how often it happens E.G. *He was not known to call anyone with great frequency.* 2 ( SCIENCE ) The frequency of a sound or radio wave is the rate at which it vibrates.

**frequent** frequents frequenting frequented
ADJECTIVE 1 often happening E.G. *His visits were frequent… They move at frequent intervals.* ▶ VERB 2 If you frequent a place, you go there often.
**frequently** ADVERB

**fresco** frescoes
NOUN a picture painted on a plastered wall while the plaster is still wet.
📖 from Italian *fresco* meaning 'fresh'

**fresh** fresher freshest
ADJECTIVE 1 A fresh thing replaces a previous one, or is added to it E.G. *footprints filled in by fresh snow… fresh evidence.* 2 Fresh food is newly made or obtained, and not tinned or frozen. 3 Fresh water is not salty, for example the water in a stream. 4 If the weather is fresh, it is fairly cold and windy. 5 If you are fresh from something, you have experienced it recently E.G. *a teacher fresh from college.*
**freshly** ADVERB **freshness** NOUN

**freshwater**
ADJECTIVE 1 A freshwater lake or pool contains water that is not salty. 2 A freshwater creature lives in a river, lake, or pool that is not salty.

**fret** frets fretting fretted
VERB 1 If you fret about something, you worry about it. ▶ NOUN 2 The frets on a stringed instrument, such as a guitar, are the metal ridges across its neck.
**fretful** ADJECTIVE

**Freudian slip** Freudian slips
NOUN something that you say or do that reveals your unconscious thoughts.

**friar** friars
NOUN a member of a Catholic religious order.

a
b
c
d
e
**f**
g
h
i
j
k
l
m
n
o
p
q
r
s
t
u
v
w
x
y
z

A
B
C
D
E
F
G
H
I
J
K
L
M
N
O
P
Q
R
S
T
U
V
W
X
Y
Z

**friction**

NOUN 1 (SCIENCE) the force that stops things from moving freely when they rub against each other.
**2** Friction between people is disagreement and quarrels.

**Friday** Fridays

NOUN the day between Thursday and Saturday.

📖 from Old English *Frigedæg* meaning 'Freya's day'. Freya was the Norse goddess of love

**fridge** fridges

NOUN the same as a **refrigerator**.

**friend** friends

NOUN Your friends are people you know well and like to spend time with.

▣ chum, companion, mate, pal

**friendly** friendlier friendliest

ADJECTIVE 1 If you are friendly to someone, you behave in a kind and pleasant way to them. **2** People who are friendly with each other like each other and enjoy spending time together.

**friendliness** NOUN

▣ (sense 1) amicable, cordial, genial

**friendship** friendships

NOUN Your friendships are the special relationships that you have with your friends. **2** Friendship is the state of being friends with someone.

▣ (sense 2) friendliness, goodwill

**frieze** friezes

NOUN 1 a strip of decoration or carving along the top of a wall or column. **2** (ART) a picture on a long strip of paper which is hung along a wall.

**frigate** frigates

NOUN a small, fast warship.

**fright**

NOUN Fright is a sudden feeling of fear.

**frighten** frightens frightening frightened

VERB If something frightens you, it makes you afraid.

**frightened** ADJECTIVE **frightening** ADJECTIVE

**frightful**

ADJECTIVE very bad or unpleasant E.G. *a frightful bully*.

**frigid**

ADJECTIVE Frigid behaviour is cold and unfriendly E.G. *frigid stares*.

**frill** frills

NOUN a strip of cloth with many folds, attached to something as a decoration.

**frilly** ADJECTIVE

**fringe** fringes

NOUN 1 the hair that hangs over a person's forehead. **2** a decoration on clothes and other objects, consisting of a row of hanging strips or threads. **3** The fringes of a place are the parts farthest from its centre E.G. *the western fringe of the Amazon basin*.

**fringed** ADJECTIVE

**frisk** frisks frisking frisked

VERB INFORMAL If someone frisks you, they search you quickly with their hands to see if you are hiding a weapon in your clothes.

**frisky** friskier friskiest

ADJECTIVE A frisky animal or child is energetic and wants to have fun.

**fritter** fritters frittering frittered

NOUN 1 Fritters consist of food dipped in batter and fried E.G. *apple fritters*.

▶ VERB **2** If you fritter away your time or money, you waste it on unimportant things.

📖 from Latin *frigere* meaning 'to fry'

**frivolous**

ADJECTIVE Someone who is frivolous

behaves in a silly or light-hearted way, especially when they should be serious or sensible.

**frivolity** NOUN
■ flippant, silly

**frizzy** frizzier frizziest
ADJECTIVE Frizzy hair has stiff, wiry curls.

**frock** frocks
NOUN; OLD-FASHIONED a dress.

**frog** frogs
NOUN a small amphibious creature with smooth skin, prominent eyes, and long back legs which it uses for jumping.

**frolic** frolics frolicking frolicked
VERB When animals or children frolic, they run around and play in a lively way.
🏛 from Dutch *vrolijk* meaning 'joyful'
■ frisk, play, romp

**from**
PREPOSITION 1 You use 'from' to say what the source, origin, or starting point of something is *E.G. a call from a public telephone… people from a city 100 miles away*. 2 If you take something from an amount, you reduce the amount by that much *E.G. A sum of money was wrongly taken from his account*. 3 You also use 'from' when stating the range of something *E.G. a score from one to five*.

**frond** fronds
NOUN Fronds are long feathery leaves.

**front** fronts fronting fronted
NOUN 1 The front of something is the part that faces forward. 2 In a war, the front is the place where two armies are fighting. 3 In meteorology, a front is the line where a mass of cold air meets a mass of warm air. 4 A front is an outward appearance, often one that is false *E.G. I put up a*

brave front… *He's no more than a respectable front for some very dubious happenings*. ▶ PHRASE 5 In front means ahead or further forward. 6 If you do something in front of someone, you do it when they are present.

**frontal** ADJECTIVE

**frontage** frontages
NOUN The frontage of a building is the wall that faces a street.

**frontier** frontiers
NOUN a border between two countries.

**frontispiece** frontispieces
NOUN a picture opposite the title page of a book.

**frost** frosts
NOUN When there is a frost, the temperature outside falls below freezing.

**frostbite**
NOUN Frostbite is damage to your fingers, toes, or ears caused by extreme cold.

**frosty** frostier frostiest
ADJECTIVE 1 If it is frosty, the temperature outside is below freezing point. 2 If someone is frosty, they are unfriendly or disapproving.

**froth** froths frothing frothed
NOUN 1 Froth is a mass of small bubbles on the surface of a liquid. ▶ VERB 2 If a liquid froths, small bubbles appear on its surface.

**frothy** ADJECTIVE

**frown** frowns frowning frowned
VERB 1 If you frown, you move your eyebrows closer together, because you are annoyed, worried, or concentrating. ▶ NOUN 2 a cross expression on someone's face.

**froze**
the past tense of **freeze**.

a
b
c
d
e
f
g
h
i
j
k
l
m
n
o
p
q
r
s
t
u
v
w
x
y
z

A
B
C
D
E
F
G
H
I
J
K
L
M
N
O
P
Q
R
S
T
U
V
W
X
Y
Z

**frozen**
1 Frozen is the past participle of **freeze**. ▶ ADJECTIVE 2 If you say are frozen, you mean you are extremely cold.
◼ chilled, ice-cold, icy

**fructose**
*Said* "fruck-toes" NOUN Fructose is a type of sugar found in many fruits and in honey.

**frugal**
ADJECTIVE 1 Someone who is frugal spends very little money. 2 A frugal meal is small and cheap.
**frugality** NOUN
◼ (sense 1) economical, thrifty

**fruit fruits**
NOUN 1 the part of a plant that develops after the flower and contains the seeds. Many fruits are edible. ▶ PLURAL NOUN 2 The fruits of something are its good results *E.G. It will be a few years before the fruits of this work are apparent.*

**fruitful**
ADJECTIVE Something that is fruitful has good and useful results *E.G. a fruitful experience.*

**fruitless**
ADJECTIVE Something that is fruitless does not achieve anything *E.G. a fruitless effort.*

**fruit machine fruit machines**
NOUN a coin-operated gambling machine which pays out money when a particular series of symbols, usually fruit, appears on a screen.

**fruit salad fruit salads**
NOUN a mixture of pieces of different fruits served in a juice as a dessert.

**fruity fruitier fruitiest**
ADJECTIVE Something that is fruity smells or tastes of fruit.

**frustrate frustrates frustrating frustrated**
VERB 1 If something frustrates you, it prevents you doing what you want and makes you upset and angry *E.G. Everyone gets frustrated with their work.* 2 To frustrate something such as a plan is to prevent it *E.G. She hopes to frustrate the engagement of her son.*
**frustrated** ADJECTIVE **frustrating** ADJECTIVE **frustration** NOUN
◼ (sense 2) foil, thwart

**fry fries frying fried**
VERB When you fry food, you cook it in a pan containing hot fat or oil.

**fuchsia fuchsias**
*Said* "fyoo-sha" NOUN a plant or small bush with pink, purple, or white flowers that hang downwards.

**fudge fudges fudging fudged**
NOUN 1 Fudge is a soft brown sweet made from butter, milk, and sugar. ▶ VERB 2 If you fudge something, you avoid making clear or definite decisions or statements about it *E.G. He was carefully fudging his message.*

**fuel fuels fuelling fuelled**
NOUN 1 Fuel is a substance such as coal or petrol that is burned to provide heat or power. ▶ VERB 2 A machine or vehicle that is fuelled by a substance works by burning the substance as a fuel *E.G. power stations fuelled by wood.*

**fug**
NOUN A fug is an airless, smoky atmosphere.

**fugitive fugitives**
*Said* "fyoo-jit-tiv" NOUN someone who is running away or hiding, especially from the police.

**fulcrum** fulcrums or fulcra
NOUN the point at which something is balancing or pivoting.

**-ful**
SUFFIX **1** '-ful' is used to form adjectives with the meaning 'full of' E.G. *careful.* **2** '-ful' is used to form nouns which mean 'the amount needed to fill' E.G. *spoonful.*
🏛 from Old English

**fulfil** fulfils fulfilling fulfilled
VERB **1** If you fulfil a promise, hope, or duty, you carry it out or achieve it. **2** If something fulfils you, it gives you satisfaction.
**fulfilling** ADJECTIVE **fulfilment** NOUN

**full** fuller fullest
ADJECTIVE **1** containing or having as much as it is possible to hold E.G. *His room is full of posters.* **2** complete or whole E.G. *They had taken a full meal… a full 20 years later.* **3** loose and made from a lot of fabric E.G. *full sleeves.* **4** rich and strong E.G. *a full, fruity wine.* ▶ ADVERB **5** completely and directly E.G. *Turn the taps full on.* ▶ PHRASE **6** Something that has been done or described **in full** has been dealt with completely.
**fullness** NOUN **fully** ADVERB
■ (sense 1) filled, loaded, packed

**full-blooded**
ADJECTIVE having great commitment and enthusiasm E.G. *a full-blooded sprint for third place.*

**full-blown**
ADJECTIVE complete and fully developed E.G. *a full-blown love of music.*

**full moon** full moons
NOUN the moon when it appears as a complete circle.

**full stop** full stops
NOUN the punctuation mark (.) used at the end of a sentence and after an abbreviation or initial.

---

| *What does the Full Stop do?* |
| --- |

The **full stop** (.) marks the end of any sentence which is not a question or an exclamation:
  E.G. *The train is leaving.*
A full stop is also used after an abbreviation or initial:
  E.G. *etc.* ■ *Dr. Jenkins* ■ *J.R. Hartley*
A full stop is also used after an expression that stands by itself but is not a complete sentence:
  E.G. *Good morning.*

---

**full-time**
ADJECTIVE **1** involving work for the whole of each normal working week. ▶ NOUN **2** In games such as football, full time is the end of the match.

**fully-fledged**
ADJECTIVE completely developed E.G. *I was a fully-fledged and mature human being.*

**fulsome**
ADJECTIVE exaggerated and elaborate, and often sounding insincere E.G. *His most fulsome praise was reserved for his mother.*

**fumble** fumbles fumbling fumbled
VERB If you fumble, you feel or handle something clumsily.

**fume** fumes fuming fumed
NOUN **1** Fumes are unpleasant-smelling gases and smoke, often toxic, that are produced by burning and by some chemicals. ▶ VERB **2** If you are fuming, you are very angry.

**fun**
NOUN **1** Fun is pleasant, enjoyable and

a b c d e f g h i j k l m n o p q r s t u v w x y z

light-hearted activity. ▶ PHRASE **2** If you **make fun** of someone, you tease them or make jokes about them.

**function** functions functioning functioned
NOUN **1** The function of something is its purpose or natural action *E.G. The function of the kidneys is to filter waste products from the blood.* **2** A person's function is the role they have in something or the job they have to do *E.G. It is one of his functions to make sure the heating system is working properly.* **3** a large formal dinner, reception, or party. ▶ VERB **4** When something functions, it operates or works.

**functional**
ADJECTIVE **1** relating to the way something works. **2** designed for practical use rather than for decoration or attractiveness *E.G. Feminine clothing has never been designed to be functional.* **3** working properly *E.G. fully functional smoke alarms.*

**fund** funds funding funded
NOUN **1** an amount of available money, usually for a particular purpose *E.G. a pension fund.* **2** A fund of something is a lot of it *E.G. He had a fund of hilarious tales on the subject.* ▶ VERB **3** Someone who funds something provides money for it *E.G. research funded by pharmaceutical companies.*
■ (sense 3) finance, subsidize

**fundamental** fundamentals
ADJECTIVE **1** basic and central *E.G. the fundamental right of freedom of choice… fundamental changes.* ▶ NOUN **2** The fundamentals of something are its most basic and important parts *E.G. teaching small*

children the fundamentals of road safety.

**funeral** funerals
*Said* "**fyoo**-ner-al" NOUN (RE) a ceremony or religious service for the burial or cremation of a dead person.

**funereal**
*Said* "few-**nee**-ree-al" ADJECTIVE depressing and gloomy.

**funfair** funfairs
NOUN a place of entertainment with things like amusement arcades and rides.

**fungicide** fungicides
NOUN a chemical used to kill or prevent fungus.

**fungus** fungi or funguses
NOUN a plant such as a mushroom or mould that does not have leaves and grows on other living things.
**fungal** ADJECTIVE

**funk** funks funking funked
VERB **1** OLD-FASHIONED If you funk something, you fail to do it because of fear. ▶ NOUN **2** Funk is a style of music with a strong rhythm based on jazz and blues.

**funnel** funnels funnelling funnelled
NOUN **1** an open cone narrowing to a tube, used to pour substances into containers. **2** a metal chimney on a ship or steam engine. ▶ VERB **3** If something is funnelled somewhere, it is directed through a narrow space into that place.

**funny** funnier funniest
ADJECTIVE **1** strange or puzzling *E.G. You get a lot of funny people coming into the libraries.* **2** causing amusement or laughter *E.G. a funny old film.*
**funnily** ADVERB
■ (sense 1) odd, peculiar, strange

■ (sense 2) amusing, comical, humorous

**fur** furs
NOUN **1** Fur is the soft thick body hair of many animals. **2** a coat made from an animal's fur.
**furry** ADJECTIVE

**furious**
ADJECTIVE **1** extremely angry. **2** involving great energy, effort, or speed E.G. *the furious speed of technological development.*
**furiously** ADVERB

**furlong** furlongs
NOUN a unit of length equal to 220 yards or about 201.2 metres. Furlong originally referred to the length of the average furrow.

**furnace** furnaces
NOUN a container for a very large, hot fire used, for example, in the steel industry for melting ore.

**furnish** furnishes furnishing furnished
VERB **1** If you furnish a room, you put furniture into it. **2** *FORMAL* If you furnish someone with something, you supply or provide it for them.

**furnishings**
PLURAL NOUN The furnishings of a room or house are the furniture and fittings in it.

**furniture**
NOUN Furniture is movable objects such as tables, chairs and wardrobes.

**furore**
*Said* "fyoo-**roh**-ree" NOUN an angry and excited reaction or protest.
▦ from Italian *furore* meaning 'rage'

**furrow** furrows furrowing furrowed
NOUN **1** a long, shallow trench made by a plough. ▶ VERB **2** When someone furrows their brow, they frown.

**further** furthers furthering furthered
**1** a comparative form of **far**.
▶ ADJECTIVE **2** additional or more E.G. *There was no further rain.* ▶ VERB **3** If you further something, you help it to progress E.G. *He wants to further his acting career.*
■ (sense 3) advance, promote

**further education**
NOUN Further education is education at a college after leaving school, but not at a university.

**furthermore**
ADVERB; *FORMAL* used to introduce additional information E.G. *There is no record of such a letter. Furthermore it is company policy never to send such letters.*

**furthest**
a superlative form of **far**.

**furtive**
ADJECTIVE secretive, sly, and cautious E.G. *a furtive smile.*
**furtively** ADVERB

**fury**
NOUN Fury is violent or extreme anger.

**fuse** fuses fusing fused
NOUN **1** a safety device in a plug or electrical appliance consisting of a piece of wire which melts to stop the electric current if a fault occurs. **2** a long cord attached to some types of simple bomb which is lit to detonate.
▶ VERB **3** When an electrical appliance fuses, it stops working because the fuse has melted to protect it. **4** If two things fuse, they join or become combined E.G. *Christianity slowly fused with existing beliefs.*

**fuselage** fuselages
*Said* "fyoo-zil-ahj" NOUN the main part of an aeroplane or rocket.

**A**
**B**
**C**
**D**
**E**
**F**
**G**
**H**
**I**
**J**
**K**
**L**
**M**
**N**
**O**
**P**
**Q**
**R**
**S**
**T**
**U**
**V**
**W**
**X**
**Y**
**Z**

## fusion

NOUN 1 Fusion is what happens when two substances join by melting together. 2 Fusion is also nuclear fusion. ▶ ADJECTIVE 3 Fusion is used to refer to food or a style of cooking that brings together ingredients or cooking techniques from several different countries.

## fuss fusses fussing fussed

NOUN 1 Fuss is unnecessarily anxious or excited behaviour. ▶ VERB 2 If someone fusses, they behave with unnecessary anxiety and concern for unimportant things.

▤ (sense 1) bother, commotion, palaver

## fussy fussier fussiest

ADJECTIVE 1 likely to fuss a lot *E.G. He was unusually fussy about keeping things perfect.* 2 with too much elaborate detail or decoration *E.G. fussy chiffon evening wear.*

▤ (sense 1) finicky, particular

## futile

ADJECTIVE having no chance of success *E.G. a futile attempt to calm the storm.*
futility NOUN

▤ useless, vain

## future futures

NOUN 1 The future is the period of time after the present. 2 Something that has a future is likely to succeed *E.G. She sees no future in a modelling career.* ▶ ADJECTIVE 3 relating to or occurring at a time after the present *E.G. to predict future events.* 4 The future tense of a verb is the form used to express something that will happen in the future.

## futuristic

ADJECTIVE very modern and strange, as if belonging to a time in the future *E.G. futuristic cars.*

## fuzz

NOUN 1 short fluffy hair. ▶ PLURAL NOUN 2 INFORMAL The fuzz are the police.

---

### Talking about the Future

There is no simple future tense in English. To talk about an event that will happen in the future, we usually use **compound tenses**.
The auxiliary verbs *will* and *shall* are used before the basic form of the verb to show that an action will happen:

*E.G. His father **will cook** the dinner.*
*I **shall cook** the dinner.*

You can also talk about the future by putting the verbs *will have* or *shall have* before the verb, and adding the ending *-ed*. This form shows that an action will be completed in the future:

*E.G. His father **will have cooked** the dinner.*
*I **shall have cooked** the dinner.*

You can also talk about the future by using the phrase *be about to* or *be going to* in front of the dictionary form of the verb. This shows that the action will take place very soon:

*E.G. He **is about to cook** the dinner.*
*I **am going to cook** the dinner.*

You can sometimes use a form of the present tense to talk about future events, but only if the sentence contains a clear reference to the future:

*E.G. His father **is cooking** the dinner tonight.*
*The plane **leaves** at three o'clock.*

Also see the grammar box at **tense**.

---

# Gg

a
b
c
d
e
f
g
h
i
j
k
l
m
n
o
p
q
r
s
t
u
v
w
x
y
z

**TIP** Some words which sound as if they might begin with *g* alone, are actually spelt with the letters *gh*, for example *ghastly* and *ghost*. Some words which sound as if they might begin with the letter *n*, are spelt with *gn*, for example *gnaw*, *gnome* and *gnu*. Also take care with the spelling of words that start with *gu-* followed by the vowels *a*, *e* or *i*, because the *u* is not pronounced, for example *guarantee*, *guard*, *guerrilla* and *guile*.

**g**
an abbreviation for 'grams'.

**gabble** gabbles gabbling gabbled
VERB If you gabble, you talk so fast that it is difficult for people to understand you.

**gable** gables
NOUN Gables are the triangular parts at the top of the outside walls at each end of a house.

**gadget** gadgets
NOUN a small machine or tool.
**gadgetry** NOUN
▬ contraption, device

**Gaelic**
*Said* "**gay**-lik" NOUN a language spoken in some parts of Scotland and Ireland.

**gaffe** gaffes
*Said* "**gaf**" NOUN a social blunder or mistake.

**gaffer** gaffers
NOUN; *INFORMAL* a boss.

**gag** gags gagging gagged
NOUN 1 a strip of cloth that is tied round someone's mouth to stop them speaking. 2 *INFORMAL* a joke told by a comedian. ▶ VERB 3 To gag someone means to put a gag round their mouth. 4 If you gag, you choke and nearly vomit.

**gaggle** gaggles
NOUN 1 a group of geese. 2 *INFORMAL* a

noisy group *E.G. a gaggle of schoolboys.*
🏛 from Old German *gagen* meaning 'to cry like a goose'

**gaiety**
*Said* "**gay**-yet-tee" NOUN liveliness and fun.

**gaily**
ADVERB in a happy and cheerful way.

**gain** gains gaining gained
VERB 1 If you gain something, you get it gradually *E.G. I spent years at night school trying to gain qualifications.* 2 If you gain from a situation, you get some advantage from it. 3 If you gain on someone, you gradually catch them up. ▶ NOUN 4 an increase *E.G. a gain in speed.* 5 an advantage that you get for yourself *E.G. People use whatever influence they have for personal gain.*

**gait** gaits
NOUN Someone's gait is their way of walking *E.G. an awkward gait.*

**gala** galas
NOUN a special public celebration or performance *E.G. the Olympics' opening gala.*

**galah** galahs
NOUN 1 an Australian cockatoo with a pink breast and a grey back and wings. 2 *INFORMAL* In Australian

English, a galah is also a stupid person.

**galaxy** galaxies
NOUN an enormous group of stars that extends over many millions of miles.
**galactic** ADJECTIVE

**gale** gales
NOUN an extremely strong wind.

**gall** galls galling galled
*Rhymes with "ball"* NOUN 1 If someone has the gall to do something, they have enough courage or impudence to do it *E.G. He even has the gall to visit her.* ▶ VERB 2 If something galls you, it makes you extremely annoyed.

**gall bladder** gall bladders
NOUN an organ in your body which stores bile and which is next to your liver.

**galleon** galleons
NOUN a large sailing ship used in the sixteenth and seventeenth centuries.

**gallery** galleries
NOUN 1 (ART) a building or room where works of art are shown. 2 In a theatre or large hall, the gallery is a raised area at the back or sides *E.G. the public gallery in Parliament.*

**galley** galleys
NOUN 1 a kitchen in a ship or aircraft. 2 a ship, driven by oars, used in ancient and medieval times.

**Gallic**
*Said "gal-lik"* ADJECTIVE; *FORMAL or LITERARY* French.

**gallon** gallons
NOUN a unit of liquid volume equal to eight pints or about 4.55 litres.

**gallop** gallops galloping galloped
VERB 1 When a horse gallops, it runs very fast, so that during each stride

all four feet are off the ground at the same time. ▶ NOUN 2 a very fast run.

**gallows**
NOUN A gallows is a framework on which criminals used to be hanged.

**gallstone** gallstones
NOUN a small painful lump that can develop in your gall bladder.

**galore**
ADJECTIVE in very large numbers *E.G. chocolates galore.*
📖 from Irish Gaelic *go leór* meaning 'to sufficiency'

**galoshes**
PLURAL NOUN Galoshes are waterproof rubber shoes which you wear over your ordinary shoes to stop them getting wet.

**galvanized** or **galvanised**
ADJECTIVE Galvanized metal has been coated with zinc by an electrical process to protect it from rust.

**gambit** gambits
NOUN something which someone does to gain an advantage in a situation *E.G. Commentators are calling the plan a clever political gambit.*
📖 from Italian *gambetto* meaning 'a tripping up'

**gamble** gambles gambling gambled
VERB 1 When people gamble, they bet money on the result of a game or race. 2 If you gamble something, you risk losing it in the hope of gaining an advantage *E.G. The company gambled everything on the new factory.* ▶ NOUN 3 If you take a gamble, you take a risk in the hope of gaining an advantage.
**gambler** NOUN **gambling** NOUN
▣ (sense 1) bet, wager

**game** games
NOUN **1** an enjoyable activity with a set of rules which is played by individuals or teams against each other. **2** an enjoyable imaginative activity played by small children E.G. childhood games of cowboys and Indians. **3** You might describe something as a game when it is designed to gain advantage E.G. the political game. **4** Game is wild animals or birds that are hunted for sport or for food. ▶ PLURAL NOUN **5** Games are sports played at school or in a competition. ▶ ADJECTIVE **6** INFORMAL Someone who is game is willing to try something unusual or difficult.
**gamely** ADVERB
■ (sense 1) amusement, pastime

**gamekeeper** gamekeepers
NOUN a person employed to look after game animals and birds on a country estate.

**gammon**
NOUN Gammon is cured meat from a pig, similar to bacon.

**gamut**
Said "**gam**-mut" NOUN; FORMAL The gamut of something is the whole range of things that can be included in it E.G. the whole gamut of human emotions.

**gander** ganders
NOUN a male goose.

**gang** gangs ganging ganged
NOUN **1** a group of people who join together for some purpose, for example to commit a crime. ▶ VERB **2** INFORMAL If people gang up on you, they join together to oppose you.

**gangplank** gangplanks
NOUN a plank used for boarding and leaving a ship or boat.

**gangrene**
Said "**gang**-green" NOUN Gangrene is decay in the tissues of part of the body, caused by inadequate blood supply.
**gangrenous** ADJECTIVE
🔲 from Greek gangraina meaning 'ulcer' or 'festering sore'

**gangster** gangsters
NOUN a violent criminal who is a member of a gang.

**gannet** gannets
NOUN a large sea bird which dives to catch fish.

**gaol**
another spelling of **jail**.

**gap** gaps
NOUN **1** a space between two things or a hole in something solid. **2** A gap between things, people, or ideas is a great difference between them E.G. the gap between fantasy and reality.
■ (sense 1) hole, opening, space

**gape** gapes gaping gaped
VERB **1** If you gape at someone or something, you stare at them with your mouth open in surprise. **2** Something that gapes is wide open E.G. gaping holes in the wall.

**garage** garages
NOUN **1** a building where a car can be kept. **2** a place where cars are repaired and where petrol is sold.

**garb**
NOUN; FORMAL Someone's garb is their clothes E.G. his usual garb of a dark suit.

**garbage**
NOUN **1** Garbage is rubbish, especially household rubbish. **2** If you say something is garbage, you mean it is nonsense.

a
b
c
d
e
f
g
h
i
j
k
l
m
n
o
p
q
r
s
t
u
v
w
x
y
z

LEt's measure the angLE (ang<u>le</u>)    SPELLING NOTE

A B C D E F **G** H I J K L M N O P Q R S T U V W X Y Z

from Anglo-French *garbelage* meaning 'removal of discarded matter'

**garbled**

ADJECTIVE Garbled messages are jumbled and the details may be wrong.

**garden gardens**

NOUN **1** an area of land next to a house, where flowers, fruit, or vegetables are grown. ► PLURAL NOUN **2** Gardens are a type of park in a town or around a large house.

**gardening** NOUN

**gardener gardeners**

NOUN a person who looks after a garden as a job or as a hobby.

**gargle gargles gargling gargled**

VERB When you gargle, you rinse the back of your throat by putting some liquid in your mouth and making a bubbling sound without swallowing the liquid.

**gargoyle gargoyles**

NOUN a stone carving below the roof of an old building, in the shape of an ugly person or animal and often having a water spout at the mouth.

**garish**

*Said "gair-rish"* ADJECTIVE bright and harsh to look at E.G. *garish bright red boots*.

**garland garlands**

NOUN a circle of flowers and leaves which is worn around the neck or head.

**garlic**

NOUN Garlic is the small white bulb of an onion-like plant which has a strong taste and smell and is used in cooking.

**garment garments**

NOUN a piece of clothing.

**garnet garnets**

NOUN a type of gemstone, usually red in colour.

**garnish garnishes garnishing garnished**

NOUN **1** something such as a a sprig of parsley, that is used in cooking for decoration. ► VERB **2** To garnish food means to decorate it with a garnish.

**garret garrets**

NOUN an attic.

**garrison garrisons**

NOUN a group of soldiers stationed in a town in order to guard it; also used of the buildings in which these soldiers live.

**garrotte garrottes garrotting garrotted**

*Said "gar-rot"*; also spelt **garotte** VERB To garrotte someone means to strangle them with a piece of wire.

**garter garters**

NOUN a piece of elastic worn round the top of a stocking to hold it up.

**gas gases; gasses gassing gassed**

NOUN **1** any airlike substance that is not liquid or solid, such as oxygen or the gas used as a fuel in heating. **2** In American English, gas is petrol. ► VERB **3** To gas people or animals means to kill them with poisonous gas.

☑ The plural of the noun *gas* is *gases*. The verb forms of *gas* are spelt with a double s.

**gas chamber gas chambers**

NOUN a room in which people or animals are killed with poisonous gas.

**gash gashes gashing gashed**

NOUN **1** a long, deep cut. ► VERB **2** If you gash something, you make a long, deep cut in it.

**gas mask** gas masks
NOUN a large mask with special filters attached which people wear over their face to protect them from poisonous gas.

**gasoline**
NOUN In American English, gasoline is petrol.

**gasp** gasps gasping gasped
VERB 1 If you gasp, you quickly draw in your breath through your mouth because you are surprised or in pain. ► NOUN 2 a sharp intake of breath through the mouth.

**gastric**
ADJECTIVE occurring in the stomach or involving the stomach E.G. *gastric pain*.

**gate** gates
NOUN 1 a barrier which can open and shut and is used to close the entrance to a garden or field. 2 The gate at a sports event is the number of people who have attended it.

**gateau** gateaux
*Said* "**gat-toe**" NOUN a rich layered cake with cream in it.

**gatecrash** gatecrashes gatecrashing gatecrashed
VERB If you gatecrash a party, you go to it when you have not been invited.

**gateway** gateways
NOUN 1 an entrance through a wall or fence where there is a gate.
2 Something that is considered to be the entrance to a larger or more important thing can be described as the gateway to the larger thing E.G. *New York is the great gateway to America*.

**gather** gathers gathering gathered
VERB 1 When people gather, they come together in a group. 2 If you gather a number of things, you bring them together in one place. 3 If something gathers speed or strength, it gets faster or stronger. 4 If you gather something, you learn it, often from what someone says.
■ (sense 1) assemble, congregate
■ (sense 2) amass, assemble, collect

**gathering** gatherings
NOUN a meeting of people who have come together for a particular purpose.

**gauche**
*Said* "**gohsh**" ADJECTIVE; *FORMAL* socially awkward.
▥ from French *gauche* meaning 'left-handed'

**gaudy** gaudier gaudiest
*Said* "**gaw-dee**" ADJECTIVE very colourful in a vulgar way.
■ bright, flashy, garish

**gauge** gauges gauging gauged
*Said* "**gayj**" VERB 1 If you gauge something, you estimate it or calculate it E.G. *He gauged the wind at over 30 knots.* ► NOUN 2 a piece of equipment that measures the amount of something E.G. *a rain gauge.* 3 something that is used as a standard by which you judge a situation E.G. *They see profit as a gauge of efficiency.* 4 On railways, the gauge is the distance between the two rails on a railway line.

**gaunt**
ADJECTIVE A person who looks gaunt is thin and bony.

**gauntlet** gauntlets
NOUN 1 Gauntlets are long thick gloves worn for protection, for example by motorcyclists. ► PHRASE

a b c d e f **g** h i j k l m n o p q r s t u v w x y z

**2** If you **throw down the gauntlet**, you challenge someone. **3** If you **run the gauntlet**, you have an unpleasant experience in which you are attacked or criticized by people.

**gave**
the past tense of **give**.

**gay gayer gayest; gays**
ADJECTIVE **1** Someone who is gay is homosexual. **2** *OLD-FASHIONED* Gay people or places are lively and full of fun. ▶ NOUN **3** a homosexual person
☑ The most common meaning of *gay* now is 'homosexual'. In some older books it may have its old-fashioned meaning of 'lively and full of fun'. The noun *gaiety* is related to this older meaning of *gay*. The noun that means 'the state of being homosexual' is *gayness*.

**gaze gazes gazing gazed**
VERB If you gaze at something, you look steadily at it for a long time.

**gazelle gazelles**
NOUN a small antelope found in Africa and Asia.

**gazette gazettes**
NOUN a newspaper or journal.

**GB**
an abbreviation for **Great Britain**.

**GCSE GCSEs**
In Britain, the GCSE is an examination taken by school students aged fifteen and sixteen. GCSE is an abbreviation for 'General Certificate of Secondary Education'.

**gear gears gearing geared**
NOUN **1** a piece of machinery which controls the rate at which energy is converted into movement. Gears in vehicles control the speed and power of the vehicle. **2** The gear for an activity is the clothes and

equipment that you need for it.
▶ VERB **3** If someone or something is geared to a particular event or purpose, they are prepared for it.

**geek geeks**; *INFORMAL*
NOUN a person who is obsessive about an interest or hobby, especially computers.

**geese**
the plural of **goose**.

**gel gels gelling gelled**
*Said* "jel" NOUN **1** a smooth soft jelly-like substance *E.G. shower gel*. ▶ VERB **2** If a liquid gels, it turns into a gel. **3** If a vague thought or plan gels, it becomes more definite.

**gelatine** or **gelatin**
*Said* "jel-lat-tin" NOUN a clear tasteless substance, obtained from meat and bones, used to make liquids firm and jelly-like.

**gelding geldings**
*Said* "gel-ding" NOUN a horse which has been castrated.

**gem gems**
NOUN **1** a jewel or precious stone. **2** You can describe something or someone that is extremely good or beautiful as a gem *E.G. A gem of a novel*.

**Gemini**
*Said* "jem-in-nye" NOUN Gemini is the third sign of the zodiac, represented by a pair of twins. People born between May 21st and June 20th are born under this sign

**gemsbok gemsbok** or **gemsboks**; also spelt **gemsbuck**
NOUN In South African English, a gemsbok is an oryx, a type of large antelope with straight horns.

**gen**
NOUN; *INFORMAL* The gen on something is information about it.

**gender** genders

NOUN 1 (PSHE) Gender is the sex of a person or animal E.G. *the female gender.* 2 the classification of nouns as masculine, feminine, and neuter in certain languages.

---

### What is Gender?

When we talk about the "gender" of a noun, we mean whether it is referred to as *he*, *she*, or *it*. There are three genders: **masculine** (things referred to as *he*), **feminine** (things referred to as *she*), and **neuter** (things referred to as *it*).

**Masculine nouns** refer to male people and animals:

E.G. *The boy put on his coat.* ➤ *boy is masculine*

**Feminine nouns** denote female people and animals:

E.G. *The girl put on her coat.* ➤ *girl is feminine*

It is customary to refer to countries and vehicles as if they were feminine:

E.G. *The ship came into view, her sails swelling in the breeze.*

**Neuter nouns** refer to inanimate objects and abstract ideas:

E.G. *The kettle will switch itself off.* ➤ *kettle is neuter*

**Common nouns** may be either masculine or feminine. Other words in the sentence may tell us if they are male or female:

E.G. *The doctor parked his car. The doctor parked her car.*

---

**gene** genes

*Said* "jeen" NOUN one of the parts of a living cell which controls the physical characteristics of an organism and which are passed on from one generation to the next.

**general** generals

ADJECTIVE 1 relating to the whole of something or to most things in a group E.G. *your general health.* 2 true, suitable, or relevant in most situations E.G. *the general truth of science.* 3 including or involving a wide range of different things E.G. *a general hospital.* 4 having complete responsibility over a wide area of work or a large number of people E.G. *the general secretary.* ➤ NOUN 5 an army officer of very high rank.

➤ PHRASE 6 In general means usually.

**generally** ADVERB

■ (sense 1) overall

■ (sense 2) common, universal, widespread

**general election** general elections

NOUN an election for a new government, which all the people of a country may vote in.

**generalize** generalizes generalizing generalized; also spelt **generalise**

VERB To generalize means to say that something is true in most cases, ignoring minor details.

**generalization** NOUN

**general practitioner** general practitioners

NOUN a doctor who works in the community rather than in a hospital.

**generate** generates generating generated

VERB To generate something means to create or produce it E.G. *using wind power to generate electricity.*

---

there's a rAKE in the brAKEs (br<u>ake</u>)    ▶ SPELLING NOTE

**generation** generations
NOUN all the people of about the same age; also the period of time between one generation and the next, usually considered to be about 25–30 years.

**generator** generators
NOUN a machine which produces electricity from another form of energy such as wind or water power.

**generic**
ADJECTIVE A generic term is a name that applies to all the members of a group of similar things.

**generous**
ADJECTIVE 1 (PSHE) A generous person is very willing to give money or time. 2 Something that is generous is very large E.G. a generous waist.
**generously** ADVERB **generosity** NOUN (PSHE)
■ (sense 1) lavish, liberal
■ (sense 2) abundant, ample, lavish

**genesis**
NOUN; FORMAL The genesis of something is its beginning.

**genetics**
NOUN Genetics is the science of the way that characteristics are passed on from generation to generation by means of genes.
**genetic** ADJECTIVE **genetically** ADVERB

**genial**
ADJECTIVE cheerful, friendly, and kind.
**genially** ADVERB

**genie** genies
Said "jee-nee" NOUN a magical being that obeys the wishes of the person who controls it.
🔲 from Arabic jinni meaning 'demon'

**genitals**
PLURAL NOUN The genitals are the reproductive organs. The technical name is genitalia.
**genital** ADJECTIVE

**genius** geniuses
NOUN 1 a highly intelligent, creative, or talented person. 2 Genius is great intelligence, creativity, or talent E.G. a poet of genius.

**genocide**
Said "jen-nos-side" NOUN; FORMAL Genocide is the systematic murder of all members of a particular race or group.

**genome** genomes
Said "jee-nome" NOUN all of the genes contained in a single cell of an organism.

**genre** genres
Said "jahn-ra" NOUN (ENGLISH) (LIBRARY) FORMAL a particular style in literature or art.

**genteel**
ADJECTIVE very polite and refined.

**Gentile** Gentiles
Said "jen-tile" NOUN a person who is not Jewish.

**gentility**
NOUN Gentility is excessive politeness and refinement.

**gentle** gentler gentlest
ADJECTIVE mild and calm; not violent or rough E.G. a gentle man.
**gently** ADVERB **gentleness** NOUN

**gentleman** gentlemen
NOUN a man who is polite and well-educated; also a polite way of referring to any man.
**gentlemanly** ADJECTIVE

**gentry**
PLURAL NOUN The gentry are people from the upper classes.

**genuine**
Said "jen-yoo-in" ADJECTIVE 1 real and

not false or pretend *E.G. a genuine smile… genuine silver.* **2** A genuine person is sincere and honest.
**genuinely** ADVERB **genuineness** NOUN

**genus genera**
*Said* "jee-nuss" NOUN In biology, a genus is a class of animals or closely related plants.

**geo-**
PREFIX 'Geo-' means 'earth' *E.G. geography… geologist.*
🔟 from Greek *gē* meaning 'earth'

**geography**
NOUN the study of the physical features of the earth, together with the climate, natural resources and population in different parts of the world.
**geographic** or **geographical** ADJECTIVE **geographically** ADVERB

**geology**
NOUN the study of the earth's structure, especially the layers of rock and soil that make up the surface of the earth.
**geological** ADJECTIVE **geologist** NOUN

**geometric** or **geometrical**
ADJECTIVE **1** consisting of regular lines and shapes, such as squares, triangles, and circles *E.G. bold geometric designs.* **2** involving geometry.

**geometry**
NOUN Geometry is the branch of mathematics that deals with lines, angles, curves, and spaces.

**Georgian**
ADJECTIVE belonging to or typical of the time from 1714 to 1830, when George I to George IV reigned in Britain.

**geranium geraniums**
NOUN a garden plant with red, pink, or white flowers.

**gerbil gerbils**
*Said* "jer-bil" NOUN a small rodent with long back legs, often kept as a pet

**geriatric**
*Said* "jer-ree-**at**-rik" ADJECTIVE **1** relating to the medical care of old people *E.G. a geriatric nurse.* **2** Someone or something that is geriatric is very old *E.G. a geriatric donkey.* ▶ NOUN **3** an old person, especially as a patient.
**geriatrics** NOUN

**germ germs**
NOUN **1** a very small organism that causes disease. **2** FORMAL The germ of an idea or plan is the beginning of it.

**German Germans**
ADJECTIVE **1** belonging or relating to Germany. ▶ NOUN **2** someone who comes from Germany. **3** German is the main language spoken in Germany and Austria and is also spoken by many people in Switzerland.

**Germanic**
ADJECTIVE **1** typical of Germany or the German people. **2** The Germanic group of languages includes English, Dutch, German, Danish, Swedish, and Norwegian.

**German measles**
NOUN German measles is a contagious disease that gives you a sore throat and red spots.

**germinate germinates germinating germinated**
VERB **1** When a seed germinates, it starts to grow. **2** When an idea or plan germinates, it starts to develop.
**germination** NOUN

**gerrymander gerrymanders gerrymandering gerrymandered**
VERB To gerrymander is to change political boundaries in an area so

a b c d e f g h i j k l m n o p q r s t u v w x y z

I always visit my FRIend on a FRIday (friend)  SPELLING NOTE that a particular party or politician gets a bigger share of votes in an election.

**gestation**
Said "jes-**tay**-shn" NOUN; TECHNICAL
Gestation is the time during which a foetus is growing inside its mother's womb.

**gesticulate gesticulates gesticulating gesticulated**
Said "jes-**stik**-yoo-late" VERB If you gesticulate, you move your hands and arms around while you are talking.
**gesticulation** NOUN

**gesture gestures gesturing gestured**
NOUN 1 a movement of your hands or head that conveys a message or feeling. 2 an action symbolizing something E.G. *a gesture of support.*
▶ VERB 3 If you gesture, you move your hands or head in order to communicate a message or feeling.

**get gets getting got**
VERB 1 Get often means the same as become E.G. *People draw the curtains once it gets dark.* 2 If you get into a particular situation, you put yourself in that situation E.G. *We are going to get into a hopeless muddle.* 3 If you get something done, you do it or you persuade someone to do it E.G. *You can get your homework done in time.* 4 If you get somewhere, you go there E.G. *I must get home.* 5 If you get something, you fetch it or are given it E.G. *I'll get us all a cup of coffee… I got your message.* 6 If you get a joke or get the point of something, you understand it. 7 If you get a train, bus, or plane, you travel on it E.G. *You can get a bus.*
▤ (sense 1) become, grow

▤ (sense 5) acquire, obtain, procure
**get across** VERB If you get an idea across, you make people understand it.
**get at** VERB 1 If someone is getting at you, they are criticizing you in an unkind way. 2 If you ask someone what they are getting at, you are asking them to explain what they mean.
**get away with** VERB If you get away with something dishonest, you are not found out or punished for doing it.
**get by** VERB If you get by, you have just enough money to live on.
**get on** VERB 1 If two people get on well together, they like each other's company. 2 If you get on with a task, you do it.
**get over with** VERB If you want to get something unpleasant over with, you want it to be finished quickly.
**get through** VERB 1 If you get through to someone, you make them understand what you are saying. 2 If you get through to someone on the telephone, you succeed in talking to them.
**getaway getaways**
NOUN an escape made by criminals.
**get-together get-togethers**
NOUN; INFORMAL an informal meeting or party.
**geyser geysers**
Said "**gee**-zer" NOUN a spring through which hot water and steam gush up in spurts.
▥ from Old Norse *geysa* meaning 'to gush'
**Ghanaian Ghanaians**
Said "gah-**nay**-an" ADJECTIVE
1 belonging or relating to Ghana.
▶ NOUN 2 someone who comes from Ghana.

**ghastly** ghastlier ghastliest
ADJECTIVE extremely horrible and
unpleasant E.G. *a ghastly crime…'
ghastly food*.

**gherkin** gherkins
NOUN a small pickled cucumber.

**ghetto** ghettoes or ghettos
NOUN a part of a city where many
poor people of a particular race live.
🏛 from Italian *borghetto* meaning
'settlement outside the city
walls'

**ghost** ghosts
NOUN the spirit of a dead person,
believed to haunt people or places.
🔲 phantom, spectre, spirit

**ghoulish**
*Said "gool-ish"* ADJECTIVE very
interested in unpleasant things such
as death and murder.

**giant** giants
NOUN 1 a huge person in a myth or
legend. ▶ ADJECTIVE 2 much larger than
other similar things E.G. *giant
prawns… a giant wave*.

**gibberish**
NOUN Gibberish is speech that makes
no sense at all.

**gibbon** gibbons
NOUN an ape with very long arms.

**gibe** gibes; also spelt **jibe**
NOUN an insulting remark.

**giddy** giddier giddiest
ADJECTIVE If you feel giddy, you feel
unsteady on your feet usually
because you are ill.
**giddily** ADVERB

**gift** gifts
NOUN 1 a present. 2 a natural skill or
ability E.G. *a gift for comedy*.

**gifted**
ADJECTIVE having a special ability E.G.
*gifted tennis players*.

**gig** gigs
NOUN a rock or jazz concert.

**gigantic**
ADJECTIVE extremely large.

**giggle** giggles giggling giggled
VERB 1 To giggle means to laugh in a
nervous or embarrassed way. ▶ NOUN
2 a short, nervous laugh.
**giggly** ADJECTIVE

**gilded**
ADJECTIVE Something which is gilded is
covered with a thin layer of gold.

**gill** gills
NOUN 1 *Said "gil"* The gills of a fish are
the organs on its sides which it uses
for breathing. 2 *Said "jil"* a unit of
liquid volume equal to one quarter
of a pint or about 0.142 litres.

**gilt** gilts
NOUN 1 a thin layer of gold. ▶ ADJECTIVE
2 covered with a thin layer of gold
E.G. *a gilt writing-table*.

**gimmick** gimmicks
NOUN a device that is not really
necessary but is used to attract interest
E.G. *All pop stars need a good gimmick*.
**gimmicky** ADJECTIVE

**gin**
NOUN Gin is a strong, colourless
alcoholic drink made from grain and
juniper berries.

**ginger**
NOUN 1 Ginger is a plant root with a
hot, spicy flavour, used in·cooking.
▶ ADJECTIVE 2 bright orange or red E.G.
*ginger hair*.

**gingerbread**
NOUN Gingerbread is a sweet, ginger-
flavoured cake.

**gingerly**
ADVERB If you move gingerly, you
move cautiously E.G. *They walked
gingerly down the stairs*.

a
b
c
d
e
f
g
h
i
j
k
l
m
n
o
p
q
r
s
t
u
v
w
x
y
z

A B C D E F G H I J K L M N O P Q R S T U V W X Y Z

**gingham**
NOUN Gingham is checked cotton cloth.
from Malay *ginggang* meaning 'striped cloth'

**gipsy**
another spelling of **gypsy**.

**giraffe** giraffes
NOUN a tall, four-legged African mammal with a very long neck.
from Arabic *zarafah* meaning 'giraffe'

**girder** girders
NOUN a large metal beam used in the construction of a bridge or a building.

**girdle** girdles
NOUN a woman's corset.

**girl** girls
NOUN a female child.
**girlish** ADJECTIVE **girlhood** NOUN

**girlfriend** girlfriends
NOUN Someone's girlfriend is the woman or girl with whom they are having a romantic or sexual relationship.

**giro** giros
*Said* "**jie-roh**" NOUN 1 Giro is a system of transferring money from one account to another through a bank or post office. 2 In Britain, a cheque received regularly from the government by unemployed or sick people.

**girth**
NOUN The girth of something is the measurement round it.

**gist**
*Said* "**jist**" NOUN the general meaning or most important points in a piece of writing or speech.

**give** gives giving gave given
VERB 1 If you give someone something, you hand it to them or provide it for them *E.G. I gave her a*
tape… *George gave me my job.*
2 'Give' is also used to express physical actions and speech *E.G. He gave a fierce smile… Rosa gave a lovely performance.* 3 If you give a party or a meal, you are the host at it. 4 If something gives, it collapses under pressure. ▶ NOUN 5 If material has give, it will bend or stretch when pulled or put under pressure. ▶ PHRASE 6 You use **give or take** to indicate that an amount you are mentioning is not exact *E.G. About two years, give or take a month or so.* 7 If something **gives way** to something else, it is replaced by it. 8 If something **gives way**, it collapses.
(sense 1) grant, present, provide

**give in** VERB If you give in, you admit that you are defeated.

**give out** VERB If something gives out, it stops working *E.G. the electricity gave out.*

**give up** VERB 1 If you give something up, you stop doing it *E.G. I can't give up my job.* 2 If you give up, you admit that you cannot do something. 3 If you give someone up, you let the police know where they are hiding.

**given**
1 the past participle of **give**.
▶ ADJECTIVE 2 fixed or specified *E.G. My style can change at any given moment.*

**glacé**
*Said* "**glass-say**" ADJECTIVE Glacé fruits are fruits soaked and coated with sugar *E.G. glacé cherries.*

**glaciation**
*Said* "**glay-see-ay-shn**" NOUN In geography, glaciation is the condition of being covered with sheet ice.

**glacier** glaciers
*Said* "**glass-yer**" NOUN a huge frozen river of slow-moving ice.

**glad** gladder gladdest

ADJECTIVE happy and pleased E.G. *They'll be glad to get away from it all.*
**gladly** ADVERB    **gladness** NOUN

**glade** glades

NOUN a grassy space in a forest.

**gladiator** gladiators

NOUN In ancient Rome, gladiators were slaves trained to fight in arenas to provide entertainment.

📖 from Latin *gladius* meaning 'sword'

**gladiolus** gladioli

NOUN a garden plant with spikes of brightly coloured flowers on a long stem.

**glamour**

NOUN The glamour of a fashionable or attractive person or place is the charm and excitement that they have E.G. *the glamour of Paris.*
**glamorous** ADJECTIVE

**glance** glances glancing glanced

VERB 1 If you glance at something, you look at it quickly. 2 If one object glances off another, it hits it at an angle and bounces away in another direction. ▶ NOUN 3 a quick look.

**gland** glands

NOUN an organs in your body, such as the thyroid gland and the sweat glands, which either produce chemical substances for your body to use, or which help to get rid of waste products from your body.
**glandular** ADJECTIVE

**glare** glares glaring glared

VERB 1 If you glare at someone, you look at them angrily. ▶ NOUN 2 a hard, angry look. 3 Glare is extremely bright light.

**glass** glasses

NOUN 1 Glass is a hard, transparent substance that is easily broken, used to make windows and bottles. 2 a container for drinking out of, made from glass.

**glasses**

PLURAL NOUN Glasses are two lenses in a frame, which some people wear over their eyes to improve their eyesight.

**glassy**

ADJECTIVE 1 smooth and shiny like glass E.G. *glassy water.* 2 A glassy look shows no feeling or expression.

**glaze** glazes glazing glazed

NOUN 1 A glaze on pottery or on food is a smooth shiny surface. ▶ VERB 2 To glaze pottery or food means to cover it with a glaze. 3 To glaze a window means to fit a sheet of glass into a window frame.

**glaze over** VERB If your eyes glaze over, they lose all expression, usually because you are bored.

**glazed**

ADJECTIVE Someone who has a glazed expression looks bored.

**gleam** gleams gleaming gleamed

VERB 1 If something gleams, it shines and reflects light. ▶ NOUN 2 a pale shining light.

**glean** gleans gleaning gleaned

VERB To glean information means to collect it from various sources.

**glee**

NOUN; OLD-FASHIONED Glee is joy and delight.
**gleeful** ADJECTIVE    **gleefully** ADVERB

**glen** glens

NOUN a deep, narrow valley, especially in Scotland or Ireland.

**glide** glides gliding glided

VERB 1 To glide means to move smoothly E.G. *cygnets gliding up the*

a
b
c
d
e
f
**g**
h
i
j
k
l
m
n
o
p
q
r
s
t
u
v
w
x
y
z

Plaice the fish has a glittering 'EYE' (I) (plaice)    SPELLING NOTE

*stream.* 2 When birds or aeroplanes glide, they float on air currents.

**glider** gliders

NOUN an aeroplane without an engine, which flies by floating on air currents.

**glimmer** glimmers glimmering glimmered

NOUN 1 a faint, unsteady light. 2 A glimmer of a feeling or quality is a faint sign of it *E.G. a glimmer of intelligence.*

**glimpse** glimpses glimpsing glimpsed

NOUN 1 a brief sight of something *E.G. They caught a glimpse of their hero.*
► VERB 2 If you glimpse something, you see it very briefly.

**glint** glints glinting glinted

VERB 1 If something glints, it reflects quick flashes of light. ► NOUN 2 a quick flash of light. 3 A glint in someone's eye is a brightness expressing some emotion *E.G. A glint of mischief in her blue-grey eyes.*

**glisten** glistens glistening glistened

*Said "gliss-sn"* VERB If something glistens, it shines or sparkles.

**glitter** glitters glittering glittered

VERB 1 If something glitters, it shines in a sparkling way *E.G. a glittering crown.* ► NOUN 2 Glitter is sparkling light.

**gloat** gloats gloating gloated

VERB If you gloat, you cruelly show your pleasure about your own success or someone else's failure. *E.G. Their rivals were gloating over their triumph.*

**global**

ADJECTIVE concerning the whole world *E.G. a global tour.*

**globalization**

NOUN 1 the process by which a company expands so that it can do business internationally. 2 the process by which cultures throughout the world become more and more similar for a variety of reasons including increased global business and better international communications.

**global warming**

NOUN an increase in the world's overall temperature believed to be caused by the greenhouse effect

**globe** globes

NOUN 1 a ball-shaped object, especially one with a map of the earth on it. 2 (GEOGRAPHY) You can refer to the world as the globe. 3 In South African, Australian, and New Zealand English, a globe is an electric light bulb.

**gloom**

NOUN 1 Gloom is darkness or dimness. 2 Gloom is also a feeling of unhappiness or despair.
**gloomy** ADJECTIVE **gloomily** ADVERB

**glorify** glorifies glorifying glorified

VERB If you glorify someone or something, you make them seem better than they really are *E.G. Their aggressive music glorifies violence.*
**glorification** NOUN

**glorious**

ADJECTIVE 1 beautiful and impressive to look at *E.G. glorious beaches.* 2 very pleasant and giving a feeling of happiness *E.G. glorious sunshine.* 3 involving great fame and success *E.G. a glorious career.*
**gloriously** ADVERB

**SPELLING NOTE** I went to see (C) the doctor's new practiCe (practice)

**glory** glories glorying gloried
NOUN **1** Glory is fame and admiration for an achievement. **2** something considered splendid or admirable *E.G. the true glories of the Alps.* ▶ VERB **3** If you glory in something, you take great delight in it.

**glory box** glory boxes
NOUN; OLD-FASHIONED In Australian and New Zealand English, a chest in which a young woman stores household goods and linen for her marriage.

**gloss** glosses glossing glossed
NOUN **1** Gloss is a bright shine on a surface. **2** Gloss is also an attractive appearance which may hide less attractive qualities *E.G. to put a positive gloss on the events.* **3** If you gloss over a problem or fault, you try to ignore it or deal with it very quickly.

**glossary** glossaries
NOUN (LIBRARY) a list of explanations of specialist words, usually found at the back of a book.

**glossy** glossier glossiest
ADJECTIVE **1** smooth and shiny *E.G. glossy lipstick.* **2** Glossy magazines and photographs are produced on expensive, shiny paper.
■ (sense 1) lustrous, shiny

**glove** gloves
NOUN Gloves are coverings which you wear over your hands for warmth or protection.

**glow** glows glowing glowed
VERB **1** If something glows, it shines with a dull, steady light *E.G. A light glowed behind the curtains.* **2** If you are glowing, you look very happy or healthy. ▶ NOUN **3** a dull, steady light. **4** a strong feeling of pleasure or happiness.

**glower** glowers glowering glowered
*Rhymes with "shower"* VERB If you glower, you stare angrily.
■ glare, scowl

**glowing**
ADJECTIVE A glowing description praises someone or something very highly. *E.G. a glowing character reference.*

**glucose**
NOUN Glucose is a type of sugar found in plants and that animals and people make in their bodies from food to provide energy.

**glue** glues gluing or glueing glued
NOUN **1** a substance used for sticking things together. ▶ VERB **2** If you glue one object to another, you stick them together using glue.

**glum** glummer glummest
ADJECTIVE miserable and depressed.
**glumly** ADVERB

**glut** gluts
NOUN a greater quantity of things than is needed.

**gluten**
*Said "gloo-ten"* NOUN a sticky protein found in cereal grains, such as wheat.

**glutton** gluttons
NOUN **1** a person who eats too much. **2** If you are a glutton for something, such as punishment or hard work, you seem very eager for it.
**gluttony** NOUN

**gnarled**
*Said "narld"* ADJECTIVE old, twisted, and rough *E.G. gnarled fingers.*

**gnat** gnats
*Said "nat"* NOUN a tiny flying insect that bites.

**gnaw** gnaws gnawing gnawed
*Said "naw"* VERB **1** To gnaw something

a b c d e f **g** h i j k l m n o p q r s t u v w x y z

A B C D E F G H I J K L M N O P Q R S T U V W X Y Z

means to bite at it repeatedly. **2** If a feeling gnaws at you, it keeps worrying you *E.G. a question gnawed at him.*

**gnome gnomes**
*Said "nome"* NOUN a tiny old man in fairy stories.

**gnu gnus**
*Said "noo"* NOUN a large African antelope.

**go goes going went gone**
VERB **1** If you go somewhere, you move or travel there. **2** You can use 'go' to mean become *E.G. She felt she was going mad.* **3** You can use 'go' to describe the state that someone or something is in *E.G. Our arrival went unnoticed.* **4** If something goes well, it is successful. If it goes badly, it is unsuccessful. **5** If you are going to do something, you will do it. **6** If a machine or clock goes, it works and is not broken. **7** You use 'go' before giving the sound something makes or before quoting a song or saying *E.G. The bell goes ding-dong.* **8** If something goes on something or to someone, it is allotted to them. **9** If one thing goes with another, they are appropriate together. **10** If one number goes into another, it can be divided into it. **11** If you go back on a promise or agreement, you do not do what you promised or agreed. **12** If someone goes for you, they attack you. **13** If you go in for something, you decide to do it as your job. **14** If you go out with someone, you have a romantic relationship with them. **15** If you go over something, you think about it or discuss it carefully. ▶ NOUN **16** an attempt at doing something. ▶ PHRASE **17** If someone is always **on the go**, they are always busy and active.

**18** To go means remaining *E.G. I've got one more year of my course to go.*

**go down** VERB **1** If something goes down well, people like it. If it goes down badly, they do not like it. **2** If you go down with an illness, you catch it.

**go off** VERB **1** If you go off someone or something, you stop liking them. **2** If a bomb goes off, it explodes.

**go on** VERB **1** If you go on doing something, you continue to do it. **2** If you go on about something, you keep talking about it in a rather boring way. **3** Something that is going on is happening.

**go through** VERB **1** If you go through an unpleasant event, you experience it. **2** If a law or agreement goes through, it is approved and becomes official. **3** If you go through with something, you do it even though it is unpleasant.

**goad goads goading goaded**
VERB If you goad someone, you encourage them to do something by making them angry or excited *E.G. He had goaded the man into near violence.*

**go-ahead**
NOUN If someone gives you the go-ahead for something, they give you permission to do it.

**goal goals**
NOUN **1** the space, in games like football or hockey, into which the players try to get the ball in order to score a point. **2** an instance of this. **3** Your goal is something that you hope to achieve.

**goalkeeper goalkeepers**
NOUN the player, in games like soccer or hockey, who stands in the goal and tries to stop the other team from scoring.

**goanna** goannas

NOUN a large Australian lizard.

**goat** goats

NOUN an animal, like a sheep, with coarse hair, a beard, and horns.

**go-away bird** go-away birds

NOUN In South Africa, a go-away bird is a grey lourie, a type of bird which lives in open grassland.

**gob** gobs

NOUN *INFORMAL* Your gob is your mouth.

**gobble** gobbles gobbling gobbled

VERB **1** If you gobble food, you eat it very quickly. **2** When a turkey gobbles, it makes a loud gurgling sound.

■ devour, guzzle, wolf

**gobbledygook** or **gobbledegook**

NOUN Gobbledygook is language that is impossible to understand because it is so formal or complicated.

**goblet** goblets

NOUN a glass with a long stem.

**goblin** goblins

NOUN an ugly, mischievous creature in fairy stories.

**god** gods

PROPER NOUN **1** The name God is given to the being who is worshipped by Christians, Jews, and Muslims as the creator and ruler of the world. ▶ NOUN **2** any of the beings that are believed in many religions to have power over an aspect of life or a part of the world *E.G. Dionysus, the Greek god of wine.* **3** If someone is your god, you admire them very much. ▶ PLURAL NOUN **4** In a theatre, the gods are the highest seats farthest from the stage.

**godchild** godchildren

NOUN If you are someone's godchild, they agreed to be responsible for your religious upbringing when you were baptized in a Christian church.

**goddaughter** NOUN **godson** NOUN

**goddess** goddesses

NOUN a female god.

**godparent** godparents

NOUN A person's godparent is someone who agrees to be responsible for their religious upbringing when they are baptized in a Christian church.

**godfather** NOUN **godmother** NOUN

**godsend** godsends

NOUN something that comes unexpectedly and helps you very much.

**goggles**

PLURAL NOUN Goggles are special glasses that fit closely round your eyes to protect them.

**going**

NOUN The going is the conditions that affect your ability to do something *E.G. He found the going very slow indeed.*

**gold**

NOUN **1** Gold is a valuable, yellow-coloured metal. It is used for making jewellery and as an international currency. **2** 'Gold' is also used to mean things that are made of gold. ▶ ADJECTIVE **3** bright yellow.

**golden**

ADJECTIVE **1** gold in colour *E.G. golden syrup.* **2** made of gold *E.G. a golden chain.* **3** excellent or ideal *E.G. a golden hero.*

**golden rule** golden rules

NOUN a very important rule to remember in order to be able to do something successfully.

**golden wedding** golden weddings

NOUN A married couple's golden wedding is their fiftieth wedding anniversary.

a b c d e f g h i j k l m n o p q r s t u v w x y z

A B C D E F **G** H I J K L M N O P Q R S T U V W X Y Z

### goldfish
NOUN a small orange-coloured fish, often kept in ponds or bowls.

### goldsmith goldsmiths
NOUN a person whose job is making jewellery out of gold.

### golf
NOUN Golf is a game in which players use special clubs to hit a small ball into holes that are spread out over a large area of grassy land.
**golfer** NOUN

### golf course golf courses
NOUN an area of grassy land where people play golf.

### gondola gondolas
*Said "gon-dol-la"* NOUN a long narrow boat used in Venice, which is propelled with a long pole.

### gone
the past participle of **go**.

### gong gongs
NOUN a flat, circular piece of metal that is hit with a hammer to make a loud sound, often as a signal for something.

### good better best; goods
ADJECTIVE 1 pleasant, acceptable, or satisfactory E.G. *good news… a good film.* 2 skilful or successful E.G. *good at art.* 3 kind, thoughtful, and loving E.G. *She was grateful to him for being so good to her.* 4 well-behaved E.G. *Have the children been good?* 5 used to emphasize something E.G. *a good few million pounds.* ▶ NOUN 6 Good is moral and spiritual justice and virtue E.G. *the forces of good and evil.* 7 Good also refers to anything that is desirable or beneficial as opposed to harmful E.G. *The break has done me good.* ▶ PLURAL NOUN 8 Goods are objects that people own or that are

sold in shops E.G. *leather goods.*
▶ PHRASE 9 For good means for ever. 10 As good as means almost E.G. *The election is as good as decided.*
☑ *Good* is an adjective, and should not be used as an adverb. You should say that *a person did well* not *did good.*

### goodbye
You say goodbye when you are leaving someone or ending a telephone conversation.

### Good Friday
NOUN Good Friday is the Friday before Easter, when Christians remember the crucifixion of Christ.

### good-natured
ADJECTIVE friendly, pleasant and even-tempered.

### goodness
NOUN 1 Goodness is the quality of being kind. ▶ INTERJECTION 2 People say 'Goodness!' or 'My goodness!' when they are surprised.

### goodwill
NOUN Goodwill is kindness and helpfulness E.G. *Messages of goodwill were exchanged.*

### goody goodies
NOUN 1 INFORMAL Goodies are enjoyable things, often food. 2 You can call a hero in a film or book a goody.

### goose geese
NOUN a fairly large bird with webbed feet and a long neck.

### gooseberry gooseberries
NOUN a round, green berry that grows on a bush and has a sharp taste.

### gore gores goring gored
VERB 1 If an animal gores someone, it wounds them badly with its horns or tusks. ▶ NOUN 2 Gore is clotted blood from a wound.

**gorge** gorges gorging gorged
NOUN 1 a deep, narrow valley. ▶ VERB
2 If you gorge yourself, you eat a lot
of food greedily.

**gorgeous**
ADJECTIVE extremely pleasant or
attractive E.G. *a gorgeous man*.

**gorilla** gorillas
NOUN a very large, strong ape with
very dark fur.
📖 from *Gorillai*, the Greek name for
an African tribe with hairy bodies

**gorse**
NOUN Gorse is a dark green wild shrub
that has sharp prickles and small
yellow flowers.

**gory** gorier goriest
ADJECTIVE Gory situations involve
people being injured in horrible ways.

**gosling** goslings
*Said* "goz-ling" NOUN a young goose.

**gospel** gospels
NOUN 1 The Gospels are the four
books in the New Testament which
describe the life and teachings of
Jesus Christ. 2 a set of ideas that
someone strongly believes in E.G. *the
so-called gospel of work*. ▶ ADJECTIVE
3 Gospel music is a style of religious
music popular among Black
Christians in the United States.

**gossip** gossips gossiping
gossiped
NOUN 1 Gossip is informal
conversation, often concerning
people's private affairs. 2 Someone
who is a gossip enjoys talking about
other people's private affairs. ▶ VERB
3 If you gossip, you talk informally
with someone, especially about
other people.

**got**
1 Got is the past tense and past

participle of **get**. 2 You can use 'have
got' instead of the more formal 'have'
when talking about possessing
things E.G. *The director has got a map*.
3 You can use 'have got to' instead of
the more formal 'have to' when
talking about something that must
be done E.G. *He has got to win*.

**gouge** gouges gouging gouged
*Said* "gowj". VERB 1 If you gouge a hole
in something, you make a hole in it
with a pointed object. 2 If you gouge
something out, you force it out of
position with your fingers or a sharp
tool.

**goulash**
*Said* "goo-lash" NOUN Goulash is a
type of rich meat stew, originally
from Hungary.

**gourd** gourds
*Said* "goord" NOUN a large fruit with a
hard outside.

**gourmet** gourmets
*Said* "goor-may" NOUN a person who
enjoys good food and drink and
knows a lot about it.

**gout**
NOUN Gout is a disease which causes
someone's joints to swell painfully,
especially in their toes.

**govern** governs governing
governed
VERB 1 To govern a country means to
control it. 2 Something that governs
a situation influences it E.G. *Our
thinking is as much governed by habit
as by behaviour*.

**governess** governesses
NOUN a woman who is employed to
teach the children in a family and
who lives with the family.

**government** governments
NOUN (HISTORY) 1 The government is

a b c d e f g h i j k l m n o p q r s t u v w x y z

the QUeen stood on the QUay (quay)    SPELLING NOTE

the group of people who govern a country. **2** Government is the control and organization of a country.
**governmental** ADJECTIVE

**governor** governors
NOUN **1** a person who controls and organizes a state or an institution. **2** In Australia, the Governor is the representative of the King or Queen in a State.

**governor-general** governors-general
NOUN the chief representative of the King or Queen in Australia, New Zealand, and other Commonwealth countries.

**gown** gowns
NOUN **1** a long, formal dress. **2** a long, dark cloak worn by people such as judges and lawyers.

**GP**
an abbreviation for **general practitioner**.

**grab** grabs grabbing grabbed
VERB **1** If you grab something, you take it or pick it up roughly. **2** If you grab an opportunity, you take advantage of it eagerly. **3** INFORMAL If an idea grabs you, it excites you.
▶ NOUN **4** A grab at an object is an attempt to grab it.
■ (senses 1 & 2) grasp, seize, snatch

**grace** graces gracing graced
NOUN **1** Grace is an elegant way of moving. **2** Grace is also a pleasant, kind way of behaving. **3** Grace is also a short prayer of thanks said before a meal. **4** Dukes and archbishops are addressed as 'Your Grace' and referred to as 'His Grace'. ▶ VERB **5** Something that graces a place makes it more attractive. **6** If someone important graces an

event, they kindly agree to be present at it.
**graceful** ADJECTIVE **gracefully** ADVERB
■ (sense 1) elegance, poise

**gracious**
ADJECTIVE **1** kind, polite, and pleasant. **2** 'Good gracious' is an exclamation of surprise.
**graciously** ADVERB

**grade** grades grading graded
VERB **1** To grade things means to arrange them according to quality.
▶ NOUN **2** The grade of something is its quality. **3** the mark that you get for an exam or piece of written work. **4** Your grade in a company or organization is your level of importance or your rank.

**gradient** gradients
NOUN a slope or the steepness of a slope.

**gradual**
ADJECTIVE happening or changing slowly over a long period of time.

**gradually**
ADVERB happening or changing slowly over a long period of time.

**graduate** graduates graduating graduated
NOUN **1** a person who has completed a first degree at a university or college. ▶ VERB **2** When students graduate, they complete a first degree at a university or college. **3** To graduate from one thing to another means to progress gradually towards the second thing.
**graduation** NOUN

**graffiti**
Said "graf-*fee*-tee" NOUN Graffiti is slogans or drawings scribbled on walls.

from Italian *graffiare* meaning 'to scratch a surface'

☑ Although *graffiti* is a plural in Italian, the language it comes from, in English it can be used as a singular noun or a plural noun.

**graft grafts grafting grafted**
NOUN **1** a piece of living tissue which is used to replace by surgery a damaged or unhealthy part of a person's body. **2** INFORMAL Graft is hard work. ▶ VERB **3** To graft one thing to another means to attach it.

**grain grains**
NOUN **1** a cereal plant, such as wheat, that is grown as a crop and used for food. **2** Grains are seeds of a cereal plant. **3** A grain of sand or salt is a tiny particle of it. **4** The grain of a piece of wood is the pattern of lines made by the fibres in it. ▶ PHRASE **5** If something **goes against the grain**, you find it difficult to accept because it is against your principles.
▣ (sense 3) bit, granule, particle

**gram grams**; also spelt **gramme**
NOUN a unit of weight equal to one thousandth of a kilogram.

**grammar**
NOUN ( ENGLISH ) Grammar is the rules of a language relating to the ways you can combine words to form sentences.

**grammar school grammar schools**
NOUN **1** a secondary school for pupils of high academic ability. **2** In Australia, a private school, usually one controlled by a church.

**grammatical**
ADJECTIVE **1** relating to grammar E.G. *grammatical knowledge*. **2** following the rules of grammar correctly E.G.

*grammatical sentences.*
**grammatically** ADVERB

**gran grans**
NOUN; INFORMAL Your gran is your grandmother.

**granary granaries**
NOUN **1** a building for storing grain.
▶ ADJECTIVE **2** TRADEMARK Granary bread contains whole grains of wheat.

**grand grander grandest**
ADJECTIVE **1** magnificent in appearance and size E.G. *a grand house*. **2** very important E.G. *the grand scheme of your life*. **3** INFORMAL very pleasant or enjoyable E.G. *It was a grand day*. **4** A grand total is the final complete amount. ▶ NOUN **5** INFORMAL a thousand pounds or dollars.
**grandly** ADVERB
▣ (sense 1) impressive, magnificent, splendid

**grandad grandads**
NOUN; INFORMAL Your grandad is your grandfather.

**grandchild grandchildren**
NOUN Someone's grandchildren are the children of their son or daughter.

**granddaughter granddaughters**
NOUN Someone's granddaughter is the daughter of their son or daughter.

**grandeur**
*Said* "grand-*yer*" NOUN Grandeur is great beauty and magnificence.

**grandfather grandfathers**
NOUN Your grandfather is your father's father or your mother's father.

**grandfather clock grandfather clocks**
NOUN a clock in a tall wooden case that stands on the floor.

**grandiose**
*Said* "gran-*dee-ose*" ADJECTIVE intended to be very impressive, but seeming

ridiculous E.G. *a grandiose gesture of love*.

**grandma** grandmas
NOUN; INFORMAL Your grandma is your grandmother.

**grandmother** grandmothers
NOUN Your grandmother is your father's mother or your mother's mother.

**grandparent** grandparents
NOUN Your grandparents are your parents' parents.

**grand piano** grand pianos
NOUN a large flat piano with horizontal strings.

**grandson** grandsons
NOUN Someone's grandson is the son of their son or daughter.

**grandstand** grandstands
NOUN a structure with a roof and seats for spectators at a sports ground.

**granite**
*Said "gran-nit"* NOUN Granite is a very hard rock used in building.

**granny** grannies
NOUN; INFORMAL Your granny is your grandmother.

**grant** grants granting granted
NOUN 1 an amount of money that an official body gives to someone for a particular purpose E.G. *a grant to carry out repairs*. ▶ VERB 2 If you grant something to someone, you allow them to have it. 3 If you grant that something is true, you admit that it is true. ▶ PHRASES 4 If you **take something for granted**, you believe it without thinking about it. If you **take someone for granted**, you benefit from them without showing that you are grateful.

**granule** granules
NOUN a very small piece of something E.G. *granules of salt*.

**grape** grapes
NOUN a small green or purple fruit, eaten raw or used to make wine.

**grapefruit** grapefruits
NOUN a large, round, yellow citrus fruit.

**grapevine** grapevines
NOUN 1 a climbing plant which grapes grow on. 2 If you hear some news on the grapevine, it has been passed on from person to person, usually unofficially or secretly.

**graph** graphs
NOUN (MATHS) a diagram in which a line shows how two sets of numbers or measurements are related.

**-graph**
SUFFIX '-graph' means a writer or recorder of some sort or something made by writing, drawing or recording E.G. *telegraph… autograph*.
🏛 from Greek *graphein* meaning 'to write'

**graphic** graphics
ADJECTIVE 1 A graphic description is very detailed and lifelike. 2 relating to drawing or painting. ▶ PLURAL NOUN 3 (ICT) Graphics are drawings and pictures composed of simple lines and strong colours E.G. *computerized graphics*.
**graphically** ADVERB

**graphite**
NOUN a black form of carbon that is used in pencil leads.

**grapple** grapples grappling grappled
VERB 1 If you grapple with someone, you struggle with them while fighting. 2 If you grapple with a problem, you try hard to solve it.

**grasp** grasps grasping grasped
VERB 1 If you grasp something, you

hold it firmly. **2** If you grasp an idea, you understand it. ▶ NOUN **3** a firm hold. **4** Your grasp of something is your understanding of it.

**grass grasses**
NOUN Grass is the common green plant that grows on lawns and in parks.
**grassy** ADJECTIVE

**grasshopper grasshoppers**
NOUN an insect with long back legs which it uses for jumping and making a high-pitched sound.

**grate grates grating grated**
NOUN **1** a framework of metal bars in a fireplace. ▶ VERB **2** To grate food means to shred it into small pieces by rubbing it against a grater. **3** When something grates on something else, it rubs against it making a harsh sound. **4** If something grates on you, it irritates you.

**grateful**
ADJECTIVE If you are grateful for something, you are glad you have it and want to thank the person who gave it to you.
**gratefully** ADVERB
■ appreciative, thankful

**grater graters**
NOUN a small metal tool used for grating food.

**gratify gratifies gratifying gratified**
VERB **1** If you are gratified by something, you are pleased by it. **2** If you gratify a wish or feeling, you satisfy it.

**grating gratings**
NOUN **1** a metal frame with bars across it fastened over a hole in a wall or in the ground. ▶ ADJECTIVE **2** A grating

sound is harsh and unpleasant E.G. *grating melodies*.

**gratis**
*Said* "**grah-tis**" ADVERB OR ADJECTIVE free E.G. *food and drink supplied gratis*.

**gratitude**
NOUN Gratitude is the feeling of being grateful.
■ appreciation, thankfulness

**gratuitous**
*Said* "**grat-yoo-it-tuss**" ADJECTIVE unnecessary E.G. *a gratuitous attack*.
**gratuitously** ADVERB

**grave graves; graver gravest**
*Rhymes with* "**save**" NOUN **1** a place where a corpse is buried. ▶ ADJECTIVE **2** FORMAL very serious E.G. *grave danger*.

**grave**
*Said* "**grahv**" ADJECTIVE In French and some other languages, a grave accent is a line sloping downwards from left to right placed over a vowel to indicate a change in pronunciation, as in the word *lèvre* (a hare).

**gravel**
NOUN Gravel is small stones used for making roads and paths.

**gravestone gravestones**
NOUN a large stone placed over someone's grave, with their name on it.

**graveyard graveyards**
NOUN an area of land where corpses are buried.

**gravitate gravitates gravitating gravitated**
VERB When people gravitate towards something, they go towards it because they are attracted by it.

**gravitation**
NOUN Gravitation is the force which causes objects to be attracted to

Eddy Ant thinks mEAt is a grEAt trEAt to EAt (-ea-)    SPELLING NOTE

A
B
C
D
E
F
G
H
I
J
K
L
M
N
O
P
Q
R
S
T
U
V
W
X
Y
Z

each other.

**gravitational** ADJECTIVE

**gravity**

NOUN 1 Gravity is the force that makes things fall when you drop them. 2 FORMAL The gravity of a situation is its seriousness.

**gravy**

NOUN Gravy is a brown sauce made from meat juices.

**graze grazes grazing grazed**

VERB 1 When animals graze, they eat grass. 2 If something grazes a part of your body, it scrapes against it, injuring you slightly. ▶ NOUN 3 a slight injury caused by something scraping against your skin.

**grease greases greasing greased**

NOUN 1 Grease is an oily substance used for lubricating machines. 2 Grease is also melted animal fat, used in cooking. 3 Grease is also an oily substance produced by your skin and found in your hair. ▶ VERB 4 If you grease something, you lubricate it with grease.

**greasy** ADJECTIVE

**great greater greatest**

ADJECTIVE 1 very large E.G. a great sea... great efforts. 2 very important E.G. a great artist. 3 INFORMAL very good E.G. Paul had a great time.

**greatly** ADVERB **greatness** NOUN

**Great Britain**

NOUN Great Britain is the largest of the British Isles, consisting of England, Scotland, and Wales.

**Great Dane Great Danes**

NOUN a very large dog with short hair.

**great-grandfather great-grandfathers**

NOUN Your great-grandfather is your

father's or mother's grandfather.

**great-grandmother great-grandmothers**

NOUN Your great-grandmother is your father's or mother's grandmother.

**greed**

NOUN Greed is a desire for more of something than you really need.

**greedy greedier greediest**

ADJECTIVE wanting more of something than you really need.

**greedily** ADVERB **greediness** NOUN

🔲 grasping, insatiable, voracious

**Greek Greeks**

ADJECTIVE 1 belonging or relating to Greece. ▶ NOUN 2 someone who comes from Greece. 3 Greek is the main language spoken in Greece.

**green greener greenest; greens**

ADJECTIVE or NOUN 1 Green is a colour between yellow and blue on the spectrum. ▶ NOUN 2 an area of grass in the middle of a village. 3 A putting green or bowling green is a grassy area on which putting or bowls is played. 4 an area of smooth short grass around each hole on a golf course. ▶ PLURAL NOUN 5 Greens are green vegetables. ▶ ADJECTIVE 6 'Green' is used to describe political movements which are concerned with environmental issues. 7 INFORMAL Someone who is green is young and inexperienced.

**greenery**

NOUN Greenery is a lot of trees, bushes, or other green plants together in one place.

**greenfly**

NOUN Greenfly are small green insects that damage plants.

**greengrocer** greengrocers
NOUN a shopkeeper who sells
vegetables and fruit.

**greenhouse** greenhouses
NOUN a glass building in which people
grow plants that need to be kept warm.

**greenhouse effect**
NOUN the gradual rise in temperature
in the earth's atmosphere due to
heat being absorbed from the sun
and being trapped by gases such as
carbon dioxide in the air around the
earth.

**green paper** green papers
NOUN In Britain, Australia, and New
Zealand, a report published by the
government containing proposals to
be discussed before decisions are
made about them.

**greenstone**
NOUN a type of jade found in New
Zealand and used for making
ornaments, weapons, and tools.

**greet** greets greeting greeted
VERB 1 If you greet someone, you say
something friendly like 'hello' to
them when you meet them. 2 If you
greet something in a particular way,
you react to it in that way E.G. He was
greeted with deep suspicion.
■ (sense 1) hail, salute

**greeting** greetings
NOUN something friendly that you say
to someone when you meet them
E.G. Her greeting was warm.

**gregarious**
Said "grig-air-ee-uss" ADJECTIVE; FORMAL
Someone who is gregarious enjoys
being with other people.

**grenade** grenades
NOUN a small bomb, containing
explosive or tear gas, which can be
thrown.

from Spanish granada meaning
'pomegranate'

**grevillea** grevilleas
NOUN an evergreen Australian tree or
shrub.

**grew**
the past tense of **grow**.

**grey** greyer greyest; greys
greying greyed
ADJECTIVE or NOUN 1 Grey is a colour
between black and white. ▶ ADJECTIVE
2 dull and boring E.G. He's a bit of a
grey man. ▶ VERB 3 If someone is
greying, their hair is going grey.
**greyness** NOUN

**greyhound** greyhounds
NOUN a thin dog with long legs that
can run very fast.

**grid** grids
NOUN 1 a pattern of lines crossing
each other to form squares. 2 The
grid is the network of wires and
cables by which electricity is
distributed throughout a country.

**grief**
NOUN 1 Grief is extreme sadness.
▶ PHRASE 2 If someone or something
**comes to grief**, they fail or are
injured.
■ (sense 1) heartache, sadness,
sorrow

**grievance** grievances
NOUN a reason for complaining.

**grieve** grieves grieving grieved
VERB 1 If you grieve, you are extremely
sad, especially because someone has
died. 2 If something grieves you, it
makes you feel very sad.
■ (sense 1) lament, mourn

**grievous**
ADJECTIVE; FORMAL extremely serious E.G.
grievous damage.
**grievously** ADVERB

'i' before 'e' except after 'c'   SPELLING NOTE

**grill** grills grilling grilled
NOUN **1** a part on a cooker where food is cooked by strong heat from above. **2** a metal frame on which you cook food over a fire. ▶ VERB **3** If you grill food, you cook it on or under a grill. **4** INFORMAL If you grill someone, you ask them a lot of questions in a very intense way.

**grille** grilles
Rhymes with "pill" NOUN a metal framework over a window or piece of machinery, used for protection.

**grim** grimmer grimmest
ADJECTIVE **1** If a situation or piece of news is grim, it is very unpleasant and worrying E.G. There are grim times ahead. **2** Grim places are unattractive and depressing. **3** If someone is grim, they are very serious or stern.
**grimly** ADVERB

**grimace** grimaces grimacing grimaced
Said "grim-mace" NOUN **1** a twisted facial expression indicating disgust or pain. ▶ VERB **2** When someone grimaces, they make a grimace.

**grime**
NOUN Grime is thick dirt which gathers on the surface of something.
**grimy** ADJECTIVE

**grin** grins grinning grinned
VERB **1** If you grin, you smile broadly. ▶ NOUN **2** a broad smile. ▶ PHRASE **3** If you **grin and bear it**, you accept a difficult situation without complaining.

**grind** grinds grinding ground
VERB **1** If you grind something such as pepper, you crush it into a fine powder. **2** If you grind your teeth, you rub your upper and lower teeth together. ▶ PHRASE **3** If something

**grinds to a halt**, it stops E.G. Progress ground to a halt.
■ (sense 1) crush, powder, pulverize

**grip** grips gripping gripped
VERB **1** If you grip something, you hold it firmly. ▶ NOUN **2** a firm hold. **3** a handle on a bat or a racket. **4** Your grip on a situation is your control over it. ▶ PHRASE **5** If you **get to grips with** a situation or problem, you start to deal with it effectively.

**grisly** grislier grisliest
ADJECTIVE very nasty and horrible E.G. a grisly murder scene.

**grit** grits gritting gritted
NOUN **1** Grit consists of very small stones. It is put on icy roads to make them less slippery. ▶ VERB **2** When workmen grit an icy road, they put grit on it. ▶ PHRASE **3** To **grit your teeth** means to decide to carry on in a difficult situation.
**gritty** ADJECTIVE

**grizzled**
ADJECTIVE Grizzled hair is grey. A grizzled person has grey hair.

**grizzly bear** grizzly bears
NOUN a large, greyish-brown bear from North America.

**groan** groans groaning groaned
VERB **1** If you groan, you make a long, low sound of pain, unhappiness, or disapproval. ▶ NOUN **2** the sound you make when you groan.

**grocer** grocers
NOUN a shopkeeper who sells many kinds of food and other household goods.

**grocery** groceries
NOUN **1** a grocer's shop. ▶ PLURAL NOUN **2** Groceries are the goods that you buy in a grocer's shop.

**grog**

NOUN; INFORMAL In Australian and New Zealand English, grog is any alcoholic drink.

**groin** groins

NOUN the area where your legs join the main part of your body at the front.

**groom** grooms grooming groomed

NOUN 1 someone who looks after horses in a stable. 2 At a wedding, the groom is the bridegroom. ▶ VERB 3 to clean an animal's fur. 4 If you groom someone for a job, you prepare them for it by teaching them the skills they will need.

**groove** grooves

NOUN a deep line cut into a surface.
**grooved** ADJECTIVE

**grope** gropes groping groped

VERB 1 If you grope for something you cannot see, you search for it with your hands. 2 If you grope for something such as the solution to a problem, you try to think of it.

**gross** grosser grossest; grosses grossing grossed

ADJECTIVE 1 extremely bad E.G. a gross betrayal. 2 Gross speech or behaviour is very rude. 3 Gross things are ugly E.G. gross holiday outfits. 4 Someone's gross income is their total income before any deductions are made. 5 The gross weight of something is its total weight including the weight of its container. ▶ VERB 6 If you gross an amount of money, you earn that amount in total.
**grossly** ADVERB

**grotesque**

Said "groh-**tesk**" ADJECTIVE

1 exaggerated and absurd E.G. It was the most grotesque thing she had ever heard. 2 very strange and ugly E.G. grotesque animal puppets.
**grotesquely** ADVERB

🔲 from Old Italian pittura grottesca meaning 'cave paintings'

**grotto** grottoes or grottos

NOUN a small cave that people visit because it is attractive.

**ground** grounds grounding grounded

NOUN 1 The ground is the surface of the earth. 2 a piece of land that is used for a particular purpose E.G. the training ground. 3 The ground covered by a book or course is the range of subjects it deals with. ▶ PLURAL NOUN 4 The grounds of a large building are the land belonging to it and surrounding it. 5 FORMAL The grounds for something are the reasons for it E.G. genuine grounds for caution. ▶ VERB 6 FORMAL If something is grounded in something else, it is based on it. 7 If an aircraft is grounded, it has to remain on the ground. 8 Ground is the past tense and past participle of **grind**.

**ground floor** ground floors

NOUN The ground floor of a building is the floor that is approximately level with the ground.

**grounding**

NOUN If you have a grounding in a skill or subject, you have had basic instruction in it.

**groundless**

ADJECTIVE not based on reason or evidence E.G. groundless accusations.

**group** groups grouping grouped

NOUN 1 A group of things or people is a number of them that are linked together in some way. 2 a number of

a b c d e f g h i j k l m n o p q r s t u v w x y z

A
B
C
D
E
F
G
H
I
J
K
L
M
N
O
P
Q
R
S
T
U
V
W
X
Y
Z

musicians who perform pop music together. ▶ VERB **3** When things or people are grouped together, they are linked together in some way. ■ (sense 1) band, bunch, crowd, set

**grouping groupings**
NOUN a number of things or people that are linked together in some way.

**grouse grouse**
NOUN a fat brown or grey bird, often shot for sport.

**grove groves**
NOUN; LITERARY a group of trees growing close together.

**grovel grovels grovelling grovelled**
VERB If you grovel, you behave in an unpleasantly humble way towards someone you regard as important.

**grow grows growing grew grown**
VERB **1** To grow means to increase in size or amount. **2** If a tree or plant grows somewhere, it is alive there. **3** When people grow plants, they plant them and look after them. **4** If a man grows a beard or moustache, he lets it develop by not shaving. **5** If you grow to have a particular feeling, you eventually have it. **6** If one thing grows from another, it develops from it. **7** INFORMAL If something grows on you, you gradually get to like it. ■ (sense 1) expand, get bigger, increase

**grow up** VERB When a child grows up, he or she becomes an adult.

**growl growls growling growled**
VERB **1** When an animal growls, it makes a low rumbling sound, usually because it is angry. **2** If you growl

something, you say it in a low, rough, rather angry voice. ▶ NOUN **3** the sound an animal makes when it growls.

**grown-up grown-ups**
NOUN **1** INFORMAL an adult. ▶ ADJECTIVE **2** Someone who is grown-up is adult, or behaves like an adult.

**growth growths**
NOUN **1** When there is a growth in something, it gets bigger E.G. the growth of the fishing industry. **2** (SCIENCE) Growth is the process by which something develops to its full size. **3** an abnormal lump that grows inside or on a person, animal, or plant. ■ (sense 1) expansion, increase

**grub grubs**
NOUN **1** a wormlike insect that has just hatched from its egg. **2** INFORMAL Grub is food.

**grubby grubbier grubbiest**
ADJECTIVE rather dirty.

**grudge grudges grudging grudged**
NOUN **1** If you have a grudge against someone, you resent them because they have harmed you in the past. ▶ VERB **2** If you grudge someone something, you give it to them unwillingly, or are displeased that they have it.

**grudging**
ADJECTIVE done or felt unwillingly E.G. grudging admiration.
**grudgingly** ADVERB

**gruel**
NOUN Gruel is oatmeal boiled in water or milk.

**gruelling**
ADJECTIVE difficult and tiring E.G. a gruelling race.

**gruesome**
ADJECTIVE shocking and horrible E.G.

*gruesome pictures.*

**gruff** gruffer gruffest
ADJECTIVE If someone's voice is gruff, it sounds rough and unfriendly.

**grumble** grumbles grumbling grumbled
VERB **1** If you grumble, you complain in a bad-tempered way. ▶ NOUN **2** a bad-tempered complaint.

**grumpy** grumpier grumpiest
ADJECTIVE bad-tempered and fed-up.
■ ill-tempered, irritable

**grunt** grunts grunting grunted
VERB **1** If a person or a pig grunts, they make a short, low, gruff sound.
▶ NOUN **2** the sound a person or a pig makes when they grunt.

**guarantee** guarantees guaranteeing guaranteed
VERB **1** If something or someone guarantees something, they make certain that it will happen E.G. *Money may not guarantee success.* ▶ NOUN **2** If something is a guarantee of something else, it makes it certain that it will happen. **3** a written promise that if a product develops a fault it will be replaced or repaired free.
**guarantor** NOUN
■ (sense 1) ensure, promise
■ (sense 2) assurance, pledge, promise

**guard** guards guarding guarded
VERB **1** If you guard a person or object, you stay near to them either to protect them or to make sure they do not escape. **2** If you guard against something, you are careful to avoid it happening. ▶ NOUN **3** a person or group of people who guard a person, object, or place. **4** a railway official in charge of a train. **5** Any

object which covers something to prevent it causing harm can be called a guard E.G. *a fire guard.*
■ (sense 1) defend, protect, watch over
■ (sense 3) protector, sentry, watchman

**guardian** guardians
NOUN **1** someone who has been legally appointed to look after an orphaned child. **2** A guardian of something is someone who protects it E.G. *a guardian of the law.*
**guardianship** NOUN

**guernsey** guernseys
NOUN **1** In Australian and New Zealand English, a jersey. **2** a sleeveless top worn by an Australian Rules football player.

**guerrilla** guerrillas
*Said "ger-rill-la"*; also spelt **guerilla**
NOUN a member of a small unofficial army fighting an official army.
▥ from Spanish *guerrilla* meaning 'little war'

**guess** guesses guessing guessed
VERB **1** If you guess something, you form or express an opinion that it is the case, without having much information. ▶ NOUN **2** (MATHS) an attempt to give the correct answer to something without having much information, or without working it out properly.
■ (sense 1) conjecture, suppose
■ (sense 2) conjecture, speculation, supposition

**guest** guests
NOUN **1** someone who stays at your home or who attends an occasion because they have been invited.
**2** The guests in a hotel are the

A
B
C
D
E
F
**G**
H
I
J
K
L
M
N
O
P
Q
R
S
T
U
V
W
X
Y
Z

people staying there.

**guffaw**
NOUN a loud, coarse laugh.

**guidance**
NOUN Guidance is help and advice.

**guide guides guiding guided**
NOUN 1 someone who shows you round places, or leads the way through difficult country. 2 a book which gives you information or instructions E.G. a Sydney street guide. 3 A Guide is a girl who is a member of an organization that encourages discipline and practical skills. ▶ VERB 4 If you guide someone in a particular direction, you lead them in that direction. 5 If you are guided by something, it influences your actions or decisions.

**guidebook guidebooks**
NOUN a book which gives information about a place.

**guide dog guide dogs**
NOUN a dog that has been trained to lead a blind person.

**guideline guidelines**
NOUN a piece of advice about how something should be done.

**guild guilds**
NOUN a society of people E.G. the Screen Writers' Guild.

**guile**
Rhymes with "mile" NOUN Guile is cunning and deceit.
**guileless** ADJECTIVE

**guillotine guillotines**
Said "gil-lot-teen" NOUN a machine used for beheading people, especially in the past in France.

**guilt**
NOUN 1 Guilt is an unhappy feeling of having done something wrong. 2 Someone's guilt is the fact that

they have done something wrong E.G. The law will decide their guilt.

**guilty guiltier guiltiest**
ADJECTIVE 1 If you are guilty of doing something wrong, you did it E.G. He was guilty of theft. 2 If you feel guilty, you are unhappy because you have done something wrong.
**guiltily** ADVERB

**guinea guineas**
Said "gin-ee" NOUN an old British unit of money, worth 21 shillings.

**guinea pig guinea pigs**
NOUN 1 a small furry animal without a tail, often kept as a pet. 2 a person used to try something out on E.G. a guinea pig for a new drug.

**guise guises**
Rhymes with "prize" NOUN a misleading appearance E.G. political statements in the guise of religious talk.

**guitar guitars**
NOUN a musical instrument with six strings which are strummed or plucked.
**guitarist** NOUN

**gulf gulfs**
NOUN 1 a very large bay. 2 a wide gap or difference between two things or people.

**gull gulls**
NOUN a sea bird with long wings, white and grey or black feathers, and webbed feet.
FROM Welsh gwylan

**gullet gullets**
NOUN the tube that goes from your mouth to your stomach.

**gullible**
ADJECTIVE easily tricked.
**gullibility** NOUN
■ credulous, naive

**gully** gullies
NOUN a long, narrow valley.

**gulp** gulps gulping gulped
VERB 1 If you gulp food or drink, you swallow large quantities of it. 2 If you gulp, you swallow air, because you are nervous. ▶ NOUN 3 A gulp of food or drink is a large quantity of it swallowed at one time.

**gum** gums
NOUN 1 Gum is a soft flavoured substance that people chew but do not swallow. 2 Gum is also glue for sticking paper. 3 Your gums are the firm flesh in which your teeth are set.

**gumboot** gumboots
NOUN Gumboots are long waterproof boots.

**gumtree** gumtrees
NOUN a eucalyptus, or other tree which produces gum.

**gun** guns
NOUN a weapon which fires bullets or shells.

**gunfire**
NOUN Gunfire is the repeated firing of guns.

**gunpowder**
NOUN Gunpowder is an explosive powder made from a mixture of potassium nitrate and other substances.

**gunshot** gunshots
NOUN the sound of a gun being fired.

**gunyah** gunyahs
NOUN In Australia, a hut or shelter in the bush.

**guppy** guppies
NOUN a small, brightly coloured tropical fish.

**gurdwara**
NOUN a Sikh place of worship.
🏛 from Sanskrit *guru* meaning 'teacher' + *dvārā* meaning 'door'

**gurgle** gurgles gurgling gurgled
VERB 1 To gurgle means to make a bubbling sound. ▶ NOUN 2 a bubbling sound.

**guru** gurus
Said "goo-rooh" NOUN a spiritual leader and teacher, especially in India.
🏛 from Sanskrit *guruh* meaning 'weighty' or 'of importance'

**gush** gushes gushing gushed
VERB 1 When liquid gushes from something, it flows out of it in large quantities. 2 When people gush, they express admiration or pleasure in an exaggerated way.
**gushing** ADJECTIVE
▦ (sense 1) flow, pour, spurt, stream

**gust** gusts
NOUN a sudden rush of wind.
**gusty** ADJECTIVE

**gusto**
NOUN Gusto is energy and enthusiasm E.G. *Her gusto for life was amazing.*

**gut** guts gutting gutted
PLURAL NOUN 1 Your guts are your internal organs, especially your intestines. ▶ VERB 2 To gut a dead fish means to remove its internal organs. 3 If a building is gutted, the inside of it is destroyed, especially by fire. ▶ NOUN 4 INFORMAL Guts is courage.
▦ (sense 1) entrails, innards, intestines

**gutter** gutters
NOUN 1 the edge of a road next to the pavement, where rain collects and flows away. 2 a channel fixed to the edge of a roof, where rain collects and flows away.
**guttering** NOUN

**guttural**
Said "gut-ter-al" ADJECTIVE Guttural

sounds are produced at the back of a person's throat and are often considered to be unpleasant.

**guy** guys

NOUN **1** INFORMAL a man or boy. **2** a crude model of Guy Fawkes, that is burnt on top of a bonfire on Guy Fawkes Day (November 5).

📖 short for *Guy* Fawkes, who plotted to blow up the British Houses of Parliament

**guzzle** guzzles guzzling guzzled

VERB To guzzle something means to drink or eat it quickly and greedily.

**gym** gyms

NOUN PE **1** a gymnasium. **2** Gym is gymnastics.

**gymkhana** gymkhanas

*Said* "jim-**kah**-na" NOUN an event in which people take part in horse-riding contests.

📖 from Hindi *gend-khana* literally meaning 'ball house', because it is where sports were held

**gymnasium** gymnasiums

NOUN a room with special equipment for physical exercises.

📖 from Greek *gumnazein* meaning 'to exercise naked'

**gymnast** gymnasts

NOUN someone who is trained in gymnastics.

**gymnastic** ADJECTIVE

**gymnastics**

NOUN PE Gymnastics is physical exercises, especially ones using equipment such as bars and ropes.

**gynaecology** or **gynecology**

*Said* "gie-nak-**kol**-loj-ee" NOUN Gynaecology is the branch of medical science concerned with the female reproductive system.

**gynaecologist** NOUN

**gynaecological** ADJECTIVE

**gypsy** gypsies; also spelt **gipsy**

NOUN a member of a race of people who travel from place to place in caravans.

from 'Egyptian', because people used to think gypsies came from Egypt

**gyrate** gyrates gyrating gyrated

*Said* "jy-**rate**" VERB To gyrate means to move round in a circle.

# Hh

a b c d e f g **h** i j k l m n o p q r s t u v w x y z

**TIP** Some words which sound as if they might begin with letter *h*, instead begin with the letters *wh*, for example *who, whole, wholly, whom, whore,* and *whose*.

**habit** habits
NOUN **1** something that you do often *E.G. He got into the habit of eating out.* **2** something that you keep doing and find it difficult to stop doing *E.G. a 20-a-day smoking habit.* **3** A monk's or nun's habit is a garment like a loose dress.
**habitual** ADJECTIVE **habitually** ADVERB

**habitat** habitats
NOUN (GEOGRAPHY) the natural home of a plant or animal.

**hack** hacks hacking hacked
VERB **1** If you hack at something, you cut it using rough strokes. ▶ NOUN **2** a writer or journalist who produces work fast without worrying about quality.

**hacker** hackers
NOUN; INFORMAL someone who uses a computer to break into the computer system of a company or government.

**hackles**
PLURAL NOUN **1** A dog's hackles are the hairs on the back of its neck which rise when it is angry. ▶ PHRASE **2** Something that **makes your hackles rise** makes you angry.

**hackneyed**
ADJECTIVE A hackneyed phrase is meaningless because it has been used too often.
■ clichéd, unoriginal

**hacksaw** hacksaws
NOUN a small saw with a narrow blade

set in a frame.

**haddock**
NOUN an edible sea fish.

**haemoglobin**
*Said* "hee-moh-**gloh**-bin" NOUN Haemoglobin is a substance in red blood cells which carries oxygen round the body.

**haemorrhage**
*Said* "**hem**-er-rij" NOUN A haemorrhage is serious bleeding especially inside a person's body.

**haemorrhoids**
*Said* "**hem**-er-roydz" PLURAL NOUN Haemorrhoids are painful lumps around the anus that are caused by swollen veins.

**hag** hags
NOUN; OFFENSIVE an ugly old woman.

**haggard**
ADJECTIVE A person who is haggard looks very tired and ill.

**haggis**
NOUN Haggis is a Scottish dish made of the internal organs of a sheep, boiled together with oatmeal and spices in a skin.

**haggle** haggles haggling haggled
VERB If you haggle with someone, you argue with them, usually about the cost of something.

**hail** hails hailing hailed
NOUN **1** Hail is frozen rain. **2** A hail of things is a lot of them falling together *E.G. a hail of bullets... a hail of protest.* ▶ VERB **3** When it is hailing,

A B C D E F G **H** I J K L M N O P Q R S T U V W X Y Z

frozen rain is falling. **4** If someone hails you, they call you to attract your attention or greet you *E.G. He hailed a taxi.*

**hair** hairs
NOUN Hair consists of the long, threadlike strands that grow from the skin of animals and humans.

**haircut** haircuts
NOUN the cutting of someone's hair; also the style in which it is cut.

**hairdo** hairdos
NOUN a hairstyle.

**hairdresser** hairdressers
NOUN someone who is trained to cut and style people's hair; also a shop where this is done.

**hairdressing** NOUN or ADJECTIVE

**hairline** hairlines
NOUN **1** the edge of the area on your forehead where your hair grows. ► ADJECTIVE **2** A hairline crack is so fine that you can hardly see it.

**hairpin** hairpins
NOUN **1** a U-shaped wire used to hold hair in position. ► ADJECTIVE **2** A hairpin bend is a U-shaped bend in the road.

**hair-raising**
ADJECTIVE very frightening or exciting.

**hairstyle** hairstyles
NOUN Someone's hairstyle is the way in which their hair is arranged or cut.

**hairy** hairier hairiest
ADJECTIVE **1** covered in a lot of hair. **2** INFORMAL difficult, exciting, and rather frightening *E.G. He had lived through many hairy adventures.*

**hajj**
*Rhymes with "badge"* NOUN The hajj is the pilgrimage to Mecca that every Muslim must make at least once in their life if they are healthy and wealthy enough to do so.

🕌 from Arabic *hajj* pilgrimage

**haka** haka or hakas
NOUN **1** In New Zealand, a haka is a ceremonial Maori dance made up of various postures and accompanied by a chant. **2** an imitation of this dance performed by New Zealand sports teams before matches as a challenge.

**hake** hakes
NOUN an edible sea fish related to the cod.

**hakea** hakeas
NOUN a large Australian shrub with bright flowers and hard, woody fruit.

**halcyon**
*Said "hal-see-on"* ADJECTIVE **1** LITERARY peaceful, gentle, and calm *E.G. halcyon colours of yellow and turquoise.* ► PHRASE **2** **Halcyon days** are a happy and carefree time in the past *E.G. halcyon days in the sun.*

**half** halves
NOUN, ADJECTIVE, OR ADVERB **1** Half refers to one of two equal parts that make up a whole *E.G. the two halves of the brain… They chatted for another half hour… The bottle was only half full.* ► ADVERB **2** You can use 'half' to say that something is only partly true *E.G. I half expected him to explode in anger.*

**half-baked**
ADJECTIVE; INFORMAL Half-baked ideas or plans have not been properly thought out.

**half board**
NOUN Half board at a hotel includes breakfast and dinner but not lunch.

**half-brother** half-brothers
NOUN Your half-brother is the son of either your mother or your father but not of your other parent.

**half-hearted**
ADJECTIVE showing no real effort or enthusiasm.

**half-pie**
ADJECTIVE; INFORMAL In New Zealand English, half-pie means incomplete or not properly done E.G. *finished in a half-pie way.*

**half-sister** half-sisters
NOUN Your half-sister is the daughter of either your mother or your father but not of your other parent.

**half-timbered**
ADJECTIVE A half-timbered building has a framework of wooden beams showing in the walls.

**half-time**
NOUN Half-time is a short break between two parts of a game when the players have a rest.

**halfway**
ADVERB at the middle of the distance between two points in place or time E.G. *He stopped halfway down the ladder… halfway through the term.*

**halibut** halibuts
NOUN a large edible flat fish.

**hall** halls
NOUN 1 the room just inside the front entrance of a house which leads into other rooms. 2 a large room or building used for public events E.G. *a concert hall.*

**hallmark** hallmarks
NOUN 1 The hallmark of a person or group is their most typical quality E.G. *A warm, hospitable welcome is the hallmark of island people.* 2 an official mark on gold or silver indicating the quality of the metal.

**hallowed**
Said "hal-lode" ADJECTIVE respected as being holy E.G. *hallowed ground.*

**Halloween**
NOUN Halloween is October 31st, and is celebrated by children dressing up, often as ghosts and witches.
📖 from Old English *halig* + *æfen* meaning 'holy evening', the evening before All Saints' Day

**hallucinate** hallucinates hallucinating hallucinated
Said "hal-**loo**-sin-ate" VERB If you hallucinate, you see strange things in your mind because of illness or drugs.
**hallucination** NOUN **hallucinatory** ADJECTIVE
📖 from Latin *alucinari* meaning 'to wander in thought'

**halo** haloes or halos
NOUN a circle of light around the head of a holy figure.
📖 from Greek *halos* meaning 'disc shape of the sun or moon'

**halt** halts halting halted
VERB 1 To halt when moving means to stop. 2 To halt development or action means to stop it. ▶ NOUN 3 a short standstill.

**halter** halters
NOUN a strap fastened round a horse's head so that it can be led easily.

**halve** halves halving halved
Said "hahv" VERB 1 If you halve something, you divide it into two equal parts. 2 To halve something also means to reduce its size or amount by half.

**ham** hams
NOUN 1 Ham is meat from the hind leg of a pig, salted and cured. 2 a bad actor who exaggerates emotions and gestures. 3 someone who is interested in amateur radio.

**hamburger** hamburgers
NOUN a flat disc of minced meat,

a b c d e f g h i j k l m n o p q r s t u v w x y z

seasoned and fried; often eaten in a bread roll.

🏛 named after its city of origin *Hamburg* in Germany

**hammer** hammers hammering hammered

NOUN **1** a tool consisting of a heavy piece of metal at the end of a handle, used for hitting nails into things. ▶ VERB **2** If you hammer something, you hit it repeatedly, with a hammer or with your fist. **3** If you hammer an idea into someone, you keep repeating it and telling them about it. **4** INFORMAL If you hammer someone, you criticize or attack them severely.

**hammock** hammocks

NOUN a piece of net or canvas hung between two supports and used as a bed.

**hamper** hampers hampering hampered

NOUN **1** a rectangular wicker basket with a lid, used for carrying food. ▶ VERB **2** If you hamper someone, you make it difficult for them to move or progress.

■ (sense 2) handicap, hinder, impede

**hamster** hamsters

NOUN a small furry rodent which is often kept as a pet.

☑ There is no *p* in *hamster*.

**hamstring** hamstrings

NOUN (PE) Your hamstring is a tendon behind your knee joining your thigh muscles to the bones of your lower leg.

**hand** hands handing handed

NOUN **1** Your hand is the part of your body beyond the wrist, with four fingers and a thumb. **2** Your hand is also your writing style. **3** The hand of

someone in a situation is their influence or the part they play in it E.G. *He had a hand in its design.* **4** If you give someone a hand, you help them to do something. **5** When an audience gives someone a big hand, they applaud. **6** The hands of a clock or watch are the pointers that point to the numbers. **7** In cards, your hand is the cards you are holding. ▶ VERB **8** If you hand something to someone, you give it to them. ▶ PHRASES **9** Something that is **at hand**, **to hand**, or **on hand** is available, close by, and ready for use. **10** You use **on the one hand** to introduce the first part of an argument or discussion with two different points of view. **11** You use **on the other hand** to introduce the second part of an argument or discussion with two different points of view. **12** If you do something **by hand**, you do it using your hands rather than a machine.

**hand down** VERB Something that is handed down is passed from one generation to another.

**handbag** handbags

NOUN a small bag used mainly by women to carry money and personal items.

**handbook** handbooks

NOUN a book giving information and instructions about something.

**handcuff** handcuffs

NOUN Handcuffs are two metal rings linked by a chain which are locked around a prisoner's wrists.

**handful** handfuls

NOUN **1** A handful of something is the amount of it you can hold in your hand E.G. *He picked up a handful of seeds.* **2** a small quantity E.G. *Only a* *handful of people knew.* **3** Someone who is a handful is difficult to control *E.G. He is a bit of a handful.*

**handicap** handicaps
**handicapping** handicapped
NOUN **1** a physical or mental disability. **2** something that makes it difficult for you to achieve something. **3** In sport, a handicap is a disadvantage or advantage given to competitors according to their skill, in order to give them an equal chance of winning. ▸ VERB **4** If something handicaps someone, it makes it difficult for them to achieve something.
▤ (sense 1) disability, impairment

**handicraft** handicrafts
NOUN Handicrafts are activities such as embroidery or pottery which involve making things with your hands; also the items produced.

**handiwork**
NOUN Your handiwork is something that you have done or made yourself.

**handkerchief** handkerchiefs
NOUN a small square of fabric used for blowing your nose.

**handle** handles handling handled
NOUN **1** The handle of an object is the part by which it is held or controlled. **2** a small lever used to open and close a door or window. ▸ VERB **3** If you handle an object, you hold it in your hands to examine it. **4** If you handle something, you deal with it or control it *E.G. I have learned how to handle pressure.*

**handlebar** handlebars
NOUN Handlebars are the bar and handles at the front of a bicycle, used for steering.

**handout** handouts
NOUN **1** a gift of food, clothing, or money given to a poor person. **2** a piece of paper giving information about something.

**hand-picked**
ADJECTIVE carefully chosen *E.G. a hand-picked team of bodyguards.*

**handset** handsets
NOUN The handset of a telephone is the part that you speak into and listen with.

**handshake** handshakes
NOUN the grasping and shaking of a person's hand by another person.

**handsome**
ADJECTIVE **1** very attractive in appearance. **2** large and generous *E.G. a handsome profit.*
**handsomely** ADVERB
▤ (sense 1) attractive, good-looking

**handwriting**
NOUN Someone's handwriting is their style of writing as it looks on the page.

**handy** handier handiest
ADJECTIVE **1** conveniently near. **2** easy to handle or use. **3** skilful.

**hang** hangs hanging hung
VERB **1** If you hang something somewhere, you attach it to a high point. If it is hanging there, it is attached by its top to something *E.G. His jacket hung from a hook behind the door.* **2** If a future event or possibility is hanging over you, it worries or frightens you *E.G. She has an eviction notice hanging over her.* **3** When you hang wallpaper, you stick it onto a wall. **4** To hang someone means to kill them by suspending them by a rope around the neck. ▸ PHRASE **5** When you **get the hang of something**, you understand it and are able to do it.

a b c d e f g h i j k l m n o p q r s t u v w x y z

A B C D E F G H I J K L M N O P Q R S T U V W X Y Z

**hang about** or **hang around**
VERB 1 *INFORMAL* To hang about or hang around means to wait somewhere. 2 To hang about or hang around with someone means to spend a lot of time with them.

**hang on** VERB 1 If you hang on to something, you hold it tightly or keep it. 2 *INFORMAL* To hang on means to wait.

**hang up** VERB When you hang up, you put down the receiver to end a telephone call

☑ When *hang* means 'kill someone by suspending them by a rope' (sense 4), the past tense and past participle are *hanged: he was hanged for murder in 1959.*

**hangar** hangars
NOUN a large building where aircraft are kept.

**hanger** hangers
NOUN a coat hanger.

**hanger-on** hangers-on
NOUN an unwelcome follower of an important person.

**hang-glider** hang-gliders
NOUN an aircraft without an engine and consisting of a large frame covered in fabric, from which the pilot hangs in a harness.

**hangi** hangi or hangis
*Said* "hung-ee" NOUN In New Zealand, a Maori oven made from a hole in the ground lined with hot stones.

**hangover** hangovers
NOUN a feeling of sickness and headache after drinking too much alcohol.

**hang-up** hang-ups
NOUN A hang-up about something is a continual feeling of embarrassment or fear about it.

**hanker** hankers hankering hankered
VERB If you hanker after something, you continually want it.
**hankering** NOUN

**hanky** hankies
NOUN a handkerchief.

**Hanukkah** or **Chanukah**
*Said* "hah-na-ka" NOUN Hanukkah is an eight-day Jewish festival of lights.
🏛 a Hebrew word meaning literally 'a dedication'

**haphazard**
*Said* "hap-haz-ard" ADJECTIVE not organized or planned.
**haphazardly** ADVERB
🏛 from Old Norse *hap* meaning 'chance' and Arabic *az-zahr* meaning 'gaming dice'

**hapless**
ADJECTIVE; *LITERARY* unlucky.

**happen** happens happening happened
VERB 1 When something happens, it occurs or takes place. 2 If you happen to do something, you do it by chance.
**happening** NOUN
▤ (sense 1) come about, occur, take place

**happiness**
NOUN a feeling of great contentment or pleasure.

**happy** happier happiest
ADJECTIVE 1 feeling, showing, or producing contentment or pleasure *E.G. a happy smile… a happy atmosphere.* 2 satisfied that something is right *E.G. I wasn't very happy about the layout.* 3 willing *E.G. I would be happy to help.* 4 fortunate or lucky *E.G. a happy coincidence.*
**happily** ADVERB

■ (sense 1) blissful, content, glad, joyful

**happy-go-lucky**
ADJECTIVE carefree and unconcerned.

**harangue** harangues haranguing harangued
Said "har-**rang**" NOUN **1** a long, forceful, passionate speech. ▶ VERB **2** To harangue someone means to talk to them at length passionately and forcefully about something.
🏛 from Old Italian *aringa* meaning 'public speech'

**harass** harasses harassing harassed
Said "har-**rass**" VERB If someone harasses you, they trouble or annoy you continually.
**harassed** ADJECTIVE **harassment** NOUN

**harbinger** harbingers
Said "har-**bin**-jer" NOUN a person or thing that announces or indicates the approach of a future event E.G. *others see the shortage of cash as a harbinger of bankruptcy*.

**harbour** harbours harbouring harboured
NOUN **1** a protected area of deep water where boats can be moored. ▶ VERB **2** To harbour someone means to hide them secretly in your house. **3** If you harbour a feeling, you have it for a long time E.G. *She's still harbouring great bitterness*.
🏛 from Old English *here* + *beorg* meaning 'army shelter'

**hard** harder hardest
ADJECTIVE or ADVERB **1** Something that is hard is firm, solid, or stiff E.G. *a hard piece of cheese… The ground was baked hard*. **2** requiring a lot of effort E.G. *hard work… They tried hard to*

*attract tourists*. ▶ ADJECTIVE **3** difficult E.G. *These are hard times*. **4** Someone who is hard has no kindness or pity E.G. *Don't be hard on him*. **5** A hard colour or voice is harsh and unpleasant. **6** Hard evidence or facts can be proved to be true. **7** Hard water contains a lot of lime and does not easily produce a lather. **8** Hard drugs are very strong illegal drugs. **9** Hard drink is strong alcohol.
▶ ADVERB **10** An event that follows hard upon something takes place immediately afterwards.
**hardness** NOUN
■ (sense 1) firm, rigid, solid, stiff

**hard and fast**
ADJECTIVE fixed and not able to be changed E.G. *hard and fast rules*.

**hardback** hardbacks
NOUN a book with a stiff cover.

**hard core**
NOUN The hard core in an organization is the group of people who most resist change.

**harden** hardens hardening hardened
VERB To harden means to become hard or get harder.
**hardening** NOUN **hardened** ADJECTIVE

**hard labour**
NOUN physical work which is difficult and tiring, used in some countries as a punishment for a crime.

**hardly**
ADVERB **1** almost not or not quite E.G. *I could hardly believe it*. **2** certainly not E.G. *It's hardly a secret*.
☑ You should not use *hardly* with a negative word like *not* or *no: he could hardly hear her* not *he could not hardly hear her*.

a b c d e f g h i j k l m n o p q r s t u v w x y z

A B C D E F G **H** I J K L M N O P Q R S T U V W X Y Z

**hard-nosed**
ADJECTIVE tough, practical, and realistic.

**hard of hearing**
ADJECTIVE not able to hear properly.

**hardship hardships**
NOUN Hardship is a time or situation of suffering and difficulty.

**hard shoulder hard shoulders**
NOUN the area at the edge of a motorway where a driver can stop in the event of a breakdown.

**hard up**
ADJECTIVE; INFORMAL having hardly any money.

**hardware**
NOUN 1 Hardware is tools and equipment for use in the home and garden. 2 (ICT) Hardware is also computer machinery rather than computer programs.

**hard-wearing**
ADJECTIVE strong, well-made, and long-lasting.

**hardwood hardwoods**
NOUN strong, hard wood from a tree such as an oak; also the tree itself.

**hardy hardier hardiest**
ADJECTIVE tough and able to endure very difficult or cold conditions E.G. a hardy race of pioneers.

**hare hares haring hared**
NOUN 1 an animal like a large rabbit, but with longer ears and legs. ► VERB 2 To hare about means to run very fast E.G. He hared off down the corridor.

**harem harems**
Said "har-reem" NOUN a group of wives or mistresses of one man, especially in Muslim societies; also the place where these women live.

**hark harks harking harked**
VERB 1 OLD-FASHIONED To hark means to listen. 2 To hark back to something in the past means to refer back to it or recall it.

**harlequin**
Said "har-lik-win" ADJECTIVE having many different colours.

**harm harms harming harmed**
VERB 1 To harm someone or something means to injure or damage them. ► NOUN 2 Harm is injury or damage.
■ (sense 1) damage, hurt, injure

**harmful**
ADJECTIVE having a bad effect on something E.G. Whilst most stress is harmful, some is beneficial.

**harmless**
ADJECTIVE 1 safe to use, or be near. 2 unlikely to cause problems or annoyance E.G. He's harmless really.
**harmlessly** ADVERB

**harmonic**
ADJECTIVE using musical harmony.

**harmonica harmonicas**
NOUN a small musical instrument which you play by blowing and sucking while moving it across your lips.

**harmonious**
Said "har-moh-nee-uss" ADJECTIVE 1 showing agreement, peacefulness, and friendship E.G. a harmonious relationship. 2 consisting of parts which blend well together making an attractive whole E.G. harmonious interior decor.
**harmoniously** ADVERB

**harmony harmonies**
NOUN 1 Harmony is a state of peaceful agreement and cooperation E.G. the promotion of racial harmony.
2 (MUSIC) Harmony is the structure and relationship of chords in a piece

of music. **3** Harmony is the pleasant combination of two or more notes played at the same time.

**harness** harnesses harnessing harnessed

NOUN **1** a set of straps and fittings fastened round a horse so that it can pull a vehicle, or fastened round someone's body to attach something E.G. *a safety harness.* ▶ VERB **2** If you harness something, you bring it under control to use it E.G. *harnessing public opinion.*

**harp** harps harping harped

NOUN **1** a musical instrument consisting of a triangular frame with vertical strings which you pluck with your fingers. ▶ VERB **2** If someone harps on something, they keep talking about it, especially in a boring way.

**harpoon** harpoons

NOUN a barbed spear attached to a rope, thrown or fired from a gun and used for catching whales or large fish.

**harpsichord** harpsichords

NOUN a musical instrument like a small piano, with strings which are plucked when the keys are pressed.

**harrowing**

ADJECTIVE very upsetting or disturbing E.G. *a harrowing experience.*

**harsh** harsher harshest

ADJECTIVE severe, difficult, and unpleasant E.G. *harsh weather conditions… harsh criticism.*
**harshly** ADVERB **harshness** NOUN
■ hard, severe, tough

**harvest** harvests harvesting harvested

NOUN **1** the cutting and gathering of a crop; also the ripe crop when it is

gathered and the time of gathering. ▶ VERB **2** To harvest food means to gather it when it is ripe.

**harvester** NOUN
▦ from Old German *herbist* meaning 'autumn'

**has-been** has-beens

NOUN; *INFORMAL* a person who is no longer important or successful.

**hash** hashes

PHRASE **1** If you **make a hash of** a job, you do it badly. ▶ NOUN **2** the name for the symbol #. **3** Hash is a dish made of small pieces of meat and vegetables cooked together.
**4** *INFORMAL* Hash is also hashish.

**hashish**

*Said* "**hash**-eesh" NOUN Hashish is a drug made from the hemp plant. It is usually smoked, and is illegal in many countries.
▦ from Arabic *hashish* meaning 'hemp' or 'dried grass'

**hassle** hassles hassling hassled

NOUN **1** *INFORMAL* Something that is a hassle is difficult or causes trouble.
▶ VERB **2** If you hassle someone, you annoy them by repeatedly asking them to do something.

**haste**

NOUN Haste is doing something quickly, especially too quickly.

**hasten** hastens hastening hastened

*Said* "**hay**-sn" VERB To hasten means to move quickly or do something quickly.

**hasty** hastier hastiest

ADJECTIVE done or happening suddenly and quickly, often without enough care or thought.
**hastily** ADVERB

**hat** hats

NOUN a covering for the head.

a b c d e f g **h** i j k l m n o p q r s t u v w x y z

**hatch** hatches hatching hatched

VERB 1 When an egg hatches, or when a bird or reptile hatches, the egg breaks open and the young bird or reptile emerges. 2 To hatch a plot means to plan it. ▸ NOUN 3 A covered opening in a floor or wall.

**hatchback** hatchbacks

NOUN a car with a door at the back which opens upwards.

**hatchet** hatchets

NOUN 1 a small axe. ▸ PHRASE 2 To **bury the hatchet** means to resolve a disagreement and become friends again.

**hate** hates hating hated

VERB 1 If you hate someone or something, you have a strong dislike for them. ▸ NOUN 2 Hate is a strong dislike.

◼ (sense 1) detest, loathe

**hatred**

Said "hay-trid" NOUN Hatred is an extremely strong feeling of dislike.

**hat trick** hat tricks

NOUN In sport, a hat trick is three achievements, for example when a footballer scores three goals in a match E.G. Crawford completed his hat trick in the 60th minute.

**haughty** haughtier haughtiest

Rhymes with "naughty" ADJECTIVE showing excessive pride E.G. He behaved in a haughty manner.

**haughtily** ADVERB

◼ disdainful, proud, supercilious

**haul** hauls hauling hauled

VERB 1 To haul something somewhere means to pull it with great effort. ▸ NOUN 2 a quantity of something obtained E.G. a good haul of fish. ▸ PHRASE 3 Something that you describe as **a long haul** takes a lot of time and effort to achieve E.G. So women began the long haul to equality.

**haulage**

Said "hawl-lij" NOUN Haulage is the business or cost of transporting goods by road.

**haunches**

PLURAL NOUN Your haunches are your buttocks and the tops of your legs E.G. He squatted on his haunches.

**haunt** haunts haunting haunted

VERB 1 If a ghost haunts a place, it is seen or heard there regularly. 2 If a memory or a fear haunts you, it continually worries you. ▸ NOUN 3 A person's favourite haunt is a place they like to visit often.

**haunted**

ADJECTIVE 1 regularly visited by a ghost E.G. a haunted house. 2 very worried or troubled E.G. a haunted expression.

**haunting**

ADJECTIVE extremely beautiful or sad so that it makes a lasting impression on you E.G. a haunting piece of music.

**have** has having had

VERB 1 Have is an auxiliary verb, used to form the past tense or to express completed actions E.G. They have never met… I have lost it. 2 If you have something, you own or possess it E.G. We have two tickets for the concert. 3 If you have something, you experience it, it happens to you, or you are affected by it E.G. I have an idea!… He had a marvellous time. 4 To have a child or baby animal means to give birth to it E.G. When is she having the baby? ▸ PHRASES 5 If you **have to** do something, you must do it. 6 If you **had better** do something, you ought to do it.

**haven** havens
*Said "hay-ven"* NOUN a safe place.

**havoc**
NOUN 1 Havoc is disorder and confusion. ▶ PHRASE 2 To **play havoc** with something means to cause great disorder and confusion. E.G. *Food allergies often play havoc with the immune system.*

**hawk** hawks hawking hawked
NOUN 1 a bird of prey with short rounded wings and a long tail. ▶ VERB 2 To hawk goods means to sell them by taking them around from place to place.

**hawthorn** hawthorns
NOUN a small, thorny tree producing white blossom and red berries.

**hay**
NOUN Hay is grass which has been cut and dried and is used as animal feed.

**hay fever**
NOUN Hay fever is an allergy to pollen and grass, causing sneezing and watering eyes.

**haystack** haystacks
NOUN a large, firmly built pile of hay, usually covered and left in the open.

**hazard** hazards hazarding hazarded
NOUN 1 (SCIENCE) a substance, object or action which could be dangerous to you. ▶ VERB 2 If you hazard something, you put it at risk E.G. *hazarding the health of his crew.* ▶ PHRASE 3 If you **hazard a guess**, you make a guess.
**hazardous** ADJECTIVE
🏛 from Arabic *az-zahr* meaning 'gaming dice'

**haze**
NOUN If there is a haze, you cannot see clearly because there is moisture or smoke in the air.

**hazel** hazels
NOUN 1 a small tree producing edible nuts. ▶ ADJECTIVE 2 greenish brown in colour.

**hazy** hazier haziest
ADJECTIVE dim or vague E.G. *hazy sunshine… a hazy memory.*

**he**
PRONOUN 'He' is used to refer to a man, boy, or male animal or to any person whose sex is not mentioned.

**head** heads heading headed
NOUN 1 Your head is the part of your body which has your eyes, brain, and mouth in it. 2 Your head is also your mind and mental abilities E.G. *He has a head for figures.* 3 The head of something is the top, start, or most important end E.G. *at the head of the table.* 4 The head of a group or organization is the person in charge. 5 The head on beer is the layer of froth on the top. 6 The head on a computer or tape recorder is the part that can read or write information. 7 When you toss a coin, the side called heads is the one with the head on it. ▶ VERB 8 To head a group or organization means to be in charge E.G. *Bryce heads the help organization.* 9 To head in a particular direction means to move in that direction E.G. *She is heading for a breakdown.* 10 To head a ball means to hit it with your head. ▶ PHRASE 11 If you **lose your head**, you panic. 12 If you say that someone is **off their head**, you mean that they are mad or very stupid. 13 If something is **over someone's head**, it is too difficult for them to understand. 14 If you **can't make head nor tail of something**, you cannot understand it.
**head off** VERB If you head off

a b c d e f g h i j k l m n o p q r s t u v w x y z

A B C D E F G **H** I J K L M N O P Q R S T U V W X Y Z

someone or something, you make them change direction or prevent something from happening E.G. *He hopes to head off a public squabble.*

**headache** headaches

NOUN **1** a pain in your head. **2** Something that is a headache is causing a lot of difficulty or worry E.G. *Delays in receiving money owed is a major headache for small firms.*

**header** headers

NOUN A header in soccer is hitting the ball with your head.

**heading** headings

NOUN a piece of writing that is written or printed at the top of a page.

**headland** headlands

NOUN a narrow piece of land jutting out into the sea.

**headlight** headlights

NOUN The headlights on a motor vehicle are the large powerful lights at the front.

**headline** headlines

NOUN **1** A newspaper headline is the title of a newspaper article printed in large, bold type. **2** The headlines are the main points of the radio or television news.

**headmaster** headmasters

NOUN a man who is the head teacher of a school.

**headmistress** headmistresses

NOUN a woman who is the head teacher of a school.

**headphones**

PLURAL NOUN Headphones are a pair of small speakers which you wear over your ears to listen to a radio without other people hearing.

**headquarters**

NOUN The headquarters of an organization is the main place or

from which it is run.

**headroom**

NOUN Headroom is the amount of space below a roof or surface under which an object must pass or fit.

**headstone** headstones

NOUN a large stone standing at one end of a grave and showing the name of the person buried there.

**headstrong**

ADJECTIVE determined to do something in your own way and ignoring other people's advice.

**head teacher** head teachers

NOUN the teacher who is in charge of a school.

**headway**

PHRASE If you are **making headway**, you are making progress.

**headwind** headwinds

NOUN a wind blowing in the opposite direction to the way you are travelling.

**heady**

ADJECTIVE extremely exciting E.G. *the heady days of the civil rights era.*

**heal** heals healing healed

VERB If something heals or if you heal it, it becomes healthy or normal again E.G. *He had a nasty wound which had not healed properly.*

**healer** NOUN

**health**

NOUN Health is the normally good condition of someone's body and the extent to which it is free from illness E.G. *Vitamins are essential for health.*

📖 from Old English *hælth* a toast drunk to a person's wellbeing

▦ fitness, wellbeing

**health food** health foods

NOUN food which is free from added chemicals and is considered to be good for your health.

**healthy** healthier healthiest

ADJECTIVE **1** Someone who is healthy is fit and strong and does not have any diseases. **2** Something that is healthy is good for you *E.G. a healthy diet.* **3** An organization or system that is healthy is successful *E.G. a healthy economy.*

**healthily** ADVERB

■ (sense 1) fit, well

**heap** heaps heaping heaped

NOUN **1** a pile of things. **2** *INFORMAL* Heaps of something means plenty of it *E.G. His performance earned him heaps of praise.* ▶ VERB **3** If you heap things up, you pile them up. **4** To heap something such as praise on someone means to give them a lot of it.

■ (sense 1) mass, mound, pile

**hear** hears hearing heard

VERB **1** When you hear sounds, you are aware of them because they reach your ears. **2** When you hear from someone, they write to you or phone you. **3** When a judge hears a case, he or she listens to it in court in order to make a decision on it. ▶ PHRASE **4** If you say that you **won't hear of** something, you mean you refuse to allow it.

**hear out** VERB If you hear someone out, you listen to all they have to say without interrupting.

**hearing** hearings

NOUN **1** Hearing is the sense which makes it possible for you to be aware of sounds *E.G. My hearing is poor.* **2** a court trial or official meeting to hear facts about an incident. **3** If someone gives you a hearing, they let you give your point of view and listen to you.

**hearsay**

NOUN Hearsay is information that you have heard from other people rather than something that you know personally to be true.

**hearse** hearses

*Rhymes with "**verse**"* NOUN a large car that carries the coffin at a funeral.

**heart** hearts

NOUN **1** the organ in your chest that pumps the blood around your body. **2** Your heart is also thought of as the centre of your emotions. **3** Heart is courage, determination, or enthusiasm *E.G. They were losing heart.* **4** The heart of something is the most central and important part of it. **5** a shape similar to a heart, used especially as a symbol of love. **6** Hearts is one of the four suits in a pack of playing cards. It is marked by a red heart-shaped symbol.

**heartache** heartaches

NOUN Heartache is very great sadness and emotional suffering.

**heart attack** heart attacks

NOUN a serious medical condition in which the heart suddenly beats irregularly or stops completely.

**heartbreak** heartbreaks

NOUN Heartbreak is great sadness and emotional suffering.

**heartbreaking** ADJECTIVE

**heartbroken**

ADJECTIVE very sad and emotionally upset *E.G. She was heartbroken at his death.*

**heartburn**

NOUN Heartburn is a painful burning sensation in your chest, caused by indigestion.

a b c d e f g h i j k l m n o p q r s t u v w x y z

**heartening**
ADJECTIVE encouraging or uplifting E.G. *heartening news.*

**heart failure**
NOUN Heart failure is a serious condition in which someone's heart does not work as well as it should, sometimes stopping completely.

**heartfelt**
ADJECTIVE sincerely and deeply felt E.G. *Our heartfelt sympathy goes out to you.*

**hearth hearths**
Said "harth" NOUN the floor of a fireplace.

**heartless**
ADJECTIVE cruel and unkind.

**heart-rending**
ADJECTIVE causing great sadness and pity E.G. *a heart-rending story.*

**heart-throb heart-throbs**
NOUN someone who is attractive to a lot of people.

**heart-to-heart heart-to-hearts**
NOUN a discussion in which two people talk about their deepest feelings.

**hearty heartier heartiest**
ADJECTIVE 1 cheerful and enthusiastic E.G. *hearty congratulations.* 2 strongly felt E.G. *a hearty dislike for her teacher.* 3 A hearty meal is large and satisfying.
**heartily** ADVERB

**heat heats heating heated**
NOUN 1 Heat is warmth or the quality of being hot; also the temperature of something that is warm or hot. 2 Heat is strength of feeling, especially of anger or excitement. 3 a contest or race in a competition held to decide who will play in the final. ▶ VERB 4 To heat something means to raise its temperature. ▶ PHRASE 5 When

a female animal is **on heat**, she is ready for mating.
**heater** NOUN

**heath heaths**
NOUN an area of open land covered with rough grass or heather.

**heathen heathens**
NOUN; OLD-FASHIONED someone who does not believe in one of the established religions.

**heather**
NOUN a plant with small purple or white flowers that grows wild on hills and moorland.

**heating**
NOUN Heating is the equipment used to heat a building; also the process and cost of running the equipment to provide heat.

**heatwave heatwaves**
NOUN a period of time during which the weather is much hotter than usual.

**heave heaves heaving heaved**
VERB 1 To heave something means to move or throw it with a lot of effort. 2 If your stomach heaves, you vomit or suddenly feel sick. 3 If you heave a sigh, you sigh loudly. ▶ NOUN 4 If you give something a heave, you move or throw it with a lot of effort.

**heaven heavens**
NOUN 1 a place of happiness where God is believed to live and where good people are believed to go when they die. 2 If you describe a situation or place as heaven, you mean that it is wonderful E.G. *The cake was pure heaven.* ▶ PHRASE 3 You say '**Good heavens**' to express surprise.

**heavenly**
ADJECTIVE 1 relating to heaven E.G. *a*

*heavenly choir.* **2** *INFORMAL* wonderful *E.G. his heavenly blue eyes.*

**heavy** **heavier heaviest; heavies**
ADJECTIVE **1** great in weight or force *E.G. How heavy are you?… a heavy blow.* **2** great in degree or amount *E.G. heavy casualties.* **3** solid and thick in appearance *E.G. heavy shoes.* **4** using a lot of something quickly *E.G. The van is heavy on petrol.* **5** serious and difficult to deal with or understand *E.G. It all got a bit heavy when the police arrived… a heavy speech.* **6** Food that is heavy is solid and difficult to digest *E.G. a heavy meal.* **7** When it is heavy, the weather is hot, humid, and still. **8** Someone with a heavy heart is very sad. ▸ NOUN **9** *INFORMAL* a large, strong man employed to protect someone or something.
**heavily** ADVERB    **heaviness** NOUN

**heavy-duty**
ADJECTIVE Heavy-duty equipment is strong and hard-wearing.

**heavy-handed**
ADJECTIVE showing a lack of care or thought and using too much authority *E.G. heavy-handed police tactics.*

**heavyweight** **heavyweights**
NOUN **1** a boxer in the heaviest weight group. **2** an important person with a lot of influence.

**Hebrew** **Hebrews**
*Said "hee-broo"* NOUN **1** Hebrew is an ancient language now spoken in Israel, where it is the official language. **2** In the past, the Hebrews were Hebrew-speaking Jews who lived in Israel. ▸ ADJECTIVE **3** relating to the Hebrews and their customs.
🏛 from Hebrew *ibhri* meaning 'one

from beyond (the river)'
**heckle** **heckles heckling heckled**
VERB If members of an audience heckle a speaker, they interrupt and shout rude remarks.
**heckler** NOUN

**hectare** **hectares**
NOUN a unit for measuring areas of land, equal to 10,000 square metres or about 2.471 acres.

**hectic**
ADJECTIVE involving a lot of rushed activity *E.G. a hectic schedule.*

**hedge** **hedges hedging hedged**
NOUN **1** a row of bushes forming a barrier or boundary. ▸ VERB **2** If you hedge against something unpleasant happening, you protect yourself. **3** If you hedge, you avoid answering a question or dealing with a problem. ▸ PHRASE **4** If you **hedge your bets**, you support two or more people or courses of action to avoid the risk of losing a lot.

**hedgehog** **hedgehogs**
NOUN a small, brown animal with sharp spikes covering its back.

**hedonism**
*Said "hee-dn-izm"* NOUN Hedonism is the belief that gaining pleasure is the most important thing in life.
**hedonistic** ADJECTIVE

**heed** **heeds heeding heeded**
VERB **1** If you heed someone's advice, you pay attention to it. ▸ NOUN **2** If you take or pay heed to something, you give it careful attention.
**▤** (sense 1) listen to, mind, pay attention to

**heel** **heels heeling heeled**
NOUN **1** the back part of your foot. **2** The heel of a shoe or sock is the part that fits over your heel. ▸ VERB

a
b
c
d
e
f
g
h
i
j
k
l
m
n
o
p
q
r
s
t
u
v
w
x
y
z

A
B
C
D
E
F
G
H
I
J
K
L
M
N
O
P
Q
R
S
T
U
V
W
X
Y
Z

**3** To heel a pair of shoes means to put a new piece on the heel. ► PHRASE **4** A person or place that looks **down at heel** looks untidy and in poor condition.

**heeler** heelers
NOUN In Australia, a dog that herds cattle by biting at their heels.

**hefty** heftier heftiest
ADJECTIVE of great size, force, or weight E.G. *a hefty fine… hefty volumes.*

**height** heights
NOUN **1** The height of an object is its measurement from the bottom to the top. **2** a high position or place E.G. *Their nesting rarely takes place at any great height.* **3** The height of something is its peak, or the time when it is most successful or intense E.G. *the height of the tourist season… at the height of his career.*

**heighten** heightens heightening heightened
VERB If something heightens a feeling or experience, it increases its intensity.

**heinous**
Said "hay-nuss or hee-nuss" ADJECTIVE evil and terrible E.G. *heinous crimes.*

**heir** heirs
Said "air" NOUN A person's heir is the person who is entitled to inherit their property or title.

**heiress** heiresses
Said "air-iss" NOUN a female with the right to inherit property or a title.

**heirloom** heirlooms
Said "air-loom" NOUN something belonging to a family that has been passed from one generation to another.

**helicopter** helicopters
NOUN an aircraft with rotating blades

above it which enable it to take off vertically, hover, and fly.
🏛 from Greek *heliko* + *pteron* meaning 'spiral wing'

**helium**
Said "hee-lee-um" NOUN Helium is a gas that is lighter than air and that is used to fill balloons.

**hell**
NOUN **1** Hell is the place where souls of evil people are believed to go to be punished after death. **2** INFORMAL If you say that something is hell, you mean it is very unpleasant.
► INTERJECTION **3** 'Hell' is also a swearword.

**hell-bent**
ADJECTIVE determined to do something whatever the consequences.

**hellish**
ADJECTIVE; INFORMAL very unpleasant.

**hello**
INTERJECTION You say 'Hello' as a greeting or when you answer the phone.

**helm** helms
NOUN **1** The helm on a boat is the position from which it is steered and the wheel or tiller. ► PHRASE **2 At the helm** means in a position of leadership or control.

**helmet** helmets
NOUN a hard hat worn to protect the head.

**help** helps helping helped
VERB **1** To help someone means to make something easier or better for them. ► NOUN **2** If you need or give help, you need or give assistance. **3** someone or something that helps you E.G. *He really is a good help.*
► PHRASE **4** If you **help yourself** to something, you take it. **5** If you **can't**

**help** something, you cannot control it or change it E.G. *I can't help feeling sorry for him.*
**helper** NOUN

**helpful**
ADJECTIVE **1** If someone is helpful, they help you by doing something for you. **2** Something that is helpful makes a situation more pleasant or easier to tolerate.
**helpfully** ADVERB
■ (sense 1) cooperative, supportive
■ (sense 2) beneficial, useful

**helping** helpings
NOUN an amount of food that you get in a single serving.

**helpless**
ADJECTIVE **1** unable to cope on your own E.G. *a helpless child.* **2** weak or powerless E.G. *helpless despair.*
**helplessly** ADVERB **helplessness** NOUN

**hem** hems hemming hemmed
NOUN **1** The hem of a garment is an edge which has been turned over and sewn in place. ▶ VERB **2** To hem something means to make a hem on it.
**hem in** VERB If someone is hemmed in, they are surrounded and prevented from moving.

**hemisphere** hemispheres
*Said "hem-iss-feer"* NOUN one half of the earth, the brain, or a sphere.

**hemp**
NOUN Hemp is a tall plant, some varieties of which are used to make rope, and others to produce the drug cannabis.

**hen** hens
NOUN a female chicken; also any female bird.

**hence**
ADVERB **1** *FORMAL* for this reason E.G. *It*
sells more papers, hence more money is made.* **2** from now or from the time mentioned E.G. *The convention is due to start two weeks hence.*

**henceforth**
ADVERB; *FORMAL* from this time onward E.G. *His life henceforth was to revolve around her.*

**henchman** henchmen
NOUN The henchmen of a powerful person are the people employed to do violent or dishonest work for that person.

**hepatitis**
NOUN Hepatitis is a serious infectious disease causing inflammation of the liver.

**her**
PRONOUN or ADJECTIVE 'Her' is used to refer to a woman, girl or female animal that has already been mentioned, or to show that something belongs to a particular female.

**herald** heralds heralding heralded
NOUN **1** In the past, a herald was a messenger. ▶ VERB **2** Something that heralds a future event is a sign of that event.

**herb** herbs
NOUN a plant whose leaves are used in medicine or to flavour food.
**herbal** ADJECTIVE **herbalist** NOUN

**herbivore** herbivores
NOUN an animal that eats only plants.

**herd** herds herding herded
NOUN **1** a large group of animals. ▶ VERB **2** To herd animals or people means to make them move together as a group.

**here**
ADVERB **1** at, to, or in the place where

a
b
c
d
e
f
g
**h**
i
j
k
l
m
n
o
p
q
r
s
t
u
v
w
x
y
z

you are, or the place mentioned or indicated. ▶ PHRASE **2 Here and there** means in various unspecified places E.G. *dense forests broken here and there by small towns.*

**hereafter**
ADVERB; FORMAL after this time or point E.G. *the South China Morning Post (referred to hereafter as SCMP).*

**hereby**
ADVERB; FORMAL used in documents and statements to indicate that a declaration is official E.G. *All leave is hereby cancelled.*

**hereditary**
ADJECTIVE passed on to a child from a parent E.G. *a hereditary disease.*

**heredity**
NOUN Heredity is the process by which characteristics are passed from parents to their children through the genes.

**herein**
ADVERB; FORMAL in this place or document.

**heresy heresies**
*Said "herr-ess-ee"* NOUN Heresy is belief or behaviour considered to be wrong because it disagrees with what is generally accepted, especially with regard to religion.
**heretic** NOUN **heretical** ADJECTIVE

**herewith**
ADVERB; FORMAL with this letter or document E.G. *I herewith return your cheque.*

**heritage**
NOUN the possessions or traditions that have been passed from one generation to another.

**hermit hermits**
NOUN a person who lives alone with a simple way of life, especially for

religious reasons.
▨ from Greek *erēmitēs* meaning 'living in the desert'

**hernia hernias**
*Said "her-nee-a"* NOUN a medical condition in which part of the intestine sticks through a weak point in the surrounding tissue.

**hero heroes**
NOUN **1** the main male character in a book, film, or play. **2** a person who has done something brave or good.

**heroic**
ADJECTIVE brave, courageous, and determined.
**heroically** ADVERB

**heroin**
*Said "herr-oh-in"* NOUN Heroin is a powerful drug formerly used as an anaesthetic and now taken illegally by some people for pleasure.

**heroine heroines**
*Said "herr-oh-in"* NOUN **1** the main female character in a book, film, or play. **2** a woman who has done something brave or good.

**heroism**
*Said "herr-oh-i-zm"* NOUN Heroism is great courage and bravery.

**heron herons**
NOUN a wading bird with very long legs and a long beak and neck.

**herpes**
*Said "her-peez"* NOUN Herpes is a virus which causes painful red spots on the skin.

**herring herrings**
NOUN a silvery fish that lives in large shoals in northern seas.

**hers**
PRONOUN 'Hers' refers to something that belongs to or relates to a woman, girl, or female animal.

## herself

PRONOUN **1** 'Herself' is used when the same woman, girl, or female animal does an action and is affected by it E.G. *She pulled herself out of the water.* **2** 'Herself' is used to emphasize 'she'.

## hertz

NOUN A hertz is a unit of frequency equal to one cycle per second.

## hesitant

ADJECTIVE If you are hesitant, you do not do something immediately because you are uncertain or worried.
**hesitantly** ADVERB
■ irresolute, uncertain, unsure

## hesitate hesitates hesitating hesitated

VERB To hesitate means to pause or show uncertainty.
**hesitation** NOUN

## hessian

NOUN Hessian is a thick, rough fabric used for making sacks.

## heterosexual heterosexuals

*Said* "het-roh-**seks**-yool" ADJECTIVE
**1** involving a sexual relationship between a man and a woman E.G. *heterosexual couples.* ► NOUN **2** a person who is sexually attracted to people of the opposite sex.

## hewn

ADJECTIVE carved from a substance E.G. *a cave, hewn out of the hillside.*

## hexagon hexagons

NOUN a shape with six straight sides.
**hexagonal** ADJECTIVE

## heyday

*Said* "**hay**-day" NOUN The heyday of a person or thing is the period when they are most successful or popular E.G. *Hollywood in its heyday.*

## hi

INTERJECTION 'Hi!' is an informal greeting.

## hiatus hiatuses

*Said* "high-**ay**-tuss" NOUN; FORMAL a pause or gap.

## hibernate hibernates hibernating hibernated

VERB Animals that hibernate spend the winter in a state like deep sleep.
**hibernation** NOUN
🔲 from Latin *hibernare* meaning 'to spend the winter'

## hibiscus hibiscuses

*Said* "hie-**bis**-kuss" NOUN a type of tropical shrub with brightly coloured flowers.

## hiccup hiccups hiccupping hiccupped

*Said* "**hik**-kup"
NOUN **1** Hiccups are short, uncontrolled choking sounds in your throat that you sometimes get if you have been eating or drinking too quickly. **2** INFORMAL a minor problem. ► VERB **3** When you hiccup, you make these little choking sounds.

## hide hides hiding hid hidden

VERB **1** To hide something means to put it where it cannot be seen, or to prevent it from being discovered E.G. *He was unable to hide his disappointment.* ► NOUN **2** the skin of a large animal.
■ (sense 1) conceal, disguise

## hideous

*Said* "**hid**-ee-uss" ADJECTIVE extremely ugly or unpleasant.
**hideously** ADVERB

## hideout hideouts

NOUN a hiding place.

## hierarchy hierarchies

*Said* "**high**-er-ar-kee" NOUN a system in

a
b
c
d
e
f
g
h
i
j
k
l
m
n
o
p
q
r
s
t
u
v
w
x
y
z

**hierarchical** ADJECTIVE

**hi-fi** hi-fis
NOUN a set of stereo equipment on which you can play compact discs and tapes.

**high** higher highest; highs
ADJECTIVE or ADVERB 1 tall or a long way above the ground. 2 great in degree, quantity, or intensity E.G. high interest rates… There is a high risk of heart disease. 3 towards the top of a scale of importance or quality E.G. high fashion. 4 close to the top of a range of sound or notes E.G. the human voice reaches a very high pitch.
▶ ADJECTIVE 5 INFORMAL Someone who is high on a drug is affected by having taken it. ▶ NOUN 6 a high point or level E.G. Morale reached a new high. 7 INFORMAL Someone who is on a high is in a very excited and optimistic mood.
■ (sense 1) lofty, tall, towering

**highbrow**
ADJECTIVE concerned with serious, intellectual subjects.

**higher education**
NOUN Higher education is education at universities and colleges.

**high jump**
NOUN The high jump is an athletics event involving jumping over a high bar.

**highlands**
PLURAL NOUN Highlands are mountainous or hilly areas of land.

**highlight** highlights highlighting highlighted
VERB 1 If you highlight a point or problem, you emphasize and draw attention to it. ▶ NOUN 2 The highlight of something is the most interesting

part of it E.G. His show was the highlight of the Festival. 3 (ART) a lighter area of a painting, showing where light shines on things. 4 Highlights are also light-coloured streaks in someone's hair.

**highly**
ADVERB 1 extremely E.G. It is highly unlikely I'll be able to replace it. 2 towards the top of a scale of importance, admiration, or respect E.G. She thought highly of him… highly qualified personnel.

**high-minded**
ADJECTIVE Someone who is high-minded has strong moral principles.

**Highness**
'Highness' is used in titles and forms of address for members of the royal family other than a king or queen E.G. Her Royal Highness, Princess Alexandra.

**high-pitched**
ADJECTIVE A high-pitched sound is high and often rather shrill.

**high-rise**
ADJECTIVE High-rise buildings are very tall.

**high school** high schools
NOUN a secondary school.

**high technology**
NOUN High technology is the development and use of advanced electronics and computers.

**high tide**
NOUN On a coast, high tide is the time, usually twice a day, when the sea is at its highest level.

**highway** highways
NOUN a road along which vehicles have the right to pass.

**highwayman** highwaymen
NOUN In the past, highwaymen were

which people or things are ranked according to how important they are.

robbers on horseback who used to rob travellers.

**hijack** hijacks hijacking hijacked
VERB If someone hijacks a plane or vehicle, they illegally take control of it during a journey.
**hijacking** NOUN

**hike** hikes hiking hiked
NOUN **1** a long country walk. ▶ VERB **2** To hike means to walk long distances in the country.
**hiker** NOUN

**hilarious**
ADJECTIVE very funny.
**hilariously** ADVERB
■ funny, humorous, uproarious

**hilarity**
NOUN Hilarity is great amusement and laughter E.G. *His antics caused great hilarity.*

**hill** hills
NOUN a rounded area of land higher than the land surrounding it.
**hilly** ADJECTIVE

**hillbilly** hillbillies
NOUN someone who lives in the country away from other people, especially in remote areas in the southern United States.

**hilt** hilts
NOUN The hilt of a sword or knife is its handle.

**him**
PRONOUN You use 'him' to refer to a man, boy, or male animal that has already been mentioned, or to any person whose sex is not known.

**himself**
PRONOUN **1** 'Himself' is used when the same man, boy, or male animal does an action and is affected by it E.G. *He discharged himself from hospital.*
**2** 'Himself' is used to emphasize 'he'.

**hind** hinds
*Rhymes with "blind"* ADJECTIVE **1** used to refer to the back part of an animal E.G. *the hind legs.* ▶ NOUN **2** a female deer.

**hinder** hinders hindering hindered
*Said* "**hin-der**" VERB If you hinder someone or something, you get in their way and make something difficult for them.

**Hindi**
*Said* "**hin-dee**" NOUN Hindi is a language spoken in northern India.
🏛 from Old Persian *Hindu* meaning 'the river Indus'

**hindrance** hindrances
NOUN **1** Someone or something that is a hindrance causes difficulties or is an obstruction. **2** Hindrance is the act of hindering someone or something.

**hindsight**
NOUN Hindsight is the ability to understand an event after it has actually taken place E.G. *With hindsight, I realized how odd he is.*

**Hindu** Hindus
*Said* "**hin-doo**" NOUN ( RE ) a person who believes in Hinduism, an Indian religion which has many gods and believes that people have another life on earth after death.
**Hinduism** NOUN

**hinge** hinges hinging hinged
NOUN **1** the movable joint which attaches a door or window to its frame. ▶ VERB **2** Something that hinges on a situation or event depends entirely on that situation or event E.G. *Victory or defeat hinged on her final putt.*

**hint** hints hinting hinted
NOUN **1** a suggestion, clue, or helpful

a
b
c
d
e
f
g
h
i
j
k
l
m
n
o
p
q
r
s
t
u
v
w
x
y
z

LEt's measure the angLE (ang*le*)    **SPELLING NOTE**

A
B
C
D
E
F
G
H
I
J
K
L
M
N
O
P
Q
R
S
T
U
V
W
X
Y
Z

piece of advice. ➤ VERB 2 If you hint at something, you suggest it indirectly.
■ (sense 1) clue, indication, suggestion
■ (sense 2) imply, insinuate, suggest

**hinterland hinterlands**
NOUN The hinterland of a coastline or a port is the area of land behind it or around it.

**hip hips**
NOUN Your hips are the two parts at the sides of your body between your waist and your upper legs.

**hippo hippos**
NOUN; INFORMAL a hippopotamus.

**hippopotamus hippopotamuses** or **hippopotami**
NOUN a large African animal with thick wrinkled skin and short legs, that lives near rivers.
🏛 from Greek *hippo* + *potamos* meaning 'river horse'

**hippy hippies**; also spelt **hippie**
NOUN In the 1960s and 1970s hippies were people who rejected conventional society and tried to live a life based on peace and love.

**hire hires hiring hired**
VERB 1 If you hire something, you pay money to be able to use it for a period of time. 2 If you hire someone, you pay them to do a job for you.
➤ PHRASE 3 Something that is **for hire** is available for people to hire.

**hirsute**
Said "hir-syoot" ADJECTIVE; FORMAL hairy.

**his**
ADJECTIVE or PRONOUN 'His' refers to something that belongs or relates to a man, boy, or male animal that has already been mentioned, or to any person whose sex is not known.

**hiss hisses hissing hissed**
VERB 1 To hiss means to make a long 's' sound, especially to show disapproval or aggression. ➤ NOUN 2 a long 's' sound.

**histogram histograms**
NOUN a graph consisting of rectangles of varying sizes, that shows the frequency of values of a quantity.

**historian historians**
NOUN a person who studies and writes about history.

**historic**
ADJECTIVE important in the past or likely to be seen as important in the future.

**historical**
ADJECTIVE 1 occurring in the past, or relating to the study of the past E.G. *historical events.* 2 describing or representing the past E.G. *historical novels.*

**historically** ADVERB

**history histories**
NOUN History is the study of the past. A history is a record of the past E.G. *The village is steeped in history… my family history.*

**histrionic histrionics**
Said "hiss-tree-on-ik" ADJECTIVE
1 Histrionic behaviour is very dramatic and full of exaggerated emotion E.G. *The setting was unbelievably histrionic.* 2 FORMAL relating to drama and acting E.G. *a young man of marked histrionic ability.* ➤ PLURAL NOUN 3 Histrionics are histrionic behaviour.

**hit hits hitting hit**
VERB 1 To hit someone or something means to strike them forcefully, usually causing hurt or damage. 2 To hit a ball or other object means to

make it move by hitting it with something. **3** If something hits you, it affects you badly and suddenly *E.G. The recession has hit the tourist industry hard.* **4** If something hits a particular point or place, it reaches it *E.G. The book hit Britain just at the right time.* **5** If you hit on an idea or solution, you suddenly think of it. ▶ NOUN **6** a person or thing that is popular and successful. **7** the action of hitting something *E.G. Give it a good hard hit with the hammer.* ▶ PHRASE **8** INFORMAL If you **hit it off** with someone, you become friendly with them the first time you meet them.

**hit and miss**
ADJECTIVE happening in an unpredictable way or without being properly organized.

**hit-and-run**
ADJECTIVE A hit-and-run car accident is one in which the person who has caused the damage drives away without stopping.

**hitch** hitches hitching hitched
NOUN **1** a slight problem or difficulty *E.G. The whole process was completed without a hitch.* ▶ VERB **2** INFORMAL If you hitch, you travel by getting lifts from passing vehicles *E.G. America is no longer a safe place to hitch round.*

**hitchhiking**
NOUN Hitchhiking is travelling by getting free lifts from passing vehicles.

**hi tech**
ADJECTIVE designed using the most modern methods and equipment, especially electronic equipment.

**hither** OLD-FASHIONED
ADVERB **1** used to refer to movement towards the place where you are. ▶ PHRASE **2** Something that moves

**hither and thither** moves in all directions.

**hitherto**
ADVERB; FORMAL until now *E.G. What he was aiming at had not hitherto been attempted.*

**HIV**
NOUN HIV is a virus that reduces people's resistance to illness and can cause AIDS. HIV is an abbreviation for 'human immunodeficiency virus'.

**hive** hives hiving hived
NOUN **1** a beehive. **2** A place that is a hive of activity is very busy with a lot of people working hard. ▶ VERB **3** If part of something such as a business is hived off, it is transferred to new ownership *E.G. The company is poised to hive off its music interests.*

**hoard** hoards hoarding hoarded
VERB **1** To hoard things means to save them even though they may no longer be useful. ▶ NOUN **2** a store of things that has been saved or hidden.
▣ (sense 1) save, stockpile, store
▣ (sense 2) cache, stash, store
☑ Do not confuse *hoard* with *horde*.

**hoarding** hoardings
NOUN a large advertising board by the side of the road.

**hoarse** hoarser hoarsest
ADJECTIVE A hoarse voice sounds rough and unclear.
**hoarsely** ADVERB

**hoax** hoaxes hoaxing hoaxed
NOUN **1** a trick or an attempt to deceive someone. ▶ VERB **2** To hoax someone means to trick or deceive them.

**hob** hobs
NOUN a surface on top of a cooker which can be heated in order to cook things.

a
b
c
d
e
f
g
h
i
j
k
l
m
n
o
p
q
r
s
t
u
v
w
x
y
z

**hobble** hobbles hobbling hobbled
VERB **1** If you hobble, you walk
awkwardly because of pain or injury.
**2** If you hobble an animal, you tie its
legs together to restrict its
movement.

**hobby** hobbies
NOUN something that you do for
enjoyment in your spare time.

**hock** hocks
NOUN The hock of a horse or other
animal is the angled joint in its back
leg.

**hockey**
NOUN Hockey is a game in which two
teams use long sticks with curved
ends to try to hit a small ball into the
other team's goal.

**hoe** hoes hoeing hoed
NOUN **1** a long-handled gardening
tool with a small square blade, used
to remove weeds and break up the
soil. ► VERB **2** To hoe the ground
means to use a hoe on it.

**hog** hogs hogging hogged
NOUN **1** a castrated male pig. ► VERB
**2** INFORMAL If you hog something, you
take more than your share of it, or
keep it for too long. ► PHRASE **3** INFORMAL
If you **go the whole hog**, you do
something completely or
thoroughly in a bold or extravagant
way.

**hoist** hoists hoisting hoisted
VERB **1** To hoist something means to
lift it, especially using a crane or
other machinery. ► NOUN **2** a machine
for lifting heavy things.

**hokey-pokey**
NOUN In New Zealand, hokey-pokey is
a kind of brittle toffee.

**hold** holds holding held
VERB **1** To hold something means to
carry or keep it in place, usually with
your hand or arms. **2** Someone who
holds power, office, or an opinion has
it or possesses it. **3** If you hold
something such as a meeting or an
election, you arrange it and cause it
to happen. **4** If something holds, it is
still available or valid E.G. The offer still
holds. **5** If you hold someone
responsible for something, you
consider them responsible for it. **6** If
something holds a certain amount, it
can contain that amount E.G. The
theatre holds 150 people. **7** If you hold
something such as theatre tickets, a
telephone call, or the price of
something, you keep or reserve it for
a period of time E.G. The line is
engaged – will you hold? **8** To hold
something down means to keep it or
to keep it under control E.G. How
could I have children and hold down a
job like this? **9** If you hold on to
something, you continue it or keep it
even though it might be difficult E.G.
They are keen to hold on to their
culture. **10** To hold something back
means to prevent it, keep it under
control, or not reveal it E.G. She failed
to hold back the tears. ► NOUN **11** If
someone or something has a hold
over you, they have power, control,
or influence over you E.G. The party
has a considerable hold over its own
leader. **12** a way of holding
something or the act of holding it
E.G. He grabbed the rope and got a
hold on it. **13** the place where cargo
or luggage is stored in a ship or a
plane.

**holder** NOUN

**holdall** holdalls
NOUN a large, soft bag for carrying
clothing.

409

## hole >> home

**hole** holes holing holed

NOUN **1** an opening or hollow in something. **2** *INFORMAL* If you are in a hole, you are in a difficult situation. **3** *INFORMAL* A hole in a theory or argument is a weakness or error in it. **4** In golf, a hole is one of the small holes into which you have to hit the ball. ▶ VERB **5** When you hole the ball in golf, you hit the ball into one of the holes.

■ (sense 1) aperture, gap, opening

**Holi**

NOUN Holi is a Hindu festival celebrated in spring.

📖 from *Holika*, a legendary female demon

**holiday** holidays holidaying holidayed

NOUN **1** a period of time spent away from home for enjoyment. **2** a time when you are not working or not at school. ▶ VERB **3** When you holiday somewhere, you take a holiday there *E.G. She is currently holidaying in Italy.*

📖 from Old English *haligdæg* meaning 'holy day'

**holidaymaker** holidaymakers

NOUN a person who is away from home on holiday.

**holiness**

NOUN **1** Holiness is the state or quality of being holy. **2** 'Your Holiness' and 'His Holiness' are titles used to address or refer to the Pope or to leaders of some other religions.

**hollow** hollows hollowing hollowed

ADJECTIVE **1** Something that is hollow has space inside it rather than being solid. **2** An opinion or situation that is hollow has no real value or worth *E.G. a hollow gesture.* **3** A hollow sound is

dull and has a slight echo *E.G. the hollow sound of his footsteps on the stairs.* ▶ NOUN **4** a hole in something or a part of a surface that is lower than the rest *E.G. It is a pleasant village in a lush hollow.* ▶ VERB **5** To hollow means to make a hollow *E.G. They hollowed out crude dwellings from the soft rock.*

**holly**

NOUN Holly is an evergreen tree or shrub with spiky leaves. It often has red berries in winter.

**holocaust** holocausts

*Said* "hol-o-kawst" NOUN **1** a large-scale destruction or loss of life, especially the result of war or fire. **2** The Holocaust was the mass murder of the Jews in Europe by the Nazis during World War II.

📖 from Greek *holos* + *kaustos* meaning 'completely burnt'

**holster** holsters

NOUN a holder for a hand gun, worn at the side of the body or under the arm.

**holy** holier holiest

ADJECTIVE **1** relating to God or to a particular religion *E.G. the holy city.* **2** Someone who is holy is religious and leads a pure and good life.

■ (sense 1) hallowed, sacred
■ (sense 2) devout, pious

**homage**

*Said* "hom-ij" NOUN Homage is an act of respect and admiration *E.G. The thronging crowds paid homage to their assassinated president.*

**home** homes

NOUN **1** Your home is the building or place in which you live or feel you belong. **2** a building in which elderly or ill people live and are looked after *E.G. He has been confined to a nursing*

there's a rAKE in the brAKEs (br**a**ke)  SPELLING NOTE

*home since his stroke.* ▶ ADJECTIVE
**3** connected with or involving your home or country *E.G. He gave them his home phone number… The government is expanding the home market.*

■ (sense 1) abode, dwelling, residence

**homeland homelands**
NOUN Your homeland is your native country.

**homeless**
ADJECTIVE **1** having no home. ▶ PLURAL NOUN **2** The homeless are people who have no home.
**homelessness** NOUN

**homely**
ADJECTIVE simple, ordinary and comfortable *E.G. The room was small and homely.*

**homeopathy**
*Said* "home-ee-**op**-path-ee" NOUN Homeopathy is a way of treating illness by giving the patient tiny amounts of a substance that would normally cause illness in a healthy person.
**homeopathic** ADJECTIVE

**homeowner homeowners**
NOUN a person who owns the home in which he or she lives.

**homesick**
ADJECTIVE unhappy because of being away from home and missing family and friends.

**homespun**
ADJECTIVE not sophisticated or complicated *E.G. The book is simple homespun philosophy.*

**homestead homesteads**
NOUN a house and its land and other buildings, especially a farm.

**home truth home truths**
NOUN Home truths are unpleasant facts about yourself that you are told by someone else.

**homeward** or **homewards**
ADJECTIVE or ADVERB towards home *E.G. the homeward journey.*

**homework**
NOUN **1** Homework is school work given to pupils to be done in the evening at home. **2** Homework is also research and preparation *E.G. You certainly need to do your homework before buying a horse.*

**homicide homicides**
NOUN Homicide is the crime of murder.
**homicidal** ADJECTIVE

**homing**
ADJECTIVE A homing device is able to guide itself to a target. An animal with a homing instinct is able to guide itself home.

**homophone homophones**
NOUN Homophones are words with different meanings which are pronounced in the same way but are spelt differently. For example, 'write' and 'right' are homophones.

**homo sapiens**
*Said* "hoh-moh **sap**-ee-enz" NOUN; *FORMAL* Homo sapiens is the scientific name for human beings.
🔒 from Latin *homo* meaning 'man' and *sapiens* meaning 'wise'

**homosexual homosexuals**
NOUN **1** a person who is sexually attracted to someone of the same sex. ▶ ADJECTIVE **2** sexually attracted to people of the same sex.
**homosexuality** NOUN

**hone hones honing honed**
VERB **1** If you hone a tool, you sharpen it. **2** If you hone a quality or ability, you develop and improve it *E.G. He had a sharply honed sense of justice.*

**honest**
ADJECTIVE truthful and trustworthy.
**honestly** ADVERB
■ honourable, trustworthy, truthful

**honesty**
NOUN Honesty is the quality of being truthful and trustworthy.
■ honour, integrity, truthfulness

**honey**
NOUN 1 Honey is a sweet, edible, sticky substance produced by bees.
2 Honey means 'sweetheart' or 'darling'. E.G. *What is it, honey?*

**honeycomb honeycombs**
NOUN a wax structure consisting of rows of six-sided cells made by bees for storage of honey and the eggs.

**honeyeater honeyeaters**
NOUN a small Australian bird that feeds on nectar from flowers.

**honeymoon honeymoons**
NOUN a holiday taken by a couple who have just got married.

**honeysuckle**
NOUN Honeysuckle is a climbing plant with fragrant pink or cream flowers.

**hongi**
*Said "hong-ee"* NOUN In New Zealand, hongi is a Maori greeting in which people touch noses.

**honk honks honking honked**
NOUN 1 a short, loud sound like that made by a car horn or a goose. ▶ VERB
2 When something honks, it makes a short, loud sound.

**honorary**
ADJECTIVE An honorary title or job is given as a mark of respect, and does not involve the usual qualifications or work. E.G. *She was awarded an honorary degree.*

**honour honours honouring honoured**

NOUN 1 Your honour is your good reputation and the respect that other people have for you E.G. *This is a war fought by men totally without honour.* 2 an award or privilege given as a mark of respect. 3 Honours is a class of university degree which is higher than a pass or ordinary degree. ▶ PHRASE 4 If something is done **in honour of** someone, it is done out of respect for them E.G. *Egypt celebrated frequent minor festivals in honour of the dead.* ▶ VERB 5 If you honour someone, you give them special praise or attention, or an award. 6 If you honour an agreement or promise, you do what was agreed or promised E.G. *There is enough cash to honour the existing pledges.*

**honourable**
ADJECTIVE worthy of respect or admiration E.G. *He should do the honourable thing and resign.*

**hood hoods**
NOUN 1 a loose covering for the head, usually part of a coat or jacket. 2 a cover on a piece of equipment or vehicle, usually curved and movable E.G. *The mechanic had the hood up to work on the engine.*
**hooded** ADJECTIVE

**-hood**
SUFFIX '-hood' is added at the end of words to form nouns that indicate a state or condition E.G. *childhood… priesthood.*
🏛 from the Old English suffix *-hād*

**hoof hooves** or **hoofs**
NOUN the hard bony part of certain animals' feet.

**hook hooks hooking hooked**
NOUN 1 a curved piece of metal or

a
b
c
d
e
f
g
h
i
j
k
l
m
n
o
p
q
r
s
t
u
v
w
x
y
z

A B C D E F G H I J K L M N O P Q R S T U V W X Y Z

plastic that is used for catching, holding, or hanging things E.G. *picture hooks*. **2** a curving movement, for example of the fist in boxing, or of a golf ball. ▶ VERB **3** If you hook one thing onto another, you attach it there using a hook. ▶ PHRASE **4** If you are **let off the hook**, something happens so that you avoid punishment or a difficult situation.

**hooked**
ADJECTIVE addicted to something; also obsessed by something E.G. *hooked on alcohol… I'm hooked on exercise*.

**hooligan hooligans**
NOUN a destructive and violent young person.

**hooliganism** NOUN
≡ delinquent, ruffian, yob

**hoop hoops**
NOUN a large ring, often used as a toy.

**hooray**
INTERJECTION another spelling of **hurray**.

**hoot hoots hooting hooted**
VERB **1** To hoot means to make a long 'oo' sound like an owl E.G. *hooting with laughter*. **2** If a car horn hoots, it makes a loud honking noise. ▶ NOUN **3** a sound like that made by an owl or a car horn.

**hoover hoovers hoovering hoovered**
NOUN **1** TRADEMARK a vacuum cleaner. ▶ VERB **2** When you hoover, you use a vacuum cleaner to clean the floor.

**hooves**
a plural of **hoof**.

**hop hops hopping hopped**
VERB **1** If you hop, you jump on one foot. **2** When animals or birds hop, they jump with two feet together. **3** INFORMAL If you hop into or out of

something, you move there quickly and easily E.G. *You only have to hop on the ferry to get there*. ▶ NOUN **4** a jump on one leg. **5** Hops are flowers of the hop plant, which are dried and used for making beer.

**hope hopes hoping hoped**
VERB **1** If you hope that something will happen or hope that it is true, you want it to happen or be true. ▶ NOUN **2** Hope is a wish or feeling of desire and expectation E.G. *There was little hope of recovery*.

**hopeful** ADJECTIVE **hopefully** ADVERB
☑ Some people do not like the use of *hopeful* to mean 'it is hoped', for example *hopefully, we can get a good result on Saturday*. Although it is very common in speech, it should be avoided in written work.

**hopeless**
ADJECTIVE **1** having no hope E.G. *She shook her head in hopeless bewilderment*. **2** certain to fail or be unsuccessful. **3** unable to do something well E.G. *I'm hopeless at remembering birthdays*.

**hopelessly** ADVERB **hopelessness** NOUN

**hopper hoppers**
NOUN a large, funnel-shaped container for storing things such as grain or sand.

**horde hordes**
*Rhymes with "bored"* NOUN a large group or number of people or animals E.G. *hordes of tourists*.
☑ Do not confuse *horde* with *hoard*.

**horizon horizons**
*Said* "hor-**eye**-zn" NOUN **1** the distant line where the sky seems to touch the land or sea. **2** Your horizons are the limits of what you want to do or

are interested in *E.G. Travel broadens your horizons.* ▶ PHRASE **3** If something is **on the horizon**, it is almost certainly going to happen or be done in the future *E.G. Political change was on the horizon.*

### horizontal
*Said* "hor-**riz**-zon-tl" ADJECTIVE (MATHS) flat and parallel with the horizon or with a line considered as a base *E.G. a patchwork of vertical and horizontal black lines.*

**horizontally** ADVERB

### hormone hormones
NOUN a chemical made by one part of your body that stimulates or has a specific effect on another part of your body.

**hormonal** ADJECTIVE

### horn horns
NOUN **1** one of the hard, pointed growths on the heads of animals such as goats. **2** a musical instrument made of brass, consisting of a pipe that is narrow at one end and wide at the other. **3** On vehicles, a horn is a warning device which makes a loud noise.

### hornet hornets
NOUN a type of very large wasp.

### horoscope horoscopes
*Said* "**hor**-ros-kope" NOUN a prediction about what is going to happen to someone, based on the position of the stars when they were born.

📖 from Greek *hora* + *skopos* meaning 'hour observer'

### horrendous
ADJECTIVE very unpleasant and shocking *E.G. horrendous injuries.*

### horrible
ADJECTIVE **1** disagreeable and unpleasant *E.G. A horrible nausea rose within him.* **2** causing shock, fear, or disgust *E.G. horrible crimes.*

**horribly** ADVERB
▣ (sense 1) disagreeable, nasty, unpleasant
▣ (sense 2) dreadful, ghastly, shocking

### horrid
ADJECTIVE very unpleasant indeed *E.G. We were all so horrid to him.*

### horrific
ADJECTIVE so bad or unpleasant that people are horrified *E.G. a horrific attack.*

### horrify horrifies horrifying horrified
VERB If something horrifies you, it makes you feel dismay or disgust *E.G. a crime trend that will horrify parents.*

**horrifying** ADJECTIVE

### horror horrors
NOUN **1** a strong feeling of alarm, dismay, and disgust *E.G. He gazed in horror at the knife.* **2** If you have a horror of something, you fear it very much *E.G. He had a horror of fire.*

### horse horses
NOUN **1** a large animal with a mane and long tail, on which people can ride. **2** a piece of gymnastics equipment with four legs, used for jumping over.

### horseback
NOUN AND ADJECTIVE You refer to someone who is riding a horse as someone **on horseback**, or a horseback rider.

### horsepower
NOUN Horsepower is a unit used for measuring how powerful an engine is, equal to about 746 watts.

### horseradish
NOUN Horseradish is the white root of

a b c d e f g **h** i j k l m n o p q r s t u v w x y z

A
B
C
D
E
F
G
**H**
I
J
K
L
M
N
O
P
Q
R
S
T
U
V
W
X
Y
Z

a plant made into a hot-tasting sauce, often served cold with beef.

**horseshoe** horseshoes
NOUN a U-shaped piece of metal, nailed to the hard surface of a horse's hoof to protect it; also anything of this shape, often regarded as a good luck symbol.

**horsey** or **horsy**
ADJECTIVE 1 very keen on horses and riding. 2 having a face similar to that of a horse.

**horticulture**
NOUN Horticulture is the study and practice of growing flowers, fruit, and vegetables.
**horticultural** ADJECTIVE

**hose** hoses hosing hosed
NOUN 1 a long flexible tube through which liquid or gas can be passed E.G. He left the garden hose on. ▶ VERB 2 If you hose something, you wash or water it using a hose E.G. The street cleaners need to hose the square down.

**hosiery**
Said "hoze-yer-ee" NOUN Hosiery consists of tights, socks, and similar items, especially in shops.

**hospice** hospices
Said "hoss-piss" NOUN a hospital which provides care for people who are dying.

**hospitable**
ADJECTIVE friendly, generous, and welcoming to guests or strangers.
**hospitality** NOUN

**hospital** hospitals
NOUN a place where sick and injured people are treated and cared for.

**host** hosts hosting hosted
NOUN 1 The host of an event is the person that welcomes guests and

provides food or accommodation for them E.G. He is a most generous host who takes his guests to the best restaurants in town. 2 a plant or animal with smaller plants or animals living on or in it. 3 A host of things is a large number of them E.G. a host of close friends. 4 In the Christian church, the Host is the consecrated bread used in Mass or Holy Communion. ▶ VERB 5 To host an event means to organize it or act as host at it.

**hostage** hostages
NOUN a person who is illegally held prisoner and threatened with injury or death unless certain demands are met by other people.

**hostel** hostels
NOUN a large building in which people can stay or live E.G. a hostel for battered women.

**hostess** hostesses
NOUN a woman who welcomes guests or visitors and provides food or accommodation for them.

**hostile**
ADJECTIVE 1 unfriendly, aggressive, and unpleasant E.G. a hostile audience. 2 relating to or involving the enemies of a country E.G. hostile territory.
**hostility** NOUN

**hot** hotter hottest
ADJECTIVE 1 having a high temperature E.G. a hot climate. 2 very spicy and causing a burning sensation in your mouth E.G. a hot curry. 3 new, recent, and exciting E.G. hot news from tinseltown. 4 dangerous or difficult to deal with E.G. Animal testing is a hot issue.
**hotly** ADVERB

**hotbed** hotbeds

NOUN A hotbed of some type of activity is a place that seems to encourage it E.G. *The city was a hotbed of rumour.*

**hot dog** hot dogs

NOUN a sausage served in a roll split lengthways.

**hotel** hotels

NOUN a building where people stay, paying for their room and meals.

**hothouse** hothouses

NOUN 1 a large heated greenhouse. 2 a place or situation of intense intellectual or emotional activity E.G. *a hothouse of radical socialist ideas.*

**hot seat**

NOUN; *INFORMAL* Someone who is in the hot seat has to make difficult decisions for which they will be held responsible.

**hound** hounds hounding hounded

NOUN 1 a dog, especially one used for hunting or racing. ▶ VERB 2 If someone hounds you, they constantly pursue or trouble you.

**hour** hours

NOUN 1 a unit of time equal to 60 minutes, of which there are 24 in a day. 2 The hour for something is the time when it happens E.G. *The hour for launching approached.* 3 The hour is also the time of day E.G. *What are you doing up at this hour?* 4 an important or difficult time E.G. *The hour has come… He is the hero of the hour.* ▶ PLURAL NOUN 5 The hours that you keep are the times that you usually go to bed and get up.

**hourly** ADJECTIVE or ADVERB

**house** houses housing housed

NOUN *Said* "hows" 1 a building where a person or family lives. 2 a building

used for a particular purpose E.G. *an auction house… the opera house.* 3 In a theatre or cinema, the house is the part where the audience sits; also the audience itself E.G. *The show had a packed house calling for more.* ▶ VERB *Said* "howz" 4 To house something means to keep it or contain it E.G. *The west wing housed a store of valuable antiques.*

**houseboat** houseboats

NOUN a small boat which people live on that is tied up at a particular place on a river or canal.

**household** households

NOUN 1 all the people who live as a group in a house or flat. ▶ PHRASE 2 Someone who is **a household name** is very well-known.

**householder** NOUN

**housekeeper** housekeepers

NOUN a person who is employed to do the cooking and cleaning in a house.

**House of Commons**

NOUN The House of Commons is the more powerful of the two parts of the British Parliament. Its members are elected by the public.

**House of Lords**

NOUN The House of Lords is the less powerful of the two parts of the British Parliament. Its members are unelected and come from noble families or are appointed by the Queen as an honour for a life of public service.

**House of Representatives**

NOUN 1 In Australia, the House of Representatives is the larger of the two parts of the Federal Parliament. 2 In New Zealand, the House of Representatives is the Parliament.

a
b
c
d
e
f
g
h
i
j
k
l
m
n
o
p
q
r
s
t
u
v
w
x
y
z

Plaïce the fish has a glittering 'EYE' (I) (plaïce)     **SPELLING NOTE**

**housewife** housewives

NOUN a married woman who does the chores in her home, and does not have a paid job.

**housing**

NOUN Housing is the buildings in which people live E.G. the serious housing shortage.

**hovel** hovels

NOUN a small hut or house that is dirty or badly in need of repair.

**hover** hovers hovering hovered

VERB 1 When a bird, insect, or aircraft hovers, it stays in the same position in the air. 2 If someone is hovering they are hesitating because they cannot decide what to do E.G. He was hovering nervously around the sick animal.

**hovercraft** hovercraft or hovercrafts

NOUN a vehicle which can travel over water or land supported by a cushion of air.

**how**

ADVERB 1 'How' is used to ask about, explain, or refer to the way in which something is done, known, or experienced E.G. How did this happen?… He knew how quickly rumours could spread. 2 'How' is used to ask about or refer to a measurement or quantity E.G. How much is it for the weekend?… I wonder how old he is. 3 'How' is used to emphasize the following word or statement E.G. How odd!

**however**

ADVERB 1 You use 'however' when you are adding a comment that seems to contradict or contrast with what has just been said E.G. For all his compassion, he is, however, surprisingly restrained. 2 You use 'however' to say that something makes no difference to a situation E.G. However hard she tried, nothing seemed to work.

**howl** howls howling howled

VERB 1 To howl means to make a long, loud wailing noise such as that made by a dog when it is upset E.G. A distant coyote howled at the moon… The wind howled through the trees. ▶ NOUN 2 a long, loud wailing noise.

**HQ**

an abbreviation for **headquarters**.

**hub** hubs

NOUN 1 the centre part of a wheel. 2 the most important or active part of a place or organization E.G. The kitchen is the hub of most households.

**hubbub**

NOUN Hubbub is great noise or confusion E.G. the general hubbub of conversation.

**huddle** huddles huddling huddled

VERB 1 If you huddle up or are huddled, you are curled up with your arms and legs close to your body. 2 When people or animals huddle together, they sit or stand close to each other, often for warmth. ▶ NOUN 3 A huddle of people or things is a small group of them.

**hue** hues

NOUN 1 LITERARY a colour or a particular shade of a colour. ▶ PHRASE 2 If people raise a **hue and cry**, they are very angry about something and protest.

**huff**

PHRASE If you are **in a huff**, you are sulking or offended about something. **huffy** ADJECTIVE

**hug** hugs hugging hugged

VERB 1 If you hug someone, you put

your arms round them and hold them close to you. **2** To hug the ground or a stretch of water or land means to keep very close to it *E.G. The road hugs the coast for hundreds of miles.* ▶ NOUN **3** If you give someone a hug, you hold them close to you.
📖 from Old Norse *hugga* meaning 'to comfort' or 'console'

**huge huger hugest**
ADJECTIVE extremely large in amount, size, or degree *E.G. a huge success… a huge crowd.*
**hugely** ADVERB
■ enormous, gigantic, vast

**hui hui or huis**
*Said "hoo-ee"* NOUN **1** In New Zealand, a meeting of Maori people. **2** INFORMAL In New Zealand English, a party.

**hulk hulks**
NOUN **1** a large, heavy person or thing. **2** the body of a ship that has been wrecked or abandoned.
**hulking** ADJECTIVE

**hull hulls**
NOUN The hull of a ship is the main part of its body that sits in the water.

**hum hums humming hummed**
VERB **1** To hum means to make a continuous low noise *E.G. The generator hummed faintly.* **2** If you hum, you sing with your lips closed. ▶ NOUN **3** a continuous low noise *E.G. the hum of the fridge.*

**human humans**
ADJECTIVE **1** relating to, concerning, or typical of people *E.G. Intolerance appears deeply ingrained in human nature.* ▶ NOUN **2** a person.
**humanly** ADVERB

**human being human beings**
NOUN a person.

**humane**
ADJECTIVE showing kindness and sympathy towards others *E.G. Medicine is regarded as the most humane of professions.*
**humanely** ADVERB

**humanism**
NOUN Humanism is the belief in mankind's ability to achieve happiness and fulfilment without the need for religion.

**humanitarian humanitarians**
NOUN **1** a person who works for the welfare of mankind. ▶ ADJECTIVE **2** concerned with the welfare of mankind *E.G. humanitarian aid.*
**humanitarianism** NOUN

**humanity**
NOUN **1** Humanity is people in general *E.G. I have faith in humanity.* **2** Humanity is also the condition of being human *E.G. He denies his humanity.* **3** Someone who has humanity is kind and sympathetic.

**human rights**
PLURAL NOUN Human rights are the rights of individuals to freedom and justice.

**humble humbler humblest; humbles humbling humbled**
ADJECTIVE **1** A humble person is modest and thinks that he or she has very little value. **2** Something that is humble is small or not very important *E.G. Just a splash of wine will transform a humble casserole.* ▶ VERB **3** To humble someone means to make them feel humiliated.
**humbly** ADVERB **humbled** ADJECTIVE
■ (sense 1) modest, unassuming

**humbug humbugs**
NOUN **1** a hard black and white striped

**humdrum**
2 Humbug is speech or writing that
is obviously dishonest or untrue E.G.
*hypocritical humbug.*

**humdrum**
ADJECTIVE ordinary, dull, and boring E.G.
*humdrum domestic tasks.*

**humid**
ADJECTIVE If it is humid, the air feels
damp, heavy, and warm.

**humidity**
NOUN Humidity is the amount of
moisture in the air, or the state of
being humid.

**humiliate** humiliates humiliating
humiliated
VERB To humiliate someone means to
make them feel ashamed or appear
stupid to other people.
**humiliation** NOUN
■ embarrass, mortify, shame

**humility**
NOUN Humility is the quality of being
modest and humble.

**hummingbird** hummingbirds
NOUN a small bird with powerful
wings that make a humming noise
as they beat.

**humour** humours humouring
humoured
NOUN 1 Humour is the quality of being
funny E.G. *They discussed it with tact
and humour.* 2 Humour is also the
ability to be amused by certain
things E.G. *Helen's got a peculiar sense
of humour.* 3 Someone's humour is
the mood they are in E.G. *He hasn't
been in a good humour lately.* ▶ VERB
4 If you humour someone, you are
especially kind to them and do
whatever they want.

**humorous** ADJECTIVE
■ (sense 1) comedy, funniness, wit

**hump** humps humping humped
NOUN 1 a small, rounded lump or
mound E.G. *a camel's hump.* ▶ VERB
2 INFORMAL If you hump something
heavy, you carry or move it with
difficulty.

**hunch** hunches hunching
hunched
NOUN 1 a feeling or suspicion
about something, not based
on facts or evidence. ▶ VERB 2 If
you hunch your shoulders, you
raise your shoulders and lean
forwards.

**hunchback** hunchbacks
NOUN; OLD-FASHIONED someone who has a
large hump on their back.

**hundred** hundreds
the number 100.
**hundredth**

**Hungarian** Hungarians
*Said* "hung-**gair**-ee-an" ADJECTIVE
1 belonging or relating to Hungary.
▶ NOUN 2 someone who comes
from Hungary. 3 Hungarian is the
main language spoken in
Hungary.

**hunger** hungers hungering
hungered
NOUN 1 Hunger is the need to eat or
the desire to eat. 2 A hunger for
something is a strong need or desire
for it E.G. *a hunger for winning.* ▶ VERB
3 If you hunger for something, you
want it very much.

**hunger strike** hunger strikes
NOUN a refusal to eat anything at all,
especially by prisoners, as a form of
protest.

**hungry** hungrier hungriest
ADJECTIVE needing or wanting to eat
E.G. *People are going hungry.*
**hungrily** ADVERB

**hunk** hunks
NOUN A hunk of something is a large piece of it.

**hunt** hunts hunting hunted
VERB 1 To hunt means to chase wild animals to kill them for food or for sport. 2 If you hunt for something, you search for it. ▶ NOUN 3 the act of hunting E.G. *Police launched a hunt for an abandoned car.*
**hunter** NOUN **hunting** ADJECTIVE or NOUN

**huntaway** huntaways
NOUN In Australia and New Zealand, a dog trained to drive sheep forward.

**hurdle** hurdles
NOUN 1 one of the frames or barriers that you jump over in an athletics race called hurdles E.G. *She won the four hundred metre hurdles.* 2 a problem or difficulty E.G. *Several hurdles exist for anyone seeking to do postgraduate study.*

**hurl** hurls hurling hurled
VERB 1 To hurl something means to throw it with great force. 2 If you hurl insults at someone, you insult them aggressively and repeatedly.

**hurray** or **hurrah** or **hooray**
INTERJECTION an exclamation of excitement or approval.

**hurricane** hurricanes
NOUN a violent wind or storm.

**hurry** hurries hurrying hurried
VERB 1 To hurry means to move or do something as quickly as possible E.G. *She hurried through the empty streets.* 2 To hurry something means to make it happen more quickly E.G. *You can't hurry nature.* ▶ NOUN 3 Hurry is the speed with which you do something quickly E.G. *He was in a hurry to leave.*

**hurried** ADJECTIVE **hurriedly** ADVERB
■ (sense 1) dash, fly, rush
■ (sense 3) haste, rush

**hurt** hurts hurting hurt
VERB 1 To hurt someone means to cause them physical pain. 2 If a part of your body hurts, you feel pain there. 3 If you hurt yourself, you injure yourself. 4 To hurt someone also means to make them unhappy by being unkind or thoughtless towards them E.G. *I didn't want to hurt his feelings.* ▶ ADJECTIVE 5 If someone feels hurt, they feel unhappy because of someone's unkindness towards them E.G. *He felt hurt by all the lies.*
**hurtful** ADJECTIVE

**hurtle** hurtles hurtling hurtled
VERB To hurtle means to move or travel very fast indeed, especially in an uncontrolled way.

**husband** husbands
NOUN A woman's husband is the man she is married to.

**husbandry**
NOUN 1 Husbandry is the art or skill of farming. 2 Husbandry is also the art or skill of managing something carefully and economically.

**hush** hushes hushing hushed
VERB 1 If you tell someone to hush, you are telling them to be quiet. 2 To hush something up means to keep it secret, especially something dishonest involving important people E.G. *The government has hushed up a series of scandals.* ▶ NOUN 3 If there is a hush, it is quiet and still E.G. *A graveyard hush fell over the group.*
**hushed** ADJECTIVE

**husk** husks
NOUN Husks are the dry outer

a
b
c
d
e
f
g
h
i
j
k
l
m
n
o
p
q
r
s
t
u
v
w
x
y
z

LEarn the principLEs (principle)    SPELLING NOTE

coverings of grain or seed.

**husky** huskier huskiest; huskies
ADJECTIVE **1** A husky voice is rough or hoarse. ▶ NOUN **2** a large, strong dog with a thick coat, often used to pull sledges across snow.

**hustle** hustles hustling hustled
VERB To hustle someone means to make them move by pushing and jostling them E.G. *The guards hustled him out of the car.*

**hut** huts
NOUN a small, simple building, with one or two rooms.

**hutch** hutches
NOUN a wooden box with wire mesh at one side, in which small pets can be kept.

**hyacinth** hyacinths
*Said* "high-as-sinth" NOUN a spring flower with many small, bell-shaped flowers.

**hybrid** hybrids
NOUN **1** a plant or animal that has been bred from two different types of plant or animal. **2** anything that is a mixture of two other things.

**hydra** hydras or hydrae
NOUN a microscopic freshwater creature that has a slender tubular body and tentacles round the mouth.

**hydrangea** hydrangeas
*Said* "high-**drain**-ja" NOUN a garden shrub with large clusters of pink or blue flowers.

**hydraulic**
*Said* "high-**drol**-lik" ADJECTIVE operated by water or other fluid which is under pressure.

**hydro-**
PREFIX 'Hydro-' means 'water'. For example, *hydroelectricity* is electricity

made using water power.
🔲 from Greek *hudōr* meaning 'water'

**hydrogen**
NOUN Hydrogen is the lightest gas and the simplest chemical element.

**hyena** hyenas
*Said* "high-ee-na"; also spelt **hyaena**
NOUN a wild doglike animal of Africa and Asia that hunts in packs.

**hygiene**
*Said* "high-jeen" NOUN D&T Hygiene is the practice of keeping yourself and your surroundings clean, especially to stop the spread of disease.
**hygienic** ADJECTIVE

**hymn** hymns
NOUN RE a Christian song in praise of God.

**hyper-**
PREFIX 'Hyper-' means 'very much' or 'excessively' E.G. *hyperactive*.
🔲 from Greek *huper* meaning 'over'

**hyperactive**
ADJECTIVE A hyperactive person is unable to relax and is always in a state of restless activity.

**hyperbole**
*Said* "high-**per**-bol-lee" NOUN Hyperbole is a style of speech or writing which uses exaggeration.

**hyperlink** hyperlinks
NOUN a word, phrase, or picture in a computer document which a user may click to move to another part of the document, or to another document.

**hypertension**
NOUN Hypertension is a medical condition in which a person has high blood pressure.

**hypertext** hypertexts
NOUN computer software that allows users to create, store, and view text

and move between related items easily.

**hyphen** hyphens

NOUN a punctuation mark used to join together words or parts of words, as for example in the word 'left-handed'.

**hyphenate** VERB    **hyphenation** NOUN

---

### What does the Hyphen do?

The **hyphen** (-) separates the different parts of certain words. A hyphen is often used when there would otherwise be an awkward combination of letters, or confusion with another word:

E.G. *Anna was re-elected president. She adopted a no-nonsense approach.*

In printed texts, the hyphen also divides a word that will not fit at the end of a line and has to be continued on the next line.

---

**hypnosis**

*Said* "hip-**noh**-siss" NOUN Hypnosis is an artificially produced state of relaxation in which the mind is very receptive to suggestion.

🔲 from Greek *hupnos* meaning 'sleep'

**hypnotize** hypnotizes hypnotizing hypnotized; also spelt **hypnotise**

VERB To hypnotize someone means to put them into a state in which they seem to be asleep but can respond to questions and suggestions.

**hypnotic** ADJECTIVE    **hypnotism** NOUN    **hypnotist** NOUN

**hypochondriac** hypochondriacs

*Said* "high-pok-**kon**-dree-ak" NOUN a person who continually worries

about their health, being convinced that they are ill when there is actually nothing wrong with them.

**hypocrisy** hypocrisies

NOUN Hypocrisy is pretending to have beliefs or qualities that you do not really have, so that you seem a better person than you are.

**hypocritical** ADJECTIVE    **hypocrite** NOUN

**hypodermic** hypodermics

NOUN a medical instrument with a hollow needle, used for giving people injections, or taking blood samples.

**hypothermia**

NOUN Hypothermia is a condition in which a person is very ill because their body temperature has been unusually low for a long time.

**hypothesis** hypotheses

NOUN an explanation or theory which has not yet been proved to be correct.

**hypothetical**

ADJECTIVE based on assumption rather than on fact or reality.

**hysterectomy** hysterectomies

*Said* "his-ter-**rek**-tom-ee" NOUN an operation to remove a woman's womb.

**hysteria**

*Said* "hiss-**teer**-ee-a" NOUN Hysteria is a state of uncontrolled excitement or panic.

**hysterical**

ADJECTIVE 1 Someone who is hysterical is in a state of uncontrolled excitement or panic. 2 INFORMAL Something that is hysterical is extremely funny.

**hysterically** ADVERB    **hysterics** NOUN

▤ (sense 1) frantic, frenzied

---

the QUeen stood on the QUay (quay)    ▶ SPELLING NOTE

a b c d e f g h i j k l m n o p q r s t u v w x y z

# I i

**I**

PRONOUN A speaker or writer uses 'I' to refer to himself or herself *E.G. I like the colour.*

**ibis ibises**

*Said "eye-biss"* NOUN a large wading bird with a long, thin, curved bill that lives in warm countries.

**-ible**

SUFFIX another form of the suffix **-able**.

**-ic** or **-ical**

SUFFIX '-ic' and '-ical' form adjectives from nouns. For example, *ironic* or *ironical* formed from *irony*.

**ice ices icing iced**

NOUN **1** water that has frozen solid. **2** an ice cream. ▶ VERB **3** If you ice cakes, you cover them with icing. **4** If something ices over or ices up, it becomes covered with a layer of ice. ▶ PHRASE **5** If you do something to **break the ice**, you make people feel relaxed and comfortable.

**Ice Age Ice Ages**

NOUN a period of time lasting thousands of years when a lot of the earth's surface was covered with ice.

**iceberg icebergs**

NOUN a large mass of ice floating in the sea.

📖 from Dutch *ijsberg* meaning 'ice mountain'

**icecap icecaps**

NOUN a layer of ice and snow that permanently covers the North or South Pole.

**ice cream ice creams**

NOUN a very cold sweet food made from frozen cream.

**ice cube ice cubes**

NOUN Ice cubes are small cubes of ice put in drinks to make them cold.

**ice hockey**

NOUN a type of hockey played on ice, with two teams of six players.

**Icelandic**

NOUN the main language spoken in Iceland.

**ice-skate ice-skates ice-skating ice-skated**

NOUN **1** a boot with a metal blade on the bottom, which you wear when skating on ice. ▶ VERB **2** If you ice-skate, you move about on ice wearing ice-skates.

**icicle icicles**

*Said "eye-sik-kl"* NOUN a piece of ice shaped like a pointed stick that hangs down from a surface.

**icing**

NOUN a mixture of powdered sugar and water or egg whites, used to decorate cakes.

**icon icons**

*Said "eye-kon"* NOUN **1** ( ICT ) a picture on a computer screen representing a program that can be activated by moving the cursor over it. **2** in the Orthodox Churches, a holy picture of Christ, the Virgin Mary, or a saint.

📖 from Greek *eikōn* meaning 'likeness' or 'image'

**ICT** an abbreviation for 'Information and Communication Technology'.

**icy icier iciest**

ADJECTIVE **1** Something which is icy is very cold *E.G. an icy wind.* **2** An icy road has ice on it.

**icily** ADVERB

# id

NOUN In psychology, your id is your basic instincts and unconscious thoughts.

## idea ideas

NOUN 1 a plan, suggestion, or thought that you have after thinking about a problem. 2 an opinion or belief *E.G. old-fashioned ideas about women.* 3 An idea of something is what you know about it *E.G. They had no idea of their position.*

■ (sense 1) impression, thought
■ (sense 2) belief, notion, opinion

## ideal ideals

NOUN 1 a principle or idea that you try to achieve because it seems perfect to you. 2 Your ideal of something is the person or thing that seems the best example of it. ► ADJECTIVE 3 The ideal person or thing is the best possible person or thing for the situation.

## idealism

*Said "eye-dee-il-izm"* NOUN behaviour that is based on a person's ideals.

**idealist** NOUN **idealistic** ADJECTIVE

## idealize idealizes idealizing idealized; also spelt idealise

VERB If you idealize someone or something, you regard them as being perfect.

**idealization** NOUN

## ideally

ADVERB 1 If you say that ideally something should happen, you mean that you would like it to happen but you know that it is not possible. 2 Ideally means perfectly *E.G. The hotel is ideally placed for business travellers.*

## identical

ADJECTIVE exactly the same *E.G. identical twins.*

**identically** ADVERB

## identification

NOUN 1 The identification of someone or something is the act of identifying them. 2 Identification is a document such as a driver's licence or passport which proves who you are.

## identify identifies identifying identified

VERB 1 recognize someone or something. 2 If you identify with someone, you understand their feelings and ideas.

**identifiable** ADJECTIVE

## identity identities

NOUN the characteristics that make you who you are.

## ideology ideologies

NOUN a set of political beliefs.

**ideological** ADJECTIVE **ideologically** ADVERB

## idiom idioms

NOUN a group of words whose meaning together is different from all the words taken individually. For example, 'It is raining cats and dogs' is an idiom.

🔟 from Greek *idíōma* meaning 'special phraseology'

## idiomatic

*Said "id-ee-om-mat-ik"* ADJECTIVE Idiomatic language is natural, fluent, and often informal.

## idiosyncrasy idiosyncrasies

*Said "id-ee-oh-sing-krass-ee"* NOUN Someone's idiosyncrasies are their own habits and likes or dislikes.

**idiosyncratic** ADJECTIVE

## idiot idiots

NOUN someone who is stupid or foolish.

🔟 from Greek *idíōtēs* meaning 'ignorant person'

■ fool, halfwit, moron

a b c d e f g h i j k l m n o p q r s t u v w x y z

**idiotic**
ADJECTIVE extremely foolish or silly.
🔳 foolish, senseless, stupid

**idle idles idling idled**
ADJECTIVE If you are idle, you are doing nothing.
**idleness** NOUN **idly** ADVERB
🏛 from Saxon *idal* meaning 'worthless' or 'empty'

**idol idols**
Said "**eye**-doll" NOUN 1 a famous person who is loved and admired by fans. 2 a picture or statue which is worshipped as if it were a god.
🏛 from Greek *eidōlon* meaning 'image' or 'phantom'

**idyll idylls**
Said "**id**-ill" NOUN a situation which is peaceful and beautiful.
**idyllic** ADJECTIVE

**i.e.**
i.e. means 'that is', and is used before giving more information. It is an abbreviation for the Latin expression 'id est'.

**if**
CONJUNCTION 1 on the condition that E.G. I shall stay if I can. 2 whether E.G. I asked her if she wanted to go.

**igloo igloos**
NOUN a dome-shaped house built out of blocks of snow by the Inuit, or Eskimo, people.
🏛 from *igdlu*, an Inuit word meaning 'house'

**igneous**
Said "**ig**-nee-uss" ADJECTIVE; TECHNICAL Igneous rocks are formed by hot liquid rock cooling and going hard.
🏛 from Latin *igneus* meaning 'fiery'

**ignite ignites igniting ignited**
VERB If you ignite something or if it ignites, it starts burning.
🏛 from Latin *ignis* meaning 'fire'

**ignition ignitions**
NOUN In a car, the ignition is the part of the engine where the fuel is ignited.

**ignominious**
ADJECTIVE shameful or considered wrong E.G. It was an ignominious end to a brilliant career.
**ignominiously** ADVERB **ignominy** NOUN

**ignoramus ignoramuses**
Said "ig-nor-**ray**-muss" NOUN an ignorant person.
🏛 from the character *Ignoramus*, an uneducated lawyer in a 17th-century play by Ruggle. In Latin *ignoramus* means 'we do not know'

**ignorant**
ADJECTIVE 1 If you are ignorant of something, you do not know about it E.G. He was completely ignorant of the rules. 2 Someone who is ignorant does not know about things in general E.G. I thought of asking, but didn't want to seem ignorant.
**ignorantly** ADVERB **ignorance** NOUN
🔳 (sense 1) unaware, unconscious, uninformed

**ignore ignores ignoring ignored**
VERB If you ignore someone or something, you deliberately do not take any notice of them.

**iguana iguanas**
Said "ig-**wah**-na" NOUN a large, tropical lizard.

**il-**
PREFIX 'Il-' means 'not' or 'the opposite of', and is the form of 'in-' that is used before the letter E.G. illegible.

**ill ills**
ADJECTIVE 1 unhealthy or sick. 2 harmful or unpleasant E.G. ill effects. ▶ PLURAL

NOUN 3 Ills are difficulties or problems.
📖 from Norse *illr* meaning 'bad'
■ (sense 1) sick, unhealthy, unwell

**ill at ease**
PHRASE If you feel **ill at ease**, you feel
unable to relax.

**illegal**
ADJECTIVE forbidden by the law.
**illegally** ADVERB **illegality** NOUN
■ criminal, illicit, unlawful

**illegible**
*Said* "il-**lej**-i-bl" ADJECTIVE Writing which
is illegible is unclear and very
difficult to read.

**illegitimate**
*Said* "il-**lij**-**it**-tim-it" ADJECTIVE A person
who is illegitimate was born to parents
who were not married at the time.
**illegitimacy** NOUN

**ill-fated**
ADJECTIVE doomed to end unhappily
E.G. *his ill-fated attempt on the world
record.*

**illicit**
*Said* "il-**liss**-it" ADJECTIVE not allowed
by law or not approved of by society
E.G. *illicit drugs.*

**illiterate**
ADJECTIVE unable to read or write.
**illiteracy** NOUN

**illness illnesses**
NOUN 1 Illness is the experience of
being ill. 2 a particular disease E.G. *the
treatment of common illnesses.*
■ (sense 2) ailment, disease, malady,
sickness

**illogical**
ADJECTIVE An illogical feeling or action
is not reasonable or sensible.
**illogically** ADVERB

**ill-treat ill-treats ill-treating ill-
treated**
VERB If you ill-treat someone or

something you hurt or damage
them or treat them cruelly.
**ill-treatment** NOUN

**illuminate illuminates
illuminating illuminated**
VERB To illuminate something is to shine
light on it to make it easier to see.

**illumination illuminations**
NOUN 1 Illumination is lighting.
2 Illuminations are the coloured
lights put up to decorate a town,
especially at Christmas.

**illusion illusions**
NOUN 1 a false belief which you think
is true E.G. *Their hopes proved to be an
illusion.* 2 (ART) a false appearance
of reality which deceives the eye E.G.
*Painters create the illusion of space.*

**illusory**
*Said* "ill-**yoo**-ser-ee" ADJECTIVE seeming
to be true, but actually false E.G. *an
illusory truce.*

**illustrate illustrates illustrating
illustrated**
VERB 1 (EXAM TERM) If you illustrate a
point, you explain it or make it clearer,
often by using examples. 2 If you
illustrate a book, you put pictures in it.
**illustrator** NOUN **illustrative**
ADJECTIVE

**illustration illustrations**
NOUN 1 an example or a story which is
used to make a point clear. 2 a
picture in a book.

**illustrious**
ADJECTIVE An illustrious person is
famous and respected.

**ill will**
NOUN Ill will is a feeling of hostility.

**im-**
PREFIX 'Im-' means 'not' or 'the
opposite of', and is the form of 'in-'
which is used before the letters b, m

a
b
c
d
e
f
g
h
**i**
j
k
l
m
n
o
p
q
r
s
t
u
v
w
x
y
z

A
B
C
D
E
F
G
H
I
J
K
L
M
N
O
P
Q
R
S
T
U
V
W
X
Y
Z

and p *E.G. imbalance... impatient... immature.*

**image** images
NOUN **1** a mental picture of someone or something. **2** the appearance which a person, group, or organization presents to the public.

**imagery**
NOUN (ENGLISH) The imagery of a poem or book is the descriptive language used in it.

**imaginary**
ADJECTIVE Something that is imaginary exists only in your mind, not in real life.

**imagination** imaginations
NOUN the ability to form new and exciting ideas.

**imaginative**
ADJECTIVE Someone who is imaginative can easily form new or exciting ideas in their mind.
**imaginatively** ADVERB

**imagine** imagines imagining imagined
VERB **1** If you imagine something, you form an idea of it in your mind, or you think you have seen or heard it but you have not really. **2** If you imagine that something is the case, you believe it is the case *E.G. I imagine that's what you aim to do.*
**imaginable** ADJECTIVE
▪ (sense 1) conceive, envisage, picture, visualize
▪ (sense 2) believe, suppose, think

**imam**
*Said "ih-mam"* NOUN a person who leads a group in prayer in a mosque.

**imbalance** imbalances
NOUN If there is an imbalance between things, they are unequal *E.G.*

*the imbalance between rich and poor.*

**imbecile** imbeciles
*Said "im-bis-seel"* NOUN a stupid person.
▥ from Latin *imbecillus* meaning 'physically or mentally feeble'

**imitate** imitates imitating imitated
VERB To imitate someone or something is to copy them.
**imitator** NOUN **imitative** ADJECTIVE
▪ copy, mimic

**imitation** imitations
NOUN a copy of something else.

**immaculate**
*Said "im-mak-yoo-lit"* ADJECTIVE
**1** completely clean and tidy *E.G. The flat was immaculate.* **2** without any mistakes at all *E.G. his usual immaculate guitar accompaniment.*
**immaculately** ADVERB

**immaterial**
ADJECTIVE Something that is immaterial is not important.

**immature**
ADJECTIVE **1** Something that is immature has not finished growing or developing. **2** A person who is immature does not behave in a sensible adult way.
**immaturity** NOUN

**immediate**
ADJECTIVE **1** Something that is immediate happens or is done without delay. **2** Your immediate relatives and friends are the ones most closely connected or related to you.

**immediately**
ADVERB **1** If something happens immediately it happens right away.
**2** Immediately means very near in time or position *E.G. immediately behind the house.*

**immemorial**

ADJECTIVE If something has been happening from time immemorial, it has been happening longer than anyone can remember.

**immense**

ADJECTIVE very large or huge.
**immensely** ADVERB  **immensity** NOUN

**immerse** immerses immersing immersed

VERB 1 If you are immersed in an activity you are completely involved in it. 2 If you immerse something in a liquid, you put it into the liquid so that it is completely covered.
**immersion** NOUN

**immigrant** immigrants

NOUN (HISTORY) someone who has come to live permanently in a new country.
**immigrate** VERB  **immigration** NOUN

**imminent**

ADJECTIVE If something is imminent, it is going to happen very soon.
**imminently** ADVERB  **imminence** NOUN

■ coming, impending, near

**immobile**

ADJECTIVE not moving.
**immobility** NOUN

**immoral**

ADJECTIVE (RE) If you describe someone or their behaviour as immoral, you mean that they do not fit in with most people's idea of what is right and proper.
**immorality** NOUN

☑ Do not confuse *immoral* and *amoral*. You use *immoral* to talk about people who are aware of moral standards, but go against

them. *Amoral* applies to people with no moral standards.

**immortal**

ADJECTIVE 1 Something that is immortal is famous and will be remembered for a long time E.G. *Emily Bronte's immortal love story.* 2 In stories, someone who is immortal will never die.

**immortality**

NOUN (RE) Immortality is never dying. In many religions, people believe that the soul or some other essential part of a person lives forever or continues to exist in some form.

**immovable** or **immoveable**

ADJECTIVE Something that is immovable is fixed and cannot be moved.
**immovably** ADVERB

**immune**

*Said* "im-**yoon**" ADJECTIVE 1 If you are immune to a particular disease, you cannot catch it. 2 If someone or something is immune to something, they are able to avoid it or are not bound by it E.G. *The captain was immune to prosecution.*
**immunity** NOUN

**immune system**

NOUN Your body's immune system consists of your white blood cells, which fight disease by producing antibodies or germs to kill germs which come into your body.

**imp** imps

NOUN a small mischievous creature in fairy stories.
**impish** ADJECTIVE

**impact** impacts

NOUN 1 The impact that someone or something has is the impression that

a
b
c
d
e
f
g
h
i
j
k
l
m
n
o
p
q
r
s
t
u
v
w
x
y
z

A
B
C
D
E
F
G
H
I
J
K
L
M
N
O
P
Q
R
S
T
U
V
W
X
Y
Z

they make or the effect that they have. **2** Impact is the action of one object hitting another, usually with a lot of force *E.G. The aircraft crashed into a ditch, exploding on impact.*

**impair impairs impairing impaired**

VERB To impair something is to damage it so that it stops working properly *E.G. Travel had made him weary and impaired his judgement.*

**impale impales impaling impaled**

VERB If you impale something, you pierce it with a sharp object.

**impart imparts imparting imparted**

VERB; FORMAL To impart information to someone is to pass it on to them.

**impartial**

ADJECTIVE Someone who is impartial has a view of something which is fair or not biased.

**impartially** ADVERB **impartiality** NOUN

■ fair, neutral, objective

**impasse**

*Said* "**am**-pass" NOUN a difficult situation in which it is impossible to find a solution.

📖 from French *impasse* meaning 'dead end'

**impassioned**

ADJECTIVE full of emotion *E.G. an impassioned plea.*

**impassive**

ADJECTIVE showing no emotion.

**impassively** ADVERB

**impasto**

NOUN (ART) a technique of painting with thick paint so that brush strokes or palette knife marks can be seen.

📖 an Italian word, from *pasta* meaning 'paste'

**impatient**

ADJECTIVE **1** Someone who is impatient becomes annoyed easily or is quick to lose their temper when things go wrong. **2** If you are impatient to do something, you are eager and do not want to wait *E.G. He was impatient to get back.*

**impatiently** ADVERB **impatience** NOUN

**impeccable**

*Said* "im-**pek**-i-bl" ADJECTIVE excellent, without any faults.

**impeccably** ADVERB

**impede impedes impeding impeded**

VERB If you impede someone, you make their progress difficult.

**impediment impediments**

NOUN something that makes it difficult to move, develop, or do something properly *E.G. a speech impediment.*

**impelled**

ADJECTIVE If you feel impelled to do something, you feel strongly that you must do it.

**impending**

ADJECTIVE; FORMAL You use 'impending' to describe something that is going to happen very soon *E.G. a sense of impending doom.*

**impenetrable**

ADJECTIVE impossible to get through.

**imperative**

ADJECTIVE **1** Something that is imperative is extremely urgent or important. ▶ NOUN **2** In grammar, an imperative is the form of a verb that is used for giving orders.

**imperfect**

ADJECTIVE **1** Something that is imperfect has faults or problems.

▶ NOUN **2** In grammar, the imperfect is a tense used to describe continuous or repeated actions which happened in the past.

**imperfectly** ADVERB **imperfection** NOUN

■ (sense 1) faulty, flawed

**imperial**

ADJECTIVE **1** (HISTORY) Imperial means relating to an empire or an emperor or empress E.G. *the Imperial Palace.* **2** The imperial system of measurement is the measuring system which uses inches, feet, and yards, ounces and pounds, and pints and gallons.

**imperialism**

NOUN (HISTORY) a system of rule in which a rich and powerful nation controls other nations.

**imperialist** ADJECTIVE or NOUN

**imperious**

ADJECTIVE proud and domineering E.G. *an imperious manner.*

**imperiously** ADVERB

**impersonal**

ADJECTIVE Something that is impersonal makes you feel that individuals and their feelings do not matter E.G. *impersonal cold rooms.*

**impersonally** ADVERB

■ detached, dispassionate, inhuman

**impersonate** impersonates impersonating impersonated

VERB If you impersonate someone, you pretend to be that person.

**impersonation** NOUN

**impersonator** NOUN

**impertinent**

ADJECTIVE disrespectful and rude E.G. *impertinent questions.*

**impertinently** ADVERB

**impertinence** NOUN

**impetuous**

ADJECTIVE If you are impetuous, you act quickly without thinking E.G. *an impetuous gamble.*

**impetuously** ADVERB **impetuosity** NOUN

**impetus**

NOUN **1** An impetus is the stimulating effect that something has on a situation, which causes it to develop more quickly. **2** In physics, impetus is the force that starts an object moving and resists changes in speed or direction.

**impinge** impinges impinging impinged

VERB If something impinges on your life, it has an effect on you and influences you E.G. *My private life doesn't impinge on my professional life.*

**implacable**

*Said* "im-**plak**-a-bl" ADJECTIVE Someone who is implacable is being harsh and refuses to change their mind.

**implacably** ADVERB

**implant** implants implanting implanted

VERB **1** To implant something into a person's body is to put it there, usually by means of an operation. ▶ NOUN **2** something that has been implanted into someone's body.

**implausible**

ADJECTIVE very unlikely E.G. *implausible stories.*

**implausibly** ADVERB

**implement** implements implementing implemented

VERB **1** If you implement something such as a plan, you carry it out E.G. *The government has failed to implement promised reforms.* ▶ NOUN

a b c d e f g h i j k l m n o p q r s t u v w x y z

**2** An implement is a tool.
**implementation** NOUN

**implicate** implicates implicating implicated
VERB If you are implicated in a crime, you are shown to be involved in it.

**implication** implications
NOUN something that is suggested or implied but not stated directly.

**implicit**
Said "im-**pliss**-it" ADJECTIVE **1** expressed in an indirect way E.G. *implicit criticism.* **2** If you have an implicit belief in something, you have no doubts about it E.G. *He had implicit faith in the noble intentions of the Emperor.*
**implicitly** ADVERB

**implore** implores imploring implored
VERB If you implore someone to do something, you beg them to do it.

**imply** implies implying implied
VERB If you imply that something is the case, you suggest it in an indirect way.

**import** imports importing imported
VERB **1** If you import something from another country, you bring it into your country or have it sent there.
▶ NOUN **2** a product that is made in another country and sent to your own country for use there.
**importation** NOUN   **importer** NOUN

**important**
ADJECTIVE **1** Something that is important is very valuable, necessary, or significant. **2** An important person has great influence or power.
**importantly** ADVERB   **importance** NOUN
■ (sense 1) momentous, significant

**impose** imposes imposing imposed
VERB **1** If you impose something on people, you force it on them E.G. *The allies had imposed a ban on all flights over Iraq.* **2** If someone imposes on you, they unreasonably expect you to do something for them.
**imposition** NOUN

**imposing**
ADJECTIVE having an impressive appearance or manner E.G. *an imposing building.*

**impossible**
ADJECTIVE Something that is impossible cannot happen, be done, or be believed.
**impossibly** ADVERB   **impossibility** NOUN

**imposter** imposters; also spelt impostor
NOUN a person who pretends to be someone else in order to get things they want.

**impotent**
ADJECTIVE **1** Someone who is impotent has no power to influence people or events. **2** A man who is impotent is unable to have or maintain an erection during sexual intercourse.
**impotently** ADVERB   **impotence** NOUN

**impound** impounds impounding impounded
VERB If something you own is impounded, the police or other officials take it.

**impoverished**
ADJECTIVE Someone who is impoverished is poor.

**impractical**
ADJECTIVE not practical, sensible, or realistic.

## impregnable
ADJECTIVE A building or other structure that is impregnable is so strong that it cannot be broken into or captured.

## impregnated
ADJECTIVE If something is impregnated with a substance, it has absorbed the substance so that it spreads right through it *E.G. sponges impregnated with detergent and water*.

## impresario impresarios
*Said "im-pris-sar-ee-oh"* NOUN a person who manages theatrical or musical events or companies.

## impress impresses impressing impressed
VERB 1 If you impress someone, you make them admire or respect you. 2 If you impress something on someone, you make them understand the importance of it.

## impression impressions
NOUN 1 An impression of someone or something is the way they look or seem to you. 2 If you **make an impression**, you have a strong effect on people you meet.

## impressionable
ADJECTIVE easy to influence *E.G. impressionable teenagers*.

## impressionism
NOUN a style of painting which is concerned with the impressions created by light and shapes, rather than with exact details.
**impressionist** NOUN

## impressive
ADJECTIVE If something is impressive, it impresses you *E.G. an impressive display of old-fashioned American cars*.

## imprint imprints imprinting imprinted
NOUN 1 If something leaves an imprint on your mind, it has a strong and lasting effect. 2 the mark left by the pressure of one object on another.
▶ VERB 3 If something is imprinted on your memory, it is firmly fixed there.

## imprison imprisons imprisoning imprisoned
VERB If you are imprisoned, you are locked up, usually in a prison.
**imprisonment** NOUN

## improbable
ADJECTIVE not probable or likely to happen.
**improbably** ADVERB
▣ doubtful, unlikely

## impromptu
*Said "im-prompt-yoo"* ADJECTIVE An impromptu action is one done without planning or organization.
▥ from Latin *in promptu* meaning 'in readiness'
▣ improvised, off the cuff, unprepared

## improper
ADJECTIVE 1 rude or shocking *E.G. improper behaviour*. 2 illegal or dishonest *E.G. improper dealings*. 3 not suitable or correct *E.G. an improper diet*.
**improperly** ADVERB

## improve improves improving improved
VERB If something improves or if you improve it, it gets better or becomes more valuable.
**improvement** NOUN
▣ better, enhance

## improvise improvises improvising improvised
VERB 1 If you improvise something, you make or do something without planning in advance, and with whatever materials are available.

a
b
c
d
e
f
g
h
i
j
k
l
m
n
o
p
q
r
s
t
u
v
w
x
y
z

A Rude Idiot Thought He Might Eat Toffee In Church (<u>arithmetic</u>)    SPELLING NOTE

A B C D E F G H I J K L M N O P Q R S T U V W X Y Z

**2** (DRAMA) When musicians or actors improvise, they make up the music or words as they go along.
**improvised** ADJECTIVE
**improvisation** NOUN

**impudent**
ADJECTIVE If someone is impudent, something they say or do is cheeky and lacking in respect.
**impudently** ADVERB **impudence** NOUN

**impulse impulses**
NOUN a strong urge to do something E.G. *She felt a sudden impulse to confide in her.*

**impulsive**
ADJECTIVE If you are impulsive, you do things suddenly, without thinking about them carefully.
**impulsively** ADVERB

**impure**
ADJECTIVE Something which is impure contains small amounts of other things, such as dirt.

**impurity impurities**
NOUN **1** Impurity is the quality of being impure E.G. *the impurity of the water.* **2** If something contains impurities, it contains small amounts of dirt or other substances that should not be there.

**in**
PREPOSITION or ADVERB 'In' is used to indicate position, direction, time, and manner E.G. *boarding schools in England… in the past few years.*

**in-**
PREFIX **1** 'In-' is added to the beginning of some words to form a word with the opposite meaning E.G. *insincere.* **2** 'In-' also means in, into, or in the course of E.G. *infiltrate.*
🏛 from a Latin prefix

**inability**
NOUN a lack of ability to do something.

**inaccessible**
ADJECTIVE impossible or very difficult to reach.

**inaccurate**
ADJECTIVE not accurate or correct.

**inadequate**
ADJECTIVE **1** If something is inadequate, there is not enough of it, or it is not good enough in quality for a particular purpose. **2** If someone feels inadequate, they feel they do not possess the skills necessary to do a particular job or to cope with life in general.
**inadequately** ADVERB **inadequacy** NOUN
▪ (sense 1) insufficient, meagre

**inadvertent**
ADJECTIVE not intentional E.G. *the murder had been inadvertent.*
**inadvertently** ADVERB

**inane**
ADJECTIVE silly or stupid.
**inanely** ADVERB **inanity** NOUN

**inanimate**
ADJECTIVE An inanimate object is not alive.

**inappropriate**
ADJECTIVE not suitable for a particular purpose or occasion E.G. *It was quite inappropriate to ask such questions.*
**inappropriately** ADVERB
▪ out of place, unfitting, unsuitable

**inarticulate**
ADJECTIVE If you are inarticulate, you are unable to express yourself well or easily in speech.

**inasmuch**
CONJUNCTION 'Inasmuch as' means to the extent that E.G. *She's giving herself*

*a hard time inasmuch as she feels guilty.*

**inaudible**
ADJECTIVE not loud enough to be heard.
**inaudibly** ADVERB

**inaugurate** inaugurates inaugurating inaugurated
*Said* "in-**awg**-yoo-rate" VERB **1** To inaugurate a new scheme is to start it. **2** To inaugurate a new leader is to officially establish them in their new position in a special ceremony *E.G. Albania's Orthodox Church inaugurated its first archbishop in 25 years.*
**inauguration** NOUN **inaugural** ADJECTIVE

**inborn**
ADJECTIVE An inborn quality is one that you were born with.

**incandescent**
ADJECTIVE Something which is incandescent gives out light when it is heated.
**incandescence** NOUN
📖 from Latin *candescere* meaning 'to glow white'

**incapable**
ADJECTIVE **1** Someone who is incapable of doing something is not able to do it *E.G. He is incapable of changing a fuse.* **2** An incapable person is weak and helpless.

**incarcerate** incarcerates incarcerating incarcerated
*Said* "in-**kar**-ser-rate" VERB To incarcerate someone is to lock them up.
**incarceration** NOUN

**Incarnation**
NOUN The Incarnation is the Christian belief that God took human form in Jesus Christ.

**incendiary**
*Said* "in-**send**-yer-ee" ADJECTIVE An incendiary weapon is one which sets fire to things *E.G. incendiary bombs.*

**incense**
NOUN Incense is a spicy substance which is burned to create a sweet smell, especially during religious services.

**incensed**
ADJECTIVE If you are incensed by something, it makes you extremely angry.

**incentive** incentives
NOUN something that encourages you to do something.
📖 from Latin *incentivus* meaning 'the beginning of a song'

**inception**
NOUN; FORMAL The inception of a project is the start of it.

**incessant**
ADJECTIVE continuing without stopping *E.G. her incessant talking.*
**incessantly** ADVERB

**incest**
NOUN Incest is the crime of two people who are closely related having sex with each other.
**incestuous** ADJECTIVE

**inch** inches inching inched
NOUN **1** a unit of length equal to about 2.54 centimetres. ▶ VERB **2** To inch forward is to move forward slowly.
📖 from Latin *uncia* meaning 'twelfth part'; there are twelve inches to the foot

**incident** incidents
NOUN an event *E.G. a shooting incident.*

**incidental**
ADJECTIVE occurring as a minor part of something *E.G. vivid incidental detail.*

a b c d e f g h i j k l m n o p q r s t u v w x y z

A B C D E F G H I J K L M N O P Q R S T U V W X Y Z

**incidentally** ADVERB

**incinerate** incinerates
incinerating incinerated
VERB If you incinerate something, you burn it.
**incineration** NOUN

**incinerator** incinerators
NOUN a furnace for burning rubbish.

**incipient**
ADJECTIVE beginning to happen or appear E.G. *incipient panic*.

**incision** incisions
NOUN a sharp cut, usually made by a surgeon operating on a patient.

**incisive**
ADJECTIVE Incisive language is clear and forceful.

**incite** incites inciting incited
VERB If you incite someone to do something, you encourage them to do it by making them angry or excited.
**incitement** NOUN
■ encourage, provoke, spur

**inclination** inclinations
NOUN If you have an inclination to do something, you want to do it.

**incline** inclines inclining inclined
VERB 1 If you are inclined to behave in a certain way, you often behave that way or you want to behave that way.
▶ NOUN 2 a slope.

**include** includes including included
VERB If one thing includes another, it has the second thing as one of its parts.
**including** PREPOSITION
■ contain, incorporate

**inclusion**
NOUN The inclusion of one thing in another is the act of making it part of the other thing.

**inclusive**
ADJECTIVE A price that is inclusive includes all the goods and services that are being offered, with no extra charge for any of them.

**incognito**
*Said* "in-kog-**nee**-toe" ADVERB If you are travelling incognito, you are travelling in disguise.
▥ from Latin *in-* + *cognitus* meaning 'not known'

**incoherent**
ADJECTIVE If someone is incoherent, they are talking in an unclear or rambling way.
**incoherently** ADVERB **incoherence** NOUN

**income** incomes
NOUN the money a person earns.

**income tax**
NOUN Income tax is a part of someone's salary which they have to pay regularly to the government.

**incoming**
ADJECTIVE coming in E.G. *incoming trains… an incoming phone call*.

**incomparable**
ADJECTIVE Something that is incomparable is so good that it cannot be compared with anything else.
**incomparably** ADVERB
■ matchless, unequalled, unparalleled

**incompatible**
ADJECTIVE Two things or people are incompatible if they are unable to live or exist together because they are completely different.
**incompatibility** NOUN

**incompetent**
ADJECTIVE Someone who is incompetent does not have the ability to do something properly.

**incompetently** ADVERB
**incompetence** NOUN
**incomplete**
ADJECTIVE not complete or finished.
**incompletely** ADVERB
**incomprehensible**
ADJECTIVE not able to be understood.
**inconceivable**
ADJECTIVE impossible to believe.
**inconclusive**
ADJECTIVE not leading to a decision or to a definite result.
**incongruous**
ADJECTIVE Something that is incongruous seems strange because it does not fit in to a place or situation.
**incongruously** ADVERB
**inconsequential**
ADJECTIVE Something that is inconsequential is not very important.
**inconsistent**
ADJECTIVE Someone or something which is inconsistent is unpredictable and behaves differently in similar situations.
**inconsistently** ADVERB
**inconsistency** NOUN
**inconspicuous**
ADJECTIVE not easily seen or obvious.
**inconspicuously** ADVERB
**incontinent**
ADJECTIVE Someone who is incontinent is unable to control their bladder or bowels.
**inconvenience** inconveniences inconveniencing inconvenienced
NOUN 1 If something causes inconvenience, it causes difficulty or problems. ▶ VERB 2 To inconvenience someone is to cause them trouble, difficulty or problems.

**inconvenient** ADJECTIVE
**inconveniently** ADVERB
**incorporate** incorporates incorporating incorporated
VERB If something is incorporated into another thing, it becomes part of that thing.
**incorporation** NOUN
**incorrect**
ADJECTIVE wrong or untrue.
**incorrectly** ADVERB
**increase** increases increasing increased
VERB 1 If something increases, it becomes larger in amount. ▶ NOUN 2 a rise in the number, level, or amount of something.
**increasingly** ADVERB
**incredible**
ADJECTIVE totally amazing or impossible to believe.
**incredibly** ADVERB
■ amazing, unbelievable
**incredulous**
ADJECTIVE If you are incredulous, you are unable to believe something because it is very surprising or shocking.
**incredulously** ADVERB  **incredulity** NOUN
**increment** increments
NOUN the amount by which something increases, or a regular increase in someone's salary.
**incremental** ADJECTIVE
**incriminate** incriminates incriminating incriminated
VERB If something incriminates you, it suggests that you are involved in a crime.
**incubate** incubates incubating incubated
*Said* "in-kyoo-bate" VERB When eggs incubate, they are kept warm until

a b c d e f g h i j k l m n o p q r s t u v w x y z

they are ready to hatch.
**incubation** NOUN

**incubator incubators**
NOUN a piece of hospital equipment in which sick or weak newborn babies are kept warm.

**incumbent incumbents** FORMAL
ADJECTIVE **1** If it is incumbent on you to do something, it is your duty to do it.
▶ NOUN **2** the person in a particular official po klklksition.

**incur incurs incurring incurred**
VERB If you incur something unpleasant, you cause it to happen.

**incurable**
ADJECTIVE **1** An incurable disease is one which cannot be cured. **2** An incurable habit is one which cannot be changed E.G. *an incurable romantic.*
**incurably** ADVERB

**indebted**
ADJECTIVE If you are indebted to someone, you are grateful to them.

**indecent**
ADJECTIVE Something that is indecent is shocking or rude, usually because it concerns nakedness or sex.
**indecently** ADVERB **indecency** NOUN

**indeed**
ADVERB You use 'indeed' to strengthen a point that you are making E.G. *The desserts are very good indeed.*
🔤 from Middle English *in dede* meaning 'in fact'

**indefatigable**
*Said* "in-dif-**fat**-ig-a-bl" ADJECTIVE
People who never get tired of doing something are indefatigable.

**indefinite**
ADJECTIVE **1** If something is indefinite, no time to finish has been decided E.G. *an indefinite strike.* **2** Indefinite

also means vague or not exact E.G.
*indefinite words and pictures.*
**indefinitely** ADVERB

**indefinite article indefinite articles**
NOUN the grammatical term for 'a' and 'an'.

**indelible**
ADJECTIVE unable to be removed E.G.
*indelible ink.*
**indelibly** ADVERB

**indemnity**
NOUN; FORMAL Indemnity is protection against damage or loss.

**indentation indentations**
NOUN a dent or a groove in a surface or on the edge of something.

**independence**
NOUN **1** Independence is not relying on anyone else. **2** ( HISTORY ) A nation or state gains its independence when it stops being ruled or governed by another country and has its own government and laws.

**independent**
ADJECTIVE **1** Something that is independent happens or exists separately from other people or things E.G. *Results are assessed by an independent panel.* **2** Someone who is independent does not need other people's help E.G. *a fiercely independent woman.* **3** An independent nation is one that is not ruled or governed by another country.
**independently** ADVERB
■ (sense 1 and 3) autonomous, self-governing

**indeterminate**
ADJECTIVE not certain or definite E.G.
*some indeterminate point in the future.*

**index** indexes

NOUN **1** an alphabetical list at the back of a book, referring to items in the book. **2** (LIBRARY) an alphabetical list of all the books in a library, arranged by title, author or subject.

**index finger** index fingers

NOUN your first finger, next to your thumb.

**Indian** Indians

ADJECTIVE **1** belonging or relating to India. ► NOUN **2** someone who comes from India. **3** someone descended from the people who lived in North, South, or Central America before Europeans arrived.

**indicate** indicates indicating indicated

VERB **1** If something indicates something, it shows that it is true E.G. *a gesture which clearly indicates his relief.* **2** If you indicate something to someone, you point to it. **3** If you indicate a fact, you mention it. **4** If the driver of a vehicle indicates, they give a signal to show which way they are going to turn.

■ (sense 1) denote, show, signify

**indication** indications

NOUN a sign of what someone feels or what is likely to happen.

**indicative**

ADJECTIVE **1** If something is indicative of something else, it is a sign of that thing E.G. *Clean, pink tongues are indicative of a good, healthy digestion.* ► NOUN **2** If a verb is used in the indicative, it is in the form used for making statements.

**indicator** indicators

NOUN **1** something which tells you what something is like or what is happening. **2** A car's indicators are the lights at the front and back which are used to show when it is turning left or right. **3** a substance used in chemistry that shows if another substance is an acid or alkali by changing colour when it comes into contact with it.

**indict** indicts indicting indicted

*Said "in-dite"* VERB; FORMAL To indict someone is to charge them officially with a crime.

**indictment** NOUN **indictable** ADJECTIVE

**indifferent**

ADJECTIVE **1** If you are indifferent to something, you have no interest in it. **2** If something is indifferent, it is of a poor quality or low standard E.G. *a pair of rather indifferent paintings.*

**indifferently** ADVERB **indifference** NOUN

**indigenous**

*Said "in-dij-in-uss"* ADJECTIVE If something is indigenous to a country, it comes from that country E.G. *a plant indigenous to Asia.*

**indigestion**

NOUN Indigestion is a pain you get when you find it difficult to digest food.

**indignant**

ADJECTIVE If you are indignant, you feel angry about something that you think is unfair.

**indignantly** ADVERB

**indignation**

NOUN Indignation is anger about something that you think is unfair.

**indignity** indignities

NOUN something that makes you feel embarrassed or humiliated E.G. *the indignity of having to flee angry protesters.*

a b c d e f g h i j k l m n o p q r s t u v w x y z

I want to see (C) your licenCe (licence)  **SPELLING NOTE**

A
B
C
D
E
F
G
H
I
J
K
L
M
N
O
P
Q
R
S
T
U
V
W
X
Y
Z

**indigo**
NOUN or ADJECTIVE dark violet-blue.

**indirect**
ADJECTIVE Something that is indirect is not done or caused directly by a particular person or thing, but by someone or something else.
**indirectly** ADVERB
■ circuitous, roundabout

**indiscriminate**
ADJECTIVE not involving careful thought or choice E.G. an indiscriminate bombing campaign.
**indiscriminately** ADVERB

**indispensable**
ADJECTIVE If something is indispensable, you cannot do without it E.G. A good pair of walking shoes is indispensable.

**indistinct**
ADJECTIVE not clear E.G. indistinct voices.
**indistinctly** ADVERB

**individual** individuals
ADJECTIVE 1 relating to one particular person or thing E.G. Each family needs individual attention. 2 Someone who is individual behaves quite differently from the way other people behave. ► NOUN 3 a person, different from any other person E.G. wealthy individuals.
**individually** ADVERB

**individualist** individualists
NOUN someone who likes to do things in their own way.
**individualistic** ADJECTIVE

**individuality**
NOUN If something has individuality, it is different from all other things, and therefore is very interesting and noticeable.

**indomitable**

ADJECTIVE; FORMAL impossible to overcome E.G. an indomitable spirit.

**Indonesian** Indonesians
Said "in-don-**nee**-zee-an" ADJECTIVE 1 belonging or relating to Indonesia. ► NOUN 2 someone who comes from Indonesia. 3 Indonesian is the official language of Indonesia.

**indoor**
ADJECTIVE situated or happening inside a building.

**indoors**
ADVERB If something happens indoors, it takes place inside a building.

**induce** induces inducing induced
VERB 1 To induce a state is to cause it E.G. His manner was rough and suspicious but he did not induce fear. 2 If you induce someone to do something, you persuade them to do it.

**inducement** inducements
NOUN something offered to encourage someone to do something.

**indulge** indulges indulging indulged
VERB 1 If you indulge in something, you allow yourself to do something that you enjoy. 2 If you indulge someone, you let them have or do what they want, often in a way that is not good for them.

**indulgence** indulgences
NOUN 1 something you allow yourself to have because it gives you pleasure. 2 Indulgence is the act of indulging yourself or another person.

**indulgent**
ADJECTIVE If you are indulgent, you treat someone with special kindness E.G. a rich, indulgent father.

**indulgently** ADJECTIVE

**industrial**

ADJECTIVE relating to industry.

**industrial action**

NOUN Industrial action is action such as striking taken by workers in protest over pay or working conditions.

**industrialist** industrialists

NOUN a person who owns or controls a lot of factories.

**Industrial Revolution**

NOUN The Industrial Revolution took place in Britain in the late eighteenth and early nineteenth century, when machines began to be used more in factories and more goods were produced as a result.

**industrious**

ADJECTIVE An industrious person works very hard.

**industry** industries

NOUN 1 Industry is the work and processes involved in manufacturing things in factories. 2 all the people and processes involved in manufacturing a particular thing.

**inedible**

ADJECTIVE too nasty or poisonous to eat.

**inefficient**

ADJECTIVE badly organized, wasteful, and slow E.G. *a corrupt and inefficient administration.*

**inefficiently** ADVERB    **inefficiency** NOUN

**inept**

ADJECTIVE without skill E.G. *an inept lawyer.*

**ineptitude** NOUN

**inequality** inequalities

NOUN a difference in size, status, wealth, or position, between different things, groups, or people.

**inert**

ADJECTIVE Something that is inert does not move and appears lifeless E.G. *an inert body lying on the floor.*

**inertia**

*Said* "in-**ner**-sha" NOUN If you have a feeling of inertia, you feel very lazy and unwilling to do anything.

**inevitable**

ADJECTIVE certain to happen.

**inevitably** ADVERB    **inevitability** NOUN

**inexhaustible**

ADJECTIVE Something that is inexhaustible will never be used up E.G. *an inexhaustible supply of ideas.*

**inexorable**

ADJECTIVE; FORMAL Something that is inexorable cannot be prevented from continuing E.G. *the inexorable increase in the number of cars.*

**inexorably** ADVERB

**inexpensive**

ADJECTIVE not costing much.

**inexperienced**

ADJECTIVE lacking experience of a situation or activity E.G. *inexperienced drivers.*

**inexperience** NOUN

■ new, raw, unpractised

**inexplicable**

ADJECTIVE If something is inexplicable, you cannot explain it E.G. *For some inexplicable reason I still felt uneasy.*

**inexplicably** ADVERB

**inextricably**

ADVERB If two or more things are inextricably linked, they cannot be separated.

**infallible**

ADJECTIVE never wrong E.G. *No machine is infallible.*

a b c d e f g h i j k l m n o p q r s t u v w x y z

**infallibility** NOUN

**infamous**
*Said* "in-fe-muss" ADJECTIVE well-known because of something bad or evil E.G. *a book about the country's most infamous murder cases.*

**infant** infants
NOUN **1** a baby or very young child. ▶ ADJECTIVE **2** designed for young children E.G. *an infant school.*
**infancy** NOUN   **infantile** ADJECTIVE
📖 from Latin *infans* meaning 'unable to speak'

**infantry**
NOUN In an army, the infantry are soldiers who fight on foot rather than in tanks or on horses.

**infatuated**
ADJECTIVE If you are infatuated with someone, you have such strong feelings of love or passion that you cannot think sensibly about them.
**infatuation** NOUN

**infect** infects infecting infected
VERB To infect someone or something is to cause disease in them.

**infection** infections
NOUN **1** a disease caused by germs E.G. *a chest infection.* **2** Infection is the state of being infected E.G. *a very small risk of infection.*

**infectious**
ADJECTIVE spreading from one person to another E.G. *an infectious disease.*
▦ catching, contagious

**infer** infers inferring inferred
VERB If you infer something, you work out that it is true on the basis of information that you already have.
**inference** NOUN
☑ Do not use *infer* to mean the same as *imply.*

**inferior** inferiors
ADJECTIVE **1** having a lower position or worth less than something else E.G. *inferior quality cassette tapes.* ▶ NOUN **2** Your inferiors are people in a lower position than you.
**inferiority** NOUN

**infernal**
ADJECTIVE very unpleasant E.G. *an infernal bore.*
📖 from Latin *infernus* meaning 'hell'

**inferno** infernos
NOUN a very large dangerous fire.

**infertile**
ADJECTIVE **1** Infertile soil is of poor quality and plants cannot grow well in it. **2** Someone who is infertile cannot have children.

**infested**
ADJECTIVE Something that is infested has a large number of animals or insects living on it and causing damage E.G. *The flats are damp and infested with rats.*
**infestation** NOUN

**infidelity** infidelities
NOUN Infidelity is being unfaithful to your husband, wife, or lover.

**infighting**
NOUN Infighting is quarrelling or rivalry between members of the same organization.

**infiltrate** infiltrates infiltrating infiltrated
VERB If people infiltrate an organization, they gradually enter it in secret to spy on its activities.
**infiltration** NOUN

**infinite**
ADJECTIVE without any limit or end E.G. *an infinite number of possibilities.*
**infinitely** ADVERB
▦ limitless, never-ending

**infinitive** infinitives
NOUN In grammar, the infinitive is the base form of the verb. It often has 'to' in front of it, for example 'to go' or 'to see'.

**infinity**
NOUN 1 Infinity is a number that is larger than any other number and can never be given an exact value. 2 Infinity is also a point that can never be reached, further away than any other point E.G. *skies stretching on into infinity*.

**infirm**
ADJECTIVE weak or ill E.G. *old and infirm*.
**infirmity** NOUN

**infirmary** infirmaries
NOUN a hospital.

**inflamed**
ADJECTIVE If part of your body is inflamed, it is red and swollen, usually because of infection.

**inflammable**
ADJECTIVE An inflammable material burns easily.
☑ Although *inflammable* and *flammable* both mean 'likely to catch fire', *flammable* is used more often as people sometimes think that *inflammable* means 'not likely to catch fire'.

**inflammation**
NOUN Inflammation is painful redness or swelling of part of the body.

**inflammatory**
ADJECTIVE Inflammatory actions are likely to make people very angry.

**inflate** inflates inflating inflated
VERB When you inflate something, you fill it with air or gas to make it swell.
**inflatable** ADJECTIVE

**inflation**
NOUN increase in the price of goods

and services in a country.
**inflationary** ADJECTIVE

**inflection** inflections; also spelt inflexion
NOUN a change in the form of a word that shows its grammatical function, for example a change that makes a noun plural.

**inflexible**
ADJECTIVE fixed and unable to be altered E.G. *an inflexible routine*.

**inflict** inflicts inflicting inflicted
VERB If you inflict something unpleasant on someone, you make them suffer it.

**influence** influences influencing influenced
NOUN 1 power that a person has over other people. 2 effect that someone or something has E.G. *under the influence of alcohol*. ▶ VERB 3 have an effect on someone or something.
🏛 from Latin *influentia* meaning 'power flowing from the stars'
▤ (sense 1) hold, power, pull

**influential**
ADJECTIVE Someone who is influential has a lot of influence over people.

**influenza**
NOUN; FORMAL Influenza is flu.

**influx**
NOUN a steady arrival of people or things E.G. *a large influx of tourists*.

**inform** informs informing informed
VERB 1 If you inform someone of something, you tell them about it. 2 If you inform on a person, you tell the police about a crime they have committed.
**informant** NOUN
▤ (sense 1) notify, tell
▤ (sense 2) betray, grass, shop

a
b
c
d
e
f
g
h
i
j
k
l
m
n
o
p
q
r
s
t
u
v
w
x
y
z

I went to see (C) the doctor's new practiCe (practice)     **SPELLING NOTE**

A
B
C
D
E
F
G
H
I
J
K
L
M
N
O
P
Q
R
S
T
U
V
W
X
Y
Z

**informal**
ADJECTIVE relaxed and casual *E.G. an informal meeting.*
**informally** ADVERB **informality** NOUN

**information**
NOUN If you have information on or about something, you know something about it.
■ data, facts

**informative**
ADJECTIVE Something that is informative gives you useful information.

**informer** informers
NOUN someone who tells the police that another person has committed a crime.

**infrastructure** infrastructures
NOUN (GEOGRAPHY) The infrastructure of a country consists of things like factories, schools, and roads, which show how much money the country has and how strong its economy is.

**infringe** infringes infringing infringed
VERB 1 If you infringe a law, you break it. 2 To infringe people's rights is to not allow them the rights to which they are entitled.
**infringement** NOUN

**infuriate** infuriates infuriating infuriated
VERB If someone infuriates you, they make you very angry.
**infuriating** ADJECTIVE

**infuse** infuses infusing infused
VERB 1 If you infuse someone with a feeling such as enthusiasm or joy, you fill them with it. 2 If you infuse a substance such as a herb or medicine, you pour hot water onto it and leave it for the water to absorb

the flavour.
**infusion** NOUN

**ingenious**
*Said* "in-jeen-yuss" ADJECTIVE very clever and using new ideas *E.G. his ingenious invention.*
**ingeniously** ADVERB

**ingenuity**
*Said* "in-jen-yoo-it-ee" NOUN Ingenuity is cleverness and skill at inventing things or working out plans.

**ingot** ingots
NOUN a brick-shaped lump of metal, especially gold.

**ingrained**
ADJECTIVE If habits and beliefs are ingrained, they are difficult to change or destroy.

**ingredient** ingredients
NOUN (D&T) Ingredients are the things that something is made from, especially in cookery.

**inhabit** inhabits inhabiting inhabited
VERB If you inhabit a place, you live there.

**inhabitant** inhabitants
NOUN The inhabitants of a place are the people who live there.
■ citizen, dweller, resident

**inhale** inhales inhaling inhaled
VERB When you inhale, you breathe in.
**inhalation** NOUN

**inherent**
ADJECTIVE Inherent qualities or characteristics in something are a natural part of it *E.G. her inherent common sense.*
**inherently** ADVERB

**inherit** inherits inheriting inherited
VERB 1 If you inherit money or property, you receive it from

someone who has died. **2** If you inherit a quality or characteristic from a parent or ancestor, it is passed on to you at birth.

**inheritance** NOUN **inheritor** NOUN

**inhibit** inhibits inhibiting inhibited

VERB If you inhibit someone from doing something, you prevent them from doing it.

**inhibited**

ADJECTIVE People who are inhibited find it difficult to relax and to show their emotions.

**inhibition** inhibitions

NOUN Inhibitions are feelings of fear or embarrassment that make it difficult for someone to relax and to show their emotions.

**inhospitable**

ADJECTIVE **1** An inhospitable place is unpleasant or difficult to live in. **2** If someone is inhospitable, they do not make people who visit them feel welcome.

**inhuman**

ADJECTIVE not human or not behaving like a human *E.G. the inhuman killing of their enemies.*

**inhumane**

ADJECTIVE extremely cruel.

**inhumanity** NOUN

**inimitable**

ADJECTIVE If you have an inimitable characteristic, no-one else can imitate it *E.G. her inimitable sense of style.*

**initial** initials

*Said* "in-**nish**-l" ADJECTIVE **1** first, or at the beginning *E.G. Shock and dismay were my initial reactions.* ▶ NOUN **2** the first letter of a name.

**initially** ADVERB

**initiate** initiates initiating initiated

*Said* "in-**nish**-ee-ate" VERB **1** If you initiate something, you make it start or happen. **2** If you initiate someone into a group or club, you allow them to become a member of it, usually by means of a special ceremony.

**initiation** NOUN

**initiative** initiatives

*Said* "in-**nish**-at-ive" NOUN **1** an attempt to get something done. **2** If you have initiative, you decide what to do and then do it, without needing the advice of other people.

**inject** injects injecting injected

VERB **1** If a doctor or nurse injects you with a substance, they use a needle and syringe to put the substance into your body. **2** If you inject something new into a situation, you add it.

**injection** NOUN

**injunction** injunctions

NOUN an order issued by a court of law to stop someone doing something.

**injure** injures injuring injured

VERB To injure someone is to damage part of their body.

**injury** injuries

NOUN ⟨PE⟩ hurt or damage, especially to part of a person's body or to their feelings *E.G. He suffered acute injury to his pride… The knee injury forced him to retire from the professional game.*

**injustice** injustices

NOUN **1** Injustice is lack of justice and fairness. **2** If you do someone an injustice, you judge them too harshly.

a b c d e f g h i j k l m n o p q r s t u v w x y z

**ink**
NOUN Ink is the coloured liquid used for writing or printing.

**inkling** inklings
NOUN a vague idea about something.

**inlaid**
ADJECTIVE decorated with small pieces of wood, metal, or stone E.G. *decorative plates inlaid with brass.*
**inlay** NOUN

**inland**
ADVERB OR ADJECTIVE towards or near the middle of a country, away from the sea.

**in-law** in-laws
NOUN Your in-laws are members of your husband's or wife's family.

**inlet** inlets
NOUN a narrow bay.

**inmate** inmates
NOUN someone who lives in a prison or psychiatric hospital.

**inn** inns
NOUN a small old country pub or hotel.

**innards**
PLURAL NOUN The innards of something are its inside parts.

**innate**
ADJECTIVE An innate quality is one that you were born with E.G. *an innate sense of fairness.*
**innately** ADVERB

**inner**
ADJECTIVE contained inside a place or object E.G. *an inner room.*

**innermost**
ADJECTIVE deepest and most secret E.G. *our innermost feelings.*

**innings**
NOUN In cricket, an innings is a period when a particular team is batting.

**innocent**
ADJECTIVE 1 not guilty of a crime.

2 without experience of evil or unpleasant things E.G. *an innocent child.*
**innocently** ADVERB  **innocence** NOUN

**innocuous**
*Said* "in-**nok**-yoo-uss" ADJECTIVE not harmful.

**innovation** innovations
NOUN (D&T) a completely new idea, product, or system of doing things.

**innuendo** innuendos or **innuendoes**
*Said* "in-yoo-**en**-doe" NOUN an indirect reference to something rude or unpleasant.
🏛 from Latin *innuendo* meaning 'by hinting'; from *innuere* meaning 'to convey by a nod'

**innumerable**
ADJECTIVE too many to be counted E.G. *innumerable cups of tea.*

**input** inputs
NOUN 1 Input consists of all the money, information, and other resources that are put into a job, project, or company to make it work.
2 (ICT) In computing, input is information which is fed into a computer.

**inquest** inquests
NOUN an official inquiry to find out what caused a person's death.

**inquire** inquires inquiring inquired; also spelt **enquire**
VERB If you inquire about something, you ask for information about it.
**inquiring** ADJECTIVE  **inquiry** NOUN

**inquisition** inquisitions
NOUN an official investigation, especially one which is very thorough and uses harsh methods of questioning.

**inquisitive**
ADJECTIVE Someone who is inquisitive is keen to find out about things.
**inquisitively** ADVERB

**inroads**
PLURAL NOUN If something makes inroads on or into something, it starts affecting it.

**insane**
ADJECTIVE Someone who is insane is mad.
**insanely** ADVERB  **insanity** NOUN

**insatiable**
Said "in-**saysh**-a-bl" ADJECTIVE A desire or urge that is insatiable is very great E.G. an insatiable curiosity.
**insatiably** ADVERB

**inscribe inscribes inscribing inscribed**
VERB If you inscribe words on an object, you write or carve them on it.

**inscription inscriptions**
NOUN the words that are written or carved on something.

**inscrutable**
Said "in-**skroot**-a-bl" ADJECTIVE Someone who is inscrutable does not show what they are really thinking.

**insect insects**
NOUN (SCIENCE) a small creature with six legs, and usually wings.

**insecticide insecticides**
NOUN a poisonous chemical used to kill insects.

**insecure**
ADJECTIVE 1 If you are insecure, you feel unsure of yourself and doubt whether other people like you.
2 Something that is insecure is not safe or well protected E.G. People still feel their jobs are insecure.
**insecurity** NOUN

**insensitive**
ADJECTIVE If you are insensitive, you do not notice when you are upsetting people.
**insensitivity** NOUN

**insert inserts inserting inserted**
VERB If you insert an object into something, you put it inside.
**insertion** NOUN

**inshore**
ADJECTIVE at sea but close to the shore E.G. inshore boats.

**inside insides**
ADVERB, PREPOSITION, or ADJECTIVE 1 Inside refers to the part of something which is surrounded by the main part and is often hidden E.G. Tom had to stay inside and work… inside the house… an inside pocket. ▶ PLURAL NOUN 2 Your insides are the parts inside your body. ▶ PHRASE 3 **Inside out** means with the inside part facing outwards
☑ Do not use of after inside. You should write she was waiting inside the school and not inside of the school.

**insider insiders**
NOUN a person who is involved in a situation and so knows more about it than other people.

**insidious**
ADJECTIVE Something that is insidious is unpleasant and develops slowly without being noticed E.G. the insidious progress of the disease.
**insidiously** ADVERB

**insight insights**
NOUN If you gain insight into a problem, you gradually get a deep and accurate understanding of it.

**insignia**
Said "in-**sig**-nee-a" NOUN the badge or a sign of a particular organization.

a b c d e f g h i j k l m n o p q r s t u v w x y z

Psychiatrists Seldom Yell Callously Hard (**psychi**atrist)  SPELLING NOTE

**insignificant**
ADJECTIVE small and unimportant.
**insignificance** NOUN

**insincere**
ADJECTIVE Someone who is insincere pretends to have feelings which they do not really have.

**insinuate** insinuates insinuating insinuated
VERB If you insinuate something unpleasant, you hint about it.
**insinuation** NOUN

**insipid**
ADJECTIVE 1 An insipid person or activity is dull and boring. 2 Food that is insipid has very little taste.
■ (sense 1) bland, colourless, uninteresting

**insist** insists insisting insisted
VERB If you insist on something, you demand it forcefully.
**insistent** ADJECTIVE **insistence** NOUN

**insolent**
ADJECTIVE very rude and disrespectful.
**insolently** ADVERB **insolence** NOUN

**insoluble**
Said "in-**sol**-yoo-bl" ADJECTIVE
1 impossible to solve E.G. an insoluble problem. 2 unable to dissolve E.G. substances which are insoluble in water.

**insolvent**
ADJECTIVE unable to pay your debts.
**insolvency** NOUN

**insomnia**
NOUN Insomnia is difficulty in sleeping.
**insomniac** NOUN

**inspect** inspects inspecting inspected
VERB To inspect something is to examine it carefully to check that

everything is all right.
**inspection** NOUN

**inspector** inspectors
NOUN 1 someone who inspects things. 2 a police officer just above a sergeant in rank.

**inspire** inspires inspiring inspired
VERB 1 (DRAMA) If something inspires you, it gives you new ideas and enthusiasm to do something. 2 To inspire an emotion in someone is to make them feel this emotion.
**inspired** ADJECTIVE **inspiring** ADJECTIVE **inspiration** NOUN

**instability**
NOUN Instability is a lack of stability in a place E.G. political instability.

**install** installs installing installed
VERB 1 If you install a piece of equipment in a place, you put it there so it is ready to be used. 2 To install someone in an important job is to officially give them that position. 3 If you install yourself in a place, you settle there and make yourself comfortable.
**installation** NOUN

**instalment** instalments
NOUN 1 If you pay for something in instalments, you pay small amounts of money regularly over a period of time. 2 one of the parts of a story or television series.

**instance** instances
NOUN 1 a particular example or occurrence of an event, situation, or person E.G. a serious instance of corruption. ▶ PHRASE 2 You use for instance to give an example of something you are talking about.

**instant** instants

NOUN **1** a moment or short period of time E.G. *In an instant they were gone.*
► ADJECTIVE **2** immediate and without delay E.G. *The record was an instant success.*
**instantly** ADVERB

**instantaneous**

ADJECTIVE happening immediately and without delay E.G. *The applause was instantaneous.*
**instantaneously** ADVERB

**instead**

ADVERB in place of something E.G. *Take the stairs instead of the lift.*

**instigate** instigates instigating instigated

VERB Someone who instigates a situation makes it happen.
**instigation** NOUN **instigator** NOUN

**instil** instils instilling instilled

VERB If you instil an idea or feeling into someone, you make them feel or think it.

**instinct** instincts

NOUN a natural tendency to do something E.G. *My first instinct was to protect myself.*
**instinctive** ADJECTIVE **instinctively** ADVERB

**institute** institutes instituting instituted

NOUN **1** an organization for teaching or research. ► VERB **2** FORMAL If you institute a rule or system, you introduce it.

**institution** institutions

NOUN **1** a custom or system regarded as an important tradition within a society E.G. *The family is an institution to be cherished.* **2** a large, important organization, for example a university or bank.

**institutional** ADJECTIVE

**instruct** instructs instructing instructed·

VERB **1** If you instruct someone to do something, you tell them to do it. **2** If someone instructs you in a subject or skill, they teach you about it.
**instructor** NOUN **instructive** ADJECTIVE **instruction** NOUN

**instrument** instruments

NOUN **1** a tool or device used for a particular job E.G. *a special instrument which cut through the metal.* **2** (MUSIC) A musical instrument is an object, such as a piano or flute, played to make music.

**instrumental**

ADJECTIVE **1** If you are instrumental in doing something, you help to make it happen. **2** (MUSIC) Instrumental music is performed using only musical instruments, and not voices.

**insufficient**

ADJECTIVE not enough for a particular purpose.
**insufficiently** ADVERB

**insular**

*Said "inss-yoo-lar"* ADJECTIVE Someone who is insular is unwilling to meet new people or to consider new ideas.
**insularity** NOUN

**insulate** insulates insulating insulated

VERB If you insulate something, you cover it with a layer to keep it warm or to stop electricity passing through it.
**insulation** NOUN **insulator** NOUN

**insulin**

*Said "inss-yoo-lin"* NOUN Insulin is a substance which controls the level of sugar in the blood. People who have

a b c d e f g h i j k l m n o p q r s t u v w x y z

A
B
C
D
E
F
G
H
I
J
K
L
M
N
O
P
Q
R
S
T
U
V
W
X
Y
Z

diabetes do not produce insulin naturally and have to take regular doses of it.

**insult insults insulting insulted**
VERB 1 If you insult someone, you offend them by being rude to them. ► NOUN 2 a rude remark which offends you.
**insulting** ADJECTIVE
☰ (sense 1) abuse, affront, offend
☰ (sense 2) abuse, affront, offence

**insure insures insuring insured**
VERB 1 If you insure something or yourself, you pay money regularly to a company so that if there is an accident or damage, the company will pay for medical treatment or repairs. 2 If you do something to insure against something unpleasant happening, you do it to prevent the unpleasant thing from happening or to protect yourself if it does happen.
**insurance** NOUN

**insurrection insurrections**
NOUN a violent action taken against the rulers of a country.

**intact**
ADJECTIVE complete, and not changed or damaged in any way E.G. *The rear of the aircraft remained intact when it crashed.*

**intake intakes**
NOUN A person's intake of food, drink, or air is the amount they take in.

**integral**
ADJECTIVE If something is an integral part of a whole thing, it is an essential part.

**integrate integrates integrating integrated**
VERB 1 If a person integrates into a group, they become part of it. 2 To

integrate things is to combine them so that they become closely linked or form one thing E.G. *his plan to integrate the coal and steel industries.*
**integration** NOUN

**integrity**
NOUN 1 Integrity is the quality of being honest and following your principles. 2 The integrity of a group of people is their being united as one whole.

**intellect intellects**
NOUN Intellect is the ability to understand ideas and information.

**intellectual intellectuals**
ADJECTIVE 1 involving thought, ideas, and understanding E.G. *an intellectual exercise.* ► NOUN 2 someone who enjoys thinking about complicated ideas.
**intellectually** ADVERB

**intelligence**
NOUN A person's intelligence is their ability to understand and learn things quickly and well.
**intelligent** ADJECTIVE **intelligently** ADVERB
☰ brains, intellect, understanding

**intelligentsia**
*Said* "in-tell-lee-**jent**-sya" NOUN The intelligentsia are intellectual people, considered as a group.

**intelligible**
ADJECTIVE able to be understood E.G. *very few intelligible remarks.*

**intend intends intending intended**
VERB 1 If you intend to do something, you have decided or planned to do it E.G. *She intended to move back to Cape Town.* 2 If something is intended for

a particular use, you have planned
that it should have this use *E.G. The
booklet is intended to be kept handy*.

**intense**
ADJECTIVE **1** very great in strength or
amount *E.G. intense heat*. **2** If a person
is intense, they take things very
seriously and have very strong
feelings.
**intensely** ADVERB **intensity** NOUN

**intensify** intensifies intensifying
intensified
VERB To intensify something is to
make it greater or stronger.

**intensive**
ADJECTIVE involving a lot of energy or
effort over a very short time *E.G. an
intensive training course*.

**intent** intents
NOUN **1** FORMAL A person's intent is their
purpose or intention. ▶ ADJECTIVE **2** If
you are intent on doing something,
you are determined to do it.
**intently** ADVERB

**intention** intentions
NOUN If you have an intention to do
something, you have a plan of what
you are going to do.

**intentional**
ADJECTIVE If something is intentional, it
is done on purpose.
**intentionally** ADVERB

**inter-**
PREFIX 'Inter-' means 'between' *E.G.
inter-school competitions*.
📖 a Latin word

**interact** interacts interacting
interacted
VERB The way two people or things
interact is the way they work
together, communicate, or react with
each other.
**interaction** NOUN

**interactive**
ADJECTIVE (ICT) Interactive television,
computers and games react to
decisions taken by the viewer, user
or player.

**intercept** intercepts
intercepting intercepted
*Said* "in-ter-**sept**" VERB If you
intercept someone or something
that is going from one place to
another, you stop them.

**interchange** interchanges
NOUN An interchange is the act or
process of exchanging things or
ideas.
**interchangeable** ADJECTIVE

**intercom** intercoms
NOUN a device consisting of a
microphone and a loudspeaker,
which you use to speak to people in
another room.

**intercourse**
NOUN Intercourse or sexual
intercourse is the act of having
sex.

**interest** interests interesting
interested
NOUN **1** If you have an interest in
something or if something is of
interest, you want to learn or hear
more about it. **2** Your interests are
your hobbies. **3** If you have an
interest in something being done,
you want it to be done because it
will benefit you. **4** Interest is an extra
payment made to the lender by
someone who has borrowed a sum
of money, or by a bank or company
to someone who has invested
money in them. Interest is worked
out as a percentage of the sum of
money borrowed or invested. ▶ VERB
**5** Something that interests you

A
B
C
D
E
F
G
H
I
J
K
L
M
N
O
P
Q
R
S
T
U
V
W
X
Y
Z

attracts your attention so that you want to learn or hear more about it.

**interesting** ADJECTIVE **interestingly** ADVERB **interested** ADJECTIVE

**interface interfaces**

NOUN 1 The interface between two subjects or systems is the area in which they affect each other or are linked. 2 (ICT) The user interface of a computer program is how it is presented on the computer screen and how easy it is to operate.

**interfere interferes interfering interfered**

VERB 1 If you interfere in a situation, you try to influence it, although it does not really concern you.
2 Something that interferes with a situation has a damaging effect on it.
**interference** NOUN **interfering** ADJECTIVE

🔲 from Old French *s'entreferir* meaning 'to collide'

▦ (sense 1) butt in, intrude, meddle

**interim**

ADJECTIVE intended for use only until something permanent is arranged E.G. *an interim government.*
from Latin *interim* meaning 'meanwhile'

**interior interiors**

NOUN 1 the inside part of something.
▶ ADJECTIVE 2 Interior means inside E.G. *They painted the interior walls white.*

**interjection interjections**

NOUN a word or phrase spoken suddenly to express surprise, pain, or anger.

---

### What is an Interjection?

An interjection is a word that expresses a strong emotion, such as anger, surprise, or excitement. Interjections often stand alone rather than as part of a sentence. Some interjections express greetings:

E.G. *Hello.* ■ *Congratulations!*

Some interjections express agreement or disagreement:

E.G. *Indeed.* ■ *No.*

Some interjections express pain, anger, or annoyance:

E.G. *Ouch!* ■ *Blast!*

Some interjections express approval, pleasure, or excitement:

E.G. *Bravo!* ■ *Hooray!*

Some interjections express surprise or relief:

E.G. *Wow!* ■ *Phew!*

Sometimes an interjection is more like a noise than a word:

E.G. *Sh!* ■ *Psst!*

A group of words can be used together as an interjection:

E.G. *Happy birthday!* ■ *Hey presto!*

When an interjection does occur within a sentence, it is usually separated by commas or dashes:

E.G. *I turned the key and, **bingo**, the engine started.*

---

**interlude interludes**

*Rhymes with* "**rude**" NOUN a short break from an activity.

**intermediary intermediaries**

*Said* "in-ter-**meed**-yer-ee" NOUN someone who tries to get two groups of people to come to an agreement.

**intermediate**
ADJECTIVE An intermediate level occurs in the middle, between two other stages E.G. *intermediate students*.

**interminable**
ADJECTIVE If something is interminable, it goes on for a very long time E.G. *an interminable wait for the bus*.
**interminably** ADVERB

**intermission intermissions**
NOUN an interval between two parts of a film or play.

**intermittent**
ADJECTIVE happening only occasionally.
**intermittently** ADVERB

**internal**
ADJECTIVE happening inside a person, place, or object.
**internally** ADVERB

**international internationals**
ADJECTIVE (GEOGRAPHY) 1 involving different countries. ▶ NOUN 2 a sports match between two countries.
**internationally** ADVERB

**Internet**
NOUN (ICT) The Internet is a worldwide communication system which people use through computers.

**interplay**
NOUN The interplay between two things is the way they react with one another.

**interpret interprets interpreting interpreted**
VERB 1 If you interpret what someone says or does, you decide what it means. 2 If you interpret a foreign language that someone is speaking, you translate it.
**interpretation** NOUN **interpreter** NOUN

**interrogate interrogates interrogating interrogated**
VERB If you interrogate someone, you question them thoroughly to get information from them.
**interrogation** NOUN **interrogator** NOUN
■ cross-examine, question

**interrupt interrupts interrupting interrupted**
VERB 1 If you interrupt someone, you start talking while they are talking. 2 If you interrupt a process or activity, you stop it continuing for a time.
**interruption** NOUN

**intersect intersects intersecting intersected**
VERB When two roads intersect, they cross each other.
**intersection** NOUN

**interspersed**
ADJECTIVE If something is interspersed with things, these things occur at various points in it.

**interval intervals**
NOUN 1 the period of time between two moments or dates. 2 a short break during a play or concert.
(MUSIC)
■ (sense 2) break, interlude, intermission

**intervene intervenes intervening intervened**
VERB If you intervene in a situation, you step in to prevent conflict between people.
**intervention** NOUN
■ mediate, step in

**intervening**
ADJECTIVE An intervening period of time is one which separates two events.

a
b
c
d
e
f
g
h
i
j
k
l
m
n
o
p
q
r
s
t
u
v
w
x
y
z

A
B
C
D
E
F
G
H
I
J
K
L
M
N
O
P
Q
R
S
T
U
V
W
X
Y
Z

**interview** interviews
interviewing interviewed
NOUN 1 a meeting at which someone
asks you questions about yourself to
see if you are suitable for a particular
job. 2 a conversation in which a
journalist asks a famous person
questions. ▶ VERB 3 If you interview
someone, you ask them questions
about themselves.

**intestine** intestines
NOUN Your intestines are a long tube
which carries food from your
stomach through to your bowels,
and in which the food is digested.
**intestinal** ADJECTIVE

**intimate** intimates intimating
intimated
ADJECTIVE 1 If two people are intimate,
there is a close relationship between
them. 2 An intimate matter is very
private and personal. 3 An intimate
knowledge of something is very
deep and detailed. ▶ VERB 4 If you
intimate something, you hint at it E.G.
*He did intimate that he is considering
legal action.*
**intimately** ADVERB **intimacy** NOUN
**intimation** NOUN

**intimidate** intimidates
intimidating intimidated
VERB If you intimidate someone, you
frighten them in a threatening way.
**intimidated** ADJECTIVE **intimidating**
ADJECTIVE **intimidation** NOUN

**into**
PREPOSITION 1 If something goes into
something else, it goes inside it. 2 If
you bump or crash into something,
you hit it. 3 *INFORMAL* If you are into
something, you like it very much E.G.
*Nowadays I'm really into healthy
food.*

**intolerable**
ADJECTIVE If something is intolerable, it
is so bad that it is difficult to put up
with it.
**intolerably** ADVERB

**intonation**
NOUN Your intonation is the way that
your voice rises and falls as you speak.

**intoxicated**
ADJECTIVE If someone is intoxicated,
they are drunk.
**intoxicating** ADJECTIVE **intoxication**
NOUN

**intra-**
PREFIX 'Intra-' means 'within' or 'inside'
E.G. *intra-European conflicts.*
🏛 from Latin *intra* meaning 'within'

**intractable**
ADJECTIVE; *FORMAL* stubborn and difficult
to deal with or control.

**intransitive**
ADJECTIVE An intransitive verb is one
that does not have a direct object.
For example, 'sings' is intransitive in
'She sings', but not in 'She sings a
song'.

**intravenous**
*Said* "in-trav-vee-nuss" ADJECTIVE
Intravenous foods or drugs are given
to sick people through their veins.
**intravenously** ADVERB

**intrepid**
ADJECTIVE not worried by danger E.G. *an
intrepid explorer.*
**intrepidly** ADVERB

**intricate**
ADJECTIVE Something that is intricate
has many fine details E.G. *walls
covered with intricate patterns.*
**intricately** ADVERB **intricacy** NOUN

**intrigue** intrigues intriguing
intrigued
NOUN 1 Intrigue is the making of

secret plans, often with the intention of harming other people E.G. *political intrigue*. ▶ VERB 2 If something intrigues you, you are fascinated by it and curious about it.

**intriguing** ADJECTIVE

**intrinsic**
ADJECTIVE; *FORMAL* The intrinsic qualities of something are its basic qualities.

**intrinsically** ADVERB

**introduce** introduces introducing introduced
VERB 1 If you introduce one person to another, you tell them each other's name so that they can get to know each other. 2 When someone introduces a radio or television show, they say a few words at the beginning to tell you about it. 3 If you introduce someone to something, they learn about it for the first time.

**introductory** ADJECTIVE

**introduction** introductions
NOUN 1 The introduction of someone or something is the act of presenting them for the first time. 2 a piece of writing at the beginning of a book, which usually tells you what the book is about.
▣ (sense 2) foreword, opening, preface

**introvert** introverts
NOUN someone who spends more time thinking about their private feelings than about the world around them, and who often finds it difficult to talk to others.

**introverted** ADJECTIVE

**intrude** intrudes intruding intruded
VERB To intrude on someone or something is to disturb them E.G. *I*

*don't want to intrude on your parents*.

**intruder** NOUN   **intrusion** NOUN

**intrusive** ADJECTIVE
▣ butt in, trespass

**intuition** intuitions
*Said* "int-yoo-**ish**-n" NOUN Your intuition is a feeling you have about something that you cannot explain E.G. *My intuition is right about him*.

**intuitive** ADJECTIVE   **intuitively** ADVERB

**Inuit** Inuits; also spelt **Innuit**
NOUN a member of a group of people who live in Northern Canada, Greenland, Alaska, and Eastern Siberia, formerly known as Eskimos.

**inundated**
ADJECTIVE If you are inundated by letters or requests, you receive so many that you cannot deal with them all.

**invade** invades invading invaded
VERB 1 If an army invades a country, it enters it by force. 2 If someone invades your privacy, they disturb you when you want to be alone.

**invader** NOUN

**invalid** invalids
*Said* "**in**-va-lid" NOUN someone who is so ill that they need to be looked after by someone else.
▦ from Latin *invalidus* meaning 'infirm'

**invalid**
*Said* "in-**val**-id" ADJECTIVE 1 If an argument or result is invalid, it is not acceptable because it is based on a mistake. 2 If a law, marriage, or election is invalid, it is illegal because it has not been carried out properly.

**invalidate** VERB
▦ from Latin *invalidus* meaning 'without legal force'

**invalidity**
*Said* "in-va-**lid**-dit-ee" NOUN Invalidity

a
b
c
d
e
f
g
h
i
j
k
l
m
n
o
p
q
r
s
t
u
v
w
x
y
z

is the condition of being very ill for a very long time.

**invaluable**

ADJECTIVE extremely useful *E.G. This book contains invaluable tips.*

**invariably**

ADVERB If something invariably happens, it almost always happens.

**invasion invasions**

NOUN ( HISTORY ) The invasion of a country or territory is the act of entering it by force. **2** an unwanted disturbance or intrusion *E.G. an invasion of her privacy.*

**invective**

NOUN; FORMAL Invective is abusive language used by someone who is angry.

**invent invents inventing invented**

VERB **1** If you invent a device or process, you are the first person to think of it or to use it. **2** If you invent a story or an excuse, you make it up.

**inventor** NOUN **invention** NOUN **inventive** ADJECTIVE **inventiveness** NOUN

■ (sense 1) conceive, create, devise

**inventory inventories**

NOUN a written list of all the objects in a place.

**inverse**

ADJECTIVE; FORMAL If there is an inverse relationship between two things, one decreases as the other increases.

**invertebrate invertebrates**

NOUN; TECHNICAL a creature which does not have a spine

**inverted**

ADJECTIVE upside down or back to front.

**inverted comma inverted commas**

NOUN Inverted commas are the punctuation marks " " or ' ', used to show where speech begins and ends.

---

#### What do Inverted Commas do?

**Inverted commas** or **quotation marks** (" " or ' ') mark the beginning and end of a speaker's exact words or thoughts:

*E.G. "I would like some more," said Matthew.*

Inverted commas are not used when a speaker's words are reported indirectly rather than in their exact form:

*E.G. Matthew said that he would like some more.*

Inverted commas can also be used to indicate the title of a book, piece of music, etc:

*E.G. The class had been reading "The Little Prince".*

Inverted commas are also used to draw attention to the fact that a word or phrase is being used in an unusual way, or that a word itself is the subject of discussion:

*E.G. Braille allows a blind person to "see" with the fingers. What rhymes with "orange"?*

---

**invest invests investing invested**

VERB **1** If you invest money, you pay it into a bank or buy shares so that you will receive a profit. **2** If you invest in something useful, you buy it because it will help you do something better. **3** If you invest money, time, or energy in something, you try to make it a success.

**investor** NOUN **investment** NOUN

**investigate** investigates
investigating investigated
VERB To investigate something is to try to find out all the facts about it.
**investigator** NOUN **investigation** NOUN
= examine, look into, study

**inveterate**
ADJECTIVE having lasted for a long time and not likely to stop *E.G. an inveterate gambler.*

**invincible**
ADJECTIVE unable to be defeated.
**invincibility** NOUN

**invisible**
ADJECTIVE If something is invisible, you cannot see it, because it is hidden, very small, or imaginary.
**invisibly** ADVERB **invisibility** NOUN

**invite** invites inviting invited
VERB 1 If you invite someone to an event, you ask them to come to it. 2 If you invite someone to do something, you ask them to do it *E.G. Andrew has been invited to speak at the conference.*
**inviting** ADJECTIVE **invitation** NOUN

**invoice** invoices
NOUN a bill for services or goods.

**invoke** invokes invoking invoked
VERB 1 FORMAL If you invoke a law, you use it to justify what you are doing.
2 If you invoke certain feelings, you cause someone to have these feelings.
🔲 from Latin *invocare* meaning 'to call upon'

**involuntary**
ADJECTIVE sudden and uncontrollable.
**involuntarily** ADVERB

**involve** involves involving involved
VERB (PSHE) If a situation involves

someone or something, it includes them as a necessary part.
**involvement** NOUN

**inward** or **inwards**
ADJECTIVE 1 Your inward thoughts and feelings are private. ▶ ADJECTIVE or ADVERB 2 If something moves inward or inwards, it moves towards the inside or centre of something.
**inwardly** ADVERB

**iodine**
*Said "eye-oh-deen"* NOUN Iodine is a bluish-black substance used in medicine and photography.

**ion** ions
*Said "eye-on"* NOUN Ions are electrically charged atoms.

**iota**
NOUN an extremely small amount *E.G. He did not have an iota of proof.*

**IQ** IQs
NOUN Your IQ is your level of intelligence shown by the results of a special test. IQ is an abbreviation for 'intelligence quotient'.

**ir-**
PREFIX 'Ir-' means 'not' or 'the opposite of', and is the form of 'in-' which is used before the letter *E.G. irrational.*

**Iranian** Iranians
*Said "ir-rain-ee-an"* ADJECTIVE
1 belonging or relating to Iran.
▶ NOUN 2 someone who comes from Iran. 3 Iranian is the main language spoken in Iran. It is also known as Farsi.

**Iraqi** Iraqis
*Said "ir-ah-kee"* ADJECTIVE 1 belonging or relating to Iraq. ▶ NOUN 2 someone who comes from Iraq.

**irate**
*Said "eye-rate"* ADJECTIVE very angry.

a b c d e f g h i j k l m n o p q r s t u v w x y z

LEt's measure the angLE (angle)    SPELLING NOTE

**iris irises**
*Said "eye-riss"* NOUN **1** the round, coloured part of your eye. **2** a tall plant with long leaves and large blue, yellow, or white flowers.
🔟 from Greek *iris* meaning 'rainbow' or 'coloured circle'

**Irish**
ADJECTIVE **1** belonging or relating to the Irish Republic, or to the whole of Ireland. ▶ NOUN **2** Irish or Irish Gaelic is a language spoken in some parts of Ireland.

**Irishman Irishmen**
NOUN a man who comes from Ireland.
**Irishwoman** NOUN

**irk irks irking irked**
VERB If something irks you, it annoys you.
**irksome** ADJECTIVE

**iron irons ironing ironed**
NOUN **1** Iron is a hard dark metal used to make steel, and things like gates and fences. Small amounts of iron are found in blood. **2** a device which heats up and which you rub over clothes to remove creases. ▶ VERB **3** If you iron clothes, you use a hot iron to remove creases from them.
**ironing** NOUN
**iron out** VERB If you iron out difficulties, you solve them.

**Iron Age**
NOUN The Iron Age was a time about three thousand years ago when people first started to make tools out of iron.

**ironbark ironbarks**
NOUN an Australian eucalypt with a hard, rough bark.

**irony**
*Said "eye-ron-ee"* NOUN **1** Irony is a form of humour in which you say the opposite of what you really mean *E.G.*

*This group could be described, without irony, as the fortunate ones.* **2** There is irony in a situation when there is an unexpected or unusual connection between things or events *E.G. It's a sad irony of life: once you are lost, a map is useless.*
**ironic** or **ironical** ADJECTIVE
**ironically** ADVERB

**irrational**
ADJECTIVE Irrational feelings are not based on logical reasons *E.G. irrational fears.*
**irrationally** ADVERB **irrationality** NOUN

**irregular**
ADJECTIVE **1** Something that is irregular is not smooth or straight, or does not form a regular pattern *E.G. irregular walls.* **2** (MATHS) Irregular things are uneven or unequal, or are not symmetrical.
**irregularly** ADVERB **irregularity** NOUN
🔲 haphazard, random, variable

**irrelevant**
ADJECTIVE (LIBRARY) not directly connected with a subject *E.G. He either ignored questions or gave irrelevant answers.*
**irrelevance** NOUN

**irrepressible**
ADJECTIVE Someone who is irrepressible is lively and cheerful.

**irresistible**
ADJECTIVE **1** unable to be controlled *E.G. an irresistible urge to yawn.* **2** extremely attractive *E.G. Women always found him irresistible.*
**irresistibly** ADVERB

**irrespective**
ADJECTIVE If you say something will be

done irrespective of certain things,
you mean it will be done without
taking those things into account.

**irresponsible**
ADJECTIVE An irresponsible person
does things without considering the
consequences E.G. *an irresponsible
driver*.

**irresponsibly** ADVERB
**irresponsibility** NOUN
■ careless, reckless, thoughtless

**irrigate** irrigates irrigating
irrigated
VERB To irrigate land is to supply it
with water brought through pipes or
ditches.

**irrigated** ADJECTIVE   **irrigation** NOUN

**irritate** irritates irritating
irritated
VERB 1 If something irritates you, it
annoys you. 2 If something irritates
part of your body, it makes it tender,
sore, or itchy.

**irritable** ADJECTIVE   **irritant** NOUN
**irritation** NOUN
■ (sense 1) annoy, get on one's
nerves

**is**
the third person, present tense of **be**.

**-ish**
SUFFIX '-ish' forms adjectives that
mean 'fairly' or 'rather' E.G. *smallish,
greenish*.
▥ from an Old English suffix

**Islam**
*Said* "iz-lahm" NOUN ( RE ) Islam is the
Muslim religion, which teaches that
there is only one God, Allah, and
Mohammed is his prophet. The holy
book of Islam is the Koran.

**Islamic** ADJECTIVE
▥ from Arabic *islam* meaning
'surrender to God'

**island** islands
*Said* "eye-land" NOUN a piece of land
surrounded on all sides by water.

**islander** NOUN

**isle** isles
*Rhymes with* "mile" NOUN; *LITERARY* an
island.

**-ism**
SUFFIX 1 '-ism' forms nouns that refer
to an action or condition E.G. *criticism,
heroism*. 2 '-ism' forms nouns that
refer to a political or economic
system or a system of beliefs E.G.
*Marxism, Sikhism*. 3 '-ism' forms nouns
that refer to a type of prejudice E.G.
*racism, sexism*.
▥ from the Greek suffix *-ismos*

**isolate** isolates isolating
isolated
VERB 1 If something isolates you or if
you isolate yourself, you are set apart
from other people. 2 If you isolate
something, you separate it from
everything else.

**isolated** ADJECTIVE   **isolation** NOUN

**isosceles**
*Said* "eye-**soss**-il-eez" ADJECTIVE ( MATHS )
An isosceles triangle has two sides of
the same length.
▥ from Greek *iso-* meaning 'equal'
and *skelos* meaning 'leg'

**ISP** an abbreviation for 'internet
service provider'.

**Israeli** Israelis
*Said* "iz-**rail**-ee" ADJECTIVE ( RE )
1 belonging or relating
to Israel. ▶ NOUN 2 someone who
comes from Israel.

**issue** issues issuing issued
*Said* "ish-yoo" NOUN 1 an important
subject that people are talking
about. 2 a particular edition of a
newspaper or magazine. ▶ VERB 3 If

a
b
c
d
e
f
g
h
i
j
k
l
m
n
o
p
q
r
s
t
u
v
w
x
y
z

you issue a statement or a warning, you say it formally and publicly. **4** If someone issues something, they officially give it *E.G. Staff were issued with plastic cards.*

◨ (sense 4) distribute, give out

## -ist

SUFFIX **1** '-ist' forms nouns and adjectives which refer to someone who is involved in a certain activity, or who believes in a certain system or religion *E.G. chemist... motorist... Buddhist.* **2** '-ist' forms nouns and adjectives which refer to someone who has a certain prejudice *E.G. racist.*

▥ from the Greek suffix *istēs*

## isthmus isthmuses

NOUN a narrow strip of land connecting two larger areas.

## it

PRONOUN **1** 'It' is used to refer to something that has already been mentioned, or to a situation or fact *E.G. It was a difficult decision.* **2** 'It' is used to refer to people or animals whose sex is not known *E.G. If a baby is thirsty, it feeds more often.* **3** You use 'it' to make statements about the weather, time, or date *E.G. It's noon.*

## Italian Italians

ADJECTIVE **1** belonging or relating to Italy. ▸ NOUN **2** someone who comes from Italy. **3** Italian is the main language spoken in Italy.

## italics

PLURAL NOUN Italics are letters printed in a special sloping way, and are often used to emphasize something. All the examples in this dictionary are in italics.

**italic** ADJECTIVE

## itch itches itching itched

VERB **1** When your skin itches, it has an

unpleasant feeling and you want to scratch it. **2** If you are itching to do something, you are impatient to do it. ▸ NOUN **3** an unpleasant feeling on your skin that you want to scratch.

**itchy** ADJECTIVE

▥ from Old English *giccean* meaning 'to itch'

## item items

NOUN **1** one of a collection or list of objects. **2** a newspaper or magazine article.

◨ (sense 2) article, feature, piece

## itinerary itineraries

NOUN a plan of a journey, showing a route to follow and places to visit.

## -itis

SUFFIX '-itis' is added to the name of a part of the body to refer to disease or inflammation in that part *E.G. appendicitis... tonsillitis.*

▥ from Greek, the feminine form of -*itēs* meaning 'belonging to'

## its

ADJECTIVE OR PRONOUN 'Its' refers to something belonging to or relating to things, children, or animals that have already been mentioned *E.G. The lion lifted its head.*

☑ Many people are confused about the difference between *its* and *it's*. *Its*, without the apostrophe, is the possessive form of *it*: *the cat has hurt its paw.* *It's*, with the apostrophe, is a short form of *it is* or *it has*: *it's green... it's been snowing again.*

## itself

PRONOUN **1** 'Itself' is used when the same thing, child, or animal does an action and is affected by it *E.G. Paris prides itself on its luxurious hotels.* **2** 'Itself' is used to emphasize 'it'.

## -ity

SUFFIX '-ity' forms nouns that refer to a state or condition *E.G. continuity… technicality.*

📖 from the Latin suffix *-itas*

## -ive

SUFFIX '-ive' forms adjectives and some nouns *E.G. massive… detective.*

📖 from Latin suffix *-īvus*

## ivory

NOUN **1** the valuable creamy-white bone which forms the tusk of an elephant. It is used to make ornaments. ▶ NOUN OR ADJECTIVE **2** creamy-white.

## ivy

NOUN an evergreen plant which creeps along the ground and up walls.

## iwi iwi or iwis

NOUN In New Zealand, a Maori tribe.

## -ize or -ise

SUFFIX '-ize' and '-ise' forms verbs. Most verbs can be spelt with either ending, though there are some that can only be spelt with '-ise', for example *advertise, improvise* and *revise.*

📖 from the Greek suffix *-izein*

a b c d e f g h i j k l m n o p q r s t u v w x y z

# Jj

> **TIP** Many words which sound as if they ought to begin with letter *j* are spelt instead with letter *g*, for example *gender*, *geranium*, *giraffe* and *gym*.

**jab jabs jabbing jabbed**
VERB **1** To jab something means to poke at it roughly. ▶ NOUN **2** a sharp or sudden poke. **3** *INFORMAL* an injection.

**jabiru jabirus**
NOUN a white-and-green Australian stork with red legs.

**jack jacks jacking jacked**
NOUN **1** a piece of equipment for lifting heavy objects, especially for lifting a car when changing a wheel. **2** In a pack of cards, a jack is a card whose value is between a ten and a queen. ▶ VERB **3** To jack up an object means to raise it, especially by using a jack.

**jackal jackals**
NOUN a wild animal related to the dog.

**jackaroo jackaroos**; also spelt **jackeroo**
NOUN In Australia, a young person learning the work of a sheep or cattle station.

**jackdaw jackdaws**
NOUN a bird like a small crow with black and grey feathers.

**jacket jackets**
NOUN **1** a short coat reaching to the waist or hips. **2** an outer covering for something *E.G. a book jacket*. **3** The jacket of a baked potato is its skin.

**jackpot jackpots**
NOUN In a gambling game, the jackpot is the top prize.

**jack up jacks up jacking up jacked up**
VERB; *INFORMAL* In New Zealand English,

to jack up is to organize or prepare something.

**jade**
NOUN Jade is a hard green stone used for making jewellery and ornaments.

**jagged**
ADJECTIVE sharp and spiky.
▣ serrated, spiked, uneven

**jaguar jaguars**
NOUN a large member of the cat family with spots on its back.

**jail jails jailing jailed**; also spelt **gaol**
NOUN **1** a building where people convicted of a crime are locked up.
▶ VERB **2** To jail someone means to lock them up in a jail.
▣ (sense 1) nick, penitentiary, prison

**jailer jailers**; also spelt **gaoler**
NOUN a person who is in charge of the prisoners in a jail.

**jam jams jamming jammed**
NOUN **1** a food, made by boiling fruit and sugar together until it sets. **2** a situation in which it is impossible to move *E.G. a traffic jam*. ▶ AN INFORMAL PHRASE **3** If someone is **in a jam**, they are in a difficult situation. ▶ VERB **4** If people or things are jammed into a place, they are squeezed together so closely that they can hardly move. **5** To jam something somewhere means to push it there roughly *E.G. He jammed his foot on the brake*. **6** If something is jammed, it is stuck or unable to work properly. **7** To jam a radio signal means to interfere with it and prevent it from

being received clearly.

■ (sense 3) fix, predicament, tight spot

**Jamaican Jamaicans**

*Said* "jam-**may**-kn" ADJECTIVE

1 belonging or relating to Jamaica.

► NOUN 2 someone who comes from Jamaica.

**jamboree jamborees**

NOUN a gathering of large numbers of people enjoying themselves.

**Jandal Jandals**

NOUN; *TRADEMARK* In New Zealand, a sandal with a strap between the big toe and other toes and over the foot.

**jangle jangles jangling jangled**

VERB 1 If something jangles, it makes a harsh metallic ringing noise. ► NOUN 2 the sound made by metal objects striking against each other.

**janitor janitors**

NOUN the caretaker of a building.

**January**

NOUN January is the first month of the year. It has 31 days.

▥ from Latin *Januarius* meaning 'the month of Janus', named after a Roman god

**Japanese**

ADJECTIVE 1 belonging or relating to Japan. ► NOUN 2 someone who comes from Japan. 3 Japanese is the main language spoken in Japan.

**jar jars jarring jarred**

NOUN 1 a glass container with a wide top used for storing food. ► VERB 2 If something jars on you, you find it unpleasant or annoying.

**jargon**

NOUN Jargon consists of words that are used in special or technical ways by particular groups of people, often

making the language difficult to understand.

**jarrah jarrahs**

NOUN an Australian eucalypt tree that produces wood used for timber.

**jasmine**

NOUN Jasmine is a climbing plant with small sweet-scented white flowers.

**jaundice**

NOUN Jaundice is an illness affecting the liver, in which the skin and the whites of the eyes become yellow.

**jaundiced**

ADJECTIVE pessimistic and lacking enthusiasm *E.G. He takes a rather jaundiced view of politicians.*

**jaunt jaunts**

NOUN a journey or trip you go on for pleasure.

**jaunty jauntier jauntiest**

ADJECTIVE expressing cheerfulness and self-confidence *E.G. a jaunty tune.*

**jauntily** ADVERB

**javelin javelins**

NOUN a long spear that is thrown in sports competitions.

**jaw jaws**

NOUN 1 A person's or animal's jaw is the bone in which the teeth are set.

2 A person's or animal's mouth and teeth are their jaws.

**jay jays**

NOUN a kind of noisy chattering bird.

**jazz jazzes jazzing jazzed**

NOUN 1 Jazz is a style of popular music with a forceful rhythm. ► VERB

2 *INFORMAL* To jazz something up means to make it more colourful or exciting.

**jazzy jazzier jazziest**

ADJECTIVE; *INFORMAL* bright and showy.

**jealous**

ADJECTIVE 1 If you are jealous, you feel

a
b
c
d
e
f
g
h
i
j
k
l
m
n
o
p
q
r
s
t
u
v
w
x
y
z

bitterness towards someone who has something that you would like to have. **2** If you are jealous of something you have, you feel you must try to keep it from other people.

**jealously** ADVERB **jealousy** NOUN
■ (sense 1) covetous, envious
■ (sense 2) possessive

**jeans**
PLURAL NOUN Jeans are casual denim trousers.

**jeep jeeps**
NOUN; TRADEMARK a small road vehicle with four-wheel drive.

**jeer jeers jeering jeered**
VERB **1** If you jeer at someone, you insult them in a loud, unpleasant way. ▸ NOUN **2** Jeers are rude and insulting remarks.
**jeering** ADJECTIVE

**Jehovah**
*Said* "ji-*hove*-ah" PROPER NOUN Jehovah is the name of God in the Old Testament.
🔲 from adding vowels to the Hebrew JHVH, the sacred name of God

**jelly jellies**
NOUN **1** a clear, sweet food eaten as a dessert. **2** a type of clear, set jam.

**jellyfish jellyfishes**
NOUN a sea animal with a clear soft body and tentacles which may sting.

**jeopardize jeopardizes jeopardizing jeopardized**
*Said* "*jep*-par-dyz"; also spelt **jeopardise**
VERB To jeopardize something means to do something which puts it at risk
E.G. *Elaine jeopardized her health.*

**jeopardy**
NOUN If someone or something is in jeopardy, they are at risk of failing or

of being destroyed.

**jerk jerks jerking jerked**
VERB **1** To jerk something means to give it a sudden, sharp pull. **2** If something jerks, it moves suddenly and sharply. ▸ NOUN **3** a sudden sharp movement. **4** INFORMAL If you call someone a jerk, you mean they are stupid.
**jerky** ADJECTIVE **jerkily** ADVERB

**jerkin jerkins**
NOUN a short sleeveless jacket.

**jersey jerseys**
NOUN **1** a knitted garment for the upper half of the body. **2** Jersey is a type of knitted woollen or cotton fabric used to make clothing.

**jest jests jesting jested**
NOUN **1** a joke. ▸ VERB **2** To jest means to speak jokingly.

**jester jesters**
NOUN In the past, a jester was a man who was kept to amuse the king or queen.

**jet jets jetting jetted**
NOUN **1** a plane which is able to fly very fast. **2** a stream of liquid, gas, or flame forced out under pressure. **3** Jet is a hard black stone, usually highly polished and used in jewellery and ornaments. ▸ VERB **4** To jet somewhere means to fly there in a plane, especially a jet.

**jet boat jet boats**
NOUN In New Zealand, a motor boat that is powered by a jet of water at the rear.

**jet lag**
NOUN Jet lag is a feeling of tiredness or confusion that people have after a long flight across different time zones.

**jettison jettisons jettisoning jettisoned**
VERB If you jettison something, you

throw it away because you no longer want it.

**jetty jetties**
NOUN a wide stone wall or wooden platform at the edge of the sea or a river, where boats can be moored.

**Jew Jews**
*Said* "joo" (RE) NOUN a person who practises the religion of Judaism, or who is of Hebrew descent.
**Jewish** ADJECTIVE
🏛 from *Judah*, the name of a Jewish patriarch

**jewel jewels**
NOUN a precious stone used to decorate valuable ornaments or jewellery.
**jewelled** ADJECTIVE

**jeweller jewellers**
NOUN a person who makes jewellery or who sells and repairs jewellery and watches.

**jewellery**
NOUN ornaments that people wear, such as rings or necklaces, made of valuable metals and sometimes decorated with precious stones.

**jib jibs**
NOUN a small sail towards the front of a sailing boat.

**jibe**
another spelling of **gibe**.

**jig jigs jigging jigged**
NOUN 1 a type of lively folk dance.
► VERB 2 If you jig, you dance around in a lively bouncy manner.

**jiggle jiggles jiggling jiggled**
VERB If you jiggle something, you move it around with quick jerky movements.

**jigsaw jigsaws**
NOUN a puzzle consisting of a picture on cardboard that has been cut up

into small pieces, which have to be put together again.

**jihad jihads**
*Said* "jee-had" NOUN 1 a holy war waged to defend or further the ideals of Islam. 2 the personal struggle of a Muslim against sin.

**jilt jilts jilting jilted**
VERB If you jilt someone, you suddenly break off your relationship with them.
**jilted** ADJECTIVE

**jingle jingles jingling jingled**
NOUN 1 a short, catchy phrase or rhyme set to music and used to advertise something on radio or television. 2 the sound of something jingling. ► VERB 3 When something jingles, it makes a tinkling sound like small bells.

**jinks**
PLURAL NOUN High jinks is boisterous and mischievous behaviour.

**jinx jinxes**
NOUN someone or something that is thought to bring bad luck *E.G. He was beginning to think he was a jinx.*

**jinxed**
ADJECTIVE If something is jinxed it is considered to be unlucky *E.G. I think this house is jinxed.*

**jitters**
PLURAL NOUN; *INFORMAL* If you have got the jitters, you are feeling very nervous.
**jittery** ADJECTIVE

**job jobs**
NOUN 1 the work that someone does to earn money. 2 a duty or responsibility. *E.G. It is a captain's job to lead from the front.* ► PHRASE 3 If something is **just the job**, it is exactly right or exactly what you wanted.

The government licenSes Schnapps (licenSes)          SPELLING NOTE

a
b
c
d
e
f
g
h
i
**j**
k
l
m
n
o
p
q
r
s
t
u
v
w
x
y
z

(sense 1) employment, occupation, work

**job centre** job centres
NOUN a government office where people can find out about job vacancies.

**jobless**
ADJECTIVE without any work.

**jockey** jockeys jockeying jockeyed
NOUN 1 someone who rides a horse in a race. ► VERB 2 To jockey for a position means to manoeuvre in order to gain an advantage over other people.

**jocular**
ADJECTIVE A jocular comment is intended to make people laugh.

**jodhpurs**
*Said* "jod-purz" PLURAL NOUN Jodhpurs are close-fitting trousers worn when riding a horse.
🗺 from *Jodhpur*, the name of a town in N. India

**joey** joeys
NOUN; INFORMAL In Australian English, a young kangaroo or other young animal.

**jog** jogs jogging jogged
VERB 1 To jog means to run slowly and rhythmically, often as a form of exercise. 2 If you jog something, you knock it slightly so that it shakes or moves. 3 If someone or something jogs your memory, they remind you of something. ► NOUN 4 a slow run.
**jogger** NOUN **jogging** NOUN

**join** joins joining joined
VERB 1 When two things join, or when one thing joins another, they come together. 2 If you join a club or organization, you become a member of it or start taking part in it. 3 To join

two things means to fasten them.
► NOUN 4 a place where two things are fastened together.
(senses 1 & 3) connect, link, unite
(sense 2) enlist, enrol, sign up

**join up** VERB If someone joins up, they become a member of the armed forces.

**joiner** joiners
NOUN a person who makes wooden window frames, doors, and furniture.

**joinery**
NOUN Joinery is the work done by a joiner.

**joint** joints jointing jointed
ADJECTIVE 1 shared by or belonging to two or more people E.G. *a joint building society account.* ► NOUN 2 a part of the body where two bones meet and are joined together so that they can move, for example a knee or hip. 3 a place where two things are fixed together. 4 a large piece of meat suitable for roasting. 5 INFORMAL any place of entertainment, such as a nightclub or pub. ► VERB 6 To joint meat means to cut it into large pieces according to where the bones are.
**jointly** ADVERB **jointed** ADJECTIVE

**joist** joists
NOUN a large beam used to support floors or ceilings.

**joke** jokes joking joked
NOUN 1 something that you say or do to make people laugh, such as a funny story. 2 anything that you think is ridiculous and not worthy of respect E.G. *The decision was a joke.*
► VERB 3 If you are joking, you are teasing someone.
**jokingly** ADVERB
(sense 1) gag, jest

A B C D E F G H I J K L M N O P Q R S T U V W X Y Z

**▣** (sense 3) jest, kid

**joker** jokers
NOUN In a pack of cards, a joker is an extra card that does not belong to any of the four suits, but is used in some games.

**jolly** jollier jolliest
ADJECTIVE 1 happy, cheerful, and pleasant. ▶ ADVERB 2 INFORMAL Jolly also means very E.G. jolly good fun.

**jolt** jolts jolting jolted
VERB 1 To jolt means to move or shake roughly and violently. 2 If you are jolted by something, it gives you an unpleasant surprise. ▶ NOUN 3 a sudden jerky movement. 4 an unpleasant shock or surprise.

**jostle** jostles jostling jostled
VERB To jostle means to push roughly against people in a crowd.

**jot** jots jotting jotted
VERB 1 If you jot something down, you write it quickly in the form of a short informal note. ▶ NOUN 2 a very small amount.
**jotting** NOUN

**jotter** jotters
NOUN a pad or notebook.

**joule** joules
Rhymes with "school" NOUN a unit of energy or work.

**journal** journals
NOUN 1 a magazine that deals with a particular subject, trade, or profession. 2 a diary which someone keeps regularly.

**journalism**
NOUN Journalism is the work of collecting, writing, and publishing news in newspapers, magazines, and on television and radio.
**journalist** NOUN **journalistic** ADJECTIVE

**journey** journeys journeying journeyed
NOUN 1 the act of travelling from one place to another. ▶ VERB 2 FORMAL To journey somewhere means to travel there E.G. He intended to journey up the Amazon.

**joust** jousts
NOUN In medieval times, a joust was a competition between knights fighting on horseback, using lances.

**jovial**
ADJECTIVE cheerful and friendly.
**jovially** ADVERB **joviality** NOUN

**joy** joys
NOUN 1 Joy is a feeling of great happiness. 2 INFORMAL Joy also means success or luck E.G. Any joy with your insurance claim? 3 something that makes you happy or gives you pleasure.

**joyful**
ADJECTIVE 1 causing pleasure and happiness. 2 Someone who is joyful is extremely happy.
**joyfully** ADVERB

**joyous**
ADJECTIVE; FORMAL joyful.
**joyously** ADVERB

**joyride** joyrides
NOUN a drive in a stolen car for pleasure.
**joyriding** NOUN **joyrider** NOUN

**joystick** joysticks
NOUN a lever in an aircraft which the pilot uses to control height and direction.

**jube** jubes
NOUN; INFORMAL In Australian and New Zealand English, a fruit-flavoured jelly sweet.

**jubilant**
ADJECTIVE feeling or expressing great happiness or triumph.
**jubilantly** ADVERB

Plaice the fish has a glittering 'EYE' (I) (plaice) ▶ SPELLING NOTE

a b c d e f g h i **j** k l m n o p q r s t u v w x y z

## jubilation

NOUN Jubilation is a feeling of great happiness and triumph.

## jubilee jubilees

NOUN a special anniversary of an event such as a coronation *E.G. Queen Elizabeth's Silver Jubilee in 1977.*

📖 from Hebrew *yobhel* meaning 'ram's horn'; rams' horns were blown during festivals and celebrations

## Judaism

*Said* "joo-day-i-zm" NOUN  ⟨RE⟩

Judaism is the religion of the Jewish people. It is based on a belief in one God, and draws its laws and authority from the Old Testament.

**Judaic** ADJECTIVE

## judder judders juddering juddered

VERB To judder means to shake and vibrate noisily and violently.

## judder bar judder bars

NOUN In New Zealand English, a bump built across a road to stop drivers from going too fast. In Britain it is called a sleeping policeman.

## judge judges judging judged

NOUN **1** the person in a law court who decides how the law should be applied to people who appear in the court. **2** someone who decides the winner in a contest or competition.

▶ VERB **3** If you judge someone or something, you form an opinion about them based on the evidence that you have. **4** To judge a contest or competition means to decide on the winner.

**judgment** or **judgement** NOUN

■ (sense 2) adjudicator, referee, umpire

■ (sense 4) adjudicate, referee, umpire

✔ *Judgment* and *judgement* are both correct spellings.

## judicial

ADJECTIVE relating to judgment or to justice *E.G. a judicial review.*

## judiciary

NOUN The judiciary is the branch of government concerned with justice and the legal system.

## judicious

ADJECTIVE sensible and showing good judgment.

**judiciously** ADVERB

## judo

NOUN Judo is a sport in which two people try to force each other to the ground using special throwing techniques.

## jug jugs

NOUN a container with a lip or spout used for holding or serving liquids.

## juggernaut juggernauts

NOUN a large heavy lorry.

📖 from Hindi *Jagannath*, the name of a huge idol of the god Krishna, which every year is wheeled through the streets of Puri in India

## juggle juggles juggling juggled

VERB To juggle means to throw objects into the air, catching them in sequence, and tossing them up again so there are several in the air at one time.

**juggler** NOUN

## jugular jugulars

NOUN The jugular or jugular vein is one of the veins in the neck which carry blood from the head back to the heart.

## juice juices

NOUN **1** Juice is the liquid that can be

squeezed or extracted from fruit or other food. **2** Juices in the body are fluids *E.G. gastric juices.*

**juicy juicier juiciest**
ADJECTIVE **1** Juicy food has a lot of juice in it. **2** Something that is juicy is interesting, exciting, or scandalous *E.G. a juicy bit of gossip.*

**jukebox jukeboxes**
NOUN a large record player found in cafés and pubs which automatically plays a selected record when coins are inserted.

**July**
NOUN July is the seventh month of the year. It has 31 days.
From Latin *Julius*, the month of July, named after Julius Caesar by the Romans

**jumble jumbles jumbling jumbled**
NOUN **1** an untidy muddle of things. **2** Jumble consists of articles for a jumble sale. ▶ VERB **3** To jumble things means to mix them up untidily.

**jumble sale jumble sales**
NOUN an event at which cheap second-hand clothes and other articles are sold to raise money, usually for a charity.

**jumbo jumbos**
NOUN **1** A jumbo or jumbo jet is a large jet aeroplane that can carry several hundred passengers.
▶ ADJECTIVE **2** very large *E.G. jumbo packs of elastic bands.*
From *Jumbo*, the name of a famous 19th-century elephant

**jumbuck jumbucks**
NOUN; *OLD-FASHIONED* In Australian English, a sheep.

**jump jumps jumping jumped**
VERB **1** To jump means to spring off the ground using your leg muscles.

**2** To jump something means to spring off the ground and move over or across it. **3** If you jump at something such as an opportunity, you accept it eagerly. **4** If you jump on someone, you criticize them suddenly and forcefully. **5** If someone jumps, they make a sudden sharp movement of surprise. **6** If an amount or level jumps, it suddenly increases. ▶ NOUN **7** a spring into the air, sometimes over an object.
■ (senses 1 & 7) bound, leap, spring

**jumper jumpers**
NOUN a knitted garment for the top half of the body.

**jumpy jumpier jumpiest**
ADJECTIVE nervous and worried.

**junction junctions**
NOUN a place where roads or railway lines meet or cross.

**June**
NOUN June is the sixth month of the year. It has 30 days.
From Latin *Junius*, the month of June, probably from the name of an important Roman family

**jungle jungles**
NOUN **1** a dense tropical forest. **2** a tangled mass of plants or other objects.

**junior juniors**
ADJECTIVE **1** Someone who is junior to other people has a lower position in an organization. **2** Junior also means younger. **3** relating to childhood *E.G. a junior school.* ▶ NOUN **4** someone who holds an unimportant position in an organization.

**juniper junipers**
NOUN an evergreen shrub with purple berries used in cooking and medicine.

**junk junks**
NOUN **1** Junk is old or second-hand

articles which are sold cheaply or thrown away. 2 If you think something is junk, you think it is worthless rubbish. 3 a Chinese sailing boat with a flat bottom and square sails.

**junk food**

NOUN Junk food is food low in nutritional value which is eaten as well as or instead of proper meals.

**junkie junkies**

NOUN; *INFORMAL* a drug addict.

**Jupiter**

NOUN Jupiter is the largest planet in the solar system and the fifth from the sun.

**jurisdiction**

NOUN 1 *FORMAL* Jurisdiction is the power or right of the courts to apply laws and make legal judgments *E.G. The Court held that it did not have the jurisdiction to examine the merits of the case.* 2 Jurisdiction is power or authority *E.G. The airport was under French jurisdiction.*

**juror jurors**

NOUN a member of a jury.

**jury juries**

NOUN a group of people in a court of law who have been selected to listen to the facts of a case on trial, and to decide whether the accused person is guilty or not.

**just**

ADJECTIVE 1 fair and impartial *E.G. She arrived at a just decision.* 2 morally right or proper *E.G. a just reward.*
► ADVERB 3 If something has just happened, it happened a very short time ago. 4 If you just do something, you do it by a very small amount *E.G. They only just won.* 5 simply or only *E.G. It was just an excuse not to mow the lawn.* 6 exactly *E.G. It's just what*

she wanted. ► PHRASE 7 In South African English, **just now** means in a little while.

**justly** ADVERB

**justice justices**

NOUN 1 Justice is fairness and reasonableness. 2 The system of justice in a country is the way in which laws are maintained by the courts. 3 a judge or magistrate.

**justify justifies justifying justified**

VERB 1 If you justify an action or idea, you prove or explain why it is reasonable or necessary. 2 *ICT* To justify text that you have typed or keyed into a computer is to adjust the spaces between the words so each full line in a paragraph fills the space between the left and right hand margins of the page.

**justification** NOUN **justifiable** ADJECTIVE

**jut juts jutting jutted**

VERB If something juts out, it sticks out beyond or above a surface or edge.
■ project, protrude, stick out

**jute**

NOUN Jute is a strong fibre made from the bark of an Asian plant, used to make rope and sacking.

**juvenile juveniles**

ADJECTIVE 1 suitable for young people. 2 childish and rather silly *E.G. a juvenile game.* ► NOUN 3 a young person not old enough to be considered an adult.

**juxtapose juxtaposes juxtaposing juxtaposed**

VERB If you juxtapose things or ideas, you put them close together, often to emphasize the difference between them.

**juxtaposition** NOUN

# Kk

**TIP** Some words that begin with a *k*- sound are spelt with the letters *ch*-, for example *chlorophyll*, *chlorine*, and *choir*. Some words that begin with a *k*-sound are spelt with letter *q*, for example *quite* and *quiet*.

**kaffir kaffirs** or **kaffir**
NOUN; *VERY OFFENSIVE* In South African English, a kaffir is a Black person.

**kaleidoscope kaleidoscopes**
*Said* "kal-**eye**-dos-skope" NOUN a toy consisting of a tube with a hole at one end. When you look through the hole and twist the other end of the tube, you can see a changing pattern of colours.
📷 from Greek *kalos* meaning 'beautiful', *eidos* meaning 'shape', and *skopein* meaning 'to look at'

**kamikaze**
NOUN In the Second World War, a kamikaze was a Japanese pilot who flew an aircraft loaded with explosives directly into an enemy target knowing he would be killed doing so.
📷 from Japanese *kami* meaning 'divine' + *kaze* meaning 'wind'

**kangaroo kangaroos**
NOUN a large Australian animal with very strong back legs which it uses for jumping.

**karate**
*Said* "kar-**rat**-ee" NOUN Karate is a sport in which people fight each other using only their hands, elbows, feet, and legs.
📷 from Japanese *kara* + *te* meaning 'empty hand'

**karma**
NOUN In Buddhism and Hinduism, karma is actions you take which affect you in your present and future lives

**Karoo Karoos**; also spelt **Karroo**
NOUN In South Africa, the Karoos are areas of very dry land.

**karri karris**
NOUN an Australian eucalypt that produces a dark red wood used for building.

**katipo katipo** or **katipos**
NOUN a small, poisonous spider with a red or orange stripe on its back, found in New Zealand.

**kauri kauri** or **kauris**
NOUN a large tree found in New Zealand which produces wood used for building and making furniture.

**kayak kayaks**
*Said* "**ky**-ak" NOUN a covered canoe with a small opening for the person sitting in it, originally used by the Inuit people.

**kea kea** or **keas**
*Said* "**kay**-ah" NOUN 1 a large, greenish parrot found in New Zealand. 2 In New Zealand, Keas are the youngest members of the Scouts.

**kebab kebabs**
NOUN pieces of meat or vegetable stuck on a stick and grilled.

**keel keels keeling keeled**
NOUN 1 the specially shaped bottom of a ship which supports the sides and sits in the water. ▶ VERB 2 If someone or something keels over, they fall down sideways.

**keen keener keenest**
ADJECTIVE 1 Someone who is keen shows great eagerness and enthusiasm. 2 If you are keen on someone or something, you are attracted to or fond of them. 3 Keen senses let you see, hear, smell, and taste things very clearly or strongly.
**keenly** ADVERB **keenness** NOUN
■ (sense 1) avid, eager, enthusiastic

**keep keeps keeping kept**
VERB 1 To keep someone or something in a particular condition means to make them stay in that condition E.G. *We'll walk to keep warm.* 2 If you keep something, you have it and look after it. 3 If you keep doing something, you do it repeatedly or continuously E.G. *I kept phoning the hospital.* 4 If you keep a promise, you do what you promised to do. 5 If you keep a secret, you do not tell anyone else. 6 If you keep a diary, you write something in it every day. 7 If you keep someone from going somewhere, you delay them so that they are late. 8 To keep someone means to provide them with money, food, and clothing. ▶ NOUN 9 Your keep is the cost of the food you eat, your housing, and your clothing E.G. *He does not contribute towards his keep.* 10 the main tower inside the walls of a castle.
■ (sense 2) hold, maintain, preserve
**keep up** VERB If you keep up with other people, you move or work at the same speed as they do.

**keeper keepers**
NOUN 1 a person whose job is to look after the animals in a zoo. 2 a goalkeeper in soccer or hockey.

**keeping**
NOUN 1 If something is in your

keeping, it has been given to you to look after for a while. ▶ PHRASE 2 If one thing is **in keeping with** another, the two things are suitable or appropriate together.

**keepsake keepsakes**
NOUN something that someone gives you to remind you of a particular person or event.
■ memento, souvenir

**keg kegs**
NOUN a small barrel.

**kelpie kelpies**; also spelt **kelpy**
NOUN a smooth-haired Australian sheepdog with upright ears.

**kennel kennels**
NOUN 1 a shelter for a dog. 2 A kennels is a place where dogs can be kept for a time, or where they are bred.

**Kenyan Kenyans**
*Said* "keen-yan" ADJECTIVE 1 belonging or relating to Kenya. ▶ NOUN 2 someone who comes from Kenya.

**kerb kerbs**
NOUN the raised edge at the point where a pavement joins onto a road.

**kernel kernels**
NOUN the part of a nut that is inside the shell.

**kerosene**
NOUN Kerosene is the same as paraffin.

**kestrel kestrels**
NOUN a type of small falcon.

**ketchup**
NOUN Ketchup is a cold sauce, usually made from tomatoes.

**kettle kettles**
NOUN a metal container with a spout, in which you boil water.

**key keys keying keyed**
NOUN 1 a shaped piece of metal that fits into a hole so that you can

A B C D E F G H I J K L M N O P Q R S T U V W X Y Z

unlock a door, wind something that is clockwork, or start a car. **2** The keys on a typewriter, piano, or cash register are the buttons that you press to use it. **3** an explanation of the symbols used in a map or diagram. **4** In music, a key is a scale of notes. ▶ VERB **5** If you key in information on a computer keyboard, you type it.

**keyboard keyboards**
NOUN (ICT) a row of levers or buttons on a piano, typewriter, or computer.

**Key Stage Key Stages**
NOUN In England and Wales, one of the four age-group divisions to which each level of the National Curriculum applies (5–7; 7–11; 11–14; 14–16).

**kg**
an abbreviation for 'kilograms'.

**khaki**
Said "kah-kee" NOUN **1** Khaki is a strong yellowish-brown material, used especially for military uniforms. ▶ NOUN or ADJECTIVE **2** yellowish-brown. from Urdu *kaki* meaning 'dusty'

**khanda khandas**
Said "kun-dah" NOUN a sword used by Sikhs in the Amrit ceremony.

**kia ora**
Said "ki-or-ah" In New Zealand, 'kia ora' is a Maori greeting.

**kibbutz kibbutzim**
Said "kib-boots" NOUN a place of work in Israel, for example a farm or factory, where the workers live together and share all the duties and income.

**kick kicks kicking kicked**
VERB **1** If you kick something, you hit it with your foot. ▶ NOUN **2** If you give something a kick, you hit it with your

foot. **3** INFORMAL If you get a kick out of doing something, you enjoy doing it very much.

**kick off** VERB When players kick off, they start a soccer or rugby match.
**kick-off** NOUN

**kid kids kidding kidded**
NOUN **1** INFORMAL a child. **2** a young goat. ▶ VERB **3** If you kid people, you tease them by deceiving them in fun.

**kidnap kidnaps kidnapping kidnapped**
VERB To kidnap someone is to take them away by force and demand a ransom in exchange for returning them.
**kidnapper** NOUN **kidnapping** NOUN
▤ abduct, seize

**kidney kidneys**
NOUN Your kidneys are two organs in your body that remove waste products from your blood.

**kill kills killing killed**
VERB **1** To kill a person, animal, or plant is to make them die. **2** If something is killing you, it is causing you severe pain or discomfort E.G. *My arms are killing me.* ▶ NOUN **3** The kill is the moment when a hunter kills an animal.
**killer** NOUN
▤ (sense 1) murder, slay

**kiln kilns**
NOUN (ART) an oven for baking china or pottery until it becomes hard and dry.

**kilo kilos**
NOUN a kilogram.

**kilogram kilograms**
NOUN (MATHS) a unit of weight equal to 1000 grams.

**kilohertz**
NOUN a unit of measurement of radio waves equal to one thousand hertz.

a b c d e f g h i j **k** l m n o p q r s t u v w x y z

A B C D E F G H I J **K** L M N O P Q R S T U V W X Y Z

**kilometre** kilometres
NOUN (MATHS) a unit of distance equal to one thousand metres.

**kilowatt** kilowatts
NOUN a unit of power equal to one thousand watts.

**kilt** kilts
NOUN a tartan skirt worn by men as part of Scottish Highland dress.

**kimono** kimonos
NOUN a long, loose garment with wide sleeves and a sash, worn in Japan.

**kin**
PLURAL NOUN Your kin are your relatives.
▤ family, kindred, relatives

**kind** kinds; kinder kindest
NOUN 1 A particular kind of thing is something of the same type or sort as other things E.G. that kind of film.
► ADJECTIVE 2 Someone who is kind is considerate and generous towards other people.

**kindly** ADVERB **kindness** NOUN
▤ (sense 1) class, sort, type
▤ (sense 2) considerate, generous
☑ When you use kind in its singular form, the adjective before it should also be singular: that kind of dog. When you use the plural form kinds, the adjective before it should be plural: those kinds of dog… those kinds of dogs.

**kindergarten** kindergartens
NOUN a school for children who are too young to go to primary school.
🏛 from German Kinder + Garten meaning 'children's garden'

**kindle** kindles kindling kindled
VERB 1 If you kindle a fire, you light it. 2 If something kindles a feeling in you, it causes you to have that feeling.

**kindling**
NOUN Kindling is bits of dry wood or paper that you use to start a fire.

**kindred**
ADJECTIVE If you say that someone is a kindred spirit, you mean that they have the same interests or opinions as you.

**kinetic energy**
NOUN Kinetic energy is the energy that is produced when something moves.

**king** kings
NOUN 1 a man who is the head of state in a country, and who inherited his position from his parents. 2 a chess piece which can only move one square at a time. 3 In a pack of cards, a king is a card with a picture of a king on it.

**kingdom** kingdoms
NOUN 1 a country that is governed by a king or queen. 2 The divisions of the natural world are called kingdoms E.G. the animal kingdom.

**kingfisher** kingfishers
NOUN a brightly coloured bird that lives near water and feeds on fish.

**king-size** or **king-sized**
ADJECTIVE larger than the normal size E.G. a king-size bed.

**kink** kinks
NOUN a dent or curve in something which is normally straight.

**kinky**
ADJECTIVE; INFORMAL having peculiar sexual tastes.

**kinship**
NOUN Kinship is a family relationship to other people.

**kiosk** kiosks
Said "kee-osk" NOUN a covered stall on a street where you can buy newspapers, sweets, or cigarettes.
🏛 from Turkish kösk meaning 'pavilion'

---

SPELLING NOTE    Rhythmical Hounds Yap To Heavy Music (<u>rhythm</u>)

**kip** kips kipping kipped *INFORMAL*
NOUN **1** a period of sleep. ▶ VERB
**2** When you kip, you sleep.

**kipper** kippers
NOUN a smoked herring.

**kirk** kirks
NOUN In Scotland, a kirk is a church.

**kiss** kisses kissing kissed
VERB **1** When you kiss someone, you
touch them with your lips as a sign
of love or affection. ▶ NOUN **2** When you
give someone a kiss, you kiss them.

**kiss of life**
NOUN The kiss of life is a method of
reviving someone by blowing air
into their lungs.

**kit** kits
NOUN **1** a collection of things that you
use for a sport or other activity. **2** a
set of parts that you put together to
make something.

**kitchen** kitchens
NOUN a room used for cooking and
preparing food.

**kite** kites
NOUN **1** a frame covered with paper or
cloth which is attached to a piece of
string, and which you fly in the air.
**2** a shape with four sides, with two
pairs of the same length, and none
of the sides parallel to each other. **3** a
large bird of prey with a long tail and
long wings.

**kitset** kitsets
NOUN In New Zealand English, a set of
parts which you have to put together
yourself to make an item such as a
house or a piece of furniture.

**kitten** kittens
NOUN a young cat.

**kitty** kitties
NOUN a fund of money that has been
given by a group of people who will

use it to pay for or do things
together.

**kiwi** kiwi or kiwis
*Said "kee-wee"* NOUN **1** a type of bird
found in New Zealand. Kiwis cannot
fly. **2** someone who comes from New
Zealand. The plural of this sense is
'kiwis'.

**kiwi fruit** kiwi fruits
NOUN a fruit with a brown hairy skin
and green flesh.

**kloof** kloofs
NOUN In South Africa, a kloof is a
narrow valley.

**km**
an abbreviation for 'kilometres'.

**knack**
NOUN an ability to do something
difficult whilst making it look easy
*E.G. the knack of making friends.*

**knead** kneads kneading kneaded
VERB If you knead dough, you press it
and squeeze it with your hands
before baking it.

**knee** knees
NOUN the joint in your leg between
your ankle and your hip.

**kneecap** kneecaps
NOUN Your kneecaps are the bones at
the front of your knees.

**kneel** kneels kneeling knelt
VERB When you kneel, you bend your
legs and lower your body until your
knees are touching the ground.

**knell** knells
NOUN; *LITERARY* the sound of a bell rung
to announce a death or at a funeral.

**knickers**
PLURAL NOUN Knickers are underpants
worn by women and girls.

**knick-knacks**
PLURAL NOUN Knick-knacks are small
ornaments.

a
b
c
d
e
f
g
h
i
j
k
l
m
n
o
p
q
r
s
t
u
v
w
x
y
z

there's SAND in my SANDwich (sandwich)    SPELLING NOTE

A
B
C
D
E
F
G
H
I
J
**K**
L
M
N
O
P
Q
R
S
T
U
V
W
X
Y
Z

**knife** knives; knifes knifing knifed
NOUN 1 D&T a sharp metal tool
that you use to cut things. ▶ VERB 2 To
knife someone is to stab them with a
knife.

**knight** knights knighting
knighted
NOUN 1 a man who has been given
the title 'Sir' by the King or Queen.
2 In medieval Europe, a knight was a
man who served a monarch or lord
as a mounted soldier. 3 a chess piece
that is usually in the shape of a
horse's head. ▶ VERB 4 To knight a man
is to give him the title 'Sir'.
**knighthood** NOUN

**knit** knits knitting knitted
VERB 1 If you knit a piece of clothing,
you make it by working lengths of
wool together, either using needles
held in the hand, or with a machine.
2 If you knit your brows, you frown.
**knitting** NOUN

**knob** knobs
NOUN 1 a round handle. 2 a round
switch on a machine E.G. the knobs of
a radio.

**knobkerrie** knobkerries
NOUN In South Africa, a knobkerrie is a
club or stick with a rounded end.

**knock** knocks knocking knocked
VERB 1 If you knock on something, you
strike it with your hand or fist. 2 If
you knock a part of your body
against something, you bump into it
quite forcefully. 3 INFORMAL To knock
someone is to criticize them. ▶ NOUN
4 a firm blow on something
solid E.G. There was a knock at the
door.

**knock out** VERB To knock someone
out is to hit them so hard that they
become unconscious.

**knocker** knockers
NOUN a metal lever attached to a
door, which you use to knock on the
door.

**knockout** knockouts
NOUN 1 a punch in boxing which
knocks a boxer unconscious. 2 a
competition in which competitors
are eliminated in each round until
only the winner is left.

**knoll** knolls
Rhymes with "roll" NOUN; LITERARY a
gently sloping hill with a rounded top.

**knot** knots knotting knotted
NOUN 1 a fastening made by looping a
piece of string around itself and
pulling the ends tight. 2 a small lump
visible on the surface of a piece of
wood. 3 A knot of people is a small
group of them. 4 TECHNICAL a unit of
speed used for ships and aircraft.
▶ VERB 5 If you knot a piece of string,
you tie a knot in it.

**know** knows knowing knew
known
VERB 1 If you know a fact, you have it
in your mind and you do not need to
learn it. 2 People you know are not
strangers because you have met
them and spoken to them. ▶ AN
INFORMAL PHRASE 3 If you are **in the
know**, you are one of a small number
of people who share a secret.

**know-how**
NOUN Know-how is the ability to do
something that is quite difficult or
technical.

**knowing**
ADJECTIVE A knowing look is one that
shows that you know or understand
something that other people do
not.
**knowingly** ADVERB

**knowledge**
NOUN Knowledge is all the information and facts that you know.

**knowledgeable**
ADJECTIVE Someone who is knowledgeable knows a lot about a subject *E.G. She was very knowledgeable about Irish mythology.*

**knuckle** knuckles
NOUN Your knuckles are the joints at the end of your fingers where they join your hand.

**koala** koalas
NOUN an Australian animal with grey fur and small tufted ears. Koalas live in trees and eat eucalyptus leaves.

**kohanga reo** or **kohanga** kohanga reo
NOUN In New Zealand, an infant class where children are taught in Maori. a Maori term meaning 'language nest'

**kookaburra** kookaburras
NOUN a large Australian kingfisher. a native Australian word

**koppie** koppies
*Said "kop-i"*; also spelt **kopje**
NOUN In South Africa, a koppie is a small hill with no other hills around it.

**Koran** or **Qur'an**
*Said "kaw-rahn"* NOUN The Koran is the holy book of Islam. from Arabic *kara'a* meaning 'to read'

**Korean** Koreans
*Said "kor-ree-an"* ADJECTIVE 1 relating or belonging to Korea. ▶ NOUN
2 someone who comes from Korea.
3 Korean is the main language spoken in Korea.

**kosher**
*Said "koh-sher"* ADJECTIVE Kosher food has been specially prepared to be eaten according to Jewish law. from Hebrew *kasher* meaning 'right' or 'proper'

**kowhai** kowhai or kowhais
*Said "ko-wigh"* a small New Zealand tree with clusters of yellow flowers.

**kraal** kraals
NOUN In South Africa, a kraal is a village in which a tribe lives and which is often surrounded by a fence.

**kudu** kudus; also spelt **koodoo**
NOUN a large African antelope with curled horns.

**kumara** or **kumera** kumara or kumaras
*Said "koo-mih-rah"* NOUN In New Zealand English, a kumara is a sweet potato, a vegetable with yellow or orange flesh.

**kumquat** kumquats
NOUN a very small round or oval citrus fruit.

**kung fu**
*Said "kung foo"* NOUN Kung fu is a Chinese style of fighting which involves using your hands and feet.

**kura kaupapa Maori** kura kaupapa Maori
*Said "koo-ra kow-puh-puh"* NOUN In New Zealand, a primary school where teaching is based on Maori language and culture.

**Kurd** Kurds
NOUN The Kurds are a group of people who live mainly in eastern Turkey, northern Iraq, and western Iran.

**Kurdish**
ADJECTIVE 1 belonging or relating to the Kurds *E.G. Kurdish culture.* ▶ NOUN
2 Kurdish is the language spoken by the Kurds.

a b c d e f g h i j **k** l m n o p q r s t u v w x y z

# LI

**I**
an abbreviation for 'litres'.

**lab labs**
NOUN; *INFORMAL* a laboratory.

**label labels labelling labelled**
NOUN 1 a piece of paper or plastic attached to something as an identification. ▶ VERB 2 If you label something, you put a label on it.

**laboratory laboratories**
NOUN (SCIENCE) a place where scientific experiments are carried out.

**laborious**
ADJECTIVE needing a lot of effort or time.
**laboriously** ADVERB

**Labor Party**
NOUN In Australia, the Labor Party is one of the major political parties.

**labour labours labouring laboured**
NOUN 1 Labour is hard work. 2 The workforce of a country or industry is sometimes called its labour *E.G. unskilled labour*. 3 In Britain, the Labour Party is a political party that believes that the government should provide free health care and education for everyone. 4 New Zealand, the Labour Party is one of the main political parties. 5 Labour is also the last stage of pregnancy when a woman gives birth to a baby. ▶ VERB 6 *OLD-FASHIONED* To labour means to work hard.

**labourer** NOUN
🔲 (sense 1) toil, work
🔲 (sense 6) slave, toil, work

**labrador labradors**
NOUN a large dog with short black or golden hair.

**labyrinth labyrinths**
*Said* "**lab**-er-inth" NOUN a complicated series of paths or passages.

**lace laces lacing laced**
NOUN 1 Lace is a very fine decorated cloth made with a lot of holes in it. 2 Laces are cords with which you fasten your shoes. ▶ VERB 3 When you lace up your shoes, you tie a bow in the laces. 4 To lace someone's food or drink means to put a small amount of alcohol, a drug, or poison in it *E.G. black coffee laced with vodka*.
**lacy** ADJECTIVE

**lack lacks lacking lacked**
NOUN 1 If there is a lack of something, it is not present when or where it is needed. ▶ VERB 2 If something is lacking, it is not present when or where it is needed. 3 If someone or something is lacking something, they do not have it or do not have enough of it *E.G. Francis was lacking in stamina*.
🔲 (sense 1) absence, scarcity, shortage

**lacklustre**
*Said* "**lak**-lus-ter" ADJECTIVE not interesting or exciting.

**laconic**
*Said* "la-**kon**-ik" ADJECTIVE using very few words.
🏛 from Greek *Lakonikas* meaning 'Spartan'. The Spartans were famous for using few words

**lacquer lacquers**
*Said* "**lak**-er" NOUN Lacquer is thin, clear paint that you put on wood to protect it and make it shiny.

**lacrosse**
NOUN Lacrosse is an outdoor ball game in which two teams try to score goals using long sticks with

nets on the end of them.

🏛 from Canadian French *la crosse* meaning 'the hooked stick'

**lad** lads
NOUN a boy or young man.

**ladder** ladders laddering laddered
NOUN 1 a wooden or metal frame used for climbing which consists of horizontal steps fixed to two vertical poles. 2 If your stockings or tights have a ladder in them, they have a vertical, ladder-like tear in them.
► VERB 3 If you ladder your stockings or tights, you get a ladder in them.

**laden**
*Said* "lay-*den*" ADJECTIVE To be laden with something means to be carrying a lot of it *E.G. bushes laden with ripe fruit.*

**ladle** ladles ladling ladled
NOUN 1 a long-handled spoon with a deep, round bowl, which you use to serve soup. ► VERB 2 If you ladle out food, you serve it with a ladle.

**lady** ladies
NOUN 1 a woman, especially one who is considered to be well mannered. 2 Lady is a title used in front of the name of a woman from the nobility, such as a lord's wife.

**ladybird** ladybirds
NOUN a small flying beetle with a round red body patterned with black spots.

**lady-in-waiting** ladies-in-waiting
NOUN a woman who acts as companion to a queen or princess.

**ladylike**
ADJECTIVE behaving in a polite and socially correct way.

**Ladyship** Ladyships
NOUN You address a woman who has the title 'Lady' as 'Your Ladyship'.

**lag** lags lagging lagged
VERB 1 To lag behind is to make slower progress than other people. 2 To lag pipes is to wrap cloth round them to stop the water inside freezing in cold weather.

**lager** lagers
NOUN Lager is light-coloured beer.
🏛 from German *Lagerbier* meaning 'beer for storing'

**lagoon** lagoons
NOUN an area of water separated from the sea by reefs or sand.

**laid**
the past tense and past participle of lay.

**lain**
the past participle of some meanings of lie.

**lair** lairs
NOUN a place where a wild animal lives.

**laird** lairds
*Rhymes with* "dared" NOUN a landowner in Scotland.

**lake** lakes
NOUN an area of fresh water surrounded by land.

**lama** lamas
NOUN a Buddhist priest or monk.

**lamb** lambs
NOUN 1 a young sheep. 2 Lamb is the meat from a lamb.

**lame**
ADJECTIVE 1 Someone who is lame has an injured leg and cannot walk easily. 2 A lame excuse is not very convincing.
**lamely** ADVERB **lameness** NOUN
■ (sense 2) feeble, flimsy, weak

**lament** laments lamenting lamented
VERB 1 To lament something means to

express sorrow or regret about it.
▶ NOUN **2** an expression of sorrow or regret. **3** a song or poem expressing grief at someone's death.

**lamentable**
ADJECTIVE disappointing and regrettable.

**laminated**
ADJECTIVE consisting of several thin sheets or layers stuck together *E.G. laminated glass*.

**lamp** lamps
NOUN a device that produces light.

**lamppost** lampposts
NOUN a tall column in a street, with a lamp at the top.

**lampshade** lampshades
NOUN a decorative covering over an electric light bulb which prevents the bulb giving out too harsh a light.

**lance** lances lancing lanced
VERB **1** To lance a boil or abscess means to stick a sharp instrument into it in order to release the fluid.
▶ NOUN **2** a long spear that used to be used by soldiers on horseback.

**land** lands landing landed
NOUN **1** Land is an area of ground. **2** Land is also the part of the earth that is not covered by water. **3** a country *E.G. our native land*. ▶ VERB **4** When a plane lands, it arrives back on the ground after a flight. **5** If you land something you have been trying to get, you succeed in getting it *E.G. She eventually landed a job with a local radio station*. **6** To land a fish means to catch it while fishing. **7** If you land someone with something unpleasant, you cause them to have to deal with it.

**landing** landings
NOUN **1** a flat area in a building at the

top of a flight of stairs. **2** The landing of an aeroplane is its arrival back on the ground after a flight *E.G. a smooth landing*.

**landlady** landladies
NOUN a woman who owns a house or small hotel and who lets rooms to people.

**landlord** landlords
NOUN a man who owns a house or small hotel and who lets rooms to people.

**landmark** landmarks
NOUN **1** a noticeable feature in a landscape, which you can use to check your position. **2** an important stage in the development of something *E.G. The play is a landmark in Japanese theatre*.

**landowner** landowners
NOUN someone who owns land, especially a large area of the countryside.

**landscape** landscapes
NOUN **1** (GEOGRAPHY) The landscape is the view over an area of open land. **2** (ART) a painting of the countryside.

**landslide** landslides
NOUN **1** a large amount of loose earth and rocks falling down a mountain side. **2** a victory in an election won by a large number of votes.

**lane** lanes
NOUN **1** a narrow road, especially in the country. **2** one of the strips on a road marked with lines to guide drivers.

**language** languages
NOUN **1** the system of words that the people of a country use to communicate with each other. **2** Your language is the style in which you

express yourself *E.G. His language is often obscure.* **3** Language is the study of the words and grammar of a particular language.

■ (sense 2) expression, speech

**languid**
*Said* "lang-gwid" ADJECTIVE slow and lacking energy.
**languidly** ADVERB

**languish** languishes languishing languished
VERB If you languish, you endure an unpleasant situation for a long time *E.G. Many languished in poverty.*

**lanky** lankier lankiest
ADJECTIVE Someone who is lanky is tall and thin and moves rather awkwardly.

**lantana** lantanas
NOUN In Australia, a shrub with yellow or orange flowers which is regarded as a pest in some areas.

**lantern** lanterns
NOUN a lamp in a metal frame with glass sides.

**lap** laps lapping lapped
NOUN **1** Your lap is the flat area formed by your thighs when you are sitting down. **2** one circuit of a running track or racecourse. ▶ VERB **3** When an animal laps up liquid, it drinks using its tongue to get the liquid into its mouth. **4** If you lap someone in a race, you overtake them when they are still on the previous lap. **5** When water laps against something, it gently moves against it in little waves.

**lapel** lapels
*Said* "lap-el" NOUN a flap which is joined on to the collar of a jacket or coat.

**lapse** lapses lapsing lapsed
NOUN **1** a moment of bad behaviour

by someone who usually behaves well. **2** a slight mistake. **3** a period of time between two events. ▶ VERB **4** If you lapse into a different way of behaving, you start behaving that way *E.G. The offenders lapsed into a sullen silence.* **5** If a legal document or contract lapses, it is not renewed on the date when it expires.

**lard**
NOUN Lard is fat from a pig, used in cooking.

**larder** larders
NOUN a room in which you store food, often next to a kitchen.

**large** larger largest
ADJECTIVE **1** Someone or something that is large is much bigger than average. ▶ PHRASE **2** If a prisoner is **at large**, he or she has escaped from prison.

**largely**
ADVERB to a great extent *E.G. The public are largely unaware of this.*

**lark** larks
NOUN **1** a small brown bird with a distinctive song. **2** If you do something for a lark, you do it in a high-spirited or mischievous way for fun.

**larrikin** larrikins
NOUN; *INFORMAL* In Australian and New Zealand English, a young person who behaves in a wild or irresponsible way.

**larva** larvae
NOUN an insect, which looks like a short, fat worm, at the stage before it becomes an adult.

**laryngitis**
*Said* "lar-in-jie-tiss" NOUN Laryngitis is an infection of the throat which causes you to lose your voice.

an ELegant angEL (angel) SPELLING NOTE

a b c d e f g h i j k l m n o p q r s t u v w x y z

A
B
C
D
E
F
G
H
I
J
K
L
M
N
O
P
Q
R
S
T
U
V
W
X
Y
Z

**larynx larynxes** or **larynges**
NOUN the part of your throat containing the vocal cords, through which air passes between your nose and lungs.

**lasagne**
*Said* "laz-**zan**-ya" NOUN Lasagne is an Italian dish made with wide flat sheets of pasta, meat, and cheese sauce.
📖 from Latin *lasanum* meaning 'cooking pot'

**laser lasers**
NOUN a machine that produces a powerful concentrated beam of light which is used to cut very hard materials and in some kinds of surgery.
📖 from the first letters of 'Light Amplification by Stimulated Emission of Radiation'

**lash lashes lashing lashed**
NOUN 1 Your lashes are the hairs growing on the edge of your eyelids. 2 a strip of leather at the end of a whip. 3 Lashes are blows struck with a whip.

**lash out** VERB To lash out at someone means to criticize them severely.

**lass lasses**
NOUN a girl or young woman.

**lasso lassoes** or **lassos lassoing lassoed**
*Said* "las-**soo**" NOUN 1 a length of rope with a noose at one end, used by cowboys to catch cattle and horses.
▶ VERB 2 To lasso an animal means to catch it by throwing the noose of a lasso around its neck.

**last lasts lasting lasted**
ADJECTIVE 1 The last thing or event is the most recent one E.G. *last year*.

2 The last thing that remains is the only one left after all the others have gone E.G. *The last family left in 1950.*
▶ ADVERB 3 If you last did something on a particular occasion, you have not done it since then E.G. *They last met in Rome.* 4 The thing that happens last in a sequence of events is the final one E.G. *He added the milk last.* ▶ VERB 5 If something lasts, it continues to exist or happen E.G. *Her speech lasted fifty minutes.* 6 To last also means to remain in good condition E.G. *The mixture will last for up to 2 weeks in the fridge.* ▶ PHRASE 7 At last means after a long time.
**lastly** ADVERB

**last-ditch**
ADJECTIVE A last-ditch attempt to do something is a final attempt to succeed when everything else has failed.

**latch latches latching latched**
NOUN 1 a simple door fastening consisting of a metal bar which falls into a hook. 2 a type of door lock which locks automatically when you close the door and which has to be opened with a key. ▶ VERB 3 INFORMAL If you latch onto someone or something, you become attached to them.

**late later latest**
ADJECTIVE OR ADVERB 1 Something that happens late happens towards the end of a period of time E.G. *the late evening… late in the morning.* 2 If you arrive late, or do something late, you arrive or do it after the time you were expected to. ▶ ADJECTIVE 3 A late event happens after the time when it usually takes place E.G. *a late breakfast.* 4 FORMAL Late means dead E.G. *my late grandmother.*

■ (sense 2) belated, overdue, tardy

**lately**
ADVERB Events that happened lately happened recently.

**latent**
ADJECTIVE A latent quality is hidden at the moment, but may emerge in the future E.G. *a latent talent for art.*

**lateral**
ADJECTIVE relating to the sides of something, or moving in a sideways direction.

**lathe** lathes
NOUN a machine which holds and turns a piece of wood or metal against a tool to cut and shape it.

**lather** lathers
NOUN Lather is the foam that you get when you rub soap in water.

**Latin** Latins
NOUN 1 Latin is the language of ancient Rome. ▶ NOUN OR ADJECTIVE 2 Latins are people who speak languages closely related to Latin, such as French, Italian, Spanish, and Portuguese.

**Latin America**
NOUN Latin America consists of the countries in North, South, and Central America where Spanish or Portuguese is the main language.
**Latin American** ADJECTIVE

**latitude** latitudes
NOUN (GEOGRAPHY) The latitude of a place is its distance north or south of the equator measured in degrees.

**latrine** latrines
*Said* "lat-**reen**" NOUN a hole or trench in the ground used as a toilet at a camp.

**latter**
ADJECTIVE OR NOUN 1 You use 'latter' to refer to the second of two things

that are mentioned E.G. *They were eating sandwiches and cakes (the latter bought from Mrs Paul's bakery).*
▶ ADJECTIVE 2 'Latter' also describes the second or end part of something E.G. *The latter part of his career.*

☑ You use *latter* to talk about the second of two items. To talk about the last of three or more items you should use *last-named.*

**latterly**
ADVERB; FORMAL Latterly means recently E.G. *It's only latterly that this has become an issue.*

**lattice** lattices
NOUN a structure made of strips which cross over each other diagonally leaving holes in between.

**laudable**
ADJECTIVE; FORMAL deserving praise E.G. *It is a laudable enough aim.*

**laugh** laughs laughing laughed
VERB 1 When you laugh, you make a noise which shows that you are amused or happy. ▶ NOUN 2 the noise you make when you laugh.
**laughter** NOUN

**laughable**
ADJECTIVE quite absurd.

**laughing stock**
NOUN someone who has been made to seem ridiculous.

**launch** launches launching launched
VERB 1 To launch a ship means to send it into the water for the first time.
2 To launch a rocket means to send it into space. 3 When a company launches a new product, they have an advertising campaign to promote it as they start to sell it. ▶ NOUN 4 a motorboat.

A Rude Idiot Thought He Might Eat Toffee In Church (<u>arithmetic</u>)    SPELLING NOTE

**launch pad** launch pads
NOUN A launch pad, or a launching pad, is the place from which space rockets take off.

**launder** launders laundering laundered
VERB; OLD-FASHIONED To launder clothes, sheets, or towels means to wash and iron them.

**laundry** laundries
NOUN 1 a business that washes and irons clothes and sheets. 2 Laundry is also the dirty clothes and sheets that are being washed, or are about to be washed.

**laurel** laurels
NOUN an evergreen tree with shiny leaves.

**lava**
NOUN Lava is the very hot liquid rock that comes shooting out of an erupting volcano, and becomes solid as it cools.

**lavatory** lavatories
NOUN a toilet.

**lavender**
NOUN 1 Lavender is a small bush with bluish-pink flowers that have a strong, pleasant scent. ▶ ADJECTIVE 2 bluish-pink.

**lavish** lavishes lavishing lavished
ADJECTIVE 1 If you are lavish, you are very generous with your time, money, or gifts. 2 A lavish amount is a large amount. ▶ VERB 3 If you lavish money or affection on someone, you give them a lot of it.
**lavishly** ADVERB

**law** laws
NOUN 1 The law is the system of rules developed by the government of a country, which regulate what people may and may not do and deals with people who break these rules. 2 The law is also the profession of people such as lawyers, whose job involves the application of the laws of a country. 3 one of the rules established by a government or a religion, which tells people what they may or may not do. 4 a scientific fact which allows you to explain how things work in the physical world.
**lawful** ADJECTIVE **lawfully** ADVERB

**law-abiding**
ADJECTIVE obeying the law and not causing any trouble.

**lawless**
ADJECTIVE having no regard for the law.

**lawn** lawns
NOUN an area of cultivated grass.

**lawnmower** lawnmowers
NOUN a machine for cutting grass.

**lawsuit** lawsuits
NOUN a civil court case between two people, as opposed to the police prosecuting someone for a criminal offence.

**lawyer** lawyers
NOUN a person who is qualified in law, and whose job is to advise people about the law and represent them in court.

**lax**
ADJECTIVE careless and not keeping up the usual standards E.G. a lax accounting system.

**laxative** laxatives
NOUN something that you eat or drink to stop you being constipated.

**lay** lays laying laid
VERB 1 When you lay something somewhere, you put it down so that it lies there. 2 If you lay the table, you put cutlery on the table ready for a meal. 3 When a bird lays an egg, it

produces the egg out of its body. **4** If you lay a trap for someone, you create a situation in which you will be able to catch them out. **5** If you lay emphasis on something, you refer to it in a way that shows you think it is very important. **6** If you lay odds on something, you bet that it will happen. ▶ ADJECTIVE **7** You use 'lay' to describe people who are involved with a Christian church but are not members of the clergy E.G. *a lay preacher.* **8** Lay is the past tense of some senses of **lie.**

**lay off** VERB **1** When workers are laid off, their employers tell them not to come to work for a while because there is a shortage of work. **2** INFORMAL If you tell someone to lay off, you want them to stop doing something annoying.

**lay on** VERB If you lay on a meal or entertainment, you provide it

☑ People often get confused about *lay* and *lie.* The verb *lay* takes an object: *lay the table please… the Queen laid a wreath.* The verb *lie* does not take an object: *the book was lying on the table… I'm going to lie down.*

**lay-by** lay-bys
NOUN **1** an area by the side of a main road where motorists can stop for a short while. **2** In Australia and New Zealand, lay-by is a system where you pay a deposit on an item in a shop so that it will be kept for you until you pay the rest of the price.

**layer** layers
NOUN a single thickness of something E.G. *layers of clothing.*

**layman** laymen
NOUN **1** someone who does not have specialized knowledge of a subject E.G. *a layman's guide to computers.*

**2** someone who belongs to the church but is not a member of the clergy.

**layout** layouts
NOUN The layout of something is the pattern in which it is arranged.

**laze** lazes lazing lazed
VERB If you laze, you relax and do no work E.G. *We spent a few days lazing around by the pool.*

**lazy** lazier laziest
ADJECTIVE idle and unwilling to work.
**lazily** ADVERB    **laziness** NOUN
▤ idle, indolent, slothful

**lb**
an abbreviation for 'pounds' E.G. *3lb of sugar.*

**lbw**
In cricket lbw is an abbreviation for 'leg before wicket', which is a way of dismissing a batsman when his legs prevent the ball from hitting the wicket.

**leach** leaches leaching leached
VERB When minerals are leached from rocks, they are dissolved by water which filters through the rock.

**lead** leads leading led
*Rhymes with "feed"* VERB **1** If you lead someone somewhere, you go in front of them in order to show them the way. **2** If one thing leads to another, it causes the second thing to happen. **3** a person who leads a group of people is in charge of them. ▶ NOUN **4** a length of leather or chain attached to a dog's collar, so that the dog can be kept under control. **5** If the police have a lead, they have a clue which might help them to solve a crime.

**leading** ADJECTIVE
▤ (sense 1) conduct, escort, guide

a b c d e f g h i j k l m n o p q r s t u v w x y z

A B C D E F G H I J K L M N O P Q R S T U V W X Y Z

**lead**

*Rhymes with "fed"* NOUN Lead is a soft, grey, heavy metal.

**leaden**

*Said "led-en"* ADJECTIVE 1 dark grey E.G. *a leaden sky.* 2 heavy and slow-moving.

**leader leaders**

NOUN 1 someone who is in charge of a country, an organization, or a group of people. 2 the person who is winning in a competition or race. 3 a newspaper article that expresses the newspaper's opinions.

**leadership**

NOUN 1 the group of people in charge of an organization. 2 Leadership is the ability to be a good leader.

**leaf leaves; leafs leafing leafed**

NOUN 1 the flat green growth on the end of a twig or branch of a tree or other plant. ► VERB 2 If you leaf through a book, magazine, or newspaper, you turn the pages over quickly.

**leafy** ADJECTIVE

**leaflet leaflets**

NOUN a piece of paper with information or advertising printed on it.

**league leagues**

*Said "leeg"* NOUN 1 ( PE ) a group of countries, clubs, or people who have joined together for a particular purpose or because they share a common interest E.G. *the League of Red Cross Societies... the Australian Football League.* 2 a unit of distance used in former times, equal to about 3 miles.

**leak leaks leaking leaked**

VERB 1 If a pipe or container leaks, it has a hole which lets gas or liquid escape. 2 If liquid or gas leaks, it

escapes from a pipe or container. 3 If someone in an organization leaks information, they give the information to someone who is not supposed to have it E.G. *The letter was leaked to the press.* ► NOUN 4 If a pipe or container has a leak, it has a hole which lets gas or liquid escape. 5 If there is a leak in an organization, someone inside the organization is giving information to people who are not supposed to have it.

**leaky** ADJECTIVE

**leakage leakages**

NOUN an escape of gas or liquid from a pipe or container.

**lean leans leaning leant or leaned; leaner leanest**

VERB 1 When you lean in a particular direction, you bend your body in that direction. 2 When you lean on something, you rest your body against it for support. 3 If you lean on someone, you depend on them. 4 If you lean towards particular ideas, you approve of them and follow them E.G. *parents who lean towards strictness.* ► ADJECTIVE 5 having little or no fat E.G. *lean cuts of meat.* 6 A lean period is a time when money or food is in short supply.

**leap leaps leaping leapt or leaped**

VERB 1 If you leap somewhere, you jump over a long distance or high in the air. ► NOUN 2 a jump over a long distance or high in the air.

**leap year leap years**

NOUN a year, occurring every four years, in which there are 366 days.

**learn learns learning learnt or learned**

VERB 1 When you learn something,

you gain knowledge or a skill through studying or training. **2** If you **learn of** something, you find out about it E.G. *She had first learnt of the bomb attack that morning.*

**learner** NOUN

■ (sense 2) discover, find out, hear

**learned**

*Said* "ler-nid" ADJECTIVE A learned person has a lot of knowledge gained from years of study.

**learning**

NOUN Learning is knowledge that has been acquired through serious study.

**lease leases leasing leased**

NOUN **1** an agreement which allows someone to use a house or flat in return for rent. ▶ VERB **2** To lease property to someone means to allow them to use it in return for rent.

**leash leashes**

NOUN a length of leather or chain attached to a dog's collar so that the dog can be controlled.

**least**

NOUN **1** The least is the smallest possible amount of something.
▶ ADJECTIVE or ADVERB **2** Least is a superlative form of **little**. ▶ PHRASE
**3** You use **at least** to show that you are referring to the minimum amount of something, and that you think the true amount is greater E.G. *At least 200 hundred people were injured.*

**leather**

NOUN Leather is the tanned skin of some animals, used to make shoes and clothes.

**leathery** ADJECTIVE

**leave leaves leaving left**

VERB **1** When you leave a place, you go

away from it. **2** If you leave someone somewhere, they stay behind after you go away. **3** If you leave a job or organization, you stop being part of it E.G. *He left his job shortly after Christmas.* **4** If someone leaves money or possessions to someone, they arrange for them to be given to them after their death. **5** In subtraction, when you take one number from another, it leaves a third number. ▶ NOUN **6** a period of holiday or absence from a job.

■ (sense 1) depart, exit, go

**Lebanese**

ADJECTIVE **1** belonging or relating to Lebanon. ▶ NOUN **2** someone who comes from Lebanon.

**lecherous**

ADJECTIVE constantly thinking about sex.

**lectern lecterns**

NOUN a sloping desk which people use to rest books or notes on.

**lecture lectures lecturing lectured**

NOUN **1** a formal talk intended to teach people about a particular subject. **2** a talk intended to tell someone off. ▶ VERB **3** Someone who lectures teaches in a college or university.

**lecturer lecturers**

NOUN a teacher in a college or university.

**led**

the past tense and past participle of **lead**.

**ledge ledges**

NOUN a narrow shelf on the side of a cliff or rock face, or on the outside of a building, directly under a window.

a
b
c
d
e
f
g
h
i
j
k
l
m
n
o
p
q
r
s
t
u
v
w
x
y
z

A B C D E F G H I J K L M N O P Q R S T U V W X Y Z

**ledger** ledgers

NOUN a book in which accounts are kept.

**lee**

NOUN 1 the sheltered side of a place E.G. *the lee of the mountain.* ▶ ADJECTIVE 2 the side of a ship away from the wind.

**leech** leeches

NOUN a small worm that lives in water and feeds by sucking the blood from other animals.

**leek** leeks

NOUN a long vegetable of the onion family, which is white at one end and has green leaves at the other.

**leer** leers leering leered

VERB 1 To leer at someone means to smile at them in an unpleasant or sexually suggestive way. ▶ NOUN 2 an unpleasant or sexually suggestive smile.

**leeway**

NOUN If something gives you some leeway, it allows you more flexibility in your plans, for example by giving you time to finish an activity.

**left**

NOUN 1 The left is one of two sides of something. For example, on a page, English writing begins on the left. 2 People and political groups who hold socialist or communist views are referred to as the Left. 3 Left is the past tense and past participle of **leave.** ▶ ADJECTIVE OR ADVERB 4 Left means on or towards the left side of something E.G. *Turn left down Govan Road.*

**left-handed**

ADJECTIVE OR ADVERB Someone who is left-handed does things such as writing with their left hand.

**leftist** leftists

NOUN OR ADJECTIVE someone who holds left-wing political views.

**leftovers**

PLURAL NOUN the bits of food which have not been eaten at the end of the meal.

**left-wing**

ADJECTIVE believing more strongly in socialism, or less strongly in capitalism or conservatism, than other members of the same party or group.

**left-winger** NOUN

**leg** legs

NOUN 1 Your legs are the two limbs which stretch from your hips to your feet. 2 The legs of a pair of trousers are the parts that cover your legs. 3 The legs of an object such as a table are the parts which rest on the floor and support the object's weight. 4 A leg of a journey is one part of it. 5 one of two matches played between two sports teams E.G. *He will miss the second leg of their UEFA Cup tie.*

**legacy** legacies

NOUN 1 property or money that someone gets in the will of a person who has died. 2 something that exists as a result of a previous event or time E.G. *the legacy of a Catholic upbringing.*

■ (sense 1) bequest, inheritance

**legal**

ADJECTIVE 1 relating to the law E.G. *the Dutch legal system.* 2 allowed by the law E.G. *The strike was perfectly legal.*

**legally** ADVERB

**legal aid**

NOUN Legal aid is a system which provides the services of a lawyer free, or very cheaply, to people who cannot afford the full fees.

**legality**
NOUN The legality of an action means whether or not it is allowed by the law E.G. *They challenged the legality of the scheme.*

**legalize legalizes legalizing legalized**; also spelt **legalise**
VERB To legalize something that is illegal means to change the law so that it becomes legal.
**legalization** NOUN

**legend legends**
NOUN **1** an old story which was once believed to be true, but which is probably untrue. **2** If you refer to someone or something as a legend, you mean they are very famous E.G. *His career has become a legend.*
**legendary** ADJECTIVE

**leggings**
PLURAL NOUN **1** Leggings are very close-fitting trousers made of stretch material, worn mainly by young women. **2** Leggings are also a waterproof covering worn over ordinary trousers to protect them.

**legible**
ADJECTIVE Writing that is legible is clear enough to be read.

**legion legions**
NOUN **1** In ancient Rome, a legion was a military unit of between 3000 and 6000 soldiers. **2** a large military force E.G. *the French Foreign Legion.* **3** Legions of people are large numbers of them.

**legislate legislates legislating legislated**
VERB; FORMAL When a government legislates, it creates new laws.

**legislation**
NOUN Legislation is a law or set of laws created by a government.

**legislative**
ADJECTIVE relating to the making of new laws E.G. *a legislative council.*

**legislator legislators**
NOUN; FORMAL a person involved in making or passing laws.

**legislature**
NOUN; FORMAL the parliament in a country, which is responsible for making new laws.

**legitimate**
*Said* "lij-**it**-tim-it" ADJECTIVE Something that is legitimate is reasonable or acceptable according to existing laws or standards E.G. *a legitimate charge for parking the car.*
**legitimacy** NOUN **legitimately** ADVERB

**leisure**
*Rhymes with* "**measure**" NOUN **1** Leisure is time during which you do not have to work, and can do what you enjoy doing. ▶ PHRASES **2** If you do something **at leisure**, or **at your leisure**, you do it at a convenient time.

**leisurely**
ADJECTIVE OR ADVERB A leisurely action is done in an unhurried and calm way.

**lekker**
ADJECTIVE; SLANG **1** In South African English, lekker means pleasant. **2** In South African English, lekker can also mean tasty.

**lemming lemmings**
NOUN a small rodent which lives in cold, northern countries. Lemmings were believed in the past to jump off cliffs to their death in large numbers.

a b c d e f g h i j k l m n o p q r s t u v w x y z

**lemon** lemons
NOUN 1 a yellow citrus fruit with a sour taste. ▶ ADJECTIVE 2 pale yellow.

**lemonade**
NOUN a sweet, fizzy drink made from lemons, water, and sugar.

**lend** lends lending lent
VERB 1 If you lend someone something, you give it to them for a period of time and then they give it back to you. 2 If a bank lends money, it gives the money to someone and the money has to be repaid in the future, usually with interest. ▶ PHRASE 3 If you lend someone a hand, you help them.
**lender** NOUN

**length** lengths
NOUN 1 The length of something is the horizontal distance from one end to the other. 2 The length of an event or activity is the amount of time it lasts for. 3 The length of something is also the fact that it is long rather than short E.G. *Despite its length, it is a rewarding read.* 4 a long piece of something.

**lengthen** lengthens lengthening lengthened
VERB To lengthen something means to make it longer.
≡ elongate, extend, prolong

**lengthways** or **lengthwise**
ADVERB If you measure something lengthways, you measure the horizontal distance from one end to the other.

**lengthy** lengthier lengthiest
ADJECTIVE Something that is lengthy lasts for a long time.

**lenient**
ADJECTIVE If someone in authority is lenient, they are less severe than expected.
**leniently** ADVERB **leniency** NOUN

**lens** lenses
NOUN 1 a curved piece of glass designed to focus light in a certain way, for example in a camera, telescope, or pair of glasses. 2 The lens in your eye is the part behind the iris, which focuses light.

**lent**
1 the past tense and past participle of **lend**. ▶ NOUN 2 Lent is the period of forty days leading up to Easter, during which Christians give up something they enjoy.

**lentil** lentils
NOUN Lentils are small dried red or brown seeds which are cooked and eaten in soups and curries.

**Leo**
NOUN Leo is the fifth sign of the zodiac, represented by a lion. People born between July 23rd and August 22nd are born under this sign.

**leopard** leopards
NOUN a wild Asian or African big cat, with yellow fur and black or brown spots.

**leotard** leotards
*Said* "lee-eh-tard" NOUN a tight-fitting costume covering the body and legs, which is worn for dancing or exercise.

**leper** lepers
NOUN someone who has leprosy.
▥ from Greek *lepros* meaning 'scaly'

**leprosy**
NOUN Leprosy is an infectious disease which attacks the skin and nerves, and which can lead to fingers or toes dropping off.

**lesbian lesbians**
NOUN a homosexual woman.
**lesbianism** NOUN

**lesion lesions**
*Said* "**lee**-zhen" NOUN a wound or injury.

**less**
ADJECTIVE or ADVERB 1 Less means a smaller amount, or not as much in quality E.G. *They left less than three weeks ago… She had become less frightened of him now.* 2 Less is a comparative form of **little**.
▶ PREPOSITION 3 You use 'less' to show that you are subtracting one number from another E.G. *Eight less two leaves six.*
✔ You use *less* to talk about things that can't be counted: *less time.* When you are talking about amounts that can be counted you should use *fewer.*

**-less**
SUFFIX '-less' means without E.G. *hopeless… fearless.*
📖 from an Old English suffix

**lessen lessens lessening lessened**
VERB If something lessens, it is reduced in amount, size, or quality.
☰ decrease, diminish, reduce

**lesser**
ADJECTIVE smaller in importance or amount than something else.

**lesson lessons**
NOUN 1 a fixed period of time during which a class of pupils is taught by a teacher. 2 an experience that makes you understand something important which you had not realized before.

**lest**
CONJUNCTION; OLD-FASHIONED as a precaution in case something

unpleasant or unwanted happens E.G. *I was afraid to open the door lest he should follow me.*

**let lets letting let**
VERB 1 If you let someone do something, you allow them to do it. 2 If someone lets a house or flat that they own, they rent it out. 3 You can say 'let's' or 'let us' when you want to suggest doing something with someone else E.G. *Let's go.* 4 If you let yourself in for something, you agree to do it although you do not really want to.

**let off** VERB 1 If someone in authority lets you off, they do not punish you for something you have done wrong. 2 If you let off a firework or explosive, you light it or detonate it.

**lethal**
*Said* "**lee**-thal" ADJECTIVE able to kill someone E.G. *a lethal weapon.*

**lethargic**
*Said* "lith-**ar**-jik" ADJECTIVE If you feel lethargic, you have no energy or enthusiasm.

**lethargy**
*Said* "**leth**-ar-jee" NOUN Lethargy is a lack of energy and enthusiasm.

**letter letters**
NOUN 1 Letters are written symbols which go together to make words. 2 a piece of writing addressed to someone, and usually sent through the post.

**letter box letter boxes**
NOUN 1 an oblong gap in the front door of a house or flat, through which letters are delivered. 2 a large metal container in the street, where you post letters.

have a plEce of plE (pie**ce**)    SPELLING NOTE

a b c d e f g h i j k m n o p q r s t u v w x y z

A B C D E F G H I J K L M N O P Q R S T U V W X Y Z

**lettering**

NOUN Lettering is writing, especially when you are describing the type of letters used *E.G. bold lettering*.

**lettuce** lettuces

NOUN a vegetable with large green leaves eaten raw in salad.

**leukaemia** or **leukemia**

*Said* "loo-kee-mee-a" NOUN Leukaemia is a serious illness which affects the blood.

**level** levels levelling levelled

ADJECTIVE 1 A surface that is level is smooth, flat, and parallel to the ground. ► VERB 2 To level a piece of land means to make it flat. 3 If you level a criticism at someone, you say or write something critical about them. ► ADVERB 4 If you draw level with someone, you get closer to them so that you are moving next to them. ► NOUN 5 a point on a scale which measures the amount, importance, or difficulty of something. 6 The level of a liquid is the height it comes up to in a container.

**▤** (sense 5) grade, position, stage

**level off** or **level out**

VERB If something levels off or levels out, it stops increasing or decreasing *E.G. Profits are beginning to level off.*

**level crossing** level crossings

NOUN a place where road traffic is allowed to drive across a railway track.

**level-headed**

ADJECTIVE Someone who is level-headed is sensible and calm in emergencies.

**lever** levers

NOUN 1 a handle on a machine that you pull in order to make the machine work. 2 a long bar that you wedge underneath a heavy object and press down on to make the object move.

**leverage**

NOUN Leverage is knowledge or influence that you can use to make someone do something.

**leveret** leverets

NOUN a young hare.

**levy** levies levying levied

*Said* "lev-ee" NOUN 1 FORMAL an amount of money that you pay in tax. ► VERB 2 When a government levies a tax, it makes people pay the tax and organizes the collection of the money.

**lewd**

*Rhymes with* "rude" ADJECTIVE sexually coarse and crude.

**lexicography**

NOUN the profession of writing dictionaries.

**lexicographer** NOUN

🏛 from Greek *lexis* meaning 'word' and *graphein* meaning 'to write'

**liability** liabilities

NOUN 1 Someone's liability is their responsibility for something they have done wrong. 2 In business, a company's liabilities are its debts. 3 INFORMAL If you describe someone as a liability, you mean that they cause a lot of problems or embarrassment.

**liable**

ADJECTIVE 1 If you say that something is liable to happen, you mean that you think it will probably happen. 2 If you are liable for something you have done, you are legally responsible for it.

☑ It used to be wrong to use *liable* to mean 'probable or likely', but that

**liaise** liaises liaising liaised
*Said "lee-**aze**"* VERB To liaise with someone or an organization means to cooperate with them and keep them informed.

**liaison** liaisons
*Said "lee-**aze**-on"* NOUN Liaison is communication between two organizations or two sections of an organization.

**liar** liars
NOUN a person who tells lies.

**libel** libels libelling libelled
*Said "**lie**-bel"* NOUN 1 Libel is something written about someone which is not true, and for which the writer can be made to pay damages in court. ▶ VERB 2 To libel someone means to write or say something untrue about them.
**libellous** ADJECTIVE

**liberal** liberals
NOUN 1 someone who believes in political progress, social welfare, and individual freedom. ▶ ADJECTIVE 2 Someone who is liberal is tolerant of a wide range of behaviour, standards, or opinions. 3 To be liberal with something means to be generous with it. 4 A liberal quantity of something is a large amount of it.
**liberally** ADVERB    **liberalism** NOUN
📖 from Latin *liberalis* meaning 'of freedom'

**Liberal Democrat** Liberal Democrats
NOUN In Britain, a member or supporter of the Liberal Democrats, a political party that believes that individuals should have more rights and freedom.

**liberate** liberates liberating liberated
VERB To liberate people means to free them from prison or from an unpleasant situation.
**liberation** NOUN    **liberator** NOUN

**liberty**
NOUN Liberty is the freedom to choose how you want to live, without government restrictions.

**libido** libidos
*Said "lib-**bee**-doe"* NOUN Someone's libido is their sexual drive.
📖 from Latin *libido* meaning 'desire'

**Libra**
NOUN Libra is the seventh sign of the zodiac, represented by a pair of scales. People born between September 23rd and October 22nd are born under this sign.

**librarian** librarians
NOUN (LIBRARY) a person who works in, or is in charge of, a library.

**library** libraries
NOUN 1 a building in which books are kept for people to come and read or borrow. 2 a collection of books, records, or videos.

**Libyan** Libyans
ADJECTIVE 1 belonging or relating to Libya. ▶ NOUN 2 someone who comes from Libya.

**lice**
the plural of **louse**.

**licence** licences
NOUN 1 an official document which entitles you to carry out a particular activity, for example to drive a car. 2 Licence is the freedom to do what you want, especially when other people consider that it is being used irresponsibly.
☑ The noun *licence* ends in *ce*.

The government licenSes Schnapps (licenSes)    SPELLING NOTE

a b c d e f g h i j k l m n o p q r s t u v w x y z

A
B
C
D
E
F
G
H
I
J
K
**L**
M
N
O
P
Q
R
S
T
U
V
W
X
Y
Z

**license** licenses licensing licensed

VERB To license an activity means to give official permission for it to be carried out

☑ The verb *license* ends in *se*.

**lichen** lichens

*Said* "**lie**-ken" NOUN Lichen is a green, moss-like growth on rocks or tree trunks.

**lick** licks licking licked

VERB 1 If you lick something, you move your tongue over it. ▶ NOUN 2 the action of licking.

**lid** lids

NOUN the top of a container, which you open in order to reach what is inside.

**lie** lies lying lay lain

VERB 1 To lie somewhere means to rest there horizontally. 2 If you say where something lies, you are describing where it is *E.G. The farm lies between two valleys.*

☑ The past tense of this verb *lie* is *lay*. Do not confuse it with the verb *lay* meaning 'put'.

**lie** lies lying lied

VERB 1 To lie means to say something that is not true. ▶ NOUN 2 something you say which is not true.

**lieu**

*Said* "**lyoo**" PHRASE If one thing happens **in lieu** of another, it happens instead of it.

**lieutenant** lieutenants

*Said* "lef-**ten**-ent" NOUN a junior officer in the army or navy.

📖 from Old French *lieutenant* meaning literally 'holding a place'

**life** lives

NOUN 1 Life is the quality of being able to grow and develop, which is

present in people, plants, and animals. 2 Your life is your existence from the time you are born until the time you die. 3 The life of a machine is the period of time for which it is likely to work. 4 If you refer to the life in a place, you are talking about the amount of activity there *E.G. The town was full of life.* 5 If criminals are sentenced to life, they are sent to prison for the rest of their lives, or until they are granted parole.

**life assurance**

NOUN Life assurance is an insurance which provides a sum of money in the event of the policy holder's death.

**lifeblood**

NOUN The lifeblood of something is the most essential part of it.

**lifeboat** lifeboats

NOUN 1 a boat kept on shore, which is sent out to rescue people who are in danger at sea. 2 a small boat kept on a ship, which is used if the ship starts to sink.

**life expectancy** life expectancies

NOUN Your life expectancy is the number of years you can expect to live.

**lifeguard** lifeguards

NOUN a person whose job is to rescue people who are in difficulty in the sea or in a swimming pool.

**life jacket** life jackets

NOUN a sleeveless inflatable jacket that keeps you afloat in water.

**lifeless**

ADJECTIVE 1 Someone who is lifeless is dead. 2 If you describe a place or person as lifeless, you mean that they are dull.

**lifelike**

ADJECTIVE A picture or sculpture that is lifelike looks very real or alive.

**lifeline** lifelines

NOUN **1** something which helps you to survive or helps an activity to continue. **2** a rope thrown to someone who is in danger of drowning.

**lifelong**

ADJECTIVE existing throughout someone's life *E.G. He had a lifelong interest in music.*

**lifesaver** lifesavers

NOUN In Australia and New Zealand, a person whose job is to rescue people who are in difficulty in the sea.

**life span** life spans

NOUN **1** Someone's life span is the length of time during which they are alive. **2** The life span of a product or organization is the length of time it exists or is useful.

**lifetime** lifetimes

NOUN Your lifetime is the period of time during which you are alive.

**lift** lifts lifting lifted

VERB **1** To lift something means to move it to a higher position. **2** When fog or mist lifts, it clears away. **3** To lift a ban on something means to remove it. **4** *INFORMAL* To lift things means to steal them. ▶ NOUN **5** a machine like a large box which carries passengers from one floor to another in a building. **6** If you give someone a lift, you drive them somewhere in a car or on a motorcycle.

■ (sense 1) elevate, raise

**ligament** ligaments

NOUN a piece of tough tissue in your body which connects your bones.

**light** lights lighting lighted or lit; lighter lightest

NOUN **1** Light is brightness from the sun, fire, or lamps, that enables you to see things. **2** a lamp or other device that gives out brightness. **3** If you give someone a light, you give them a match or lighter to light their cigarette. ▶ ADJECTIVE **4** A place that is light is bright because of the sun or the use of lamps. **5** A light colour is pale. **6** A light object does not weigh much. **7** A light task is fairly easy. **8** Light books or music are entertaining and are not intended to be serious. ▶ VERB **9** To light a place means to cause it to be filled with light. **10** To light a fire means to make it start burning. **11** To light upon something means to find it by accident.

**lightly** ADVERB    **lightness** NOUN

**lighten** lightens lightening lightened

VERB **1** When something lightens, it becomes less dark. **2** To lighten a load means to make it less heavy.

**lighter** lighters

NOUN a device for lighting a cigarette or cigar.

**light-headed**

ADJECTIVE If you feel light-headed, you feel slightly dizzy or drunk.

**light-hearted**

ADJECTIVE Someone who is light-hearted is cheerful and has no worries.

■ blithe, carefree, happy-go-lucky

**lighthouse** lighthouses

NOUN a tower by the sea, which sends out a powerful light to guide ships and warn them of danger.

## lighting
NOUN **1** The lighting in a room or building is the way that it is lit.
**2** (**DRAMA**) Lighting in the theatre or for a film is the special lights that are directed on the performers or scene.

## lightning
NOUN Lightning is the bright flashes of light in the sky which are produced by natural electricity during a thunder storm.

## lightweight lightweights
NOUN **1** a boxer in one of the lighter weight groups. ▶ ADJECTIVE **2** Something that is lightweight does not weigh very much E.G. *a lightweight jacket.*

## light year light years
NOUN a unit of distance equal to the distance that light travels in a year.

## likable or likeable
ADJECTIVE Someone who is likable is very pleasant and friendly.

## like likes liking liked
PREPOSITION **1** If one thing is like another, it is similar to it. ▶ NOUN **2** 'The like' means other similar things of the sort just mentioned E.G. *nappies, prams, cots, and the like.*
▶ PHRASE **3** If you **feel like** something, you want to do it or have it E.G. *I feel like a walk.* ▶ VERB **4** If you like something or someone, you find them pleasant.

## -like
SUFFIX '-like' means resembling or similar to E.G. *a balloonlike object.*

## likelihood
NOUN If you say that there is a likelihood that something will happen, you mean that you think it will probably happen.

## likely likelier likeliest
ADJECTIVE Something that is likely will probably happen or is probably true.

## liken likens likening likened
VERB If you liken one thing to another, you say that they are similar.

## likeness likenesses
NOUN If two things have a likeness to each other, they are similar in appearance.

## likewise
ADVERB Likewise means similarly E.G. *She sat down and he did likewise.*

## liking
NOUN If you have a liking for someone or something, you like them.

## lilac
NOUN **1** a shrub with large clusters of pink, white, or mauve flowers.
▶ ADJECTIVE **2** pale mauve.

## lilt lilts
NOUN A lilt in someone's voice is a pleasant rising and falling sound in it.

## lilting ADJECTIVE

## lily lilies
NOUN a plant with trumpet-shaped flowers of various colours.

## limb limbs
NOUN **1** Your limbs are your arms and legs. **2** The limbs of a tree are its branches. ▶ PHRASE **3** If you have gone **out on a limb**, you have said or done something risky.

## limber up limbers up limbering up limbered up
VERB If you limber up, you stretch your muscles before doing a sport.

## limbo
NOUN **1** If you are in limbo, you are in an uncertain situation over which you feel you have no control. **2** The limbo is a West Indian dance in

which the dancer has to pass under a low bar while leaning backwards. 🔲 sense 1 is from Latin *in limbo* meaning 'on the border (of Hell)'

**lime** limes

NOUN **1** a small, green citrus fruit, rather like a lemon. **2** A lime tree is a large tree with pale green leaves. **3** Lime is a chemical substance that is used in cement and as a fertilizer.

**limelight**

NOUN If someone is in the limelight, they are getting a lot of attention.

**limerick** limericks

NOUN an amusing nonsense poem of five lines.

**limestone**

NOUN Limestone is a white rock which is used for building and making cement.

**limit** limits limiting limited

NOUN **1** a boundary or an extreme beyond which something cannot go *E.G. the speed limit.* ▸ VERB **2** To limit something means to prevent it from becoming bigger, spreading, or making progress *E.G. He did all he could to limit the damage.*

**limitation** limitations

NOUN **1** The limitation of something is the reducing or controlling of it. **2** If you talk about the limitations of a person or thing, you are talking about the limits of their abilities.

**limited**

ADJECTIVE Something that is limited is rather small in amount or extent *E.G. a limited number of bedrooms.*

**limousine** limousines

*Said* "**lim**-o-zeen" NOUN a large, luxurious car, usually driven by a chauffeur.

**limp** limps limping limped; limper limpest

VERB **1** If you limp, you walk unevenly because you have hurt your leg or foot. ▸ NOUN **2** an uneven way of walking. ▸ ADJECTIVE **3** Something that is limp is soft and floppy, and not stiff or firm *E.G. a limp lettuce.*

**limpet** limpets

NOUN a shellfish with a pointed shell, that attaches itself very firmly to rocks.

**line** lines lining lined

NOUN **1** a long, thin mark. **2** a number of people or things positioned one behind the other. **3** a route along which someone or something moves *E.G. a railway line.* **4** In a piece of writing, a line is a number of words together *E.G. I often used to change my lines as an actor.* **5** Someone's line of work is the kind of work they do. **6** The line someone takes is the attitude they have towards something *E.G. He took a hard line with terrorism.* **7** In a shop or business, a line is a type of product *E.G. That line has been discontinued.* ▸ VERB **8** To line something means to cover its inside surface or edge with something *E.G. Cottages lined the edge of the harbour.*

**line up** VERB **1** When people line up, they stand in a line. **2** When you line something up, you arrange it for a special occasion *E.G. A tour is being lined up for July.*

**lineage** lineages

*Said* "**lin**-ee-ij" NOUN Someone's lineage is all the people from whom they are directly descended.

**linear**

*Said* "**lin**-ee-ar" ADJECTIVE arranged in a

a
b
c
d
e
f
g
h
i
j
k
l
m
n
o
p
q
r
s
t
u
v
w
x
y
z

A
B
C
D
E
F
G
H
I
J
K
**L**
M
N
O
P
Q
R
S
T
U
V
W
X
Y
Z

line or in a strict sequence, or happening at a constant rate.

**line dancing**

NOUN a type of dancing performed by rows of people to country music.

**linen**

NOUN ( D & T ) 1 Linen is a type of cloth made from a plant called flax. 2 Linen is also household goods made of cloth, such as sheets and tablecloths.

**liner liners**

NOUN a large passenger ship that makes long journeys.

**linesman linesmen**

NOUN an official at a sports match who watches the lines of the field or court and indicates when the ball goes outside them.

**-ling**

SUFFIX '-ling' means 'small' E.G. duckling.
📖 from an Old English suffix

**linger lingers lingering lingered**

VERB To linger means to remain for a long time E.G. Economic problems lingered in the background.

**lingerie**

Said "lan-jer-ee" NOUN Lingerie is women's nightclothes and underclothes.

**lingo lingoes**

NOUN; INFORMAL a foreign language.

**linguist linguists**

NOUN someone who studies foreign languages or the way in which language works.

**lining linings**

NOUN any material used to line the inside of something.

**link links linking linked**

NOUN 1 a relationship or connection between two things E.G. the link between sunbathing and skin cancer.

2 a physical connection between two things or places E.G. a high-speed rail link between the cities. 3 one of the rings in a chain. ▶ VERB 4 To link people, places, or things means to join them together.

**linkage** NOUN

**lino**

NOUN Lino is the same as linoleum.

**linoleum**

NOUN a floor covering with a shiny surface.

**lint**

NOUN soft cloth made from linen, used to dress wounds.

**lion lions**

NOUN a large member of the cat family which comes from Africa. Lions have light brown fur, and the male has a long mane. A female lion is called a lioness.

**lip lips**

NOUN 1 Your lips are the edges of your mouth. 2 The lip of a jug is the slightly pointed part through which liquids are poured out.

**lip-read lip-reads lip-reading lip-read**

VERB To lip-read means to watch someone's lips when they are talking in order to understand what they are saying. Deaf people often lip-read.

**lipstick lipsticks**

NOUN a coloured substance which women wear on their lips.

**liqueur liqueurs**

Said "lik-yoor" NOUN a strong sweet alcoholic drink, usually drunk after a meal.

**liquid liquids** ( SCIENCE )

NOUN 1 any substance which is not a solid or a gas, and which can be poured. ▶ ADJECTIVE 2 Something that is liquid is in the form of a liquid *E.G. liquid nitrogen.* **3** In commerce and finance a person's or company's liquid assets are the things that can be sold quickly to raise cash.

**liquidate** liquidates liquidating liquidated
VERB **1** To liquidate a company means to close it down and to use its assets to pay off its debts. **2** *INFORMAL* To liquidate a person means to murder them.
**liquidation** NOUN  **liquidator** NOUN

**liquor**
NOUN Liquor is any strong alcoholic drink.

**liquorice**
*Said* "lik-ker-iss" NOUN Liquorice is a root used to flavour sweets; also the sweets themselves.

**lira** lire
NOUN a unit of currency formerly used in Italy.

**lisp** lisps lisping lisped
NOUN **1** Someone who has a lisp pronounces the sounds 's' and 'z' like 'th'. ► VERB **2** To lisp means to speak with a lisp.

**list** lists listing listed
NOUN **1** a set of words or items written one below the other. ► VERB **2** If you list a number of things, you make a list of them.

**listen** listens listening listened
VERB If you listen to something, you hear it and pay attention to it.
**listener** NOUN

**listless**
ADJECTIVE lacking energy and enthusiasm.
**listlessly** ADVERB
from Old English *list* meaning 'desire'

**lit**
a past tense and past participle of **light**.

**litany** litanies
NOUN **1** a part of a church service in which the priest says or chants prayers and the people give responses. **2** something, especially a list of things, that is repeated often or in a boring or insincere way *E.G. a tedious litany of complaints.*

**literacy**
NOUN Literacy is the ability to read and write.
**literate** ADJECTIVE

**literal**
ADJECTIVE **1** The literal meaning of a word is its most basic meaning. **2** A literal translation from a foreign language is one that has been translated exactly word for word.
**literally** ADVERB
✔ Be careful where you use *literally*. It can emphasize something without changing the meaning: *the house was literally only five minutes walk away.* However, it can make nonsense of some things: *he literally swept me off my feet.* This sentence is ridiculous unless *he* actually took a broom and swept the speaker over.

**literary**
ADJECTIVE connected with literature *E.G. literary critics.*

**literature**
NOUN **1** Literature consists of novels, plays, and poetry. **2** The literature on a subject is everything that has been written about it.

**lithe**
ADJECTIVE supple and graceful.

**litmus**
NOUN In chemistry, litmus is a

substance that turns red under acid and blue under alkali conditions.

**litmus test** litmus tests

NOUN something which is regarded as a simple and accurate test of a particular thing, such as a person's attitude to an issue E.G. *The conflict was seen as a litmus test of Britain's will to remain a major power.*

**litre** litres

NOUN (MATHS) a unit of liquid volume equal to about 1.76 pints.

**litter** litters littering littered

NOUN 1 Litter is rubbish in the street and other public places. 2 Cat litter is a gravelly substance you put in a container where you want your cat to urinate and defecate. 3 a number of baby animals born at the same time to the same mother. ► VERB 4 If things litter a place, they are scattered all over it.

**little** less lesser least

ADJECTIVE 1 small in size or amount. ► NOUN OR ADVERB 2 A little is a small amount or degree E.G. *Would you like a little fruit juice?* 3 Little also means not much E.G. *He has little to say.*

**live** lives living lived

VERB 1 If you live in a place, that is where your home is. 2 To live means to be alive. 3 If something lives up to your expectations, it is as good as you thought it would be. ► ADJECTIVE OR ADVERB 4 Live television or radio is broadcast while the event is taking place E.G. *a live football match… The concert will go out live.* ► ADJECTIVE 5 Live animals or plants are alive, rather than dead or artificial E.G. *a live spider.* 6 Something is live if it is directly connected to an electricity supply E.G. *Careful – those wires are*

*live.* 7 Live bullets or ammunition have not yet been exploded.

**live down** VERB If you cannot live down a mistake or failure, you cannot make people forget it.

**livelihood** livelihoods

NOUN Someone's livelihood is their job or the source of their income.

**lively**

ADJECTIVE full of life and enthusiasm E.G. *lively conversation.*

**liveliness** NOUN

▤ brisk, energetic, vigorous

**liven** livens livening livened

VERB To liven things up means to make them more lively or interesting.

**liver** livers

NOUN 1 Your liver is a large organ in your body which cleans your blood and helps digestion. 2 Liver is also the liver of some animals, which may be cooked and eaten.

▥ from Greek *liparos* meaning 'fat'

**livestock**

NOUN Livestock is farm animals.

**livid**

ADJECTIVE 1 extremely angry. 2 dark purple or bluish E.G. *livid bruises.*

**living**

ADJECTIVE 1 If someone is living, they are alive E.G. *her only living relative.* ► NOUN 2 The work you do for a living is the work you do in order to earn money to live.

**living room** living rooms

NOUN the room where people relax and entertain in their homes.

**lizard** lizards

NOUN a long, thin, dry-skinned reptile found in hot, dry countries.

**llama** llamas

NOUN a South American animal related to the camel.

**load** loads loading loaded
NOUN **1** something being carried.
**2** *INFORMAL* Loads means a lot *E.G. loads of work.* ▶ VERB **3** To load a vehicle or animal means to put a large number of things into it or onto it.

**loaf** loaves; loafs loafing loafed
NOUN **1** a large piece of bread baked in a shape that can be cut into slices. ▶ VERB **2** To loaf around means to be lazy and not do any work.

**loan** loans loaning loaned
NOUN **1** a sum of money that you borrow. **2** the act of borrowing or lending something *E.G. I am grateful to Jane for the loan of her book.* ▶ VERB **3** If you loan something to someone, you lend it to them.

**loath**
*Rhymes with "both"* ADJECTIVE If you are loath to do something, you are very unwilling to do it
☑ Do not confuse *loath* with *loathe*.

**loathe** loathes loathing loathed
VERB To loathe someone or something means to feel strong dislike for them.

**loathing** NOUN **loathsome** ADJECTIVE
☑ Do not confuse *loathe* with *loath*.

**lob** lobs lobbing lobbed
VERB **1** If you lob something, you throw it high in the air. ▶ NOUN **2** In tennis, a lob is a stroke in which the player hits the ball high in the air.

**lobby** lobbies lobbying lobbied
NOUN **1** The lobby in a building is the main entrance area with corridors and doors leading off it. **2** a group of people trying to persuade an organization that something should be done *E.G. the environmental lobby.* ▶ VERB **3** To lobby an MP or an organization means to try to

persuade them to do something, for example by writing them lots of letters.

**lobe** lobes
NOUN **1** The lobe of your ear is the rounded soft part at the bottom. **2** any rounded part of something *E.G. the frontal lobe of the brain.*

**lobster** lobsters
NOUN an edible shellfish with two front claws and eight legs.

**local** locals
ADJECTIVE **1** Local means in, near, or belonging to the area in which you live *E.G. the local newspaper.* **2** A local anaesthetic numbs only one part of your body and does not send you to sleep. ▶ NOUN **3** The locals are the people who live in a particular area. **4** *INFORMAL* Someone's local is the pub nearest their home.

**locally** ADVERB
≡ (sense 1) provincial, regional

**locality** localities
NOUN an area of a country or city *E.G. a large map of the locality.*

**localized** or **localised**
ADJECTIVE existing or happening in only one place *E.G. localized pain.*

**locate** locates locating located
VERB **1** To locate someone or something means to find out where they are. **2** If something is located in a place, it is in that place

**location** locations
NOUN **1** ( GEOGRAPHY ) a place, or the position of something. **2** In South Africa, a location was a small town where only Black people or Coloured people were allowed to live. ▶ PHRASE **3** If a film is made **on location**, it is made away from a studio.
≡ (sense 1) place, position

a
b
c
d
e
f
g
h
i
j
k
l
m
n
o
p
q
r
s
t
u
v
w
x
y
z

A
B
C
D
E
F
G
H
I
J
K
**L**
M
N
O
P
Q
R
S
T
U
V
W
X
Y
Z

**loch** lochs

NOUN In Scottish English, a loch is a lake.

**lock** locks locking locked

VERB 1 If you lock something, you close it and fasten it with a key. 2 If something locks into place, it moves into place and becomes firmly fixed there. ► NOUN 3 a device on something which fastens it and prevents it from being opened except with a key. 4 A lock on a canal is a place where the water level can be raised or lowered to allow boats to go between two parts of the canal which have different water levels. 5 A lock of hair is a small bunch of hair.

**locker** lockers

NOUN a small cupboard for your personal belongings, for example in a changing room.

**locket** lockets

NOUN a piece of jewellery consisting of a small case which you can keep a photograph in, and which you wear on a chain round your neck.

**locksmith** locksmiths

NOUN a person who makes or mends locks.

**locomotive** locomotives

NOUN a railway engine.

**locust** locusts

NOUN an insect like a large grasshopper, which travels in huge swarms and eats crops.

**lodge** lodges lodging lodged

NOUN 1 a small house in the grounds of a large country house, or a small house used for holidays. ► VERB 2 If you lodge in someone else's house, you live there and pay them rent. 3 If something lodges somewhere, it gets stuck there E.G. The bullet lodged in his pelvis. 4 If you lodge a

complaint, you formally make it.

**lodger** lodgers

NOUN a person who lives in someone's house and pays rent.

**lodgings**

PLURAL NOUN If you live in lodgings, you live in someone else's house and pay them rent.

**loft** lofts

NOUN the space immediately under the roof of a house, often used for storing things.

**lofty** loftier loftiest

ADJECTIVE 1 very high E.G. a lofty hall. 2 very noble and important E.G. lofty ideals. 3 proud and superior E.G. her lofty manner.

**log** logs logging logged

NOUN 1 a thick branch or piece of tree trunk which has fallen or been cut down. 2 the captain's official record of everything that happens on board a ship. ► VERB 3 If you log something, you officially make a record of it, for example in a ship's log. 4 To log into a computer system means to gain access to it, usually by giving your name and password. To log out means to finish using the system.

**logic**

NOUN Logic is a way of reasoning involving a series of statements, each of which must be true if the statement before it is true.

**logical**

ADJECTIVE 1 A logical argument uses logic. 2 A logical course of action or decision is sensible or reasonable in the circumstances E.G. the logical conclusion.

**logically** ADVERB

**logistics**

NOUN; FORMAL The logistics of a

complicated undertaking is the skilful organization of it.

**logo logos**
*Said* "loh-goh" NOUN The logo of an organization is a special design that is put on all its products.
🔲 from Greek *logos* meaning 'word'

**-logy**
SUFFIX '-logy' is used to form words that refer to the study of something *E.G. biology… geology*
🔲 from Greek *logos* meaning 'reason', 'speech', or 'discourse'

**loin loins**
NOUN 1 OLD-FASHIONED Your loins are the front part of your body between your waist and your thighs, especially your sexual parts. 2 Loin is a piece of meat from the back or sides of an animal *E.G. loin of pork*.

**loiter loiters loitering loitered**
VERB To loiter means stand about idly with no real purpose.

**loll lolls lolling lolled**
VERB 1 If you loll somewhere, you sit or lie there in an idle, relaxed way. 2 If your head or tongue lolls, it hangs loosely.

**lollipop lollipops**
NOUN a hard sweet on the end of a stick.

**lolly lollies**
NOUN 1 a lollipop. 2 a piece of flavoured ice or ice cream on a stick. 3 In Australian and New Zealand English, a sweet.

**lolly scramble lolly scrambles**
NOUN In New Zealand, a lolly scramble is a lot of sweets thrown on the ground for children to pick up.

**lone**
ADJECTIVE A lone person or thing is the only one in a particular place *E.G. a lone climber*.
▣ single, solitary

**lonely lonelier loneliest**
ADJECTIVE 1 If you are lonely, you are unhappy because you are alone. 2 A lonely place is an isolated one which very few people visit *E.G. a lonely hillside*.
**loneliness** NOUN

**loner loners**
NOUN a person who likes to be alone.

**lonesome**
ADJECTIVE lonely and sad.

**long longer longest; longs longing longed**
ADJECTIVE or ADVERB 1 continuing for a great amount of time *E.G. There had been no rain for a long time… The equipment will not last much longer.*
▶ ADJECTIVE 2 great in length or distance *E.G. a long dress… a long road.* ▶ PHRASE 3 If something **no longer** happens, it does not happen any more. 4 **Before long** means soon. 5 If one thing is true **as long as** another thing is true, it is true only if the other thing is true. ▶ VERB 6 If you long for something, you want it very much.
**longing** NOUN

**longevity**
*Said* "lon-jev-it-ee" NOUN; FORMAL Longevity is long life.

**longhand**
NOUN If you write something in longhand, you do it in your own handwriting rather than using shorthand or a typewriter.

**longitude longitudes**
NOUN (GEOGRAPHY) The longitude of a place is its distance east or west of a line passing through Greenwich,

a
b
c
d
e
f
g
h
i
j
k
l
m
n
o
p
q
r
s
t
u
v
w
x
y
z

measured in degrees.

**long jump**
NOUN The long jump is an athletics event in which you jump as far as possible after taking a long run.

**long-range**
ADJECTIVE 1 able to be used over a great distance E.G. *long-range artillery*. 2 extending a long way into the future E.G. *a long-range weather forecast*.

**long-sighted**
ADJECTIVE If you are long-sighted, you have difficulty seeing things that are close.

**long-standing**
ADJECTIVE having existed for a long time E.G. *a long-standing tradition*.

**long-suffering**
ADJECTIVE very patient E.G. *her long-suffering husband*.

**long-term**
ADJECTIVE extending a long way into the future E.G. *a long-term investment*.

**long-winded**
ADJECTIVE long and boring E.G. *a long-winded letter*.

**loo** loos
NOUN; INFORMAL a toilet.

**look** looks looking looked
VERB 1 If you look at something, you turn your eyes towards it so that you can see it. 2 If you look for someone or something, you try to find them. 3 If you look at a subject or situation, you study it or judge it. 4 If you look down on someone, you think that they are inferior to you. 5 If you are looking forward to something, you want it to happen because you think you will enjoy it. 6 If you look up to someone, you admire and respect them. 7 If you describe the way that

something looks, you are describing its appearance. ▶ NOUN 8 If you have a look at something, you look at it. 9 The look on your face is the expression on it. 10 If you talk about someone's looks, you are talking about how attractive they are.
▶ INTERJECTION 11 You say 'look out' to warn someone of danger.
■ (sense 1) gaze, glance, see, watch
■ (sense 8) glance, glimpse, peek
■ (sense 9) appearance, expression

**look after** VERB If you look after someone or something, you take care of them.

**look up** VERB 1 To look up information means to find it out in a book. 2 If you look someone up, you go to see them after not having seen them for a long time. 3 If a situation is looking up, it is improving.

**lookalike** lookalikes
NOUN a person who looks very like someone else E.G. *an Elvis lookalike*.

**lookout** lookouts
NOUN 1 someone who is watching for danger, or a place where they watch for danger. ▶ PHRASE 2 If you are **on the lookout** for something, you are watching for it or waiting expectantly for it.

**loom** looms looming loomed
NOUN 1 a machine for weaving cloth.
▶ VERB 2 If something looms in front of you, it suddenly appears as a tall, unclear, and sometimes frightening shape. 3 If a situation or event is looming, it is likely to happen soon and is rather worrying.

**loony** loonies INFORMAL
ADJECTIVE 1 People or behaviour can be described as loony if they are mad or eccentric. ▶ NOUN 2 a mad or eccentric person.

A B C D E F G H I J K L M N O P Q R S T U V W X Y Z

**loop** loops looping looped

NOUN 1 a curved or circular shape in something long such as a piece of string. ► VERB 2 If you loop rope or string around an object, you place it in a loop around the object.

**loophole** loopholes

NOUN a small mistake or omission in the law which allows you to do something that the law really intends that you should not do.

**loose** looser loosest

ADJECTIVE 1 If something is loose, it is not firmly held, fixed, or attached. 2 Loose clothes are rather large and do not fit closely. ► ADVERB 3 To set animals loose means to set them free after they have been tied up or kept in a cage.

**loosely** ADVERB

☑ The adjective and adverb *loose* is spelt with two *o*s. Do not confuse it with the verb *lose*.

**loosen** loosens loosening loosened

VERB To loosen something means to make it looser. *E.G. He loosened his tie.*

**loot** loots looting looted

VERB 1 To loot shops and houses means to steal goods from them during a battle or riot. ► NOUN 2 Loot is stolen money or goods.

🏛 from Hindi *lut*

▤ (sense 1) pillage, plunder, ransack

▤ (sense 2) booty, plunder, spoils

**lop** lops lopping lopped

VERB If you lop something off, you cut it off with one quick stroke.

**lopsided**

ADJECTIVE Something that is lopsided is uneven because its two sides are different sizes or shapes.

**lord** lords

NOUN 1 a nobleman. 2 Lord is a title used in front of the names of some noblemen, and of bishops, archbishops, judges, and some high-ranking officials *E.G. the Lord Mayor of London*. 3 In Christianity, Lord is a name given to God and Jesus Christ.

**Lordship** Lordships

NOUN You address a lord, judge, or bishop as Your Lordship.

**lore**

NOUN The lore of a place, people, or subject is all the traditional knowledge and stories about it.

**lorikeet** lorikeets

NOUN a type of small parrot found in Australia.

**lorry** lorries

NOUN a large vehicle for transporting goods by road.

**lory** lories

*Said "law-ree"* NOUN a small, brightly coloured parrot found in Australia.

**lose** loses losing lost

VERB 1 If you lose something, you cannot find it, or you no longer have it because it has been taken away from you *E.G. I lost my airline ticket.* 2 If you lose a relative or friend, they die *E.G. She lost her brother in the war.* 3 If you lose a fight or an argument, you are beaten. 4 If a business loses money, it is spending more money than it is earning.

**loser** NOUN

☑ The verb *lose* is spelt with one *o*. Do not confuse it with the adjective and adverb *loose*.

**loss** losses

NOUN 1 The loss of something is the losing of it. ► PHRASE 2 If you are **at a loss**, you do not know what to do.

a
b
c
d
e
f
g
h
i
j
k
l
m
n
o
p
q
r
s
t
u
v
w
x
y
z

## lost
ADJECTIVE **1** If you are lost, you do not know where you are. **2** If something is lost, you cannot find it. ▶ **3** Lost is the past tense and past participle of **lose**.

## lot lots
NOUN **1** A lot of something, or lots of something, is a large amount of it. **2** A lot means very much or very often *E.G. I love him a lot.* **3** an amount of something or a number of things *E.G. He bet all his wages and lost the lot.* **4** In an auction, a lot is one of the things being sold.

■ (sense 1) abundance, load(s), plenty

## lotion lotions
NOUN a liquid that you put on your skin to protect or soften it *E.G. suntan lotion.*

## lottery lotteries
NOUN a method of raising money by selling tickets by which a winner is selected at random.

## lotus lotuses
NOUN a large water lily, found in Africa and Asia.

## loud louder loudest
ADJECTIVE or ADVERB **1** A loud noise has a high volume of sound *E.G. a loud explosion.* **2** If you describe clothing as loud, you mean that it is too bright *E.G. a loud tie.*

**loudly** ADVERB

## loudspeaker loudspeakers
NOUN a piece of equipment that makes your voice louder when you speak into a microphone connected to it.

## lounge lounges lounging lounged
NOUN **1** a room in a house or hotel with comfortable chairs where people can relax. **2** The lounge or lounge bar in a pub or hotel is a more expensive and comfortably furnished bar. ▶ VERB **3** If you lounge around, you lean against something or sit or lie around in a lazy and comfortable way.

## lourie louries
*Rhymes with "Maori"* NOUN one of two types of bird found in South Africa. The grey lourie lives in open grassland and the other more brightly coloured species lives in forests and wooded areas.

## louse lice
NOUN Lice are small insects that live on people's bodies *E.G. head lice.*

## lousy lousier lousiest
ADJECTIVE *INFORMAL* **1** of bad quality or very unpleasant *E.G. The weather is lousy.* **2** ill or unhappy.

## lout louts
NOUN a young man who behaves in an aggressive and rude way.

## lovable or loveable
ADJECTIVE having very attractive qualities and therefore easy to love *E.G. a lovable black mongrel.*

## love loves loving loved
VERB **1** If you love someone, you have strong emotional feelings of affection for them. **2** If you love something, you like it very much *E.G. We both love fishing.* **3** If you would love to do something, you want very much to do it *E.G. I would love to live there.* ▶ NOUN **4** Love is a strong emotional feeling of affection for someone or something. **5** In tennis, love is a score of zero. ▶ PHRASE **6** If you are **in love** with someone, you feel strongly attracted to them romantically or sexually. **7** When two

people **make love**, they have sex.
**loving** ADJECTIVE   **lovingly** ADVERB
■ (sense 1) adore, dote on

**love affair** love affairs
NOUN a romantic and often sexual relationship between two people who are not married to each other.

**love life** love lives
NOUN a person's romantic and sexual relationships.

**lovely** lovelier loveliest
ADJECTIVE very beautiful, attractive, and pleasant.
**loveliness** NOUN

**lover** lovers
NOUN 1 A person's lover is someone that they have a sexual relationship with but are not married to.
2 Someone who is a lover of something, for example art or music, is very fond of it.

**low** lower lowest
ADJECTIVE OR ADVERB 1 Something that is low is close to the ground, or measures a short distance from the ground to the top E.G. *a low stool.*
2 'Low' is used to describe people who are considered not respectable E.G. *mixing with low company.* ► NOUN
3 a level or amount that is less than before E.G. *Sales hit a new low.*

**lowboy** lowboys
NOUN In Australian and New Zealand English, a small wardrobe or chest of drawers.

**lower** lowers lowering lowered
VERB To lower something means to move it downwards or to make it less in value or amount.

**lowlands**
PLURAL NOUN Lowlands are an area of flat, low land.
**lowland** ADJECTIVE

**lowly** lowlier lowliest
ADJECTIVE low in importance, rank or status.

**low tide**
NOUN On a coast, low tide is the time, usually twice a day, when the sea is at its lowest level.

**loyal**
ADJECTIVE firm in your friendship or support for someone or something.
**loyally** ADVERB   **loyalty** NOUN

**loyalist** loyalists
NOUN a person who remains firm in their support for a government or ruler.

**lozenge** lozenges
NOUN 1 a type of sweet with medicine in it, which you suck to relieve a sore throat or cough. 2 a diamond shape.

**LP** LPs
NOUN a long-playing record. LP is short for 'long-playing record'.

**LSD**
NOUN LSD is a very powerful drug which causes hallucinations. LSD is an abbreviation for 'lysergic acid diethylamide'.

**Ltd**
an abbreviation for 'limited'; used after the names of limited companies.

**lubra** lubras
NOUN an Australian Aboriginal woman.

**lubricate** lubricates lubricating lubricated
VERB To lubricate something such as a machine means to put oil or an oily substance onto it, so that it moves smoothly and friction is reduced.
**lubrication** NOUN   **lubricant** NOUN

**lucid**
ADJECTIVE 1 Lucid writing or speech is

a
b
c
d
e
f
g
h
i
j
k
l
m
n
o
p
q
r
s
t
u
v
w
x
y
z

A B C D E F G H I J K L M N O P Q R S T U V W X Y Z

clear and easy to understand.
**2** Someone who is lucid after having been ill or delirious is able to think clearly again.

**luck**
NOUN Luck is anything that seems to happen by chance and not through your own efforts.
■ chance, fortune

**luckless**
ADJECTIVE unsuccessful or unfortunate E.G. *We reduced our luckless opponents to shattered wrecks.*

**lucky luckier luckiest**
ADJECTIVE **1** Someone who is lucky has a lot of good luck. **2** Something that is lucky happens by chance and has good effects or consequences.
**luckily** ADVERB

**lucrative**
ADJECTIVE Something that is lucrative earns you a lot of money E.G. *a lucrative sponsorship deal.*

**ludicrous**
ADJECTIVE completely foolish, unsuitable, or ridiculous.

**lug lugs lugging lugged**
VERB If you lug a heavy object around, you carry it with difficulty.

**luggage**
NOUN Your luggage is the bags and suitcases that you take with you when you travel.

**lukewarm**
ADJECTIVE **1** slightly warm E.G. *a mug of lukewarm tea.* **2** not very enthusiastic or interested E.G. *The report was given a polite but lukewarm response.*

**lull lulls lulling lulled**
NOUN **1** a pause in something, or a short time when it is quiet and nothing much happens E.G. *There was*

*a temporary lull in the fighting.* ▶ VERB **2** If you are lulled into feeling safe, someone or something causes you to feel safe at a time when you are not safe E.G. *We had been lulled into a false sense of security.*

**lullaby lullabies**
NOUN a song used for sending a baby or child to sleep.

**lumber lumbers lumbering lumbered**
NOUN **1** Lumber is wood that has been roughly cut up. **2** Lumber is also old unwanted furniture and other items. ▶ VERB **3** If you lumber around, you move heavily and clumsily. **4** INFORMAL If you are lumbered with something, you are given it to deal with even though you do not want it E.G. *Women are still lumbered with the housework.*

**luminary luminaries**
NOUN; LITERARY a person who is famous or an expert in a particular subject.

**luminous**
ADJECTIVE Something that is luminous glows in the dark, usually because it has been treated with a special substance E.G. *The luminous dial on her clock.*
**luminosity** NOUN

**lump lumps lumping lumped**
NOUN **1** A lump of something is a solid piece of it, of any shape or size E.G. *a big lump of dough.* **2** a bump on the surface of something. ▶ VERB **3** If you lump people or things together, you combine them into one group or consider them as being similar in some way.
**lumpy** ADJECTIVE

**lump sum lump sums**
NOUN a large sum of money given or

received all at once.

**lunacy**

NOUN **1** Lunacy is extremely foolish or eccentric behaviour. **2** *OLD-FASHIONED* Lunacy is also severe mental illness.

**lunar**

ADJECTIVE relating to the moon.

📖 from Latin *luna* meaning 'moon'

**lunatic** lunatics

NOUN **1** If you call someone a lunatic, you mean that they are very foolish *E.G. He drives like a lunatic!* **2** someone who is insane. ▶ ADJECTIVE **3** Lunatic behaviour is very stupid, foolish, or dangerous.

**lunch** lunches lunching lunched

NOUN **1** a meal eaten in the middle of the day. ▶ VERB **2** When you lunch, you eat lunch.

**luncheon** luncheons

*Said* "lun-shen" NOUN; *FORMAL* Luncheon is lunch.

**lung** lungs

NOUN Your lungs are the two organs inside your ribcage with which you breathe.

**lunge** lunges lunging lunged

NOUN **1** a sudden forward movement *E.G. He made a lunge for her.* ▶ VERB **2** To lunge means to make a sudden movement in a particular direction.

**lurch** lurches lurching lurched

VERB **1** To lurch means to make a sudden, jerky movement. ▶ NOUN **2** a sudden, jerky movement.

**lure** lures luring lured

VERB **1** To lure someone means to attract them into going somewhere or doing something. ▶ NOUN **2** something that you find very attractive.

**lurid**

*Said* "loo-rid" ADJECTIVE **1** involving a lot

of sensational detail *E.G. lurid stories in the press.* **2** very brightly coloured or patterned.

**lurk** lurks lurking lurked

VERB To lurk somewhere means to remain there hidden from the person you are waiting for.

**luscious**

ADJECTIVE very tasty *E.G. luscious fruit.*

**lush** lusher lushest

ADJECTIVE In a lush field or garden, the grass or plants are healthy and growing thickly.

**lust** lusts lusting lusted

NOUN **1** Lust is a very strong feeling of sexual desire for someone. **2** A lust for something is a strong desire to have it *E.G. a lust for money.* ▶ VERB **3** To lust for or after someone means to desire them sexually. **4** If you lust for or after something, you have a very strong desire to possess it *E.G. She lusted after fame.*

**lustre**

*Said* "lus-ter" NOUN Lustre is soft shining light reflected from the surface of something *E.G. the lustre of silk.*

**lute** lutes

NOUN an old-fashioned stringed musical instrument which is plucked like a guitar.

**luxuriant**

ADJECTIVE Luxuriant plants, trees, and gardens are large, healthy and growing strongly.

**luxurious**

ADJECTIVE very expensive and full of luxury.

**luxuriously** ADVERB

🔲 opulent, splendid, sumptuous

**luxury** luxuries

NOUN **1** Luxury is great comfort in expensive and beautiful

a
b
c
d
e
f
g
h
i
j
k
l
m
n
o
p
q
r
s
t
u
v
w
x
y
z

A
B
C
D
E
F
G
H
I
J
K
L
M
N
O
P
Q
R
S
T
U
V
W
X
Y
Z

surroundings *E.G. a life of luxury.*
**2** something that you enjoy very
much but do not have very often,
usually because it is expensive.
■ (sense 1) extravagance,
indulgence, treat

**-ly**
SUFFIX **1** '-ly' forms adjectives that
describe a quality *E.G. friendly.* **2** '-ly'
forms adjectives that refer to how
often something happens or is done
*E.G. yearly.* **3** '-ly' forms adverbs that
refer to how or in what way
something is done *E.G. quickly… nicely.*

**lying**
NOUN **1** Lying is telling lies. **2** Lying is
also the present participle of **lie.**

**lynch** lynches lynching lynched
VERB If a crowd lynches someone, it

kills them in a violent way without
first holding a legal trial.

**lynx** lynxes
NOUN a wildcat with a short tail and
tufted ears.

**lyre** lyres
NOUN a stringed instrument rather
like a small harp, which was used in
ancient Greece.

**lyric** lyrics
NOUN **1** (MUSIC) The lyrics of a song
are the words. ► ADJECTIVE **2** Lyric
poetry is written in a simple and
direct style, and is usually about
love.

**lyrical**
ADJECTIVE poetic and romantic.

# Mm

**m**
an abbreviation for 'metres' or 'miles'.

**macabre**
Said "mak-**kahb**-ra" ADJECTIVE A macabre event is strange and horrible E.G. a macabre horror story.

**macadamia macadamias**
Said "ma-ka-**dame**-ee-a" NOUN an Australian tree, also grown in New Zealand, that produces edible nuts.

**macaroni**
NOUN Macaroni is short hollow tubes of pasta.
📖 an Italian word; from Greek makaria meaning 'food made from barley'

**macaroon macaroons**
NOUN a sweet biscuit flavoured with almonds or coconut.

**mace maces**
NOUN an ornamental pole carried by an official during ceremonies as a symbol of authority.

**machete machetes**
Said "mash-**ett**-ee" NOUN a large, heavy knife with a big blade.

**machine machines machining machined**
NOUN 1 ( D & T ) a piece of equipment which uses electricity or power from an engine to make it work. ▶ VERB 2 If you machine something, you make it or work on it using a machine.

**machine-gun machine-guns**
NOUN a gun that works automatically, firing bullets one after the other.

**machinery**
NOUN Machinery is machines in general.

**machismo**
Said "mak-**kiz**-moe" NOUN Machismo is exaggerated aggressive male behaviour.

**macho**
Said "**mat**-shoh" ADJECTIVE A man who is described as macho behaves in an aggressively masculine way.
📖 from Spanish macho meaning 'male'

**mackerel mackerels**
NOUN a sea fish with blue and silver stripes.

**mackintosh mackintoshes**
NOUN a raincoat made from specially treated waterproof cloth.

**mad madder maddest**
ADJECTIVE 1 Someone who is mad has a mental illness which often causes them to behave in strange ways. 2 If you describe someone as mad, you mean that they are very foolish E.G. He said we were mad to share a flat. 3 INFORMAL Someone who is mad is angry. 4 If you are mad about someone or something, you like them very much E.G. Alan was mad about golf.

**madness** NOUN **madman** NOUN
▣ (sense 1) crazy, deranged, insane
▣ (sense 2) daft, foolish

**madam**
'Madam' is a very formal way of addressing a woman.

**maddening**
ADJECTIVE irritating or frustrating E.G. She had many maddening habits.

**madly**
ADVERB If you do something madly, you do it in a fast, excited way.

**madrigal madrigals**
NOUN a song sung by several people without instruments.

**Mafia**
NOUN The Mafia is a large crime

A
B
C
D
E
F
G
H
I
J
K
L
M
N
O
P
Q
R
S
T
U
V
W
X
Y
Z

organization operating in Sicily, Italy, and the USA.

**magazine magazines**
NOUN 1 (LIBRARY) a weekly or monthly publication with articles and photographs. 2 a compartment in a gun for cartridges.
📖 from Arabic *makhzan* meaning 'storehouse'

**magenta**
*Said* "maj-jen-ta" NOUN or ADJECTIVE dark reddish-purple.

**maggot maggots**
NOUN a creature that looks like a small worm and lives on decaying things. Maggots turn into flies.

**magic**
NOUN 1 In fairy stories, magic is a special power that can make impossible things happen. 2 Magic is the art of performing tricks to entertain people.
**magical** ADJECTIVE **magically** ADVERB

**magician magicians**
NOUN 1 a person who performs tricks as entertainment. 2 In fairy stories, a magician is a man with magical powers.

**magistrate magistrates**
NOUN an official who acts as a judge in a law court that deals with less serious crimes.

**magnanimous**
ADJECTIVE generous and forgiving.

**magnate magnates**
NOUN someone who is very rich and powerful in business.

**magnet magnets**
NOUN a piece of iron which attracts iron or steel towards it, and which points towards north if allowed to swing freely.
**magnetic** ADJECTIVE **magnetism** NOUN

**magnificent**
ADJECTIVE extremely beautiful or impressive.
**magnificently** ADVERB
**magnificence** NOUN

**magnify magnifies magnifying magnified**
VERB When a microscope or lens magnifies something, it makes it appear bigger than it actually is.
**magnification** NOUN

**magnifying glass magnifying glasses**
NOUN a lens which makes things appear bigger than they really are.

**magnitude**
NOUN The magnitude of something is its great size or importance.

**magnolia magnolias**
NOUN a tree which has large white or pink flowers in spring.

**magpie magpies**
NOUN a large black and white bird with a long tail.

**mahogany**
NOUN Mahogany is a hard reddish brown wood used for making furniture.

**maid maids**
NOUN a female servant.

**maiden maidens**
NOUN 1 *LITERARY* a young woman.
► ADJECTIVE 2 first *E.G. a maiden voyage.*

**maiden name maiden names**
NOUN the surname a woman had before she married.

**mail mails mailing mailed**
NOUN 1 Your mail is the letters and parcels delivered to you by the post office. ► VERB 2 If you mail a letter, you send it by post.

**mail order**

NOUN Mail order is a system of buying goods by post.

**maim** maims maiming maimed

VERB To maim someone is to injure them very badly for life.

**main** mains

ADJECTIVE **1** most important *E.G. the main event.* ► NOUN **2** The mains are large pipes or wires that carry gas, water or electricity.

**mainly** ADVERB

■ (sense 1) chief, major, principal

**mainframe** mainframes

NOUN a large computer which can be used by many people at the same time.

**mainland**

NOUN The mainland is the main part of a country in contrast to islands around its coast.

**mainstay**

NOUN The mainstay of something is the most important part of it.

**mainstream**

NOUN The mainstream is the most ordinary and conventional group of people or ideas in a society.

**maintain** maintains maintaining maintained

VERB **1** If you maintain something, you keep it going or keep it at a particular rate or level *E.G. I wanted to maintain our friendship.* **2** If you maintain someone, you provide them regularly with money for what they need. **3** To maintain a machine or a building is to keep it in good condition. **4** If you maintain that something is true, you believe it is true and say so.

**maintenance**

NOUN **1** Maintenance is the process of keeping something in good condition. **2** Maintenance is also money that a person sends regularly to someone to provide for the things they need.

**maize**

NOUN Maize is a tall plant which produces sweet corn.

**majesty** majesties **1** You say 'His Majesty' when you are talking about a king, and 'Her Majesty' when you are talking about a queen.
NOUN **2** Majesty is great dignity and impressiveness.

**majestic** ADJECTIVE **majestically** ADVERB

**major** majors

ADJECTIVE **1** more important or more significant than other things *E.G. There were over fifty major injuries.* **2** (MUSIC) A major key is one of the keys in which most European music is written. ► NOUN **3** an army officer of the rank immediately above captain.

**majority** majorities

NOUN **1** The majority of people or things in a group is more than half of the group. **2** In an election, the majority is the difference between the number of votes gained by the winner and the number gained by the runner-up

☑ You should use *majority* only to talk about things that can be counted: *the majority of car owners.* To talk about an amount that cannot be counted you should use *most*: *most of the harvest was saved.*

**make** makes making made

VERB **1** To make something is to produce or construct it, or to cause it

A
B
C
D
E
F
G
H
I
J
K
L
**M**
N
O
P
Q
R
S
T
U
V
W
X
Y
Z

to happen. **2** To make something is to do it *E.G. He was about to make a speech.* **3** To make something is to prepare it *E.G. I'll make some salad dressing.* **4** If someone makes you do something, they force you to do it *E.G. Mum made me clean the bathroom.* ► NOUN **5** The make of a product is the name of the company that manufactured it *E.G. 'What make of car do you drive?' – 'Toyota'.*

■ (sense 1) create, fashion, form, produce

■ (sense 5) brand, kind, type

**make up** VERB **1** If a number of things make up something, they form that thing. **2** If you make up a story, you invent it. **3** If you make yourself up, you put make-up on. **4** If two people make it up, they become friends again after a quarrel.

**make-up**
NOUN **1** Make-up is coloured creams and powders which women put on their faces to make themselves look more attractive. **2** Someone's make-up is their character or personality.

**making**
NOUN **1** The making of something is the act or process of creating or producing it. ► PHRASE **2** When you describe someone as something **in the making**, you mean that they are gradually becoming that thing *E.G. a captain in the making.*

**maladjusted**
ADJECTIVE A maladjusted person has psychological or behaviour problems.

**malaise**
*Said "mal-laze"* NOUN; *FORMAL* Malaise is a feeling of dissatisfaction or unhappiness.

**malaria**
*Said "mal-lay-ree-a"* NOUN Malaria is a tropical disease caught from mosquitoes which causes fever and shivering.

**Malaysian** Malaysians
ADJECTIVE **1** belonging or relating to Malaysia. ► NOUN **2** someone who comes from Malaysia.

**male** males
NOUN **1** a person or animal belonging to the sex that cannot give birth or lay eggs. ► ADJECTIVE **2** concerning or affecting men rather than women.

**male chauvinist** male chauvinists
NOUN a man who thinks that men are better than women.

**malevolent**
*Said "mal-lev-oh-lent"* ADJECTIVE; *FORMAL* wanting or intending to cause harm. **malevolence** NOUN

■ malicious, spiteful, vindictive

**malfunction** malfunctions malfunctioning malfunctioned
VERB **1** If a machine malfunctions, it fails to work properly. ► NOUN **2** the failure of a machine to work properly.

**malice**
NOUN Malice is a desire to cause harm to people.

**malicious**
ADJECTIVE Malicious talk or behaviour is intended to harm someone.

**malign** maligns maligning maligned
VERB; *FORMAL* To malign someone is to say unpleasant and untrue things about them.

**malignant**
ADJECTIVE **1** harmful and cruel. **2** A malignant disease or tumour could

cause death if it is allowed to
continue.

**mallard** mallards
NOUN a kind of wild duck. The male
has a green head.

**mallee** mallees
NOUN a eucalypt that grows close to
the ground in dry areas of Australia.

**mallet** mallets
NOUN a wooden hammer with a
square head.

**malnutrition**
NOUN Malnutrition is not eating
enough healthy food.

**malodorous**
ADJECTIVE If you describe something as
malodorous, you means it smells
bad.

**malpractice**
NOUN If someone such as a doctor or
lawyer breaks the rules of their
profession, their behaviour is called
malpractice.

**malt**
NOUN Malt is roasted grain, usually
barley, that is used in making beer
and whisky.

**mammal** mammals
NOUN (SCIENCE) Animals that give birth
to live babies and feed their young
with milk from the mother's body
are called mammals. Human beings,
dogs, and whales are all mammals.

**mammoth** mammoths
ADJECTIVE **1** very large indeed E.G. a
mammoth outdoor concert. ▶ NOUN **2** a
huge animal that looked like a hairy
elephant with long tusks. Mammoths
became extinct a long time ago.

**man** men; mans manning
manned
NOUN **1** an adult male human being.
▶ PLURAL NOUN **2** Human beings in

general are sometimes referred to as
men E.G. All men are equal. ▶ VERB **3** To
man something is to be in charge of
it or operate it E.G. Two officers were
manning the radar screens.
■ (sense 1) bloke, chap, guy
■ (sense 2) humanity, mankind

**mana**
NOUN Mana is authority and influence
such as that held by a New Zealand
Maori chief.

**manacle** manacles
NOUN Manacles are metal rings or
clamps attached to a prisoner's
wrists or ankles.

**manage** manages managing
managed
VERB **1** If you manage to do
something, you succeed in doing it
E.G. We managed to find somewhere to
sit. **2** If you manage an organization
or business, you are responsible for
controlling it.
■ (sense 1) accomplish, succeed

**manageable**
ADJECTIVE able to be dealt with.

**management**
NOUN **1** The management of a
business is the controlling and
organizing of it. **2** The people who
control an organization are called
the management.
■ (sense 1) administration, control,
running

**manager** managers
NOUN a person responsible for
running a business or organization
E.G. a bank manager.
☑ In business, the word manager
can apply to either a man or a
woman.

**manageress** manageresses
NOUN a woman responsible for

a
b
c
d
e
f
g
h
i
j
k
l
**m**
n
o
p
q
r
s
t
u
v
w
x
y
z

running a business or organization.

**managing director** managing
directors

NOUN a company director who is
responsible for the way the company
is managed.

**mandarin** mandarins

NOUN a type of small orange which is
easy to peel.

**mandate** mandates

NOUN FORMAL A government's mandate
is the authority it has to carry out
particular policies as a result of
winning an election.

**mandatory**

ADJECTIVE If something is mandatory,
there is a law or rule stating that it
must be done E.G. a mandatory life
sentence for murder.

**mandir** mandirs

Said "mun-dir" NOUN a Hindu temple.
📖 a Hindi word

**mandolin** mandolins

NOUN a musical instrument like a
small guitar with a deep, rounded
body.

**mane** manes

NOUN the long hair growing from the
neck of a lion or horse.

**manger** mangers

NOUN a feeding box in a barn or
stable.

**mangle** mangles mangling
mangled

VERB 1 If something is mangled, it is
crushed and twisted. ▶ NOUN 2 an old-
fashioned piece of equipment
consisting of two large rollers
which squeeze water out of wet
clothes.

**mango** mangoes or mangos

NOUN a sweet yellowish fruit which
grows in tropical countries.

**manhole** manholes

NOUN a covered hole in the ground
leading to a drain or sewer.

**manhood**

NOUN Manhood is the state of being a
man rather than a boy.

**mania** manias

NOUN 1 a strong liking for something
E.G. my wife's mania for plant
collecting. 2 a mental illness.
📖 from Greek mania meaning
'madness'

**maniac** maniacs

NOUN a mad person who is violent
and dangerous.

**manic**

ADJECTIVE energetic and excited E.G. a
manic attack.

**manicure** manicures

NOUN a special treatment for the
hands and nails.
**manicurist** NOUN

**manifest** manifests manifesting
manifested FORMAL

ADJECTIVE 1 obvious or easily seen E.G.
his manifest enthusiasm. ▶ VERB 2 To
manifest something is to make
people aware of it E.G. Fear can
manifest itself in many ways.

**manifestation** manifestations

NOUN; FORMAL A manifestation of
something is a sign that it is
happening or exists E.G. The illness
may be a manifestation of stress.

**manifesto** manifestoes or
manifestos

NOUN a published statement of the
aims and policies of a political party.

**manipulate** manipulates
manipulating manipulated

VERB 1 To manipulate people or
events is to control or influence
them to produce a particular result.

**2** If you **manipulate** a piece of equipment, you control it in a skilful way.

**manipulation** NOUN **manipulator** NOUN **manipulative** ADJECTIVE

**mankind**
NOUN 'Mankind' is used to refer to all human beings E.G. *a threat to mankind.*

**manly** manlier manliest
ADJECTIVE having qualities that are typically masculine E.G. *He laughed a deep, manly laugh.*

**manna**
NOUN If something appears like manna from heaven, it appears suddenly as if by a miracle and helps you in a difficult situation.

**manner** manners
NOUN **1** The manner in which you do something is the way you do it. **2** Your manner is the way in which you behave and talk E.G. *his kind manner.* ► PLURAL NOUN **3** If you have good manners, you behave very politely.

**mannerism** mannerisms
NOUN a gesture or a way of speaking which is characteristic of a person.

**manoeuvre** manoeuvres manoeuvring manoeuvred
*Said* "man-**noo**-ver" VERB **1** If you manoeuvre something into a place, you skilfully move it there E.G. *It took expertise to manoeuvre the boat so close to the shore.* ► NOUN **2** a clever move you make in order to change a situation to your advantage.

**manor**
NOUN a large country house with land.

**manpower**
NOUN Workers can be referred to as manpower.

**mansion** mansions
NOUN a very large house.

**manslaughter**
NOUN; LEGAL Manslaughter is the accidental killing of a person.

**mantelpiece** mantelpieces
NOUN a shelf over a fireplace.

**mantle** mantles
NOUN LITERARY To take on the mantle of something is to take on responsibility for it E.G. *He has taken over the mantle of England's greatest living poet.*

**mantra** mantras
NOUN a word or short piece of sacred text or prayer continually repeated to help concentration.

**manual** manuals
ADJECTIVE **1** Manual work involves physical strength rather than mental skill. **2** operated by hand rather than by electricity or by motor E.G. *a manual typewriter.* ► NOUN **3** an instruction book which tells you how to use a machine.

**manually** ADVERB

**manufacture** manufactures manufacturing manufactured
(D&T) VERB **1** To manufacture goods is to make them in a factory. ► NOUN **2** The manufacture of goods is the making of them in a factory E.G. *the manufacture of nuclear weapons.*

**manufacturer** NOUN

**manure**
NOUN Manure is animal faeces used to fertilize the soil.

**manuscript** manuscripts
NOUN a handwritten or typed document, especially a version of a book before it is printed.

a
b
c
d
e
f
g
h
i
j
k
l
**m**
n
o
p
q
r
s
t
u
v
w
x
y
z

Plaice the fish has a glittering 'EYE' (I) (plaice)        SPELLING NOTE

**Manx**

ADJECTIVE belonging or relating to the Isle of Man.

**many**

ADJECTIVE 1 If there are many people or things, there are a large number of them. 2 You also use 'many' to ask how great a quantity is or to give information about it E.G. *How many tickets do you require?* ▸ PRONOUN 3 a large number of people or things E.G. *Many are too weak to walk.*

**Maori** Maoris

NOUN 1 someone descended from the people who lived in New Zealand before Europeans arrived. 2 Maori is a language spoken by Maoris.

**map** maps mapping mapped

NOUN 1 a detailed drawing of an area as it would appear if you saw it from above. ▸ VERB 2 If you map out a plan, you work out in detail what you will do.

**maple** maples

NOUN a tree that has large leaves with five points.

**mar** mars marring marred

VERB To mar something is to spoil it E.G. *The game was marred by violence.*

**marae** marae or maraes

NOUN *Said* "ma-**rye**" In New Zealand, a Maori meeting house; also the enclosed space in front of it.

**marathon** marathons

NOUN 1 a race in which people run 26 miles along roads. ▸ ADJECTIVE 2 A marathon task is a large one that takes a long time.

**marble** marbles

NOUN 1 Marble is a very hard, cold stone which is often polished to show the coloured patterns in it. 2 Marbles is a children's game played with small coloured glass balls. These balls are also called marbles.

**march** marches marching marched

NOUN 1 March is the third month of the year. It has 31 days. 2 an organized protest in which a large group of people walk somewhere together. ▸ VERB 3 When soldiers march, they walk with quick regular steps in time with each other. 4 To march somewhere is to walk quickly in a determined way E.G. *He marched out of the room.*

📖 sense 1 is from Latin *Martius* (month) of Mars, the Roman god of war

**mare** mares

NOUN an adult female horse.

**margarine**

*Said* "mar-jar-reen" margarines

NOUN Margarine is a substance that is similar to butter but is made from vegetable oil and animal fats.

**margin** margins

NOUN 1 If you win a contest by a large or small margin, you win it by a large or small amount. 2 an extra amount that allows you more freedom in doing something E.G. *a small margin of error.* 3 the blank space at each side on a written or printed page.

**marginal**

ADJECTIVE 1 small and not very important E.G. *a marginal increase.* 2 A marginal seat or constituency is a political constituency where the previous election was won by a very small majority.

**marginally** ADVERB

**marigold** marigolds

NOUN a type of yellow or orange garden flower.

**marijuana**

*Said* "mar-rih-**hwan**-a" NOUN Marijuana is an illegal drug which is smoked in cigarettes.

**marina** marinas

NOUN a harbour for pleasure boats and yachts.

**marinate** marinates marinating marinated; also spelt **marinade**

VERB To marinate food is to soak it in a mixture of oil and vinegar to flavour it before cooking.

**marine** marines

NOUN **1** a soldier who serves with the navy. ► ADJECTIVE **2** relating to or involving the sea *E.G. marine life*.

**marital**

ADJECTIVE relating to or involving marriage *E.G. marital problems*.

**maritime**

ADJECTIVE relating to the sea and ships *E.G. maritime trade*.

**marjoram**

NOUN Marjoram is a herb with small, rounded leaves and tiny, pink flowers.

**mark** marks marking marked

NOUN **1** a small stain or damaged area on a surface *E.G. I can't get this mark off the curtain*. **2** a written or printed symbol *E.G. He made a few marks with his pen*. **3** a letter or number showing how well you have done in homework or in an exam. **4** a unit of currency formerly used in Germany. ► VERB **5** If something marks a surface, it damages it in some way. **6** If you mark something, you write a symbol on it or identify it in some other way. **7** When a teacher marks your work, he or she decides how good it is and gives it a mark. **8** To mark something is to be a sign of it *E.G. The accident marked a tragic end to the day*. **9** In

soccer or hockey, if you mark your opposing player, you stay close to them, trying to prevent them from getting the ball.

**marked**

ADJECTIVE very obvious *E.G. a marked improvement*.

**markedly** ADVERB

**market** markets marketing marketed

NOUN **1** a place where goods or animals are bought and sold. **2** a place with many small stalls selling different goods. **3** The market for a product is the number of people who want to buy it *E.G. the market for cars*. ► VERB **4** To market a product is to sell it in an organized way.

◼ (sense 1) bazaar, fair, mart

**marketing**

NOUN Marketing is the part of a business concerned with the way a product is sold.

**market research**

NOUN Market research is research into what people want and buy.

**marksman** marksmen

NOUN someone who can shoot very accurately.

**marlin** marlins

NOUN a large fish found in tropical seas which has a very long upper jaw.

**marmalade**

NOUN Marmalade is a jam made from citrus fruit, usually eaten at breakfast.

🏛 from Latin *marmelo* meaning 'quince'

**maroon**

NOUN OR ADJECTIVE dark reddish-purple.

**marooned**

ADJECTIVE If you are marooned in a place, you are stranded there and cannot leave it.

A
B
C
D
E
F
G
H
I
J
K
L
M
N
O
P
Q
R
S
T
U
V
W
X
Y
Z

**marquee** marquees
*Said* "mar-**kee**" NOUN a very large tent used at a fair or other outdoor entertainment.

**marquis** marquises
*Said* "mar-**kwiss**"; also spelt **marquess**
NOUN a male member of the nobility of the rank between duke and earl.

**marriage** marriages
NOUN 1 the relationship between a husband and wife. 2 ( RE ) Marriage is the act of marrying someone.
■ (sense 1) matrimony, wedlock

**marrow** marrows
NOUN a long, thick green-skinned fruit with cream-coloured flesh eaten as a vegetable.

**marry** marries marrying married
VERB 1 When a man and a woman marry, they become each other's husband and wife during a special ceremony. 2 When a clergyman or registrar marries a couple, he or she is in charge of their marriage ceremony.
**married** ADJECTIVE

**Mars**
NOUN Mars is the planet in the solar system which is fourth from the sun.

**marsh** marshes
NOUN an area of land which is permanently wet.

**marshal** marshals marshalling marshalled
VERB 1 If you marshal things or people, you gather them together and organize them E.G. Shipping was being marshalled into convoys. ▶ NOUN 2 an official who helps to organize a public event.

**marshmallow** marshmallows
NOUN a soft, spongy, pink or white sweet made using gelatine.

**marsupial** marsupials
*Said* "mar-**syoo**-pee-al" NOUN an animal that carries its young in a pouch. Koalas and kangaroos are marsupials.
🔲 from Greek *marsupion* meaning 'purse'

**martial**
*Said* "mar-shal" ADJECTIVE relating to or involving war or soldiers E.G. martial music.

**martial arts**
PLURAL NOUN The martial arts are the techniques of self-defence that come from the Far East, for example karate or judo.

**Martian** Martians
*Said* "mar-shan" NOUN an imaginary creature from the planet Mars.

**martyr** martyrs martyring martyred
NOUN 1 someone who suffers or is killed rather than change their beliefs. ▶ VERB 2 If someone is martyred, they are killed because of their beliefs.
**martyrdom** NOUN

**marvel** marvels marvelling marvelled
VERB 1 If you marvel at something, it fills you with surprise or admiration E.G. Modern designers can only marvel at his genius. ▶ NOUN 2 something that makes you feel great surprise or admiration E.G. a marvel of high technology.

**marvellous**
ADJECTIVE wonderful or excellent.
**marvellously** ADVERB

**Marxism**
NOUN Marxism is a political philosophy based on the writings of

Karl Marx. It states that society will develop towards communism through the struggle between different social classes.

**Marxist** ADJECTIVE or NOUN

**marzipan**

NOUN Marzipan is a paste made of almonds, sugar, and egg. It is put on top of cakes or used to make small sweets.

**mascara**

NOUN Mascara is a substance that can be used to colour eyelashes and make them look longer.

**mascot** mascots

NOUN a person, animal, or toy which is thought to bring good luck E.G. *Celtic's mascot, Hoopy the Huddle Hound.*

**masculine**

ADJECTIVE 1 typical of men, rather than women E.G. *the masculine world of motorsport.* 2 belonging to a particular class of nouns in some languages, such as French, German, and Latin.

**masculinity** NOUN

---

### What is Masculine?

**Masculine nouns** refer to male people and animals:

E.G. *The boy put on his coat.* ➤ *boy* is **masculine**

**Common nouns** may be either masculine or feminine. Other words in the sentence may tell us if they are male or female:

E.G. *The doctor parked <u>his</u> car.*
*The doctor parked <u>her</u> car.*

Also look at the grammar boxes at **gender**, **feminine** and **neuter**.

---

**mash** mashes mashing mashed

VERB If you mash vegetables, you crush them after they have been cooked.

**mask** masks masking masked

NOUN 1 something you wear over your face for protection or disguise E.G. *a surgical mask.* ➤ VERB 2 If you mask something, you cover it so that it is protected or cannot be seen.

**masochist** masochists

*Said "mass-so-kist"* NOUN someone who gets pleasure from their own suffering.

**masochism** NOUN

📖 named after the Austrian novelist Leopold von Sacher Masoch (1836–1895), who wrote about masochism

**mason** masons

NOUN a person who is skilled at making things with stone.

**masonry**

NOUN Masonry is pieces of stone which form part of a wall or building.

**masquerade** masquerades masquerading masqueraded

*Said "mass-ker-raid"* VERB If you masquerade as something, you pretend to be it E.G. *He masqueraded as a doctor.*

**mass** masses massing massed

NOUN 1 a large amount of something. 2 The masses are the ordinary people in society considered as a group E.G. *opera for the masses.* 3 In physics, the mass of an object is the amount of physical matter that it has. 4 In the Roman Catholic Church, Mass is a religious service in which people share bread and wine in remembrance of the death and resurrection of Jesus Christ.

a
b
c
d
e
f
g
h
i
j
k
l
m
n
o
p
q
r
s
t
u
v
w
x
y
z

LEarn the principLEs (princip<u>le</u>)    **SPELLING NOTE**

▶ ADJECTIVE **5** involving a large number of people E.G. *mass unemployment*.
▶ VERB **6** When people mass, they gather together in a large group.

**massacre** massacres massacring massacred
*Said "mass-ik-ker"* NOUN **1** the killing of a very large number of people in a violent and cruel way. ▶ VERB **2** To massacre people is to kill large numbers of them in a violent and cruel way.

**massage** massages massaging massaged
VERB **1** To massage someone is to rub their body in order to help them relax or to relieve pain. ▶ NOUN **2** A massage is treatment which involves rubbing the body.

**massive**
ADJECTIVE extremely large E.G. *a massive iceberg*.
**massively** ADVERB

**mass-produce** mass-produces mass-producing mass-produced
VERB To mass-produce something is to make it in large quantities E.G. *They began mass-producing cameras after the war*.

**mast** masts
NOUN the tall upright pole that supports the sails of a boat.

**master** masters mastering mastered
NOUN **1** a man who has authority over others, such as the employer of servants, or the owner of slaves or animals. **2** If you are master of a situation, you have control over it E.G. *He was master of his own destiny*. **3** a male teacher at some schools. ▶ VERB **4** If you master a difficult situation, you succeed in controlling it. **5** If you

master something, you learn how to do it properly E.G. *She found it easy to master the typewriter*.

**masterful**
ADJECTIVE showing control and authority.

**masterly**
ADJECTIVE extremely clever or well done E.G. *a masterly exhibition of batting*.

**mastermind** masterminds masterminding masterminded
VERB **1** If you mastermind a complicated activity, you plan and organize it. ▶ NOUN **2** The mastermind behind something is the person responsible for planning it.

**masterpiece** masterpieces
NOUN an extremely good painting or other work of art.

**masturbate** masturbates masturbating masturbated
VERB If someone masturbates, they stroke or rub their own genitals in order to get sexual pleasure.
**masturbation** NOUN

**mat** mats
NOUN **1** a small round or square piece of cloth, card, or plastic that is placed on a table to protect it from plates or glasses. **2** a small piece of carpet or other thick material that is placed on the floor.

**matador** matadors
NOUN a man who fights and tries to kill bulls as part of a public entertainment, especially in Spain. 🏛 from Spanish *matar* meaning 'to kill'

**match** matches matching matched
NOUN **1** an organized game of football, cricket, or some other sport.

**2** a small, thin stick of wood that produces a flame when you strike it against a rough surface. ▶ VERB **3** If one thing matches another, the two things look the same or have similar qualities.

**mate** mates mating mated
NOUN **1** INFORMAL Your mates are your friends. **2** The first mate on a ship is the officer who is next in importance to the captain. **3** An animal's mate is its sexual partner. ▶ VERB **4** When a male and female animal mate, they come together sexually in order to breed.

**material** materials
NOUN **1** Material is cloth. **2** a substance from which something is made E.G. *the materials to make red dye.* **3** The equipment for a particular activity can be referred to as materials E.G. *building materials.* **4** Material for a book, play, or film is the information or ideas on which it is based.
▶ ADJECTIVE **5** involving possessions and money E.G. *concerned with material comforts.*
**materially** ADVERB

**materialism**
NOUN Materialism is thinking that money and possessions are the most important things in life.
**materialistic** ADJECTIVE

**materialize** materializes materializing materialized; also spelt **materialise**
VERB If something materializes, it actually happens or appears E.G. *Fortunately, the attack did not materialize.*

**maternal**
ADJECTIVE relating to or involving a mother E.G. *her maternal instincts.*

**maternity**
ADJECTIVE relating to or involving pregnant women and birth E.G. *a maternity hospital.*

**mathematics**
NOUN Mathematics is the study of numbers, quantities, and shapes.
**mathematical** ADJECTIVE
**mathematically** ADVERB
**mathematician** NOUN

**maths**
NOUN Maths is mathematics.

**Matilda**
NOUN; OLD-FASHIONED In Australia, Matilda is the pack of belongings carried by a swagman in the bush. The word is now used only in the phrase 'waltzing Matilda', meaning to travel in the bush with few possessions.

**matinee** matinees
*Said* "mat-in-nay"; also spelt **matinée**
NOUN an afternoon performance of a play or film.

**matrimony**
NOUN; FORMAL Matrimony is marriage.
**matrimonial** ADJECTIVE

**matrix** matrices
*Said* "may-trix" NOUN **1** FORMAL the framework in which something grows and develops. **2** In maths, a matrix is a set of numbers or elements set out in rows and columns.

**matron** matrons
NOUN In a hospital, a senior nurse in charge of all the nursing staff used to be known as matron.

**matt**
ADJECTIVE A matt surface is dull rather than shiny E.G. *matt black plastic.*

a
b
c
d
e
f
g
h
i
j
k
l
m
n
o
p
q
r
s
t
u
v
w
x
y
z

**A B C D E F G H I J K L M N O P Q R S T U V W X Y Z**

**matted**
ADJECTIVE Hair that is matted is tangled with the strands sticking together.

**matter matters mattering mattered**
NOUN 1 something that you have to deal with. 2 Matter is any substance E.G. *The atom is the smallest divisible particle of matter.* 3 Books and magazines are reading matter. ▶ VERB 4 If something matters to you, it is important. ▶ PHRASE 5 If you ask **What's the matter?**, you are asking what is wrong.
▣ (sense 1) affair, business, situation, subject

**matter-of-fact**
ADJECTIVE showing no emotion.

**matting**
NOUN Matting is thick woven material such as rope or straw, used as a floor covering.

**mattress mattresses**
NOUN a large thick pad filled with springs or feathers that is put on a bed to make it comfortable.

**mature matures maturing matured**
VERB 1 When a child or young animal matures, it becomes an adult. 2 When something matures, it reaches complete development. ▶ ADJECTIVE 3 Mature means fully developed and emotionally balanced.
**maturely** ADVERB **maturity** NOUN

**maudlin**
ADJECTIVE Someone who is maudlin is sad and sentimental when they are drunk.

**maul mauls mauling mauled**
VERB If someone is mauled by an animal, they are savagely attacked

and badly injured by it.

**mausoleum mausoleums**
*Said* "maw-sal-lee-um" NOUN a building which contains the grave of a famous person.

**mauve**
*Rhymes with* "**grove**" NOUN or ADJECTIVE pale purple.

**maxim maxims**
NOUN a short saying which gives a rule for good or sensible behaviour E.G. *Instant action: that's my maxim.*

**maximize maximizes maximizing maximized;** also spelt **maximise**
VERB To maximize something is to make it as great or effective as possible E.G. *Their objective is to maximize profits.*

**maximum**
ADJECTIVE 1 The maximum amount is the most that is possible E.G. *the maximum recommended intake.* ▶ NOUN 2 The maximum is the most that is possible E.G. *a maximum of fifty men.*

**may**
VERB 1 If something may happen, it is possible that it will happen E.G. *It may happen quite soon.* 2 If someone may do something, they are allowed to do it E.G. *Please may I be excused?* 3 You can use 'may' when saying that, although something is true, something else is also true E.G. *This may be true, but it is only part of the story.* 4 FORMAL You also use 'may' to express a wish that something will happen E.G. *May you live to be a hundred.* ▶ NOUN 5 May is the fifth month of the year. It has 31 days.
▣ sense 5 is probably from *Maia*, a Roman goddess
☑ It used to be that you used *may*

instead of *can* when asking for or giving someone permission to do something: *you may leave the table.* Nowadays *may* is usually only used in polite questions: *may I open the window?*

**maybe**

ADVERB You use 'maybe' when you are stating a possibility that you are not certain about *E.G. Maybe I should lie about my age.*

**mayhem**

NOUN You can refer to a confused and chaotic situation as mayhem *E.G. There was complete mayhem in the classroom.*

**mayonnaise**

*Said* "may-on-**nayz**" NOUN Mayonnaise is a thick salad dressing made with egg yolks and oil.

**mayor mayors**

NOUN a person who has been elected to lead and represent the people of a town.

**maze mazes**

NOUN a system of complicated passages which it is difficult to find your way through *E.G. a maze of dark tunnels.*

**MBE MBEs**

NOUN a British honour granted by the King or Queen. MBE is an abbreviation for 'Member of the Order of the British Empire' *E.G. Ally McCoist, MBE.*

**MD**

an abbreviation for 'Doctor of Medicine' or 'Managing Director'.

**me**

PRONOUN A speaker or writer uses 'me' to refer to himself or herself.

**meadow meadows**

NOUN a field of grass.

**meagre**

*Said* "**mee**-ger" ADJECTIVE very small and poor *E.G. his meagre pension.*

**meal meals**

NOUN an occasion when people eat, or the food they eat at that time

**mealie mealies**; also spelt **mielie**

NOUN In South African English, mealie is maize or an ear of maize.

**mean means meaning meant; meaner meanest**

VERB 1 If you ask what something means, you want it explained to you. 2 If you mean what you say, you are serious *E.G. The boss means what he says.* 3 If something means a lot to you, it is important to you. 4 If one thing means another, it shows that the second thing is true or will happen *E.G. Major roadworks will mean long delays.* 5 If you mean to do something, you intend to do it *E.G. I meant to phone you, but didn't have time.* 6 If something is meant to be true, it is supposed to be true *E.G. I found a road that wasn't meant to be there.* ▶ ADJECTIVE 7 Someone who is mean is unwilling to spend much money. 8 Someone who is mean is unkind or cruel *E.G. He apologized for being so mean to her.* ▶ NOUN 9 A means of doing something is a method or object which makes it possible *E.G. The tests were marked by means of a computer.* ▶ PLURAL NOUN 10 Someone's means are their money and income *E.G. He's obviously a man of means.* ▶ NOUN 11 In mathematics, the mean is the average of a set of numbers.

**meanness** NOUN

▤ (sense 5) aim, intend, plan
▤ (sense 7) miserly, parsimonious, stingy, tight-fisted

a b c d e f g h i j k l **m** n o p q r s t u v w x y z

A
B
C
D
E
F
G
H
I
J
K
**M**
N
O
P
Q
R
S
T
U
V
W
X
Y
Z

**meander** meanders meandering meandered

*Said "mee-an-der"* VERB If a road or river meanders, it has a lot of bends in it.

**meaning** meanings

NOUN 1 The meaning of a word, expression, or gesture is what it refers to or expresses. 2 The meaning of what someone says, or of a book or a film, is the thoughts or ideas that it is intended to express. 3 If something has meaning, it seems to be worthwhile and to have real purpose.

**meaningful** ADJECTIVE **meaningfully** ADVERB **meaningless** ADJECTIVE

■ (sense 1) gist, sense, significance

**means test** means tests

NOUN a check of a person's money and income to see whether they need money or benefits from the government or other organization.

**meantime**

PHRASE **In the meantime** means in the period of time between two events E.G. I'll call the nurse; in the meantime, you must rest.

**meanwhile**

ADVERB 1 Meanwhile means while something else is happening. ▶ NOUN 2 Meanwhile also means the time between two events.

**measles**

NOUN Measles is an infectious illness in which you have red spots on your skin.

**measly**

ADJECTIVE; *INFORMAL* very small or inadequate E.G. a measly ten cents.

**measure** measures measuring measured

VERB 1 (MATHS) When you measure

something, you find out how big it is by using a ruler or tape measure. 2 (MATHS) If something measures a particular distance, its length or depth is that distance E.G. slivers of glass measuring a few millimetres across. ▶ NOUN 3 A measure of something is a certain amount of it E.G. There has been a measure of agreement. 4 (MATHS) a unit in which size, speed, or depth is expressed. 5 Measures are actions carried out to achieve a particular result E.G. Tough measures are needed to maintain order.

**measurement** NOUN

**measured**

ADJECTIVE careful and deliberate E.G. walking at the same measured pace.

**measurement** measurements

NOUN 1 the result that you obtain when you measure something. 2 Measurement is the activity of measuring something. 3 Your measurements are the sizes of your chest, waist, and hips that you use to buy the correct size of clothes.

**meat** meats

NOUN Meat is the flesh of animals that is cooked and eaten.

**meaty** ADJECTIVE

**Mecca**

NOUN 1 Mecca is the holiest city of Islam, to which many Muslims make pilgrimages. 2 If a place is a mecca for people of a particular kind, many of them go there because it is of special interest to them E.G. The island is a mecca for bird lovers.

☑ Most Muslims dislike this form and use the Arabic *Makkah*.

**mechanic** mechanics

NOUN 1 a person who repairs and

maintains engines and machines.
▶ PLURAL NOUN **2** The mechanics of
something are the way in which it
works or is done E.G. *the mechanics of
accounting.* ▶ NOUN **3** Mechanics is,
also the scientific study of movement
and the forces that affect objects.

**mechanical**
ADJECTIVE **1** A mechanical device has
moving parts and is used to do a
physical task. **2** A mechanical action
is done automatically without
thinking about it E.G. *He gave a
mechanical smile.*
**mechanically** ADVERB

**mechanism mechanisms**
NOUN **1** a part of a machine that does
a particular task E.G. *a locking
mechanism.* **2** part of your behaviour
that is automatic E.G. *the body's
defence mechanisms.*

**medal medals**
NOUN a small disc of metal given as an
award for bravery or as a prize for sport.

**medallion medallions**
NOUN a round piece of metal worn as
an ornament on a chain round the
neck.

**medallist medallists**
NOUN a person who has won a medal
in sport E.G. *a gold medallist at the
Olympics.*

**meddle meddles meddling
meddled**
VERB To meddle is to interfere and try
to change things without being
asked.

**media**
PLURAL NOUN You can refer to the
television, radio, and newspapers as
the media.

☑ Although *media* is a plural noun, it
is becoming more common for it

to be used as a singular: *the media is
obsessed with violence.*

**mediaeval**
another spelling of **medieval**.

**median medians**
*Said "**mee-dee-an**"* ADJECTIVE **1** The
median value of a set is the middle
value when the set is arranged in
order. ▶ NOUN **2** In geometry, a straight
line drawn from one of the angles of
a triangle to the middle point of the
opposite side.

**mediate mediates mediating
mediated**
VERB If you mediate between two
groups, you try to settle a dispute
between them.
**mediation** NOUN    **mediator** NOUN

**medical medicals**
ADJECTIVE **1** relating to the prevention
and treatment of illness and injuries.
▶ NOUN **2** a thorough examination of
your body by a doctor.
**medically** ADVERB

**medication medications**
NOUN Medication is a substance that
is used to treat illness.

**medicinal**
ADJECTIVE relating to the treatment of
illness E.G. *a valuable medicinal herb.*

**medicine medicines**
NOUN ⟨PE⟩ **1** Medicine is the
treatment of illness and injuries by
doctors and nurses. **2** a substance
that you drink or swallow to help
cure an illness.

**medieval** or **mediaeval**
*Said "**med-dee-ee-vul**"* ADJECTIVE
relating to the period between
about 1100 AD and 1500 AD,
especially in Europe.
📖 from Latin *medium aevum*
meaning 'the middle age'

a b c d e f g h i j k l **m** n o p q r s t u v w x y z

A B C D E F G H I J K L **M** N O P Q R S T U V W X Y Z

**mediocre**
Said "meed-dee-oh-ker" ADJECTIVE of rather poor quality E.G. a mediocre string of performances.
**mediocrity** NOUN

**meditate meditates meditating meditated**
VERB 1 If you meditate on something, you think about it very deeply. 2 If you meditate, you remain in a calm, silent state for a period of time, often as part of a religious training.
**meditation** NOUN

**Mediterranean**
NOUN 1 The Mediterranean is the large sea between southern Europe and northern Africa. ► ADJECTIVE 2 relating to or typical of the Mediterranean or the European countries adjoining it.

**medium mediums** or **media**
ADJECTIVE 1 If something is of medium size or degree, it is neither large nor small E.G. a medium sized hotel. ► NOUN 2 a means that you use to communicate something E.G. the medium of television. 3 a person who claims to be able to speak to the dead and to receive messages from them.

**medley medleys**
NOUN 1 a mixture of different things creating an interesting effect. 2 a number of different songs or tunes sung or played one after the other.

**meek meeker meekest**
ADJECTIVE A meek person is timid and does what other people say.
**meekly** ADVERB
■ submissive, timid

**meet meets meeting met**
VERB 1 If you meet someone, you happen to be in the same place as them. 2 If you meet a visitor you go

to be with them when they arrive. 3 When a group of people meet, they gather together for a purpose. 4 If something meets a need, it can fulfil it E.G. services intended to meet the needs of the elderly. 5 If something meets with a particular reaction, it gets that reaction from people E.G. I was met with silence.

**meeting meetings**
NOUN 1 an event in which people discuss proposals and make decisions together. 2 what happens when you meet someone.

**megabyte megabytes**
NOUN (ICT) a unit of storage in a computer, equal to 1 048 576 bytes.

**melaleuca melaleucas**
Said "mel-a-loo-ka" NOUN an Australian tree or shrub that has black branches and a white trunk.

**melancholy**
ADJECTIVE or NOUN If you feel melancholy, you feel sad.

**mêlée mêlées**
Said "mel-lay" NOUN a situation where there are a lot of people rushing around.

**mellow mellower mellowest; mellows mellowing mellowed**
ADJECTIVE 1 Mellow light is soft and golden. 2 A mellow sound is smooth and pleasant to listen to E.G. his mellow clarinet. ► VERB 3 If someone mellows, they become more pleasant or relaxed E.G. He certainly hasn't mellowed with age.

**melodic**
ADJECTIVE relating to melody.

**melodious**
ADJECTIVE pleasant to listen to E.G. soft melodious music.

# melodrama >> memory

**melodrama melodramas**
NOUN a story or play in which people's emotions are exaggerated.

**melodramatic**
ADJECTIVE behaving in an exaggerated, emotional way.
■ histrionic, overdramatic, theatrical

**melody melodies**
NOUN (MUSIC) a tune.

**melon melons**
NOUN a large, juicy fruit with a green or yellow skin and many seeds inside.

**melt melts melting melted**
VERB 1 When something melts or when you melt it, it changes from a solid to a liquid because it has been heated. 2 If something melts, it disappears E.G. *The crowd melted away… Her inhibitions melted.*

**member members**
NOUN 1 A member of a group is one of the people or things belonging to the group E.G. *members of the family.* 2 A member of an organization is a person who has joined the organization. ▶ ADJECTIVE 3 A country belonging to an international organization is called a member country or a member state.

**Member of Parliament Members of Parliament**
NOUN a person who has been elected to represent people in a country's parliament.

**membership**
NOUN 1 Membership of an organization is the state of being a member of it. 2 The people who belong to an organization are its membership.

**membrane membranes**
NOUN a very thin piece of skin or tissue which connects or covers plant or animal organs or cells E.G. *the nasal membrane.*

**memento mementos**
NOUN an object which you keep because it reminds you of a person or a special occasion E.G. *a lasting memento of their romance.*

**memo memos**
NOUN a note from one person to another within the same organization. Memo is short for 'memorandum'.

**memoirs**
*Said* "**mem**-wahrz" PLURAL NOUN If someone writes their memoirs, they write a book about their life and experiences.

**memorable**
ADJECTIVE If something is memorable, it is likely to be remembered because it is special or unusual E.G. *a memorable victory.*
**memorably** ADVERB

**memorandum memorandums or memoranda**
NOUN a memo.

**memorial memorials**
NOUN 1 a structure built to remind people of a famous person or event E.G. *a war memorial.* ▶ ADJECTIVE 2 A memorial event or prize is in honour of someone who has died, so that they will be remembered.

**memory memories**
NOUN 1 Your memory is your ability to remember things. 2 something you remember about the past E.G. *memories of their school days.* 3 (ICT) the part in which information is stored in a computer.
■ (sense 1) recall, recollection, remembrance

a b c d e f g h i j k l **m** n o p q r s t u v w x y z

'i' before 'e' except after 'c' **SPELLING NOTE**

**men**
the plural of **man**.

**menace** menaces menacing menaced
NOUN **1** someone or something that is likely to cause serious harm E.G. *the menace of drugs in sport*. **2** Menace is the quality of being threatening E.G. *an atmosphere of menace*. ▶ VERB **3** If someone or something menaces you, they threaten to harm you.
**menacingly** ADVERB

**menagerie** menageries
*Said* "men-**naj**-er-ree" NOUN a collection of different wild animals.
📖 from French *menagerie* meaning 'household management', which used to include the care of domestic animals

**mend** mends mending mended
VERB If you mend something that is broken, you repair it.

**menial**
ADJECTIVE Menial work is boring and tiring and the people who do it have low status.

**meningitis**
NOUN Meningitis is a serious infectious illness which affects your brain and spinal cord.

**menopause**
NOUN The menopause is the time during which a woman gradually stops menstruating. This usually happens when she is about fifty.

**menorah** menorahs
*Said* "mi-**naw**-rah" NOUN a candelabra that usually has seven parts and is used in Jewish temples.

**menstruate** menstruates menstruating menstruated
VERB When a woman menstruates, blood comes from her womb. This normally happens once a month.

**menstruation** NOUN **menstrual** ADJECTIVE

**-ment**
SUFFIX '-ment' forms nouns which refer to a state or a feeling E.G. *contentment… resentment*.
📖 from Latin suffix *-mentum*

**mental**
ADJECTIVE **1** relating to the process of thinking or intelligence E.G. *mental arithmetic*. **2** relating to the health of the mind E.G. *mental health*.
**mentally** ADVERB

**mentality** mentalities
NOUN an attitude or way of thinking E.G. *the traditional military mentality*.

**mention** mentions mentioning mentioned
VERB **1** If you mention something, you talk about it briefly. ▶ NOUN **2** a brief comment about someone or something E.G. *He made no mention of his criminal past*.
■ (sense 1) bring up, refer to, touch upon

**mentor** mentors
NOUN Someone's mentor is a person who teaches them and gives them advice.

**menu** menus
NOUN **1** a list of the foods you can eat in a restaurant. **2** a list of different options shown on a computer screen which the user must choose from.

**MEP** MEPs
NOUN an abbreviation for 'Member of the European Parliament': a person who has been elected to represent people in the European Parliament.

**mercenary** mercenaries
NOUN **1** a soldier who is paid to fight for a foreign country. ▶ ADJECTIVE **2** Someone who is mercenary is mainly interested in getting money.

**merchandise**

NOUN; *FORMAL* Merchandise is goods that are sold *E.G. He had left me with more merchandise than I could sell.*

**merchant** merchants

NOUN a trader who imports and exports goods *E.G. a coal merchant.*

**merchant navy**

NOUN The merchant navy is the boats and sailors involved in carrying goods for trade.

**merciful**

ADJECTIVE **1** considered to be fortunate as a relief from suffering *E.G. Death came as a merciful release.* **2** showing kindness and forgiveness.

**mercifully** ADVERB

■ (sense 2) compassionate, humane, kind

**merciless**

ADJECTIVE showing no kindness or forgiveness.

**mercilessly** ADVERB

■ cruel, heartless, ruthless

**mercury**

NOUN **1** Mercury is a silver-coloured metallic element that is liquid at room temperature. It is used in thermometers. **2** Mercury is also the planet in the solar system which is nearest to the sun.

**mercy** mercies

NOUN If you show mercy, you show kindness and forgiveness and do not punish someone as severely as you could.

■ compassion, kindness, pity

**mere** merest

ADJECTIVE used to emphasize how unimportant or small something is *E.G. It's a mere 7-minute journey by boat.*

**merely** ADVERB

**merge** merges merging merged

VERB When two things merge, they combine together to make one thing *E.G. The firms merged in 1983.*

**merger** NOUN

**meringue** meringues

*Said* "mer-**rang**" NOUN a type of crisp, sweet cake made with egg whites and sugar.

**merino** merinos

*Said* "mer-**ree**-no" NOUN a breed of sheep, common in Australia and New Zealand, with long, fine wool.

**merit** merits meriting merited

NOUN **1** If something has merit, it is good or worthwhile. **2** The merits of something are its advantages or good qualities. ► VERB **3** If something merits a particular treatment, it deserves that treatment *E.G. He merits a place in the team.*

**mermaid** mermaids

NOUN In stories, a mermaid is a woman with a fish's tail instead of legs, who lives in the sea.

**merry** merrier merriest

ADJECTIVE happy and cheerful *E.G. He was, for all his shyness, a merry man.*

**merrily** ADVERB

**merry-go-round** merry-go-rounds

NOUN a large rotating platform with models of animals or vehicles on it, on which children ride at a fair.

**mesh**

NOUN Mesh is threads of wire or plastic twisted together like a net *E.G. a fence made of wire mesh.*

**mess** messes messing messed

NOUN **1** something untidy. **2** a situation which is full of problems and trouble. **3** a room or building in which members of the armed forces

an E**L**egant ang**EL** (ang**el**)    SPELLING NOTE

eat *E.G. the officers' mess.* ▶ VERB **4** If you mess about or mess around, you do things without any particular purpose. **5** If you mess something up, you spoil it or do it wrong.
**messy** ADJECTIVE

**message messages**
NOUN **1** a piece of information or a request that you send someone or leave for them. **2** an idea that someone tries to communicate to people, for example in a play or a speech *E.G. the story's anti-drugs message.*

**messaging**
NOUN Messaging or text messaging is the sending and receiving of short pieces of information between mobile phones, using both letters and numbers to produce shortened forms of words.

**messenger messengers**
NOUN someone who takes a message to someone for someone else.
⬛ courier, emissary, envoy

**Messiah**
*Said* "miss-**eye**-ah" PROPER NOUN **1** For Jews, the Messiah is the king of the Jews who will be sent by God. **2** For Christians, the Messiah is Jesus Christ.
🔲 from Hebrew *mashiach* meaning 'anointed'

**Messrs**
*Said* "**mes**-serz" Messrs is the plural of **Mr.** It is often used in the names of businesses *E.G. Messrs Brown and Humberley, Solicitors.*

**met**
the past tense and past participle of **meet**.

**metabolism metabolisms**
NOUN Your metabolism is the chemical processes in your body that use food for growth and energy.

**metabolic** ADJECTIVE

**metal metals**
NOUN Metal is a chemical element such as iron, steel, copper, or lead. Metals are good conductors of heat and electricity.
**metallic** ADJECTIVE

**metamorphic**
ADJECTIVE Metamorphic rock is rock that has been altered from its original state by heat or pressure.

**metamorphosis**
**metamorphoses**
*Said* "met-am-**mor**-fiss-iss" NOUN; FORMAL When a metamorphosis occurs, a person or thing changes into something completely different *E.G. the metamorphosis of a larva into an insect.*

**metaphor metaphors**
NOUN ( ENGLISH ) an imaginative way of describing something as another thing, and so suggesting that it has the typical qualities of that other thing. For example, if you wanted to say that someone is shy, you might say they are a mouse.
**metaphorical** ADJECTIVE
**metaphorically** ADVERB

**meteor meteors**
NOUN a piece of rock or metal that burns very brightly when it enters the earth's atmosphere from space.

**meteoric**
ADJECTIVE A meteoric rise to power or success happens very quickly.

**meteorite meteorites**
NOUN a piece of rock from space that has landed on earth.

**meteorological**
ADJECTIVE relating to or involving the weather or weather forecasting.
**meteorology** NOUN

**meter** meters

NOUN a device that measures and records something E.G. *a gas meter.*

**methane**

*Said "mee-thane"* NOUN Methane is a colourless gas with no smell that is found in coal gas and produced by decaying vegetable matter. It burns easily and can be used as a fuel.

**method** methods

NOUN 1 a particular way of doing something E.G. *the traditional method of making wine.* 2 (SCIENCE) a way that an experiment or test is carried out E.G. *Describe the method as well as the result obtained.*

**methodical**

ADJECTIVE Someone who is methodical does things carefully and in an organized way.

**methodically** ADVERB

**Methodist** Methodists

NOUN or ADJECTIVE someone who belongs to the Methodist Church, a Protestant church whose members worship God in a way begun by John Wesley and his followers.

**meticulous**

ADJECTIVE A meticulous person does things very carefully and with great attention to detail.

**meticulously** ADVERB

**metre** metres

NOUN 1 (MATHS) a unit of length equal to 100 centimetres. 2 In poetry, metre is the rhythmic arrangement of words and syllables.

**metric**

ADJECTIVE relating to the system of measurement that uses metres, grams, and litres.

**metropolis** metropolises

NOUN a very large city.

🔲 from Greek *mētēr* + *polis* meaning 'mother city'

**metropolitan**

ADJECTIVE relating or belonging to a large, busy city E.G. *metropolitan districts.*

**mettle**

NOUN If you are on your mettle, you are ready to do something as well as you can because you know you are being tested or challenged.

**mew** mews mewing mewed

VERB 1 When a cat mews, it makes a short high-pitched noise. ▶ NOUN 2 the short high-pitched sound that a cat makes. 3 A mews is a quiet yard or street surrounded by houses.

**Mexican** Mexicans

ADJECTIVE 1 belonging or relating to Mexico. ▶ NOUN 2 someone who comes from Mexico.

**mg**

an abbreviation for 'milligrams'.

**miasma** miasmas or miasmata

NOUN an unhealthy or unpleasant atmosphere, especially one caused by decaying things.

**mice**

the plural of mouse.

**micro-**

PREFIX 'Micro-' means very small.

🔲 from Greek *micros* meaning 'small'

**microchip** microchips

NOUN a small piece of silicon on which electronic circuits for a computer are printed.

**microphone** microphones

NOUN a device that is used to make sounds louder or to record them on a tape recorder.

**microprocessor** microprocessors

NOUN a microchip which can be

A Rude Idiot Thought He Might Eat Toffee In Church (<u>arithmetic</u>)     SPELLING NOTE

A
B
C
D
E
F
G
H
I
J
K
L
**M**
N
O
P
Q
R
S
T
U
V
W
X
Y
Z

programmed to do a large number of tasks or calculations.

**microscope microscopes**
NOUN a piece of equipment which magnifies very small objects so that you can study them.

**microscopic**
ADJECTIVE very small indeed E.G. *microscopic parasites.*

**microwave microwaves**
NOUN A microwave or microwave oven is a type of oven which cooks food very quickly by radiation.

**mid-**
PREFIX 'Mid-' is used to form words that refer to the middle part of a place or period of time E.G. *mid-Atlantic… the mid-70s.*
▨ from Old English

**midday**
NOUN Midday is twelve o'clock in the middle of the day.

**middle middles**
NOUN 1 The middle of something is the part furthest from the edges, ends, or outside surface. ▶ ADJECTIVE
2 The middle one in a series or a row is the one that has an equal number of people or things each side of it E.G. *the middle house.*

**middle age**
NOUN Middle age is the period of your life when you are between about 40 and 60 years old.
**middle-aged** ADJECTIVE

**Middle Ages**
PLURAL NOUN In European history, the Middle Ages were the period between about 1100 AD and 1500 AD.

**middle class middle classes**
NOUN The middle classes are the people in a society who are not working class or upper class, for

example managers and lawyers.

**Middle East**
NOUN The Middle East consists of Iran and the countries in Asia to the west and south-west of Iran.

**Middle English**
NOUN Middle English was the English language from about 1100 AD until about 1450 AD.

**middle-of-the-road**
ADJECTIVE Middle-of-the-road opinions are moderate.

**middle school middle schools**
NOUN In England and Wales, a middle school is for children aged between about 8 and 12.

**middling**
ADJECTIVE of average quality or ability.

**midge midges**
NOUN a small flying insect which can bite people.

**midget midgets**
NOUN a very short person.

**midnight**
NOUN Midnight is twelve o'clock at night.

**midriff midriffs**
NOUN the middle of your body between your waist and your chest.

**midst**
NOUN If you are in the midst of a crowd or an event, you are in the middle of it.

**midsummer**
ADJECTIVE relating to the period in the middle of summer E.G. *a lovely midsummer morning in July.*

**midway**
ADVERB in the middle of a distance or period of time E.G. *They scored midway through the second half.*

**midwife midwives**
NOUN a nurse who is trained to help

women at the birth of a baby.
**midwifery** NOUN
**might**
VERB 1 If you say something might happen, you mean that it is possible that it will happen E.G. *I might stay a while.* 2 If you say that someone might do something, you are suggesting that they do it E.G. *You might like to go and see it.* 3 Might is also the past tense of **may.** ▶ NOUN 4 LITERARY Might is strength or power E.G. *the full might of the Navy.*
☑ You can use **might** or **may** to make a very polite request: *might I ask a favour?… may I ask a favour?*
**mightily**
ADVERB; LITERARY to a great degree or extent E.G. *I was mightily relieved by the decision.*
**mighty mightier mightiest**
ADJECTIVE; LITERARY very powerful or strong E.G. *a mighty army on the march.*
**migraine migraines**
*Said "mee-grane or my-grane"* NOUN a severe headache that makes you feel very ill.
🏛 from Latin *hemicrania* meaning 'pain in half the head'
**migrate migrates migrating migrated**
VERB 1 If people migrate, they move from one place to another, especially to find work. 2 When birds or animals migrate, they move at a particular season to a different place, usually to breed or to find new feeding grounds E.G. *the birds migrate each year to Mexico.*
**migration** NOUN **migratory** ADJECTIVE **migrant** NOUN or ADJECTIVE

**mike mikes**
NOUN; INFORMAL a microphone.
**mild milder mildest**
ADJECTIVE 1 Something that is mild is not strong and does not have any powerful or damaging effects E.G. *a mild shampoo.* 2 Someone who is mild is gentle and kind. 3 Mild weather is warmer than usual E.G. *The region has mild winters and hot summers.* 4 Mild emotions or attitudes are not very great or extreme E.G. *mild surprise.*
**mildly** ADVERB
**mildew**
NOUN Mildew is a soft white fungus that grows on things when they are warm and damp.
**mile miles**
NOUN a unit of distance equal to 1760 yards or about 1.6 kilometres.
🏛 from Latin *milia passuum* meaning 'a thousand paces'
**mileage mileages**
NOUN 1 Your mileage is the distance that you have travelled, measured in miles. 2 The amount of mileage that you get out of something is how useful it is to you.
**militant militants**
ADJECTIVE 1 A militant person is very active in trying to bring about extreme political or social change E.G. *a militant socialist.* ▶ NOUN 2 a person who tries to bring about extreme political or social change.
**militancy** NOUN
**military**
ADJECTIVE 1 related to or involving the armed forces of a country E.G. *military bases.* ▶ NOUN 2 The military are the armed forces of a country.
**militarily** ADVERB

a b c d e f g h i j k l m n o p q r s t u v w x y z

A
B
C
D
E
F
G
H
I
J
K
L
**M**
N
O
P
Q
R
S
T
U
V
W
X
Y
Z

**militia** militias
*Said* "mil-*lish-a*" NOUN an organization that operates like an army but whose members are not professional soldiers.

**milk** milks milking milked
NOUN **1** Milk is the white liquid produced by female cows, goats, and some other animals to feed their young. People drink milk and use it to make butter, cheese, and yogurt. **2** Milk is also the white liquid that a baby drinks from its mother's breasts. ▶ VERB **3** When someone milks a cow or a goat, they get milk from it by pulling its udders. **4** If you milk a situation, you get as much personal gain from it as possible *E.G. They milked money from a hospital charity.*

**milk tooth** milk teeth
NOUN Your milk teeth are your first teeth which fall out and are replaced by the permanent set.

**milky** milkier milkiest
ADJECTIVE **1** pale creamy white *E.G. milky white skin.* **2** containing a lot of milk *E.G. a large mug of milky coffee.*

**Milky Way**
NOUN The Milky Way is a strip of stars clustered closely together, appearing as a pale band in the sky.

**mill** mills
NOUN **1** a building where grain is crushed to make flour. **2** a factory for making materials such as steel, wool, or cotton. **3** a small device for grinding coffee or spices into powder *E.G. a pepper mill.*

**millennium** millennia or millenniums
NOUN; FORMAL a period of 1000 years.

**millennium bug**
NOUN a computer software problem

caused by the change of date at the start of the year 2000.

**miller** millers
NOUN the person who operates a flour mill.

**milligram** milligrams
NOUN a unit of weight equal to one thousandth of a gram.

**millilitre** millilitres
NOUN a unit of liquid volume equal to one thousandth of a litre.

**millimetre** millimetres
NOUN a unit of length equal to a tenth of a centimetre or one thousandth of a metre.

**million** millions
the number 1,000,000.
**millionth**

**millionaire** millionaires
NOUN a very rich person who has property worth millions of pounds or dollars.

**millstone** millstones
PHRASE If something is **a millstone round your neck**, it is an unpleasant problem or responsibility you cannot escape from.

**mime** mimes miming mimed
NOUN **1** Mime is the use of movements and gestures to express something or to tell a story without using speech. ▶ VERB **2** If you mime something, you describe or express it using mime.

**mimic** mimics mimicking mimicked
VERB **1** If you mimic someone's actions or voice, you imitate them in an amusing way. ▶ NOUN **2** a person who can imitate other people.
**mimicry** NOUN

**minaret** minarets
NOUN a tall, thin tower on a mosque.

**mince** minces mincing minced

NOUN **1** Mince is meat which has been chopped into very small pieces in a special machine. ▶ VERB **2** If you mince meat, you chop it into very small pieces. **3** To mince about is to walk with small quick steps in an affected, effeminate way.

**mind** minds minding minded

NOUN **1** Your mind is your ability to think, together with all the thoughts you have and your memory. ▶ PHRASE **2** If you **change your mind**, you change a decision that you have made or an opinion that you have. ▶ VERB **3** If you do not mind something, you are not annoyed by it or bothered about it. **4** If you say that you wouldn't mind something, you mean that you would quite like it E.G. *I wouldn't mind a drink*. **5** If you mind a child or mind something for someone, you look after it for a while E.G. *My mother is minding the office*.

**mindful**

ADJECTIVE; FORMAL If you are mindful of something, you think about it carefully before taking action E.G. *mindful of their needs*.

**mindless**

ADJECTIVE **1** Mindless actions are regarded as stupid and destructive E.G. *mindless violence*. **2** A mindless job or activity is simple and repetitive.

**mine** mines mining mined

PRONOUN **1** 'Mine' refers to something belonging or relating to the person who is speaking or writing E.G. *a friend of mine*. ▶ NOUN **2** a series of holes or tunnels in the ground from which diamonds, coal, or other

minerals are dug out E.G. *a diamond mine*. **3** a bomb hidden in the ground or underwater, which explodes when people or things touch it. ▶ VERB **4** To mine diamonds, coal, or other minerals is to obtain these substances from underneath the ground.

**miner** NOUN **mining** NOUN

**minefield** minefields

NOUN an area of land or water where mines have been hidden.

**mineral** minerals

NOUN ( D & T ) a substance such as tin, salt, or coal that is formed naturally in rocks and in the earth E.G. *rich mineral deposits*.

**mineral water**

NOUN Mineral water is water which comes from a natural spring.

**minestrone**

*Said* "min-nes-**strone**-ee" NOUN Minestrone is soup containing small pieces of vegetable and pasta.
🏛 from Italian *minestrare* meaning 'to serve'

**minesweeper** minesweepers

NOUN a ship for clearing away underwater mines.

**mingle** mingles mingling mingled

VERB If things mingle, they become mixed together E.G. *His cries mingled with theirs*.

**mini-**

PREFIX 'Mini-' is used to form nouns referring to something smaller or less important than similar things E.G. *a TV mini-series*.

**miniature** miniatures

*Said* "min-nit-cher" ADJECTIVE **1** a tiny copy of something much larger. ▶ NOUN **2** a very small detailed painting, often of a person.

a
b
c
d
e
f
g
h
i
j
k
l
**m**
n
o
p
q
r
s
t
u
v
w
x
y
z

A
B
C
D
E
F
G
H
I
J
K
L
M
N
O
P
Q
R
S
T
U
V
W
X
Y
Z

**minibus** minibuses
NOUN a van with seats in the back which is used as a small bus.

**minim** minims
NOUN (MUSIC) a musical note (♩) that has a time value equal to half a semibreve. In the United States and Canada, a minim is called a half note.

**minimal**
ADJECTIVE very small in quality, quantity, or degree E.G. *He has minimal experience.*
**minimally** ADVERB

**minimize** minimizes minimizing minimized; also spelt **minimise**.
VERB If you minimize something, you reduce it to the smallest amount possible E.G. *His route was changed to minimize jet lag.*

**minimum**
ADJECTIVE 1 The minimum amount is the smallest amount that is possible E.G. *a minimum wage.* ▶ NOUN 2 The minimum is the smallest amount that is possible E.G. *a minimum of three weeks.*

**minister** ministers
NOUN 1 A minister is a person who is in charge of a particular government department E.G. *Portugal's deputy foreign minister.* 2 A minister in a Protestant church is a member of the clergy.

**ministerial**
ADJECTIVE relating to a government minister or ministry E.G. *ministerial duties.*

**ministry** ministries
NOUN 1 a government department that deals with a particular area of work E.G. *the Ministry of Defence.* 2 Members of the clergy can be referred to as the ministry E.G. *Her son is in the ministry.*

**mink** minks
NOUN Mink is an expensive fur used to make coats or hats.

**minnow** minnows
NOUN a very small freshwater fish.

**minor** minors
ADJECTIVE 1 not as important or serious as other things E.G. *a minor injury.* 2 (MUSIC) A minor key is one of the keys in which most European music is written. ▶ NOUN 3 FORMAL a young person under the age of 18 E.G. *laws concerning the employment of minors.*

**minority** minorities
NOUN 1 The minority of people or things in a group is a number of them forming less than half of the whole E.G. *Only a minority of people want this.* 2 A minority is a group of people of a particular race or religion living in a place where most people are of a different race or religion E.G. *ethnic minorities.*

**minstrel** minstrels
NOUN a singer and entertainer in medieval times.

**mint** mints minting minted
NOUN 1 Mint is a herb used for flavouring in cooking. 2 a peppermint-flavoured sweet. 3 The mint is the place where the official coins of a country are made. ▶ VERB 4 When coins or medals are minted, they are made. ▶ ADJECTIVE 5 If something is in mint condition, it is in very good condition, like new.

**minus** (MATHS) 1 You use 'minus' to show that one number is being subtracted from another E.G. *Ten minus six equals four.* ADJECTIVE 2 'Minus' is used when

talking about temperatures below
0°C or 0°F.

**minuscule**
Said "min-nus-kyool" ADJECTIVE very
small indeed.

**minute** minutes minuting
minuted
Said "min-nit" NOUN 1 a unit of time
equal to sixty seconds. 2 The minutes
of a meeting are the written records
of what was said and decided. ▶ VERB
3 To minute a meeting is to write the
official notes of it.

**minute**
Said "my-nyoot" ADJECTIVE extremely
small E.G. a minute amount of
pesticide.
**minutely** ADVERB

**minutiae**
Said "my-nyoo-shee-aye" PLURAL NOUN;
FORMAL Minutiae are small,
unimportant details.

**miracle** miracles
NOUN 1 RE a wonderful and
surprising event, believed to have
been caused by God. 2 any very
surprising and fortunate event E.G.
My father got a job. It was a miracle.
**miraculous** ADJECTIVE
**miraculously** ADVERB

**mirage** mirages
Said "mir-ahj" NOUN an image which
you can see in the distance in very
hot weather, but which does not
actually exist.

**mire**
NOUN; LITERARY Mire is swampy ground
or mud.

**mirror** mirrors mirroring
mirrored
NOUN 1 a piece of glass which reflects
light and in which you can see your
reflection. ▶ VERB 2 To mirror

something is to have similar features
to it E.G. His own shock was mirrored
on her face.

**mirth**
NOUN; LITERARY Mirth is great
amusement and laughter.

**mis-**
PREFIX 'Mis-' means 'wrong' or 'false' E.G.
misbehaviour… misconception.
🔲 from Old English

**misbehave** misbehaves
misbehaving misbehaved
VERB If a child misbehaves, he or she is
naughty or behaves badly.
**misbehaviour** NOUN

**miscarriage** miscarriages
NOUN 1 If a woman has a miscarriage
she gives birth to a baby before it is
properly formed and it dies. 2 A
miscarriage of justice is a wrong
decision made by a court, which
causes an innocent person to be
punished.

**miscellaneous**
ADJECTIVE A miscellaneous group is
made up of people or things that are
different from each other.

**mischief**
NOUN Mischief is eagerness to have
fun by teasing people or playing tricks.
**mischievous** ADJECTIVE

**misconception** misconceptions
NOUN a wrong idea about something
E.G. Another misconception is that
cancer is infectious.

**misconduct**
NOUN Misconduct is bad or
unacceptable behaviour by a
professional person E.G. The Football
Association found him guilty of
misconduct.

**misdemeanour** misdemeanours
Said "miss-dem-mee-ner" NOUN; FORMAL

a
b
c
d
e
f
g
h
i
j
k
l
m
n
o
p
q
r
s
t
u
v
w
x
y
z

I want to see (C) your licenCe (licence)    **SPELLING NOTE**

**miser** misers
NOUN a person who enjoys saving money but hates spending it.
**miserly** ADJECTIVE

**miserable**
ADJECTIVE 1 If you are miserable, you are very unhappy. 2 If a place or a situation is miserable, it makes you feel depressed E.G. *a miserable little flat*.
**miserably** ADVERB
■ (sense 1) dejected, unhappy, wretched
■ (sense 2) gloomy, wretched

**misery** miseries
NOUN Misery is great unhappiness.

**misfire** misfires misfiring misfired
VERB If a plan misfires, it goes wrong.

**misfit** misfits
NOUN a person who is not accepted by other people because of being rather strange or eccentric.

**misfortune** misfortunes
NOUN an unpleasant occurrence that is regarded as bad luck E.G. *I had the misfortune to fall off my bike.*

**misgiving** misgivings
NOUN If you have misgivings, you are worried or unhappy about something E.G. *I had misgivings about his methods.*

**misguided**
ADJECTIVE A misguided opinion or action is wrong because it is based on a misunderstanding or bad information.

**misinform** misinforms misinforming misinformed
VERB If you are misinformed, you are given wrong or inaccurate information.
**misinformation** NOUN

**misinterpret** misinterprets misinterpreting misinterpreted
VERB To misinterpret something is to understand it wrongly E.G. *You completely misinterpreted what I wrote.*

**misjudge** misjudges misjudging misjudged
VERB If you misjudge someone or something, you form an incorrect idea or opinion about them.

**mislay** mislays mislaying mislaid
VERB If you mislay something, you lose it because you have forgotten where you put it.

**mislead** misleads misleading misled
VERB To mislead someone is to make them believe something which is not true.

**misplaced**
ADJECTIVE A misplaced feeling is inappropriate or directed at the wrong thing or person E.G. *misplaced loyalty.*

**misprint** misprints
NOUN a mistake such as a spelling mistake in something that has been printed.

**misrepresent** misrepresents misrepresenting misrepresented
VERB To misrepresent someone is to give an inaccurate or misleading account of what they have said or done.
**misrepresentation** NOUN

**miss** misses missing missed
VERB 1 If you miss something, you do not notice it E.G. *You can't miss it. It's*

an act that is shocking or unacceptable.

*on the second floor.* **2** If you miss someone or something, you feel sad that they are no longer with you *E.G. The boys miss their father.* **3** If you miss a chance or opportunity, you fail to take advantage of it. **4** If you miss a bus, plane, or train, you arrive too late to catch it. **5** If you miss something, you fail to hit it when you aim at it *E.G. His shot missed the target and went wide.* ▶ NOUN **6** an act of missing something that you were aiming at. **7** 'Miss' is used before the name of a woman or girl who is not married as a form of address *E.G. Did you know Miss Smith?*

**missile** missiles
NOUN a weapon that moves long distances through the air and explodes when it reaches its target; also used of any object thrown as a weapon.

**mission** missions
NOUN **1** an important task that you have to do. **2** a group of people who have been sent to a foreign country to carry out an official task *E.G. He became head of the Israeli mission.* **3** a journey made by a military aeroplane or space rocket to carry out a task. **4** If you have a mission, there is something that you believe it is your duty to try to achieve. **5** the workplace of a group of Christians who are working for the Church.

**missionary** missionaries
NOUN a Christian who has been sent to a foreign country to work for the Church.

**missive** missives
NOUN; *OLD-FASHIONED* a letter or message.

**mist** mists misting misted
NOUN **1** Mist consists of a large number of tiny drops of water in the

air, which make it hard to see clearly. ▶ VERB **2** If your eyes mist, you cannot see very far because there are tears in your eyes. **3** If glass mists over or mists up, it becomes covered with condensation so that you cannot see through it.

**mistake** mistakes mistaking mistook mistaken
NOUN **1** an action or opinion that is wrong or is not what you intended. ▶ VERB **2** If you mistake someone or something for another person or thing, you wrongly think that they are the other person or thing *E.G. I mistook him for the owner of the house.*
■ (sense 1) blunder, error, miscalculation, slip

**mistaken**
ADJECTIVE **1** If you are mistaken about something, you are wrong about it. **2** If you have a mistaken belief or opinion, you believe something which is not true.
**mistakenly** ADVERB

**mister**
A man is sometimes addressed in a very informal way as 'mister' *E.G. Where do you live, mister?*

**mistletoe**
*Said* "mis-sel-toe" NOUN Mistletoe is a plant which grows on trees and has white berries on it. It is used as a Christmas decoration.

**mistook**
the past tense of **mistake**.

**mistreat** mistreats mistreating mistreated
VERB To mistreat a person or animal is to treat them badly and make them suffer.

**mistress** mistresses
NOUN **1** A married man's mistress is a

woman who is not his wife and who he is having a sexual relationship with. **2** A school mistress is a female teacher. **3** A servant's mistress is the woman who is the servant's employer.

**mistrust mistrusts mistrusting mistrusted**
VERB **1** If you mistrust someone, you do not feel that you can trust them. ▶ NOUN **2** Mistrust is a feeling that you cannot trust someone.

**misty mistier mistiest**
ADJECTIVE full of or covered with mist.

**misunderstand misunderstands misunderstanding misunderstood**
VERB If you misunderstand someone, you do not properly understand what they say or do E.G. *He misunderstood the problem.*

**misunderstanding misunderstandings**
NOUN If two people have a misunderstanding, they have a slight quarrel or disagreement.

**misuse misuses misusing misused**
*Said* "mis-**yooz**" NOUN The misuse of something is the incorrect or dishonest use of it E.G. *the misuse of public money. Said* "mis-**yoos**" VERB To misuse something is to use it incorrectly or dishonestly.

**mite mites**
NOUN a very tiny creature that lives in the fur of animals.

**mitigating**
ADJECTIVE; *FORMAL* Mitigating circumstances make a crime easier to understand, and perhaps justify it.

**mitten mittens**
NOUN Mittens are gloves which have

one section that covers your thumb and another section for the rest of your fingers together.

**mix mixes mixing mixed**
VERB If you mix things, you combine them or shake or stir them together.
■ blend, combine, merge, mingle

**mix up** VERB If you mix up two things or people, you confuse them E.G. *People often mix us up and greet us by each other's names.*

**mixed**
ADJECTIVE **1** consisting of several things of the same general kind E.G. *a mixed salad.* **2** involving people from two or more different races E.G. *mixed marriages.* **3** Mixed education or accommodation is for both males and females E.G. *a mixed comprehensive.*

**mixed up**
ADJECTIVE **1** If you are mixed up, you are confused E.G. *I'm mixed up about which country I want to play for.* **2** If you are mixed up in a crime or a scandal, you are involved in it.

**mixer mixers**
NOUN a machine used for mixing things together E.G. *a cement mixer.*

**mixture mixtures**
NOUN several different things mixed together. a substance that consists of other substances which have been stirred or shaken together E.G. *Spoon the mixture into serving glasses.*
■ blend, medley, mix

**mix-up mix-ups**
NOUN a mistake in something that was planned E.G. *a mix-up with the bookings.*

**ml**
an abbreviation for 'millilitres'.

**mm**
an abbreviation for 'millimetres'.

**moa** moa or moas
NOUN a large, flightless bird that lived in New Zealand and which became extinct in the late 18th century.

**moan** moans moaning moaned
VERB 1 If you moan, you make a low, miserable sound because you are in pain or suffering. 2 INFORMAL If you moan about something, you complain about it. ▶ NOUN 3 a low cry of pain or misery.

**moat** moats
NOUN a wide, water-filled ditch around a building such as a castle.

**mob** mobs mobbing mobbed
NOUN 1 a large, disorganized crowd of people E.G. *A violent mob attacked the team bus.* ▶ VERB 2 If a lot of people mob someone, they crowd around the person in a disorderly way E.G. *The band was mobbed by over a thousand fans.*
🔲 from Latin *mobile vulgus* meaning 'the fickle public'

**mobile** mobiles
ADJECTIVE 1 able to move or be moved freely and easily E.G. *a mobile phone.* 2 ⬭ PE If you are mobile, you are able to travel or move about from one place to another E.G. *a mobile workforce.* ▶ NOUN 3 a decoration consisting of several small objects which hang from threads and move around when a breeze blows. 4 a mobile phone.
**mobility** NOUN

**mobile phone** mobile phones
NOUN a small portable telephone.

**moccasin** moccasins
NOUN Moccasins are flat, soft leather shoes with a raised seam above the toe.

🔲 from *mocussin*, a North American Indian word meaning 'shoe'

**mock** mocks mocking mocked
VERB 1 If you mock someone, you say something scornful or imitate their foolish behaviour. ▶ ADJECTIVE 2 not genuine E.G. *mock surprise… a mock Tudor house.* 3 A mock examination is one that you do as a practice before the real examination.
🔳 (sense 1) laugh at, make fun of, ridicule

**mockery**
NOUN Mockery is the expression of scorn or ridicule of someone.
🔳 derision, ridicule

**mode** modes
NOUN 1 A mode of life or behaviour is a particular way of living or behaving. 2 In mathematics, the mode is the biggest in a set of groups.

**model** models modelling modelled
NOUN or ADJECTIVE 1 a copy of a something that shows what it looks like or how it works E.G. *a model aircraft.* ▶ NOUN 2 Something that is described as, for example, a model of clarity or a model of perfection, is extremely clear or absolutely perfect. 3 a type or version of a machine E.G. *Which model of washing machine did you choose?* 4 a person who poses for a painter or a photographer. 5 a person who wears the clothes that are being displayed at a fashion show. ▶ ADJECTIVE 6 Someone who is described as, for example, a model wife or a model student is an excellent wife or student. ▶ VERB 7 If you model yourself on someone, you copy their behaviour because you admire them. 8 To model clothes is

a b c d e f g h i j k l **m** n o p q r s t u v w x y z

to display them by wearing them.
**9** To model shapes or figures is to
make them out of clay or wood.
■ (sense 2) example, ideal,
pattern

**modem** modems
Said "**moe**-dem" NOUN (ICT) a piece
of equipment that links a computer
to the telephone system so that data
can be transferred from one
machine to another via the
telephone line.

**moderate** moderates
moderating moderated
ADJECTIVE **1** Moderate views are not
extreme, and usually favour gradual
changes rather than major ones. **2** A
moderate amount of something is
neither large not small. ▶ NOUN **3** a
person whose political views are not
extreme. ▶ VERB **4** If you moderate
something or if it moderates, it
becomes less extreme or violent E.G.
*The weather moderated.*
**moderately** ADVERB

**moderation**
NOUN Moderation is control of your
behaviour that stops you acting in
an extreme way E.G. *a man of fairness
and moderation.*

**modern**
ADJECTIVE **1** relating to the present time
E.G. *modern society.* **2** new and
involving the latest ideas and
equipment E.G. *modern technology.*
**modernity** NOUN
■ (sense 1) contemporary, current,
present-day

**modernize** modernizes
modernizing modernized; also
spelt **modernise**
VERB To modernize something is to
introduce new methods or

equipment to it.

**modest**
ADJECTIVE **1** quite small in size or
amount. **2** Someone who is modest
does not boast about their abilities
or possessions. **3** shy and easily
embarrassed.
**modestly** ADVERB **modesty** NOUN

**modification** modifications
NOUN a small change made to
improve something E.G. *Modifications
to the undercarriage were made.*

**modify** modifies modifying
modified
VERB If you modify something, you
change it slightly in order to improve
it.

**module** modules
NOUN **1** one of the parts which when
put together form a whole unit or
object E.G. *The college provides
modules for trainees.* **2** (ICT) a part
of a machine or system that does a
particular task. **3** a part of a
spacecraft which can do certain
things away from the main body E.G.
*the lunar module.*
**modular** ADJECTIVE

**mohair**
NOUN Mohair is very soft, fluffy wool
obtained from angora goats.

**moist** moister moistest
ADJECTIVE slightly wet.

**moisten** moistens moistening
moistened
VERB If you moisten something, you
make it slightly wet.

**moisture**
NOUN Moisture is tiny drops of water
in the air or on the ground.

**molar** molars
NOUN Your molars are the large teeth
at the back of your mouth.

**mole** moles

NOUN **1** a dark, slightly raised spot on your skin. **2** a small animal with black fur. Moles live in tunnels underground. **3** INFORMAL a member of an organization who is working as a spy for a rival organization.

**molecule** molecules

NOUN the smallest amount of a substance that can exist.

**molecular** ADJECTIVE

**molest** molests molesting molested

VERB To molest a child is to touch the child in a sexual way. This is illegal.

**molester** NOUN

**mollify** mollifies mollifying mollified

VERB To mollify someone is to do something to make them less upset or angry.

**mollusc** molluscs

NOUN an animal with a soft body and no backbone. Snails, slugs, clams, and mussels are all molluscs.

**molten**

ADJECTIVE Molten rock or metal has been heated to a very high temperature and has become a thick liquid.

**moment** moments

NOUN **1** a very short period of time E.G. *He paused for a moment.* **2** The moment at which something happens is the point in time at which it happens E.G. *At that moment, the doorbell rang.* ▶ PHRASE **3** If something is happening **at the moment**, it is happening now.

■ (sense 1) instant, second

**momentary**

ADJECTIVE Something that is momentary lasts for only a few seconds E.G. *a momentary lapse of concentration.*

**momentarily** ADVERB

☑ Some Americans say *momentarily* when they mean 'very soon', rather than 'for a moment'.

**momentous**

ADJECTIVE; FORMAL very important, often because of its future effect E.G. *a momentous occasion.*

**momentum**

NOUN **1** Momentum is the ability that something has to keep developing E.G. *The campaign is gaining momentum.* **2** Momentum is also the ability that an object has to continue moving as a result of the speed it already has.

**monarch** monarchs

*Said* "**mon-nark**" NOUN a queen, king, or other royal person who reigns over a country.

**monarchy** monarchies

NOUN a system in which a queen or king reigns in a country.

**monastery** monasteries

NOUN a building in which monks live.

**monastic** ADJECTIVE

**Monday** Mondays

NOUN Monday is the day between Sunday and Tuesday.

🏛 from Old English *monandæg* meaning 'moon's day'

**money**

NOUN Money is the coins or banknotes that you use to buy something.

**mongrel** mongrels

NOUN a dog with parents of different breeds.

**monitor** monitors monitoring monitored

VERB **1** If you monitor something, you

a
b
c
d
e
f
g
h
i
j
k
l
**m**
n
o
p
q
r
s
t
u
v
w
x
y
z

A
B
C
D
E
F
G
H
I
J
K
L
M
N
O
P
Q
R
S
T
U
V
W
X
Y
Z

regularly check its condition and progress E.G. *Her health will be monitored daily.* ▶ NOUN **2** a machine used to check or record things. **3** ICT the visual display unit of a computer. **4** a school pupil chosen to do special duties by the teacher.

**monk monks**
NOUN a member of a male religious community.

**monkey monkeys**
NOUN an animal which has a long tail and climbs trees. Monkeys live in hot countries.

**mono-**
PREFIX 'Mono-' is used at the beginning of nouns and adjectives that have 'one' as part of their meaning E.G. *monopoly… monogamy.* 🔲 from Greek *monos* meaning 'single'

**monocle monocles**
NOUN a glass lens worn in front of one eye only and held in place by the curve of the eye socket.

**monogamy**
NOUN; FORMAL Monogamy is the custom of being married to only one person at a time.
**monogamous** ADJECTIVE

**monologue monologues**
*Said* "mon-nol-og" NOUN a long speech by one person during a play or a conversation.

**monopoly monopolies**
NOUN control of most of an industry by one or a few large firms.

**monotone monotones**
NOUN a tone which does not vary E.G. *He droned on in a boring monotone.*

**monotonous**
ADJECTIVE having a regular pattern which is very dull and boring E.G.

*monotonous work.*
**monotony** NOUN

**monotreme monotremes**
NOUN an Australian mammal that has a single opening in its body.

**monounsaturated**
ADJECTIVE Monounsaturated oils are made mainly from vegetable fats and are considered to be healthier than saturated oils.
**monounsaturate** NOUN

**monsoon monsoons**
NOUN the season of very heavy rain in South-east Asia.

**monster monsters**
NOUN **1** a large, imaginary creature that looks very frightening. **2** a cruel or frightening person. ▶ ADJECTIVE **3** extremely large E.G. *a monster truck.* 🔲 from Latin *monstrum* meaning 'omen' or 'warning'

**monstrosity monstrosities**
NOUN something that is large and extremely ugly E.G. *a concrete monstrosity in the middle of the city.*

**monstrous**
ADJECTIVE extremely shocking or unfair E.G. *a monstrous crime.*
**monstrously** ADVERB

**montage montages**
*Said* "mon-tahj" NOUN a picture or film consisting of a combination of several different items arranged to produce an unusual effect.

**month months**
NOUN one of the twelve periods that a year is divided into.

**monthly monthlies**
ADJECTIVE Monthly describes something that happens or appears once a month E.G. *monthly staff meetings.*

**monument** monuments

NOUN a large stone structure built to remind people of a famous person or event E.G. *a monument to the dead.*

**monumental**

ADJECTIVE **1** A monumental building or sculpture is very large and important. **2** very large or extreme E.G. *We face a monumental task.*

**moo** moos mooing mooed

VERB When a cow moos, it makes a long, deep sound.

**mood** moods

NOUN the way you are feeling at a particular time E.G. *She was in a really cheerful mood.*

■ humour, state of mind, temper

**moody** moodier moodiest

ADJECTIVE **1** Someone who is moody is depressed or unhappy E.G. *Tony, despite his charm, could sulk and be moody.* **2** Someone who is moody often changes their mood for no apparent reason.

■ (sense 1) morose, sulky, sullen
■ (sense 2) mercurial, temperamental

**moon** moons

NOUN The moon is an object moving round the earth which you see as a shining circle or crescent in the sky at night. Some other planets have moons.

**moonlight** moonlights moonlighting moonlighted

NOUN **1** Moonlight is the light that comes from the moon at night. ▶ VERB **2** INFORMAL If someone is moonlighting, they have a second job that they have not informed the tax office about.

**moonlit** ADJECTIVE

**moor** moors mooring moored

NOUN **1** a high area of open land.
▶ VERB **2** If a boat is moored, it is attached to the land with a rope.

**mooring** moorings

NOUN a place where a boat can be tied.

**moose**

NOUN a large North American deer with flat antlers.

**moot** moots mooting mooted

VERB; FORMAL When something is mooted, it is suggested for discussion E.G. *The project was first mooted in 1988.*

**mop** mops mopping mopped

NOUN **1** a tool for washing floors, consisting of a sponge or string head attached to a long handle. **2** a large amount of loose or untidy hair. ▶ VERB **3** To mop a floor is to clean it with a mop. **4** To mop a surface is to wipe it with a dry cloth to remove liquid.

**mope** mopes moping moped

VERB If you mope, you feel miserable and not interested in anything.

**moped** mopeds

*Said* "moe-ped" NOUN a type of small motorcycle.

**mopoke** mopokes

NOUN a small, spotted owl found in Australia and New Zealand. In New Zealand it is called a **morepork**

**moral** morals

PLURAL NOUN **1** ⟨RE⟩ Morals are values based on beliefs about the correct and acceptable way to behave.
▶ ADJECTIVE **2** concerned with whether behaviour is right or acceptable E.G. *moral values.*

**morality** NOUN    **morally** ADVERB

**morale**

*Said* "mor-rahl" NOUN Morale is the

**morbid**

ADJECTIVE having a great interest in unpleasant things, especially death.

**more**

ADJECTIVE or PRONOUN 1 More means a greater number or extent than something else *E.G. He's got more chips than me... I've got more than you.* 2 used to refer to an additional thing or amount of something *E.G. He found some more clues.* ► ADVERB 3 to a greater degree or extent *E.G. more amused than concerned.* 4 You can use 'more' in front of adjectives and adverbs to form comparatives *E.G. You look more beautiful than ever.*

**moreover**

ADVERB used to introduce a piece of information that supports or expands the previous statement *E.G. They have accused the government of corruption. Moreover, they have named names.*

**morepork** moreporks

NOUN In New Zealand English, the same as a mopoke.

**morgue** morgues

*Said "morg"* NOUN a building where dead bodies are kept before being buried or cremated.

**moribund**

ADJECTIVE no longer having a useful function and about to come to an end *E.G. a moribund industry.*

**morning** mornings

NOUN 1 the early part of the day until lunchtime. 2 the part of the day between midnight and noon *E.G. He was born at three in the morning.*

"amount of confidence and optimism that you have *E.G. The morale of the troops was high.*"

**Moroccan** Moroccans

*Said "mor-rok-an"* ADJECTIVE 1 belonging or relating to Morocco. ► NOUN 2 someone who comes from Morocco.

**moron** morons

NOUN; *INFORMAL* a very stupid person. **moronic** ADJECTIVE

**morose**

ADJECTIVE miserable and bad-tempered.

**morphine**

NOUN Morphine is a drug which is used to relieve pain.

**Morse** or **Morse code**

NOUN Morse or Morse code is a code used for sending messages in which each letter is represented by a series of dots and dashes.

**morsel** morsels

NOUN a small piece of food.

**mortal** mortals

ADJECTIVE 1 unable to live forever *E.G. Remember that you are mortal.* 2 A mortal wound is one that causes death. ► NOUN 3 an ordinary person.

**mortality**

NOUN 1 Mortality is the fact that all people must die. 2 Mortality also refers to the number of people who die at any particular time *E.G. a low infant mortality rate.*

**mortar** mortars

NOUN 1 a short cannon which fires missiles high into the air for a short distance. 2 Mortar is a mixture of sand, water, and cement used to hold bricks firmly together.

**mortgage** mortgages mortgaging mortgaged

*Said "mor-gij"* NOUN 1 a loan which you get from a bank or a building society in order to buy a house.

► VERB **2** If you mortgage your house, you use it as a guarantee to a company in order to borrow money from them. They can take the house from you if you do not pay back the money you have borrowed.

**mortifying**

ADJECTIVE embarrassing or humiliating E.G. *There were some mortifying setbacks.*

**mortuary mortuaries**

NOUN a special room in a hospital where dead bodies are kept before being buried or cremated.

**mosaic mosaics**

*Said* "moe-**zay**-yik" NOUN a design made of small coloured stones or pieces of coloured glass set into concrete or plaster.

**Moslem**

another spelling of **Muslim**.

**mosque mosques**

*Said* "**mosk**" NOUN a building where Muslims go to worship.

🏛 from Arabic *masjid* meaning 'temple'

**mosquito mosquitoes** or **mosquitos**

*Said* "moss-**skee**-toe" NOUN Mosquitoes are small insects which bite people in order to suck their blood.

🏛 from Spanish *mosquito* meaning 'little fly'

**moss mosses**

NOUN Moss is a soft, low-growing, green plant which grows on damp soil or stone.

**mossy** ADJECTIVE

**most**

ADJECTIVE or PRONOUN **1** Most of a group of things or people means nearly all of them E.G. *Most people don't share*

your views. **2** The most means a larger amount than anyone or anything else E.G. *She has the most talent.* ► ADVERB **3** You can use 'most' in front of adjectives or adverbs to form superlatives E.G. *the most beautiful women in the world.*

**mostly**

ADVERB 'Mostly' is used to show that a statement is generally true E.G. *Her friends are mostly men.*

**MOT MOTs**

NOUN In Britain, an annual test for road vehicles to check that they are safe to drive.

**motel motels**

NOUN a hotel providing overnight accommodation for people in the middle of a car journey.

**moth moths**

NOUN an insect like a butterfly which usually flies at night.

**mother mothers mothering mothered**

NOUN **1** Your mother is the woman who gave birth to you. **2** Your mother could also be the woman who has looked after them and brought you up. ► VERB **3** To mother someone is to look after them and bring them up.

**motherhood**

NOUN Motherhood is the state of being a mother.

**mother-in-law mothers-in-law**

NOUN Someone's mother-in-law is the mother of their husband or wife.

**motif motifs**

*Said* "moe-**teef**" NOUN a design which is used as a decoration.

**motion motions motioning motioned**

NOUN **1** Motion is the process of continually moving or changing

a b c d e f g h i j k l **m** n o p q r s t u v w x y z

A
B
C
D
E
F
G
H
I
J
K
L
M
N
O
P
Q
R
S
T
U
V
W
X
Y
Z

position *E.G. the motion of the ship.*
**2** an action or gesture *E.G. Apply with a brush using circular motions.* **3** a proposal which people discuss and vote on at a meeting. ► VERB **4** If you motion to someone, you make a movement with your hand in order to show them what they should do *E.G. I motioned him to proceed.*

**motionless**
ADJECTIVE not moving at all *E.G. He sat motionless.*

**motivate** motivates motivating motivated
VERB **1** If you are motivated by something, it makes you behave in a particular way *E.G. He is motivated by duty rather than ambition.* **2** If you motivate someone, you make them feel determined to do something. **motivated** ADJECTIVE **motivation** NOUN
■ (sense 1) drive, inspire, prompt

**motive** motives
NOUN (HISTORY) a reason or purpose for doing something *E.G. There was no motive for the attack.*

**motley**
ADJECTIVE A motley collection is made up of people or things of very different types.

**motor** motors
NOUN **1** a part of a vehicle or a machine that uses electricity or fuel to produce movement so that the machine can work. ► ADJECTIVE **2** concerned with or relating to vehicles with a petrol or diesel engine *E.G. the motor industry.*

**motorboat** motorboats
NOUN a boat with an engine.

**motorcycle** motorcycles
NOUN a two-wheeled vehicle with an

engine which is ridden like a bicycle.
**motorcyclist** NOUN

**motoring**
ADJECTIVE relating to cars and driving *E.G. a motoring correspondent.*

**motorist** motorists
NOUN a person who drives a car.

**motorway** motorways
NOUN a wide road built for fast travel over long distances.

**mottled**
ADJECTIVE covered with patches of different colours *E.G. mottled leaves.*

**motto** mottoes or mottos
NOUN a short sentence or phrase that is a rule for good or sensible behaviour.

**mould** moulds moulding moulded
VERB **1** To mould someone or something is to influence and change them so they develop in a particular way *E.G. Early experiences mould our behaviour for life.* **2** To mould a substance is to make it into a particular shape *E.G. Mould the mixture into flat round cakes.* ► NOUN **3** a container used to make something into a particular shape *E.G. a jelly mould.* **4** Mould is a soft grey or green substance that can form on old food or damp walls.
**mouldy** ADJECTIVE

**moult** moults moulting moulted
VERB When an animal or bird moults, it loses its hair or feathers so new ones can grow.

**mound** mounds
NOUN **1** a small man-made hill. **2** a large, untidy pile *E.G. a mound of blankets.*

**mount** mounts mounting mounted
VERB **1** To mount a campaign or event

is to organize it and carry it out. **2** If something is mounting, it is increasing *E.G. Economic problems are mounting.* **3** FORMAL To mount something is to go to the top of it *E.G. He mounted the steps.* **4** If you mount a horse, you climb on its back. **5** If you mount an object in a particular place, you fix it there to display it. ▶ NOUN **6** 'Mount' is also used as part of the name of a mountain *E.G. Mount Everest.*

**mountain mountains**
NOUN **1** a very high piece of land with steep sides. **2** a large amount of something *E.G. mountains of paperwork.*

**mountaineer mountaineers**
NOUN a person who climbs mountains.

**mountainous**
ADJECTIVE A mountainous area has a lot of mountains.

**mourn mourns mourning mourned**
VERB **1** If you mourn for someone who has died, you are very sad and think about them a lot. **2** If you mourn something, you are sad because you no longer have it *E.G. He mourned the end of his marriage.*

**mourner mourners**
NOUN a person who attends a funeral.

**mournful**
ADJECTIVE very sad.

**mourning**
NOUN If someone is in mourning, they wear special black clothes or behave in a quiet and restrained way because a member of their family has died.

**mouse mice**
NOUN **1** a small rodent with a long tail. **2** a small device moved by hand to control the position of the cursor on a computer screen.

**mousse mousses**
*Said "moos"* NOUN Mousse is a light, fluffy food made from whipped eggs and cream.

**moustache moustaches**
*Said "mus-stahsh"* NOUN A man's moustache is hair growing on his upper lip.
🔤 from Greek *mustax* meaning 'upper lip'

**mouth mouths mouthing mouthed**
NOUN **1** your lips, or the space behind them where your tongue and teeth are. **2** The mouth of a cave or a hole is the entrance to it. **3** The mouth of a river is the place where it flows into the sea. ▶ VERB **4** If you mouth something, you form words with your lips without making any sound *E.G. He mouthed 'Thank you' to the jurors.*

**mouthful** NOUN

**mouthpiece mouthpieces**
NOUN **1** the part you speak into on a telephone. **2** the part of a musical instrument you put to your mouth. **3** The mouthpiece of an organization is the person who publicly states its opinions and policies.

**movable**
ADJECTIVE Something that is movable can be moved from one place to another.

**move moves moving moved**
VERB **1** To move means to go to a different place or position. To move something means to change its place or position. **2** If you move, or move house, you go to live in a different house. **3** If something

A B C D E F G H I J K L M N O P Q R S T U V W X Y Z

moves you, it causes you to feel a deep emotion E.G. *Her story moved us to tears.* ▶ NOUN 4 a change from one place or position to another E.G. *We were watching his every move.* 5 an act of moving house. 6 the act of putting a piece or counter in a game in a different position E.G. *It's your move next.*

■ (sense 1) budge, go, shift, stir

**movement** movements

NOUN 1 (DRAMA) Movement involves changing position or going from one place to another. ▶ PLURAL NOUN 2 FORMAL Your movements are everything you do during a period of time E.G. *They asked him for an account of his movements during the previous morning.* ▶ NOUN 3 a group of people who share the same beliefs or aims E.G. *the peace movement.* 4 one of the major sections of a piece of classical music.

**moving**

ADJECTIVE Something that is moving makes you feel deep sadness or emotion.

**movingly** ADVERB

**mow** mows mowing mowed mown

VERB 1 To mow grass is to cut it with a lawnmower. 2 To mow down a large number of people is to kill them all violently.

**mower** mowers

NOUN a machine for cutting grass.

**MP** MPs

NOUN a person who has been elected to represent people in a country's parliament. MP is an abbreviation for 'Member of Parliament'.

**MP3 player** MP3 players

NOUN a device that plays audio or video files, often used for listening to music downloaded from the Internet.

**mpg**

an abbreviation for 'miles per gallon'.

**mph**

an abbreviation for 'miles per hour'.

**Mr**

*Said* "**miss-ter**" 'Mr' is used before a man's name when you are speaking or referring to him.

**Mrs**

*Said* "**miss-iz**" 'Mrs' is used before the name of a married woman when you are speaking or referring to her.

**Ms**

*Said* "**miz**" 'Ms' is used before a woman's name when you are speaking or referring to her. Ms does not specify whether a woman is married or not.

**MSP** MSPs

NOUN an abbreviation for 'Member of the Scottish Parliament': a person who has been elected to represent people in the Scottish Parliament.

**much**

ADVERB 1 You use 'much' to emphasize that something is true to a great extent E.G. *I feel much better now.* 2 If something does not happen much, it does not happen very often.

▶ ADJECTIVE or PRONOUN 3 You use 'much' to ask questions or give information about the size or amount of something E.G. *How much money do you need?*

**muck** mucks mucking mucked

NOUN 1 INFORMAL Muck is dirt or some other unpleasant substance. 2 Muck is also manure. ▶ VERB 3 INFORMAL If you muck about, you behave stupidly and waste time.

**mucky** ADJECTIVE

## mucus

*Said* "myoo-kuss" NOUN Mucus is a liquid produced in parts of your body, for example in your nose.

## mud

NOUN Mud is wet, sticky earth.

## muddle muddles muddling muddled

NOUN 1 A muddle is a state of disorder or untidiness E.G. *Our finances are in a muddle.* ▶ VERB 2 If you muddle things, you mix them up.

(sense 2) jumble, mix up

## muddy muddier muddiest

ADJECTIVE 1 covered in mud. 2 A muddy colour is dull and not clear E.G. *a mottled, muddy brown.*

## muesli

*Said* "myooz-lee" NOUN Muesli is a mixture of chopped nuts, cereal flakes, and dried fruit that you can eat for breakfast with milk.

## muffin muffins

NOUN a small, round cake which you eat hot.

## muffled

ADJECTIVE A muffled sound is quiet or difficult to hear E.G. *a muffled explosion.*

## mug mugs mugging mugged

NOUN 1 a large, deep cup. 2 INFORMAL someone who is stupid and easily deceived. ▶ VERB 3 INFORMAL If someone mugs you, they attack you in order to steal your money.

mugging NOUN    mugger NOUN

## muggy muggier muggiest

ADJECTIVE Muggy weather is unpleasantly warm and damp.

## mule mules

NOUN the offspring of a female horse and a male donkey.

## mulga

NOUN 1 Mulga are acacia shrubs that are found in the desert regions of Australia. 2 INFORMAL In Australian English, mulga is also the bush or outback.

## mull mulls mulling mulled

VERB If you mull something over, you think about it for a long time before making a decision.

## mullet mullets

NOUN a common edible fish found in Australian and New Zealand waters.

## mulloway mulloways

NOUN a large edible fish found in Australian waters.

## multi-

PREFIX 'Multi-' is used to form words that refer to something that has many parts or aspects E.G. *a multistorey car park.*

from Latin *multus* meaning 'much' or 'many'

## multimedia

NOUN 1 ( ICT ) in computing, you use multimedia to refer to products which use sound, pictures, film and ordinary text to convey information. 2 in the classroom, all the things like TV, computers, and books which are used as teaching aids are called multimedia.

## multinational multinationals

NOUN a very large company with branches in many countries.

## multiple multiples

ADJECTIVE 1 having or involving many different functions or things E.G. *He died from multiple injuries in the crash.* ▶ NOUN 2 The multiples of a number are other numbers that it will divide into exactly. For example, 6, 9, and 12 are multiples of 3.

## multiple sclerosis

*Said* "skler-**roe**-siss" NOUN Multiple

a b c d e f g h i j k l **m** n o p q r s t u v w x y z

A
B
C
D
E
F
G
H
I
J
K
L
**M**
N
O
P
Q
R
S
T
U
V
W
X
Y
Z

sclerosis is a serious disease which attacks the nervous system, affecting your ability to move.

**multiplication**

NOUN 1 (MATHS) Multiplication is the process of multiplying one number by another. 2 The multiplication of things is a large increase in their number E.G. *the multiplication of universities*.

**multiplicity**

NOUN If there is a multiplicity of things, there is a large number or variety of them.

**multiply** multiplies multiplying multiplied

VERB 1 When something multiplies, it increases greatly in number E.G. *The trip wore on and the hazards multiplied*. 2 (MATHS) When you multiply one number by another, you calculate the total you would get if you added the first number to itself a particular number of times. For example, two multiplied by three is equal to two plus two plus two, which equals six.

**multitude** multitudes

NOUN; FORMAL a very large number of people or things.

**mum** mums

NOUN; INFORMAL Your mum is your mother.

**mumble** mumbles mumbling mumbled

VERB If you mumble, you speak very quietly and indistinctly.

**mummy** mummies

NOUN 1 AN INFORMAL USE, USED ESPECIALLY BY CHILDREN Your mummy is your mother. 2 a dead body which was preserved long ago by being rubbed with special oils and wrapped in cloth.

**mumps**

NOUN Mumps is a disease that causes painful swelling in the neck glands.

**munch** munches munching munched

VERB If you munch something, you chew it steadily and thoroughly.

**mundane**

ADJECTIVE very ordinary and not interesting or unusual E.G. *a mundane job*.

**municipal**

*Said* "myoo-**nis**-si-pl" ADJECTIVE belonging to a city or town which has its own local government E.G. *a municipal golf course*.

🏛 from Latin *municipium* meaning 'free town'

**munitions**

PLURAL NOUN Munitions are bombs, guns, and other military supplies.

**mural** murals

NOUN a picture painted on a wall.

**murder** murders murdering murdered

NOUN 1 Murder is the deliberate killing of a person. ▶ VERB 2 To murder someone is to kill them deliberately. **murderer** NOUN

▦ (sense 1) homicide, killing

**murderous**

ADJECTIVE 1 likely to murder someone E.G. *murderous gangsters*. 2 A murderous attack or other action results in the death of many people E.G. *murderous acts of terrorism*.

**murky** murkier murkiest

ADJECTIVE dark or dirty and unpleasant E.G. *He rushed through the murky streets*.

**murmur** murmurs murmuring murmured

VERB 1 If you murmur, you say

something very softly. ▶ NOUN
**2** something that someone says which can hardly be heard.

**muscle muscles muscling muscled**
NOUN **1** ( PE ) Your muscles are pieces of flesh which you can expand or contract in order to move parts of your body. ▶ VERB **2** *INFORMAL* If you muscle in on something, you force your way into a situation in which you are not welcome.
from Latin *musculus* meaning 'little mouse', because muscles were thought to look like mice

**muscular**
*Said* "musk-yool-lar" ADJECTIVE
**1** involving or affecting your muscles *E.G. muscular strength.* **2** Someone who is muscular has strong, firm muscles.

**muse muses musing mused**
VERB *LITERARY* To muse is to think about something for a long time.

**museum museums**
NOUN a building where many interesting or valuable objects are kept and displayed.

**mush**
NOUN A mush is a thick, soft paste.

**mushroom mushrooms mushrooming mushroomed**
NOUN **1** a fungus with a short stem and a round top. Some types of mushroom are edible. ▶ VERB **2** If something mushrooms, it appears and grows very quickly *E.G. The mill towns mushroomed into cities.*

**mushy mushier mushiest**
ADJECTIVE **1** Mushy fruits or vegetables are too soft *E.G. mushy tomatoes.*
**2** *INFORMAL* Mushy stories are too sentimental.

**music**
NOUN **1** Music is a pattern of sounds performed by people singing or playing instruments. **2** Music is also the written symbols that represent musical sounds *E.G. I taught myself to read music.*

**musical musicals**
ADJECTIVE **1** relating to playing or studying music *E.G. a musical instrument.* ▶ NOUN **2** a play or film that uses songs and dance to tell the story.
**musically** ADVERB

**musician musicians**
NOUN ( MUSIC ) a person who plays a musical instrument as their job or hobby.

**musk**
NOUN Musk is a substance with a strong, sweet smell. It is used to make perfume.
**musky** ADJECTIVE

**musket muskets**
NOUN an old-fashioned gun with a long barrel.

**Muslim Muslims**; also spelt **Moslem**
NOUN ( RE ) **1** a person who believes in Islam and lives according to its rules. ▶ ADJECTIVE **2** relating to Islam.

**muslin**
NOUN Muslin is a very thin cotton material.

**mussel mussels**
NOUN Mussels are a kind of shellfish with black shells.

**must**
VERB **1** If something must happen, it is very important or necessary that it happens *E.G. You must be over 18.* **2** If you tell someone they must do something, you are suggesting that

a
b
c
d
e
f
g
h
i
j
k
l
**m**
n
o
p
q
r
s
t
u
v
w
x
y
z

A B C D E F G H I J K L **M** N O P Q R S T U V W X Y Z

they do it E.G. *You must try this pudding: it's delicious.* ▶ NOUN
**3** something that is absolutely necessary E.G. *The museum is a must for all visitors.*

**mustard**
NOUN Mustard is a spicy-tasting yellow or brown paste made from seeds.

**muster** musters mustering mustered
VERB If you muster something such as energy or support, you gather it together E.G. *as much calm as he could muster.*

**musty** mustier mustiest
ADJECTIVE smelling stale and damp E.G. *musty old books.*

**mutate** mutates mutating mutated
VERB; TECHNICAL If something mutates, its structure or appearance alters in some way E.G. *Viruses react to change and can mutate fast.*
**mutation** NOUN **mutant** NOUN or ADJECTIVE

**mute**
ADJECTIVE; FORMAL not giving out sound or speech E.G. *mute amazement.*

**muted**
ADJECTIVE **1** Muted colours or sounds are soft and gentle. **2** A muted reaction is not very strong

**muti**
*Said* "**moo-ti**" NOUN; INFORMAL In South African English, muti is medicine.

**mutilate** mutilates mutilating mutilated
VERB **1** If someone is mutilated, their body is badly injured E.G. *His leg was badly mutilated.* **2** If you mutilate something, you deliberately damage

or spoil it E.G. *Almost every book had been mutilated.*
**mutilation** NOUN

**mutiny** mutinies
NOUN A mutiny is a rebellion against someone in authority.

**mutter** mutters muttering muttered
VERB To mutter is to speak in a very low and perhaps cross voice E.G. *Rory muttered something under his breath.*

**mutton**
NOUN Mutton is the meat of an adult sheep.

**muttonbird** muttonbirds
NOUN a seabird in the Pacific Ocean that is often hunted for its flesh, which is said to taste like mutton.

**mutual**
ADJECTIVE used to describe something that two or more people do to each other or share E.G. *They had a mutual interest in rugby.*
☑ It used to be that *mutual* could only be used of something that was shared between two people or groups. Nowadays you can use it to mean 'shared between two or more people or groups'.

**mutually**
ADVERB Mutually describes a situation in which two or more people feel the same way about each other E.G. *a mutually supportive relationship.*

**muzzle** muzzles muzzling muzzled
NOUN **1** the nose and mouth of an animal. **2** a cover or a strap for a dog's nose and mouth to prevent it from biting. **3** the open end of a gun through which the bullets come out.
▶ VERB **4** To muzzle a dog is to put a muzzle on it.

## my
ADJECTIVE 'My' refers to something belonging or relating to the person speaking or writing E.G. *I held my breath.*

## mynah bird mynah birds
NOUN a tropical bird which can mimic speech and sounds.

## myriad myriads
*Said* "mir-*ree*-ad" NOUN or ADJECTIVE; *LITERARY* a very large number of people or things.

## myrrh
*Rhymes with* "**purr**" NOUN Myrrh is a fragrant substance used in perfume and incense.

## myself
PRONOUN 1 'Myself' is used when the person speaking or writing does an action and is affected by it E.G. *I was ashamed of myself.* 2 'Myself' is also used to emphasize 'I' E.G. *I find it a bit odd myself.*

## mysterious
ADJECTIVE 1 strange and not well understood. 2 secretive about something E.G. *Stop being so mysterious.*

**mysteriously** ADVERB
■ (sense 2) enigmatic, secretive

## mystery mysteries
NOUN something that is not understood or known about.

## mystic mystics
NOUN 1 a religious person who spends

long hours meditating. ▶ ADJECTIVE 2 Mystic means the same as mystical.

## mystical
ADJECTIVE involving spiritual powers and influences E.G. *a mystical experience.*

**mysticism** NOUN

## mystify mystifies mystifying mystified
VERB If something mystifies you, you find it impossible to understand.

## mystique
*Said* "mis-*steek*" NOUN Mystique is an atmosphere of mystery and importance associated with a particular person or thing.

## myth myths
NOUN 1 an untrue belief or explanation. 2 (ENGLISH) a story which was made up long ago to explain natural events and religious beliefs E.G. *Viking myths.*

## mythical
ADJECTIVE imaginary, untrue, or existing only in myths E.G. *a mythical beast.*

## mythology
NOUN Mythology refers to stories that have been made up in the past to explain natural events or justify religious beliefs.

**mythological** ADJECTIVE

LEt's measure the angLE (angle)    SPELLING NOTE

# Nn

> **TIP** Some words which sound as if they should begin with letter *n*, are spelt with *gn*, for example *gnaw*, *gnome* and *gnu*. Other words that sound as if they ought to begin with letter *n* are actually spelt with *kn*, for example *knee*, *knight*, *knock* and *knot*. Other words that sound as if they ought to begin with letter *n* are actually spelt with *pn*, for example *pneumatic* and *pneumonia*.

**naartjie naartjies**
*Said* "**nar-**chi" NOUN In South African English, a tangerine.

**nag nags nagging nagged**
VERB **1** If you nag someone, you keep complaining to them about something. **2** If something nags at you, it keeps worrying you.

**nail nails nailing nailed**
NOUN **1** a small piece of metal with a sharp point at one end, which you hammer into objects to hold them together. **2** Your nails are the thin hard areas covering the ends of your fingers and toes. ▸ VERB **3** If you nail something somewhere, you fit it there using a nail.

**naive** or **naïve**
*Said* "ny-**eev**" ADJECTIVE foolishly believing that things are easier or less complicated than they really are.
**naively** ADVERB **naivety** NOUN

**naked**
ADJECTIVE **1** not wearing any clothes or not covered by anything. **2** shown openly E.G. *naked aggression*.
**nakedness** NOUN

**name names naming named**
NOUN **1** a word that you use to identify a person, place, or thing. **2** Someone's name is also their reputation E.G. *My only wish now is to clear my name.* ▸ VERB **3** If you name someone or something, you give them a name or you say their name. **4** If you name a price or a date, you say what you want it to be.

**nameless**
ADJECTIVE You describe someone or something as nameless when you do not know their name, or when a name has not yet been given to them.

**namely**
ADVERB that is; used to introduce more detailed information about what you have just said E.G. *The state stripped them of their rights, namely the right to own land.*

**namesake namesakes**
NOUN Your namesake is someone with the same name as you E.G. *Audrey Hepburn and her namesake Katharine.*

**nanny nannies**
NOUN a woman whose job is looking after young children.

**nap naps napping napped**
NOUN **1** a short sleep. ▸ VERB **2** When you nap, you have a short sleep.

**nape napes**
NOUN The nape of your neck is the back of it.

**napkin napkins**
NOUN a small piece of cloth or paper used to wipe your hands and mouth after eating.

**nappy** nappies

NOUN a piece of towelling or paper worn round a baby's bottom.

**narcotic** narcotics

NOUN a drug which makes you sleepy and unable to feel pain.

🔲 from Greek *narkoun* meaning 'to make numb'

**narrate** narrates narrating narrated

VERB If you narrate a story, you tell it. **narration** NOUN

**narrative** narratives

*Said* "nar-rat-tiv" NOUN (ENGLISH) a story or an account of events.

**narrator** narrators

NOUN **1** a person who is reading or telling a story out loud. **2** (ENGLISH) a character in a novel who tells the story.

**narrow** narrower narrowest; narrows narrowing narrowed

ADJECTIVE **1** having a small distance from one side to the other *E.G. a narrow stream*. **2** concerned only with a few aspects of something and ignoring the important points *E.G. people with a narrow point of view*. **3** A narrow escape or victory is one that you only just achieve. ▶ VERB **4** To narrow means to become less wide *E.G. The road narrowed*.

**narrowly** ADVERB

**narrow-minded**

ADJECTIVE unwilling to consider new ideas or opinions.

▪ bigoted, intolerant

**nasal**

*Said* "nay-zal" ADJECTIVE **1** relating to the nose *E.G. the nasal passages*. **2** Nasal sounds are made by breathing out through your nose as you speak.

**nasty** nastier nastiest

ADJECTIVE very unpleasant *E.G. a nasty shock*.

**nastily** ADVERB **nastiness** NOUN

**nation** nations

NOUN (GEOGRAPHY) a large group of people sharing the same history and language and usually inhabiting a particular country.

**national** nationals (GEOGRAPHY)

ADJECTIVE **1** relating to the whole of a country *E.G. a national newspaper*. **2** typical of a particular country *E.G. women in Polish national dress*. ▶ NOUN **3** A national of a country is a citizen of that country *E.G. Turkish nationals*.

**nationally** ADVERB

**national anthem** national anthems

NOUN A country's national anthem is its official song.

**nationalism**

NOUN **1** Nationalism is a desire for the independence of a country; also a political movement aiming to achieve such independence. **2** Nationalism is also love of your own country.

**nationalist** NOUN **nationalistic** ADJECTIVE

**nationality** nationalities

NOUN Nationality is the fact of belonging to a particular country.

**nationalize** nationalizes nationalizing nationalized; also spelt **nationalise**

VERB To nationalize an industry means to bring it under the control and ownership of the state.

**nationalization** NOUN

**National Party**

NOUN In Australia and New Zealand,

a b c d e f g h i j k l m n o p q r s t u v w x y z

the National Party is a major political party.

**national service**

NOUN National service is a compulsory period of service in the armed forces.

**nationwide**

ADJECTIVE or ADVERB happening all over a country E.G. *a nationwide search.*

**native natives**

ADJECTIVE 1 Your native country is the country where you were born. 2 Your native language is the language that you first learned to speak. 3 Animals or plants that are native to a place live or grow there naturally and have not been brought there by people.
▶ NOUN 4 A native of a place is someone who was born there.

**Nativity**

NOUN In Christianity, the Nativity is the birth of Christ or the festival celebrating this.

**natter natters nattering nattered**

VERB; INFORMAL If you natter, you talk about unimportant things.

**natural naturals**

ADJECTIVE 1 normal and to be expected E.G. *It was only natural that he was tempted.* 2 not trying to pretend or hide anything E.G. *Caitlin's natural manner reassured her.* 3 (D&T) existing or happening in nature E.G. *natural disasters.* 4 A natural ability is one you were born with. 5 Your natural mother or father is your real mother or father and not someone who has adopted you. ▶ NOUN 6 someone who is born with a particular ability E.G. *She's a natural at bridge.* 7 In music, a natural is a note that is not a sharp or a flat. It is

represented by the symbol (♮).

**naturally** ADVERB

■ (sense 4) inborn, inherent, innate

**nature natures**

NOUN 1 Nature is animals, plants, and all the other things in the world not made by people. 2 The nature of a person or thing is their basic character E.G. *She liked his warm, generous nature.*

📖 from Latin *natura* meaning 'birth'

**naughty naughtier naughtiest**

ADJECTIVE 1 behaving badly. 2 rude or indecent E.G. *naughty films.*

**naughtiness** NOUN

**nausea**

*Said* "naw-zee-ah" NOUN Nausea is a feeling in your stomach that you are going to be sick.

**nauseous** ADJECTIVE

**nautical**

*Said* "naw-tik-kl" ADJECTIVE relating to ships or navigation.

**naval**

ADJECTIVE relating to or having a navy E.G. *naval officers… naval bases.*

**navel navels**

NOUN the small hollow on the front of your body just below your waist.

**navigate navigates navigating navigated**

VERB 1 When someone navigates, they work out the direction in which a ship, plane, or car should go, using maps and sometimes instruments. 2 To navigate a stretch of water means to travel safely across it E.G. *It was the first time I had navigated the ocean.*

**navigation** NOUN **navigator** NOUN

**navy navies**

NOUN 1 the part of a country's armed

forces that fights at sea. ▶ ADJECTIVE
**2** dark blue.

**Nazi** Nazis

*Said* "**naht-see**" NOUN The Nazis were
members of the National Socialist
German Workers' Party, which was
led by Adolf Hitler.

**NB**

You write NB to draw attention to
what you are going to write next. NB
is an abbreviation for the Latin 'nota
bene', which means 'note well'.

**near** nearer nearest; nears
nearing neared

PREPOSITION or ADVERB **1** not far from.
▶ ADJECTIVE **2** You can also use 'near' to
mean almost *E.G. a night of near
disaster.* ▶ VERB **3** When you are
nearing something, you are
approaching it and will soon reach it
*E.G. The dog began to bark as he
neared the porch.*

**nearby**

ADJECTIVE or ADVERB only a short
distance away.

**nearly**

ADVERB not completely but almost.

**neat** neater neatest

ADJECTIVE **1** tidy and smart. **2** A neat
alcoholic drink does not have
anything added to it *E.G. a small glass
of neat vodka.*
**neatly** ADVERB **neatness** NOUN

**necessarily**

ADVERB Something that is not
necessarily the case is not always or
inevitably the case.

**necessary**

ADJECTIVE **1** Something that is
necessary is needed or must be
done. **2** FORMAL Necessary also means
certain or inevitable *E.G. a necessary
consequence of war.*

■ (sense 1) essential, needed,
requisite

**necessity** necessities

NOUN **1** Necessity is the need to do
something *E.G. There is no necessity for
any of this.* **2** Necessities are things
needed in order to live.

**neck** necks

NOUN **1** the part of your body which
joins your head to the rest of your
body. **2** the long narrow part at the
top of a bottle.

**necklace** necklaces

NOUN **1** a piece of jewellery which a
woman wears around her neck. **2** In
South Africa, a name for a tyre filled
with petrol which is placed round a
person's neck and set on fire in order
to kill that person.

**nectar**

NOUN Nectar is a sweet liquid produced
by flowers and attractive to insects.

**nectarine** nectarines

NOUN a kind of peach with a smooth
skin.

**née**

*Rhymes with* "**day**" 'Née' is used to
indicate what a woman's surname
was before she got married *E.G. Sara
Black, née Wells.*

**need** needs needing needed

VERB **1** If you need something, you
believe that you must have it or do
it. ▶ NOUN **2** Your needs are the things
that you need to have. **3** a strong
feeling that you must have or do
something *E.G. I just felt the need to
write about it.*

■ (sense 2) necessity, requirement

**needle** needles needling needled

NOUN **1** a small thin piece of metal
with a pointed end and a hole at the
other, which is used for sewing.

a
b
c
d
e
f
g
h
i
j
k
l
m
**n**
o
p
q
r
s
t
u
v
w
x
y
z

**2** Needles are also long thin pieces of steel or plastic, used for knitting. **3** the small pointed part in a record player that touches the record and picks up the sound signals. **4** the part of a syringe which a doctor or nurse sticks into your body. **5** the thin piece of metal or plastic on a dial which moves to show a measurement. **6** The needles of a pine tree are its leaves. ▶ VERB **7** INFORMAL If someone needles you, they annoy or provoke you.

## needless
ADJECTIVE unnecessary.
**needlessly** ADVERB

## needy needier neediest
ADJECTIVE very poor.

## negative ➤
ADJECTIVE **1** A negative answer means 'no'. **2** Someone who is negative sees only problems and disadvantages E.G. Why are you so negative about everything? **3** If a medical or scientific test is negative, it shows that something has not happened or is not present E.G. The pregnancy test came back negative. **4** (MATHS) A negative number is less than zero. ▶ NOUN **5** the image that is first produced when you take a photograph.
**negatively** ADVERB

## neglect neglects neglecting neglected
VERB **1** If you neglect something, you do not look after it properly. **2** FORMAL If you neglect to do something, you fail to do it E.G. He had neglected to give her his address. ▶ NOUN **3** Neglect is failure to look after something or someone properly E.G. Most of her plants died from neglect.
**neglectful** ADJECTIVE

## negligent
ADJECTIVE not taking enough care E.G. her negligent driving.
**negligence** NOUN

## negligible
ADJECTIVE very small and unimportant E.G. a negligible amount of fat.

## negotiable
ADJECTIVE able to be changed or agreed by discussion E.G. All contributions are negotiable.

## negotiate negotiates negotiating negotiated
VERB **1** When people negotiate, they have formal discussions in order to reach an agreement about something. **2** If you negotiate an obstacle, you manage to get over it or round it.
**negotiation** NOUN **negotiator** NOUN

## Negro Negroes
NOUN; OLD-FASHIONED a person with black skin who comes from Africa or whose ancestors came from Africa.

## neigh neighs neighing neighed
Rhymes with "day" VERB **1** When a horse neighs, it makes a loud high-pitched sound. ▶ NOUN **2** a loud sound made by a horse.

## neighbour neighbours
NOUN **1** Your neighbour is someone who lives next door to you or near you. **2** Your neighbour is also someone standing or sitting next to you E.G. I got chatting with my neighbour in the studio.

## neighbourhood neighbourhoods
NOUN a district where people live E.G. a safe neighbourhood.

## neighbouring
ADJECTIVE situated nearby E.G. schools in neighbouring areas.

## neither
ADJECTIVE or PRONOUN used to indicate that a negative statement refers to two or more things or people E.G. *It's neither a play nor a musical… Neither of them spoke.*

☑ When *neither* is followed by a plural noun, the verb can be plural too: *neither of these books are useful.* When you have two singular subjects the verb should be singular too: *neither Jack nor John has done the work.*

## neo-
PREFIX new or modern E.G. *neo-fascism.*
📖 from Greek *neos* meaning 'new'

## nephew nephews
NOUN Someone's nephew is the son of their sister or brother.

## Neptune
NOUN Neptune is the planet in the solar system which is eighth from the sun.
📖 from *Neptune*, the Roman god of the sea

## nerve nerves
NOUN 1 a long thin fibre that sends messages between your brain and other parts of your body. 2 If you talk about someone's nerves, you are referring to how able they are to remain calm in a difficult situation E.G. *It needs confidence and strong nerves.* 3 Nerve is courage E.G. *O'Meara held his nerve to sink the putt.* 4 INFORMAL Nerve is boldness or rudeness E.G. *He had the nerve to swear at me.* ▶ AN INFORMAL PHRASE 5 If someone **gets on your nerves**, they irritate you.

## nerve-racking
ADJECTIVE making you feel very worried and tense E.G. *a nerve-racking experience.*

## nervous
ADJECTIVE 1 worried and frightened. 2 A nervous illness affects your emotions and mental health.
**nervously** ADVERB **nervousness** NOUN
🔲 (sense 1) apprehensive, edgy, jumpy

## nervous breakdown nervous breakdowns
NOUN an illness in which someone suffers from deep depression and needs psychiatric treatment.

## nervous system nervous systems
NOUN Your nervous system is the nerves in your body together with your brain and spinal cord.

## -ness
SUFFIX '-ness' forms nouns from adjectives E.G. *tenderness… happiness.*
📖 from an Old English suffix

## nest nests nesting nested
NOUN 1 a place that a bird makes to lay its eggs in; also a place that some insects and other animals make to rear their young in. ▶ VERB 2 When birds nest, they build a nest and lay eggs in it.

## nestle nestles nestling nestled
Said "**ness**-əl" VERB If you nestle somewhere, you settle there comfortably, often pressing up against someone else E.G. *A new puppy nestled in her lap.*

## nestling nestlings
NOUN a young bird that has not yet learned to fly and so has not left the nest.

## net nets
NOUN 1 a piece of material made of

a b c d e f g h i j k l m **n** o p q r s t u v w x y z

threads woven together with small spaces in between. **2** The net is the same as the **Internet**. ▶ ADJECTIVE **3** A net result or amount is final, after everything has been considered E.G. *a net profit of 171 million.* **4** The net weight of something is its weight without its wrapping.

### netball
NOUN Netball is a game played by two teams of seven players in which each team tries to score goals by throwing a ball through a net at the top of a pole.

### netting
NOUN Netting is material made of threads or metal wires woven together with small spaces in between.

### nettle nettles
NOUN a wild plant covered with little hairs that sting.

### network networks
NOUN **1** a large number of lines or roads which cross each other at many points E.G. *a small network of side roads.* **2** A network of people or organizations is a large number of them that work together as a system E.G. *the public telephone network.* **3** A television network is a group of broadcasting stations that all transmit the same programmes at the same time. **4** ( ICT ) a group of computers connected to each other.

### neuron neurons
NOUN a cell that is part of the nervous system and conducts messages to and from the brain.

### neurone neurones
NOUN the same as a **neuron**.

### neurosis neuroses
Said "nyoor-**roh**-siss" NOUN Neurosis is

mental illness which causes people to have strong and unreasonable fears and worries.

### neurotic
Said "nyoor-**rot**-ik" ADJECTIVE having strong and unreasonable fears and worries E.G. *He was almost neurotic about being followed.*

### neuter neuters neutering neutered
Said "**nyoo**-ter" VERB **1** When an animal is neutered, its reproductive organs are removed. ▶ ADJECTIVE **2** In some languages, a neuter noun or pronoun is one which is not masculine or feminine.

---

#### What is Neuter?

**Neuter nouns** refer to inanimate objects and abstract ideas:
E.G. *The kettle will switch itself off.* ▶ *kettle is* **neuter**

Also look at the grammar boxes at **gender**, **masculine** and **feminine**.

---

### neutral neutrals
ADJECTIVE **1** People who are neutral do not support either side in a disagreement or war. **2** The neutral wire in an electric plug is the one that is not earth or live. **3** A neutral colour is not definite or striking, for example pale grey. **4** In chemistry, a neutral substance is neither acid nor alkaline. ▶ NOUN **5** a person or country that does not support either side in a disagreement or war. **6** Neutral is the position between the gears of a vehicle in which the gears are not connected to the engine and so the vehicle cannot move.

### neutrality NOUN

**neutron** neutrons
NOUN an atomic particle that has no
electrical charge.

**never**
ADVERB at no time in the past, present,
or future
☑ Do not use *never* to mean 'not' in
writing. You should say *I didn't see her*
not *I never saw her.*

**nevertheless**
ADVERB in spite of what has just been
said E.G. *They dress rather plainly but
nevertheless look quite smart.*

**new** newer newest
ADJECTIVE 1 recently made or created
E.G. *a new house… a new plan.* 2 only
recently discovered E.G. *a new virus.*
3 not used or owned before E.G. *We've
got a new car.* 4 different or
unfamiliar E.G. *a name which was new
to me.*
■ (sense 1) latest, modern, recent

**newborn**
ADJECTIVE born recently.

**newcomer** newcomers
NOUN someone who has recently
arrived in a place.

**newly**
ADVERB recently E.G. *the newly born baby.*

**new moon** new moons
NOUN The moon is a new moon when
it is a thin crescent shape at the start
of its four-week cycle.

**news**
NOUN News is information about
things that have happened.

**newsagent** newsagents
NOUN a person or shop that sells
newspapers and magazines.

**newspaper** newspapers
NOUN a publication, on large sheets of
paper, that is produced regularly and
contains news and articles.

**newt** newts
NOUN a small amphibious creature
with a moist skin, short legs, and a
long tail.
▥ from a mistaken division of
Middle English *an ewt*

**New Testament**
NOUN The New Testament is the
second part of the Bible, which deals
with the life of Jesus Christ and with
the early Church.

**New Year**
NOUN New Year is the time when
people celebrate the start of a year.

**New Zealander** New
Zealanders
NOUN someone who comes from New
Zealand.

**next**
ADJECTIVE or ADVERB 1 coming
immediately after something else E.G.
*They lived in the next street.* ▶ PHRASE
2 If one thing is **next to** another, it is
at the side of it.
■ (sense 1) following, subsequent

**next door**
ADJECTIVE or ADVERB in the house next to
yours.

**NHS**
In Britain, an abbreviation for
'National Health Service'.

**nib** nibs
NOUN the pointed end of a pen.

**nibble** nibbles nibbling nibbled
VERB 1 When you nibble something,
you take small bites of it. ▶ NOUN 2 a
small bite of something.

**nice** nicer nicest
ADJECTIVE pleasant or attractive.
**nicely** ADVERB

**nicety** niceties
*Said* "nigh-se-tee" NOUN a small detail
E.G. *the social niceties.*

a
b
c
d
e
f
g
h
i
j
k
l
m
n
o
p
q
r
s
t
u
v
w
x
y
z

The government licenSes Schnapps (licenses)   SPELLING NOTE

A B C D E F G H I J K L M **N** O P Q R S T U V W X Y Z

**niche** niches
*Said "neesh"* NOUN 1 a hollow area in a wall. 2 If you say that you have found your niche, you mean that you have found a job or way of life that is exactly right for you.

**nick** nicks nicking nicked
VERB 1 If you nick something, you make a small cut in its surface *E.G. He nicked his chin.* 2 *INFORMAL* To nick something also means to steal it.
▶ NOUN 3 a small cut in the surface of something.

**nickel**
NOUN Nickel is a silver-coloured metal that is used in making steel.

**nickname** nicknames nicknaming nicknamed
NOUN 1 an informal name given to someone. ▶ VERB 2 If you nickname someone, you give them a nickname.
📖 from Middle English *an ekename* meaning 'an additional name'

**nicotine**
NOUN Nicotine is an addictive substance found in tobacco.

**niece** nieces
NOUN Someone's niece is the daughter of their sister or brother.

**nifty**
ADJECTIVE neat and pleasing or cleverly done.

**Nigerian** Nigerians
*Said "nie-jeer-ee-an"* ADJECTIVE
1 belonging or relating to Nigeria.
▶ NOUN 2 someone from Nigeria.

**niggle** niggles niggling niggled
VERB 1 If something niggles you, it worries you slightly. ▶ NOUN 2 a small worry that you keep thinking about.

**night** nights
NOUN Night is the time between sunset and sunrise when it is dark.

**nightclub** nightclubs
NOUN a place where people go late in the evening to drink and dance.

**nightdress** nightdresses
NOUN a loose dress that a woman or girl wears to sleep in.

**nightfall**
NOUN Nightfall is the time of day when it starts to get dark.

**nightie** nighties
NOUN; *INFORMAL* a nightdress.

**nightingale** nightingales
NOUN a small brown European bird, the male of which sings very beautifully, especially at night.

**nightly**
ADJECTIVE or ADVERB happening every night *E.G. the nightly news programme.*

**nightmare** nightmares
NOUN a very frightening dream; also used of any very unpleasant or frightening situation *E.G. The meal itself was a nightmare.*
**nightmarish** ADJECTIVE
📖 from *night* + Middle English *mare* meaning 'evil spirit'

**nil**
NOUN Nil means zero or nothing. It is used especially in sports scores.

**nimble** nimbler nimblest
ADJECTIVE 1 able to move quickly and easily. 2 able to think quickly and cleverly.
**nimbly** ADVERB

**nine**
the number 9.
**ninth**

**nineteen**
the number 19.
**nineteenth**

**ninety** nineties
the number 90.
**ninetieth**

**nip** nips nipping nipped
VERB **1** INFORMAL If you nip somewhere, you go there quickly. **2** To nip someone or something means to pinch or them slightly. ▶ NOUN **3** a light pinch.

**nipple** nipples
NOUN Your nipples are the two small pieces of projecting flesh on your chest. Babies suck milk through the nipples on their mothers' breasts.

**nirvana**
*Said* "neer-**vah**-na" NOUN Nirvana is the ultimate state of spiritual enlightenment which can be achieved in the Hindu and Buddhist religions.

**nit** nits
NOUN Nits are the eggs of a kind of louse that sometimes lives in people's hair.

**nitrogen**
NOUN Nitrogen is a chemical element usually found as a gas. It forms about 78% of the earth's atmosphere.

**no**
INTERJECTION **1** used to say that something is not true or to refuse something. ▶ ADJECTIVE **2** none at all or not at all E.G. *She gave no reason… You're no friend of mine.* ▶ ADVERB **3** used with a comparative to mean 'not' E.G. *no later than 24th July.*

**no.**
a written abbreviation for **number.**

**nobility**
NOUN **1** Nobility is the quality of being noble E.G. *the unmistakable nobility of his character.* **2** The nobility of a society are all the people who have titles and high social rank.

**noble** nobler noblest; nobles
ADJECTIVE **1** honest and brave, and

deserving admiration. **2** very impressive E.G. *broad cheekbones which gave them a noble appearance.* ▶ NOUN **3** a member of the nobility.
**nobly** ADVERB

**nobleman** noblemen
NOUN a man who is a member of the nobility.
**noblewoman** NOUN

**nobody** nobodies
PRONOUN **1** not a single person. ▶ NOUN **2** Someone who is a nobody is not at all important
☑ *Nobody* and *no-one* mean the same.

**nocturnal**
ADJECTIVE **1** happening at night E.G. *a nocturnal journey through New York.* **2** active at night E.G. *a nocturnal animal.*

**nod** nods nodding nodded
VERB **1** When you nod, you move your head up and down, usually to show agreement. ▶ NOUN **2** a movement of your head up and down.
**nod off** VERB If you nod off, you fall asleep.

**noise** noises
NOUN a sound, especially one that is loud or unpleasant.
◧ din, racket, sound

**noisy** noisier noisiest
ADJECTIVE making a lot of noise or full of noise E.G. *a noisy crowd.*
**noisily** ADVERB **noisiness** NOUN

**nomad** nomads
NOUN a person who belongs to a tribe which travels from place to place rather than living in just one place.
**nomadic** ADJECTIVE

**nominal**
ADJECTIVE **1** Something that is nominal is supposed to have a particular

a b c d e f g h i j k l m n o p q r s t u v w x y z

identity or status, but in reality does not have it *E.G. the nominal leader of his party.* **2** A nominal amount of money is very small compared to the value of something *E.G. I am prepared to sell my shares at a nominal price.*
**nominally** ADVERB

**nominate** nominates nominating nominated
VERB If you nominate someone for a job or position, you formally suggest that they have it.
**nomination** NOUN
■ name, propose, suggest

**non-**
PREFIX not *E.G. non-smoking.*
from Latin

**nonchalant**
*Said* "**non**-shal-nt" ADJECTIVE seeming calm and not worried.
**nonchalance** NOUN   **nonchalantly** ADVERB

**noncommissioned officer** noncommissioned officers
NOUN an officer such as a sergeant or corporal who has been promoted from the lower ranks.

**nondescript**
ADJECTIVE Someone or something nondescript has no special or interesting qualities or details *E.G. a nondescript coat.*

**none**
PRONOUN not a single thing or person, or not even a small amount of something.

**nonfiction**
NOUN (LIBRARY) Nonfiction is writing that gives facts and information rather than telling a story.

**nonplussed**
ADJECTIVE confused and unsure about how to react.

**nonsense**
NOUN Nonsense is foolish and meaningless words or behaviour.
**nonsensical** ADJECTIVE

**nonstop**
ADJECTIVE OR ADVERB continuing without any pauses or breaks *E.G. nonstop excitement.*

**noodle** noodles
NOUN Noodles are a kind of pasta shaped into long, thin pieces.

**nook** nooks
NOUN; *LITERARY* a small sheltered place.

**noon**
NOUN Noon is midday.

**no-one** or **no one**
PRONOUN not a single person
☑ *No-one* and *nobody* mean the same.

**noose** nooses
NOUN a loop at the end of a piece of rope, with a knot that tightens when the rope is pulled.

**nor**
CONJUNCTION used after 'neither' or after a negative statement, to add something else that the negative statement applies to *E.G. They had neither the time nor the money for the sport.*

**norm**
NOUN If something is the norm, it is the usual and expected thing *E.G. cultures where large families are the norm.*
rom Latin *norma* meaning 'carpenter's rule'

**normal**
ADJECTIVE usual and ordinary *E.G. I try to lead a normal life.*
**normality** NOUN
■ conventional, ordinary, usual

**normally**
ADVERB **1** usually *E.G. I don't normally*

*like dancing.* **2** in a way that is normal *E.G. The foetus is developing normally.*

**north**
NOUN **1** The north is the direction to your left when you are looking towards the place where the sun rises. **2** The north of a place or country is the part which is towards the north when you are in the centre. ► ADVERB OR ADJECTIVE **3** North means towards the north *E.G. The helicopter took off and headed north.* ► ADJECTIVE **4** A north wind blows from the north.

**North America**
NOUN North America is the third largest continent, consisting of Canada, the United States, and Mexico.
**North American** ADJECTIVE

**north-east**
NOUN, ADVERB, OR ADJECTIVE North-east is halfway between north and east.

**north-easterly**
ADJECTIVE **1** North-easterly means to or towards the north-east. **2** A north-easterly wind blows from the north-east.

**north-eastern**
ADJECTIVE in or from the north-east.

**northerly**
ADJECTIVE **1** Northerly means to or towards the north *E.G. travelling in a northerly direction.* **2** A northerly wind blows from the north.

**northern**
ADJECTIVE in or from the north *E.G. the mountains of northern Italy.*

**North Pole**
NOUN The North Pole is the most northerly point of the earth's surface.

**northward** or **northwards**
ADVERB **1** Northward or northwards means towards the north *E.G. We continued northwards.* ► ADJECTIVE **2** The northward part of something is the north part.

**north-west**
NOUN, ADVERB, OR ADJECTIVE North-west is halfway between north and west.

**north-westerly**
ADJECTIVE **1** North-westerly means to or towards the north-west. **2** A north-westerly wind blows from the north-west.

**north-western**
ADJECTIVE in or from the north-west.

**Norwegian Norwegians**
*Said "nor-wee-jn"* ADJECTIVE **1** belonging or relating to Norway. ► NOUN **2** someone who comes from Norway. **3** Norwegian is the main language spoken in Norway.

**nose noses**
NOUN **1** the part of your face above your mouth which you use for smelling and breathing. **2** the front part of a car or plane.

**nostalgia**
*Said "nos-tal-ja"* NOUN Nostalgia is a feeling of affection for the past, and sadness that things have changed.
**nostalgic** ADJECTIVE

**nostril nostrils**
NOUN Your nostrils are the two openings in your nose which you breathe through.

**nosy nosier nosiest**; also spelt **nosey**
ADJECTIVE trying to find out about things that do not concern you.

**not**
ADVERB used to make a sentence negative, to refuse something, or to deny something.

### What does 'not' do?

You can turn most sentences into negatives if you want to express the opposite meaning.

You can usually make a sentence into a negative by adding the word *not*:

*E.G. Robbie was **not** feeling tired.*

If a sentence already contains an auxiliary verb, such as *have*, *will*, *be*, or *must*, the word *not* should go after this verb:

*E.G. She has **not** gone to the shops.*

If the sentence does not already contain an auxiliary verb, a form of the verb *do* is added, and the word *not* is placed after this:

*E.G. We **do** not expect to win.*

In spoken and informal English, the ending *-n't* may be added to an auxiliary verb in place of *not*:

*E.G. She **hasn't** gone to the shops.*

## notable
ADJECTIVE important or interesting *E.G. The production is notable for some outstanding performances.*
**notably** ADVERB

## notch notches
NOUN a small V-shaped cut in a surface.
rom a mistaken division of Middle English *an otch*

## note notes noting noted
NOUN 1 a short letter. 2 a written piece of information that helps you to remember something *E.G. You should make a note of that.* 3 In music, a note is a musical sound of a particular pitch, or a written symbol that represents it. 4 a banknote. 5 an atmosphere, feeling, or quality *E.G. There was a note of regret in his voice… I'm determined to close on an optimistic note.* ▶ VERB 6 If you note a fact, you become aware of it or you mention it *E.G. I noted that the rain had stopped.* ▶ PHRASE 7 If you **take note** of something, you pay attention to it *E.G. The world hardly took note of this crisis.*

**note down** VERB If you note something down, you write it down so that you will remember it.

## notebook notebooks
NOUN a small book for writing notes in.

## noted
ADJECTIVE well-known and admired *E.G. a noted Hebrew scholar.*

## nothing
PRONOUN not anything *E.G. There was nothing to do.*
▤ nil, nought, zero
☑ *Nothing* is usually followed by a singular verb: *nothing was in the bag.* If the expression *nothing but* is followed by a plural noun, the verb should be plural too: *a large room where nothing but souvenirs were sold.*

## notice notices noticing noticed
VERB 1 If you notice something, you become aware of it. ▶ NOUN 2 Notice is attention or awareness *E.G. I'm glad he brought it to my notice.* 3 a written announcement. 4 Notice is also advance warning about something *E.G. We were lucky to get you at such short notice.* ▶ PHRASE 5 If you **hand in your notice**, you tell your employer that you intend to leave your job after a fixed period of time.
▤ (sense 1) detect, observe, perceive

**noticeable**

ADJECTIVE obvious and easy to see E.G. *a noticeable improvement.*
noticeably ADVERB

**noticeboard** noticeboards
NOUN a board for notices.

**notify** notifies notifying notified
VERB To notify someone of something means to officially inform them of it E.G. *You must notify us of any change of address.*
notification NOUN

**notion** notions
NOUN an idea or belief.

**notorious**
ADJECTIVE well-known for something bad E.G. *The area has become notorious for violence against tourists.*
notoriously ADVERB notoriety NOUN

**notwithstanding**
PREPOSITION; FORMAL in spite of E.G. *Notwithstanding his age, Sikorski had an important job.*

**nougat**
Said "noo-gah" NOUN Nougat is a kind of chewy sweet containing nuts and sometimes fruit.
🏛 from Provençal *noga* meaning 'nut'

**nought**
the number 0.

**noun** nouns
NOUN a word which refers to a person, thing, or idea. Examples of nouns are 'president', 'table', 'sun', and 'beauty'. → SEE BOX OPPOSITE

**nourish** nourishes nourishing nourished
Said "nur-rish" VERB To nourish people or animals means to provide them with food.

---

### What is a Noun?

A noun is a word that labels a person, a thing or an idea. In any sentence, the nouns will tell you which people or things are involved. They are sometimes called "naming words".

**Common nouns** are words which indicate every example of a certain type of thing. They begin with small letters:
E.G. *girl* ■ *city* ■ *picture*

**Proper nouns** are words which give the name of a particular person, place, or object. They begin with capital letters:
E.G. *Anna Jamieson* ■ *Los Angeles* *The Mona Lisa*

Some common nouns are **concrete nouns**. These are words that indicate things that you *can* touch:
E.G. *cat* ■ *pen* ■ *apple*

Other common nouns are **abstract nouns**. These are words that indicate things that you *cannot* touch:
E.G. *beauty* ■ *ambition* ■ *popularity*

Some common nouns are **collective nouns**. These are words that indicate a group or collection of things:
E.G. *pack* ■ *bunch* ■ *flock*

**nourishing**
ADJECTIVE Food that is nourishing makes you strong and healthy.

**nourishment**
NOUN Nourishment is food that your body needs in order to remain healthy E.G. *poor nourishment.*

A
B
C
D
E
F
G
H
I
J
K
L
M
N
O
P
Q
R
S
T
U
V
W
X
Y
Z

**novel** novels
NOUN 1 (LIBRARY) a book that tells an invented story. ▶ ADJECTIVE 2 new and interesting E.G. *a very novel experience*.

**novelist** novelists
NOUN a person who writes novels.

**novelty** novelties
NOUN 1 Novelty is the quality of being new and interesting E.G. *The novelty had worn off*. 2 something new and interesting E.G. *Steam power was still a bit of a novelty*. 3 a small, unusual object sold as a gift or souvenir.

**November**
NOUN November is the eleventh month of the year. It has 30 days.
🏛 from Latin *November* meaning 'the ninth month'

**novice** novices
NOUN 1 someone who is not yet experienced at something.
2 someone who is preparing to become a monk or nun.

**now**
ADVERB 1 at the present time or moment. ▶ CONJUNCTION 2 as a result or consequence of a particular fact E.G. *Things have got better now there is a new board*. ▶ PHRASE 3 Just now means very recently E.G. *I drove Brenda back to the camp just now*. 4 If something happens now and then, it happens sometimes but not regularly.

**nowadays**
ADVERB at the present time E.G. *Nowadays most fathers choose to be present at the birth*.

**nowhere**
ADVERB not anywhere.

**noxious**
Said "**nok**-shus" ADJECTIVE harmful or

poisonous E.G. *a noxious gas*.

**nozzle** nozzles
NOUN a spout fitted onto the end of a pipe or hose to control the flow of a liquid.

**nuance** nuances
Said "**nyoo**-ahnss" NOUN a small difference in sound, colour, or meaning E.G. *the nuances of his music*.

**nubile**
Said "**nyoo**-bile" ADJECTIVE A woman who is nubile is young and sexually attractive.
🏛 from Latin *nubere* meaning 'to take a husband'

**nuclear**
ADJECTIVE 1 relating to the energy produced when the nuclei of atoms are split E.G. *nuclear power… the nuclear industry*. 2 relating to weapons that explode using the energy released by atoms E.G. *nuclear war*. 3 relating to the structure and behaviour of the nuclei of atoms E.G. *nuclear physics*.

**nuclear reactor** nuclear reactors
NOUN A nuclear reactor is a device which is used to obtain nuclear energy.

**nucleus** nuclei
Said "**nyoo**-klee-uss" NOUN 1 the central part of an atom or cell. 2 The nucleus of something is the basic central part of it to which other things are added E.G. *They have retained the nucleus of the team that won the World Cup*.
🏛 from Latin *nucleus* meaning 'kernel'

**nude** nudes
ADJECTIVE 1 naked. ▶ NOUN 2 a picture or

statue of a naked person.

**nudity** NOUN

**nudge** nudges nudging nudged
VERB **1** If you nudge someone, you push them gently, usually with your elbow. ▶ NOUN **2** a gentle push.

**nudist** nudists
NOUN a person who believes in wearing no clothes.

**nugget** nuggets
NOUN a small rough lump of something, especially gold.

**nuisance** nuisances
NOUN someone or something that is annoying or inconvenient.
■ bother, inconvenience, problem

**null**
PHRASE **Null and void** means not legally valid E.G. *Other documents were declared to be null and void.*

**nulla-nulla** nulla-nullas
NOUN a thick heavy stick used as a weapon by Australian Aborigines.

**numb** numbs numbing numbed
ADJECTIVE **1** unable to feel anything E.G. *My legs felt numb… numb with grief.*
▶ VERB **2** If something numbs you, it makes you unable to feel anything E.G. *The cold numbed my fingers.*

**numbat** numbats
NOUN a small Australian marsupial with a long snout and tongue and strong claws which it uses for hunting and eating insects.

**number** numbers numbering numbered
NOUN **1** a word or a symbol used for counting or calculating. **2** Someone's number is the series of numbers that you dial when you telephone them. **3** A number of things is a quantity of them E.G. *Adrian has introduced me to*

a large number of people. **4** a song or piece of music. ▶ VERB **5** If things number a particular amount, there are that many of them E.G. *At that time London's population numbered about 460,000.* **6** If you number something, you give it a number E.G. *The picture is signed and numbered by the artist.* **7** To be numbered among a particular group means to belong to it E.G. *Only the best are numbered among their champions.*
■ (sense 1) digit, figure, numeral

---

### What do Numbers do?

**Numbers** tell you how many of a thing there are.

**Cardinal numbers** tell you the total number of a thing:

E.G. **Three** figures huddled in the doorway.

**Ordinal numbers** tell you the order of something. They often end with the letters *-th*:

E.G. Her **sixth** novel was the most successful yet.

---

**numeral** numerals
NOUN a symbol that represents a number E.G. *a wristwatch with Roman numerals.*

**numerator** numerators
NOUN (MATHS) In maths, the numerator is the top part of a fraction.

**numerical**
ADJECTIVE expressed in numbers or relating to numbers E.G. *a numerical value.*

**numerous**
ADJECTIVE existing or happening in large numbers.

the QUeen stood on the QUay (quay)    SPELLING NOTE

A
B
C
D
E
F
G
H
I
J
K
L
M
N
O
P
Q
R
S
T
U
V
W
X
Y
Z

**nun** nuns
NOUN a woman who has taken religious vows and lives in a convent.

**nurse** nurses nursing nursed
NOUN 1 a person whose job is to look after people who are ill. ▶ VERB 2 If you nurse someone, you look after them when they are ill. 3 If you nurse a feeling, you feel it strongly for a long time E.G. He nursed a grudge against the USA.

**nursery** nurseries
NOUN 1 a place where young children are looked after while their parents are working. 2 a room in which young children sleep and play. 3 a place where plants are grown and sold.

**nursery school** nursery schools
NOUN a school for children from three to five years old.

**nursing home** nursing homes
NOUN a privately run hospital, especially for old people.

**nurture** nurtures nurturing nurtured
VERB; FORMAL If you nurture a young child or a plant, you look after it carefully.

**nut** nuts
NOUN 1 a fruit with a hard shell and an edible centre that grows on certain trees. 2 a piece of metal with a hole in the middle which a bolt screws into.

**nutmeg**
NOUN Nutmeg is a spice used for flavouring in cooking.

**nutrient** nutrients
NOUN (SCIENCE) Nutrients are substances that help plants or animals to grow E.G. the nutrients in the soil.

**nutrition**
NOUN (D & T) Nutrition is the food that you eat, considered from the point of view of how it helps you to grow and remain healthy E.G. The effects of poor nutrition are evident.
**nutritional** ADJECTIVE **nutritionist** NOUN

**nutritious**
ADJECTIVE containing substances that help you to grow and remain healthy.

**nutty** nuttier nuttiest
ADJECTIVE 1 INFORMAL mad or very foolish. 2 tasting of nuts.

**nylon** nylons
NOUN 1 Nylon is a type of strong artificial material E.G. nylon stockings. 2 Nylons are stockings or tights.

# Oo

**oaf** oafs
NOUN a clumsy and stupid person.
📖 from Old Norse *alfr* meaning 'elf'

**oak** oaks
NOUN a large tree which produces acorns. It has a hard wood which is often used to make furniture.

**OAP** OAPs
NOUN In Britain, a man over the age of 65 or a woman over the age of 60 who receives a pension. OAP is an abbreviation for 'old age pensioner'.

**oar** oars
NOUN a wooden pole with a wide, flat end, used for rowing a boat.

**oasis** oases
*Said* "oh-ay-siss" NOUN a small area in a desert where water and plants are found.

**oat** oats
NOUN Oats are a type of grain.

**oath** oaths
NOUN a formal promise, especially a promise to tell the truth in a court of law.
📧 pledge, promise, vow

**oatmeal**
NOUN Oatmeal is a rough flour made from oats.

**OBE** OBEs
NOUN a British honour awarded by the King or Queen. OBE is an abbreviation for 'Officer of the Order of the British Empire'.

**obedient**
ADJECTIVE If you are obedient, you do what you are told to do.
**obediently** ADVERB **obedience** NOUN

**obelisk** obelisks
NOUN a stone pillar built in honour of a person or an event.

**obese**
*Said* "oh-**bees**" ADJECTIVE extremely fat.
**obesity** NOUN
📖 from Latin *ob-* meaning 'much' and *edere* meaning 'to eat'

**obey** obeys obeying obeyed
VERB If you obey a person or an order, you do what you are told to do.

**obituary** obituaries
NOUN a piece of writing about the life and achievements of someone who has just died.

**object** objects objecting objected
NOUN 1 anything solid that you can touch or see, and that is not alive. 2 an aim or purpose. 3 The object of your feelings or actions is the person that they are directed towards. 4 In grammar, the object of a verb or preposition is the word or phrase which follows it and describes the person or thing affected. ▶ VERB 5 If you object to something, you dislike it or disapprove of it.
📧 (sense 5) oppose, protest, take exception

**objection** objections
NOUN If you have an objection to something, you dislike it or disapprove of it.

**objectionable**
ADJECTIVE unpleasant and offensive.

**objective** objectives
NOUN 1 an aim *E.G. The protection of the countryside is their main objective.*
▶ ADJECTIVE 2 If you are objective, you are not influenced by personal feelings or prejudices *E.G. an objective approach.*
**objectively** ADVERB **objectivity** NOUN

**obligation** obligations
NOUN something that you must do
because it is your duty.

**obligatory**
Said "ob-lig-a-tree" ADJECTIVE required
by a rule or law E.G. Religious
education was made obligatory.

**oblige** obliges obliging obliged
VERB 1 If you are obliged to do
something, you have to do it. 2 If you
oblige someone, you help them.
**obliging** ADJECTIVE

**oblique**
Said "o-bleek" ADJECTIVE 1 An oblique
remark is not direct, and is therefore
difficult to understand. 2 An oblique
line slopes at an angle.

**obliterate** obliterates
obliterating obliterated
VERB To obliterate something is to
destroy it completely.
**obliteration** NOUN

**oblivion**
NOUN Oblivion is unconsciousness or
complete lack of awareness of your
surroundings.
**oblivious** ADJECTIVE **obliviously**
ADVERB

**oblong** oblongs
NOUN 1 a four-sided shape with two
parallel short sides, two parallel long
sides, and four right angles.
▶ ADJECTIVE 2 shaped like an oblong.

**obnoxious**
Said "ob-nok-shuss" ADJECTIVE
extremely unpleasant.

**oboe** oboes
NOUN a woodwind musical
instrument with a double reed.
**oboist** NOUN
▥ from French haut bois meaning
literally 'high wood', a reference to
the instrument's pitch

**obscene**
ADJECTIVE indecent and likely to upset
people E.G. obscene pictures.
**obscenely** ADVERB **obscenity** NOUN
▣ filthy, indecent, pornographic

**obscure** obscures obscuring
obscured
ADJECTIVE 1 Something that is obscure
is known by only a few people E.G. an
obscure Mongolian dialect.
2 Something obscure is difficult to
see or to understand E.G. The news
was shrouded in obscure language.
▶ VERB 3 To obscure something is to
make it difficult to see or understand
E.G. His view was obscured by trees.
**obscurity** NOUN
▣ (sense 2) cryptic, unclear, vague

**observance**
NOUN The observance of a law or
custom is the practice of obeying or
following it.

**observant**
ADJECTIVE Someone who is observant
notices things that are not easy to
see.

**observation** observations
NOUN 1 Observation is the act of
watching something carefully E.G.
Success hinges on close observation.
2 something that you have seen or
noticed. 3 a remark. 4 Observation is
the ability to notice things that are
not easy to see.

**observatory** observatories
NOUN a room or building containing
telescopes and other equipment for
studying the sun, moon, and stars.

**observe** observes observing
observed
VERB 1 To observe something is to
watch it carefully. 2 To observe
something is to notice it. 3 If you

observe that something is the case, you make a comment about it. **4** To observe a law or custom is to obey or follow it.
**observer** NOUN **observable** ADJECTIVE

**obsession obsessions**
NOUN If someone has an obsession about something, they cannot stop thinking about that thing.
**obsessional** ADJECTIVE **obsessed** ADJECTIVE **obsessive** ADJECTIVE

**obsolete**
ADJECTIVE out of date and no longer used.
▪ outmoded, passé

**obstacle obstacles**
NOUN something which is in your way and makes it difficult to do something.
▪ difficulty, stumbling block

**obstetrics**
NOUN Obstetrics is the branch of medicine concerned with pregnancy and childbirth.
**obstetrician** NOUN

**obstinate**
ADJECTIVE Someone who is obstinate is stubborn and unwilling to change their mind.
**obstinately** ADVERB **obstinacy** NOUN

**obstruct obstructs obstructing obstructed**
VERB If something obstructs a road or path, it blocks it.
**obstruction** NOUN **obstructive** ADJECTIVE

**obtain obtains obtaining obtained**
VERB If you obtain something, you get it.
**obtainable** ADJECTIVE

**obtrusive**
ADJECTIVE noticeable in an unpleasant way E.G. *a remarkably obtrusive cigar.*

**obtuse**
ADJECTIVE **1** Someone who is obtuse is stupid or slow to understand things. **2** An obtuse angle is an angle between 90° and 180°.

**obvious**
ADJECTIVE easy to see or understand.
**obviously** ADVERB
▪ clear, evident, plain

**occasion occasions occasioning occasioned**
NOUN **1** a time when something happens. **2** an important event. **3** An occasion for doing something is an opportunity for doing it. ▶ VERB **4** FORMAL To occasion something is to cause it E.G. *damage occasioned by fire.*

**occasional**
ADJECTIVE happening sometimes but not often E.G. *an occasional outing.*
**occasionally** ADVERB

**occult**
NOUN The occult is the knowledge and study of supernatural and magical forces or powers.

**occupancy**
NOUN The occupancy of a building is the act of living or working in it.

**occupant occupants**
NOUN The occupants of a building are the people who live or work in it.

**occupation occupations**
NOUN **1** a job or profession. **2** a hobby or something you do for pleasure. **3** The occupation of a country is the act of invading it and taking control of it.
**occupational** ADJECTIVE

a b c d e f g h i j k l m n o p q r s t u v w x y z

A B C D E F G H I J K L M N O P Q R S T U V W X Y Z

**occupy** occupies occupying occupied

VERB **1** The people who occupy a building are the people who live or work there. **2** When people occupy a place, they move into it and take control of it E.G. *Demonstrators occupied the building.* **3** To occupy a position in a system or plan is to have that position E.G. *His phone-in show occupies a daytime slot.* **4** If something occupies you, you spend your time doing it E.G. *That problem occupies me night and day.*
**occupier** NOUN

**occur** occurs occurring occurred

VERB **1** If something occurs, it happens or exists E.G. *The second attack occurred at a swimming pool.* **2** If something occurs to you, you suddenly think of it

☑ If an event has been planned, you should not say that it *occurred* or *happened*: the wedding took place on Saturday. Only something unexpected *occurs* or *happens*: an accident has occurred; the burglary happened last night.

**occurrence** occurrences

NOUN **1** an event. **2** The occurrence of something is the fact that it happens or exists E.G. *the occurrence of diseases.*

**ocean** oceans

NOUN **1** LITERARY the sea. **2** The five oceans are the five very large areas of sea E.G. *the Atlantic Ocean.*
**oceanic** ADJECTIVE

**o'clock**

ADVERB You use 'o'clock' after the number of the hour to say what the time is.

**octagon** octagons

NOUN a shape with eight straight sides.
**octagonal** ADJECTIVE

**octave** octaves

NOUN (MUSIC) the difference in pitch between the first note and the eighth note of a musical scale.

**October**

NOUN October is the tenth month of the year. It has 31 days.
📖 from Latin *october* meaning 'the eighth month'

**octopus** octopuses

NOUN a sea creature with eight long tentacles which it uses to catch food.
📖 from Greek *okto* + *pous* meaning 'eight feet'

**odd** odder oddest; odds

ADJECTIVE **1** Something odd is strange or unusual. **2** Odd things do not match each other E.G. *odd socks.* **3** Odd numbers are numbers that cannot be divided exactly by two.
▶ ADVERB **4** You use 'odd' after a number to say that it is approximate E.G. *I've written twenty odd plays.*
▶ PLURAL NOUN **5** In gambling, the probability of something happening is called the odds E.G. *The odds are against the record being beaten.*
**oddly** ADVERB  **oddness** NOUN

**oddity** oddities

NOUN something very strange.

**oddments**

PLURAL NOUN Oddments are things that are left over after other things have been used.

**odds and ends**

PLURAL NOUN You can refer to a collection of small unimportant things as odds and ends.

**ode** odes
NOUN a poem written in praise of someone or something.

**odious**
ADJECTIVE extremely unpleasant.

**odour** odours
NOUN; FORMAL a strong smell.
**odorous** ADJECTIVE

**odyssey** odysseys
Said "od-i-see" NOUN a long and eventful journey.

**oesophagus** oesophaguses
Said "ee-**sof**-fag-uss" NOUN the tube that carries food from your throat to your stomach.

**oestrogen**
another spelling of **estrogen**.

**of**
PREPOSITION 1 consisting of or containing E.G. a collection of short stories… a cup of tea. 2 used when naming something or describing a characteristic of something E.G. the city of Canberra… a woman of great power and influence. 3 belonging to or connected with E.G. a friend of Rachel… the cover of the book.
☑ Where of means 'belonging to', it can be replaced by an apostrophe: the cover of the book is the same as the book's cover.

**off**
PREPOSITION or ADVERB 1 indicating movement away from or out of a place E.G. They had just stepped off the plane… She got up and marched off. 2 indicating separation or distance from a place E.G. some islands off the coast of Australia… The whole crescent has been fenced off. 3 not working E.G. It was Frank's night off.
▸ ADVERB or ADJECTIVE 4 not switched on E.G. He turned the radio off, the off

switch. ▸ ADJECTIVE 5 cancelled or postponed E.G. The concert was off. 6 Food that is off has gone sour or bad. ▸ PREPOSITION 7 not liking or not using something E.G. He went right off alcohol.
☑ Do not use of after off. You should say he stepped off the bus not he stepped off of the bus. It is very informal to use off where you mean 'from': they bought milk off a farmer instead of they bought milk from a farmer. Always use from in written work.

**offal**
NOUN Offal is liver, kidneys, and other parts of animals, which can be eaten.

**offence** offences
NOUN 1 a crime E.G. a drink-driving offence. ▸ PHRASES 2 If something gives offence, it upsets people. If you take offence, you are upset by someone or something.

**offend** offends offending offended
VERB 1 If you offend someone, you upset them. 2 FORMAL To offend or to offend a law is to commit a crime.
**offender** NOUN

**offensive** offensives
ADJECTIVE 1 Something offensive is rude and upsetting E.G. offensive behaviour. 2 Offensive actions or weapons are used in attacking someone. ▸ NOUN 3 an attack E.G. a full-scale offensive against the rebels.
**offensively** ADVERB

**offer** offers offering offered
VERB 1 If you offer something to someone, you ask them if they would like it. ▸ NOUN 2 something that someone says they will give you or do for you if you want them to E.G. He

a b c d e f g h i j k l m n **o** p q r s t u v w x y z

*refused the offer of a drink.* **3** a specially low price for a product in a shop *E.G. You will need a voucher to qualify for the special offer.*

**offering** offerings
NOUN something that is offered or given to someone.

**offhand**
ADJECTIVE **1** If someone is offhand, they are unfriendly and slightly rude. ▶ ADVERB **2** If you know something offhand, you know it without having to think very hard *E.G. I couldn't tell you offhand how long he's been here.*

**office** offices
NOUN **1** a room where people work at desks. **2** a government department *E.G. the Office of Fair Trading.* **3** a place where people can go for information, tickets, or other services. **4** Someone who holds office has an important job or position in government or in an organization.

**officer** officers
NOUN a person with a position of authority in the armed forces, the police, or a government organization.

**official** officials
ADJECTIVE **1** approved by the government or by someone in authority *E.G. the official figures.* **2** done or used by someone in authority as part of their job *E.G. official notepaper.* ▶ NOUN **3** a person who holds a position of authority in an organization.
**officially** ADVERB

**officialdom**
NOUN You can refer to officials in government or other organizations as officialdom, especially when you find them difficult to deal with.

**officiate** officiates officiating officiated
VERB To officiate at a ceremony is to be in charge and perform the official part of the ceremony.

**offing**
PHRASE If something is **in the offing**, it is likely to happen soon *E.G. A change is in the offing.*

**off-licence** off-licences
NOUN a shop which sells alcoholic drinks.

**offline**
ADJECTIVE **1** If a computer is offline, it is switched off or not connected to the Internet. ▶ ADVERB **2** If you do something offline, you do it while not connected to the Internet.

**offset** offsets offsetting offset
VERB If one thing is offset by another thing, its effect is reduced or cancelled out by that thing *E.G. This tedium can be offset by watching the television.*

**offshoot** offshoots
NOUN something that has developed from another thing *E.G. The technology we use is an offshoot of the motor industry.*

**offshore**
ADJECTIVE OR ADVERB in or from the part of the sea near the shore *E.G. an offshore wind… a wreck fifteen kilometres offshore.*

**offside**
ADJECTIVE **1** If a soccer, rugby, or hockey player is offside, they have broken the rules by moving too far forward. ▶ NOUN **2** the side of a vehicle that is furthest from the pavement.

**offspring**
NOUN A person's or animal's offspring are their children.

**often**
ADVERB happening many times or a lot of the time.

**ogle** ogles ogling ogled
*Said "oh-gl"* VERB To ogle someone is to stare at them in a way that indicates a sexual interest.

**ogre** ogres
*Said "oh-gur"* NOUN a cruel, frightening giant in a fairy story.

**ohm** ohms
*Rhymes with "home"* NOUN In physics, an ohm is a unit used to measure electrical resistance.

**oil** oils oiling oiled
NOUN 1 Oil is a thick, sticky liquid used as a fuel and for lubrication. 2 Oil is also a thick, greasy liquid made from plants or animals *E.G. cooking oil… bath oil.* ► VERB 3 If you oil something, you put oil in it or on it.

**oil painting** oil paintings
NOUN a picture that has been painted with thick paints used with coloured powder and a kind of oil.

**oilskin** oilskins
NOUN a piece of clothing made from a thick, waterproof material, worn especially by fishermen.

**oily**
ADJECTIVE Something that is oily is covered with or contains oil *E.G. an oily rag… oily skin.*

**ointment** ointments
NOUN a smooth, thick substance that you put on sore skin to heal it

**okay** or **OK**
ADJECTIVE or ADVERB; *INFORMAL* Okay means all right *E.G. Tell me if this sounds okay.*
■ acceptable, all right, satisfactory

**old** older oldest
ADJECTIVE 1 having lived or existed for a long time *E.G. an old lady… old*
clothes. 2 'Old' is used to give the age of someone or something *E.G. This photo is five years old.* 3 'Old' also means former *E.G. my old art teacher.*

**olden**
PHRASE **In the olden days** means long ago.

**Old English**
NOUN Old English was the English language from the fifth century AD until about 1100. Old English is also known as Anglo-Saxon.

**old-fashioned**
ADJECTIVE 1 Something which is old-fashioned is no longer fashionable *E.G. old-fashioned shoes.* 2 Someone who is old-fashioned believes in the values and standards of the past.
■ (sense 1) dated, outmoded, passé

**Old Norse**
NOUN Old Norse was a language spoken in Scandinavia and Iceland from about 700 AD to about 1350 AD. Many English words are derived from Old Norse.

**Old Testament**
NOUN The Old Testament is the first part of the Christian Bible. It is also the holy book of the Jewish religion and contains writings which relate to the history of the Jews.

**oleander** oleanders
NOUN an evergreen shrub with fragrant white, pink, or purple flowers.

**olive** olives
NOUN 1 a small green or black fruit containing a stone. Olives are usually pickled and eaten as a snack or crushed to produce oil. ► ADJECTIVE or NOUN 2 dark yellowish-green.

**-ology**
SUFFIX -ology is used to form words

a
b
c
d
e
f
g
h
i
j
k
l
m
n
o
p
q
r
s
t
u
v
w
x
y
z

an ELegant angEL (angel)    SPELLING NOTE

A
B
C
D
E
F
G
H
I
J
K
L
M
N
O
P
Q
R
S
T
U
V
W
X
Y
Z

that refer to the study of something
*E.G. biology… geology.*
🔳 from Greek *logos* meaning
'reason', 'speech', or 'discourse'

**Olympic Games**
*Said* "ol-**lim**-pik" PLURAL NOUN The
Olympic Games are a set of sporting
contests held in a different city every
four years.

**ombudsman** ombudsmen
NOUN The ombudsman is a person
who investigates complaints against
the government or a public
organization.

**omelette** omelettes
*Said* "**om**-lit" NOUN a dish made by
beating eggs together and cooking
them in a flat pan.

**omen** omens
NOUN something that is thought to be
a sign of what will happen in the
future *E.G. John saw this success as a
good omen for his trip.*
🔳 portent, sign

**ominous**
ADJECTIVE suggesting that something
unpleasant is going to happen *E.G. an
ominous sign.*
**ominously** ADVERB
🔳 sinister, threatening

**omission** omissions
NOUN 1 something that has not been
included or done *E.G. There are some
striking omissions in the survey.*
2 Omission is the act of not including
or not doing something *E.G.
controversy over the omission of
female novelists.*

**omit** omits omitting omitted
VERB 1 If you omit something, you do
not include it. 2 *FORMAL* If you omit to
do something, you do not do it.

**omnibus** omnibuses

NOUN 1 a book containing a collection
of stories or articles by the same
author or about the same subject.
▶ ADJECTIVE 2 An omnibus edition of a
radio or television show contains
two or more programmes that were
originally broadcast separately.

**omnipotent**
*Said* "om-**nip**-a-tent" ADJECTIVE having
very great or unlimited power *E.G.
omnipotent emperors.*
**omnipotence** NOUN

**omnivore**
NOUN An omnivore is an animal that
eats all kinds of food, including meat
and plants.
**omnivorous** ADJECTIVE

**on**
PREPOSITION 1 touching or attached to
something *E.G. The woman was sitting
on the sofa.* 2 If you are on a bus,
plane, or train, you are inside it. 3 If
something happens on a particular
day, that is when it happens *E.G. It is
his birthday on Monday.* 4 If
something is done on an instrument
or machine, it is done using that
instrument or machine *E.G. He
preferred to play on his computer.* 5 A
book or talk on a particular subject is
about that subject. ▶ ADVERB 6 If you
have a piece of clothing on, you are
wearing it. ▶ ADJECTIVE 7 A machine or
switch that is on is working. 8 If an
event is on, it is happening or taking
place *E.G. The race is definitely on.*

**once**
ADVERB 1 If something happens once,
it happens one time only. 2 If
something was once true, it was true
in the past, but is no longer true.
▶ CONJUNCTION 3 If something happens
once another thing has happened, it
happens immediately afterwards *E.G.*

*Once you get used to working for yourself, it's tough working for anybody else.* ► PHRASES **4** If you do something **at once**, you do it immediately. If several things happen **at once**, they all happen at the same time.

**one** ones **1** One is the number 1. ADJECTIVE **2** If you refer to the one person or thing of a particular kind, you mean the only person or thing of that kind *E.G. My one aim is to look after the horses well.* **3** One also means 'a'; used when emphasizing something *E.G. They got one almighty shock.* ► PRONOUN **4** One refers to a particular thing or person *E.G. Alf Brown's business was a good one.* **5** One also means people in general *E.G. One likes to have the opportunity to chat.*

**one-off** one-offs
NOUN something that happens or is made only once.

**onerous**
*Said "ohn-er-uss"* ADJECTIVE; FORMAL difficult or unpleasant *E.G. an onerous task.*

**oneself**
PRONOUN 'Oneself' is used when you are talking about people in general *E.G. One could hardly hear oneself talk.*

**one-sided**
ADJECTIVE **1** If an activity or relationship is one-sided, one of the people has a lot more success or involvement than the other *E.G. a one-sided contest.* **2** A one-sided argument or report considers the facts or a situation from only one point of view.

**one-way**
ADJECTIVE **1** One-way streets are streets along which vehicles can drive in only one direction. **2** A one-way ticket is one that you can use to travel to a place, but not to travel back again.

**ongoing**
ADJECTIVE continuing to happen *E.G. an ongoing process of learning.*

**onion** onions
NOUN a small, round vegetable with a brown skin like paper and a very strong taste.

**online**
ADJECTIVE **1** If a computer is online, it is switched on or connected to the Internet. ► ADVERB **2** If you do something online, you do it while connected to the Internet.

**onlooker** onlookers
NOUN someone who is watching an event.

**only**
ADVERB **1** You use 'only' to indicate the one thing or person involved *E.G. Only Keith knows whether he will continue.* **2** You use 'only' to emphasize that something is unimportant or small *E.G. He's only a little boy.* **3** You can use 'only' to introduce something which happens immediately after something else *E.G. She had thought of one plan, only to discard it for another.* ► ADJECTIVE **4** If you talk about the only thing or person, you mean that there are no others *E.G. their only hit single.* **5** If you are an only child, you have no brothers or sisters. ► CONJUNCTION **6** 'Only' also means but or except *E.G. He was like you, only blond.* ► PHRASE **7** Only too means extremely *E.G. I would be only too happy to swap places.*

A Rude Idiot Thought He Might Eat Toffee In Church (<u>arithmetic</u>)                    SPELLING NOTE

A B C D E F G H I J K L M N O P Q R S T U V W X Y Z

**onomatopoeia**
*Said "on-o-mat-o-pee-a"* NOUN
(ENGLISH) the use of words which sound like the thing that they represent. 'Hiss' and 'buzz' are examples of onomatopoeia.
**onomatopoeic** ADJECTIVE
🏛 from Greek *onoma* meaning 'name' and *poiein* meaning 'to make'

**onset**
NOUN The onset of something unpleasant is the beginning of it *E.G. the onset of war.*

**onslaught** onslaughts
*Said "on-slawt"* NOUN a violent attack.

**onto** or **on to**
PREPOSITION If you put something onto an object, you put it on it.

**onus**
*Rhymes with "bonus"* NOUN; FORMAL If the onus is on you to do something, it is your duty to do it.

**onwards** or **onward**
ADVERB 1 continuing to happen from a particular time *E.G. He could not speak a word from that moment onwards.* 2 travelling forwards *E.G. Duncliffe escorted the pair onwards to his own room.*

**onyx**
*Said "on-iks"* NOUN Onyx is a semiprecious stone used for making ornaments and jewellery.

**ooze** oozes oozing oozed
VERB When a thick liquid oozes, it flows slowly *E.G. The cold mud oozed over her new footwear.*

**opal** opals
NOUN a pale or whitish semiprecious stone used for making jewellery.

**opaque**
*Said "oh-pake"* ADJECTIVE If something is opaque, you cannot see through it *E.G. opaque glass windows.*

**open** opens opening opened
VERB 1 When you open something, or when it opens, you move it so that it is no longer closed *E.G. She opened the door.* 2 When a shop or office opens, people are able to go in. 3 To open something also means to start it *E.G. He tried to open a bank account.* ▶ ADJECTIVE 4 Something that is open is not closed or fastened *E.G. an open box of chocolates.* 5 If you have an open mind, you are willing to consider new ideas or suggestions. 6 Someone who is open is honest and frank. 7 When a shop or office is open, people are able to go in. 8 An open area of sea or land is a large, empty area *E.G. open country.* 9 If something is open to you, it is possible for you to do it *E.G. There is no other course open to us but to fight it out.* 10 If a situation is still open, it is still being considered *E.G. Even if the case remains open, the full facts may never be revealed.* ▶ PHRASE 11 In the open means outside. 12 In the open also means not secret.
**openly** ADVERB

**opening** openings
ADJECTIVE 1 Opening means coming first *E.G. the opening day of the season.* ▶ NOUN 2 The opening of a book or film is the first part of it. 3 a hole or gap. 4 an opportunity *E.G. The two men circled around, looking for an opening to attack.*
📄 (sense 3) aperture, gap, hole

**open-minded**
ADJECTIVE willing to consider new ideas and suggestions.

**open-plan**
ADJECTIVE An open-plan office or building has very few dividing walls inside.

**opera** operas
NOUN a play in which the words are sung rather than spoken.
**operatic** ADJECTIVE
🏛 from Latin *opera* meaning 'works'

**operate** operates operating operated
VERB **1** To operate is to work *E.G. We are shocked at the way that businesses operate.* **2** When you operate a machine, you make it work. **3** When surgeons operate, they cut open a patient's body to remove or repair a damaged part.

**operation** operations
NOUN **1** a complex, planned event *E.G. a full-scale military operation.* **2** a form of medical treatment in which a surgeon cuts open a patient's body to remove or repair a damaged part.
▶ PHRASE **3** If something is **in operation**, it is working or being used *E.G. The system is in operation from April to the end of September.*

**operational**
ADJECTIVE working or able to be used *E.G. an operational aircraft.*

**operative**
ADJECTIVE Something that is operative is working or having an effect.

**operator** operators
NOUN **1** someone who works at a telephone exchange or on a switchboard. **2** someone who operates a machine *E.G. a computer operator.* **3** someone who runs a business *E.G. a tour operator.*

**opinion** opinions
NOUN a belief or view.
▤ belief, judgment, view

**opinionated**
ADJECTIVE Someone who is opinionated has strong views and

refuses to accept that they might be wrong.

**opium**
NOUN Opium is a drug made from the seeds of a poppy. It is used in medicine to relieve pain.
🏛 from Latin *opium* meaning 'poppy juice'

**opponent** opponents
NOUN someone who is against you in an argument or a contest.

**opportune**
ADJECTIVE; *FORMAL* happening at a convenient time *E.G. The king's death was opportune for the prince.*

**opportunism**
NOUN Opportunism is taking advantage of any opportunity to gain money or power for yourself.
**opportunist** NOUN

**opportunity** opportunities
NOUN a chance to do something.

**oppose** opposes opposing opposed
VERB If you oppose something, you disagree with it and try to prevent it.

**opposed**
ADJECTIVE **1** If you are opposed to something, you disagree with it *E.G. He was totally opposed to bullying in schools.* **2** Opposed also means opposite or very different *E.G. two opposed schools of thought.* ▶ PHRASE **3** If you refer to one thing **as opposed to** another, you are emphasizing that it is the first thing rather than the second which concerns you *E.G. Real spectators, as opposed to invited guests, were hard to spot.*

**opposite** opposites
PREPOSITION or ADVERB **1** If one thing is opposite another, it is facing it *E.G. the*

shop opposite the station… the house opposite. ▸ ADJECTIVE **2** The opposite part of something is the part farthest away from you E.G. the opposite side of town. **3** If things are opposite, they are completely different E.G. I take the opposite view to you. ▸ NOUN **4** If two things are completely different, they are opposites.

■ (sense 4) antithesis, contrary, reverse

**opposition**
NOUN **1** If there is opposition to something, people disagree with it and try to prevent it. **2** The political parties who are not in power are referred to as the Opposition. **3** In a game or sports event, the opposition is the person or team that you are competing against.

**oppressed**
ADJECTIVE People who are oppressed are treated cruelly or unfairly.
**oppress** VERB **oppression** NOUN
**oppressor** NOUN

**oppressive**
ADJECTIVE **1** If the weather is oppressive, it is hot and humid. **2** An oppressive situation makes you feel depressed or concerned E.G. The silence became oppressive. **3** An oppressive system treats people cruelly or unfairly E.G. Married women were subject to oppressive laws.
**oppressively** ADVERB

**opt** opts opting opted
VERB If you opt for something, you choose it. If you opt out of something, you choose not to be involved in it.

**optical**
ADJECTIVE **1** concerned with vision, light, or images E.G. an optical

scanner. **2** relating to the appearance of things E.G. an optical illusion.
**optic** ADJECTIVE

**optician** opticians
NOUN someone who tests people's eyes, and makes and sells glasses and contact lenses.

**optimism**
NOUN Optimism is a feeling of hopefulness about the future.
**optimist** NOUN **optimistic** ADJECTIVE
**optimistically** ADVERB

**optimum**
ADJECTIVE the best that is possible E.G. Six is the optimum number of participants for a good meeting.

**option** options
NOUN a choice between two or more things.
**optional** ADJECTIVE

**opulent**
Said "op-yool-nt" ADJECTIVE grand and expensive-looking E.G. an opulent seafront estate.

**opus** opera
NOUN an artistic work, especially a piece of music.

**or**
CONJUNCTION **1** used to link two different things E.G. I didn't know whether to laugh or cry. **2** used to introduce a warning E.G. Do what I say or else I will fire.

**-or**
SUFFIX '-or' is used to form nouns from verbs E.G. actor… conductor.
▥ from Latin

**oracle** oracles
NOUN **1** In ancient Greece, an oracle was a place where a priest or priestess made predictions about the future. **2** a prophecy made by a

priest or other person with great
authority or wisdom.

**oral orals**
ADJECTIVE **1** spoken rather than written
*E.G. oral history*. **2** Oral describes
things that are used in your mouth
or done with your mouth *E.G. an oral
vaccine*. ▶ NOUN **3** an examination that
is spoken rather than written.
**orally** ADVERB
■ (sense 1) spoken, verbal

**orange oranges**
NOUN **1** a round citrus fruit that is juicy
and sweet and has a thick reddish-
yellow skin. ▶ ADJECTIVE or NOUN
**2** reddish-yellow.
▥ from Sanskrit *naranga* meaning
'orange'

**orang-utan orang-utans**; also
spelt **orang-utang**
NOUN a large ape with reddish-brown
hair.

**orator orators**
NOUN someone who is good at
making speeches.

**oratory**
NOUN Oratory is the art and skill of
making formal public speeches.

**orbit orbits orbiting orbited**
NOUN **1** the curved path followed by
an object going round a planet or
the sun. ▶ VERB **2** If something orbits a
planet or the sun, it goes round and
round it.

**orchard orchards**
NOUN a piece of land where fruit trees
are grown.

**orchestra orchestras**
*Said "or-kess-tra"* NOUN (MUSIC) a
large group of musicians who play
musical instruments together.
**orchestral** ADJECTIVE
▥ from Greek *orkhestra* meaning

'the area in a theatre reserved for
musicians'

**orchestrate orchestrates
orchestrating orchestrated**
VERB **1** To orchestrate something is to
organize it very carefully in order to
produce a particular result. **2** To
orchestrate a piece of music is to
rewrite it so that it can be played by
an orchestra.
**orchestration** NOUN

**orchid orchids**
*Said "or-kid"* NOUN Orchids are plants
with beautiful and unusual
flowers.

**ordain ordains ordaining
ordained**
VERB When someone is ordained, they
are made a member of the clergy.

**ordeal ordeals**
NOUN a difficult and extremely
unpleasant experience *E.G. the ordeal
of being arrested and charged with
attempted murder.*
■ hardship, torture, tribulation

**order orders ordering ordered**
NOUN **1** a command given by
someone in authority. **2** If things are
arranged or done in a particular
order, they are arranged or done in
that sequence *E.G. in alphabetical
order*. **3** Order is a situation in which
everything is in the correct place or
done at the correct time.
**4** something that you ask to be
brought to you or sent to you. ▶ VERB
**5** To order someone to do something
is to tell them firmly to do it. **6** When
you order something, you ask for it
to be brought or sent to you. ▶ PHRASE
**7** If you do something **in order to**
achieve a particular thing, you do it
because you want to achieve that thing.

a
b
c
d
e
f
g
h
i
j
k
l
m
n
**o**
p
q
r
s
t
u
v
w
x
y
z

A B C D E F G H I J K L M N **O** P Q R S T U V W X Y Z

**orderly**
ADJECTIVE Something that is orderly is well organized or arranged.
■ methodical, well-organized

**ordinarily**
ADVERB If something ordinarily happens, it usually happens.

**ordinary**
ADJECTIVE Ordinary means not special or different in any way.
■ conventional, normal, usual

**ordination**
NOUN When someone's ordination takes place, they are made a member of the clergy.

**ordnance**
NOUN Weapons and other military supplies are referred to as ordnance.

**ore** ores
NOUN Ore is rock or earth from which metal can be obtained.

**oregano**
*Said* "or-rig-**garh**-no" NOUN Oregano is a herb used for flavouring in cooking.

**organ** organs
NOUN 1 Your organs are parts of your body that have a particular function, for example your heart or lungs. 2 a large musical instrument with pipes of different lengths through which air is forced. It has various keyboards which are played like a piano.

**organic**
ADJECTIVE 1 Something that is organic is produced by or found in plants or animals *E.G. decaying organic matter.* 2 Organic food is produced without the use of artificial fertilizers or pesticides.
**organically** ADVERB

**organism** organisms
NOUN (SCIENCE) any living animal or plant.

**organist** organists
NOUN someone who plays the organ.

**organization** organizations; also spelt **organisation**
NOUN 1 any group or business. 2 The organization of something is the act of planning and arranging it.
**organizational** ADJECTIVE
■ (sense 1) body, company, group

**organize** organizes organizing organized; also spelt **organise**
VERB 1 If you organize an event, you plan and arrange it. 2 If you organize things, you arrange them in a sensible order.
**organized** ADJECTIVE **organizer** NOUN

**orgasm** orgasms
NOUN the moment of greatest pleasure and excitement during sexual activity.

**orgy** orgies
*Said* "**or**-jee" NOUN 1 a wild, uncontrolled party involving a lot of drinking and sexual activity. 2 You can refer to a period of intense activity as an orgy of that activity *E.G. an orgy of violence.*
📖 from Greek *orgia* meaning 'nocturnal festival'

**orient**
NOUN *LITERARY* The Orient is eastern and south-eastern Asia.

**oriental**
ADJECTIVE relating to eastern or south-eastern Asia.

**orientated**
ADJECTIVE If someone is interested in a particular thing, you can say that they are orientated towards it *E.G. These men are very career-orientated.*

**orientation**
NOUN You can refer to an

organization's activities and aims as its orientation *E.G. Poland's political and military orientation.*

**oriented**
ADJECTIVE Oriented means the same as orientated.

**orienteering**
NOUN Orienteering is a sport in which people run from one place to another in the countryside, using a map and compass to guide them.

**origin origins**
NOUN 1 You can refer to the beginning or cause of something as its origin or origins. 2 You can refer to someone's family background as their origin or origins *E.G. She was of Swedish origin.*
■ (sense 1) root, source

**original originals**
ADJECTIVE 1 Original describes things that existed at the beginning, rather than being added later, or things that were the first of their kind to exist *E.G. the original owner of the cottage.* 2 Original means imaginative and clever *E.G. a stunningly original idea.* ► NOUN 3 a work of art or a document that is the one that was first produced, and not a copy.
**originally** ADVERB **originality** NOUN

**originate originates originating originated**
VERB When something originates, or you originate it, it begins to happen or exist.
**originator** NOUN

**ornament ornaments**
NOUN a small, attractive object that you display in your home or that you wear in order to look attractive.

**ornamental**
ADJECTIVE designed to be attractive

rather than useful *E.G. an ornamental lake.*

**ornamentation**
NOUN Ornamentation is decoration on a building, a piece of furniture, or a work of art.

**ornate**
ADJECTIVE Something that is ornate has a lot of decoration on it.

**ornithology**
NOUN Ornithology is the study of birds.
**ornithologist** NOUN
▥ from Greek *ornis* meaning 'bird' and *-logia* meaning 'study of'

**orphan orphans orphaning orphaned**
NOUN 1 a child whose parents are dead. ► VERB 2 If a child is orphaned, its parents die.

**orphanage orphanages**
NOUN a place where orphans are looked after.

**orthodox**
ADJECTIVE 1 Orthodox beliefs or methods are the ones that most people have or use and that are considered standard. 2 People who are orthodox believe in the older, more traditional ideas of their religion or political party. 3 The Orthodox church is the part of the Christian church which separated from the western European church in the 11th century and is the main church in Greece and Russia.
**orthodoxy** NOUN

**osmosis**
*Said* "oz-moh-siss" NOUN TECHNICAL Osmosis is the process by which a liquid moves through a semipermeable membrane from a weaker solution to a more concentrated one.

a
b
c
d
e
f
g
h
i
j
k
l
m
n
o
p
q
r
s
t
u
v
w
x
y
z

I want to see (C) your licenCe (licen*c*e)    ▶ SPELLING NOTE

A B C D E F G H I J K L M N O P Q R S T U V W X Y Z

**osprey** ospreys
*Said* "**oss-pree**" NOUN a large bird of prey which catches fish with its feet.

**ostensibly**
ADVERB If something is done ostensibly for a reason, that seems to be the reason for it *E.G. Byrnes submitted his resignation, ostensibly on medical grounds.*

**ostentatious**
ADJECTIVE 1 Something that is ostentatious is intended to impress people, for example by looking expensive *E.G. ostentatious sculptures.* 2 People who are ostentatious try to impress other people with their wealth or importance.
**ostentatiously** ADVERB
**ostentation** NOUN

**ostinato** ostinatos (MUSIC)
NOUN 1 a musical phrase that is continuously repeated throughout a piece. ▶ ADJECTIVE 2 continuously repeated *E.G. an ostinato passage.*

**ostrich** ostriches
NOUN The ostrich is the largest bird in the world. Ostriches cannot fly.

**other** others
ADJECTIVE OR PRONOUN 1 Other people or things are different people or things *E.G. All the other children had gone home… One of the cabinets came from the palace; the other is a copy.* ▶ PHRASES 2 **The other day** or the **other week** means recently *E.G. She had bought four pairs of shoes the other day.*

**otherwise**
ADVERB 1 You use 'otherwise' to say a different situation would exist if a particular fact or occurrence was not the case *E.G. You had to learn to swim pretty quickly, otherwise you sank.*

2 'Otherwise' means apart from the thing mentioned *E.G. She had written to her daughter, but otherwise refused to take sides.* 3 'Otherwise' also means in a different way *E.G. The majority voted otherwise.*

**otter** otters
NOUN a small, furry animal with a long tail. Otters swim well and eat fish.

**ouch**
INTERJECTION You say ouch when you suddenly feel pain.

**ought**
*Said* "**awt**" VERB If you say that someone ought to do something, you mean that they should do it *E.G. He ought to see a doctor.*
☑ Do not use *did* and *had* with *ought*: he ought not to come is correct: *he didn't ought to come* is not correct.

**ounce** ounces
NOUN a unit of weight equal to one sixteenth of a pound or about 28.35 grams.

**our**
ADJECTIVE 'Our' refers to something belonging or relating to the speaker or writer and one or more other people *E.G. We recently sold our house.*
☑ Some people pronounce *our* and *are* in the same way, so do not confuse the spellings of these words.

**ours**
PRONOUN 'Ours' refers to something belonging or relating to the speaker or writer and one or more other people *E.G. a friend of ours from Korea.*

**ourselves**
PRONOUN 1 'Ourselves' is used when the same speaker or writer and one or more other people do an action and are affected by it *E.G. We haven't*

damaged ourselves too badly.
**2** 'Ourselves' is used to emphasize 'we'.

**oust** ousts ousting ousted
VERB If you oust someone, you force them out of a job or a place E.G. *Cole was ousted from the board.*

**out**
ADVERB **1** towards the outside of a place E.G. *Two dogs rushed out of the house.* **2** not at home E.G. *She was out when I rang last night.* **3** in the open air E.G. *They are playing out in bright sunshine.* **4** no longer shining or burning E.G. *The lights went out.*
▶ ADJECTIVE **5** on strike E.G. *1000 construction workers are out in sympathy.* **6** unacceptable or unfashionable E.G. *Miniskirts are out.* **7** incorrect E.G. *Logan's timing was out in the first two rounds.*

**out-**
PREFIX **1** 'Out-' means 'exceeding' or 'going beyond'. E.G. *outdo… outclass.* **2** 'Out-' also means on the outside or away from the centre E.G. *outback… outpost.*

**out-and-out**
ADJECTIVE entire or complete E.G. *an out-and-out lie.*

**outback**
NOUN In Australia, the outback is the remote parts where very few people live.

**outboard motor** outboard motors
NOUN a motor that can be fixed to the back of a small boat.

**outbreak** outbreaks
NOUN If there is an outbreak of something unpleasant, such as war, it suddenly occurs.

**outburst** outbursts
NOUN **1** a sudden, strong expression of

an emotion, especially anger E.G. *John broke into an angry outburst about how unfairly the work was divided.* **2** a sudden occurrence of violent activity E.G. *an outburst of gunfire.*

**outcast** outcasts
NOUN someone who is rejected by other people.

**outclassed**
ADJECTIVE If you are outclassed, you are much worse than your opponent at a particular activity.

**outcome** outcomes
NOUN a result E.G. *the outcome of the election.*

**outcrop** outcrops
NOUN a large piece of rock that sticks out of the ground.

**outcry** outcries
NOUN If there is an outcry about something, a lot of people are angry about it E.G. *a public outcry over alleged fraud.*

**outdated**
ADJECTIVE no longer in fashion.

**outdo** outdoes outdoing outdid outdone
VERB If you outdo someone, you do a particular thing better than they do.

**outdoor**
ADJECTIVE happening or used outside E.G. *outdoor activities.*

**outdoors**
ADVERB outside E.G. *It was too chilly to sit outdoors.*

**outer**
ADJECTIVE The outer parts of something are the parts furthest from the centre E.G. *the outer door of the office.*

**outer space**
NOUN Outer space is everything beyond the Earth's atmosphere.

A B C D E F G H I J K L M N O P Q R S T U V W X Y Z

**outfit** outfits
NOUN **1** a set of clothes. **2** INFORMAL an organization.

**outgoing** outgoings
ADJECTIVE **1** Outgoing describes someone who is leaving a job or place E.G. the outgoing President. **2** Someone who is outgoing is friendly and not shy. ▶ PLURAL NOUN **3** Your outgoings are the amount of money that you spend.

**outgrow** outgrows outgrowing outgrew outgrown
VERB **1** If you outgrow a piece of clothing, you grow too big for it. **2** If you outgrow a way of behaving, you stop it because you have grown older and more mature.

**outhouse** outhouses
NOUN a small building in the grounds of a house to which it belongs.

**outing** outings
NOUN a trip made for pleasure.

**outlandish**
ADJECTIVE very unusual or odd E.G. outlandish clothes.

**outlaw** outlaws outlawing outlawed
VERB **1** If something is outlawed, it is made illegal. ▶ NOUN **2** In the past, an outlaw was a criminal.

**outlay** outlays
NOUN an amount of money spent on something E.G. a cash outlay of 300 dollars.

**outlet** outlets
NOUN **1** An outlet for your feelings or ideas is a way of expressing them. **2** a hole or pipe through which water or air can flow away. **3** a shop which sells goods made by a particular manufacturer.

**outline** outlines outlining outlined
VERB **1** If you outline a plan or idea, you explain it in a general way. **2** You say that something is outlined when you can see its shape because there is a light behind it. ▶ NOUN **3** a general explanation or description of something. **4** The outline of something is its shape.

**outlive** outlives outliving outlived
VERB To outlive someone is to live longer than they do.

**outlook**
NOUN **1** Your outlook is your general attitude towards life. **2** The outlook of a situation is the way it is likely to develop E.G. The Japanese economy's outlook is uncertain.

**outlying**
ADJECTIVE Outlying places are far from cities.

**outmoded**
ADJECTIVE old-fashioned and no longer useful E.G. an outmoded form of transport.

**outnumber** outnumbers outnumbering outnumbered
VERB If there are more of one group than of another, the first group outnumbers the second.

**out of**
PREPOSITION **1** If you do something out of a particular feeling, you are motivated by that feeling E.G. Out of curiosity she went along. **2** 'Out of' also means from E.G. old instruments made out of wood. **3** If you are out of something, you no longer have any of it E.G. I do hope we're not out of fuel again. **4** If you are out of the rain, sun, or wind, you are sheltered from it. **5** You also use 'out of' to indicate proportion. For example, one out of five means one in every five.

**out of date**

ADJECTIVE old-fashioned and no longer useful.

**out of doors**

ADVERB outside E.G. *Sometimes we eat out of doors.*

**outpatient** outpatients

NOUN Outpatients are people who receive treatment in hospital without staying overnight.

**outpost** outposts

NOUN a small collection of buildings a long way from a main centre E.G. *a remote mountain outpost.*

**output** outputs

NOUN 1 Output is the amount of something produced by a person or organization. 2 (ICT) The output of a computer is the information that it produces.

**outrage** outrages outraging outraged

VERB 1 If something outrages you, it angers and shocks you E.G. *I was outraged at what had happened to her.* ► NOUN 2 Outrage is a feeling of anger and shock. 3 something very shocking or violent.

**outrageous** ADJECTIVE
**outrageously** ADVERB

**outright**

ADJECTIVE 1 absolute E.G. *an outright rejection.* ► ADVERB 2 in an open and direct way E.G. *Have you asked him outright?* 3 completely and totally E.G. *I own the company outright.*

**outset**

NOUN The outset of something is the beginning of it E.G. *the outset of his journey.*

**outshine** outshines outshining outshone

VERB If you outshine someone, you

perform better than they do.

**outside**

NOUN 1 The outside of something is the part which surrounds or encloses the rest of it. ► ADVERB, ADJECTIVE, or PREPOSITION 2 Outside means not inside E.G. *houses just outside the airport… He stood outside and shouted… an outside toilet.* 3 Outside also means not included in something E.G. *outside office hours.*

✔ Do not use *of* after *outside*. You should write *she was waiting outside the school* and not *outside of the school*.

**outsider** outsiders

NOUN 1 someone who does not belong to a particular group. 2 a competitor considered unlikely to win in a race.

**outsize** or **outsized**

ADJECTIVE much larger than usual E.G. *outsize feet.*

**outskirts**

PLURAL NOUN The outskirts of a city or town are the parts around the edge of it.

**outspoken**

ADJECTIVE Outspoken people give their opinions openly, even if they shock other people.

**outstanding**

ADJECTIVE 1 extremely good E.G. *The collection contains hundreds of outstanding works of art.* 2 Money that is outstanding is still owed E.G. *an outstanding mortgage of 46,000 pounds.*

**outstretched**

ADJECTIVE If your arms are outstretched, they are stretched out as far as possible.

**outstrip** outstrips outstripping outstripped

VERB If one thing outstrips another

a b c d e f g h i j k l m n o p q r s t u v w x y z

A
B
C
D
E
F
G
H
I
J
K
L
M
N
**O**
P
Q
R
S
T
U
V
W
X
Y
Z

thing, it becomes bigger or more successful or moves faster than the other thing.

**outward**
ADJECTIVE or ADVERB **1** Outward means away from a place or towards the outside E.G. *the outward journey.*
▶ ADJECTIVE **2** The outward features of someone are the ones they appear to have, rather than the ones they actually have E.G. *He never showed any outward signs of emotion.*
**outwardly** ADVERB

**outwards**
ADVERB away from a place or towards the outside E.G. *The door opened outwards.*

**outweigh** outweighs outweighing outweighed
VERB If you say that the advantages of something outweigh its disadvantages, you mean that the advantages are more important than the disadvantages.

**outwit** outwits outwitting outwitted
VERB If you outwit someone, you use your intelligence to defeat them.

**oval** ovals
NOUN **1** a round shape, similar to a circle but wider in one direction than the other. ▶ ADJECTIVE **2** shaped like an oval E.G. *an oval table.*

**ovary** ovaries
*Said* "oh-var-ree" NOUN A woman's ovaries are the two organs in her body that produce eggs.

**ovation** ovations
NOUN a long burst of applause.

**oven** ovens
NOUN the part of a cooker that you use for baking or roasting food.

**over** overs
PREPOSITION **1** Over something means directly above it or covering it E.G. *the picture over the fireplace... He put his hands over his eyes.* **2** A view over an area is a view across that area E.G. *The pool and terrace look out over the sea.* **3** If something is over a road or river it is on the opposite side of the road or river. **4** Something that is over a particular amount is more than that amount. **5** 'Over' indicates a topic which is causing concern E.G. *An American was arguing over the bill.* **6** If something happens over a period of time, it happens during that period E.G. *I went to New Zealand over Christmas.* ▶ ADVERB or PREPOSITION **7** If you lean over, you bend your body in a particular direction E.G. *He bent over and rummaged in a drawer... She was hunched over her typewriter.* ▶ ADVERB **8** 'Over' is used to indicate a position E.G. *over by the window... Come over here.* **9** If something rolls or turns over, it is moved so that its other side is facing upwards E.G. *He flipped over the envelope.* ▶ ADJECTIVE **10** Something that is over is completely finished. ▶ PHRASE **11 All over** a place means everywhere in that place E.G. *studios all over America.* ▶ NOUN **12** In cricket, an over is a set of six balls bowled by a bowler from the same end of the pitch.

**over-**
PREFIX 'Over' means to too great an extent or too much E.G. *overprotective... overindulge... overact.*
📖 from Old English *ofer*

**overall** overalls
ADJECTIVE or ADVERB **1** Overall means taking into account all the parts or

aspects of something E.G. *The overall quality of pupils' work had shown a marked improvement… Overall, things are not really too bad.* ▸ PLURAL NOUN **2** Overalls are a piece of clothing that looks like trousers and a jacket combined. You wear overalls to protect your other clothes when you are working. ▸ NOUN **3** An overall is a piece of clothing like a coat that you wear to protect your other clothes when you are working.

**overawed**
ADJECTIVE If you are overawed by something, you are very impressed by it and a little afraid of it.

**overbearing**
ADJECTIVE trying to dominate other people E.G. *Mozart had a difficult relationship with his overbearing father.*

**overboard**
ADVERB If you fall overboard, you fall over the side of a ship into the water.

**overcast**
ADJECTIVE If it is overcast, the sky is covered by cloud.

**overcoat** overcoats
NOUN a thick, warm coat.

**overcome** overcomes overcoming overcame overcome
VERB **1** If you overcome a problem or a feeling, you manage to deal with it or control it. ▸ ADJECTIVE **2** If you are overcome by a feeling, you feel it very strongly.

**overcrowded**
ADJECTIVE If a place is overcrowded, there are too many things or people in it.

**overdo** overdoes overdoing overdid overdone
VERB If you overdo something, you do it too much or in an exaggerated

way E.G. *It is important never to overdo new exercises.*

**overdose** overdoses
NOUN a larger dose of a drug than is safe.

**overdraft** overdrafts
NOUN an agreement with a bank that allows someone to spend more money than they have in their account.

**overdrawn**
ADJECTIVE If someone is overdrawn, they have taken more money from their bank account than the account has in it.

**overdrive**
NOUN Overdrive is an extra, higher gear in a vehicle, which is used at high speeds to reduce engine wear and save petrol.

**overdue**
ADJECTIVE If someone or something is overdue, they are late E.G. *The payments are overdue.*

**overestimate** overestimates overestimating overestimated
VERB If you overestimate something, you think that it is bigger, more important, or better than it really is E.G. *We had overestimated his popularity.*

**overflow** overflows overflowing overflowed overflown
VERB If a liquid overflows, it spills over the edges of its container. If a river overflows, it flows over its banks.

**overgrown**
ADJECTIVE A place that is overgrown is covered with weeds because it has not been looked after E.G. *an overgrown path.*

**overhang** overhangs overhanging overhung
VERB If one thing overhangs another,

a
b
c
d
e
f
g
h
i
j
k
l
m
n
o
p
q
r
s
t
u
v
w
x
y
z

A
B
C
D
E
F
G
H
I
J
K
L
M
N
O
P
Q
R
S
T
U
V
W
X
Y
Z

it sticks out sideways above it *E.G. old trees whose branches overhang a footpath.*

**overhaul** overhauls overhauling overhauled

VERB **1** If you overhaul something, you examine it thoroughly and repair any faults. ▶ NOUN **2** If you give something an overhaul, you examine it and repair or improve it.

**overhead** overheads

ADVERB or ADJECTIVE **1** Overhead means above you *E.G. seagulls flying overhead.* ▶ PLURAL NOUN **2** The overheads of a business are the costs of running it.

**overhear** overhears overhearing overheard

VERB If you overhear someone's conversation, you hear what they are saying to someone else.

**overjoyed**

ADJECTIVE extremely pleased *E.G. Colm was overjoyed to see me.*
■ delighted, over the moon

**overlaid**

ADJECTIVE If something is overlaid by something else, it is covered by it.

**overland**

ADJECTIVE or ADVERB travelling across land rather than going by sea or air *E.G. an overland trek to India… Wray was returning to England overland.*

**overlander** overlanders

NOUN In Australian history, an overlander was a man who drove cattle or sheep long distances through the outback.

**overlap** overlaps overlapping overlapped

VERB If one thing overlaps another, one part of it covers part of the other thing.

**overleaf**

ADVERB on the next page *E.G. Write to us at the address shown overleaf.*

**overload** overloads overloading overloaded

VERB If you overload someone or something, you give them too much to do or to carry.

**overlook** overlooks overlooking overlooked

VERB **1** If a building or window overlooks a place, it has a view over that place. **2** If you overlook something, you ignore it or do not notice it.

**overly**

ADVERB excessively *E.G. I'm not overly fond of jazz.*

**overnight**

ADJECTIVE or ADVERB **1** during the night *E.G. Further rain was forecast overnight.* **2** sudden or suddenly *E.G. an overnight success… Good players don't become bad ones overnight.* ▶ ADJECTIVE **3** for use when you go away for one or two nights *E.G. an overnight bag.*

**overpower** overpowers overpowering overpowered

VERB **1** If you overpower someone, you seize them despite their struggles, because you are stronger than them. **2** If a feeling overpowers you, it affects you very strongly. **overpowering** ADJECTIVE

**overrate** overrates overrating overrated

VERB If you overrate something, you think that it is better or more important than it really is. **overrated** ADJECTIVE

**overreact** overreacts overreacting overreacted
VERB If you overreact, you react in an extreme way.

**overriding**
ADJECTIVE more important than anything else E.G. *an overriding duty*.

**overrule** overrules overruling overruled
VERB To overrule a person or their decisions is to decide that their decisions are incorrect.
■ countermand, override, reverse

**overrun** overruns overrunning overran overrun
VERB 1 If an army overruns a country, it occupies it very quickly. 2 If animals or plants overrun a place, they spread quickly over it. 3 If an event overruns, it continues for longer than it was meant to.

**overseas**
ADJECTIVE or ADVERB 1 abroad E.G. *an overseas tour… travelling overseas.*
► ADJECTIVE 2 from abroad E.G. *overseas students.*

**oversee** oversees overseeing oversaw overseen
VERB To oversee a job is to make sure it is done properly.
**overseer** NOUN

**overshadow** overshadows overshadowing overshadowed
VERB If something is overshadowed, it is made unimportant by something else that is better or more important.

**oversight** oversights
NOUN something which you forget to do or fail to notice.

**overspill**
NOUN or ADJECTIVE Overspill refers to the moving of people from overcrowded cities to houses in smaller towns E.G. *an East End overspill… overspill estates.*

**overstate** overstates overstating overstated
VERB If you overstate something, you exaggerate its importance.

**overstep** oversteps overstepping overstepped
PHRASE If you **overstep the mark**, you behave in an unacceptable way.

**overt**
ADJECTIVE open and obvious E.G. *overt signs of stress.*
**overtly** ADVERB

**overtake** overtakes overtaking overtook overtaken
VERB If you overtake someone, you pass them because you are moving faster than them.

**overthrow** overthrows overthrowing overthrew overthrown
VERB If a government is overthrown, it is removed from power by force.

**overtime**
NOUN 1 Overtime is time that someone works in addition to their normal working hours. ► ADVERB 2 If someone works overtime, they do work in addition to their normal working hours.

**overtones**
PLURAL NOUN If something has overtones of an emotion or attitude, it suggests it without showing it openly E.G. *the political overtones of the trial.*

**overture** overtures
NOUN 1 a piece of music that is the introduction to an opera or play. 2 If you make overtures to someone, you approach them because you want to start a friendly or business relationship with them.

a b c d e f g h i j k l m n o p q r s t u v w x y z

**overturn** overturns overturning overturned
VERB **1** To overturn something is to turn it upside down or onto its side. **2** If someone overturns a legal decision, they change it by using their higher authority.

**overview** overviews
NOUN a general understanding or description of a situation.

**overweight**
ADJECTIVE too fat, and therefore unhealthy E.G. *overweight businessmen.*

**overwhelm** overwhelms overwhelming overwhelmed
VERB **1** If you are overwhelmed by something, it affects you very strongly E.G. *The priest appeared overwhelmed by the news.* **2** If one group of people overwhelm another, they gain complete control or victory over them.
**overwhelming** ADJECTIVE
**overwhelmingly** ADVERB

**overwork** overworks overworking overworked
VERB If you overwork, you work too hard.

**overwrought**
*Said* "oh-ver-**rawt**" ADJECTIVE extremely upset E.G. *He didn't get angry or overwrought.*

**ovulate** ovulates ovulating ovulated
*Said* "**ov**-yool-late" VERB When a woman or female animal ovulates, she produces ova or eggs from her ovary.

**ovum** ova
*Said* "**oh**-vum" NOUN a reproductive cell of a woman or female animal. The ovum is fertilized by a male sperm to produce young.
📖 a Latin word meaning 'egg'

**owe** owes owing owed
VERB **1** If you owe someone money, they have lent it to you and you have not yet paid it back. **2** If you owe a quality or skill to someone, they are responsible for giving it to you E.G. *He owes his success to his mother.* **3** If you say that you owe someone gratitude or loyalty, you mean that they deserve it from you.

**owl** owls
NOUN Owls are birds of prey that hunt at night. They have large eyes and short, hooked beaks.

**own** owns owning owned
ADJECTIVE **1** If something is your own, it belongs to you or is associated with you E.G. *She stayed in her own house.* ▶ VERB **2** If you own something, it belongs to you. ▶ PHRASE **3 On your own** means alone.

**owner** owners
NOUN The owner of something is the person it belongs to.

**ownership**
NOUN If you have ownership of something, you own it E.G. *He shared the ownership of a sailing dinghy.*

**ox** oxen
NOUN Oxen are cattle which are used for carrying or pulling things.

**oxide** oxides
NOUN a compound of oxygen and another chemical element.

**oxidize** oxidizes oxidizing oxidized; also spelt **oxidise**
VERB When a substance oxidizes, it changes chemically by reacting with oxygen.
**oxidation** NOUN

**SPELLING NOTE**   the QUeen stood on the QUay (quay)

## oxygen

NOUN (SCIENCE) a colourless and odourless gas in the air. It makes up about 21% of the Earth's atmosphere. With an extremely small number of exceptions, living things need oxygen to survive, and things cannot burn without it.

## oxymoron oxymora or oxymorons

NOUN two words that contradict each other placed beside each other, for example 'deafening silence'.

## oyster oysters

NOUN Oysters are large, flat shellfish. Some oysters can be eaten, and others produce pearls.

🏛 from Greek *ostrakon* meaning 'shell'

## oz

an abbreviation for 'ounces'.

## ozone

NOUN Ozone is a form of oxygen that is poisonous and has a strong smell. There is a layer of ozone high above the Earth's surface.

## ozone layer

NOUN The ozone layer is that part of the Earth's atmosphere that protects living things from the harmful radiation of the sun.

a
b
c
d
e
f
g
h
i
j
k
l
m
n
o
p
q
r
s
t
u
v
w
x
y
z

# Pp

**p**
1 p is an abbreviation for 'pence'. 2 p is also a written abbreviation for 'page'. The plural is pp.

**pa** pa or pas
NOUN In New Zealand, a Maori village or settlement.

**pace** paces pacing paced
NOUN 1 The pace of something is the speed at which it moves or happens. 2 a step; also used as a measurement of distance. ▶ VERB 3 If you pace up and down, you continually walk around because you are anxious or impatient.

**pacemaker** pacemakers
NOUN a small electronic device put into someone's heart to control their heartbeat.

**Pacific**
*Said* "pas-**sif**-ik" NOUN The Pacific is the ocean separating North and South America from Asia and Australia.

**pacifist** pacifists
NOUN someone who is opposed to all violence and war.
**pacifism** NOUN

**pacify** pacifies pacifying pacified
VERB If you pacify someone who is angry, you calm them.
■ appease, calm, placate

**pack** packs packing packed
VERB 1 If you pack, you put things neatly into a suitcase, bag, or box. 2 If people pack into a place, it becomes crowded with them. ▶ NOUN 3 a bag or rucksack carried on your back. 4 a packet or collection of something *E.G. a pack of cigarettes.* 5 A pack of playing cards is a complete set. 6 A

pack of dogs or wolves is a group of them.

**pack up** VERB If you pack up your belongings, you put them in a bag because you are leaving.

**package** packages
NOUN 1 a small parcel. 2 a set of proposals or offers presented as a whole *E.G. a package of beauty treatments.*
**packaged** ADJECTIVE

**packaging**
NOUN Packaging is the container or wrapping in which an item is sold or sent.

**packed**
ADJECTIVE very full *E.G. The church was packed with people.*

**packet** packets
NOUN a thin cardboard box or paper container in which something is sold.

**pact** pacts
NOUN a formal agreement or treaty.

**pad** pads padding padded
NOUN 1 a thick, soft piece of material. 2 a number of pieces of paper fixed together at one end. 3 The pads of an animal such as a cat or dog are the soft, fleshy parts on the bottom of its paws. 4 a flat surface from which helicopters take off or rockets are launched. ▶ VERB 5 If you pad something, you put a pad inside it or over it to protect it or change its shape. 6 If you pad around, you walk softly.
**padding** NOUN

**paddle** paddles paddling paddled
NOUN 1 a short pole with a broad blade at one or both ends, used to

move a small boat or a canoe. ▸ VERB **2** If someone paddles a boat, they move it using a paddle. **3** If you paddle, you walk in shallow water.

**paddock** paddocks
NOUN a small field where horses are kept.

**paddy** paddies
NOUN A paddy or paddy field is an area in which rice is grown.

**padlock** padlocks padlocking padlocked
NOUN **1** a lock made up of a metal case with a U-shaped bar attached to it, which can be put through a metal loop and then closed. It is unlocked by turning a key in the lock on the case. ▸ VERB **2** If you padlock something, you lock it with a padlock.

**padre** padres
Said "**pah**-dray" NOUN a priest, especially a chaplain to the armed forces.
🏛 from Italian or Spanish *padre* meaning 'father'

**paediatrician** paediatricians
Said "pee-dee-ya-**trish**-n"; also spelt pediatrician
NOUN a doctor who specializes in treating children.
🏛 from Greek *pais* meaning 'child' and *iatros* meaning 'physician'

**paediatrics**
Said "pee-dee-ya-**triks**"; also spelt pediatrics
NOUN Paediatrics is the area of medicine which deals with children's diseases.
**paediatric** ADJECTIVE

**pagan** pagans
Said "**pay**-gan" ADJECTIVE **1** involving beliefs and worship outside the main religions of the world *E.G. pagan myths and cults.* ▸ NOUN **2** someone who believes in a pagan religion.
**paganism** NOUN

**page** pages paging paged
NOUN **1** one side of one of the pieces of paper in a book or magazine; also the sheet of paper itself. **2** In medieval times, a page was a young boy servant who was learning to be a knight. ▸ VERB **3** To page someone is to send a signal or message to a small electronic device which they are carrying.

**pageant** pageants
Said "**paj**-jent" NOUN a grand, colourful show or parade.

**pagoda** pagodas
NOUN a tall, elaborately decorated Buddhist or Hindu temple.

**pail** pails
NOUN a bucket.

**pain** pains paining pained
NOUN **1** Pain is an unpleasant feeling of physical hurt or deep unhappiness. ▸ VERB **2** If something pains you, it makes you very unhappy.
**painless** ADJECTIVE **painlessly** ADVERB
▤ (sense 1) ache, hurt, pang, twinge

**painful**
ADJECTIVE causing emotional or physical pain.
**painfully** ADVERB

**painkiller** painkillers
NOUN a drug that reduces or stops pain.

**painstaking**
ADJECTIVE very careful and thorough *E.G. years of painstaking research.*

**paint** paints painting painted
NOUN **1** Paint is a coloured liquid used

to decorate buildings, or to make a picture. ▶ VERB 2 If you paint something or paint a picture of it, you make a picture of it using paint. 3 When you paint something such as a wall, you cover it with paint.

**painter** NOUN **painting** NOUN

**pair** pairs pairing paired
NOUN 1 two things of the same type or that do the same thing E.G. *a pair of earrings*. 2 You use 'pair' when referring to certain objects which have two main matching parts E.G. *a pair of scissors*. ▶ VERB 3 When people pair off, they become grouped in pairs. 4 If you pair up with someone, you agree to do something together
☑ The verb following *pair* can be singular or plural. If *pair* refers to a unit, the verb is singular: *a pair of good shoes is essential*. If *pair* refers to two individual things, the verb is plural: *the pair are said to dislike each other*.

**pakeha** pakeha or pakehas
*Said* "pa-ki-ha" NOUN In New Zealand English, someone who is of European rather than Maori descent.

**Pakistani** Pakistanis
*Said* "pah-kiss-**tah**-nee" ADJECTIVE
1 belonging or relating to Pakistan.
▶ NOUN 2 someone who comes from Pakistan.

**pal** pals
NOUN; *INFORMAL* a friend.

**palace** palaces
NOUN a large, grand house, especially the official home of a king or queen.

**palagi** palagi or palagis
*Said* "pa-**lang**-ee" NOUN a Samoan name for a New Zealander of European descent.

**palatable**
ADJECTIVE Palatable food tastes pleasant.

**palate** palates
*Said* "**pall**-lat" NOUN 1 the top of the inside of your mouth. 2 Someone's palate is their ability to judge good food and wine E.G. *dishes to tempt every palate*.

**pale** paler palest
ADJECTIVE rather white and without much colour or brightness.

**Palestinian** Palestinians
NOUN an Arab from the region formerly called Palestine situated between the River Jordan and the Mediterranean.

**palette** palettes
NOUN (ART) a flat piece of wood on which an artist mixes colours.

**pall** palls palling palled
*Rhymes with* "fall" VERB 1 If something palls, it becomes less interesting or less enjoyable E.G. *This record palls after ten minutes*. ▶ NOUN 2 a thick cloud of smoke. 3 a cloth covering a coffin.

**palm** palms
NOUN 1 A palm or palm tree is a tropical tree with no branches and a crown of long leaves. 2 the flat surface of your hand which your fingers bend towards.

**Palm Sunday**
NOUN Palm Sunday is the Sunday before Easter.

**palpable**
ADJECTIVE obvious and easily sensed E.G. *Happiness was palpable in the air*.

**palpably** ADVERB
▥ from Latin *palpabilis* meaning 'able to be touched'

**paltry**
*Said* "pawl-tree" ADJECTIVE A paltry sum of money is a very small amount.
■ insignificant, trifling, trivial

**pamper** pampers pampering pampered
VERB If you pamper someone, you give them too much kindness and comfort.

**pamphlet** pamphlets
NOUN (ENGLISH) a very thin book in paper covers giving information about something.

**pan** pans panning panned
NOUN 1 a round metal container with a long handle, used for cooking things in on top of a cooker. ▶ VERB 2 When a film camera pans, it moves in a wide sweep. 3 *INFORMAL* To pan something is to criticize it strongly.

**panacea** panaceas
*Said* "pan-nass-**see**-ah" NOUN something that is supposed to cure everything.

**panache**
*Said* "pan-**nash**" NOUN Something that is done with panache is done confidently and stylishly.

**pancake** pancakes
NOUN a thin, flat piece of fried batter which can be served with savoury or sweet fillings.

**pancreas** pancreases
*Said* "**pang**-kree-ass" NOUN an organ in the body situated behind the stomach. It helps the body to digest food.

**panda** pandas
NOUN A panda or giant panda is a large animal rather like a bear that lives in China. It has black fur with large patches of white.

**panda car** panda cars
NOUN In Britain, a police patrol car.

**pandemonium**
*Said* "pan-dim-**moan**-ee-um" NOUN Pandemonium is a state of noisy confusion *E.G. scenes of pandemonium.*
🏛 from *Pandemonium*, the capital of Hell in Milton's 'Paradise Lost'

**pander** panders pandering pandered
VERB If you pander to someone, you do everything they want.

**pane** panes
NOUN a sheet of glass in a window or door.

**panel** panels
NOUN 1 a small group of people who are chosen to do something *E.G. a panel of judges.* 2 a flat piece of wood that is part of a larger object *E.G. door panels.* 3 A control panel is a surface containing switches and instruments to operate a machine.
**panelled** ADJECTIVE

**panelling**
NOUN Panelling is rectangular pieces of wood covering an inside wall.

**pang** pangs
NOUN a sudden strong feeling of sadness or pain.

**panic** panics panicking panicked
NOUN 1 Panic is a sudden overwhelming feeling of fear or anxiety. ▶ VERB 2 If you panic, you become so afraid or anxious that you cannot act sensibly.

**panorama** panoramas
NOUN an extensive view over a wide area of land *E.G. a fine panorama over the hills.*
**panoramic** ADJECTIVE

**pansy** pansies
NOUN a small garden flower with large round petals.

Elaine and Emily shout EE when they mEEt to grEEt each other (-ee-)   SPELLING NOTE

A
B
C
D
E
F
G
H
I
J
K
L
M
N
O
P
Q
R
S
T
U
V
W
X
Y
Z

**pant** pants panting panted
VERB If you pant, you breathe quickly and loudly through your mouth.

**panther** panthers
NOUN a large wild animal belonging to the cat family, especially the black leopard.

**pantomime** pantomimes
NOUN a musical play, usually based on a fairy story and performed at Christmas.

**pantry** pantries
NOUN a small room where food is kept.
🔲 from Old French *paneterie* meaning 'bread store'

**pants**
PLURAL NOUN 1 Pants are a piece of underwear with holes for your legs and elastic around the waist or hips. 2 Pants are also trousers.

**papaya** papayas
NOUN a fruit with sweet yellow flesh that grows in the West Indies and tropical Australia.

**paper** papers papering papered
NOUN 1 Paper is a material made from wood pulp and used for writing on or wrapping things. 2 a newspaper. ▶ PLURAL NOUN 3 Papers are official documents, for example a passport for identification. ▶ NOUN 4 part of a written examination. ▶ VERB 5 If you paper a wall, you put wallpaper on it.
🔲 from *papyrus*, the plant from which paper was made in ancient Egypt, Greece, and Rome

**paperback** paperbacks
NOUN a book with a thin cardboard cover.

**paperwork**
NOUN Paperwork is the part of a job that involves dealing with letters and records.

**papier-mâché**
*Said* "pap-yay **mash**-shay" NOUN Papier-mâché is a hard substance made from mashed wet paper mixed with glue and moulded when moist to make things such as bowls and ornaments.
🔲 from French *papier-mâché* meaning literally 'chewed paper'

**paprika**
NOUN Paprika is a red powder made from a kind of pepper.
🔲 a Hungarian word

**par**
PHRASE 1 Something that is **on a par** with something else is similar in quality or amount *E.G. This match was on a par with the German Cup Final.* 2 Something that is **below par** or **under par** is below its normal standard. ▶ NOUN 3 In golf, par is the number of strokes which it is thought a good player should take for a hole or all the holes on a particular golf course.

**parable** parables
NOUN (RE) a short story which makes a moral or religious point.

**parachute** parachutes
*Said* "par-rash-oot" NOUN a circular piece of fabric attached by lines to a person or package so that they can fall safely to the ground from an aircraft.

**parade** parades parading paraded
NOUN 1 a line of people or vehicles standing or moving together as a display. ▶ VERB 2 When people parade, they walk together in a group as a display.

**Paradise**
NOUN According to some religions,

Paradise is a wonderful place where good people go when they die.
📖 from Greek *paradeisos* meaning 'garden'

**paradox** paradoxes
NOUN something that contains two ideas that seem to contradict each other E.G. *the paradox of having to drink in order to stay sober.*
**paradoxical** ADJECTIVE

**paraffin**
NOUN Paraffin is a strong-smelling liquid which is used as a fuel.

**paragon** paragons
NOUN someone whose behaviour is perfect in some way E.G. *a paragon of elegance.*

**paragraph** paragraphs
NOUN (ENGLISH) a section of a piece of writing. Paragraphs begin on a new line.

**parallel** parallels
NOUN 1 Something that is a parallel to something else has similar qualities or features to it. ► ADJECTIVE 2 (MATHS) If two lines are parallel, they are the same distance apart along the whole of their length.

**parallelogram** parallelograms
NOUN (MATHS) a four-sided shape in which each side is parallel to the opposite side.

**paralyse** paralyses paralysing paralysed
VERB If something paralyses you, it causes loss of feeling and movement in your body.
▪ freeze, immobilize, numb

**paralysis**
Said "par-**ral**-liss-iss" NOUN Paralysis is loss of the power to move.

**paramedic** paramedics
Said "par-ram-**med**-dik" NOUN a person

who does some types of medical work, for example for the ambulance service.

**parameter** parameters
Said "par-**ram**-met-ter" NOUN a limit which affects the way something is done E.G. *the general parameters set by the president.*

**paramilitary**
ADJECTIVE A paramilitary organization has a military structure but is not the official army of a country.

**paramount**
ADJECTIVE more important than anything else E.G. *Safety is paramount.*

**paranoia**
Said "par-ran-**noy**-ah" NOUN Paranoia is a mental illness in which someone believes that other people are trying to harm them.

**paranoid**
Said "**par**-ran-noyd" ADJECTIVE Someone who is paranoid believes wrongly that other people are trying to harm them.

**parapet** parapets
NOUN a low wall along the edge of a bridge or roof.
📖 from Italian *parapetto* meaning 'chest-high wall'

**paraphernalia**
Said "par-raf-fan-**ale**-yah" NOUN Someone's paraphernalia is all their belongings or equipment.
📖 from Latin *parapherna* meaning 'personal property of a married woman'

**paraphrase** paraphrases paraphrasing paraphrased
NOUN 1 A paraphrase of a piece of writing or speech is the same thing said in a different way E.G. *a paraphrase of the popular song.* ► VERB

a
b
c
d
e
f
g
h
i
j
k
l
m
n
o
p
q
r
s
t
u
v
w
x
y
z

**2** If you paraphrase what someone has said, you express it in a different way.

**parasite** parasites
NOUN a small animal or plant that lives on or inside a larger animal or plant.
**parasitic** ADJECTIVE
📖 from Greek *parasitos* meaning 'someone who eats at someone else's table'

**parasol** parasols
NOUN an object like an umbrella that provides shelter from the sun.

**paratroops** or **paratroopers**
PLURAL NOUN Paratroops are soldiers trained to be dropped by parachute.

**parcel** parcels parcelling parcelled
NOUN **1** something wrapped up in paper. ▶ VERB **2** If you parcel something up, you make it into a parcel.

**parched**
ADJECTIVE **1** If the ground is parched, it is very dry and in need of water. **2** If you are parched, you are very thirsty.

**parchment**
NOUN Parchment is thick yellowish paper of very good quality.

**pardon** pardons pardoning pardoned **1** You say **pardon** or **beg your pardon** to express surprise or apology, or when you have not heard what someone has said.
VERB **2** If you pardon someone, you forgive them for doing something wrong.

**pare** pares paring pared
VERB When you pare fruit or vegetables, you cut off the skin.

**parent** parents
NOUN Your parents are your father and mother.
**parental** ADJECTIVE

**parentage**
NOUN A person's parentage is their parents and ancestors.

**parish** parishes
NOUN an area with its own church and clergyman, and often its own elected council.

**parishioner** parishioners
NOUN A clergyman's parishioners are the people who live in his parish and attend his church.

**parity**
NOUN; FORMAL If there is parity between things, they are equal *E.G. By 1943 the USA had achieved a rough parity of power with the British.*

**park** parks parking parked
NOUN **1** a public area with grass and trees. **2** a private area of grass and trees around a large country house. ▶ VERB **3** When someone parks a vehicle, they drive it into a position where it can be left.
**parked** ADJECTIVE  **parking** NOUN

**parliament** parliaments
NOUN (HISTORY) the group of elected representatives who make the laws of a country.
**parliamentary** ADJECTIVE

**parlour** parlours
NOUN; OLD-FASHIONED a sitting room.
📖 from Old French *parleur* meaning 'room for talking to visitors (in a convent)'

**parochial**
*Said* "par-**roe**-key-yal" ADJECTIVE concerned only with local matters *E.G. narrow parochial interests.*

**parody** parodies parodying parodied

NOUN **1** an amusing imitation of the style of an author or of a familiar situation. ▶ VERB **2** If you parody something, you make a parody of it.

■ (sense 1) send-up, spoof, takeoff

**parole**

NOUN When prisoners are given parole, they are released early on condition that they behave well.

📖 from French *parole d'honneur* meaning 'word of honour'

**parrot** parrots

NOUN a brightly coloured tropical bird with a curved beak.

**parry** parries parrying parried

VERB **1** If you parry a question, you cleverly avoid answering it *E.G. My searching questions are simply parried with evasions.* **2** If you parry a blow, you push aside your attacker's arm to defend yourself.

**parsley**

NOUN Parsley is a herb with curly leaves used for flavouring in cooking.

**parsnip** parsnips

NOUN a long, pointed, cream-coloured root vegetable.

**parson** parsons

NOUN a vicar or other clergyman.

**part** parts parting parted

NOUN **1** one of the pieces or aspects of something. **2** one of the roles in a play or film, played by an actor or actress. **3** Someone's part in something is their involvement in it *E.G. He was jailed for eleven years for his part in the plot.* ▶ PHRASE **4** If you take part in an activity, you do it together with other people. ▶ VERB **5** If things that are next to each other part, they move away from each other. **6** If two people part, they leave each other.

■ (sense 1) bit, component, constituent, piece

**partake** partakes partaking partook partaken

VERB; FORMAL If you partake of food, you eat it *E.G. She partook of the refreshments offered.*

**partial**

ADJECTIVE **1** not complete or whole *E.G. a partial explanation… partial success.* **2** liking something very much *E.G. I'm very partial to marigolds.* **3** supporting one side in a dispute, rather than being fair and without bias.

**partially** ADVERB

**participate** participates participating participated

VERB If you participate in an activity, you take part in it.

**participant** NOUN **participation** NOUN

■ be involved in, join in, take part

**participle** participles

NOUN In grammar, a participle is a form of a verb used with an auxiliary verb in compound tenses and often as an adjective. English has two participles: the past participle, which describes a completed action, and the present participle, which describes a continuing action. For example in 'He has gone', 'gone' is a past participle and in 'She was winning', 'winning' is a present participle.

**particle** particles

NOUN **1** (SCIENCE) a basic unit of matter, such as an atom, molecule or electron. **2** a very small piece of something.

LEt's measure the angLE (ang<u>le</u>)     SPELLING NOTE

**particular** particulars
ADJECTIVE 1 relating or belonging to only one thing or person E.G. *That particular place is dangerous.*
2 especially great or intense E.G. *Pay particular attention to the forehead.*
3 Someone who is particular has high standards and is not easily satisfied. ▶ PLURAL NOUN 4 Particulars are facts or details.
**particularly** ADVERB

**parting** partings
NOUN an occasion when one person leaves another.

**partisan** partisans
ADJECTIVE 1 favouring or supporting one person or group E.G. *a partisan crowd.* ▶ NOUN 2 a member of an unofficial armed force fighting to free their country from enemy occupation E.G. *Norwegian partisans.*

**partition** partitions partitioning partitioned
NOUN 1 a screen separating one part of a room or vehicle from another.
2 Partition is the division of a country into independent areas. ▶ VERB 3 To partition something is to divide it into separate parts.

**partly**
ADVERB to some extent but not completely.

**partner** partners partnering partnered
NOUN 1 Someone's partner is the person they are married to or are living with. 2 Your partner is the person you are doing something with, for example in a dance or a game. 3 Business partners are joint owners of their business. ▶ VERB 4 If you partner someone, you are their partner for a game or social occasion.

**partnership** NOUN

**part of speech** parts of speech
NOUN a particular grammatical class of word, such as 'noun' or 'adjective'.

---

### What is a Part of Speech?

Every word in the dictionary can be classified into a group. These groups are known as **parts of speech**. If we know which group a word belongs to, we can understand what sort of idea the word represents, and how it can be combined with other words to produce meaningful statements. You can check the part of speech of any word by looking it up in the dictionary. The part of speech is given after the main entry word. The most common parts of speech in this dictionary are noun, verb, adjective, adverb, pronoun, preposition, interjection and conjunction. There are grammar boxes for all of these.

---

**partook**
the past tense of **partake**.

**partridge** partridges
NOUN a brown game bird with a round body and a short tail.

**part-time**
ADJECTIVE involving work for only a part of the working day or week.

**party** parties
NOUN 1 a social event held for people to enjoy themselves. 2 an organization whose members share the same political beliefs and campaign for election to government. 3 a group who are doing something together.
4 FORMAL one of the people involved in a legal agreement or dispute.

**pass** passes passing passed
VERB 1 To pass something is to move past it. 2 To pass in a particular direction is to move in that direction E.G. *We passed through the gate.* 3 If you pass something to someone, you hand it to them or transfer it to them. 4 If you pass a period of time doing something, you spend it that way E.G. *He hoped to pass the long night in meditation.* 5 When a period of time passes, it happens and finishes. 6 If you pass a test, you are considered to be of an acceptable standard. 7 When a new law or proposal is passed, it is formally approved. 8 When a judge passes sentence on someone, the judge states what the punishment will be. 9 If you pass the ball in a ball game, you throw, kick, or hit it to another player in your team. ▶ NOUN 10 the transfer of the ball in a ball game to another player in the same team. 11 an official document that allows you to go somewhere. 12 a narrow route between mountains.
■ (sense 1) go past, overtake
■ (sense 5) elapse, go by, lapse

**pass away** or **pass on**
VERB Someone who has passed away has died.

**pass out** VERB If someone passes out, they faint.

**passable**
ADJECTIVE of an acceptable standard E.G. *a passable imitation of his dad.*

**passage** passages
NOUN 1 a long, narrow corridor or space that connects two places. 2 a section of a book or piece of music.

**passé**
*Said "pas-say"* ADJECTIVE no longer fashionable.

**passenger** passengers
NOUN a person travelling in a vehicle, aircraft, or ship.

**passer-by** passers-by
NOUN someone who is walking past someone or something.

**passing**
ADJECTIVE lasting only for a short time E.G. *a passing phase.*
■ brief, fleeting, momentary

**passion** passions
NOUN Passion is a very strong feeling, especially of sexual attraction.
■ emotion, fervour, intensity

**passionate**
ADJECTIVE expressing very strong feelings about something.
**passionately** ADVERB
■ emotional, fervent, intense

**passive**
ADJECTIVE 1 remaining calm and showing no feeling when provoked. ▶ NOUN 2 In grammar, the passive or passive voice is the form of the verb in which the person or thing to which an action is being done is the grammatical subject of the sentence, and is given more emphasis as a result. For example, the passive of *The committee rejected your application* is *Your application was rejected by the committee.*
**passively** ADVERB   **passivity** NOUN
■ (sense 1) inactive, submissive

---

### The Passive Voice

The **passive** voice and the **active** voice are two different ways of presenting information in a sentence. The **passive** always uses a form of the auxiliary verb *to be* with the past participle of the verb.

CONTINUED ON NEXT PAGE →

a b c d e f g h i j k l m n o p q r s t u v w x y z

---

Beautiful Elephants Are Usually Tiny (b<u>eau</u>tiful)        SPELLING NOTE

When a sentence is in the passive voice, the subject of the verb is affected by the action, rather than doing it:

*E.G. The cat **is being fed** by Anna. The mouse **was chased** by a cat.*

It usually sounds more natural to use the active rather than the passive. However, it is sometimes better to use the passive if you want to avoid giving blame or if the name of the subject is not known:

*E.G. The book has been mislaid. We are being followed.*

Also look at the grammar box at **active**.

**Passover**
NOUN The Passover is an eight day Jewish festival held in spring.

**passport** passports
NOUN an official identification document which you need to show when you travel abroad.

**password** passwords
NOUN 1 a secret word known to only a few people. It allows people on the same side to recognize a friend.
2 (ICT) a word you need to know to get into some computers or computer files.

**past**
NOUN 1 The past is the period of time before the present. ▶ ADJECTIVE 2 Past things are things that happened or existed before the present *E.G. the past 30 years.* ▶ PREPOSITION OR ADVERB
3 You use 'past' when you are telling the time *E.G. It was ten past eleven.* 4 If you go past something, you move

towards it and continue until you are on the other side *E.G. They drove rapidly past their cottage.* ▶ PREPOSITION
5 Something that is past a place is situated on the other side of it *E.G. It's just past the church there.*

### Talking about the Past

You can talk about events that have already happened by using **simple past tenses** or **compound tenses**.

The **simple past tense** is formed without any auxiliary verbs. It is usually formed by taking the dictionary form of the verb and adding the ending *-ed*. (If the verb already ends in *-e*, then you only need to add *-d*.)

*E.G. I **cooked** the dinner. She **liked** fish.*

You can also use **compound tenses** to talk about actions that have happened.

One compound past tense is formed by using *was* or *were* in front of the main verb, and adding the ending *-ing*. This shows that an action happening in the past was continuous:

*E.G. I **was cooking** the dinner. We **were dining**.*

Notice that if the verb ends in *e*, the *e* is dropped.

Another compound past tense is formed by using a form of the verb *to have* in front of the main verb, and adding the ending *-ed*. This shows that an action has been completed:

*E.G. I **have cooked** the dinner. We **have dined**.*

CONTINUED ON NEXT PAGE →

Notice that if the verb already ends in e you don't need to add one. Another compound past tense is formed by using *had* in front of the main verb, and adding the ending -ed. This form shows that an action in the past had been completed before something else took place:

*E.G.* I **had cooked** the dinner. We **had dined**.

Another compound past tense is formed by using *did* in front of the basic form of the verb. This can add emphasis:

*E.G.* We **did enjoy** that!

## pasta
NOUN Pasta is a dried mixture of flour, eggs, and water, formed into different shapes.

## paste pastes pasting pasted
NOUN 1 Paste is a soft, rather sticky mixture that can be easily spread *E.G. tomato paste.* ▶ VERB 2 If you paste something onto a surface, you stick it with glue.

## pastel
ADJECTIVE Pastel colours are pale and soft. (ART)

## pasteurized
*Said "past-yoor-ized"; also spelt* **pasteurised**
ADJECTIVE Pasteurized milk has been treated with a special heating process to kill bacteria.

## pastime pastimes
NOUN a hobby or something you do just for pleasure.
▦ activity, hobby, recreation

## pastor pastors
NOUN a clergyman in charge of a congregation.

## pastoral
ADJECTIVE 1 characteristic of peaceful country life and landscape *E.G. pastoral scenes.* 2 relating to the duties of the clergy in caring for the needs of their parishioners *E.G. a pastoral visit.*

## past participle past participles
NOUN In grammar, the past participle of a verb is the form, usually ending in 'ed' or 'en', that is used to make some past tenses and the passive. For example 'killed' in 'She has killed the goldfish' and 'broken' in 'My leg was broken' are past participles.

## pastry pastries
NOUN 1 Pastry is a mixture of flour, fat, and water, rolled flat and used for making pies. 2 a small cake.

## past tense
NOUN In grammar, the past tense is the tense of a verb that you use mainly to refer to things that happened or existed before the time of writing or speaking.

## pasture pastures
NOUN Pasture is an area of grass on which farm animals graze.

## pasty pasties
ADJECTIVE 1
*Rhymes with "hasty"* Someone who is pasty looks pale and unhealthy.
▶ NOUN 2
*Said "pass-tee"* a small pie containing meat and vegetables.

## pat pats patting patted
VERB 1 If you pat something, you tap it lightly with your hand held flat.
▶ NOUN 2 a small lump of butter.

## patch patches patching patched
NOUN 1 a piece of material used to cover a hole in something. 2 an area of a surface that is different in

appearance from the rest *E.G. a bald patch.* ▸ VERB **3** If you patch something, you mend it by fixing a patch over the hole.

**patch up** VERB If you patch something up, you mend it hurriedly or temporarily.

**patchwork**
ADJECTIVE **1** A patchwork quilt is made from many small pieces of material sewn together. ▸ NOUN **2** Something that is a patchwork is made up of many parts.

**patchy** patchier patchiest
ADJECTIVE Something that is patchy is unevenly spread or incomplete in parts *E.G. patchy fog on the hills.*

**pâté**
*Said "pa-tay"* NOUN Pâté is a mixture of meat, fish, or vegetables blended into a paste and spread on bread or toast.

**patent** patents patenting patented
NOUN **1** an official right given to an inventor to be the only person or company allowed to make or sell a new product. ▸ VERB **2** If you patent something, you obtain a patent for it. ▸ ADJECTIVE **3** obvious *E.G. This was patent nonsense.*
**patently** ADVERB

**paternal**
ADJECTIVE relating to a father *E.G. paternal pride.*

**paternity**
NOUN Paternity is the state or fact of being a father.

**path** paths
NOUN **1** a strip of ground for people to walk on. **2** Your path is the area ahead of you and the direction in which you are moving.

**pathetic**
ADJECTIVE **1** If something is pathetic, it makes you feel pity. **2** Pathetic also means very poor or unsuccessful *E.G. a pathetic attempt.*
**pathetically** ADVERB
■ (sense 1) heart-rending, moving, sad

**pathological**
ADJECTIVE extreme and uncontrollable *E.G. a pathological fear of snakes.*
**pathologically** ADVERB

**pathology**
NOUN Pathology is the study of diseases and the way they develop.
**pathologist** NOUN

**pathos**
*Said "pay-thoss"* NOUN Pathos is a quality in literature or art that causes great sadness or pity.

**pathway** pathways
NOUN a path.

**patience**
NOUN Patience is the ability to stay calm in a difficult or irritating situation.
■ forbearance, tolerance

**patient** patients
ADJECTIVE **1** If you are patient, you stay calm in a difficult or irritating situation. ▸ NOUN **2** a person receiving medical treatment from a doctor or in a hospital.
**patiently** ADVERB

**patio** patios
NOUN a paved area close to a house.

**patriarch** patriarchs
*Said "pay-tree-ark"* NOUN the male head of a family or tribe.
**patriarchal** ADJECTIVE

**patrician**
ADJECTIVE; *FORMAL* belonging to a family of high rank.

**patriot** patriots

NOUN someone who loves their country and feels very loyal towards it.

**patriotic** ADJECTIVE **patriotism** NOUN

**patrol** patrols patrolling patrolled

VERB 1 When soldiers, police, or guards patrol an area, they walk or drive around to make sure there is no trouble. ▶ NOUN 2 a group of people patrolling an area.

🏛 from French *patouiller* meaning 'to flounder in mud'

**patron** patrons

NOUN 1 a person who supports or gives money to artists, writers, or musicians. 2 The patrons of a hotel, pub, or shop are the people who use it.

**patronage** NOUN

**patronize** patronizes patronizing patronized; also spelt **patronise**

VERB 1 If someone patronizes you, they treat you kindly, but in a way that suggests that you are less intelligent than them or inferior to them. 2 If you patronize a hotel, pub, or shop, you are a customer there.

**patronizing** ADJECTIVE

**patron saint** patron saints

NOUN The patron saint of a group of people or place is a saint who is believed to look after them.

**patter** patters pattering pattered

VERB 1 If something patters on a surface, it makes quick, light, tapping sounds. ▶ NOUN 2 a series of light tapping sounds E.G. *a patter of light rain*.

**pattern** patterns

NOUN 1 a decorative design of repeated shapes. 2 The pattern of something is the way it is usually done or happens E.G. *a perfectly normal pattern of behaviour*. 3 a diagram or shape used as a guide for making something, for example clothes.

**patterned** ADJECTIVE

**paunch** paunches

NOUN If a man has a paunch, he has a fat stomach.

**pauper** paupers

NOUN; OLD-FASHIONED a very poor person.

**pause** pauses pausing paused

VERB 1 If you pause, you stop what you are doing for a short time. ▶ NOUN 2 a short period when you stop what you are doing. 3 a short period of silence.

**pave** paves paving paved

VERB When an area of ground is paved, it is covered with flat blocks of stone or concrete.

**pavement** pavements

NOUN a path with a hard surface at the side of a road.

**pavilion** pavilions

NOUN a building at a sports ground where players can wash and change.

**paw** paws pawing pawed

NOUN 1 The paws of an animal such as a cat or bear are its feet with claws and soft pads. ▶ VERB 2 If an animal paws something, it hits it or scrapes at it with its paws.

**pawn** pawns pawning pawned

VERB 1 If you pawn something, you leave it with a pawnbroker in exchange for money. ▶ NOUN 2 the smallest and least valuable playing piece in chess.

a b c d e f g h i j k l m n o **p** q r s t u v w x y z

I always visit my FRIend on a FRIday (<u>friend</u>)     ▶ SPELLING NOTE

**pawnbroker** pawnbrokers
NOUN a dealer who lends money in return for personal property left with him or her, which may be sold if the loan is not repaid on time.

**pawpaw** pawpaws
NOUN the same as a papaya.

**pay** pays paying paid
VERB 1 When you pay money to someone, you give it to them because you are buying something or owe it to them. 2 If it pays to do something, it is to your advantage to do it *E.G. They say it pays to advertise.* 3 If you pay for something that you have done, you suffer as a result. 4 If you pay attention to something, you give it your attention. 5 If you pay a visit to someone, you visit them.
▶ NOUN 6 Someone's pay is their salary or wages.
■ (sense 1) give, reimburse, settle

**payable**
ADJECTIVE 1 An amount of money that is payable has to be paid or can be paid *E.G. All fees are payable in advance.* 2 If a cheque is made payable to you, you are the person who should receive the money.

**payment** payments
NOUN 1 Payment is the act of paying money. 2 a sum of money paid.

**payroll** payrolls
NOUN Someone who is on an organization's payroll is employed and paid by them.

**PC** PCs
NOUN 1 In Britain, a police constable. 2 a personal computer. ▶ ADJECTIVE 3 short for politically correct.

**PE**
NOUN PE is a lesson in which gymnastics or sports are taught. PE is an abbreviation for 'physical education'.

**pea** peas
NOUN Peas are small round green seeds that grow in pods and are eaten as a vegetable.

**peace**
NOUN 1 Peace is a state of calm and quiet when there is no disturbance of any kind. 2 When a country is at peace, it is not at war.
**peaceable** ADJECTIVE
■ (sense 1) stillness, tranquillity

**peaceful**
ADJECTIVE quiet and calm.
**peacefully** ADVERB
■ serene, tranquil

**peach** peaches
NOUN 1 a soft, round fruit with yellow flesh and a yellow and red skin.
▶ ADJECTIVE 2 pale pink with a hint of orange.

**peacock** peacocks
NOUN a large bird with green and blue feathers. The male has a long tail which it can spread out in a fan.

**peak** peaks peaking peaked
NOUN 1 The peak of an activity or process is the point at which it is strongest or most successful. 2 the pointed top of a mountain. ▶ VERB 3 When something peaks, it reaches its highest value or its greatest level of success.
**peaked** ADJECTIVE
■ (sense 1) climax, culmination, high point

**peal** peals pealing pealed
NOUN 1 A peal of bells is the musical sound made by bells ringing one after another. ▶ VERB 2 When bells peal, they ring one after the other.

**peanut** peanuts
NOUN Peanuts are small oval nuts that grow under the ground.

**pear** pears
NOUN a fruit which is narrow at the top and wide and rounded at the bottom.

**pearl** pearls
NOUN a hard, round, creamy-white object used in jewellery. Pearls grow inside the shell of an oyster.

**peasant** peasants
NOUN a person who works on the land, especially in a poor country.

**peat**
NOUN Peat is dark-brown decaying plant material found in cool, wet regions. Dried peat can be used as fuel.

**pebble** pebbles
NOUN a smooth, round stone.

**peck** pecks pecking pecked
VERB 1 If a bird pecks something, it bites at it quickly with its beak. 2 If you peck someone on the cheek, you give them a quick kiss. ▶ NOUN 3 a quick bite by a bird. 4 a quick kiss on the cheek.

**peculiar**
ADJECTIVE 1 strange and perhaps unpleasant. 2 relating or belonging only to a particular person or thing E.G. a gesture peculiar to her.
**peculiarly** ADVERB **peculiarity** NOUN

**pedal** pedals pedalling pedalled
NOUN 1 a control lever on a machine or vehicle that you press with your foot. ▶ VERB 2 When you pedal a bicycle, you push the pedals round with your feet to move along.

**pedantic**
ADJECTIVE If a person is pedantic, they are too concerned with unimportant details and traditional rules.

**peddle** peddles peddling peddled
VERB Someone who peddles something sells it.

**pedestal** pedestals
NOUN a base on which a statue stands.

**pedestrian** pedestrians
NOUN 1 someone who is walking. ▶ ADJECTIVE 2 Pedestrian means ordinary and rather dull E.G. a pedestrian performance.

**pedestrian crossing**
pedestrian crossings
NOUN a specially marked place where you can cross the road safely.

**pediatrician**
another spelling of **paediatrician**.

**pediatrics**
another spelling of **paediatrics**.

**pedigree** pedigrees
ADJECTIVE 1 A pedigree animal is descended from a single breed and its ancestors are known and recorded. ▶ NOUN 2 Someone's pedigree is their background or ancestry.

**peek** peeks peeking peeked
VERB 1 If you peek at something, you have a quick look at it E.G. I peeked round the corner. ▶ NOUN 2 a quick look at something.

**peel** peels peeling peeled
NOUN 1 The peel of a fruit is the skin when it has been removed. ▶ VERB 2 When you peel fruit or vegetables, you remove the skin. 3 If a surface is peeling, it is coming off in thin layers.
**peelings** PLURAL NOUN

**peep** peeps peeping peeped
VERB 1 If you peep at something, you have a quick look at it. 2 If something peeps out from behind something

A
B
C
D
E
F
G
H
I
J
K
L
M
N
O
**P**
Q
R
S
T
U
V
W
X
Y
Z

else, a small part of it becomes visible *E.G. a handkerchief peeping out of his breast pocket.* ▶ NOUN 3 a quick look at something.

**peer** peers peering peered
VERB 1 If you peer at something, you look at it very hard. ▶ NOUN 2 a member of the nobility. 3 Your peers are the people who are of the same age and social status as yourself.

**peerage** peerages
NOUN 1 The peers in a country are called the peerage. 2 A peerage is also the rank of being a peer.

**peer group** peer groups
NOUN Your peer group is the people who are of the same age and social status as yourself.

**peerless**
ADJECTIVE so magnificent or perfect that nothing can equal it *E.G. peerless wines.*

**peewee** peewees
NOUN a small black-and-white Australian bird with long, thin legs.

**peg** pegs pegging pegged
NOUN 1 a plastic or wooden clip used for hanging wet clothes on a line. 2 a hook on a wall where you can hang things. ▶ VERB 3 If you peg clothes on a line, you fix them there with pegs. 4 If a price is pegged at a certain level, it is fixed at that level.

**peggy square** peggy squares
NOUN In New Zealand, a small square of knitted wool which is sewn together with others to make a rug.

**pejorative**
*Said* "pej-**jor**-ra-tiv" ADJECTIVE A pejorative word expresses criticism.

**pekinese** pekineses
*Said* "pee-kin-**eez**"; also spelt pekingese

NOUN a small long-haired dog with a flat nose.

**pelican** pelicans
NOUN a large water bird with a pouch beneath its beak in which it stores fish.

**pellet** pellets
NOUN a small ball of paper, lead, or other material.

**pelt** pelts pelting pelted
VERB 1 If you pelt someone with things, you throw the things with force at them. 2 If you pelt along, you run very fast. ▶ NOUN 3 the skin and fur of an animal.

**pelvis** pelvises
NOUN the wide, curved group of bones at hip-level at the base of your spine.
**pelvic** ADJECTIVE

**pen** pens penning penned
NOUN 1 a long, thin instrument used for writing with ink. 2 a small fenced area in which farm animals are kept for a short time. ▶ VERB 3 LITERARY If someone pens a letter or article, they write it. 4 If you are penned in or penned up, you have to remain in an uncomfortably small area.
▥ from Latin *penna* meaning 'feather'; pens used to be made from feathers

**penal**
ADJECTIVE relating to the punishment of criminals.

**penalize** penalizes penalizing penalized; also spelt penalise
VERB If you are penalized, you are made to suffer some disadvantage as a punishment for something.

**penalty** penalties
NOUN 1 a punishment or disadvantage that someone is made to suffer. 2 In soccer, a penalty is a free kick at goal

that is given to the attacking team if the defending team have committed a foul near their goal.

**penance**
NOUN If you do penance, you do something unpleasant to show that you are sorry for something wrong that you have done.

**pence**
a plural form of **penny**.

**penchant**
*Said "pon-shon"* NOUN; FORMAL If you have a penchant for something, you have a particular liking for it E.G. *a penchant for crime*.

**pencil pencils**
NOUN a long thin stick of wood with graphite in the centre, used for drawing or writing.

**pendant pendants**
NOUN a piece of jewellery attached to a chain and worn round the neck.

**pending** FORMAL
ADJECTIVE **1** Something that is pending is waiting to be dealt with or will happen soon. ▶ PREPOSITION **2** Something that is done pending a future event is done until the event happens E.G. *The army should stay in the west pending a future war*.

**pendulum pendulums**
NOUN a rod with a weight at one end in a clock which swings regularly from side to side to control the clock.

**penetrate penetrates penetrating penetrated**
VERB To penetrate an area that is difficult to get into is to succeed in getting into it.
**penetration** NOUN

**penetrating**
ADJECTIVE **1** loud and high-pitched E.G. *a penetrating voice*. **2** having or

showing deep understanding E.G. *penetrating questions*.

**pen friend pen friends**
NOUN someone living in a different place or country whom you write to regularly, although you may never have met each other.

**penguin penguins**
NOUN a black and white bird with webbed feet and small wings like flippers.

**penicillin**
NOUN Penicillin is a powerful antibiotic obtained from fungus and used to treat infections.

**peninsula peninsulas**
NOUN an area of land almost surrounded by water.

**penis penises**
NOUN A man's penis is the part of his body that he uses when urinating and having sexual intercourse.

**penitent**
ADJECTIVE Someone who is penitent is deeply sorry for having done something wrong.
**penitence** NOUN

**penknife penknives**
NOUN a small knife with a blade that folds back into the handle.

**pennant pennants**
NOUN a triangular flag, especially one used by ships as a signal.

**penniless**
ADJECTIVE Someone who is penniless has no money.

**penny pennies** or **pence**
NOUN a unit of currency in Britain and some other countries. In Britain a penny is worth one-hundredth of a pound.

**pension pensions**
*Said "pen-shn"* NOUN a regular sum of

a b c d e f g h i j k l m n o **p** q r s t u v w x y z

A B C D E F G H I J K L M N O P Q R S T U V W X Y Z

money paid to an old or retired person.

**pensioner** pensioners
NOUN an old retired person who gets a pension paid by the state.

**pensive**
ADJECTIVE deep in thought.
▪ dreamy, meditative, thoughtful

**pentagon** pentagons
NOUN a shape with five straight sides.

**pentathlon** pentathlons
Said "pen-**tath**-lon" NOUN a sports contest in which athletes compete in five different events.

**penthouse** penthouses
NOUN a luxurious flat at the top of a building.

**pent-up**
ADJECTIVE Pent-up emotions have been held back for a long time without release.
▪ bottled up, suppressed

**penultimate**
ADJECTIVE The penultimate thing in a series is the one before the last.

**peony** peonies
Said "**pee**-yon-ee"
NOUN a garden plant with large pink, white, or red flowers.

**people** peoples peopling peopled
PLURAL NOUN 1 People are men, women, and children. ▶ NOUN 2 all the men, women, and children of a particular country or race. ▶ VERB 3 If an area is peopled by a particular group, that group of people live there.
▪ (sense 1) humanity, mankind, persons
▪ (sense 2) nation, population, race

**pepper** peppers
NOUN 1 a hot-tasting powdered spice used for flavouring in cooking. 2 a hollow green, red, or yellow fruit

eaten as a vegetable, with sweet-flavoured flesh.

**peppermint** peppermints
NOUN Peppermint is a plant with a strong taste. It is used for making sweets and in medicine.

**per**
PREPOSITION 'Per' is used to mean 'each' when expressing rates and ratios E.G. The class meets two evenings per week.

**perceive** perceives perceiving perceived
VERB If you perceive something that is not obvious, you see it or realize it.
▪ notice, see, spot

**per cent**
PHRASE You use **per cent** to talk about amounts as a proportion of a hundred. An amount that is 10 per cent (10%) of a larger amount is equal to 10 hundredths of the larger amount E.G. 86 per cent of Americans believe Presley is alive.
▥ from Latin per meaning 'each' and centum meaning 'hundred'

**percentage** percentages
NOUN (MATHS) a fraction expressed as a number of hundredths E.G. the high percentage of failed marriages.

**perceptible**
ADJECTIVE Something that is perceptible can be seen E.G. a barely perceptible nod.

**perception** perceptions
NOUN 1 Perception is the recognition of things using the senses, especially the sense of sight. 2 Someone who has perception realizes or notices things that are not obvious. 3 Your perception of something or someone is your understanding of them.

---

SPELLING NOTE    I went to see (C) the doctor's new practiCe (practice)

**perceptive**

ADJECTIVE Someone who is perceptive realizes or notices things that are not obvious.

**perceptively** ADVERB
■ astute, observant, sharp

**perch** perches perching perched

VERB 1 If you perch on something, you sit on the edge of it. 2 When a bird perches on something, it stands on it. ▶ NOUN 3 a short rod for a bird to stand on. 4 an edible freshwater fish.

**percolator** percolators

NOUN a special pot for making and serving coffee.

**percussion**

NOUN OR ADJECTIVE (MUSIC) Percussion instruments are musical instruments that you hit to produce sounds.

**percussionist** NOUN

**perennial**

ADJECTIVE continually occurring or never ending E.G. The damp cellar was a perennial problem.

**perfect** perfects perfecting perfected

ADJECTIVE 1 of the highest standard and without fault E.G. His English was perfect. 2 complete or absolute E.G. They have a perfect right to say so. 3 In English grammar, the perfect tense of a verb is formed with the present tense of 'have' and the past participle of the main verb E.G. I have lost my home. ▶ VERB 4 If you perfect something, you make it as good as it can possibly be.

**perfectly** ADVERB **perfection** NOUN
■ (sense 1) faultless, flawless
■ (sense 4) improve, refine

**perfectionist** perfectionists

NOUN someone who always tries to do everything perfectly.

**perforated**

ADJECTIVE Something that is perforated has had small holes made in it.

**perforation** NOUN

**perform** performs performing performed

VERB 1 To perform a task or action is to do it. 2 (DRAMA) To perform is to act, dance, or play music in front of an audience.

**performer** NOUN

**performance** performances

NOUN 1 (DRAMA) an entertainment provided for an audience. 2 The performance of a task or action is the doing of it. 3 Someone's or something's performance is how successful they are E.G. the poor performance of the American economy.

**perfume** perfumes

NOUN 1 Perfume is a pleasant-smelling liquid which women put on their bodies. 2 The perfume of something is its pleasant smell.

**perfumed** ADJECTIVE

**perfunctory**

ADJECTIVE done quickly without interest or care E.G. a perfunctory kiss.

**perhaps**

ADVERB You use 'perhaps' when you are not sure whether something is true or possible.

**peril** perils

NOUN; FORMAL Peril is great danger.

**perilous** ADJECTIVE **perilously** ADVERB

**perimeter** perimeters

NOUN (MATHS) The perimeter of an area or figure is the whole of its outer edge.

**period** periods

NOUN 1 a particular length of time.

a
b
c
d
e
f
g
h
i
j
k
l
m
n
o
p
q
r
s
t
u
v
w
x
y
z

A
B
C
D
E
F
G
H
I
J
K
L
M
N
O
P
Q
R
S
T
U
V
W
X
Y
Z

**2** one of the parts the day is divided into at school. **3** A woman's period is the monthly bleeding from her womb. ▶ ADJECTIVE **4** relating to a historical period of time *E.G. period furniture*.
**periodic** ADJECTIVE   **periodically** ADVERB

**periodical** periodicals
NOUN a magazine.

**peripheral**
Said "per-**rif**-fer-ral" ADJECTIVE **1** of little importance in comparison with other things *E.G. a peripheral activity*. **2** on or relating to the edge of an area.

**periphery** peripheries
NOUN The periphery of an area is its outside edge.

**perish** perishes perishing perished
VERB **1** FORMAL If someone or something perishes, they are killed or destroyed. **2** If fruit or fabric perishes, it rots.
**perishable** ADJECTIVE

**perjury**
NOUN; A FORMAL OR LEGAL WORD If someone commits perjury, they tell a lie in court while under oath.
**perjure** VERB

**perk** perks perking perked
NOUN **1** an extra, such as a company car, offered by an employer in addition to a salary. Perk is an abbreviation of 'perquisite'. ▶ VERB **2** INFORMAL When someone perks up, they become more cheerful.
**perky** ADJECTIVE

**perm** perms perming permed
NOUN **1** If you have a perm, your hair is curled and treated with chemicals to keep the curls for several months.

▶ VERB **2** To perm someone's hair means to put a perm in it.

**permanent**
ADJECTIVE lasting for ever, or present all the time.
**permanently** ADVERB   **permanence** NOUN

**permeable**
Said "**per**-mee-a-bl" ADJECTIVE; FORMAL If something is permeable, liquids are able to pass through it *E.G. permeable rock*.

**permeate** permeates permeating permeated
VERB To permeate something is to spread through it and affect every part of it *E.G. The feeling of failure permeates everything I do*.

**permissible**
ADJECTIVE allowed by the rules.
■ allowable, permitted

**permission**
NOUN If you have permission to do something, you are allowed to do it.
■ authorization, go-ahead

**permissive**
ADJECTIVE A permissive society allows things which some people disapprove of, especially freedom in sexual behaviour.
**permissiveness** NOUN

**permit** permits permitting permitted
VERB **1** To permit something is to allow it or make it possible. ▶ NOUN **2** an official document which says that you are allowed to do something.
■ (sense 1) allow, give permission, let

**permutation** permutations
NOUN one possible arrangement of a number of things.

**pernicious**
ADJECTIVE; FORMAL very harmful E.G. *the pernicious influence of television.*

**peroxide**
NOUN Peroxide is a chemical used for bleaching hair or as an antiseptic.

**perpendicular**
ADJECTIVE (MATHS) upright, or at right angles to a horizontal line.
📖 from Latin *perpendiculum* meaning 'plumb line'

**perpetrate** perpetrates perpetrating perpetrated
VERB; FORMAL To perpetrate a crime is to commit it.
**perpetrator** NOUN

**perpetual**
ADJECTIVE never ending E.G. *a perpetual toothache.*
**perpetually** ADVERB  **perpetuity** NOUN

**perpetuate** perpetuates perpetuating perpetuated
VERB To perpetuate a situation or belief is to cause it to continue E.G. *The television series will perpetuate the myths.*

**perplexed**
ADJECTIVE If you are perplexed, you are puzzled and do not know what to do.

**persecute** persecutes persecuting persecuted
VERB To persecute someone is to treat them cruelly and unfairly over a long period of time.
**persecution** NOUN  **persecutor** NOUN
▤ pick on, victimize

**persevere** perseveres persevering persevered
VERB If you persevere, you keep trying to do something and do not give up.

**perseverance** NOUN
▤ carry on, continue, keep going

**Persian**
*Said* "per-shn" ADJECTIVE or NOUN an old word for **Iranian**, used especially when referring to the older forms of the language.

**persimmon** persimmons
NOUN a sweet, red, tropical fruit.

**persist** persists persisting persisted
VERB 1 If something undesirable persists, it continues to exist. 2 If you persist in doing something, you continue in spite of opposition or difficulty.
**persistence** NOUN  **persistent** ADJECTIVE

**person** people or persons
NOUN 1 a man, woman, or child. 2 In grammar, the first person is the speaker (I), the second person is the person being spoken to (you), and the third person is anyone else being referred to (he, she, they).
▤ (sense 1) human being, individual
✔ The usual plural of *person* is *people*. *Persons* is much less common, and is used only in formal or official English.

**personal**
ADJECTIVE 1 Personal means belonging or relating to a particular person rather than to people in general E.G. *my personal feeling.* 2 (PE) Personal matters relate to your feelings, relationships, and health which you may not wish to discuss with other people.
**personally** ADVERB
▤ (sense 1) individual, own, private

**personality** personalities
NOUN 1 Your personality is your

a b c d e f g h i j k l m n o p q r s t u v w x y z

character and nature. **2** a famous person in entertainment or sport.

## personification

NOUN **1** (ENGLISH) Personification is a form of imagery in which something inanimate is described as if it has human qualities E.G. *The trees sighed and whispered as the impatient breeze stirred their branches.* **2** Someone who is the personification of some quality is a living example of that quality E.G. *He was the personification of evil.*

## personify personifies personifying personified

VERB Someone who personifies a particular quality seems to be a living example of it. If you personify a thing or concept, you write or speak of it as if it has human abilities or qualities, for example 'The sun is trying to come out'.

## personnel

*Said* "per-son-**nell**" NOUN The personnel of an organization are the people who work for it.

## perspective perspectives

NOUN **1** A particular perspective is one way of thinking about something. **2** (ART) Perspective is a method artists use to make some people and things seem further away than others.

## perspiration

NOUN Perspiration is the moisture that appears on your skin when you are hot or frightened.

## perspire perspires perspiring perspired

VERB If someone perspires, they sweat.

## persuade persuades persuading persuaded

VERB If someone persuades you to do

something or persuades you that something is true, they make you do it or believe it by giving you very good reasons.

**persuasion** NOUN **persuasive** ADJECTIVE

■ convince, talk into

## pertaining

ADJECTIVE; *FORMAL* If information or questions are pertaining to a place or thing, they are about that place or thing E.G. *issues pertaining to women.*

## pertinent

ADJECTIVE especially relevant to the subject being discussed E.G. *He asks pertinent questions.*

## perturbed

ADJECTIVE Someone who is perturbed is worried.

## Peruvian Peruvians

*Said* "per-**roo**-vee-an" ADJECTIVE **1** belonging or relating to Peru. ▶ NOUN **2** someone who comes from Peru.

## pervade pervades pervading pervaded

VERB Something that pervades a place is present and noticeable throughout it E.G. *a fear that pervades the community.*

**pervasive** ADJECTIVE

## perverse

ADJECTIVE Someone who is perverse deliberately does things that are unreasonable or harmful.

**perversely** ADVERB **perversity** NOUN

## pervert perverts perverting perverted

VERB **1** *FORMAL* To pervert something is to interfere with it so that it is no longer what it should be E.G. *a conspiracy to pervert the course of* *justice.* ▶ NOUN 2 a person whose sexual behaviour is disgusting or harmful.

**perversion** NOUN

🏛 from Latin *pervertere* meaning 'to turn the wrong way'

**perverted**

ADJECTIVE 1 Someone who is perverted has disgusting or unacceptable behaviour or ideas, especially sexual behaviour or ideas. 2 Something that is perverted is completely wrong *E.G. a perverted sense of value.*

**peseta** pesetas

*Said* "pes-**say**-ta" NOUN a unit of currency formerly used in Spain.

**peso** pesos

*Said* "**pay**-soh" NOUN the main unit of currency in several South American countries.

**pessimism**

NOUN Pessimism is the tendency to believe that bad things will happen.

**pessimist** NOUN **pessimistic** ADJECTIVE

**pest** pests

NOUN 1 an insect or small animal which damages plants or food supplies. 2 someone who keeps bothering or annoying you.

**pester** pesters pestering pestered

VERB If you pester someone, you keep bothering them or asking them to do something.

📰 annoy, badger, hassle

**pesticide** pesticides

NOUN Pesticides are chemicals sprayed onto plants to kill insects and grubs.

**pet** pets petting petted

NOUN 1 a tame animal kept at home.
▶ ADJECTIVE 2 Someone's pet theory or pet project is something that they particularly support or feel strongly about. ▶ VERB 3 If you pet a person or animal, you stroke them affectionately.

**petal** petals

NOUN The petals of a flower are the coloured outer parts.

**peter out** peters out petering out petered out

VERB If something peters out, it gradually comes to an end.

**petite**

*Said* "pet-**teet**" ADJECTIVE A woman who is petite is small and slim.

**petition** petitions petitioning petitioned

NOUN 1 a document demanding official action which is signed by a lot of people. 2 an formal request to a court for legal action to be taken.
▶ VERB 3 If you petition someone in authority, you make a formal request to them *E.G. I petitioned the Chinese government for permission to visit its country.*

**petrified**

ADJECTIVE If you are petrified, you are very frightened.

**petrol**

NOUN Petrol is a liquid obtained from petroleum and used as a fuel for motor vehicles.

**petroleum**

NOUN Petroleum is thick, dark oil found under the earth or under the sea bed.

🏛 from Latin *petra* meaning 'rock' and *oleum* meaning 'oil'

**petticoat** petticoats

NOUN a piece of women's underwear like a very thin skirt.

**petty** pettier pettiest

ADJECTIVE 1 Petty things are small and

a b c d e f g h i j k l m n o **p** q r s t u v w x y z

the QUeen stood on the QUay (quay)     SPELLING NOTE

unimportant. **2** Petty behaviour consists of doing small things which are selfish and unkind.

**petulant**
ADJECTIVE showing unreasonable and childish impatience or anger.
**petulantly** ADVERB **petulance** NOUN

**petunia** petunias
*Said* "pit-**yoon**-nee-ah" NOUN a garden plant with large trumpet-shaped flowers.

**pew** pews
NOUN a long wooden seat with a back, which people sit on in church.

**pewter**
NOUN Pewter is a silvery-grey metal made from a mixture of tin and lead.

**pH**
NOUN The pH of a solution or of the soil is a measurement of how acid or alkaline it is. Acid solutions have a pH of less than 7 and alkaline solutions have a pH greater than 7. pH is an abbreviation for 'potential hydrogen'.

**phalanger** phalangers
*Said* "fal-**lan**-jer" NOUN an Australian marsupial with thick fur and a long tail. In Australia and New Zealand, it is also called a possum.

**phallus** phalluses
NOUN a penis or a symbolic model of a penis.
**phallic** ADJECTIVE

**phantom** phantoms
NOUN **1** a ghost. ▶ ADJECTIVE **2** imagined or unreal *E.G. a phantom pregnancy.*

**pharaoh** pharaohs
*Said* "**fair**-oh" NOUN The pharaohs were kings of ancient Egypt.

**pharmaceutical**
*Said* "far-mass-**yoo**-tik-kl" ADJECTIVE connected with the industrial production of medicines.

**pharmacist** pharmacists
NOUN a person who is qualified to prepare and sell medicines.

**pharmacy** pharmacies
NOUN a shop where medicines are sold.

**phase** phases phasing phased
NOUN **1** a particular stage in the development of something. ▶ VERB **2** To phase something is to cause it to happen gradually in stages.

**PhD** PhDs
NOUN a degree awarded to someone who has done advanced research in a subject. PhD is an abbreviation for 'Doctor of Philosophy'.

**pheasant** pheasants
NOUN a large, long-tailed game bird.

**phenomenal**
*Said* "fin-**nom**-in-nal" ADJECTIVE extraordinarily great or good.
**phenomenally** ADVERB

**phenomenon** phenomena
NOUN something that happens or exists, especially something remarkable or something being considered in a scientific way *E.G. a well-known geographical phenomenon.*
☑ The word *phenomenon* is singular. The plural form is *phenomena*.

**philanthropist** philanthropists
*Said* "fil-**lan**-throp-pist" NOUN someone who freely gives help or money to people in need.
**philanthropic** ADJECTIVE
**philanthropy** NOUN

**philistine** philistines
NOUN If you call someone a philistine, you mean that they do not like art, literature, or music.

**philosophical** or **philosophic**
ADJECTIVE Someone who is philosophical does not get upset when disappointing things happen.

A B C D E F G H I J K L M N O P Q R S T U V W X Y Z

**philosophy** philosophies
NOUN **1** Philosophy is the study or creation of ideas about existence, knowledge or beliefs. **2** a set of beliefs that a person has.
**philosopher** NOUN
📖 from Greek *philosophos* meaning 'lover of wisdom'

**phlegm**
*Said* "flem" NOUN Phlegm is a thick mucus which you get in your throat when you have a cold.

**phobia** phobias
NOUN an great fear or hatred of something E.G. *The man had a phobia about flying.*
**phobic** ADJECTIVE

**-phobia**
SUFFIX '-phobia' means 'fear of' E.G. *claustrophobia.*
📖 from Greek *phobos* meaning 'fear'

**phoenix** phoenixes
*Said* "fee-niks" NOUN an imaginary bird which, according to myth, burns itself to ashes every five hundred years and rises from the fire again.

**phone** phones phoning phoned
NOUN **1** a piece of electronic equipment which allows you to speak to someone in another place by keying in or dialling their number. ▶ VERB **2** If you phone someone, you key in or dial their number and speak to them using a phone.

**-phone**
SUFFIX '-phone' means 'giving off sound' E.G. *telephone… gramophone.*
📖 from Greek *phōnē* meaning 'voice' or 'sound'

**phoney** phonier phoniest; also spelt **phony**
ADJECTIVE; INFORMAL false and intended to deceive.

**photo** photos
NOUN; INFORMAL a photograph.

**photo-**
PREFIX 'Photo-' means 'light' or 'using light' E.G. *photography.*

**photocopier** photocopiers
NOUN a machine which makes instant copies of documents by photographing them.

**photocopy** photocopies photocopying photocopied
(LIBRARY)
NOUN **1** a copy of a document produced by a photocopier. ▶ VERB **2** If you photocopy a document, you make a copy of it using a photocopier.

**photogenic**
ADJECTIVE Someone who is photogenic always looks nice in photographs.

**photograph** photographs photographing photographed
NOUN **1** a picture made using a camera. ▶ VERB **2** When you photograph someone, you take a picture of them by using a camera.
**photographer** NOUN
**photography** NOUN

**photographic**
ADJECTIVE connected with photography.

**photosynthesis**
NOUN Photosynthesis is the process by which the action of sunlight on the chlorophyll in plants produces the substances that keep the plants alive.

**phrasal verb** phrasal verbs
NOUN a verb such as 'take over' or 'break in', which is made up of a verb and an adverb or preposition.

**phrase** phrases phrasing phrased
NOUN **1** a group of words considered

a
b
c
d
e
f
g
h
i
j
k
l
m
n
o
p
q
r
s
t
u
v
w
x
y
z

A B C D E F G H I J K L M N O P Q R S T U V W X Y Z

as a unit. ▶ VERB **2** If you phrase something in a particular way, you choose those words to express it *E.G. I should have phrased that better.*

---

### What is a Phrase?

A **phrase** is a group of words which combine together but is not usually capable of standing on its own to describe an idea or situation. It requires additional words to form a meaningful sentence:

*E.G. She drank **a cup of tea**.*
*I **was reading** a book.*

Some phrases act as nouns:

*E.G. **A stack of newspapers** lay on the floor.*
***My sister's friend** lives in Canada.*

Some phrases act as verbs. Verb phrases often contain an auxiliary verb. They may also contain adverbs.

*E.G. She **was always complaining** about the buses.*
*He **used to play** the piano.*

Some phrases act as adjectives. When words combine to act as an adjective, they are usually hyphenated if they occur before the noun:

*E.G. The food here is **of the highest quality**.*
*He asked for an **up-to-the-minute** report.*

Some phrases act as adverbs. Adverb phrases often begin with a preposition.

*E.G. She disappeared **in the blink of an eye**.*
*They played **with great gusto**.*

CONTINUED →

---

Some phrases are acceptable as substitutes for sentences. Although they do not contain a subject and a verb, they can be understood on their own:

*E.G. Happy Birthday!* ■ *Good morning.* ■ *All right?*

---

**physical**
ADJECTIVE **1** concerning the body rather than the mind. **2** (GEOGRAPHY) relating to things that can be touched or seen, especially with regard to their size or shape *E.G. the physical characteristics of their machinery… the physical world.*
**physically** ADVERB

**physical education**
NOUN Physical education consists of the sport that you do at school.

**physician** physicians
NOUN a doctor.

**physics**
NOUN Physics is the scientific study of matter, energy, gravity, electricity, heat, and sound.
**physicist** NOUN

**physio-**
PREFIX 'Physio-' means to do with the body or natural functions *E.G. physiotherapy.*
🏛 from Greek *physio*, from *phuein* meaning 'to make grow'

**physiology**
NOUN Physiology is the scientific study of the way the bodies of living things work.

**physiotherapy**
NOUN Physiotherapy is medical treatment which involves exercise and massage.
**physiotherapist** NOUN

---

**physique** physiques
*Said* "fiz-**zeek**" NOUN A person's physique is the shape and size of their body.

**pi**
*Rhymes with* "**fly**" NOUN Pi is a number, approximately 3.142 and symbolized by the Greek letter π. Pi is the ratio of the circumference of a circle to its diameter.

**piano** pianos
NOUN a large musical instrument with a row of black and white keys. When the keys are pressed, little hammers hit wires to produce the different notes.
**pianist** NOUN
🏛 originally called 'pianoforte', from Italian *gravecembalo col piano e forte* meaning 'harpsichord with soft and loud (sounds)'

**piccolo** piccolos
NOUN a high-pitched wind instrument like a small flute.
🏛 from Italian *piccolo* meaning 'small'

**pick** picks picking picked
VERB 1 To pick something is to choose it. 2 If you pick a flower or fruit, or pick something from a place, you remove it with your fingers. 3 If someone picks a lock, they open it with a piece of wire instead of a key. ▶ NOUN 4 a pickaxe.

**pick on** VERB If you pick on someone, you criticize them unfairly or treat them unkindly.

**pick up** VERB If you pick someone or something up, you collect them from the place where they are waiting.

**pickaxe** pickaxes
NOUN a tool consisting of a curved pointed iron bar attached in the middle to a long handle.

**picket** pickets picketing picketed
VERB 1 When a group of people picket a place of work, they stand outside to persuade other workers to join a strike. ▶ NOUN 2 someone who is picketing a place.

**pickings**
PLURAL NOUN Pickings are goods or money that can be obtained very easily *E.G. rich pickings*.

**pickle** pickles pickling pickled
NOUN 1 Pickle or pickles consists of vegetables or fruit preserved in vinegar or salt water. ▶ VERB 2 To pickle food is to preserve it in vinegar or salt water.

**pickpocket** pickpockets
NOUN a thief who steals from people's pockets or handbags.

**picnic** picnics picnicking picnicked
NOUN 1 a meal eaten out of doors. ▶ VERB 2 People who are picnicking are having a picnic.

**pictorial**
ADJECTIVE relating to or using pictures *E.G. a pictorial record of the railway*.

**picture** pictures picturing pictured
NOUN 1 a drawing, painting, or photograph of someone or something. 2 If you have a picture of something in your mind, you have an idea or impression of it. ▶ PLURAL NOUN 3 If you go to the pictures, you go to see a film at the cinema. ▶ VERB 4 If someone is pictured in a newspaper or magazine, a photograph of them is printed in it. 5 If you picture something, you think of it and

a
b
c
d
e
f
g
h
i
j
k
l
m
n
o
**p**
q
r
s
t
u
v
w
x
y
z

imagine it clearly E.G. *That is how I always picture him.*

**picturesque**
*Said* "pik-chur-**esk**" ADJECTIVE A place that is picturesque is very attractive and unspoiled.

**pie** pies
NOUN a dish of meat, vegetables, or fruit covered with pastry.

**piece** pieces piecing pieced
NOUN **1** a portion or part of something. **2** something that has been written or created, such as a work of art or a musical composition. **3** a coin E.G. *a 50 pence piece.* ▶ VERB **4** If you piece together a number of things, you gradually put them together to make something complete.

**piecemeal**
ADVERB or ADJECTIVE done gradually and at irregular intervals E.G. *a piecemeal approach to career management.*

**pier** piers
NOUN a large structure which sticks out into the sea at a seaside town, and which people can walk along.

**pierce** pierces piercing pierced
VERB If a sharp object pierces something, it goes through it, making a hole.
■ penetrate, puncture

**piercing**
ADJECTIVE **1** A piercing sound is high-pitched and unpleasant. **2** Someone with piercing eyes seems to look at you very intensely.
■ (sense 1) penetrating, shrill

**piety**
*Said* "**pie**-it-tee" NOUN Piety is strong and devout religious belief or behaviour.

**pig** pigs
NOUN a farm animal kept for its meat.

It has pinkish skin, short legs, and a snout.

**pigeon** pigeons
NOUN a largish bird with grey feathers, often seen in towns.

**pigeonhole** pigeonholes
NOUN one of the sections in a frame on a wall where letters can be left.

**piggyback** piggybacks
NOUN If you give someone a piggyback, you carry them on your back, supporting them under their knees.

**piglet** piglets
NOUN a young pig.

**pigment** pigments
NOUN a substance that gives something a particular colour.
**pigmentation** NOUN

**pigsty** pigsties
NOUN a hut with a small enclosed area where pigs are kept.

**pigtail** pigtails
NOUN a length of plaited hair.

**pike** pikes
NOUN **1** a large freshwater fish of northern countries with strong teeth. **2** a medieval weapon consisting of a pointed metal blade attached to a long pole.

**pilchard** pilchards
NOUN a small sea fish.

**pile** piles piling piled
NOUN **1** a quantity of things lying one on top of another. **2** the soft surface of a carpet consisting of many threads standing on end. ▶ PLURAL NOUN **3** Piles are painful swellings that appear in the veins inside or just outside a person's anus. ▶ VERB **4** If you pile things somewhere, you put them one on top of the other.

**pile-up** pile-ups
NOUN; INFORMAL a road accident

**pilfer** pilfers pilfering pilfered
VERB Someone who pilfers steals small things over a period of time. 📖 from Old French *pelfre* meaning 'booty'

**pilgrim** pilgrims
NOUN (RE) a person who travels to a holy place for religious reasons.
**pilgrimage** NOUN

**pill** pills
NOUN 1 a small, hard tablet of medicine that you swallow. 2 The pill is a type of drug that women can take regularly to prevent pregnancy. 📖 from Latin *pilula* meaning 'little ball'

**pillage** pillages pillaging pillaged
VERB If a group of people pillage a place, they steal from it using violence.

**pillar** pillars
NOUN 1 a tall, narrow, solid structure, usually supporting part of a building. 2 Someone who is described as a pillar of a particular group is an active and important member of it E.G. *a pillar of the Church*.

**pillar box** pillar boxes
NOUN a red cylinder or box in which you post letters.

**pillory** pillories pillorying pilloried
VERB If someone is pilloried, they are criticized severely by a lot of people.

**pillow** pillows
NOUN a rectangular cushion which you rest your head on when you are in bed.

**pillowcase** pillowcases
NOUN a cover for a pillow which can be removed and washed.

**pilot** pilots piloting piloted
NOUN 1 a person who is trained to fly an aircraft. 2 a person who goes on board ships to guide them through local waters to a port. ▶ VERB 3 To pilot something is to control its movement or to guide it. ▶ ADJECTIVE 4 a small test of a scheme or product, done to see if it would be successful.

**pimp** pimps
NOUN a man who finds clients for prostitutes and takes a large part of their earnings.

**pimple** pimples
NOUN a small spot on the skin.
**pimply** ADJECTIVE

**PIN** PINs
NOUN an abbreviation for 'personal identification number': a number used by the holder of a cash card or credit card.

**pin** pins pinning pinned
NOUN 1 a thin, pointed piece of metal used to fasten together things such as pieces of fabric or paper. ▶ VERB 2 If you pin something somewhere, you fasten it there with a pin or a drawing pin. 3 If someone pins you in a particular position, they hold you there so that you cannot move. 4 If you try to pin something down, you try to get or give a clear and exact description of it or statement about it.

**pinafore** pinafores
NOUN a dress with no sleeves, worn over a blouse.

**pincers**
PLURAL NOUN 1 Pincers are a tool used for gripping and pulling things. They consist of two pieces of metal hinged in the middle. 2 The pincers of a crab or lobster are its front claws.

a b c d e f g h i j k l m n o p q r s t u v w x y z

'i' before 'e' except after 'c'    SPELLING NOTE

A B C D E F G H I J K L M N O P Q R S T U V W X Y Z

**pinch** pinches pinching pinched
VERB **1** If you pinch something, you squeeze it between your thumb and first finger. **2** INFORMAL If someone pinches something, they steal it. ▸ NOUN **3** A pinch of something is the amount that you can hold between your thumb and first finger E.G. *a pinch of salt.*

**pinched**
ADJECTIVE If someone's face is pinched, it looks thin and pale.

**pine** pines pining pined
NOUN **1** A pine or pine tree is an evergreen tree with very thin leaves. ▸ VERB **2** If you pine for something, you are sad because you cannot have it.

**pineapple** pineapples
NOUN a large, oval fruit with sweet, yellow flesh and a thick, lumpy brown skin.

**ping-pong**
NOUN the same as **table tennis.**

**pink** pinker pinkest
ADJECTIVE pale reddish-white.

**pinnacle** pinnacles
NOUN **1** a tall pointed piece of stone or rock. **2** The pinnacle of something is its best or highest level E.G. *the pinnacle of his career.*

**pinpoint** pinpoints pinpointing pinpointed
VERB If you pinpoint something, you explain or discover exactly what or where it is.

**pinstripe**
ADJECTIVE Pinstripe cloth has very narrow vertical stripes.

**pint** pints
NOUN a unit of liquid volume equal to one eighth of a gallon or about 0.568 litres.

**pioneer** pioneers pioneering pioneered
*Said* "pie-on-**ear**" NOUN **1** Someone who is a pioneer in a particular activity is one of the first people to develop it. ▸ VERB **2** Someone who pioneers a new process or invention is the first person to develop it.

**pious**
*Said* "**pie**-uss" ADJECTIVE very religious and moral.

**pip** pips
NOUN Pips are the hard seeds in a fruit.

**pipe** pipes piping piped
NOUN **1** a long, hollow tube through which liquid or gas can flow. **2** an object used for smoking tobacco. It consists of a small hollow bowl attached to a tube. ▸ VERB **3** To pipe a liquid or gas somewhere is to transfer it through a pipe.

**pipeline** pipelines
NOUN a large underground pipe that carries oil or gas over a long distance.

**piper** pipers
NOUN a person who plays the bagpipes.

**piping**
NOUN Piping consists of pipes and tubes.

**piranha** piranhas
*Said* "pir-**rah**-nah" NOUN a small, fierce fish with sharp teeth.
🏛 a Portuguese word

**pirate** pirates
NOUN Pirates were sailors who attacked and robbed other ships.

**pirouette** pirouettes
*Said* "pir-roo-**et**" NOUN In ballet, a pirouette is a fast spinning step done on the toes.

## Pisces
*Said* "**pie**-seez" NOUN Pisces is the twelfth sign of the zodiac, represented by two fish. People born between February 19th and March 20th are born under this sign. 🏛 the plural of Latin *piscis* meaning 'a fish'

## pistil pistils
NOUN in a flower, the pistil is the female reproductive part made up of the carpel or two or more carpels fused together.

## pistol pistols
NOUN a small gun held in the hand.

## piston pistons
NOUN a cylinder or disc that slides up and down inside a tube. Pistons make parts of engines move.

## pit pits
NOUN **1** a large hole in the ground. **2** a small hollow in the surface of something. **3** a coal mine.

## pitch pitches pitching pitched
NOUN **1** ( PE ) an area of ground marked out for playing a game such as football. **2** ( MUSIC ) The pitch of a sound is how high or low it is. **3** a black substance used in road tar and also for making boats and roofs waterproof. ▶ VERB **4** If you pitch something somewhere, you throw it with a lot of force. **5** If you pitch something at a particular level of difficulty, you set it at that level *E.G. Any film must be pitched at a level to suit its intended audience.* **6** When you pitch a tent, you fix it in an upright position.

## pitcher pitchers
NOUN a large jug.

## pitfall pitfalls
NOUN The pitfalls of a situation are its difficulties or dangers.

## pith
NOUN the white substance between the outer skin and the flesh of an orange or lemon.

## pitiful
ADJECTIVE Someone or something that is pitiful is in such a sad or weak situation that you feel pity for them.

## pittance
NOUN a very small amount of money.

## pitted
ADJECTIVE covered in small hollows *E.G. Nails often become pitted.*

## pity pities pitying pitied
VERB **1** If you pity someone, you feel very sorry for them. ▶ NOUN **2** Pity is a feeling of being sorry for someone. **3** If you say that it is a pity about something, you are expressing your disappointment about it.

## pivot pivots pivoting pivoted
VERB **1** If something pivots, it balances or turns on a central point *E.G. The keel pivots on a large stainless steel pin.* ▶ NOUN **2** the central point on which something balances or turns.
**pivotal** ADJECTIVE

## pixie pixies
NOUN an imaginary little creature in fairy stories.

## pizza pizzas
*Said* "**peet**-sah" NOUN a flat piece of dough covered with cheese, tomato, and other savoury food.

## placard placards
NOUN a large notice carried at a demonstration or displayed in a public place.

## placate placates placating placated
VERB If you placate someone, you stop them feeling angry by doing something to please them.

a b c d e f g h i j k l m n o **p** q r s t u v w x y z

A
B
C
D
E
F
G
H
I
J
K
L
M
N
O
**P**
Q
R
S
T
U
V
W
X
Y
Z

**place** places placing placed
NOUN 1 any point, building, or area.
2 the position where something
belongs E.G. *She set the holder in its
place on the table.* 3 a space at a table
set with cutlery where one person
can eat. 4 If you have a place in a
group or at a college, you are a
member or are accepted as a
student. 5 a particular point or stage
in a sequence of things E.G. *second
place in the race.* ▶ PHRASE 6 When
something **takes place**, it happens.
▶ VERB 7 If you place something
somewhere, you put it there. 8 If you
place an order, you order something.
■ (sense 1) location, site, spot

**placebo** placebos
*Said* "plas-**see**-boh" NOUN a substance
given to a patient in place of a drug
and from which, though it has no
active ingredients, the patient
may imagine they get some
benefit.

**placenta** placentas
*Said* "plas-**sen**-tah" NOUN The
placenta is the mass of veins and
tissues in the womb of a pregnant
woman or animal. It gives the foetus
food and oxygen.

**placid**
ADJECTIVE calm and not easily excited
or upset.
**placidly** ADVERB
■ even-tempered, unexcitable

**plagiarism**
*Said* "**play**-jer-rizm" NOUN Plagiarism is
copying someone else's work or
ideas and pretending that it is your
own.
**plagiarist** NOUN **plagiarize** VERB
▥ from Latin *plagiarus* meaning
'plunderer'

**plague** plagues plaguing plagued
*Said* "playg" NOUN 1 Plague is a very
infectious disease that kills large
numbers of people. 2 A plague of
unpleasant things is a large number
of them occurring at the same time
E.G. *a plague of rats.* ▶ VERB 3 If
problems plague you, they keep
causing you trouble.

**plaice**
NOUN an edible European flat fish.

**plaid** plaids
*Said* "plad" NOUN Plaid is woven
material with a tartan design.

**plain** plainer plainest; plains
ADJECTIVE 1 very simple in style with no
pattern or decoration E.G. *plain walls.*
2 obvious and easy to recognize or
understand E.G. *plain language.* 3 A
person who is plain is not at all
beautiful or attractive. ▶ ADVERB 4 You
can use 'plain' before a noun or
adjective to emphasize it E.G. *You
were just plain stupid.* ▶ NOUN 5 a large,
flat area of land with very few trees.
**plainly** ADVERB
■ (sense 1) bare, simple, unadorned

**plaintiff** plaintiffs
NOUN a person who has brought a
court case against another person.

**plait** plaits plaiting plaited
VERB 1 If you plait three lengths of hair
or rope together, you twist them
over each other in turn to make one
thick length. ▶ NOUN 2 a length of hair
that has been plaited.

**plan** plans planning planned
NOUN 1 a method of achieving
something that has been worked
out beforehand. 2 a detailed diagram
or drawing of something that is to
be made. ▶ VERB 3 If you plan
something, you decide in detail what

it is to be and how to do it. **4** If you are planning to do something, you intend to do it *E.G. They plan to marry in the summer*.

■ (sense 1) scheme, strategy
■ (sense 3) devise, scheme, think out
■ (sense 4) intend, mean, propose

**plane** planes planing planed
NOUN **1** a vehicle with wings and engines that enable it to fly. **2** a flat surface. **3** You can refer to a particular level of something as a particular plane *E.G. to take the rock and roll concert to a higher plane*. **4** a tool with a flat bottom with a sharp blade in it. You move it over a piece of wood to remove thin pieces from the surface. ► VERB **5** If you plane a piece of wood, you smooth its surface with a plane.

**planet** planets
NOUN a round object in space which moves around the sun or a star and is lit by light from it.
**planetary** ADJECTIVE

**plank** planks
NOUN a long rectangular piece of wood.

**plankton**
NOUN Plankton is a layer of tiny plants and animals that live just below the surface of a sea or lake.

**plant** plants planting planted
NOUN **1** a living thing that grows in the earth and has stems, leaves, and roots. **2** a factory or power station *E.G. a giant bottling plant*. ► VERB **3** When you plant a seed or plant, you put it into the ground. **4** If you plant something somewhere, you put it there firmly or secretly.

**plantation** plantations
NOUN **1** a large area of land where

crops such as tea, cotton, or sugar are grown. **2** a large number of trees planted together.

**plaque** plaques
*Rhymes with "black"* NOUN **1** a flat piece of metal which is fixed to a wall and has an inscription in memory of a famous person or event. **2** Plaque is a substance which forms around your teeth and consists of bacteria, saliva, and food.

**plasma**
*Said "plaz-mah"* NOUN Plasma is the clear fluid part of blood.

**plaster** plasters plastering plastered
NOUN **1** Plaster is a paste made of sand, lime, and water, which is used to form a smooth surface for inside walls and ceilings. **2** a strip of sticky material with a small pad, used for covering cuts on your body. ► VERB **3** To plaster a wall is to cover it with a layer of plaster. ► PHRASE **4** If your arm or leg is **in plaster**, it has a plaster cast on it to protect a broken bone.
**plasterer** NOUN

**plastered**
ADJECTIVE **1** If something is plastered to a surface, it is stuck there. **2** If something is plastered with things, they are all over its surface.

**plastic** plastics
NOUN **1** Plastic is a substance made by a chemical process that can be moulded when soft to make a wide range of objects. ► ADJECTIVE **2** made of plastic.

**plastic surgery**
NOUN Plastic surgery is surgery to replace or repair damaged skin or to improve a person's appearance by changing the shape of their features.

A B C D E F G H I J K L M N O P Q R S T U V W X Y Z

**plate** plates
NOUN **1** a flat dish used to hold food.
**2** a flat piece of metal or other hard material used for various purposes in machinery or building *E.G. heavy steel plates used in shipbuilding.*

**plateau** plateaus or plateaux
*Rhymes with "snow"* NOUN a large area of high and fairly flat land.

**plated**
ADJECTIVE Metal that is plated is covered with a thin layer of silver or gold.

**platform** platforms
NOUN **1** a raised structure on which someone or something can stand.
**2** the raised area in a railway station where passengers get on and off trains.

**platinum**
NOUN Platinum is a valuable silver-coloured metal.

**platitude** platitudes
NOUN a statement made as if it were significant but which has become meaningless or boring because it has been used so many times before.

**platonic**
ADJECTIVE A platonic relationship is simply one of friendship and does not involve sexual attraction.
🏛 from the name of the Greek philospher Plato

**platoon** platoons
NOUN a small group of soldiers, commanded by a lieutenant.

**platter** platters
NOUN a large serving plate.

**platypus** platypuses
NOUN A platypus or duck-billed platypus is an Australian mammal which lives in rivers. It has brown fur,

webbed feet, and a snout like a duck.
🏛 from Greek *platus* meaning 'flat' and *pous* meaning 'foot'

**plaudits**
PLURAL NOUN; *FORMAL* Plaudits are expressions of admiration.

**plausible**
ADJECTIVE An explanation that is plausible seems likely to be true.
**plausibility** NOUN

**play** plays playing played
VERB **1** When children play, they take part in games or use toys. **2** When you play a sport or match, you take part in it. **3** If an actor plays a character in a play or film, he or she performs that role. **4** If you play a musical instrument, you produce music from it: **5** If you play a record or tape, you listen to it. ▶ NOUN **6** a piece of drama performed in the theatre or on television.
**player** NOUN

**playboy** playboys
NOUN a rich man who spends his time enjoying himself.

**playful**
ADJECTIVE **1** friendly and light-hearted *E.G. a playful kiss on the tip of his nose.*
**2** lively *E.G. a playful puppy.*
**playfully** ADVERB

**playground** playgrounds
NOUN a special area for children to play in.

**playgroup** playgroups
NOUN an informal kind of school for very young children where they learn by playing.

**playing card** playing cards
NOUN Playing cards are cards printed with numbers or pictures which are used to play various games.

**playing field** playing fields
NOUN an area of grass where people play sports.

**playwright** playwrights
NOUN (DRAMA) (ENGLISH) a person who writes plays.

**plaza** plazas
*Said* "plah-za" NOUN an open square in a city.

**plea** pleas
NOUN 1 an emotional request *E.G. a plea for help.* 2 In a court of law, someone's plea is their statement that they are guilty or not guilty.

**plead** pleads pleading pleaded
VERB 1 If you plead with someone, you ask them in an intense emotional way to do something. 2 When a person pleads guilty or not guilty, they state in court that they are guilty or not guilty of a crime.

**pleasant**
ADJECTIVE enjoyable, likable, or attractive.
**pleasantly** ADVERB
▪ agreeable, nice, pleasing

**please** pleases pleasing pleased
1 You say please when you are asking someone politely to do something.
VERB 2 If something pleases you, it makes you feel happy and satisfied.
**pleased** ADJECTIVE
▪ (sense 2) delight, gladden, satisfy

**pleasing**
ADJECTIVE attractive, satisfying, or enjoyable *E.G. a pleasing appearance.*

**pleasure** pleasures
NOUN 1 Pleasure is a feeling of happiness, satisfaction, or enjoyment. 2 an activity that you enjoy.
**pleasurable** ADJECTIVE

**pleat** pleats
NOUN a permanent fold in fabric made by folding one part over another.

**plebiscite** plebiscites
*Said* "pleb-iss-ite" NOUN; FORMAL a vote on a matter of national importance in which all the voters in a country can take part.
▦ from Latin *plebiscitum* meaning 'decree of the people'

**pledge** pledges pledging pledged
NOUN 1 a solemn promise. ▶ VERB 2 If you pledge something, you promise that you will do it or give it.

**plentiful**
ADJECTIVE existing in large numbers or amounts and readily available *E.G. Fruit and vegetables were plentiful.*
**plentifully** ADVERB

**plenty**
NOUN If there is plenty of something, there is a lot of it.

**plethora**
*Said* "pleth-thor-ah" NOUN A plethora of something is an amount that is greater than you need.

**pleurisy**
*Said* "ploor-ris-see" NOUN Pleurisy is a serious illness in which a person's lungs become inflamed and breathing is difficult.

**pliable**
ADJECTIVE 1 If something is pliable, you can bend it without breaking it. 2 Someone who is pliable can be easily influenced or controlled.
▪ (sense 1) bendy, flexible, supple

**pliers**
PLURAL NOUN Pliers are a small tool with metal jaws for holding small objects and bending wire.

a
b
c
d
e
f
g
h
i
j
k
l
m
n
o
p
q
r
s
t
u
v
w
x
y
z

Betty Eats Cakes And Uses Seven Eggs (<u>because</u>)          SPELLING NOTE

A B C D E F G H I J K L M N O P Q R S T U V W X Y Z

**plight**

NOUN Someone's plight is the very difficult or dangerous situation that they are in *E.G. the plight of the refugees.*

**plinth plinths**

NOUN a block of stone on which a statue or pillar stands.

**plod plods plodding plodded**

VERB If you plod somewhere, you walk there slowly and heavily.

**plonk plonks plonking plonked**

VERB If you plonk something down, you put it down heavily and carelessly.

**plop plops plopping plopped**

NOUN **1** a gentle sound made by something light dropping into a liquid. ▶ VERB **2** If something plops into a liquid, it drops into it with a gentle sound.

**plot plots plotting plotted**

NOUN **1** a secret plan made by a group of people. **2** The plot of a novel or play is the story. **3** a small piece of land. ▶ VERB **4** If people plot to do something, they plan it secretly *E.G. His family is plotting to disinherit him.* **5** If someone plots the course of a plane or ship on a map, or plots a graph, they mark the points in the correct places.

⬛ (sense 1) conspiracy, scheme
⬛ (sense 4) conspire, plan, scheme

**plough ploughs ploughing ploughed**

*Rhymes with "cow"* NOUN **1** a large farming tool that is pulled across a field to turn the soil over before planting seeds. ▶ VERB **2** When someone ploughs land, they use a plough to turn over the soil.

**ploy ploys**

NOUN a clever plan or way of behaving in order to get something that you want.

**pluck plucks plucking plucked**

VERB **1** To pluck a fruit or flower is to remove it with a sharp pull. **2** To pluck a chicken or other dead bird means to pull its feathers out before cooking it. **3** When you pluck a stringed instrument, you pull the strings and let them go. ▶ NOUN **4** Pluck is courage.

**plucky** ADJECTIVE

**plug plugs plugging plugged**

NOUN **1** a plastic object with metal prongs that can be pushed into a socket to connect an appliance to the electricity supply. **2** a disc of rubber or metal with which you block up the hole in a sink or bath. ▶ VERB **3** If you plug a hole, you block it with something.

**plum plums**

NOUN a small fruit with a smooth red or yellow skin and a large stone in the middle.

**plumage**

*Said "ploom-mage"* NOUN A bird's plumage is its feathers.

**plumber plumbers**

NOUN a person who connects and repairs water pipes.

🏛 from Old French *plommier* meaning 'worker in lead'

**plumbing**

NOUN The plumbing in a building is the system of water pipes, sinks, and toilets.

**plume plumes**

NOUN a large, brightly coloured feather.

**plummet** plummets plummeting plummeted
VERB If something plummets, it falls very quickly E.G. *Sales have plummeted.*

**plump** plumper plumpest
ADJECTIVE rather fat E.G. *a small plump baby.*
■ chubby, podgy, tubby

**plunder** plunders plundering plundered
VERB If someone plunders a place, they steal things from it.

**plunge** plunges plunging plunged
VERB 1 If something plunges, it falls suddenly. 2 If you plunge an object into something, you push it in quickly. 3 If you plunge into an activity or state, you suddenly become involved in it or affected by it E.G. *The United States had just plunged into the war.* ▶ NOUN 4 a sudden fall.
■ (sense 1) dive, drop, fall, plummet

**Plunket Society**
NOUN In New Zealand, the Plunket Society was an organization for the care of mothers and babies. It is now called the Royal New Zealand Society for the Health of Women and Children.

**plural** plurals
NOUN (ENGLISH) the form of a word that is used to refer to two or more people or things, for example the plural of 'chair' is 'chairs', and the plural of 'mouse' is 'mice'.
→ SEE BOX ON NEXT PAGE

**pluralism**
NOUN Pluralism is the belief that it is possible for different social and religious groups to live together peacefully while keeping their own beliefs and traditions.

**pluralist** ADJECTIVE OR NOUN

**plural noun** plural nouns
NOUN In this dictionary, 'plural noun' is the name given to a noun that is normally used only in the plural, for example 'scissors' or 'police'.
See box on p 636

**plus** 1 You use 'plus' to show that one number is being added to another E.G. *Two plus two equals four.*
ADJECTIVE 2 slightly more than the number mentioned E.G. *a career of 25 years plus.* ▶ PREPOSITION 3 You can use 'plus' when you mention an additional item E.G. *He wrote a history of Scotland plus a history of British literature.*
☑ Although you can use *plus* to mean 'additionally' in spoken language, you should avoid it in written work: *plus, you could win a holiday in Florida.*

**plush**
ADJECTIVE very expensive and smart E.G. *a plush hotel.*

**Pluto**
NOUN Pluto is the smallest planet in the solar system and the furthest from the sun.

**ply** plies plying plied
VERB 1 If you ply someone with things or questions, you keep giving them things or asking them questions. 2 To ply a trade is to do a particular job as your work. ▶ NOUN 3 Ply is the thickness of wool or thread, measured by the number of strands it is made from.

**plywood**
NOUN Plywood is wooden board made from several thin sheets of wood glued together under pressure.

a
b
c
d
e
f
g
h
i
j
k
l
m
n
o
p
q
r
s
t
u
v
w
x
y
z

## What is a Plural?

Most nouns can exist in either the singular or plural.

The **singular** form of the noun is used to mean only one instance of a thing. This is the main form given in the dictionary:

*E.G.* one book ■ a raven

The **plural** form of the noun is used to mean more than one instance of a thing. The plural form is given in the dictionary in smaller type after the main form:

*E.G.* two books ■ some ravens

The plural form of the noun is usually formed by adding the letter *-s* to the singular:

*E.G.* book ➤ books ■ raven ➤ ravens

Words that end in *-s*, *-z*, *-x*, *-ch*, or *-sh* in the singular are made plural by adding the letters *-es*:

*E.G.* cross ➤ crosses ■ box ➤ boxes

Words that end in a consonant + *-y* in the singular are made plural by removing the *-y* and adding *-ies*:

*E.G.* pony ➤ ponies ■ party ➤ parties

Words that end in *-ife* in the singular are made plural by removing the *-fe* and adding *-ves*:

*E.G.* knife ➤ knives ■ life ➤ lives

Some words that end in *-f* in the singular are made plural by removing the *-f* and adding *-ves*. Other words that end in *-f* in the singular are made plural by simply adding *-s*:

*E.G.* hoof ➤ hooves ■ roof ➤ roofs

**BE CAREFUL** not to use an apostrophe (') when you add an *-s* to make a plural.

## Irregular Plurals

Some words that have come to English from a foreign language have plurals that do not end in *-s*.

Some words that came into English from French have plurals ending in *-x*:

*E.G.* bureau ➤ bureaux ■ gateau ➤ gateaux

Some words that came into English from Italian have plurals ending in *-i*:

*E.G.* paparazzo ➤ paparazzi graffito ➤ graffiti

Some words that came into English from Hebrew have plurals ending in *-im*:

*E.G.* cherub ➤ cherubim ■ kibbutz ➤ kibbutzim

Some words that came into English from Latin have plurals ending in *-i*, *-a*, or *-ae*:

*E.G.* cactus ➤ cacti ■ medium ➤ media ■ formula ➤ formulae

Some words that came into English from Ancient Greek have plurals ending in *-a*:

*E.G.* phenomenon ➤ phenomena criterion ➤ criteria

The plural forms of a few words are not formed according to any regular rule. However, there are very few words like this. Here are some of the most common ones: *child, children; deer, deer; fish, fish or fishes; foot, feet; man, men; mouse, mice; ox, oxen; sheep, sheep; woman, women.*

## p.m.
used to specify times between 12 noon and 12 midnight, eg *He went to bed at 9 p.m.* It is an abbreviation for the Latin phrase 'post meridiem', which means 'after noon'.

## pneumatic
*Said* "new-**mat**-ik" ADJECTIVE operated by or filled with compressed air *E.G. a pneumatic drill.*
🔲 from Latin *pneumaticus* meaning 'of air or wind'

## pneumonia
*Said* "new-**moan**-ee-ah" NOUN Pneumonia is a serious disease which affects a person's lungs and makes breathing difficult.

## poach poaches poaching poached
VERB 1 If someone poaches animals from someone else's land, they illegally catch the animals for food. 2 When you poach food, you cook it gently in hot liquid.
**poacher** NOUN

## pocket pockets
NOUN 1 a small pouch that forms part of a piece of clothing. 2 A pocket of something is a small area of it *E.G. There are still pockets of resistance.*

## pocket money
NOUN Pocket money is an amount of money given regularly to children by their parents.

## pod pods
NOUN a long narrow seed container that grows on plants such as peas or beans.

## poddy poddies
NOUN In Australian English, a calf or lamb that is being fed by hand.

## podium podiums
NOUN a small platform, often one on which someone stands to make a speech.

## poem poems
NOUN a piece of writing in which the words are arranged in short rhythmic lines, often with a rhyme.

## poet poets
NOUN a person who writes poems.

## poetic
ADJECTIVE 1 very beautiful and expressive *E.G. a pure and poetic love.* 2 relating to poetry.
**poetically** ADVERB

## poetry
NOUN Poetry is poems, considered as a form of literature.

## poignant
*Said* "**poyn**-yant" ADJECTIVE Something that is poignant has a strong emotional effect on you, often making you feel sad *E.G. a moving and poignant moment.*
**poignancy** NOUN

## point points pointing pointed
NOUN 1 an opinion or fact expressed by someone *E.G. You've made a good point.* 2 a quality *E.G. Tact was never her strong point.* 3 the purpose or meaning something has *E.G. He completely missed the point in most of his argument.* 4 a position or time *E.G. At some point during the party, a fight erupted.* 5 a single mark in a competition. 6 the thin, sharp end of something such as a needle or knife. 7 The points of a compass are the 32 directions indicated on it. 8 The decimal point in a number is the dot separating the whole number from the fraction. 9 On a railway track, the points are the levers and rails which enable a train to move from one track to another. ▶ VERB 10 If you point

a
b
c
d
e
f
g
h
i
j
k
l
m
n
o
p
q
r
s
t
u
v
w
x
y
z

at something, you stick out your finger to show where it is. **11** If something points in a particular direction, it faces that way.

**point-blank**
ADJECTIVE **1** Something that is shot at point-blank range is shot with a gun held very close to it. ▶ ADVERB **2** If you say something point-blank, you say it directly without explanation or apology.

**pointed**
ADJECTIVE **1** A pointed object has a thin, sharp end. **2** Pointed comments express criticism.
**pointedly** ADVERB

**pointer** pointers
NOUN a piece of information which helps you to understand something E.G. *Here are a few pointers to help you make a choice.*

**pointless**
ADJECTIVE Something that is pointless has no purpose.
**pointlessly** ADVERB

**point of view** points of view
NOUN Your point of view is your opinion about something or your attitude towards it.

**poise**
NOUN Someone who has poise is calm and dignified.

**poised**
ADJECTIVE If you are poised to do something, you are ready to do it at any moment.

**poison** poisons poisoning poisoned
NOUN **1** Poison is a substance that can kill people or animals if they swallow it or absorb it. ▶ VERB **2** To poison someone is to try to kill them with poison.
**poisonous** ADJECTIVE

**poke** pokes poking poked
VERB **1** If you poke someone or something, you push at them quickly with your finger or a sharp object. **2** Something that pokes out of another thing appears from underneath or behind it E.G. *roots poking out of the earth.*
■ (sense 1) dig, jab, prod

**poker** pokers
NOUN **1** Poker is a card game in which the players make bets on the cards dealt to them. **2** a long metal rod used for moving coals or logs in a fire.

**polar**
ADJECTIVE relating to the area around the North and South Poles.

**polar bear** polar bears
NOUN a large white bear which lives in the area around the North Pole.

**pole** poles
NOUN **1** a long rounded piece of wood or metal. **2** The earth's poles are the two opposite ends of its axis E.G. *the North Pole.*

**Pole** Poles
NOUN someone who comes from Poland.

**pole vault**
NOUN The pole vault is an athletics event in which contestants jump over a high bar using a long flexible pole to lift themselves into the air.

**police** polices policing policed
PLURAL NOUN **1** The police are the people who are officially responsible for making sure that people obey the law. ▶ VERB **2** To police an area is to keep law and order there by means of the police or an armed force.

**policeman** policemen
NOUN a man who is a member of a

police force.
**policewoman** NOUN

**policy** policies
NOUN **1** a set of plans, especially in politics or business *E.G. the new economic policy.* **2** An insurance policy is a document which shows an agreement made with an insurance company.

**polio**
NOUN Polio is an infectious disease that is caused by a virus and often results in paralysis. Polio is short for 'poliomyelitis'.

**polish** polishes polishing polished
VERB **1** If you polish something, you put polish on it or rub it with a cloth to make it shine. ▶ NOUN **2** Polish is a substance that you put on an object to clean it and make it shine *E.G. shoe polish.*
**polished** ADJECTIVE

**Polish**
*Said "pole-ish"* ADJECTIVE **1** belonging or relating to Poland. ▶ NOUN **2** Polish is the main language spoken in Poland.

**polite**
ADJECTIVE Someone who is polite has good manners and behaves considerately towards other people.
**politely** ADVERB **politeness** NOUN
◼ civil, courteous, well-mannered

**political**
ADJECTIVE **1** relating to the state, government, or public administration. **2** relating to or interested in politics.
**politically** ADVERB

**politically correct**
ADJECTIVE careful not to offend or designed not to offend minority or

disadvantaged groups.

**politician** politicians
NOUN a person involved in the government of a country.

**politics**
NOUN (HISTORY) Politics is the activity and planning concerned with achieving power and control in a country or organization. ▶ PLURAL NOUN Your politics are your beliefs about how a country ought to be governed.

**polka** polkas
NOUN a fast dance in which couples dance together in circles around the room.

**poll** polls polling polled
NOUN **1** a survey in which people are asked their opinions about something. ▶ PLURAL NOUN **2** A political election can be referred to as the polls. ▶ VERB **3** If you are polled on something, you are asked your opinion about it as part of a survey.

**pollen**
NOUN Pollen is a fine yellow powder produced by flowers in order to fertilize other flowers of the same species.

**pollinate** pollinates pollinating pollinated
VERB To pollinate a plant is to fertilize it with pollen.
**pollination** NOUN

**pollutant** pollutants
NOUN a substance that causes pollution.

**pollute** pollutes polluting polluted
VERB To pollute water or air is to make it dirty and dangerous to use or live in.
**polluted** ADJECTIVE
◼ contaminate, foul, poison

a
b
c
d
e
f
g
h
i
j
k
l
m
n
o
p
q
r
s
t
u
v
w
x
y
z

A
B
C
D
E
F
G
H
I
J
K
L
M
N
O
P
Q
R
S
T
U
V
W
X
Y
Z

**pollution**

NOUN (GEOGRAPHY) Pollution of the environment happens when dirty or dangerous substances get into the air, water or soil.

**polo**

NOUN Polo is a game played between two teams of players on horseback. The players use wooden hammers with long handles to hit a ball.

**polo-necked**

ADJECTIVE A polo-necked jumper has a deep fold of material at the neck.

**polyester**

NOUN (D & T) a man-made fibre, used especially to make clothes.

**polygamy**

Said "pol-**lig**-gam-ee" NOUN Polygamy is having more than one wife at the same time.

**polygamous** ADJECTIVE

**polygon** polygons

NOUN any two-dimensional shape whose sides are all straight.

**polystyrene**

NOUN Polystyrene is a very light plastic, used especially as insulating material or to make containers.

**polythene**

NOUN Polythene is a type of plastic that is used to make thin sheets or bags.

**polyunsaturated**

ADJECTIVE Polyunsaturated oils and margarines are made mainly from vegetable fats and are considered to be healthier than saturated oils.

**polyunsaturate** NOUN

**pomegranate** pomegranates

NOUN a round fruit with a thick reddish skin. It contains a lot of small seeds.

📖 from Latin *pomum granatum* meaning 'apple full of seeds'

**pomp**

NOUN Pomp is the use of ceremony, fine clothes, and decorations on special occasions *E.G. Sir Patrick was buried with much pomp.*

**pompous**

ADJECTIVE behaving in a way that is too serious and self-important.

**pomposity** NOUN

**pond** ponds

NOUN a small, usually man-made area of water.

**ponder** ponders pondering pondered

VERB If you ponder, you think about something deeply *E.G. He was pondering the problem when Phillipson drove up.*

■ consider, mull over, think

**ponderous**

ADJECTIVE dull, slow, and serious *E.G. the ponderous commentary.*

**pong** pongs

NOUN; *INFORMAL* an unpleasant smell.

**pontiff** pontiffs

NOUN; *FORMAL* The pontiff is the Pope.

**pony** ponies

NOUN a small horse.

**ponytail** ponytails

NOUN a hairstyle in which long hair is tied at the back of the head and hangs down like a tail.

**pony trekking**

NOUN Pony trekking is a leisure activity in which people ride across country on ponies.

**poodle** poodles

NOUN a type of dog with curly hair.

**pool** pools pooling pooled

NOUN 1 a small area of still water.
2 Pool is a game in which players try to hit coloured balls into pockets around the table using long sticks

called cues. **3** A pool of people, money, or things is a group or collection used or shared by several people. ▶ PLURAL NOUN **4** The pools are a competition in which people try to guess the results of football matches. ▶ VERB **5** If people pool their resources, they gather together the things they have so that they can be shared or used by all of them.

**poor poorer poorest**
ADJECTIVE **1** Poor people have very little money and few possessions. **2** Poor places are inhabited by people with little money and show signs of neglect. **3** You use 'poor' to show sympathy E.G. *Poor you!* **4** 'Poor' also means of a low quality or standard E.G. *a poor performance.*
■ (sense 1) impoverished, penniless, poverty-stricken

**poorly**
ADJECTIVE **1** feeling unwell or ill. ▶ ADVERB **2** badly E.G. *a poorly planned operation.*

**pop pops popping popped**
NOUN **1** Pop is modern music played and enjoyed especially by young people. **2** You can refer to fizzy, nonalcoholic drinks as pop. **3** a short, sharp sound. ▶ VERB **4** If something pops, it makes a sudden sharp sound. **5** If you pop something somewhere, you put it there quickly E.G. *I'd just popped the pie in the oven.* **6** If you pop somewhere, you go there quickly E.G. *His mother popped out to buy him an ice cream.*

**popcorn**
NOUN Popcorn is a snack consisting of grains of maize heated until they puff up and burst.

**Pope Popes**
NOUN The Pope is the head of the Roman Catholic Church.
▥ from Latin *Papa* meaning 'bishop' or 'father'

**poplar poplars**
NOUN a type of tall thin tree.

**poppy poppies**
NOUN a plant with a large red flower on a hairy stem.

**populace**
NOUN; FORMAL The populace of a country is its people.

**popular**
ADJECTIVE **1** liked or approved of by a lot of people. **2** involving or intended for ordinary people E.G. *the popular press.*
**popularly** ADVERB **popularity** NOUN
**popularize** VERB
■ (sense 1) fashionable, well-liked

**populate populates populating populated**
VERB The people or animals that populate an area live there.

**population populations**
NOUN The population of a place is the people who live there, or the number of people living there.

**porcelain**
NOUN Porcelain is a delicate, hard material used to make crockery and ornaments.

**porch porches**
NOUN a covered area at the entrance to a building.

**porcupine porcupines**
NOUN a large rodent with long spines covering its body.
▥ from Old French *porc d'espins* meaning 'pig with spines'

**pore pores poring pored**
NOUN **1** The pores in your skin or on the surface of a plant are very small holes which allow moisture to pass through. ▶ VERB **2** If you pore over a

a b c d e f g h i j k l m n o **p** q r s t u v w x y z

A B C D E F G H I J K L M N O P Q R S T U V W X Y Z

piece of writing or a diagram, you study it carefully.

**pork**
NOUN Pork is meat from a pig which has not been salted or smoked.

**pornography**
NOUN Pornography refers to magazines and films that are designed to cause sexual excitement by showing naked people and sexual acts.
**pornographic** ADJECTIVE
📖 from Greek *pornos* meaning 'prostitute' and *graphein* meaning 'to write' .

**porpoise** porpoises
*Said* "por-pus" NOUN a sea mammal related to the dolphin.
📖 from Latin *porcus* meaning 'pig' and *piscis* meaning 'fish'

**porridge**
NOUN Porridge is a thick, sticky food made from oats cooked in water or milk.

**port** ports
NOUN 1 a town or area which has a harbour or docks. 2 Port is a kind of strong, sweet red wine. ▶ ADJECTIVE 3 The port side of a ship is the left side when you are facing the front.

**-port**
SUFFIX '-port' comes at the end of words that have something to do with 'carrying' in their meaning *E.G. transport.*
📖 from Latin *portāre* meaning 'to carry'

**portable**
ADJECTIVE designed to be easily carried *E.G. a portable television.*

**porter** porters
NOUN 1 a person whose job is to be in charge of the entrance of a building, greeting and directing visitors. 2 A porter in a railway station or hospital is a person whose job is to carry or move things.

**portfolio** portfolios
NOUN 1 a thin, flat case for carrying papers. 2 D&T A portfolio is also a group of selected duties, investments, or items of artwork.
📖 from Italian *portafoglio* meaning 'carrier for papers'

**porthole** portholes
NOUN a small window in the side of a ship or aircraft.

**portion** portions
NOUN a part or amount of something *E.G. a portion of fresh fruit.*
📶 bit, part, piece

**portrait** portraits
NOUN ART a picture or photograph of someone.

**portray** portrays portraying portrayed
VERB When an actor, artist, or writer portrays someone or something, they represent or describe them.
**portrayal** NOUN

**Portuguese**
*Said* "por-tyoo-**geez**" ADJECTIVE 1 belonging or relating to Portugal. ▶ NOUN 2 someone who comes from Portugal. 3 Portuguese is the main language spoken in Portugal and Brazil.

**pose** poses posing posed
VERB 1 If something poses a problem, it is the cause of the problem. 2 If you pose a question, you ask it. 3 If you pose as someone else, you pretend to be that person in order to deceive people. ▶ NOUN 4 a way of standing, sitting, or lying *E.G. Mr Clark assumes a pose for the photographer.*
📶 (sense 4) attitude, posture

**poser** posers
NOUN 1 someone who behaves or dresses in an exaggerated way in order to impress people. 2 a difficult problem.

**SPELLING NOTE** You must practiSe your Ss (practiSe)

## posh posher poshest

ADJECTIVE 1 *INFORMAL* smart, fashionable, and expensive *E.G. a posh restaurant.* 2 upper class *E.G. the man with the posh voice.*

## position positions positioning positioned

NOUN 1 (DRAMA) The position of someone or something is the place where they are or ought to be *E.G. Would the cast take their positions, please.* 2 When someone or something is in a particular position, they are sitting or lying in that way *E.G. I raised myself to a sitting position.* 3 a job or post in an organization. 4 The position that you are in at a particular time is the situation that you are in *E.G. This puts the president in a difficult position.* ▶ VERB 5 To position something somewhere is to put it there *E.G. Llewelyn positioned a cushion behind Joanna's back.*

## positive

ADJECTIVE 1 completely sure about something *E.G. I was positive he'd known about that money.* 2 confident and hopeful *E.G. I felt very positive about everything.* 3 showing approval or encouragement *E.G. I anticipate a positive response.* 4 providing definite proof of the truth or identity of something *E.G. positive evidence.* 5 (MATHS) A positive number is greater than zero.
**positively** ADVERB
■ (sense 4) absolute, certain, definite

## possess possesses possessing possessed

VERB 1 If you possess something, you own it or have it. 2 If a feeling or belief possesses you, it strongly influences you *E.G. Absolute terror possessed her.*
**possessor** NOUN

## possession possessions

NOUN 1 If something is in your possession or if you are in possession of it, you have it. 2 Your possessions are the things that you own or that you have with you.
■ (sense 2) belongings, property

## possessive

ADJECTIVE 1 A person who is possessive about someone or something wants to keep them to themselves. ▶ NOUN 2 In grammar, the possessive is the form of a noun or pronoun used to show possession *E.G. my car… That's hers.*

---

### What is the Possessive?

The possessive case is formed by adding an apostrophe (') and the letter *s* to the dictionary form of the word.

The **possessive** is used when a noun indicates a person or thing that owns another person or thing:

> *E.G. The **cat's** fur was wet.*
> *The **doctor's** cat was called Joey.*

If the noun is plural and already ends in -*s*, the possessive is formed by simply adding an apostrophe:

> *E.G. The vet often trims **cats'** claws.*
> ***Doctors'** surgeries make me nervous.*

The possessive can also be shown by using the word *of* in front of the noun. This is usually used when you are talking about something that is not alive or cannot be touched:

> *E.G. We climbed to the top **of the hill**.*
> *He is a master **of disguise**.*

When a possessive is not followed by another noun, it refers to the place where that person lives or works:

> *E.G. I am going to stay at my **aunt's**.*
> *I bought a loaf at the **baker's**.*

---

a b c d e f g h i j k l m n o p q r s t u v w x y z

A
B
C
D
E
F
G
H
I
J
K
L
M
N
O
**P**
Q
R
S
T
U
V
W
X
Y
Z

**possibility** possibilities
NOUN something that might be true or might happen E.G. the possibility of a ban.
■ chance, likelihood, probability

**possible**
ADJECTIVE 1 likely to happen or able to be done. 2 likely or capable of being true or correct.
**possibly** ADVERB
■ (sense 1) feasible, practicable

**possum** possums
NOUN In Australian and New Zealand English, a possum is a phalanger, a marsupial with thick fur and a long tail.

**post** posts posting posted
NOUN 1 The post is the system by which letters and parcels are collected and delivered. 2 a job or official position in an organization. 3 a strong upright pole fixed into the ground E.G. They are tied to a post.
▶ VERB 4 If you post a letter, you send it to someone by putting it into a postbox. 5 If you are posted somewhere, you are sent by your employers to work there.
**postal** ADJECTIVE

**post-**
PREFIX after a particular time or event E.G. his postwar career.
▥ from Latin post meaning 'after'

**postage**
NOUN Postage is the money that you pay to send letters and parcels by post.

**postal order** postal orders
NOUN a piece of paper representing a sum of money which you can buy at a post office.

**postbox** postboxes
NOUN a metal box with a hole in it

which you put letters into for collection by the postman.

**postcard** postcards
NOUN a card, often with a picture on one side, which you write on and send without an envelope.

**postcode** postcodes
NOUN a short sequence of letters and numbers at the end of an address which helps the post office to sort the mail.

**poster** posters
NOUN a large notice or picture that is stuck on a wall as an advertisement or for decoration.

**posterior** posteriors
NOUN; A HUMOROUS USE A person's posterior is their bottom.

**posterity**
NOUN; FORMAL You can refer to the future and the people who will be alive then as posterity E.G. to record the voyage for posterity.
▥ from Latin posteritas meaning 'future generations'

**posthumous**
Said "**poss**-tyum-uss" ADJECTIVE happening or awarded after a person's death E.G. a posthumous medal.
**posthumously** ADVERB

**postman** postmen
NOUN someone who collects and delivers letters and parcels sent by post.

**postmortem** postmortems
NOUN a medical examination of a dead body to find out how the person died.

**post office** post offices
NOUN 1 The Post Office is the national organization responsible for postal services. 2 a building where you can

buy stamps and post letters.

**postpone** postpones postponing postponed

VERB If you postpone an event, you arrange for it to take place at a later time than was originally planned.

**postponement** NOUN

📰 put off, shelve

**posture** postures

NOUN Your posture is the position or manner in which you hold your body.

**posy** posies

NOUN a small bunch of flowers.

**pot** pots

NOUN a deep round container; also used to refer to its contents.

**potassium nitrate**

NOUN a white chemical compound used to make gunpowder, fireworks and fertilizers. Potassium nitrate is also called saltpetre.

**potato** potatoes

NOUN a white vegetable that has a brown or red skin and grows underground.

**potent**

ADJECTIVE effective or powerful E.G. a potent cocktail.

**potency** NOUN

**potential**

ADJECTIVE 1 capable of becoming the thing mentioned E.G. potential customers… potential sources of finance. ▶ NOUN 2 Your potential is your ability to achieve success in the future.

**potentially** ADVERB

**potential energy**

NOUN Potential energy is the energy stored in something.

**pothole** potholes

NOUN 1 a hole in the surface of a road

caused by bad weather or traffic. 2 an underground cavern.

**potion** potions

NOUN a drink containing medicine, poison, or supposed magical powers.

🏛 from Latin potio meaning 'a drink'

**potted**

ADJECTIVE Potted meat or fish is cooked and put into a small sealed container to preserve it.

**potter** potters pottering pottered

NOUN 1 a person who makes pottery. ▶ VERB 2 If you potter about, you pass the time doing pleasant, unimportant things.

**pottery**

NOUN 1 Pottery is pots, dishes, and other items made from clay and fired in a kiln. 2 Pottery is also the craft of making pottery.

**potty** potties; pottier pottiest

NOUN 1 a bowl which a small child can sit on and use instead of a toilet. ▶ ADJECTIVE 2 INFORMAL crazy or foolish.

**pouch** pouches

NOUN 1 a small, soft container with a fold-over top E.G. a tobacco pouch. 2 Animals like kangaroos have a pouch, which is a pocket of skin in which they carry their young.

**poultry**

NOUN Chickens, turkeys, and other birds kept for their meat or eggs are referred to as poultry.

**pounce** pounces pouncing pounced

VERB If an animal or person pounces on something, they leap and grab it.

**pound** pounds pounding pounded

NOUN 1 The pound is the main unit of currency in Britain and in some other

A B C D E F G H I J K L M N O P Q R S T U V W X Y Z

countries. **2** a unit of weight equal to 16 ounces or about 0.454 kilograms. ▸ VERB **3** If you pound something, you hit it repeatedly with your fist *E.G. Someone was pounding on the door.* **4** If you pound a substance, you crush it into a powder or paste *E.G. Wooden mallets were used to pound the meat.* **5** If your heart is pounding, it is beating very strongly and quickly. **6** If you pound somewhere, you run there with heavy noisy steps.

**pour pours pouring poured**
VERB **1** If you pour a liquid out of a container, you make it flow out by tipping the container. **2** If something pours somewhere, it flows there quickly and in large quantities *E.G. Sweat poured down his face.* **3** When it is raining heavily, you can say that it is pouring.

**pout pouts pouting pouted**
VERB If you pout, you stick out your lips or bottom lip.

**poverty**
NOUN (GEOGRAPHY) the state of being very poor.
☰ destitution, pennilessness, want

**powder powders powdering powdered**
NOUN **1** Powder consists of many tiny particles of a solid substance. ▸ VERB **2** If you powder a surface, you cover it with powder.
**powdery** ADJECTIVE

**power powers powering powered**
NOUN **1** Someone who has power has a lot of control over people and activities. **2** Someone who has the power to do something has the ability to do it *E.G. the power of*

*speech.* **3** The power of something is the physical strength that it has to move things. **4** Power is energy obtained, for example, by burning fuel or using the wind or waves. **5** In physics, power is the energy transferred from one thing to another in one second. It is measured in watts. ▸ VERB **6** Something that powers a machine provides the energy for it to work.
**powerful** ADJECTIVE **powerfully** ADVERB
☰ (sense 3) force, strength

**powerless**
ADJECTIVE unable to control or influence events *E.G. I was powerless to save her.*
☰ helpless, impotent, incapable

**power station power stations**
NOUN a place where electricity is generated.

**practicable**
ADJECTIVE If a task or plan is practicable, it can be carried out successfully *E.G. a practicable option.*

**practical practicals**
ADJECTIVE **1** The practical aspects of something are those that involve experience and real situations rather than ideas or theories *E.G. the practical difficulties of teaching science.* **2** sensible and likely to be effective *E.G. practical low-heeled shoes.* **3** Someone who is practical is able to deal effectively and sensibly with problems. ▸ NOUN **4** an examination in which you make or perform something rather than simply write.
**practicality** NOUN
☰ (sense 2) functional, utilitarian

**practically**
ADVERB **1** almost but not completely or

exactly *E.G. The house was practically a wreck.* **2** in a practical way *E.G. practically minded.*

**practice** practices

NOUN **1** You can refer to something that people do regularly as a practice *E.G. the practice of kissing hands.* **2** Practice is regular training or exercise *E.G. I need more practice.* **3** A doctor's or lawyer's practice is his or her business.

☑ The noun *practice* ends in *ice.*

**practise** practises practising practised

VERB **1** If you practise something, you do it regularly in order to improve. **2** People who practise a religion, custom, or craft regularly take part in the activities associated with it *E.G. a practising Buddhist.* **3** Someone who practises medicine or law works as a doctor or lawyer

☑ The verb *practise* ends in *ise.*

**practised**

ADJECTIVE Someone who is practised at doing something is very skilful at it *E.G. a practised performer.*

**practitioner** practitioners

NOUN You can refer to someone who works in a particular profession as a practitioner *E.G. a medical practitioner.*

**pragmatic**

ADJECTIVE A pragmatic way of considering or doing something is a practical rather than theoretical way *E.G. He is pragmatic about the risks involved.*

**pragmatically** ADVERB
**pragmatism** NOUN

**prairie** prairies

NOUN a large area of flat, grassy land in North America.

**praise** praises praising praised

VERB **1** If you praise someone or something, you express strong approval of their qualities or achievements. ▶ NOUN **2** Praise is what is said or written in approval of someone's qualities or achievements.

🔳 (sense 1) acclaim, approve, compliment

🔳 (sense 2) acclaim, approval, commendation

**pram** prams

NOUN a baby's cot on wheels.

**prance** prances prancing pranced

VERB Someone who is prancing around is walking with exaggerated movements.

**prank** pranks

NOUN a childish trick.

**prattle** prattles prattling prattled

VERB If someone prattles on, they talk a lot without saying anything important.

**prawn** prawns

NOUN a small, pink, edible shellfish with a long tail.

**pray** prays praying prayed

VERB ( RE ) When someone prays, they speak to God to give thanks or to ask for help.

**prayer** prayers

NOUN ( RE ) **1** Prayer is the activity of praying. **2** the words said when someone prays.

**pre-**

PREFIX 'Pre-' means before a particular time or event *E.G. pre-war.*

🔳 from Latin *prae* meaning 'before'

**preach** preaches preaching preached

VERB When someone preaches, they

give a short talk on a religious or moral subject as part of a church service.

**preacher** NOUN

**precarious**

ADJECTIVE **1** If your situation is precarious, you may fail in what you are doing at any time. **2** Something that is precarious is likely to fall because it is not well balanced or secured.

**precariously** ADVERB

■ (sense 2) insecure, shaky, unsafe

**precaution** precautions

NOUN an action that is intended to prevent something from happening E.G. *It's still worth taking precautions against accidents.*

**precautionary** ADJECTIVE

**precede** precedes preceding preceded

VERB **1** Something that precedes another thing happens or occurs before it. **2** If you precede someone somewhere, you go in front of them.

**preceding** ADJECTIVE

**precedence**

Said "press-id-ens" NOUN If something takes precedence over other things, it is the most important thing and should be dealt with first.

**precedent** precedents

NOUN An action or decision that is regarded as a precedent is used as a guide in taking similar action or decisions later.

**precinct** precincts

NOUN **1** A shopping precinct is a pedestrian shopping area. ▶ PLURAL NOUN **2** The precincts of a place are its buildings and land.

**precious**

ADJECTIVE Something that is precious is

valuable or very important and should be looked after or used carefully.

**precipice** precipices

Said "press-sip-piss" NOUN a very steep rock face.

**precipitate** precipitates precipitating precipitated

VERB FORMAL If something precipitates an event or situation, it causes it to happen suddenly.

**precipitation**

NOUN; FORMAL Precipitation is rain, snow, or hail; used especially when stating the amount that falls during a particular period.

**precise**

ADJECTIVE exact and accurate in every detail E.G. *precise measurements.*

**precisely** ADVERB **precision** NOUN

**preclude** precludes precluding precluded

VERB; FORMAL If something precludes an event or situation, it prevents it from happening E.G. *The meal precluded serious conversation.*

**precocious**

ADJECTIVE Precocious children behave in a way that seems too advanced for their age.

**preconceived**

ADJECTIVE Preconceived ideas about something have been formed without any real experience or information.

**preconception** NOUN

**precondition** preconditions

NOUN If something is a precondition for another thing, it must happen before the second thing can take place.

**precursor** precursors

NOUN A precursor of something that

exists now is a similar thing that existed at an earlier time *E.G. real tennis, an ancient precursor of the modern game.*

**predator** predators
*Said "pred-dat-tor"* NOUN (SCIENCE) an animal that kills and eats other animals.
**predatory** ADJECTIVE

**predecessor** predecessors
NOUN Someone's predecessor is a person who used to do their job before.

**predetermined**
ADJECTIVE decided in advance or controlled by previous events rather than left to chance.

**predicament** predicaments
NOUN a difficult situation.
≡ dilemma, fix, jam

**predict** predicts predicting predicted
VERB If someone predicts an event, they say that it will happen in the future.
**prediction** NOUN
≡ forecast, foretell, prophesy

**predominant**
ADJECTIVE more important or more noticeable than anything else in a particular set of people or things *E.G. Yellow is the predominant colour in the house.*
**predominantly** ADVERB
≡ chief, main, prevailing

**predominate** predominates predominating predominated
VERB If one type of person or thing predominates, it is the most common, frequent, or noticeable *E.G. Fresh flowers predominate in the bouquet.*
**predominance** NOUN

**pre-eminent**
ADJECTIVE recognized as being the most important in a particular group *E.G. the pre-eminent experts in the area.*
**pre-eminence** NOUN

**pre-empt** pre-empts pre-empting pre-empted
VERB; *FORMAL* If you pre-empt something, you prevent it by doing something else which makes it pointless or impossible *E.G. a wish to pre-empt any further publicity.*

**preen** preens preening preened
VERB When a bird preens its feathers, it cleans them using its beak.

**preface** prefaces
*Said "pref-fiss"* NOUN an introduction at the beginning of a book explaining what the book is about or why it was written.

**prefect** prefects
NOUN a pupil who has special duties at a school.
🖼 from Latin *praefectus* meaning 'someone put in charge'

**prefer** prefers preferring preferred
VERB If you prefer one thing to another, you like it better than the other thing.
**preferable** ADJECTIVE **preferably** ADVERB

**preference** preferences
*Said "pref-fer-enss"* NOUN 1 If you have a preference for something, you like it more than other things *E.G. a preference for white.* 2 When making a choice, if you give preference to one type of person or thing, you try to choose that type.

**preferential**
ADJECTIVE A person who gets

a
b
c
d
e
f
g
h
i
j
k
l
m
n
o
**p**
q
r
s
t
u
v
w
x
y
z

A
B
C
D
E
F
G
H
I
J
K
L
M
N
O
**P**
Q
R
S
T
U
V
W
X
Y
Z

preferential treatment is treated better than others.

**prefix** prefixes
NOUN (ENGLISH) a letter or group of letters added to the beginning of a word to make a new word, for example 'semi-', 'pre-', and 'un-'.

**pregnant**
ADJECTIVE A woman who is pregnant has a baby developing in her womb.
**pregnancy** NOUN

**prehistoric**
ADJECTIVE existing at a time in the past before anything was written down.

**prejudice** prejudices
NOUN (RE) Prejudice is an unreasonable and unfair dislike of, or preference for, a particular type of person or thing.
**prejudiced** ADJECTIVE **prejudicial** ADJECTIVE

**preliminary**
ADJECTIVE Preliminary activities take place before something starts, in preparation for it E.G. the preliminary rounds of the competition.
■ first, initial, preparatory

**prelude** preludes
NOUN Something that is an introduction to a more important event can be described as a prelude to that event.

**premature**
ADJECTIVE happening too early, or earlier than expected E.G. premature baldness.
**prematurely** ADVERB

**premeditated**
ADJECTIVE planned in advance E.G. a premeditated attack.

**premier** premiers
NOUN 1 The leader of a government is sometimes referred to as the

premier. 2 In Australia, the leader of a State government. ▶ ADJECTIVE 3 considered to be the best or most important E.G. Wellington's premier jewellers.

**premiere** premieres
Said "prem-mee-er" NOUN the first public performance of a new play or film.

**premise** premises
Said "prem-iss" PLURAL NOUN 1 The premises of an organization are all the buildings it occupies on one site.
▶ NOUN 2 a statement which you suppose is true and use as the basis for an idea or argument.

**premium** premiums
NOUN an extra sum of money that has to be paid E.G. Paying a premium for space is worthwhile.

**premonition** premonitions
Said "prem-on-ish-on" NOUN a feeling that something unpleasant is going to happen.
■ (sense 1) feeling, foreboding, presentiment

**preoccupation** preoccupations
NOUN If you have a preoccupation with something, it is very important to you and you keep thinking about it.

**preoccupied**
ADJECTIVE Someone who is preoccupied is deep in thought or totally involved with something.

**preparatory**
ADJECTIVE Preparatory activities are done before doing something else in order to prepare for it.

**prepare** prepares preparing prepared
VERB If you prepare something, you make it ready for a particular

purpose or event *E.G. He was preparing the meal.*
**preparation** NOUN

**prepared**
ADJECTIVE If you are prepared to do something, you are willing to do it.

**preposition** prepositions
NOUN (ENGLISH) a word such as 'by', 'for', 'into', or 'with', which usually has a noun as its object.

---

### What is a Preposition?

A preposition is a word that is used before a noun or pronoun to relate it to other words.
Prepositions may tell you the **place** of something in relation to another thing:
> *E.G. She saw the cat **in** the garden.*
> *The cat was sheltering **under** a bench.*

Prepositions may also indicate **movement**:
> *E.G. The train came **into** the station.*
> *We pushed **through** the crowd.*

Prepositions may indicate **time**:
> *E.G. They will arrive **on** Friday.*
> *They will stay **for** two days.*

---

**preposterous**
ADJECTIVE extremely unreasonable and ridiculous *E.G. a preposterous statement.*

**prerequisite** prerequisites
Said "pree-**rek**-wiz-zit" NOUN; *FORMAL*
Something that is a prerequisite for another thing must happen or exist before the other thing is possible *E.G. Self-esteem is a prerequisite for a happy life.*

**prerogative** prerogatives
Said "prir-**rog**-at-tiv" NOUN; *FORMAL*
Something that is the prerogative of a person is their special privilege or right.

**prescribe** prescribes
prescribing prescribed
VERB When a doctor prescribes treatment, he or she states what treatment a patient should have.

**prescription** prescriptions
NOUN a piece of paper on which the doctor has written the name of a medicine needed by a patient.

**presence**
NOUN **1** Someone's presence in a place is the fact of their being there *E.G. His presence made me happy.* **2** If you are in someone's presence, you are in the same place as they are. **3** Someone who has presence has an impressive appearance or manner.

**present** presents presenting presented
ADJECTIVE
Said "**prez**-ent" **1** If someone is present somewhere, they are there *E.G. He had been present at the birth of his son.* **2** A present situation is one that exists now rather than in the past or the future. ▶ NOUN
Said "**prez**-ent" **3** The present is the period of time that is taking place now. **4** something that you give to someone for them to keep. ▶ VERB
Said "pri-**zent**" **5** If you present someone with something, you give it to them *E.G. She presented a bravery award to the girl.* **6** Something that presents a difficulty or a challenge causes it or provides it. **7** The person who presents a radio or television

a b c d e f g h i j k l m n o **p** q r s t u v w x y z

A
B
C
D
E
F
G
H
I
J
K
L
M
N
O
**P**
Q
R
S
T
U
V
W
X
Y
Z

show introduces each part or each guest.

**presenter** NOUN

■ (sense 2) contemporary, current, existing

**presentable**

ADJECTIVE neat or attractive and suitable for people to see.

**presentation** presentations

NOUN 1 the act of presenting or a way of presenting something. 2 The presentation of a piece of work is the way it looks or the impression it gives. 3 (D&T) To give a presentation is to give a talk or demonstration to an audience of something you have been studying or working on.

**present-day**

ADJECTIVE existing or happening now E.G. *present-day farming practices.*

**presently**

ADVERB 1 If something will happen presently, it will happen soon E.G. *I'll finish the job presently.* 2 Something that is presently happening is happening now E.G. *Some progress is presently being made.*

**present participle** present participles

NOUN In grammar, the present participle of an English verb is the form that ends in '-ing'. It is used to form some tenses, and can be used to form adjectives and nouns from a verb.

**present tense**

NOUN In grammar, the present tense is the tense of a verb that you use mainly to talk about things that happen or exist at the time of writing or speaking.

---

### Talking about the Present

You can talk about events that are happening now by using **simple tenses** or **compound tenses**.

The **simple present tense** is formed by using the verb on its own, without any auxiliary verbs. For the first and second person, and for all plural forms, the simple present tense of the verb is the same as the main form given in the dictionary:

E.G. *I **cook** the dinner.*

For the third person singular, however, you need to add an *-s* to the dictionary form to make the simple present tense:

E.G. *He **cooks** the dinner.*

You can also talk about an event that is happening in the present by using **compound tenses**. Compound tenses are formed by adding an auxiliary verb to a form of the main verb.

The most common compound present tense is formed by putting a form of the verb *to be* in front of the main verb, and adding the ending *-ing*. This shows that the action is going on at the present time and is continuous:

E.G. *I **am listening** to the radio.*

You can also talk about the present using a form of the verb *to do* in front of the basic form of the verb. This can add emphasis:

E.G. *I **do like** fish.*

**preservative** preservatives

NOUN a substance or chemical that stops things decaying.

**preserve** preserves preserving preserved

VERB **1** If you preserve something, you take action so that it remains as it is. **2** If you preserve food, you treat it to prevent it from decaying. ▶ NOUN **3** Preserves are foods such as jam or chutney that have been made with a lot of sugar or vinegar.

**preservation** NOUN

**preside** presides presiding presided

VERB A person who presides over a formal event is in charge of it.

**president** presidents

NOUN **1** In a country which has no king or queen, the president is the elected leader *E.G. the President of the United States of America.* **2** The president of an organization is the person who has the highest position.

**presidency** NOUN    **presidential** ADJECTIVE

**press** presses pressing pressed

VERB **1** If you press something, you push it or hold it firmly against something else *E.G. Lisa pressed his hand… Press the blue button.* **2** If you press clothes, you iron them. **3** If you press for something, you try hard to persuade someone to agree to it *E.G. She was pressing for improvements to the education system.* **4** If you press charges, you make an accusation against someone which has to be decided in a court of law. ▶ NOUN **5** Newspapers and the journalists who work for them are called the press.

**press conference** press conferences

NOUN When someone gives a press conference, they have a meeting to answer questions put by reporters.

**pressing**

ADJECTIVE Something that is pressing needs to be dealt with immediately *E.G. pressing needs.*

**pressure** pressures pressuring pressured

NOUN **1** (SCIENCE) Pressure is the force that is produced by pushing on something. **2** (PSHE) If you are under pressure, you have too much to do and not enough time, or someone is trying hard to persuade you to do something. ▶ VERB **3** If you pressure someone, you try hard to persuade them to do something.

**pressurize** pressurizes pressurizing pressurized; also spelt **pressurise**

VERB If you pressurize someone, you try hard to persuade them to do something.

**prestige**

*Said "press-**teezh**"* NOUN If you have prestige, people admire you because of your position.

**prestigious** ADJECTIVE

■ honour, standing, status

**presumably**

ADVERB If you say that something is presumably the case, you mean you assume that it is *E.G. Your audience, presumably, are younger.*

**presume** presumes presuming presumed

*Said "priz-**yoom**"* VERB If you presume something, you think that it is the case although you have no proof.

**presumption** NOUN

■ assume, believe, suppose

**presumptuous**

ADJECTIVE Someone who behaves in a presumptuous way does things that they have no right to do.

a
b
c
d
e
f
g
h
i
j
k
l
m
n
o
p
q
r
s
t
u
v
w
x
y
z

A
B
C
D
E
F
G
H
I
J
K
L
M
N
O
P
Q
R
S
T
U
V
W
X
Y
Z

**pretence** pretences
NOUN a way of behaving that is false and intended to deceive people.

**pretend** pretends pretending pretended
VERB If you pretend that something is the case, you try to make people believe that it is, although in fact it is not E.G. *Latimer pretended not to notice.*
■ affect, feign, sham

**pretender** pretenders
NOUN A pretender to a throne or title is someone who claims it but whose claim is being questioned.

**pretension** pretensions
NOUN Someone with pretensions claims that they are more important than they really are.

**pretentious**
ADJECTIVE Someone or something that is pretentious is trying to seem important when in fact they are not.

**pretext** pretexts
NOUN a false reason given to hide the real reason for doing something.

**pretty** prettier prettiest
ADJECTIVE 1 attractive in a delicate way.
► ADVERB 2 INFORMAL quite or rather E.G. *He spoke pretty good English.*
**prettily** ADVERB  **prettiness** NOUN

**prevail** prevails prevailing prevailed
VERB 1 If a custom or belief prevails in a particular place, it is normal or most common there E.G. *This attitude has prevailed in Britain for many years.*
2 If someone or something prevails, they succeed in their aims E.G. *In recent years better sense has prevailed.*
**prevailing** ADJECTIVE

**prevalent**
ADJECTIVE very common or widespread E.G. *the hooliganism so prevalent today.*
**prevalence** NOUN

**prevent** prevents preventing prevented
VERB If you prevent something, you stop it from happening or being done.
**preventable** ADJECTIVE  **prevention** NOUN
■ avert, forestall, stop

**preventive** or **preventative**
ADJECTIVE intended to help prevent things such as disease or crime E.G. *preventive health care.*

**preview** previews
NOUN 1 an opportunity to see something, such as a film or exhibition, before it is shown to the public. 2 (ICT) a part of a computer program which allows you to look at what you have keyed or added to a document or spreadsheet as it will appear when it is printed.

**previous**
ADJECTIVE happening or existing before something else in time or position E.G. *previous reports… the previous year.*
**previously** ADVERB
■ earlier, former, preceding

**prey** preys preying preyed
*Rhymes with "say"* NOUN 1 The creatures that an animal hunts and eats are called its prey. ► VERB 2 An animal that preys on a particular kind of animal lives by hunting and eating it.

**price** prices pricing priced
NOUN 1 The price of something is the amount of money you have to pay to

buy it. ▶ VERB 2 To price something at
a particular amount is to fix its price
at that amount.

■ (sense 1) charge, cost, expense

**priceless**
ADJECTIVE Something that is priceless is
so valuable that it is difficult to work
out how much it is worth.

**pricey** pricier priciest
ADJECTIVE; INFORMAL expensive.

**prick** pricks pricking pricked
VERB 1 If you prick something, you
stick a sharp pointed object into it.
▶ NOUN 2 a small, sharp pain caused
when something pricks you.

**prickle** prickles prickling
prickled
NOUN 1 Prickles are small sharp points
or thorns on plants. ▶ VERB 2 If your
skin prickles, it feels as if a lot of
sharp points are being stuck into it.
**prickly** ADJECTIVE

**pride** prides priding prided
NOUN 1 Pride is a feeling of
satisfaction you have when you have
done something well. 2 Pride is also
a feeling of being better than other
people. 3 A pride of lions is a group
of them. ▶ VERB 4 If you pride yourself
on a quality or skill, you are proud of
it E.G. She prides herself on punctuality.

■ (sense 1) gratification, pleasure,
satisfaction

**priest** priests
NOUN ( RE ) 1 a member of the clergy
in some Christian Churches. 2 In
many non-Christian religions, a priest
is a man who has special duties in
the place where people worship.
**priestly** ADJECTIVE

**priestess** priestesses
NOUN a female priest in a non-
Christian religion.

**priesthood**
NOUN The priesthood is the position
of being a priest.

**prim** primmer primmest
ADJECTIVE Someone who is prim
always behaves very correctly and is
easily shocked by anything rude.

■ priggish, prudish, strait-laced

**primaeval**
another spelling of **primeval**.

**primarily**
ADVERB You use 'primarily' to indicate
the main or most important feature
of something E.G. I still rated people
primarily on their looks.

**primary**
ADJECTIVE 'Primary' is used to describe
something that is extremely
important for someone or
something E.G. the primary aim of his
research.

**primary colour** primary colours
NOUN In art, the primary colours are
red, yellow, and blue, from which
other colours can be obtained by
mixing.

**primary school** primary schools
NOUN a school for children aged up to
11.

**primate** primates
NOUN 1 an archbishop. 2 a member of
the group of animals which includes
humans, monkeys, and apes.

**prime** primes priming primed
ADJECTIVE 1 main or most important E.G.
a prime cause of brain damage. 2 of
the best quality E.G. in prime
condition. ▶ NOUN 3 Someone's prime
is the stage when they are at their
strongest, most active, or most
successful. ▶ VERB 4 If you prime
someone, you give them information
about something in advance to

a
b
c
d
e
f
g
h
i
j
k
l
m
n
o
p
q
r
s
t
u
v
w
x
y
z

A
B
C
D
E
F
G
H
I
J
K
L
M
N
O
**P**
Q
R
S
T
U
V
W
X
Y
Z

prepare them E.G. *We are primed for every lesson.*

■ (sense 3) height, heyday, peak

**prime minister** prime ministers

NOUN The prime minister is the leader of the government.

**primeval** or **primaeval**

*Said* "pry-**mee**-vl" ADJECTIVE belonging to a very early period in the history of the world.

**primitive**

ADJECTIVE **1** connected with a society that lives very simply without industries or a writing system E.G. *the primitive peoples of the world.* **2** very simple, basic, or old-fashioned E.G. *a very small primitive cottage.*

**primrose** primroses

NOUN a small plant that has pale yellow flowers in spring.

📖 from Latin *prima rosa* meaning 'first rose'

**prince** princes

NOUN a male member of a royal family, especially the son of a king or queen.

**princely** ADJECTIVE

📖 from Latin *princeps* meaning 'chief' or 'ruler'

**princess** princesses

NOUN a female member of a royal family, usually the daughter of a king or queen, or the wife of a prince.

**principal** principals

ADJECTIVE **1** main or most important E.G. *the principal source of food.* ▶ NOUN **2** the person in charge of a school or college.

**principally** ADVERB

☑ Do not confuse *principal* with *principle*: *my principal objection.*

**principality** principalities

NOUN a country ruled by a prince.

**principle** principles

NOUN **1** a belief you have about the way you should behave E.G. *a woman of principle.* **2** a general rule or scientific law which explains how something happens or works E.G. *the principle of evolution in nature.*

■ (sense 1) precept, standard, rule

☑ Do not confuse *principle* with *principal*: *a man with no principles.*

**print** prints printing printed

VERB **1** To print a newspaper or book is to reproduce it in large quantities using a mechanical or electronic copying process. **2** If you print when you are writing, you do not join the letters together. ▶ NOUN **3** The letters and numbers on the pages of a book or newspaper are referred to as the print. **4** a photograph, or a printed copy of a painting. **5** Footprints and fingerprints can be referred to as prints.

**printer** NOUN

**print-out** print-outs

NOUN a printed copy of information from a computer.

**prior** priors

ADJECTIVE **1** planned or done at an earlier time E.G. *I have a prior engagement.* ▶ PHRASE **2** Something that happens **prior to** a particular time or event happens before it. ▶ NOUN **3** a monk in charge of a small group of monks in a priory.

**prioress** NOUN

**priority** priorities

NOUN something that needs to be dealt with first E.G. *The priority is building homes.*

**prioritize** prioritizes prioritizing prioritized or prioritise

VERB To prioritize things is to decide

which is the most important and deal with it first.

**priory** priories
NOUN a place where a small group of monks live under the charge of a prior.

**prise** prises prising prised
VERB If you prise something open or away from a surface, you force it open or away E.G. *She prised his fingers loose.*

**prism** prisms
NOUN 1 an object made of clear glass with many flat sides. It separates light passing through it into the colours of the rainbow. 2 In maths, a prism is any polyhedron with two identical parallel ends and sides which are parallelograms.

**prison** prisons
NOUN a building where criminals are kept in captivity.

**prisoner** prisoners
NOUN someone who is kept in prison or held in captivity against their will.

**pristine**
*Said* "priss-teen" ADJECTIVE; FORMAL very clean or new and in perfect condition.

**private** privates
ADJECTIVE 1 for the use of one person rather than people in general E.G. *a private bathroom.* 2 taking place between a small number of people and kept secret from others E.G. *a private conversation.* 3 owned or run by individuals or companies rather than by the state E.G. *a private company.* ▶ NOUN 4 a soldier of the lowest rank.
**privacy** NOUN   **privately** ADVERB

**private school** private schools
NOUN a school that does not receive

money from the government, and parents pay for their children to attend.

**privatize** privatizes privatizing privatized; also spelt **privatise**
VERB If the government privatizes a state-owned industry or organization, it allows it to be bought and owned by a private individual or group.

**privilege** privileges
NOUN a special right or advantage given to a person or group E.G. *the privileges of monarchy.*
**privileged** ADJECTIVE

**privy**
ADJECTIVE FORMAL If you are privy to something secret, you have been told about it.

**prize** prizes prizing prized
NOUN 1 a reward given to the winner of a competition or game. ▶ ADJECTIVE 2 of the highest quality or standard E.G. *his prize dahlia.* 3 Something that is prized is wanted and admired for its value or quality.
■ (sense 1) award, reward, trophy

**pro** pros
NOUN 1 INFORMAL a professional. ▶ PHRASE 2 The **pros and cons** of a situation are its advantages and disadvantages.
▥ sense 2 is from Latin *pro* meaning 'for' and *contra* meaning 'against'

**pro-**
PREFIX 'Pro-' means supporting or in favour of E.G. *pro-democracy protests.*

**probability** probabilities
NOUN 1 The probability of something happening is how likely it is to happen E.G. *the probability of success.* 2 If something is a probability, it is likely to happen E.G. *The probability is*

Beautiful Elephants Are Usually Tiny (<u>beautiful</u>)   ▶ SPELLING NOTE

A
B
C
D
E
F
G
H
I
J
K
L
M
N
O
P
Q
R
S
T
U
V
W
X
Y
Z

*that you will be feeling better.*
■ (sense 1) chance(s), likelihood, odds

**probable**
ADJECTIVE Something that is probable is likely to be true or correct, or likely to happen *E.G. the most probable outcome.*

**probably**
ADVERB Something that is probably the case is likely but not certain.

**probation**
NOUN Probation is a period of time during which a person convicted of a crime is supervised by a probation officer instead of being sent to prison.
**probationary** ADJECTIVE

**probe** probes probing probed
VERB 1 If you probe, you ask a lot of questions to discover the facts about something. ► NOUN 2 a long thin instrument used by doctors and dentists when examining a patient.

**problem** problems
NOUN 1 an unsatisfactory situation that causes difficulties. 2 a puzzle or question that you solve using logical thought or mathematics.
**problematic** ADJECTIVE
■ (sense 1) difficulty, predicament

**procedure** procedures
NOUN a way of doing something, especially the correct or usual way *E.G. It's standard procedure.*
**procedural** ADJECTIVE

**proceed** proceeds proceeding proceeded
VERB 1 If you proceed to do something, you start doing it, or continue doing it *E.G. She proceeded to tell them.* 2 FORMAL If you proceed in a particular direction, you move in

that direction *E.G. The taxi proceeded along a lonely road.* ► PLURAL NOUN 3 The proceeds from a fund-raising event are the money obtained from it.

**proceedings**
PLURAL NOUN 1 You can refer to an organized and related series of events as the proceedings *E.G. She was determined to see the proceedings from start to finish.* 2 Legal proceedings are legal action taken against someone.

**process** processes processing processed
NOUN 1 a series of actions intended to achieve a particular result or change.
► PHRASE 2 If you are **in the process** of doing something, you have started doing it but have not yet finished.
► VERB 3 When something such as food or information is processed, it is treated or dealt with.

**procession** processions
NOUN a group of people or vehicles moving in a line, often as part of a ceremony.

**processor** processors
NOUN (ICT) In computing, a processor is the central chip in a computer which controls its operations.

**proclaim** proclaims proclaiming proclaimed
VERB If someone proclaims something, they announce it or make it known *E.G. You have proclaimed your innocence.*
**proclamation** NOUN

**procure** procures procuring procured
VERB; FORMAL If you procure something, you obtain it.

**prod** prods prodding prodded

VERB If you prod something, you give it a push with your finger or with something pointed.

**prodigy** prodigies
*Said "prod-dij-ee"* NOUN someone who shows an extraordinary natural ability at an early age.

**produce** produces producing produced
VERB 1 To produce something is to make it or cause it E.G. *a white wine produced mainly from black grapes.* 2 If you produce something from somewhere, you bring it out so it can be seen. ▶ NOUN 3 Produce is food that is grown to be sold E.G. *fresh produce.*

**producer** producers
NOUN The producer of a record, film, or show is the person in charge of making it or putting it on.

**product** products
NOUN 1 something that is made to be sold E.G. *high-quality products.* 2 In maths, the product of two or more numbers or quantities is the result of multiplying them together.

**production** productions
NOUN ⟨D&T⟩ 1 Production is the process of manufacturing or growing something in large quantities E.G. *modern methods of production.* 2 Production is also the amount of goods manufactured or food grown by a country or company E.G. *Production has fallen by 13.2%.* 3 A production of a play, opera, or other show is a series of performances of it.

**productive**
ADJECTIVE 1 To be productive means to produce a large number of things E.G. *Farms were more productive in these*

*areas.* 2 If something such as a meeting is productive, good or useful things happen as a result of it. ■ (sense 2) beneficial, useful, worthwhile

**productivity**
NOUN Productivity is the rate at which things are produced or dealt with.

**profane**
ADJECTIVE *FORMAL* showing disrespect for a religion or religious things E.G. *profane language.*

**profess** professes professing professed
VERB 1 *FORMAL* If you profess to do or have something, you claim to do or have it. 2 If you profess a feeling or opinion, you express it E.G. *He professes a lasting affection for Trinidad.*

**profession** professions
NOUN 1 a type of job that requires advanced education or training. 2 You can use 'profession' to refer to all the people who have a particular profession E.G. *the medical profession.*

**professional** professionals
ADJECTIVE 1 Professional means relating to the work of someone who is qualified in a particular profession E.G. *I think you need professional advice.* 2 Professional also describes activities when they are done to earn money rather than as a hobby E.G. *professional football.* 3 A professional piece of work is of a very high standard. ▶ NOUN 4 a person who has been trained in a profession. 5 someone who plays a sport to earn money rather than as a hobby.

**professor** professors
NOUN the senior teacher in a

a b c d e f g h i j k l m n o p q r s t u v w x y z

there's a rAKE in the brAKEs (br<u>a</u>ke)    **SPELLING NOTE**

A
B
C
D
E
F
G
H
I
J
K
L
M
N
O
**P**
Q
R
S
T
U
V
W
X
Y
Z

department of a British university.
**professorial** ADJECTIVE

**proficient**
ADJECTIVE If you are proficient at something, you can do it well.
**proficiency** NOUN

**profile** profiles
NOUN 1 Your profile is the outline of your face seen from the side. 2 A profile of someone is a short description of their life and character.

📖 from Italian *profilare* meaning 'to sketch lightly'

**profit** profits profiting profited
NOUN 1 When someone sells something, the profit is the amount they gain by selling it for more than it cost them to buy or make. ► VERB 2 If you profit from something, you gain or benefit from it.
**profitable** ADJECTIVE

■ (sense 1) gain, proceeds, return

**profound**
ADJECTIVE 1 great in degree or intensity *E.G. a profound need to please.*
2 showing great and deep intellectual understanding *E.G. a profound question.*
**profoundly** ADVERB   **profundity** NOUN

**profuse**
*Said "prof-yooss"* ADJECTIVE very large in quantity or number *E.G. There were profuse apologies for his absence.*
**profusely** ADVERB

**program** programs programming programmed
(ICT) NOUN 1 a set of instructions that a computer follows to perform a particular task. ► VERB 2 When

someone programs a computer, they write a program and put it into the computer.

**programmer** NOUN

**programme** programmes
NOUN 1 a planned series of events *E.G. a programme of official engagements.*
2 a particular piece presented as a unit on television or radio, such as a play, show, or discussion. 3 a booklet giving information about a play, concert, or show that you are attending.

■ (sense 1) agenda, plan, schedule

**progress** progresses progressing progressed
NOUN 1 Progress is the process of gradually improving or getting near to achieving something *E.G. Gerry is now making some real progress towards fitness.* 2 The progress of something is the way in which it develops or continues *E.G. news on the progress of the war.* ► PHRASE
3 Something that is **in progress** is happening *E.G. A cricket match was in progress.* ► VERB 4 If you progress, you become more advanced or skilful.
5 To progress is to continue *E.G. As the evening progressed, sadness turned to rage.*

**progression** NOUN
■ (sense 1) advance, headway
■ (sense 2) course, movement

**progressive**
ADJECTIVE 1 having modern ideas about how things should be done.
2 happening gradually *E.G. a progressive illness.*

**prohibit** prohibits prohibiting prohibited
VERB If someone prohibits something, they forbid it or make it illegal.
**prohibition** NOUN

☑ You *prohibit* a person *from* doing something.

**prohibitive**

ADJECTIVE If the cost of something is prohibitive, it is so high that people cannot afford it.

**project** projects projecting projected

NOUN **1** a carefully planned attempt to achieve something or to study something over a period of time. ▶ VERB **2** Something that is projected is planned or expected to happen in the future E.G. *The population aged 65 or over is projected to increase.* **3** To project an image onto a screen is to make it appear there using equipment such as a projector. **4** Something that projects sticks out beyond a surface or edge.

**projection** NOUN

**projector** projectors

NOUN a piece of equipment which produces a large image on a screen by shining light through a photographic slide or film strip.

**proletariat**

NOUN; FORMAL Working-class people are sometimes referred to as the proletariat.

**proletarian** ADJECTIVE

**proliferate** proliferates proliferating proliferated

VERB If things proliferate, they quickly increase in number.

**proliferation** NOUN

🔟 from Latin *prolifer* meaning 'having children'

**prolific**

ADJECTIVE producing a lot of something E.G. *this prolific artist.*

**prologue** prologues

NOUN a speech or section that

introduces a play or book.

**prolong** prolongs prolonging prolonged

VERB If you prolong something, you make it last longer.

**prolonged** ADJECTIVE

**prom** proms

NOUN; INFORMAL a concert at which some of the audience stand.

**promenade** promenades

*Said "prom-min-ahd"* NOUN a road or path next to the sea at a seaside resort.

🔟 a French word, from *se promener* meaning 'to go for a walk'

**prominent**

ADJECTIVE **1** Prominent people are important. **2** Something that is prominent is very noticeable E.G. *a prominent nose.*

**prominence** NOUN **prominently** ADVERB

**promiscuous**

*Said "prom-**misk**-yoo-uss"* ADJECTIVE Someone who is promiscuous has sex with many different people.

**promiscuity** NOUN

**promise** promises promising promised

VERB **1** If you promise to do something, you say that you will definitely do it. **2** Something that promises to have a particular quality shows signs that it will have that quality E.G. *This promised to be a very long night.* ▶ NOUN **3** a statement made by someone that they will definitely do something E.G. *He made a promise to me.* **4** Someone or something that shows promise seems likely to be very successful.

**promising** ADJECTIVE

I always visit my FRIend on a FRIday (<u>fri</u>end)    **SPELLING NOTE**

a b c d e f g h i j k l m n o p q r s t u v w x y z

A
B
C
D
E
F
G
H
I
J
K
L
M
N
O
**P**
Q
R
S
T
U
V
W
X
Y
Z

■ (sense 1) guarantee, pledge, vow
■ (sense 3) guarantee, oath, vow

**promontory** promontories
*Said "prom-mon-tree"* NOUN an area
of high land sticking out into the
sea.

**promote** promotes promoting
promoted
VERB **1** If someone promotes
something, they try to make it
happen or become more popular E.G.
*to promote their latest film.* **2** If
someone is promoted, they are given
a more important job at work.
**promoter** NOUN **promotion** NOUN

**prompt** prompts prompting
prompted
VERB **1** If something prompts
someone to do something, it makes
them decide to do it E.G. *Curiosity
prompted him to push at the door.* **2** If
you prompt someone when they
stop speaking, you tell them what to
say next or encourage them to
continue. ▶ ADVERB **3** exactly at the
time mentioned E.G. *Wednesday
morning at 10.40 prompt.* ▶ ADJECTIVE
**4** A prompt action is done without
any delay E.G. *a prompt reply.*
**promptly** ADVERB

**prone**
ADJECTIVE **1** If you are prone to
something, you have a tendency to
be affected by it or to do it E.G. *She is
prone to depression.* **2** If you are
prone, you are lying flat and face
downwards E.G. *lying prone on the
grass.*
■ (sense 1) inclined, liable,
subject

**prong** prongs
NOUN The prongs of a fork are the
long, narrow, pointed parts.

**pronoun** pronouns
NOUN In grammar, a pronoun is a
word that is used to replace a noun.
'He', 'she', and 'them' are all pronouns.

---

#### What is a Pronoun?

A **pronoun** is a word that is used in
place of a noun. Pronouns may be
used instead of naming a person
or thing.

**Personal pronouns** replace the
subject or object of a sentence:
> E.G. **She** caught a fish.
> The nurse reassured **him**.

**Reflexive pronouns** replace the
object when it is the same person
or thing as the subject:
> E.G. Matthew saw **himself** in the
> mirror.

**Demonstrative pronouns** replace
the subject or object when you
want to show where something is:
> E.G. **That** is a nice jacket.
> Have you seen **this**?

**Possessive** pronouns replace the
subject or object when you want
to show who owns it:
> E.G. The blue car is **mine**.
> **Hers** is a strange story.

**Relative pronouns** replace a noun
to link two different parts of the
sentence:
> E.G. Do you know the man **who**
> lives next door?
> I watched a programme **that** I
> had recorded yesterday.

**Interrogative pronouns** ask
questions:
> E.G. **What** are you doing?

**Indefinite pronouns** replace a

CONTINUED ON NEXT PAGE →

---

subject or object to talk about a broad or vague range of people or things:

> E.G. **Everybody** knew the exercise was a waste of time.
> **Some** say he cheats at cards.

Also look at the grammar box at **relative pronoun**.

**pronounce** pronounces pronouncing pronounced
VERB When you pronounce a word, you say it.
☑ There is an *o* before the *u* in *pronounce*. Compare this spelling with *pronunciation*.

**pronounced**
ADJECTIVE very noticeable E.G. *He talks with a pronounced lowland accent*.

**pronouncement** pronouncements
NOUN a formal statement.

**pronunciation** pronunciations
*Said* "pron-nun-*see*-**ay**-shn" NOUN the way a word is usually said
☑ There is no *o* before the *u* in *pronunciation*. Compare this spelling with *pronounce*.

**proof**
NOUN If you have proof of something, you have evidence which shows that it is true or exists.
☰ confirmation, evidence, verification

**prop** props propping propped
VERB 1 If you prop an object somewhere, you support it or rest it against something E.G. *The barman propped himself against the counter*.
▶ NOUN 2 a stick or other object used to support something. 3 The props in a play are all the objects and furniture used by the actors.

**propaganda**
NOUN (HISTORY) Propaganda is exaggerated or false information that is published or broadcast in order to influence people.

**propagate** propagates propagating propagated
VERB 1 If people propagate an idea, they spread it to try to influence many other people. 2 If you propagate plants, you grow more of them from an original one.
**propagation** NOUN

**propel** propels propelling propelled
VERB To propel something is to cause it to move in a particular direction.

**propeller** propellers
NOUN a device on a boat or aircraft with rotating blades which make the boat or aircraft move.

**propensity** propensities
NOUN; FORMAL a tendency to behave in a particular way.

**proper**
ADJECTIVE 1 real and satisfactory E.G. *He was no nearer having a proper job*. 2 correct or suitable E.G. *Put things in their proper place*.
**properly** ADVERB

**proper noun** proper nouns
NOUN the name of a person, place, or institution.

**property** properties
NOUN 1 A person's property is the things that belong to them. 2 a building and the land belonging to it. 3 a characteristic or quality E.G. *Mint has powerful healing properties*.

**prophecy** prophecies
NOUN a statement about what

The government licenSes Schnapps (licenSes)    ◀ SPELLING NOTE

A
B
C
D
E
F
G
H
I
J
K
L
M
N
O
P
Q
R
S
T
U
V
W
X
Y
Z

someone believes will happen in the future

☑ The noun *prophecy* ends in *cy*.

**prophesy** prophesies
prophesying prophesied

VERB If someone prophesies something, they say it will happen

☑ The verb *prophesy* ends in *sy*.

**prophet** prophets

NOUN (RE) a person who predicts what will happen in the future.

**prophetic**

ADJECTIVE correctly predicting what will happen E.G. *It was a prophetic warning.*

**proportion** proportions

NOUN 1 A proportion of an amount or group is a part of it E.G. *a tiny proportion of the population.* 2 The proportion of one amount to another is its size in comparison with the other amount E.G. *the highest proportion of single women to men.*

▶ PLURAL NOUN 3 You can refer to the size of something as its proportions E.G. *a red umbrella of vast proportions.*

**proportional** or **proportionate**

ADJECTIVE If one thing is proportional to another, it remains the same size in comparison with the other E.G. *proportional increases in profit.*

**proportionally** or **proportionately**
ADVERB

**proportional representation**

NOUN Proportional representation is a system of voting in elections in which the number of representatives of each party is in proportion to the number of people who voted for it.

**proposal** proposals

NOUN a plan that has been suggested E.G. *business proposals.*

**propose** proposes proposing
proposed

VERB 1 If you propose a plan or idea, you suggest it. 2 If you propose to do something, you intend to do it E.G. *And how do you propose to do that?* 3 When someone proposes a toast to a particular person, they ask people to drink a toast to that person. 4 If someone proposes to another person, they ask that person to marry them.

**proposition** propositions

NOUN 1 a statement expressing a theory or opinion. 2 an offer or suggestion E.G. *I made her a proposition.*

**proprietor** proprietors

NOUN The proprietor of a business is the owner.

**propriety**

NOUN; FORMAL Propriety is what is socially or morally acceptable E.G. *a model of propriety.*

**propulsion**

NOUN Propulsion is the power that moves something.

**prose**

NOUN Prose is ordinary written language in contrast to poetry.

🏛 from Latin *prosa oratorio* meaning 'straightforward speech'

**prosecute** prosecutes
prosecuting prosecuted

VERB If someone is prosecuted, they are charged with a crime and have to stand trial.

**prosecutor** NOUN

**prosecution**

NOUN The lawyers who try to prove that a person on trial is guilty are called the prosecution.

**prospect** prospects prospecting prospected

NOUN **1** If there is a prospect of something happening, there is a possibility that it will happen *E.G. There was little prospect of going home.* **2** Someone's prospects are their chances of being successful in the future. ▶ VERB **3** If someone prospects for gold or oil, they look for it.

**prospector** NOUN

**prospective**

ADJECTIVE 'Prospective' is used to say that someone wants to be or is likely to be something. For example, the prospective owner of something is the person who wants to own it.

**prospectus** prospectuses

NOUN a booklet giving details about a college or a company.

**prosper** prospers prospering prospered

VERB When people or businesses prosper, they are successful and make a lot of money.

**prosperous** ADJECTIVE **prosperity** NOUN

**prostitute** prostitutes

NOUN a person, usually a woman, who has sex with men in exchange for money.

**prostitution** NOUN

**prostrate**

ADJECTIVE lying face downwards on the ground.

**protagonist** protagonists

NOUN *FORMAL* **1** Someone who is a protagonist of an idea or movement is a leading supporter of it. **2** a main character in a play or story.

📖 from Greek *prōtagonistēs* meaning 'main actor in a play'

**protea** proteas

NOUN an evergreen African shrub with colourful flowers.

**protect** protects protecting protected

VERB To protect someone or something is to prevent them from being harmed or damaged.

**protection** NOUN **protective** ADJECTIVE **protector** NOUN

**protégé** protégés

*Said* "proh-tij-ay" NOUN Someone who is the protégé of an older, more experienced person is helped and guided by that person.

**protein** proteins

NOUN (D&T) Protein is a substance that is found in meat, eggs, and milk and that is needed by bodies for growth.

**protest** protests protesting protested

VERB **1** If you protest about something, you say or demonstrate publicly that you disagree with it *E.G. They protested against the killing of a teenager.* ▶ NOUN **2** a demonstration or statement showing that you disagree with something.

**Protestant** Protestants

NOUN OR ADJECTIVE (HISTORY) a member of one of the Christian Churches which separated from the Catholic Church in the sixteenth century.

**protestation** protestations

NOUN a strong declaration that something is true or not true *E.G. his protestations of love.*

**protocol**

NOUN Protocol is the system of rules about the correct way to behave in formal situations.

a
b
c
d
e
f
g
h
i
j
k
l
m
n
o
**p**
q
r
s
t
u
v
w
x
y
z

A
B
C
D
E
F
G
H
I
J
K
L
M
N
O
P
Q
R
S
T
U
V
W
X
Y
Z

**proton** protons

NOUN a particle which forms part of the nucleus of an atom and has a positive electrical charge.

**prototype** prototypes

NOUN a first model of something that is made so that the design can be tested and improved.

**protracted**

ADJECTIVE lasting longer than usual E.G. a protracted dispute.

**protractor** protractors

NOUN a flat, semicircular piece of plastic used for measuring angles.

**protrude** protrudes protruding protruded

VERB; FORMAL If something is protruding from a surface or edge, it is sticking out.

**protrusion** NOUN

**proud** prouder proudest

ADJECTIVE 1 feeling pleasure and satisfaction at something you own or have achieved E.G. I was proud of our players today. 2 having great dignity and self-respect E.G. too proud to ask for money.

**proudly** ADVERB

**prove** proves proving proved or proven

VERB 1 To prove that something is true is to provide evidence that it is definitely true E.G. A letter from Kathleen proved that he lived there. 2 If something proves to be the case, it becomes clear that it is so E.G. His first impressions of her proved wrong.

■ (sense 1) confirm, show, verify

**proverb** proverbs

NOUN a short sentence which gives advice or makes a comment about life.

**proverbial** ADJECTIVE

**provide** provides providing provided

VERB 1 If you provide something for someone, you give it to them or make it available for them. 2 If you provide for someone, you give them the things they need.

■ (sense 1) furnish, supply

**provided** or **providing**

CONJUNCTION If you say that something will happen provided something else happens, you mean that the first thing will happen only if the second thing does

✔ Provided is followed by that, but providing is not: I'll come, providing he doesn't… You can go, provided that you phone as soon as you get there.

**providence**

NOUN Providence is God or a force which is believed to arrange the things that happen to us.

**province** provinces

NOUN 1 one of the areas into which some large countries are divided, each province having its own administration. 2 You can refer to the parts of a country which are not near the capital as the provinces.

🏛 from Latin provincia meaning 'a conquered territory'

**provincial**

ADJECTIVE 1 connected with the parts of a country outside the capital E.G. a provincial theatre. 2 narrow-minded and lacking sophistication.

**provision** provisions

NOUN (GEOGRAPHY) 1 The provision of something is the act of making it available to people E.G. the provision of health care. ▶ PLURAL NOUN 2 Provisions are supplies of food.

**provisional**

ADJECTIVE A provisional arrangement has not yet been made definite and so might be changed.

**proviso** provisos

*Said "prov-eye-zoh"* NOUN a condition in an agreement.

**provocation** provocations

NOUN an act done deliberately to annoy someone.

**provocative**

ADJECTIVE **1** intended to annoy people or make them react *E.G. a provocative speech.* **2** intended to make someone feel sexual desire *E.G. provocative poses.*

**provoke** provokes provoking provoked

VERB **1** If you provoke someone, you deliberately try to make them angry. **2** If something provokes an unpleasant reaction, it causes it *E.G. illness provoked by tension or worry.*

**prow** prows

NOUN the front part of a boat.

**prowess**

NOUN Prowess is outstanding ability *E.G. his prowess at tennis.*

**prowl** prowls prowling prowled

VERB If a person or animal prowls around, they move around quietly and secretly, as if hunting.

**proximity**

NOUN, *FORMAL* Proximity is nearness to someone or something.

**proxy**

PHRASE If you do something **by proxy**, someone else does it on your behalf *E.G. voting by proxy.*

**prude** prudes

NOUN someone who is too easily shocked by sex or nudity.

**prudish** ADJECTIVE

📖 from Old French *prode femme* meaning 'respectable woman'

**prudent**

ADJECTIVE behaving in a sensible and cautious way *E.G. It is prudent to plan ahead.*

**prudence** NOUN **prudently** ADVERB

**prune** prunes pruning pruned

NOUN **1** a dried plum. ▶ VERB **2** When someone prunes a tree or shrub, they cut back some of the branches.

**pry** pries prying pried

VERB If someone is prying, they are trying to find out about something secret or private.

**PS**

PS is written before an additional message at the end of a letter. PS is an abbreviation for 'postscript'.

**psalm** psalms

*Said "sahm"* NOUN one of the 150 songs, poems, and prayers which together form the Book of Psalms in the Bible.

**pseudo-**

*Said "syoo-doh"* PREFIX 'Pseudo-' is used to form adjectives and nouns indicating that something is not what it is claimed to be *E.G. pseudo-scientific theories.*

📖 from Greek *pseudēs* meaning 'false'

**pseudonym** pseudonyms

*Said "syoo-doe-nim"* NOUN a name an author uses rather than their real name.

**PSHE**

NOUN an abbreviation for 'Personal, Social, and Health Education': a lesson in which students are taught about social and personal issues.

a
b
c
d
e
f
g
h
i
j
k
l
m
n
o
**p**
q
r
s
t
u
v
w
x
y
z

Psychiatrists Seldom Yell Callously Hard (psychiatrist)　　**SPELLING NOTE**

A
B
C
D
E
F
G
H
I
J
K
L
M
N
O
**P**
Q
R
S
T
U
V
W
X
Y
Z

**psyche psyches**
*Said* "**sigh**-kee" NOUN your mind and your deepest feelings.

**psychiatry**
NOUN Psychiatry is the branch of medicine concerned with mental illness.
**psychiatrist** NOUN **psychiatric** ADJECTIVE

**psychic**
ADJECTIVE having unusual mental powers such as the ability to read people's minds or predict the future.

**psychoanalysis**
NOUN Psychoanalysis is the examination and treatment of someone who is mentally ill by encouraging them to talk about their feelings and past events in order to discover the cause of the illness.
**psychoanalyst** NOUN
**psychoanalyse** VERB

**psychology**
NOUN Psychology is the scientific study of the mind and of the reasons for people's behaviour.
**psychological** ADJECTIVE
**psychologist** NOUN

**psychopath psychopaths**
NOUN a mentally ill person who behaves violently without feeling guilt.
**psychopathic** ADJECTIVE

**psychosis psychoses**
*Said* "sigh-**koe**-siss" NOUN a severe mental illness.
**psychotic** ADJECTIVE

**pterodactyl pterodactyls**
*Said* "ter-rod-**dak**-til" NOUN Pterodactyls were flying reptiles in prehistoric times.

▦ from Greek *pteron* meaning 'wing' and *daktulos* meaning 'finger'

**PTO**
PTO is an abbreviation for 'please turn over'. It is written at the bottom of a page to indicate that the writing continues on the other side.

**pub pubs**
NOUN a building where people go to buy and drink alcoholic or soft drinks and talk with their friends.

**puberty**
*Said* "**pyoo**-ber-tee" NOUN Puberty is the stage when a person's body changes from that of a child into that of an adult.

**pubic**
*Said* "**pyoo**-bik" ADJECTIVE relating to the area around and above a person's genitals.

**public**
NOUN 1 You can refer to people in general as the public. ▶ ADJECTIVE 2 relating to people in general *E.G. There was some public support for the idea.* 3 provided for everyone to use, or open to anyone *E.G. public transport.*
**publicly** ADVERB

**publican publicans**
NOUN a person who owns or manages a pub.

**publication publications**
NOUN 1 The publication of a book is the act of printing it and making it available. 2 a book or magazine *E.G. medical publications.*

**publicity**
NOUN Publicity is information or advertisements about an item or event.

**publicize publicizes publicizing publicized**; also spelt **publicise**

VERB When someone publicizes a fact or event, they advertise it and make it widely known.

**public school** public schools
NOUN In Britain, a public school is a school that is privately run and that charges fees for the pupils to attend.

**public servant** public servants
NOUN In Australia and New Zealand, someone who works in the public service.

**public service**
NOUN In Australia and New Zealand, the public service is the government departments responsible for the administration of the country.

**publish** publishes publishing published
VERB When a company publishes a book, newspaper, or magazine, they print copies of it and distribute it.
**publishing** NOUN

**publisher** publishers
NOUN (LIBRARY) The publisher of a book, newspaper or magazine is the person or company that prints copies of it and distributes it.

**pudding** puddings
NOUN **1** a sweet cake mixture cooked with fruit or other flavouring and served hot. **2** You can refer to the sweet course of a meal as the pudding.

**puddle** puddles
NOUN a small shallow pool of liquid.

**puerile**
Said "pyoo-rile" ADJECTIVE Puerile behaviour is silly and childish.
📖 from Latin puerilis, from puer meaning 'boy'

**puff** puffs puffing puffed
VERB **1** To puff a cigarette or pipe is to smoke it. **2** If you are puffing, you are breathing loudly and quickly with your mouth open. **3** If something puffs out or puffs up, it swells and becomes larger and rounder. ▶ NOUN **4** a small amount of air or smoke that is released.

**puffin** puffins
NOUN a black and white sea bird with a large brightly coloured beak.

**pug** pugs
NOUN a small, short-haired dog with a flat nose.

**puja**
Said "poo-jah" NOUN Puja is a variety of practices which make up Hindu worship.

**puke** pukes puking puked
VERB; INFORMAL If someone pukes, they vomit.

**pull** pulls pulling pulled
VERB **1** When you pull something, you hold it and move it towards you. **2** When something is pulled by a vehicle or animal, it is attached to it and moves along behind it E.G. Four oxen can pull a single plough. **3** When you pull a curtain or blind, you move it so that it covers or uncovers the window. **4** If you pull a muscle, you injure it by stretching it too far or too quickly. **5** When a vehicle pulls away, pulls out, or pulls in, it moves in that direction. ▶ NOUN **6** The pull of something is its attraction or influence E.G. the pull of the past.

**pull down** VERB When a building is pulled down, it is deliberately destroyed.

**pull out** VERB If you pull out of something, you leave it or decide not to continue with it E.G. The German government has pulled out of the project.

a
b
c
d
e
f
g
h
i
j
k
l
m
n
o
p
q
r
s
t
u
v
w
x
y
z

LEarn the princip**L**Es (princip**le**)    SPELLING NOTE

**pull through** VERB When someone pulls through, they recover from a serious illness.

**pulley** pulleys
NOUN a device for lifting heavy weights. The weight is attached to a rope which passes over a wheel or series of wheels.

**pullover** pullovers
NOUN a woollen piece of clothing that covers the top part of your body.

**pulmonary**
ADJECTIVE; FORMAL relating to the lungs or to the veins and arteries carrying blood between the lungs and the heart.

**pulp**
NOUN If something is turned into a pulp, it is crushed until it is soft and moist.

**pulpit** pulpits
Said "pool-pit" NOUN the small raised platform in a church where a member of the clergy stands to preach.

**pulse** pulses pulsing pulsed
NOUN 1 Your pulse is the regular beating of blood through your body, the rate of which you can feel at your wrists and elsewhere. 2 The seeds of beans, peas, and lentils are called pulses when they are used for food. ▶ VERB 3 If something is pulsing, it is moving or vibrating with rhythmic, regular movements E.G. She could feel the blood pulsing in her eardrums.

**puma** pumas
Said "pyoo-mah" NOUN a wild animal belonging to the cat family.

**pumice**
Said "pum-miss" NOUN Pumice stone is very light-weight grey stone that can be used to soften areas of hard skin.

**pummel** pummels pummelling pummelled
VERB If you pummel something, you beat it with your fists.

**pump** pumps pumping pumped
NOUN 1 a machine that is used to force a liquid or gas to move in a particular direction. 2 Pumps are light shoes with flat soles which people wear for sport or leisure. ▶ VERB 3 To pump a liquid or gas somewhere is to force it to flow in that direction, using a pump. 4 If you pump money into something, you put a lot of money into it.

**pumpkin** pumpkins
NOUN a very large, round, orange fruit eaten as a vegetable.

**pun** puns
NOUN a clever and amusing use of words so that what you say has two different meanings, such as my dog's a champion boxer.

**punch** punches punching punched
VERB 1 If you punch someone, you hit them hard with your fist. ▶ NOUN 2 a hard blow with the fist. 3 a tool used for making holes. 4 Punch is a drink made from a mixture of wine, spirits, and fruit.

**punctual**
ADJECTIVE arriving at the correct time. **punctually** ADVERB **punctuality** NOUN
■ on time, prompt

**punctuate** punctuates punctuating punctuated
VERB 1 Something that is punctuated by a particular thing is interrupted

by it at intervals *E.G. a grey day punctuated by bouts of rain.* **2** When you punctuate a piece of writing, you put punctuation into it.

**punctuation**
NOUN The marks in writing such as full stops, question marks, and commas are called punctuation or punctuation marks.

---

> ### What does Punctuation do?
> Punctuation marks are essential parts of written language. They help the reader to understand what is being read.
> Look at the grammar boxes at **apostrophe, bracket, colon, comma, dash, exclamation mark, full stop, hyphen, inverted comma, question mark,** and **semicolon**.

---

**puncture** punctures puncturing punctured
NOUN **1** If a tyre has a puncture, a small hole has been made in it and it has become flat. ▸ VERB **2** To puncture something is to make a small hole in it.

**pungent**
ADJECTIVE having a strong, unpleasant smell or taste.
**pungency** NOUN

**punish** punishes punishing punished
VERB To punish someone who has done something wrong is to make them suffer because of it.
🔲 chastise, discipline, penalize

**punishment** punishments
NOUN something unpleasant done to someone because they have done something wrong.

**punitive**
*Said "pyoo-*nit*-tiv"* ADJECTIVE harsh and intended to punish people *E.G. punitive military action.*

**Punjabi** Punjabis
*Said "pun-jah-bee"* ADJECTIVE
**1** belonging or relating to the Punjab, a state in north-western India. ▸ NOUN **2** someone who comes from the Punjab. **3** Punjabi is a language spoken in the Punjab.

**punk**
NOUN Punk or punk rock is an aggressive style of rock music.

**punt** punts
NOUN a long, flat-bottomed boat. You move it along by pushing a pole against the river bottom.

**puny** punier puniest
ADJECTIVE very small and weak.

**pup** pups
NOUN a young dog. Some other young animals such as seals are also called pups.

**pupil** pupils
NOUN **1** The pupils at a school are the children who go there. **2** Your pupils are the small, round, black holes in the centre of your eyes.

**puppet** puppets
NOUN a doll or toy animal that is moved by pulling strings or by putting your hand inside its body.

**puppy** puppies
NOUN a young dog.

**purchase** purchases purchasing purchased
VERB **1** When you purchase something, you buy it. ▸ NOUN **2** something you have bought.
**purchaser** NOUN

**pure** purer purest
ADJECTIVE **1** Something that is pure is

a b c d e f g h i j k l m n o p q r s t u v w x y z

A
B
C
D
E
F
G
H
I
J
K
L
M
N
O
P
Q
R
S
T
U
V
W
X
Y
Z

not mixed with anything else E.G. *pure wool… pure white*. **2** Pure also means clean and free from harmful substances E.G. *The water is pure enough to drink*. **3** People who are pure have not done anything considered to be sinful. **4** Pure also means complete and total E.G. *a matter of pure luck*.

**purity** NOUN
■ (sense 2) clean, uncontaminated
■ (sense 3) chaste, innocent, virtuous

**purée purées**
*Said "pyoo-ray"* NOUN a food which has been mashed or blended to a thick, smooth consistency.

**purely**
ADVERB involving only one feature and not including anything else E.G. *purely professional*.

**Purgatory**
NOUN Roman Catholics believe that Purgatory is a place where spirits of the dead are sent to suffer for their sins before going to Heaven.

**purge purges purging purged**
VERB To purge something is to remove undesirable things from it E.G. *to purge the country of criminals*.

**purify purifies purifying purified**
VERB To purify something is to remove all dirty or harmful substances from it.
**purification** NOUN

**purist purists**
NOUN someone who believes that something should be done in a particular, correct way E.G. *a football purist*.

**puritan puritans**
NOUN someone who believes in strict

moral principles and avoids physical pleasures.
**puritanical** ADJECTIVE

**purple**
NOUN or ADJECTIVE reddish-blue.

**purport purports purporting purported**
*Said "pur-**port**"* VERB; FORMAL Something that purports to be or have a particular thing is claimed to be or have it E.G. *a country which purports to disapprove of smokers*.

**purpose purposes**
NOUN **1** The purpose of something is the reason for it E.G. *the purpose of the meeting*. **2** If you have a particular purpose, this is what you want to achieve E.G. *To make music is my purpose in life*. ▶ PHRASE **3** If you do something **on purpose**, you do it deliberately.
**purposely** ADVERB **purposeful** ADJECTIVE

**purr purrs purring purred**
VERB When a cat purrs, it makes a low vibrating sound because it is contented.

**purse purses pursing pursed**
NOUN **1** a small leather or fabric container for carrying money. ▶ VERB **2** If you purse your lips, you move them into a tight, rounded shape.

**purser pursers**
NOUN the officer responsible for the paperwork and the welfare of passengers on a ship.

**pursue pursues pursuing pursued**
VERB **1** If you pursue an activity or plan, you do it or make efforts to achieve it E.G. *I decided to pursue a career in photography*. **2** If you pursue

someone, you follow them to try to catch them.

**pursuer** NOUN   **pursuit** NOUN

**purveyor** purveyors

NOUN; FORMAL A purveyor of goods or services is a person who sells them or provides them.

**pus**

NOUN Pus is a thick yellowish liquid that forms in an infected wound.

**push** pushes pushing pushed

VERB **1** When you push something, you press it using force in order to move it. **2** If you push someone into doing something, you force or persuade them to do it E.G. *His mother pushed him into auditioning for a part.* **3** INFORMAL Someone who pushes drugs sells them illegally.

■ (sense 1) shove, thrust

**push off** VERB; INFORMAL If you tell someone to push off, you are telling them rudely to go away.

**pushchair** pushchairs

NOUN a small folding chair on wheels in which a baby or toddler can be wheeled around.

**pusher** pushers

NOUN; INFORMAL someone who sells illegal drugs.

**pushing**

PREPOSITION Someone who is pushing a particular age is nearly that age E.G. *pushing sixty.*

**pushover**

NOUN INFORMAL **1** something that is easy. **2** someone who is easily persuaded or defeated.

**pushy** pushier pushiest

ADJECTIVE; INFORMAL behaving in a forceful and determined way.

**pussy** pussies

NOUN; INFORMAL a cat.

**put** puts putting put

VERB **1** When you put something somewhere, you move it into that place or position. **2** If you put an idea or remark in a particular way, you express it that way E.G. *I think you've put that very well.* **3** To put someone or something in a particular state or situation means to cause them to be in it E.G. *It puts us both in an awkward position.* **4** You can use 'put' to express an estimate of the size or importance of something E.G. *Her wealth is now put at 290 million.*

■ (sense 1) place, position, set

**put down** VERB **1** To put someone down is to criticize them and make them appear foolish. **2** If an animal is put down, it is killed because it is very ill or dangerous.

**put off** VERB **1** If you put something off, you delay doing it. **2** To put someone off is to discourage them.

**put out** VERB **1** If you put a fire out or put the light out, you make it stop burning or shining. **2** If you are put out, you are annoyed or upset.

**put up** VERB **1** If you put up resistance to something, you argue or fight against it E.G. *She put up a tremendous struggle.* **2** If you put up with something, you tolerate it even though you disagree with it or dislike it.

**putt** putts

NOUN In golf, a putt is a gentle stroke made when the ball is near the hole.

**putting**

NOUN Putting is a game played on a small grass course with no obstacles. You hit a ball gently with a club so that it rolls towards one of a series of holes around the course.

a
b
c
d
e
f
g
h
i
j
k
l
m
n
o
**p**
q
r
s
t
u
v
w
x
y
z

A
B
C
D
E
F
G
H
I
J
K
L
M
N
O
**P**
Q
R
S
T
U
V
W
X
Y
Z

**putty**
NOUN Putty is a paste used to fix panes of glass into frames.

**puzzle** puzzles puzzling puzzled
VERB **1** If something puzzles you, it confuses you and you do not understand it *E.G. There was something about her that puzzled me.*
▶ NOUN **2** A puzzle is a game or question that requires a lot of thought to complete or solve.
**puzzled** ADJECTIVE **puzzlement** NOUN
**☰** (sense 1) baffle, mystify, perplex

**PVC**
NOUN PVC is a plastic used for making clothing, pipes, and many other things. PVC is an abbreviation for 'polyvinyl chloride'.

**pygmy** pygmies
*Said* "pig-mee"; also spelt **pigmy**
NOUN a very small person, especially one who belongs to a racial group in which all the people are small.
**🏛** from Greek *pugmaios* meaning 'undersized'

**pyjamas**
PLURAL NOUN Pyjamas are loose trousers and a jacket or top that you wear in bed.
**🏛** from Persian *pay jama* meaning 'leg clothing'

**pylon** pylons
NOUN a very tall metal structure which carries overhead electricity cables.

**pyramid** pyramids
NOUN **1** a three-dimensional shape with a flat base and flat triangular sides sloping upwards to a point.
**2** The Pyramids are ancient stone structures built over the tombs of Egyptian kings and queens.

**pyre** pyres
NOUN a high pile of wood on which a dead body or religious offering is burned.

**python** pythons
NOUN a large snake that kills animals by squeezing them with its body.
**🏛** from Greek *Puthon*, a huge mythical serpent

# Qq

**quack** quacks quacking quacked
VERB When a duck quacks, it makes a loud harsh sound.

**quad** quads
*Said "kwod"* NOUN Quad is the same as quadruplet.

**quadrangle** quadrangles
*Said "kwod-rang-gl"* NOUN a courtyard with buildings all round it.

**quadri-**
PREFIX 'Quadri-' means 'four'.
📖 a Latin word

**quadriceps**
NOUN (PE) a large muscle in four parts at the front of your thigh.

**quadrilateral** quadrilaterals
*Said "kwod-ril-lat-ral"* NOUN (MATHS) a shape with four straight sides.

**quadruped** quadrupeds
*Said "kwod-roo-ped"* NOUN any animal with four legs.

**quadruple** quadruples quadrupling quadrupled
*Said "kwod-roo-pl"* VERB When an amount or number quadruples, it becomes four times as large as it was.

**quadruplet** quadruplets
*Said "kwod-roo-plet"* NOUN Quadruplets are four children born at the same time to the same mother.

**quagmire** quagmires
*Said "kwag-mire"* NOUN a soft, wet area of land which you sink into if you walk on it.

**quail** quails quailing quailed
NOUN 1 a type of small game bird with a round body and short tail. ▶ VERB 2 If you quail, you feel or look afraid.

**quaint** quainter quaintest
ADJECTIVE attractively old-fashioned or unusual E.G. *quaint customs.*
**quaintly** ADVERB

**quake** quakes quaking quaked
VERB If you quake, you shake and tremble because you are very frightened.

**Quaker** Quakers
NOUN a member of a Christian group, the Society of Friends.

**qualification** qualifications
NOUN 1 Your qualifications are your skills and achievements, especially as officially recognized at the end of a course of training or study.
2 something you add to a statement to make it less strong E.G. *It is a good novel and yet cannot be recommended without qualification.*

**qualify** qualifies qualifying qualified
VERB 1 (PE) When you qualify, you pass the examinations or tests that you need to pass to do a particular job or to take part in a sporting event. 2 If you qualify a statement, you add a detail or explanation to make it less strong E.G. *I would qualify that by putting it into context.* 3 If you qualify for something, you become entitled to have it E.G. *You qualify for a discount.*
**qualified** ADJECTIVE

**quality** qualities
NOUN 1 The quality of something is how good it is E.G. *The quality of food is very poor.* 2 a characteristic E.G. *These qualities are essential for success.*

**qualm** qualms
*Said "kwahm"* NOUN If you have

a b c d e f g h i j k l m n o p **q** r s t u v w x y z

qualms about what you are doing, you worry that it might not be right.

**quandary** quandaries

*Said* "kwon-dree" NOUN If you are in a quandary, you cannot decide what to do.

**quango** quangos

NOUN a body responsible for a particular area of public administration, which is financed by the government but is outside direct government control. Quango is short for quasi-autonomous non-governmental organization.

**quantity** quantities

NOUN 1 an amount you can measure or count E.G. *a small quantity of alcohol.* 2 Quantity is the amount of something that there is E.G. *emphasis on quantity rather than quality.*

**quarantine**

*Said* "kwor-an-teen" NOUN If an animal is in quarantine, it is kept away from other animals for a time because it might have an infectious disease.

📖 from Italian *quarantina* meaning 'forty days'

**quarrel** quarrels quarrelling quarrelled

NOUN 1 an angry argument. ▶ VERB 2 If people quarrel, they have an angry argument.

📄 (sense 1) argument, disagreement, fight

📄 (sense 2) argue, disagree, fall out

**quarry** quarries quarrying quarried

*Said* "kwor-ree" NOUN 1 a place where stone is removed from the ground by digging or blasting. 2 A person's or animal's quarry is the animal that they are hunting. ▶ VERB 3 To quarry stone means to remove it from a quarry by digging or blasting.

📖 sense 2 is from Middle English *quirre* meaning 'entrails given to the hounds to eat'

**quart** quarts

*Said* "kwort" NOUN a unit of liquid volume equal to two pints or about 1.136 litres.

**quarter** quarters

NOUN 1 one of four equal parts. 2 an American coin worth 25 cents. 3 You can refer to a particular area in a city as a quarter E.G. *the French quarter.* 4 You can use 'quarter' to refer vaguely to a particular person or group of people E.G. *You are very popular in certain quarters.* ▶ PLURAL NOUN 5 A soldier's or a servant's quarters are the rooms that they live in.

**quarterly** quarterlies

ADJECTIVE or ADVERB 1 Quarterly means happening regularly every three months E.G. *my quarterly report.*
▶ NOUN 2 a magazine or journal published every three months.

**quartet** quartets

*Said* "kwor-tet" NOUN a group of four musicians who sing or play together; also a piece of music written for four instruments or singers.

**quartz**

NOUN Quartz is a kind of hard, shiny crystal used in making very accurate watches and clocks.

**quash** quashes quashing quashed

*Said* "kwosh" VERB To quash a decision or judgment means to reject it officially E.G. *The judges quashed their convictions.*

**quasi-**

*Said* "kway-sie" PREFIX Quasi- means resembling something but not actually being that thing *E.G. a quasi-religious order.*

🏛 a Latin word meaning 'as if'

**quaver** quavers quavering quavered

*Said "kway-ver"* VERB **1** If your voice quavers, it sounds unsteady, usually because you are nervous. NOUN **2** (MUSIC) a musical note (♩) that has a time value of an eighth of a semibreve. In the United States and Canada, a quaver is known as an eighth note.

**quay** quays

*Said "kee"* NOUN a place where boats are tied up and loaded or unloaded.

**queasy** queasier queasiest

*Said "kwee-zee"* ADJECTIVE feeling slightly sick.

**queen** queens

NOUN **1** a female monarch or a woman married to a king. **2** a female bee or ant which can lay eggs. **3** In chess, the queen is the most powerful piece, which can move in any direction. **4** In a pack of cards, a queen is a card with a picture of a queen on it.

**queen mother** queen mothers

NOUN the widow of a king and the mother of the reigning monarch.

**queer** queerer queerest

ADJECTIVE Queer means very strange.

**quell** quells quelling quelled

VERB **1** To quell a rebellion or riot means to put an end to it by using force. **2** If you quell a feeling such as fear or grief, you stop yourself from feeling it *E.G. trying to quell the loneliness.*

**quench** quenches quenching quenched

VERB If you quench your thirst, you have a drink so that you are no longer thirsty.

**query** queries querying queried

*Said "qweer-ree"* NOUN **1** a question. ► VERB **2** If you query something, you ask about it because you think it might not be right *E.G. No-one queried my decision.*

**quest** quests

NOUN a long search for something.

**question** questions questioning questioned

NOUN **1** a sentence which asks for information. **2** If there is some question about something, there is doubt about it. **3** a problem that needs to be discussed *E.G. Can we get back to the question of the car?* ► VERB **4** If you question someone, you ask them questions. **5** If you question something, you express doubts about it *E.G. He never stopped questioning his own beliefs.* ► PHRASE **6** If something is **out of the question**, it is impossible.

📋 (sense 1) inquiry, query
📋 (sense 5) challenge, dispute

---

### What is a Question?

Questions are used to ask for information.

A question has a question mark at the end of the sentence:

  *E.G. What is your name?*

Questions are often introduced by a questioning word such as *what, who, where, when, why,* or *how*:

  *E.G. **Where** do you live?*

If a sentence does not already contain an auxiliary verb, a form of the auxiliary verb *do* may be placed at the start to turn it into a question:

  *E.G. **Does** Anna have a sister?*

CONTINUED ON NEXT PAGE →

---

the QUeen stood on the QUay (quay)    **SPELLING NOTE**

a b c d e f g h i j k l m n o p **q** r s t u v w x y z

A
B
C
D
E
F
G
H
I
J
K
L
M
N
O
P
Q
R
S
T
U
V
W
X
Y
Z

If there is already an auxiliary verb in the sentence, you can turn it into a question by reversing the word order so the auxiliary verb comes before the subject instead of after it:

E.G. **Are** you going to the swimming baths?
**Must** they keep doing that?

A question can also be made by adding a phrase, such as *isn't it?* or *don't you?*, on to the end of a statement:

E.G. It is hot today, **isn't it?**
You like chocolate, **don't you?**

**questionable**
ADJECTIVE possibly not true or not honest.

**question mark** question marks
NOUN the punctuation mark (?) which is used at the end of a question.

---

*What does the Question Mark do?*

The **question mark** (?) marks the end of a question:

E.G. When is the train leaving?

After an indirect question or a polite request, a full stop is used rather than a question mark:

E.G. Anna asked when the train was leaving.
Will you please send me an application form.

---

**questionnaire** questionnaires
NOUN (MATHS) a list of questions which asks for information for a survey.

**queue** queues queuing or queueing queued
*Said* "kyoo" NOUN 1 a line of people or vehicles waiting for something. ▶ VERB 2 When people queue, they stand in a line waiting for something.

**quibble** quibbles quibbling quibbled
VERB 1 If you quibble, you argue about something unimportant. ▶ NOUN 2 a minor objection.

**quiche** quiches
*Said* "keesh" NOUN a tart with a savoury filling.
📖 a French word, originally from German *Kuchen* meaning 'cake'

**quick** quicker quickest
ADJECTIVE 1 moving with great speed. 2 lasting only a short time E.G. a quick chat. 3 happening without any delay E.G. a quick response. 4 intelligent and able to understand things easily.
**quickly** ADVERB

**quicksand** quicksands
NOUN an area of deep wet sand that you sink into if you walk on it.

**quid**
NOUN; INFORMAL In British English, a pound in money.

**quiet** quieter quietest
ADJECTIVE 1 Someone or something that is quiet makes very little noise or no noise at all. 2 Quiet also means peaceful E.G. a quiet evening at home. 3 A quiet event happens with very little fuss or publicity E.G. a quiet wedding. ▶ NOUN 4 Quiet is silence.
**quietly** ADVERB
☑ Do not confuse the spellings of *quiet* and the adverb *quite*.

SPELLING NOTE    King IAn went to ParlIAment in a carrIAge for his marrIAge (-ia-)

**quieten** quietens quietening quietened
VERB To quieten someone means to make them become quiet.

**quill** quills
NOUN **1** a pen made from a feather. **2** A bird's quills are the large feathers on its wings and tail. **3** A porcupine's quills are its spines.

**quilt** quilts
NOUN A quilt for a bed is a cover, especially a cover that is padded.

**quilted**
ADJECTIVE Quilted clothes or coverings are made of thick layers of material sewn together.

**quin** quins
NOUN Quin is the same as **quintuplet**.

**quince** quinces
NOUN an acid-tasting fruit used for making jam and marmalade.

**quintessential**
ADJECTIVE; *FORMAL* A person or thing that is quintessential seems to represent the basic nature of something in a pure, concentrated form E.G. *It was the quintessential Hollywood party.*

**quintet** quintets
*Said* "kwin-**tet**" NOUN a group of five musicians who sing or play together; also a piece of music written for five instruments or singers.

**quintuplet** quintuplets
*Said* "kwin-**tyoo**-plit" NOUN Quintuplets are five children born at the same time to the same mother.

**quip** quips quipping quipped
NOUN **1** an amusing or clever remark. ▶ VERB **2** To quip means to make an amusing or clever remark.

**quirk** quirks
NOUN **1** an odd habit or characteristic E.G. *an interesting quirk of human* nature. **2** an unexpected event or development E.G. *a quirk of fate.*

**quirky** ADJECTIVE

**quit** quits quitting quit
VERB If you quit something, you leave it or stop doing it E.G. *Leigh quit his job as a salesman.*

**quite**
ADVERB **1** fairly but not very E.G. *quite old.* **2** completely E.G. *Jane lay quite still.* ▶ PHRASE **3** You use **quite a** to emphasize that something is large or impressive E.G. *It was quite a party.*
☑ You should be careful about using *quite.* It can mean 'completely': *quite amazing.* It can also mean 'fairly but not very': *quite friendly.* Do not confuse the spellings of *quite* and the adjective *quiet.*

**quiver** quivers quivering quivered
VERB **1** If something quivers, it trembles. ▶ NOUN **2** a trembling movement E.G. *a quiver of panic.*

**quiz** quizzes quizzing quizzed
NOUN **1** a game in which the competitors are asked questions to test their knowledge. ▶ VERB **2** If you quiz someone, you question them closely about something.

**quizzical**
*Said* "**kwiz**-ik-kl" ADJECTIVE amused and questioning E.G. *a quizzical smile.*

**quota** quotas
NOUN a number or quantity of something which is officially allowed E.G. *a quota of three foreign players allowed in each team.*

**quotation** quotations
NOUN an extract from a book or speech which is quoted.
→ *SEE BOX ON NEXT PAGE*

A B C D E F G H I J K L M N O P Q R S T U V W X Y Z

### What is a Quotation?

There are two ways of writing what people say. You can write down the exact words that are spoken. This is called **direct speech**. The second way is to write down the meaning of what they say without using the exact words. This is called **indirect speech** or **reported speech**.

When you use direct speech, the exact words spoken go into quotation marks:

*E.G. Robbie said, **"Thank you very much for the prize."***

The sentence will contain a main verb which indicates speaking, such as *say, tell, ask,* or *answer*. The words contained in quotation marks begin with a capital letter. If there is no other punctuation, they are separated from the rest of the sentence by a comma:

*E.G. "This is the best picture," said the judge.*

When you use indirect or reported speech, there is a subordinate clause which reports the meaning of what was said.

*E.G. The judge said **that Robbie's picture was the best**.*

When the reported words are a statement, the clause that reports them is usually introduced by *that*. The main clause usually contains a verb such as *say, tell, explain,* or *reply*:

*E.G. The judge said **that** Robbie should win first prize.*

Sometimes the word *that* can be left out.

*E.G. The judge said Robbie should win first prize.*

**quote** quotes quoting quoted
VERB **1** If you quote something that someone has written or said, you repeat their exact words. **2** If you quote a fact, you state it because it supports what you are saying. ▶ NOUN **3** an extract from a book or speech. **4** an estimate of how much a piece of work will cost.

**Qur'an**
another spelling of **Koran**.

# Rr

**TIP** Some words which sound as if they should begin with letter *r* are spelt with *wr*, for example *wrangle, wretch, write* and *wrong*. Other words which sound as if they ought to begin with letter *r* alone are actually spelt with *rh*, for example *rhapsody, rheumatism, rhino* and *rhododendron*.

**RAAF**
In Australia, an abbreviation for 'Royal Australian Air Force'.

**rabbi** rabbis
*Said "rab-by"* NOUN a Jewish religious leader.
🏛 from Hebrew *rabh* + *-i* meaning 'my master'

**rabbit** rabbits
NOUN a small animal with long ears.

**rabble**
NOUN a noisy, disorderly crowd.

**rabid**
ADJECTIVE 1 used to describe someone with strong views that you do not approve of *E.G. a rabid Nazi.* 2 A rabid dog or other animal has rabies.

**rabies**
*Said "ray-beez"* NOUN an infectious disease which causes people and animals, especially dogs, to go mad and die.

**raccoon** raccoons; also spelt **racoon**
NOUN a small North American animal with a long striped tail.

**race** races racing raced
NOUN 1 a competition to see who is fastest, for example in running or driving. 2 one of the major groups that human beings can be divided into according to their physical features. ▶ VERB 3 If you race someone, you compete with them in a race. 4 If you race something or if it races, it goes at its greatest rate *E.G. Her heart raced uncontrollably.* 5 If you race somewhere, you go there as quickly as possible *E.G. The hares raced away out of sight.*
**racing** NOUN

**racecourse** racecourses
NOUN a grass track, sometimes with jumps, along which horses race.

**racehorse** racehorses
NOUN a horse trained to run in races.

**racial**
ADJECTIVE relating to the different races that people belong to *E.G. racial harmony.*
**racially** ADVERB

**racism** or **racialism**
NOUN (PSHE) Racism or racialism is the treatment of some people as inferior because of their race.
**racist** NOUN or ADJECTIVE

**rack** racks racking racked
NOUN 1 a piece of equipment for holding things or hanging things on. ▶ VERB 2 If you are racked by something, you suffer because of it *E.G. She was racked by guilt.* ▶ AN INFORMAL PHRASE 3 If you **rack your brains**, you try hard to think of or remember something.

**racket** rackets
NOUN 1 If someone is making a racket, they are making a lot of noise. 2 an illegal way of making money *E.G. a*

---

A Rude Idiot Thought He Might Eat Toffee In Church (<u>arithmetic</u>)     ▶ SPELLING NOTE *drugs racket.* **3** Racket is another spelling of **racquet**.

**racquet racquets**; also spelt **racket**
NOUN a bat with strings across it used in tennis and similar games.
from Arabic *rahat* meaning 'palm of the hand'

**radar**
NOUN Radar is equipment used to track ships or aircraft that are out of sight by using radio signals that are reflected back from the object and shown on a screen.
from *RA(dio) D(etecting) A(nd) R(anging)*

**radiant**
ADJECTIVE **1** Someone who is radiant is so happy that it shows in their face. **2** glowing brightly.
**radiance** NOUN

**radiate radiates radiating radiated**
VERB **1** If things radiate from a place, they form a pattern like lines spreading out from the centre of a circle. **2** If you radiate a quality or emotion, it shows clearly in your face and behaviour *E.G. He radiated health.*

**radiation**
NOUN the stream of particles given out by a radioactive substance.

**radiator radiators**
NOUN **1** a hollow metal device for heating a room, usually connected to a central heating system. **2** the part of a car that is filled with water to cool the engine.

**radical radicals**
NOUN **1** Radicals are people who think there should be great changes in society, and try to make them

happen. ▶ ADJECTIVE **2** very significant, important, or basic *E.G. a radical change in the law.*
**radically** ADVERB **radicalism** NOUN

**radii**
the plural of **radius**.

**radio radios radioing radioed**
NOUN **1** Radio is a system of sending sound over a distance by transmitting electrical signals. **2** Radio is also the broadcasting of programmes to the public by radio. **3** a piece of equipment for listening to radio programmes. ▶ VERB **4** To radio someone means to send them a message by radio *E.G. The pilot radioed that a fire had started.*

**radioactive**
ADJECTIVE giving off powerful and harmful rays.
**radioactivity** NOUN

**radiotherapy**
NOUN the treatment of diseases such as cancer using radiation.
**radiotherapist** NOUN

**radish radishes**
NOUN a small salad vegetable with a red skin and white flesh and a hot taste.

**radium**
NOUN a radioactive element which is used in the treatment of cancer.

**radius radii**
NOUN (MATHS) The radius of a circle is the length of a straight line drawn from its centre to its circumference.

**RAF**
In Britain, an abbreviation for 'Royal Air Force'.

**raffia**
NOUN a material made from palm leaves and used for making mats and baskets.

**raffle** raffles
NOUN a competition in which people buy numbered tickets and win a prize if they have the ticket that is chosen.

**raft** rafts
NOUN a floating platform made from long pieces of wood tied together.

**rafter** rafters
NOUN Rafters are the sloping pieces of wood that support a roof.

**rag** rags
NOUN 1 a piece of old cloth used to clean or wipe things. 2 If someone is dressed in rags, they are wearing old torn clothes.

**rage** rages raging raged
NOUN 1 Rage is great anger. ▶ VERB 2 To rage about something means to speak angrily about it. 3 If something such as a storm or battle is raging, it is continuing with great force or violence E.G. *The fire still raged out of control.*
■ (sense 1) anger, fury, wrath

**ragged**
ADJECTIVE Ragged clothes are old and torn.

**raid** raids raiding raided
VERB 1 To raid a place means to enter it by force to attack it or steal something. ▶ NOUN 2 the raiding of a building or a place E.G. *an armed raid on a bank.*

**rail** rails
NOUN 1 a fixed horizontal bar used as a support or for hanging things on. 2 Rails are the steel bars which trains run along. 3 Rail is the railway considered as a means of transport E.G. *I plan to go by rail.*

**railing** railings
NOUN Railings are a fence made from metal bars.

**railway** railways
NOUN a route along which trains travel on steel rails.

**rain** rains raining rained
NOUN 1 water falling from the clouds in small drops. ▶ VERB 2 When it is raining, rain is falling.
**rainy** ADJECTIVE

**rainbird** rainbirds
NOUN a bird whose call is believed to be a sign that it will rain.

**rainbow** rainbows
NOUN an arch of different colours that sometimes appears in the sky after it has been raining.

**raincoat** raincoats
NOUN a waterproof coat.

**rainfall**
NOUN the amount of rain that falls in a place during a particular period.

**rainforest** rainforests
NOUN a dense forest of tall trees in a tropical area where there is a lot of rain.

**rainwater**
NOUN rain that has been stored.

**raise** raises raising raised
VERB 1 If you raise something, you make it higher E.G. *She went to the window and raised the blinds… a drive to raise standards of literacy.* 2 If you raise your voice, you speak more loudly. 3 To raise money for a cause means to get people to donate money towards it. 4 To raise a child means to look after it until it is grown up. 5 If you raise a subject, you mention it.

**raisin** raisins
NOUN Raisins are dried grapes.

**rake** rakes raking raked
NOUN a garden tool with a row of

a b c d e f g h i j k l m n o p q r s t u v w x y z

A
B
C
D
E
F
G
H
I
J
K
L
M
N
O
P
Q
R
S
T
U
V
W
X
Y
Z

metal teeth and a long handle.

**rake up** VERB If you rake up something embarrassing from the past, you remind someone about it.

**rally** rallies rallying rallied
NOUN **1** a large public meeting held to show support for something. **2** a competition in which vehicles are raced over public roads. **3** In tennis or squash, a rally is a continuous series of shots exchanged by the players. ▶ VERB **4** When people rally to something, they gather together to continue a struggle or to support something.

**ram** rams ramming rammed
VERB **1** If one vehicle rams another, it crashes into it. **2** To ram something somewhere means to push it there firmly *E.G. He rammed his key into the lock.* ▶ NOUN **3** an adult male sheep.

**RAM**
NOUN In computing, RAM is a storage space which can be filled with data but which loses its contents when the machine is switched off. RAM stands for 'random access memory'.

**Ramadan**
NOUN the ninth month of the Muslim year, during which Muslims eat and drink nothing during daylight.
📖 from Arabic *Ramadan* meaning literally 'the hot month'

**ramble** rambles rambling rambled
NOUN **1** a long walk in the countryside. ▶ VERB **2** To ramble means to go for a ramble. **3** To ramble also means to talk in a confused way *E.G. He then started rambling and repeating himself.*
**rambler** NOUN

**ramification** ramifications
NOUN The ramifications of a decision or plan are all its consequences and effects.

**ramp** ramps
NOUN a sloping surface connecting two different levels.

**rampage** rampages rampaging rampaged
VERB **1** To rampage means to rush about wildly causing damage.
▶ PHRASE **2** To **go on the rampage** means to rush about in a wild or violent way.
📰 (sense 1) go berserk, run amok

**rampant**
ADJECTIVE If something such as crime or disease is rampant, it is growing or spreading uncontrollably.

**rampart** ramparts
NOUN Ramparts are earth banks, often with a wall on top, built to protect a castle or city.

**ramshackle**
ADJECTIVE A ramshackle building is in very poor condition.

**ranch** ranches
NOUN a large farm where cattle or horses are reared, especially in the USA.
📖 from Mexican Spanish *rancho* meaning 'small farm'

**rancid**
*Said "ran-sid"* ADJECTIVE Rancid food has gone bad.
📖 from Latin *rancere* meaning 'to stink'

**rancour**
*Said "rang-kur"* NOUN; FORMAL Rancour is bitter hatred.
**rancorous** ADJECTIVE

**rand**
NOUN The rand is the main unit of currency in South Africa.

## random

ADJECTIVE **1** A random choice or arrangement is not based on any definite plan. ▶ PHRASE **2** If you do something **at random**, you do it without any definite plan *E.G. He chose his victims at random.*

**randomly** ADVERB

▣ (sense 1) chance, haphazard, incidental

## range ranges ranging ranged

NOUN **1** The range of something is the maximum distance over which it can reach things or detect things *E.G. This mortar has a range of 15,000 metres.* **2** a number of different things of the same kind *E.G. A wide range of colours are available.* **3** a set of values on a scale *E.G. The average age range is between 35 and 55.* **4** A range of mountains is a line of them. **5** A rifle range or firing range is a place where people practise shooting at targets. ▶ VERB **6** When a set of things ranges between two points, they vary within these points on a scale *E.G. prices ranging between 370 and 1200 pounds.*

▣ (sense 2) series, variety

## ranger rangers

NOUN someone whose job is to look after a forest or park.

## rank ranks ranking ranked

NOUN **1** Someone's rank is their official level in a job or profession. **2** The ranks are the ordinary members of the armed forces, rather than the officers. **3** The ranks of a group are its members *E.G. We welcomed five new members to our ranks.* **4** a row of people or things. ▶ VERB **5** To rank as something means to have that status or position on a scale *E.G. His dismissal ranks as the worst*

humiliation he has ever known. ▶ ADJECTIVE **6** complete and absolute *E.G. rank stupidity.* **7** having a strong, unpleasant smell *E.G. the rank smell of unwashed clothes.*

## ransack ransacks ransacking ransacked

VERB To ransack a place means to disturb everything and leave it in a mess, in order to search for or steal something.

🏛 from Old Norse *rann* meaning 'house' and *saka* meaning 'to search'

## ransom ransoms

NOUN money that is demanded to free someone who has been kidnapped.

## rant rants ranting ranted

VERB To rant means to talk loudly in an excited or angry way.

## rap raps rapping rapped

VERB **1** If you rap something, you hit it with a series of quick blows. ▶ NOUN **2** a quick knock or blow on something *E.G. A rap on the door signalled his arrival.* **3** Rap is a style of poetry spoken to music with a strong rhythmic beat.

## rape rapes raping raped

VERB **1** If a man rapes a woman, he violently forces her to have sex with him against her will. ▶ NOUN **2** Rape is the act or crime of raping a woman *E.G. victims of rape.* **3** Rape is a plant with yellow flowers that is grown as a crop for oil and fodder.

**rapist** NOUN

## rapid rapids

ADJECTIVE **1** happening or moving very quickly *E.G. rapid industrial expansion… He took a few rapid steps.* ▶ PLURAL NOUN **2** An area of a river where the water moves extremely

a b c d e f g h i j k l m n o p q **r** s t u v w x y z

A
B
C
D
E
F
G
H
I
J
K
L
M
N
O
P
Q
**R**
S
T
U
V
W
X
Y
Z

fast over rocks is referred to as rapids.
**rapidly** ADVERB   **rapidity** NOUN

**rapier** rapiers
NOUN a long thin sword with a sharp point.

**rapport**
*Said* "rap-**por**" NOUN; *FORMAL* If there is a rapport between two people, they find it easy to understand each other's feelings and attitudes.

**rapt**
ADJECTIVE If you are rapt, you are so interested in something that you are not aware of other things *E.G. sitting with rapt attention in front of the screen.*

**rapture**
NOUN Rapture is a feeling of extreme delight.
**rapturous** ADJECTIVE   **rapturously** ADVERB

**rare** rarer rarest
ADJECTIVE 1 Something that is rare is not common or does not happen often *E.G. a rare flower… Such major disruptions are rare.* 2 Rare meat has been lightly cooked.
**rarely** ADVERB

**rarefied**
*Said* "**rare**-if-eyed" ADJECTIVE seeming to have little connection with ordinary life *E.G. He grew up in a rarefied literary atmosphere.*

**raring**
ADJECTIVE If you are raring to do something, you are very eager to do it.

**rarity** rarities
NOUN 1 something that is interesting or valuable because it is unusual. 2 The rarity of something is the fact that it is not common.

**rascal** rascals
NOUN If you refer to someone as a

rascal, you mean that they do bad or mischievous things.

**rash** rashes
ADJECTIVE 1 If you are rash, you do something hasty and foolish. ▶ NOUN 2 an area of red spots that appear on your skin when you are ill or have an allergy. 3 A rash of events is a lot of them happening in a short time *E.G. a rash of strikes.*
**rashly** ADVERB
■ (sense 1) foolhardy, reckless

**rasher** rashers
NOUN a thin slice of bacon.

**rasp** rasps rasping rasped
VERB 1 To rasp means to make a harsh unpleasant sound. ▶ NOUN 2 a coarse file with rows of raised teeth, used for smoothing wood or metal.

**raspberry** raspberries
NOUN a small soft red fruit that grows on a bush.

**rat** rats
NOUN a long-tailed animal which looks like a large mouse.

**rate** rates rating rated
NOUN 1 The rate of something is the speed or frequency with which it happens *E.G. New diet books appear at the rate of nearly one a week.* 2 The rate of interest is its level *E.G. a further cut in interest rates.* 3 Rates are a local tax paid by people who own buildings. ▶ PHRASE 4 If you say **at this rate** something will happen, you mean it will happen if things continue in the same way *E.G. At this rate we'll be lucky to get home before six.* 5 You say **at any rate** when you want to add to or amend what you have just said *E.G. He is the least appealing character, to me at any rate.* ▶ VERB 6 The way you rate someone or

something is your opinion of them *E.G. He was rated as one of England's top young players.*

## rather

ADVERB **1** Rather means to a certain extent *E.G. We got along rather well… The reality is rather more complex.* ▶ PHRASE **2** If you **would rather** do a particular thing, you would prefer to do it. **3** If you do one thing **rather than** another, you choose to do the first thing instead of the second.

■ (sense 1) quite, relatively, somewhat

■ (sense 2) preferably, sooner

## ratify ratifies ratifying ratified

VERB; *FORMAL* To ratify a written agreement means to approve it formally, usually by signing it.

**ratification** NOUN

## rating ratings

NOUN **1** a score based on the quality or status of something. **2** The ratings are statistics showing how popular each television programme is.

## ratio ratios

NOUN a relationship which shows how many times one thing is bigger than another *E.G. The adult to child ratio is 1 to 6.*

## ration rations rationing rationed

NOUN **1** Your ration of something is the amount you are allowed to have. **2** Rations are the food given each day to a soldier or member of an expedition. ▶ VERB **3** When something is rationed, you are only allowed a limited amount of it, because there is a shortage.

## rational

ADJECTIVE When people are rational,

their judgments are based on reason rather than emotion.

**rationally** ADVERB **rationality** NOUN

## rationale

*Said* "rash-on-**nahl**" NOUN The rationale for a course of action or for a belief is the set of reasons on which it is based.

## rattle rattles rattling rattled

VERB **1** When something rattles, it makes short, regular knocking sounds. **2** If something rattles you, it upsets you *E.G. He was obviously rattled by events.* ▶ NOUN **3** the noise something makes when it rattles. **4** a baby's toy which makes a noise when it is shaken.

## rattlesnake rattlesnakes

NOUN a poisonous American snake.

## raucous

*Said* "**raw**-kuss" ADJECTIVE A raucous voice is loud and rough.

## ravage ravages ravaging ravaged

*FORMAL*

VERB **1** To ravage something means to seriously harm or damage it *E.G. a country ravaged by floods.* ▶ NOUN **2** The ravages of something are its damaging effects *E.G. the ravages of two world wars.*

## rave raves raving raved

VERB **1** If someone raves, they talk in an angry, uncontrolled way *E.G. He started raving about being treated badly.* **2** *INFORMAL* If you rave about something, you talk about it very enthusiastically. ▶ ADJECTIVE **3** *INFORMAL* If something gets a rave review, it is praised enthusiastically. ▶ NOUN **4** *INFORMAL* a large party with electronic dance music.

## raven ravens

NOUN **1** a large black bird with a deep,

I want to see (C) your licenCe (lice**n**ce)      SPELLING NOTE

A B C D E F G H I J K L M N O P Q **R** S T U V W X Y Z

harsh call. ► ADJECTIVE **2** Raven hair is black and shiny.

**ravenous**
ADJECTIVE very hungry.

**ravine** ravines
NOUN a deep, narrow valley with steep sides.

**raving** ravings
ADJECTIVE **1** If someone is raving, they are mad E.G. *a raving lunatic.* ► NOUN **2** Someone's ravings are crazy things they write or say.

**ravioli**
*Said* "rav-ee-oh-lee" NOUN Ravioli consists of small squares of pasta filled with meat and served with a sauce.

**ravishing**
ADJECTIVE Someone or something that is ravishing is very beautiful E.G. *a ravishing landscape.*

**raw**
ADJECTIVE **1** Raw food has not been cooked. **2** A raw substance is in its natural state E.G. *raw sugar.* **3** If part of your body is raw, the skin has come off or been rubbed away. **4** Someone who is raw is too young or too new in a job or situation to know how to behave.

**raw material** raw materials
NOUN Raw materials are the natural substances used to make something.

**ray** rays
NOUN **1** a beam of light or radiation. **2** A ray of hope is a small amount that makes an unpleasant situation seem slightly better. **3** a large sea fish with eyes on the top of its body, and a long tail.

**raze** razes razing razed
VERB To raze a building, town, or forest means to completely destroy it E.G. *The town was razed to the ground during the occupation.*

**razor** razors
NOUN a tool that people use for shaving.

**razor blade** razor blades
NOUN a small, sharp, flat piece of metal fitted into a razor for shaving.

**re-**
PREFIX **1** 'Re-' is used to form nouns and verbs that refer to the repetition of an action or process E.G. *reread… remarry.* **2** 'Re-' is also used to form verbs that refer to going back to a previous condition E.G. *refresh… renew.* 📖 from a Latin prefix

**reach** reaches reaching reached
VERB **1** When you reach a place, you arrive there. **2** When you reach for something, you stretch out your arm to it. **3** If something reaches a place or point, it extends as far as that place or point E.G. *She has a cloak that reaches to the ground.* **4** If something or someone reaches a stage or level, they get to it E.G. *Unemployment has reached record levels.* **5** To reach an agreement or decision means to succeed in achieving it. ► PHRASE **6** If a place is **within reach**, you can get there E.G. *a cycle route well within reach of most people.* **7** If something is **out of reach**, you cannot get it to it by stretching out your arm E.G. *Store out of reach of children.*

**react** reacts reacting reacted
VERB **1** When you react to something, you behave in a particular way because of it E.G. *He reacted badly to the news.* **2** If one substance reacts with another, a chemical change takes place when they are put together.

**reaction** reactions
NOUN **1** Your reaction to something is what you feel, say, or do because of it

*E.G. Reaction to the visit is mixed.* **2** Your reactions are your ability to move quickly in response to something that happens *E.G. Squash requires fast reactions.* **3** If there is a reaction against something, it becomes unpopular *E.G. a reaction against Christianity.* **4** In a chemical reaction, a chemical change takes place when two substances are put together.

**reactionary reactionaries**
ADJECTIVE **1** Someone who is reactionary tries to prevent political or social change. ▸ NOUN **2** Reactionaries are reactionary people.

**reactor reactors**
NOUN a device which is used to produce nuclear energy.

**read reads reading read**
VERB **1** When you read, you look at something written and follow it or say it aloud. **2** If you can read someone's moods or mind, you can judge what they are feeling or thinking. **3** When you read a meter or gauge, you look at it and record the figure on it. **4** If you read a subject at university, you study it.

**reader readers**
NOUN **1** The readers of a newspaper or magazine are the people who read it regularly. **2** At a university, a reader is a senior lecturer just below the rank of professor.

**readership**
NOUN The readership of a newspaper or magazine consists of the people who read it regularly.

**readily**
ADVERB **1** willingly and eagerly *E.G. She readily agreed to see Alex.* **2** easily done or quickly obtainable *E.G. Help is readily available.*

**reading readings**
NOUN **1** Reading is the activity of reading books. **2** The reading on a meter or gauge is the figure or measurement it shows.

**readjust readjusts readjusting readjusted**
*Said "ree-aj-just"* VERB **1** If you readjust, you adapt to a new situation. **2** If you readjust something, you alter it to a different position.

**ready**
ADJECTIVE **1** having reached the required stage, or prepared for action or use *E.G. In a few days time the plums will be ready to eat.* **2** willing or eager to do something *E.G. She says she's not ready for marriage.* **3** If you are ready for something, you need it *E.G. I'm ready for bed.* **4** easily produced or obtained *E.G. ready cash.*
**readiness** NOUN

**ready-made**
ADJECTIVE already made and therefore able to be used immediately.

**reaffirm reaffirms reaffirming reaffirmed**
VERB To reaffirm something means to state it again *E.G. He reaffirmed his support for the campaign.*

**real**
ADJECTIVE **1** actually existing and not imagined or invented. **2** genuine and not imitation *E.G. Who's to know if they're real guns?* **3** true or actual and not mistaken *E.G. This was the real reason for her call.*
■ (sense 1) authentic, genuine, true

**real estate**
NOUN Real estate is property in the form of land and buildings rather than personal possessions.

a b c d e f g h i j k l m n o p q r s t u v w x y z

have a pIEce of pIE (pi<u>e</u>ce) **SPELLING NOTE**

A
B
C
D
E
F
G
H
I
J
K
L
M
N
O
P
Q
R
S
T
U
V
W
X
Y
Z

**realism**
NOUN Realism is the recognition of the true nature of a situation E.G. *a triumph of muddled thought over realism and common sense.*
**realist** NOUN

**realistic**
ADJECTIVE **1** recognizing and accepting the true nature of a situation. **2** representing things in a way that is true to real life E.G. *His novels are more realistic than his short stories.*
**realistically** ADVERB

**reality**
NOUN (PSHE) **1** Reality is the real nature of things, rather than the way someone imagines it E.G. *Fiction and reality were increasingly blurred.* **2** If something has become reality, it actually exists or is actually happening. ▇ (sense 1) fact, truth

**realize** realizes realizing realized; also spelt **realise**
VERB **1** If you realize something, you become aware of it. **2** FORMAL If your hopes or fears are realized, what you hoped for or feared actually happens E.G. *Our worst fears were realized.* **3** To realize a sum of money means to receive it as a result of selling goods or shares.
**realization** NOUN

**really**
ADVERB **1** used to add emphasis to what is being said E.G. *I'm not really surprised.* **2** used to indicate that you are talking about the true facts about something E.G. *What was really going on?*
☑ If you want to emphasize an adjective you should always use *really* rather than *real*: *really interesting.*

**realm** realms
*Said* "relm" NOUN FORMAL **1** You can refer to any area of thought or activity as a realm E.G. *the realm of politics.* **2** a country with a king or queen E.G. *defence of the realm.*

**reap** reaps reaping reaped
VERB **1** To reap a crop such as corn means to cut and gather it. **2** When people reap benefits or rewards, they get them as a result of hard work or careful planning.
**reaper** NOUN

**reappear** reappears reappearing reappeared
VERB When people or things reappear, you can see them again, because they have come back E.G. *The stolen ring reappeared three years later in a pawn shop.*
**reappearance** NOUN

**reappraisal** reappraisals
NOUN; FORMAL If there is a reappraisal, people think about something and decide whether they want to change it E.G. *a reappraisal of the government's economic policies.*

**rear** rears rearing reared
NOUN **1** The rear of something is the part at the back. ▶ VERB **2** To rear children or young animals means to bring them up until they are able to look after themselves. **3** When a horse rears, it raises the front part of its body, so that its front legs are in the air.

**rear admiral** rear admirals
NOUN a senior officer in the navy.

**rearrange** rearranges rearranging rearranged
VERB To rearrange something means to organize or arrange it in a different way.

**reason** reasons reasoning reasoned
NOUN **1** The reason for something is

the fact or situation which explains why it happens or which causes it to happen. **2** If you have reason to believe or feel something, there are definite reasons why you believe it or feel it *E.G. He had every reason to be upset.* **3** Reason is the ability to think and make judgments. ▶ VERB **4** If you reason that something is true, you decide it is true after considering all the facts. **5** If you reason with someone, you persuade them to accept sensible arguments.

■ (sense 1) cause, motive
■ (sense 3) rationality, sense(s), understanding

## reasonable
ADJECTIVE **1** Reasonable behaviour is fair and sensible. **2** If an explanation is reasonable, there are good reasons for thinking it is correct. **3** A reasonable amount is a fairly large amount. **4** A reasonable price is fair and not too high.
**reasonably** ADVERB

## reasoning
NOUN Reasoning is the process by which you reach a conclusion after considering all the facts.

## reassess reassesses reassessing reassessed
VERB If you reassess something, you consider whether it still has the same value or importance.
**reassessment** NOUN

## reassure reassures reassuring reassured
VERB If you reassure someone, you say or do things that make them less worried.
**reassurance** NOUN

## rebate rebates
NOUN money paid back to someone

who has paid too much tax or rent.

## rebel rebels rebelling rebelled
NOUN **1** (HISTORY) Rebels are people who are fighting their own country's army to change the political system. **2** Someone who is a rebel rejects society's values and behaves differently from other people. ▶ VERB **3** To rebel means to fight against authority and reject accepted values.

## rebellion rebellions
NOUN (HISTORY) A rebellion is organized and often violent opposition to authority.
■ mutiny, revolution, uprising

## rebellious
ADJECTIVE unwilling to obey and likely to rebel against authority.

## rebuff rebuffs rebuffing rebuffed
VERB **1** If you rebuff someone, you reject what they offer *E.G. She rebuffed their offers of help.* ▶ NOUN **2** a rejection of an offer.

## rebuild rebuilds rebuilding rebuilt
VERB When a town or building is rebuilt, it is built again after being damaged or destroyed.

## rebuke rebukes rebuking rebuked
*Said "rib-yook"* VERB To rebuke someone means to speak severely to them about something they have done.

## recall recalls recalling recalled
VERB **1** To recall something means to remember it. **2** If you are recalled to a place, you are ordered to return there. **3** If a company recalls products, it asks people to return them because they are faulty.

## recap recaps recapping recapped
VERB To recap means to repeat and

a
b
c
d
e
f
g
h
i
j
k
l
m
n
o
p
q
r
s
t
u
v
w
x
y
z

summarize the main points of an explanation or discussion.

**recapture** recaptures recapturing recaptured

VERB **1** When you recapture a pleasant feeling, you experience it again *E.G. She may never recapture that past assurance*. **2** When soldiers recapture a place, they capture it from the people who took it from them. **3** When animals or prisoners are recaptured, they are caught after they have escaped.

**recede** recedes receding receded

VERB **1** When something recedes, it moves away into the distance. **2** If a man's hair is receding, he is starting to go bald at the front.

**receipt** receipts

*Said* "ris-**seet**" NOUN **1** a piece of paper confirming that money or goods have been received. **2** In a shop or theatre, the money received is often called the receipts *E.G. Box-office receipts were down last month*. **3** *FORMAL* The receipt of something is the receiving of it *E.G. You have to sign here and acknowledge receipt*.

**receive** receives receiving received

VERB **1** When you receive something, someone gives it to you, or you get it after it has been sent to you. **2** To receive something also means to have it happen to you *E.G. injuries she received in a car crash*. **3** When you receive visitors or guests, you welcome them. **4** If something is received in a particular way, that is how people react to it *E.G. The decision has been received with great disappointment*.

**receiver** receivers

NOUN the part of a telephone you hold near to your ear and mouth.

**recent**

ADJECTIVE Something recent happened a short time ago.

**recently** ADVERB

**reception** receptions

NOUN **1** In a hotel or office, reception is the place near the entrance where appointments or enquiries are dealt with. **2** a formal party. **3** The reception someone or something gets is the way people react to them *E.G. Her tour met with a rapturous reception*. **4** If your radio or television gets good reception, the sound or picture is clear.

**receptionist** receptionists

NOUN The receptionist in a hotel or office deals with people when they arrive, answers the telephone, and arranges appointments.

**receptive**

ADJECTIVE Someone who is receptive to ideas or suggestions is willing to consider them.

**recess** recesses

NOUN **1** a period when no work is done by a committee or parliament *E.G. the Christmas recess*. **2** a place where part of a wall has been built further back than the rest.

**recession** recessions

NOUN a period when a country's economy is less successful and more people become unemployed.

**recharge** recharges recharging recharged

VERB To recharge a battery means to charge it with electricity again after it has been used.

**recipe** recipes
*Said "res-sip-ee"* NOUN **1** (D&T) a list of ingredients and instructions for cooking something. **2** If something is a recipe for disaster or for success, it is likely to result in disaster or success.

**recipient** recipients
NOUN The recipient of something is the person receiving it.

**reciprocal**
ADJECTIVE A reciprocal agreement involves two people, groups, or countries helping each other in a similar way *E.G. a reciprocal agreement on trade.*

**reciprocate** reciprocates reciprocating reciprocated
VERB If you reciprocate someone's feelings or behaviour, you feel or behave in the same way towards them.

**recital** recitals
NOUN a performance of music or poetry, usually by one person.

**recite** recites reciting recited
VERB If you recite a poem or something you have learnt, you say it aloud.
**recitation** NOUN

**reckless**
ADJECTIVE showing a complete lack of care about danger or damage *E.G. a reckless tackle.*
**recklessly** ADVERB **recklessness** NOUN

**reckon** reckons reckoning reckoned
VERB **1** *INFORMAL* If you reckon that something is true, you think it is true *E.G. I reckoned he was still fond of her.* **2** *INFORMAL* If someone reckons to do something, they claim or expect to do it *E.G. Officers on the case are reckoning to charge someone shortly.* **3** To reckon an amount means to calculate it. **4** If you reckon on something, you rely on it happening when making your plans *E.G. He reckons on being world champion.* **5** If you had not reckoned with something, you had not expected it and therefore were unprepared when it happened *E.G. Giles had not reckoned with the strength of Sally's feelings.*

**reckoning** reckonings
NOUN a calculation *E.G. There were a thousand or so, by my reckoning.*

**reclaim** reclaims reclaiming reclaimed
VERB **1** When you reclaim something, you collect it after leaving it somewhere or losing it. **2** To reclaim land means to make it suitable for use, for example by draining it.
**reclamation** NOUN

**recline** reclines reclining reclined
VERB To recline means to lie or lean back at an angle *E.G. a photo of him reclining on his bed.*

**recluse** recluses
NOUN Someone who is a recluse lives alone and avoids other people.
**reclusive** ADJECTIVE ♪

**recognize** recognizes recognizing recognized; also spelt recognise
VERB **1** If you recognize someone or something, you realize that you know who or what they are *E.G. The receptionist recognized me at once.* **2** To recognize something also means to accept and acknowledge it *E.G. The RAF*

a
b
c
d
e
f
g
h
i
j
k
l
m
n
o
p
q
r
s
t
u
v
w
x
y
z

recognized him as an outstanding pilot.

**recognition** NOUN **recognizable** ADJECTIVE **recognizably** ADVERB
■ (sense 1) identify, know, place

**recommend** recommends recommending recommended
VERB If you recommend something to someone, you praise it and suggest they try it.

**recommendation** NOUN

**reconcile** reconciles reconciling reconciled
VERB 1 To reconcile two things that seem to oppose one another, means to make them work or exist together successfully *E.G. The designs reconciled style with comfort.* 2 When people are reconciled, they become friendly again after a quarrel. 3 If you reconcile yourself to an unpleasant situation, you accept it.

**reconciliation** NOUN

**reconnaissance**
*Said* "rik-kon-iss-sanss" NOUN
Reconnaissance is the gathering of military information by soldiers, planes, or satellites.

**reconsider** reconsiders reconsidering reconsidered
VERB To reconsider something means to think about it again to decide whether to change it.

**reconsideration** NOUN

**reconstruct** reconstructs reconstructing reconstructed
VERB 1 To reconstruct something that has been damaged means to build it again. 2 To reconstruct a past event means to get a complete description of it from small pieces of information.

**reconstruction** NOUN

**record** records recording recorded
NOUN 1 If you keep a record of something, you keep a written account or store information in a computer *E.G. medical records.* 2 a round, flat piece of plastic on which music has been recorded. 3 an achievement which is the best of its type. 4 Your record is what is known about your achievements or past activities *E.G. He had a distinguished war record.* ▶ VERB 5 If you record information, you write it down or put it into a computer. 6 To record sound means to put it on tape, record, or compact disc. ▶ ADJECTIVE 7 higher, lower, better, or worse than ever before *E.G. Profits were at a record level.*
■ (sense 1) document, file, register
■ (sense 5) note, register, write down

**recorder** recorders
NOUN a small woodwind instrument.

**recording** recordings
NOUN A recording of something is a record, tape, or video of it.

**recount** recounts recounting recounted
VERB 1 If you recount a story, you tell it. ▶ NOUN 2 a second count of votes in an election when the result is very close.

**recoup** recoups recouping recouped
*Said* "rik-koop" VERB If you recoup money that you have spent or lost, you get it back.

**recourse**
NOUN; FORMAL If you have recourse to something, you use it to help you *E.G. The members settled their differences without recourse to war.*

**recover** recovers recovering recovered

VERB **1** To recover from an illness or unhappy experience means to get well again or get over it. **2** If you recover a lost object or your ability to do something, you get it back.
**recovery** NOUN

■ (sense 1) convalesce, get better, recuperate

■ (sense 2) regain, retrieve

**recreate** recreates recreating recreated

VERB To recreate something means to succeed in making it happen or exist again E.G. *a museum that faithfully recreates an old farmhouse.*

**recreation** recreations
Said "rek-kree-**ay-shn**" NOUN
Recreation is all the things that you do for enjoyment in your spare time.
**recreational** ADJECTIVE

**recrimination** recriminations
NOUN Recriminations are accusations made by people about each other.

**recruit** recruits recruiting recruited

VERB **1** To recruit people means to get them to join a group or help with something. ▶ NOUN **2** someone who has joined the army or some other organization.
**recruitment** NOUN

**rectangle** rectangles
NOUN a four-sided shape with four right angles.
**rectangular** ADJECTIVE

**rectify** rectifies rectifying rectified

VERB; FORMAL If you rectify something that is wrong, you put it right.

**rector** rectors
NOUN a Church of England priest in charge of a parish.

**rectory** rectories
NOUN a house where a rector lives.

**rectum** rectums
NOUN; MEDICAL the bottom end of the tube down which waste food passes out of your body.
**rectal** ADJECTIVE

**recuperate** recuperates recuperating recuperated
VERB When you recuperate, you gradually recover after being ill or injured.
**recuperation** NOUN

**recur** recurs recurring recurred
VERB If something recurs, it happens or occurs again E.G. *His hamstring injury recurred after the first game.*
**recurrence** NOUN **recurrent** ADJECTIVE

**recurring**
ADJECTIVE **1** happening or occurring many times E.G. *a recurring dream.* **2** (MATHS) In maths, a recurring digit is one that is repeated over and over again after the decimal point in a decimal fraction.

**recycle** recycles recycling recycled
VERB To recycle used products means to process them so that they can be used again E.G. *recycled glass.*

**red** redder reddest; reds
NOUN OR ADJECTIVE **1** Red is the colour of blood or of a ripe tomato. ▶ ADJECTIVE **2** Red hair is between orange and brown in colour.

**redback** redbacks
NOUN a small Australian spider with a poisonous bite.

**redcurrant** redcurrants
NOUN Redcurrants are very small,

a
b
c
d
e
f
g
h
i
j
k
l
m
n
o
p
q
**r**
s
t
u
v
w
x
y
z

bright red fruits that grow in bunches on a bush.

**redeem** redeems redeeming redeemed

VERB **1** If a feature redeems an unpleasant thing or situation, it makes it seem less bad. **2** If you redeem yourself, you do something that gives people a good opinion of you again. **3** If you redeem something, you get it back by paying for it. **4** In Christianity, to redeem someone means to free them from sin by giving them faith in Jesus Christ.

**redemption**

NOUN Redemption is the state of being redeemed.

**red-handed**

PHRASE To **catch someone red-handed** means to catch them doing something wrong.

**red-hot**

ADJECTIVE Red-hot metal has been heated to such a high temperature that it has turned red.

**redress** redresses redressing redressed *FORMAL*

VERB **1** To redress a wrong means to put it right. ▶ NOUN **2** If you get redress for harm done to you, you are compensated for it.

**red tape**

NOUN Red tape is official rules and procedures that seem unnecessary and cause delay.

**reduce** reduces reducing reduced

VERB **1** To reduce something means to make it smaller in size or amount. **2** You can use 'reduce' to say that someone or something is changed to a weaker or inferior state *E.G. She reduced them to tears… The village*

*was reduced to rubble.*

▣ (sense 1) cut, decrease, lessen

**reduction** reductions

NOUN When there is a reduction in something, it is made smaller.

**redundancy** redundancies

NOUN **1** Redundancy is the state of being redundant. **2** The number of redundancies is the number of people made redundant.

**redundant**

ADJECTIVE **1** When people are made redundant, they lose their jobs because there is no more work for them or no money to pay them. **2** When something becomes redundant, it is no longer needed.

**reed** reeds

NOUN **1** Reeds are hollow stemmed plants that grow in shallow water or wet ground. **2** a thin piece of cane or metal inside some wind instruments which vibrates when air is blown over it.

**reef** reefs

NOUN a long line of rocks or coral close to the surface of the sea.

**reek** reeks reeking reeked

VERB **1** To reek of something means to smell strongly and unpleasantly of it. ▶ NOUN **2** If there is a reek of something, there is a strong unpleasant smell of it.

**reel** reels reeling reeled

NOUN **1** a cylindrical object around which you wrap something; often part of a device which you turn as a control. **2** a fast Scottish dance. ▶ VERB **3** When someone reels, they move unsteadily as if they are going to fall. **4** If your mind is reeling, you are confused because you have too much to think about.

A B C D E F G H I J K L M N O P Q R S T U V W X Y Z

**reel off** VERB If you reel off information, you repeat it from memory quickly and easily.

**re-elect** re-elects re-electing re-elected
VERB When someone is re-elected, they win an election again and are able to stay in power.

**refer** refers referring referred
VERB 1 If you refer to something, you mention it. 2 If you refer to a book or record, you look at it to find something out. 3 When a problem or issue is referred to someone, they are formally asked to deal with it E.G. The case was referred to the European Court.

🏛 from Latin *referre* meaning 'to carry back'

✔ The word *refer* contains the sense 'back' in its meaning. Therefore, you should not use *back* after *refer*: this *refers to what has already been said* not *refers back*.

**referee** referees
NOUN 1 the official who controls a football game or a boxing or wrestling match. 2 someone who gives a reference to a person who is applying for a job.

**reference** references
NOUN 1 A reference to something or someone is a mention of them. 2 Reference is the act of referring to something or someone for information or advice E.G. He makes that decision without reference to her. 3 a number or name that tells you where to find information or identifies a document. 4 If someone gives you a reference when you apply for a job, they write a letter about your abilities.

**referendum** referendums or referenda
NOUN a vote in which all the people in a country are officially asked whether they agree with a policy or proposal.

**refine** refines refining refined
VERB To refine a raw material such as oil or sugar means to process it to remove impurities.

**refined**
ADJECTIVE very polite and well-mannered.

**refinement** refinements
NOUN 1 Refinements are minor improvements. 2 Refinement is politeness and good manners.

**refinery** refineries
NOUN a factory where substances such as oil or sugar are refined.

**reflect** reflects reflecting reflected
VERB 1 If something reflects an attitude or situation, it shows what it is like E.G. His off-duty hobbies reflected his maritime interests. 2 If something reflects light or heat, the light or heat bounces off it. 3 When something is reflected in a mirror or water, you can see its image in it. 4 (MATHS) If something reflects, its direction is reversed. 5 When you reflect, you think about something.

**reflective** ADJECTIVE **reflectively** ADVERB

**reflection** reflections
NOUN 1 If something is a reflection of something else, it shows what it is like E.G. This is a terrible reflection of the times. 2 an image in a mirror or water. 3 Reflection is the process by which light and heat are bounced off a surface. 4 (MATHS) In maths, reflection is also the turning back of something on itself E.G. reflection of

abcdefghijklmnopqrstuvwxyz

an axis. **5** Reflection is also thought
E.G. *After days of reflection she decided
to leave.*

## reflex reflexes

NOUN **1** A reflex or reflex action is a
sudden uncontrollable movement
that you make as a result of pressure
or a blow. **2** If you have good
reflexes, you respond very quickly
when something unexpected
happens. ▶ ADJECTIVE **3** A reflex angle is
between 180° and 360°.

## reflexive reflexives

ADJECTIVE or NOUN In grammar, a
reflexive verb or pronoun is one that
refers back to the subject of the
sentence E.G. *She washed herself.*

## reform reforms reforming reformed

NOUN **1** Reforms are major changes to
laws or institutions E.G. *a programme
of economic reform.* ▶ VERB **2** When
laws or institutions are reformed,
major changes are made to them.
**3** When people reform, they stop
committing crimes or doing other
unacceptable things.
**reformer** NOUN

## Reformation

NOUN The Reformation was a religious
and political movement in Europe in
the 16th century that began as an
attempt to reform the Roman
Catholic Church, but ended in the
establishment of the Protestant
Churches.

## refraction

NOUN Refraction is the bending of a
ray of light, for example when it
enters water or glass.

## refrain refrains refraining refrained

VERB **1** FORMAL If you refrain from doing

something, you do not do it E.G.
*Please refrain from smoking in the
hall.* ▶ NOUN **2** The refrain of a song is
a short, simple part, repeated many
times.

## refresh refreshes refreshing refreshed

VERB **1** If something refreshes you
when you are hot or tired, it makes
you feel cooler or more energetic E.G.
*A glass of fruit juice will refresh you.*
▶ PHRASE **2** To **refresh someone's
memory** means to remind them of
something they had forgotten.

## refreshing

ADJECTIVE You say that something is
refreshing when it is pleasantly
different from what you are used to
E.G. *She is a refreshing contrast to her
father.*

## refreshment refreshments

NOUN Refreshments are drinks and
small amounts of food provided at
an event.

## refrigerator refrigerators

NOUN an electrically cooled container
in which you store food to keep it fresh.

## refuel refuels refuelling refuelled

VERB When an aircraft or vehicle is
refuelled, it is filled with more fuel.

## refuge refuges

NOUN **1** a place where you go for
safety. **2** If you take refuge, you go
somewhere for safety or behave in a
way that will protect you E.G. *They
took refuge in a bomb shelter…
Father Rowan took refuge in silence.*
■ (sense 1) haven, sanctuary, shelter

## refugee refugees

NOUN Refugees are people who have
been forced to leave their country
and live elsewhere.

**refund refunds refunding refunded**
NOUN 1 money returned to you because you have paid too much for something or because you have returned goods. ▶ VERB 2 To refund someone's money means to return it to them after they have paid for something with it.

**refurbish refurbishes refurbishing refurbished**
VERB; FORMAL To refurbish a building means to decorate it and repair damage.
**refurbishment** NOUN

**refusal refusals**
NOUN A refusal is when someone says firmly that they will not do, allow, or accept something.

**refuse refuses refusing refused**
Said "rif-**yooz**" VERB 1 If you refuse to do something, you say or decide firmly that you will not do it. 2 If someone refuses something, they do not allow it or do not accept it E.G. The United States has refused him a visa… He offered me a second drink which I refused.

**refuse**
Said "**ref**-yoos" NOUN Refuse is rubbish or waste.

**refute refutes refuting refuted**
VERB; FORMAL To refute a theory or argument means to prove that it is wrong.

☑ Refute does not mean the same as deny. If you refute something, you provide evidence to show that it is not true. If you deny something, you say that it is not true.

**regain regains regaining regained**
VERB To regain something means to get it back.

**regal**
ADJECTIVE very grand and suitable for a king or queen E.G. regal splendour.
**regally** ADVERB

**regard regards regarding regarded**
VERB 1 To regard someone or something in a particular way means to think of them in that way or have that opinion of them E.G. We all regard him as a friend… Many disapprove of the tax, regarding it as unfair. 2 LITERARY To regard someone in a particular way also means to look at them in that way E.G. She regarded him curiously for a moment. ▶ NOUN 3 If you have a high regard for someone, you have a very good opinion of them. ▶ PHRASES 4 **Regarding, as regards, with regard to,** and **in regard to** are all used to indicate what you are talking or writing about E.G. There was always some question regarding education… As regards the war, he believed in victory at any price. 5 'Regards' is used in various expressions to express friendly feelings E.G. Give my regards to your husband.

**regardless**
PREPOSITION or ADVERB done or happening in spite of something else E.G. He led from the front, regardless of the danger.

**regatta regattas**
NOUN a race meeting for sailing or rowing boats.

**regency regencies**
NOUN a period when a country is ruled by a regent.

**regenerate regenerates regenerating regenerated**
VERB; FORMAL To regenerate something

a b c d e f g h i j k l m n o p q r s t u v w x y z

means to develop and improve it after it has been declining *E.G. a scheme to regenerate the docks area of the city*.

**regeneration** NOUN

**regent** regents

NOUN someone who rules in place of a king or queen who is ill or too young to rule.

**reggae**

NOUN Reggae is a type of music, originally from the West Indies, with a strong beat.

**regime** regimes

*Said "ray-jeem"* NOUN a system of government, and the people who are ruling a country *E.G. a communist regime*.

**regiment** regiments

NOUN a large group of soldiers commanded by a colonel.

**regimental** ADJECTIVE

**regimented**

ADJECTIVE very strictly controlled *E.G. the regimented life of the orphanage*.

**regimentation** NOUN

**region** regions

NOUN 1 ( GEOGRAPHY ) a large area of land. 2 You can refer to any area or part as a region *E.G. the pelvic region*. ▶ PHRASE 3 **In the region of** means approximately *E.G. The scheme will cost in the region of six million*.

**regional** ADJECTIVE **regionally** ADVERB

■ (sense 1) area, district, territory

**register** registers registering registered

NOUN 1 an official list or record of things *E.G. the electoral register*. 2 *TECHNICAL* a style of speaking or writing used in particular circumstances or social occasions. ▶ VERB 3 When something is

registered, it is recorded on an official list *E.G. The car was registered in my name*. 4 If an instrument registers a measurement, it shows it. 5 If your face registers a feeling, it expresses it.

**registration** NOUN

**registrar** registrars

NOUN 1 a person who keeps official records of births, marriages, and deaths. 2 At a college or university, the registrar is a senior administrative official. 3 a senior hospital doctor.

**registration number** registration numbers

NOUN the sequence of letters and numbers on the front and back of a motor vehicle that identify it.

**registry** registries

NOUN a place where official records are kept.

**registry office** registry offices

NOUN a place where births, marriages, and deaths are recorded, and where people can marry without a religious ceremony.

**regret** regrets regretting regretted

VERB 1 If you regret something, you are sorry that it happened. 2 You can say that you regret something as a way of apologizing *E.G. We regret any inconvenience to passengers*. ▶ NOUN 3 If you have regrets, you are sad or sorry about something.

**regretful** ADJECTIVE **regretfully** ADVERB

■ (sense 1) repent, rue

**regrettable**

ADJECTIVE unfortunate and undesirable *E.G. a regrettable accident*.

**regrettably** ADVERB

**regular** regulars

ADJECTIVE **1** even and equally spaced
*E.G. soft music with a regular beat.*
**2** (MATHS) A regular shape has equal
angles and equal sides *E.G. a regular
polygon.* **3** Regular events or
activities happen often and
according to a pattern, for example
each day or each week *E.G. The trains
to London are fairly regular.* **4** If you
are a regular customer or visitor
somewhere, you go there often.
**5** usual or normal *E.G. I was filling in
for the regular bartender.* **6** having a
well balanced appearance *E.G. a
regular geometrical shape.* ▶ NOUN
**7** People who go to a place often are
known as its regulars.
**regularly** ADVERB **regularity** NOUN
■ (sense 1) even, steady, uniform

**regulate** regulates regulating
regulated

VERB To regulate something means to
control the way it operates *E.G. Sweating
helps to regulate the body's temperature.*
**regulator** NOUN

**regulation** regulations

NOUN **1** Regulations are official rules.
**2** Regulation is the control of
something *E.G. regulation of the
betting industry.*

**regurgitate** regurgitates
regurgitating regurgitated

*Said "rig-gur-jit-tate"* VERB To
regurgitate food means to bring it
back from the stomach before it is
digested.

**rehabilitate** rehabilitates
rehabilitating rehabilitated

VERB To rehabilitate someone who
has been ill or in prison means to
help them lead a normal life.
**rehabilitation** NOUN

**rehearsal** rehearsals

NOUN (DRAMA) a practice of a
performance in preparation for the
actual event.

**rehearse** rehearses rehearsing
rehearsed

VERB (DRAMA) To rehearse a
performance means to practise it in
preparation for the actual event.

**reign** reigns reigning reigned

*Said "rain"* VERB **1** When a king or
queen reigns, he or she rules a
country. **2** You can say that
something reigns when it is a
noticeable feature of a situation or
period of time *E.G. Panic reigned after
his assassination.* ▶ NOUN **3** (HISTORY)
The reign of a king or queen is the
period during which he or she
reigns.

**rein** reins

NOUN **1** Reins are the thin leather
straps which you hold when you are
riding a horse. ▶ PHRASE **2** To **keep a
tight rein on** someone or
something means to control them
firmly.

**reincarnation**

NOUN People who believe in
reincarnation believe that when you
die, you are born again as another
creature.

**reindeer**

NOUN Reindeer are deer with large
antlers, that live in northern
regions.

**reinforce** reinforces reinforcing
reinforced

VERB **1** To reinforce something means
to strengthen it *E.G. a reinforced steel
barrier.* **2** If something reinforces an
idea or claim, it provides evidence to
support it.

a
b
c
d
e
f
g
h
i
j
k
l
m
n
o
p
q
r
s
t
u
v
w
x
y
z

A
B
C
D
E
F
G
H
I
J
K
L
M
N
O
P
Q
R
S
T
U
V
W
X
Y
Z

**reinforcement** reinforcements
NOUN 1 Reinforcements are additional soldiers sent to join an army in battle. 2 Reinforcement is the reinforcing of something.

**reinstate** reinstates reinstating reinstated
VERB 1 To reinstate someone means to give them back a position they have lost. 2 To reinstate something means to bring it back E.G. *Parliament voted against reinstating capital punishment.*
**reinstatement** NOUN

**reiterate** reiterates reiterating reiterated
*Said "ree-it-er-ate"* VERB; *FORMAL* If you reiterate something, you say it again.
**reiteration** NOUN

**reject** rejects rejecting rejected
VERB 1 If you reject a proposal or request, you do not accept it or agree to it. 2 If you reject a belief, political system, or way of life, you decide that it is not for you. ▶ NOUN 3 a product that cannot be used, because there is something wrong with it.
**rejection** NOUN
🔳 (sense 1) decline, refuse, turn down

**rejoice** rejoices rejoicing rejoiced
VERB To rejoice means to be very pleased about something E.G. *The whole country rejoiced after his downfall.*

**rejoin** rejoins rejoining rejoined
VERB If you rejoin someone, you go back to them soon after leaving them E.G. *She rejoined her friends in the bar.*

**rejuvenate** rejuvenates rejuvenating rejuvenated
*Said "ree-joo-vin-ate"* VERB To rejuvenate someone means to make them feel young again.
**rejuvenation** NOUN

**relapse** relapses
NOUN If a sick person has a relapse, their health suddenly gets worse after improving.

**relate** relates relating related
VERB 1 If something relates to something else, it is connected or concerned with it E.G. *The statistics relate only to western Germany.* 2 If you can relate to someone, you can understand their thoughts and feelings. 3 To relate a story means to tell it.

**relation** relations
NOUN 1 If there is a relation between two things, they are similar or connected in some way E.G. *This theory bears no relation to reality.* 2 Your relations are the members of your family. 3 Relations between people are their feelings and behaviour towards each other E.G. *Relations between husband and wife had not improved.*

**relationship** relationships
NOUN (PSHE) 1 The relationship between two people or groups is the way they feel and behave towards each other. 2 a close friendship, especially one involving romantic or sexual feelings. 3 The relationship between two things is the way in which they are connected E.G. *the relationship between slavery and the sugar trade.*

**relative** relatives
ADJECTIVE 1 compared to other things

or people of the same kind *E.G. The fighting resumed after a period of relative calm… He is a relative novice.* **2** You use 'relative' when comparing the size or quality of two things *E.G. the relative strengths of the British and German forces.* ▶ NOUN **3** Your relatives are the members of your family.

**relative pronoun relative pronouns**

NOUN a pronoun that replaces a noun that links two parts of a sentence.

---

### What is a Relative Pronoun?

Relative pronouns are used to replace a noun which links two different parts of a sentence. The relative pronouns are *who, whom, whose, which,* and *that.*

Relative pronouns always refer back to a word in the earlier part of the sentence. The word they refer to is called the **antecedent**. (In the examples that follow, the antecedents are underlined.)

*E.G. I have <u>a friend</u> **who** lives in Rome.*
*We could go to <u>a place</u> **that** I know.*

The forms *who, whom,* and *whose* are used when the antecedent is a person. *Who* indicates the subject of the verb, while *whom* indicates the object of the verb:

*E.G. It was <u>the same person</u> **who** saw me yesterday.*
*It was <u>the person</u> **whom** I saw yesterday.*

The distinction between *who* and *whom* is often ignored in everyday English, and *who* is often used as the object:

CONTINUED →

---

*E.G. It was <u>the person</u> **who** I saw yesterday.*

*Whom* is used immediately after a preposition. However, if the preposition is separated from the relative pronoun, *who* is usually used:

*E.G. He is <u>a man</u> **in whom** I have great confidence.*
*He is <u>a man</u> **who** I have great confidence **in**.*

*Whose* is the possessive form of the relative pronoun. It can refer to things as well as people:

*E.G. Anna has <u>a sister</u> **whose** name is Rosie.*
*I found <u>a book</u> **whose** pages were torn.*

*Which* is only used when the antecedent is not a person:

*E.G. We took <u>the road</u> **which** leads to the sea.*

*That* refers to things or people. It is never used immediately after a preposition, but it can be used if the preposition is separated from the relative pronoun:

*E.G. It was <u>a film</u> **that** I had little interest **in**.*

---

**relax relaxes relaxing relaxed**

VERB **1** If you relax, you become calm and your muscles lose their tension. **2** If you relax your hold, you hold something less tightly. **3** To relax something also means to make it less strict or controlled *E.G. The rules governing student conduct were relaxed.*

**relaxation** NOUN
■ (sense 1) rest, take it easy, unwind
■ (sense 2) lessen, loosen, slacken

---

a b c d e f g h i j k l m n o p q r s t u v w x y z

A
B
C
D
E
F
G
H
I
J
K
L
M
N
O
P
Q
R
S
T
U
V
W
X
Y
Z

**relay** relays relaying relayed

NOUN 1 (PE) A relay race or relay is a race between teams, with each team member running one part of the race. ▸ VERB 2 To relay a television or radio signal means to send it on. 3 If you relay information, you tell it to someone else.

**release** releases releasing released

VERB 1 To release someone or something means to set them free or remove restraints from them. 2 To release something also means to issue it or make it available E.G. *He is releasing an album of love songs.* ▸ NOUN 3 When the release of someone or something takes place, they are set free. 4 A press release or publicity release is an official written statement given to reporters. 5 A new release is a new record or video that has just become available.

**relegate** relegates relegating relegated

VERB To relegate something or someone means to give them a less important position or status. **relegation** NOUN

**relent** relents relenting relented

VERB If someone relents, they agree to something they had previously not allowed.

**relentless**

ADJECTIVE never stopping and never becoming less intense E.G. *the relentless rise of business closures.* **relentlessly** ADVERB

**relevant**

ADJECTIVE (LIBRARY) If something is relevant, it is connected with and is appropriate to what is being discussed E.G. *We have passed all*

*relevant information on to the police.*
**relevance** NOUN

■ appropriate, pertinent, significant

**reliable**

ADJECTIVE 1 Reliable people and things can be trusted to do what you want. 2 If information is reliable, you can assume that it is correct. **reliably** ADVERB **reliability** NOUN

**reliant**

ADJECTIVE If you are reliant on someone or something, you depend on them E.G. *They are not wholly reliant on charity.* **reliance** NOUN

**relic** relics

NOUN 1 Relics are objects or customs that have survived from an earlier time. 2 an object regarded as holy because it is thought to be connected with a saint.

**relief**

NOUN 1 If you feel relief, you are glad and thankful because a bad situation is over or has been avoided. 2 Relief is also money, food, or clothing provided for poor or hungry people.

**relief map** relief maps

NOUN a map showing the shape of mountains and hills by shading.

**relieve** relieves relieving relieved

VERB 1 If something relieves an unpleasant feeling, it makes it less unpleasant E.G. *Drugs can relieve much of the pain.* 2 FORMAL If you relieve someone, you do their job or duty for a period. 3 If someone is relieved of their duties, they are dismissed from their job. 4 If you relieve yourself, you urinate.

**religion** religions

NOUN (RE) 1 Religion is the belief in a god or gods and all the activities connected with such beliefs. **2** a system of religious belief.

**religious**

ADJECTIVE **1** (HISTORY) connected with religion E.G. *religious worship.* **2** (RE) Someone who is religious has a strong belief in a god or gods.

■ (sense 2) devout, pious

**religiously**

ADVERB If you do something religiously, you do it regularly as a duty E.G. *He stuck religiously to the rules.*

**relinquish** relinquishes relinquishing relinquished

*Said* "ril-**ling**-kwish" VERB; FORMAL If you relinquish something, you give it up.

**relish** relishes relishing relished

VERB **1** If you relish something, you enjoy it E.G. *He relished the idea of getting some cash.* ▸ NOUN **2** Relish is enjoyment E.G. *He told me with relish of the wonderful times he had.* **3** Relish is also a savoury sauce or pickle.

**relive** relives reliving relived

VERB If you relive a past experience, you remember it and imagine it happening again.

**relocate** relocates relocating relocated

VERB If people or businesses are relocated, they are moved to a different place.

**relocation** NOUN

**reluctant**

ADJECTIVE If you are reluctant to do something, you are unwilling to do it.

**reluctance** NOUN

**reluctantly**

ADVERB If you do something reluctantly, you do it although you do not want to.

**rely** relies relying relied

VERB **1** If you rely on someone or something, you need them and depend on them E.G. *She has to rely on hardship payments.* **2** If you can rely on someone to do something, you can trust them to do it E.G. *They can always be relied on to turn up.*

**remain** remains remaining remained

VERB **1** If you remain in a particular place or state, you stay there or stay the same and do not change E.G. *The three men remained silent.* **2** Something that remains still exists or is left over E.G. *Huge amounts of weapons remain to be collected.* ▸ PLURAL NOUN **3** The remains of something are the parts that are left after most of it has been destroyed E.G. *the remains of an ancient mosque.* **4** You can refer to a dead body as remains E.G. *More human remains have been unearthed today.*

■ (sense 3) debris, remnants

**remainder**

NOUN The remainder of something is the part that is left E.G. *He gulped down the remainder of his coffee.*

**remand** remands remanding remanded

VERB **1** If a judge remands someone who is accused of a crime, the trial is postponed and the person is ordered to come back at a later date. ▸ PHRASE **2** If someone is **on remand**, they are in prison waiting for their trial to begin.

**remark** remarks remarking remarked

VERB **1** If you remark on something, you mention it or comment on it E.G. *She had remarked on the boy's improvement.* ▸ NOUN **2** something you say, often in a casual way.

a
b
c
d
e
f
g
h
i
j
k
l
m
n
o
p
q
r
s
t
u
v
w
x
y
z

LEt's measure the angLE (an**g**le)    **SPELLING NOTE**

**remarkable**

ADJECTIVE impressive and unexpected E.G. *It was a remarkable achievement.*
**remarkably** ADVERB

■ extraordinary, outstanding, wonderful

**remarry remarries remarrying remarried**

VERB If someone remarries, they get married again.

**remedial**

ADJECTIVE 1 Remedial activities are to help someone improve their health after they have been ill. 2 Remedial exercises are designed to improve someone's ability in something E.G. *the remedial reading class.*

**remedy remedies remedying remedied**

NOUN 1 a way of dealing with a problem E.G. *a remedy for colic.* ▶ VERB 2 If you remedy something that is wrong, you correct it E.G. *We have to remedy the situation immediately.*

**remember remembers remembering remembered**

VERB 1 If you can remember someone or something from the past, you can bring them into your mind or think about them. 2 If you remember to do something, you do it when you intended to E.G. *Ben had remembered to book reservations.*

■ (sense 1) recall, recollect

**remembrance**

NOUN If you do something in remembrance of a dead person, you are showing that they are remembered with respect and affection.

**remind reminds reminding reminded**

VERB 1 If someone reminds you of a fact, they say something to make you think about it E.G. *Remind me to buy a bottle of wine, will you?* 2 If someone reminds you of another person, they look similar and make you think of them.

**reminder reminders**

NOUN 1 If one thing is a reminder of another, the first thing makes you think of the second E.G. *a reminder of better times.* 2 a note sent to tell someone they have forgotten to do something.

**reminiscent**

ADJECTIVE Something that is reminiscent of something else reminds you of it.

**remission**

NOUN When prisoners get remission for good behaviour, their sentences are reduced.

**remit remits**

NOUN; FORMAL The remit of a person or committee is the subject or task they are responsible for E.G. *Their remit is to research into a wide range of health problems.*

**remittance remittances**

NOUN; FORMAL payment for something sent through the post.

**remnant remnants**

NOUN a small part of something left after the rest has been used or destroyed.

**remorse**

NOUN; FORMAL Remorse is a strong feeling of guilt.
**remorseful** ADJECTIVE

■ contrition, regret, repentance

**remote remoter remotest**

ADJECTIVE 1 Remote areas are far away from places where most people live. 2 far away in time E.G. *the remote past.* 3 If you say a person is remote, you mean they do not want to be friendly E.G. *She is severe, solemn, and remote.* 4 If there is only a remote possibility of something happening, it is unlikely to happen.
**remoteness** NOUN

**remote control**

NOUN Remote control is a system of controlling a machine or vehicle from a distance using radio or electronic signals.

**remotely**

ADVERB used to emphasize a negative statement E.G. *He isn't remotely keen.*

**removal**

NOUN 1 The removal of something is the act of taking it away. 2 A removal company transports furniture from one building to another.

**remove removes removing removed**

VERB 1 If you remove something from a place, you take it off or away. 2 If you are removed from a position of authority, you are not allowed to continue your job. 3 If you remove an undesirable feeling or attitude, you get rid of it E.G. *Most of her fears had been removed.*
**removable** ADJECTIVE
■ (sense 1) extract, take away, withdraw

**Renaissance**

Said "ren-**nay**-sonss" NOUN The Renaissance was a period from the 14th to 16th centuries in Europe when there was a great revival in the arts and learning.

🏛 a French word, meaning literally 'rebirth'

**renal**

ADJECTIVE; TECHNICAL concerning the kidneys E.G. *renal failure.*

**rename renames renaming renamed**

VERB If you rename something, you give it a new name.

**render renders rendering rendered**

VERB You can use 'render' to say that something is changed into a different state E.G. *The bomb was quickly rendered harmless.*

**rendezvous**

Said "**ron**-day-voo" NOUN 1 a meeting E.G. *Baxter arranged a six o'clock rendezvous.* 2 a place where you have arranged to meet someone E.G. *The pub became a popular rendezvous.*

**rendition renditions**

NOUN; FORMAL a performance of a play, poem, or piece of music.

**renew renews renewing renewed**

VERB 1 To renew an activity or relationship means to begin it again. 2 To renew a licence or contract means to extend the period of time for which it is valid.
**renewal** NOUN

**renewable renewables**

ADJECTIVE 1 able to be renewed. ▶ NOUN 2 a renewable form of energy, such as wind power or solar power.

**renounce renounces renouncing renounced**

VERB; FORMAL If you renounce something, you reject it or give it up.
**renunciation** NOUN

**renovate renovates renovating renovated**

a b c d e f g h i j k l m n o p q r s t u v w x y z

**A B C D E F G H I J K L M N O P Q R S T U V W X Y Z**

VERB If you renovate an old building or machine, you repair it and restore it to good condition.

**renovation** NOUN

**renowned**

ADJECTIVE well-known for something good E.G. *He is not renowned for his patience.*

**renown** NOUN

**rent rents renting rented**

VERB 1 If you rent something, you pay the owner a regular sum of money in return for being able to use it. ► NOUN 2 Rent is the amount of money you pay regularly to rent land or accommodation.

**rental**

ADJECTIVE 1 concerned with the renting out of goods and services E.G. *Scotland's largest video rental company.* ► NOUN 2 the amount of money you pay when you rent something.

**reorganize reorganizes reorganizing reorganized**; also spelt **reorganise**

VERB To reorganize something means to organize it in a new way in order to make it more efficient or acceptable.

**reorganization** NOUN

**rep reps**

NOUN; INFORMAL a travelling salesman or saleswoman. Rep is an abbreviation for representative.

**repair repairs repairing repaired**

NOUN 1 something you do to mend something that is damaged or broken. ► VERB 2 If you repair something, you mend it.

**repay repays repaying repaid**

VERB 1 To repay money means to give it back to the person who lent it. 2 If you repay a favour, you do

something to help the person who helped you.

**repayment** NOUN

**repeal repeals repealing repealed**

VERB If the government repeals a law, it cancels it so that it is no longer valid.

**repeat repeats repeating repeated**

VERB 1 If you repeat something, you say, write, or do it again. 2 If you repeat what someone has said, you tell someone else about it E.G. *I trust you not to repeat that to anyone.* ► NOUN 3 something which is done or happens again E.G. *the number of repeats shown on TV.*

**repeated** ADJECTIVE **repeatedly** ADVERB

**repel repels repelling repelled**

VERB 1 If something repels you, you find it horrible and disgusting. 2 When soldiers repel an attacking force, they successfully defend themselves against it. 3 When a magnetic pole repels an opposite pole, it forces the opposite pole away.

▪ (sense 1) disgust, revolt, sicken

**repellent repellents**

ADJECTIVE 1 FORMAL horrible and disgusting E.G. *I found him repellent.* ► NOUN 2 Repellents are chemicals used to keep insects or other creatures away.

**repent repents repenting repented**

VERB; FORMAL If you repent, you are sorry for something bad you have done.

**repentance** NOUN **repentant** ADJECTIVE

**repercussion repercussions**

NOUN The repercussions of an event

are the effects it has at a later time.

**repertoire repertoires**
*Said "rep-et-twar"* NOUN A performer's repertoire is all the pieces of music or dramatic parts he or she has learned and can perform

**repertory repertories**
NOUN 1 Repertory is the practice of performing a small number of plays in a theatre for a short time, using the same actors in each play. 2 In Australian, New Zealand and South African English, repertory is the same as **repertoire**.

**repetition repetitions**
NOUN If there is a repetition of something, it happens again *E.G. We don't want a repetition of last week's fiasco.*

**repetitive**
ADJECTIVE A repetitive activity involves a lot of repetition and is boring *E.G. dull and repetitive work.*

**replace replaces replacing replaced**
VERB 1 When one thing replaces another, the first thing takes the place of the second. 2 If you replace something that is damaged or lost, you get a new one. 3 If you replace something, you put it back where it was before *E.G. She replaced the receiver.*
■ (sense 1) supersede, supplant

**replacement replacements**
NOUN 1 The replacement for someone or something is the person or thing that takes their place. 2 The replacement of a person or thing happens when they are replaced by another person or thing.

**replay replays replaying replayed**
VERB 1 If a match is replayed, the teams play it again. 2 If you replay a tape or film, you play it again *E.G. Replay the first few seconds of the tape please.* ▶ NOUN 3 a match that is played for a second time.

**replenish replenishes replenishing replenished**
VERB; FORMAL If you replenish something, you make it full or complete again.

**replica replicas**
NOUN an accurate copy of something *E.G. a replica of Columbus's ship.*
**replicate** VERB

**reply replies replying replied**
VERB 1 If you reply to something, you say or write an answer. ▶ NOUN 2 what you say or write when you answer someone.

**report reports reporting reported**
VERB 1 If you report that something has happened, you tell someone about it or give an official account of it *E.G. He reported the theft to the police.* 2 To report someone to an authority means to make an official complaint about them. 3 If you report to a person or place, you go there and say you have arrived.
▶ NOUN 4 an account of an event or situation.
■ (sense 4) account, description

**reported speech**
NOUN a report of what someone said that gives the content of the speech without repeating the exact words.

**reporter reporters**
NOUN someone who writes news articles or broadcasts news reports.

**repossess repossesses repossessing repossessed**
VERB If a shop or company

a
b
c
d
e
f
g
h
i
j
k
l
m
n
o
p
q
r
s
t
u
v
w
x
y
z

repossesses goods that have not been paid for, they take them back.

**represent** represents representing represented
VERB (PSHE) 1 If you represent someone, you act on their behalf E.G. *lawyers representing relatives of the victims.* 2 If a sign or symbol represents something, it stands for it. 3 To represent something in a particular way means to describe it in that way E.G. *The popular press tends to represent him as a hero.*

**representation** representations
NOUN 1 Representation is the state of being represented by someone E.G. *Was there any student representation?* 2 You can describe a picture or statue as a representation of them.

**representative** representatives
NOUN 1 (PSHE) a person chosen to act on behalf of another person or a group. ▶ ADJECTIVE 2 A representative selection is typical of the group it belongs to E.G. *The photos chosen are not representative of his work.*

**repress** represses repressing repressed
VERB 1 If you repress a feeling, you succeed in not showing or feeling it E.G. *I couldn't repress my anger any longer.* 2 To repress people means to restrict their freedom and control them by force.
**repression** NOUN

**repressive**
ADJECTIVE Repressive governments use force and unjust laws to restrict and control people.

**reprieve** reprieves reprieving reprieved
Said "rip-**preev**" VERB 1 If someone who has been sentenced to death is reprieved, their sentence is changed and they are not killed. ▶ NOUN 2 a delay before something unpleasant happens E.G. *The zoo won a reprieve from closure.*

**reprimand** reprimands reprimanding reprimanded
VERB 1 If you reprimand someone, you officially tell them that they should not have done something. ▶ NOUN 2 something said or written by a person in authority when they are reprimanding someone.

**reprisal** reprisals
NOUN Reprisals are violent actions taken by one group of people against another group that has harmed them.

**reproach** reproaches reproaching reproached FORMAL
NOUN 1 If you express reproach, you show that you feel sad and angry about what someone has done E.G. *a long letter of reproach.* ▶ VERB 2 If you reproach someone, you tell them, rather sadly, that they have done something wrong.
**reproachful** ADJECTIVE

**reproduce** reproduces reproducing reproduced
VERB (SCIENCE) 1 To reproduce something means to make a copy of it. 2 When living things reproduce, they produce more of their own kind E.G. *Bacteria reproduce by splitting into two.*

**reproduction** reproductions
NOUN 1 a modern copy of a painting or piece of furniture. 2 Reproduction is the process by which a living thing produces more of its kind E.G. *the study of animal reproduction.*

**reproductive**

ADJECTIVE relating to the reproduction of living things E.G. *the female reproductive system.*

**reptile** reptiles

NOUN a cold-blooded animal, such as a snake or a lizard, which has scaly skin and lays eggs.

**reptilian** ADJECTIVE

📖 from Latin *reptilis* meaning 'creeping'

**republic** republics

NOUN a country which has a president rather than a king or queen.

**republican** NOUN or ADJECTIVE

**republicanism** NOUN

📖 from Latin *res publica* meaning literally 'public thing'

**repulse** repulses repulsing repulsed

VERB 1 If you repulse someone who is being friendly, you put them off by behaving coldly towards them E.G. *He repulses friendly advances.* 2 To repulse an attacking force means to fight it and cause it to retreat. 3 If something repulses you, you find it horrible and disgusting and you want to avoid it.

**repulsion**

NOUN 1 Repulsion is a strong feeling of disgust. 2 Repulsion is a force separating two objects, such as the force between two like electric charges.

**repulsive**

ADJECTIVE horrible and disgusting.

**reputable**

ADJECTIVE known to be good and reliable E.G. *a well-established and reputable firm.*

**reputation** reputations

NOUN The reputation of something or someone is the opinion that people

have of them E.G. *The college had a good reputation.*

■ name, renown, standing

**reputed**

ADJECTIVE If something is reputed to be true, some people say that it is true E.G. *the reputed tomb of Christ.*

**reputedly** ADVERB

**request** requests requesting requested

VERB 1 If you request something, you ask for it politely or formally. ▶ NOUN 2 If you make a request for something, you request it.

**requiem** requiems

*Said* "rek-wee-em" NOUN 1 A requiem or requiem mass is a mass celebrated for someone who has recently died. 2 a piece of music for singers and an orchestra, originally written for a requiem mass E.G. *Mozart's Requiem.*

📖 from Latin *requies* meaning 'rest'

**require** requires requiring required

VERB 1 If you require something, you need it. 2 If you are required to do something, you have to do it because someone says you must E.G. *The rules require employers to provide safety training.*

**requirement** requirements

NOUN something that you must have or must do E.G. *A good degree is a requirement for entry.*

**requisite** requisites FORMAL

ADJECTIVE 1 necessary for a particular purpose E.G. *She filled in the requisite paperwork.* ▶ NOUN 2 something that is necessary for a particular purpose.

**rescue** rescues rescuing rescued

VERB 1 If you rescue someone, you

a
b
c
d
e
f
g
h
i
j
k
l
m
n
o
p
q
**r**
s
t
u
v
w
x
y
z

save them from a dangerous or unpleasant situation. ▶ NOUN **2** Rescue is help which saves someone from a dangerous or unpleasant situation.

**rescuer** NOUN

**research** researches researching researched

NOUN **1** Research is work that involves studying something and trying to find out facts about it. ▶ VERB **2** If you research something, you try to discover facts about it.

**researcher** NOUN

**resemblance**

NOUN If there is a resemblance between two things, they are similar to each other *E.G. There was a remarkable resemblance between them.*

■ likeness, similarity

**resemble** resembles resembling resembled

VERB To resemble something means to be similar to it.

**resent** resents resenting resented

VERB If you resent something, you feel bitter and angry about it.

**resentment** NOUN

**resentful**

ADJECTIVE bitter and angry *E.G. He felt very resentful about losing his job.*

**resentfully** ADVERB

**reservation** reservations

NOUN **1** If you have reservations about something, you are not sure that it is right. **2** If you make a reservation, you book a place in advance. **3** an area of land set aside for American Indian peoples *E.G. a Cherokee reservation.*

**reserve** reserves reserving reserved

VERB **1** If something is reserved for a

particular person or purpose, it is kept specially for them. ▶ NOUN **2** a supply of something for future use. **3** In sport, a reserve is someone who is available to play in case one of the team is unable to play. **4** A nature reserve is an area of land where animals, birds, or plants are officially protected. **5** If someone shows reserve, they keep their feelings hidden.

**reserved** ADJECTIVE

■ (sense 1) put by, save, set aside

**reservoir** reservoirs

*Said* "**rez**-ev-wahr" NOUN a lake used for storing water before it is supplied to people.

**reshuffle** reshuffles

NOUN a reorganization of people or things.

**reside** resides residing resided

*Said* "riz-**zide**" VERB; FORMAL If a quality resides in something, the quality is in that thing.

**residence** residence

NOUN; FORMAL a house.

**resident** residents

NOUN **1** A resident of a house or area is someone who lives there. ▶ ADJECTIVE **2** If someone is resident in a house or area, they live there.

**residential**

ADJECTIVE **1** A residential area contains mainly houses rather than offices or factories. **2** providing accommodation *E.G. residential care for the elderly.*

**residue** residues

NOUN a small amount of something that remains after most of it has gone *E.G. an increase in toxic residues found in drinking water.*

**residual** ADJECTIVE

**resign resigns resigning resigned**
VERB 1 If you resign from a job, you formally announce that you are leaving it. 2 If you resign yourself to an unpleasant situation, you realize that you have to accept it.
**resigned** ADJECTIVE

**resignation resignations**
NOUN 1 Someone's resignation is a formal statement of their intention to leave a job. 2 Resignation is the reluctant acceptance of an unpleasant situation or fact.

**resilient**
ADJECTIVE able to recover quickly from unpleasant or damaging events.
**resilience** NOUN

**resin resins**
NOUN 1 Resin is a sticky substance produced by some trees. 2 Resin is also a substance produced chemically and used to make plastics.

**resist resists resisting resisted**
VERB 1 If you resist something, you refuse to accept it and try to prevent it E.G. *The pay squeeze will be fiercely resisted by the unions.* 2 If you resist someone, you fight back against them.
■ (sense 1) fight, oppose

**resistance resistances**
NOUN 1 Resistance to something such as change is a refusal to accept it. 2 Resistance to an attack consists of fighting back E.G. *The demonstrators offered no resistance.* 3 Your body's resistance to germs or disease is its power to not be harmed by them. 4 Resistance is also the power of a substance to resist the flow of an electrical current through it.

**resistant**
ADJECTIVE 1 opposed to something and wanting to prevent it E.G. *People were very resistant to change.* 2 If something is resistant to a particular thing, it is not harmed or affected by it E.G. *Certain insects are resistant to this spray.*

**resolute**
*Said* "**rez**-ol-loot" ADJECTIVE; FORMAL Someone who is resolute is determined not to change their mind.
**resolutely** ADVERB

**resolution resolutions**
NOUN 1 Resolution is determination. 2 If you make a resolution, you promise yourself to do something. 3 a formal decision taken at a meeting. 4 (ENGLISH) FORMAL The resolution of a problem is the solving of it.

**resolve resolves resolving resolved**
VERB 1 If you resolve to do something, you firmly decide to do it. 2 If you resolve a problem, you find a solution to it. ▶ NOUN 3 Resolve is absolute determination.

**resonance resonances**
NOUN 1 Resonance is sound produced by an object vibrating as a result of another sound nearby. 2 Resonance is also a deep, clear, and echoing quality of sound.

**resonate resonates resonating resonated**
VERB If something resonates, it vibrates and produces a deep, strong sound.

**resort resorts resorting resorted**
VERB 1 If you resort to a course of

a b c d e f g h i j k l m n o p q **r** s t u v w x y z

A B C D E F G H I J K L M N O P Q R S T U V W X Y Z

action, you do it because you have no alternative. ▶ NOUN 2 a place where people spend their holidays. ▶ PHRASE 3 If you do something **as a last resort**, you do it because you can find no other way of solving a problem.

**resounding**
ADJECTIVE 1 loud and echoing E.G. *a resounding round of applause.* 2 A resounding success is a great success.

**resource resources**
NOUN The resources of a country, organization, or person are the materials, money, or skills they have.

**resourceful**
ADJECTIVE A resourceful person is good at finding ways of dealing with problems.
**resourcefulness** NOUN

**respect respects respecting respected**
VERB 1 If you respect someone, you have a good opinion of their character or ideas. 2 If you respect someone's rights or wishes, you do not do things that they would not like, or would consider wrong E.G. *It is about time they started respecting the law.* ▶ NOUN 3 If you have respect for someone, you respect them. ▶ PHRASE 4 You can say **in this respect** to refer to a particular feature E.G. *At least in this respect we are equals.*

**respectable**
ADJECTIVE 1 considered to be acceptable and morally correct E.G. *respectable families.* 2 adequate or reasonable E.G. *a respectable rate of economic growth.*
**respectability** NOUN **respectably** ADVERB

**respectful**
ADJECTIVE showing respect for someone E.G. *Our children are always respectful to their elders.*
**respectfully** ADVERB

**respective**
ADJECTIVE belonging or relating individually to the people or things just mentioned E.G. *They went into their respective rooms to pack.*

**respectively**
ADVERB in the same order as the items just mentioned E.G. *They finished first and second respectively.*

**respiration**
NOUN (SCIENCE) TECHNICAL Your respiration is your breathing.

**respiratory**
ADJECTIVE; TECHNICAL relating to breathing E.G. *respiratory diseases.*

**respire respires respiring respired**
VERB (SCIENCE) To respire is to breathe.

**respite**
NOUN; FORMAL a short rest from something unpleasant.

**respond responds responding responded**
VERB When you respond to something, you react to it by doing or saying something.

**respondent respondents**
NOUN 1 a person who answers a questionnaire or a request for information. 2 In a court case, the respondent is the defendant.

**response responses**
NOUN Your response to an event is your reaction or reply to it E.G. *There has been no response to his remarks yet.*

**responsibility responsibilities**
NOUN 1 If you have responsibility for

**SPELLING NOTE** have a pIEce of pIE (pi<u>e</u>ce)

something, it is your duty to deal with it or look after it *E.G. The garden was to have been his responsibility.* **2** If you accept responsibility for something that has happened, you agree that you caused it or were to blame *E.G. We must all accept responsibility for our own mistakes.*

**responsible**
ADJECTIVE **1** If you are responsible for something, it is your duty to deal with it and you are to blame if it goes wrong. **2** If you are responsible to someone, that person is your boss and tells you what you have to do. **3** A responsible person behaves properly and sensibly without needing to be supervised. **4** A responsible job involves making careful judgments about important matters.
**responsibly** ADVERB
■ (sense 1) accountable, answerable, liable

**responsive**
ADJECTIVE **1** quick to show interest and pleasure. **2** taking notice of events and reacting in an appropriate way *E.G. The course is responsive to students' needs.*

**rest rests resting rested**
NOUN **1** The rest of something is all the remaining parts of it. **2** If you have a rest, you sit or lie quietly and relax.
▶ VERB **3** If you rest, you relax and do not do anything active for a while.

**restaurant restaurants**
*Said "rest-ront"* NOUN a place where you can buy and eat a meal.
🔢 a French word; from *restaurer* meaning 'to restore'

**restaurateur restaurateurs**
*Said "rest-er-a-tur"* NOUN someone

who owns or manages a restaurant.

**restful**
ADJECTIVE Something that is restful helps you feel calm and relaxed.

**restless**
ADJECTIVE finding it hard to remain still or relaxed because of boredom or impatience.
**restlessness** NOUN **restlessly** ADVERB

**restore restores restoring restored**
VERB **1** To restore something means to cause it to exist again or to return to its previous state *E.G. He was anxious to restore his reputation.* **2** To restore an old building or work of art means to clean and repair it.
**restoration** NOUN
■ (sense 2) refurbish, renovate

**restrain restrains restraining restrained**
VERB To restrain someone or something means to hold them back or prevent them from doing what they want to.

**restrained**
ADJECTIVE behaving in a controlled way.

**restraint restraints**
NOUN **1** Restraints are rules or conditions that limit something *E.G. wage restraints.* **2** Restraint is calm, controlled behaviour.

**restrict restricts restricting restricted**
VERB **1** If you restrict something, you prevent it becoming too large or varied. **2** To restrict people or animals means to limit their movement or actions.
**restrictive** ADJECTIVE

**restriction restrictions**
NOUN a rule or situation that limits

a b c d e f g h i j k l m n o p q **r** s t u v w x y z

Plaice the fish has a glittering 'EYE' (I) (plaice)        SPELLING NOTE

what you can do *E.G. financial restrictions*.

**result** results resulting resulted

NOUN **1** The result of an action or situation is the situation that is caused by it *E.G. As a result of the incident he got a two-year suspension*. **2** The result is also the final marks, figures, or situation at the end of an exam, calculation, or contest *E.G. election results… The result was calculated to three decimal places*.

▶ VERB **3** If something results in a particular event, it causes that event to happen. **4** If something results from a particular event, it is caused by that event *E.G. The fire had resulted from carelessness*.

**resultant** ADJECTIVE

■ (sense 1) consequence, outcome, upshot

**resume** resumes resuming resumed

*Said* "riz-**yoom**" VERB If you resume an activity or position, you return to it after a break.

**resumption** NOUN

**resurgence**

NOUN If there is a resurgence of an attitude or activity, it reappears and grows stronger.

**resurgent** ADJECTIVE

**resurrect** resurrects resurrecting resurrected

VERB If you resurrect something, you make it exist again after it has disappeared or ended.

**resurrection** NOUN

**Resurrection**

NOUN In Christian belief, the Resurrection is the coming back to life of Jesus Christ three days after he had been killed.

**resuscitate** resuscitates resuscitating resuscitated

*Said* "ris-**suss**-it-tate" VERB If you resuscitate someone, you make them conscious again after an accident.

**resuscitation** NOUN

**retail**

NOUN The retail price is the price at which something is sold in the shops.

**retailer** NOUN

**retain** retains retaining retained

VERB To retain something means to keep it.

**retention** NOUN

**retaliate** retaliates retaliating retaliated

VERB If you retaliate, you do something to harm or upset someone because they have already acted in a similar way against you.

**retaliation** NOUN

**retarded**

ADJECTIVE If someone is retarded, their mental development is much less advanced than average.

**rethink** rethinks rethinking rethought

VERB If you rethink something, you think about how it should be changed *E.G. We have to rethink our strategy*.

**reticent**

ADJECTIVE Someone who is reticent is unwilling to tell people about things.

**reticence** NOUN

**retina** retinas

NOUN the light-sensitive part at the back of your eyeball, which receives an image and sends it to your brain.

**retinue** retinues

NOUN a group of helpers or friends travelling with an important person.

**SPELLING NOTE** I went to see (C) the doctor's new practiCe (practice)

**retire** retires retiring retired

VERB **1** When older people retire, they give up work. **2** *FORMAL* If you retire, you leave to go into another room, or to bed *E.G. She retired early with a good book.*

**retired** ADJECTIVE   **retirement** NOUN

**retort** retorts retorting retorted

VERB **1** To retort means to reply angrily. ▶ NOUN **2** a short, angry reply.

**retract** retracts retracting retracted

VERB **1** If you retract something you have said, you say that you did not mean it. **2** When something is retracted, it moves inwards or backwards *E.G. The undercarriage was retracted shortly after takeoff.*

**retraction** NOUN   **retractable** ADJECTIVE

**retreat** retreats retreating retreated

VERB **1** To retreat means to move backwards away from something or someone. **2** If you retreat from something difficult or unpleasant, you avoid doing it. ▶ NOUN **3** If an army moves away from the enemy, this is referred to as a retreat. **4** a quiet place that you can go to rest or do things in private.

**retribution**

NOUN; *FORMAL* Retribution is punishment *E.G. the threat of retribution.*

**retrieve** retrieves retrieving retrieved

VERB If you retrieve something, you get it back.

**retrieval** NOUN

**retriever** retrievers

NOUN a large dog often used by hunters to bring back birds and animals which have been shot.

**retro-**

PREFIX 'Retro-' means 'back' or 'backwards' *E.G. retrospective.*

🔲 from Latin *retrō* meaning 'behind' or 'backwards'

**retrospect**

NOUN When you consider something in retrospect, you think about it afterwards and often have a different opinion from the one you had at the time *E.G. In retrospect, I probably shouldn't have resigned.*

**retrospective**

ADJECTIVE **1** concerning things that happened in the past. **2** taking effect from a date in the past.

**retrospectively** ADVERB

**return** returns returning returned

VERB **1** When you return to a place, you go back after you have been away. **2** If you return something to someone, you give it back to them. **3** When you return a ball during a game, you hit it back to your opponent. **4** When a judge or jury returns a verdict, they announce it. ▶ NOUN **5** Your return is your arrival back at a place. **6** The return on an investment is the profit or interest you get from it. **7** a ticket for the journey to a place and back again. ▶ PHRASE **8** If you do something in return for a favour, you do it to repay the favour.

**reunion** reunions

NOUN a party or meeting for people who have not seen each other for a long time.

**reunite** reunites reuniting reunited

VERB If people are reunited, they meet

You must practi**S**e your Ss (practi**s**e)   **SPELLING NOTE**

**rev** revs revving revved *INFORMAL*

VERB 1 When you rev the engine of a vehicle, you press the accelerator to increase the engine speed. ▶ NOUN 2 The speed of an engine is measured in revolutions per minute, referred to as revs *E.G. I noticed that the engine revs had dropped.*

**Rev** or **Revd**

abbreviations for **Reverend**.

**revamp** revamps revamping revamped

VERB To revamp something means to improve or repair it.

**reveal** reveals revealing revealed

VERB 1 To reveal something means to tell people about it *E.G. They were not ready to reveal any of the details.* 2 If you reveal something that has been hidden, you uncover it.

**revel** revels revelling revelled

VERB If you revel in a situation, you enjoy it very much.

**revelry** NOUN

**revelation** revelations

NOUN 1 a surprising or interesting fact made known to people. 2 If an experience is a revelation, it makes you realize or learn something.

**revenge** revenges revenging revenged

NOUN 1 Revenge involves hurting someone who has hurt you. ▶ VERB 2 If you revenge yourself on someone who has hurt you, you hurt them in return.

☰ (sense 1) retaliation, vengeance
☰ (sense 2) avenge, retaliate

**revenue** revenues

NOUN Revenue is money that a government, company, or organization receives *E.G. government tax revenues.*

**revered**

ADJECTIVE If someone is revered, he or she is respected and admired *E.G. He is still revered as the father of the nation.*

**reverence**

NOUN Reverence is a feeling of great respect. *E.G. The prince was treated with great reverence on the royal visit.*

**Reverend**

Reverend is a title used before the name of a member of the clergy *E.G. the Reverend George Young.*

**reversal** reversals

NOUN If there is a reversal of a process or policy, it is changed to the opposite process or policy.

**reverse** reverses reversing reversed

VERB 1 When someone reverses a process, they change it to the opposite process *E.G. They won't reverse the decision to increase prices.* 2 If you reverse the order of things, you arrange them in the opposite order. 3 When you reverse a car, you drive it backwards. ▶ NOUN 4 The reverse is the opposite of what has just been said or done. ▶ ADJECTIVE 5 Reverse means opposite to what is usual or to what has just been described.

**reversible**

ADJECTIVE Reversible clothing can be worn with either side on the outside.

**revert** reverts reverting reverted

VERB; *FORMAL* To revert to a former state or type of behaviour means to go back to it.

again after they have been separated for some time.

**review** reviews reviewing reviewed

NOUN **1** an article or an item on television or radio, giving an opinion of a new book or play. **2** When there is a review of a situation or system, it is examined to decide whether changes are needed. ▶ VERB **3** To review a play or book means to write an account expressing an opinion of it. **4** To review something means to examine it to decide whether changes are needed.

**reviewer** NOUN

≡ (sense 2) examination, survey
≡ (sense 4) reassess, reconsider, revise

**revise** revises revising revised

VERB **1** If you revise something, you alter or correct it. **2** When you revise for an examination, you go over your work to learn things thoroughly.

**revision** NOUN

**revive** revives reviving revived

VERB **1** When a feeling or practice is revived, it becomes active or popular again. **2** When you revive someone who has fainted, they become conscious again.

**revival** NOUN

**revolt** revolts revolting revolted

NOUN (HISTORY) **1** a violent attempt by a group of people to change their country's political system. ▶ VERB **2** When people revolt, they fight against the authority that governs them. **3** If something revolts you, it is so horrible that you feel disgust.

**revolting**

ADJECTIVE horrible and disgusting E.G. The smell in the cell was revolting.

**revolution** revolutions

NOUN **1** (HISTORY) a violent attempt by a large group to change the political

system of their country. **2** an important change in an area of human activity E.G. the Industrial Revolution. **3** one complete turn in a circle.

**revolutionary** revolutionaries

ADJECTIVE **1** involving great changes E.G. a revolutionary new cooling system. ▶ NOUN **2** a person who takes part in a revolution.

**revolve** revolves revolving revolved

VERB **1** If something revolves round something else, it centres on that as the most important thing E.G. My job revolves around the telephone. **2** When something revolves, it turns in a circle around a central point E.G. The moon revolves round the earth.

**revolver** revolvers

NOUN a small gun held in the hand.

**revulsion**

NOUN Revulsion is a strong feeling of disgust or disapproval.

**reward** rewards rewarding rewarded (PSHE)

NOUN **1** something you are given because you have done something good. ▶ VERB **2** If you reward someone, you give them a reward.

**rewarding**

ADJECTIVE Something that is rewarding gives you a lot of satisfaction.

**rewind** rewinds rewinding rewound

VERB To make the tape go backwards on a tape recorder or video.

**rhapsody** rhapsodies

Said "rap-sod-ee" NOUN a short piece of music which is very passionate and flowing.

**rhetoric**

NOUN Rhetoric is speech or writing that is intended to impress people.

a
b
c
d
e
f
g
h
i
j
k
l
m
n
o
p
q
r
s
t
u
v
w
x
y
z

LEarn the principLEs (principle)    SPELLING NOTE

A B C D E F G H I J K L M N O P Q R S T U V W X Y Z

**rhetorical**

ADJECTIVE **1** A rhetorical question is one which is asked in order to make a statement rather than to get an answer. **2** Rhetorical language is intended to be grand and impressive.

**rheumatism**

*Said "room-at-izm"* NOUN Rheumatism is an illness that makes your joints and muscles stiff and painful.
**rheumatic** ADJECTIVE

**rhino rhinos**

NOUN; *INFORMAL* a rhinoceros.

**rhinoceros rhinoceroses**

NOUN a large African or Asian animal with one or two horns on its nose. 📖 from Greek *rhin* meaning 'of the nose' and *keras* meaning 'horn'

**rhododendron rhododendrons**

NOUN an evergreen bush with large coloured flowers.

**rhombus rhombuses or rhombi**

NOUN (MATHS) a shape with four equal sides and no right angles.

**rhubarb**

NOUN Rhubarb is a plant with long red stems which can be cooked with sugar and eaten.

**rhyme rhymes rhyming rhymed**

(ENGLISH) VERB **1** If two words rhyme, they have a similar sound *E.G. Sally rhymes with valley.* ▶ NOUN **2** a word that rhymes with another. **3** a short poem with rhyming lines.

**rhythm rhythms**

NOUN **1** (MUSIC) Rhythm is a regular movement or beat. **2** a regular pattern of changes, for example, in the seasons.
**rhythmic** ADJECTIVE **rhythmically** ADVERB

**rib ribs**

NOUN Your ribs are the curved bones that go from your backbone to your chest.
**ribbed** ADJECTIVE

**ribbon ribbons**

NOUN a long, narrow piece of cloth used for decoration.

**ribcage ribcages**

NOUN Your ribcage is the framework of bones made up of your ribs which protects your internal organs like your heart and lungs.

**rice**

NOUN Rice is a tall grass that produces edible grains. Rice is grown in warm countries on wet ground.

**rich richer richest; riches**

ADJECTIVE **1** Someone who is rich has a lot of money and possessions. **2** Something that is rich in something contains a large amount of it *E.G. Liver is particularly rich in vitamin A.* **3** Rich food contains a large amount of fat, oil, or sugar. **4** Rich colours, smells, and sounds are strong and pleasant. ▶ PLURAL NOUN **5** Riches are valuable possessions or large amounts of money *E.G. the oil riches of the Middle East.*
**richness** NOUN

**richly**

ADVERB **1** If someone is richly rewarded, they are rewarded well with something valuable. **2** If you feel strongly that someone deserves something, you can say it is richly deserved.

**rick ricks**

NOUN a large pile of hay or straw.

**rickets**

NOUN Rickets is a disease that causes soft bones in children if they do not get enough vitamin D.

**rickety**

ADJECTIVE likely to collapse or break E.G. *a rickety wooden jetty*.

**rickshaw** rickshaws

NOUN a hand-pulled cart used in Asia for carrying passengers.

**ricochet** ricochets ricocheting or ricochetting ricocheted or ricochetted

*Said* "rik-osh-ay" VERB When a bullet ricochets, it hits a surface and bounces away from it.

**rid** rids ridding rid

PHRASE 1 When you **get rid** of something you do not want, you remove or destroy it. ▶ VERB 2 FORMAL To rid a place of something unpleasant means to succeed in removing it.

**riddle** riddles

NOUN 1 a puzzle which seems to be nonsense, but which has an entertaining solution. 2 Something that is a riddle puzzles and confuses you.

■ (sense 2) enigma, mystery

**riddled**

ADJECTIVE full of something undesirable E.G. *The report was riddled with errors*.

🏛 from Old English *hriddel* meaning 'sieve'

**ride** rides riding rode ridden

VERB 1 When you ride a horse or a bike, you sit on it and control it as it moves along. 2 When you ride in a car, you travel in it. ▶ NOUN 3 a journey on a horse or bike or in a vehicle.

**rider** riders

NOUN 1 a person riding on a horse or bicycle. 2 an additional statement which changes or puts a condition

on what has already been said.

**ridge** ridges

NOUN 1 a long, narrow piece of high land. 2 a raised line on a flat surface.

**ridicule** ridicules ridiculing ridiculed

VERB 1 To ridicule someone means to make fun of them in an unkind way. ▶ NOUN 2 Ridicule is unkind laughter and mockery.

**ridiculous**

ADJECTIVE very foolish.

**ridiculously** ADVERB

**rife**

ADJECTIVE; FORMAL very common E.G. *Unemployment was rife*.

**rifle** rifles rifling rifled

NOUN 1 a gun with a long barrel. ▶ VERB 2 When someone rifles something, they make a quick search through it to steal things.

**rift** rifts

NOUN 1 a serious quarrel between friends that damages their friendship. 2 a split in something solid, especially in the ground.

**rig** rigs rigging rigged

VERB 1 If someone rigs an election or contest, they dishonestly arrange for a particular person to succeed. ▶ NOUN 2 a large structure used for extracting oil or gas from the ground or sea bed.

**rig up** VERB If you rig up a device or structure, you make it quickly and fix it in place E.G. *They had even rigged up a makeshift aerial*.

**right** rights righting righted

ADJECTIVE or ADVERB 1 correct and in accordance with the facts E.G. *That clock never tells the right time… That's absolutely right*. 2 'Right' means on or towards the right side of something.

a
b
c
d
e
f
g
h
i
j
k
l
m
n
o
p
q
r
s
t
u
v
w
x
y
z

A B C D E F G H I J K L M N O P Q **R** S T U V W X Y Z

▶ ADJECTIVE **3** The right choice or decision is the best or most suitable one. **4** The right people or places are those that have influence or are socially admired E.G. *He was always to be seen in the right places.* **5** The right side of something is the side intended to be seen and to face outwards. ▶ NOUN **6** 'Right' is used to refer to principles of morally correct behaviour E.G. *At least he knew right from wrong.* **7** If you have a right to do something, you are morally or legally entitled to do it. **8** The right is one of the two sides of something. For example, when you look at the word 'to', the 'o' is to the right of the 't'. **9** The Right refers to people who support the political ideas of capitalism and conservatism rather than socialism. ▶ ADVERB **10** 'Right' is used to emphasize a precise place E.G. *I'm right here.* **11** 'Right' means immediately E.G. *I had to decide right then.* ▶ VERB **12** If you right something, you correct it or put it back in an upright position.

**rightly** ADVERB
■ (sense 3) appropriate, proper, suitable
■ (sense 7) prerogative, privilege

**right angle right angles**
NOUN an angle of 90°.

**righteous**
ADJECTIVE Righteous people behave in a way that is morally good and religious.

**rightful**
ADJECTIVE Someone's rightful possession is one which they have a moral or legal right to.
**rightfully** ADVERB

**right-handed**
ADJECTIVE or ADVERB Someone who is

right-handed does things such as writing and painting with their right hand.

**right-wing**
ADJECTIVE believing more strongly in capitalism or conservatism, or less strongly in socialism, than other members of the same party or group.
**right-winger** NOUN

**rigid**
ADJECTIVE **1** Rigid laws or systems cannot be changed and are considered severe. **2** A rigid object is stiff and does not bend easily.
**rigidly** ADVERB **rigidity** NOUN
■ (sense 1) inflexible, strict

**rigorous**
ADJECTIVE very careful and thorough.
**rigorously** ADVERB

**rigour rigours**
NOUN; FORMAL The rigours of a situation are the things which make it hard or unpleasant E.G. *the rigours of childbirth.*

**rim rims**
NOUN the outside or top edge of an object such as a wheel or a cup.

**rimu rimu or rimus**
*Said "ree-moo"* NOUN a New Zealand tree with narrow, pointed leaves, which produces wood used for furniture.

**rind rinds**
NOUN Rind is the thick outer skin of fruit, cheese, or bacon.

**ring rings ringing rang rung**
VERB **1** If you ring someone, you phone them. **2** When a bell rings, it makes a clear, loud sound. **3** To ring something means to draw a circle around it. **4** If something is ringed with something else, it has that thing

all the way around it E.G. *The courthouse was ringed with police.*
► NOUN **5** the sound made by a bell. **6** a small circle of metal worn on your finger. **7** an object or group of things in the shape of a circle. **8** At a boxing match or circus, the ring is the place where the fight or performance takes place. **9** an organized group of people who are involved in an illegal activity E.G. *an international spy ring.*

☑ The past tense of *ring* is *rang*, and the past participle is *rung*. Do not confuse these words: *she rang the bell… I had rung the police.*

**ringbark** ringbarks ringbarking ringbarked
VERB If you ringbark a tree, you kill it by cutting away a strip of bark from around its trunk.

**ringer** ringers
NOUN **1** a person or thing that is almost identical to another. **2** In Australian English, someone who works on a sheep farm. **3** In Australian and New Zealand English, the fastest shearer in a woolshed.

**ring-in** ring-ins
NOUN *INFORMAL* **1** In Australian English, a person or thing that is not normally a member of a particular group. **2** In Australian and New Zealand English, someone who is brought in at the last minute as a replacement for someone else.

**ringleader** ringleaders
NOUN the leader of a group of people who get involved in mischief or crime.

**rink** rinks
NOUN a large indoor area for ice-skating or roller-skating.

**rinse** rinses rinsing rinsed
VERB **1** When you rinse something, you wash it in clean water. ► NOUN **2** a liquid you can put on your hair to give it a different colour.

**riot** riots rioting rioted
NOUN **1** When there is a riot, a crowd of people behave noisily and violently. ► VERB **2** To riot means to behave noisily and violently. ► PHRASE **3** To **run riot** means to behave in a wild and uncontrolled way.

**rip** rips ripping ripped
VERB **1** When you rip something, you tear it violently. **2** If you rip something away, you remove it quickly and violently. ► NOUN **3** a long split in cloth or paper.

**rip off** VERB; *INFORMAL* If someone rips you off, they cheat you by charging you too much money.

**RIP**
RIP is an abbreviation often written on gravestones, meaning 'rest in peace'.

**ripe** riper ripest
ADJECTIVE **1** When fruit or grain is ripe, it is fully developed and ready to be eaten. **2** If a situation is ripe for something to happen, it is ready for it.

**ripeness** NOUN

**ripen** ripens ripening ripened
VERB When crops ripen, they become ripe.

**ripper** rippers
NOUN; *INFORMAL* In Australia and New Zealand English, an excellent person or thing.

**ripple** ripples rippling rippled
NOUN **1** Ripples are little waves on the surface of calm water. **2** If there is a ripple of laughter or applause,

there's SAND in my SANDwich (<u>sand</u>wich)    SPELLING NOTE

A
B
C
D
E
F
G
H
I
J
K
L
M
N
O
P
Q
R
S
T
U
V
W
X
Y
Z

people laugh or applaud gently for a short time. ▶ VERB **3** When the surface of water ripples, little waves appear on it.

**rise** rises rising rose risen
VERB **1** If something rises, it moves upwards. **2** *FORMAL* When you rise, you stand up. **3** To rise also means to get out of bed. **4** When the sun rises, it first appears. **5** The place where a river rises is where it begins. **6** If land rises, it slopes upwards. **7** If a sound or wind rises, it becomes higher or stronger. **8** If an amount rises, it increases. **9** If you rise to a challenge or a remark, you respond to it rather than ignoring it *E.G. He rose to the challenge with enthusiasm.* **10** When people rise up, they start fighting against people in authority. ▶ NOUN **11** an increase. **12** Someone's rise is the process by which they become more powerful or successful *E.G. his rise to fame.*
■ (sense 1) ascend, climb, go up

**riser** risers
NOUN An early riser is someone who likes to get up early in the morning.

**risk** risks risking risked
NOUN **1** a chance that something unpleasant or dangerous might happen. ▶ VERB **2** If you risk something unpleasant, you do something knowing that the unpleasant thing might happen as a result *E.G. If he doesn't play, he risks losing his place in the team.* **3** If you risk someone's life, you put them in a dangerous situation in which they might be killed.

**risky** ADJECTIVE
📖 from Italian *rischiare* meaning 'to be in danger'

**rite** rites
NOUN a religious ceremony.

**ritual** rituals
NOUN **1** a series of actions carried out according to the custom of a particular society or group *E.G. This is the most ancient of the Buddhist rituals.* ▶ ADJECTIVE **2** Ritual activities happen as part of a tradition or ritual *E.G. fasting and ritual dancing.*
**ritualistic** ADJECTIVE

**rival** rivals rivalling rivalled
NOUN **1** Your rival is the person you are competing with. ▶ VERB **2** If something rivals something else, it is of the same high standard or quality *E.G. As a holiday destination, South Africa rivals Kenya for weather.*
■ (sense 1) adversary, opponent

**rivalry** rivalries
NOUN Rivalry is active competition between people.

**river** rivers
NOUN a natural feature consisting of water flowing for a long distance between two banks.

**rivet** rivets
NOUN a short, round pin with a flat head which is used to fasten sheets of metal together.

**riveting**
ADJECTIVE If you find something riveting, you find it fascinating and it holds your attention *E.G. I find tennis riveting.*

**road** roads
NOUN a long piece of hard ground specially surfaced so that people and vehicles can travel along it easily.

**road map** road maps
NOUN **1** a map intended for drivers. **2** a plan or guide for future actions *E.G. a road map for peace.*

**road rage**
NOUN Road rage is aggressive behaviour by a driver as a reaction to the behaviour of another driver.

**road train** road trains
NOUN In Australia, a line of linked trailers pulled by a truck, used for transporting cattle or sheep.

**roadworks**
PLURAL NOUN Roadworks are repairs being done on a road.

**roam** roams roaming roamed
VERB If you roam around, you wander around without any particular purpose E.G. *Hens were roaming around the yard.*

**roar** roars roaring roared
VERB 1 If something roars, it makes a very loud noise. 2 To roar with laughter or anger means to laugh or shout very noisily. 3 When a lion roars, it makes a loud, angry sound. ▶ NOUN 4 a very loud noise.

**roast** roasts roasting roasted
VERB 1 When you roast meat or other food, you cook it using dry heat in an oven or over a fire. ▶ ADJECTIVE 2 Roast meat has been roasted. ▶ NOUN 3 a piece of meat that has been roasted.

**rob** robs robbing robbed
VERB 1 If someone robs you, they steal your possessions. 2 If you rob someone of something they need or deserve, you deprive them of it E.G. *He robbed me of my childhood.*

**robber** robbers
NOUN Robbers are people who steal money or property using force or threats E.G. *bank robbers.*
**robbery** NOUN

**robe** robes
NOUN a long, loose piece of clothing which covers the body E.G. *He knelt in his white robes before the altar.*

**robin** robins
NOUN a small bird with a red breast.

**robot** robots
NOUN a machine which is programmed to move and perform tasks automatically.
📖 from Czech *robota* meaning 'work'

**robust**
ADJECTIVE very strong and healthy.
**robustly** ADVERB

**rock** rocks rocking rocked
NOUN 1 Rock is the hard mineral substance that forms the surface of the earth. 2 a large piece of rock E.G. *She picked up a rock and threw it into the lake.* 3 Rock or rock music is music with simple tunes and a very strong beat. 4 Rock is also a sweet shaped into long, hard sticks, sold in holiday resorts. ▶ VERB 5 When something rocks or when you rock it, it moves regularly backwards and forwards or from side to side E.G. *She rocked the baby.* 6 If something rocks people, it shocks and upsets them E.G. *Palermo was rocked by a crime wave.* 7 If someone's marriage or relationship is **on the rocks**, it is unsuccessful and about to end.

**rock and roll**
NOUN Rock and roll is a style of music with a strong beat that was especially popular in the 1950s.

**rocket** rockets rocketing rocketed
NOUN 1 a space vehicle, usually shaped like a long pointed tube. 2 an explosive missile E.G. *They fired rockets into a number of government buildings.* 3 a firework that explodes when it is high in the air. ▶ VERB 4 If

a b c d e f g h i j k l m n o p q r s t u v w x y z

prices rocket, they increase very quickly.

**rocking chair rocking chairs**
NOUN a chair on two curved pieces of wood that rocks backwards and forwards when you sit in it.

**rock melon rock melons**
NOUN In Australian, New Zealand, and American English a rock melon is a cantaloupe, a melon with orange flesh and a hard, lumpy skin.

**rocky**
ADJECTIVE covered with rocks.

**rod rods**
NOUN a long, thin pole or bar, usually made of wood or metal E.G. *a fishing rod*.

**rodent rodents**
NOUN a small mammal with sharp front teeth which it uses for gnawing.
from Latin *rodere* meaning 'to gnaw'

**rodeo rodeos**
NOUN a public entertainment in which cowboys show different skills.

**roe**
NOUN Roe is the eggs of a fish.

**rogue rogues**
NOUN 1 You can refer to a man who behaves dishonestly as a rogue. ▶ ADJECTIVE 2 a vicious animal that lives apart from its herd or pack.

**role roles**; also spelt **rôle**
NOUN 1 Someone's role is their position and function in a situation or society. 2 (DRAMA) An actor's role is the character that he or she plays E.G. *her first leading role*.

**roll rolls rolling rolled**
VERB 1 When something rolls or when you roll it, it moves along a surface, turning over and over. 2 When

vehicles roll along, they move E.G. *Tanks rolled into the village.* 3 If you roll your eyes, you make them turn up or go from side to side. 4 If you roll something flexible into a cylinder or ball, you wrap it several times around itself E.G. *He rolled up the bag with the money in it.* ▶ NOUN 5 A roll of paper or cloth is a long piece of it that has been rolled into a tube E.G. *a roll of film.* 6 a small, rounded, individually baked piece of bread. 7 an official list of people's names E.G. *the electoral roll.* 8 A roll on a drum is a long, rumbling sound made on it.

**roll-call roll-calls**
NOUN If you take a roll-call, you call a register of names to see who is present.

**roller rollers**
NOUN 1 a cylinder that turns round in a machine or piece of equipment. 2 Rollers are tubes which you can wind your hair around to make it curly.

**Rollerblade Rollerblades**
NOUN; TRADEMARK Rollerblades are roller-skates which have the wheels set in one straight line on the bottom of the boot.

**roller-coaster roller-coasters**
NOUN a pleasure ride at a fair, consisting of a small railway that goes up and down very steep slopes.

**roller-skate roller-skates roller-skating roller-skated**
NOUN 1 Roller-skates are shoes with four small wheels underneath. ▶ VERB 2 If you roller-skate, you move along wearing roller-skates.

**rolling pin rolling pins**
NOUN a wooden cylinder used for rolling pastry dough to make it flat.

## ROM

NOUN In computing, ROM is a storage device that holds data permanently and cannot be altered by the programmer. ROM stands for 'read only memory'.

## Roman Catholic Roman Catholics

ADJECTIVE 1 relating or belonging to the branch of the Christian church that accepts the Pope in Rome as its leader. ▶ NOUN 2 someone who belongs to the Roman Catholic church. **Roman Catholicism** NOUN

## romance romances

NOUN 1 a relationship between two people who are in love with each other. 2 Romance is the pleasure and excitement of doing something new and unusual E.G. *the romance of foreign travel*. 3 (LIBRARY) a novel about a love affair.

## Romanian Romanians

*Said* "roe-**may**-nee-an"; also spelt **Rumanian**

ADJECTIVE 1 belonging or relating to Romania. 2 someone who comes from Romania. 3 Romanian is the main language spoken in Romania.

## romantic romantics

ADJECTIVE or NOUN 1 A romantic person has ideas that are not realistic, for example about love or about ways of changing society E.G. *a romantic idealist*. ▶ ADJECTIVE 2 connected with sexual love E.G. *a romantic relationship*. 3 Something that is romantic is beautiful in a way that strongly affects your feelings E.G. *It is one of the most romantic ruins in Scotland*. 4 Romantic describes a style of music, literature, and art popular in Europe in the late 18th and early 19th centuries, which emphasized feeling and imagination rather than order and form. **romantically** ADVERB **romanticism** NOUN

## rondavel rondavels

NOUN In South Africa, a rondavel is a small circular building with a conical roof.

## roo roos

NOUN; *INFORMAL* In Australian English, a kangaroo.

## roof roofs

NOUN 1 The roof of a building or car is the covering on top of it. 2 The roof of your mouth or of a cave is the highest part.

## roofing

NOUN Roofing is material used for covering roofs.

## rooftop rooftops

NOUN the outside part of the roof of a building.

## rook rooks

NOUN 1 a large black bird. 2 a chess piece which can move any number of squares in a straight but not diagonal line.

## room rooms

NOUN 1 a separate section in a building, divided from other rooms by walls. 2 If there is plenty of room, there is a lot of space E.G. *There wasn't enough room for his gear*.

## roost roosts roosting roosted

NOUN 1 a place where birds rest or build their nests. ▶ VERB 2 When birds roost, they settle somewhere for the night.

## root roots rooting rooted

NOUN 1 The roots of a plant are the

*'i' before 'e' except after 'c'*    **SPELLING NOTE**

a b c d e f g h i j k l m n o p q r s t u v w x y z

A
B
C
D
E
F
G
H
I
J
K
L
M
N
O
P
Q
R
S
T
U
V
W
X
Y
Z

parts that grow under the ground.
**2** The root of a hair is the part beneath the skin. **3** You can refer to the place or culture that you grew up in as your roots. **4** The root of something is its original cause or basis E.G. *We got to the root of the problem.* ▶ VERB **5** To root through things means to search through them, pushing them aside E.G. *She rooted through his bag.*

**root out** VERB If you root something or someone out, you find them and force them out E.G. *a major drive to root out corruption.*

**rooted**
ADJECTIVE developed from or strongly influenced by something E.G. *songs rooted in traditional African music.*

**rope** ropes roping roped
NOUN **1** a thick, strong length of twisted cord. ▶ VERB **2** If you rope one thing to another, you tie them together with rope.

**rosary** rosaries
NOUN a string of beads that Catholics use for counting prayers.

**rose** roses
NOUN **1** a large garden flower which has a pleasant smell and grows on a bush with thorns. ▶ NOUN OR ADJECTIVE **2** reddish-pink.

**rosella** rosellas
NOUN a brightly coloured Australian parrot.

**rosemary**
NOUN Rosemary is a herb with fragrant spiky leaves, used for flavouring in cooking.

**rosette** rosettes
NOUN a large badge of coloured ribbons gathered into a circle, which

is worn as a prize in a competition or to support a political party.

**Rosh Hashanah** or **Rosh Hashana**
NOUN the festival celebrating the Jewish New Year.
📖 a Hebrew phrase meaning 'head of the year'

**roster** rosters
NOUN a list of people who take it in turn to do a particular job E.G. *He put himself first on the new roster for domestic chores.*

**rostrum** rostrums or rostra
NOUN a raised platform on which someone stands to speak to an audience or conduct an orchestra.
📖 from Latin *rostrum* meaning 'ship's prow'; Roman orators' platforms were decorated with the prows of captured ships

**rosy** rosier rosiest
ADJECTIVE **1** reddish-pink. **2** If a situation seems rosy, it is likely to be good or successful. **3** If a person looks rosy, they have pink cheeks and look healthy.

**rot** rots rotting rotted
VERB **1** When food or wood rots, it decays and can no longer be used. **2** When something rots another substance, it causes it to decay E.G. *Sugary drinks rot your teeth.* ▶ NOUN **3** Rot is the condition that affects things when they rot E.G. *The timber frame was not protected against rot.*
📖 (sense 1) decay, decompose

**rota** rotas
NOUN a list of people who take turns to do a particular job.

**rotate** rotates rotating rotated
VERB (MATHS) When something rotates, it turns with a circular movement E.G.

*He rotated the camera 180°.*
**rotation** NOUN

**rotor** rotors
NOUN **1** The rotor is the part of a machine that turns. **2** The rotors or rotor blades of a helicopter are the four long flat pieces of metal on top of it which rotate and lift it off the ground.

**rotten**
ADJECTIVE **1** decayed and no longer of use E.G. *The front bay window is rotten.* **2** *INFORMAL* of very poor quality E.G. *I think it's a rotten idea.* **3** *INFORMAL* very unfair, unkind, or unpleasant E.G. *That's a rotten thing to say!*

**rouble** roubles
*Said* "roo-bl" NOUN the main unit of currency in Russia.
📖 In Russian *rubl* means literally 'silver bar'

**rough** rougher roughest; roughs
*Said* "ruff" ADJECTIVE **1** uneven and not smooth. **2** not using enough care or gentleness E.G. *Don't be so rough or you'll break it.* **3** difficult or unpleasant E.G. *Teachers have been given a rough time.* **4** approximately correct E.G. *At a rough guess it is five times more profitable.* **5** If the sea is rough, there are large waves because of bad weather. **6** A rough town or area has a lot of crime or violence.
▶ NOUN OR ADJECTIVE **7** A rough or a rough sketch is a drawing or description that shows the main features but does not show the details. **8** On a golf course, the rough is the part of the course next to a fairway where the grass has not been cut.
**roughly** ADVERB **roughness** NOUN

**roulette**
*Said* "roo-let" NOUN Roulette is a

gambling game in which a ball is dropped onto a revolving wheel with numbered holes in it.

**round** rounder roundest; rounds rounding rounded
ADJECTIVE **1** Something round is shaped like a ball or a circle. **2** complete or whole E.G. *round numbers.* ▶ PREPOSITION OR ADVERB **3** If something is round something else, it surrounds it. **4** The distance round something is the length of its circumference or boundary E.G. *I'm about two inches larger round the waist.* **5** You can refer to an area near a place as the area round it E.G. *There's nothing to do round here.*
▶ PREPOSITION **6** If something moves round you, it keeps moving in a circle with you in the centre. **7** When someone goes to the other side of something, they have gone round it.
▶ ADVERB OR PREPOSITION **8** If you go round a place, you go to different parts of it to look at it E.G. *We went round the museum.* ▶ ADVERB **9** If you turn or look round, you turn so you are facing in a different direction. **10** When someone comes round, they visit you E.G. *He came round with a bottle of wine.* ▶ NOUN **11** one of a series of events E.G. *After round three, two Americans shared the lead.* **12** If you buy a round of drinks, you buy a drink for each member of the group you are with.
■ (sense 1) globular, spherical
**round up** VERB If you round up people or animals, you gather them together.

**roundabout** roundabouts
NOUN **1** a meeting point of several roads with a circle in the centre

an ELegant angEL (ang**e**l)　▶ SPELLING NOTE

a b c d e f g h i j k l m n o p q **r** s t u v w x y z

which vehicles have to travel around. **2** a circular platform which rotates and which children can ride on in a playground. **3** the same as a merry-go-round.

**rounded**

ADJECTIVE curved in shape, without any points or sharp edges.

**rounders**

NOUN a game played by two teams, in which a player scores points by hitting a ball and running around four sides of a square pitch.

**round-the-clock**

ADJECTIVE happening continuously.

**rouse** rouses rousing roused

VERB **1** If someone rouses you, they wake you up. **2** If you rouse yourself to do something, you make yourself get up and do it. **3** If something rouses you, it makes you feel very emotional and excited.

**rouseabout** rouseabouts

NOUN In Australian and New Zealand English, an unskilled worker who does odd jobs, especially on a farm.

**rout** routs routing routed

*Rhymes with "***out***"* VERB To rout your opponents means to defeat them completely and easily.

**route** routes

*Said "***root***"* NOUN a way from one place to another.

**routine** routines

ADJECTIVE **1** Routine activities are done regularly. ▶ NOUN **2** the usual way or order in which you do things. **3** a boring repetition of tasks.

**routinely** ADVERB

**roving**

ADJECTIVE **1** wandering or roaming *E.G. roving gangs of youths.* **2** not restricted to any particular location

or area *E.G. a roving reporter.*

**row** rows rowing rowed

*Rhymes with "***snow***"* NOUN **1** A row of people or things is several of them arranged in a line. ▶ VERB **2** When you row a boat, you use oars to make it move through the water.

**row** rows rowing rowed

*Rhymes with "***now***"* NOUN **1** a serious argument. **2** If someone is making a row, they are making too much noise. ▶ VERB **3** If people are rowing, they are quarrelling noisily.

**rowdy** rowdier rowdiest

ADJECTIVE rough and noisy.

**royal** royals

ADJECTIVE **1** belonging to or involving a queen, a king, or a member of their family. **2** 'Royal' is used in the names of organizations appointed or supported by a member of a royal family. ▶ NOUN **3** *INFORMAL* Members of the royal family are sometimes referred to as the royals.

◼ (sense 1) imperial, regal

**royalist** royalists

NOUN someone who supports their country's royal family.

**royalty** royalties

NOUN **1** The members of a royal family are sometimes referred to as royalty. **2** Royalties are payments made to authors and musicians from the sales of their books or records.

**rub** rubs rubbing rubbed

VERB If you rub something, you move your hand or a cloth backwards and forwards over it.

**rub out** VERB To rub out something written means to remove it by rubbing it with a rubber or a cloth.

**rubber** rubbers

NOUN **1** Rubber is a strong, elastic

substance used for making tyres, boots, and other products. **2** a small piece of rubber used to rub out pencil mistakes.

**rubbish**

NOUN **1** Rubbish is unwanted things or waste material. **2** You can refer to nonsense or something of very poor quality as rubbish.

◼ (sense 1) garbage, refuse, trash, waste

◼ (sense 2) garbage, nonsense, twaddle

**rubble**

NOUN Bits of old brick and stone are referred to as rubble.

**rubric** rubrics

*Said* "**roo**-brik" NOUN; *FORMAL* a set of instructions at the beginning of an official document.

**ruby** rubies

NOUN a type of red jewel.

**rucksack** rucksacks

NOUN a bag with shoulder straps for carrying things on your back.

**rudder** rudders

NOUN a piece of wood or metal at the back of a boat or plane which is moved to make the boat or plane turn.

**rude** ruder rudest

ADJECTIVE **1** not polite. **2** embarrassing or offensive because of reference to sex or other bodily functions *E.G. rude jokes.* **3** unexpected and unpleasant *E.G. a rude awakening.*

**rudely** ADVERB **rudeness** NOUN

◼ (sense 1) discourteous, ill-mannered, impolite, uncivil

**rudimentary**

ADJECTIVE; *FORMAL* very basic or not developed *E.G. He had only a rudimentary knowledge of French.*

**rudiments**

PLURAL NOUN When you learn the rudiments of something, you learn only the simplest and most basic things about it.

▥ from Latin *rudimentum* meaning 'beginning'

**ruff** ruffs

NOUN **1** a stiff circular collar with many pleats in it, worn especially in the 16th century. **2** a thick band of fur or feathers around the neck of a bird or animal.

**ruffle** ruffles ruffling ruffled

VERB **1** If you ruffle someone's hair, you move your hand quickly backwards and forwards over their head. **2** If something ruffles you, it makes you annoyed or upset. ▶ NOUN **3** Ruffles are small folds made in a piece of material for decoration.

**rug** rugs

NOUN **1** a small, thick carpet. **2** a blanket which you can use to cover your knees or for sitting on outdoors.

**rugby**

NOUN Rugby is a game played by two teams, who try to kick and throw an oval ball to their opponents' end of the pitch. Rugby League is played with 13 players in each side, Rugby Union is played with 15 players in each side.

**rugged**

ADJECTIVE **1** rocky and wild *E.G. the rugged west coast of Ireland.* **2** having strong features *E.G. his rugged good looks.*

**rugger**

NOUN Rugger is the same as rugby.

**ruin** ruins ruining ruined

VERB **1** If you ruin something, you

destroy or spoil it completely. **2** If someone is ruined, they have lost all their money. ► NOUN **3** Ruin is the state of being destroyed or completely spoilt. **4** A ruin or the ruins of something refers to the parts that are left after it has been severely damaged E.G. *the ruins of a thirteenth-century monastery.*

**rule rules ruling ruled**
NOUN **1** Rules are statements which tell you what you are allowed to do. ► VERB **2** To rule a country or group of people means to have power over it and be in charge of its affairs. **3** FORMAL When someone in authority rules on a particular matter, they give an official decision about it. ► PHRASE **4 As a rule,** means usually or generally E.G. *As a rule, I eat my meals in front of the TV.*

▤ (sense 1) law, regulation

**rule out** VERB **1** If you rule out an idea or course of action, you reject it. **2** If one thing rules out another, it prevents it from happening or being possible E.G. *The accident ruled out a future for him in football.*

**ruler rulers**
NOUN **1** a person who rules a country. **2** a long, flat piece of wood or plastic with straight edges marked in centimetres or inches, used for measuring or drawing straight lines.

**rum**
NOUN Rum is a strong alcoholic drink made from sugar cane juice.

**Rumanian**
*Said* "roo-may-nee-an" another spelling of **Romanian.**

**rumble rumbles rumbling rumbled**
VERB **1** If something rumbles, it makes a continuous low noise E.G. *Another train rumbled past the house.* ► NOUN **2** a continuous low noise E.G. *the distant rumble of traffic.*

**rummage rummages rummaging rummaged**
VERB If you rummage somewhere, you search for something, moving things about carelessly.

**rumour rumours rumoured**
NOUN **1** a story that people are talking about, which may or may not be true. ► VERB **2** If something is rumoured, people are suggesting that it is has happened.
▣ from Latin *rumor* meaning 'common talk'
▤ (sense 1) gossip, hearsay, story

**rump rumps**
NOUN **1** An animal's rump is its rear end. **2** Rump or rump steak is meat cut from the rear end of a cow.

**run runs running ran**
VERB **1** When you run, you move quickly, leaving the ground during each stride. **2** If you run away from a place, you leave it suddenly and secretly. **3** If you say that a road or river runs in a particular direction, you are describing its course. **4** If you run your hand or an object over something, you move it over it. **5** If someone runs in an election, they stand as a candidate E.G. *He announced he would run for President.* **6** If you run a business or an activity, you are in charge of it. **7** If you run an experiment, a computer program, or tape, you start it and let it continue E.G. *He ran a series of computer checks.* **8** To run a car means to have it and use it. **9** If you run someone somewhere in a car, you drive them there E.G. *Could you run me up to*

*town?* **10** If you run water, you turn on a tap to make it flow *E.G. We heard him running the kitchen tap.* **11** If your nose is running, it is producing a lot of mucus. **12** If the dye in something runs, the colour comes out when it is washed. **13** If a feeling runs through your body, it affects you quickly and strongly. **14** If an amount is running at a particular level, it is at that level *E.G. Inflation is currently running at 2.6%.* **15** If someone or something is running late, they have taken more time than was planned. **16** If an event or contract runs for a particular time, it lasts for that time. ▶ NOUN **17** If you go for a run, you run for pleasure or exercise. **18** a journey somewhere *E.G. It was quite a run to the village.* **19** If a play or show has a run of a particular length of time, it is on for that time. **20** A run of success or failure is a series of successes or failures. **21** In cricket or baseball, a player scores one run by running between marked places on the pitch after hitting the ball.

▤ (sense 1) dash, race, sprint
▤ (sense 2) bolt, flee

**run out** VERB If you run out of something, you have no more left.
**run over** VERB If someone is run over, they are hit by a moving vehicle.

**runaway runaways**
NOUN a person who has escaped from a place or left it secretly and hurriedly.

**rundown**
ADJECTIVE **1** tired and not well. **2** neglected and in poor condition. ▶ NOUN **3** *INFORMAL* If you give someone the rundown on a situation, you tell them the basic, important facts about it.

**rung rungs**
NOUN The rungs on a ladder are the bars that form the steps.

**runner runners**
NOUN **1** a person who runs, especially as a sport. **2** a person who takes messages or runs errands. **3** A runner on a plant such as a strawberry is a long shoot from which a new plant develops. **4** The runners on drawers and ice skates are the thin strips on which they move.

**runner bean runner beans**
NOUN Runner beans are long green pods eaten as a vegetable, which grow on a climbing plant.

**runner-up runners-up**
NOUN a person or team that comes second in a race or competition.

**running**
ADJECTIVE **1** continuing without stopping over a period of time *E.G. a running commentary.* **2** Running water is flowing rather than standing still.

**runny runnier runniest**
ADJECTIVE **1** more liquid than usual *E.G. Warm the honey until it becomes runny.* **2** If someone's nose or eyes are runny, liquid is coming out of them.

**runt runts**
NOUN The runt of a litter of animals is the smallest and weakest.

**runway runways**
NOUN a long strip of ground used by aeroplanes for taking off or landing.

**rupee rupees**
*Said* "roo-**pee**" NOUN the main unit of currency in India, Pakistan, and some other countries.

**rupture ruptures rupturing ruptured**
NOUN **1** a severe injury in which part

a b c d e f g h i j k l m n o p q **r** s t u v w x y z

of your body tears or bursts open. ▸ VERB 2 To rupture part of the body means to cause it to tear or burst E.G. *a ruptured spleen*.

**rural**
ADJECTIVE (GEOGRAPHY) relating to or involving the countryside.

**ruse** ruses
NOUN; *FORMAL* an action which is intended to trick someone.

**rush** rushes rushing rushed
VERB 1 To rush means to move fast or do something quickly. 2 If you rush someone into doing something, you make them do it without allowing them enough time to think. ▸ NOUN 3 If you are in a rush, you are busy and do not have enough time to do things. 4 If there is a rush for something, there is a sudden increase in demand for it E.G. *There was a rush for tickets*. 5 Rushes are plants with long, thin stems that grow near water.

**rush hour** rush hours
NOUN The rush hour is one of the busy parts of the day when most people are travelling to or from work.

**rusk** rusks
NOUN a hard, dry biscuit given to babies.

**Russian** Russians
ADJECTIVE 1 belonging or relating to Russia. ▸ NOUN 2 someone who comes from Russia. 3 Russian is the main language spoken in Russia.

**rust** rusts rusting rusted
NOUN 1 Rust is a reddish-brown substance that forms on iron or steel which has been in contact with water and which is decaying gradually. ▸ NOUN or ADJECTIVE 2 reddish-brown. ▸ VERB 3 When a metal object rusts, it becomes covered in rust.

**rustic**
ADJECTIVE simple in a way considered to be typical of the countryside E.G. *a rustic old log cabin*.

**rustle** rustles rustling rustled
VERB When something rustles, it makes soft sounds as it moves.
**rustling** ADJECTIVE or NOUN

**rusty** rustier rustiest
ADJECTIVE 1 affected by rust E.G. *a rusty iron gate*. 2 If someone's knowledge is rusty, it is not as good as it used to be because they have not used it for a long time E.G. *My German is a bit rusty these days*.

**rut** ruts
NOUN 1 a deep, narrow groove in the ground made by the wheels of a vehicle. ▸ PHRASE 2 If someone is in a rut, they have become fixed in their way of doing things.

**ruthless**
ADJECTIVE very harsh or cruel E.G. *a ruthless drug dealer*.
**ruthlessness** NOUN **ruthlessly** ADVERB

**rye**
NOUN a type of grass that produces light brown grain.

A B C D E F G H I J K L M N O P Q **R** S T U V W X Y Z

# S s

a
b
c
d
e
f
g
h
i
j
k
l
m
n
o
p
q
r
s
t
u
v
w
x
y
z

> **TIP** Some words which sound as if they begin with *s* actually begin with *c*, for example *city*. Some words which sound as if they begin with *sh* actually begin with *ch*, for example *chivalry*. Other words which sound as if they begin with *s* actually begin with the letters *ps*, for example *psychiatry* and *psychology*.

**Sabbath**
NOUN The Sabbath is the day of the week when members of some religious groups, especially Jews and Christians, do not work.
📖 from Hebrew *shabbath* meaning 'to rest'

**sable** sables
NOUN a very expensive fur used for making coats and hats; also the wild animal from which this fur is obtained.

**sabotage** sabotages sabotaging sabotaged
*Said* "sab-ot-ahj" NOUN 1 the deliberate damaging of things such as machinery and railway lines. ▶ VERB 2 If something is sabotaged, it is deliberately damaged.

**saboteur** NOUN
📖 from French *saboter* meaning 'to spoil through clumsiness'

**sabre** sabres
NOUN 1 a heavy curved sword. 2 a light sword used in fencing.

**saccharine** or **saccharin**
*Said* "sak-er-rine" NOUN a chemical used instead of sugar to sweeten things.

**sachet** sachets
*Said* "sash-ay" NOUN a small closed packet, containing a small amount of something such as sugar or shampoo.

**sack** sacks sacking sacked
NOUN 1 a large bag made of rough material used for carrying or storing goods. ▶ VERB 2 INFORMAL If someone is sacked, they are dismissed from their job by their employer. ▶ PHRASE 3 INFORMAL If someone **gets the sack**, they are sacked by their employer.
🟰 (sense 2) dismiss, fire

**sacrament** sacraments
NOUN an important Christian ceremony such as communion, baptism, or marriage.

**sacred**
*Said* "say-krid" ADJECTIVE holy, or connected with religion or religious ceremonies *E.G. sacred ground.*

**sacrifice** sacrifices sacrificing sacrificed
*Said* "sak-riff-ice" VERB 1 If you sacrifice something valuable or important, you give it up. 2 To sacrifice an animal means to kill it as an offering to a god. ▶ NOUN 3 the killing of an animal as an offering to a god or gods.

**sacrificial** ADJECTIVE
🟰 (sense 1) forfeit, give up

**sacrilege**
*Said* "sak-ril-ij" NOUN Sacrilege is behaviour that shows great disrespect for something holy.

**sacrilegious** ADJECTIVE

you'll brEAK that Electrical Aerial, Kitty (br**eak**)    SPELLING NOTE

**sacrosanct**
*Said* "**sak**-roe-sangkt" ADJECTIVE
regarded as too important to be
criticized or changed E.G. *Freedom of
the press is sacrosanct.*

**sad sadder saddest**
ADJECTIVE **1** If you are sad, you feel
unhappy. **2** Something sad makes
you feel unhappy E.G. *a sad story.*
**sadly** ADVERB **sadness** NOUN
▣ (sense 1) low, melancholy,
unhappy

**sadden saddens saddening
saddened**
VERB If something saddens you, it
makes you feel sad.

**saddle saddles saddling saddled**
NOUN **1** a leather seat that you sit on
when you are riding a horse. **2** The
saddle on a bicycle is the seat. ▶ VERB
**3** If you saddle a horse, you put a
saddle on it.

**sadism**
*Said* "**say**-diz-m" NOUN Sadism is the
obtaining of pleasure, especially
sexual pleasure, from making people
suffer pain or humiliation.
**sadist** NOUN **sadistic** ADJECTIVE
▣ from the Marquis de Sade
(1740–1814), who got his pleasure in
this way

**safari safaris**
NOUN an expedition for hunting or
observing wild animals.
▣ from Swahili *safari* meaning
'journey'

**safari park safari parks**
NOUN a large park where wild animals
such as lions and elephants roam
freely.

**safe safer safest; safes**
ADJECTIVE **1** Something that is safe
does not cause harm or danger. **2** If

you are safe, you are not in any
danger. **3** If it is safe to say
something, you can say it with little
risk of being wrong. ▶ NOUN **4** a strong
metal box with special locks, in
which you can keep valuable things.
**safely** ADVERB **safety** NOUN
▣ (sense 2) out of danger, secure

**safeguard safeguards
safeguarding safeguarded**
VERB **1** To safeguard something means
to protect it. ▶ NOUN **2** a rule or law
designed to protect something or
someone.

**safekeeping**
NOUN If something is given to you for
safekeeping, it is given to you to look
after.

**sag sags sagging sagged**
VERB When something sags, it hangs
down loosely or sinks downwards in
the middle.
**sagging** ADJECTIVE

**saga sagas**
*Said* "**sah**-ga" NOUN a very long story,
usually with many different
adventures E.G. *a saga of rivalry,
honour and love.*
▣ from Old Norse *saga* meaning
'story'

**sage sages**
NOUN **1** LITERARY a very wise person.
**2** Sage is also a herb used for
flavouring in cooking.
▣ sense 1 is from Latin *sapere*
meaning 'to be wise'; sense 2 is from
Latin *salvus* meaning 'healthy',
because of the supposed medicinal
properties of the plant

**Sagittarius**
*Said* "saj-it-**tair**-ee-uss" NOUN
Sagittarius is the ninth sign of the
zodiac, represented by a creature

half-horse, half-man holding a bow and arrow. People born between November 22nd and December 21st are born under this sign.

🏛 from Latin *sagittarius* meaning 'archer'

**sail** sails sailing sailed

NOUN 1 Sails are large pieces of material attached to a ship's mast. The wind blows against the sail and moves the ship. ▸ VERB 2 When a ship sails, it moves across water. 3 If you sail somewhere, you go there by ship.

**sailor** sailors

NOUN a member of a ship's crew.

**saint** saints

NOUN a person who after death is formally recognized by a Christian Church as deserving special honour because of having lived a very holy life.

🏛 from Latin *sanctus* meaning 'holy'

**saintly**

ADJECTIVE behaving in a very good or holy way.

**sake** sakes

PHRASE 1 If you do something **for someone's sake**, you do it to help or please them. 2 You use **for the sake of** to say why you are doing something *E.G. a one-off expedition for interest's sake.*

**salad** salads

NOUN a mixture of raw vegetables.

🏛 from Old Provençal *salar* meaning 'to season with salt'

**salami**

*Said* "sal-**lah**-mee" NOUN Salami is a kind of spicy sausage.

**salary** salaries

NOUN a regular monthly payment to an employee.

🏛 from Latin *salarium* meaning 'money given to soldiers to buy salt'

**sale** sales

NOUN 1 The sale of goods is the selling of them. 2 an occasion when a shop sells things at reduced prices.

▸ PLURAL NOUN 3 The sales of a product are the numbers that are sold.

**salesman** salesmen

NOUN someone who sells products for a company.

**saleswoman** NOUN

**salient**

*Said* "**say**-lee-ent" ADJECTIVE; FORMAL The salient points or facts are the important ones.

**saliva**

*Said* "sal-**live**-a" NOUN Saliva is the watery liquid in your mouth that helps you chew and digest food.

**sallow**

ADJECTIVE Sallow skin is pale and unhealthy.

**salmon** salmons or salmon

*Said* "**sam**-on" NOUN a large edible silver-coloured fish with pink flesh.

**salmonella**

*Said* "sal-mon-**nell**-a" NOUN Salmonella is a kind of bacteria which can cause severe food poisoning.

**salon** salons

NOUN a place where hairdressers work.

**saloon** saloons

NOUN 1 a car with a fixed roof and a separate boot. 2 In America, a place where alcoholic drinks are sold and drunk.

**salt** salts

NOUN 1 Salt is a white substance found naturally in sea water. It is used to flavour and preserve food. 2 a chemical compound formed from an acid base.

a b c d e f g h i j k l m n o p q r **s** t u v w x y z

I want to see (C) your licenCe (licen<u>c</u>e)    SPELLING NOTE

A B C D E F G H I J K L M N O P Q R S T U V W X Y Z

**salty** saltier saltiest
ADJECTIVE containing salt or tasting of salt.

**salute** salutes saluting saluted
NOUN 1 a formal sign of respect. Soldiers give a salute by raising their right hand to their forehead. ▶ VERB 2 If you salute someone, you give them a salute.

**salvage** salvages salvaging salvaged
VERB 1 If you salvage things, you save them, for example from a wrecked ship or a destroyed building. ▶ NOUN 2 You refer to things saved from a wrecked ship or destroyed building as salvage.

**salvation**
NOUN 1 When someone's salvation takes place, they are saved from harm or evil. 2 To be someone's salvation means to save them from harm or evil.

**salvo** salvos or salvoes
NOUN the firing of several guns or missiles at the same time.

**same**
ADJECTIVE OR PRONOUN 1 If two things are the same, they look like one another. 2 Same means just one thing and not two different ones E.G. They were born in the same town.

**Samoan** Samoans
ADJECTIVE 1 belonging or relating to Samoa. ▶ NOUN 2 someone who comes from Samoa.

**sample** samples sampling sampled
NOUN 1 A sample of something is a small amount of it that you can try or test E.G. a sample of new wine.
▶ VERB 2 If you sample something, you try it E.G. I sampled his cooking.

**samurai**
Said "**sam**-oor-eye" NOUN A samurai was a member of an ancient Japanese warrior class.

**sanctimonious**
Said "sank-tim-**moan**-ee-uss" ADJECTIVE pretending to be very religious and virtuous.

**sanction** sanctions sanctioning sanctioned
VERB (PSHE) 1 To sanction something means to officially approve of it or allow it. ▶ NOUN 2 Sanction is official approval of something. 3 a severe punishment or penalty intended to make people obey the law.
4 Sanctions are sometimes taken by countries against a country that has broken international law.

**sanctity**
NOUN If you talk about the sanctity of something, you are saying that it should be respected because it is very important E.G. the sanctity of marriage.

**sanctuary** sanctuaries
NOUN 1 a place where you are safe from harm or danger. 2 a place where wildlife is protected E.G. a bird sanctuary.

**sand** sands sanding sanded
NOUN 1 Sand consists of tiny pieces of stone. Beaches are made of sand.
▶ VERB 2 If you sand something, you rub sandpaper over it to make it smooth.

**sandal** sandals
NOUN Sandals are light shoes with straps, worn in warm weather.

**sandpaper**
NOUN Sandpaper is strong paper with a coating of sand on it, used for rubbing surfaces to make them smooth.

**sandshoe** sandshoes
NOUN In British, Australian, and New Zealand English, a light canvas shoe with a rubber sole.

**sandstone**
NOUN Sandstone is a type of rock formed from sand, often used for building.

**sandwich** sandwiches sandwiching sandwiched
NOUN **1** two slices of bread with a filling between them. ▶ VERB **2** If one thing is sandwiched between two others, it is in a narrow space between them E.G. *a small shop sandwiched between a bar and an office.*
🏛 sense 1 is named after the 4th Earl of Sandwich (1718–1792), for whom they were invented so that he could eat and gamble at the same time

**sandy** sandier sandiest
ADJECTIVE **1** A sandy area is covered with sand. **2** Sandy hair is light orange-brown.

**sane** saner sanest
ADJECTIVE **1** If someone is sane, they have a normal and healthy mind. **2** A sane action is sensible and reasonable.

**sanguine**
*Said* "sang-gwin" ADJECTIVE; FORMAL cheerful and confident.

**sanitary**
ADJECTIVE Sanitary means concerned with keeping things clean and hygienic E.G. *improving the sanitary conditions.*

**sanitary towel** sanitary towels
NOUN Sanitary towels are pads of thick, soft material which women wear during their periods.

**sanitation**
NOUN Sanitation is the process of keeping places clean and hygienic, especially by providing a sewage system and clean water supply.

**sanity**
NOUN Your sanity is your ability to think and act normally and reasonably.

**sap** saps sapping sapped
VERB **1** If something saps your strength or confidence, it gradually weakens and destroys it. ▶ NOUN **2** Sap is the watery liquid in plants.

**sapling** saplings
NOUN a young tree.

**sapphire** sapphires
NOUN a blue precious stone.

**sarcastic**
ADJECTIVE saying or doing the opposite of what you really mean in order to mock or insult someone E.G. *a sarcastic remark.*
**sarcasm** NOUN **sarcastically** ADVERB
🏛 from Greek *sarkazein* meaning 'to tear the flesh'

**sarcophagus** sarcophagi or sarcophaguses
*Said* "sar-kof-fag-uss" NOUN a stone coffin used in ancient times.

**sardine** sardines
NOUN a small edible sea fish.

**sardonic**
ADJECTIVE mocking or scornful E.G. *a sardonic grin.*
**sardonically** ADVERB

**sari** saris
*Said* "sah-ree" NOUN a piece of clothing worn especially by Indian women, consisting of a long piece of material folded around the body.
🏛 a Hindi word

a
b
c
d
e
f
g
h
i
j
k
l
m
n
o
p
q
r
s
t
u
v
w
x
y
z

## sarmie sarmies
NOUN; SLANG In South African English, a sarmie is a sandwich.

## sartorial
ADJECTIVE; FORMAL relating to clothes E.G. sartorial elegance.

## sash sashes
NOUN a long piece of cloth worn round the waist or over one shoulder.
📖 from Arabic *shash* meaning 'muslin'

## Satan
NOUN Satan is the Devil.
📖 from Hebrew *satan* meaning 'to plot against'

## satanic
Said "sa-**tan**-ik" ADJECTIVE caused by or influenced by Satan E.G. satanic forces.

## satchel satchels
NOUN a leather or cloth bag with a long strap.

## satellite satellites
NOUN 1 a spacecraft sent into orbit round the earth to collect information or as part of a communications system. 2 a natural object in space that moves round a planet or star.

## satin satins
NOUN Satin is a kind of smooth, shiny silk.

## satire satires
NOUN Satire is the use of mocking or ironical humour, especially in literature, to show how foolish or wicked some people are.
**satirical** ADJECTIVE

## satisfaction
NOUN Satisfaction is the feeling of pleasure you get when you do something you wanted or needed to do.

## satisfactory
ADJECTIVE acceptable or adequate E.G. a satisfactory explanation.
**satisfactorily** ADVERB

## satisfy satisfies satisfying satisfied
VERB 1 To satisfy someone means to give them enough of something to make them pleased or contented. 2 To satisfy someone that something is the case means to convince them of it. 3 To satisfy the requirements for something means to fulfil them.
**satisfied** ADJECTIVE
■ (sense 1) content, indulge, please

## satisfying
ADJECTIVE Something that is satisfying gives you a feeling of pleasure and fulfilment.

## satsuma satsumas
Said "sat-**soo**-ma" NOUN a fruit like a small orange.

## saturated
ADJECTIVE 1 very wet. 2 If a place is saturated with things, it is completely full of them.
**saturation** NOUN

## Saturday Saturdays
NOUN the day between Friday and Sunday.
📖 from Latin *Saturni dies* meaning 'day of Saturn'

## Saturn
NOUN Saturn is the planet in the solar system which is sixth from the sun.

## sauce sauces
NOUN a liquid eaten with food to give it more flavour.
☑ Do not confuse the spellings of *sauce* and *source*, which can sound very similar.

**saucepan saucepans**
NOUN a deep metal cooking pot with a handle and a lid.

**saucer saucers**
NOUN a small curved plate for a cup.

**saucy saucier sauciest**
ADJECTIVE cheeky in an amusing way.

**Saudi Saudis**
*Rhymes with "cloudy"* ADJECTIVE 1 belonging or relating to Saudi Arabia. ▶ NOUN 2 someone who comes from Saudi Arabia.

**sauna saunas**
*Said "saw-na"* NOUN If you have a sauna, you go into a very hot room in order to sweat, then have a cold bath or shower.
▦ a Finnish word

**saunter saunters sauntering sauntered**
VERB To saunter somewhere means to walk there slowly and casually.

**sausage sausages**
NOUN a mixture of minced meat and herbs formed into a tubular shape and served cooked.

**sauté sautés sautéing or sautéeing sautéed**
*Said "soh-tay"* VERB To sauté food means to fry it quickly in a small amount of oil or butter.

**savage savages savaging savaged**
ADJECTIVE 1 cruel and violent E.G. *savage fighting.* ▶ NOUN 2 If you call someone a savage, you mean that they are violent and uncivilized. ▶ VERB 3 If an animal savages you, it attacks you and bites you.

**savagely** ADVERB
▬ (sense 1) brutal, cruel, vicious

**savagery**
NOUN Savagery is cruel and violent behaviour.

**save saves saving saved**
VERB 1 If you save someone, you rescue them or help to keep them safe E.G. *He saved my life.* 2 If you save something, you keep it so that you can use it later E.G. *He'd saved up enough money for the deposit.* 3 To save time, money, or effort means to prevent it from being wasted E.G. *You could have saved us the trouble.*
▶ PREPOSITION 4 FORMAL Save means except E.G. *I was alone in the house save for a very old woman.*

**saving savings**
NOUN 1 a reduction in the amount of time or money used. ▶ PLURAL NOUN 2 Your savings are the money you have saved.

**saviour saviours**
NOUN 1 If someone saves you from danger, you can refer to them as your saviour. ▶ PROPER NOUN 2 In Christianity, the Saviour is Jesus Christ.

**savour savours savouring savoured**
VERB If you savour something, you take your time with it and enjoy it fully E.G. *These spirits should be sipped and savoured like fine whiskies.*

**savoury**
ADJECTIVE 1 Savoury is salty or spicy. 2 Something that is not very savoury is not very pleasant or respectable E.G. *the less savoury places.*

**saw saws sawing sawed sawn**
1 Saw is the past tense of **see**. NOUN 2 a tool, with a blade with sharp teeth along one edge, for cutting wood. ▶ VERB 3 If you saw something, you cut it with a saw.

I went to see (C) the doctor's new practiCe (practice)　　**SPELLING NOTE**

**sawdust**

NOUN Sawdust is the fine powder produced when you saw wood.

**saxophone saxophones**

NOUN a curved metal wind instrument often played in jazz bands.
🏛 named after Adolphe Sax (1814–1894), who invented the instrument

**say says saying said**

VERB 1 When you say something, you speak words. 2 'Say' is used to give an example E.G. *a maximum fee of, say, a million.* ▶ NOUN 3 If you have a say in something, you can give your opinion and influence decisions.
▤ (sense 1) remark, speak, utter

**saying sayings**

NOUN a well-known sentence or phrase that tells you something about human life.
▤ adage, proverb

**scab scabs**

NOUN a hard, dry covering that forms over a wound.

**scabby** ADJECTIVE

**scaffolding**

NOUN Scaffolding is a framework of poles and boards that is used by workmen to stand on while they are working on the outside structure of a building.

**scald scalds scalding scalded**

*Said "skawld"* VERB 1 If you scald yourself, you burn yourself with very hot liquid or steam. ▶ NOUN 2 a burn caused by scalding.

**scale scales scaling scaled**

NOUN 1 The scale of something is its size or extent E.G. *the sheer scale of the disaster.* 2 a set of levels or numbers used for measuring things. 3 The scale of a map, plan, or model

is the relationship between the size of something in the map, plan, or model and its size in the real world E.G. *a scale of 1:10,000.* 4 (MUSIC) an upward or downward sequence of musical notes. 5 The scales of a fish or reptile are the small pieces of hard skin covering its body. ▶ PLURAL NOUN 6 Scales are a piece of equipment used for weighing things. ▶ VERB 7 If you scale something high, you climb it.

**scalene**

ADJECTIVE A scalene triangle has sides which are all of different lengths.

**scallop scallops**

NOUN Scallops are edible shellfish with two flat fan-shaped shells.

**scalp scalps scalping scalped**

NOUN 1 Your scalp is the skin under the hair on your head. 2 the piece of skin and hair removed when someone is scalped. ▶ VERB 3 To scalp someone means to remove the skin and hair from their head in one piece.

**scalpel scalpels**

NOUN a knife with a thin, sharp blade, used by surgeons.

**scaly**

ADJECTIVE covered with scales.

**scamper scampers scampering scampered**

VERB To scamper means to move quickly and lightly.

**scampi**

PLURAL NOUN Scampi are large prawns often eaten fried in breadcrumbs.

**scan scans scanning scanned**

VERB 1 If you scan something, you look at all of it carefully E.G. *I scanned the horizon to the north-east.* 2 If a machine scans something, it examines it by means of a beam of light or X-rays. ➤ NOUN **3** an examination or search by a scanner *E.G. a brain scan.*

**scandal scandals**
NOUN a situation or event that people think is shocking and immoral.
**scandalous** ADJECTIVE

**Scandinavia**
*Said* "skan-din-**nay**-vee-a" NOUN Scandinavia is the name given to a group of countries in Northern Europe, including Norway, Sweden, Denmark, and sometimes Finland and Iceland.
**Scandinavian** NOUN OR ADJECTIVE

**scanner scanners**
NOUN **1** a machine which is used to examine, identify, or record things by means of a beam of light or X-rays. **2** ICT a machine which converts text or images into a form that can be stored on a computer.

**scant scanter scantest**
ADJECTIVE If something receives scant attention, it does not receive enough attention.

**scapegoat scapegoats**
NOUN If someone is made a scapegoat, they are blamed for something, although it may not be their fault.

**scar scars scarring scarred**
NOUN **1** a mark left on your skin after a wound has healed. **2** a permanent effect on someone's mind that results from a very unpleasant experience *E.G. the scars of war.* ➤ VERB **3** If an injury scars you, it leaves a permanent mark on your skin. **4** If an unpleasant experience scars you, it has a permanent effect on you.

**scarce scarcer scarcest**
ADJECTIVE If something is scarce, there is not very much of it.
**scarcity** NOUN

**scarcely**
ADVERB Scarcely means hardly *E.G. I can scarcely hear her.*
✔ As *scarcely* already has a negative sense, it is followed by *ever* or *any*, and not by *never* or *no*.

**scare scares scaring scared**
VERB **1** If something scares you, it frightens you. ➤ NOUN **2** If something gives you a scare, it scares you. **3** If there is a scare about something, a lot of people are worried about it *E.G. an AIDS scare.*
**scared** ADJECTIVE
▤ (sense 1) alarm, frighten, startle

**scarecrow scarecrows**
NOUN an object shaped like a person put in a field to scare birds away.

**scarf scarfs** OR **scarves**
NOUN a piece of cloth worn round your neck or head to keep you warm.

**scarlet**
NOUN OR ADJECTIVE bright red.

**scary scarier scariest**
ADJECTIVE; INFORMAL frightening.

**scathing**
*Said* "**skayth**-ing" ADJECTIVE harsh and scornful *E.G. They were scathing about his job.*

**scatter scatters scattering scattered**
VERB **1** To scatter things means to throw or drop them all over an area. **2** If people scatter, they suddenly move away in different directions.
▤ (sense 1) sprinkle, strew, throw about

a
b
c
d
e
f
g
h
i
j
k
l
m
n
o
p
q
r
s
t
u
v
w
x
y
z

**scattering**

NOUN A scattering of things is a small number of them spread over a large area E.G. *the scattering of islands*.

**scavenge** scavenges scavenging scavenged

VERB If you scavenge for things, you search for them among waste and rubbish.

**scavenger** NOUN

**scenario** scenarios

Said "sin-**nar**-ee-oh" NOUN 1 (DRAMA) The scenario of a film or play is a summary of its plot. 2 the way a situation could possibly develop in the future E.G. *the worst possible scenario*.

**scene** scenes

NOUN 1 (ENGLISH) (DRAMA) part of a play or film in which a series of events happen in one place. 2 Pictures and views are sometimes called scenes E.G. *a village scene*. 3 The scene of an event is the place where it happened. 4 an area of activity E.G. *the music scene*.

**scenery**

NOUN 1 In the countryside, you can refer to everything you see as the scenery. 2 In a theatre, the scenery is the painted cloth on the stage which represents the place where the action is happening.

**scenic**

ADJECTIVE A scenic place or route has nice views.

**scent** scents scenting scented

NOUN 1 a smell, especially a pleasant one. 2 Scent is perfume. ► VERB 3 When an animal scents something, it becomes aware of it by smelling it.

**sceptic** sceptics

Said "**skep**-tik" NOUN someone who

has doubts about things that other people believe.

**sceptical** ADJECTIVE **scepticism** NOUN

**sceptre** sceptres

Said "**sep**-ter" NOUN an ornamental rod carried by a king or queen as a symbol of power.

**schedule** schedules scheduling scheduled

Said "**shed**-yool" NOUN 1 a plan that gives a list of events or tasks, together with the times at which each thing should be done. ► VERB 2 If something is scheduled to happen, it has been planned and arranged E.G. *Their journey was scheduled for the beginning of May*.

**schema** schemata

Said "**skee**-ma" NOUN 1 TECHNICAL an outline of a plan or theory. 2 a mental model which the mind uses to understand new experiences or to view the world.

**scheme** schemes scheming schemed

NOUN 1 a plan or arrangement E.G. *a five-year development scheme*. ► VERB 2 When people scheme, they make secret plans.

**schism** schisms

Said "**skizm**" NOUN a split or division within a group or organization.

**schizophrenia**

Said "skit-soe-**free**-nee-a" NOUN Schizophrenia is a serious mental illness which prevents someone relating their thoughts and feelings to what is happening around them.

**schizophrenic** NOUN OR ADJECTIVE
🔲 from Greek *skhizein* meaning 'to split' and *phren* meaning 'mind'

**scholar** scholars

NOUN 1 a person who studies an

A B C D E F G H I J K L M N O P Q R S T U V W X Y Z

academic subject and knows a lot about it. **2** In South African English, a scholar is a school pupil.

**scholarly**
ADJECTIVE having or showing a lot of knowledge.

**scholarship scholarships**
NOUN **1** If you get a scholarship to a school or university, your studies are paid for by the school or university or by some other organization. **2** Scholarship is academic study and knowledge.

**school schools schooling schooled**
NOUN **1** a place where children are educated. **2** University departments and colleges are sometimes called schools E.G. *My oldest son is in medical school.* **3** You can refer to a large group of dolphins or fish as a school. ▶ VERB **4** When someone is schooled in something, they are taught it E.G. *They were schooled in the modern techniques.*

**schoolchild schoolchildren**
NOUN Schoolchildren are children who go to school.

**schoolboy** NOUN **schoolgirl** NOUN

**schooling**
NOUN Your schooling is the education you get at school.

**schooner schooners**
NOUN a sailing ship.

**science sciences**
NOUN **1** Science is the study of the nature and behaviour of natural things and the knowledge obtained about them. **2** a branch of science, for example physics or biology.

**science fiction**
NOUN Stories about events happening in the future or in other parts of the universe are called science fiction.

**scientific**
ADJECTIVE **1** relating to science or to a particular science E.G. *scientific knowledge.* **2** done in a systematic way, using experiments or tests E.G. *this scientific method.*
**scientifically** ADVERB

**scientist scientists**
NOUN an expert in one of the sciences who does work connected with it.

**scintillating**
*Said "sin-til-late-ing"* ADJECTIVE lively and witty E.G. *scintillating conversation.*

**scissors**
PLURAL NOUN Scissors are a cutting tool with two sharp blades.

**scoff scoffs scoffing scoffed**
VERB **1** If you scoff, you speak in a scornful, mocking way about something. **2** *INFORMAL* If you scoff food, you eat it quickly and greedily.

**scold scolds scolding scolded**
VERB If you scold someone, you tell them off.
▪ rebuke, reprimand, tell off

**scone scones**
*Said "skon or skone"* NOUN Scones are small cakes made from flour and fat and usually eaten with butter.

**scoop scoops scooping scooped**
VERB **1** If you scoop something up, you pick it up using a spoon or the palm of your hand. ▶ NOUN **2** an object like a large spoon which is used for picking up food such as ice cream.

**scooter scooters**
NOUN **1** a small, light motorcycle. **2** a simple cycle which a child rides by standing on it and pushing the ground with one foot.

**scope**
NOUN **1** If there is scope for doing

a
b
c
d
e
f
g
h
i
j
k
l
m
n
o
p
q
r
**s**
t
u
v
w
x
y
z

something, the opportunity to do it exists. **2** The scope of something is the whole subject area which it deals with or includes.

**-scope**

SUFFIX '-scope' is used to form nouns which refer to an instrument used for observing or detecting E.G. *microscope… telescope.*

🔲 from Greek *skopein* meaning 'to look at'

**scorch scorches scorching scorched** ▸ VERB To scorch something means to burn it slightly.

**scorching**

ADJECTIVE extremely hot E.G. *another scorching summer.*

**score scores scoring scored**

VERB **1** If you score in a game, you get a goal, run, or point. **2** To score in a game also means to record the score obtained by the players. **3** If you score a success or victory, you achieve it. **4** To score a surface means to cut a line into it. ▸ NOUN **5** The score in a game is the number of goals, runs, or points obtained by the two teams. **6** Scores of things means very many of them E.G. *Ros entertained scores of celebrities.* **7** OLD-FASHIONED A score is twenty. **8** (MUSIC) The score of a piece of music is the written version of it.

**scorer** NOUN

**scorn scorns scorning scorned**

NOUN **1** Scorn is great contempt E.G. *a look of scorn.* ▸ VERB **2** FORMAL If you scorn something, you refuse to accept it.

**scornful**

ADJECTIVE showing contempt E.G. *his scornful comment.*

**scornfully** ADVERB

▣ contemptuous, disdainful, sneering

**Scorpio**

NOUN Scorpio is the eighth sign of the zodiac, represented by a scorpion. People born between October 23rd and November 21st are born under this sign.

🔲 from Latin *scorpio* meaning 'scorpion'

**scorpion scorpions**

NOUN an animal that looks like a small lobster, with a long tail with a poisonous sting on the end.

**Scot Scots**

NOUN **1** a person who comes from Scotland. ▸ ADJECTIVE **2** Scots means the same as **Scottish.**

**scotch scotches**

NOUN Scotch is whisky made in Scotland.

**Scotsman Scotsmen**

NOUN a man who comes from Scotland.

**Scotswoman** NOUN

**Scottish**

ADJECTIVE belonging or relating to Scotland.

**scoundrel scoundrels**

NOUN; OLD-FASHIONED a man who cheats and deceives people.

**scour scours scouring scoured**

VERB **1** If you scour a place, you look all over it in order to find something E.G. *The police scoured the area.* **2** If you scour something such as a pan, you clean it by rubbing it with something rough.

**scourge scourges**

*Rhymes with "*u**rge***"* NOUN something that causes a lot of suffering E.G. *hay fever, that scourge of summer.*

**scout** scouts scouting scouted
NOUN **1** a boy who is a member of the Scout Association, an organization for boys which aims to develop character and responsibility. **2** someone who is sent to an area to find out the position of an enemy army. ▶ VERB **3** If you scout around for something, you look around for it.

**scowl** scowls scowling scowled
VERB **1** If you scowl, you frown because you are angry E.G. *They were scowling at me.* ▶ NOUN **2** an angry expression.

**scrabble** scrabbles scrabbling scrabbled
VERB If you scrabble at something, you scrape at it with your hands or feet.
📖 from Old Dutch *schrabbelen* meaning 'to scrape repeatedly'

**scramble** scrambles scrambling scrambled
VERB **1** If you scramble over something, you climb over it using your hands to help you. ▶ NOUN **2** a motorcycle race over rough ground.

**scrap** scraps scrapping scrapped
NOUN **1** A scrap of something is a very small piece of it E.G. *a scrap of cloth.*
▶ PLURAL NOUN **2** Scraps are pieces of leftover food. ▶ ADJECTIVE OR NOUN **3** Scrap metal or scrap is metal from old machinery or cars that can be re-used. ▶ VERB **4** If you scrap something, you get rid of it E.G. *They considered scrapping passport controls.*

**scrapbook** scrapbooks
NOUN a book in which you stick things such as pictures or newspaper articles.

**scrape** scrapes scraping scraped
VERB **1** If you scrape something off a surface, you remove it by pulling a rough or sharp object over it E.G. *to scrape the fallen snow off the track.* **2** If something scrapes, it makes a harsh noise by rubbing against something E.G. *his shoes scraping across the stone ground.*

**scratch** scratches scratching scratched
VERB **1** To scratch something means to make a small cut on it accidentally E.G. *They were always getting scratched by cats.* **2** If you scratch, you rub your skin with your nails because it is itching. ▶ NOUN **3** a small cut.

**scratchcard** scratchcards
NOUN a ticket in a competition with a surface that you scratch off to show whether or not you have won a prize.

**scrawl** scrawls scrawling scrawled
VERB **1** If you scrawl something, you write it in a careless and untidy way.
▶ NOUN **2** You can refer to careless and untidy writing as a scrawl.

**scrawny** scrawnier scrawniest
ADJECTIVE thin and bony E.G. *a small scrawny man.*

**scream** screams screaming screamed
VERB **1** If you scream, you shout or cry in a loud, high-pitched voice. ▶ NOUN **2** a loud, high-pitched cry.
📔 cry, shriek, yell

**screech** screeches screeching screeched
VERB **1** To screech means to make an unpleasant high-pitched noise E.G.

a
b
c
d
e
f
g
h
i
j
k
l
m
n
o
p
q
r
s
t
u
v
w
x
y
z

*The car wheels screeched.* ► NOUN **2** an unpleasant high-pitched noise.

**screen screens screening screened**

NOUN **1** a flat vertical surface on which a picture is shown *E.G. a television screen.* **2** a vertical panel used to separate different parts of a room or to protect something. ► VERB **3** To screen a film or television programme means to show it. **4** If you screen someone, you put something in front of them to protect them.

**screenplay screenplays**

NOUN The screenplay of a film is the script.

**screw screws screwing screwed**

NOUN **1** a small, sharp piece of metal used for fixing things together or for fixing something to a wall. ► VERB **2** If you screw things together, you fix them together using screws. **3** If you screw something onto something else, you fix it there by twisting it round and round *E.G. He screwed the top on the ink bottle.*

**screw up** VERB If you screw something up, you twist it or squeeze it so that it no longer has its proper shape *E.G. Amy screwed up her face.*

**screwdriver screwdrivers**

NOUN a tool for turning screws.

**scribble scribbles scribbling scribbled**

VERB **1** If you scribble something, you write it quickly and roughly. **2** To scribble also means to make meaningless marks *E.G. When Caroline was five she scribbled on a wall.* ► NOUN **3** You can refer to something written or drawn quickly and roughly as a scribble.

**scrimp scrimps scrimping scrimped**

VERB If you scrimp, you live cheaply and spend as little money as you can.

**script scripts**

NOUN (DRAMA) the written version of a play or film.

**scripture scriptures**

NOUN Scripture refers to sacred writings, especially the Bible. **scriptural** ADJECTIVE

**scroll scrolls**

NOUN a long roll of paper or parchment with writing on it.

**scrounge scrounges scrounging scrounged**

VERB; *INFORMAL* If you scrounge something, you get it by asking for it rather than by earning or buying it. **scrounger** NOUN

■ cadge, sponge

**scrub scrubs scrubbing scrubbed**

VERB **1** If you scrub something, you clean it with a stiff brush and water. ► NOUN **2** If you give something a scrub, you scrub it. **3** Scrub consists of low trees and bushes.

**scruff**

NOUN The scruff of your neck is the back of your neck or collar.

**scruffy scruffier scruffiest**

ADJECTIVE dirty and untidy *E.G. four scruffy youths.*

■ tatty, unkempt

**scrum scrums**

NOUN When rugby players form a scrum, they form a group and push against each other with their heads down in an attempt to get the ball.

A B C D E F G H I J K L M N O P Q R S T U V W X Y Z

**scrunchie** scrunchies
NOUN a loop of elastic loosely covered with material which is used to hold hair in a ponytail.

**scruple** scruples
*Said* "**skroo**-pl" NOUN Scruples are moral principles that make you unwilling to do something that seems wrong E.G. *The West must drop its scruples and fight back.*

**scrupulous**
ADJECTIVE 1 always doing what is honest or morally right. 2 paying very careful attention to detail E.G. *a long and scrupulous search.*
**scrupulously** ADVERB

**scrutiny**
NOUN If something is under scrutiny, it is being observed very carefully.

**scuba diving**
NOUN Scuba diving is the sport of swimming underwater with tanks of compressed air on your back.

**scuff** scuffs scuffing scuffed
VERB 1 If you scuff your feet, you drag them along the ground when you are walking. 2 If you scuff your shoes, you mark them by scraping or rubbing them.

**scuffle** scuffles scuffling scuffled
NOUN 1 a short, rough fight. ▶ VERB 2 When people scuffle, they fight roughly.

**scullery** sculleries
NOUN a small room next to a kitchen where washing and cleaning are done.

**sculpt** sculpts sculpting sculpted
VERB When something is sculpted, it is carved or shaped in stone, wood, or clay.

**sculptor** sculptors
NOUN someone who makes sculptures.

**sculpture** sculptures
NOUN 1 a work of art produced by carving or shaping stone or clay. 2 Sculpture is the art of making sculptures.

**scum**
NOUN Scum is a layer of a dirty substance on the surface of a liquid.

**scurrilous**
*Said* "**skur**-ril-luss" ADJECTIVE abusive and damaging to someone's good name E.G. *scurrilous stories.*

**scurry** scurries scurrying scurried
VERB To scurry means to run quickly with short steps.

**scurvy**
NOUN Scurvy is a disease caused by a lack of vitamin C.

**scuttle** scuttles scuttling scuttled
VERB 1 To scuttle means to run quickly. 2 To scuttle a ship means to sink it deliberately by making holes in the bottom. ▶ NOUN 3 a container for coal.

**scythe** scythes
NOUN a tool with a long handle and a curved blade used for cutting grass or grain.

**sea** seas
NOUN 1 The sea is the salty water that covers much of the earth's surface. 2 A sea of people or things is a very large number of them E.G. *a sea of red flags.*

**seagull** seagulls
NOUN Seagulls are common white, grey, and black birds that live near the sea.

**seahorse** seahorses
NOUN a small fish which swims upright, with a head that resembles a horse's head.

a
b
c
d
e
f
g
h
i
j
k
l
m
n
o
p
q
r
s
t
u
v
w
x
y
z

On WEDNESday Wayne WED NESta (<u>Wednes</u>day)    **SPELLING NOTE**

A
B
C
D
E
F
G
H
I
J
K
L
M
N
O
P
Q
R
**S**
T
U
V
W
X
Y
Z

**seal** seals sealing sealed
NOUN **1** an official mark on a document which shows that it is genuine. **2** a piece of wax fixed over the opening of a container. **3** a large mammal with flippers, that lives partly on land and partly in the sea. ▶ VERB **4** If you seal an envelope, you stick down the flap. **5** If you seal an opening, you cover it securely so that air, gas, or liquid cannot get through.

**sea lion** sea lions
NOUN a type of large seal.

**seam** seams
NOUN **1** a line of stitches joining two pieces of cloth. **2** A seam of coal is a long, narrow layer of it beneath the ground.

**seaman** seamen
NOUN a sailor.

**seance** seances
Said "**say-ahnss**"; also spelt **séance**
NOUN a meeting in which people try to communicate with the spirits of dead people.

**search** searches searching searched
VERB **1** If you search for something, you look for it in several places. **2** If a person is searched their body and clothing is examined to see if they are hiding anything. ▶ NOUN **3** an attempt to find something.
■ (sense 1) hunt, look, scour
■ (sense 3) look, hunt, quest

**search engine** search engines
NOUN a service on the Internet which enables users to search for items of interest.

**searching**
ADJECTIVE intended to discover the truth about something E.G. searching questions.

**searchlight** searchlights
NOUN a powerful light whose beam can be turned in different directions.

**searing**
ADJECTIVE A searing pain is very sharp.

**seashore**
NOUN The seashore is the land along the edge of the sea.

**seasick**
ADJECTIVE feeling sick because of the movement of a boat.
**seasickness** NOUN

**seaside**
NOUN The seaside is an area next to the sea.

**season** seasons seasoning seasoned
NOUN **1** The seasons are the periods into which a year is divided and which have their own typical weather conditions. The seasons are spring, summer, autumn, and winter. **2** a period of the year when something usually happens E.G. the football season… the hunting season. ▶ VERB **3** If you season food, you add salt, pepper, or spices to it.

**seasonal**
ADJECTIVE happening during one season or one time of the year E.G. seasonal work.

**seasoned**
ADJECTIVE very experienced E.G. a seasoned professional.

**seasoning**
NOUN Seasoning is flavouring such as salt and pepper.

**season ticket** season tickets
NOUN a train or bus ticket that you can use as many times as you like within a certain period.

**seat** seats seating seated
NOUN **1** something you can sit on.

**2** The seat of a piece of clothing is the part that covers your bottom. **3** If someone wins a seat in parliament, they are elected. ▶ VERB **4** If you seat yourself somewhere, you sit down. **5** If a place seats a particular number of people, it has enough seats for that number E.G. *The theatre seats 570 people*.

**seat belt** seat belts
NOUN a strap that you fasten across your body for safety when travelling in a car or an aircraft.

**seating**
NOUN The seating in a place is the number or arrangement of seats there.

**seaweed**
NOUN Plants that grow in the sea are called seaweed.

**secateurs**
*Said "sek-at-turz"* PLURAL NOUN Secateurs are small shears for pruning garden plants.

**secluded**
ADJECTIVE quiet and hidden from view E.G. *a secluded beach*.
**seclusion** NOUN

**second** seconds seconding seconded
ADJECTIVE **1** The second item in a series is the one counted as number two. ▶ NOUN **2** one of the sixty parts that a minute is divided into. ▶ PLURAL NOUN **3** Seconds are goods that are sold cheaply because they are slightly faulty. ▶ VERB **4** If you second a proposal, you formally agree with it so that it can be discussed or voted on. **5** If you are seconded somewhere, you are sent there temporarily to work.
**secondly** ADVERB

☑ Senses 1–4 are pronounced "**seck**-ond", but sense 5 is pronounced "sick-**kond**".

**secondary**
ADJECTIVE **1** Something that is secondary is less important than something else. **2** Secondary education is education for pupils between the ages of eleven and eighteen.

**secondary school** secondary schools
NOUN a school for pupils between the ages of eleven and eighteen.

**second-class**
ADJECTIVE **1** Second-class things are regarded as less important than other things of the same kind E.G. *He has been treated as a second-class citizen*. ▶ ADJECTIVE OR ADVERB **2** Second-class services are cheaper and therefore slower or less comfortable than first-class ones.

**second cousin** second cousins
NOUN Your second cousins are the children of your parents' cousins.

**second-hand**
ADJECTIVE OR ADVERB **1** Something that is second-hand has already been owned by someone else E.G. *a second-hand car*. **2** If you hear a story second-hand, you hear it indirectly, rather than from the people involved.

**second-rate**
ADJECTIVE of poor quality E.G. *a second-rate movie*.

**secret** secrets
ADJECTIVE **1** Something that is secret is told to only a small number of people and hidden from everyone else E.G. *a secret meeting*. ▶ NOUN **2** a fact told to only a small number of

**secretly** ADVERB   **secrecy** NOUN ■ (sense 1) confidential, concealed, hidden

**secret agent** secret agents
NOUN a spy.

**secretary** secretaries
NOUN 1 a person employed by an organization to keep records, write letters, and do office work. 2 Ministers in charge of some government departments are also called secretaries E.G. the Health Secretary.
**secretarial** ADJECTIVE

**secrete** secretes secreting secreted
Said "sik-**kreet**" VERB 1 When part of a plant or animal secretes a liquid, it produces it. 2 FORMAL If you secrete something somewhere, you hide it.
**secretion** NOUN

**secretive**
ADJECTIVE Secretive people tend to hide their feelings and intentions. ■ reticent, tight-lipped

**secret service**
NOUN A country's secret service is the government department in charge of espionage.

**sect** sects
NOUN a religious or political group which has broken away from a larger group.

**sectarian**
Said "sek-**tair**-ee-an" ADJECTIVE strongly supporting a particular sect E.G. sectarian violence.

**section** sections
NOUN (LIBRARY) A section of something is one of the parts it is divided into E.G. this section of the motorway.

■ part, portion, segment

**sector** sectors
NOUN 1 A sector of something, especially a country's economy, is one part of it E.G. the private sector. 2 A sector of a circle is one of the two parts formed when you draw two straight lines from the centre to the circumference.

**secular**
ADJECTIVE having no connection with religion E.G. secular education.

**secure** secures securing secured
VERB 1 FORMAL If you secure something, you manage to get it E.G. They secured the rights to her story. 2 If you secure a place, you make it safe from harm or attack. 3 To secure something also means to fasten it firmly E.G. One end was secured to the pier. ▶ ADJECTIVE 4 If a place is secure, it is tightly locked or well protected. 5 If an object is secure, it is firmly fixed in place. 6 If you feel secure, you feel safe and confident.
**securely** ADVERB

**security**
NOUN OR ADJECTIVE 1 Security means all the precautions taken to protect a place E.G. Security forces arrested one member. ▶ NOUN 2 A feeling of security is a feeling of being safe.

**sedate** sedates sedating sedated
Said "sid-**date**" ADJECTIVE 1 quiet and dignified. ▶ VERB 2 To sedate someone means to give them a drug to calm them down or make them sleep.
**sedately** ADVERB

**sedative** sedatives
Said "**sed**-at-tiv" NOUN 1 a drug that calms you down or makes you sleep.

ABCDEFGHIJKLMNOPQRSTUVWXYZ

▶ ADJECTIVE **2** having a calming or soothing effect E.G. *antihistamines which have a sedative effect.*
**sedation** NOUN

**sedentary**
*Said "sed-en-tree"* ADJECTIVE A sedentary occupation is one in which you spend most of your time sitting down.

**sediment**
NOUN **1** Sediment is solid material that settles at the bottom of a liquid E.G. *a bottle of beer with sediment in it is usually a guarantee of quality.* **2** Sediment is also small particles of rock that have been worn down and deposited together by water, ice, and wind.

**sedimentary**
ADJECTIVE Sedimentary rocks are formed from fragments of shells or rocks that have become compressed. Sandstone and limestone are sedimentary rocks.

**seduce seduces seducing seduced**
VERB **1** To seduce someone means to persuade them to have sex. **2** If you are seduced into doing something, you are persuaded to do it because it seems very attractive.

**seductive**
ADJECTIVE **1** A seductive person is sexually attractive. **2** Something seductive is very attractive and tempting.
**seductively** ADVERB

**see sees seeing saw seen**
VERB **1** If you see something, you are looking at it or you notice it. **2** If you see someone, you visit them or meet them E.G. *I went to see my dentist.* **3** If you see someone to a place, you accompany them there. **4** To see something also means to realize or understand it E.G. *I see what you mean.* **5** If you say you will see what is happening, you mean you will find out. **6** If you say you will see if you can do something, you mean you will try to do it. **7** If you see that something is done, you make sure that it is done. **8** If you see to something, you deal with it. **9** 'See' is used to say that an event takes place during a particular period of time E.G. *The next couple of years saw two momentous developments.* ▶ PHRASES **10** INFORMAL **Seeing that** or **seeing as** means because E.G. *I took John for lunch, seeing as it was his birthday.* ▶ NOUN **11** A bishop's see is his diocese.
■ (sense 1) notice, perceive, spot

**seed seeds**
NOUN **1** The seeds of a plant are the small, hard parts from which new plants can grow. **2** The seeds of a feeling or process are its beginning or origins E.G. *the seeds of mistrust.*

**seedling seedlings**
NOUN a young plant grown from a seed.

**seedy seedier seediest**
ADJECTIVE untidy and shabby E.G. *a seedy hotel.*

**seek seeks seeking sought**
VERB FORMAL **1** To seek something means to try to find it, obtain it, or achieve it E.G. *The police were still seeking information.* **2** If you seek to do something, you try to do it E.G. *De Gaulle sought to reunite the country.*

**seem seems seeming seemed**
VERB If something seems to be the

a b c d e f g h i j k l m n o p q r s t u v w x y z

case, it appears to be the case or you think it is the case E.G. *He seemed such a quiet chap.*

**seeming**

ADJECTIVE appearing to be real or genuine E.G. *this seeming disregard for human life.*

**seemingly** ADVERB

**seep** seeps seeping seeped

VERB If a liquid or gas seeps through something, it flows through very slowly.

**seesaw** seesaws

NOUN a long plank, supported in the middle, on which two children sit, one on each end, and move up and down in turn.

**seething**

ADJECTIVE If you are seething about something, you are very angry but it does not show.

**segment** segments

NOUN 1 A segment of something is one part of it. 2 The segments of an orange or grapefruit are the sections which you can divide it into. 3 A segment of a circle is one of the two parts formed when you draw a straight line across it.

**segregate** segregates segregating segregated

VERB To segregate two groups of people means to keep them apart from each other.

**segregated** ADJECTIVE **segregation** NOUN

**seize** seizes seizing seized

VERB 1 If you seize something, you grab it firmly E.G. *He seized the phone.* 2 To seize a place or to seize control of it means to take control of it quickly and suddenly. 3 If you seize an opportunity, you take advantage

of it. 4 If you seize on something, you immediately show great interest in it E.G. *MPs have seized on a new report.*

**seizure** seizures

Said "*seez-yer*" NOUN 1 a sudden violent attack of an illness, especially a heart attack or a fit. 2 If there is a seizure of power, a group of people suddenly take control using force.

**seldom**

ADVERB not very often E.G. *They seldom speak to each other.*

**select** selects selecting selected

VERB 1 If you select something, you choose it. ▶ ADJECTIVE 2 of good quality E.G. *a select gentlemen's club.*

**selector** NOUN

**selection** selections

NOUN 1 Selection is the choosing of people or things E.G. *the selection of parliamentary candidates.* 2 A selection of people or things is a set of them chosen from a larger group. 3 The selection of goods in a shop is the range of goods available E.G. *a good selection of wines.*

**selective**

ADJECTIVE choosing things carefully E.G. *I am selective about what I eat.*

**selectively** ADVERB

**self** selves

NOUN Your self is your basic personality or nature E.G. *Hershey is her normal dependable self.*

**self-**

PREFIX 1 done to yourself or by yourself E.G. *self-help… self-control.* 2 doing something automatically E.G. *a self-loading rifle.*

**self-assured**

ADJECTIVE behaving in a way that shows confidence in yourself.

**self-centred**

ADJECTIVE thinking only about yourself and not about other people.

**self-confessed**

ADJECTIVE admitting to having bad habits or unpopular opinions E.G. *a self-confessed liar*.

**self-confident**

ADJECTIVE confident of your own abilities or worth.
self-confidence NOUN

**self-conscious**

ADJECTIVE nervous and easily embarrassed, and worried about what other people think of you.
self-consciously ADVERB

**self-control**

NOUN Self-control is the ability to restrain yourself and not show your feelings.

**self-defence**

NOUN Self-defence is the use of special physical techniques to protect yourself when someone attacks you.

**self-employed**

ADJECTIVE working for yourself and organizing your own finances, rather than working for an employer.

**self-esteem**

NOUN Your self-esteem is your good opinion of yourself.

**self-evident**

ADJECTIVE Self-evident facts are completely obvious and need no proof or explanation.

**self-indulgent**

ADJECTIVE allowing yourself to do or have things you enjoy, especially as a treat.

**self-interest**

NOUN If you do something out of self-interest, you do it for your own benefit rather than to help other people.

**selfish**

ADJECTIVE caring only about yourself, and not about other people.
selfishly ADVERB selfishness NOUN

**selfless**

ADJECTIVE putting other people's interests before your own.

**self-made**

ADJECTIVE rich and successful through your own efforts E.G. *a self-made man*.

**self-raising**

ADJECTIVE Self-raising flour contains baking powder to make it rise.

**self-respect**

NOUN Self-respect is a feeling of confidence and pride in your own abilities and worth.

**self-righteous**

ADJECTIVE convinced that you are better or more virtuous than other people.
self-righteousness NOUN
▤ holier-than-thou, sanctimonious

**self-service**

ADJECTIVE A self-service shop or restaurant is one where you serve yourself.

**self-sufficient**

ADJECTIVE 1 producing or making everything you need, and so not needing to buy things. 2 able to live in a way in which you do not need other people.

**sell sells selling sold**

VERB 1 If you sell something, you let someone have it in return for money. 2 If a shop sells something, it has it available for people to buy E.G. *a tobacconist that sells stamps*. 3 If something sells, people buy it E.G. *This book will sell*.

a
b
c
d
e
f
g
h
i
j
k
l
m
n
o
p
q
r
s
t
u
v
w
x
y
z

LEt's measure the angLE (ang*le*)  SPELLING NOTE

A
B
C
D
E
F
G
H
I
J
K
L
M
N
O
P
Q
R
**S**
T
U
V
W
X
Y
Z

■ (sense 2) deal in, retail, stock

**sell out** VERB If a shop has sold out of something, it has sold it all.
**seller** NOUN

**Sellotape**
NOUN; _TRADEMARK_ Sellotape is a transparent sticky tape.

**semblance**
NOUN If there is a semblance of something, it seems to exist, although it might not really exist _E.G. an effort to restore a semblance of normality._

**semen**
_Said "see-men"_ NOUN Semen is the liquid containing sperm produced by a man's or male animal's sex organs.

**semi-**
PREFIX 'Semi-' means half or partly _E.G. semiskilled workers._
▥ from Latin _semi-_ meaning 'half' or 'partly'

**semibreve semibreves**
NOUN (MUSIC) a musical note (𝅝) which can be divided by any power of 2 to give all other notes. In the United States and Canada, a semibreve is known as a whole note.

**semicircle semicircles**
NOUN a half of a circle, or something with this shape.
**semicircular** ADJECTIVE

**semicolon semicolons**
NOUN the punctuation mark (;), used to separate different parts of a sentence or to indicate a pause. → SEE BOX OPPOSITE

**semidetached**
ADJECTIVE A semidetached house is joined to another house on one side.

**semifinal semifinals**
NOUN The semifinals are the two

matches in a competition played to decide who plays in the final.
**semifinalist** NOUN

---

### What does the Semicolon do?

The **semicolon** (;) and the **colon** (:) are often confused and used incorrectly.

The **semicolon** is stronger than a comma, but weaker than a full stop. It can be used to mark the break between two main clauses, especially where there is balance or contrast between them:

> _E.G. I'm not that interested in jazz; I prefer classical music._

The semicolon can also be used instead of a comma to separate clauses or items in a long list:

> _E.G. They did not enjoy the meal: the food was cold; the service was poor; and the music was too loud._

Also look at the grammar box at **colon**.

---

**seminar seminars**
NOUN a meeting of a small number of university students or teachers to discuss a particular topic.

**semipermeable**
ADJECTIVE A semipermeable material is one that certain substances with small enough molecules can pass through but which others with larger molecules can not.

**semiprecious**
ADJECTIVE Semiprecious stones are stones such as opals or turquoises that are used in jewellery. They are less valuable than precious stones.

**semitone** semitones

NOUN (MUSIC) an interval representing the difference in pitch between a note and its sharpened or flattened equivalent. Two semitones are equal to one tone.

**Senate** Senates

NOUN The Senate is the smaller, more important of the two councils in the government of some countries, for example Australia, Canada, and the USA.

**senator** senators

NOUN a member of a Senate.

**send** sends sending sent

VERB 1 If you send something to someone, you arrange for it to be delivered to them. 2 To send a radio signal or message means to transmit it. 3 If you send someone somewhere, you tell them to go there or arrange for them to go. 4 If you send for someone, you send a message asking them to come and see you. 5 If you send off for something, you write and ask for it to be sent to you. 6 To send people or things in a particular direction means to make them move in that direction E.G. It should have sent him tumbling from the saddle.

■ (sense 1) direct, dispatch, forward

**senile**

ADJECTIVE If old people become senile, they become confused and cannot look after themselves.

**senility** NOUN

**senior** seniors

ADJECTIVE 1 The senior people in an organization or profession have the highest and most important jobs. ▶ NOUN 2 Someone who is your senior is older than you.

**seniority** NOUN

**senior citizen** senior citizens

NOUN an elderly person, especially one receiving an old-age pension.

**sensation** sensations

NOUN 1 a feeling, especially a physical feeling. 2 If something is a sensation, it causes great excitement and interest.

**sensational**

ADJECTIVE 1 causing great excitement and interest. 2 INFORMAL extremely good E.G. a sensational party.

**sensationally** ADVERB

**sense** senses sensing sensed

NOUN 1 Your senses are the physical abilities of sight, hearing, smell, touch, and taste. 2 a feeling E.G. a sense of guilt. 3 A sense of a word is one of its meanings. 4 Sense is the ability to think and behave sensibly. ▶ VERB 5 If you sense something, you become aware of it. ▶ PHRASE 6 If something makes sense, you can understand it or it seems sensible E.G. It makes sense to find out as much as you can.

**senseless**

ADJECTIVE 1 A senseless action has no meaning or purpose E.G. senseless destruction. 2 If someone is senseless, they are unconscious.

**sensibility** sensibilities

NOUN Your sensibility is your ability to experience deep feelings E.G. a man of sensibility rather than reason.

**sensible**

ADJECTIVE showing good sense and judgment.

**sensibly** ADVERB

■ prudent, rational, wise

**sensitive**

ADJECTIVE 1 If you are sensitive to other

a b c d e f g h i j k l m n o p q r s t u v w x y z

people's feelings, you understand them. **2** If you are sensitive about something, you are worried or easily upset about it *E.G. He was sensitive about his height.* **3** A sensitive subject or issue needs to be dealt with carefully because it can make people angry or upset. **4** Something that is sensitive to a particular thing is easily affected or harmed by it.
**sensitively** ADVERB **sensitivity** NOUN

**sensor** sensors
NOUN (ICT) an instrument which reacts to physical conditions such as light or heat.

**sensual**
*Said "senss-yool"* ADJECTIVE **1** showing or suggesting a liking for sexual pleasures *E.G. He was a very sensual person.* **2** giving pleasure to your physical senses rather than to your mind *E.G. the sensual rhythm of his voice.*
**sensuality** NOUN

**sensuous**
ADJECTIVE giving pleasure through the senses.
**sensuously** ADVERB

**sentence** sentences sentencing sentenced
NOUN **1** a group of words which make a statement, question, or command. When written down a sentence begins with a capital letter and ends with a full stop. **2** In a law court, a sentence is a punishment given to someone who has been found guilty. ▶ VERB **3** When a guilty person is sentenced, they are told officially what their punishment will be.
→ SEE BOX OPPOSITE.

**sentiment** sentiments
NOUN **1** a feeling, attitude, or opinion *E.G. I doubt my parents share my sentiments.* **2** Sentiment consists of feelings such as tenderness or sadness *E.G. There's no room for sentiment in business.*

**sentimental**
ADJECTIVE **1** feeling or expressing tenderness or sadness to an exaggerated extent *E.G. sentimental love stories.* **2** relating to a person's emotions *E.G. things of sentimental value.*
**sentimentality** NOUN
◾ (sense 1) emotional, romantic, slushy

**sentinel** sentinels
NOUN; *OLD-FASHIONED* a sentry.

**sentry** sentries
NOUN a soldier who keeps watch and guards a camp or building.

**separate** separates separating separated
ADJECTIVE **1** If something is separate from something else, the two things are not connected. ▶ VERB **2** To separate people or things means to cause them to be apart from each other. **3** If people or things separate, they move away from each other. **4** If a married couple separate, they decide to live apart.
**separately** ADVERB **separation** NOUN
◾ (sense 2) divide, split, part
◾ (sense 3) diverge, part, part company

**sepia**
*Said "see-pee-a"* ADJECTIVE or NOUN deep brown, like the colour of old photographs.
▦ from Latin *sepia* meaning 'cuttlefish', because the brown dye is obtained from the ink of this fish

### What is a Sentence?

The different types of word can go together to make sentences. A sentence is a group of words which expresses an idea or describes a situation.

Sentences begin with a **capital letter**:

*E.G. The child was sleeping.*

Sentences usually end with a **full stop**:

*E.G. Anna lives in Lisbon.*

If a sentence is a question, it ends with a **question mark** instead of a full stop:

*E.G. Where is my purse?*

If a sentence is an exclamation of surprise, anger, or excitement, it ends with an **exclamation mark** instead of a full stop:

*E.G. You must be joking!*

Sentences have a **subject**, which indicates a person or thing. The rest of the sentence usually says something about the subject. The subject is usually the first word or group of words in a sentence:

*E.G. **Anna** laughed.*
*    **Robbie** likes bananas.*

Most sentences have a **verb**. The verb says what the subject of the sentence is doing or what is happening to the subject. The verb usually follows immediately after the subject:

*E.G. Matthew **smiled**.*

### Simple, Compound and Complex Sentences

**Simple sentences** consist of only one main clause, and no subordinate clause:

*E.G. Anna fed the cat.*

The **subject** of a simple sentence is the person or thing that the sentence is about. It usually comes at the start of the sentence. The subject may be a noun, a pronoun, or a noun phrase:

*E.G. **We** often go to the cinema.*

The remaining part of the sentence is called the **predicate**. The predicate says something about the subject:

*E.G. Anna **likes to go swimming**.*
*    She **is a strong swimmer**.*
*    A ginger cat **was sitting on the stair**.*

**Compound sentences** consist of two or more main clauses joined together by a conjunction. Both clauses are equally important:

*E.G. Anna likes to go swimming, but Matthew likes to go fishing.*

**Complex sentences** consist of a main clause with one or more subordinate clauses joined to it. Numerous subordinate clauses can be added to a main clause:

*E.G. **After looking at all the pictures**, the judges gave the first prize, **which was a silver trophy**, to Robbie, **because his work was the best**.*

a b c d e f g h i j k l m n o p q r **s** t u v w x y z

## September

NOUN September is the ninth month of the year. It has 30 days.
🏛 from Latin *September* meaning 'the seventh month'

## septic

ADJECTIVE If a wound becomes septic, it becomes infected with poison.

there's a rAKE in the brAKEs (br<u>ake</u>)    **SPELLING NOTE**

**sepulchre** sepulchres
*Said* "**sep**-pul-ka" NOUN; *LITERARY* a large tomb.

**sequel** sequels
NOUN **1** A sequel to a book or film is another book or film which continues the story. **2** The sequel to an event is a result or consequence of it *E.G. There's a sequel to my egg story.*

**sequence** sequences
NOUN **1** A sequence of events is a number of them coming one after the other *E.G. the whole sequence of events that had brought me to this place.* **2** The sequence in which things are arranged is the order in which they are arranged *E.G. Do things in the right sequence.*

**sequin** sequins
NOUN Sequins are small, shiny, coloured discs sewn on clothes to decorate them.

**Serbian** Serbians
ADJECTIVE **1** belonging to or relating to Serbia. ▶ NOUN **2** someone who comes from Serbia. **3** Serbian is the form of Serbo-Croat spoken in Serbia.

**Serbo-Croat**
*Said* "ser-boh-**kroh**-at" NOUN Serbo-Croat is the main language spoken in Serbia and Croatia.

**serenade** serenades serenading serenaded
VERB **1** If you serenade someone you love, you sing or play music to them outside their window. ▶ NOUN **2** a song sung outside a woman's window by a man who loves her.

**serene**
ADJECTIVE peaceful and calm *E.G. She had a serene air.*
**serenely** ADVERB **serenity** NOUN

**serf** serfs
NOUN Serfs were servants in medieval Europe who had to work on their master's land and could not leave without his permission.

**sergeant** sergeants
NOUN **1** a noncommissioned officer of middle rank in the army or air force. **2** a police officer just above a constable in rank.

**sergeant major** sergeant majors
NOUN a noncommissioned army officer of the highest rank.

**serial** serials
NOUN a story which is broadcast or published in a number of parts over a period of time *E.G. a television serial.*

**serial number** serial numbers
NOUN An object's serial number is a number you can see on it which identifies it and distinguishes it from other objects of the same kind.

**series**
NOUN **1** (LIBRARY) A series of things is a number of them coming one after the other *E.G. a series of loud explosions.* **2** A radio or television series is a set of programmes with the same title.
■ (sense 1) sequence, set, succession

**serious**
ADJECTIVE **1** A serious problem or situation is very bad and worrying. **2** Serious matters are important and should be thought about carefully. **3** If you are serious about something, you are sincere about it *E.G. You are really serious about having a baby.* **4** People who are serious are

thoughtful, quiet, and do not laugh much.

**seriousness** NOUN

■ (sense 1) grave, severe

■ (sense 4) grave, solemn

**seriously**

ADVERB **1** You say seriously to emphasize that you mean what you say *E.G. Seriously, though, something must be done.* ▶ PHRASE **2** If you **take something seriously**, you regard it as important.

**sermon** sermons

NOUN a talk on a religious or moral subject given as part of a church service.

**serpent** serpents

NOUN; *LITERARY* a snake.

**serrated**

ADJECTIVE having a row of V-shaped points along the edge, like a saw *E.G. green serrated leaves.*

**servant** servants

NOUN someone who is employed to work in another person's house.

**serve** serves serving served

VERB **1** If you serve a country, an organization, or a person, you do useful work for them. **2** To serve as something means to act or be used as that thing *E.G. the room that served as their office.* **3** If something serves people in a particular place, it provides them with something they need *E.G. a recycling plant which serves the whole of the county.* **4** If you serve food or drink to people, you give it to them. **5** To serve customers in a shop means to help them and provide them with what they want. **6** To serve a prison sentence or an apprenticeship means to spend time doing it. **7** When you serve in tennis

or badminton, you throw the ball or shuttlecock into the air and hit it over the net to start playing. ▶ NOUN **8** the act of serving in tennis or badminton.

**server** servers

NOUN (ICT) a computer or computer program which supplies information or resources to a number of computers on a network.

**service** services servicing serviced

NOUN **1** a system organized to provide something for the public *E.G. the bus service.* **2** Some government organizations are called services *E.G. the diplomatic service.* **3** The services are the army, the navy, and the air force. **4** If you give your services to a person or organization, you work for them or help them in some way *E.G. services to the community.* **5** In a shop or restaurant, service is the process of being served. **6** a religious ceremony. **7** When it is your service in a game of tennis or badminton, it is your turn to serve. ▶ PLURAL NOUN **8** Motorway services consist of a garage, restaurant, shop, and toilets. ▶ VERB **9** When a machine or vehicle is serviced, it is examined and adjusted so that it will continue working efficiently.

**serviceman** servicemen

NOUN a man in the army, navy, or air force.

**servicewoman** NOUN

**service station** service stations

NOUN a garage that sells petrol, oil, spare parts, and snacks.

**servile**

ADJECTIVE too eager to obey people.

**servility** NOUN

■ obsequious, subservient

A
B
C
D
E
F
G
H
I
J
K
L
M
N
O
P
Q
R
S
T
U
V
W
X
Y
Z

**serving** servings
NOUN **1** a helping of food. ▶ ADJECTIVE
**2** A serving spoon or dish is used for serving food.

**session** sessions
NOUN **1** a meeting of an official group E.G. *the emergency session of the Indiana Supreme Court.* **2** a period during which meetings are held regularly E.G. *the end of the parliamentary session.* **3** The period during which an activity takes place can also be called a session E.G. *a drinking session.*

**set** sets setting set
NOUN **1** Several things make a set when they belong together or form a group E.G. *a set of weights.* **2** In maths, a set is a collection of numbers or other things which are treated as a group. **3** A television set is a television. **4** The set for a play or film is the scenery or furniture on the stage or in the studio. **5** In tennis, a set is a group of six or more games. There are usually several sets in a match. ▶ VERB **6** If something is set somewhere, that is where it is E.G. *The house was set back from the beach.* **7** When the sun sets, it goes below the horizon. **8** When you set the table, you prepare it for a meal by putting plates and cutlery on it. **9** When you set a clock or a control, you adjust it to a particular point or position. **10** If you set someone a piece of work or a target, you give it to them to do or to achieve. **11** When something such as jelly or cement sets, it becomes firm or hard.
▶ ADJECTIVE **12** Something that is set is fixed and not varying E.G. *a set charge.* **13** If you are set to do something, you are ready or likely to

do it. **14** If you are set on doing something, you are determined to do it. **15** If a play or story is set at a particular time or in a particular place, the events in it take place at that time or in that place.
■ (sense 12) fixed, hard and fast, inflexible

**set about** VERB If you set about doing something, you start doing it.

**set back** VERB If something sets back a project or scheme, it delays it.

**set off** VERB **1** When you set off, you start a journey. **2** To set something off means to cause it to start.

**set out** VERB **1** When you set out, you start a journey. **2** If you set out to do something, you start trying to do it.

**set up** VERB If you set something up, you make all the necessary preparations for it E.G. *We have done all we can about setting up a system of communication.*

**setback** setbacks
NOUN something that delays or hinders you.

**settee** settees
NOUN a long comfortable seat for two or three people to sit on.

**setter** setters
NOUN a long-haired breed of dog originally used in hunting.

**setting** settings
NOUN **1** The setting of something is its surroundings or circumstances E.G. *The Irish setting made the story realistic.* **2** The settings on a machine are the different positions to which the controls can be adjusted.

**settle** settles settling settled
VERB **1** To settle an argument means to put an end to it E.G. *The dispute*

*was settled.* **2** If something is settled, it has all been decided and arranged. **3** If you settle on something or settle for it, you choose it *E.G. We settled for orange juice and coffee.* **4** When you settle a bill, you pay it. **5** If you settle in a place, you make it your permanent home. **6** If you settle yourself somewhere, you sit down and make yourself comfortable. **7** If something settles, it sinks slowly down and comes to rest *E.G. A black dust settled on the walls.*

**settle down** VERB **1** When someone settles down, they start living a quiet life in one place, especially when they get married. **2** To settle down means to become quiet or calm.

**settlement** settlements
NOUN **1** an official agreement between people who have been involved in a conflict *E.G. the last chance for a peaceful settlement.* **2** (GEOGRAPHY) a place where people have settled and built homes.

**settler** settlers
NOUN someone who settles in a new country *E.G. the first settlers in Cuba.*

**seven**
the number 7.

**seventeen**
the number 17.
**seventeenth**

**seventh** sevenths
**1** The seventh item in a series is the one counted as number seven. NOUN **2** one of seven equal parts.

**seventy** seventies
the number 70.
**seventieth**

**sever** severs severing severed
VERB **1** To sever something means to

cut it off or cut right through it. **2** If you sever a connection with someone or something, you end it completely *E.G. She severed her ties with England.*

**several**
ADJECTIVE or PRONOUN Several people or things means a small number of them.

**severe**
ADJECTIVE **1** extremely bad or unpleasant *E.G. severe stomach pains.* **2** stern and harsh *E.G. Perhaps I was too severe with that young man.*
**severely** ADVERB **severity** NOUN

**sew** sews sewing sewed sewn
*Said "so"* VERB (D&T) When you sew things together, you join them using a needle and thread.
**sewing** NOUN

**sewage**
NOUN Sewage is dirty water and waste which is carried away in sewers.

**sewer** sewers
NOUN an underground channel that carries sewage to a place where it is treated to make it harmless.

**sewerage**
NOUN Sewerage is the system by which sewage is carried away and treated.

**sex** sexes
NOUN **1** The sexes are the two groups, male and female, into which people and animals are divided. **2** The sex of a person or animal is their characteristic of being either male or female. **3** Sex is the physical activity by which people and animals produce young.

**sexism**
NOUN (PSHE) Sexism is discrimination against the members of one sex, usually women.
**sexist** ADJECTIVE or NOUN

**sextet** sextets
NOUN a group of six musicians who sing or play together; also a piece of music written for six instruments or singers.

**sextuplet** sextuplets
NOUN Sextuplets are six children born at the same time to the same mother.

**sexual**
ADJECTIVE 1 connected with the act of sex or with people's desire for sex E.G. *sexual attraction.* 2 relating to the difference between males and females E.G. *sexual equality.* 3 relating to the biological process by which people and animals produce young E.G. *sexual reproduction.*
**sexually** ADVERB

**sexual intercourse**
NOUN Sexual intercourse is the physical act of sex between two people.

**sexuality**
Said "seks-yoo-**al**-it-ee" NOUN A person's sexuality is their ability to experience sexual feelings.

**sexy** sexier sexiest
ADJECTIVE sexually attractive or exciting E.G. *these sexy blue eyes.*

**shabby** shabbier shabbiest
ADJECTIVE 1 old and worn in appearance E.G. *a shabby overcoat.* 2 dressed in old, worn-out clothes E.G. *a shabby figure crouching in a doorway.* 3 behaving in a mean or unfair way E.G. *shabby treatment.*
**shabbily** ADVERB
■ (sense 1) tatty, threadbare, worn

**shack** shacks
NOUN a small hut.

**shackle** shackles shackling shackled
NOUN 1 In the past, shackles were two metal rings joined by a chain fastened around a prisoner's wrists or ankles. ▶ VERB 2 To shackle someone means to put shackles on them. 3 LITERARY If you are shackled by something, it restricts or hampers you.

**shade** shades shading shaded
NOUN 1 Shade is an area of darkness and coolness which the sun does not reach E.G. *The table was in the shade.* 2 a lampshade. 3 The shades of a colour are its different forms. For example, olive green is a shade of green. ▶ VERB 4 If a place is shaded by trees or buildings, they prevent the sun from shining on it. 5 If you shade your eyes, you put your hand in front of them to protect them from a bright light.

**shadow** shadows shadowing shadowed
NOUN 1 the dark shape made when an object prevents light from reaching a surface. 2 Shadow is darkness caused by light not reaching a place. ▶ VERB 3 To shadow someone means to follow them and watch them closely.

**shadow cabinet**
NOUN The shadow cabinet consists of the leaders of the main opposition party, each of whom is concerned with a particular policy.

**shadowy**
ADJECTIVE 1 A shadowy place is dark and full of shadows. 2 A shadowy figure or shape is difficult to see because it is dark or misty.

**shady** shadier shadiest
ADJECTIVE A shady place is sheltered from sunlight by trees or buildings.

**shaft shafts**

NOUN **1** a vertical passage, for example one for a lift or one in a mine. **2** A shaft of light is a beam of light. **3** A shaft in a machine is a rod which revolves and transfers movement in the machine E.G. *the drive shaft*.

**shaggy shaggier shaggiest**

ADJECTIVE Shaggy hair or fur is long and untidy.

**shake shakes shaking shook shaken**

VERB **1** To shake something means to move it quickly from side to side or up and down. **2** If something shakes, it moves from side to side or up and down with small, quick movements. **3** If your voice shakes, it trembles because you are nervous or angry. **4** If something shakes you, it shocks and upsets you. **5** When you shake your head, you move it from side to side in order to say 'no'. ‣ NOUN **6** If you give something a shake, you shake it. ‣ PHRASE **7** When you **shake hands** with someone, you grasp their hand as a way of greeting them.

■ (sense 2) quiver, tremble, vibrate

**shaky shakier shakiest**

ADJECTIVE rather weak and unsteady E.G. *Confidence in the economy is still shaky*.

**shakily** ADVERB

**shall**

VERB **1** If I say I shall do something, I mean that I intend to do it. **2** If I say something shall happen, I am emphasizing that it will definitely happen, or I am ordering it to happen E.G. *There shall be work and security!* **3** 'Shall' is also used in questions when you are asking what

to do, or making a suggestion E.G. *Shall we sit down… Shall I go and check for you?*

---

### The verbs Shall and Will

The verbs *shall* and *will* have only one form. They do not have a present form ending in *-s*, and they do not have a present participle, a past tense, or a past participle. These verbs are used as auxiliary verbs to form the future tense:

> E.G. We **shall** arrive on Thursday.
> She **will** give a talk about Chinese history.

People used to use *shall* to indicate the first person, and *will* to indicate the second person and the third person. However, this distinction is often ignored now:

> E.G. I **shall** see you on Sunday.
> I **will** see you on Sunday.

*Shall* is always used in questions involving *I* and *we*. *Will* is avoided in these cases:

> E.G. **Shall** I put the cat out?
> **Shall** we dance?

*Will* is always used when making polite requests, giving orders, and indicating persistence. *Shall* is avoided in these cases:

> E.G. **Will** you please help me?
> **Will** you be quiet!
> She **will** keep going on about Al Pacino.

---

**shallow shallower shallowest; shallows**

ADJECTIVE **1** Shallow means not deep. **2** Shallow also means not involving serious thought or sincere feelings E.G. *a well-meaning but shallow man*.

a b c d e f g h i j k l m n o p q r s t u v w x y z

---

Plaice the fish has a glittering 'EYE' (I) (plaice)    **SPELLING NOTE**

A
B
C
D
E
F
G
H
I
J
K
L
M
N
O
P
Q
R
**S**
T
U
V
W
X
Y
Z

▶ PLURAL NOUN **3** The shallows are the shallow part of a river or lake.

**sham** shams
NOUN **1** Something that is a sham is not real or genuine. ▶ ADJECTIVE **2** not real or genuine E.G. *a sham display of affection*.

**shambles**
NOUN If an event is a shambles, it is confused and badly organized

**shame** shames shaming shamed
NOUN **1** Shame is the feeling of guilt or embarrassment you get when you know you have done something wrong or foolish. **2** To bring shame on someone means to make people lose respect for them E.G. *the scenes that brought shame to English soccer.* **3** If you say something is a shame, you mean you are sorry about it E.G. *It's a shame you can't come round.*
▶ INTERJECTION **4** INFORMAL In South African English, you say 'Shame!' to show sympathy. ▶ VERB **5** If something shames you, it makes you feel ashamed. **6** If you shame someone into doing something, you force them to do it by making them feel ashamed not to E.G. *Two children shamed their parents into giving up cigarettes.*

**shameful**
ADJECTIVE If someone's behaviour is shameful, they ought to be ashamed of it.
**shamefully** ADVERB

**shameless**
ADJECTIVE behaving in an indecent or unacceptable way, but showing no shame E.G. *shameless dishonesty*.
**shamelessly** ADVERB
▤ barefaced, brazen, flagrant

**shampoo** shampoos shampooing shampooed

NOUN **1** Shampoo is a soapy liquid used for washing your hair. ▶ VERB **2** When you shampoo your hair, you wash it with shampoo.
▦ from Hindi *champna* meaning 'to knead'

**shamrock** shamrocks
NOUN a plant with three round leaves on each stem which is the national emblem of Ireland.
▦ from Irish Gaelic *seamrog* meaning 'little clover'

**shanghai** shanghais shanghaiing shanghaied INFORMAL
VERB **1** If someone is shanghaied, they are kidnapped and forced to work on a ship. **2** If you shanghai someone, you trick or force them into doing something. ▶ NOUN **3** In Australian and New Zealand English, a catapult.

**shanty** shanties
NOUN **1** a small, rough hut. **2** A sea shanty is a song sailors used to sing.

**shape** shapes shaping shaped
NOUN **1** The shape of something is the form or pattern of its outline, for example whether it is round or square. **2** something with a definite form, for example a circle or triangle. **3** The shape of something such as an organization is its structure and size.
▶ VERB **4** If you shape an object, you form it into a particular shape E.G. *Shape the dough into an oblong.* **5** To shape something means to cause it to develop in a particular way E.G. *events that shaped the lives of some of the leading characters.*
▤ (sense 1) figure, form, outline

**shapeless**
ADJECTIVE not having a definite shape.

**shapely** shapelier shapeliest
ADJECTIVE A shapely woman has an attractive figure.

**shard** shards
NOUN a small fragment of pottery, glass, or metal.

**share** shares sharing shared
VERB (DRAMA) 1 If two people share something, they both use it, do it, or have it E.G. We shared a bottle of champagne. 2 If you share an idea or a piece of news with someone, you tell it to them. ▶ NOUN 3 A share of something is a portion of it. 4 The shares of a company are the equal parts into which its ownership is divided. People can buy shares as an investment.
■ (sense 3) lot, part, portion

**share out** VERB If you share something out, you give it out equally among a group of people.

**shareholder** shareholders
NOUN a person who owns shares in a company.

**share-milker** share-milkers
NOUN In New Zealand, someone who works on a dairy farm and shares the profit from the sale of its produce.

**shark** sharks
NOUN 1 Sharks are large, powerful fish with sharp teeth. 2 a person who cheats people out of money.

**sharp** sharper sharpest; sharps
ADJECTIVE 1 A sharp object has a fine edge or point that is good for cutting or piercing things. 2 A sharp outline or distinction is easy to see. 3 A sharp person is quick to notice or understand things. 4 A sharp change is sudden and significant E.G. a sharp rise in prices. 5 If you say something in a sharp way, you say it firmly and

rather angrily. 6 A sharp sound is short, sudden, and quite loud. 7 A sharp pain is sudden and painful. 8 A sharp taste is slightly sour. 9 A musical instrument or note that is sharp is slightly too high in pitch.
▶ ADVERB 10 If something happens at a certain time sharp, it happens at that time precisely E.G. You'll begin at eight o'clock sharp. ▶ NOUN 11 In music, a sharp is a note or key a semitone higher than that described by the same letter. It is represented by the symbol (♯).
**sharply** ADVERB **sharpness** NOUN
■ (sense 3) astute, perceptive, quick-witted

**sharpen** sharpens sharpening sharpened
VERB 1 To sharpen an object means to make its edge or point sharper. 2 If your senses or abilities sharpen, you become quicker at noticing or understanding things.
**sharpener** NOUN

**shatter** shatters shattering shattered
VERB 1 If something shatters, it breaks into a lot of small pieces. 2 If something shatters your hopes or beliefs, it destroys them completely. 3 If you are shattered by an event or piece of news, you are shocked and upset by it.

**shattered**
ADJECTIVE; INFORMAL completely exhausted E.G. He must be absolutely shattered after all his efforts.

**shattering**
ADJECTIVE making you feel shocked and upset E.G. a shattering event.

**shave** shaves shaving shaved
VERB 1 When a man shaves, he

a
b
c
d
e
f
g
h
i
j
k
l
m
n
o
p
q
r
s
t
u
v
w
x
y
z

A B C D E F G H I J K L M N O P Q R S T U V W X Y Z

removes hair from his face with a razor. **2** If you shave off part of a piece of wood, you cut thin pieces from it. ▶ NOUN **3** When a man has a shave, he shaves.

**shaven**
ADJECTIVE If part of someone's body is shaven, it has been shaved E.G. *a shaven head.*

**shaver shavers**
NOUN an electric razor.

**shavings**
PLURAL NOUN Shavings are small, very thin pieces of wood which have been cut from a larger piece.

**shawl shawls**
NOUN a large piece of woollen cloth worn round a woman's head or shoulders or used to wrap a baby in.

**she**
PRONOUN 'She' is used to refer to a woman or girl whose identity is clear. 'She' is also used to refer to a country, a ship, or a car.

**sheaf sheaves**
NOUN **1** A sheaf of papers is a bundle of them. **2** A sheaf of corn is a bundle of ripe corn tied together.

**shear shears shearing sheared shorn**
VERB **1** To shear a sheep means to cut the wool off it. ▶ PLURAL NOUN **2** Shears are a tool like a large pair of scissors, used especially for cutting hedges.

**shearer shearers**
NOUN someone whose job is to shear sheep.

**sheath sheaths**
NOUN **1** a covering for the blade of a knife. **2** a condom.

**shed sheds shedding shed**
NOUN **1** a small building used for storing things. ▶ VERB **2** When an

animal sheds hair or skin, some of its hair or skin drops off. When a tree sheds its leaves, its leaves fall off. **3** FORMAL To shed something also means to get rid of it E.G. *The firm is to shed 700 jobs.* **4** If a lorry sheds its load, the load falls off the lorry onto the road. **5** If you shed tears, you cry.

**sheen**
NOUN a gentle brightness on the surface of something.

**sheep**
NOUN A sheep is a farm animal with a thick woolly coat. Sheep are kept for meat and wool
☑ The plural of *sheep* is *sheep*.

**sheep-dip sheep-dips**
NOUN a liquid disinfectant used to keep sheep clean and free of pests.

**sheepdog sheepdogs**
NOUN a breed of dog often used for controlling sheep.

**sheepish**
ADJECTIVE If you look sheepish, you look embarrassed because you feel shy or foolish.

**sheepishly** ADVERB

**sheepskin**
NOUN Sheepskin is the skin and wool of a sheep, used for making rugs and coats.

**sheer sheerer sheerest**
ADJECTIVE **1** Sheer means complete and total E.G. *sheer exhaustion.* **2** A sheer cliff or drop is vertical. **3** Sheer fabrics are very light and delicate.

**sheet sheets**
NOUN **1** a large rectangular piece of cloth used to cover a bed. **2** A sheet of paper is a rectangular piece of it. **3** A sheet of glass or metal is a large, flat piece of it.

**sheik** sheiks
*Said "shake"; also spelt* **sheikh**
NOUN an Arab chief or ruler.
📖 from Arabic *shaykh* meaning 'old man'

**shelf** shelves
NOUN a flat piece of wood, metal, or glass fixed to a wall and used for putting things on.

**shell** shells shelling shelled
NOUN 1 The shell of an egg or nut is its hard covering. 2 The shell of a tortoise, snail, or crab is the hard protective covering on its back. 3 The shell of a building or other structure is its frame *E.G. The room was just an empty shell.* 4 a container filled with explosives that can be fired from a gun. ▶ VERB 5 If you shell peas or nuts, you remove their natural covering. 6 To shell a place means to fire large explosive shells at it.

**shellfish** shellfish or shellfishes
NOUN a small sea creature with a shell.

**shelter** shelters sheltering sheltered
NOUN 1 a small building made to protect people from bad weather or danger. 2 If a place provides shelter, it provides protection from bad weather or danger. ▶ VERB 3 If you shelter in a place, you stay there and are safe. 4 If you shelter someone, you provide them with a place to stay when they are in danger.

**sheltered**
ADJECTIVE 1 A sheltered place is protected from wind and rain. 2 If you lead a sheltered life, you do not experience unpleasant or upsetting things. 3 Sheltered accommodation is accommodation designed for old or handicapped people.

**shelve** shelves shelving shelved
VERB If you shelve a plan, you decide to postpone it for a while.

**shepherd** shepherds shepherding shepherded
NOUN 1 a person who looks after sheep. ▶ VERB 2 If you shepherd someone somewhere, you accompany them there.

**sheriff** sheriffs
NOUN 1 In America, a sheriff is a person elected to enforce the law in a county. 2 In Australia, an administrative officer of the Supreme Court who carries out writs and judgments.
📖 from Old English *scir* meaning 'shire' and *gerefa* meaning 'reeve', an official

**sherry** sherries
NOUN Sherry is a kind of strong wine.
📖 from the Spanish town *Jerez* where it was first made

**shield** shields shielding shielded
NOUN 1 a large piece of a strong material like metal or plastic which soldiers or policeman carry to protect themselves. 2 If something is a shield against something, it gives protection from it. ▶ VERB 3 To shield someone means to protect them from something.

**shift** shifts shifting shifted
VERB 1 If you shift something, you move it. If something shifts, it moves *E.G. to shift the rubble.* 2 If an opinion or situation shifts, it changes slightly. ▶ NOUN 3 A shift in an opinion or situation is a slight change. 4 a set period during which people work in a factory *E.G. the night shift.*

**shilling** shillings
NOUN a former British, Australian, and

a b c d e f g h i j k l m n o p q r **s** t u v w x y z

New Zealand coin worth one-twentieth of a pound.

**shimmer** shimmers shimmering shimmered

VERB 1 If something shimmers, it shines with a faint, flickering light. ▶ NOUN 2 a faint, flickering light.

**shin** shins shinning shinned

NOUN 1 Your shin is the front part of your leg between your knee and your ankle. ▶ VERB 2 If you shin up a tree or pole, you climb it quickly by gripping it with your hands and legs.

**shine** shines shining shone

VERB 1 When something shines, it gives out or reflects a bright light E.G. *The stars shone brilliantly.* 2 If you shine a torch or lamp somewhere, you point it there.

**shingle** shingles

NOUN 1 Shingle consists of small pebbles on the seashore. 2 Shingles are small wooden roof tiles. 3 Shingles is a disease that causes a painful red rash, especially around the waist.

**shining**

ADJECTIVE 1 Shining things are very bright, usually because they are reflecting light E.G. *shining stainless steel tables.* 2 A shining example of something is a very good or typical example of that thing E.G. *a shining example of courage.*

■ (sense 1) bright, gleaming

**shiny** shinier shiniest

ADJECTIVE Shiny things are bright and look as if they have been polished E.G. *a shiny brass plate.*

**ship** ships shipping shipped

NOUN 1 a large boat which carries passengers or cargo. ▶ VERB 2 If people or things are shipped somewhere, they are transported there.

**-ship**

SUFFIX '-ship' is used to form nouns that refer to a condition or position E.G. *fellowship.*
🔢 from Old English

**shipment** shipments

NOUN 1 a quantity of goods that are transported somewhere E.G. *a shipment of olive oil.* 2 The shipment of goods is the transporting of them.

**shipping**

NOUN 1 Shipping is the transport of cargo on ships. 2 You can also refer to ships generally as shipping E.G. *Attention all shipping!*

**shipwreck** shipwrecks

NOUN When there is a shipwreck, a ship is destroyed in an accident at sea E.G. *He was drowned in a shipwreck.*

**shipyard** shipyards

NOUN a place where ships are built and repaired.

**shiralee** shiralees

NOUN; *OLD-FASHIONED* In Australian English, the bundle of possessions carried by a swagman.

**shire** shires

NOUN 1 *OLD-FASHIONED* In Britain, a county. 2 In Australia, a rural district with its own local council.

**shirk** shirks shirking shirked

VERB To shirk a task means to avoid doing it.

**shirt** shirts

NOUN a piece of clothing worn on the upper part of the body, having a collar, sleeves, and buttons down the front.

**shiver** shivers shivering shivered

VERB 1 When you shiver, you tremble

slightly because you are cold or scared. ▶ NOUN 2 a slight trembling caused by cold or fear.

**shoal** shoals
NOUN A shoal of fish is a large group of them swimming together.

**shock** shocks shocking shocked
NOUN 1 If you have a shock, you have a sudden upsetting experience. 2 Shock is a person's emotional and physical condition when something very unpleasant or upsetting has happened to them. 3 In medicine, shock is a serious physical condition in which the blood cannot circulate properly because of an injury. 4 a slight movement in something when it is hit by something else E.G. *The straps help to absorb shocks.* 5 A shock of hair is a thick mass of it. ▶ VERB 6 If something shocks you, it upsets you because it is unpleasant and unexpected E.G. *I was shocked by his appearance.* 7 You can say that something shocks you when it offends you because it is rude or immoral.
**shocked** ADJECTIVE
▣ (sense 6) appal, horrify
▣ (sense 7) disgust, scandalize

**shock absorber** shock absorbers
NOUN Shock absorbers are devices fitted near the wheels of a vehicle. They help to prevent the vehicle from bouncing up and down.

**shocking**
ADJECTIVE 1 INFORMAL very bad E.G. *It's been a shocking year.* 2 rude or immoral E.G. *a shocking video.*

**shoddy** shoddier shoddiest
ADJECTIVE badly made or done E.G. *a shoddy piece of work.*

**shoe** shoes shoeing shod
NOUN 1 Shoes are strong coverings for your feet. They cover most of your foot, but not your ankle. ▶ VERB 2 To shoe a horse means to fix horseshoes onto its hooves.

**shoestring**
NOUN If you do something on a shoestring, you do it using very little money.

**shoot** shoots shooting shot
VERB 1 To shoot a person or animal means to kill or injure them by firing a gun at them. 2 To shoot an arrow means to fire it from a bow. 3 If something shoots in a particular direction, it moves there quickly and suddenly E.G. *They shot back into Green Street.* 4 When a film is shot, it is filmed E.G. *The whole film was shot in California.* 5 In games such as football or hockey, to shoot means to kick or hit the ball towards the goal. ▶ NOUN 6 an occasion when people hunt animals or birds with guns. 7 a plant that is beginning to grow, or a new part growing from a plant.

**shooting** shootings
NOUN an incident in which someone is shot.

**shooting star** shooting stars
NOUN a meteor.

**shop** shops shopping shopped
NOUN 1 a place where things are sold. 2 a place where a particular type of work is done E.G. *a bicycle repair shop.* ▶ VERB 3 When you shop, you go to the shops to buy things.
**shopper** NOUN

**shopkeeper** shopkeepers
NOUN someone who owns or manages a small shop.

a b c d e f g h i j k l m n o p q r s t u v w x y z

**shoplifting**

NOUN Shoplifting is stealing goods from shops.

**shoplifter** NOUN

**shopping**

NOUN Your shopping is the goods you have bought from the shops.

**shop steward** shop stewards

NOUN a trade union member elected to represent the workers in a factory or office.

**shore** shores shoring shored

NOUN 1 The shore of a sea, lake, or wide river is the land along the edge of it. ▶ VERB 2 If you shore something up, you reinforce it or strengthen it E.G. *a short-term solution to shore up the worst defence in the League.*

**shoreline** shorelines

NOUN the edge of a sea, lake, or wide river.

**shorn**

1 Shorn is the past participle of **shear.** ▶ ADJECTIVE 2 Grass or hair that is shorn is cut very short.

**short** shorter shortest; shorts

ADJECTIVE 1 not lasting very long. 2 small in length, distance, or height E.G. *a short climb… the short road.* 3 If you are short with someone, you speak to them crossly. 4 If you have a short temper, you get angry very quickly. 5 If you are short of something, you do not have enough of it. 6 If a name is short for another name, it is a short version of it. ▶ PLURAL NOUN 7 Shorts are trousers with short legs. ▶ ADVERB 8 If you stop short of a place, you do not quite reach it. ▶ PHRASE 9 Short of is used to say that a level or amount has not quite been reached E.G. *a hundred votes short of a majority.* ▣ (sense 3) abrupt, curt, sharp

**shortage** shortages

NOUN If there is a shortage of something, there is not enough of it.

**shortbread**

NOUN Shortbread is a crumbly biscuit made from flour and butter.
🏛 from an old-fashioned use of *short* meaning 'crumbly'

**short circuit** short circuits

NOUN a fault in an electrical system when two points accidentally become connected and the electricity travels directly between them rather than through the complete circuit.

**shortcoming** shortcomings

NOUN Shortcomings are faults or weaknesses.

**shortcut** shortcuts

NOUN 1 a quicker way of getting somewhere than the usual route. 2 a quicker way of doing something E.G. *Stencils have been used as a shortcut to hand painting.*

**shorten** shortens shortening shortened

VERB If you shorten something or if it shortens, it becomes shorter E.G. *This might help to shorten the conversation.*

**shortfall** shortfalls

NOUN If there is a shortfall in something, there is less than you need.

**shorthand**

NOUN Shorthand is a way of writing in which signs represent words or syllables. It is used to write down quickly what someone is saying.

**short-list** short-lists short-listing short-listed

NOUN 1 a list of people selected from a larger group, from which one person is finally selected for a job or prize. ▶ VERB **2** If someone is short-listed for a job or prize, they are put on a short-list.

**shortly**

ADVERB **1** Shortly means soon *E.G. I'll be back shortly*. **2** If you speak to someone shortly, you speak to them in a cross and impatient way.

**short-sighted**

ADJECTIVE **1** If you are short-sighted, you cannot see things clearly when they are far away. **2** A short-sighted decision does not take account of the way things may develop in the future.

**short-term**

ADJECTIVE happening or having an effect within a short time or for a short time.

**shot shots**

**1** Shot is the past tense and past participle of **shoot**. NOUN **2** the act of firing a gun. **3** Someone who is a good shot can shoot accurately. **4** In football, golf, and tennis, a shot is the act of kicking or hitting the ball. **5** a photograph or short film sequence *E.G. I'd like to get some shots of the river*. **6** INFORMAL If you have a shot at something, you try to do it.

**shotgun shotguns**

NOUN a gun that fires a lot of small pellets all at once.

**shot put**

NOUN In athletics, the shot put is an event in which the contestants throw a heavy metal ball called a shot as far as possible.

**shot putter** NOUN

**should**

VERB **1** You use 'should' to say that something ought to happen *E.G.*

*Ward should have done better*. **2** You also use 'should' to say that you expect something to happen *E.G. He should have heard by now*. **3** FORMAL You can use 'should' to announce that you are about to do or say something *E.G. I should like to express my thanks to the Professor*. **4** 'Should' is used in conditional sentences *E.G. If they should discover the fact, what use would the knowledge be to them?* **5** 'Should' is sometimes used in 'that' clauses *E.G. It is inevitable that you should go*. **6** If you say that you should think something, you mean that it is probably true *E.G. I should think that's unlikely*.

**shoulder shoulders shouldering shouldered**

NOUN **1** Your shoulders are the parts of your body between your neck and the tops of your arms. ▶ VERB **2** If you shoulder something heavy, you put it across one of your shoulders to carry it. **3** If you shoulder the responsibility or blame for something, you accept it.

**shoulder blade shoulder blades**

NOUN Your shoulder blades are the two large, flat bones in the upper part of your back, below your shoulders.

**shout shouts shouting shouted**

NOUN **1** a loud call or cry. ▶ VERB **2** If you shout something, you say it very loudly *E.G. He shouted something to his brother*.

■ call, cry, yell

**shove shoves shoving shoved**

VERB **1** If you shove someone or something, you push them roughly *E.G. He shoved his wallet into a back pocket*. ▶ NOUN **2** a rough push.

**shove off** VERB; INFORMAL If you tell

A

B

C

D

E

F

G

H

I

J

K

L

M

N

O

P

Q

R

S

T

U

V

W

X

Y

Z

someone to shove off, you are telling them angrily and rudely to go away.

**shovel** shovels shovelling shovelled

NOUN **1** a tool like a spade, used for moving earth or snow. ► VERB **2** If you shovel earth or snow, you move it with a shovel.

**show** shows showing showed shown

VERB **1** To show that something exists or is true means to prove it *E.G. The survey showed that 29 per cent would now approve the treaty.* **2** If a picture shows something, it represents it *E.G. The painting shows supporters and crowd scenes.* **3** If you show someone something, you let them see it *E.G. Show me your passport.* **4** If you show someone to a room or seat, you lead them there. **5** If you show someone how to do something, you demonstrate it to them. **6** If something shows, it is visible. **7** If something shows a quality or characteristic, you can see that it has it *E.G. Her sketches and watercolours showed promise.* **8** If you show your feelings, you let people see them *E.G. She was flustered, but too proud to show it.* **9** If you show affection or mercy, you behave in an affectionate or merciful way *E.G. the first person who showed me some affection.* **10** To show a film or television programme means to let the public see it. ► NOUN **11** a form of light entertainment at the theatre or on television. **12** an exhibition *E.G. the Napier Antiques Show.* **13** A show of a feeling or attitude is behaviour in which you show it *E.G. a show of optimism.* ► PHRASE **14** If something is **on show**, it is being exhibited for the

public to see.

**目** (sense 1) demonstrate, prove

**目** (sense 7) display, indicate, reveal

**目** (sense 12) display, exhibition

**show off** VERB *INFORMAL* If someone is showing off, they are trying to impress people.

**show up** VERB **1** *INFORMAL* If you show up, you arrive at a place where you are expected. **2** If something shows up, it can be seen clearly *E.G. Her bones were too soft to show up on an X-ray.*

**show business**

NOUN Show business is entertainment in the theatre, films, and television.

**showdown** showdowns

NOUN; *INFORMAL* a major argument or conflict intended to end a dispute.

**shower** showers showering showered

NOUN **1** a device which sprays you with water so that you can wash yourself. **2** If you have a shower, you wash yourself by standing under a shower. **3** a short period of rain. **4** You can refer to a lot of things falling at once as a shower *E.G. a shower of confetti.* ► VERB **5** If you shower, you have a shower. **6** If you are showered with a lot of things, they fall on you.

**showing** showings

NOUN A showing of a film or television programme is a presentation of it so that the public can see it.

**showjumping**

NOUN Showjumping is a horse-riding competition in which the horses jump over a series of high fences.

**show-off** show-offs

NOUN; *INFORMAL* someone who tries to impress people with their knowledge or skills.

**showroom** showrooms

NOUN a shop where goods such as cars or electrical appliances are displayed.

**showy** showier showiest

ADJECTIVE large or bright and intended to impress people E.G. *a showy house.*

▤ flamboyant, flashy, ostentatious

**shrapnel**

NOUN Shrapnel consists of small pieces of metal scattered from an exploding shell.

🏛 named after General Henry *Shrapnel* (1761–1842), who invented it

**shred** shreds shredding shredded

VERB 1 If you shred something, you cut or tear it into very small pieces. ▶ NOUN 2 A shred of paper or material is a small, narrow piece of it. 3 If there is not a shred of something, there is absolutely none of it E.G. *He was left without a shred of self-esteem.*

**shrew** shrews

Said "**shroo**" NOUN a small mouse-like animal with a long pointed nose.

**shrewd** shrewder shrewdest

ADJECTIVE Someone who is shrewd is intelligent and makes good judgments.

**shrewdly** ADVERB  **shrewdness** NOUN

▤ astute, clever, sharp

**shriek** shrieks shrieking shrieked

NOUN 1 a high-pitched scream. ▶ VERB 2 If you shriek, you make a high-pitched scream.

**shrift**

NOUN If you give someone or something short shrift, you pay very little attention to them.

🏛 from Old English *scrift* meaning 'confession'; 'short shrift' referred to the short time allowed to prisoners before they were put to death to make their confession

**shrill** shriller shrillest

ADJECTIVE A shrill sound is unpleasantly high-pitched and piercing.

**shrilly** ADVERB

**shrimp** shrimps

NOUN a small edible shellfish with a long tail and many legs.

**shrine** shrines

NOUN ( RE ) a place of worship associated with a sacred person or object.

**shrink** shrinks shrinking shrank shrunk

VERB 1 If something shrinks, it becomes smaller. 2 If you shrink from something, you move away from it because you are afraid of it.

**shrinkage** NOUN

**shrivel** shrivels shrivelling shrivelled

VERB When something shrivels, it becomes dry and withered.

**shroud** shrouds shrouding shrouded

NOUN 1 a cloth in which a dead body is wrapped before it is buried. ▶ VERB 2 If something is shrouded in darkness or fog, it is hidden by it.

**shrub** shrubs

NOUN a low, bushy plant.

**shrug** shrugs shrugging shrugged

VERB 1 If you shrug your shoulders, you raise them slightly as a sign of indifference. ▶ NOUN 2 If you give a shrug of your shoulders, you shrug them.

a b c d e f g h i j k l m n o p q r s t u v w x y z

A
B
C
D
E
F
G
H
I
J
K
L
M
N
O
P
Q
R
S
T
U
V
W
X
Y
Z

**shrunken**

ADJECTIVE; *FORMAL* Someone or
something that is shrunken has
become smaller than it used to be
*E.G. a shrunken old man.*

**shudder** shudders shuddering
shuddered

VERB 1 If you shudder, you tremble
with fear or horror. 2 If a machine or
vehicle shudders, it shakes violently.
▶ NOUN 3 a shiver of fear or horror.

**shuffle** shuffles shuffling
shuffled

VERB 1 If you shuffle, you walk without
lifting your feet properly off the
ground. 2 If you shuffle about, you
move about and fidget because you
feel uncomfortable or embarrassed.
3 If you shuffle a pack of cards, you
mix them up before you begin a
game. ▶ NOUN 4 the way someone
walks when they shuffle.

**shun** shuns shunning shunned

VERB If you shun someone or
something, you deliberately avoid
them.

**shunt** shunts shunting shunted

VERB; *INFORMAL* If you shunt people or
things to a place, you move them
there *E.G. You are shunted from room
to room.*

**shut** shuts shutting shut

VERB 1 If you shut something, you
close it. 2 When a shop or pub shuts,
it is closed and you can no longer go
into it. ▶ ADJECTIVE 3 If something is
shut, it is closed.

**shut up** VERB; *INFORMAL* If you shut up,
you stop talking.

**shutter** shutters

NOUN Shutters are hinged wooden or
metal covers fitted on the outside or
inside of a window.

**shuttle** shuttles

ADJECTIVE 1 A shuttle service is an air,
bus, or train service which makes
frequent journeys between two
places. ▶ NOUN 2 a plane used in a
shuttle service.

**shuttlecock** shuttlecocks

NOUN the feathered object used as a
ball in the game of badminton.

**shy** shyer shyest; shies shying
shied

ADJECTIVE 1 A shy person is nervous
and uncomfortable in the company
of other people. ▶ VERB 2 When a
horse shies, it moves away suddenly
because something has frightened
it. 3 If you shy away from doing
something, you avoid doing it
because you are afraid or nervous.
**shyly** ADVERB **shyness** NOUN
■ (sense 1) bashful, self-conscious,
timid

**sibling** siblings

NOUN; *FORMAL* Your siblings are your
brothers and sisters.

**sick** sicker sickest

ADJECTIVE 1 If you are sick, you are ill.
2 If you feel sick, you feel as if you are
going to vomit. If you are sick, you
vomit. 3 *INFORMAL* If you are sick of
doing something, you feel you have
been doing it too long. 4 *INFORMAL* A
sick joke or story deals with death or
suffering in an unpleasantly frivolous
way. ▶ PHRASE 5 If something **makes
you sick**, it makes you angry.
**sickness** NOUN
■ (sense 2) nauseous, queasy

**sicken** sickens sickening
sickened

VERB If something sickens you, it
makes you feel disgusted.
**sickening** ADJECTIVE

**sickle** sickles
NOUN a tool with a short handle and a curved blade used for cutting grass or grain.

**sickly** sicklier sickliest
ADJECTIVE **1** A sickly person or animal is weak and unhealthy. **2** Sickly also means very unpleasant to smell or taste.

**side** sides siding sided
NOUN **1** Side refers to a position to the left or right of something E.G. *the two armchairs on either side of the fireplace.* **2** The sides of a boundary or barrier are the two areas it separates E.G. *this side of the border.* **3** Your sides are the parts of your body from your armpits down to your hips. **4** The sides of something are its outside surfaces, especially the surfaces which are not its front or back. **5** The sides of a hill or valley are the parts that slope. **6** The two sides in a war, argument, or relationship are the two people or groups involved. **7** A particular side of something is one aspect of it E.G. *the sensitive, caring side of human nature.* ▶ ADJECTIVE **8** situated on a side of a building or vehicle E.G. *the side door.* **9** A side road is a small road leading off a larger one. **10** A side issue is an issue that is less important than the main one. ▶ VERB **11** If you side with someone in an argument, you support them.

**sideboard** sideboards
NOUN **1** a long, low cupboard for plates and glasses. ▶ PLURAL NOUN **2** A man's sideboards are his sideburns.

**sideburns**
PLURAL NOUN A man's sideburns are areas of hair growing on his cheeks in front of his ears.
📖 from a 19th century US army general called *Burnside* who wore his whiskers like this

**side effect** side effects
NOUN The side effects of a drug are the effects it has in addition to its main effects.

**sidekick** sidekicks
NOUN; *INFORMAL* Someone's sidekick is their close friend who spends a lot of time with them.

**sideline** sidelines
NOUN an extra job in addition to your main job.

**sideshow** sideshows
NOUN Sideshows are stalls at a fairground.

**sidestep** sidesteps sidestepping sidestepped
VERB If you sidestep a difficult problem or question, you avoid dealing with it.

**sidewalk** sidewalks
NOUN In American English, a sidewalk is a pavement.

**sideways**
ADVERB from or towards the side of something or someone.

**siding** sidings
NOUN a short railway track beside the main tracks, where engines and carriages are left when not in use.

**sidle** sidles sidling sidled
VERB If you sidle somewhere, you walk there cautiously and slowly, as if you do not want to be noticed.

**siege** sieges
*Said "seej"* NOUN (HISTORY) a military operation in which an army surrounds a place and prevents food or help from reaching the people inside.

'i' before 'e' except after 'c'   SPELLING NOTE

A B C D E F G H I J K L M N O P Q R S T U V W X Y Z

**sieve** sieves sieving sieved
*Said* "siv" NOUN **1** a kitchen tool made of mesh, used for sifting or straining things. ▶ VERB **2** If you sieve a powder or liquid, you pass it through a sieve.

**sift** sifts sifting sifted
VERB **1** If you sift a powdery substance, you pass it through a sieve to remove lumps. **2** If you sift through something such as evidence, you examine it all thoroughly.

**sigh** sighs sighing sighed
VERB **1** When you sigh, you let out a deep breath. ▶ NOUN **2** the breath you let out when you sigh.

**sight** sights sighting sighted
NOUN **1** Sight is the ability to see E.G. *His sight was so poor that he could not follow the cricket.* **2** something you see E.G. *It was a ghastly sight.* ▶ PLURAL NOUN **3** Sights are interesting places which tourists visit. ▶ VERB **4** If you sight someone or something, you see them briefly or suddenly E.G. *He had been sighted in Cairo.* ▶ PHRASES **5** If something is **in sight**, you can see it. If it is **out of sight**, you cannot see it. ✔ Do not confuse the spellings of *sight* and *site*.

**sighted**
ADJECTIVE Someone who is sighted can see.

**sighting** sightings
NOUN A sighting of something rare or unexpected is an occasion when it is seen.

**sightseeing**
NOUN Sightseeing is visiting the interesting places that tourists usually visit.
**sightseer** NOUN

**sign** signs signing signed
NOUN **1** a mark or symbol that always

has a particular meaning, for example in mathematics or music. **2** a gesture with a particular meaning. **3** A sign can also consist of words, a picture, or a symbol giving information or a warning. **4** ⟨RE⟩ A sign is an event or happening that some people believe God has sent as a warning or instruction to an individual or to people in general. **5** If there are signs of something, there is evidence that it exists or is happening E.G. *We are now seeing the first signs of recovery.* ▶ VERB **6** If you sign a document, you write your name on it E.G. *He hurriedly signed the death certificate.* **7** If you sign, you communicate by using sign language. ■ (sense 2) gesture, signal

**sign on** VERB **1** If you sign on for a job or course, you officially agree to do it by signing a contract. **2** When people sign on, they officially state that they are unemployed and claim benefit from the state.

**sign up** VERB If you sign up for a job or course, you officially agree to do it by signing a contract.

**signal** signals signalling signalled
NOUN **1** a gesture, sound, or action intended to give a message to someone. **2** A railway signal is a piece of equipment beside the track which tells train drivers whether to stop or not. ▶ VERB **3** If you signal to someone, you make a gesture or sound to give them a message.

**signature** signatures
NOUN If you write your signature, you write your name the way you usually write it.

**significant**
ADJECTIVE **1** A significant amount is a

large amount. **2** Something that is significant is important *E.G. a significant victory.*

**significance** NOUN   **significantly** ADVERB

**signify** signifies signifying signified

VERB A gesture that signifies something has a particular meaning *E.G. They signified a desire to leave.*

**sign language**

NOUN Sign language is a way of communicating using your hands, used especially by deaf people.

**signpost** signposts

NOUN a road sign with information on it such as the name of a town and how far away it is.

**Sikh** Sikhs

*Said* "*seek*" NOUN (RE) a person who believes in Sikhism, an Indian religion which separated from Hinduism in the sixteenth century and which teaches that there is only one God.

**Sikhism** NOUN

🏛 from Hindi *sikh* meaning 'disciple'

**silence** silences silencing silenced

NOUN **1** Silence is quietness. **2** Someone's silence about something is their failure or refusal to talk about it. ▶ VERB **3** To silence someone or something means to stop them talking or making a noise.

**silent**

ADJECTIVE **1** If you are silent, you are not saying anything. **2** If you are silent about something, you do not tell people about it. **3** When something is silent, it makes no noise. **4** A silent film has only pictures and no sound.

**silently** ADVERB

◼ (sense 1) dumb, mute, speechless

**silhouette** silhouettes

*Said* "*sil-loo-ett*" NOUN the outline of a dark shape against a light background.

**silhouetted** ADJECTIVE

**silicon**

NOUN Silicon is an element found in sand, clay, and stone. It is used to make parts of computers.

**silk** silks

NOUN Silk is a fine, soft cloth made from a substance produced by silkworms.

🏛 from Chinese *ssu* meaning 'silk'

**silkworm** silkworms

NOUN Silkworms are the larvae of a particular kind of moth.

**silky** silkier silkiest

ADJECTIVE smooth and soft.

**sill** sills

NOUN a ledge at the bottom of a window.

**silly** sillier silliest

ADJECTIVE foolish or childish.

◼ daft, foolish, stupid

**silt**

NOUN Silt is fine sand or soil which is carried along by a river.

**silver**

NOUN **1** Silver is a valuable greyish-white metallic element used for making jewellery and ornaments. **2** Silver is also coins made from silver or from silver-coloured metal. ▶ ADJECTIVE OR NOUN **3** greyish-white.

**silver beet** silver beets

NOUN a type of beet grown in Australia and New Zealand.

**silver fern**

NOUN a tall fern that is found in New Zealand. It is the symbol of New Zealand national sports teams.

an ELegant angEL (angel)   ▶ **SPELLING NOTE**

**silverfish** silverfishes or silverfish

NOUN a small silver insect with no wings that eats paper and clothing.

**silver jubilee** silver jubilees

NOUN the 25th anniversary of an important event.

**silver medal** silver medals

NOUN a medal made from silver awarded to the competitor who comes second in a competition.

**silver wedding** silver weddings

NOUN A couple's silver wedding is the 25th anniversary of their wedding.

**silvery**

ADJECTIVE having the appearance or colour of silver E.G. the silvery moon.

**similar**

ADJECTIVE 1 If one thing is similar to another, or if two things are similar, they are like each other. 2 In maths, two triangles are similar if the angles in one correspond exactly to the angles in the other.

**similarly** ADVERB

☑ Be careful when deciding whether to use similar or same. Similar means 'alike but not identical', and same means 'identical'. Do not put as after similar: her dress was similar to mine.

**similarity** similarities

NOUN If there is a similarity between things, they are similar in some way.

☰ likeness, resemblance

**simile** similes

Said "sim-ill-ee" NOUN (ENGLISH) an expression in which a person or thing is described as being similar to someone or something else. Examples of similes are She runs like a deer and He's as white as a sheet.

**simmer** simmers simmering simmered

VERB When food simmers, it cooks gently at just below boiling point.

**simple** simpler simplest

ADJECTIVE 1 Something that is simple is uncomplicated and easy to understand or do. 2 Simple also means plain and not elaborate in style E.G. a simple coat. 3 A simple way of life is uncomplicated. 4 Someone who is simple is mentally retarded. 5 You use 'simple' to emphasize that what you are talking about is the only important thing E.G. simple stubbornness.

**simplicity** NOUN

**simple-minded**

ADJECTIVE not very intelligent or sophisticated E.G. simple-minded pleasures.

**simplify** simplifies simplifying simplified

VERB To simplify something means to make it easier to do or understand.

**simplification** NOUN

**simplistic**

ADJECTIVE too simple or naive E.G. a rather simplistic approach to the subject.

**simply**

ADVERB 1 Simply means merely E.G. It was simply a question of making the decision. 2 You use 'simply' to emphasize what you are saying E.G. It is simply not true. 3 If you say or write something simply, you do it in a way that makes it easy to understand.

**simulate** simulates simulating simulated

VERB To simulate something means to

A B C D E F G H I J K L M N O P Q R S T U V W X Y Z

imitate it *E.G. The wood has been painted to simulate stone.*
**simulation** NOUN

**simultaneous**
ADJECTIVE Things that are simultaneous happen at the same time.
**simultaneously** ADVERB

**sin** sins sinning sinned
NOUN **1** Sin is wicked and immoral behaviour. ▶ VERB **2** To sin means to do something wicked and immoral.
**目** (sense 1) evil, iniquity, wrongdoing
**目** (sense 2) lapse, transgress

**since**
PREPOSITION, CONJUNCTION, or ADVERB **1** Since means from a particular time until now *E.G. I've been waiting patiently since half past three.* ▶ ADVERB **2** Since also means at some time after a particular time in the past *E.G. They split up and he has since remarried.* ▶ CONJUNCTION **3** Since also means because *E.G. I'm forever on a diet, since I put on weight easily.*
**✓** Do not put *ago* before *since*, as it is not needed: *it is ten years since she wrote her book* not *ten years ago since*.

**sincere**
ADJECTIVE If you are sincere, you say things that you really mean *E.G. a sincere expression of friendliness.*
**sincerity** NOUN
**目** genuine, honest

**sincerely**
ADVERB **1** If you say or feel something sincerely, you mean it or feel it genuinely. ▶ PHRASE **2** You write **Yours sincerely** before your signature at the end of a letter in which you have named the person you are writing to in the greeting at the beginning of

the letter. For example, if you began your letter 'Dear Mr Brown' you would use 'Yours sincerely'.

**sinew** sinews
*Said* "**sin**-yoo" NOUN a tough cord in your body that connects a muscle to a bone.

**sinful**
ADJECTIVE wicked and immoral.

**sing** sings singing sang sung
VERB **1** When you sing, you make musical sounds with your voice, usually producing words that fit a tune. **2** When birds or insects sing, they make pleasant sounds.
**singer** NOUN
**✓** The past tense of *sing* is *sang*, and the past participle is *sung*. Do not confuse these words: *the team sang the national anthem; we have sung together many times.*

**singe** singes singeing singed
VERB **1** To singe something means to burn it slightly so that it goes brown but does not catch fire. ▶ NOUN **2** a slight burn.

**single** singles singling singled
ADJECTIVE **1** Single means only one and not more *E.G. A single shot was fired.* **2** People who are single are not married. **3** A single bed or bedroom is for one person. **4** A single ticket is a one-way ticket. ▶ NOUN **5** a recording of one or two short pieces of music on a small record, CD, or cassette. **6** Singles is a game of tennis, badminton, or squash between just two players.

**single out** VERB If you single someone out from a group, you give them special treatment *E.G. He'd been singled out for some special award.*

a
b
c
d
e
f
g
h
i
j
k
l
m
n
o
p
q
r
**s**
t
u
v
w
x
y
z

**single-handed**

ADVERB If you do something single-handed, you do it on your own, without any help.

**single-minded**

ADJECTIVE A single-minded person has only one aim and is determined to achieve it.

**singly**

ADVERB If people do something singly, they do it on their own or one by one.

**singular**

NOUN **1** In grammar, the singular is the form of a word that refers to just one person or thing. ▶ ADJECTIVE **2** FORMAL unusual and remarkable E.G. *her singular beauty*.

**singularity** NOUN **singularly** ADVERB

**sinister**

ADJECTIVE seeming harmful or evil E.G. *something cold and sinister about him*.

📖 from Latin *sinister* meaning 'left-hand side', because the left side was considered unlucky

**sink** sinks sinking sank sunk

NOUN **1** a basin with taps supplying water, usually in a kitchen or bathroom. ▶ VERB **2** If something sinks, it moves downwards, especially through water E.G. *An Indian cargo ship sank in icy seas*. **3** To sink a ship means to cause it to sink by attacking it. **4** If an amount or value sinks, it decreases. **5** If you sink into an unpleasant state, you gradually pass into it E.G. *He sank into black despair*. **6** To sink something sharp into an object means to make it go deeply into it E.G. *The tiger sank its teeth into his leg*.

**sink in** VERB When a fact sinks in, you fully understand it or realize it E.G. *The truth was at last sinking in*.

**sinner** sinners

NOUN someone who has committed a sin.

**sinus** sinuses

NOUN Your sinuses are the air passages in the bones of your skull, just behind your nose.

**sip** sips sipping sipped

VERB **1** If you sip a drink, you drink it by taking a small amount at a time. ▶ NOUN **2** a small amount of drink that you take into your mouth.

**siphon** siphons siphoning siphoned

*Said* "**sigh**-fn"; also spelt **syphon**
VERB If you siphon off a liquid, you draw it out of a container through a tube and transfer it to another place.

**sir**

NOUN **1** Sir is a polite, formal way of addressing a man. **2** Sir is also the title used in front of the name of a knight or baronet.

**siren** sirens

NOUN a warning device, for example on a police car, which makes a loud, wailing noise.

📖 the Sirens in Greek mythology were sea nymphs who had beautiful voices and sang in order to lure sailors to their deaths on the rocks where the nymphs lived

**sirloin**

NOUN Sirloin is a prime cut of beef from the lower part of a cow's back.

📖 from Old French *sur* meaning 'above' and *longe* meaning 'loin'

**sis** or **sies**

*Said* "**sies**" INTERJECTION; *INFORMAL* In South African English, you say 'Sis!' to show disgust.

**sister** sisters

NOUN **1** Your sister is a girl or woman

who has the same parents as you. **2** a member of a female religious order. **3** In a hospital, a sister is a senior nurse who supervises a ward. ▶ ADJECTIVE **4** Sister means closely related to something or very similar to it *E.G. Citroen and its sister company Peugeot.*

**sisterhood**

NOUN Sisterhood is a strong feeling of companionship between women.

**sister-in-law** sisters-in-law

NOUN Your sister-in-law is the wife of your brother, the sister of your husband or wife, or the woman married to your wife's or husband's brother.

**sit** sits sitting sat

VERB **1** If you are sitting, your weight is supported by your buttocks rather than your feet. **2** When you sit or sit down somewhere, you lower your body until you are sitting. **3** If you sit an examination, you take it. **4** FORMAL When a parliament, law court, or other official body sits, it meets and officially carries out its work.

**sitcom** sitcoms

NOUN; INFORMAL a television comedy series which shows characters in amusing situations that are similar to everyday life.

🔲 shortened from *situation comedy*

**site** sites siting sited

NOUN **1** a piece of ground where a particular thing happens or is situated *E.G. a building site.* ▶ VERB **2** If something is sited in a place, it is built or positioned there.

☑ Do not confuse the spellings of *site* and *sight*.

**sitting** sittings

NOUN **1** one of the times when a meal is served. **2** one of the occasions when a parliament or law court meets and carries out its work.

**sitting room** sitting rooms

NOUN a room in a house where people sit and relax.

**situated**

ADJECTIVE If something is situated somewhere, that is where it is *E.G. a town situated 45 minutes from Geneva.*

**situation** situations

NOUN **1** what is happening in a particular place at a particular time *E.G. the political situation.*
**2** ( GEOGRAPHY ) The situation of a building or town is its surroundings *E.G. a beautiful situation.*

🔳 (sense 1) circumstances, condition, state of affairs

**Siva**

PROPER NOUN Siva is a Hindu god and is one of the Trimurti.

🔳 from a Sanskrit word meaning 'auspicious'

**six**

Six is the number 6.

**sixteen**

the number 16.

**sixteenth**

**sixth** sixths

**1** The sixth item in a series is the one counted as number six.
NOUN **2** one of six equal parts.

**sixth sense**

NOUN You say that someone has a sixth sense when they know something instinctively, without having any evidence of it.

**sixty** sixties

the number 60.

**sixtieth**

**sizable** or **sizeable**

ADJECTIVE fairly large *E.G. a sizable amount of money.*

Betty Eats Cakes And Uses Seven Eggs (<u>because</u>) ▶ SPELLING NOTE

A
B
C
D
E
F
G
H
I
J
K
L
M
N
O
P
Q
R
**S**
T
U
V
W
X
Y
Z

**size** sizes

NOUN **1** The size of something is how big or small it is E.G. *the size of the audience.* **2** The size of something is also the fact that it is very large E.G. *the sheer size of Australia.* **3** one of the standard graded measurements of clothes and shoes.

■ (sense 1) dimensions, magnitude, proportions

**sizzle** sizzles sizzling sizzled

VERB If something sizzles, it makes a hissing sound like the sound of frying food

**sjambok** sjamboks

*Said "sham-bok"* NOUN In South African English, a sjambok is a long whip made from animal hide.

**skate** skates skating skated

NOUN **1** Skates are ice skates or roller skates. **2** a flat edible sea fish. ► VERB **3** If you skate, you move about on ice wearing ice skates. **4** If you skate round a difficult subject, you avoid discussing it.

**skateboard** skateboards

NOUN a narrow board on wheels which you stand on and ride for fun.

**skeleton** skeletons

NOUN Your skeleton is the framework of bones in your body.

**sketch** sketches sketching sketched

NOUN **1** (ART) a quick, rough drawing. **2** A sketch of a situation or incident is a brief description of it. **3** a short, humorous piece of acting, usually forming part of a comedy show. ► VERB **4** If you sketch something, you draw it quickly and roughly.

**sketchy** sketchier sketchiest

ADJECTIVE giving only a rough description or account E.G. *Details* surrounding his death are sketchy.

**skew** or **skewed**

*Said "skyoo"* ADJECTIVE in a slanting position, rather than straight or upright.

**skewer** skewers skewering skewered

NOUN **1** a long metal pin used to hold pieces of food together during cooking. ► VERB **2** If you skewer something, you push a skewer through it.

**ski** skis skiing skied

NOUN **1** Skis are long pieces of wood, metal, or plastic that you fasten to special boots so you can move easily on snow. ► VERB **2** When you ski, you move on snow wearing skis, especially as a sport.

▥ from Old Norse *skith* meaning 'snowshoes'

**skid** skids skidding skidded

VERB If a vehicle skids, it slides in an uncontrolled way, for example because the road is wet or icy.

**skilful**

ADJECTIVE If you are skilful at something, you can do it very well. **skilfully** ADVERB

■ able, expert, proficient

**skill** skills

NOUN **1** Skill is the knowledge and ability that enables you to do something well. **2** a type of work or technique which requires special training and knowledge.

■ (sense 1) ability, expertise, proficiency

**skilled**

ADJECTIVE **1** A skilled person has the knowledge and ability to do something well. **2** Skilled work is work which can only be done by people who have had special training.

**skim** skims skimming skimmed

VERB 1 If you skim something from the surface of a liquid, you remove it. 2 If something skims a surface, it moves along just above it *E.G. seagulls skimming the waves*.

**skimmed milk**

NOUN Skimmed milk has had the cream removed.

**skin** skins skinning skinned

NOUN 1 Your skin is the natural covering of your body. An animal skin is the skin and fur of a dead animal. 2 The skin of a fruit or vegetable is its outer covering. 3 a solid layer which forms on the surface of a liquid. ▶ VERB 4 If you skin a dead animal, you remove its skin. 5 If you skin a part of your body, you accidentally graze it.

**skinny** skinnier skinniest

ADJECTIVE extremely thin.

**skip** skips skipping skipped

VERB 1 If you skip along, you move along jumping from one foot to the other. 2 If you skip something, you miss it out or avoid doing it *E.G. It is all too easy to skip meals*. ▶ NOUN 3 Skips are the movements you make when you skip. 4 a large metal container for holding rubbish and rubble.

**skipper** skippers

NOUN; INFORMAL The skipper of a ship or boat is its captain.

📖 from Old Dutch *schipper* meaning 'shipper'

**skirmish** skirmishes

NOUN a short, rough fight.

**skirt** skirts skirting skirted

NOUN 1 A woman's skirt is a piece of

clothing which fastens at her waist and hangs down over her legs. ▶ VERB 2 Something that skirts an area is situated around the edge of it. 3 If you skirt something, you go around the edge of it *E.G. We skirted the town*. 4 If you skirt a problem, you avoid dealing with it *E.G. He was skirting the real question*.

📖 from Old Norse *skyrta* meaning 'shirt'

**skirting** skirtings

NOUN A skirting or skirting board is a narrow strip of wood running along the bottom of a wall in a room.

**skite** skites skiting skited INFORMAL

VERB 1 In Australian and New Zealand English, to skite is to talk in a boastful way about something that you own or that you have done. ▶ NOUN 2 In Australian and New Zealand English, someone who boasts.

**skittle** skittles

NOUN Skittles is a game in which players roll a ball and try to knock down wooden objects called skittles.

**skull** skulls

NOUN Your skull is the bony part of your head which surrounds your brain.

**skunk** skunks

NOUN a small black and white animal from North America which gives off an unpleasant smell when it is frightened.

📖 a North American Indian word

**sky** skies

NOUN The sky is the space around the earth which you can see when you look upwards.

📖 from Old Norse *sky* meaning 'cloud'

A
B
C
D
E
F
G
H
I
J
K
L
M
N
O
P
Q
R
**S**
T
U
V
W
X
Y
Z

**skylight** skylights
NOUN a window in a roof or ceiling.

**skyline** skylines
NOUN The skyline is the line where the sky meets buildings or the ground E.G. *the New York City skyline.*

**skyscraper** skyscrapers
NOUN a very tall building.

**slab** slabs
NOUN a thick, flat piece of something.

**slack** slacker slackest; slacks
ADJECTIVE **1** Something that is slack is loose and not firmly stretched or positioned. **2** A slack period is one in which there is not much work to do. ► NOUN **3** The slack in a rope is the part that hangs loose. ► PLURAL NOUN **4** Slacks are casual trousers.
**slackness** NOUN

**slacken** slackens slackening slackened
VERB **1** If something slackens, it becomes slower or less intense E.G. *The rain had slackened to a drizzle.* **2** To slacken also means to become looser E.G. *Her grip slackened on Arnold's arm.*

**slag** slags slagging slagged
NOUN **1** Slag is the waste material left when ore has been melted down to remove the metal E.G. *a slag heap.* ► VERB **2** INFORMAL To slag someone off means to criticize them in an unpleasant way, usually behind their back.

**slalom** slaloms
*Said "slah-lom"* NOUN a skiing competition in which the competitors have to twist and turn quickly to avoid obstacles.
📖 from Norwegian *slad* + *lom* meaning 'sloping path'

**slam** slams slamming slammed
VERB **1** If you slam a door or if it slams,

it shuts noisily and with great force. **2** If you slam something down, you throw it down violently E.G. *She slammed the phone down.*

**slander** slanders slandering slandered
NOUN **1** Slander is something untrue and malicious said about someone. ► VERB **2** To slander someone means to say untrue and malicious things about them.
**slanderous** ADJECTIVE
■ (sense 1) defamation, smear

**slang**
NOUN Slang consists of very informal words and expressions.

**slant** slants slanting slanted
VERB **1** If something slants, it slopes E.G. *The back can be adjusted to slant into the most comfortable position.* **2** If news or information is slanted, it is presented in a biased way. ► NOUN **3** a slope. **4** A slant on a subject is one way of looking at it, especially a biased one.

**slap** slaps slapping slapped
VERB **1** If you slap someone, you hit them with the palm of your hand. **2** If you slap something onto a surface, you put it there quickly and noisily. ► NOUN **3** If you give someone a slap, you slap them.
📖 from German *Schlappe* an imitation of the sound

**slash** slashes slashing slashed
VERB **1** If you slash something, you make a long, deep cut in it. **2** INFORMAL To slash money means to reduce it greatly E.G. *Car makers could be forced to slash prices.* ► NOUN **3** a diagonal line that separates letters, words, or numbers, for example in the number 340/21/K.

**slat** slats
NOUN Slats are the narrow pieces of wood or metal plastic in things such as Venetian blinds.
**slatted** ADJECTIVE

**slate** slates slating slated
NOUN **1** Slate is a dark grey rock that splits easily into thin layers. **2** Slates are small, flat pieces of slate used for covering roofs. ▶ VERB **3** INFORMAL If critics slate a play, film, or book, they criticize it severely.

**slaughter** slaughters slaughtering slaughtered
VERB **1** To slaughter a large number of people means to kill them unjustly or cruelly. **2** To slaughter farm animals means to kill them for meat. ▶ NOUN **3** Slaughter is the killing of many people.
⬛ (sense 3) carnage, massacre, murder

**slave** slaves slaving slaved
NOUN **1** someone who is owned by another person and must work for them. ▶ VERB **2** If you slave for someone, you work very hard for them.
**slavery** NOUN
🏛 from Latin *Sclavus* meaning 'a Slav', because the Slavonic races were frequently conquered and made into slaves

**slay** slays slaying slew slain
VERB; LITERARY To slay someone means to kill them.

**sleazy** sleazier sleaziest
ADJECTIVE A sleazy place looks dirty, run-down, and not respectable.

**sled** sleds
NOUN a sledge.

**sledge** sledges
NOUN a vehicle on runners used for travelling over snow.

**sledgehammer** sledgehammers
NOUN a large, heavy hammer.

**sleek** sleeker sleekest
ADJECTIVE **1** Sleek hair is smooth and shiny. **2** Someone who is sleek looks rich and dresses elegantly.

**sleep** sleeps sleeping slept
NOUN **1** Sleep is the natural state of rest in which your eyes are closed and you are unconscious. **2** If you have a sleep, you sleep for a while E.G. *He'll be ready for a sleep soon.* ▶ VERB **3** When you sleep, you rest in a state of sleep. ▶ PHRASE **4** If a sick or injured animal **is put to sleep**, it is painlessly killed.
⬛ (sense 2) doze, nap, slumber

**sleeper** sleepers
NOUN **1** You use 'sleeper' to say how deeply someone sleeps E.G. *I'm a very heavy sleeper.* **2** a bed on a train, or a train which has beds on it. **3** Railway sleepers are the large beams that support the rails of a railway track.

**sleeping bag** sleeping bags
NOUN a large, warm bag for sleeping in, especially when you are camping.

**sleeping pill** sleeping pills
NOUN A sleeping pill or a sleeping tablet is a pill which you take to help you sleep.

**sleepout** sleepouts
NOUN **1** In Australia, an area of veranda or porch which has been closed off to be used as a bedroom. **2** In New Zealand, a small building outside a house, used for sleeping.

**sleepover** sleepovers
NOUN a gathering or party at which friends spend the night at another friend's house.

**sleepwalk** sleepwalks sleepwalking sleepwalked

a b c d e f g h i j k l m n o p q r s t u v w x y z

A
B
C
D
E
F
G
H
I
J
K
L
M
N
O
P
Q
R
S
T
U
V
W
X
Y
Z

VERB If you sleepwalk, you walk around while you are asleep.

**sleepy** sleepier sleepiest
ADJECTIVE **1** tired and ready to go to sleep. **2** A sleepy town or village is very quiet.

**sleepily** ADVERB **sleepiness** NOUN

**sleet**
NOUN Sleet is a mixture of rain and snow.

**sleeve** sleeves
NOUN The sleeves of a piece of clothing are the parts that cover your arms.

**sleeveless** ADJECTIVE

**sleigh** sleighs
Said "slay" NOUN a sledge.

**slender**
ADJECTIVE **1** attractively thin and graceful. **2** small in amount or degree E.G. the first slender hopes of peace.
■ (sense 1) slim, willowy

**sleuth** sleuths
Said "slooth" NOUN; OLD-FASHIONED a detective.
🔒 a shortened form of *sleuthhound*, a tracker dog, from Old Norse *sloth* meaning 'track'

**slew** slews slewing slewed
**1** Slew is the past tense of **slay**.
▶ VERB **2** If a vehicle slews, it slides or skids E.G. The bike slewed into the crowd.

**slice** slices slicing sliced
NOUN **1** A slice of cake, bread, or other food is a piece of it cut from a larger piece. **2** a kitchen tool with a broad, flat blade E.G. a fish slice. **3** In sport, a slice is a stroke in which the player makes the ball go to one side, rather than straight ahead. ▶ VERB **4** If you slice food, you cut it into thin pieces. **5** To slice through something means to cut or move through it quickly,

like a knife E.G. The ship sliced through the water.

**slick** slicker slickest; slicks
ADJECTIVE **1** A slick action is done quickly and smoothly E.G. slick passing and strong running. **2** A slick person speaks easily and persuasively but is not sincere E.G. a slick TV presenter. ▶ NOUN **3** An oil slick is a layer of oil floating on the surface of the sea or a lake.

**slide** slides sliding slid
VERB **1** When something slides, it moves smoothly over or against something else. ▶ NOUN **2** a small piece of photographic film which can be projected onto a screen so that you can see the picture. **3** a small piece of glass on which you put something that you want to examine through a microscope. **4** In a playground, a slide is a structure with a steep, slippery slope for children to slide down.

**slight** slighter slightest; slights slighting slighted
ADJECTIVE **1** Slight means small in amount or degree E.G. a slight dent.
**2** A slight person has a slim body.
▶ PHRASE **3** Not in the slightest means not at all E.G. This doesn't surprise me in the slightest. ▶ VERB **4** If you slight someone, you insult them by behaving rudely towards them.
▶ NOUN **5** A slight is rude or insulting behaviour.

**slightly** ADVERB

**slim** slimmer slimmest; slims slimming slimmed
ADJECTIVE **1** A slim person is attractively thin. **2** A slim object is thinner than usual E.G. a slim book. **3** If there is only a slim chance that something will happen, it is unlikely

to happen. ▸ VERB **4** If you are slimming, you are trying to lose weight.

**slimmer** NOUN

**slime**

NOUN Slime is an unpleasant, thick, slippery substance.

🏛 from Old English *slim* meaning 'soft sticky mud'

**slimy** slimier slimiest

ADJECTIVE **1** covered in slime. **2** Slimy people are friendly and pleasant in an insincere way *E.G. a slimy business partner.*

**sling** slings slinging slung

VERB **1** INFORMAL If you sling something somewhere, you throw it there. **2** If you sling a rope between two points, you attach it so that it hangs loosely between them. ▸ NOUN **3** a piece of cloth tied round a person's neck to support a broken or injured arm. **4** a device made of ropes or cloth used for carrying things.

**slip** slips slipping slipped

VERB **1** If you slip, you accidentally slide and lose your balance. **2** If something slips, it slides out of place accidentally *E.G. One of the knives slipped from her grasp.* **3** If you slip somewhere, you go there quickly and quietly *E.G. She slipped out of the house.* **4** If you slip something somewhere, you put it there quickly and quietly. **5** If something slips to a lower level or standard, it falls to that level or standard *E.G. The shares slipped to an all-time low.* ▸ NOUN **6** a small mistake. **7** A slip of paper is a small piece of paper. **8** a piece of clothing worn under a dress or skirt.

**slipped disc** slipped discs

NOUN a painful condition in which

one of the discs in your spine has moved out of its proper position.

**slipper** slippers

NOUN Slippers are loose, soft shoes that you wear indoors.

**slippery**

ADJECTIVE **1** smooth, wet, or greasy, and difficult to hold or walk on. **2** You describe a person as slippery when they cannot be trusted.

**slippery dip** slippery dips

NOUN; INFORMAL In Australian English, a children's slide at a playground or funfair.

**slip rail** slip rails

NOUN In Australian and New Zealand English, a rail in a fence that can be slipped out of place to make an opening.

**slipstream** slipstreams

NOUN The slipstream of a car or plane is the flow of air directly behind it.

**slit** slits slitting slit

VERB **1** If you slit something, you make a long, narrow cut in it. ▸ NOUN **2** a long, narrow cut or opening.

**slither** slithers slithering slithered

VERB To slither somewhere means to move there by sliding along the ground in an uneven way *E.G. The snake slithered into the water.*

**sliver** slivers

NOUN a small, thin piece of something.

**slob** slobs

NOUN; INFORMAL a lazy, untidy person.

**slog** slogs slogging slogged

VERB; INFORMAL If you slog at something, you work hard and steadily at it *E.G. They are still slogging away at algebra.*

**slogan** slogans

NOUN a short, easily-remembered

a
b
c
d
e
f
g
h
i
j
k
l
m
n
o
p
q
r
s
t
u
v
w
x
y
z

A
B
C
D
E
F
G
H
I
J
K
L
M
N
O
P
Q
R
S
T
U
V
W
X
Y
Z

phrase used in advertising or by a political party.

🔲 from Gaelic *sluagh-ghairm* meaning 'war cry'

🟦 catch-phrase, motto

**slop** slops slopping slopped
VERB **1** If a liquid slops, it spills over the edge of a container in a messy way. ▶ PLURAL NOUN **2** You can refer to dirty water or liquid waste as slops.

**slope** slopes sloping sloped
NOUN **1** a flat surface that is at an angle, so that one end is higher than the other. **2** The slope of something is the angle at which it slopes. ▶ VERB **3** If a surface slopes, it is at an angle. **4** If something slopes, it leans to one side rather than being upright E.G. *sloping handwriting.*

🟦 (sense 1) incline, slant, tilt
🟦 (sense 2) gradient, inclination

**sloppy** sloppier sloppiest
ADJECTIVE *INFORMAL* **1** very messy or careless E.G. *two sloppy performances.* **2** foolishly sentimental E.G. *some sloppy love story.*

**sloppily** ADVERB **sloppiness** NOUN

**slot** slots slotting slotted
NOUN **1** a narrow opening in a machine or container, for example for putting coins in. ▶ VERB **2** When you slot something into something else, you put it into a space where it fits.

**sloth** sloths
*Rhymes with "growth"* NOUN **1** *FORMAL* Sloth is laziness. **2** a South and Central American animal that moves very slowly and hangs upside down from the branches of trees.

**slouch** slouches slouching slouched
VERB If you slouch, you stand or sit

with your shoulders and head drooping forwards.

**slouch hat** slouch hats
NOUN a hat with a wide, flexible brim, especially an Australian army hat with the left side of the brim turned up.

**Slovak** Slovaks
ADJECTIVE **1** belonging to or relating to Slovakia. ▶ NOUN **2** someone who comes from Slovakia. **3** Slovak is the language spoken in Slovakia.

**slow** slower slowest; slows slowing slowed
ADJECTIVE **1** moving, happening, or doing something with very little speed E.G. *His progress was slow.* **2** Someone who is slow is not very clever. **3** If a clock or watch is slow, it shows a time earlier than the correct one. ▶ VERB **4** If something slows, slows down, or slows up, it moves or happens more slowly.

**slowly** ADVERB **slowness** NOUN

**slow motion**
NOUN Slow motion is movement which is much slower than normal, especially in a film E.G. *It all seemed to happen in slow motion.*

**sludge**
NOUN Sludge is thick mud or sewage.

**slug** slugs
NOUN **1** a small, slow-moving creative with a slimy body, like a snail without a shell. **2** *INFORMAL* A slug of a strong alcoholic drink is a mouthful of it.

**sluggish**
ADJECTIVE moving slowly and without energy E.G. *the sluggish waters.*

**sluice** sluices sluicing sluiced
*Said "sloose"* NOUN **1** a channel which carries water, with an opening called a sluicegate which can be opened or

closed to control the flow of water.
► VERB **2** If you sluice something, you wash it by pouring water over it E.G. *He had sluiced his hands under a tap.*
🏛 from Latin *exclusa aqua* meaning 'water shut out'

**slum** slums
NOUN a poor, run-down area of a city.

**slumber** slumbers slumbering slumbered *LITERARY*
NOUN **1** Slumber is sleep. ► VERB **2** When you slumber, you sleep.

**slump** slumps slumping slumped
VERB **1** If an amount or a value slumps, it falls suddenly by a large amount. **2** If you slump somewhere, you fall or sit down heavily E.G. *He slumped against the side of the car.* ► NOUN **3** a sudden, severe drop in an amount or value E.G. *the slump in house prices.* **4** a time when there is economic decline and high unemployment.

**slur** slurs slurring slurred
NOUN **1** an insulting remark. ► VERB **2** When people slur their speech, they do not say their words clearly, often because they are drunk or ill.

**slurp** slurps slurping slurped
VERB If you slurp a drink, you drink it noisily.
🏛 from Old Dutch *slorpen* meaning 'to sip'

**slush**
NOUN **1** Slush is wet melting snow. **2** *INFORMAL* You can refer to sentimental love stories as slush.
**slushy** ADJECTIVE

**slut** sluts
NOUN; *OFFENSIVE* a dirty, untidy woman, or one considered to be immoral.

**sly** slyer or slier slyest or sliest
ADJECTIVE **1** A sly expression or remark shows that you know something

other people do not know E.G. *a sly smile.* **2** A sly person is cunning and good at deceiving people.
**slyly** ADVERB
▦ (sense 2) crafty, cunning, devious

**smack** smacks smacking smacked
VERB **1** If you smack someone, you hit them with your open hand. **2** If something smacks of something else, it reminds you of it E.G. *His tale smacks of fantasy.* ► NOUN **3** If you give someone a smack, you smack them. **4** a loud, sharp noise E.G. *He landed with a smack on the tank.*

**small** smaller smallest; smalls
ADJECTIVE **1** Small means not large in size, number, or amount. **2** Small means not important or significant E.G. *small changes.* ► NOUN **3** The small of your back is the narrow part where your back curves slightly inwards.
▦ (sense 1) little, tiny
▦ (sense 2) insignificant, minor, trivial

**smallpox**
NOUN Smallpox is a serious contagious disease that causes a fever and a rash.

**small talk**
NOUN Small talk is conversation about unimportant things.

**smart** smarter smartest; smarts smarting smarted
ADJECTIVE **1** A smart person is clean and neatly dressed. **2** Smart means clever E.G. *a smart idea.* **3** A smart movement is quick and sharp. ► VERB **4** If a wound smarts, it stings. **5** If you are smarting from criticism or unkindness, you are feeling upset by it.
**smartly** ADVERB

a b c d e f g h i j k l m n o p q r s t u v w x y z

A
B
C
D
E
F
G
H
I
J
K
L
M
N
O
P
Q
R
**S**
T
U
V
W
X
Y
Z

**smarten** smartens smartening smartened

VERB If you smarten something up, you make it look neater and tidier.

**smash** smashes smashing smashed

VERB 1 If you smash something, you break it into a lot of pieces by hitting it or dropping it. 2 To smash through something such as a wall means to go through it by breaking it. 3 To smash against something means to hit it with great force E.G. *An immense wave smashed against the hull.* ▶ NOUN 4 INFORMAL If a play or film is a smash or a smash hit, it is very successful. 5 a car crash. 6 In tennis, a smash is a stroke in which the player hits the ball downwards very hard.

**smashing**

ADJECTIVE; INFORMAL If you describe something as smashing, you mean you like it very much.

**smattering**

NOUN A smattering of knowledge or information is a very small amount of it E.G. *a smattering of Russian.*

**smear** smears smearing smeared

NOUN 1 a dirty, greasy mark on a surface E.G. *a smear of pink lipstick.* 2 an untrue and malicious rumour. ▶ VERB 3 If something smears a surface, it makes dirty, greasy marks on it E.G. *The blade was chipped and smeared.* 4 If you smear a surface with a greasy or sticky substance, you spread a layer of the substance over the surface.

**smell** smells smelling smelled or smelt

NOUN 1 The smell of something is a quality it has which you perceive

through your nose E.G. *a smell of damp wood.* 2 Your sense of smell is your ability to smell things. ▶ VERB 3 If something smells or if you can smell it, it has a quality you can perceive through your nose E.G. *He smelled of tobacco and garlic.* 4 If you can smell something such as danger or trouble, you feel it is present or likely to happen.

■ (sense 1) odour, scent

**smelly** smellier smelliest

ADJECTIVE having a strong, unpleasant smell.

**smelt** smelts smelting smelted

VERB To smelt a metal ore means to heat it until it melts, so that the metal can be extracted.

**smile** smiles smiling smiled

VERB 1 When you smile, the corners of your mouth move outwards and slightly upwards because you are pleased or amused. ▶ NOUN 2 the expression you have when you smile.

**smirk** smirks smirking smirked

VERB 1 When you smirk, you smile in a sneering or sarcastic way E.G. *The boy smirked and turned the volume up.* ▶ NOUN 2 a sneering or sarcastic smile.

**smith** smiths

NOUN someone who makes things out of iron, gold, or another metal.

**smitten**

ADJECTIVE If you are smitten with someone or something, you are very impressed with or enthusiastic about them E.G. *They were totally smitten with each other.*

**smock** smocks

NOUN a loose garment like a long blouse.

**smog**

NOUN Smog is a mixture of smoke and fog which occurs in some industrial cities.

**smoke** smokes smoking smoked

NOUN 1 Smoke is a mixture of gas and small particles sent into the air when something burns. ► VERB 2 If something is smoking, smoke is coming from it. 3 When someone smokes a cigarette or pipe, they suck smoke from it into their mouth and blow it out again. 4 To smoke fish or meat means to hang it over burning wood so that the smoke preserves it and gives it a pleasant flavour E.G. smoked bacon.

**smoker** NOUN **smoking** NOUN

**smoky** smokier smokiest

ADJECTIVE A smoky place is full of smoke.

**smooth** smoother smoothest; smooths smoothing smoothed

ADJECTIVE 1 A smooth surface has no roughness and no holes in it. 2 A smooth liquid or mixture has no lumps in it. 3 A smooth movement or process happens evenly and steadily E.G. smooth acceleration. 4 Smooth also means successful and without problems E.G. staff responsible for the smooth running of the hall. ► VERB 5 If you smooth something, you move your hands over it to make it smooth and flat.

**smoothly** ADVERB **smoothness** NOUN

**smoothie** smoothies

NOUN a thick type of drink made in an electric blender from milk, fruit and crushed ice.

**smother** smothers smothering smothered

VERB 1 If you smother a fire, you cover it with something to put it out. 2 To smother a person means to cover their face with something so that they cannot breathe. 3 To smother someone also means to give them too much love and protection E.G. She loved her own children, almost smothering them with love. 4 If you smother an emotion, you control it so that people do not notice it E.G. They tried to smother their glee.

**smothered**

ADJECTIVE completely covered with something E.G. a spectacular trellis smothered in climbing roses.

**smoulder** smoulders smouldering smouldered

VERB 1 When something smoulders, it burns slowly, producing smoke but no flames. 2 If a feeling is smouldering inside you, you feel it very strongly but do not show it E.G. smouldering with resentment.

**smudge** smudges smudging smudged

NOUN 1 a dirty or blurred mark or a smear on something. ► VERB 2 If you smudge something, you make it dirty or messy by touching it or marking it.

**smug** smugger smuggest

ADJECTIVE Someone who is smug is very pleased with how good or clever they are.

**smugly** ADVERB **smugness** NOUN

**smuggle** smuggles smuggling smuggled

VERB To smuggle things or people into or out of a place means to take them there illegally or secretly.

**smuggler** smugglers

NOUN someone who smuggles goods illegally into a country.

A
B
C
D
E
F
G
H
I
J
K
L
M
N
O
P
Q
R
**S**
T
U
V
W
X
Y
Z

**snack** snacks
NOUN a light, quick meal.

**snag** snags snagging snagged
NOUN 1 a small problem or disadvantage E.G. *There is one snag: it is not true.* ▶ VERB 2 If you snag your clothing, you damage it by catching it on something sharp. ▶ NOUN; *INFORMAL* 3 In Australian and New Zealand English, a sausage.

**snail** snails
NOUN a small, slow-moving creature with a long, shiny body and a shell on its back.

**snail mail**
NOUN; *INFORMAL* the conventional postal system, as opposed to email.

**snake** snakes snaking snaked
NOUN 1 a long, thin, scaly reptile with no legs. ▶ VERB 2 Something that snakes moves in long winding curves E.G. *The queue snaked out of the shop.*

**snap** snaps snapping snapped
VERB 1 If something snaps or if you snap it, it breaks with a sharp cracking noise. 2 If you snap something into a particular position, you move it there quickly with a sharp sound. 3 If an animal snaps at you, it shuts its jaws together quickly as if to bite you. 4 If someone snaps at you, they speak in a sharp, unfriendly way. 5 If you snap someone, you take a quick photograph of them. ▶ NOUN 6 the sound of something snapping. 7 *INFORMAL* a photograph taken quickly and casually. ▶ ADJECTIVE 8 A snap decision or action is taken suddenly without careful thought.

**snapper** snappers
NOUN a fish with edible pink flesh,

found in waters around Australia and New Zealand.

**snapshot** snapshots
NOUN a photograph taken quickly and casually.

**snare** snares snaring snared
NOUN 1 a trap for catching birds or small animals. ▶ VERB 2 To snare an animal or bird means to catch it using a snare.

**snarl** snarls snarling snarled
VERB 1 When an animal snarls, it bares its teeth and makes a fierce growling noise. 2 If you snarl, you say something in a fierce, angry way. ▶ NOUN 3 the noise an animal makes when it snarls.

**snatch** snatches snatching snatched
VERB 1 If you snatch something, you reach out for it quickly and take it. 2 If you snatch an amount of time or an opportunity, you quickly make use of it. ▶ NOUN 3 If you make a snatch at something, you reach out for it quickly to try to take it. 4 A snatch of conversation or song is a very small piece of it.

**sneak** sneaks sneaking sneaked
VERB 1 If you sneak somewhere, you go there quickly trying not to be seen or heard. 2 If you sneak something somewhere, you take it there secretly. ▶ NOUN 3 *INFORMAL* someone who tells people in authority that someone else has done something wrong.

**sneaker** sneakers
NOUN Sneakers are casual shoes with rubber soles.

**sneaking**
ADJECTIVE If you have a sneaking feeling about something or

someone, you have this feeling rather reluctantly *E.G. I had a sneaking suspicion that she was enjoying herself.*

**sneaky** sneakier sneakiest
ADJECTIVE; *INFORMAL* Someone who is sneaky does things secretly rather than openly.

**sneer** sneers sneering sneered
VERB **1** If you sneer at someone or something, you show by your expression and your comments that you think they are stupid or inferior. ▶ NOUN **2** the expression on someone's face when they sneer.

**sneeze** sneezes sneezing sneezed
VERB **1** When you sneeze, you suddenly take in breath and blow it down your nose noisily, because there is a tickle in your nose. ▶ NOUN **2** an act of sneezing.

**snide**
ADJECTIVE A snide comment or remark criticizes someone in a nasty and unfair way.

**sniff** sniffs sniffing sniffed
VERB **1** When you sniff, you breathe in air through your nose hard enough to make a sound. **2** If you sniff something, you smell it by sniffing. **3** You can say that a person sniffs at something when they do not think very much of it *E.G. Bessie sniffed at his household arrangements.* ▶ NOUN **4** the noise you make when you sniff. **5** A sniff of something is a smell of it *E.G. a sniff at the flowers.*

**snigger** sniggers sniggering sniggered
VERB **1** If you snigger, you laugh in a quiet, sly way *E.G. They were sniggering at her accent.* ▶ NOUN **2** a

quiet, disrespectful laugh.

**snip** snips snipping snipped
VERB **1** If you snip something, you cut it with scissors or shears in a single quick action. ▶ NOUN **2** a small cut made by scissors or shears.

**snippet** snippets
NOUN A snippet of something such as information or news is a small piece of it.

**snob** snobs
NOUN **1** someone who admires upper-class people and looks down on lower-class people. **2** someone who believes that they are better than other people.
**snobbery** NOUN    **snobbish** ADJECTIVE

**snooker**
NOUN Snooker is a game played on a large table covered with smooth green cloth. Players score points by hitting different coloured balls into side pockets using a long stick called a cue.

**snoop** snoops snooping snooped
VERB; *INFORMAL* Someone who is snooping is secretly looking round a place to find out things.
📖 from Dutch *snoepen* meaning 'to eat furtively'

**snooze** snoozes snoozing snoozed *INFORMAL*
VERB **1** If you snooze, you sleep lightly for a short time, especially during the day. ▶ NOUN **2** a short, light sleep.

**snore** snores snoring snored
VERB **1** When a sleeping person snores, they make a loud noise each time they breathe. ▶ NOUN **2** the noise someone makes when they snore.

**snorkel** snorkels
NOUN a tube you can breathe through when you are swimming just under

a b c d e f g h i j k l m n o p q r s t u v w x y z

the surface of the sea.

**snorkelling** NOUN

🔲 from German *Schnorchel*, originally an air pipe for a submarine

**snort snorts snorting snorted**
VERB 1 When people or animals snort, they force breath out through their nose in a noisy way E.G. *Sarah snorted with laughter.* ▶ NOUN 2 the noise you make when you snort.

**snout snouts**
NOUN An animal's snout is its nose.

**snow snows snowing snowed**
NOUN 1 Snow consists of flakes of ice crystals which fall from the sky in cold weather. ▶ VERB 2 When it snows, snow falls from the sky.

**snowball snowballs snowballing snowballed**
NOUN 1 a ball of snow for throwing. ▶ VERB 2 When something such as a project snowballs, it grows rapidly.

**snowdrift snowdrifts**
NOUN a deep pile of snow formed by the wind.

**snowdrop snowdrops**
NOUN a small white flower which appears in early spring.

**snowman snowmen**
NOUN a large mound of snow moulded into the shape of a person.

**snub snubs snubbing snubbed**
VERB 1 To snub someone means to behave rudely towards them, especially by making an insulting remark or ignoring them. ▶ NOUN 2 an insulting remark or a piece of rude behaviour. ▶ ADJECTIVE 3 A snub nose is short and turned-up.
▣ (sense 2) affront, insult, slap in the face

**snuff**
NOUN Snuff is powdered tobacco

which people take by sniffing it up their noses.

**snug**
ADJECTIVE A snug place is warm and comfortable. If you are snug, you are warm and comfortable.

**snugly** ADVERB

**snuggle snuggles snuggling snuggled**
VERB If you snuggle somewhere, you cuddle up more closely to something or someone.

**so**
ADVERB 1 'So' is used to refer back to what has just been mentioned E.G. *Had he locked the car? If so, where were the keys?* 2 'So' is used to mean also E.G. *He laughed, and so did Jarvis.* 3 'So' can be used to mean 'therefore' E.G. *It's a bit expensive, so I don't think I will get one.* 4 'So' is used when you are talking about the degree or extent of something E.G. *Why are you so cruel?* 5 'So' is used before words like 'much' and 'many' to say that there is a definite limit to something E.G. *There are only so many questions that can be asked about the record.*
▶ CONJUNCTION 6 'So that' and 'so as' are used to introduce the reason for doing something E.G. *to die so that you might live.*

**soak soaks soaking soaked**
VERB 1 To soak something or leave it to soak means to put it in a liquid and leave it there. 2 When a liquid soaks something, it makes it very wet. 3 When something soaks up a liquid, the liquid is drawn up into it.
▣ (sense 2) saturate, wet

**soaked**
ADJECTIVE extremely wet.

A B C D E F G H I J K L M N O P Q R S T U V W X Y Z

**soaking**
ADJECTIVE If something is soaking, it is very wet.

**soap soaps**
NOUN Soap is a substance made of natural oils and fats and used for washing yourself.
**soapy** ADJECTIVE

**soap opera soap operas**
NOUN a popular television drama serial about people's daily lives.

**soar soars soaring soared**
VERB 1 If an amount soars, it quickly increases by a great deal E.G. *Property prices soared.* 2 If something soars into the air, it quickly goes up into the air.
**soaring** ADJECTIVE

**sob sobs sobbing sobbed**
VERB 1 When someone sobs, they cry in a noisy way, breathing in short breaths. ▶ NOUN 2 the noise made when you cry.

**sober soberer soberest; sobers sobering sobered**
ADJECTIVE 1 If someone is sober, they are not drunk. 2 Sober also means serious and thoughtful. 3 Sober colours are plain and rather dull.
▶ VERB 4 To sober up means to become sober after being drunk.
**soberly** ADVERB

**sobering**
ADJECTIVE Something which is sobering makes you serious and thoughtful E.G. *the sobering lesson of the last year.*

**so-called**
ADJECTIVE You use 'so-called' to say that the name by which something is called is incorrect or misleading E.G. *so-called environmentally-friendly products.*

**soccer**
NOUN Soccer is a game played by two teams of eleven players kicking a ball in an attempt to score goals.
▤ formed from *Association Football*

**sociable**
ADJECTIVE Sociable people are friendly and enjoy talking to other people.
**sociability** NOUN
▤ friendly, gregarious, outgoing

**social**
ADJECTIVE 1 to do with society or life within a society E.G. *women from similar social backgrounds.* 2 to do with leisure activities that involve meeting other people.
**socially** ADVERB

**socialism**
NOUN Socialism is the political belief that the state should own industries on behalf of the people and that everyone should be equal.
**socialist** ADJECTIVE or NOUN

**socialize socializes socializing socialized; also spelt socialise**
VERB When people socialize, they meet other people socially, for example at parties.

**social security**
NOUN Social security is a system by which the government pays money regularly to people who have no other income or only a very small income.

**social work**
NOUN Social work involves giving help and advice to people with serious financial or family problems.
**social worker** NOUN

**society societies**
NOUN 1 Society is the people in a particular country or region E.G. *a major problem in society.* 2 an

a b c d e f g h i j k l m n o p q r **s** t u v w x y z

organization for people who have the same interest or aim *E.G. the school debating society.* **3** Society is also rich, upper-class, fashionable people.

■ (sense 1) civilization, culture

**sociology**

NOUN Sociology is the study of human societies and the relationships between groups in these societies.

**sociological** ADJECTIVE **sociologist** NOUN

**sock socks**

NOUN Socks are pieces of clothing covering your foot and ankle.

🏛 from Old English *socc* meaning 'light shoe'

**socket sockets**

NOUN **1** a place on a wall or on a piece of electrical equipment into which you can put a plug or bulb. **2** Any hollow part or opening into which another part fits can be called a socket *E.G. eye sockets.*

**sod**

NOUN; *LITERARY* The sod is the surface of the ground, together with the grass and roots growing in it.

**soda sodas**

NOUN **1** Soda is the same as **soda water. 2** Soda is also sodium in the form of crystals or a powder, and is used for baking or cleaning.

**soda water soda waters**

NOUN Soda water is fizzy water used for mixing with alcoholic drinks or fruit juice.

**sodden**

ADJECTIVE soaking wet.

**sodium**

NOUN Sodium is a silvery-white chemical element which combines

with other chemicals. Salt is a sodium compound.

**sofa sofas**

NOUN a long comfortable seat with a back and arms for two or three people.

🏛 from Arabic *suffah* meaning 'an upholstered raised platform'

**soft softer softest**

ADJECTIVE **1** Something soft is not hard, stiff, or firm. **2** Soft also means very gentle *E.G. a soft breeze.* **3** A soft sound or voice is quiet and not harsh. **4** A soft colour or light is not bright.

**softly** ADVERB

**soft drink soft drinks**

NOUN any cold, nonalcoholic drink.

**soften softens softening softened**

VERB **1** If something is softened or softens, it becomes less hard, stiff, or firm. **2** If you soften, you become more sympathetic and less critical *E.G. Phillida softened as she spoke.*

**software**

NOUN ( ICT ) Computer programs are known as software.

**soggy soggier soggiest**

ADJECTIVE unpleasantly wet or full of water.

🏛 from American dialect *sog* meaning 'marsh'

**soil soils soiling soiled**

NOUN **1** Soil is the top layer on the surface of the earth in which plants grow. ► VERB **2** If you soil something, you make it dirty.

**soiled** ADJECTIVE

■ (sense 1) earth, ground

**solace**

NOUN; *LITERARY* Solace is something that

makes you feel less sad *E.G. I found solace in writing*.

**solar**

ADJECTIVE **1** relating or belonging to the sun. **2** using the sun's light and heat as a source of energy *E.G. a solar-powered calculator*.

**solar system**

NOUN The solar system is the sun and all the planets, comets, and asteroids that orbit round it.

**solder** solders soldering soldered

VERB **1** To solder two pieces of metal together means to join them with molten metal. ▸ NOUN **2** Solder is the soft metal used for soldering.

**soldier** soldiers

NOUN a person in an army.

**sole** soles soling soled

ADJECTIVE **1** The sole thing or person of a particular type is the only one of that type. ▸ NOUN **2** The sole of your foot or shoe is the underneath part. **3** a flat sea-water fish which you can eat. ▸ VERB **4** When a shoe is soled, a sole is fitted to it.

**solely**

ADVERB If something involves solely one thing, it involves that thing and nothing else.

**solemn**

ADJECTIVE Solemn means serious rather than cheerful or humorous.

**solemnly** ADVERB    **solemnity** NOUN

**solicitor** solicitors

NOUN a lawyer who gives legal advice and prepares legal documents and cases.

**solid** solids

ADJECTIVE **1** A solid substance or object is hard or firm, and not in the form of a liquid or gas. **2** You say that

something is solid when it is not hollow *E.G. solid steel*. **3** You say that a structure is solid when it is strong and not likely to fall down *E.G. solid fences*. **4** You use 'solid' to say that something happens for a period of time without interruption *E.G. I cried for two solid days*. ▸ NOUN **5** a solid substance or object.

**solidly** ADVERB

**solidarity**

NOUN If a group of people show solidarity, they show unity and support for each other.

**soliloquy** soliloquies

*Said* "sol-**lill**-ok-wee" NOUN (ENGLISH) a speech in a play made by a character who is alone on the stage.

🏛 from Latin *solus* meaning 'alone' and *loqui* meaning 'to speak'

**solitary**

ADJECTIVE **1** A solitary activity is one that you do on your own. **2** A solitary person or animal spends a lot of time alone. **3** If there is a solitary person or object somewhere, there is only one.

**solitary confinement**

NOUN A prisoner in solitary confinement is being kept alone in a prison cell.

**solitude**

NOUN Solitude is the state of being alone.

🟰 isolation, seclusion

**solo** solos

NOUN **1** a piece of music played or sung by one person alone. ▸ ADJECTIVE **2** A solo performance or activity is done by one person alone *E.G. my first solo flight*. ▸ ADVERB **3** Solo means alone *E.G. to sail solo around the world*.

a b c d e f g h i j k l m n o p q r s t u v w x y z

**soloist soloists**
NOUN a person who performs a solo.

**solstice solstices**
NOUN one of the two times in the year when the sun is at its furthest point south or north of the equator.
📖 from Latin *sol* meaning 'sun' and *sistere* meaning 'to stand still'

**soluble**
ADJECTIVE A soluble substance is able to dissolve in liquid.

**solution solutions**
NOUN 1 a way of dealing with a problem or difficult situation E.G. *a quick solution to our problem*. 2 The solution to a riddle or a puzzle is the answer. 3 (SCIENCE) a liquid in which a solid substance has been dissolved.

**solve solves solving solved**
VERB If you solve a problem or a question, you find a solution or answer to it.
■ answer, resolve, work out

**solvent solvents**
ADJECTIVE 1 If a person or company is solvent, they have enough money to pay all their debts. ▶ NOUN 2 a liquid that can dissolve other substances.
**solvency** NOUN

**Somali Somalis**
ADJECTIVE 1 belonging or relating to Somalia. ▶ NOUN 2 The Somalis are a group of people who live in Somalia. 3 Somali is the language spoken by Somalis.

**sombre**
ADJECTIVE 1 Sombre colours are dark and dull. 2 A sombre person is serious, sad, or gloomy.

**some** 1 You use 'some' to refer to a quantity or number when you are not stating the quantity or number exactly E.G. *There's some money on the table*. 2 You use 'some' to emphasize that a quantity or number is fairly large E.G. *She had been there for some days*.
ADVERB 3 You use 'some' in front of a number to show that it is not exact E.G. *a fishing village some seven miles north*.

**somebody**
PRONOUN Somebody means someone
✔ *Somebody* and *someone* mean the same.

**some day**
ADVERB Some day means at a date in the future that is unknown or that has not yet been decided.

**somehow**
ADVERB 1 You use 'somehow' to say that you do not know how something was done or will be done E.G. *You'll find a way of doing it somehow*. 2 You use 'somehow' to say that you do not know the reason for something E.G. *Somehow it didn't feel quite right*.

**someone**
PRONOUN You use 'someone' to refer to a person without saying exactly who you mean
✔ *Someone* and *somebody* mean the same.

**somersault somersaults**
NOUN a forwards or backwards roll in which the head is placed on the ground and the body is brought over it.
📖 from Old Provençal *sobre* meaning 'over' and *saut* meaning 'jump'

**something**
PRONOUN You use 'something' to refer to anything that is not a person without saying exactly what you mean.

**sometime**

ADVERB **1** at a time in the future or the past that is unknown or that has not yet been fixed *E.G. He has to find out sometime.* ▶ ADJECTIVE **2** FORMAL 'Sometime' is used to say that a person had a particular job or role in the past *E.G. a sometime actress, dancer and singer.*

**sometimes**

ADVERB occasionally, rather than always or never.

**somewhat**

ADVERB to some extent or degree *E.G. The future seemed somewhat bleak.*

**somewhere**

ADVERB **1** 'Somewhere' is used to refer to a place without stating exactly where it is *E.G. There has to be a file somewhere.* **2** 'Somewhere' is used when giving an approximate amount, number, or time *E.G. somewhere between the winter of 1989 and the summer of 1991.*

**son** sons

NOUN Someone's son is their male child.

**sonar**

NOUN Sonar is equipment on a ship which calculates the depth of the sea or the position of an underwater object using sound waves. 🏛 from *So(und) Na(vigation) R(anging)*

**sonata** sonatas

NOUN a piece of classical music, usually in three or more movements, for piano or for another instrument with or without piano.

**song** songs

NOUN a piece of music with words that are sung to the music.

**songbird** songbirds

NOUN a bird that produces musical sounds like singing.

**son-in-law** sons-in-law

NOUN Someone's son-in-law is the husband of their daughter.

**sonnet** sonnets

NOUN a poem with 14 lines, in which lines rhyme according to fixed patterns. 🏛 from Old Provençal *sonet* meaning 'little poem'

**soon** sooner soonest

ADVERB If something is going to happen soon, it will happen in a very short time.

**soot**

NOUN Soot is black powder which rises in the smoke from a fire.

**sooty** ADJECTIVE

**soothe** soothes soothing soothed

VERB **1** If you soothe someone who is angry or upset, you make them calmer. **2** Something that soothes pain makes the pain less severe.

**soothing** ADJECTIVE

**sophisticated**

ADJECTIVE **1** Sophisticated people have refined or cultured tastes or habits. **2** A sophisticated machine or device is made using advanced and complicated methods.

**sophistication** NOUN

■ (sense 1) cultured, urbane

**soppy** soppier soppiest

ADJECTIVE; INFORMAL silly or foolishly sentimental.

**soprano** sopranos

NOUN a woman, girl, or boy with a singing voice in the highest range of musical notes.

**sorcerer** sorcerers

*Said "sor-ser-er"* NOUN a person who

a b c d e f g h i j k l m n o p q r s t u v w x y z

A
B
C
D
E
F
G
H
I
J
K
L
M
N
O
P
Q
R
**S**
T
U
V
W
X
Y
Z

performs magic by using the power of evil spirits.

**sorceress** sorceresses
NOUN a female sorcerer.

**sorcery**
NOUN Sorcery is magic that uses the power of evil spirits.

**sordid**
ADJECTIVE 1 dishonest or immoral *E.G. a rather sordid business*. 2 dirty, unpleasant, or depressing *E.G. the sordid guest house*.
■ (sense 2) seedy, sleazy, squalid

**sore** sorer sorest; sores
ADJECTIVE 1 If part of your body is sore, it causes you pain and discomfort. 2 LITERARY 'Sore' is used to emphasize something *E.G. The President is in sore need of friends.* ► NOUN 3 a painful place where your skin has become infected.
**sorely** ADVERB **soreness** NOUN
■ (sense 1) painful, sensitive, tender

**sorghum**
*Said "saw-gum"* NOUN a type of tropical grass that is grown for hay, grain, and syrup.

**sorrow** sorrows
NOUN 1 Sorrow is deep sadness or regret. 2 Sorrows are things that cause sorrow *E.G. the sorrows of this world*.

**sorry** sorrier sorriest
ADJECTIVE 1 If you are sorry about something, you feel sadness, regret, or sympathy because of it *E.G. I was so sorry to hear about your husband.* 2 'Sorry' is used to describe people and things that are in a bad physical or mental state *E.G. She was in a pretty sorry state when we found her.*
■ (sense 1) apologetic, contrite, regretful

**sort** sorts sorting sorted
NOUN 1 The different sorts of something are the different types of it. ► VERB 2 To sort things means to arrange them into different groups or sorts.
■ (sense 1) kind, type, variety
**sort out** VERB If you sort out a problem or misunderstanding, you deal with it and find a solution to it.
☑ When you use *sort* in its singular form, the adjective before it should also be singular: *that sort of car.* When you use the plural form *sorts*, the adjective before it should be plural: *those sorts of shop; those sorts of shops.*

**SOS**
NOUN An SOS is a signal that you are in danger and need help.

**so-so**
ADJECTIVE neither good nor bad *E.G. The food is so-so.*

**soufflé** soufflés
*Said "soo-flay"; also spelt* **souffle**
NOUN a light, fluffy food made from beaten egg whites and other ingredients that is baked in the oven.

**sought**
the past tense and past participle of **seek**.

**soul** souls
NOUN 1 A person's soul is the spiritual part of them that is supposed to continue after their body is dead. 2 People also use 'soul' to refer to a person's mind, character, thoughts, and feelings. 3 'Soul' can be used to mean person *E.G. There was not a soul there.* 4 Soul is a type of pop music.

**sound** sounds sounding sounded; sounder soundest
NOUN 1 Sound is everything that can

be heard. **2** A particular sound is something that you hear. **3** The sound of someone or something is the impression you have of them *E.G. I like the sound of your father's grandfather.* ▶ VERB **4** If something sounds or if you sound it, it makes a noise. **5** To sound something deep, such as a well or the sea, means to measure how deep it is using a weighted line or sonar. ▶ ADJECTIVE **6** in good condition *E.G. a guarantee that a house is sound.* **7** reliable and sensible *E.G. The logic behind the argument seems sound.*

**soundly** ADVERB

**sound bite** sound bites

NOUN a short and memorable sentence or phrase extracted from a longer speech for use on radio or television.

**sound effect** sound effects

NOUN Sound effects are sounds created artificially to make a play more realistic, especially a radio play.

**soundproof**

ADJECTIVE If a room is soundproof, sound cannot get into it or out of it.

**soundtrack** soundtracks

NOUN The soundtrack of a film is the part you hear.

**soup** soups

NOUN Soup is liquid food made by boiling meat, fish, or vegetables in water.

**sour** sours souring soured

ADJECTIVE **1** If something is sour, it has a sharp, acid taste. **2** Sour milk has an unpleasant taste because it is no longer fresh. **3** A sour person is bad-tempered and unfriendly. ▶ VERB **4** If a friendship, situation, or attitude sours or if something sours it, it becomes

less friendly, enjoyable, or hopeful.

**source** sources

NOUN **1** The source of something is the person, place, or thing that it comes from *E.G. the source of his confidence.* **2** (HISTORY) **3** The source of a river or stream is the place where it begins.

☑ Do not confuse the spellings of *source* and *sauce*, which can sound very similar.

**sour grapes**

PLURAL NOUN You describe someone's behaviour as sour grapes when they say something is worthless but secretly want it and cannot have it.

**south**

NOUN **1** The south is the direction to your right when you are looking towards the place where the sun rises. **2** The south of a place or country is the part which is towards the south when you are in the centre. ▶ ADVERB OR ADJECTIVE **3** South means towards the south *E.G. The taxi headed south… the south end of the site.* ▶ ADJECTIVE **4** A south wind blows from the south.

**South America**

NOUN South America is the fourth largest continent. It has the Pacific Ocean on its west side, the Atlantic on the east, and the Antarctic to the south. South America is joined to North America by the Isthmus of Panama.

**South American** ADJECTIVE

**south-east**

NOUN, ADVERB, OR ADJECTIVE South-east is halfway between south and east.

**south-easterly**

ADJECTIVE **1** South-easterly means to or towards the south-east. **2** A south-easterly wind blows from the south-east.

**south-eastern**

ADJECTIVE in or from the south-east.

**southerly**

ADJECTIVE 1 Southerly means to or towards the south. 2 A southerly wind blows from the south.

**southern**

ADJECTIVE in or from the south.

**Southern Cross**

NOUN The Southern Cross is a small group of stars which can be seen from the southern part of the earth, and which is represented on the national flags of Australia and New Zealand.

**South Pole**

NOUN The South Pole is the place on the surface of the earth that is farthest towards the south.

**southward** or **southwards**

ADVERB 1 Southward or southwards means towards the south E.G. *the dusty road which led southwards.* ▸ ADJECTIVE 2 The southward part of something is the south part.

**south-west**

NOUN, ADVERB, or ADJECTIVE South-west is halfway between south and west.

**south-westerly**

ADJECTIVE 1 South-westerly means to or towards the south-west. 2 A south-westerly wind blows from the south-west.

**south-western**

ADJECTIVE in or from the south-west.

**souvenir souvenirs**

NOUN something you keep to remind you of a holiday, place, or event.
📖 from French *se souvenir* meaning 'to remember'

**sovereign sovereigns**

*Said* "**sov**-rin" NOUN 1 a king, queen, or royal ruler of a country. 2 In the past, a sovereign was a British gold coin worth one pound. ▸ ADJECTIVE 3 A sovereign state or country is independent and not under the authority of any other country.

**sovereignty**

*Said* "**sov**-rin-tee" NOUN Sovereignty is the political power that a country has to govern itself.

**Soviet Soviets**

*Said* "**soe**-vee-et" ADJECTIVE 1 belonging or relating to the country that used to be the Soviet Union. ▸ NOUN 2 The people and the government of the country that used to be the Soviet Union were sometimes referred to as the Soviets.

**sow sows sowing sowed sown**

*Said* "**soh**" VERB 1 To sow seeds or sow an area of land with seeds means to plant them in the ground. 2 To sow undesirable feelings or attitudes means to cause them E.G. *You have sown discontent.*

**sow sows**

*Rhymes with* "**now**" NOUN an adult female pig.

**soya**

NOUN Soya flour, margarine, oil, and milk are made from soya beans.
📖 from Chinese *chiang yu* meaning 'paste sauce'

**soya bean soya beans**

NOUN Soya beans are a type of edible Asian bean.

**spa spas**

NOUN a place where water containing minerals bubbles out of the ground, at which people drink or bathe in the water to improve their health.

**SPELLING NOTE**    an ELegant angEL (angel)

🏛 from the Belgian town *Spa* where there are mineral springs

**space** spaces spacing spaced
NOUN **1** Space is the area that is empty or available in a place, building, or container. **2** Space is the area beyond the earth's atmosphere surrounding the stars and planets. **3** a gap between two things *E.G. the space between the tables.* **4** Space can also refer to a period of time *E.G. two incidents in the space of a week.* ▸ VERB **5** If you space a series of things, you arrange them with gaps between them.

**spacecraft**
NOUN a rocket or other vehicle that can travel in space.

**spaceman** spacemen
NOUN someone who travels in space.

**spaceship** spaceships
NOUN a spacecraft that carries people through space.

**space shuttle** space shuttles
NOUN a spacecraft designed to be used many times for travelling out into space and back again.

**spacious**
ADJECTIVE having or providing a lot of space *E.G. the spacious living room.*
▪ capacious, commodious, roomy

**spade** spades
NOUN **1** a tool with a flat metal blade and a long handle used for digging. **2** Spades is one of the four suits in a pack of playing cards. It is marked by a black symbol in the shape of a heart-shaped leaf with a stem.

**spaghetti**
*Said "spag-get-ee"* NOUN Spaghetti consists of long, thin pieces of pasta.

**spam**
NOUN unwanted e-mails, usually containing advertising.

**span** spans spanning spanned
NOUN **1** the period of time during which something exists or functions *E.G. looking back today over a span of forty years.* **2** The span of something is the total length of it from one end to the other. ▸ VERB **3** If something spans a particular length of time, it lasts throughout that time *E.G. a career that spanned 50 years.* **4** A bridge that spans something stretches right across it.

**spangle** spangles spangling spangled
VERB **1** If something is spangled, it is covered with small, sparkling objects. ▸ NOUN **2** Spangles are small sparkling pieces of metal or plastic used to decorate clothing or hair.

**Spaniard** Spaniards
*Said "span-yard"* NOUN someone who comes from Spain.

**spaniel** spaniels
NOUN a dog with long drooping ears and a silky coat.
🏛 from Old French *espaigneul* meaning 'Spanish dog'

**Spanish**
ADJECTIVE **1** belonging or relating to Spain. ▸ NOUN **2** Spanish is the main language spoken in Spain, and is also spoken by many people in Central and South America.

**spank** spanks spanking spanked
VERB If a child is spanked, it is punished by being slapped, usually on its leg or bottom.

**spanner** spanners
NOUN a tool with a specially shaped end that fits round a nut to turn it.

**spar** spars sparring sparred
VERB **1** When boxers spar, they hit each other with light punches for

a
b
c
d
e
f
g
h
i
j
k
l
m
n
o
p
q
r
**s**
t
u
v
w
x
y
z

LEt's measure the angLE (ang**le**)  ▸ SPELLING NOTE

practice. **2** To spar with someone also means to argue with them, but not in an unpleasant or serious way.
▶ NOUN **3** a strong pole that a sail is attached to on a yacht or ship.

## spare spares sparing spared
ADJECTIVE **1** extra to what is needed *E.G. What does she do in her spare time?*
▶ NOUN **2** a thing that is extra to what is needed. ▶ VERB **3** If you spare something for a particular purpose, you make it available *E.G. Few troops could be spared to go abroad.* **4** If someone is spared an unpleasant experience, they are prevented from suffering it *E.G. The capital was spared the misery of an all-out train strike.*

## sparing
ADJECTIVE If you are sparing with something, you use it in very small quantities.
**sparingly** ADVERB

## spark sparks sparking sparked
NOUN **1** a tiny, bright piece of burning material thrown up by a fire. **2** a small flash of light caused by electricity. **3** A spark of feeling is a small amount of it *E.G. that tiny spark of excitement.* ▶ VERB **4** If something sparks, it throws out sparks. **5** If one thing sparks another thing off, it causes the second thing to start happening *E.G. The tragedy sparked off a wave of sympathy among staff.*

## sparkle sparkles sparkling sparkled
VERB **1** If something sparkles, it shines with a lot of small, bright points of light. ▶ NOUN **2** Sparkles are small, bright points of light.
**sparkling** ADJECTIVE
▪ (sense 1) gleam, glitter, twinkle

## sparrow sparrows
NOUN a common, small bird with brown and grey feathers.

## sparse sparser sparsest
ADJECTIVE small in number or amount and spread out over an area *E.G. the sparse audience.*
**sparsely** ADVERB

## spartan
ADJECTIVE A spartan way of life is very simple with no luxuries *E.G. spartan accommodation.*
▦ from *Sparta*, a city in Ancient Greece, whose inhabitants were famous for their discipline, military skill, and stern and plain way of life

## spasm spasms
NOUN **1** a sudden tightening of the muscles. **2** a sudden, short burst of something *E.G. a spasm of fear.*

## spasmodic
ADJECTIVE happening suddenly for short periods of time at irregular intervals *E.G. spasmodic movements.*

## spastic spastics
ADJECTIVE **1** A spastic person is born with a disability which makes it difficult for them to control their muscles. ▶ NOUN **2** a spastic person.
▦ from Greek *spasmos* meaning 'cramp' or 'convulsion'

## spate
NOUN A spate of things is a large number of them that happen or appear in a rush *E.G. a recent spate of first novels from older writers.*

## spatial
*Said "spay-shl"* ADJECTIVE to do with size, area, or position.

## spatter spatters spattering spattered
VERB **1** If something spatters a surface, it covers the surface with drops of

liquid. ▶ NOUN **2** A spatter of
something is a small amount of it in
drops or tiny pieces.

**spawn** spawns spawning
spawned
NOUN **1** Spawn is a jelly-like substance
containing the eggs of fish or
amphibians. ▶ VERB **2** When fish or
amphibians spawn, they lay their
eggs. **3** If something spawns
something else, it causes it E.G. *The
depressed economy spawned the riots.*

**speak** speaks speaking spoke
spoken
VERB **1** When you speak, you use your
voice to say words. **2** If you speak a
foreign language, you know it and
can use it.
■ (sense 1) say, talk, utter

**speak out** VERB To speak out about
something means to publicly state
an opinion about it.

**speaker** speakers
NOUN **1** a person who is speaking,
especially someone making a
speech. **2** A speaker on a radio or hi-
fi is a loudspeaker.

**spear** spears spearing speared
NOUN **1** a weapon consisting of a long
pole with a sharp point. ▶ VERB **2** To
spear something means to push or
throw a spear or other pointed
object into it.

**spearhead** spearheads
spearheading spearheaded
VERB If someone spearheads a
campaign, they lead it.

**spec** specs INFORMAL
PLURAL NOUN **1** Someone's specs are
their glasses. ▶ PHRASE **2** If you do something
**on spec**, you do it hoping for a result
but without any certainty E.G. *He
turned up at the same event on spec.*

**special**
ADJECTIVE ( RE ) **1** Something special is
more important or better than other
things of its kind. **2** Special describes
someone who is officially appointed,
or something that is needed for a
particular purpose E.G. *Karen actually
had to get special permission to go
there.* **3** Special also describes
something that belongs or relates to
only one particular person, group, or
place E.G. *the special needs of the
chronically sick.*

**specialist** specialists
NOUN **1** someone who has a particular
skill or who knows a lot about a
particular subject E.G. *a skin specialist.*
▶ ADJECTIVE **2** having a skill or knowing
a lot about a particular subject E.G. *a
specialist teacher.*
**specialism** NOUN

**speciality** specialities
NOUN A person's speciality is something
they are especially good at or know a
lot about E.G. *Roses are her speciality.*

**specialize** specializes
specializing specialized; also spelt
specialise
VERB If you specialize in something,
you make it your speciality E.G. *a shop
specializing in ceramics.*
**specialization** NOUN

**specialized** or **specialised**
ADJECTIVE developed for a particular
purpose or trained in a particular area
of knowledge E.G. *a specialized sales team.*

**specially**
ADVERB If something has been done
specially for a particular person or
purpose, it has been done only for
that person or purpose.

**species**
Said "**spee**-sheez" NOUN a class of

a
b
c
d
e
f
g
h
i
j
k
l
m
n
o
p
q
r
s
t
u
v
w
x
y
z

A
B
C
D
E
F
G
H
I
J
K
L
M
N
O
P
Q
R
S
T
U
V
W
X
Y
Z

plants or animals whose members have the same characteristics and are able to breed with each other.

**specific**

ADJECTIVE **1** particular E.G. *specific areas of difficulty.* **2** precise and exact E.G. *She will ask for specific answers.*
**specifically** ADVERB

**specification** specifications

NOUN (D&T) a detailed description of what is needed for something, such as the necessary features in the design of something E.G. *I like to build it to my own specifications.*

**specify** specifies specifying specified

VERB To specify something means to state or describe it precisely E.G. *In his will he specified that these documents were never to be removed.*

**specimen** specimens

NOUN A specimen of something is an example or small amount of it which gives an idea of what the whole is like E.G. *a specimen of your writing.*

**speck** specks

NOUN a very small stain or amount of something.

**speckled**

ADJECTIVE Something that is speckled is covered in very small marks or spots.

**spectacle** spectacles

PLURAL NOUN **1** Someone's spectacles are their glasses. ▶ NOUN **2** a strange or interesting sight or scene E.G. *an astonishing spectacle.* **3** a grand and impressive event or performance.

**spectacular** spectaculars

ADJECTIVE **1** Something spectacular is very impressive or dramatic. ▶ NOUN **2** a grand and impressive show or performance.

■ (sense 1) impressive, sensational, stunning

**spectator** spectators

NOUN a person who is watching something.

■ observer, onlooker, watcher

**spectra**

the plural of **spectrum**.

**spectre** spectres

NOUN **1** a frightening idea or image E.G. *the spectre of war.* **2** a ghost.

**spectrum** spectra or spectrums

NOUN **1** (ART) The spectrum is the range of different colours produced when light passes through a prism or a drop of water. A rainbow shows the colours in a spectrum. **2** A spectrum of opinions or emotions is a range of them.

**speculate** speculates speculating speculated

VERB If you speculate about something, you think about it and form opinions about it.
**speculation** NOUN

**speculative**

ADJECTIVE **1** A speculative piece of information is based on guesses and opinions rather than known facts. **2** Someone with a speculative expression seems to be trying to guess something E.G. *His mother regarded him with a speculative eye.*

**speech** speeches

NOUN **1** Speech is the ability to speak or the act of speaking. **2** a formal talk given to an audience. **3** In a play, a speech is a group of lines spoken by one of the characters.

■ (sense 2) address, talk

**speechless**

ADJECTIVE Someone who is speechless is unable to speak for a short time because something has shocked them.

**speed** speeds speeding sped or speeded
NOUN **1** The speed of something is the rate at which it moves or happens. **2** Speed is very fast movement or travel. ▶ VERB **3** If you speed somewhere, you move or travel there quickly. **4** Someone who is speeding is driving a vehicle faster than the legal speed limit.
≣ (sense 2) rapidity, swiftness, velocity

**speedboat** speedboats
NOUN a small, fast motorboat.

**speed limit** speed limits
NOUN The speed limit is the maximum speed at which vehicles are legally allowed to drive on a particular road.

**speedway**
NOUN Speedway is the sport of racing lightweight motorcycles on special tracks.

**speedy** speedier speediest
ADJECTIVE done very quickly.
**speedily** ADVERB

**spell** spells spelling spelt or spelled
VERB **1** When you spell a word, you name or write its letters in order. **2** When letters spell a word, they form that word when put together in a particular order. **3** If something spells a particular result, it suggests that this will be the result E.G. *This haphazard method could spell disaster for you.* ▶ NOUN **4** A spell of something is a short period of it E.G. *a spell of rough weather.* **5** a word or sequence of words used to perform magic.
**spell out** VERB If you spell

something out, you explain it in detail E.G. *I don't have to spell it out, do I?*

**spellbound**
ADJECTIVE so fascinated by something that you cannot think about anything else E.G. *She had sat spellbound through the film.*

**spelling** spellings
NOUN The spelling of a word is the correct order of letters in it.

**spend** spends spending spent
VERB **1** When you spend money, you buy things with it. **2** To spend time or energy means to use it.

**spent**
ADJECTIVE **1** Spent describes things which have been used and therefore cannot be used again E.G. *spent matches.* **2** If you are spent, you are exhausted and have no energy left.

**sperm** sperms
NOUN a cell produced in the sex organ of a male animal which can enter a female animal's egg and fertilize it.

**spew** spews spewing spewed
VERB **1** When things spew from something or when it spews them out, they come out of it in large quantities. **2** INFORMAL To spew up means to vomit.

**sphere** spheres
NOUN **1** a perfectly round object, such as a ball. **2** An area of activity or interest can be referred to as a sphere of activity or interest.
**spherical** ADJECTIVE

**sphinx** sphinxes
*Said "sfingks"* NOUN In mythology, the sphinx was a monster with a person's head and a lion's body.

**spice** spices spicing spiced
NOUN **1** Spice is powder or seeds from

a
b
c
d
e
f
g
h
i
j
k
l
m
n
o
p
q
r
s
t
u
v
w
x
y
z

A B C D E F G H I J K L M N O P Q R S T U V W X Y Z

a plant added to food to give it flavour. **2** Spice is something which makes life more exciting *E.G. Variety is the spice of life.* ▶ VERB **3** To spice food means to add spice to it. **4** If you spice something up, you make it more exciting or lively.

**spicy** spicier spiciest
ADJECTIVE strongly flavoured with spices.

**spider** spiders
NOUN a small insect-like creature with eight legs that spins webs to catch insects for food.
📖 from Old English *spinnan* meaning 'to spin'

**spike** spikes
NOUN **1** a long pointed piece of metal. **2** The spikes on a sports shoe are the pointed pieces of metal attached to the sole. **3** Some other long pointed objects are called spikes *E.G. beautiful pink flower spikes.*

**spiky** spikier spikiest
ADJECTIVE Something spiky has sharp points.

**spill** spills spilling spilled or spilt
VERB **1** If you spill something or if it spills, it accidentally falls or runs out of a container. **2** If people or things spill out of a place, they come out of it in large numbers.

**spillage** spillages
NOUN the spilling of something, or something that has been spilt *E.G. the oil spillage in the Shetlands.*

**spin** spins spinning spun
VERB **1** If something spins, it turns quickly around a central point. **2** When spiders spin a web, they give out a sticky substance and make it into a web. **3** When people spin, they make thread by twisting together

pieces of fibre using a machine. **4** If your head is spinning, you feel dizzy or confused. ▶ NOUN **5** a rapid turn around a central point *E.G. a golf club which puts more spin on the ball.*

**spinach**
*Said "spin-ij"* NOUN Spinach is a vegetable with large green leaves.

**spinal**
ADJECTIVE to do with the spine.

**spine** spines
NOUN **1** Your spine is your backbone. **2** Spines are long, sharp points on an animal's body or on a plant.

**spinifex**
NOUN Spinifex is a coarse, spiny Australian grass.

**spinning wheel** spinning wheels
NOUN a wooden machine for spinning flax or wool.

**spin-off** spin-offs
NOUN something useful that unexpectedly results from an activity.

**spinster** spinsters
NOUN a woman who has never married.
📖 originally a person whose occupation was spinning; later, the official label of an unmarried woman

**spiny**
ADJECTIVE covered with spines.

**spiral** spirals spiralling spiralled
NOUN **1** a continuous curve which winds round and round, with each curve above or outside the previous one. ▶ ADJECTIVE **2** in the shape of a spiral *E.G. a spiral staircase.* ▶ VERB **3** If something spirals, it moves up or down in a spiral curve *E.G. The aircraft spiralled down.* **4** If an amount or level spirals, it rises or falls quickly at an increasing rate *E.G.*

*Prices have spiralled recently.*

**spire** spires

NOUN The spire of a church is the tall cone-shaped structure on top.

**spirit** spirits spiriting spirited

NOUN 1 Your spirit is the part of you that is not physical and that is connected with your deepest thoughts and feelings. 2 ( RE ) The spirit of a dead person is a nonphysical part that is believed to remain alive after death. 3 a supernatural being, such as a ghost. 4 Spirit is liveliness, energy, and self-confidence *E.G. a band full of spirit.* 5 Spirit can refer to an attitude *E.G. his old fighting spirit.* ▶ PLURAL NOUN 6 Spirits can describe how happy or unhappy someone is *E.G. in good spirits.* 7 Spirits are strong alcoholic drinks such as whisky and gin. ▶ VERB 8 If you spirit someone or something into or out of a place, you get them in or out quickly and secretly.

**spirited**

ADJECTIVE showing energy and courage.

**spirit level** spirit levels

NOUN a device for finding out if a surface is level, consisting of a bubble of air sealed in a tube of liquid in a wooden or metal frame.

**spiritual** spirituals

ADJECTIVE ( RE ) 1 to do with people's thoughts and beliefs, rather than their bodies and physical surroundings. 2 to do with people's religious beliefs *E.G. spiritual guidance.* ▶ NOUN 3 a religious song originally sung by Black slaves in America.

**spiritually** ADVERB **spirituality** NOUN

**spit** spits spitting spat

NOUN 1 Spit is saliva. 2 a long stick made of metal or wood which is pushed through a piece of meat so that it can be hung over a fire and cooked. 3 a long, flat, narrow piece of land sticking out into the sea. ▶ VERB 4 If you spit, you force saliva or some other substance out of your mouth. 5 When it is spitting, it is raining very lightly.

**spite** spites spiting spited

PHRASE 1 In spite of is used to introduce a statement which makes the rest of what you are saying seem surprising *E.G. In spite of all the gossip, Virginia stayed behind.* ▶ VERB 2 If you do something to spite someone, you do it deliberately to hurt or annoy them. ▶ NOUN 3 If you do something out of spite, you do it to spite someone.

**spiteful**

ADJECTIVE A spiteful person does or says nasty things to people deliberately to hurt them.

■ malicious, nasty, vindictive

**spitting image**

NOUN If someone is the spitting image of someone else, they look just like them.

**splash** splashes splashing splashed

VERB 1 If you splash around in water, your movements disturb the water in a noisy way. 2 If liquid splashes something, it scatters over it in a lot of small drops. ▶ NOUN 3 A splash is the sound made when something hits or falls into water. 4 A splash of liquid is a small quantity of it that has been spilt on something.

A
B
C
D
E
F
G
H
I
J
K
L
M
N
O
P
Q
R
S
T
U
V
W
X
Y
Z

**splatter** splatters splattering splattered

VERB When something is splattered with a substance, the substance is splashed all over it *E.G. fur coats splattered with paint.*

**spleen** spleens

NOUN Your spleen is an organ near your stomach which controls the quality of your blood.

**splendid**

ADJECTIVE **1** very good indeed *E.G. a splendid career.* **2** beautiful and impressive *E.G. a splendid old mansion.*

**splendidly** ADVERB

▇ (sense 2) grand, magnificent

**splendour** splendours

NOUN **1** If something has splendour, it is beautiful and impressive. ▶ PLURAL NOUN **2** The splendours of something are its beautiful and impressive features.

**splint** splints

NOUN a long piece of wood or metal fastened to a broken limb to hold it in place.

**splinter** splinters splintering splintered

NOUN **1** a thin, sharp piece of wood or glass which has broken off a larger piece. ▶ VERB **2** If something splinters, it breaks into thin, sharp pieces.

**split** splits splitting split

VERB **1** If something splits or if you split it, it divides into two or more parts. **2** If something such as wood or fabric splits, a long crack or tear appears in it. **3** If people split something, they share it between them. ▶ NOUN **4** A split in a piece of wood or fabric is a crack or tear. **5** A split between two things is a division

or difference between them *E.G. the split between rugby league and rugby union.*

▇ (sense 1) break, divide, separate
▇ (sense 5) division, schism

**split up** VERB If two people split up, they end their relationship or marriage.

**split second**

NOUN an extremely short period of time.

**splitting**

ADJECTIVE A splitting headache is very painful.

**splutter** splutters spluttering spluttered

VERB **1** If someone splutters, they speak in a confused way because they are embarrassed. **2** If something splutters, it makes a series of short, sharp sounds.

**spoil** spoils spoiling spoiled or spoilt

VERB **1** If you spoil something, you prevent it from being successful or satisfactory. **2** To spoil children means to give them everything they want, with harmful effects on their character. **3** To spoil someone also means to give them something nice as a treat. ▶ PLURAL NOUN **4** Spoils are valuable things obtained during war or as a result of violence *E.G. the spoils of war.*

▇ (sense 1) mess up, ruin, wreck
▇ (sense 2) overindulge, pamper

**spoilsport** spoilsports

NOUN someone who spoils people's fun.

**spoke** spokes

NOUN The spokes of a wheel are the bars which connect the hub to the rim.

**spokesperson** spokespersons

NOUN someone who speaks on behalf of another person or a group.
**spokesman** NOUN **spokeswoman** NOUN

**sponge** sponges sponging sponged

NOUN **1** a sea creature with a body made up of many cells. **2** part of the very light skeleton of a sponge, used for bathing and cleaning. **3** A sponge or sponge cake is a very light cake. ▶ VERB **4** If you sponge something, you clean it by wiping it with a wet sponge.

**sponsor** sponsors sponsoring sponsored

VERB **1** To sponsor something, such as an event or someone's training, means to support it financially E.G. The visit was sponsored by the London Natural History Society. **2** If you sponsor someone who is doing something for charity, you agree to give them a sum of money for the charity if they manage to do it. **3** If you sponsor a proposal or suggestion, you officially put it forward and support it E.G. the MP who sponsored the Bill. ▶ NOUN **4** a person or organization sponsoring something or someone.
**sponsorship** NOUN

**spontaneous**

ADJECTIVE **1** Spontaneous acts are not planned or arranged, but are done because you feel like it. **2** A spontaneous event happens because of processes within something rather than being caused by things outside it E.G. spontaneous bleeding.
**spontaneously** ADVERB
**spontaneity** NOUN

**spoof** spoofs

NOUN something such as an article or television programme that seems to be about a serious matter but is actually a joke.

**spooky** spookier spookiest

ADJECTIVE eerie and frightening.

**spool** spools

NOUN a cylindrical object onto which thread, tape, or film can be wound.

**spoon** spoons

NOUN an object shaped like a small shallow bowl with a long handle, used for eating, stirring, and serving food.

**spoonful** spoonfuls or spoonsful

NOUN the amount held by a spoon.

**sporadic**

ADJECTIVE happening at irregular intervals E.G. a few sporadic attempts at keeping a diary.
**sporadically** ADVERB

**spore** spores

NOUN; TECHNICAL Spores are cells produced by bacteria and nonflowering plants such as fungi which develop into new bacteria or plants.

**sporran** sporrans

NOUN a large purse made of leather or fur, worn by a Scotsman over his kilt. 🔢 from Scottish Gaelic sporan meaning 'purse'

**sport** sports sporting sported

NOUN **1** Sports are games and other enjoyable activities which need physical effort and skill. **2** You say that someone is a sport when they accept defeat or teasing cheerfully E.G. Be a sport, Minister! ▶ VERB **3** If you sport something noticeable or unusual, you wear it E.G. A German boy sported a ponytail.

a
b
c
d
e
f
g
h
i
j
k
l
m
n
o
p
q
r
s
t
u
v
w
x
y
z

The government licenSes Schnapps (licenses)   SPELLING NOTE

A
B
C
D
E
F
G
H
I
J
K
L
M
N
O
P
Q
R
S
T
U
V
W
X
Y
Z

**sporting**

ADJECTIVE 1 relating to sport.

2 behaving in a fair and decent way.

**sports car** sports cars

NOUN a low, fast car, usually with room for only two people.

**sportsman** sportsmen

NOUN a man who takes part in sports and is good at them.

**sportswoman** sportswomen

NOUN a woman who takes part in sports and is good at them.

**sporty** sportier sportiest

ADJECTIVE 1 A sporty car is fast and flashy. 2 A sporty person is good at sports.

**spot** spots spotting spotted

NOUN 1 Spots are small, round, coloured areas on a surface. 2 Spots on a person's skin are small lumps, usually caused by an infection or allergy. 3 A spot of something is a small amount of it *E.G. spots of rain*. 4 A place can be called a spot *E.G. the most beautiful spot in the garden*. ▶ VERB 5 If you spot something, you notice it. ▶ PHRASE 6 If you do something **on the spot**, you do it immediately.

**spot check** spot checks

NOUN a random examination made without warning on one of a group of things or people *E.G. spot checks by road safety officers*.

**spotless**

ADJECTIVE perfectly clean.

**spotlessly** ADVERB

■ clean, immaculate, impeccable

**spotlight** spotlights spotlighting spotlit or spotlighted

NOUN 1 (*DRAMA*) a powerful light which can be directed to light up a small area. ▶ VERB 2 If something spotlights

a situation or problem, it draws the public's attention to it *E.G. a national campaign to spotlight the problem*.

**spot-on**

ADJECTIVE; *INFORMAL* exactly correct or accurate.

**spotted**

ADJECTIVE Something spotted has a pattern of spots on it.

**spotter** spotters

NOUN a person whose hobby is looking out for things of a particular kind *E.G. a train spotter*.

**spotty** spottier spottiest

ADJECTIVE Someone who is spotty has spots or pimples on their skin, especially on their face.

**spouse** spouses

NOUN Someone's spouse is the person they are married to.

**spout** spouts spouting spouted

VERB 1 When liquid or flame spouts out of something, it shoots out in a long stream. 2 When someone spouts what they have learned, they say it in a boring way. ▶ NOUN 3 a tube with a lip-like end for pouring liquid *E.G. a teapot with a long spout*.

**sprain** sprains spraining sprained

VERB 1 If you sprain a joint, you accidentally damage it by twisting it violently. ▶ NOUN 2 the injury caused by spraining a joint.

**sprawl** sprawls sprawling sprawled

VERB 1 If you sprawl somewhere, you sit or lie there with your legs and arms spread out. 2 A place that sprawls is spread out over a large area *E.G. a Monday market which sprawls all over town*. ▶ NOUN 3 anything that spreads in an untidy and uncontrolled way *E.G. a sprawl of skyscrapers.*

**sprawling** ADJECTIVE

**spray** sprays spraying sprayed

NOUN **1** Spray consists of many drops of liquid splashed or forced into the air *E.G. The salt spray stung her face.* **2** Spray is also a liquid kept under pressure in a can or other container *E.G. hair spray.* **3** a piece of equipment for spraying liquid *E.G. a garden spray.* **4** A spray of flowers or leaves consists of several of them on one stem. ▸ VERB **5** To spray a liquid over something means to cover it with drops of the liquid.

**spread** spreads spreading spread

VERB **1** If you spread something out, you open it out or arrange it so that it can be seen or used easily *E.G. He spread the map out on his knees.* **2** If you spread a substance on a surface, you put a thin layer on the surface. **3** If something spreads, it gradually reaches or affects more people *E.G. The news spread quickly.* **4** If something spreads over a period of time, it happens regularly or continuously over that time *E.G. His four international appearances were spread over eight years.* **5** If something such as work is spread, it is distributed evenly. ▸ NOUN **6** The spread of something is the extent to which it gradually reaches or affects more people *E.G. the spread of Buddhism.* **7** A spread of ideas, interests, or other things is a wide variety of them. **8** soft food put on bread *E.G. cheese spread.*

**spread-eagled**

ADJECTIVE Someone who is spread-eagled is lying with their arms

and legs spread out.

**spreadsheet** spreadsheets

NOUN (ICT) a computer program that is used for entering and arranging figures, used mainly for financial planning.

**spree** sprees

NOUN a period of time spent doing something enjoyable *E.G. a shopping spree.*

**sprig** sprigs

NOUN **1** a small twig with leaves on it. **2** In Australian and New Zealand English, sprigs are studs on the sole of a football boot.

**sprightly** sprightlier sprightliest

ADJECTIVE lively and active.

**spring** springs springing sprang sprung

NOUN **1** Spring is the season between winter and summer. **2** a coil of wire which returns to its natural shape after being pressed or pulled. **3** a place where water comes up through the ground. **4** an act of springing *E.G. With a spring he had opened the door.* ▸ VERB **5** To spring means to jump upwards or forwards *E.G. Martha sprang to her feet.* **6** If something springs in a particular direction, it moves suddenly and quickly *E.G. The door sprang open.* **7** If one thing springs from another, it is the result of it *E.G. The failures sprang from three facts.*

**springboard** springboards

NOUN **1** a flexible board on which a diver or gymnast jumps to gain height. **2** If something is a springboard for an activity or enterprise, it makes it possible for it to begin.

**springbok** springboks

NOUN **1** a small South African antelope

a
b
c
d
e
f
g
h
i
j
k
l
m
n
o
p
q
r
**s**
t
u
v
w
x
y
z

Plaice the fish has a glittering 'EYE' (I) (plaice)     **SPELLING NOTE**

which moves in leaps. **2** a Springbok is a person who has represented South Africa in a sports team.

**spring-clean** spring-cleans spring-cleaning spring-cleaned
VERB To spring-clean a house means to clean it thoroughly throughout.

**spring onion** spring onions
NOUN a small onion with long green shoots, often eaten raw in salads.

**sprinkle** sprinkles sprinkling sprinkled
VERB If you sprinkle a liquid or powder over something, you scatter it over it.

**sprinkling** sprinklings
NOUN A sprinkling of something is a small quantity of it E.G. *a light sprinkling of snow.*

**sprint** sprints sprinting sprinted
NOUN **1** a short, fast race. ▶ VERB **2** To sprint means to run fast over a short distance.

**sprinter** sprinters
NOUN an athlete who runs fast over short distances.

**sprite** sprites
NOUN a type of fairy.

**sprout** sprouts sprouting sprouted
VERB **1** When something sprouts, it grows. **2** If things sprout up, they appear rapidly E.G. *Their houses sprouted up in that region.* ▶ NOUN **3** Sprouts are the same as **brussels sprouts**.

**spruce** spruces; sprucer sprucest; spruces sprucing spruced
NOUN **1** an evergreen tree with needle-like leaves. ▶ ADJECTIVE **2** Someone who is spruce is very neat and smart. ▶ VERB **3** To spruce

something up means to make it neat and smart.

**spunk** spunks
NOUN *INFORMAL* **1** *OLD-FASHIONED* Spunk is courage. **2** In Australian and New Zealand English, someone who is good-looking.

**spur** spurs spurring spurred
VERB **1** If something spurs you to do something or spurs you on, it encourages you to do it. ▶ NOUN **2** Something that acts as a spur encourages a person to do something. **3** Spurs are sharp metal points attached to the heels of a rider's boots and used to urge a horse on. ▶ PHRASE **4** If you do something **on the spur of the moment**, you do it suddenly, without planning it.

**spurious**
*Said "spyoor-ee-uss"* ADJECTIVE not genuine or real.

**spurn** spurns spurning spurned
VERB If you spurn something, you refuse to accept it E.G. *You spurned his last offer.*

**spurt** spurts spurting spurted
VERB **1** When a liquid or flame spurts out of something, it comes out quickly in a thick, powerful stream. ▶ NOUN **2** A spurt of liquid or flame is a thick powerful stream of it E.G. *a small spurt of blood.* **3** A spurt of activity or effort is a sudden, brief period of it.

**spy** spies spying spied
NOUN **1** a person sent to find out secret information about a country or organization. ▶ VERB **2** Someone who spies tries to find out secret information about another country or organization. **3** If you spy on

someone, you watch them secretly.
**4** If you spy something, you notice it.

**squabble** squabbles squabbling squabbled

VERB **1** When people squabble, they quarrel about something trivial.
▶ NOUN **2** a quarrel.

**squad** squads

NOUN (PE) a small group chosen to do a particular activity *E.G. the fraud squad… the England football squad.*
🏛 from Old Spanish *escuadra* meaning 'square', because of the square formation used by soldiers

**squadron** squadrons

NOUN a section of one of the armed forces, especially the air force.
🏛 from Italian *squadrone* meaning 'soldiers drawn up in a square formation'

**squalid**

ADJECTIVE **1** dirty, untidy, and in bad condition. **2** Squalid activities are unpleasant and often dishonest.

**squall** squalls

NOUN a brief, violent storm.

**squalor**

NOUN Squalor consists of bad or dirty conditions or surroundings.

**squander** squanders squandering squandered

VERB To squander money or resources means to waste them *E.G. They have squandered huge amounts of money.*

**square** squares squaring squared

NOUN **1** (MATHS) a shape with four equal sides and four right angles. **2** In a town or city, a square is a flat, open place, bordered by buildings or streets. **3** The square of a number is the number multiplied by itself. For example, the square of 3, written $3^2$, is $3 \times 3$. ▶ ADJECTIVE **4** shaped like a square *E.G. her delicate square face.* **5** 'Square' is used before units of length when talking about the area of something *E.G. $24m^2$.* **6** 'Square' is used after units of length when you are giving the length of each side of something square *E.G. a towel measuring a foot square.* ▶ VERB **7** If you square a number, you multiply it by itself.

**squarely**

ADVERB **1** Squarely means directly rather than indirectly or at an angle *E.G. I looked squarely in the mirror.* **2** If you approach a subject squarely, you consider it fully, without trying to avoid unpleasant aspects of it.

**square root** square roots

NOUN A square root of a number is a number that makes the first number when it is multiplied by itself. For example, the square roots of 25 are 5 and –5.

**squash** squashes squashing squashed

VERB **1** If you squash something, you press it, so that it becomes flat or loses its shape. ▶ NOUN **2** If there is a squash in a place, there are a lot of people squashed in it. **3** Squash is a game in which two players hit a small rubber ball against the walls of a court using rackets. **4** Squash is a drink made from fruit juice, sugar, and water.

**squat** squats squatting squatted; squatter squattest

VERB **1** If you squat down, you crouch, balancing on your feet with your legs bent. **2** A person who squats in an unused building lives there as a squatter. ▶ NOUN **3** a building used by squatters. ▶ ADJECTIVE **4** short and thick.

a
b
c
d
e
f
g
h
i
j
k
l
m
n
o
p
q
r
s
t
u
v
w
x
y
z

A
B
C
D
E
F
G
H
I
J
K
L
M
N
O
P
Q
R
S
T
U
V
W
X
Y
Z

**squatter** squatters

NOUN **1** a person who lives in an unused building without permission and without paying rent. **2** In Australian English, someone who owns a large amount of land for sheep or cattle farming. **3** In Australia and New Zealand in the past, someone who rented land from the King or Queen.

**squawk** squawks squawking squawked

VERB **1** When a bird squawks, it makes a loud, harsh noise. ▶ NOUN **2** a loud, harsh noise made by a bird.

**squeak** squeaks squeaking squeaked

VERB **1** If something squeaks, it makes a short high-pitched sound. ▶ NOUN **2** a short, high-pitched sound. **squeaky** ADJECTIVE

**squeal** squeals squealing squealed

VERB **1** When things or people squeal, they make long, high-pitched sounds. ▶ NOUN **2** a long, high-pitched sound.

**squeamish**

ADJECTIVE easily upset by unpleasant sights or situations.

**squeeze** squeezes squeezing squeezed

VERB **1** When you squeeze something, you press it firmly from two sides. **2** If you squeeze something into a small amount of time or space, you manage to fit it in. ▶ NOUN **3** If you give something a squeeze, you squeeze it E.G. *She gave my hand a quick squeeze.* **4** If getting into something is a squeeze, it is just possible to fit into it E.G. *It would take four comfortably, but six*

*would be a squeeze.*

**squelch** squelches squelching squelched

VERB **1** To squelch means to make a wet, sucking sound. ▶ NOUN **2** a wet, sucking sound.

**squid** squids

NOUN a sea creature with a long soft body and many tentacles.

**squiggle** squiggles

NOUN a wriggly line.

**squint** squints squinting squinted

VERB **1** If you squint at something, you look at it with your eyes screwed up. ▶ NOUN **2** If someone has a squint, their eyes look in different directions from each other.

**squire** squires

NOUN In a village, the squire was a gentleman who owned a large house with a lot of land.

**squirm** squirms squirming squirmed

VERB If you squirm, you wriggle and twist your body about, usually because you are nervous or embarrassed.

**squirrel** squirrels

NOUN a small furry animal with a long bushy tail.

📖 from Greek *skia* meaning 'shadow' and *oura* meaning 'tail'

**squirt** squirts squirting squirted

VERB **1** If a liquid squirts, it comes out of a narrow opening in a thin, fast stream. ▶ NOUN **2** a thin, fast stream of liquid.

**Sri Lankan** Sri Lankans

*Said* "sree-**lang**-kan" ADJECTIVE
**1** belonging or relating to Sri Lanka.
▶ NOUN **2** someone who comes from Sri Lanka.

**stab** stabs stabbing stabbed
VERB **1** To stab someone means to wound them by pushing a knife into their body. **2** To stab at something means to push at it sharply with your finger or with something long and narrow. ▶ PHRASE **3** INFORMAL If you **have a stab** at something, you try to do it. ▶ NOUN **4** You can refer to a sudden unpleasant feeling as a stab of something E.G. *He felt a stab of guilt.*

**stable** stables
ADJECTIVE **1** not likely to change or come to an end suddenly E.G. *I am in a stable relationship.* **2** firmly fixed or balanced and not likely to move, wobble, or fall. ▶ NOUN **3** a building in which horses are kept.
**stability** NOUN   **stabilize** VERB

**staccato**
*Said* "stak-kah-toe" ADJECTIVE consisting of a series of short, sharp, separate sounds.

**stack** stacks stacking stacked
NOUN **1** A stack of things is a pile of them, one on top of the other. ▶ PLURAL NOUN **2** INFORMAL If someone has stacks of something, they have a lot of it. ▶ VERB **3** If you stack things, you arrange them one on top of the other in a pile.

**stadium** stadiums
NOUN a sports ground with rows of seats around it.
🏛 from Greek *stadion* meaning 'racecourse'

**staff** staffs staffing staffed
NOUN **1** The staff of an organization are the people who work for it. ▶ VERB **2** To staff an organization means to find and employ people to work in it. **3** If an organization is staffed by

particular people, they are the people who work for it.

**stag** stags
NOUN an adult male deer.

**stage** stages staging staged
NOUN **1** a part of a process that lasts for a period of time. **2** (DRAMA) In a theatre, the stage is a raised platform where the actors or entertainers perform. **3** (DRAMA) You can refer to the profession of acting as the stage. ▶ VERB **4** If someone stages a play or event, they organize it and present it or take part in it.
▦ (sense 1) period, phase, point

**stagecoach** stagecoaches
NOUN a large carriage pulled by horses which used to carry passengers and mail.

**stagger** staggers staggering staggered
VERB **1** If you stagger, you walk unsteadily because you are ill or drunk. **2** If something staggers you, it amazes you. **3** If events are staggered, they are arranged so that they do not all happen at the same time.
**staggering** ADJECTIVE
▦ (sense 1) lurch, reel, totter

**stagnant**
ADJECTIVE Stagnant water is not flowing and is unhealthy and dirty.

**stag night** stag nights
NOUN a party for a man who is about to get married, which only men go to.

**staid**
ADJECTIVE serious and dull.

**stain** stains staining stained
NOUN **1** a mark on something that is difficult to remove. ▶ VERB **2** If a substance stains something, the

a
b
c
d
e
f
g
h
i
j
k
l
m
n
o
p
q
r
s
t
u
v
w
x
y
z

thing becomes marked or coloured by it.

**stained glass**

NOUN Stained glass is coloured pieces of glass held together with strips of lead.

**stainless steel**

NOUN Stainless steel is a metal made from steel and chromium which does not rust.

**stair stairs**

NOUN Stairs are a set of steps inside a building going from one floor to another.

**staircase staircases**

NOUN a set of stairs.

**stairway stairways**

NOUN a set of stairs.

**stake stakes staking staked**

PHRASE 1 If something is **at stake**, it might be lost or damaged if something else is not successful E.G. *The whole future of the company was at stake.* ▶ PLURAL NOUN 2 The stakes involved in something are the things that can be lost or gained. ▶ VERB 3 If you say you would stake your money, life, or reputation on the success or truth of something, you mean you would risk it E.G. *He is prepared to stake his own career on this.* ▶ NOUN 4 If you have a stake in something such as a business, you own part of it and its success is important to you. 5 a pointed wooden post that can be hammered into the ground and used as a support.

**stale staler stalest**

ADJECTIVE 1 Stale food or air is no longer fresh. 2 If you feel stale, you have no new ideas and are bored.

■ (sense 1) fusty, musty, old

**stalemate**

NOUN 1 Stalemate is a situation in which neither side in an argument or contest can win. 2 In chess, stalemate is a situation in which a player cannot make any move permitted by the rules, so that the game ends and no-one wins.

**stalk stalks stalking stalked**

*Said "stawk"* NOUN 1 The stalk of a flower or leaf is its stem. ▶ VERB 2 To stalk a person or animal means to follow them quietly in order to catch, kill, or observe them. 3 If someone stalks into a room, they walk in a stiff, proud, or angry way.

**stall stalls stalling stalled**

NOUN 1 a large table containing goods for sale or information. ▶ PLURAL NOUN 2 In a theatre, the stalls are the seats at the lowest level, in front of the stage. ▶ VERB 3 When a vehicle stalls, the engine suddenly stops. 4 If you stall when someone asks you to do something, you try to avoid doing it until a later time.

**stallion stallions**

NOUN an adult male horse that can be used for breeding.

**stamina**

NOUN Stamina is the physical or mental energy needed to do something for a very long time.

**stammer stammers stammering stammered**

VERB 1 When someone stammers, they speak with difficulty, repeating words and sounds and hesitating awkwardly. ▶ NOUN 2 Someone who has a stammer tends to stammer when they speak.

**stamp** stamps stamping stamped

NOUN **1** a small piece of gummed paper which you stick on a letter or parcel before posting it. **2** a small block with a pattern cut into it, which you press onto an inky pad and make a mark with it on paper; also the mark made by the stamp. **3** If something bears the stamp of a particular quality or person, it shows clear signs of that quality or of the person's style or characteristics. ► VERB **4** If you stamp a piece of paper, you make a mark on it using a stamp. **5** If you stamp, you lift your foot and put it down hard on the ground.

**stamp out** VERB To stamp something out means to put an end to it *E.G. the battle to stamp out bullying in schools.*

**stampede** stampedes stampeding stampeded

VERB **1** When a group of animals stampede, they run in a wild, uncontrolled way. ► NOUN **2** a group of animals stampeding.

🏛 from Spanish *estampida* meaning 'crash' or 'din'

**stance** stances

NOUN Your stance on a particular matter is your attitude and way of dealing with it *E.G. He takes no particular stance on animal rights.*

**stand** stands standing stood

VERB **1** If you are standing, you are upright, your legs are straight, and your weight is supported by your feet. When you stand up, you get into a standing position. **2** If something stands somewhere, that is where it is *E.G. The house stands alone on the top of a small hill.* **3** If you stand something somewhere, you put it there in an upright position *E.G. Stand the containers on bricks.* **4** If a decision or offer stands, it is still valid *E.G. My offer still stands.* **5** You can use 'stand' when describing the state or condition of something *E.G. Youth unemployment stands at 35%.* **6** If a letter stands for a particular word, it is an abbreviation for that word. **7** If you say you will not stand for something, you mean you will not tolerate it. **8** If something can stand a situation or test, it is good enough or strong enough not to be damaged by it. **9** If you cannot stand something, you cannot bear it *E.G. I can't stand that woman.* **10** If you stand in an election, you are one of the candidates. ► PHRASE **11** When someone **stands trial**, they are tried in a court of law. ► NOUN **12** a stall or very small shop outdoors or in a large public building. **13** a large structure at a sports ground, where the spectators sit to watch what is happening. **14** a piece of furniture designed to hold something *E.G. an umbrella stand.*

**stand by** VERB **1** If you stand by to provide help or take action, you are ready to do it if necessary. **2** If you stand by while something happens, you do nothing to stop it.

**stand down** VERB If someone stands down, they resign from their job or position.

**stand in** VERB If you stand in for someone, you take their place while they are ill or away.

**stand out** VERB If something stands out, it can be easily noticed or is more important than other similar things.

the QUeen stood on the QUay (quay)   SPELLING NOTE

a b c d e f g h i j k l m n o p q r **s** t u v w x y z

**stand up** VERB 1 If something stands up to rough treatment, it is not damaged or harmed. 2 If you stand up to someone who is criticizing or attacking you, you defend yourself.

**standard** standards
NOUN 1 a level of quality or achievement that is considered acceptable E.G. *The work is not up to standard.* ▶ PLURAL NOUN 2 Standards are moral principles of behaviour. ▶ ADJECTIVE 3 usual, normal, and correct E.G. *The practice became standard procedure for most motor companies.*

**standard English**
NOUN Standard English is the form of English taught in schools, used in text books and broadsheet newspapers, and spoken and written by most educated people.

**standardize** standardizes standardizing standardized; also spelt **standardise**
VERB To standardize things means to change them so that they all have a similar set of features E.G. *We have decided to standardize our equipment.*

**stand-by** stand-bys
NOUN 1 something available for use when you need it E.G. *a useful stand-by.* ▶ ADJECTIVE 2 A stand-by ticket is a cheap ticket that you buy just before a theatre performance or a flight if there are any seats left.

**stand-in** stand-ins
NOUN someone who takes a person's place while the person is ill or away E.G. *stand-in teachers.*

**standing**
ADJECTIVE 1 permanently in existence or used regularly E.G. *a standing joke.* ▶ NOUN 2 A person's standing is their status and reputation. 3 'Standing' is used to say how long something has existed E.G. *a friend of 20 years' standing.*

**standpoint** standpoints
NOUN If you consider something from a particular standpoint, you consider it from that point of view E.G. *from a military standpoint.*

**standstill**
NOUN If something comes to a standstill, it stops completely.

**stanza** stanzas
NOUN a verse of a poem.
🏛 from Italian *stanza* meaning 'stopping place'

**staple** staples stapling stapled
NOUN 1 Staples are small pieces of wire that hold sheets of paper firmly together. ▶ VERB 2 If you staple sheets of paper, you fasten them together with staples. ▶ ADJECTIVE 3 A staple food forms a regular and basic part of someone's everyday diet.

**star** stars starring starred
NOUN 1 a large ball of burning gas in space that appears as a point of light in the sky at night. 2 a shape with four, five, or more points sticking out in a regular pattern. 3 Famous actors, sports players, and musicians are referred to as stars. ▶ PLURAL NOUN 4 The horoscope in a newspaper or magazine can be referred to as the stars E.G. *I'm a Virgo, but don't read my stars every day.* ▶ VERB 5 If an actor or actress stars in a film or if the film stars that person, he or she has one of the most important parts in it.

**starboard**
ADJECTIVE OR NOUN The starboard side of a ship is the right-hand side when you are facing the front.

🏛 from Old English *steorbord* meaning 'steering side', because boats were formerly steered with a paddle over the right-hand side

**starch** starches starching starched

NOUN **1** Starch is a substance used for stiffening fabric such as cotton and linen. **2** Starch is a carbohydrate found in foods such as bread and potatoes. ▶ VERB **3** To starch fabric means to stiffen it with starch.

**stare** stares staring stared

VERB **1** If you stare at something, you look at it for a long time. ▶ NOUN **2** a long fixed look at something.

■ (sense 1) gawp, gaze, goggle

**starfish** starfishes or starfish

NOUN a flat, star-shaped sea creature with five limbs.

**stark** starker starkest

ADJECTIVE **1** harsh, unpleasant and plain *E.G. the stark choice.* ▶ PHRASE **2** If someone is **stark-naked**, they have no clothes on at all.

**starling** starlings

NOUN a common European bird with shiny dark feathers.

**start** starts starting started

VERB **1** To start means to begin. To start doing something means to begin doing it *E.G. School starts next week… Suzy started crying.* **2** If you start a machine or car, you operate the controls to make it work. **3** If you start, your body suddenly jerks because of surprise or fear. ▶ NOUN **4** The start of something is the point or time at which it begins. **5** If you do something with a start, you do it with a sudden jerky movement because of surprise or fear *E.G. I awoke with a start.*

**starter** starters

NOUN a small quantity of food served as the first part of a meal.

**startle** startles startling startled

VERB If something sudden and unexpected startles you, it surprises you and makes you slightly frightened.

**startled** ADJECTIVE    **startling** ADJECTIVE

**starve** starves starving starved

VERB **1** If people are starving, they are suffering from a serious lack of food and are likely to die. **2** To starve a person or animal means to prevent them from having any food. **3** *INFORMAL* If you say you are starving, you mean you are very hungry. **4** If someone or something is starved of something they need, they are suffering because they are not getting enough of it *E.G. The hospital was starved of cash.*

**starvation** NOUN

**stash** stashes stashing stashed

VERB; *INFORMAL* If you stash something away in a secret place, you store it there to keep it safe.

**state** states stating stated

NOUN **1** The state of something is its condition, what it is like, or its circumstances. **2** Countries are sometimes referred to as states *E.G. the state of Denmark.* **3** Some countries are divided into regions called states which make some of their own laws *E.G. the State of Vermont.* **4** You can refer to the government or administration of a country as the state. ▶ PHRASE **5** If you are **in a state**, you are nervous or upset and unable to control your

a b c d e f g h i j k l m n o p q r **s** t u v w x y z

emotions. ▶ ADJECTIVE **6** A state ceremony involves the ruler or leader of a country. ▶ VERB **7** If you state something, you say it or write it, especially in a formal way.

**state house** state houses
NOUN In New Zealand, a house built and owned by the government and rented out.

**stately home** stately homes
NOUN In Britain, a very large old house which belongs to an upper-class family.

**statement** statements
NOUN **1** something you say or write when you give facts or information in a formal way. **2** a document provided by a bank showing all the money paid into and out of an account during a period of time.

**state school** state schools
NOUN a school maintained and financed by the government in which education is free.

**statesman** statesmen
NOUN an important and experienced politician.

**static**
ADJECTIVE **1** never moving or changing E.G. *The temperature remains fairly static.* ▶ NOUN **2** Static is an electrical charge caused by friction. It builds up in metal objects.

**station** stations stationing stationed
NOUN **1** a building and platforms where trains stop for passengers. **2** A bus or coach station is a place where some buses start their journeys. **3** A radio station is the frequency on which a particular company broadcasts. **4** In Australian and New Zealand English, a large sheep or

cattle farm. **5** OLD-FASHIONED A person's station is their position or rank in society. ▶ VERB **6** Someone who is stationed somewhere is sent there to work or do a particular job E.G. *Her husband was stationed in Vienna.*

**stationary**
ADJECTIVE not moving E.G. *a stationary car.*
■ fixed, motionless

**stationery**
NOUN Stationery is paper, pens, and other writing equipment.

**statistic** statistics
NOUN **1** Statistics are facts obtained by analysing numerical information. **2** Statistics is the branch of mathematics that deals with the analysis of numerical information.
**statistical** ADJECTIVE

**statistician** statisticians
*Said "stat-iss-tish-an"* NOUN a person who studies or works with statistics.

**statue** statues
NOUN a sculpture of a person.

**stature**
NOUN **1** Someone's stature is their height and size. **2** Someone's stature is also their importance and reputation E.G. *the desire to gain international stature.*

**status** statuses
*Said "stay-tuss"* NOUN **1** A person's status is their position and importance in society. **2** Status is also the official classification given to someone or something E.G. *I am not sure what your legal status is.*
■ (sense 1) position, prestige, standing

**status quo**
*Said "stay-tuss kwoh"* NOUN The status quo is the situation that exists

at a particular time *E.G. They want to keep the status quo.*

🔤 a Latin expression, meaning literally 'the state in which'

**statute statutes**

NOUN a law.

**statutory** ADJECTIVE

**staunch stauncher staunchest**

ADJECTIVE A staunch supporter is a strong and loyal supporter.

**stave staves staving staved**

NOUN 1 In music, a stave is the five lines that music is written on. ▶ VERB 2 If you stave something off, you try to delay or prevent it

**stay stays staying stayed**

VERB 1 If you stay in a place, you do not move away from it *E.G. She stayed in bed until noon.* 2 If you stay at a hotel or a friend's house, you spend some time there as a guest or visitor. 3 If you stay in a particular state, you continue to be in it *E.G. I stayed awake the first night.* 4 In Scottish and South African English, to stay in a place can also mean to live there. ▶ NOUN 5 a short time spent somewhere *E.G. a very pleasant stay in Cornwall.*

🔲 (sense 1) linger, remain

**stead**

NOUN; *FORMAL* Something that will stand someone in good stead will be useful to them in the future.

**steady steadier steadiest; steadies steadying steadied**

ADJECTIVE 1 continuing or developing gradually without major interruptions or changes *E.G. a steady rise in profits.* 2 firm and not shaking or wobbling *E.G. O'Brien held out a steady hand.* 3 A steady look or voice is calm and controlled. 4 Someone who is steady is sensible and reliable.

▶ VERB 5 When you steady something, you hold on to prevent it from shaking or wobbling. 6 When you steady yourself, you control and calm yourself.

**steadily** ADVERB

🔲 (sense 2) firm, secure, stable

**steak steaks**

NOUN 1 Steak is good-quality beef without much fat. 2 A fish steak is a large piece of fish.

🔤 from Old Norse *steik* meaning 'roast'

**steal steals stealing stole stolen**

VERB 1 To steal something means to take it without permission and without intending to return it. 2 To steal somewhere means to move there quietly and secretively.

🔲 (sense 1) nick, purloin, take

**stealth**

*Rhymes with* "**health**" NOUN If you do something with stealth, you do it quietly and secretively.

**stealthy** ADJECTIVE    **stealthily** ADVERB

**steam steams steaming steamed**

NOUN 1 Steam is the hot vapour formed when water boils. ▶ ADJECTIVE 2 Steam engines are operated using steam as a means of power. ▶ VERB 3 If something steams, it gives off steam. 4 To steam food means to cook it in steam.

**steamy** ADJECTIVE

**steam-engine steam-engines**

NOUN any engine that uses the energy of steam to produce mechanical work.

**steamer steamers**

NOUN 1 a ship powered by steam. 2 a container with small holes in the

a b c d e f g h i j k l m n o p q r **s** t u v w x y z

bottom in which you steam food.

**steed** steeds

NOUN; *LITERARY* a horse.

**steel** steels steeling steeled

NOUN **1** Steel is a very strong metal containing mainly iron with a small amount of carbon. ▸ VERB **2** To steel yourself means to prepare to deal with something unpleasant.

**steel band** steel bands

NOUN a group of people who play music on special metal drums.

**steep** steeper steepest; steeps steeping steeped

ADJECTIVE **1** A steep slope rises sharply and is difficult to go up. **2** A steep increase is large and sudden. ▸ VERB **3** To steep something in a liquid means to soak it thoroughly.

**steeply** ADVERB

▦ (sense 1) precipitous, sheer

**steeped**

ADJECTIVE If a person or place is steeped in a particular quality, they are deeply affected by it *E.G. an industry steeped in tradition.*

**steeple** steeples

NOUN a tall pointed structure on top of a church tower.

**steeplechase** steeplechases

NOUN a long horse race in which the horses jump over obstacles such as hedges and water jumps.

▦ originally a race with a church steeple in sight as the goal

**steer** steers steering steered

VERB **1** To steer a vehicle or boat means to control it so that it goes in the right direction. **2** To steer someone towards a particular course of action means to influence and direct their behaviour or thoughts. ▸ NOUN **3** a castrated bull.

▦ (sense 1) direct, guide, pilot

**stem** stems stemming stemmed

NOUN **1** The stem of a plant is the long thin central part above the ground that carries the leaves and flowers. **2** The stem of a glass is the long narrow part connecting the bowl to the base. ▸ VERB **3** If a problem stems from a particular situation, that situation is the original starting point or cause of the problem. **4** If you stem the flow of something, you restrict it or stop it from spreading *E.G. to stem the flow of refugees.*

**stench** stenches

NOUN a very strong, unpleasant smell.

**stencil** stencils stencilling stencilled

NOUN **1** a thin sheet with a cut-out pattern through which ink or paint passes to form the pattern on the surface below. ▸ VERB **2** To stencil a design on a surface means to create it using a stencil.

▦ from Middle English *stanselen* meaning 'to decorate with bright colours'

**step** steps stepping stepped

NOUN **1** If you take a step, you lift your foot and put it down somewhere else. **2** one of a series of actions that you take in order to achieve something. **3** a raised flat surface, usually one of a series that you can walk up or down. ▸ VERB **4** If you step in a particular direction, you move your foot in that direction. **5** If someone steps down or steps aside from an important position, they resign.

**step-**

PREFIX If a word like 'father' or 'sister' has 'step-' in front of it, it shows that the family relationship has come about because a parent has married again *E.G. stepfather… stepsister.*

**steppe** steppes
*Said* "**step**" NOUN a large area of open grassland with no trees.
📖 from Old Russian *step* meaning 'lowland'

**stepping stone** stepping stones
NOUN **1** Stepping stones are a line of large stones that you walk on to cross a shallow river. **2** a job or event that is regarded as a stage in your progress, especially in your career.

**stereo** stereos
ADJECTIVE **1** A stereo recording or music system is one in which the sound is directed through two speakers. ▶ NOUN **2** a piece of equipment that reproduces sound from records, tapes, or CDs directing the sound through two speakers.

**stereotype** stereotypes
**stereotyping** stereotyped (PSHE)
NOUN **1** a fixed image or set of characteristics that people consider to represent a particular type of person or thing *E.G. the stereotype of the polite, industrious Japanese.* ▶ VERB **2** If you stereotype someone, you assume they are a particular type of person and will behave in a particular way.

**sterile**
ADJECTIVE **1** Sterile means completely clean and free from germs. **2** A sterile person or animal is unable to produce offspring.
**sterility** NOUN
▤ (sense 1) germ-free, sterilized

**sterilize** sterilizes sterilizing sterilized; also spelt **sterilise**
VERB **1** To sterilize something means to make it completely clean and free

from germs, usually by boiling it or treating it with an antiseptic. **2** If a person or animal is sterilized, they have an operation that makes it impossible for them to produce offspring.

**sterling**
NOUN **1** Sterling is the money system of Great Britain. ▶ ADJECTIVE **2** excellent in quality *E.G. Volunteers are doing sterling work.*

**stern** sterner sternest; sterns
ADJECTIVE **1** very serious and strict *E.G. a stern father… a stern warning.* ▶ NOUN **2** The stern of a boat is the back part.

**steroid** steroids
NOUN Steroids are chemicals that occur naturally in your body. Sometimes sportsmen illegally take them as drugs to improve their performance.

**stethoscope** stethoscopes
NOUN a device used by doctors to listen to a patient's heart and breathing, consisting of earpieces connected to a hollow tube and a small disc.
📖 from Greek *stēthos* meaning 'chest' and *skopein* meaning 'to look at'

**stew** stews stewing stewed
NOUN **1** a dish of small pieces of savoury food cooked together slowly in a liquid. ▶ VERB **2** To stew meat, vegetables, or fruit means to cook them slowly in a liquid.
📖 from Middle English *stuen* meaning 'to take a very hot bath'

**steward** stewards
NOUN **1** a man who works on a ship or plane looking after passengers and serving meals. **2** a person who helps

a
b
c
d
e
f
g
h
i
j
k
l
m
n
o
p
q
r
**s**
t
u
v
w
x
y
z

A
B
C
D
E
F
G
H
I
J
K
L
M
N
O
P
Q
R
S
T
U
V
W
X
Y
Z

to direct the public at a race, march, or other event.

🏛 from Old English *stigweard* meaning 'hall protector'

**stewardess** stewardesses

NOUN a woman who works on a ship or plane looking after passengers and serving meals.

**stick** sticks sticking stuck

NOUN **1** a long, thin piece of wood. **2** A stick of something is a long, thin piece of it *E.G. a stick of celery*. ▶ VERB **3** If you stick a long or pointed object into something, you push it in. **4** If you stick one thing to another, you attach it with glue or sticky tape. **5** If one thing sticks to another, it becomes attached and is difficult to remove. **6** If a movable part of something sticks, it becomes fixed and will no longer move or work properly *E.G. My gears keep sticking*. **7** INFORMAL If you stick something somewhere, you put it there. **8** If you stick by someone, you continue to help and support them. **9** If you stick to something, you keep to it and do not change to something else *E.G. He should have stuck to the old ways of doing things*. **10** When people stick together, they stay together and support each other.

**stick out** VERB **1** If something sticks out, it projects from something else. **2** To stick out also means to be very noticeable.

**stick up** VERB **1** If something sticks up, it points upwards from a surface. **2** INFORMAL If you stick up for a person or principle, you support or defend them.

**sticker** stickers

NOUN a small piece of paper or plastic with writing or a picture on it, that

you stick onto a surface.

**sticking plaster** sticking plasters

NOUN a small piece of fabric that you stick over a cut or sore to protect it.

**stick insect** stick insects

NOUN an insect with a long cylindrical body and long legs, which looks like a twig.

**sticky** stickier stickiest

ADJECTIVE **1** A sticky object is covered with a substance that can stick to other things *E.G. sticky hands*. **2** Sticky paper or tape has glue on one side so that you can stick it to a surface. **3** INFORMAL A sticky situation is difficult or embarrassing to deal with. **4** Sticky weather is unpleasantly hot and humid.

**stiff** stiffer stiffest

ADJECTIVE **1** Something that is stiff is firm and not easily bent. **2** If you feel stiff, your muscles or joints ache when you move. **3** Stiff behaviour is formal and not friendly or relaxed. **4** Stiff also means difficult or severe *E.G. stiff competition for places*. **5** A stiff drink contains a large amount of alcohol. **6** A stiff breeze is blowing strongly. ▶ ADVERB **7** INFORMAL If you are bored stiff or scared stiff, you are very bored or very scared.

**stiffly** ADVERB **stiffness** NOUN

**stiffen** stiffens stiffening stiffened

VERB **1** If you stiffen, you suddenly stop moving and your muscles become tense *E.G. I stiffened with tension*. **2** If your joints or muscles stiffen, they become sore and difficult to bend or move. **3** If fabric or material is stiffened, it is made firmer so that it does not bend easily.

**stifle** stifles stifling stifled
*Said "sty-fl"* VERB **1** If the atmosphere stifles you, you feel you cannot breathe properly. **2** To stifle something means to stop it from happening or continuing *E.G. Martin stifled a yawn.*
**stifling** ADJECTIVE

**stigma** stigmas
NOUN If something has a stigma attached to it, people consider it unacceptable or a disgrace *E.G. the stigma of mental illness.*

**stile** stiles
NOUN a step on either side of a wall or fence to enable you to climb over.

**stiletto** stilettos
NOUN Stilettos are women's shoes with very high, narrow heels.
▨ from Italian *stilo* meaning 'dagger', because of the shape of the heels

**still** stiller stillest; stills
ADVERB **1** If a situation still exists, it has continued to exist and it exists now. **2** If something could still happen, it might happen although it has not happened yet. **3** 'Still' emphasizes that something is the case in spite of other things *E.G. Whatever you think of him, he's still your father.* ▶ ADVERB or ADJECTIVE **4** Still means staying in the same position without moving *E.G. Sit still… The air was still.* ▶ ADJECTIVE **5** A still place is quiet and peaceful with no signs of activity. ▶ NOUN **6** a photograph taken from a cinema film or video.
**stillness** NOUN

**stillborn**
ADJECTIVE A stillborn baby is dead when it is born.

**stilt** stilts
NOUN **1** Stilts are long upright poles on which a building is built, for example on wet land. **2** Stilts are also two long pieces of wood or metal on which people balance and walk.

**stilted**
ADJECTIVE formal, unnatural, and rather awkward *E.G. a stilted conversation.*

**stimulant** stimulants
NOUN a drug or other substance that makes your body work faster, increasing your heart rate and making it difficult to sleep.

**stimulate** stimulates stimulating stimulated
VERB **1** To stimulate something means to encourage it to begin or develop *E.G. to stimulate discussion.* **2** If something stimulates you, it gives you new ideas and enthusiasm.
**stimulating** ADJECTIVE **stimulation** NOUN
▤ (sense 1) arouse, encourage, inspire

**stimulus** stimuli
NOUN something that causes a process or event to begin or develop.

**sting** stings stinging stung
VERB **1** If a creature or plant stings you, it pricks your skin and injects a substance which causes pain. **2** If a part of your body stings, you feel a sharp tingling pain there. **3** If someone's remarks sting you, they make you feel upset and hurt. ▶ NOUN **4** A creature's sting is the part it stings you with.
▤ (sense 2) hurt, smart

**stink** stinks stinking stank stunk
VERB **1** Something that stinks smells very unpleasant. ▶ NOUN **2** a very unpleasant smell.
▤ (sense 2) pong, stench

a
b
c
d
e
f
g
h
i
j
k
l
m
n
o
p
q
r
**s**
t
u
v
w
x
y
z

an ELegant angEL (ange**l**)        SPELLING NOTE

A
B
C
D
E
F
G
H
I
J
K
L
M
N
O
P
Q
R
S
T
U
V
W
X
Y
Z

**stint** stints

NOUN a period of time spent doing a particular job E.G. *a three-year stint in the army*.

**stipulate** stipulates stipulating stipulated

VERB; FORMAL If you stipulate that something must be done, you state clearly that it must be done.

**stipulation** NOUN

**stir** stirs stirring stirred

VERB 1 When you stir a liquid, you move it around using a spoon or a stick. 2 To stir means to move slightly. 3 If something stirs you, it makes you feel strong emotions E.G. *The power of the singing stirred me.* ▸ NOUN 4 If an event causes a stir, it causes general excitement or shock E.G. *two books which have caused a stir*.

**stirring** stirrings

ADJECTIVE 1 causing excitement, emotion, and enthusiasm E.G. *a stirring account of the action.* ▸ NOUN 2 If there is a stirring of emotion, people begin to feel it.

**stirrup** stirrups

NOUN Stirrups are two metal loops hanging by leather straps from a horse's saddle, which you put your feet in when riding.

**stitch** stitches stitching stitched

VERB 1 When you stitch pieces of material together, you use a needle and thread to sew them together. 2 To stitch a wound means to use a special needle and thread to hold the edges of skin together. ▸ NOUN 3 one of the pieces of thread that can be seen where material has been sewn. 4 one of the pieces of thread that can be seen where a

wound has been stitched E.G. *He had eleven stitches in his lip.* 5 If you have a stitch, you feel a sharp pain at the side of your abdomen, usually because you have been running or laughing.

**stoat** stoats

NOUN a small wild animal with a long body and brown fur.

**stock** stocks stocking stocked

NOUN 1 Stocks are shares bought as an investment in a company; also the amount of money raised by the company through the issue of shares. 2 A shop's stock is the total amount of goods it has for sale. 3 If you have a stock of things, you have a supply ready for use. 4 The stock an animal or person comes from is the type of animal or person they are descended from E.G. *She was descended from Scots Highland stock.* 5 Stock is farm animals. 6 Stock is a liquid made from boiling meat, bones, or vegetables together in water. Stock is used as a base for soups, stews, and sauces. ▸ VERB 7 A shop that stocks particular goods keeps a supply of them to sell. 8 If you stock a shelf or cupboard, you fill it with food or other things. ▸ ADJECTIVE 9 A stock expression or way of doing something is one that is commonly used.

**stock up** VERB If you stock up with something, you buy a supply of it.

**stockbroker** stockbrokers

NOUN A stockbroker is a person whose job is to buy and sell shares for people who want to invest money.

**stock exchange** stock exchanges

NOUN a place where there is trading in

stocks and shares E.G. *the New York Stock Exchange.*

**stocking** stockings

NOUN Stockings are long pieces of thin clothing that cover a woman's leg.

**stockman** stockmen

NOUN a man who looks after sheep or cattle on a farm.

**stock market** stock markets

NOUN The stock market is the organization and activity involved in buying and selling stocks and shares.

**stockpile** stockpiles stockpiling stockpiled

VERB 1 If someone stockpiles something, they store large quantities of it for future use. ▶ NOUN 2 a large store of something.

**stocktaking**

NOUN Stocktaking is the counting and checking of all a shop's or business's goods.

**stocky** stockier stockiest

ADJECTIVE A stocky person is rather short, but broad and solid-looking.

**stoke** stokes stoking stoked

VERB To stoke a fire means to keep it burning by moving or adding fuel.

**stomach** stomachs stomaching stomached

NOUN 1 Your stomach is the organ inside your body where food is digested. 2 You can refer to the front part of your body below your waist as your stomach. ▶ VERB 3 If you cannot stomach something, you strongly dislike it and cannot accept it.

**stone** stones stoning stoned

NOUN 1 Stone is the hard solid substance found in the ground and used for building. 2 a small piece of rock. 3 The stone in a fruit such as a plum or cherry is the large seed in the centre. 4 a unit of weight equal to 14 pounds or about 6.35 kilograms. 5 You can refer to a jewel as a stone E.G. *a diamond ring with three stones.* ▶ VERB 6 To stone something or someone means to throw stones at them.

**stoned**

ADJECTIVE; *INFORMAL* affected by drugs.

**stony** stonier stoniest

ADJECTIVE 1 Stony ground is rough and contains a lot of stones or rocks. 2 If someone's expression is stony, it shows no friendliness or sympathy.

**stool** stools

NOUN 1 a seat with legs but no back or arms. 2 a lump of faeces.

**stoop** stoops stooping stooped

VERB 1 If you stoop, you stand or walk with your shoulders bent forwards. 2 If you would not stoop to something, you would not disgrace yourself by doing it.

**stop** stops stopping stopped

VERB 1 If you stop doing something, you no longer do it. 2 If an activity or process stops, it comes to an end or no longer happens. 3 If a machine stops, it no longer functions or it is switched off. 4 To stop something means to prevent it. 5 If people or things that are moving stop, they no longer move. 6 If you stop somewhere, you stay there for a short while. ▶ PHRASE 7 To **put a stop to** something means to prevent it from happening or continuing. ▶ NOUN 8 a place where a bus, train, or other vehicle stops during a journey. 9 If something that is moving comes to a stop, it no longer moves.

■ (sense 1) cease, desist, halt

a
b
c
d
e
f
g
h
i
j
k
l
m
n
o
p
q
r
s
t
u
v
w
x
y
z

A B C D E F G H I J K L M N O P Q R S T U V W X Y Z

**stoppage** stoppages
NOUN If there is a stoppage, people stop work because of a disagreement with their employer.

**stopper** stoppers
NOUN a piece of glass or cork that fits into the neck of a jar or bottle.

**stopwatch** stopwatches
NOUN a watch that can be started and stopped by pressing buttons, which is used to time events.

**storage**
NOUN The storage of something is the keeping of it somewhere until it is needed.

**store** stores storing stored
NOUN 1 a shop. 2 A store of something is a supply kept for future use. 3 a place where things are kept while they are not used. ▶ VERB 4 When you store something somewhere, you keep it there until it is needed.
▶ PHRASE 5 Something that is **in store for** you is going to happen to you in the future.
■ (sense 1) hoard, stockpile, supply

**storeroom** storerooms
NOUN a room where things are kept until they are needed.

**storey** storeys
NOUN A storey of a building is one of its floors or levels.

**stork** storks
NOUN a very large white and black bird with long red legs and a long bill.

**storm** storms storming stormed
NOUN 1 When there is a storm, there is heavy rain, a strong wind, and often thunder and lightning. 2 If something causes a storm, it causes an angry or excited reaction E.G. *His*

*words caused a storm of protest.* ▶ VERB 3 If someone storms out, they leave quickly, noisily, and angrily. 4 To storm means to say something in a loud, angry voice E.G. *'It's a fiasco!' he stormed.* 5 If people storm a place, they attack it.
**stormy** ADJECTIVE

**story** stories
NOUN 1 a description of imaginary people and events written or told to entertain people. 2 The story of something or someone is an account of the important events that have happened to them E.G. *his life story.*
■ anecdote, tale, yarn

**stout** stouter stoutest
ADJECTIVE 1 rather fat. 2 thick, strong, and sturdy E.G. *stout walking shoes.* 3 determined, firm, and strong E.G. *He can outrun the stoutest opposition.*
**stoutly** ADVERB

**stove** stoves
NOUN a piece of equipment for heating a room or for cooking.

**stow** stows stowing stowed
VERB 1 If you stow something somewhere or stow it away, you store it until it is needed. 2 If someone stows away in a ship or plane, they hide in it to go somewhere secretly without paying.

**straddle** straddles straddling straddled
VERB 1 If you straddle something, you stand or sit with one leg on either side of it. 2 If something straddles a place, it crosses it, linking different parts together E.G. *The town straddles a river.*

**straight** straighter straightest
ADJECTIVE OR ADVERB 1 continuing in the same direction without curving or

bending E.G. *the straight path… Amy stared straight ahead of her.* **2** upright or level rather than sloping or bent E.G. *Keep your arms straight.* ▶ ADVERB **3** immediately and directly E.G. *We will go straight to the hotel.* ▶ ADJECTIVE **4** neat and tidy E.G. *Get this room straight.* **5** honest, frank, and direct E.G. *They wouldn't give me a straight answer.* **6** A straight choice involves only two options.

**straightaway**
ADVERB If you do something straightaway, you do it immediately.

**straighten straightens straightening straightened**
VERB **1** To straighten something means to remove any bends or curves from it. **2** To straighten something also means to make it neat and tidy. **3** To straighten out a confused situation means to organize and deal with it.

**straightforward**
ADJECTIVE **1** easy and involving no problems. **2** honest, open, and frank.

**strain strains straining strained**
NOUN **1** Strain is worry and nervous tension. **2** If a strain is put on something, it is affected by a strong force which may damage it. **3** You can refer to an aspect of someone's character, remarks, or work as a strain E.G. *There was a strain of bitterness in his voice.* **4** You can refer to distant sounds of music as strains of music. **5** A particular strain of plant is a variety of it E.G. *strains of rose.* ▶ VERB **6** To strain something means to force it or use it more than is reasonable or normal. **7** If you strain a muscle, you injure it by moving awkwardly. **8** To strain food means to pour away the liquid from it.

◼ (sense 1) anxiety, stress
◼ (sense 6) overexert, tax

**strained**
ADJECTIVE **1** worried and anxious. **2** If a relationship is strained, people feel unfriendly and do not trust each other.

**strait straits**
NOUN **1** You can refer to a narrow strip of sea as a strait or the straits E.G. *the Straits of Hormuz.* ▶ PLURAL NOUN **2** If someone is in a bad situation, you can say they are in difficult straits.

**straitjacket straitjackets**
NOUN A special jacket used to tie the arms of a violent person tightly around their body.

**strait-laced**
ADJECTIVE having a very strict and serious attitude to moral behaviour.

**strand strands**
NOUN **1** A strand of thread or hair is a single long piece of it. **2** You can refer to a part of a situation or idea as a strand of it E.G. *the different strands of the problem.*

**stranded**
ADJECTIVE If someone or something is stranded somewhere, they are stuck and cannot leave.

**strange stranger strangest**
ADJECTIVE **1** unusual or unexpected. **2** not known, seen, or experienced before E.G. *alone in a strange country.*
**strangely** ADVERB **strangeness**
NOUN
◼ (sense 1) curious, odd, peculiar
◼ (sense 2) alien, new, unfamiliar

**stranger strangers**
NOUN **1** someone you have never met before. **2** If you are a stranger to a place or situation, you have not been there or experienced it before.

a
b
c
d
e
f
g
h
i
j
k
l
m
n
o
p
q
r
s
t
u
v
w
x
y
z

Betty Eats Cakes And Uses Seven Eggs (because)    SPELLING NOTE

A
B
C
D
E
F
G
H
I
J
K
L
M
N
O
P
Q
R
**S**
T
U
V
W
X
Y
Z

**strangle** strangles strangling
strangled
VERB To strangle someone means to
kill them by squeezing their throat.
**strangulation** NOUN

**strangled**
ADJECTIVE A strangled sound is unclear
and muffled.

**stranglehold** strangleholds
NOUN To have a stranglehold on
something means to have control
over it and prevent it from developing.

**strap** straps strapping
strapped
NOUN 1 a narrow piece of leather or
cloth, used to fasten or hold things
together. ▶ VERB 2 To strap something
means to fasten it with a strap.

**strapping**
ADJECTIVE tall, strong, and healthy-
looking.

**strata**
the plural of **stratum**.

**strategic**
Said "strat-**tee**-jik" ADJECTIVE planned
or intended to achieve something or
to gain an advantage E.G. a strategic
plan.
**strategically** ADVERB

**strategy** strategies
NOUN 1 a plan for achieving
something. 2 Strategy is the skill of
planning the best way to achieve
something, especially in war.
**strategist** NOUN

**stratum** strata
NOUN The strata in the earth's surface
are the different layers of rock.

**straw** straws
NOUN 1 Straw is the dry, yellowish
stalks from cereal crops. 2 a hollow
tube of paper or plastic which you
use to suck a drink into your mouth.

▶ PHRASE 3 If something is **the last
straw**, it is the latest in a series of
bad events and makes you feel you
cannot stand any more.

**strawberry** strawberries
NOUN a small red fruit with tiny seeds
in its skin.

**stray** strays straying strayed
VERB 1 When people or animals stray,
they wander away from where they
should be. 2 If your thoughts stray,
you stop concentrating. ▶ ADJECTIVE
3 A stray dog or cat is one that has
wandered away from home. 4 Stray
things are separated from the main
group of things of their kind E.G. a
stray piece of lettuce. ▶ NOUN 5 a stray
dog or cat.

**streak** streaks streaking
streaked
NOUN 1 a long mark or stain. 2 If
someone has a particular streak, they
have that quality in their character.
3 A lucky or unlucky streak is a series
of successes or failures. ▶ VERB 4 If
something is streaked with a colour,
it has lines of the colour in it. 5 To
streak somewhere means to move
there very quickly.
**streaky** ADJECTIVE

**stream** streams streaming
streamed
NOUN 1 a small river. 2 You can refer to
a steady flow of something as a
stream E.G. a constant stream of
people. 3 In a school, a stream is a
group of children of the same age
and ability. ▶ VERB 4 To stream
somewhere means to move in a
continuous flow in large quantities
E.G. Rain streamed down the
windscreen.

**streamer** streamers

NOUN a long, narrow strip of coloured paper used for decoration.

**streamline** streamlines streamlining streamlined

VERB 1 To streamline a vehicle, aircraft, or boat means to improve its shape so that it moves more quickly and efficiently. 2 To streamline an organization means to make it more efficient by removing parts of it.

**street** streets

NOUN a road in a town or village, usually with buildings along it.

**strength** strengths

NOUN 1 Your strength is your physical energy and the power of your muscles. 2 Strength can refer to the degree of someone's confidence or courage. 3 You can refer to power or influence as strength E.G. *The campaign against factory closures gathered strength.* 4 Someone's strengths are their good qualities and abilities. 5 The strength of an object is the degree to which it can stand rough treatment. 6 The strength of a substance is the amount of other substances that it contains E.G. *coffee with sugar and milk in it at the correct strength.* 7 The strength of a feeling or opinion is the degree to which it is felt or supported. 8 The strength of a relationship is its degree of closeness or success. 9 The strength of a group is the total number of people in it.
► PHRASE 10 If people do something **in strength**, a lot of them do it together E.G. *The press were here in strength.*
≣ (sense 1) might, muscle
≣ (sense 3) force, intensity, power

**strengthen** strengthens strengthening strengthened

VERB 1 To strengthen something means to give it more power, influence, or support and make it more likely to succeed. 2 To strengthen an object means to improve it or add to its structure so that it can withstand rough treatment.
≣ fortify, reinforce

**strenuous**

*Said "stren-yoo-uss"* ADJECTIVE involving a lot of effort or energy.
**strenuously** ADVERB

**stress** stresses stressing stressed

NOUN 1 Stress is worry and nervous tension. 2 Stresses are strong physical forces applied to an object. 3 Stress is emphasis put on a word or part of a word when it is pronounced, making it slightly louder. ► VERB 4 If you stress a point, you emphasize it and draw attention to its importance.
**stressful** ADJECTIVE
≣ (sense 1) anxiety, pressure, strain
≣ (sense 3) accent, emphasis
≣ (sense 4) accentuate, emphasize

**stretch** stretches stretching stretched

VERB 1 Something that stretches over an area extends that far. 2 When you stretch, you hold out part of your body as far as you can. 3 To stretch something soft or elastic means to pull it to make it longer or bigger.
► NOUN 4 A stretch of land or water is an area of it. 5 A stretch of time is a period of time.

**stretcher** stretchers

NOUN a long piece of material with a

a b c d e f g h i j k l m n o p q r s t u v w x y z

A B C D E F G H I J K L M N O P Q R S T U V W X Y Z

pole along each side, used to carry an injured person.

**strewn**

ADJECTIVE If things are strewn about, they are scattered about untidily *E.G. The costumes were strewn all over the floor.*

**stricken**

ADJECTIVE severely affected by something unpleasant.

**strict stricter strictest**

ADJECTIVE 1 Someone who is strict controls other people very firmly. 2 A strict rule must always be obeyed absolutely. 3 The strict meaning of something is its precise and accurate meaning. 4 You can use 'strict' to describe someone who never breaks the rules or principles of a particular belief *E.G. a strict Muslim.*

▤ (sense 1) severe, stern
▤ (sense 2) stringent

**strictly**

ADVERB 1 Strictly means only for a particular purpose *E.G. I was in it strictly for the money.* ▶ PHRASE 2 You say **strictly speaking** to correct a statement or add more precise information *E.G. Somebody pointed out that, strictly speaking, electricity was a discovery, not an invention.*

**stride strides striding strode stridden**

VERB 1 To stride along means to walk quickly with long steps. ▶ NOUN 2 a long step; also the length of a step.

**strident**

*Said "stry-dent"* ADJECTIVE loud, harsh, and unpleasant.

**strife**

NOUN; FORMAL Strife is trouble, conflict, and disagreement.

**strike strikes striking struck**

NOUN 1 If there is a strike, people stop working as a protest. 2 A hunger strike is a refusal to eat anything as a protest. A rent strike is a refusal to pay rent. 3 a military attack *E.G. the threat of American air strikes.* ▶ VERB 4 To strike someone or something means to hit them. 5 If an illness, disaster, or enemy strikes, it suddenly affects or attacks someone. 6 If a thought strikes you, it comes into your mind. 7 If you are struck by something, you are impressed by it. 8 When a clock strikes, it makes a sound to indicate the time. 9 To strike a deal with someone means to come to an agreement with them. 10 If someone strikes oil or gold, they discover it in the ground. 11 If you strike a match, you rub it against something to make it burst into flame.

**strike off** VERB If a professional person is struck off for bad behaviour, their name is removed from an official register and they are not allowed to practise their profession.

**strike up** VERB To strike up a conversation or friendship means to begin it.

**striker strikers**

NOUN 1 Strikers are people who are refusing to work as a protest. 2 In soccer, a player whose function is to attack and score goals.

**striking**

ADJECTIVE very noticeable because of being unusual or very attractive.
**strikingly** ADVERB

**string strings stringing strung**

NOUN 1 String is thin cord made of twisted threads. 2 You can refer to a row or series of similar things as a string of them *E.G. a string of islands… a string of injuries.* **3** The strings of a musical instrument are tightly stretched lengths of wire or nylon which vibrate to produce the notes. ► PLURAL NOUN **4** The section of an orchestra consisting of stringed instruments is called the strings.

**string along** VERB *INFORMAL* To string someone along means to deceive them.

**string out** VERB **1** If things are strung out, they are spread out in a long line. **2** To string something out means to make it last longer than necessary.

**stringed**

ADJECTIVE A stringed instrument is one with strings, such as a guitar or violin.

**stringent**

ADJECTIVE Stringent laws conditions are very severe or are strictly controlled *E.G. stringent financial checks.*

**stringy-bark** stringy-barks

NOUN any Australian eucalypt that has bark that peels off in long, tough strands.

**strip** strips stripping stripped

NOUN **1** A strip of something is a long, narrow piece of it. **2** A comic strip is a series of drawings which tell a story. **3** A sports team's strip is the clothes worn by the team when playing a match. ► VERB **4** If you strip, you take off all your clothes. **5** To strip something means to remove whatever is covering its surface. **6** To strip someone of their property or rights means to take their property or rights away from them officially.

**stripe** stripes

NOUN Stripes are long, thin lines,

usually of different colours.

**striped** ADJECTIVE

**stripper** strippers

NOUN an entertainer who does striptease.

**striptease**

NOUN Striptease is a form of entertainment in which someone takes off their clothes gradually to music.

**strive** strives striving strove striven

VERB If you strive to do something, you make a great effort to achieve it.

**stroke** strokes stroking stroked

VERB **1** If you stroke something, you move your hand smoothly and gently over it. ► NOUN **2** If someone has a stroke, they suddenly lose consciousness as a result of a blockage or rupture in a blood vessel in the brain. A stroke can result in damage to speech and paralysis. **3** The strokes of a brush or pen are the movements that you make with it. **4** The strokes of a clock are the sounds that indicate the hour. **5** A swimming stroke is a particular style of swimming. ► PHRASE **6** If you have **a stroke of luck**, then you are lucky and something good happens to you.

**stroll** strolls strolling strolled

VERB **1** To stroll along means to walk slowly in a relaxed way. ► NOUN **2** a slow, pleasurable walk.

■ amble, saunter, walk

**stroller** strollers

NOUN In Australian English, a stroller is a pushchair.

**strong** stronger strongest

ADJECTIVE **1** Someone who is strong has powerful muscles. **2** You also say

a b c d e f g h i j k l m n o p q r **s** t u v w x y z

A B C D E F G H I J K L M N O P Q R S T U V W X Y Z

that someone is strong when they are confident and have courage. **3** Strong objects are able to withstand rough treatment. **4** Strong also means great in degree or intensity *E.G. a strong wind.* **5** A strong argument or theory is supported by a lot of evidence. **6** If a group or organization is strong, it has a lot of members or influence. **7** You can use 'strong' to say how many people there are in a group *E.G. The audience was about two dozen strong.* **8** Your strong points are the things you are good at. **9** A strong economy or currency is stable and successful. **10** A strong liquid or drug contains a lot of a particular substance. ▶ ADVERB **11** If someone or something is still going strong, they are still healthy or working well after a long time.
**strongly** ADVERB
■ (sense 1) muscular, powerful
■ (sense 4) acute, intense

**stronghold** strongholds
NOUN **1** a place that is held and defended by an army. **2** A stronghold of an attitude or belief is a place in which the attitude or belief is strongly held *E.G. Europe's last stronghold of male dominance.*

**structure** structures structuring structured
NOUN **1** The structure of something is the way it is made, built, or organized. **2** something that has been built or constructed. **3** If something has structure, it is properly organized *E.G. The days have no real structure.* ▶ VERB **4** To structure something means to arrange it into an organized pattern or system.

**structural** ADJECTIVE **structurally** ADVERB
■ (sense 1) arrangement, construction, make-up

**struggle** struggles struggling struggled
VERB **1** If you struggle to do something, you try hard to do it in difficult circumstances. **2** When people struggle, they twist and move violently during a fight. ▶ NOUN **3** Something that is a struggle is difficult to achieve and takes a lot of effort. **4** a fight.

**strum** strums strumming strummed
VERB To strum a guitar means to play it by moving your fingers backwards and forwards across all the strings.

**strut** struts strutting strutted
VERB **1** To strut means to walk in a stiff, proud way with your chest out and your head high. ▶ NOUN **2** a piece of wood or metal which strengthens or supports part of a building or structure.

**Stuart** Stuarts
NOUN Stuart was the family name of the monarchs who ruled Scotland from 1371 to 1714 and England from 1603 to 1714.

**stub** stubs stubbing stubbed
NOUN **1** The stub of a pencil or cigarette is the short piece that remains when the rest has been used. **2** The stub of a cheque or ticket is the small part that you keep. ▶ VERB **3** If you stub your toe, you hurt it by accidentally kicking something.

**stubble**
NOUN **1** The short stalks remaining in the ground after a crop is harvested are called stubble. **2** If a man has

stubble on his face, he has very short hair growing there because he has not shaved recently.

## stubborn

ADJECTIVE **1** Someone who is stubborn is determined not to change their opinion or course of action. **2** A stubborn stain is difficult to remove.

**stubbornly** ADVERB    **stubbornness** NOUN

▬ (sense 1) inflexible, obstinate, pig-headed

## stuck

ADJECTIVE **1** If something is stuck in a particular position, it is fixed or jammed and cannot be moved *E.G. His car's stuck in a snowdrift.* **2** If you are stuck, you are unable to continue what you were doing because it is too difficult. **3** If you are stuck somewhere, you are unable to get away.

## stuck-up

ADJECTIVE; *INFORMAL* proud and conceited.

## stud studs

NOUN **1** a small piece of metal fixed into something. **2** A male horse or other animal that is kept for stud is kept for breeding purposes.

## studded

ADJECTIVE decorated with small pieces of metal or precious stones.

## student students

NOUN a person studying at university or college.

## studied

ADJECTIVE A studied action or response has been carefully planned and is not natural *E.G. She sipped her glass of white wine with studied boredom.*

## studio studios

NOUN **1** a room where a photographer or painter works. **2** a room

containing special equipment where records, films, or radio or television programmes are made.

## studious

*Said "styoo-dee-uss"* ADJECTIVE spending a lot of time studying.

## studiously

ADVERB carefully and deliberately *E.G. She was studiously ignoring me.*

## study studies studying studied

VERB **1** If you study a particular subject, you spend time learning about it. **2** If you study something, you look at it carefully *E.G. He studied the map in silence.* ▶ NOUN **3** Study is the activity of studying a subject *E.G. the serious study of medieval archaeology.* **4** Studies are subjects which are studied *E.G. media studies.* **5** a piece of research on a particular subject *E.G. a detailed study of the world's most violent people.* **6** a room used for writing and studying.

## stuff stuffs stuffing stuffed

NOUN **1** You can refer to a substance or group of things as stuff. ▶ VERB **2** If you stuff something somewhere, you push it there quickly and roughly. **3** If you stuff something with a substance or objects, you fill it with the substance or objects.

## stuffing

NOUN Stuffing is a mixture of small pieces of food put inside poultry or a vegetable before it is cooked.

## stuffy stuffier stuffiest

ADJECTIVE **1** very formal and old-fashioned. **2** If it is stuffy in a room, there is not enough fresh air.

▬ (sense 2) airless, close, fusty

## stumble stumbles stumbling stumbled

VERB **1** If you stumble while you are

have a pIEce of pIE (pie<u>ce</u>)    **SPELLING NOTE**

a
b
c
d
e
f
g
h
i
j
k
l
m
n
o
p
q
r
**s**
t
u
v
w
x
y
z

A B C D E F G H I J K L M N O P Q R S T U V W X Y Z

walking or running, you trip and almost fall. **2** If you stumble when speaking, you make mistakes when pronouncing the words. **3** If you stumble across something or stumble on it, you find it unexpectedly.

**stump** stumps stumping stumped
NOUN **1** a small part of something that is left when the rest has been removed E.G. *the stump of a dead tree.* **2** In cricket, the stumps are the three upright wooden sticks that support the bails, forming the wicket. ► VERB **3** If a question or problem stumps you, you cannot think of an answer or solution.

**stun** stuns stunning stunned
VERB **1** If you are stunned by something, you are very shocked by it. **2** To stun a person or animal means to knock them unconscious with a blow to the head.

**stunning**
ADJECTIVE very beautiful or impressive E.G. *a stunning first novel.*

**stunt** stunts stunting stunted
NOUN **1** an unusual or dangerous and exciting action that someone does to get publicity or as part of a film. ► VERB **2** To stunt the growth or development of something means to prevent it from developing as it should.

**stupendous**
ADJECTIVE very large or impressive E.G. *a stupendous amount of money.*

**stupid** stupider stupidest
ADJECTIVE showing lack of good judgment or intelligence and not at all sensible.

**stupidity** NOUN

■ foolish, obtuse, unintelligent

**sturdy** sturdier sturdiest
ADJECTIVE strong and firm and unlikely to be damaged or injured E.G. *a sturdy chest of drawers.*

**sturgeon**
*Said "stur-jon"* NOUN a large edible fish, the eggs of which are also eaten and are known as caviar.

**stutter** stutters stuttering stuttered
NOUN **1** Someone who has a stutter finds it difficult to speak smoothly and often repeats sounds through being unable to complete a word. ► VERB **2** When someone stutters, they hesitate or repeat sounds when speaking.

**sty** sties
NOUN a pigsty.

**stye** styes
NOUN an infection in the form of a small red swelling on a person's eyelid.

**style** styles styling styled
NOUN **1** The style of something is the general way in which it is done or presented, often showing the attitudes of the people involved. **2** A person or place that has style is smart, elegant, and fashionable. **3** The style of something is its design E.G. *new windows that fit in with the style of the house.* ► VERB **4** To style a piece of clothing or a person's hair means to design and create its shape.

■ (sense 2) elegance, flair, panache

**stylish**
ADJECTIVE smart, elegant, and fashionable.

**stylishly** ADVERB

■ chic, smart

**suave**

*Said "swahv"* ADJECTIVE **charming, polite, and confident** *E.G. a suave Italian.*

**sub-**

PREFIX **1** 'Sub-' is used at the beginning of words that have 'under' as part of their meaning *E.G. submarine.* **2** 'Sub-' is also used to form nouns that refer to the parts into which something is divided *E.G. Subsection 2 of section 49… a particular subgroup of citizens.*

🔲 from Latin *sub* meaning 'under' or 'below'

**subconscious**

NOUN **1** Your subconscious is the part of your mind that can influence you without your being aware of it. ▸ ADJECTIVE **2** happening or existing in someone's subconscious and therefore not directly realized or understood by them *E.G. a subconscious fear of rejection.*
**subconsciously** ADVERB

**subcontinent subcontinents**

NOUN a large mass of land, often consisting of several countries, and forming part of a continent *E.G. the Indian subcontinent.*

**subdue subdues subduing subdued**

VERB **1** If soldiers subdue a group of people, they bring them under control by using force *E.G. It would be quite impossible to subdue the whole continent.* **2** To subdue a colour, light, or emotion means to make it less bright or strong.

■ (sense 1) control, overcome, quell

**subdued**

ADJECTIVE **1** rather quiet and sad. **2** not very noticeable or bright.

**subject subjects subjecting subjected**

NOUN **1** The subject of writing or a conversation is the thing or person being discussed. **2** In grammar, the subject is the word or words representing the person or thing doing the action expressed by the verb. For example, in the sentence 'My cat keeps catching birds', 'my cat' is the subject. **3** an area of study. **4** The subjects of a country are the people who live there. ▸ VERB **5** To subject someone to something means to make them experience it *E.G. He was subjected to constant interruption.* ▸ ADJECTIVE **6** Someone or something that is subject to something is affected by it *E.G. He was subject to attacks at various times.*

**subjective**

ADJECTIVE influenced by personal feelings and opinion rather than based on fact or rational thought.

**subjunctive**

NOUN In grammar, the subjunctive or subjunctive mood is one of the forms a verb can take. It is used to express attitudes such as wishing and doubting.

**sublime**

ADJECTIVE Something that is sublime is wonderful and affects people emotionally *E.G. sublime music.*

**submarine submarines**

NOUN a ship that can travel beneath the surface of the sea.

**submerge submerges submerging submerged**

VERB **1** To submerge means to go beneath the surface of a liquid. **2** If you submerge yourself in an activity, you become totally involved in it.

a b c d e f g h i j k l m n o p q r **s** t u v w x y z

I went to see (C) the doctor's new practiCe (practice)    ◀ SPELLING NOTE

A
B
C
D
E
F
G
H
I
J
K
L
M
N
O
P
Q
R
**S**
T
U
V
W
X
Y
Z

**submission** submissions
NOUN 1 Submission is a state in which someone accepts the control of another person E.G. *Now he must beat us into submission.* 2 The submission of a proposal or application is the act of sending it for consideration.

**submissive**
ADJECTIVE behaving in a quiet, obedient way.

**submit** submits submitting submitted
VERB 1 If you submit to something, you accept it because you are not powerful enough to resist it. 2 If you submit an application or proposal, you send it to someone for consideration.

**subordinate** subordinates subordinating subordinated
NOUN 1 A person's subordinate is someone who is in a less important position than them. ► ADJECTIVE 2 If one thing is subordinate to another, it is less important E.G. *Non-elected officials are subordinate to elected leaders.* ► VERB 3 To subordinate one thing to another means to treat it as being less important.

**subordinate clause** subordinate clauses
NOUN (ENGLISH) In grammar, a subordinate clause is a clause which adds details to the main clause of a sentence.

**subscribe** subscribes subscribing subscribed
VERB 1 If you subscribe to a particular belief or opinion, you support it or agree with it. 2 If you subscribe to a magazine, you pay to receive regular copies.

**subscriber** NOUN

**subscription** subscriptions
NOUN a sum of money that you pay regularly to belong to an organization or to receive regular copies of a magazine.

**subsequent**
ADJECTIVE happening or coming into existence at a later time than something else E.G. *the December uprising and the subsequent political violence.*

**subsequently** ADVERB

**subservient**
ADJECTIVE Someone who is subservient does whatever other people want them to do.

**subside** subsides subsiding subsided
VERB 1 To subside means to become less intense or quieter E.G. *Her excitement suddenly subsided.* 2 If water or the ground subsides, it sinks to a lower level.

**subsidence**
NOUN If a place is suffering from subsidence, parts of the ground have sunk to a lower level.

**subsidiary** subsidiaries
Said "sub-**sid**-yer-ee" NOUN 1 a company which is part of a larger company. ► ADJECTIVE 2 treated as being of less importance and additional to another thing E.G. *Drama is offered as a subsidiary subject.*

**subsidize** subsidizes subsidizing subsidized; also spelt **subsidise**
VERB To subsidize something means to provide part of the cost of it E.G. *He feels the government should do much more to subsidize films.*

**subsidized** ADJECTIVE

**SPELLING NOTE** You must practiSe your Ss (practise)

**subsidy** subsidies

NOUN a sum of money paid to help support a company or provide a public service.

**substance** substances

NOUN 1 Anything which is a solid, a powder, a liquid, or a paste can be referred to as a substance. 2 If a speech or piece of writing has substance, it is meaningful or important E.G. *a good speech, but there was no substance.*

■ (sense 1) material, stuff

**substantial**

ADJECTIVE 1 very large in degree or amount E.G. *a substantial pay rise.* 2 large and strongly built E.G. *a substantial stone building.*

**substantially**

ADVERB Something that is substantially true is generally or mostly true.

**substitute** substitutes substituting substituted

VERB 1 To substitute one thing for another means to use it instead of the other thing or to put it in the other thing's place. ► NOUN 2 If one thing is a substitute for another, it is used instead of it or put in its place. **substitution** NOUN

■ (sense 1) exchange, replace
■ (sense 2) alternative, replacement, surrogate

**subterfuge** subterfuges

*Said "sub-ter-fyooj"* NOUN Subterfuge is the use of deceitful or dishonest methods.

🏛 from Latin *subterfugere* meaning 'to escape by stealth'

**subtitle** subtitles

NOUN A film with subtitles has a printed translation of the dialogue at the bottom of the screen.

**subtle** subtler subtlest

*Said "sut-tl"* ADJECTIVE 1 very fine, delicate, or small in degree E.G. *a subtle change.* 2 using indirect methods to achieve something. **subtly** ADVERB **subtlety** NOUN

**subtract** subtracts subtracting subtracted

VERB If you subtract one number from another, you take away the first number from the second.

**subtraction** subtractions

NOUN (MATHS) Subtraction is subtracting one number from another, or a sum in which you do this.

**suburb** suburbs

NOUN an area of a town or city that is away from its centre.

**suburban**

ADJECTIVE 1 relating to a suburb or suburbs. 2 dull and conventional.

**suburbia**

NOUN You can refer to the suburbs of a city as suburbia.

**subversive** subversives

ADJECTIVE 1 intended to destroy or weaken a political system E.G. *subversive activities.* ► NOUN 2 Subversives are people who try to destroy or weaken a political system. **subversion** NOUN

**subvert** subverts subverting subverted

VERB; FORMAL To subvert something means to cause it to weaken or fail E.G. *a cunning campaign to subvert the music industry.*

**subway** subways

NOUN 1 a footpath that goes underneath a road. 2 an underground railway.

a b c d e f g h i j k l m n o p q r s t u v w x y z

A
B
C
D
E
F
G
H
I
J
K
L
M
N
O
P
Q
R
**S**
T
U
V
W
X
Y
Z

**succeed** succeeds succeeding succeeded

VERB **1** To succeed means to achieve the result you intend. **2** To succeed someone means to be the next person to have their job. **3** If one thing succeeds another, it comes after it in time E.G. *The explosion was succeeded by a crash.*

**succeeding** ADJECTIVE

■ (sense 1) be successful, do well, make it

**success** successes

NOUN **1** Success is the achievement of something you have been trying to do. **2** Someone who is a success has achieved an important position or made a lot of money.

**successful** ADJECTIVE   **successfully** ADVERB

**succession** successions

NOUN **1** A succession of things is a number of them occurring one after the other. **2** When someone becomes the next person to have an important position, you can refer to this event as their succession to this position E.G. *his succession to the throne.* ▶ PHRASE **3** If something happens a number of weeks, months, or years **in succession**, it happens that number of times without a break E.G. *Borg won Wimbledon five years in succession.*

**successive**

ADJECTIVE occurring one after the other without a break E.G. *three successive victories.*

**successor** successors

NOUN Someone's successor is the person who takes their job when they leave.

**succinct**

*Said* "suk-**singkt**" ADJECTIVE expressing something clearly and in very few words.

**succinctly** ADVERB

**succulent**

ADJECTIVE Succulent food is juicy and delicious.

**succumb** succumbs succumbing succumbed

VERB If you succumb to something, you are unable to resist it any longer E.G. *She never succumbed to his charms.*

**such**

ADJECTIVE or PRONOUN **1** You use 'such' to refer to the person or thing you have just mentioned, or to someone or something similar E.G. *Naples or Palermo or some such place.* ▶ PHRASE **2** You can use **such as** to introduce an example of something E.G. *herbal teas such as camomile.* **3** You can use **such as it is** to indicate that something is not great in quality or quantity E.G. *The action, such as it is, is set in Egypt.* **4** You can use **such and such** when you want to refer to something that is not specific E.G. *A good trick is to ask whether they have seen such and such a film.* ▶ ADJECTIVE **5** 'Such' can be used for emphasizing E.G. *I have such a terrible sense of guilt.*

**suchlike**

ADJECTIVE or PRONOUN used to refer to things similar to those already mentioned E.G. *shampoos, talcs, toothbrushes, and suchlike.*

**suck** sucks sucking sucked

VERB **1** If you suck something, you hold it in your mouth and pull at it with your cheeks and tongue, usually to get liquid out of it. **2** To suck something in a particular direction means to draw it there with a powerful force. **3** *INFORMAL* To suck up to someone means to do things to please them in order to obtain praise or approval.

**sucker** suckers

NOUN **1** *INFORMAL* If you call someone a sucker, you mean that they are easily fooled or cheated. **2** Suckers are pads on the bodies of some animals and insects which they use to cling to a surface.

**suckle** suckles suckling suckled

VERB When a mother suckles a baby, she feeds it with milk from her breast.

**sucrose**

*Said "syoo-kroze"* NOUN; *TECHNICAL* Sucrose is sugar in crystalline form found in sugar cane and sugar beet.

**suction**

NOUN **1** Suction is the force involved when a substance is drawn or sucked from one place to another. **2** Suction is the process by which two surfaces stick together when the air between them is removed *E.G. They stay there by suction.*

**Sudanese**

*Said "soo-dan-neez"* ADJECTIVE **1** belonging or relating to the Sudan. ▶ NOUN **2** someone who comes from the Sudan.

**sudden**

ADJECTIVE happening quickly and unexpectedly *E.G. a sudden cry.*
**suddenly** ADVERB **suddenness** NOUN

**sudoku**

NOUN a puzzle in which you have to enter numbers in a square made up of nine three-by-three grids, so that every column, row, and grid contains

the numbers one to nine.
🔳 Japanese for 'numbers singly'

**sue** sues suing sued

VERB To sue someone means to start a legal case against them, usually to claim money from them.

**suede**

*Said "swayd"* NOUN Suede is a thin, soft leather with a rough surface.
🔳 from French *gants de Suède* meaning 'gloves from Sweden'

**suffer** suffers suffering suffered

VERB **1** If someone is suffering pain, or suffering as a result of an unpleasant situation, they are badly affected by it. **2** If something suffers as a result of neglect or a difficult situation, its condition or quality becomes worse *E.G. The bus service is suffering.*
**sufferer** NOUN **suffering** NOUN

**suffice** suffices sufficing sufficed

VERB; *FORMAL* If something suffices, it is enough or adequate for a purpose.

**sufficient**

ADJECTIVE If a supply or quantity is sufficient for a purpose, there is enough of it available.
**sufficiently** ADVERB

**suffix** suffixes

NOUN (ENGLISH) a group of letters which is added to the end of a word to form a new word, for example '-ology' or '-itis'.

**suffocate** suffocates suffocating suffocated

VERB To suffocate means to die as a result of having too little air or oxygen to breathe.
**suffocation** NOUN

**suffrage**

NOUN Suffrage is the right to vote in political elections.

a
b
c
d
e
f
g
h
i
j
k
l
m
n
o
p
q
r
s
t
u
v
w
x
y
z

A B C D E F G H I J K L M N O P Q R S T U V W X Y Z

**suffragette** suffragettes

NOUN a woman who, at the beginning of the 20th century, campaigned for women to be given the right to vote.

**suffused**

ADJECTIVE; LITERARY If something is suffused with light or colour, light or colour has gradually spread over it.

**sugar**

NOUN Sugar is a sweet substance used to sweeten food and drinks.

**suggest** suggests suggesting suggested

VERB 1 If you suggest a plan or idea to someone, you mention it as a possibility for them to consider. 2 If something suggests a particular thought or impression, it makes you think in that way or gives you that impression E.G. *Nothing you say suggests he is mentally ill.*

■ (sense 1) advocate, propose, recommend

■ (sense 2) hint, imply

**suggestion** suggestions

NOUN 1 a plan or idea that is mentioned as a possibility for someone to consider. 2 A suggestion of something is a very slight indication or faint sign of it E.G. *a suggestion of dishonesty.*

■ (sense 1) proposal, recommendation

**suggestive**

ADJECTIVE 1 Something that is suggestive of a particular thing gives a slight hint or sign of it. 2 Suggestive remarks or gestures make people think about sex.

■ (sense 2) risqué, smutty

**suicidal**

ADJECTIVE 1 People who are suicidal want to kill themselves. 2 Suicidal behaviour is so dangerous that it is likely to result in death E.G. *a mad suicidal attack.*

**suicide**

NOUN People who commit suicide deliberately kill themselves.

▥ from Latin *sui* meaning 'of oneself' and *caedere* meaning 'to kill'

**suicide bomber** suicide bombers

NOUN a terrorist who carries out a bomb attack, knowing that he or she will be killed in the explosion.

**suicide bombing** NOUN

**suit** suits suiting suited

NOUN 1 a matching jacket and trousers or skirt. 2 In a court of law, a suit is a legal action taken by one person against another. 3 one of four different types of card in a pack of playing cards. The four suits are hearts, clubs, diamonds, and spades.

▶ VERB 4 If a situation or course of action suits you, it is appropriate or acceptable for your purpose. 5 If a piece of clothing or a colour suits you, you look good when you are wearing it. 6 If you do something to suit yourself, you do it because you want to and without considering other people.

**suitable**

ADJECTIVE right or acceptable for a particular purpose or occasion.

**suitability** NOUN **suitably** ADVERB

■ appropriate, apt, fitting

**suitcase** suitcases

NOUN a case in which you carry your clothes when you are travelling.

**suite** suites

*Said* "**sweet**" NOUN 1 In a hotel, a suite is a set of rooms. 2 a set of matching furniture or bathroom fittings.

**suited**

ADJECTIVE right or appropriate for a particular purpose or person E.G. *He is well suited to be minister for the arts.*

**suitor** suitors

NOUN; *OLD-FASHIONED* A woman's suitor is a man who wants to marry her.

**sulk** sulks sulking sulked

VERB Someone who is sulking is showing their annoyance by being silent and moody.

**sulky** ADJECTIVE

**sullen**

ADJECTIVE behaving in a bad-tempered and disagreeably silent way E.G. *a sullen and resentful workforce.*

**sulphur**

NOUN Sulphur is a pale yellow nonmetallic element which burns with a very unpleasant smell.

**sultan** sultans

NOUN In some Muslim countries, the ruler of the country is called the sultan.

🏛 from Arabic *sultan* meaning 'rule'

**sultana** sultanas

NOUN 1 a dried grape. 2 the wife of a sultan.

**sum** sums summing summed

NOUN 1 an amount of money. 2 In arithmetic, a sum is a calculation. 3 The sum of something is the total amount of it.

**sum up** VERB If you sum something up, you briefly describe its main points.

**summarize** summarizes summarizing summarized; also spelt **summarise**

VERB (EXAM TERM) To summarize something means to give a short account of its main points.

**summary** summaries

NOUN 1 A summary of something is a short account of its main points.

▶ ADJECTIVE 2 A summary action is done without delay or careful thought E.G. *Summary executions are common.*

**summarily** ADVERB

▤ (sense 1) précis, résumé, synopsis

**summer** summers

NOUN Summer is the season between spring and autumn.

**summit** summits

NOUN 1 The summit of a mountain is its top. 2 a meeting between leaders of different countries to discuss particular issues.

**summon** summons summoning summoned

VERB 1 If someone summons you, they order you to go to them. 2 If you summon up strength or energy, you make a great effort to be strong or energetic.

**summons** summonses

NOUN 1 an official order to appear in court. 2 an order to go to someone E.G. *The result was a summons to headquarters.*

**sumptuous**

ADJECTIVE Something that is sumptuous is magnificent and obviously very expensive.

**sum total**

NOUN The sum total of a number of things is all of them added or considered together.

**sun** suns sunning sunned

NOUN 1 The sun is the star providing heat and light for the planets revolving around it in our solar system. 2 You refer to heat and light from the sun as sun E.G. *We need a bit of sun.* ▶ VERB 3 If you sun yourself, you sit in the sunshine.

**sunbathe** sunbathes sunbathing sunbathed

VERB If you sunbathe, you sit in the sunshine to get a suntan.

**sunburn**

NOUN Sunburn is sore red skin on someone's body due to too much exposure to the rays of the sun.
**sunburnt** ADJECTIVE

**sundae** sundaes

*Said "sun-day"* NOUN A dish of ice cream with cream and fruit or nuts.

**Sunday** Sundays

NOUN Sunday is the day between Saturday and Monday.

📖 from Old English *sunnandæg* meaning 'day of the sun'

**Sunday school** Sunday schools

NOUN Sunday school is a special class held on Sundays to teach children about Christianity.

**sundial** sundials

NOUN An object used for telling the time, consisting of a pointer which casts a shadow on a flat base marked with the hours.

**sundry**

ADJECTIVE 1 'Sundry' is used to refer to several things or people of various sorts E.G. *sundry journalists and lawyers.* ► PHRASE 2 **All and sundry** means everyone.

**sunflower** sunflowers

NOUN A tall plant with very large yellow flowers.

**sunglasses**

PLURAL NOUN Sunglasses are spectacles with dark lenses that you wear to protect your eyes from the sun.

**sunken**

ADJECTIVE 1 having sunk to the bottom of the sea, a river, or lake E.G. *sunken ships.* 2 A sunken object or area has been constructed below the level of the surrounding area E.G. *a sunken garden.* 3 curving inwards E.G. *Her cheeks were sunken.*

**sunlight**

NOUN Sunlight is the bright light produced when the sun is shining.
**sunlit** ADJECTIVE

**sunny** sunnier sunniest

ADJECTIVE When it is sunny, the sun is shining.

**sunrise** sunrises

NOUN Sunrise is the time in the morning when the sun first appears, and the colours produced in the sky at that time.

**sunset** sunsets

NOUN Sunset is the time in the evening when the sun disappears below the horizon, and the colours produced in the sky at that time.

**sunshine**

NOUN Sunshine is the bright light produced when the sun is shining.

**sunstroke**

NOUN Sunstroke is an illness caused by spending too much time in hot sunshine.

**suntan** suntans

NOUN If you have a suntan, the sun has turned your skin brown.
**suntanned** ADJECTIVE

**super**

ADJECTIVE very nice or very good E.G. *a super party.*

**super-**

PREFIX 'Super-' is used to describe something that is larger or better than similar things E.G. *a European superstate.*

📖 from Latin *super* meaning 'above'

**superb**

ADJECTIVE very good indeed.
**superbly** ADVERB

**supercilious**
*Said* "soo-per-**sill**-ee-uss" ADJECTIVE If you are supercilious, you behave in a scornful way towards other people because you think they are inferior to you.

**superego**
NOUN; *TECHNICAL* Your superego is the part of your mind that controls your ideas of right and wrong and produces feelings of guilt.

**superficial**
ADJECTIVE 1 involving only the most obvious or most general aspects of something *E.G. a superficial knowledge of music.* 2 not having a deep, serious, or genuine interest in anything *E.G. a superficial and rather silly woman.* 3 Superficial wounds are not very deep or severe.
**superficially** ADVERB

**superfluous**
*Said* "soo-per-**floo**-uss" ADJECTIVE; *FORMAL* unnecessary or no longer needed.

**superhuman**
ADJECTIVE having much greater power or ability than is normally expected of humans *E.G. superhuman strength.*

**superimpose** superimposes superimposing superimposed
VERB To superimpose one image on another means to put the first image on top of the other so that they are seen as one image.

**superintendent** superintendents
NOUN 1 a police officer above the rank of inspector. 2 a person whose job is to be responsible for a particular thing *E.G. the superintendent of prisons.*

**superior** superiors
ADJECTIVE 1 better or of higher quality than other similar things. 2 in a position of higher authority than another person. 3 showing too much pride and self-importance *E.G. Jerry smiled in a superior way.* ▶ NOUN 4 Your superiors are people who are in a higher position than you in society or an organization.
**superiority** NOUN

**superlative** superlatives
*Said* "soo-per-**lat**-tiv" NOUN 1 In grammar, the superlative is the form of an adjective which indicates that the person or thing described has more of a particular quality than anyone or anything else. For example, 'quickest', 'best', and 'easiest' are all superlatives. ▶ ADJECTIVE 2 *FORMAL* very good indeed *E.G. a superlative performance.*

---

### What is a Superlative?

Many adjectives have three different forms. These are known as the **positive**, the **comparative**, and the **superlative**. The comparative and superlative are used when you make comparisons.

The **positive** form of an adjective is given as the entry in the dictionary. It is used when there is no comparison between different objects:

*E.G. Matthew is tall.*

The **superlative** form is usually made by adding the ending -est to the positive form of the adjective. It shows that something possesses a quality to a greater extent than all the others in its class or group:

CONTINUED ON NEXT PAGE →

On WEDNESday Wayne WED NESta (<u>Wednes</u>day)     **SPELLING NOTE**

a b c d e f g h i j k l m n o p q r s t u v w x y z

A
B
C
D
E
F
G
H
I
J
K
L
M
N
O
P
Q
R
S
T
U
V
W
X
Y
Z

> *E.G. Matthew is the **tallest** boy in his class.*
> You can also express superlatives by using the words *most* or *least* with the positive (not the superlative) form of the adjective:
> *E.G. Matthew is the **most energetic** member of the family.*
> Also look at the grammar box at **comparative**.

**supermarket** supermarkets
NOUN a shop selling food and household goods arranged so that you can help yourself and pay for everything at a till by the exit.

**supernatural**
ADJECTIVE 1 Something that is supernatural, for example ghosts or witchcraft, cannot be explained by normal scientific laws. ▶ NOUN 2 You can refer to supernatural things as the supernatural.

**superpower** superpowers
NOUN a very powerful and influential country such as the USA.

**supersede** supersedes superseding superseded
*Said* "soo-per-**seed**" VERB If something supersedes another thing, it replaces it because it is more modern *E.G. New York superseded Paris as the centre for modern art.*

**supersonic**
ADJECTIVE A supersonic aircraft can travel faster than the speed of sound.

**superstar** superstars
NOUN You can refer to a very famous entertainer or sports player as a superstar.

**superstition** superstitions
NOUN Superstition is a belief in things like magic and powers that bring good or bad luck.
**superstitious** ADJECTIVE
🏛 from Latin *superstitio* meaning 'dread of the supernatural'

**supervise** supervises supervising supervised
VERB To supervise someone means to check and direct what they are doing to make sure that they do it correctly. **supervision** NOUN **supervisor** NOUN
▤ oversee, superintend

**supper** suppers
NOUN Supper is a meal eaten in the evening or a snack eaten before you go to bed.

**supplant** supplants supplanting supplanted
VERB; *FORMAL* To supplant someone or something means to take their place *E.G. By the 1930s the wristwatch had supplanted the pocket watch.*

**supple**
ADJECTIVE able to bend and move easily.

**supplement** supplements supplementing supplemented
VERB 1 To supplement something means to add something to it to improve it *E.G. Many village men supplemented their wages by fishing for salmon.* ▶ NOUN 2 something that is added to something else to improve it.

**supplementary**
ADJECTIVE added to something else to improve it *E.G. supplementary doses of vitamin E.*

**supplier** suppliers
NOUN a firm which provides particular goods.

**supply** supplies supplying supplied

VERB **1** To supply someone with something means to provide it or send it to them. ► NOUN **2** A supply of something is an amount available for use E.G. *the world's supply of precious metals.* ► PLURAL NOUN **3** Supplies are food and equipment for a particular purpose.

**support** supports supporting supported

VERB **1** If you support someone, you agree with their aims and want them to succeed. **2** If you support someone who is in difficulties, you are kind, encouraging, and helpful to them. **3** If something supports an object, it is underneath it and holding it up. **4** To support someone or something means to prevent them from falling by holding them. **5** To support someone financially means to provide them with money. ► NOUN **6** an object that is holding something up. **7** Moral support is encouragement given to someone to help them do something difficult. **8** Financial support is money that is provided for someone or something. **supporter** NOUN **supportable** ADJECTIVE

**supportive**

ADJECTIVE A supportive person is encouraging and helpful to someone who is in difficulties.

**suppose** supposes supposing supposed

VERB **1** If you suppose that something is the case, you think that it is likely E.G. *I supposed that would be too obvious.* ► PHRASE **2** You can say **I suppose** when you are not entirely certain or enthusiastic about

something E.G. *Yes, I suppose he could come.* **3** If something **is supposed** to be done, it should be done E.G. *You are supposed to report it to the police.* **4** If something **is supposed** to happen, it is planned or expected to happen E.G. *It was supposed to be this afternoon.* **5** Something that **is supposed** to be the case is generally believed or thought to be so E.G. *Wimbledon is supposed to be the best tournament of them all.* ► CONJUNCTION **6** You can use 'suppose' or 'supposing' when you are considering or suggesting a possible situation or action E.G. *Supposing he were to break down under interrogation?*

**supposed**

ADJECTIVE 'Supposed' is used to express doubt about something that is generally believed E.G. *the supposed culprit.*

**supposedly** ADVERB

**supposition** suppositions

NOUN something that is believed or assumed to be true E.G. *the supposition that science requires an ordered universe.*

**suppress** suppresses suppressing suppressed

VERB **1** If an army or government suppresses an activity, it prevents people from doing it. **2** If someone suppresses a piece of information, they prevent it from becoming generally known. **3** If you suppress your feelings, you stop yourself expressing them.

**suppression** NOUN

■ (sense 1) crush, quell, stop

**supremacy**

*Said* "soo-**prem**-mass-ee" NOUN If a group of people has supremacy over

a b c d e f g h i j k l m n o p q r **s** t u v w x y z

others, it is more powerful than the others.

**supreme**

ADJECTIVE 1 'Supreme' is used as part of a title to indicate the highest level of an organization or system *E.G. the Supreme Court.* 2 'Supreme' is used to emphasize the greatness of something *E.G. the supreme achievement of the human race.*

**supremely** ADVERB

≡ (sense 2) greatest, highest, paramount

**surcharge surcharges**

NOUN an additional charge.

**sure surer surest**

ADJECTIVE 1 If you are sure about something, you have no doubts about it. 2 If you are sure of yourself, you are very confident. 3 If something is sure to happen, it will definitely happen. 4 Sure means reliable or accurate *E.G. a sure sign that something is wrong.* ▶ PHRASE 5 If you **make sure** about something, you check it or take action to see that it is done. ▶ INTERJECTION 6 Sure is an informal way of saying 'yes' *E.G. 'Can I come too?' – 'Sure'.*

**surely**

ADVERB 'Surely' is used to emphasize the belief that something is the case *E.G. Surely these people here knew that?*

**surf surfs surfing surfed**

VERB 1 When you surf, you go surfing. 2 When you surf the Internet, you go from website to website reading the information. ▶ NOUN 3 Surf is the white foam that forms on the top of waves when they break near the shore.

**surface surfaces surfacing surfaced**

NOUN 1 The surface of something is the top or outside area of it. 2 The surface of a situation is what can be seen easily rather than what is hidden or not immediately obvious. ▶ VERB 3 If someone surfaces, they come up from under water to the surface.

**surfboard surfboards**

NOUN a long narrow lightweight board used for surfing.

**surf club surf clubs**

NOUN In Australia, a surf club is an organization of lifesavers in charge of safety on a particular beach, and which often provides leisure facilities.

**surfeit**

*Said* "**sur**-fit" NOUN If there is a surfeit of something, there is too much of it.

**surfing**

NOUN Surfing is a sport which involves riding towards the shore on the top of a large wave while standing on a surfboard.

**surge surges surging surged**

NOUN 1 a sudden great increase in the amount of something *E.G. a surge of panic.* ▶ VERB 2 If something surges, it moves suddenly and powerfully *E.G. The soldiers surged forwards.*

**surgeon surgeons**

NOUN a doctor who performs operations.

**surgery surgeries**

NOUN 1 Surgery is medical treatment involving cutting open part of the patient's body to treat the damaged part. 2 The room or building where a doctor or dentist works is called a surgery. 3 A period of time during which a doctor is available to see patients is called surgery *E.G. evening surgery.*

**SPELLING NOTE**      'i' before 'e' except after 'c'

**surgical**
ADJECTIVE used in or involving a medical operation *E.G. surgical gloves.*
**surgically** ADVERB

**surly** surlier surliest
ADJECTIVE rude and bad-tempered.
**surliness** NOUN

**surmise** surmises surmising surmised
VERB; FORMAL To surmise something means to guess it *E.G. I surmised it was of French manufacture.*

**surmount** surmounts surmounting surmounted
VERB 1 To surmount a difficulty means to manage to solve it. 2 FORMAL If something is surmounted by a particular thing, that thing is on top of it *E.G. The island is surmounted by a huge black castle.*

**surname** surnames
NOUN Your surname is your last name which you share with other members of your family.

**surpass** surpasses surpassing surpassed
VERB; FORMAL To surpass someone or something means to be better than them.

**surplus** surpluses
NOUN If there is a surplus of something there is more of it than is needed.
**≡** excess, surfeit

**surprise** surprises surprising surprised
NOUN 1 an unexpected event. 2 Surprise is the feeling caused when something unexpected happens. ► VERB 3 If something surprises you, it gives you a feeling of surprise. 4 If you surprise someone, you do something they were not expecting.

**surprising** ADJECTIVE

**surreal**
ADJECTIVE very strange and dreamlike.

**surrender** surrenders surrendering surrendered
VERB 1 To surrender means to stop fighting and agree that the other side has won. 2 If you surrender to a temptation or feeling, you let it take control of you. 3 To surrender something means to give it up to someone else *E.G. The gallery director surrendered his keys.* ► NOUN 4 Surrender is a situation in which one side in a fight agrees that the other side has won and gives in.
**≡** (sense 1) give in, submit, yield
**≡** (sense 4) capitulation, submission

**surreptitious**
*Said* "sur-rep-**tish**-uss" ADJECTIVE A surreptitious action is done secretly or so that no-one will notice *E.G. a surreptitious glance.*
**surreptitiously** ADVERB

**surrogate** surrogates
ADJECTIVE 1 acting as a substitute for someone or something. ► NOUN 2 a person or thing that acts as a substitute.

**surround** surrounds surrounding surrounded
VERB 1 To surround someone or something means to be situated all around them. ► NOUN 2 The surround of something is its outside edge or border.
**≡** (sense 1) encircle, enclose

**surrounding** surroundings
ADJECTIVE 1 The surrounding area of a particular place is the area around it *E.G. the surrounding countryside.*
► PLURAL NOUN 2 You can refer to the area and environment around a

a
b
c
d
e
f
g
h
i
j
k
l
m
n
o
p
q
r
**s**
t
u
v
w
x
y
z

place or person as their surroundings *E.G. very comfortable surroundings.*

**surveillance**
*Said "sur-vay-lanss"* NOUN Surveillance is the close watching of a person's activities by the police or army.
🏛 from French *surveiller* meaning 'to watch over'

**survey** surveys surveying surveyed
VERB **1** To survey something means to look carefully at the whole of it. **2** To survey a building or piece of land means to examine it carefully in order to make a report or plan of its structure and features. ➤ NOUN **3** A survey of something is a detailed examination of it, often in the form of a report.
■ (sense 1) look over, scan, view

**surveyor** surveyors
NOUN a person whose job is to survey buildings or land.

**survival** survivals
NOUN Survival is being able to continue living or existing in spite of great danger or difficulties *E.G. There was no hope of survival.*

**survive** survives surviving survived
VERB To survive means to continue to live or exist in spite of a great danger or difficulties *E.G. a German monk who survived the shipwreck.*
**survivor** NOUN

**sus-**
PREFIX 'Sus-' is another form of **sub-**.

**susceptible**
ADJECTIVE If you are susceptible to something, you are likely to be influenced or affected by it *E.G.*

*Elderly people are more susceptible to infection.*
**susceptibility** NOUN

**suspect** suspects suspecting suspected
VERB **1** If you suspect something, you think that it is likely or is probably true *E.G. I suspected that the report would be sent.* **2** If you suspect something, you have doubts about its reliability *E.G. He suspected her intent.* **3** If you suspect someone of doing something wrong, you think that they have done it. ➤ NOUN **4** someone who is thought to be guilty of a crime. ➤ ADJECTIVE **5** If something is suspect, it cannot be trusted or relied upon *E.G. a rather suspect holy man.*

**suspend** suspends suspending suspended
VERB **1** If something is suspended, it is hanging from somewhere *E.G. the television set suspended above the bar.* **2** To suspend an activity or event means to delay it or stop it for a while. **3** If someone is suspended from their job, they are told not to do it for a period of time, usually as a punishment.

**suspender** suspenders
NOUN Suspenders are fastenings which hold up a woman's stockings.

**suspense**
NOUN Suspense is a state of excitement or anxiety caused by having to wait for something.

**suspension**
NOUN **1** The suspension of something is the delaying or stopping of it. **2** A person's suspension is their removal from a job for a period of time, usually as a punishment. **3** The

suspension of a vehicle consists of springs and shock absorbers which provide a smooth ride. **4** a liquid mixture in which very small bits of a solid material are contained and are not dissolved.

**suspicion** suspicions
NOUN **1** Suspicion is the feeling of not trusting someone or the feeling that something is wrong. **2** a feeling that something is likely to happen or is probably true *E.G. the suspicion that more could have been achieved.*
■ (sense 1) distrust, misgiving, scepticism

**suspicious**
ADJECTIVE **1** If you are suspicious of someone, you do not trust them. **2** 'Suspicious' is used to describe things that make you think that there is something wrong with a situation *E.G. suspicious circumstances.*
**suspiciously** ADVERB
■ (sense 2) dubious, questionable, suspect

**sustain** sustains sustaining sustained
VERB **1** To sustain something means to continue it for a period of time *E.G. Their team-mates were unable to sustain the challenge.* **2** If something sustains you, it gives you energy and strength. **3** *FORMAL* To sustain an injury or loss means to suffer it.

**sustainable**
ADJECTIVE **1** capable of being sustained. **2** If economic development or energy resources are sustainable they are capable of being maintained at a steady level without exhausting natural resources or causing ecological damage *E.G. sustainable forestry.*

**sustenance**
NOUN; *FORMAL* Sustenance is food and drink.

**swab** swabs swabbing swabbed
NOUN **1** a small piece of cotton wool used for cleaning a wound. ▶ VERB **2** To swab something means to clean it using a large mop and a lot of water. **3** To swab a wound means to clean it or take specimens from it using a swab.

**swag** swags
NOUN *INFORMAL* **1** goods or valuables, especially ones which have been gained dishonestly. **2** In Australian and New Zealand English, the bundle of possessions belonging to a tramp. **3** In Australian and New Zealand English, swags of something is lots of it.

**swagger** swaggers swaggering swaggered
VERB **1** To swagger means to walk in a proud, exaggerated way. ▶ NOUN **2** an exaggerated walk.

**swagman** swagmen
NOUN; *INFORMAL* In Australia and New Zealand in the past, a tramp who carried his possessions on his back.

**swallow** swallows swallowing swallowed
VERB **1** If you swallow something, you make it go down your throat and into your stomach. **2** When you swallow, you move your throat muscles as if you were swallowing something, especially when you are nervous. ▶ NOUN **3** a bird with pointed wings and a long forked tail.

**swamp** swamps swamping swamped
NOUN **1** an area of permanently wet land. ▶ VERB **2** If something is

LEt's measure the angLE (ang<u>le</u>)　　SPELLING NOTE

swamped, it is covered or filled with water. **3** If you are swamped by things, you have more than you are able to deal with E.G. *She was swamped with calls.*

**swampy** ADJECTIVE

**swan swans**

NOUN a large, usually white, bird with a long neck that lives on rivers or lakes.

**swap swaps swapping swapped**

*Rhymes with "stop"* VERB To swap one thing for another means to replace the first thing with the second, often by making an exchange with another person E.G. *Webb swapped shirts with a Leeds player.*

■ exchange, switch, trade

**swarm swarms swarming swarmed**

NOUN **1** A swarm of insects is a large group of them flying together. ▶ VERB **2** When bees or other insects swarm, they fly together in a large group. **3** If people swarm somewhere, a lot of people go there quickly and at the same time E.G. *the crowds of office workers who swarm across the bridge.* **4** If a place is swarming with people, there are a lot of people there.

**swarthy swarthier swarthiest**

ADJECTIVE A swarthy person has a dark complexion.

**swashbuckling**

ADJECTIVE 'Swashbuckling' is used to describe people who have the exciting behaviour or appearance of pirates.

▥ from Middle English *swashbuckling* meaning 'making a noise by striking your sword against a shield'

**swastika swastikas**

*Said "swoss-tik-ka"* NOUN a symbol in the shape of a cross with each arm bent over at right angles. It was the official symbol of the Nazis in Germany, but in India it is a good luck sign.

▥ from Sanskrit *svasti* meaning 'prosperity'

**swat swats swatting swatted**

VERB To swat an insect means to hit it sharply in order to kill it.

**swathe swathes**

*Rhymes with "bathe"* NOUN **1** a long strip of cloth that is wrapped around something E.G. *swathes of white silk.* **2** A swathe of land is a long strip of it.

**swathed**

ADJECTIVE If someone is swathed in something, they are wrapped in it E.G. *She was swathed in towels.*

**sway sways swaying swayed**

VERB **1** To sway means to lean or swing slowly from side to side. **2** If something sways you, it influences your judgment. ▶ NOUN **3** LITERARY Sway is the power to influence people E.G. *under the sway of more powerful neighbours.*

**swear swears swearing swore sworn**

VERB **1** To swear means to say words that are considered to be very rude or blasphemous. **2** If you swear to something, you state solemnly that you will do it or that it is true. **3** If you swear by something, you firmly believe that it is a reliable cure or solution E.G. *Some women swear by extra vitamins.*

**swearword swearwords**

NOUN a word which is considered to be rude or blasphemous, which people use when they are angry.

**sweat** sweats sweating sweated

NOUN **1** Sweat is the salty liquid produced by your sweat glands when you are hot or afraid. ▶ VERB **2** When you sweat, sweat comes through the pores in your skin in order to lower the temperature of your body.

**sweater** sweaters

NOUN a knitted piece of clothing covering your upper body and arms.

**sweatshirt** sweatshirts

NOUN a piece of clothing made of thick cotton, covering your upper body and arms.

**sweaty**

ADJECTIVE covered or soaked with sweat.

**swede** swedes

NOUN a large round root vegetable with yellow flesh and a brownish-purple skin.

🎦 from *Swedish turnip* because it was introduced from Sweden in the 18th century

**Swede** Swedes

NOUN someone who comes from Sweden.

**Swedish**

ADJECTIVE **1** belonging or relating to Sweden. ▶ NOUN **2** Swedish is the main language spoken in Sweden.

**sweep** sweeps sweeping swept

VERB **1** If you sweep the floor, you use a brush to gather up dust or rubbish from it. **2** To sweep things off a surface means to push them all off with a quick, smooth movement. **3** If something sweeps from one place to another, it moves there very quickly *E.G. A gust of wind swept over the terrace.* **4** If an attitude or new fashion sweeps a place, it spreads rapidly through it *E.G. a phenomenon that is sweeping America.* ▶ NOUN **5** If you do something with a sweep of your arm, you do it with a wide curving movement of your arm.

**sweeping**

ADJECTIVE **1** A sweeping curve or movement is long and wide. **2** A sweeping statement is based on a general assumption rather than on careful thought. **3** affecting a lot of people to a great extent *E.G. sweeping changes.*

**sweet** sweeter sweetest; sweets

ADJECTIVE **1** containing a lot of sugar *E.G. a mug of sweet tea.* **2** pleasant and satisfying *E.G. sweet success.* **3** A sweet smell is soft and fragrant. **4** A sweet sound is gentle and tuneful. **5** attractive and delightful *E.G. a sweet little baby.* ▶ NOUN **6** Things such as toffees, chocolates, and mints are sweets. **7** a dessert.

**sweetly** ADVERB **sweetness** NOUN

■ (sense 5) charming, cute, delightful

**sweet corn**

NOUN Sweet corn is a long stalk covered with juicy yellow seeds that can be eaten as a vegetable.

**sweeten** sweetens sweetening sweetened

VERB To sweeten food means to add sugar or another sweet substance to it.

**sweetener** sweeteners

NOUN a very sweet, artificial substance that can be used instead of sugar.

**sweetheart** sweethearts

NOUN **1** You can call someone who you are very fond of 'sweetheart'. **2** A

a b c d e f g h i j k l m n o p q r s t u v w x y z

# sweet pea >> swindle

**sweet pea** sweet peas
NOUN Sweet peas are delicate, very fragrant climbing flowers.

**sweet tooth**
NOUN If you have a sweet tooth, you like sweet food very much.

**swell** swells swelling swelled swollen
VERB 1 If something swells, it becomes larger and rounder E.G. It causes the abdomen to swell. 2 If an amount swells, it increases in number. ▸ NOUN 3 The regular up and down movement of the waves at sea can be called a swell.

**swelling** swellings
NOUN 1 an enlarged area on your body as a result of injury or illness. 2 The swelling of something is an increase in its size.

**sweltering**
ADJECTIVE If the weather is sweltering, it is very hot.

**swerve** swerves swerving swerved
VERB To swerve means to suddenly change direction to avoid colliding with something.

**swift** swifter swiftest; swifts
ADJECTIVE 1 happening or moving very quickly E.G. a swift glance. ▸ NOUN 2 a bird with narrow crescent-shaped wings.
**swiftly** ADVERB

**swig** swigs swigging swigged
INFORMAL
VERB 1 To swig a drink means to drink it in large mouthfuls, usually from a bottle. ▸ NOUN 2 If you have a swig of a drink, you take a large mouthful of it.

**swill** swills swilling swilled
VERB 1 To swill something means to pour water over it to clean it E.G. Swill the can out thoroughly. ▸ NOUN 2 Swill is a liquid mixture containing waste food that is fed to pigs.

**swim** swims swimming swam swum
VERB 1 To swim means to move through water using various movements with parts of the body. 2 If things are swimming, it seems as if everything you see is moving and you feel dizzy. ▸ NOUN 3 If you go for a swim, you go into water to swim for pleasure.
**swimmer** NOUN

**swimming**
NOUN Swimming is the activity of moving through water using your arms and legs.

**swimming bath** swimming baths
NOUN a public swimming pool.

**swimming costume** swimming costumes
NOUN the clothing worn by a woman when she goes swimming.

**swimming pool** swimming pools
NOUN a large hole that has been tiled and filled with water for swimming.

**swimming trunks**
PLURAL NOUN Swimming trunks are shorts worn by a man when he goes swimming.

**swimsuit** swimsuits
NOUN a swimming costume.

**swindle** swindles swindling swindled
VERB 1 To swindle someone means to deceive them to obtain money or property. ▸ NOUN 2 a trick in which

SPELLING NOTE Betty Eats Cakes And Uses Seven Eggs (because)

858

someone is cheated out of money or property.

**swindler** NOUN

📖 from German *Schwindler* meaning 'cheat'

**swine** swines

NOUN **1** *OLD-FASHIONED* Swine are pigs. **2** *INFORMAL* If you call someone a swine, you mean they are nasty and spiteful.

**swing** swings swinging swung

VERB **1** If something swings, it moves repeatedly from side to side from a fixed point. **2** If someone or something swings in a particular direction, they turn quickly or move in a sweeping curve in that direction. ▶ NOUN **3** a seat hanging from a frame or a branch, which moves backwards and forwards when you sit on it. **4** A swing in opinion is a significant change in people's opinion.

**swipe** swipes swiping swiped

VERB **1** To swipe at something means to try to hit it making a curving movement with the arm. **2** *INFORMAL* To swipe something means to steal it. **3** To swipe a credit card means to pass it through a machine that electronically reads the information stored in the card. ▶ NOUN **4** To take a swipe at something means to swipe at it.

**swirl** swirls swirling swirled

VERB To swirl means to move quickly in circles *E.G. The black water swirled around his legs.*

**swish** swishes swishing swished

VERB **1** To swish means to move quickly through the air making a soft sound *E.G. The curtains swished back.* ▶ NOUN **2** the sound made when something swishes.

**Swiss**

ADJECTIVE **1** belonging or relating to Switzerland. ▶ NOUN **2** someone who comes from Switzerland.

**switch** switches switching switched

NOUN **1** a small control for an electrical device or machine. **2** a change *E.G. a switch in routine.* ▶ VERB **3** To switch to a different task or topic means to change to it. **4** If you switch things, you exchange one for the other.

**switch off** VERB To switch off a light or machine means to stop it working by pressing a switch.

**switch on** VERB To switch on a light or machine means to start it working by pressing a switch.

**switchboard** switchboards

NOUN The switchboard in an organization is the part where all telephone calls are received.

**swivel** swivels swivelling swivelled

VERB **1** To swivel means to turn round on a central point. ▶ ADJECTIVE **2** A swivel chair or lamp is made so that you can move the main part of it while the base remains in a fixed position.

**swollen**

ADJECTIVE Something that is swollen has swelled up.

📖 distended, enlarged, puffed up

**swoon** swoons swooning swooned

VERB; *LITERARY* To swoon means to faint as a result of strong emotion.

**swoop** swoops swooping swooped

VERB To swoop means to move downwards through the air in a fast curving movement *E.G. A flock of*

A
B
C
D
E
F
G
H
I
J
K
L
M
N
O
P
Q
R
**S**
T
U
V
W
X
Y
Z

*pigeons swooped low over the square.*

**swop**
another spelling of **swap**.

**sword swords**
NOUN a weapon consisting of a very long blade with a short handle.

**swordfish swordfishes** or **swordfish**
NOUN a large sea fish with a long upper jaw.

**sworn**
ADJECTIVE If you make a sworn statement, you swear that everything in it is true.

**swot swots swotting swotted**
INFORMAL
VERB 1 To swot means to study or revise very hard. 2 If you swot up on a subject you find out as much about it as possible in a short time.
▶ NOUN 3 someone who spends too much time studying.

**sycamore sycamores**
*Said* "sik-am-mor" NOUN a tree that has large leaves with five points.

**syllable syllables**
NOUN a part of a word that contains a single vowel sound and is pronounced as a unit. For example, 'book' has one syllable and 'reading' has two.

**syllabus syllabuses** or **syllabi**
NOUN The subjects that are studied for a particular course or examination are called the syllabus
☑ The plural *syllabuses* is much more common than *syllabi*.

**symbol symbols**
NOUN ( RE ) a shape, design, or idea that is used to represent something
E.G. *The fish has long been a symbol of Christianity.*
∎ emblem, representation, sign

**symbolic**
ADJECTIVE Something that is symbolic has a special meaning that is considered to represent something else E.G. *Six tons of ivory were burned in a symbolic ceremony.*

**symbolize symbolizes symbolizing symbolized**; also spelt **symbolise**
VERB If a shape, design, or idea symbolizes something, it is regarded as being a symbol of it E.G. *In China and Japan the carp symbolizes courage.*
**symbolism** NOUN

**symmetrical**
ADJECTIVE ( MATHS ) If something is symmetrical, it has two halves which are exactly the same, except that one half is like a reflection of the other half.
**symmetrically** ADVERB

**symmetry**
NOUN ( MATHS ) Something that has symmetry is symmetrical.

**sympathetic**
ADJECTIVE 1 A sympathetic person shows kindness and understanding to other people. 2 If you are sympathetic to a proposal or an idea, you approve of it.

**sympathize sympathizes sympathizing sympathized**; also spelt **sympathise**
VERB To sympathize with someone who is in difficulties means to show them understanding and care.

**sympathizer sympathizers**; also spelt **sympathiser**
NOUN People who support a particular cause can be referred to as sympathizers.

**sympathy sympathies**
NOUN 1 Sympathy is kindness and

understanding towards someone who is in difficulties. **2** If you have sympathy with someone's ideas or actions, you agree with them.
▶ PHRASE **3** If you do something **in sympathy** with someone, you do it to show your support for them.
■ (sense 1) compassion, pity

**symphony** symphonies
NOUN a piece of music for an orchestra, usually in four movements.
▥ from Greek *sumphōnos* meaning 'harmonious'

**symptom** symptoms
NOUN **1** something wrong with your body that is a sign of an illness. **2** Something that is considered to be a sign of a bad situation can be referred to as a symptom of it *E.G. another symptom of the racism sweeping across the country.*
**symptomatic** ADJECTIVE

**synagogue** synagogues
*Said "**sin**-a-gog"* NOUN RE a building where Jewish people meet for worship and religious instruction.
▥ from Greek *sunagōgē* meaning 'meeting'

**synchronize** synchronizes synchronizing synchronized
*Said "**sing**-kron-nize"; also spelt **synchronise**
VERB **1** MUSIC To synchronize two actions means to do them at the same time and speed. **2** To synchronize watches means to set them to show exactly the same time as each other.

**syncopation**
NOUN MUSIC Syncopation in rhythm is the stressing of weak beats instead of the usual strong ones.

▥ from Greek *suncopē* meaning 'cutting off'

**syndicate** syndicates
NOUN an association of business people formed to carry out a particular project.

**syndrome** syndromes
NOUN **1** a medical condition characterized by a particular set of symptoms *E.G. Down's syndrome.* **2** You can refer to a typical set of characteristics as a syndrome *E.G. the syndrome of skipping from one wonder diet to the next.*

**synod** synods
NOUN a council of church leaders which meets regularly to discuss religious and moral issues.
▥ from Greek *sunodos* meaning 'meeting'

**synonym** synonyms
NOUN ENGLISH If two words have the same or a very similar meaning, they are synonyms.

**synonymous**
ADJECTIVE **1** Two words that are synonymous have the same or very similar meanings. **2** If two things are closely associated, you can say that one is synonymous with the other *E.G. New York is synonymous with the Statue of Liberty.*

**synopsis** synopses
NOUN a summary of a book, play, or film.

**syntax**
NOUN The syntax of a language is its grammatical rules and the way its words are arranged.

**synthetic**
ADJECTIVE made from artificial substances rather than natural ones.

**syphon**
another spelling of **siphon**.

a b c d e f g h i j k l m n o p q r **s** t u v w x y z

A
B
C
D
E
F
G
H
I
J
K
L
M
N
O
P
Q
R
S
T
U
V
W
X
Y
Z

**Syrian** Syrians
*Said* "sirr-ee-an" ADJECTIVE **1** belonging
or relating to Syria. ▶ NOUN **2** someone
who comes from Syria.

**syringe** syringes
*Said* "sir-rinj" NOUN a hollow tube
with a part which is pushed down
inside and a fine hollow needle at
one end, used for injecting or
extracting liquids.

**syrup** syrups
NOUN a thick sweet liquid made by
boiling sugar with water.
🏛 from Arabic *sharab* meaning
'drink'

**system** systems
NOUN **1** (LIBRARY) an organized way of
doing or arranging something

according to a fixed plan or set of
rules. **2** People sometimes refer to
the government and administration
of the country as the system. **3** You
can also refer to a set of equipment
as a system *E.G. an old stereo system.*
**4** In biology, a system of a particular
kind is the set of organs that
perform that function *E.G. the
immune system.*
▤ (sense 1) method, procedure,
routine

**systematic**
ADJECTIVE following a fixed plan and
done in an efficient way *E.G. a
systematic study.*
**systematically** ADVERB

# Tt

**tab** tabs
NOUN a small extra piece that is attached to something, for example on a curtain so it can be hung on a pole.

**tabby** tabbies
NOUN a cat whose fur has grey, brown, or black stripes.
🏛 from Old French *tabis* meaning 'striped silk cloth'

**tabernacle** tabernacles
*Said* "**tab**-er-nak-kl" NOUN 1 a place of worship for certain Christian groups. 2 a sanctuary in which the ancient Hebrews carried the Ark of the Covenant as they wandered from place to place. 3 a Jewish temple.
🏛 from Latin *tabernaculum* meaning 'tent'

**table** tables tabling tabled
NOUN 1 a piece of furniture with a flat horizontal top supported by one or more legs. 2 a set of facts or figures arranged in rows or columns. ▶ VERB 3 If you table something such as a proposal, you say formally that you want it to be discussed.

**tablecloth** tablecloths
NOUN a cloth used to cover a table and keep it clean.

**tablespoon** tablespoons
NOUN a large spoon used for serving food; also the amount that a tablespoon contains.

**tablet** tablets
NOUN 1 any small, round pill made of powdered medicine. 2 a slab of stone with words cut into it.

**table tennis**
NOUN Table tennis is a game for two or four people in which you use bats

to hit a small hollow ball over a low net across a table.

**tabloid** tabloids
NOUN (ENGLISH) a newspaper with small pages, short news stories, and lots of photographs.

**taboo** taboos
NOUN 1 a social custom that some words, subjects, or actions must be avoided because they are considered embarrassing or offensive *E.G. We have a powerful taboo against boasting.* 2 a religious custom that forbids people to do something. ▶ ADJECTIVE 3 forbidden or disapproved of *E.G. a taboo subject.*

**tacit**
*Said* "**tass**-it" ADJECTIVE understood or implied without actually being said or written.

**tacitly** ADVERB

**taciturn**
*Said* "**tass**-it-urn" ADJECTIVE Someone who is taciturn does not talk very much and so seems unfriendly.

**tack** tacks tacking tacked
NOUN 1 a short nail with a broad, flat head. 2 If you change tack, you start to use a different method for dealing with something. ▶ VERB 3 If you tack something to a surface, you nail it there with tacks. 4 If you tack a piece of fabric, you sew it with long loose stitches.

**tackies** or **takkies**
PLURAL NOUN; *INFORMAL* In South African English, tackies are tennis shoes or plimsolls.

**tackle** tackles tackling tackled
VERB 1 If you tackle a difficult task, you start dealing with it in a determined

A B C D E F G H I J K L M N O P Q R S T U V W X Y Z

way. **2** If you tackle someone in a game such as soccer, you try to get the ball away from them. **3** If you tackle someone about something, you talk to them about it in order to get something changed or dealt with. ▶ NOUN **4** A tackle in sport is an attempt to get the ball away from your opponent. **5** Tackle is the equipment used for fishing.

■ (sense 1) deal with, undertake

**tacky** tackier tackiest
ADJECTIVE **1** slightly sticky to touch E.G. *The cream feels tacky to the touch.* **2** INFORMAL badly made and in poor taste E.G. *tacky furniture.*

**tact**
NOUN Tact is the ability to see when a situation is difficult or delicate and to handle it without upsetting people.
**tactful** ADJECTIVE **tactfully** ADVERB
**tactless** ADJECTIVE **tactlessly** ADVERB

■ delicacy, diplomacy, discretion

**tactic** tactics
NOUN **1** (PE) Tactics are the methods you use to achieve what you want, especially to win a game. **2** Tactics are also the ways in which troops and equipment are used in order to win a battle.
**tactical** ADJECTIVE **tactically** ADVERB

**tactile**
ADJECTIVE involving the sense of touch.

**tadpole** tadpoles
NOUN Tadpoles are the larvae of frogs and toads. They are black with round heads and long tails and live in water.

🔠 from Middle English *tadde* meaning 'toad' and *pol* meaning 'head'

**taffeta**
*Said "taf-fit-a"* NOUN Taffeta is a stiff, shiny fabric that is used mainly for making women's clothes.

**tag** tags tagging tagged
NOUN **1** a small label made of cloth, paper, or plastic. **2** If you tag along with someone, you go with them or behind them.

**tail** tails tailing tailed
NOUN **1** The tail of an animal, bird, or fish is the part extending beyond the end of its body. **2** Tail can be used to mean the end part of something E.G. *the tail of the plane.* ▶ PLURAL NOUN **3** If a man is wearing tails, he is wearing a formal jacket which has two long pieces hanging down at the back. ▶ VERB **4** INFORMAL If you tail someone, you follow them in order to find out where they go and what they do. ▶ ADJECTIVE or ADVERB **5** The tails side of a coin is the side which does not have a person's head.

**tail off** VERB If something tails off, it becomes gradually less.

**tailback** tailbacks
NOUN a long queue of traffic stretching back from whatever is blocking the road.

**tailor** tailors tailoring tailored
NOUN **1** a person who makes, alters, and repairs clothes, especially for men. ▶ VERB **2** If something is tailored for a particular purpose, it is specially designed for it.

**tailor-made**
ADJECTIVE suitable for a particular person or purpose, or specifically designed for them.

**taint** taints tainting tainted
VERB **1** To taint something is to spoil it by adding something undesirable to

it. ▶ NOUN **2** an undesirable quality in something which spoils it.

**taipan** taipans

NOUN a large and very poisonous Australian snake.

**take** takes taking took taken

VERB **1** 'Take' is used to show what action or activity is being done E.G. *Amy took a bath… She took her driving test*. **2** If something takes a certain amount of time, or a particular quality or ability, it requires it E.G. *He takes three hours to get ready*. **3** If you take something, you put your hand round it and hold it or carry it E.G. *Here, let me take your coat*. **4** If you take someone somewhere, you drive them there by car or lead them there. **5** If you take something that is offered to you, you accept it E.G. *He had to take the job.* **6** If you take the responsibility or blame for something, you accept responsibility or blame. **7** If you take something that does not belong to you, you steal it. **8** If you take pills or medicine, you swallow them. **9** If you can take something painful, you can bear it E.G. *We can't take much more of this.* **10** If you take someone's advice, you do what they say you should do. **11** If you take a person's temperature or pulse, you measure it. **12** If you take a car or train, or a road or route, you use it to go from one place to another.

**take after** VERB If you take after someone in your family, you look or behave like them.

**take down** VERB If you take down what someone is saying, you write it down.

**take in** VERB **1** If someone is taken in, they are deceived. **2** If you take

something in, you understand it.

**take off** VERB When an aeroplane takes off, it leaves the ground and begins to fly.

**takeoff** NOUN

**take over** VERB To take something over means to start controlling it.

**takeover** NOUN

**take to** VERB If you take to someone or something, you like them immediately.

**takeaway** takeaways

NOUN **1** a shop or restaurant that sells hot cooked food to be eaten elsewhere. **2** a hot cooked meal bought from a takeaway.

**takings**

PLURAL NOUN Takings are the money that a shop or cinema gets from selling its goods or tickets.

**talc**

NOUN Talc is the same as talcum powder.

**talcum powder**

NOUN Talcum powder is a soft perfumed powder used for absorbing moisture on the body.

**tale** tales

NOUN a story.

**talent** talents

NOUN Talent is the natural ability to do something well.

**talented** ADJECTIVE

▪ ability, flair, gift

**talisman** talismans

*Said* "**tal**-iz-man" NOUN an object which you believe has magic powers to protect you or bring luck.

▥ from Greek *telesma* meaning 'holy object'

**talk** talks talking talked

VERB **1** When you talk, you say things to someone. **2** If people talk,

a
b
c
d
e
f
g
h
i
j
k
l
m
n
o
p
q
r
s
**t**
u
v
w
x
y
z

especially about other people's private affairs, they gossip about them E.G. *the neighbours might talk.* **3** If you talk on or about something, you make an informal speech about it. ▶ NOUN **4** Talk is discussion or gossip. **5** an informal speech about something.

**talk down** VERB If you talk down to someone, you talk to them in a way that shows that you think you are more important or clever than them.

**talkative**
ADJECTIVE talking a lot.
■ chatty, garrulous, loquacious

**tall** taller tallest
ADJECTIVE **1** of more than average or normal height. **2** having a particular height E.G. *a wall ten metres tall.*
▶ PHRASE **3** If you describe something as **a tall story**, you mean that it is difficult to believe because it is so unlikely.

**tally** tallies tallying tallied
NOUN **1** an informal record of amounts which you keep adding to as you go along E.G. *He ended with a reasonable goal tally last season.*
▶ VERB **2** If numbers or statements tally, they are exactly the same or they give the same results or conclusions.

**Talmud**
*Said* "**t**al-*mood*" NOUN The Talmud consists of the books containing the ancient Jewish ceremonies and civil laws.
🔲 a Hebrew word meaning literally 'instruction'

**talon** talons
NOUN Talons are sharp, hooked claws, especially of a bird of prey.

**tambourine** tambourines
NOUN a percussion instrument made of a skin stretched tightly over a circular frame, with small round pieces of metal around the edge with the tambourine is beaten or shaken.

**tame** tamer tamest; tames taming tamed
ADJECTIVE **1** A tame animal or bird is not afraid of people and is not violent towards them. **2** Something that is tame is uninteresting and lacks excitement or risk E.G. *The report was pretty tame.* ▶ VERB **3** If you tame people or things, you bring them under control. **4** To tame a wild animal or bird is to train it to be obedient and live with humans.

**tamper** tampers tampering tampered
VERB If you tamper with something, you interfere or meddle with it.

**tampon** tampons
NOUN a firm, specially shaped piece of cotton wool that a woman places inside her vagina to absorb the blood during her period.

**tan** tans tanning tanned
NOUN **1** If you have a tan, your skin is darker than usual because you have been in the sun. ▶ VERB **2** To tan an animal's hide is to turn it into leather by treating it with chemicals.
▶ ADJECTIVE **3** Something that is tan is of a light yellowish-brown colour E.G. *a tan dress.*

**tandem** tandems
NOUN a bicycle designed for two riders sitting one behind the other.

**tang** tangs
NOUN a strong, sharp smell or flavour E.G. *the tang of lemon.*
**tangy** ADJECTIVE

**tangata whenua**
*Said "**tang**-ah-tah **feh**-noo-ah"* NOUN
Tangata whenua is a Maori term for the original Polynesian settlers in New Zealand, and their descendants.

**tangent** tangents
NOUN **1** A tangent of a curve is any straight line that touches the curve at one point only. ▶ PHRASE **2** If you **go off at a tangent**, you start talking or thinking about something that is not completely relevant to what has gone before.

**tangerine** tangerines
NOUN **1** a type of small sweet orange with a loose rind. ▶ NOUN OR ADJECTIVE **2** reddish-orange.

**tangible**
*Said "tan-jib-bl"* ADJECTIVE clear or definite enough to be easily seen or felt *E.G. tangible proof.*

**tangle** tangles tangling tangled
NOUN **1** a mass of things such as hairs or fibres knotted or coiled together and difficult to separate. ▶ VERB **2** If you are tangled in wires or ropes, you are caught or trapped in them so that it is difficult to get free.

**tango** tangos
NOUN A tango is a Latin American dance using long gliding steps and sudden pauses; also a piece of music composed for this dance.

**taniwha** taniwha or taniwhas
*Said "tun-ee-fah"* NOUN In New Zealand, a monster of Maori legends that lives in water.

**tank** tanks
NOUN **1** a large container for storing liquid or gas. **2** an armoured military vehicle which moves on tracks and is equipped with guns or rockets.

**tankard** tankards
NOUN a large metal mug used for drinking beer.

**tanker** tankers
NOUN a ship or lorry designed to carry large quantities of gas or liquid *E.G. a petrol tanker.*

**tannin**
NOUN a brown or yellow substance found in plants and used in making leather.

**tantalizing** or **tantalising**
ADJECTIVE Something that is tantalizing makes you feel hopeful and excited, although you know that you probably will not be able to have what you want *E.G. a tantalizing glimpse of riches to come.*

**tantamount**
ADJECTIVE If you say that something is tantamount to something else, you mean that it is almost the same as it *E.G. That would be tantamount to treason.*

**tantrum** tantrums
NOUN a noisy and sometimes violent outburst of temper, especially by a child.

**Tanzanian** Tanzanians
*Said "tan-zan-**nee**-an"* ADJECTIVE
**1** belonging or relating to Tanzania. ▶ NOUN **2** someone who comes from Tanzania.

**tap** taps tapping tapped
NOUN **1** a device that you turn to control the flow of liquid or gas from a pipe or container. **2** the action of hitting something lightly; also the sound that this action makes. ▶ VERB **3** If you tap something or tap on it, you hit it lightly. **4** If a telephone is tapped, a device is fitted to it so that someone can listen secretly to the calls.

a
b
c
d
e
f
g
h
i
j
k
l
m
n
o
p
q
r
s
t
u
v
w
x
y
z

**tap-dancing**

NOUN Tap-dancing is a type of dancing in which the dancers wear special shoes with pieces of metal on the toes and heels which click against the floor.

**tape** tapes taping taped

NOUN 1 Tape is plastic ribbon covered with a magnetic substance and used to record sounds, pictures, and computer information. 2 a cassette or spool with magnetic tape wound round it. 3 Tape is a long, thin strip of fabric that is used for binding or fastening. 4 Tape is also a strip of sticky plastic which you use for sticking things together. ▶ VERB 5 If you tape sounds or television pictures, you record them using a tape recorder or a video recorder. 6 If you tape one thing to another, you attach them using sticky tape.

**tape measure** tape measures

NOUN a strip of plastic or metal that is marked off in inches or centimetres and used for measuring things.

**taper** tapers tapering tapered

VERB 1 Something that tapers becomes thinner towards one end. ▶ NOUN 2 a thin candle.

**tape recorder** tape recorders

NOUN a machine used for recording sounds onto magnetic tape, and for playing these sounds back.

**tapestry** tapestries

NOUN a piece of heavy cloth with designs embroidered on it.

**tar**

NOUN Tar is a thick, black, sticky substance which is used in making roads.

**tarantula** tarantulas

Said "tar-**rant**-yoo-la" NOUN a large,

hairy poisonous spider.

**target** targets

NOUN 1 something which you aim at when firing weapons. 2 The target of an action or remark is the person or thing at which it is directed E.G. You become a target for our hatred. 3 Your target is the result that you are trying to achieve.

**tariff** tariffs

NOUN 1 a tax that a government collects on imported goods. 2 any list of prices or charges.

**tarmac**

NOUN Tarmac is a material used for making road surfaces. It consists of crushed stones mixed with tar. 🏛 short for *tarmacadam*, from the name of John McAdam, the Scottish engineer who invented it

**tarnish** tarnishes tarnishing tarnished

VERB 1 If metal tarnishes, it becomes stained and loses its shine. 2 If something tarnishes your reputation, it spoils it and causes people to lose their respect for you.

**tarot**

Said "**tar**-roh" NOUN A tarot card is one of a special pack of cards used for fortune-telling.

**tarpaulin** tarpaulins

NOUN a sheet of heavy waterproof material used as a protective covering.

**tarragon**

NOUN Tarragon is a herb with narrow green leaves used in cooking.

**tarry** tarries tarrying tarried

VERB; OLD-FASHIONED To tarry is to wait, or to stay somewhere for a little longer.

**tarseal**

NOUN In New Zealand English, tarseal

is the tarmac surface of a road.

**tart tarts; tarter tartest**
NOUN 1 a pastry case with a sweet filling. ▶ ADJECTIVE 2 Something that is tart is sour or sharp to taste. 3 A tart remark is unpleasant and cruel.

**tartan tartans**
NOUN Tartan is a woollen fabric from Scotland with checks of various colours and sizes, depending on which clan it belongs to.

**tartar**
NOUN Tartar is a hard, crusty substance that forms on teeth.

**tarwhine tarwhines**
NOUN an edible Australian marine fish, especially a sea bream.

**task tasks**
NOUN any piece of work which has to be done.
■ chore, duty, job

**Tasmanian devil Tasmanian devils**
NOUN a black-and-white marsupial of Tasmania, which eats flesh.

**tassel tassels**
NOUN a tuft of loose threads tied by a knot and used for decoration.

**taste tastes tasting tasted**
NOUN 1 Your sense of taste is your ability to recognize the flavour of things in your mouth. 2 The taste of something is its flavour. 3 If you have a taste of food or drink, you have a small amount of it to see what it is like. 4 If you have a taste for something, you enjoy it E.G. *a taste for publicity.* 5 If you have a taste of something, you experience it E.G. *my first taste of defeat.* 6 A person's taste is their choice in the things they like to buy or have around them E.G. *His taste in music is great.* ▶ VERB 7 When

you can taste something in your mouth, you are aware of its flavour. 8 If you taste food or drink, you have a small amount of it to see what it is like. 9 If food or drink tastes of something, it has that flavour.

**taste bud taste buds**
NOUN Your taste buds are the little points on the surface of your tongue which enable you to taste things.

**tasteful**
ADJECTIVE attractive and elegant.
**tastefully** ADVERB

**tasteless**
ADJECTIVE 1 vulgar and unattractive. 2 A tasteless remark or joke is offensive. 3 Tasteless food has very little flavour.

**tasty tastier tastiest**
ADJECTIVE having a pleasant flavour.

**tatters**
PLURAL NOUN Clothes that are in tatters are badly torn.
**tattered** ADJECTIVE

**tattoo tattoos tattooing tattooed**
VERB 1 If someone tattoos you or tattoos a design on you, they draw it on your skin by pricking little holes and filling them with coloured dye. ▶ NOUN 2 a picture or design tattooed on someone's body. 3 a public military display of exercises and music.

**tatty tattier tattiest**
ADJECTIVE worn out or untidy and rather dirty.

**taught**
the past tense and past participle of teach.

**taunt taunts taunting taunted**
VERB 1 To taunt someone is to speak to them about their weaknesses or

a
b
c
d
e
f
g
h
i
j
k
l
m
n
o
p
q
r
s
**t**
u
v
w
x
y
z

failures in order to make them angry
or upset. ➤ NOUN **2** an offensive
remark intended to make a person
angry or upset.

**Taurus**

NOUN Taurus is the second sign of the
zodiac, represented by a bull. People
born between April 20th and May
20th are born under this sign.
🎴 from Latin *taurus* meaning 'bull'

**taut**

ADJECTIVE stretched very tight *E.G. taut
wires.*

**tavern taverns**

NOUN; *OLD-FASHIONED* a pub.

**tawdry tawdrier tawdriest**

*Said* "**taw-***dree*" ADJECTIVE cheap,
gaudy, and of poor quality.

**tawny**

NOUN or ADJECTIVE brownish-yellow.

**tax taxes taxing taxed**

NOUN **1** Tax is an amount of money
that the people in a country have to
pay to the government so that it can
provide public services such as
health care and education. ➤ VERB **2** If
a sum of money is taxed, a certain
amount of it has to be paid to the
government. **3** If goods are taxed, a
certain amount of their price has to
be paid to the government. **4** If a
person or company is taxed, they
have to pay a certain amount of their
income to the government. **5** If
something taxes you, it makes
heavy demands on you *E.G. They must
be told not to tax your
patience.*

**taxation** NOUN

**taxi taxis taxiing taxied**

NOUN **1** a car with a driver which you
hire to take you to where you want
to go. ➤ VERB **2** When an aeroplane

taxis, it moves slowly along the
runway before taking off or after
landing.

**tea teas**

NOUN **1** Tea is the dried leaves of an
evergreen shrub found in Asia. **2** Tea
is a drink made by brewing the
leaves of the tea plant in hot water;
also a cup of this. **3** Tea is also any
drink made with hot water and
leaves or flowers *E.G. peppermint tea.*
**4** Tea is a meal taken in the late
afternoon or early evening.

**tea bag tea bags**

NOUN a small paper bag with tea
leaves in it which is placed in boiling
water to make tea.

**teach teaches teaching taught**

VERB **1** If you teach someone
something, you give them
instructions so that they know about
it or know how to do it. **2** If you teach
a subject, you help students learn
about a subject at school, college, or
university.

**teacher** NOUN **teaching** NOUN

■ (sense 1) educate, instruct, train,
tutor

**teak**

NOUN Teak is a hard wood which
comes from a large Asian tree.

**team teams teaming teamed**

NOUN **1** a group of people who play
together against another group in a
sport or game. ➤ VERB **2** If you team up
with someone, you join them and
work together with them.

**teamwork**

NOUN Teamwork is the ability of a
group of people to work well
together.

**teapot teapots**

NOUN a round pot with a handle, a lid,

A
B
C
D
E
F
G
H
I
J
K
L
M
N
O
P
Q
R
S
T
U
V
W
X
Y
Z

and a spout, used for brewing and pouring tea.

**tear** tears tearing tore torn
NOUN 1 Tears are the drops of salty liquid that come out of your eyes when you cry. 2 a hole that has been made in something. ▶ VERB 3 If you tear something, it is damaged by being pulled so that a hole appears in it. 4 If you tear somewhere, you rush there *E.G. He tore through busy streets in a high-speed chase.*
■ (sense 2) hole, rip, rupture
✓ When *tear* means 'a drop of salty water' (sense 1), it rhymes with *fear*. For all the other senses it rhymes with *hair*.

**tearaway** tearaways
NOUN someone who is wild and uncontrollable.

**tearful**
ADJECTIVE about to cry or crying gently.
**tearfully** ADVERB

**tease** teases teasing teased
VERB 1 If you tease someone, you deliberately make fun of them or embarrass them because it amuses you. ▶ NOUN 2 someone who enjoys teasing people.

**teaspoon** teaspoons
NOUN a small spoon used for stirring drinks; also the amount that a teaspoon holds.

**teat** teats
NOUN 1 a nipple on a female animal. 2 a piece of rubber or plastic that is shaped like a nipple and fitted to a baby's feeding bottle.

**tea tree** tea trees
NOUN a tree found in Australia and New Zealand with leaves that contain tannin, like tea leaves.

**tech** techs NOUN; *INFORMAL* a technical college.

**technical**
ADJECTIVE 1 involving machines, processes, and materials used in industry, transport, and communications. 2 skilled in practical and mechanical things rather than theories and ideas. 3 involving a specialized field of activity *E.G. I never understood the technical jargon.*

**technical college** technical colleges
NOUN a college where you can study subjects like technology and secretarial skills.

**technicality** technicalities
NOUN 1 The technicalities of a process or activity are the detailed methods used to do it. 2 an exact detail of a law or a set of rules, especially one some people might not notice *E.G. The verdict may have been based on a technicality.*

**technically**
ADVERB If something is technically true or correct, it is true or correct when you consider only the facts, rules, or laws, but may not be important or relevant in a particular situation *E.G. Technically, they were not supposed to drink on duty.*

**technician** technicians
NOUN someone whose job involves skilled practical work with scientific equipment.

**technique** techniques
NOUN 1 a particular method of doing something *E.G. these techniques of manufacture.* 2 Technique is skill and ability in an activity which is developed through training and

a b c d e f g h i j k l m n o p q r s **t** u v w x y z

A
B
C
D
E
F
G
H
I
J
K
L
M
N
O
P
Q
R
S
**T**
U
V
W
X
Y
Z

practice E.G. *Jim's unique vocal technique.*

**techno-**

PREFIX 'Techno-' means a craft or art E.G. *technology.*

📖 from Greek *tekhnē* meaning 'a skill'

**technology technologies**

NOUN 1 (D&T) Technology is the study of the application of science and scientific knowledge for practical purposes in industry, farming, medicine, or business. 2 a particular area of activity that requires scientific methods and knowledge E.G. *computer technology.*
**technological** ADJECTIVE
**technologically** ADVERB

**teddy teddies**

NOUN A teddy or teddy bear is a stuffed toy that looks like a friendly bear.

📖 named after the American President Theodore (Teddy) Roosevelt, who hunted bears

**tedious**

*Said "tee-dee-uss"* ADJECTIVE boring and lasting for a long time E.G. *the tedious task of clearing up.*

**tedium**

*Said "tee-dee-um"* NOUN the quality of being boring and lasting for a long time E.G. *the tedium of unemployment.*

**tee tees teeing teed**

NOUN 1 the small wooden or plastic peg on which a golf ball is placed before the golfer first hits it. ▶ VERB 2 To tee off is to hit the golf ball from the tee, or to start a round of golf.

**teem teems teeming teemed**

VERB 1 If a place is teeming with people or things, there are a lot of

them moving about. 2 If it teems, it rains very heavily E.G. *The rain was teeming down.*

**teenage**

ADJECTIVE 1 aged between thirteen and nineteen. 2 typical of people aged between thirteen and nineteen E.G. *teenage fashion.*
**teenager** NOUN

**teens**

PLURAL NOUN Your teens are the period of your life when you are between thirteen and nineteen years old.

**tee shirt**

another spelling of **T-shirt**.

**teeter teeters teetering teetered**

VERB To teeter is to shake or sway slightly in an unsteady way and seem about to fall over.

**teeth**

the plural of **tooth**.

**teethe teethes teething teethed**

*Rhymes with "breathe"* VERB When babies are teething, their teeth are starting to come through, usually causing them pain.

**teetotal**

*Said "tee-toe-tl"* ADJECTIVE Someone who is teetotal never drinks alcohol.
**teetotaller** NOUN

**tele-**

PREFIX 'Tele-' means at or over a distance E.G. *telegraph.*

📖 from Greek *tele* meaning 'far'

**telecommunications**

NOUN Telecommunications is the science and activity of sending signals and messages over long distances using electronic equipment.

**telegram telegrams**

NOUN a message sent by telegraph.

**telegraph**

NOUN The telegraph is a system of sending messages over long distances using electrical or radio signals.

**telepathy**

Said "til-**lep**-ath-ee" NOUN Telepathy is direct communication between people's minds.

**telepathic** ADJECTIVE

**telephone** telephones telephoning telephoned

NOUN 1 a piece of electrical equipment for talking directly to someone who is in a different place. ► VERB 2 If you telephone someone, you speak to them using a telephone.

**telephone box** telephone boxes

NOUN a small shelter in the street where there is a public telephone.

**telescope** telescopes

NOUN a long instrument shaped like a tube which has lenses which make distant objects appear larger and nearer.

**teletext**

NOUN Teletext is an electronic system that broadcasts pages of information onto a television set.

**televise** televises televising televised

VERB If an event is televised, it is filmed and shown on television.

**television** televisions

NOUN a piece of electronic equipment which receives pictures and sounds by electrical signals over a distance.

**tell** tells telling told

VERB 1 If you tell someone something, you let them know about it. 2 If you tell someone to do something, you order or advise them to do it. 3 If you can tell something, you are able to

judge correctly what is happening or what the situation is E.G. I could tell he was scared. 4 If an unpleasant or tiring experience begins to tell, it begins to have a serious effect E.G. The pressure began to tell.

■ (sense 1) inform, notify

**teller** tellers

NOUN a person who receives or gives out money in a bank.

**telling**

ADJECTIVE Something that is telling has an important effect, often because it shows the true nature of a situation E.G. a telling account of the war.

**telltale**

ADJECTIVE A telltale sign reveals information E.G. the sad, telltale signs of a recent accident.

**telly** tellies

NOUN; INFORMAL a television.

**temerity**

Said "tim-**mer**-it-ee" NOUN If someone has the temerity to do something, they do it even though it upsets or annoys other people E.G. She had the temerity to call him Bob.

**temp** temps

NOUN; INFORMAL a secretary who works for short periods of time in different places.

**temper** tempers tempering tempered

NOUN 1 Your temper is the frame of mind or mood you are in. 2 a sudden outburst of anger. ► PHRASE 3 If you **lose your temper**, you become very angry. ► VERB 4 To temper something is to make it more acceptable or suitable E.G. curiosity tempered with some caution.

**temperament** temperaments

Said "**tem**-pra-ment" NOUN Your

a
b
c
d
e
f
g
h
i
j
k
l
m
n
o
p
q
r
s
t
u
v
w
x
y
z

temperament is your nature or personality, shown in the way you react towards people and situations *E.G. an artistic temperament.*

**temperamental**
ADJECTIVE Someone who is temperamental has moods that change often and suddenly.

**temperate**
ADJECTIVE A temperate place has weather that is neither extremely hot nor extremely cold.

**temperature temperatures**
NOUN 1 (SCIENCE) The temperature of something is how hot or cold it is. 2 Your temperature is the temperature of your body. ► PHRASE 3 If you **have a temperature**, the temperature of your body is higher than it should be, because you are ill.

**tempest tempests**
NOUN; *LITERARY* a violent storm.

**tempestuous**
*Said "tem-pest-yoo-uss"* ADJECTIVE violent or strongly emotional *E.G. a tempestuous relationship.*

**template templates**
NOUN a shape or pattern cut out in wood, metal, plastic, or card which you draw or cut around to reproduce that shape or pattern.

**temple temples**
NOUN 1 (RE) a building used for the worship of a god in various religions *E.G. a Buddhist temple.* 2 Your temples are the flat parts on each side of your forehead.

**tempo tempos or tempi**
NOUN 1 The tempo of something is the speed at which it happens *E.G. the slow tempo of change.* 2 (MUSIC); *TECHNICAL* The tempo of a piece of music is its speed.

**temporary**
ADJECTIVE lasting for only a short time.
**temporarily** ADVERB

**tempt tempts tempting tempted**
VERB 1 If you tempt someone, you try to persuade them to do something by offering them something they want. 2 If you are tempted to do something, you want to do it but you think it might be wrong or harmful *E.G. He was tempted to reply with sarcasm.*
■ (sense 1) entice, lure

**temptation temptations**
NOUN 1 Temptation is the state you are in when you want to do or have something, even though you know it might be wrong or harmful. 2 something that you want to do or have, even though you know it might be wrong or harmful *E.G. There is a temptation to ignore the problem.*

**ten**
the number 10.
**tenth**

**tenacious**
*Said "tin-nay-shuss"* ADJECTIVE determined and not giving up easily.
**tenaciously** ADVERB  **tenacity** NOUN

**tenant tenants**
NOUN someone who pays rent for the place they live in, or for land or buildings that they use.
**tenancy** NOUN

**tend tends tending tended**
VERB 1 If something tends to happen, it happens usually or often. 2 If you tend someone or something, you look after them *E.G. the way we tend our cattle.*
■ (sense 1) be apt to, be inclined to, be liable to

**tendency** tendencies

NOUN a trend or type of behaviour that happens very often *E.G. a tendency to be critical.*

**tender** tenderest; tenders tendering tendered

ADJECTIVE **1** Someone who is tender has gentle and caring feelings. **2** If someone is at a tender age, they are young and do not know very much about life. **3** Tender meat is easy to cut or chew. **4** If a part of your body is tender, it is painful and sore. ▶ VERB **5** If someone tenders an apology or their resignation, they offer it. ▶ NOUN **6** a formal offer to supply goods or to do a job for a particular price.

■ (sense 1) affectionate, gentle, loving

**tendon** tendons

NOUN a strong cord of tissue which joins a muscle to a bone.

**tendril** tendrils

NOUN Tendrils are short, thin stems which grow on climbing plants and attach them to walls.

**tenement** tenements

*Said "ten-em-ent"* NOUN a large house or building divided into many flats.

**tenet** tenets

NOUN The tenets of a theory or belief are the main ideas it is based upon.

**tenner** tenners

NOUN; *INFORMAL* a ten-pound or ten-dollar note.

**tennis**

NOUN Tennis is a game played by two or four players on a rectangular court in which a ball is hit by players over a central net.

**tenor** tenors

NOUN **1** a man who sings in a fairly high voice. **2** The tenor of something is the general meaning or mood that it expresses *E.G. the whole tenor of his poetry had changed.* ▶ ADJECTIVE **3** A tenor recorder, saxophone, or other musical instrument has a range of notes of a fairly low pitch.

**tense** tenser tensest; tenses tensing tensed

ADJECTIVE **1** If you are tense, you are nervous and cannot relax. **2** A tense situation or period of time is one that makes people nervous and worried. **3** If your body is tense, your muscles are tight. ▶ VERB **4** If you tense, or if your muscles tense, your muscles become tight and stiff. ▶ NOUN **5** The tense of a verb is the form which shows whether you are talking about the past, present, or future.

■ (sense 1) anxious, nervous, uptight

---

### What is a Tense?

The "tense" of the verb tells us whether the action is in the past, the present or the future.

Some forms of the verb indicate that the action has already happened. These forms are **past tenses**:

*E.G. The captain **asked** Matthew for advice.*
*The captain **has asked** Matthew for advice.*
*The captain **was asking** Matthew for advice this morning.*
*The captain **had asked** Matthew for advice that morning.*

Some forms of the verb indicate that the action is happening at the present time. These forms are **present tenses**:

CONTINUED ON NEXT PAGE →

---

a
b
c
d
e
f
g
h
i
j
k
l
m
n
o
p
q
r
s
t
u
v
w
x
y
z

Eddy Ant thinks mEAt is a grEAt trEAt to EAt (-ea-)    SPELLING NOTE

E.G. *I* **see** *some cause for optimism.*
*I* **do see** *some cause for optimism.*

Some forms of the verb indicate that the action will happen in the future. These forms are **future tenses:**

E.G. *They* **will go** *to Fiji in September.*
*They* **will have gone** *to Fiji by the end of September.*

Also look at the grammar boxes at **future**, **past tense**, and **present tense**.

## tension tensions
NOUN **1** Tension is the feeling of nervousness or worry that you have when something dangerous or important is happening. **2** (D&T) The tension in a rope or wire is how tightly it is stretched.

## tent tents
NOUN a shelter made of canvas or nylon held up by poles and pinned down with pegs and ropes.

## tentacle tentacles
NOUN The tentacles of an animal such as an octopus are the long, thin parts that it uses to feel and hold things.

## tentative
ADJECTIVE acting or speaking cautiously because of being uncertain or afraid.
**tentatively** ADVERB

## tenterhooks
PLURAL NOUN If you are on tenterhooks, you are nervous and excited about something that is going to happen. 🔒 from the hooks called *tenterhooks* which were used to stretch cloth tight while it was drying

## tenuous
*Said* "**ten**-yoo-uss" ADJECTIVE If an idea or connection is tenuous, it is so slight and weak that it may not really exist or may easily cease to exist E.G. *a very tenuous friendship.*

## tenure tenures
*Said* "**ten**-yoor" NOUN **1** Tenure is the legal right to live in a place or to use land or buildings for a period of time. **2** Tenure is the period of time during which someone holds an important job E.G. *His tenure ended in 1998.*

## tepee tepees
*Said* "**tee**-pee" NOUN a cone-shaped tent of animal skins used by North American Indians.

## tepid
ADJECTIVE Tepid liquid is only slightly warm.

## term terms terming termed
NOUN **1** a fixed period of time E.G. *her second term of office.* **2** one of the periods of time that each year is divided into at a school or college. **3** a name or word used for a particular thing. ▶ PLURAL NOUN **4** The terms of an agreement are the conditions that have been accepted by the people involved in it. **5** If you express something in particular terms, you express it using a particular type of language or in a way that clearly shows your attitude E.G. *The young priest spoke of her in glowing terms.* ▶ PHRASE **6** If you **come to terms with** something difficult or unpleasant, you learn to accept it. ▶ VERB **7** To term something is to give it a name or to describe it E.G. *He termed my performance memorable.*

**terminal terminals**

ADJECTIVE **1** A terminal illness or disease cannot be cured and causes death gradually. ▶ NOUN **2** a place where vehicles, passengers, or goods begin or end a journey. **3** A computer terminal is a keyboard and a visual display unit that is used to put information into or get information out of a computer. **4** one of the parts of an electrical device through which electricity enters or leaves.

**terminally** ADVERB

**terminate terminates terminating terminated**

VERB When you terminate something or when it terminates, it stops or ends.

**termination** NOUN

**terminology terminologies**

NOUN The terminology of a subject is the set of special words and expressions used in it.

**terminus terminuses**

*Said* "**ter-min-uss**" NOUN a place where a bus or train route ends.

**termite termites**

NOUN Termites are small white insects that feed on wood.

**tern terns**

NOUN a small black and white sea bird with long wings and a forked tail.

**ternary**

ADJECTIVE (MUSIC) Ternary form is a musical structure of three sections, the first and the second contrasting with each other and the third being a repetition of the first.

**terrace terraces**

NOUN **1** a row of houses joined together. **2** a flat area of stone next to a building where people can sit.

**terracotta**

NOUN a type of brown pottery with no glaze.

🏛 from Italian *terra cotta* meaning 'baked earth'

**terrain**

NOUN The terrain of an area is the type of land there *E.G. the region's hilly terrain.*

**terrapin terrapins**

NOUN a small North American freshwater turtle.

**terrestrial**

ADJECTIVE involving the earth or land.

**terrible**

ADJECTIVE **1** serious and unpleasant *E.G. a terrible illness.* **2** INFORMAL very bad or of poor quality *E.G. Paddy's terrible haircut.*

**terribly**

ADVERB very or very much *E.G. I was terribly upset.*

**terrier terriers**

NOUN a small, short-bodied dog.

**terrific**

ADJECTIVE **1** INFORMAL very pleasing or impressive *E.G. a terrific film.* **2** great in amount, degree, or intensity *E.G. a terrific blow on the head.*

**terrifically** ADVERB

**terrify terrifies terrifying terrified**

VERB If something terrifies you, it makes you feel extremely frightened.

**territorial**

ADJECTIVE involving or relating to the ownership of a particular area of land or water *E.G. a territorial dispute.*

**territory territories**

NOUN **1** The territory of a country is the land that it controls. **2** An animal's territory is an area which it

a b c d e f g h i j k l m n o p q r s t u v w x y z

regards as its own and defends when other animals try to enter it.

**terror** terrors

NOUN 1 Terror is great fear or panic. 2 something that makes you feel very frightened.

**terrorism**

NOUN Terrorism is the use of violence for political reasons.

**terrorist** NOUN OR ADJECTIVE

**terrorize** terrorizes terrorizing terrorized; also spelt **terrorise**

VERB If someone terrorizes you, they frighten you by threatening you or being violent to you.

**terse** terser tersest

ADJECTIVE A terse statement is short and rather unfriendly.

**tertiary**

Said "**ter**-shar-ee" ADJECTIVE 1 third in order or importance. 2 Tertiary education is education at university or college level.

**test** tests testing tested

VERB 1 When you test something, you try it to find out what it is, what condition it is in, or how well it works. 2 If you test someone, you ask them questions to find out how much they know. ▶ NOUN 3 a deliberate action or experiment to find out whether something works or how well it works. 4 a set of questions or tasks given to someone to find out what they know or can do.

**testament** testaments

NOUN 1 LEGAL a will. 2 a copy of either the Old or the New Testament of the Bible.

**test case** test cases

NOUN a legal case that becomes an example for deciding other similar cases.

**testicle** testicles

NOUN A man's testicles are the two sex glands that produce sperm.

**testify** testifies testifying testified

VERB 1 When someone testifies, they make a formal statement, especially in a court of law E.G. Ismay later testified at the British inquiry. 2 To testify to something is to show that it is likely to be true E.G. a consultant's certificate testifying to her good health.

**testimonial** testimonials

Said "tess-tim-**moh**-nee-al" NOUN a statement saying how good someone or something is.

**testimony** testimonies

NOUN A person's testimony is a formal statement they make, especially in a court of law.

**testing**

ADJECTIVE Testing situations or problems are very difficult to deal with E.G. It is a testing time for his team.

**testis** testes

NOUN A man's testes are his testicles.

**test match** test matches

NOUN one of a series of international cricket or rugby matches.

**testosterone**

Said "tess-**toss**-ter-rone" NOUN Testosterone is a male hormone that produces male characteristics.

**test tube** test tubes

NOUN a small cylindrical glass container that is used in chemical experiments.

**tetanus**

Said "**tet**-nuss" NOUN Tetanus is a painful infectious disease caused by germs getting into wounds.

**tether** tethers tethering tethered
VERB **1** If you tether an animal, you tie it to a post. ▶ PHRASE **2** If you are **at the end of your tether**, you are extremely tired and have no more patience or energy left.

**Teutonic**
*Said* "tyoo-**tonn**-ik" ADJECTIVE; FORMAL involving or related to German people.

**text** texts texting texted
NOUN **1** The text of a book is the main written part of it, rather than the pictures or index. **2** Text is any written material. **3** a book or other piece of writing used for study or an exam at school or college. **4** Text is short for 'text message'. ▶ VERB **5** If you text someone, you send them a text message.
**textual** ADJECTIVE

**textbook** textbooks
NOUN a book about a particular subject for students to use.

**textile** textiles
NOUN (D&T) a woven cloth or fabric.

**text message** text messages
NOUN a written message sent using a mobile phone.

**texture** textures
NOUN The texture of something is the way it feels when you touch it.
▣ consistency, feel

**Thai** Thais
ADJECTIVE **1** belonging or relating to Thailand. ▶ NOUN **2** someone who comes from Thailand. **3** Thai is the main language spoken in Thailand.

**than**
PREPOSITION or CONJUNCTION **1** You use 'than' to link two parts of a comparison E.G. *She was older than*

*me.* **2** You use 'than' to link two parts of a contrast E.G. *Players would rather play than train.*

**thank** thanks thanking thanked
VERB When you thank someone, you show them that you are grateful.

**thankful**
ADJECTIVE happy and relieved that something has happened.
**thankfully** ADVERB

**thankless**
ADJECTIVE A thankless job or task involves doing a lot of hard work that other people do not notice or are not grateful for E.G. *Referees have a thankless task.*

**thanks**
PLURAL NOUN **1** When you express your thanks to someone, you tell or show them how grateful you are for something. ▶ PHRASE **2** If something happened **thanks to** someone or something, it happened because of them E.G. *I'm as prepared as I can be, thanks to you.* ▶ INTERJECTION **3** You say 'thanks' to show that you are grateful for something.

**thanksgiving**
NOUN **1** Thanksgiving is an act of thanking God, especially in prayer or in a religious ceremony. **2** In the United States, Thanksgiving is a public holiday in the autumn.

**thank you**
You say 'thank you' to show that you are grateful to someone for something.

**that** those
ADJECTIVE or PRONOUN **1** 'That' or 'those' is used to refer to things or people already mentioned or known about E.G. *That man was waving.*
▶ CONJUNCTION **2** 'That' is used to introduce a clause E.G. *I said that I was coming home.* ▶ PRONOUN **3** 'That' is

a b c d e f g h i j k l m n o p q r s **t** u v w x y z

an ELegant angEL (ang**e**l)    SPELLING NOTE

also used to introduce a relative clause *E.G. I followed Alex to a door that led inside.*

☑ You can use either *that* or *which* in clauses known as defining clauses. These are clauses that identify the object you are talking about. In the sentence *The book that is on the table is mine*, '*that' is on the table* is a defining clause which distinguishes the book from other books that are not on the table. Some people think these types of clause should only be introduced by *that*, and *which* should be kept for nondefining clauses. These nondefining clauses add extra information about the object, but do not identify it. In the sentence *The book, which is on the table, is mine*, '*which' is on the table* is a nondefining clause which gives the reader extra detail about the book.

**thatch** thatches thatching thatched

NOUN **1** Thatch is straw and reeds used to make roofs. ▶ VERB **2** To thatch a roof is to cover it with thatch.

**thaw** thaws thawing thawed

VERB **1** When snow or ice thaws, it melts. **2** When you thaw frozen food, or when it thaws, it returns to its normal state in a warmer atmosphere. **3** When people who are unfriendly thaw, they begin to be more friendly and relaxed. ▶ NOUN **4** a period of warmer weather in winter when snow or ice melts.

**the**

ADJECTIVE The definite article 'the' is used when you are talking about something that is known about, that has just been mentioned, or that you are going to give details about.

---

### The Definite Article

The word *the* is known as the **definite article**. You use it before a noun to refer to a specific example of that noun:

*E.G. the kitchen table*
    *the school I attend*

The definite article *the* may be used before singular and plural nouns. However, you cannot use the indefinite article *a* or *an* before a plural noun. You need to use the word *some* in this case:

*E.G. the tables* ➤ *some tables*
*E.G. the schools* ➤ *some schools*

Also look at the grammar box at **a.**

---

**theatre** theatres

*Said* "**theer**-ter" NOUN **1** (DRAMA) a building where plays and other entertainments are performed on a stage. **2** Theatre is work such as writing, producing, and acting in plays. **3** An operating theatre is a room in a hospital designed and equipped for surgical operations.

🏛 from Greek *theatron* meaning 'viewing place'

**theatrical**

*Said* "thee-**at**-rik-kl" ADJECTIVE **1** (DRAMA) involving the theatre or performed in a theatre *E.G. his theatrical career.* **2** Theatrical behaviour is exaggerated, unnatural, and done for effect.

**theatrically** ADVERB

**thee**

PRONOUN; *OLD-FASHIONED* Thee means you.

**theft** thefts

NOUN Theft is the crime of stealing.

▤ robbery, stealing

**their**

ADJECTIVE 'Their' refers to something belonging or relating to people or things, other than yourself or the person you are talking to, which have already been mentioned *E.G. It was their fault.*

☑ Be careful not to confuse *their* with *there*.

**theirs**

PRONOUN 'Theirs' refers to something belonging or relating to people or things, other than yourself or the person you are talking to, which have already been mentioned *E.G. Amy had been Helen's friend, not theirs.*

**them**

PRONOUN 'Them' refers to things or people, other than yourself or the people you are talking to, which have already been mentioned *E.G. He picked up the pillows and threw them to the floor.*

**theme** themes

NOUN 1 a main idea or topic in a piece of writing, painting, film, or music *E.G. the main theme of the book.* 2 a tune, especially one played at the beginning and end of a television or radio programme.

**themselves**

PRONOUN 1 'Themselves' is used when people, other than yourself or the person you are talking to, do an action and are affected by it *E.G. They think they've made a fool of themselves.* 2 'Themselves' is used to emphasize 'they' *E.G. He was as excited as they themselves were.*

**then**

ADVERB at a particular time in the past or future *E.G. I'd left home by then.*

**theologian** theologians

*Said "thee-ol-loe-jee-an"* NOUN someone who studies religion and the nature of God.

**theology**

NOUN Theology is the study of religion and God.

**theological** ADJECTIVE

**theoretical**

ADJECTIVE 1 based on or to do with ideas of a subject rather than the practical aspects. 2 not proved to exist or be true.

**theoretically** ADVERB

**theory** theories

NOUN 1 an idea or set of ideas that is meant to explain something *E.G. Darwin's theory of evolution.* 2 Theory is the set of rules and ideas that a particular subject or skill is based upon. ▶ PHRASE 3 You use **in theory** to say that although something is supposed to happen, it may not in fact happen *E.G. In theory, prices should rise by 2%.*

▤ (sense 1) conjecture, hypothesis

**therapeutic**

*Said "ther-ap-yoo-tik"* ADJECTIVE 1 If something is therapeutic, it helps you to feel happier and more relaxed *E.G. Laughing is therapeutic.* 2 In medicine, therapeutic treatment is designed to treat a disease or to improve a person's health.

**therapy**

NOUN Therapy is the treatment of mental or physical illness, often without the use of drugs or operations.

**therapist** NOUN

**there**

ADVERB 1 in, at, or to that place, point, or case *E.G. He's sitting over there.*

a b c d e f g h i j k l m n o p q r s **t** u v w x y z

A B C D E F G H I J K L M N O P Q R S T U V W X Y Z

▶ PRONOUN 2 'There' is used to say that something exists or does not exist, or to draw attention to something E.G. *There are flowers on the table.*

☑ Be careful not to confuse *there* with *their*. A good way to remember that *there* is connected to the idea of place is by remembering the spelling of two other place words, *here* and *where*.

**thereby**
ADVERB; FORMAL as a result of the event or action mentioned E.G. *They had recruited 200 new members, thereby making the day worthwhile.*

**therefore**
ADVERB as a result.

**thermal**
ADJECTIVE 1 to do with or caused by heat E.G. *thermal energy.* 2 Thermal clothes are specially designed to keep you warm in cold weather.

**thermometer** thermometers
NOUN (SCIENCE) an instrument for measuring the temperature of a room or a person's body.

**thermostat** thermostats
NOUN a device used to control temperature, for example on a central heating system.

**thesaurus** thesauruses
Said "this-**saw**-russ" NOUN (LIBRARY) a reference book in which words with similar meanings are grouped together.
📖 from Greek *thēsauros* meaning 'treasure'

**these**
the plural of *this.*

**thesis** theses
Said "**thee**-siss" NOUN a long piece of writing, based on research, that is done as part of a university degree.

**they**
PRONOUN 1 'They' refers to people or things, other than you or the people you are talking to, that have already been mentioned E.G. *They married two years later.* 2 'They' is sometimes used instead of 'he' or 'she' where the sex of the person is unknown or unspecified. Some people consider this to be incorrect E.G. *Someone could have a nasty accident if they tripped over that.*

**thick** thicker thickest
ADJECTIVE 1 Something thick has a large distance between its two opposite surfaces. 2 If something is a particular amount thick, it measures that amount between its two sides. 3 Thick means growing or grouped closely together and in large quantities E.G. *thick dark hair.* 4 Thick liquids contain little water and do not flow easily E.G. *thick soup.*
5 INFORMAL A thick person is stupid or slow to understand things.

**thicken** thickens thickening thickened
VERB If something thickens, it becomes thicker E.G. *The clouds thickened.*

**thicket** thickets
NOUN a small group of trees growing closely together.

**thief** thieves
NOUN a person who steals.

**thieving**
NOUN Thieving is the act of stealing.

**thigh** thighs
NOUN Your thighs are the top parts of your legs, between your knees and your hips.

**thimble** thimbles
NOUN a small metal or plastic cap that you put on the end of your finger to protect it when you are sewing.

**thin** thinner thinnest; thins thinning thinned
ADJECTIVE **1** Something that is thin is much narrower than it is long. **2** A thin person or animal has very little fat on their body. **3** Thin liquids contain a lot of water *E.G. thin soup*.
▶ VERB **4** If you thin something such as paint or soup, you add water or other liquid to it.
■ (sense 2) lean, skinny, slim

**thing** things
NOUN **1** an object, rather than a plant, an animal, a human being. ▶ PLURAL NOUN **2** Your things are your clothes or possessions.
■ (sense 1) article, object

**think** thinks thinking thought
VERB **1** When you think about ideas or problems, you use your mind to consider them. **2** If you think something, you have the opinion that it is true or the case *E.G. I think she has a secret boyfriend*. **3** If you think of something, you remember it or it comes into your mind. **4** If you think a lot of someone or something, you admire them or think they are good.

**third** thirds
ADJECTIVE **1** The third item in a series is the one counted as number three.
▶ NOUN **2** one of three equal parts.

**Third World**
NOUN The poorer countries of Africa, Asia, and South America can be referred to as the Third World.

**thirst** thirsts
NOUN **1** If you have a thirst, you feel a need to drink something. **2** A thirst for something is a very strong desire for it *E.G. a thirst for money*.

**thirsty** ADJECTIVE     **thirstily** ADVERB

**thirteen**
the number 13.
**thirteenth**

**thirty** thirties
the number 30.
**thirtieth**

**this** these
ADJECTIVE OR PRONOUN **1** 'This' is used to refer to something or someone that is nearby or has just been mentioned *E.G. This is Robert*. **2** 'This' is used to refer to the present time or place *E.G. this week*.

**thistle** thistles
NOUN a wild plant with prickly-edged leaves and purple flowers.

**thong** thongs
NOUN a long narrow strip of leather.

**thorn** thorns
NOUN one of many sharp points growing on some plants and trees.

**thorny** thornier thorniest
ADJECTIVE **1** covered with thorns. **2** A thorny subject or question is difficult to discuss or answer.

**thorough**
*Said "thur-ruh"* ADJECTIVE **1** done very carefully and completely *E.G. a thorough examination*. **2** A thorough person is very careful in what they do and makes sure nothing has been missed out.
**thoroughly** ADVERB

**thoroughbred** thoroughbreds
NOUN an animal that has parents that are of the same high quality breed.

**thoroughfare** thoroughfares
NOUN a main road in a town.

**those**
the plural of **that**.

**thou**
PRONOUN; *OLD-FASHIONED* Thou means you.

a
b
c
d
e
f
g
h
i
j
k
l
m
n
o
p
q
r
s
**t**
u
v
w
x
y
z

Betty Eats Cakes And Uses Seven Eggs (<u>because</u>)     ▶ SPELLING NOTE

A
B
C
D
E
F
G
H
I
J
K
L
M
N
O
P
Q
R
S
T
U
V
W
X
Y
Z

**though**
*Rhymes with "show"* CONJUNCTION
**1** despite the fact that *E.G. Meg felt better, even though she knew it was the end.* **2** if *E.G. It looks as though you were right.*

**thought** thoughts
**1** Thought is the past tense and past participle of **think**. ▶ NOUN **2** an idea that you have in your mind. **3** Thought is the activity of thinking *E.G. She was lost in thought.* **4** Thought is a particular way of thinking or a particular set of ideas *E.G. this school of thought.*
◼ (sense 3) consideration, reflection, thinking

**thoughtful**
ADJECTIVE **1** When someone is thoughtful, they are quiet and serious because they are thinking about something. **2** A thoughtful person remembers what other people want or need, and tries to be kind to them.
**thoughtfully** ADVERB
◼ (sense 1) meditative, pensive, reflective
◼ (sense 2) caring, considerate, kind

**thoughtless**
ADJECTIVE A thoughtless person forgets or ignores what other people want, need, or feel.
**thoughtlessly** ADVERB

**thousand** thousands
the number 1000.
**thousandth**

**thrash** thrashes thrashing thrashed
VERB **1** To thrash someone is to beat them by hitting them with something. **2** To thrash someone in a contest or fight is to defeat them completely. **3** To thrash out a problem or an idea is to discuss it in detail until a solution is reached.

**thread** threads threading threaded
NOUN **1** a long, fine piece of cotton, silk, nylon, or wool. **2** The thread on something such as a screw or the top of a container is the raised spiral line of metal or plastic round it. **3** The thread of an argument or story is an idea or theme that connects the different parts of it. ▶ VERB **4** When you thread something, you pass thread, tape, or cord through it. **5** If you thread your way through people or things, you carefully make your way through them.

**threadbare**
ADJECTIVE Threadbare cloth or clothing is old and thin.

**threat** threats
NOUN **1** a statement that someone will harm you, especially if you do not do what they want. **2** anything or anyone that seems likely to harm you. **3** If there is a threat of something unpleasant happening, it is very possible that it will happen.

**threaten** threatens threatening threatened
VERB **1** If you threaten to harm someone or threaten to do something that will upset them, you say that you will do it. **2** If someone or something threatens a person or thing, they are likely to harm them.
◼ (sense 2) endanger, jeopardize

**three**
the number 3.

**three-dimensional**
ADJECTIVE A three-dimensional object or shape is not flat, but has height or

depth as well as length and width.

**threesome** threesomes
NOUN a group of three.

**threshold** thresholds
*Said* "thresh-hold" NOUN **1** the doorway or the floor in the doorway of a building or room. **2** The threshold of something is the lowest amount, level, or limit at which something happens or changes *E.G. the tax threshold… His boredom threshold was exceptionally low.*

**thrice**
ADVERB; *OLD-FASHIONED* If you do something thrice, you do it three times.

**thrift**
NOUN Thrift is the practice of saving money and not wasting things.

**thrifty** thriftier thriftiest
ADJECTIVE A thrifty person saves money and does not waste things.

**thrill** thrills thrilling thrilled
NOUN **1** a sudden feeling of great excitement, pleasure, or fear; also any event or experience that gives you such a feeling. ▶ VERB **2** If something thrills you, or you thrill to it, it gives you a feeling of great pleasure and excitement.
**thrilled** ADJECTIVE   **thrilling** ADJECTIVE
■ (sense 1) buzz, kick

**thriller** thrillers
NOUN a book, film, or play that tells an exciting story about dangerous or mysterious events.

**thrive** thrives thriving thrived or throve
VERB When people or things thrive, they are healthy, happy, or successful.
**thriving** ADJECTIVE

**throat** throats
NOUN **1** the back of your mouth and the top part of the passages inside your neck. **2** the front part of your neck.

**throb** throbs throbbing throbbed
VERB **1** If a part of your body throbs, you feel a series of strong beats or dull pains. **2** If something throbs, it vibrates and makes a loud, rhythmic noise *E.G. The engines throbbed.*

**throes**
PLURAL NOUN **1** Throes are a series of violent pangs or movements *E.G. death throes.* ▶ PHRASE **2** If you are **in the throes** of something, you are deeply involved in it.

**thrombosis** thromboses
*Said* "throm-**boe**-siss" NOUN a blood clot which blocks the flow of blood in the body. Thromboses are dangerous and often fatal.

**throne** thrones
NOUN **1** a ceremonial chair used by a king or queen on important official occasions. **2** The throne is a way of referring to the position of being king or queen.

**throng** throngs thronging thronged
NOUN **1** a large crowd of people. ▶ VERB **2** If people throng somewhere or throng a place, they go there in great numbers *E.G. Hundreds of city workers thronged the scene.*

**throttle** throttles throttling throttled
VERB To throttle someone is to kill or injure them by squeezing their throat.

**through**
*Said* "threw" PREPOSITION **1** moving all the way from one side of something to the other *E.G. a path through the*

woods. **2** because of *E.G. He had been exhausted through lack of sleep.* **3** during *E.G. He has to work through the summer.* **4** If you go through an experience, it happens to you *E.G. I don't want to go through that again.* ► ADJECTIVE **5** If you are through with something, you have finished doing it or using it

☑ Do not confuse the spellings of *through* and *threw*, the past tense of *throw*.

**throughout**
PREPOSITION **1** during *E.G. I stayed awake throughout the night.* ► ADVERB **2** happening or existing through the whole of a place *E.G. The house was painted brown throughout.*

**throve**
the past tense of **thrive**.

**throw throws throwing threw thrown**
VERB **1** When you throw something you are holding, you move your hand quickly and let it go, so that it moves through the air. **2** If you throw yourself somewhere, you move there suddenly and with force *E.G. We threw ourselves on the ground.* **3** To throw someone into an unpleasant situation is to put them there *E.G. It threw them into a panic.* **4** If something throws light or shadow on something else, it makes that thing have light or shadow on it. **5** If you throw yourself into an activity, you become actively and enthusiastically involved in it. **6** If you throw a fit or tantrum, you suddenly begin behaving in an uncontrolled way.

■ (sense 1) chuck, fling, hurl

**throwback throwbacks**
NOUN something which has the

characteristics of something that existed a long time ago *E.G. Everything about her was a throwback to the fifties.*

**thrush thrushes**
NOUN **1** a small brown songbird. **2** Thrush is a disease of the mouth or of the vagina, caused by a fungus.

**thrust thrusts thrusting thrust**
VERB **1** If you thrust something somewhere, you push or move it there quickly with a lot of force. **2** If you thrust your way somewhere, you move along, pushing between people or things. ► NOUN **3** a sudden forceful movement. **4** The main thrust of an activity or idea is the most important part of it *E.G. the general thrust of his argument.*

**thud thuds thudding thudded**
NOUN **1** a dull sound, usually made by a solid, heavy object hitting something soft. ► VERB **2** If something thuds somewhere, it makes a dull sound, usually by hitting something else.

**thug thugs**
NOUN a very rough and violent person.
📖 from Hindi *thag* meaning 'thief'

**thumb thumbs thumbing thumbed**
NOUN **1** the short, thick finger on the side of your hand. ► VERB **2** If someone thumbs a lift, they stand at the side of the road and stick out their thumb until a driver stops and gives them a lift.

**thump thumps thumping thumped**
VERB **1** If you thump someone or something, you hit them hard with your fist. **2** If something thumps

somewhere, it makes a fairly loud, dull sound, usually when it hits something else. **3** When your heart thumps, it beats strongly and quickly. ▶ NOUN **4** a hard hit *E.G. a great thump on the back*. **5** a fairly loud, dull sound.

**thunder** thunders thundering thundered

NOUN **1** Thunder is a loud cracking or rumbling noise caused by expanding air which is suddenly heated by lightning. **2** Thunder is any loud rumbling noise *E.G. the distant thunder of bombs*. ▶ VERB **3** When it thunders, a loud cracking or rumbling noise occurs in the sky after a flash of lightning. **4** If something thunders, it makes a loud continuous noise *E.G. The helicopter thundered low over the trees*.

**thunderbolt** thunderbolts

NOUN a flash of lightning, accompanied by thunder.

**thunderous**

ADJECTIVE A thunderous noise is very loud *E.G. thunderous applause*.

**Thursday** Thursdays

NOUN Thursday is the day between Wednesday and Friday.
🔲 from Old English *Thursdæg* meaning 'Thor's day'; Thor was the Norse god of thunder

**thus**

ADVERB FORMAL **1** in this way *E.G. I sat thus for nearly half an hour*. **2** therefore *E.G. Critics were thus able to denounce him*.

**thwart** thwarts thwarting thwarted

VERB To thwart someone or their plans is to prevent them from doing or getting what they want.

**thy**

ADJECTIVE; OLD-FASHIONED Thy means your.

**thyme**

*Said "time"* NOUN Thyme is a bushy herb with very small leaves.

**thyroid gland** thyroid glands

NOUN Your thyroid gland is situated at the base of your neck. It releases hormones which control your growth and your metabolism.

**tiara** tiaras

*Said "tee-ah-ra"* NOUN a semicircular crown of jewels worn by a woman on formal occasions.

**Tibetan** Tibetans

ADJECTIVE **1** belonging or relating to Tibet. ▶ NOUN **2** someone who comes from Tibet.

**tic** tics

NOUN a twitching of a group of muscles, especially the muscles in the face.

**tick** ticks ticking ticked

NOUN **1** a written mark to show that something is correct or has been dealt with. **2** The tick of a clock is the series of short sounds it makes when it is working. **3** a tiny, blood-sucking, insect-like creature that usually lives on the bodies of people or animals. ▶ VERB **4** To tick something written on a piece of paper is to put a tick next to it. **5** When a clock ticks, it makes a regular series of short sounds as it works.

**tick off** VERB INFORMAL If you tick someone off, you speak angrily to them because they have done something wrong.

**ticking** NOUN

**ticket** tickets

NOUN a piece of paper or card which shows that you have paid for a

I want to see (C) your licenCe (licence)      ▶ **SPELLING NOTE**

A B C D E F G H I J K L M N O P Q R S T U V W X Y Z

journey or have paid to enter a place of entertainment.

**tickle** tickles tickling tickled
VERB 1 When you tickle someone, you move your fingers lightly over their body in order to make them laugh. 2 If something tickles you, it amuses you or gives you pleasure E.G. *Simon is tickled by the idea*.

**tidal**
ADJECTIVE to do with or produced by tides E.G. *a tidal estuary*.

**tidal wave** tidal waves
NOUN a very large wave, often caused by an earthquake, that comes over land and destroys things.

**tide** tides tiding tided
NOUN 1 The tide is the regular change in the level of the sea on the shore, caused by the gravitational pull of the sun and the moon. 2 The tide of opinion or fashion is what the majority of people think or do at a particular time. 3 A tide of something is a large amount of it E.G. *the tide of anger and bitterness*.

**tide over** VERB If something will tide someone over, it will help them through a difficult period of time.

**tidings**
PLURAL NOUN; FORMAL Tidings are news.

**tidy** tidier tidiest; tidies tidying tidied
ADJECTIVE 1 Something that is tidy is neat and arranged in an orderly way. 2 Someone who is tidy always keeps their things neat and arranged in an orderly way. 3 INFORMAL A tidy amount of money is a fairly large amount of it. ▶ VERB 4 To tidy a place is to make it neat by putting things in their proper place.

**tie** ties tying tied
VERB 1 If you tie one thing to another or tie it in a particular position, you fasten it using cord of some kind. 2 If you tie a knot or a bow in a piece of cord or cloth, you fasten the ends together to make a knot or bow. 3 Something or someone that is tied to something else is closely linked with it E.G. *40,000 jobs are tied to the project*. 4 If you tie with someone in a competition or game, you have the same number of points. ▶ NOUN 5 a long, narrow piece of cloth worn around the neck under a shirt collar and tied in a knot at the front. 6 a connection or feeling that links you with a person, place, or organization E.G. *I had very close ties with the family*.
■ (sense 1) bind, fasten

**tied up**
ADJECTIVE If you are tied up, you are busy.

**tier** tiers
NOUN one of a number of rows or layers of something E.G. *Take the stairs to the upper tier*.

**tiff** tiffs
NOUN a small unimportant quarrel.

**tiger** tigers
NOUN a large meat-eating animal of the cat family. It comes from Asia and has an orange coloured coat with black stripes.

**tiger snake** tiger snakes
NOUN a fierce, very poisonous Australian snake with dark stripes across its back.

**tight** tighter tightest
ADJECTIVE 1 fitting closely E.G. *The shoes are too tight*. 2 firmly fastened and difficult to move E.G. *a tight knot*. 3 stretched or pulled so as not to be

slack E.G. *a tight cord.* **4** A tight plan or arrangement allows only the minimum time or money needed to do something E.G. *Our schedule tonight is very tight.* ▶ ADVERB **5** held firmly and securely E.G. *He held me tight.*

**tightly** ADVERB **tightness** NOUN
■ (sense 3) stretched, taut

**tighten** tightens tightening tightened
VERB **1** If you tighten your hold on something, you hold it more firmly. **2** If you tighten a rope or chain, or if it tightens, it is stretched or pulled until it is straight. **3** If someone tightens a rule or system, they make it stricter or more efficient.

**tightrope** tightropes
NOUN a tightly-stretched rope on which an acrobat balances and performs tricks.

**tights**
PLURAL NOUN Tights are a piece of clothing made of thin stretchy material that fit closely round a person's hips, legs, and feet.

**tiki** tiki or tikis
NOUN In New Zealand, a small carving of an ancestor worn as a pendant in some Maori cultures.

**tile** tiles tiling tiled
NOUN **1** a small flat square piece of something, for example slate or carpet, that is used to cover surfaces. ▶ VERB **2** To tile a surface is to fix tiles to it.

**tiled** ADJECTIVE

**till** tills tilling tilled
PREPOSITION or CONJUNCTION **1** Till means the same as until. ▶ NOUN **2** a drawer or box in a shop where money is kept, usually in a cash register. ▶ VERB

**3** To till the ground is to plough it for raising crops.

**tiller** tillers
NOUN the handle fixed to the top of the rudder for steering a boat.

**tilt** tilts tilting tilted
VERB **1** If you tilt an object or it tilts, it changes position so that one end or side is higher than the other. ▶ NOUN **2** a position in which one end or side of something is higher than the other.
■ (sense 1) incline, lean, tip

**timber** timbers
NOUN **1** Timber is wood that has been cut and prepared ready for building and making furniture. **2** The timbers of a ship or house are the large pieces of wood that have been used to build it.

**time** times timing timed
NOUN **1** Time is what is measured in hours, days, and years E.G. *What time is it?* **2** 'Time' is used to mean a particular period or point E.G. *I enjoyed my time in Durban.* **3** If you say it is time for something or it is time to do it, you mean that it ought to happen or be done now E.G. *It is time for a change.* **4** 'Times' is used after numbers to indicate how often something happens E.G. *I saw my father four times a year.* **5** 'Times' is used after numbers when you are saying how much bigger, smaller, better, or worse one thing is compared to another E.G. *The Belgians drink three times as much beer as the French.* **6** 'Times' is used in arithmetic to link numbers that are multiplied together E.G. *Two times three is six.* ▶ VERB **7** If you time something for a particular time, you plan that it should happen then E.G.

have a pIEce of pIE (pie̱ce)    ◀ SPELLING NOTE

A B C D E F G H I J K L M N O P Q R S T U V W X Y Z

*We could not have timed our arrival better.* **8** If you time an activity or action, you measure how long it lasts.

■ (sense 2) interval, period, spell

**timeless**

ADJECTIVE Something timeless is so good or beautiful that it cannot be affected by the passing of time or by changes in fashion.

**timely**

ADJECTIVE happening at just the right time *E.G. a timely appearance.*

■ opportune, well-timed

**timer timers**

NOUN a device that measures time, especially one that is part of a machine.

**timescale timescales**

NOUN The timescale of an event is the length of time during which it happens.

**timetable timetables**

NOUN **1** a plan of the times when particular activities or jobs should be done. **2** a list of the times when particular trains, boats, buses, or aeroplanes arrive and depart.

**timid**

ADJECTIVE shy and having no courage or self-confidence.

**timidly** ADVERB **timidity** NOUN

■ fearful, shy, timorous

**timing**

NOUN **1** Someone's timing is their skill in judging the right moment at which to do something. **2** The timing of an event is when it actually happens.

**timpani**

*Said "tim-pan-ee"* PLURAL NOUN Timpani are large drums with curved bottoms that are played in an

orchestra.

**tin tins**

NOUN **1** Tin is a soft silvery-white metal. **2** a metal container which is filled with food and then sealed in order to preserve the food. **3** a small metal container which may have a lid *E.G. a cake tin.*

**tinder**

NOUN Tinder is small pieces of dry wood or grass that burn easily and can be used for lighting a fire.

**tinge tinges**

NOUN a small amount of something *E.G. a tinge of envy.*

**tinged** ADJECTIVE

**tingle tingles tingling tingled**

VERB **1** When a part of your body tingles, you feel a slight prickling feeling in it. ▶ NOUN **2** a slight prickling feeling.

**tingling** NOUN or ADJECTIVE

**tinker tinkers tinkering tinkered**

NOUN **1** a person who travels from place to place mending metal pots and pans or doing other small repair jobs. ▶ VERB **2** If you tinker with something, you make a lot of small changes to it in order to repair or improve it *E.G. All he wanted was to tinker with engines.*

**tinkle tinkles tinkling tinkled**

VERB **1** If something tinkles, it makes a sound like a small bell ringing. ▶ NOUN **2** a sound like that of a small bell ringing.

**tinned**

ADJECTIVE Tinned food has been preserved by being sealed in a tin.

**tinsel**

NOUN Tinsel is long threads with strips of shiny paper attached, used as a decoration at Christmas.

**tint** tints tinting tinted

NOUN 1 a small amount of a particular colour E.G. *a distinct tint of green.*
▶ VERB 2 If a person tints their hair, they change its colour by adding a weak dye to it.
**tinted** ADJECTIVE

**tiny** tinier tiniest

ADJECTIVE extremely small.
◼ diminutive, minute

**tip** tips tipping tipped

NOUN 1 the end of something long and thin E.G. *a fingertip.* 2 a place where rubbish is dumped. 3 If you give someone such as a waiter a tip, you give them some money to thank them for their services. 4 a useful piece of advice or information. ▶ VERB 5 If you tip an object, you move it so that it is no longer horizontal or upright. 6 If you tip something somewhere, you pour it there quickly or carelessly.
**tipped** ADJECTIVE

**tipple** tipples

NOUN A person's tipple is the alcoholic drink that they normally drink.

**tipsy** tipsier tipsiest

ADJECTIVE slightly drunk.

**tiptoe** tiptoes tiptoeing tiptoed

VERB If you tiptoe somewhere, you walk there very quietly on your toes.

**tirade** tirades

*Said "tie-rade"* NOUN a long, angry speech in which you criticize someone or something.
▦ from Italian *tirata* meaning 'volley of shots'

**tire** tires tiring tired

VERB 1 If something tires you, it makes you use a lot of energy so that you want to rest or sleep. 2 If you tire of something, you become bored with it.

**tired** ADJECTIVE **tiredness** NOUN
◼ (sense 1) exhaust, fatigue, weary

**tireless**

ADJECTIVE Someone who is tireless has a lot of energy and never seems to need a rest.

**tiresome**

ADJECTIVE A person or thing that is tiresome makes you feel irritated or bored.

**tiring**

ADJECTIVE Something that is tiring makes you tired.

**tissue** tissues

*Said "tiss-yoo"* NOUN 1 The tissue in plants and animals consists of cells that are similar in appearance and function E.G. *scar tissue… dead tissue.* 2 Tissue is thin paper that is used for wrapping breakable objects. 3 a small piece of soft paper that you use as a handkerchief.

**tit** tits

NOUN a small European bird E.G. *a blue tit.*

**titanic**

ADJECTIVE very big or important.
▦ in Greek legend, the *Titans* were a family of giants

**titillate** titillates titillating titillated

VERB If something titillates someone, it pleases and excites them, especially in a sexual way.
**titillation** NOUN

**title** titles

NOUN 1 the name of a book, play, or piece of music. 2 a word that describes someone's rank or job E.G. *My official title is Design Manager.* 3 the position of champion in a

I went to see (C) the doctor's new practiCe (practice) ◀ SPELLING NOTE

**titled**

ADJECTIVE Someone who is titled has a high social rank and has a title such as 'Princess', 'Lord', 'Lady', or 'Sir'.

**titter titters tittering tittered**

VERB If you titter, you laugh in a way that shows you are nervous or embarrassed.

**TNT**

NOUN TNT is a type of powerful explosive. It is an abbreviation for 'trinitrotoluene'.

**to**

PREPOSITION 1 'To' is used to indicate the place that someone or something is moving towards or pointing at E.G. *They are going to China.* 2 'To' is used to indicate the limit of something E.G. *Goods to the value of 500 pounds.* 3 'To' is used in ratios and rates when saying how many units of one type there are for each unit of another E.G. *I only get about 30 kilometres to the gallon from it.* ▶ ADVERB 4 If you push or shut a door to, you close it but do not shut it completely.

✓ The preposition *to* is spelt with one *o*, the adverb *too* has two *o*s, and the number *two* is spelt with *wo*.

**toad toads**

NOUN an amphibian that looks like a frog but has a drier skin and lives less in the water.

**toadstool toadstools**

NOUN a type of poisonous fungus.

**toast toasts toasting toasted**

NOUN 1 Toast is slices of bread made brown and crisp by cooking at a high temperature. 2 To drink a toast to someone is to drink an alcoholic drink in honour of them. ▶ VERB 3 If

you toast bread, you cook it at a high temperature so that it becomes brown and crisp. 4 If you toast yourself, you sit in front of a fire so that you feel pleasantly warm. 5 To toast someone is to drink an alcoholic drink in honour of them. 🔟 from Latin *tostus* meaning 'parched'

**toaster toasters**

NOUN a piece of electrical equipment used for toasting bread.

**tobacco**

NOUN Tobacco is the dried leaves of the tobacco plant which people smoke in pipes, cigarettes, and cigars.

**tobacconist tobacconists**

NOUN a shop where tobacco, cigarettes, and cigars are sold.

**toboggan toboggans**

NOUN a flat seat with two wooden or metal runners, used for sliding over the snow.

🔟 an American Indian word

**today**

ADVERB OR NOUN 1 Today means the day on which you are speaking or writing. 2 Today also means the present period of history E.G. *the challenges of teaching in today's schools.*

**toddle toddles toddling toddled**

VERB To toddle is to walk in short, quick steps, as a very young child does.

**toddler toddlers**

NOUN a small child who has just learned to walk.

**to-do to-dos**

NOUN A to-do is a situation in which people are very agitated or confused E.G. *It's just like him to make such a to-do about a baby.*

A B C D E F G H I J K L M N O P Q R S T U V W X Y Z

**toe toes**

NOUN **1** Your toes are the five movable parts at the end of your foot. **2** The toe of a shoe or sock is the part that covers the end of your foot.

**toff toffs**

NOUN; *AN INFORMAL, OLD-FASHIONED WORD* a rich person or one from an aristocratic family.

**toffee toffees**

NOUN Toffee is a sticky, chewy sweet made by boiling sugar and butter together with water.

**toga togas**

NOUN a long loose robe worn in ancient Rome.

**together**

ADVERB **1** If people do something together, they do it with each other. **2** If two things happen together, they happen at the same time. **3** If things are joined or fixed together, they are joined or fixed to each other. **4** If things or people are together, they are very near to each other.

■ (sense 1) collectively, jointly

■ (sense 2) concurrently, simultaneously

☑ Two nouns joined by *together with* do not make a plural subject, so the following verb is not plural: *Jones, together with his partner, has had great success.*

**togetherness**

NOUN Togetherness is a feeling of closeness and friendship.

**toil toils toiling toiled**

VERB **1** When people toil, they work hard doing unpleasant, difficult, or tiring tasks or jobs. ▶ NOUN **2** Toil is unpleasant, difficult, or tiring work.

**toilet toilets**

NOUN **1** a large bowl, connected by a pipe to the drains, which you use when you want to get rid of urine or faeces. **2** a small room containing a toilet.

**toiletries**

PLURAL NOUN Toiletries are the things you use when cleaning and taking care of your body, such as soap and talc.

**token tokens**

NOUN **1** a piece of paper or card that is worth a particular amount of money and can be exchanged for goods *E.G. record tokens.* **2** a flat round piece of metal or plastic that can sometimes be used instead of money. **3** If you give something to someone as a token of your feelings for them, you give it to them as a way of showing those feelings. ▶ ADJECTIVE **4** If something is described as token, it shows that it is not being treated as important *E.G. a token contribution to your fees.*

**told**

Told is the past tense and past participle of **tell**.

**tolerable**

ADJECTIVE **1** able to be put up with. **2** fairly satisfactory or reasonable *E.G. a tolerable salary.*

**tolerance**

NOUN **1** A person's tolerance is their ability to accept or put up with something which may not be enjoyable or pleasant for them. **2** Tolerance is the quality of allowing other people to have their own attitudes or beliefs, or to behave in a particular way, even if you do not agree or approve *E.G. religious tolerance.*

**tolerant** ADJECTIVE

a b c d e f g h i j k l m n o p q r s t u v w x y z

pAL up with the principAL and principAL staff (princip**al**)    SPELLING NOTE

A
B
C
D
E
F
G
H
I
J
K
L
M
N
O
P
Q
R
S
T
U
V
W
X
Y
Z

**tolerate tolerates tolerating tolerated**

VERB **1** If you tolerate things that you do not approve of or agree with, you allow them. **2** If you can tolerate something, you accept it, even though it is unsatisfactory or unpleasant.

**toleration** NOUN

■ (sense 2) bear, endure, stand

**toll tolls tolling tolled**

NOUN **1** The death toll in an accident is the number of people who have died in it. **2** a sum of money that you have to pay in order to use a particular bridge or road. ▶ VERB **3** When someone tolls a bell, it is rung slowly, often as a sign that someone has died.

**tom toms**

NOUN a male cat.

**tomahawk tomahawks**

NOUN a small axe used by North American Indians.

**tomato tomatoes**

NOUN a small round red fruit, used as a vegetable and often eaten raw in salads.

**tomb tombs**

NOUN a large grave for one or more corpses.

**tomboy tomboys**

NOUN a girl who likes playing rough or noisy games.

**tome tomes**

NOUN; *FORMAL* a very large heavy book.

**tomorrow**

ADVERB or NOUN **1** Tomorrow means the day after today. **2** You can refer to the future, especially the near future, as tomorrow.

**ton tons**

NOUN **1** a unit of weight equal to 2240 pounds or about 1016 kilograms. ▶ PLURAL NOUN **2** *INFORMAL* If you have tons of something, you have a lot of it.

**tonal**

ADJECTIVE involving the quality or pitch of a sound or of music.

**tone tones toning toned**

NOUN **1** Someone's tone is a quality in their voice which shows what they are thinking or feeling. **2** The tone of a musical instrument or a singer's voice is the kind of sound it has. **3** The tone of a piece of writing is its style and the ideas or opinions expressed in it *E.G. I was shocked at the tone of your leading article.* **4** a lighter, darker, or brighter shade of the same colour *E.G. The whole room is painted in two tones of orange.*

**tone down** VERB If you tone down something, you make it less forceful or severe.

**tone-deaf**

ADJECTIVE unable to sing in tune or to recognize different tunes.

**tongs**

PLURAL NOUN Tongs consist of two long narrow pieces of metal joined together at one end. You press the pieces together to pick an object up.

**tongue tongues**

NOUN **1** Your tongue is the soft part in your mouth that you can move and use for tasting, licking, and speaking. **2** a language. **3** Tongue is the cooked tongue of an ox. **4** The tongue of a shoe or boot is the piece of leather underneath the laces.

**tonic tonics**

NOUN **1** Tonic or tonic water is a colourless, fizzy drink that has a slightly bitter flavour and is often mixed with alcoholic drinks. **2** a medicine that makes you feel stronger, healthier, and less tired. **3** anything that makes you feel stronger or more cheerful *E.G. It was a tonic just being with her*.

**tonight**
ADVERB or NOUN Tonight is the evening or night that will come at the end of today.

**tonne tonnes**
*Said "tun"* NOUN (MATHS) a unit of weight equal to 1000 kilograms.

**tonsil tonsils**
NOUN Your tonsils are the two small, soft lumps in your throat at the back of your mouth.

**tonsillitis**
*Said "ton-sil-lie-tiss"* NOUN Tonsillitis is a painful swelling of your tonsils caused by an infection.

**too**
ADVERB **1** also or as well *E.G. You were there too*. **2** more than a desirable, necessary, or acceptable amount *E.G. a man who had taken too much to drink*.
☑ The adverb *too* has two *o*s, the preposition *to* is spelt with one *o*, and the number *two* is spelt with *wo*.

**tool tools**
NOUN **1** any hand-held instrument or piece of equipment that you use to help you do a particular kind of work. **2** an object, skill, or idea that is needed or used for a particular purpose *E.G. You can use the survey as a bargaining tool in the negotiations*.
▤ (sense 1) implement, instrument, utensil

**toot toots tooting tooted**
VERB If a car horn toots, it produces a short sound.

**tooth teeth**
NOUN **1** Your teeth are the hard enamel-covered objects in your mouth that you use for biting and chewing food. **2** The teeth of a comb, saw, or zip are the parts that stick out in a row on its edge.

**toothpaste**
NOUN Toothpaste is a substance which you use to clean your teeth.

**top tops topping topped**
NOUN **1** The top of something is its highest point, part, or surface. **2** The top of a bottle, jar, or tube is its cap or lid. **3** a piece of clothing worn on the upper half of your body. **4** a toy with a pointed end on which it spins.
▶ ADJECTIVE **5** The top thing of a series of things is the highest one *E.G. the top floor of the building*. ▶ VERB **6** If someone tops a poll or popularity chart, they do better than anyone else in it *E.G. It has topped the bestseller lists in almost every country*. **7** If something tops a particular amount, it is greater than that amount *E.G. The temperature topped 90°*.

**top up** VERB To top something up is to add something to it in order to keep it at an acceptable or usable level.

**top hat top hats**
NOUN a tall hat with a narrow brim that men wear on special occasions.

**topic topics**
NOUN a particular subject that you write about or discuss.

**topical**
ADJECTIVE involving or related to events that are happening at the time you are speaking or writing.

a b c d e f g h i j k l m n o p q r s **t** u v w x y z

A
B
C
D
E
F
G
H
I
J
K
L
M
N
O
P
Q
R
S
T
U
V
W
X
Y
Z

**topping toppings**
NOUN food that is put on top of other food in order to decorate it or add to its flavour.

**topple topples toppling toppled**
VERB If something topples, it becomes unsteady and falls over.

**top-secret**
ADJECTIVE meant to be kept completely secret.

**topsy-turvy**
ADJECTIVE in a confused state E.G. *My life was truly topsy-turvy.*

**top-up card top-up cards**
NOUN a card that you use to add credit to your mobile phone.

**Torah**
NOUN The Torah is Jewish law and teaching.

**torch torches**
NOUN 1 a small electric light carried in the hand and powered by batteries. 2 a long stick with burning material wrapped around one end.

**torment torments tormenting tormented**
NOUN 1 Torment is extreme pain or unhappiness. 2 something that causes extreme pain and unhappiness E.G. *It's a torment to see them staring at me.* ▶ VERB 3 If something torments you, it causes you extreme unhappiness.

**torn**
1 Torn is the past participle of **tear**. ▶ ADJECTIVE 2 If you are torn between two or more things, you cannot decide which one to choose and this makes you unhappy E.G. *torn between duty and pleasure.*

**tornado tornadoes** or **tornados**
*Said "tor-nay-doh"* NOUN a violent storm with strong circular winds

around a funnel-shaped cloud.

**torpedo torpedoes torpedoing torpedoed**
*Said "tor-pee-doh"* NOUN 1 a tube-shaped bomb that travels underwater and explodes when it hits a target. ▶ VERB 2 If a ship is torpedoed, it is hit, and usually sunk, by a torpedo.

**torrent torrents**
NOUN 1 When a lot of water is falling very rapidly, it can be said to be falling in torrents. 2 A torrent of speech is a lot of it directed continuously at someone E.G. *torrents of abuse.*

**torrential**
ADJECTIVE Torrential rain pours down very rapidly and in great quantities.

**torrid**
ADJECTIVE 1 Torrid weather is very hot and dry. 2 A torrid love affair is one in which people show very strong emotions.

**torso torsos**
NOUN the main part of your body, excluding your head, arms, and legs.

**tortoise tortoises**
NOUN a slow-moving reptile with a large hard shell over its body into which it can pull its head and legs for protection.

**tortuous**
ADJECTIVE 1 A tortuous road is full of bends and twists. 2 A tortuous piece of writing is long and complicated.

**torture tortures torturing tortured**
NOUN 1 Torture is great pain that is deliberately caused to someone to punish them or get information from them. ▶ VERB 2 If someone tortures another person, they deliberately cause that person great pain to

punish them or get information. **3** To torture someone is also to cause them to suffer mentally *E.G. Memory tortured her.*

**torturer** NOUN

**Tory** Tories

NOUN In Britain, a member or supporter of the Conservative Party. 📖 from Irish *toraidhe* meaning 'outlaw'

**toss** tosses tossing tossed

VERB **1** If you toss something somewhere, you throw it there lightly and carelessly. **2** If you toss a coin, you decide something by throwing a coin into the air and guessing which side will face upwards when it lands. **3** If you toss your head, you move it suddenly backwards, especially when you are angry, annoyed, or want your own way. **4** To toss is to move repeatedly from side to side *E.G. We tossed and turned and tried to sleep.*

■ (sense 1) fling, sling, throw

**tot** tots totting totted

NOUN **1** a very young child. **2** a small amount of strong alcohol such as whisky. ▶ VERB **3** To tot up numbers is to add them together.

**total** totals totalling totalled

NOUN **1** the number you get when you add several numbers together. ▶ VERB **2** When you total a set of numbers or objects, you add them all together. **3** If several numbers total a certain figure, that is the figure you get when all the numbers are added together *E.G. Their debts totalled over 300,000 dollars.* ▶ ADJECTIVE **4** Total means complete *E.G. a total failure.*

**totally** ADVERB

■ (sense 1) aggregate, sum, whole

**totalitarian**

*Said* "toe-tal-it-**tair**-ee-an" ADJECTIVE A totalitarian political system is one in which one political party controls everything and does not allow any other parties to exist.

**totalitarianism** NOUN

**tote** totes toting toted

VERB; *INFORMAL* To tote a gun is to carry it.

**totem pole** totem poles

NOUN a long wooden pole with symbols and pictures carved and painted on it. Totem poles are made by some North American Indians.

**totter** totters tottering tottered

VERB When someone totters, they walk in an unsteady way.

**toucan** toucans

*Said* "**too**-kan" NOUN a large tropical bird with a very large beak.

**touch** touches touching touched

VERB **1** If you touch something, you put your fingers or hand on it. **2** When two things touch, their surfaces come into contact *E.G. Their knees were touching.* **3** If you are touched by something, you are emotionally affected by it *E.G. I was touched by his thoughtfulness.* ▶ NOUN **4** Your sense of touch is your ability to tell what something is like by touching it. **5** a detail which is added to improve something *E.G. finishing touches.* **6** a small amount of something *E.G. a touch of mustard.* ▶ PHRASE **7** If you are **in touch** with someone, you are in contact with them.

**touchdown** touchdowns

NOUN Touchdown is the landing of an aircraft.

**touching**

ADJECTIVE causing feelings of sadness

a b c d e f g h i j k l m n o p q r s t u v w x y z

A
B
C
D
E
F
G
H
I
J
K
L
M
N
O
P
Q
R
S
T
U
V
W
X
Y
Z

and sympathy.

■ moving, poignant, sad

**touchy touchier touchiest**
ADJECTIVE **1** If someone is touchy, they are easily upset or irritated. **2** A touchy subject is one that needs to be dealt with carefully, because it might upset or offend people.

**tough tougher toughest**
Said "tuff" ADJECTIVE **1** A tough person is strong and independent and able to put up with hardship. **2** A tough substance is difficult to break. **3** A tough task, problem, or way of life is difficult or full of hardship. **4** Tough policies or actions are strict and firm E.G. tough measures against organized crime.

**toughly** ADVERB   **toughness** NOUN
**toughen** VERB
■ (sense 2) durable, resilient, strong

**toupee toupees**
Said "too-pay" NOUN a small wig worn by a man to cover a bald patch on his head.

**tour tours touring toured**
NOUN **1** a long journey during which you visit several places. **2** a short trip round a place such as a city or famous building. ▶ VERB **3** If you tour a place, you go on a journey or a trip round it.

**tourism**
NOUN (GEOGRAPHY) Tourism is the business of providing services for people on holiday, for example hotels and sightseeing trips.

**tourist tourists** (GEOGRAPHY)
NOUN a person who visits places for pleasure or interest.

**tournament tournaments**
NOUN (PE) a sports competition in which players who win a match play

further matches, until just one person or team is left.

**tourniquet tourniquets**
Said "toor-nik-kay" NOUN a strip of cloth tied tightly round a wound to stop it bleeding.

**tousled**
ADJECTIVE Tousled hair is untidy.

**tout touts touting touted**
VERB **1** If someone touts something, they try to sell it. **2** If someone touts for business or custom, they try to obtain it in a very direct way E.G. volunteers who spend days touting for donations. ▶ NOUN **3** someone who sells tickets outside a sports ground or theatre, charging more than the original price.

**tow tows towing towed**
VERB **1** If a vehicle tows another vehicle, it pulls it along behind it. ▶ NOUN **2** To give a vehicle a tow is to tow it. ▶ PHRASE **3** If you have someone **in tow**, they are with you because you are looking after them.

**towards**
PREPOSITION **1** in the direction of E.G. He turned towards the door. **2** about or involving E.G. My feelings towards Susan have changed. **3** as a contribution for E.G. a huge donation towards the new opera house. **4** near to E.G. We sat towards the back.

**towel towels**
NOUN a piece of thick, soft cloth that you use to dry yourself with.

**towelling**
NOUN Towelling is thick, soft cloth that is used for making towels.

**tower towers towering towered**
NOUN **1** a tall, narrow building, sometimes attached to a larger building such as a castle or church.

▶ VERB **2** Someone or something that towers over other people or things is much taller than them.
**towering** ADJECTIVE

**town** towns
NOUN **1** a place with many streets and buildings where people live and work. **2** Town is the central shopping and business part of a town rather than the suburbs E.G. *She has gone into town.*

**township** townships
NOUN a small town in South Africa where only Black people or Coloured people were allowed to live.

**towpath** towpaths
NOUN a path along the side of a canal or river.

**toxic**
ADJECTIVE poisonous E.G. *toxic waste.*
📖 from Greek *toxikon* meaning 'poison used on arrows' from *toxon* meaning 'arrow'

**toxin** toxins
NOUN a poison, especially one produced by bacteria and very harmful to living creatures.

**toy** toys toying toyed
NOUN **1** any object made to play with. ▶ VERB **2** If you toy with an idea, you consider it without being very serious about it E.G. *She toyed with the idea of telephoning him.* **3** If you toy with an object, you fiddle with it E.G. *Jessica was toying with her glass.*

**toyi-toyi** or **toy-toy**
NOUN In South Africa, a toyi-toyi is a dance performed to protest about something.

**trace** traces tracing traced
VERB **1** If you trace something, you find it after looking for it E.G. *Police are trying to trace the owner.*

**2** (EXAM TERM) To trace the development of something is to find out or describe how it developed. **3** If you trace a drawing or a map, you copy it by covering it with a piece of transparent paper and drawing over the lines underneath. ▶ NOUN **4** a sign which shows you that someone or something has been in a place E.G. *No trace of his father had been found.* **5** a very small amount of something.
**tracing** NOUN

**track** tracks tracking tracked
NOUN **1** a narrow road or path. **2** a strip of ground with rails on it that a train travels along. **3** a piece of ground, shaped like a ring, which horses, cars, or athletes race around. ▶ PLURAL NOUN **4** Tracks are marks left on the ground by a person or animal E.G. *the deer tracks by the side of the path.*
▶ ADJECTIVE **5** In an athletics competition, the track events are the races on a running track. ▶ VERB **6** If you track animals or people, you find them by following their footprints or other signs that they have left behind.

**track down** VERB If you track down someone or something, you find them by searching for them.

**track record** track records
NOUN The track record of a person or a company is their past achievements or failures E.G. *the track record of the film's star.*

**tracksuit** tracksuits
NOUN a loose, warm suit of trousers and a top, worn for outdoor sports.

**tract** tracts
NOUN **1** A tract of land or forest is a large area of it. **2** a pamphlet which expresses a strong opinion on a

a b c d e f g h i j k l m n o p q r s **t** u v w x y z

On WEDNESday Wayne WED NESta (Wednesday)　　　SPELLING NOTE

A B C D E F G H I J K L M N O P Q R S T U V W X Y Z

religious, moral, or political subject.
**3** a system of organs and tubes in an
animal's or person's body that has a
particular function E.G. the digestive
tract.

**traction**
NOUN Traction is a form of medical
treatment given to an injured limb
which involves pulling it gently for
long periods of time using a system
of weights and pulleys.

**tractor tractors**
NOUN a vehicle with large rear wheels
that is used on a farm for pulling
machinery and other heavy loads.

**trade trades trading traded**
NOUN **1** (HISTORY) Trade is the activity
of buying, selling, or exchanging
goods or services between people,
firms, or countries. **2** Someone's trade
is the kind of work they do,
especially when it requires special
training in practical skills E.G. a joiner
by trade. ▶ VERB **3** When people, firms,
or countries trade, they buy, sell, or
exchange goods or services. **4** If you
trade things, you exchange them E.G.
Their mother had traded her rings for
a few potatoes.
 ▤ (sense 1) business, commerce
 ▤ (sense 3) deal, do business,
traffic

**trademark trademarks**
NOUN a name or symbol that a
manufacturer always uses on its
products. Trademarks are usually
protected by law so that no-one else
can use them.

**trader traders**
NOUN a person whose job is to trade
in goods E.G. a timber trader.

**tradesman tradesmen**
NOUN a person, for example a

shopkeeper, whose job is to sell
goods.

**trade union trade unions**
NOUN an organization of workers that
tries to improve the pay and
conditions in a particular industry.

**tradition traditions**
NOUN a custom or belief that has
existed for a long time without
changing.
 ▤ convention, custom

**traditional**
ADJECTIVE **1** Traditional customs or
beliefs have existed for a long time
without changing E.G. her traditional
Indian dress. **2** A traditional
organization or institution is one in
which older methods are used rather
than modern ones E.G. a traditional
school.

**traditionally** ADVERB

**traditionalist traditionalists**
NOUN someone who supports the
established customs and beliefs of
their society, and does not want to
change them.

**traffic traffics trafficking
trafficked**
NOUN **1** Traffic is the movement of
vehicles or people along a route at a
particular time. **2** Traffic in something
such as drugs is an illegal trade in
them. ▶ VERB **3** Someone who traffics
in drugs or other goods buys and
sells them illegally.

**traffic light traffic lights**
NOUN Traffic lights are the set of red,
amber, and green lights at a road
junction which control the flow of
traffic.

**traffic warden traffic wardens**
NOUN a person whose job is to make
sure that cars are not parked in the

wrong place or for longer than is allowed.

**tragedy tragedies**
Said "**traj-id-ee**" NOUN 1 an event or situation that is disastrous or very sad. 2 a serious story or play, that usually ends with the death of the main character.

**tragic**
ADJECTIVE 1 Something tragic is very sad because it involves death, suffering, or disaster E.G. *a tragic accident.* 2 Tragic films, plays, and books are sad and serious E.G. *a tragic love story.*

**tragically** ADVERB

**trail trails trailing trailed**
NOUN 1 a rough path across open country or through forests. 2 a series of marks or other signs left by someone or something as they move along. ▶ VERB 3 If you trail something or it trails, it drags along behind you as you move, or it hangs down loosely E.G. *a small plane trailing a banner.* 4 If someone trails along, they move slowly, without any energy or enthusiasm. 5 If a voice trails away or trails off, it gradually becomes more hesitant until it stops completely.

**trailer trailers**
NOUN a small vehicle which can be loaded with things and pulled behind a car.

**train trains training trained**
NOUN 1 a number of carriages or trucks which are pulled by a railway engine. 2 A train of thought is a connected series of thoughts. 3 A train of vehicles or people is a line or group following behind something or someone E.G. *a train of wives and*

*girlfriends.* ▶ VERB 4 If you train, you learn how to do a particular job E.G. *She trained as a serious actress.* 5 If you train for a sports match or a race, you prepare for it by doing exercises.

**training** NOUN

**trainee trainees**
NOUN someone who is being taught how to do a job.

**trainers**
PLURAL NOUN Trainers are special shoes worn for running or jogging.

**trait traits**
NOUN a particular characteristic or tendency E.G. *a very English trait.*

**traitor traitors**
NOUN (HISTORY) someone who betrays their country or the group which they belong to.

**trajectory trajectories**
Said "**traj-jek-tor-ee**" NOUN The trajectory of an object moving through the air is the curving path that it follows.

**tram trams**
NOUN a vehicle which runs on rails along the street and is powered by electricity from an overhead wire.

**tramp tramps tramping tramped**
NOUN 1 a person who has no home, no job, and very little money. 2 a long country walk E.G. *I took a long, wet tramp through the fine woodlands.* ▶ VERB 3 If you tramp from one place to another, you walk with slow, heavy footsteps.

**trample tramples trampling trampled**
VERB 1 If you trample on something, you tread heavily on it so that it is damaged. 2 If you trample on

someone or on their rights or feelings, you behave in a way that shows you don't care about them.

**trampoline** trampolines
NOUN a piece of gymnastic equipment consisting of a large piece of strong cloth held taut by springs in a frame, on which a gymnast jumps to help them jump high.

**trance** trances
NOUN a mental state in which someone seems to be asleep but is conscious enough to be aware of their surroundings and to respond to questions and commands.

**tranquil**
Said "**trang**-kwil" ADJECTIVE calm and peaceful E.G. tranquil lakes… I have a tranquil mind.
**tranquillity** NOUN

**tranquillizer** tranquillizers; also spelt tranquilliser
NOUN a drug that makes people feel less anxious or nervous.

**trans-**
PREFIX Trans- means across, through, or beyond E.G. transatlantic.

**transaction** transactions
NOUN a business deal which involves buying and selling something.

**transcend** transcends transcending transcended
VERB If one thing transcends another, it goes beyond it or is superior to it E.G. Her beauty transcends all barriers.

**transcribe** transcribes transcribing transcribed
VERB If you transcribe something that is spoken or written, you write it down, copy it, or change it into a different form of writing E.G. These letters were often transcribed by his wife Patti.

**transcript** transcripts
NOUN a written copy of of something that is spoken.

**transfer** transfers transferring transferred
VERB 1 If you transfer something from one place to another, you move it E.G. They transferred the money to the Swiss account. 2 If you transfer to a different place or job, or are transferred to it, you move to a different place or job within the same organization. ▶ NOUN 3 the movement of something from one place to another. 4 a piece of paper with a design on one side which can be ironed or pressed onto cloth, paper, or china.
**transferable** ADJECTIVE

**transfixed**
ADJECTIVE If a person is transfixed by something, they are so impressed or frightened by it that they cannot move E.G. Price stood transfixed at the sight of that tiny figure.

**transform** transforms transforming transformed
VERB If something is transformed, it is changed completely E.G. The frown is transformed into a smile.
**transformation** NOUN

**transfusion** transfusions
NOUN A transfusion or blood transfusion is a process in which blood from a healthy person is injected into the body of another person who is badly injured or ill.

**transient**
Said "**tran**-zee-ent" ADJECTIVE Something transient does not stay or exist for very long E.G. transient emotions.
**transience** NOUN

SPELLING NOTE    'i' before 'e' except after 'c'

**transistor transistors**

NOUN **1** a small electrical device in something such as a television or radio which is used to control electric currents. **2** A transistor or a transistor radio is a small portable radio.

**transit**

NOUN **1** Transit is the carrying of goods or people by vehicle from one place to another. ▶ PHRASE **2** People or things that are **in transit** are travelling or being taken from one place to another E.G. *damage that had occurred in transit.*

**transition transitions**

NOUN a change from one form or state to another E.G. *the transition from war to peace.*

**transitional**

ADJECTIVE A transitional period or stage is one during which something changes from one form or state to another.

**transitive**

ADJECTIVE In grammar, a transitive verb is a verb which has an object.

**transitory**

ADJECTIVE lasting for only a short time.

**translate translates translating translated**

VERB To translate something that someone has said or written is to say it or write it in a different language. **translation** NOUN    **translator** NOUN

**translucent**

ADJECTIVE If something is translucent, light passes through it so that it seems to glow E.G. *translucent petals.*

**transmission transmissions**

NOUN **1** The transmission of something involves passing or sending it to a different place or person E.G. *the transmission of infectious diseases.* **2** The transmission of television or radio programmes is the broadcasting of them. **3** a broadcast.

**transmit transmits transmitting transmitted**

VERB **1** When a message or an electronic signal is transmitted, it is sent by radio waves. **2** To transmit something to a different place or person is to pass it or send it to the place or person E.G. *the clergy's role in transmitting knowledge.* **transmitter** NOUN

**transparency transparencies**

NOUN **1** a small piece of photographic film which can be projected onto a screen. **2** Transparency is the quality that an object or substance has if you can see through it.

**transparent**

ADJECTIVE If an object or substance is transparent, you can see through it. **transparently** ADVERB

■ clear, limpid, see-through

**transpire transpires transpiring transpired**

VERB **1** FORMAL When it transpires that something is the case, people discover that it is the case E.G. *It transpired that he had flown off on holiday.* **2** When something transpires, it happens E.G. *You start to wonder what transpired between them.*

☑ Some people think that it is wrong to use *transpire* to mean 'happen'. However, it is very widely used in this sense, especially in spoken English.

**transplant transplants transplanting transplanted**

NOUN **1** a process of removing something from one place and

a
b
c
d
e
f
g
h
i
j
k
l
m
n
o
p
q
r
s
t
u
v
w
x
y
z

A
B
C
D
E
F
G
H
I
J
K
L
M
N
O
P
Q
R
S
T
U
V
W
X
Y
Z

putting it in another E.G. *a man who needs a heart transplant.* ▶ VERB **2** When something is transplanted, it is moved to a different place.

**transport** transports transporting transported

NOUN (GEOGRAPHY) **1** Vehicles that you travel in are referred to as transport E.G. *public transport.* **2** Transport is the moving of goods or people from one place to another E.G. *The prices quoted include transport costs.* ▶ VERB **3** When goods or people are transported from one place to another, they are moved there.

▣ (sense 3) carry, convey, transfer

**transportation**

NOUN (GEOGRAPHY) Transportation is the transporting of people and things from one place to another.

**transvestite** transvestites

NOUN a person who enjoys wearing clothes normally worn by people of the opposite sex.

▥ from *trans-* and Latin *vestitus* meaning 'clothed'

**trap** traps trapping trapped

NOUN **1** a piece of equipment or a hole that is carefully positioned in order to catch animals or birds. **2** a trick that is intended to catch or deceive someone. ▶ VERB **3** Someone who traps animals catches them using traps. **4** If you trap someone, you trick them so that they do or say something which they did not want to. **5** If you are trapped somewhere, you cannot move or escape because something is blocking your way or holding you down. **6** If you are trapped, you are in an unpleasant situation that you cannot easily change E.G. *I'm trapped in an unhappy marriage.*

▣ (sense 3) catch, snare
▣ (sense 4) dupe, trick

**trap door** trap doors

NOUN a small horizontal door in a floor, ceiling, or stage.

**trapeze** trapezes

NOUN a bar of wood or metal hanging from two ropes on which acrobats and gymnasts swing and perform skilful movements.

**trapezium** trapeziums or trapezia

*Said* "trap-**pee**-zee-um" NOUN a four-sided shape with two sides parallel to each other.

**trappings**

PLURAL NOUN The trappings of a particular rank, position, or state are the clothes or equipment that go with it.

**trash**

NOUN **1** Trash is rubbish E.G. *He picks up your trash on Mondays.* **2** If you say that something such as a book, painting, or film is trash, you mean that it is not very good.

**trauma** traumas

*Said* "**traw**-ma" NOUN a very upsetting experience which causes great stress E.G. *the trauma of his mother's death.*
▥ from Greek *trauma* meaning 'wound'

**traumatic**

ADJECTIVE A traumatic experience is very upsetting.

**travel** travels travelling travelled

VERB **1** To travel is to go from one place to another. **2** When something reaches one place from another, you say that it travels there E.G. *Gossip travels fast.* ▶ NOUN **3** Travel is the act of travelling E.G. *air travel.* ▶ PLURAL

NOUN **4** Someone's travels are the journeys that they make to places a long way from their home E.G. *my travels in the Himalayas.*

**traveller** NOUN **travelling** ADJECTIVE

■ (sense 1) go, journey

**traveller's cheque** traveller's cheques
NOUN Traveller's cheques are cheques for use abroad. You buy them at home and then exchange them when you are abroad for foreign currency.

**traverse** traverses traversing traversed
VERB; FORMAL If you traverse an area of land or water, you go across it or over it E.G. *They have traversed the island from the west coast.*

**travesty** travesties
NOUN a very bad or ridiculous representation or imitation of something E.G. *British salad is a travesty of freshness.*

**trawl** trawls trawling trawled
VERB When fishermen trawl, they drag a wide net behind a ship in order to catch fish.

**trawler** trawlers
NOUN a fishing boat that is used for trawling.

**tray** trays
NOUN a flat object with raised edges which is used for carrying food or drinks.

**treacherous**
ADJECTIVE **1** A treacherous person is likely to betray you and cannot be trusted. **2** The ground or the sea can be described as treacherous when it is dangerous or unreliable E.G. *treacherous mountain roads.*

**treacherously** ADVERB

■ (sense 1) disloyal, untrustworthy

**treachery**

NOUN Treachery is behaviour in which someone betrays their country or a person who trusts them.

**treacle**
NOUN Treacle is a thick, sweet syrup used to make cakes and toffee E.G. *treacle tart.*

**tread** treads treading trod trodden
VERB **1** If you tread on something, you walk on it or step on it. **2** If you tread something into the ground or into a carpet, you crush it in by stepping on it E.G. *bubblegum that has been trodden into the pavement.* ▶ NOUN **3** A person's tread is the sound they make with their feet as they walk E.G. *his heavy tread.* **4** The tread of a tyre or shoe is the pattern of ridges on it that stops it slipping.

**treadmill** treadmills
NOUN Any task or job that you must keep doing even though it is unpleasant or tiring can be referred to as a treadmill E.G. *My life is one constant treadmill of making music.*

**treason**
NOUN Treason is the crime of betraying your country, for example by helping its enemies.

**treasure** treasures treasuring treasured
NOUN **1** Treasure is a collection of gold, silver, jewels, or other precious objects, especially one that has been hidden E.G. *buried treasure.*
**2** Treasures are valuable works of art E.G. *the finest art treasures in the world.*
▶ VERB **3** If you treasure something, you are very pleased that you have it and regard it as very precious E.G. *He treasures his friendship with her.*
**treasured** ADJECTIVE

LEt's measure the angLE (angle)    **SPELLING NOTE**

a
b
c
d
e
f
g
h
i
j
k
l
m
n
o
p
q
r
s
t
u
v
w
x
y
z

**treasurer treasurers**
NOUN a person who is in charge of the finance and accounts of an organization.

**Treasury**
NOUN The Treasury is the government department that deals with the country's finances.

**treat treats treating treated**
VERB 1 If you treat someone in a particular way, you behave that way towards them. 2 If you treat something in a particular way, you deal with it that way or see it that way E.G. *We are now treating this case as murder.* 3 When a doctor treats a patient or an illness, he or she gives them medical care and attention. 4 If something such as wood or cloth is treated, a special substance is put on it in order to protect it or give it special properties E.G. *The carpet's been treated with a stain protector.* 5 If you treat someone, you buy or arrange something special for them which they will enjoy. ▶ NOUN 6 If you give someone a treat, you buy or arrange something special for them which they will enjoy E.G. *my birthday treat.*

**treatment** NOUN

**treatise treatises**
*Said "tree-tiz"* NOUN a long formal piece of writing about a particular subject.

**treaty treaties**
NOUN a written agreement between countries in which they agree to do something or to help each other.

**treble trebles trebling trebled**
VERB 1 If something trebles or is trebled, it becomes three times greater in number or amount.

▶ ADJECTIVE 2 Treble means three times as large or three times as strong as previously E.G. *Next year we can raise treble that amount.*

**tree trees**
NOUN a large plant with a hard woody trunk, branches, and leaves.

**trek treks trekking trekked**
VERB 1 If you trek somewhere, you go on a long and difficult journey. ▶ NOUN 2 a long and difficult journey, especially one made by walking.
🏛 an Afrikaans word

**trellis trellises**
NOUN a frame made of horizontal and vertical strips of wood or metal and used to support plants.

**tremble trembles trembling trembled**
VERB 1 If you tremble, you shake slightly, usually because you are frightened or cold. 2 If something trembles, it shakes slightly. 3 If your voice trembles, it sounds unsteady, usually because you are frightened or upset.

**trembling** ADJECTIVE

**tremendous**
ADJECTIVE 1 large or impressive E.G. *It was a tremendous performance.* 2 INFORMAL very good or pleasing E.G. *tremendous fun.*

**tremendously** ADVERB

**tremor tremors**
NOUN 1 a shaking movement of your body which you cannot control. 2 an unsteady quality in your voice, for example when you are upset. 3 a small earthquake.

**trench trenches**
NOUN a long narrow channel dug into the ground.

**trenchant**
Said "**trent**-shent" ADJECTIVE Trenchant writing or comments are bold and firmly expressed.

**trend** trends
NOUN a change towards doing or being something different.

**trendy** trendier trendiest
ADJECTIVE; INFORMAL Trendy things or people are fashionable.

**trepidation**
NOUN; FORMAL Trepidation is fear or anxiety E.G. He saw the look of trepidation on my face.

**trespass** trespasses trespassing trespassed
VERB If you trespass on someone's land or property, you go onto it without their permission.
**trespasser** NOUN

**tresses**
PLURAL NOUN; OLD-FASHIONED A woman's tresses are her long flowing hair.

**trestle** trestles
NOUN a wooden or metal structure that is used as one of the supports for a table.

**trevally** trevallies
NOUN an Australian and New Zealand fish that is caught for both food and sport.

**tri-**
PREFIX three E.G. tricycle.

**triad** triads
Said "**try**-ad" NOUN 1 FORMAL a group of three similar things. 2 (MUSIC) TECHNICAL In music, a triad is a chord of three notes consisting of the tonic and the third and fifth above it.

**trial** trials
NOUN 1 the legal process in which a judge and jury decide whether a person is guilty of a particular crime after listening to all the evidence about it. 2 an experiment in which something is tested E.G. Trials of the drug start next month.

**triangle** triangles
NOUN 1 (MATHS) a shape with three straight sides. 2 a percussion instrument consisting of a thin steel bar bent in the shape of a triangle.
**triangular** ADJECTIVE

**triathlon** triathlons
Said "tri-**ath**-lon" NOUN a sports contest in which athletes compete in three different events.

**tribe** tribes
NOUN a group of people of the same race, who have the same customs, religion, language, or land, especially when they are thought to be primitive.
**tribal** ADJECTIVE

**tribulation** tribulations
NOUN; FORMAL Tribulation is trouble or suffering E.G. the tribulations of a female football star.

**tribunal** tribunals
Said "try-**byoo**-nl" NOUN a special court or committee appointed to deal with particular problems E.G. an industrial tribunal.

**tributary** tributaries
NOUN a stream or river that flows into a larger river.

**tribute** tributes
NOUN 1 A tribute is something said or done to show admiration and respect for someone E.G. Police paid tribute to her courage. 2 If one thing is a tribute to another, it is the result of the other thing and shows how good it is E.G. His success has been a tribute to hard work.

a b c d e f g h i j k l m n o p q r s t u v w x y z

Beautiful Elephants Are Usually Tiny (<u>beaut</u>iful)    SPELLING NOTE

**trice**

NOUN If someone does something in a trice, they do it very quickly.

**triceps**

*Said* "**try**-*seps*" NOUN ( PE ) Your triceps is the large muscle at the back of your upper arm that straightens your arm.

**trick tricks tricking tricked**

VERB **1** If someone tricks you, they deceive you. ▸ NOUN **2** an action done to deceive someone. **3** Tricks are clever or skilful actions done in order to entertain people *E.G. magic tricks*.

**trickery**

NOUN Trickery is deception *E.G. He accused the Serbs of trickery.*

**trickle trickles trickling trickled**

VERB **1** When a liquid trickles somewhere, it flows slowly in a thin stream. **2** When people or things trickle somewhere, they move there slowly in small groups or amounts. ▸ NOUN **3** a thin stream of liquid. **4** A trickle of people or things is a small number or quantity of them.

**tricky trickier trickiest**

ADJECTIVE difficult to do or deal with.

**tricycle tricycles**

NOUN a vehicle similar to a bicycle but with two wheels at the back and one at the front.

**trifle trifles trifling trifled**

NOUN **1** A trifle means a little *E.G. He seemed a trifle annoyed.* **2** Trifles are things that are not very important or valuable. **3** a cold pudding made of layers of sponge cake, fruit, jelly, and custard. ▸ VERB **4** If you trifle with someone or something, you treat them in a disrespectful way *E.G. He was not to be trifled with.*

**trifling**

ADJECTIVE small and unimportant.

**trigger triggers triggering triggered**

NOUN **1** the small lever on a gun which is pulled in order to fire it. ▸ VERB **2** If something triggers an event or triggers it off, it causes it to happen.

📖 from Dutch *trekken* meaning 'to pull'

**trigonometry**

*Said* "*trig*-*gon*-**nom**-*it*-*ree*" NOUN Trigonometry is the branch of mathematics that is concerned with calculating the angles of triangles or the lengths of their sides.

**trill trills trilling trilled**

VERB If a bird trills, it sings with short high-pitched repeated notes.

**trillion trillions**

NOUN; *INFORMAL* Trillions of things means an extremely large number of them. Formerly, a trillion meant a million million million.

**trilogy trilogies**

NOUN a series of three books or plays that have the same characters or are on the same subject.

**trim trimmer trimmest; trims trimming trimmed**

ADJECTIVE **1** neat, tidy, and attractive. ▸ VERB **2** To trim something is to clip small amounts off it. **3** If you trim off parts of something, you cut them off because they are not needed *E.G. Trim off the excess marzipan.* ▸ NOUN **4** If something is given a trim, it is cut a little *E.G. All styles need a trim every six to eight weeks.* **5** a decoration on something, especially along its edges *E.G. a fur trim.*

**trimmed** ADJECTIVE

A B C D E F G H I J K L M N O P Q R S T U V W X Y Z

**trimming** trimmings
NOUN Trimmings are extra parts added to something for decoration or as a luxury *E.G. bacon and eggs with all the trimmings.*

**Trimurti**
NOUN In the Hindu religion, the Trimurti are the three deities Brahma, Vishnu, and Siva.

**Trinity**
NOUN In the Christian religion, the Trinity is the joining of God the Father, God the Son, and God the Holy Spirit.

**trinket** trinkets
NOUN a cheap ornament or piece of jewellery.

**trio** trios
NOUN 1 a group of three musicians who sing or play together; also a piece of music written for three instruments or singers. 2 any group of three things or people together *E.G. a trio of children's tales.*

**trip** trips tripping tripped
NOUN 1 a journey made to a place.
▶ VERB 2 If you trip, you catch your foot on something and fall over. 3 If you trip someone or trip them up, you make them fall over by making them catch their foot on something.
■ (sense 1) excursion, journey, outing

**tripe**
NOUN Tripe is the stomach lining of a pig, cow, or ox, which is cooked and eaten.

**triple** triples tripling tripled
ADJECTIVE 1 consisting of three things or three parts *E.G. the Triple Alliance.*
▶ VERB 2 If you triple something or if it triples, it becomes three times greater in number or size.

**triplet** triplets
NOUN Triplets are three children born at the same time to the same mother.

**tripod** tripods
*Said "try-pod"* NOUN a stand with three legs used to support something like a camera or telescope.

**tripper** trippers
NOUN a tourist or someone on an excursion.

**trite**
ADJECTIVE dull and not original *E.G. his trite novels.*

**triumph** triumphs triumphing triumphed
NOUN 1 a great success or achievement. 2 Triumph is a feeling of great satisfaction when you win or achieve something. ▶ VERB 3 If you triumph, you win a victory or succeed in overcoming something.

**triumphal**
ADJECTIVE done or made to celebrate a victory or great success *E.G. a triumphal return to Rome.*

**triumphant**
ADJECTIVE Someone who is triumphant feels very happy because they have won a victory or have achieved something *E.G. a triumphant shout.*

**trivia**
PLURAL NOUN Trivia are unimportant things.

**trivial**
ADJECTIVE Something trivial is unimportant.
🏛 from Latin *trivialis* meaning 'found everywhere'

**troll** trolls
NOUN an imaginary creature in Scandinavian mythology that lives in caves or mountains and is believed

a
b
c
d
e
f
g
h
i
j
k
l
m
n
o
p
q
r
s
t
u
v
w
x
y
z

A
B
C
D
E
F
G
H
I
J
K
L
M
N
O
P
Q
R
S
T
U
V
W
X
Y
Z

to turn to stone at daylight.

**trolley** trolleys
NOUN **1** a small table on wheels. **2** a small cart on wheels used for carrying heavy objects *E.G. a supermarket trolley.*

**trombone** trombones
NOUN a brass wind instrument with a U-shaped slide which you move to produce different notes.

**troop** troops trooping trooped
NOUN **1** Troops are soldiers. **2** A troop of people or animals is a group of them. ▶ VERB **3** If people troop somewhere, they go there in a group.

**trooper** troopers
NOUN a low-ranking soldier in the cavalry.

**trophy** trophies
NOUN **1** a cup or shield given as a prize to the winner of a competition. **2** something you keep to remember a success or victory.
🏛 from Greek *trope* meaning 'defeat of the enemy'

**tropical**
ADJECTIVE belonging to or typical of the tropics *E.G. a tropical island.*

**tropics**
PLURAL NOUN The tropics are the hottest parts of the world between two lines of latitude, the Tropic of Cancer, 232° north of the equator, and the Tropic of Capricorn, 232° south of the equator.

**trot** trots trotting trotted
VERB **1** When a horse trots, it moves at a speed between a walk and a canter, lifting its feet quite high off the ground. **2** If you trot, you run or jog using small quick steps. ▶ NOUN **3** When a horse breaks into a trot, it starts trotting.

**trotter** trotters
NOUN A pig's trotters are its feet.

**trouble** troubles troubling troubled
NOUN **1** Troubles are difficulties or problems. **2** If there is trouble, people are quarrelling or fighting *E.G. There was more trouble after the match.*
▶ PHRASE **3** If you are **in trouble**, you are in a situation where you may be punished because you have done something wrong. ▶ VERB **4** If something troubles you, it makes you feel worried or anxious. **5** If you trouble someone for something, you disturb them in order to ask them for it *E.G. Can I trouble you for milk?*

**troubling** ADJECTIVE **troubled** ADJECTIVE
▤ (sense 1) difficulty, problem, worry
▤ (sense 5) bother, inconvenience

**troublesome**
ADJECTIVE causing problems or difficulties *E.G. a troublesome teenager.*

**trough** troughs
*Said* "troff" NOUN a long, narrow container from which animals drink or feed.

**trounce** trounces trouncing trounced
VERB If you trounce someone, you defeat them completely.

**troupe** troupes
*Said* "troop" NOUN a group of actors, singers, or dancers who work together and often travel around together.

**trousers**
PLURAL NOUN Trousers are a piece of clothing covering the body from the

waist down, enclosing each leg separately.

🖾 from Gaelic *triubhas*

**trout**

NOUN a type of freshwater fish.

**trowel trowels**

NOUN **1** a small garden tool with a curved, pointed blade used for planting or weeding. **2** a small tool with a flat blade used for spreading cement or plaster.

**truant truants**

NOUN **1** a child who stays away from school without permission. ► PHRASE **2** If children **play truant**, they stay away from school without permission.

**truancy** NOUN

**truce truces**

NOUN an agreement between two people or groups to stop fighting for a short time.

**truck trucks**

NOUN **1** a large motor vehicle used for carrying heavy loads. **2** an open vehicle used for carrying goods on a railway.

**truculent**

*Said* "truk-*yoo*-lent" ADJECTIVE bad-tempered and aggressive.

**truculence** NOUN

**trudge trudges trudging trudged**

VERB **1** If you trudge, you walk with slow, heavy steps. ► NOUN **2** a slow tiring walk *E.G. the long trudge home.*

**true truer truest**

ADJECTIVE **1** A true story or statement is based on facts and is not made up. **2** 'True' is used to describe things or people that are genuine *E.G. She was a true friend.* **3** True feelings are sincere and genuine. ► PHRASE **4** If

something **comes true**, it actually happens.

**truly** ADVERB

📘 (sense 1) accurate, correct, factual

**truffle truffles**

NOUN **1** a soft, round sweet. **2** a round mushroom-like fungus which grows underground and is considered very good to eat.

**trump trumps**

NOUN In a game of cards, trumps is the suit with the highest value.

**trumpet trumpets trumpeting trumpeted**

NOUN **1** a brass wind instrument with a narrow tube ending in a bell-like shape. ► VERB **2** When an elephant trumpets, it makes a sound like a very loud trumpet.

**truncated**

ADJECTIVE Something that is truncated is made shorter.

**truncheon truncheons**

*Said* "**trunt**-shn" NOUN a stick carried by police officers as a weapon, especially the short, thick kind formerly used by British police.

🖾 from Old French *tronchon* meaning 'stump'

**trundle trundles trundling trundled**

VERB If you trundle something or it trundles somewhere, it moves or rolls along slowly.

**trunk trunks**

NOUN **1** the main stem of a tree from which the branches and roots grow. **2** the main part of your body, excluding your head, neck, arms, and legs. **3** the long flexible nose of an elephant. **4** a large, strong case or box with a hinged lid used for storing things. ► PLURAL NOUN **5** A man's

a b c d e f g h i j k l m n o p q r s **t** u v w x y z

I always visit my FRIend on a FRIday (**fri**end)    SPELLING NOTE trunks are his bathing pants or shorts.

**truss trusses trussing trussed**
VERB **1** To truss someone or truss them up is to tie them up so that they cannot move. ▶ NOUN **2** a supporting belt with a pad worn by a man with a hernia.

**trust trusts trusting trusted**
VERB **1** If you trust someone, you believe that they are honest and will not harm you. **2** If you trust someone to do something, you believe they will do it successfully or properly. **3** If you trust someone with something, you give it to them or tell it to them E.G. *One member of the group cannot be trusted with the secret.* **4** If you do not trust something, you feel that it is not safe or reliable E.G. *I didn't trust my arms and legs to work.* ▶ NOUN **5** Trust is the responsibility you are given to deal with or look after important or secret things E.G. *He had built up a position of trust.* **6** a financial arrangement in which an organization looks after and invests money for someone.
**trusting** ADJECTIVE

**trustee trustees**
NOUN someone who is allowed by law to control money or property they are keeping or investing for another person.

**trustworthy**
ADJECTIVE A trustworthy person is reliable and responsible and can be trusted.

**trusty trustier trustiest**
ADJECTIVE Trusty things and animals are considered to be reliable because they have always worked well in the past E.G. *a trusty black labrador.*

**truth truths**
NOUN **1** The truth is the facts about something, rather than things that are imagined or made up E.G. *I know she was telling the truth.* **2** an idea or principle that is generally accepted to be true E.G. *the basic truths in life.*
■ (sense 1) fact, reality

**truthful**
ADJECTIVE A truthful person is honest and tells the truth.
**truthfully** ADVERB

**try tries trying tried**
VERB **1** To try to do something is to make an effort to do it. **2** If you try something, you use it or do it to test how useful or enjoyable it is E.G. *Howard wanted me to try the wine.* **3** When a person is tried, they appear in court and a judge and jury decide if they are guilty after hearing the evidence. ▶ NOUN **4** an attempt to do something. **5** a test of something E.G. *You gave it a try.* **6** In rugby, a try is scored when someone carries the ball over the goal line of the opposing team and touches the ground with it.
■ (sense 1) attempt, endeavour, strive
■ (sense 4) attempt, go, shot
☑ You can use *try to* in speech and writing: *try to get here on time for once.* Try and is very common is speech, but you should avoid it in written work: *just try and stop me!.*

**trying**
ADJECTIVE Something or someone trying is difficult to deal with and makes you feel impatient or annoyed.

**tryst trysts**
*Said* "**trist**" NOUN an appointment or

A B C D E F G H I J K L M N O P Q R S T U V W X Y Z

meeting, especially between lovers in a quiet, secret place.

**tsar tsars**
*Said* "zar"; also spelt **czar**
NOUN a Russian emperor or king between 1547 and 1917.

**tsarina tsarinas**
*Said* "zah-**ree**-na"; also spelt **czarina**
NOUN a female tsar or the wife of a tsar.

**tsetse fly tsetse flies**
*Said* "**tset**-tsee" NOUN an African fly that feeds on blood and causes serious diseases in people and animals.

**T-shirt T-shirts**; also spelt **tee shirt**
NOUN a simple short-sleeved cotton shirt with no collar.

**tsunami tsunamis**
NOUN a large, often destructive sea wave, caused by an earthquake or volcanic eruption under the sea.
▣ from Japanese *tsunami* meaning 'harbour wave'

**tuatara tuatara** or **tuataras**
*Said* "too-ah-**tah**-rah" NOUN a large, lizard-like reptile found on certain islands off the coast of New Zealand.

**tub tubs**
NOUN a wide circular container.

**tuba tubas**
NOUN a large brass musical instrument that can produce very low notes.

**tubby tubbier tubbiest**
ADJECTIVE rather fat.

**tube tubes**
NOUN 1 a round, hollow pipe. 2 a soft metal or plastic cylindrical container with a screw cap at one end *E.G. a tube of toothpaste.*

**tubing** NOUN

**tuberculosis**
*Said* "tyoo-ber-kyoo-**low**-siss" NOUN Tuberculosis is a serious infectious disease affecting the lungs.

**tubular**
ADJECTIVE in the shape of a tube.

**TUC**
In Britain, an abbreviation for 'Trades Union Congress', which is an association of trade unions.

**tuck tucks tucking tucked**
VERB 1 If you tuck something somewhere, you put it there so that it is safe or comfortable *E.G. She tucked the letter into her handbag.* 2 If you tuck a piece of fabric into or under something, you push the loose ends inside or under it to make it tidy. 3 If something is tucked away, it is in a quiet place where few people go *E.G. a little house tucked away in a valley.*

**tucker tuckers tuckering tuckered** INFORMAL
NOUN 1 In Australian and New Zealand English, tucker is food. ▶ VERB 2 In Australian and New Zealand English, if you are tuckered out you are tired out.

**Tudor Tudors**
NOUN Tudor was the family name of the English monarchs who reigned from 1485 to 1603.

**Tuesday Tuesdays**
NOUN Tuesday is the day between Monday and Wednesday.
▣ from Old English *tiwesdæg* meaning 'Tiw's day'; Tiw was the Scandinavian god of war and the sky

**tuft tufts**
NOUN A tuft of something such as hair is a bunch of it growing closely together.

a
b
c
d
e
f
g
h
i
j
k
l
m
n
o
p
q
r
s
t
u
v
w
x
y
z

The government licenSes Schnapps (licenses)    SPELLING NOTE

A
B
C
D
E
F
G
H
I
J
K
L
M
N
O
P
Q
R
S
T
U
V
W
X
Y
Z

**tug** tugs tugging tugged
VERB **1** To tug something is to give it a quick, hard pull. ▶ NOUN **2** a quick, hard pull *E.G. He felt a tug at his arm.* **3** a small, powerful boat which tows large ships.

**tug of war**
NOUN A tug of war is a sport in which two teams test their strength by pulling against each other on opposite ends of a rope.

**tuition**
NOUN Tuition is the teaching of a subject, especially to one person or to a small group.

**tulip** tulips
NOUN a brightly coloured spring flower.
🏛 from Turkish *tulbend* meaning 'turban', because of its shape

**tumble** tumbles tumbling tumbled
VERB **1** To tumble is to fall with a rolling or bouncing movement. ▶ NOUN **2** a fall.

**tumbler** tumblers
NOUN a drinking glass with straight sides.

**tummy** tummies
NOUN; *INFORMAL* Your tummy is your stomach.

**tumour** tumours
*Said* "tyoo-mur" NOUN a mass of diseased or abnormal cells that has grown in a person's or animal's body.

**tumultuous**
ADJECTIVE A tumultuous event or welcome is very noisy because people are happy or excited.

**tuna**
*Said* "tyoo-na" NOUN Tuna are large fish that live in warm seas and are caught for food.

**tundra**
NOUN The tundra is a vast treeless Arctic region.
🏛 a Russian word

**tune** tunes tuning tuned
NOUN **1** a series of musical notes arranged in a particular way. ▶ VERB **2** To tune a musical instrument is to adjust it so that it produces the right notes. **3** To tune an engine or machine is to adjust it so that it works well. **4** If you tune to a particular radio or television station you turn or press the controls to select the station you want to listen to or watch. ▶ PHRASE **5** If your voice or an instrument is **in tune**, it produces the right notes.

**tuneful**
ADJECTIVE having a pleasant and easily remembered tune.

**tuner** tuners
NOUN A piano tuner is a person whose job it is to tune pianos.

**tunic** tunics
NOUN a sleeveless garment covering the top part of the body and reaching to the hips, thighs, or knees.

**Tunisian** Tunisians
*Said* "tyoo-**niz**-ee-an" ADJECTIVE **1** belonging or relating to Tunisia. ▶ NOUN **2** someone who comes from Tunisia.

**tunnel** tunnels tunnelling tunnelled
NOUN **1** a long underground passage. ▶ VERB **2** To tunnel is to make a tunnel.

**turban** turbans
NOUN a head-covering worn by a Hindu, Muslim, or Sikh man, consisting of a long piece of cloth wound round his head.

**turbine** turbines
NOUN a machine or engine in which power is produced when a stream of air, gas, water, or steam pushes the blades of a wheel and makes it turn round.
🏛 from Latin *turbo* meaning 'whirlwind'

**turbot**
*Said* "**tur**-bot" NOUN a large European flat fish that is caught for food.

**turbulent**
ADJECTIVE 1 A turbulent period of history is one where there is much uncertainty, and possibly violent change. 2 Turbulent air or water currents make sudden changes of direction.
**turbulence** NOUN

**tureen** tureens
*Said* "tur-**reen**" NOUN a large dish with a lid for serving soup.

**turf** turves; turfs turfing turfed
NOUN Turf is short thick even grass and the layer of soil beneath it.
**turf out** VERB; *INFORMAL* To turf someone out is to force them to leave a place.

**turgid**
*Said* "**tur**-jid" ADJECTIVE *LITERARY* A turgid play, film, or piece of writing is difficult to understand and rather boring.

**Turk** Turks
NOUN someone who comes from Turkey.

**turkey** turkeys
NOUN a large bird kept for food; also the meat of this bird.

**Turkish**
ADJECTIVE 1 belonging or relating to Turkey. ► NOUN 2 Turkish is the main language spoken in Turkey.

**turmoil**
NOUN Turmoil is a state of confusion, disorder, or great anxiety *E.G. Europe is in a state of turmoil.*

**turn** turns turning turned
VERB 1 When you turn, you move so that you are facing or going in a different direction. 2 When you turn something or when it turns, it moves or rotates so that it faces in a different direction or is in a different position. 3 If you turn your attention or thoughts to someone or something, you start thinking about them or discussing them. 4 When something turns or is turned into something else, it becomes something different *E.G. A hobby can be turned into a career.* ► NOUN 5 an act of turning something so that it faces in a different direction or is in a different position. 6 a change in the way something is happening or being done *E.G. Her career took a turn for the worse.* 7 If it is your turn to do something, you have the right, chance, or duty to do it. ► PHRASE 8 **In turn** is used to refer to people, things, or actions that are in sequence one after the other.
📊 (sense 7) chance, go, opportunity

**turn down** VERB If you turn down someone's request or offer, you refuse or reject it.

**turn up** VERB 1 If someone or something turns up, they arrive or appear somewhere. 2 If something turns up, it is found or discovered.

**turncoat** turncoats
NOUN a person who leaves one political party or group for an opposing one.

**turning** turnings
NOUN a road which leads away from

a b c d e f g h i j k l m n o p q r s t u v w x y z

Plaice the fish has a glittering 'EYE' (I) (plaice)  **SPELLING NOTE**

A B C D E F G H I J K L M N O P Q R S T U V W X Y Z

the side of another road.

**turning point** turning points

NOUN the moment when decisions are taken and events start to move in a different direction.

**turnip** turnips

NOUN a round root vegetable with a white or yellow skin.

**turnout** turnouts

NOUN The turnout at an event is the number of people who go to it.

**turnover** turnovers

NOUN 1 The turnover of people in a particular organization or group is the rate at which people leave it and are replaced by others. 2 The turnover of a company is the value of the goods or services sold during a particular period.

**turnstile** turnstiles

NOUN a revolving mechanical barrier at the entrance to places like football grounds or zoos.

**turpentine**

NOUN Turpentine is a strong-smelling colourless liquid used for cleaning and for thinning paint.

**turps**

NOUN Turps is turpentine.

**turquoise**

Said "tur-kwoyz" NOUN or ADJECTIVE 1 light bluish-green. ▶ NOUN 2 Turquoise is a bluish-green stone used in jewellery.

**turret** turrets

NOUN a small narrow tower on top of a larger tower or other buildings.

**turtle** turtles

NOUN a large reptile with a thick shell covering its body and flippers for swimming. It lays its eggs on land but lives the rest of its life in the sea.

**tusk** tusks

NOUN The tusks of an elephant, wild boar, or walrus are the pair of long curving pointed teeth it has.

**tussle** tussles

NOUN an energetic fight or argument between two people, especially about something they both want.

**tutor** tutors tutoring tutored

NOUN 1 a teacher at a college or university. 2 a private teacher. ▶ VERB 3 If someone tutors a person or subject, they teach that person or subject.

**tutorial** tutorials

NOUN a teaching session involving a tutor and a small group of students.

**tutu** tutus

Said "too-too" NOUN a short stiff skirt worn by female ballet dancers.

**TV** TVs

NOUN 1 TV is television. 2 a television set.

**twang** twangs twanging twanged

NOUN 1 a sound like the one made by pulling and then releasing a tight wire. 2 A twang is a nasal quality in a person's voice. ▶ VERB 3 If a tight wire or string twangs or you twang it, it makes a sound as it is pulled and then released.

**tweak** tweaks tweaking tweaked

VERB 1 If you tweak something, you twist it or pull it. ▶ NOUN 2 a short twist or pull of something.

**twee**

ADJECTIVE sweet and pretty but in bad taste or sentimental.

**tweed** tweeds

NOUN Tweed is a thick woollen cloth.

**tweet** tweets tweeting tweeted

VERB 1 When a small bird tweets, it makes a short, high-pitched sound.

SPELLING NOTE    I went to see (C) the doctor's new practiCe (practice)

▶ NOUN **2** a short high-pitched sound made by a small bird.

**tweezers**

PLURAL NOUN Tweezers are a small tool with two arms which can be closed together and are used for pulling out hairs or picking up small objects.

**twelve**

the number 12.

**twelfth**

**twenty twenties**

the number 20.

**twentieth**

**twice**

ADVERB Twice means two times.

**twiddle twiddles twiddling twiddled**

VERB To twiddle something is to twist it or turn it quickly.

**twig twigs**

NOUN a very small thin branch growing from a main branch of a tree or bush.

**twilight**

Said "twy-lite" NOUN **1** Twilight is the time after sunset when it is just getting dark. **2** The twilight of something is the final stages of it E.G. the twilight of his career.

**twin twins**

NOUN **1** If two people are twins, they have the same mother and were born on the same day. **2** 'Twin' is used to describe two similar things that are close together or happen together E.G. the little twin islands.

**twine twines twining twined**

NOUN **1** Twine is strong smooth string. ▶ VERB **2** If you twine one thing round another, you twist or wind it round.

**twinge twinges**

NOUN a sudden, unpleasant feeling E.G. a twinge of jealousy.

**twinkle twinkles twinkling twinkled**

VERB **1** If something twinkles, it sparkles or seems to sparkle with an unsteady light E.G. Her green eyes twinkled. ▶ NOUN **2** a sparkle or brightness that something has.

**twirl twirls twirling twirled**

VERB If something twirls, or if you twirl it, it spins or twists round and round.

**twist twists twisting twisted**

VERB **1** When you twist something you turn one end of it in one direction while holding the other end or turning it in the opposite direction. **2** When something twists or is twisted, it moves or bends into a strange shape. **3** If you twist a part of your body, you injure it by turning it too sharply or in an unusual direction E.G. I've twisted my ankle. **4** If you twist something that someone has said, you change the meaning slightly. ▶ NOUN **5** a twisting action or motion. **6** an unexpected development or event in a story or film, especially at the end E.G. Each day now seemed to bring a new twist to the story.

■ (sense 1) coil, wind
■ (sense 2) contort, distort

**twisted**

ADJECTIVE **1** Something twisted has been bent or moved into a strange shape E.G. a tangle of twisted metal. **2** If someone's mind or behaviour is twisted, it is unpleasantly abnormal E.G. He's bitter and twisted.

**twit twits**

NOUN; INFORMAL a silly person.

**twitch twitches twitching twitched**

VERB **1** If you twitch, you make little

A
B
C
D
E
F
G
H
I
J
K
L
M
N
O
P
Q
R
S
T
U
V
W
X
Y
Z

jerky movements which you cannot control. **2** If you twitch something, you give it a little jerk in order to move it. ▶ NOUN **3** a little jerky movement.

**twitter** twitters twittering twittered
VERB When birds twitter, they make short high-pitched sounds.

**two**
the number 2
☑ Do not confuse the spelling of the preposition *to*, the adverb *too*, and the number *two*.

**two-faced**
ADJECTIVE A two-faced person is not honest in the way they behave towards other people.

**twofold**
ADJECTIVE Something twofold has two equally important parts or reasons E.G. *Their concern was twofold: personal and political.*

**twosome** twosomes
*Said* "**too**-sum" NOUN two people or things that are usually seen together.

**two-time** two-times two-timing two-timed
VERB; *INFORMAL* If you two-time your boyfriend or girlfriend, you deceive them, by having a romantic relationship with someone else without telling them.

**two-up**
NOUN In Australia and New Zealand, two-up is a popular gambling game in which two coins are tossed and bets are placed on whether they land heads or tails.

**tycoon** tycoons
NOUN a person who is successful in business and has become rich and powerful.

🈺 from Chinese *ta* + *chun* meaning 'great ruler'

**type** types typing typed
NOUN **1** A type of something is a class of it that has common features and belongs to a larger group of related things E.G. *What type of dog should we get?* **2** A particular type of person has a particular appearance or quality E.G. *Andrea is the type who likes to play safe.* ▶ VERB **3** If you type something, you use a typewriter or word processor to write it.

**typewriter** typewriters
NOUN a machine with a keyboard with individual keys which are pressed to produce letters and numbers on a page.

**typhoid**
*Said* "**tie**-foyd" NOUN Typhoid, or typhoid fever, is an infectious disease caused by dirty water or food. It produces fever and can kill.

**typhoon** typhoons
NOUN a very violent tropical storm.
🈺 from Chinese *tai fung* meaning 'great wind'

**typhus**
NOUN Typhus is an infectious disease transmitted by lice or mites. It results in fever, severe headaches, and a skin rash.

**typical**
ADJECTIVE showing the most usual characteristics or behaviour.
**typically** ADVERB
🔲 characteristic, standard, usual

**typify** typifies typifying typified
VERB If something typifies a situation or thing, it is characteristic of it or a typical example of it E.G. *This story is one that typifies our times.*

**typing**

NOUN Typing is the work or activity of producing something on a typewriter.

**typist** typists

NOUN a person whose job is typing.

**tyrannosaurus** tyrannosauruses

*Said* "tir-ran-oh-**saw**-russ" NOUN a very large meat-eating dinosaur which walked upright on its hind legs.

📖 from Greek *turannos* meaning 'tyrant' and Latin *saurus* meaning 'lizard'

**tyranny** tyrannies

NOUN **1** A tyranny is cruel and unjust rule of people by a person or group *E.G. the evils of Nazi tyranny.* **2** You can refer to something which is not human but is harsh as tyranny *E.G. the tyranny of drugs.*

**tyrannical** ADJECTIVE

**tyrant** tyrants

NOUN a person who treats the people he or she has authority over cruelly and unjustly.

**tyre** tyres

NOUN a thick ring of rubber fitted round each wheel of a vehicle and filled with air.

a b c d e f g h i j k l m n o p q r s t u v w x y z

LEarn the principLEs (principLe)   **SPELLING NOTE**

# Uu

## ubiquitous
*Said* "yoo-**bik**-wit-tuss" ADJECTIVE
Something that is ubiquitous seems
to be everywhere at the same time
*E.G. the ubiquitous jeans.*
📖 from Latin *ubique* meaning
'everywhere'

## udder udders
NOUN the baglike organ that hangs
below a cow's body and produces
milk.

## UFO UFOs
NOUN a strange object seen in the sky,
which some people believe to be a
spaceship from another planet. UFO
is an abbreviation for 'unidentified
flying object'.

## Ugandan Ugandans
*Said* "yoo-**gan**-dan" ADJECTIVE
1 belonging or relating to Uganda.
▶ NOUN 2 someone who comes from
Uganda.

## ugly uglier ugliest
ADJECTIVE very unattractive in
appearance.
📖 from Old Norse *uggligr* meaning
'terrifying'
🔳 plain, unattractive, unsightly

## UK
an abbreviation for United
Kingdom.

## ulcer ulcers
NOUN a sore area on the skin or inside
the body, which takes a long time to
heal *E.G. stomach ulcers.*

## ulterior
*Said* "ul-**teer**-ee-or" ADJECTIVE If you
have an ulterior motive for doing
something, you have a hidden
reason for it.

## ultimate
ADJECTIVE 1 final or eventual *E.G.
Olympic gold is the ultimate goal.*
2 most important or powerful *E.G. the
ultimate ambition of any player.*
▶ NOUN 3 You can refer to the best or
most advanced example of
something as the ultimate *E.G. This
hotel is the ultimate in luxury.*
**ultimately** ADVERB

## ultimatum ultimatums
*Said* "ul-tim-**may**-tum" NOUN a
warning stating that unless someone
meets your conditions, you will take
action against them.

## ultra-
PREFIX 'Ultra-' is used to form
adjectives describing something as
having a quality to an extreme
degree *E.G. the ultra-competitive world
of sport today.*

## ultramarine
NOUN OR ADJECTIVE bright blue.
📖 from Latin *ultramarinus* meaning
'beyond the sea', because the
pigment was imported from abroad

## ultrasonic
ADJECTIVE An ultrasonic sound has a
very high frequency that cannot be
heard by the human ear.

## ultrasound
NOUN sound which cannot be heard
by the human ear because its
frequency is too high.

## ultraviolet
ADJECTIVE Ultraviolet light is not visible
to the human eye. It is a form of
radiation that causes your skin to
darken after being exposed to the sun.

## umbilical cord umbilical cords
*Said* "um-**bil**-lik-kl" NOUN the tube of

blood vessels which connects an unborn baby to its mother and through which the baby receives nutrients and oxygen.

**umbrella** umbrellas
NOUN a device that you use to protect yourself from the rain. It consists of a folding frame covered in cloth attached to a long stick.

**umpire** umpires umpiring umpired
NOUN 1 The umpire in cricket or tennis is the person who makes sure that the game is played according to the rules and who makes a decision if there is a dispute. ▶ VERB 2 If you umpire a game, you are the umpire.

**umpteen**
ADJECTIVE; INFORMAL very many E.G. tomatoes and umpteen other plants. **umpteenth** ADJECTIVE

**un-**
PREFIX Un- is added to the beginning of many words to form a word with the opposite meaning E.G. an uncomfortable chair… He unlocked the door.

**unabashed**
ADJECTIVE not embarrassed or discouraged by something E.G. Samuel was continuing unabashed.

**unabated**
ADJECTIVE or ADVERB continuing without any reduction in intensity or amount E.G. The noise continued unabated.

**unable**
ADJECTIVE If you are unable to do something, you cannot do it.

**unacceptable**
ADJECTIVE very bad or of a very low standard.

**unaccompanied**
ADJECTIVE alone.

**unaccustomed**
ADJECTIVE If you are unaccustomed to something, you are not used to it.

**unaffected**
ADJECTIVE 1 not changed in any way by a particular thing E.G. unaffected by the recession. 2 behaving in a natural and genuine way E.G. the most down-to-earth unaffected person I've ever met.

**unaided**
ADVERB or ADJECTIVE without help E.G. He was incapable of walking unaided.

**unambiguous**
ADJECTIVE An unambiguous statement has only one meaning.

**unanimous**
Said "yoon-**nan**-nim-mus" ADJECTIVE When people are unanimous, they all agree about something.
**unanimously** ADVERB    **unanimity** NOUN
📖 from Latin unanimus meaning 'of one mind'

**unannounced**
ADJECTIVE happening unexpectedly and without warning.

**unarmed**
ADJECTIVE not carrying any weapons.

**unassuming**
ADJECTIVE modest and quiet.

**unattached**
ADJECTIVE An unattached person is not married and is not having a steady relationship with someone.

**unattended**
ADJECTIVE not being watched or looked after E.G. an unattended handbag.

**unauthorized** or **unauthorised**
ADJECTIVE done without official permission E.G. unauthorized parking.

a b c d e f g h i j k l m n o p q r s t u v w x y z

A
B
C
D
E
F
G
H
I
J
K
L
M
N
O
P
Q
R
S
T
U
V
W
X
Y
Z

**unavoidable**
ADJECTIVE unable to be prevented or
avoided.

**unaware**
ADJECTIVE If you are unaware of
something, you do not know about
it
☑ *Unaware* is usually followed by *of*
or *that*. Do not confuse it with the
adverb *unawares*.

**unawares**
ADVERB If something catches you
unawares, it happens when you are
not expecting it
☑ Do not confuse *unawares* with
the adjective *unaware*.

**unbalanced**
ADJECTIVE 1 with more weight or
emphasis on one side than the other
*E.G. an unbalanced load… an
unbalanced relationship.* 2 slightly
mad. 3 made up of parts that do not
work well together *E.G. an
unbalanced lifestyle.* 4 An unbalanced
account of something is an unfair
one because it emphasizes some
things and ignores others.

**unbearable**
ADJECTIVE Something unbearable is so
unpleasant or upsetting that you feel
you cannot stand it *E.G. The pain was
unbearable.*
**unbearably** ADVERB
▤ insufferable, intolerable

**unbeatable**
ADJECTIVE Something that is
unbeatable is the best thing of its
kind.

**unbelievable**
ADJECTIVE 1 extremely great or
surprising *E.G. unbelievable courage.*
2 so unlikely that you cannot believe it.
**unbelievably** ADVERB

▤ (sense 1) astonishing, incredible
▤ (sense 2) far-fetched, implausible

**unborn**
ADJECTIVE not yet born.

**unbroken**
ADJECTIVE continuous or complete *E.G.
ten days of almost unbroken sunshine.*

**uncanny**
ADJECTIVE strange and difficult to
explain *E.G. an uncanny resemblance.*
🔳 from Scottish *uncanny* meaning
'unreliable' or 'not safe to deal with'

**uncertain**
ADJECTIVE 1 not knowing what to do
*E.G. For a minute he looked uncertain.*
2 doubtful or not known *E.G. The
outcome of the war was uncertain.*
**uncertainty** NOUN

**unchallenged**
ADJECTIVE accepted without any
questions being asked *E.G. We can't
let this enormous theft go
unchallenged.*

**uncharacteristic**
ADJECTIVE not typical or usual *E.G. My
father reacted with uncharacteristic
speed.*

**uncivilized** or **uncivilised**
ADJECTIVE unacceptable, for example
by being very cruel or rude *E.G. the
uncivilized behaviour of football
hooligans.*

**uncle** uncles
NOUN the brother of your mother or
father or the husband of your aunt.

**unclean**
ADJECTIVE dirty *E.G. unclean water.*

**unclear**
ADJECTIVE confusing and not obvious.

**uncomfortable**
ADJECTIVE 1 If you are uncomfortable,
you are not physically relaxed and
feel slight pain or discomfort.

SPELLING NOTE    Rhythmical Hounds Yap To Heavy Music (<u>rhythm</u>)

**2** Uncomfortable also means slightly worried or embarrassed.
**uncomfortably** ADVERB

**uncommon**
ADJECTIVE **1** not happening often or not seen often. **2** unusually great *E.G. She had read Cecilia's last letter with uncommon interest.*
**uncommonly** ADVERB

**uncompromising**
ADJECTIVE determined not to change an opinion or aim in any way *E.G. an uncompromising approach to life.*
**uncompromisingly** ADVERB

**unconcerned**
ADJECTIVE not interested in something or not worried about it.

**unconditional**
ADJECTIVE with no conditions or limitations *E.G. a full three-year unconditional guarantee.*
**unconditionally** ADVERB

**unconscious**
ADJECTIVE **1** Someone who is unconscious is asleep or in a state similar to sleep as a result of a shock, accident, or injury. **2** If you are unconscious of something, you are not aware of it.
**unconsciously** ADVERB

**uncontrollable**
ADJECTIVE If someone or something is uncontrollable, they or it cannot be controlled or stopped *E.G. uncontrollable anger.*
**uncontrollably** ADVERB

**unconventional**
ADJECTIVE not behaving in the same way as most other people.

**unconvinced**
ADJECTIVE not at all certain that something is true or right *E.G. Some critics remain unconvinced by the*

*plan.*

**uncouth**
*Said "un-**kooth**"* ADJECTIVE bad-mannered and unpleasant.
■ boorish, coarse, vulgar

**uncover** uncovers uncovering uncovered
VERB **1** If you uncover a secret, you find it out. **2** To uncover something is to remove the cover or lid from it.

**undaunted**
ADJECTIVE If you are undaunted by something disappointing, you are not discouraged by it.

**undecided**
ADJECTIVE If you are undecided, you have not yet made a decision about something.

**undemanding**
ADJECTIVE not difficult to do or deal with *E.G. undemanding work.*

**undeniable**
ADJECTIVE certainly true *E.G. undeniable evidence.*
**undeniably** ADVERB

**under**
PREPOSITION **1** below or beneath. **2** You can use 'under' to say that a person or thing is affected by a particular situation or condition *E.G. The country was under threat… Animals are kept under unnatural conditions.* **3** If someone studies or works under a particular person, that person is their teacher or their boss. **4** less than *E.G. under five kilometres… children under the age of 14.* ▶ PHRASE **5** **Under way** means already started *E.G. A murder investigation is already under way.*

**under-**
PREFIX 'Under-' is used in words that describe something as not being

a
b
c
d
e
f
g
h
i
j
k
l
m
n
o
p
q
r
s
**u**
v
w
x
y
z

A B C D E F G H I J K L M N O P Q R S T U V W X Y Z

provided to a sufficient extent or not having happened to a sufficient extent.

**underarm**
ADJECTIVE **1** under your arm *E.G. underarm hair.* ► ADVERB **2** If you throw a ball underarm, you throw it without raising your arm over your shoulder.

**undercarriage** undercarriages
NOUN The part of an aircraft, including the wheels, that supports the aircraft when it is on the ground.

**underclass**
NOUN The underclass is the people in society who are the most poor and whose situation is unlikely to improve.

**underclothes**
PLURAL NOUN Your underclothes are the clothes that you wear under your other clothes and next to your skin.

**undercover**
ADJECTIVE involving secret work to obtain information *E.G. a police undercover operation.*

**undercurrent** undercurrents
NOUN a weak, partly hidden feeling that may become stronger later.

**undercut** undercuts undercutting undercut
VERB **1** To undercut someone's prices is to sell a product more cheaply than they do. **2** If something undercuts your attempts to achieve something, it prevents them from being effective.

**underdeveloped**
ADJECTIVE An underdeveloped country does not have modern industries, and usually has a low standard of living.

**underdog** underdogs
NOUN The underdog in a competition is the person who seems likely to lose.

**underestimate** underestimates underestimating underestimated
VERB If you underestimate something or someone, you do not realize how large, great, or capable they are.

**underfoot**
ADJECTIVE OR ADVERB under your feet *E.G. the icy ground underfoot.*

**undergo** undergoes undergoing underwent undergone
VERB If you undergo something unpleasant, it happens to you.

**underground**
ADJECTIVE **1** below the surface of the ground. **2** secret, unofficial, and usually illegal. ► NOUN **3** The underground is a railway system in which trains travel in tunnels below ground.

**undergrowth**
NOUN Small bushes and plants growing under trees are called the undergrowth.

**underhand**
ADJECTIVE secret and dishonest *E.G. underhand behaviour.*

**underlie** underlies underlying underlay underlain
VERB The thing that underlies a situation is the cause or basis of it. **underlying** ADJECTIVE

**underline** underlines underlining underlined
VERB **1** If something underlines a feeling or a problem, it emphasizes it. **2** If you underline a word or sentence, you draw a line under it.

**underling** underlings
NOUN someone who is less important than someone else in rank or status.

**undermine** undermines
undermining undermined
VERB To undermine an idea, feeling, or
system is to make it less strong or
secure *E.G. You're trying to undermine
my confidence again.*
⛏ from the practice in warfare of
digging tunnels under enemy
fortifications in order to make them
collapse
🔲 subvert, weaken

**underneath**
PREPOSITION **1** below or beneath.
▶ ADVERB or PREPOSITION **2** Underneath
describes feelings and qualities that
do not show in your behaviour *E.G.
Alex knew that underneath she was
shattered.* ▶ ADJECTIVE **3** The
underneath part of something is the
part that touches or faces the
ground.

**underpants**
PLURAL NOUN Underpants are a piece of
clothing worn by men and boys
under their trousers.

**underpass** underpasses
NOUN a road or footpath that goes
under a road or railway.

**underpin** underpins
underpinning underpinned
VERB If something underpins
something else, it helps it to
continue by supporting and
strengthening it *E.G. Australian skill is
usually underpinned by an immense
team spirit.*

**underprivileged**
ADJECTIVE Underprivileged people
have less money and fewer
opportunities than other people.

**underrate** underrates
underrating underrated
VERB If you underrate someone, you

do not realize how clever or valuable
they are.

**understand** understands
understanding understood
VERB **1** If you understand what
someone says, you know what they
mean. **2** If you understand a
situation, you know what is
happening and why. **3** If you say that
you understand that something is
the case, you mean that you have
heard that it is the case *E.G. I
understand that she's a lot better now.*
🔲 comprehend, follow, grasp, see

**understandable**
ADJECTIVE If something is
understandable, people can easily
understand it.
**understandably** ADVERB

**understanding** understandings
NOUN **1** If you have an understanding
of something, you have some
knowledge about it. **2** an informal
agreement between people.
▶ ADJECTIVE **3** kind and sympathetic.
🔲 (sense 1) comprehension, grasp,
perception

**understatement**
understatements
NOUN a statement that does not say
fully how true something is *E.G. To say
I was pleased was an
understatement.*

**understudy** understudies
NOUN someone who has learnt a part
in a play so that they can act it if the
main actor or actress is ill.

**undertake** undertakes
undertaking undertook
undertaken
VERB When you undertake a task or
job, you agree to do it.
**undertaking** NOUN

a b c d e f g h i j k l m n o p q r s t u v w x y z

A B C D E F G H I J K L M N O P Q R S T U V W X Y Z

**undertaker** undertakers

NOUN someone whose job is to prepare bodies for burial and arrange funerals.

**undertone** undertones

NOUN **1** If you say something in an undertone, you say it very quietly. **2** If something has undertones of a particular kind, it indirectly suggests ideas of this kind E.G. *unsettling undertones of violence.*

**undervalue** undervalues undervaluing undervalued

VERB If you undervalue something, you think it is less important than it really is.

**underwater**

ADVERB OR ADJECTIVE **1** beneath the surface of the sea, a river, or a lake.
► ADJECTIVE **2** designed to work in water E.G. *an underwater camera.*

**underwear**

NOUN Your underwear is the clothing that you wear under your other clothes, next to your skin.

**underwent**

the past tense of undergo.

**undesirable**

ADJECTIVE unwelcome and likely to cause harm E.G. *undesirable behaviour.*

**undid**

the past tense of undo.

**undisputed**

ADJECTIVE definite and without any doubt E.G. *the undisputed champion.*

**undivided**

ADJECTIVE If you give something your undivided attention, you concentrate on it totally.

**undo** undoes undoing undid undone

VERB **1** If you undo something that is tied up, you untie it. **2** If you undo something that has been done, you reverse the effect of it.

**undoing**

NOUN If something is someone's undoing, it is the cause of their failure.

**undoubted**

ADJECTIVE You use 'undoubted' to emphasize something E.G. *The event was an undoubted success.*
**undoubtedly** ADVERB

**undress** undresses undressing undressed

VERB When you undress, you take off your clothes.

**undue**

ADJECTIVE greater than is reasonable E.G. *undue violence.*
**unduly** ADVERB

**undulating**

ADJECTIVE; *FORMAL* moving gently up and down E.G. *undulating hills.*

**undying**

ADJECTIVE lasting forever E.G. *his undying love for his wife.*

**unearth** unearths unearthing unearthed

VERB If you unearth something that is hidden, you discover it.

**unearthly**

ADJECTIVE strange and unnatural.

**uneasy**

ADJECTIVE If you are uneasy, you feel worried that something may be wrong.
**unease** NOUN **uneasily** ADVERB
**uneasiness** NOUN

**unemployed**

ADJECTIVE **1** without a job E.G. *an unemployed mechanic.* ► NOUN **2** The unemployed are all the people who are without a job.

**unemployment**

NOUN Unemployment is the state of being without a job.

**unending**

ADJECTIVE Something unending has continued for a long time and seems as if it will never stop *E.G. unending joy*.

**unenviable**

ADJECTIVE An unenviable situation is one that you would not like to be in.

**unequal**

ADJECTIVE 1 An unequal society does not offer the same opportunities and privileges to all people. 2 Unequal things are different in size, strength, or ability.

**uneven**

ADJECTIVE 1 An uneven surface is not level or smooth. 2 not the same or consistent *E.G. six lines of uneven length*.

**unevenly** ADVERB

**uneventful**

ADJECTIVE An uneventful period of time is one when nothing interesting happens.

**unexpected**

ADJECTIVE Something unexpected is surprising because it was not thought likely to happen.

**unexpectedly** ADVERB

**unfailing**

ADJECTIVE continuous and not weakening as time passes *E.G. his unfailing cheerfulness*.

**unfair**

ADJECTIVE not right or just.

**unfairly** ADVERB

**unfaithful**

ADJECTIVE If someone is unfaithful to their lover or the person they are married to, they have a sexual relationship with someone else.

**unfamiliar**

ADJECTIVE If something is unfamiliar to you, or if you are unfamiliar with it, you have not seen or heard it before.

**unfashionable**

ADJECTIVE Something that is unfashionable is not popular or is no longer used by many people.

**unfavourable**

ADJECTIVE not encouraging or promising, or not providing any advantage.

**unfit**

ADJECTIVE 1 If you are unfit, your body is not in good condition because you have not been taking enough exercise. 2 Something that is unfit for a particular purpose is not suitable for that purpose.

**unfold** unfolds unfolding unfolded

VERB 1 When a situation unfolds, it develops and becomes known. 2 If you unfold something that has been folded, you open it out so that it is flat.

**unforeseen**

ADJECTIVE happening unexpectedly.

**unforgettable**

ADJECTIVE Something unforgettable is so good or so bad that you are unlikely to forget it.

**unforgettably** ADVERB

**unforgivable**

ADJECTIVE Something unforgivable is so bad or cruel that it can never be forgiven or justified.

**unforgivably** ADVERB

**unfortunate**

ADJECTIVE 1 Someone who is unfortunate is unlucky. 2 If you describe an event as unfortunate,

a
b
c
d
e
f
g
h
i
j
k
l
m
n
o
p
q
r
s
t
u
v
w
x
y
z

'i' before 'e' except after 'c'　　　SPELLING NOTE

A B C D E F G H I J K L M N O P Q R S T U V W X Y Z

you mean that it is a pity that it happened *E.G. an unfortunate accident.*

**unfortunately** ADVERB

**unfounded**

ADJECTIVE Something that is unfounded has no evidence to support it *E.G. unfounded allegations.*

**unfriendly**

ADJECTIVE **1** A person who is unfriendly is not pleasant to you. **2** A place that is unfriendly makes you feel uncomfortable or is not welcoming.

**ungainly**

ADJECTIVE moving in an awkward or clumsy way.

🏛 from Old Norse *ungegn* meaning 'not straight'

**unhappy** unhappier unhappiest

ADJECTIVE **1** sad and depressed. **2** not pleased or satisfied *E.G. I am unhappy at being left out.* **3** If you describe a situation as an unhappy one, you are sorry that it exists *E.G. an unhappy state of affairs.*

**unhappily** ADVERB **unhappiness** NOUN

**unhealthy**

ADJECTIVE **1** likely to cause illness *E.G. an unhealthy lifestyle.* **2** An unhealthy person is often ill.

**unheard-of**

ADJECTIVE never having happened before and therefore surprising or shocking.

**unhinged**

ADJECTIVE Someone who is unhinged is mentally ill.

**unhurried**

ADJECTIVE Unhurried is used to describe actions or movements that are slow and relaxed.

**unicorn** unicorns

NOUN an imaginary animal that looks like a white horse with a straight horn growing from its forehead.

🏛 from Latin *unicornis* meaning 'having one horn'

**unidentified**

ADJECTIVE You say that someone or something is unidentified when nobody knows who or what they are.

**uniform** uniforms

NOUN **1** a special set of clothes worn by people at work or school.
▶ ADJECTIVE **2** Something that is uniform does not vary but is even and regular throughout.

**uniformity** NOUN

**unify** unifies unifying unified

VERB If you unify a number of things, you bring them together.

**unification** NOUN

**unilateral**

ADJECTIVE A unilateral decision or action is one taken by only one of several groups involved in a particular situation.

**unilaterally** ADVERB

**unimaginable**

ADJECTIVE impossible to imagine or understand properly *E.G. a fairyland of unimaginable beauty.*

**unimportant**

ADJECTIVE having very little significance or importance.

▤ insignificant, minor, trivial

**uninhabited**

ADJECTIVE An uninhabited place is a place where nobody lives.

**uninhibited**

ADJECTIVE If you are uninhibited, you behave freely and naturally and show your true feelings.

**unintelligible**

ADJECTIVE; *FORMAL* impossible to understand.

**uninterested**

ADJECTIVE If you are uninterested in something, you are not interested in it.

**uninterrupted**

ADJECTIVE continuing without breaks or interruptions *E.G. uninterrupted views.*

**union** unions

NOUN 1 an organization of workers that aims to improve the working conditions, pay, and benefits of its members. 2 When the union of two things takes place, they are joined together to become one thing.

**unique**

*Said* "yoo-**neek**" ADJECTIVE 1 being the only one of its kind. 2 If something is unique to one person or thing, it concerns or belongs to that person or thing only *E.G. trees and vegetation unique to the Canary islands.*

**uniquely** ADVERB    **uniqueness** NOUN

☑ Something is either *unique* or *not unique*, so you should avoid saying things like *rather unique* or *very unique.*

**unisex**

ADJECTIVE designed to be used by both men and women *E.G. unisex clothing.*

**unison**

NOUN If a group of people do something in unison, they all do it together at the same time.

📖 from Latin *unisonus* meaning 'making the same musical sound'

**unit** units

NOUN 1 If you consider something as a unit, you consider it as a single complete thing. 2 a group of people who work together at a particular job *E.G. the Police Support Unit.* 3 a machine or piece of equipment which has a particular function *E.G. a remote control unit.* 4 A unit of measurement is a fixed standard that is used for measuring things.

**unite** unites uniting united

VERB If a number of people unite, they join together and act as a group.

**United Kingdom**

NOUN The United Kingdom consists of Great Britain and Northern Ireland.

**United Nations**

NOUN The United Nations is an international organization which tries to encourage peace, cooperation, and friendship between countries.

**unity**

NOUN Where there is unity, people are in agreement and act together for a particular purpose.

**universal**

ADJECTIVE concerning or relating to everyone in the world or every part of the universe *E.G. Music and sports programmes have a universal appeal… universal destruction.*

**universally** ADVERB

**universe** universes

NOUN The universe is the whole of space, including all the stars and planets.

**university** universities

NOUN a place where students study for degrees.

📖 from Latin *universitas* meaning 'group of scholars'

**unjust**

ADJECTIVE not fair or reasonable.

**unjustly** ADVERB

an ELegant angEL (ang*el*)     SPELLING NOTE

**unjustified**

ADJECTIVE If a belief or action is unjustified, there is no good reason for it.

**unkempt**

ADJECTIVE untidy and not looked after properly *E.G. unkempt hair*.

**unkind**

ADJECTIVE unpleasant and rather cruel. **unkindly** ADVERB **unkindness** NOUN
◼ cruel, nasty, uncharitable

**unknown**

ADJECTIVE 1 If someone or something is unknown, people do not know about them or have not heard of them. ▶ NOUN 2 You can refer to the things that people in general do not know about as the unknown.

**unlawful**

ADJECTIVE not legal *E.G. the unlawful use of drugs*.

**unleaded**

ADJECTIVE Unleaded petrol has a reduced amount of lead in it in order to reduce the pollution from cars.

**unleash** unleashes unleashing unleashed

VERB When a powerful or violent force is unleashed, it is released.

**unless**

CONJUNCTION You use 'unless' to introduce the only circumstances in which something will not take place or is not true *E.G. Unless it was raining, they played in the little garden*.

**unlike**

PREPOSITION If one thing is unlike another, the two things are different.

**unlikely**

ADJECTIVE 1 If something is unlikely, it is probably not true or probably will not happen. 2 strange and

unexpected *E.G. There are riches in unlikely places*.

**unlimited**

ADJECTIVE If a supply of something is unlimited, you can have as much as you want or need.

**unload** unloads unloading unloaded

VERB If you unload things from a container or vehicle, you remove them.

**unlock** unlocks unlocking unlocked

VERB If you unlock a door or container, you open it by turning a key in the lock.

**unlucky**

ADJECTIVE Someone who is unlucky has bad luck. **unluckily** ADVERB
◼ hapless, unfortunate

**unmarked**

ADJECTIVE 1 with no marks of damage or injury. 2 with no signs or marks of identification *E.G. unmarked police cars*.

**unmistakable** or **unmistakeable**

ADJECTIVE Something unmistakable is so obvious that it cannot be mistaken for something else. **unmistakably** ADVERB

**unmitigated**

ADJECTIVE; FORMAL You use 'unmitigated' to describe a situation or quality that is completely bad *E.G. an unmitigated disaster*.

**unmoved**

ADJECTIVE not emotionally affected *E.G. He is unmoved by criticism*.

**unnatural**

ADJECTIVE 1 strange and rather frightening because it is not usual

A B C D E F G H I J K L M N O P Q R S T U V W X Y Z

E.G. *There was an unnatural stillness.*
**2** artificial and not typical E.G. *My voice sounded high-pitched and unnatural.*
**unnaturally** ADVERB

**unnecessary**
ADJECTIVE If something is unnecessary, there is no need for it to happen or be done.
**unnecessarily** ADVERB

**unnerve unnerves unnerving unnerved**
VERB If something unnerves you, it frightens or startles you.
**unnerving** ADJECTIVE

**unobtrusive**
ADJECTIVE Something that is unobtrusive does not draw attention to itself.

**unoccupied**
ADJECTIVE If a house is unoccupied, there is nobody living in it.

**unofficial**
ADJECTIVE without the approval or permission of a person in authority E.G. *unofficial strikes.*
**unofficially** ADVERB

**unorthodox**
ADJECTIVE unusual and not generally accepted E.G. *an unorthodox theory.*

**unpack unpacks unpacking unpacked**
VERB When you unpack, you take everything out of a suitcase or bag.

**unpaid**
ADJECTIVE **1** If you do unpaid work, you do not receive any money for doing it. **2** An unpaid bill has not yet been paid.

**unpalatable**
ADJECTIVE **1** Unpalatable food is so unpleasant that you can hardly eat it. **2** An unpalatable idea is so

unpleasant that it is difficult to accept.

**unparalleled**
ADJECTIVE greater than anything else of its kind E.G. *an unparalleled success.*

**unpleasant**
ADJECTIVE **1** Something unpleasant causes you to have bad feelings, for example by making you uncomfortable or upset. **2** An unpleasant person is unfriendly or rude.
**unpleasantly** ADVERB
**unpleasantness** NOUN

**unpopular**
ADJECTIVE disliked by most people E.G. *an unpopular idea.*

**unprecedented**
*Said* "un-**press**-id-en-tid" ADJECTIVE; FORMAL Something that is unprecedented has never happened before or is the best of its kind so far.

**unpredictable**
ADJECTIVE If someone or something is unpredictable, you never know how they will behave or react.

**unprepared**
ADJECTIVE If you are unprepared for something, you are not ready for it and are therefore surprised or at a disadvantage when it happens.

**unproductive**
ADJECTIVE not producing anything useful.
▤ fruitless, useless

**unqualified**
ADJECTIVE **1** having no qualifications or not having the right qualifications for a particular job E.G. *dangers posed by unqualified doctors.* **2** total E.G. *an unqualified success.*

**unquestionable**
ADJECTIVE so obviously true or real that

a
b
c
d
e
f
g
h
i
j
k
l
m
n
o
p
q
r
s
t
u
v
w
x
y
z

A Rude Idiot Thought He Might Eat Toffee In Church (<u>arithmetic</u>)     SPELLING NOTE

nobody can doubt it *E.G. His devotion is unquestionable.*

**unquestionably** ADVERB

**unravel** unravels unravelling unravelled

VERB **1** If you unravel something such as a twisted and knotted piece of string, you unwind it so that it is straight. **2** If you unravel a mystery, you work out the answer to it. 📖 from Dutch *ravelen* meaning 'to unpick'

**unreal**

ADJECTIVE so strange that you find it difficult to believe.

**unrealistic**

ADJECTIVE **1** An unrealistic person does not face the truth about something or deal with it in a practical way. **2** Something unrealistic is not true to life *E.G. an unrealistic picture.*

**unreasonable**

ADJECTIVE unfair and difficult to deal with or justify *E.G. an unreasonable request.*

**unreasonably** ADVERB

**unrelated**

ADJECTIVE Things that are unrelated have no connection with each other.

**unrelenting**

ADJECTIVE continuing in a determined way without caring about any hurt that is caused *E.G. unrelenting criticism.*

**unreliable**

ADJECTIVE If people, machines, or methods are unreliable, you cannot rely on them.

**unremitting**

ADJECTIVE continuing without stopping.

**unrest**

NOUN If there is unrest, people are angry and dissatisfied.

**unrivalled**

ADJECTIVE better than anything else of its kind *E.G. an unrivalled range of health and beauty treatments.*

**unroll** unrolls unrolling unrolled

VERB If you unroll a roll of cloth or paper, you open it up and make it flat.

**unruly**

ADJECTIVE difficult to control or organize *E.G. unruly children… unruly hair.*

**unsatisfactory**

ADJECTIVE not good enough.

**unsaturated**

ADJECTIVE Unsaturated oils and fats are made mainly from vegetable fats and are considered to be healthier than saturated oils.

**unscathed**

ADJECTIVE not injured or harmed as a result of a dangerous experience.

**unscrew** unscrews unscrewing unscrewed

VERB If you unscrew something, you remove it by turning it or by removing the screws that are holding it.

**unscrupulous**

ADJECTIVE willing to behave dishonestly in order to get what you want.

**unseemly**

ADJECTIVE Unseemly behaviour is not suitable for a particular situation and shows a lack of control and good manners *E.G. an unseemly squabble.*

**unseen**

ADJECTIVE You use 'unseen' to describe things that you cannot see or have not seen.

**unsettle** unsettles unsettling unsettled
VERB If something unsettles you, it makes you restless or worried.

**unshakable** or **unshakeable**
ADJECTIVE An unshakable belief is so strong that it cannot be destroyed.

**unsightly**
ADJECTIVE very ugly E.G. *an unsightly scar.*

**unskilled**
ADJECTIVE Unskilled work does not require any special training.

**unsolicited**
ADJECTIVE given or happening without being asked for.

**unsound**
ADJECTIVE 1 If a conclusion or method is unsound, it is based on ideas that are likely to be wrong. 2 An unsound building is likely to collapse.

**unspeakable**
ADJECTIVE very unpleasant.

**unspecified**
ADJECTIVE You say that something is unspecified when you are not told exactly what it is E.G. *It was being stored in some unspecified place.*

**unspoilt** or **unspoiled**
ADJECTIVE If you describe a place as unspoilt or spoiled, you mean it has not been changed and it is still in its natural or original state.

**unspoken**
ADJECTIVE An unspoken wish or feeling is one that is not mentioned to other people.

**unstable**
ADJECTIVE 1 likely to change suddenly and create difficulty or danger E.G. *The political situation in Moscow is unstable.* 2 not firm or fixed properly and likely to wobble or fall.

**unsteady**
ADJECTIVE 1 having difficulty in controlling the movement of your legs or hands E.G. *unsteady on her feet.* 2 not held or fixed securely and likely to fall over.
**unsteadily** ADVERB

**unstuck**
ADJECTIVE If something comes unstuck, it becomes separated from the thing that it was stuck to.

**unsuccessful**
ADJECTIVE If you are unsuccessful, you do not succeed in what you are trying to do.
**unsuccessfully** ADVERB

**unsuitable**
ADJECTIVE not right or appropriate for a particular purpose.
**unsuitably** ADVERB

**unsuited**
ADJECTIVE not appropriate for a particular task or situation E.G. *He's totally unsuited to the job.*

**unsung**
ADJECTIVE You use 'unsung' to describe someone who is not appreciated or praised for their good work E.G. *George is the unsung hero of the club.*
🏛 from the custom of celebrating in song the exploits of heroes

**unsure**
ADJECTIVE uncertain or doubtful.

**unsuspecting**
ADJECTIVE having no idea of what is happening or going to happen E.G. *His horse escaped and collided with an unsuspecting cyclist.*

**untangle** untangles untangling untangled
VERB If you untangle something that is twisted together, you undo the twists.

a
b
c
d
e
f
g
h
i
j
k
l
m
n
o
p
q
r
s
**u**
v
w
x
y
z

Betty Eats Cakes And Uses Seven Eggs (<u>because</u>)   SPELLING NOTE

A
B
C
D
E
F
G
H
I
J
K
L
M
N
O
P
Q
R
S
T
U
V
W
X
Y
Z

**untenable**

ADJECTIVE; FORMAL A theory, argument, or position that is untenable cannot be successfully defended.

**unthinkable**

ADJECTIVE so shocking or awful that you cannot imagine it to be true.

**untidy** untidier untidiest

ADJECTIVE not neat or well arranged. **untidily** ADVERB

**untie** unties untying untied

VERB If you untie something, you undo the knots in the string or rope around it.

**until**

PREPOSITION or CONJUNCTION **1** If something happens until a particular time, it happens before that time and stops at that time E.G. *The shop stayed open until midnight… She waited until her husband was asleep.* **2** If something does not happen until a particular time, it does not happen before that time and only starts happening at that time E.G. *It didn't rain until the middle of the afternoon… It was not until they arrived that they found out who he was.*

**untimely**

ADJECTIVE happening too soon or sooner than expected E.G. *his untimely death.*

**unto**

PREPOSITION; OLD-FASHIONED Unto means the same as to E.G. *Nation shall speak peace unto nation.*

**untold**

ADJECTIVE You use 'untold' to emphasize how great or extreme something is E.G. *The island possessed untold wealth.*

**untouched**

ADJECTIVE **1** not changed, moved, or

damaged E.G. *a small village untouched by tourism.* **2** If a meal is untouched, none of it has been eaten.

**untoward**

ADJECTIVE unexpected and causing difficulties E.G. *no untoward problems.*

**untrue**

ADJECTIVE not true.

**unused**

*Said* "un-yoozd" ADJECTIVE not yet used. *Said* "un-yoost" ADJECTIVE If you are unused to something, you have not often done or experienced it.

**unusual**

ADJECTIVE Something that is unusual does not occur very often. **unusually** ADVERB

■ exceptional, extraordinary, rare

**unveil** unveils unveiling unveiled

VERB When someone unveils a new statue or plaque, they draw back a curtain that is covering it.

**unwanted**

ADJECTIVE Unwanted things are not desired or wanted, either by a particular person or by people in general E.G. *He felt lonely and unwanted.*

**unwarranted**

ADJECTIVE; FORMAL not justified or not deserved E.G. *unwarranted fears.*

**unwelcome**

ADJECTIVE not wanted E.G. *an unwelcome visitor… unwelcome news.*

**unwell**

ADJECTIVE If you are unwell, you are ill.

**unwieldy**

ADJECTIVE difficult to move or carry because of being large or an awkward shape.

## unwilling
ADJECTIVE If you are unwilling to do something, you do not want to do it.
**unwillingly** ADVERB
■ averse, loath, reluctant

## unwind unwinds unwinding unwound
VERB 1 When you unwind after working hard, you relax. 2 If you unwind something that is wrapped round something else, you undo it.

## unwise
ADJECTIVE foolish or not sensible.

## unwitting
ADJECTIVE Unwitting describes someone who becomes involved in something without realizing what is really happening E.G. her unwitting victims.
**unwittingly** ADVERB

## unworthy
ADJECTIVE; FORMAL Someone who is unworthy of something does not deserve it.

## unwrap unwraps unwrapping unwrapped
VERB When you unwrap something, you take off the paper or covering around it.

## unwritten
ADJECTIVE An unwritten law is one which is generally understood and accepted without being officially laid down.

## up
ADVERB or PREPOSITION 1 towards or in a higher place E.G. He ran up the stairs, high up in the mountains. 2 towards or in the north E.G. I'm flying up to Darwin. ► PREPOSITION 3 If you go up a road or river, you go along it. 4 You use 'up to' to say how large something can be or what level it

has reached E.G. traffic jams up to 15 kilometres long. 5 INFORMAL If someone is up to something, they are secretly doing something they should not be doing. 6 If it is up to someone to do something, it is their responsibility. ► ADJECTIVE 7 If you are up, you are not in bed. 8 If a period of time is up, it has come to an end. ► ADVERB 9 If an amount of something goes up, it increases.

## up-and-coming
ADJECTIVE Up-and-coming people are likely to be successful.

## upbringing
NOUN Your upbringing is the way that your parents have taught you to behave.

## update updates updating updated
VERB If you update something, you make it more modern or add new information to it E.G. He had failed to update his will.

## upgrade upgrades upgrading upgraded
VERB If a person or their job is upgraded, they are given more responsibility or status and usually more money.

## upheaval upheavals
NOUN a big change which causes a lot of trouble.

## uphill
ADVERB 1 If you go uphill, you go up a slope. ► ADJECTIVE 2 An uphill task requires a lot of effort and determination.

## uphold upholds upholding upheld
VERB If someone upholds a law or a decision, they support and maintain it.

## upholstery
NOUN Upholstery is the soft covering

you'll brEAK that Electrical Aerial, Kitty (br<u>eak</u>)    **SPELLING NOTE**

A
B
C
D
E
F
G
H
I
J
K
L
M
N
O
P
Q
R
S
T
U
V
W
X
Y
Z

on chairs and sofas that makes them comfortable.

**upkeep**
NOUN The upkeep of something is the continual process and cost of keeping it in good condition.

**upland** uplands
ADJECTIVE 1 An upland area is an area of high land. ▶ NOUN 2 Uplands are areas of high land.

**uplifting**
ADJECTIVE making you feel happy.

**upload** uploads uploading uploaded
VERB If you upload a computer file or program, you transfer it from your computer into the memory of another computer.

**up-market**
ADJECTIVE sophisticated and expensive.

**upon**
PREPOSITION 1 *FORMAL* Upon means on *E.G. I stood upon the stair.* 2 You use 'upon' when mentioning an event that is immediately followed by another *E.G. Upon entering the hall he took a quick glance round.* 3 If an event is upon you, it is about to happen *E.G. The football season is upon us once more.*

**upper** uppers
ADJECTIVE 1 referring to something that is above something else, or the higher part of something *E.G. the upper arm.* ▶ NOUN 2 the top part of a shoe.

**upper class** upper classes
NOUN The upper classes are people who belong to a very wealthy or aristocratic group in a society.

**uppermost**
ADJECTIVE or ADVERB 1 on top or in the highest position *E.G. the uppermost*

*leaves… Lay your arms beside your body with the palms turned uppermost.* ▶ ADJECTIVE 2 most important *E.G. His family is now uppermost in his mind.*

**upright**
ADJECTIVE or ADVERB 1 standing or sitting up straight, rather than bending or lying down. 2 behaving in a very respectable and moral way.

**uprising** uprisings
NOUN If there is an uprising, a large group of people begin fighting against the existing government to bring about political changes.

**uproar**
NOUN If there is uproar or an uproar, there is a lot of shouting and noise, often because people are angry.
🔲 from Dutch *oproer* meaning 'revolt'
🟰 commotion, furore, pandemonium

**uproot** uproots uprooting uprooted
VERB 1 If someone is uprooted, they have to leave the place where they have lived for a long time. 2 If a tree is uprooted, it is pulled out of the ground.

**upset** upsets upsetting upset
ADJECTIVE 1 unhappy and disappointed. ▶ VERB 2 If something upsets you, it makes you feel worried or unhappy. 3 If you upset something, you turn it over or spill it accidentally. ▶ NOUN 4 A stomach upset is a slight stomach illness caused by an infection or by something you have eaten.

**upshot**
NOUN The upshot of a series of events is the final result.

**upside down**

ADJECTIVE or ADVERB the wrong way up.

**upstage** upstages upstaging upstaged

VERB If someone upstages you, they draw people's attention away from you by being more attractive or interesting.

**upstairs**

ADVERB 1 If you go upstairs in a building, you go up to a higher floor. ► NOUN 2 The upstairs of a building is its upper floor or floors.

**upstart** upstarts

NOUN someone who has risen too quickly to an important position and are too arrogant.

**upstream**

ADVERB towards the source of a river E.G. *They made their way upstream.*

**upsurge**

NOUN An upsurge of something is a sudden large increase in it.

**uptake**

NOUN You can say that someone is quick on the uptake if they understand things quickly.
🏛 from Scottish *uptake* meaning 'to understand'

**uptight**

ADJECTIVE; INFORMAL tense or annoyed.

**up-to-date**

ADJECTIVE 1 being the newest thing of its kind. 2 having the latest information.

**up-to-the-minute**

ADJECTIVE Up-to-the-minute information is the latest available information.

**upturn** upturns

NOUN an improvement in a situation.

**upturned**

ADJECTIVE 1 pointing upwards E.G. *rain*

*splashing down on her upturned face.*
2 upside down E.G. *an upturned bowl.*

**upwards**

ADVERB 1 towards a higher place E.G. *People stared upwards and pointed.*
2 to a higher level or point on a scale E.G. *The world population is rocketing upwards.*

**upward** ADJECTIVE

**uranium**

*Said "yoo-**ray**-nee-um"* NOUN Uranium is a radioactive metal used to produce nuclear energy and weapons.

**Uranus**

NOUN Uranus is the planet in the solar system which is seventh from the sun.
🏛 named after the Greek god *Ouranos* who ruled the universe

**urban**

ADJECTIVE (GEOGRAPHY) relating to a town or city E.G. *urban development.*

**urbane**

ADJECTIVE well-mannered, and comfortable in social situations.

**Urdu**

*Said "**oor**-doo"* NOUN Urdu is the official language of Pakistan. It is also spoken by many people in India.

**urge** urges urging urged

NOUN 1 If you have an urge to do something, you have a strong wish to do it. ► VERB 2 If you urge someone to do something, you try hard to persuade them to do it.
🟰 (sense 1) compulsion, desire, impulse
🟰 (sense 2) beg, implore

**urgent**

ADJECTIVE needing to be dealt with as soon as possible.

**urgently** ADVERB   **urgency** NOUN
🟰 crucial, pressing

a b c d e f g h i j k l m n o p q r s t u v w x y z

I want to see (C) your licenCe (licence)    SPELLING NOTE

**urinal** urinals
*Said* "yoor-**rye**-nl" NOUN a bowl or trough fixed to the wall in a men's public toilet for men to urinate in.

**urinate** urinates urinating urinated
*Said* "yoor-rin-ate" VERB When you urinate, you go to the toilet and get rid of urine from your body.

**urine**
*Said* "yoor-rin" NOUN the waste liquid that you get rid of from your body when you go to the toilet.

**URL** URLs
NOUN an abbreviation for 'uniform resource locator': a technical name for an Internet address.

**urn** urns
NOUN a decorated container, especially one that is used to hold the ashes of a person who has been cremated.

**us**
PRONOUN A speaker or writer uses 'us' to refer to himself or herself and one or more other people E.G. *Why don't you tell us?*

**US** or **USA**
an abbreviation for 'United States of America'.

**usage**
NOUN 1 the degree to which something is used, or the way in which it is used. 2 the way in which words are actually used E.G. *The terms soon entered common usage.*

**use** uses using used
*Said* "yooz" VERB 1 If you use something, you do something with it in order to do a job or achieve something E.G. *May I use your phone?* 2 If you use someone, you take advantage of them by making them do things for you. *Said* "yoos" ▶ NOUN 3 The use of something is the act of using it E.G. *the use of force.* 4 If you have the use of something, you have the ability or permission to use it. 3 If you find a use for something, you find a purpose for it.

**usable** or **useable** ADJECTIVE

**user** NOUN
▣ (sense 1) apply, employ, utilize
▣ (sense 3) application, employment, usage

**used**
*Said* "yoost" VERB 1 Something that used to be done or used to be true was done or was true in the past. ▶ PHRASE 2 If you are **used to** something, you are familiar with it and have often experienced it. *Said* "yoozd" ▶ 3 ADJECTIVE A used object has had a previous owner.

**useful**
ADJECTIVE If something is useful, you can use it in order to do something or to help you in some way.
**usefully** ADVERB **usefulness** NOUN

**useless**
ADJECTIVE 1 If something is useless, you cannot use it because it is not suitable or helpful. 2 If a course of action is useless, it will not achieve what is wanted.

**username** usernames
NOUN a name that someone uses when logging into a computer or website.

**usher** ushers ushering ushered
VERB 1 If you usher someone somewhere, you show them where to go by going with them. ▶ NOUN 2 a person who shows people where to sit at a wedding or a concert.

## USSR

an abbreviation for 'Union of Soviet Socialist Republics', a country which was made up of a lot of smaller countries including Russia, but which is now broken up.

## usual

ADJECTIVE **1** happening, done, or used most often E.G. *his usual seat.* ▶ PHRASE **2** If you do something **as usual**, you do it in the way that you normally do it.

**usually** ADVERB

■ (sense 1) customary, normal, regular

## usurp usurps usurping usurped

*Said* "yoo-**zerp**" VERB; FORMAL If someone usurps another person's job or title they take it when they have no right to do so.

## ute utes

*Said* "**yoot**" NOUN; INFORMAL In Australian and New Zealand English, a utility truck.

## utensil utensils

*Said* "yoo-**ten**-sil" NOUN Utensils are tools E.G. *cooking utensils.*

🏛 from Latin *utensilis* meaning 'available for use'

## uterus uteruses

*Said* "**yoo**-ter-russ" NOUN; FORMAL A woman's uterus is her womb.

## utility utilities

NOUN **1** The utility of something is its usefulness. **2** a service, such as water or gas, that is provided for everyone.

## utility truck utility trucks

NOUN In Australian and New Zealand English, a small motor vehicle with an open body and low sides.

## utilize utilizes utilizing utilized; also spelt utilise

VERB; FORMAL To utilize something is to use it.

**utilization** NOUN

## utmost

ADJECTIVE used to emphasize a particular quality E.G. *I have the utmost respect for Richard.*

## utter utters uttering uttered

VERB **1** When you utter sounds or words, you make or say them. ▶ ADJECTIVE **2** Utter means complete or total E.G. *scenes of utter chaos.*

**utterly** ADVERB

## utterance utterances

NOUN something that is said E.G. *his first utterance.*

a b c d e f g h i j k l m n o p q r s t u v w x y z

have a plEce of plE (pie<u>ce</u>)  SPELLING NOTE

# Vv

**v**
an abbreviation for **versus**.

**vacant**
ADJECTIVE **1** If something is vacant, it is not occupied or being used. **2** If a job or position is vacant, no-one holds it at present. **3** A vacant look suggests that someone does not understand something or is not very intelligent.

**vacancy** NOUN **vacantly** ADVERB

**vacate vacates vacating vacated**
VERB; *FORMAL* If you vacate a room or job, you leave it and it becomes available for someone else.

**vacation vacations**
NOUN **1** the period between academic terms at a university or college *E.G. the summer vacation*. **2** a holiday.

**vaccinate vaccinates vaccinating vaccinated**
*Said "vak-sin-ate"* VERB To vaccinate someone means to give them a vaccine, usually by injection, to protect them against a disease.

**vaccination** NOUN

**vaccine vaccines**
*Said "vak-seen"* NOUN a substance made from the germs that cause a disease and is given to people to make them immune to that disease.
🏛 from Latin *vacca* meaning 'cow', because smallpox vaccine is based on cowpox, a disease of cows

**vacuum vacuums vacuuming vacuumed**
*Said "vak-yoom"* NOUN **1** a space containing no air, gases, or other matter. ▶ VERB **2** If you vacuum something, you clean it using a vacuum cleaner.

**vacuum cleaner vacuum cleaners**
NOUN an electric machine which cleans by sucking up dirt.

**vagina vaginas**
*Said "vaj-jie-na"* NOUN A woman's vagina is the passage that connects her outer sex organs to her womb.
🏛 from Latin *vagina* meaning 'sheath'

**vagrant vagrants**
NOUN a person who moves from place to place, and has no home or regular job.

**vagrancy** NOUN

**vague vaguer vaguest**
*Said "vayg"* ADJECTIVE **1** If something is vague, it is not expressed or explained clearly, or you cannot see or remember it clearly *E.G. vague statements*. **2** Someone looks or sounds vague if they are not concentrating or thinking clearly.

**vaguely** ADVERB **vagueness** NOUN
📰 (sense 1) imprecise, indefinite, unclear

**vain vainer vainest**
ADJECTIVE **1** A vain action or attempt is one which is not successful *E.G. He made a vain effort to cheer her up*. **2** A vain person is very proud of their looks, intelligence, or other qualities.
▶ PHRASE **3** If you do something **in vain**, you do not succeed in achieving what you intend.

**vainly** ADVERB

**vale vales**
NOUN; *LITERARY* a valley.

**valentine valentines**
NOUN **1** Your valentine is someone you love and send a card to on Saint Valentine's Day, February 14th. **2** A

valentine or a valentine card is the card you send to the person you love on Saint Valentine's Day.

🏛 Saint Valentine was a 3rd century martyr

**valet** valets
*Said* "**val**-lit *or* val-lay" NOUN a male servant who is employed to look after another man, particularly caring for his clothes.

**valiant**
ADJECTIVE very brave.
**valiantly** ADVERB

**valid**
ADJECTIVE 1 Something that is valid is based on sound reasoning. 2 A valid ticket or document is one which is officially accepted.
**validity** NOUN

**validate** validates validating validated
VERB If something validates a statement or claim, it proves that it is true or correct.

**valley** valleys
NOUN a long stretch of land between hills, often with a river flowing through it.

**valour**
NOUN Valour is great bravery.

**valuable** valuables
ADJECTIVE 1 Something that is valuable has great value. ▶ PLURAL NOUN
2 Valuables are things that you own that cost a lot of money.
■ (sense 1) costly, expensive, precious

**valuation** valuations
NOUN a judgment about how much money something is worth or how good it is.

**value** values valuing valued
NOUN 1 The value of something is its

importance or usefulness *E.G. information of great value.* 2 The value of something you own is the amount of money that it is worth. 3 The values of a group or a person are the moral principles and beliefs that they think are important *E.G. the values of liberty and equality.* ▶ VERB 4 If you value something, you think it is important and you appreciate it. 5 When experts value something, they decide how much money it is worth.

**valued** ADJECTIVE **valuer** NOUN

**valve** valves
NOUN 1 a part attached to a pipe or tube which controls the flow of gas or liquid. 2 a small flap in your heart or in a vein which controls the flow and direction of blood.

**vampire** vampires
NOUN In horror stories, vampires are corpses that come out of their graves at night and suck the blood of living people.

**van** vans
NOUN a covered vehicle larger than a car but smaller than a lorry, used for carrying goods.

**vandal** vandals
NOUN someone who deliberately damages or destroys things, particularly public property.
**vandalize** or **vandalise** VERB
**vandalism** NOUN

**vane** vanes
NOUN a flat blade that is part of a mechanism for using the energy of the wind or water to drive a machine.

**vanguard**
*Said* "**van**-gard" NOUN If someone is in the vanguard of something, they are in the most advanced part of it.

a
b
c
d
e
f
g
h
i
j
k
l
m
n
o
p
q
r
s
t
u
w
x
y
z

A
B
C
D
E
F
G
H
I
J
K
L
M
N
O
P
Q
R
S
T
U
V
W
X
Y
Z

**vanilla**

NOUN Vanilla is a flavouring for food such as ice cream, which comes from the pods of a tropical plant.

**vanish** vanishes vanishing vanished

VERB If something vanishes, it disappears or ceases to exist E.G. *The moon vanished behind a cloud.*

**vanity**

NOUN Vanity is a feeling of excessive pride about your looks or abilities.

**vanquish** vanquishes vanquishing vanquished

*Said* "vang-kwish" VERB; LITERARY To vanquish someone means to defeat them completely.

**vapour**

NOUN Vapour is a mass of tiny drops of water or other liquids in the air, which looks like mist.

**variable** variables

ADJECTIVE **1** Something that is variable is likely to change at any time. ▶ NOUN **2** In any situation, a variable is something in it that can change. **3** In maths, a variable is a symbol such as x which can represent any value or any one of a set of values.

**variability** NOUN

**variance**

NOUN If one thing is at variance with another, the two seem to contradict each other.

**variant** variants

NOUN **1** A variant of something has a different form from the usual one, for example *gaol* is a variant of *jail*. ▶ ADJECTIVE **2** alternative or different.

**variation** variations

NOUN **1** a change from the normal or usual pattern E.G. *a variation of the same route.* **2** a change in level,

amount, or quantity E.G. *a large variation in demand.*

**varicose veins**

PLURAL NOUN Varicose veins are swollen painful veins in the legs.

**varied**

ADJECTIVE of different types, quantities, or sizes.

**variety** varieties

NOUN **1** If something has variety, it consists of things which are not all the same. **2** A variety of things is a number of different kinds of them E.G. *a wide variety of readers.* **3** A variety of something is a particular type of it E.G. *a new variety of celery.* **4** Variety is a form of entertainment consisting of short unrelated acts, such as singing, dancing, and comedy.

■ (sense 2) assortment, mixture, range

**various**

ADJECTIVE Various means of several different types E.G. *trees of various sorts.*

**variously** ADVERB

■ different, miscellaneous, sundry

✔ You should avoid putting *different* after *various*: *the disease exists in various forms* not *various different forms.*

**varnish** varnishes varnishing varnished

NOUN **1** a liquid which when painted onto a surface gives it a hard clear shiny finish. ▶ ▶ VERB **2** If you varnish something, you paint it with varnish.

**vary** varies varying varied

VERB **1** If things vary, they change E.G. *Weather patterns vary greatly.* **2** If you vary something, you introduce

changes in it E.G. *Vary your routes as much as possible.*
**varied** ADJECTIVE

**vascular**
ADJECTIVE relating to tubes or ducts that carry fluids within animals or plants.

**vase vases**
NOUN a glass or china jar for flowers.

**vasectomy vasectomies**
*Said "vas-**sek**-tom-ee"* NOUN an operation to sterilize a man by cutting the tube that carries the sperm.

**Vaseline**
NOUN; TRADEMARK Vaseline is a soft clear jelly made from petroleum and used as an ointment or as grease.

**vast**
ADJECTIVE extremely large.
**vastly** ADVERB **vastness** NOUN

**vat vats**
NOUN a large container for liquids.

**VAT**
NOUN In Britain, VAT is a tax which is added to the costs of making or providing goods and services. VAT is an abbreviation for 'value-added tax'.

**vault vaults vaulting vaulted**
*Rhymes with "**salt**"* NOUN **1** a strong secure room, often underneath a building, where valuables are stored, or underneath a church where people are buried. **2** an arched roof, often found in churches. ► VERB **3** If you vault over something, you jump over it using your hands or a pole to help.

**VCR**
an abbreviation for 'video cassette recorder'.

**VDU VDUs**
NOUN a monitor screen attached to a computer or word processor. VDU is an abbreviation for 'visual display unit'.

**veal**
NOUN Veal is the meat from a calf.

**Veda Vedas**
*Said "**vay**-da"* NOUN an ancient sacred text of the Hindu religion; also these texts as a collection.
**Vedic** ADJECTIVE

**veer veers veering veered**
VERB If something which is moving veers in a particular direction, it suddenly changes course E.G. *The aircraft veered sharply to one side.*

**vegan vegans**
*Said "**vee**-gn"* NOUN someone who does not eat any food made from animal products, such as meat, eggs, cheese, or milk.

**vegetable vegetables**
NOUN **1** Vegetables are edible roots or leaves such as carrots or cabbage. ► ADJECTIVE **2** 'Vegetable' is used to refer to any plants in contrast to animals or minerals E.G. *vegetable life.*
📖 from Latin *vegetabilis* meaning 'enlivening'

**vegetarian vegetarians**
NOUN a person who does not eat meat, poultry, or fish.
**vegetarianism** NOUN

**vegetation**
NOUN Vegetation is the plants in a particular area.

**vehement**
*Said "**vee**-im-ent"* ADJECTIVE Someone who is vehement has strong feelings or opinions and expresses them forcefully E.G. *He wrote a letter of vehement protest.*
**vehemence** NOUN **vehemently** ADVERB

a b c d e f g h i j k l m n o p q r s t u v w x y z

A
B
C
D
E
F
G
H
I
J
K
L
M
N
O
P
Q
R
S
T
U
V
W
X
Y
Z

**vehicle** vehicles

*Said "vee-ik-kl"* NOUN **1** a machine, often with an engine, used for transporting people or goods. **2** something used to achieve a particular purpose or as a means of expression E.G. *The play seemed an ideal vehicle for his music.*
**vehicular** ADJECTIVE

**veil** veils

*Rhymes with "male"* NOUN a piece of thin, soft cloth that women sometimes wear over their heads.

**vein** veins

*Rhymes with "rain"* NOUN **1** Your veins are the tubes in your body through which your blood flows to your heart. **2** Veins are the thin lines on leaves or on insects' wings. **3** A vein of a metal or a mineral is a layer of it in rock. **4** Something that is in a particular vein is in that style or mood E.G. *in a more serious vein.*

**veld**

*Said "felt"* NOUN The veld is flat high grassland in Southern Africa.

**veldskoen** veldskoens

*Said "felt-skoon"* NOUN In South Africa, a veldskoen is a tough ankle-length boot.

**velocity**

NOUN; TECHNICAL Velocity is the speed at which something is moving in a particular direction.

**velvet**

NOUN Velvet is a very soft material which has a thick layer of fine short threads on one side.
**velvety** ADJECTIVE
📖 from Latin *villus* meaning 'shaggy hair'

**vendetta** vendettas

NOUN a long-lasting bitter quarrel

which results in people trying to harm each other.

**vending machine** vending machines

NOUN a machine which provides things such as drinks or sweets when you put money in it.

**vendor** vendors

NOUN a person who sells something.

**veneer**

NOUN **1** You can refer to a superficial quality that someone has as a veneer of that quality E.G. *a veneer of calm.* **2** Veneer is a thin layer of wood or plastic used to cover a surface.

**venerable**

ADJECTIVE **1** A venerable person is someone you treat with respect because they are old and wise. **2** Something that is venerable is impressive because it is old and important historically.

**venerate** venerates venerating venerated

VERB; FORMAL If you venerate someone, you feel great respect for them.
**veneration** NOUN

**vengeance**

NOUN **1** Vengeance is the act of harming someone because they have harmed you. ▶ PHRASE **2** If something happens **with a vengeance**, it happens to a much greater extent than was expected E.G. *It began to rain again with a vengeance.*

**venison**

NOUN Venison is the meat from a deer.
📖 from Latin *venatio* meaning 'hunting'

**venom**

NOUN **1** The venom of a snake, scorpion, or spider is its poison.

**2** Venom is a feeling of great bitterness or spitefulness towards someone *E.G. He was glaring at me with venom.*

**venomous** ADJECTIVE

**vent** vents venting vented
NOUN **1** a hole in something through which gases and smoke can escape and fresh air can enter *E.G. air vents.*
▶ VERB **2** If you vent strong feelings, you express them *E.G. She wanted to vent her anger upon me.* ▶ PHRASE **3** If you **give vent** to strong feelings, you express them *E.G. Pamela gave vent to a lot of bitterness.*

**ventilate** ventilates ventilating ventilated
VERB To ventilate a room means to allow fresh air into it.
**ventilated** ADJECTIVE

**ventilation**
NOUN **1** Ventilation is the process of breathing air in and out of the lungs. **2** A ventilation system supplies fresh air into a building.

**ventilator** ventilators
NOUN a machine that helps people breathe when they cannot breathe naturally, for example if they are very ill.

**ventriloquist** ventriloquists
*Said "ven-**trill**-o-kwist"* NOUN an entertainer who can speak without moving their lips so that the words seem to come from a dummy.
**ventriloquism** NOUN
🔲 from Latin *venter* meaning 'belly' and *loqui* meaning 'to speak'

**venture** ventures venturing ventured
NOUN **1** something new which involves the risk of failure or of losing money *E.G. a successful venture in television films.* ▶ VERB **2** If you

venture something such as an opinion, you say it cautiously or hesitantly because you are afraid it might be foolish or wrong *E.G. I would not venture to agree.* **3** If you venture somewhere that might be dangerous, you go there.
🔳 (sense 1) enterprise, undertaking

**venue** venues
*Said "**ven**-yoo"* NOUN The venue for an event is the place where it will happen.

**Venus**
NOUN Venus is the planet in the solar system which is second from the sun.
🔲 named after the Roman goddess of love

**veranda** verandas
*Said "ver-**ran**-da"; also spelt* **verandah**
NOUN a platform with a roof that is attached to an outside wall of a house at ground level.

**verb** verbs
NOUN In grammar, a verb is a word that expresses actions and states, for example 'be', 'become', 'take', and 'run'.
→ SEE BOX ON NEXT PAGE

**verbal**
ADJECTIVE **1** You use 'verbal' to describe things connected with words and their use *E.G. verbal attacks on referees.* **2** 'Verbal' describes things which are spoken rather than written *E.G. a verbal agreement.*
**verbally** ADVERB

**verdict** verdicts
NOUN **1** In a law court, a verdict is the decision which states whether a prisoner is guilty or not guilty. **2** If you give a verdict on something, you give your opinion after thinking about it.

a
b
c
d
e
f
g
h
i
j
k
l
m
n
o
p
q
r
s
t
u
w
x
y
z

A
B
C
D
E
F
G
H
I
J
K
L
M
N
O
P
Q
R
S
T
U
V
W
X
Y
Z

### What Is a Verb?

A verb is a word that describes an action or a state of being. Verbs are sometimes called "doing words".
**Verbs of state** indicate the way things are:

> E.G. Robert **is** a Taurus.
> Anna **has** one sister.

**Verbs of action** indicate specific events that happen, have happened or will happen:

> E.G. Anna **visits** the dentist.
> The man **faxed** his order.

**Auxiliary verbs** are used in combination with other verbs to allow the user to distinguish between different times, different degrees of completion, and different amounts of certainty:

> E.G. Anna **will** visit the dentist.
> The man **is** faxing his order.
> They **may** talk for up to three hours.

A **phrasal verb** consists of a verb followed by either an adverb or a preposition. The two words taken together have a special meaning which could not be deduced from their literal meanings:

> E.G. The car **broke down** again.
> When did you **take up** croquet?

An **impersonal verb** is a verb that does not have a subject and is only used after *it* or *there*:

> E.G. It **rains** here every day.

### Modal Verbs

*Can, could, may, might, must, should, would,* and *ought* are called "modal verbs". They are usually used as auxiliary verbs to change the tone of the meaning of another verb:

> E.G. I wonder if you **can come.**

Even when they are used on their own, they *suggest* another verb:

> E.G. I certainly **can**. (i.e. I certainly **can come**)

There is no difference between the third person present and the other forms of the present tense. No form of the verb ends in -s:

> E.G. I **can** speak German.
> She **can** speak German.

These verbs do not have a present participle or a past participle.
The verb *could* may be used as the past tense of *can*:

> E.G. I **could** speak German when I was younger.

You can talk about past time by using *could have, may have, might have, must have, should have, would have,* and *ought to have*:

> E.G. We **may have** taken a wrong turning.
> She **must have** thought I was stupid.

**verge verges verging verged**
NOUN 1 The verge of a road is the narrow strip of grassy ground at the side. ▶ PHRASE 2 If you are **on the verge** of something, you are going to do it soon or it is likely to happen soon E.G. on the verge of crying. ▶ VERB 3 Something that verges on

something else is almost the same as it E.G. dark blue that verged on purple.
**verify verifies verifying verified**
VERB If you verify something, you check that it is true E.G. None of his statements could be verified.
**verifiable** ADJECTIVE **verification** NOUN

**veritable**

ADJECTIVE You use 'veritable' to emphasize that something is really true, even if it seems as if you are exaggerating *E.G. a veritable jungle of shops.*

**vermin**

PLURAL NOUN Vermin are small animals or insects, such as rats and cockroaches, which carry disease and damage crops.

**vernacular** vernaculars

*Said* "ver-**nak**-yoo-lar" NOUN The vernacular of a particular country or district is the language widely spoken there.

**verruca** verrucas

*Said* "ver-**roo**-ka" NOUN a small hard infectious growth rather like a wart, occurring on the sole of the foot.

**versatile**

ADJECTIVE If someone is versatile, they have many different skills.
**versatility** NOUN

**verse** verses

NOUN 1 Verse is another word for poetry. 2 one part of a poem, song, or chapter of the Bible.

**versed**

ADJECTIVE If you are versed in something, you know a lot about it.

**version** versions

NOUN 1 A version of something is a form of it in which some details are different from earlier or later forms *E.G. a cheaper version of the aircraft.* 2 Someone's version of an event is their personal description of what happened.

**versus**

PREPOSITION 'Versus' is used to indicate that two people or teams are competing against each other.

**vertebra** vertebrae

*Said* "**ver**-tib-bra" NOUN Vertebrae are the small bones which form a person's or animal's backbone.

**vertebrate** vertebrates

NOUN (SCIENCE) Vertebrates are any creatures which have a backbone.

**vertex** vertexes or vertices

NOUN (MATHS) The vertex of something such as a triangle or pyramid is the point opposite the base.

**vertical**

ADJECTIVE (MATHS) Something that is vertical points straight up and forms a ninety-degree angle with the surface on which it stands.
**vertically** ADVERB

**vertigo**

NOUN Vertigo is a feeling of dizziness caused by looking down from a high place.

**verve**

NOUN Verve is lively and forceful enthusiasm.

**very**

ADJECTIVE or ADVERB 1 'Very' is used before words to emphasize them *E.G. very bad dreams… the very end of the book.* ▶ PHRASE 2 You use **not very** to mean that something is the case only to a small degree *E.G. You're not very like your sister.*

■ (sense 1) extremely, greatly, really

**vessel** vessels

NOUN 1 a ship or large boat. 2 *LITERARY* any bowl or container in which a liquid can be kept. 3 (SCIENCE) a thin tube along which liquids such as blood or sap move in animals and plants.

**vest** vests

NOUN a piece of underwear worn for warmth on the top half of the body.

a
b
c
d
e
f
g
h
i
j
k
l
m
n
o
p
q
r
s
t
u
w
x
y
z

A
B
C
D
E
F
G
H
I
J
K
L
M
N
O
P
Q
R
S
T
U
V
W
X
Y
Z

**vestige** vestiges

*Said "vest-ij"* NOUN; *FORMAL* If there is not a vestige of something, then there is not even a little of it left *E.G. They have a vestige of strength left.*

**vestry** vestries

NOUN The vestry is the part of the church building where a priest or minister changes into their official clothes.

**vet** vets vetting vetted

NOUN 1 a doctor for animals. ▶ VERB 2 If you vet someone or something, you check them carefully to see if they are acceptable *E.G. He refused to let them vet his speeches.*

**veteran** veterans

NOUN 1 someone who has served in the armed forces, particularly during a war. 2 someone who has been involved in a particular activity for a long time *E.G. a veteran of 25 political campaigns.*

**veterinary**

*Said "vet-er-in-ar-ee"* ADJECTIVE 'Veterinary' is used to describe the work of a vet and the medical treatment of animals.

🏛 from Latin *veterinae* meaning 'animals used for pulling carts and ploughs'

**veterinary surgeon** veterinary surgeons

NOUN the same as a **vet**.

**veto** vetoes vetoing vetoed

VERB 1 If someone in authority vetoes something, they say no to it. ▶ NOUN 2 Veto is the right that someone in authority has to say no to something *E.G. Dr Baker has the power of veto.*

**vexed**

ADJECTIVE If you are vexed, you are annoyed, worried, or puzzled.

**VHF**

NOUN VHF is a range of high radio frequencies. VHF is an abbreviation for 'very high frequency'.

**via**

PREPOSITION 1 If you go to one place via another, you travel through that place to get to your destination *E.G. He drove directly from Bonn via Paris.* 2 Via also means done or achieved by making use of a particular thing or person *E.G. to follow proceedings via newspapers or television.*

**viable**

*Said "vy-a-bl"* ADJECTIVE Something that is viable is capable of doing what it is intended to do without extra help or financial support *E.G. a viable business.*

**viability** NOUN

**viaduct** viaducts

NOUN a long high bridge that carries a road or railway across a valley.

🏛 from Latin *via* meaning 'road' and *ducere* meaning 'to bring'

**vibrant**

ADJECTIVE Something or someone that is vibrant is full of life, energy, and enthusiasm.

**vibrantly** ADVERB  **vibrancy** NOUN

**vibrate** vibrates vibrating vibrated

VERB If something vibrates, it moves a tiny amount backwards and forwards very quickly.

**vibration** NOUN

**vicar** vicars

NOUN a priest in the Church of England.

**vicarage** vicarages

NOUN a house where a vicar lives.

**vice** vices

NOUN 1 a serious moral fault in someone's character, such as greed,

or a weakness, such as smoking.
**2** Vice is criminal activities connected with prostitution and pornography. **3** a tool with a pair of jaws that hold an object tightly while it is being worked on.

**vice-**

PREFIX 'Vice-' is used before a title or position to show that the holder is the deputy of the person with that title or position E.G. *vice-president*.

**viceregal**

ADJECTIVE **1** of or concerning a viceroy. **2** In Australia and New Zealand, viceregal means of or concerning a governor or governor-general.

**viceroy** viceroys

NOUN A viceroy is someone who has been appointed to govern a place as a representative of a monarch.

**vice versa**

'Vice versa' is used to indicate that the reverse of what you have said is also true E.G. *Wives criticize their husbands, and vice versa.*

**vicinity**

*Said* "vis-**sin**-it-ee" NOUN If something is in the vicinity of a place, it is in the surrounding or nearby area.

**vicious**

ADJECTIVE cruel and violent.
**viciously** ADVERB **viciousness** NOUN

**victim** victims

NOUN someone who has been harmed or injured by someone or something.

**victor** victors

NOUN The victor in a fight or contest is the person who wins.

**Victorian**

ADJECTIVE **1** Victorian describes things that happened or were made during the reign of Queen Victoria.

**2** Victorian also describes people or things connected with the state of Victoria in Australia.

**victory** victories

NOUN a success in a battle or competition.
**victorious** ADJECTIVE

■ conquest, triumph, win

**video** videos videoing videoed

NOUN **1** Video is the recording and showing of films and events using a video recorder, video tape, and a television set. **2** a sound and picture recording which can be played back on a television set. **3** a video recorder. ▶ VERB **4** If you video something, you record it on magnetic tape for later viewing.

**video recorder** video recorders

NOUN A video recorder or video cassette recorder is a machine for recording and playing back programmes from television.

**vie** vies vying vied

VERB; *FORMAL* If you vie with someone, you compete to do something sooner than or better than they do.

**Vietnamese**

*Said* "vyet-nam-**meez**" ADJECTIVE
**1** belonging or relating to Vietnam.
▶ NOUN **2** someone who comes from Vietnam. **3** Vietnamese is the main language spoken in Vietnam.

**view** views viewing viewed

NOUN **1** Your views are your personal opinions E.G. *his political views.*
**2** everything you can see from a particular place. ▶ VERB **3** If you view something in a particular way, you think of it in that way E.G. *They viewed me with contempt.* ▶ PHRASE **4** You use **in view of** to specify the main fact or event influencing your actions or opinions E.G. *He wore a lighter suit in*

a b c d e f g h i j k l m n o p q r s t u w x y z

A
B
C
D
E
F
G
H
I
J
K
L
M
N
O
P
Q
R
S
T
U
V
W
X
Y
Z

*view of the heat.* **5** If something is **on view**, it is being shown or exhibited to the public.

■ (sense 2) prospect, scene, vista

**viewer** viewers

NOUN Viewers are the people who watch television.

**viewpoint** viewpoints

NOUN **1** Your viewpoint is your attitude towards something. **2** a place from which you get a good view of an area or event.

**vigil** vigils

*Said* "vij-jil" NOUN a period of time, especially at night, when you stay quietly in one place, for example because you are making a political protest or praying.

**vigilant**

ADJECTIVE careful and alert to danger or trouble.

**vigilante** vigilantes

*Said* "vij-il-**ant**-ee" NOUN Vigilantes are unofficially organized groups of people who try to protect their community and catch and punish criminals.

**vigorous**

ADJECTIVE energetic or enthusiastic.
**vigorously** ADVERB **vigour** NOUN

**Viking** Vikings

NOUN The Vikings were seamen from Scandinavia who attacked villages in parts of north-western Europe from the 8th to the 11th centuries.

**vile** viler vilest

ADJECTIVE unpleasant or disgusting *E.G. a vile accusation… a vile smell.*

**villa** villas

NOUN a house, especially a pleasant holiday home in a country with a warm climate.

**village** villages

NOUN a collection of houses and other buildings in the countryside.
**villager** NOUN

**villain** villains

NOUN someone who harms others or breaks the law.
**villainous** ADJECTIVE **villainy** NOUN

■ criminal, evildoer, rogue

**vindicate** vindicates vindicating vindicated

VERB; *FORMAL* If someone is vindicated, their views or ideas are proved to be right *E.G. My friend's instincts have been vindicated.*

**vindictive**

ADJECTIVE Someone who is vindictive is deliberately hurtful towards someone, often as an act of revenge.
**vindictiveness** NOUN

**vine** vines

NOUN a trailing or climbing plant which winds itself around and over a support, especially one which produces grapes.

**vinegar**

NOUN Vinegar is a sharp-tasting liquid made from sour wine, beer, or cider, which is used for salad dressing.
**vinegary** ADJECTIVE

▥ from French *vin* meaning 'wine' and *aigre* meaning 'sour'

**vineyard** vineyards

NOUN an area of land where grapes are grown.

**vintage** vintages

ADJECTIVE **1** A vintage wine is a good quality wine which has been stored for a number of years to improve its quality. **2** Vintage describes something which is the best or most typical of its kind *E.G. a vintage guitar.* **3** A vintage car is one made between 1918 and 1930. ▶ NOUN **4** a grape harvest of one particular year and the wine produced from it.

**vinyl**

NOUN Vinyl is a strong plastic used to make things such as furniture and floor coverings.

**viola** violas

*Said "vee-oh-la"* NOUN a musical instrument like a violin, but larger and with a lower pitch.

**violate** violates violating violated

VERB **1** If you violate an agreement, law, or promise, you break it. **2** If you violate someone's peace or privacy, you disturb it. **3** If you violate a place, especially a holy place, you treat it with disrespect or violence.

**violation** NOUN

**violence**

NOUN **1** Violence is behaviour which is intended to hurt or kill people. **2** If you do or say something with violence, you use a lot of energy in doing or saying it, often because you are angry.

**violent**

ADJECTIVE **1** If someone is violent, they try to hurt or kill people. **2** A violent event happens unexpectedly and with great force. **3** Something that is violent is said, felt, or done with great force.

**violently** ADVERB

**violet** violets

NOUN **1** a plant with dark purple flowers. ▶ NOUN OR ADJECTIVE **2** bluish purple.

**violin** violins

NOUN a musical instrument with four strings that is held under the chin and played with a bow.

**violinist** NOUN

**VIP** VIPs

NOUN VIPs are famous or important people. VIP is an abbreviation for

'very important person'.

**viper** vipers

NOUN Vipers are types of poisonous snakes.

**virgin** virgins

NOUN **1** someone who has never had sexual intercourse. ▶ PROPER NOUN **2** The Virgin, or the Blessed Virgin, is a name given to Mary, the mother of Jesus Christ. ▶ ADJECTIVE **3** Something that is virgin is fresh and unused *E.G. virgin land.*

**virginity** NOUN

**virginal** virginals

ADJECTIVE **1** Someone who is virginal looks young and innocent. **2** Something that is virginal is fresh and clean and looks as if it has never been used. ▶ NOUN **3** a keyboard instrument popular in the 16th and 17th centuries.

**Virgo**

NOUN Virgo is the sixth sign of the zodiac, represented by a girl. People born between August 23rd and September 22nd are born under this sign.

**virile**

ADJECTIVE A virile man has all the qualities that a man is traditionally expected to have, such as strength and sexuality.

**virility** NOUN

**virtual**

*Said "vur-tyool"* ADJECTIVE Virtual means that something has all the characteristics of a particular thing, but it is not formally recognized as being that thing *E.G. The country is in a virtual state of war.*

**virtually** ADVERB

**virtual reality**

NOUN Virtual reality is a situation or

Elaine and Emily shout EE when they mEEt to grEEt each other (-ee-)     ▶ SPELLING NOTE

**virtue** virtues

NOUN **1** Virtue is thinking and doing what is morally right and avoiding what is wrong. **2** a good quality in someone's character. **3** A virtue of something is an advantage E.G. *the virtue of neatness.* ▶ A FORMAL PHRASE

**4 By virtue of** means because of E.G. *The article stuck in my mind by virtue of one detail.*

■ (sense 1) goodness, integrity, morality

**virtuoso** virtuosos or virtuosi
*Said* "vur-*tyoo*-**oh**-zoh" NOUN someone who is exceptionally good at something, particularly playing a musical instrument.

🏛 from Italian *virtuoso* meaning 'skilled'

**virtuous**

ADJECTIVE behaving with or showing moral virtue.

■ good, moral, upright

**virus** viruses
*Said* "vie-*russ*" NOUN **1** a kind of germ that can cause disease. **2** ( ICT ) a program that alters or damages the information stored in a computer system.

**viral** ADJECTIVE

**visa** visas

NOUN an official stamp, usually put in your passport, that allows you to visit a particular country.

**viscount** viscounts
*Said* "vie-*kount*" NOUN a British nobleman.

**viscountess** NOUN

**Vishnu**

PROPER NOUN Vishnu is a Hindu god and is one of the Trimurti.

**visibility**

NOUN You use 'visibility' to say how far or how clearly you can see in particular weather conditions.

**visible**

ADJECTIVE **1** able to be seen.
**2** noticeable or evident E.G. *There was little visible excitement.*

**visibly** ADVERB

**vision** visions

NOUN **1** Vision is the ability to see clearly. **2** a mental picture, in which you imagine how things might be different E.G. *the vision of a possible future.* **3** Vision is also imaginative insight E.G. *a total lack of vision and imagination.* **4** an unusual experience that you have, in which you see things that other people cannot see, as a result of madness, divine inspiration, or taking drugs.

**visionary** NOUN OR ADJECTIVE

**visit** visits visiting visited

VERB **1** If you visit someone, you go to see them and spend time with them. **2** If you visit a place, you go to see it. ▶ NOUN **3** a trip to see a person or place.

**visitor** NOUN

**visor** visors
*Said* "vie-*zor*" NOUN a transparent movable shield attached to a helmet, which can be pulled down to protect the eyes or face.

**visual**

ADJECTIVE relating to sight E.G. *visual problems.*

**visualize** visualizes visualizing visualized
*Said* "viz-*yool*-eyes"; also spelt **visualise**

VERB If you visualize something, you form a mental picture of it.

# vital

ADJECTIVE **1** necessary or very important *E.G. vital evidence.* **2** energetic, exciting, and full of life *E.G. an active and vital life outside school.*

**vitally** ADVERB

■ (sense 1) essential, necessary

# vitality

NOUN People who have vitality are energetic and lively.

# vitamin vitamins

NOUN (D&T) Vitamins are organic compounds which you need in order to remain healthy. They occur naturally in food.

# vitriolic

ADJECTIVE; *FORMAL* Vitriolic language or behaviour is full of bitterness and hate.

# vivacious

*Said* "viv-**vay**-shuss" ADJECTIVE A vivacious person is attractively lively and high-spirited.

**vivacity** NOUN

# vivid

ADJECTIVE very bright in colour or clear in detail *E.G. vivid red paint… vivid memories.*

**vividly** ADVERB   **vividness** NOUN

■ intense, powerful

# vivisection

NOUN Vivisection is the act of cutting open living animals for medical research.

# vixen vixens

NOUN a female fox.

# vocabulary vocabularies

NOUN (ENGLISH) **1** Someone's vocabulary is the total number of words they know in a particular language. **2** The vocabulary of a language is all the words in it.

# vocal

ADJECTIVE You say that someone is vocal if they express their opinions strongly and openly. (MUSIC)

# vocation vocations

NOUN **1** a strong wish to do a particular job, especially one which involves serving other people. **2** a profession or career.

# vocational

ADJECTIVE 'Vocational' is used to describe the skills needed for a particular job or profession *E.G. vocational training.*

# vociferous

*Said* "voe-**sif**-fer-uss" ADJECTIVE; *FORMAL* Someone who is vociferous speaks a lot, or loudly, because they want to make a point strongly *E.G. vociferous critics.*

**vociferously** ADVERB

# vodka vodkas

NOUN a strong clear alcoholic drink which originally came from Russia.

▥ from Russian *vodka* meaning 'little water'

# vogue

*Said* "vohg" PHRASE If something is **the vogue** or **in vogue**, it is fashionable and popular *E.G. Colour photographs became the vogue.*

# voice voices voicing voiced

NOUN **1** Your voice is the sounds produced by your vocal cords, or the ability to make such sounds. ▶ VERB **2** If you voice an opinion or an emotion, you say what you think or feel *E.G. A range of opinions were voiced.*

# void voids

NOUN **1** a situation which seems empty because it has no interest or excitement *E.G. Cats fill a very large void in your life.* **2** a large empty hole or space *E.G. His feet dangled in the void.*

a
b
c
d
e
f
g
h
i
j
k
l
m
n
o
p
q
r
s
t
u
w
x
y
z

A
B
C
D
E
F
G
H
I
J
K
L
M
N
O
P
Q
R
S
T
U
V
W
X
Y
Z

**volatile**

ADJECTIVE liable to change often and unexpectedly *E.G. The situation at work is volatile.*

**volcanic**

ADJECTIVE A volcanic region has many volcanoes or was created by volcanoes.

**volcano volcanoes**

NOUN a hill with an opening through which lava, gas, and ash burst out from inside the earth onto the surface.

📖 named after *Vulcan*, the Roman god of fire

**vole voles**

NOUN a small mammal like a mouse with a short tail, which lives in fields and near rivers.

**volition**

NOUN; FORMAL If you do something of your own volition, you do it because you have decided for yourself, without being persuaded by others *E.G. He attended of his own volition.*

**volley volleys**

NOUN 1 A volley of shots or gunfire is a lot of shots fired at the same time. 2 In tennis, a volley is a stroke in which the player hits the ball before it bounces.

**volleyball**

NOUN Volleyball is a game in which two teams hit a large ball back and forth over a high net with their hands. The ball is not allowed to bounce on the ground.

**volt volts**

NOUN a unit used to measure the force of an electric current.

**voltage voltages**

NOUN The voltage of an electric current is its force measured in volts.

**volume volumes**

NOUN 1 (MATHS) The volume of something is the amount of space it contains or occupies. 2 The volume of something is also the amount of it that there is *E.G. a large volume of letters.* 3 The volume of a radio, TV, or record player is the strength of the sound that it produces. 4 a book, or one of a series of books.

**voluminous**

*Said* "vol-**loo**-min-uss" ADJECTIVE very large or full in size or quantity *E.G. voluminous skirts.*

**voluntary**

ADJECTIVE 1 Voluntary actions are ones that you do because you choose to do them and not because you have been forced to do them. 2 Voluntary work is done by people who are not paid for what they do.

**voluntarily** ADVERB

**volunteer volunteers volunteering volunteered**

NOUN 1 someone who does work for which they are not paid *E.G. a volunteer for Greenpeace.* 2 someone who chooses to join the armed forces, especially during wartime.

▶ VERB 3 If you volunteer to do something, you offer to do it rather than being forced into it. 4 If you volunteer information, you give it without being asked.

**voluptuous**

*Said* "vol-**lupt**-yoo-uss" ADJECTIVE A voluptuous woman has a figure which is considered to be sexually exciting.

**voluptuously** ADVERB

**voluptuousness** NOUN

**vomit vomits vomiting vomited**

VERB 1 If you vomit, food and drink comes back up from your stomach

and out through your mouth. ▶ NOUN
**2** Vomit is partly digested food and
drink that has come back up from
someone's stomach and out through
their mouth.

**voodoo**

NOUN Voodoo is a form of magic
practised in the Caribbean, especially
in Haiti.

**vote** votes voting voted

NOUN **1** Someone's vote is their choice
in an election, or at a meeting where
decisions are taken. **2** When a group
of people have a vote, they make a
decision by allowing each person in
the group to say what they would
prefer. **3** In an election, the vote is the
total number of people who have
made their choice *E.G. the average
Liberal vote.* **4** If people have the
vote, they have the legal right to
vote in an election. ▶ VERB **5** When
people vote, they indicate their
choice or opinion, usually by writing
on a piece of paper or by raising
their hand. **6** If you vote that a
particular thing should happen, you
are suggesting it should happen *E.G. I
vote that we all go to Holland.*

**voter** NOUN

**vouch** vouches vouching
vouched

VERB **1** If you say that you can vouch
for something, you mean that you
have evidence from your own
experience that it is true or correct.
**2** If you say that you can vouch for
someone, you mean that you are
sure that you can guarantee their
good behaviour or support *E.G. Her
employer will vouch for her.*

**voucher** vouchers

NOUN a piece of paper that can be
used instead of money to pay for
something.

**vow** vows vowing vowed

VERB **1** If you vow to do something,
you make a solemn promise to do it
*E.G. He vowed to do better in future.*
▶ NOUN **2** a solemn promise.

**vowel** vowels

NOUN (ENGLISH) a sound made without
your tongue touching the roof of
your mouth or your teeth, or one of
the letters a, e, i, o, u, which represent
such sounds.

**voyage** voyages

NOUN a long journey on a ship or in a
spacecraft.

**voyager** NOUN

**vulgar**

ADJECTIVE **1** socially unacceptable or
offensive *E.G. vulgar language.*
**2** showing a lack of taste or quality
*E.G. the most vulgar person who ever
existed.*

**vulgarity** NOUN    **vulgarly** ADVERB

**vulnerable**

ADJECTIVE weak and without
protection.

**vulnerably** ADVERB    **vulnerability**
NOUN

▪ defenceless, susceptible, weak

**vulture** vultures

NOUN a large bird which lives in hot
countries and eats the flesh of dead
animals.

**vying**

the present participle of **vie**.

a b c d e f g h i j k l m n o p q r s t u w x y z

# Ww

**wacky wackier wackiest**

ADJECTIVE; INFORMAL odd or crazy E.G. *wacky clothes*.

**wad wads**

NOUN 1 A wad of papers or banknotes is a thick bundle of them. 2 A wad of something is a lump of it E.G. *a wad of cotton wool*.

**waddle waddles waddling waddled**

VERB When a duck or a fat person waddles, they walk with short, quick steps, swaying slightly from side to side.

**waddy waddies**

NOUN a heavy, wooden club used by Australian Aborigines as a weapon in war.

**wade wades wading waded**

VERB 1 If you wade through water or mud, you walk slowly through it. 2 If you wade through a book or document, you spend a lot of time and effort reading it because you find it dull or difficult.

**wader waders**

NOUN Waders are long waterproof rubber boots worn by fishermen.

**wafer wafers**

NOUN 1 a thin, crisp, sweet biscuit often eaten with ice cream. 2 a thin disc of special bread used in the Christian service of Holy Communion.

**waffle waffles waffling waffled**

*Said "wof-fl"* VERB 1 When someone waffles, they talk or write a lot without being clear or without saying anything of importance. ▶ NOUN 2 Waffle is vague and lengthy speech or writing. 3 a thick, crisp

pancake with squares marked on it often eaten with syrup poured over it.

**waft wafts wafting wafted**

*Said "wahft"* VERB If a sound or scent wafts or is wafted through the air, it moves gently through it.

**wag wags wagging wagged**

VERB 1 When a dog wags its tail, it shakes it repeatedly from side to side. 2 If you wag your finger, you move it repeatedly up and down.

**wage wages waging waged**

NOUN 1 A wage or wages is the regular payment made to someone each week for the work they do, especially for manual or unskilled work. ▶ VERB 2 If a person or country wages a campaign or war, they start it and carry it on over a period of time.

**wager wagers**

NOUN a bet.

**wagon wagons**; also spelt **waggon**

NOUN 1 a strong four-wheeled vehicle for carrying heavy loads, usually pulled by a horse or tractor. 2 Wagons are also the containers for freight pulled by a railway engine.

**waif waifs**

*Said "wayf"* NOUN a young, thin person who looks hungry and homeless.

**wail wails wailing wailed**

VERB 1 To wail is to cry loudly with sorrow or pain. ▶ NOUN 2 a long, unhappy cry.

**waist waists**

NOUN the middle part of your body where it narrows slightly above your hips.

**waistcoat waistcoats**

NOUN a sleeveless piece of clothing,

often worn under a suit or jacket, which buttons up the front.

**wait** waits waiting waited

VERB **1** If you wait, you spend time, usually doing little or nothing, before something happens. **2** If something can wait, it is not urgent and can be dealt with later. **3** If you wait on people in a restaurant, it is your job to serve them food. ▶ NOUN **4** A period of time before something happens.
▶ PHRASE **5** If you **can't wait** to do something, you are very excited and eager to do it.

**waiter** waiters

NOUN a man who works in a restaurant, serving people with food and drink.

**waiting list** waiting lists

NOUN a list of people who have asked for something which cannot be given to them immediately, for example medical treatment.

**waitress** waitresses

NOUN a woman who works in a restaurant, serving people with food and drink.

**waive** waives waiving waived

*Said* "wave" VERB If someone waives something such as a rule or a right, they decide not to insist on it being applied.

**wake** wakes waking woke woken

VERB **1** When you wake or when something wakes you, you become conscious again after being asleep.
▶ NOUN **2** The wake of a boat or other object moving in water is the track of waves it leaves behind it. **3** A gathering of people who have got together to mourn someone's death.
▶ PHRASE **4** If one thing follows **in the wake of** another, it follows it as a

result of it, or in imitation of it *E.G. a project set up in the wake of last year's riots.*

■ (sense 1) awaken, rouse

**wake up** VERB **1** When you wake up or something wakes you up, you become conscious again after being asleep. **2** If you wake up to a dangerous situation, you become aware of it.

**waken** wakens wakening wakened

VERB; *LITERARY* When you waken someone, you wake them up.

**walk** walks walking walked

VERB **1** When you walk, you move along by putting one foot in front of the other on the ground. **2** If you walk away with or walk off with something such as a prize, you win it or achieve it easily. ▶ NOUN **3** a journey made by walking *E.G. We'll have a quick walk.* **4** Your walk is the way you walk *E.G. his rolling walk.*

**walk out** VERB **1** If you walk out on someone, you leave them suddenly. **2** If workers walk out, they go on strike.

**walkabout** walkabouts

NOUN **1** an informal walk amongst crowds in a public place by royalty or by some other well-known person. **2** Walkabout is when an Australian Aborigine goes off to live and wander in the bush for a period of time.

**walker** walkers

NOUN a person who walks, especially for pleasure or to keep fit.

**walking stick** walking sticks

NOUN a wooden stick which people can lean on while walking.

**Walkman**

NOUN; *TRADEMARK* a small cassette player

a b c d e f g h i j k l m n o p q r s t u v **w** x y z

with lightweight headphones, which people carry around so that they can listen to music while they are doing something like walking.

**walk of life** walks of life

NOUN The walk of life that you come from is the position you have in society and the kind of job you have.

**walkover** walkovers

NOUN; INFORMAL a very easy victory in a competition or contest.

**walkway** walkways

NOUN a passage between two buildings for people to walk along.

**wall** walls

NOUN **1** one of the vertical sides of a building or a room. **2** a long, narrow vertical structure made of stone or brick that surrounds or divides an area of land. **3** a lining or membrane enclosing a bodily cavity or structure E.G. the wall of the womb.

**wallaby** wallabies

NOUN an animal like a small kangaroo.
📖 from wolaba, an Australian Aboriginal word

**wallaroo** wallaroos

NOUN a large, stocky kangaroo that lives in rocky or mountainous regions of Australia.

**wallet** wallets

NOUN a small, flat case made of leather or plastic, used for keeping paper money and sometimes credit cards.

**wallop** wallops walloping walloped

VERB; INFORMAL If you wallop someone, you hit them very hard.

**wallow** wallows wallowing wallowed

VERB **1** If you wallow in an unpleasant feeling or situation, you allow it to continue longer than is reasonable

or necessary because you are getting a kind of enjoyment from it E.G. We're wallowing in misery. **2** When an animal wallows in mud or water, it lies or rolls about in it slowly for pleasure.

**wallpaper** wallpapers

NOUN Wallpaper is thick coloured or patterned paper for pasting onto the walls of rooms in order to decorate them.

**walnut** walnuts

NOUN **1** an edible nut with a wrinkled shape and a hard, round, light-brown shell. **2** Walnut is wood from the walnut tree which is often used for making expensive furniture.
📖 from Old English walh-hnutu meaning 'foreign nut'

**walrus** walruses

NOUN an animal which lives in the sea and which looks like a large seal with a tough skin, coarse whiskers, and two tusks.

**waltz** waltzes waltzing waltzed

NOUN **1** a dance which has a rhythm of three beats to the bar. ▶ VERB **2** If you waltz with someone, you dance a waltz with them. **3** INFORMAL If you waltz somewhere, you walk there in a relaxed and confident way.
📖 from Old German walzen meaning 'to revolve'

**wan**

Rhymes with "on" ADJECTIVE pale and tired-looking.

**wand** wands

NOUN a long, thin rod that magicians wave when they are performing tricks and magic.

**wander** wanders wandering wandered

VERB **1** If you wander in a place, you

walk around in a casual way. **2** If your mind wanders or your thoughts wander, you lose concentration and start thinking about other things.
**wanderer** NOUN
▪ (sense 1) ramble, roam, stroll

**wane** wanes waning waned
VERB If a condition, attitude, or emotion wanes, it becomes gradually weaker.

**wangle** wangles wangling wangled
VERB; *INFORMAL* If you wangle something that you want, you manage to get it by being crafty or persuasive.

**want** wants wanting wanted
VERB **1** If you want something, you feel a desire to have it or a need for it to happen. **2** *INFORMAL* If something wants doing, there is a need for it to be done *E.G. Her hair wants cutting.* **3** If someone is wanted, the police are searching for them *E.G. John was wanted for fraud.* ▶ NOUN **4** *FORMAL* A want of something is a lack of it.

**wanting**
ADJECTIVE If you find something wanting or if it proves wanting, it is not as good in some way as you think it should be.

**wanton**
ADJECTIVE A wanton action deliberately causes unnecessary harm or waste *E.G. wanton destruction.*

**war** wars warring warred
NOUN **1** a period of fighting between countries or states when weapons are used and many people may be killed. **2** a competition between groups of people, or a campaign against something *E.G. a trade war… the war against crime.* ▶ VERB **3** When two countries war with each other,

they are fighting a war against each other.
**warring** ADJECTIVE
▪ (sense 1) battle, fighting, hostilities
▪ (sense 3) battle, fight

**waratah** waratahs
*Said "wor-ra-tah"* NOUN an Australian shrub with dark green leaves and large clusters of crimson flowers.

**warble** warbles warbling warbled
VERB When a bird warbles, it sings pleasantly with high notes.

**ward** wards warding warded
NOUN **1** a room in a hospital which has beds for several people who need similar treatment. **2** an area or district which forms a separate part of a political constituency or local council. **3** A ward or a ward of court is a child who is officially put in the care of an adult or a court of law, because their parents are dead or because they need protection. ▶ VERB **4** If you ward off a danger or an illness, you do something to prevent it from affecting or harming you.

**-ward** or **-wards**
SUFFIX -ward and -wards form adverbs or adjectives that show the way something is moving or facing *E.G. homeward… westwards.*

**warden** wardens
NOUN **1** a person in charge of a building or institution such as a youth hostel or prison. **2** an official who makes sure that certain laws or rules are obeyed in a particular place or activity *E.G. a traffic warden.*

**warder** warders
NOUN a person who is in charge of prisoners in a jail.

a b c d e f g h i j k l m n o p q r s t u v w x y z

**wardrobe** wardrobes

NOUN **1** a tall cupboard in which you can hang your clothes. **2** Someone's wardrobe is their collection of clothes.

**ware** wares

NOUN **1** Ware is manufactured goods of a particular kind E.G. *kitchenware*. **2** Someone's wares are the things they sell, usually in the street or in a market.

**warehouse** warehouses

NOUN a large building where raw materials or manufactured goods are stored.

**warfare**

NOUN Warfare is the activity of fighting a war.

**warhead** warheads

NOUN the front end of a bomb or missile, where the explosives are carried.

**warlock** warlocks

NOUN a male witch.

**warm** warmer warmest; warms warming warmed

ADJECTIVE **1** Something that is warm has some heat, but not enough to be hot E.G. *a warm day*. **2** Warm clothes or blankets are made of a material which protects you from the cold. **3** Warm colours or sounds are pleasant and make you feel comfortable and relaxed. **4** A warm person is friendly and affectionate.
▸ VERB **5** If you warm something, you heat it up gently so that it stops being cold.

**warmly** ADVERB

**warm up** VERB If you warm up for an event or an activity, you practise or exercise gently to prepare for it.

**warmth**

NOUN **1** Warmth is a moderate amount of heat. **2** Someone who has warmth is friendly and affectionate.

**warn** warns warning warned

VERB **1** If you warn someone about a possible problem or danger, you tell them about it in advance so that they are aware of it E.G. *I warned him what it would be like*. **2** If you warn someone not to do something, you advise them not to do it, in order to avoid possible danger or punishment E.G. *I have warned her not to train for 10 days*.
■ (sense 1) alert, caution, notify

**warn off** VERB If you warn someone off, you tell them to go away or to stop doing something.

**warning** warnings

NOUN something said or written to tell people of a possible problem or danger.

**warp** warps warping warped

VERB **1** If something warps or is warped, it becomes bent, often because of the effect of heat or water. **2** If something warps someone's mind or character, it makes them abnormal or corrupt. **3** The warp in a piece of cloth is the stronger lengthwise threads.

**warrant** warrants warranting warranted

VERB **1** FORMAL If something warrants a particular action, it makes the action seem necessary E.G. *no evidence to warrant a murder investigation*.
▸ NOUN **2** an official document which gives permission to the police to do something E.G. *a warrant for his arrest*.

**warranty warranties**

NOUN a guarantee E.G. *a three-year warranty.*

**warren warrens**

NOUN a group of holes under the ground connected by tunnels, which rabbits live in.

**warrigal warrigals**

*Said "wor-rih-gl"* NOUN **1** In Australian English, a dingo. **2** In Australian English, a wild horse or other wild creature. ▶ ADJECTIVE **3** In Australian English, wild.

**warrior warriors**

NOUN a fighting man or soldier, especially in former times.

**warship warships**

NOUN a ship built with guns and used for fighting in wars.

**wart warts**

NOUN a small, hard piece of skin which can grow on someone's face or hands.

**wartime**

NOUN Wartime is a period of time during which a country is at war.

**wary warier wariest**

ADJECTIVE cautious and on one's guard E.G. *Michelle is wary of marriage.*

**warily** ADVERB

**was**

a past tense of **be**.

**wash washes washing washed**

VERB **1** If you wash something, you clean it with water and soap. **2** If you wash, you clean yourself using soap and water. **3** If something is washed somewhere, it is carried there gently by water E.G. *The infant Arthur was washed ashore.* ▶ NOUN **4** The wash is all the clothes and bedding that are washed together at one time E.G. *a typical family's weekly wash.* **5** The wash in water is the disturbance and waves produced at the back of a moving boat. ▶ PHRASE **6** If you **wash your hands of** something, you refuse to have anything more to do with it.

**wash up** VERB **1** If you wash up, you wash the dishes, pans, and cutlery used in preparing and eating a meal. **2** If something is washed up on land, it is carried by a river or sea and left there E.G. *A body had been washed up on the beach.*

**washbasin washbasins**

NOUN a deep bowl, usually fixed to a wall, with taps for hot and cold water.

**washer washers**

NOUN **1** a thin, flat ring of metal or plastic which is placed over a bolt before the nut is screwed on, so that it is fixed more tightly. **2** In Australian English, a small piece of towelling for washing yourself.

**washing**

NOUN Washing consists of clothes and bedding which need to be washed or are in the process of being washed and dried.

**washing machine washing machines**

NOUN a machine for washing clothes in.

**washing-up**

NOUN If you do the washing-up, you wash the dishes, pans, and cutlery which have been used in the cooking and eating of a meal.

**wasp wasps**

NOUN an insect with yellow and black stripes across its body, which can sting like a bee.

**wastage**

NOUN Wastage is loss and misuse of something E.G. *wastage of resources.*

I always visit my FRIend on a FRIday (friend)    SPELLING NOTE

a b c d e f g h i j k l m n o p q r s t u v **w** x y z

ABCDEFGHIJKLMNOPQRSTUVWXYZ

**waste** wastes wasting wasted

VERB **1** If you waste time, money, or energy, you use too much of it on something that is not important or necessary. **2** If you waste an opportunity, you do not take advantage of it when it is available. **3** If you say that something is wasted on someone, you mean that it is too good, too clever, or too sophisticated for them *E.G. This book is wasted on us.* ▶ NOUN **4** If an activity is a waste of time, money, or energy, it is not important or necessary. **5** Waste is the use of more money or some other resource than is necessary. **6** Waste is also material that is no longer wanted, or material left over from a useful process *E.G. nuclear waste.* ▶ ADJECTIVE **7** unwanted in its present form *E.G. waste paper.* **8** Waste land is land which is not used or looked after by anyone.

≡ (sense 1) fritter away, misuse, squander

≡ (sense 5) misuse, squandering

**waste away** VERB If someone is wasting away, they are becoming very thin and weak because they are ill or not eating properly.

**wasted**

ADJECTIVE unnecessary *E.G. a wasted journey.*

**wasteful**

ADJECTIVE extravagant or causing waste by using something in a careless and inefficient way.

≡ extravagant, prodigal, spendthrift

**wasteland** wastelands

NOUN A wasteland is land which is of no use because it is infertile or has been misused.

**wasting**

ADJECTIVE A wasting disease is one that gradually reduces the strength and health of the body.

**watch** watches watching watched

NOUN **1** a small clock usually worn on a strap on the wrist. **2** a period of time during which a guard is kept over something. ▶ VERB **3** If you watch something, you look at it for some time and pay close attention to what is happening. **4** If you watch a situation, you pay attention to it or are aware of it *E.G. I had watched Jimmy's progress with interest.* **5** If you watch over someone or something, you care for them.

**watch out** VERB **1** If you watch out for something, you keep alert to see if it is near you *E.G. Watch out for more fog and ice.* **2** If you tell someone to watch out, you are warning them to be very careful.

**watchdog** watchdogs

NOUN **1** a dog used to guard property. **2** a person or group whose job is to make sure that companies do not act illegally or irresponsibly.

**watchful**

ADJECTIVE careful to notice everything that is happening *E.G. the watchful eye of her father.*

**watchman** watchmen

NOUN a person whose job is to guard property.

**water** waters watering watered

NOUN **1** Water is a clear, colourless, tasteless, and odourless liquid that is necessary for all plant and animal life. **2** You use water or waters to refer to a large area of water, such as a lake or sea *E.G. the black waters of the* *lake.* ▶ VERB **3** If you water a plant or an animal, you give it water to drink. **4** If your eyes water, you have tears in them because they are hurting. **5** If your mouth waters, it produces extra saliva, usually because you think of or can smell something appetizing.

**water down** VERB If you water something down, you make it weaker.

**watercolour watercolours**
NOUN **1** Watercolours are paints for painting pictures, which are diluted with water and put on the paper using a wet brush. **2** a picture which has been painted using watercolours.

**watercress**
NOUN Watercress is a small plant which grows in streams and pools. Its leaves taste hot and are eaten in salads.

**waterfall waterfalls**
NOUN A waterfall is water from a river or stream as it flows over the edge of a steep cliff in hills or mountains and falls to the ground below.

**waterfront waterfronts**
NOUN a street or piece of land next to an area of water such as a river or harbour.

**watering can watering cans**
NOUN a container with a handle and a long spout, which you use to water plants.

**waterlogged**
ADJECTIVE Land that is waterlogged is so wet that the soil cannot contain any more water, so that some water remains on the surface of the ground.

**watermelon watermelons**
NOUN a large, round fruit which has a hard green skin and red juicy flesh.

**waterproof waterproofs**
ADJECTIVE **1** not letting water pass through E.G. *waterproof clothing*. ▶ NOUN **2** a coat which keeps water out.

**watershed watersheds**
NOUN an event or period which marks a turning point or the beginning of a new way of life E.G. *a watershed in European history*.

**watersider watersiders**
NOUN In Australian and New Zealand English, a person who loads and unloads the cargo from ships.

**water-skiing**
NOUN Water-skiing is the sport of skimming over the water on skis while being pulled by a boat.

**water table water tables**
NOUN The water table is the level below the surface of the ground at which water can be found.

**watertight**
ADJECTIVE **1** Something that is watertight does not allow water to pass through. **2** An agreement or an argument that is watertight has been so carefully put together that nobody should be able to find a fault in it.

**waterway waterways**
NOUN a canal, river, or narrow channel of sea which ships or boats can sail along.

**waterworks**
NOUN A waterworks is the system of pipes, filters, and tanks where the public supply of water is stored and cleaned, and from where it is distributed.

**watery**
ADJECTIVE **1** pale or weak E.G. *a watery smile*. **2** Watery food or drink

a b c d e f g h i j k l m n o p q r s t u v w x y z

A
B
C
D
E
F
G
H
I
J
K
L
M
N
O
P
Q
R
S
T
U
V
W
X
Y
Z

contains a lot of water or is thin like water.

**watt** watts
Said "**wot**" NOUN a unit of measurement of electrical power.

**wattle** wattles
Said "**wot**-tl" NOUN an Australian acacia tree with spikes of brightly coloured flowers.

**wave** waves waving waved
VERB 1 If you wave your hand, you move it from side to side, usually to say hello or goodbye. 2 If you wave someone somewhere or wave them on, you make a movement with your hand to tell them which way to go. 3 If you wave something, you hold it up and move it from side to side E.G. *The doctor waved a piece of paper at him.* ▶ NOUN 4 a ridge of water on the surface of the sea caused by wind or by tides. 5 A wave is the form in which some types of energy such as heat, light, or sound travel through a substance. 6 A wave of sympathy, alarm, or panic is a steady increase in it which spreads through you or through a group of people. 7 an increase in a type of activity or behaviour E.G. *the crime wave.*
■ (sense 3) brandish, flourish

**wavelength** wavelengths
NOUN 1 the distance between the same point on two adjacent waves of energy. 2 the size of radio wave which a particular radio station uses to broadcast its programmes.

**waver** wavers wavering wavered
VERB 1 If you waver or if your confidence or beliefs waver, you are no longer as firm, confident, or sure in your beliefs E.G. *Ben has never wavered from his belief.* 2 If

something wavers, it moves slightly E.G. *The gun did not waver in his hand.*

**wavy** wavier waviest
ADJECTIVE having waves or regular curves E.G. *wavy hair.*

**wax** waxes waxing waxed
NOUN 1 Wax is a solid, slightly shiny substance made of fat or oil and used to make candles and polish. 2 Wax is also the sticky yellow substance in your ears. ▶ VERB 3 If you wax a surface, you treat it or cover it with a thin layer of wax, especially to polish it. 4 FORMAL If you wax eloquent, you talk in an eloquent way.

**way** ways
NOUN 1 A way of doing something is the manner of doing it E.G. *an excellent way of cooking meat.* 2 The ways of a person or group are their customs or their normal behaviour E.G. *Their ways are certainly different.* 3 The way you feel about something is your attitude to it or your opinion about it. 4 If you have a way with people or things, you are very skilful at dealing with them. 5 The way to a particular place is the route that you take to get there. 6 If you go or look a particular way, you go or look in that direction E.G. *She glanced the other way.* 7 If you divide something a number of ways, you divide it into that number of parts. 8 'Way' is used with words such as 'little' or 'long' to say how far off in distance or time something is E.G. *They lived a long way away.* ▶ PHRASE 9 If something or someone is **in the way**, they prevent you from moving freely or seeing clearly. 10 You say **by the way** when adding something to what you are saying E.G. *By the way, I asked Brad to drop in.* 11 If you **go out of your way**

to do something, you make a special effort to do it.

■ (sense 5) course, path, route

**wayside**

PHRASE If someone or something **falls by the wayside**, they fail in what they are trying to do, or become forgotten and ignored.

**wayward**

ADJECTIVE difficult to control and likely to change suddenly E.G. *your wayward husband.*

**WC WCs**

NOUN a toilet. WC is an abbreviation for 'water closet'.

**we**

PRONOUN A speaker or writer uses 'we' to refer to himself or herself and one or more other people E.G. *We are going to see Eddie.*

**weak weaker weakest**

ADJECTIVE **1** not having much strength E.G. *weak from lack of sleep.* **2** If something is weak, it is likely to break or fail E.G. *Russia's weak economy.* **3** If you describe someone as weak, you mean they are easily influenced by other people.

**weakly** ADVERB

■ (sense 1) feeble, frail, puny

**weaken weakens weakening weakened**

VERB **1** If someone weakens something, they make it less strong or certain. **2** If someone weakens, they become less certain about something.

**weakling weaklings**

NOUN a person who lacks physical strength or who is weak in character or health.

**weakness weaknesses**

NOUN **1** Weakness is lack of moral or

physical strength. **2** If you have a weakness for something, you have a great liking for it E.G. *a weakness for whisky.*

▶ **wealth**

NOUN **1** (GEOGRAPHY) Wealth is the large amount of money or property which someone owns. **2** A wealth of something is a lot of it E.G. *a wealth of information.*

■ (sense 1) fortune, prosperity, riches

**wealthy wealthier wealthiest**

ADJECTIVE having a large amount of money, property, or other valuable things.

■ affluent, rich, well-off

**wean weans weaning weaned**

VERB To wean a baby or animal is to start feeding it food other than its mother's milk.

**weapon weapons**

NOUN **1** an object used to kill or hurt people in a fight or war. **2** anything which can be used to get the better of an opponent E.G. *Surprise was his only weapon.*

**weaponry** NOUN

**wear wears wearing wore worn**

VERB **1** When you wear something such as clothes, make-up, or jewellery, you have them on your body or face. **2** If you wear a particular expression, it shows on your face. **3** If something wears, it becomes thinner or worse in condition. ▶ NOUN **4** You can refer to clothes that are suitable for a particular time or occasion as a kind of wear E.G. *beach wear.* **5** Wear is the amount or type of use that something has and which causes damage or change to it E.G. *signs of*

a
b
c
d
e
f
g
h
i
j
k
l
m
n
o
p
q
r
s
t
u
v
**w**
x
y
z

*wear.*

**wear down** VERB If you wear people down, you weaken them by repeatedly doing something or asking them to do something.

**wear off** VERB If a feeling such as pain wears off, it gradually disappears.

**wear out** VERB When something wears out or when you wear it out, it is used so much that it becomes thin, weak, and no longer usable.

**wear and tear**
NOUN Wear and tear is the damage caused to something by normal use.

**wearing**
ADJECTIVE Someone or something that is wearing makes you feel extremely tired.

**weary** wearier weariest; wearies wearying wearied
ADJECTIVE 1 very tired. ▶ VERB 2 If you weary of something, you become tired of it.
**wearily** ADVERB **weariness** NOUN

**weasel** weasels
NOUN a small wild animal with a long, thin body and short legs.

**weather** weathers weathering weathered
NOUN 1 (GEOGRAPHY) The weather is the condition of the atmosphere at any particular time and the amount of rain, wind, or sunshine occurring. ▶ VERB 2 If something such as rock or wood weathers, it changes colour or shape as a result of being exposed to the wind, rain, or sun. 3 If you weather a problem or difficulty, you come through it safely. ▶ PHRASE 4 If you are **under the weather**, you feel slightly ill.

**weather forecast** weather forecasts
NOUN a statement saying what the weather will be like the next day or for the next few days.

**weather vane** weather vanes
NOUN a metal object on the roof of a building which turns round in the wind and shows which way the wind is blowing.

**weave** weaves weaving wove woven
VERB 1 To weave cloth is to make it by crossing threads over and under each other, especially by using a machine called a loom. 2 If you weave your way somewhere, you go there by moving from side to side through and round the obstacles. ▶ NOUN 3 The weave of cloth is the way in which the threads are arranged and the pattern that they form E.G. *a tight weave.*

**weaver** weavers
NOUN a person who weaves cloth.

**web** webs
NOUN 1 a fine net of threads that a spider makes from a sticky substance which it produces in its body. 2 something that has a complicated structure or pattern E.G. *a web of lies.* 3 The Web is the same as the **World Wide Web**.

**webbed**
ADJECTIVE Webbed feet have the toes connected by a piece of skin.

**weblog** weblogs
NOUN a person's online diary or journal that he or she puts on the Internet so that other people can read it. It is also shortened to **blog**.

**website** websites
NOUN a publication on the World

Wide Web which contains information about a particular subject.

**wed** weds wedding wedded or wed

VERB; *OLD-FASHIONED* If you wed someone or if you wed, you get married.

**wedding** weddings

NOUN (RE) a marriage ceremony.

**wedge** wedges wedging wedged

VERB 1 If you wedge something, you force it to remain there by holding it there tightly, or by fixing something next to it to prevent it from moving *E.G. I shut the shed door and wedged it with a log of wood.* ▶ NOUN 2 a piece of something such as wood, metal, or rubber with one pointed edge and one thick edge which is used to wedge something. 3 a piece of something that has a thick triangular shape *E.G. a wedge of cheese.*

**wedlock**

NOUN; *OLD-FASHIONED* Wedlock is the state of being married.

**Wednesday** Wednesdays

NOUN Wednesday is the day between Tuesday and Thursday.
🏛 from Old English *Wodnes dæg* meaning 'Woden's day'

**wee** weer weest

ADJECTIVE; *A SCOTTISH WORD* very small.

**weed** weeds weeding weeded

NOUN 1 a wild plant that prevents cultivated plants from growing properly. ▶ VERB 2 If you weed a place, you remove the weeds from it.

**weed out** VERB If you weed out unwanted things, you get rid of them.

**week** weeks

NOUN 1 a period of seven days, especially one beginning on a

Sunday and ending on a Saturday. 2 A week is also the number of hours you spend at work during a week *E.G. a 35-hour week.* 3 The week can refer to the part of a week that does not include Saturday and Sunday *E.G. They are working during the week.*

**weekday** weekdays

NOUN any day except Saturday and Sunday.

**weekend** weekends

NOUN Saturday and Sunday.

**weekly** weeklies

ADJECTIVE OR ADVERB 1 happening or appearing once a week. ▶ NOUN 2 a newspaper or magazine that is published once a week.

**weep** weeps weeping wept

VERB 1 If someone weeps, they cry. 2 If something such as a wound weeps, it oozes blood or other liquid.

**weevil** weevils

NOUN a type of beetle which eats grain, seeds, or plants.

**weft**

NOUN The weft of a piece of woven material is the threads which are passed sideways in and out of the threads held in a loom.

**weigh** weighs weighing weighed

VERB 1 If something weighs a particular amount, that is how heavy it is. 2 If you weigh something, you measure how heavy it is using scales. 3 If you weigh facts or words, you think about them carefully before coming to a decision or before speaking. 4 If a problem weighs on you or weighs upon you, it makes you very worried.

**weigh down** VERB 1 If a load weighs you down, it stops you moving easily. 2 If you are weighed down by

a b c d e f g h i j k l m n o p q r s t u v w x y z

a difficulty, it is making you very worried.

**weigh up** VERB If you weigh up a person or a situation, you make an assessment of them.

**weight** weights weighting weighted

NOUN 1 (MATHS) The weight of something is its heaviness. 2 a metal object which has a certain known heaviness. Weights are used with sets of scales in order to weigh things. 3 any heavy object. 4 The weight of something is its large amount or importance which makes it hard to fight against or contradict E.G. the weight of the law. ► VERB 5 If you weight something or weight it down, you make it heavier, often so that it cannot move. ► PHRASE 6 If you **pull your weight**, you work just as hard as other people involved in the same activity.

**weighted**

ADJECTIVE A system that is weighted in favour of a particular person or group is organized in such a way that this person or group will have an advantage.

**weightlifting**

NOUN Weightlifting is the sport of lifting heavy weights in competition or for exercise.

**weightlifter** NOUN

**weighty** weightier weightiest

ADJECTIVE serious or important E.G. a weighty problem.

**weir** weirs

Rhymes with "near" NOUN a low dam which is built across a river to raise the water level, control the flow of water, or change its direction.

**weird** weirder weirdest

Said "weerd" ADJECTIVE strange or odd.

**weirdly** ADVERB

■ bizarre, odd, strange

**weirdo** weirdos

Said "weer-doe" NOUN; INFORMAL If you call someone a weirdo, you mean they behave in a strange way.

**welcome** welcomes welcoming welcomed

VERB 1 If you welcome a visitor, you greet them in a friendly way when they arrive. 2 'Welcome' can be said as a greeting to a visitor who has just arrived. 3 If you welcome something, you approve of it and support it E.G. He welcomed the decision. ► NOUN 4 a greeting to a visitor E.G. a warm welcome. ► ADJECTIVE 5 If someone is welcome at a place, they will be warmly received there. 6 If something is welcome, it brings pleasure or is accepted gratefully E.G. a welcome rest. 7 If you tell someone they are welcome to something or welcome to do something, you mean you are willing for them to have or to do it.

**welcoming** ADJECTIVE

**weld** welds welding welded

VERB To weld two pieces of metal together is to join them by heating their edges and fixing them together so that when they cool they harden into one piece.

**welder** NOUN

**welfare**

NOUN 1 The welfare of a person or group is their general state of health and comfort. 2 Welfare services are provided to help with people's living conditions and financial problems E.G. welfare workers.

**welfare state**

NOUN The welfare state is a system in which the government uses money from taxes to provide health care and education services, and to give benefits to people who are old, unemployed, or sick.

**well** better best; wells welling welled

ADVERB **1** If something goes well, it happens in a satisfactory way E.G. *The interview went well.* **2** in a good, skilful, or pleasing way E.G. *He draws well.* **3** thoroughly and completely E.G. *well established.* **4** kindly E.G. *We treat our employees well.* **5** If something may well or could well happen, it is likely to happen. **6** You use 'well' to emphasize an adjective, adverb, or phrase E.G. *He was well aware of that.* ► ADJECTIVE **7** If you are well, you are healthy. ► PHRASE **8** As well means also E.G. *He was a bus driver as well.* **9** As well as means in addition to E.G. *a meal which includes meat or fish, as well as rice.* **10** If you say you may as well or might as well do something, you mean you will do it although you are not keen to do it. ► NOUN **11** a hole drilled in the ground from which water, oil, or gas is obtained. ► VERB **12** If tears well or well up, they appear in someone's eyes.

**well-advised**

ADJECTIVE sensible or wise E.G. *Bill would be well-advised to retire.*

**well-balanced**

ADJECTIVE sensible and without serious emotional problems E.G. *a well-balanced happy teenager.*

**wellbeing**

NOUN Someone's wellbeing is their health and happiness.

**well-earned**

ADJECTIVE thoroughly deserved.

**well-heeled**

ADJECTIVE; *INFORMAL* wealthy.

**well-informed**

ADJECTIVE having a great deal of knowledge about a subject or subjects.

**wellington** wellingtons

NOUN Wellingtons or wellington boots are long waterproof rubber boots.

**well-meaning**

ADJECTIVE A well-meaning person tries to be helpful but is often unsuccessful.

**well-off**

ADJECTIVE; *INFORMAL* quite wealthy.

**well-to-do**

ADJECTIVE quite wealthy.

**well-worn**

ADJECTIVE **1** A well-worn expression or saying has been used too often and has become boring. **2** A well-worn object or piece of clothing has been used and worn so much that it looks old and shabby.

**welly** wellies

NOUN; *INFORMAL* Wellies are wellingtons.

**Welsh**

ADJECTIVE **1** belonging or relating to Wales. ► NOUN **2** Welsh is a language spoken in parts of Wales.

**Welshman** Welshmen

NOUN a man who comes from Wales.
**Welshwoman** NOUN

**welt** welts

NOUN a raised mark on someone's skin made by a blow from something like a whip or a stick.

**welter**

NOUN; *FORMAL* A welter of things is a large number of them that happen or appear together in a state

a b c d e f g h i j k l m n o p q r s t u v w x y z

LEarn the principLEs (princip**le**)    ▸ **SPELLING NOTE**

of confusion *E.G. a welter of rumours.*

**wench** wenches

NOUN; *OLD-FASHIONED* a woman or young girl.

**wept**
the past tense and past participle of **weep.**

**were**
a past tense of **be.**

**werewolf** werewolves

NOUN In horror stories, a werewolf is a person who changes into a wolf.
🔲 from Old English *wer + wulf* meaning 'man wolf'

**Wesak**
*Said* "**wess**-suck" NOUN Wesak is the Buddhist festival celebrating the Buddha, held in May.

**west**
NOUN **1** The west is the direction in which you look to see the sun set. **2** The west of a place or country is the part which is towards the west when you are in the centre *E.G. the west of America.* **3** The West refers to the countries of North America and western and southern Europe.
▶ ADVERB or ADJECTIVE **4** West means towards the west. ▶ ADJECTIVE **5** A west wind blows from the west.

**westerly**
ADJECTIVE Westerly means to or towards the west *E.G. France's most westerly region.*

**western** westerns
ADJECTIVE **1** in or from the west. **2** coming from or associated with the countries of North America and western and southern Europe *E.G. western dress.* ▶ NOUN **3** A book or film about life in the west of America in the nineteenth century.

**West Indian** West Indians

NOUN someone who comes from the West Indies.

**westward** or **westwards**
ADVERB Westward or westwards means towards the west *E.G. He stared westwards towards the clouds.*

**wet** wetter wettest; wets wetting wet or wetted

ADJECTIVE **1** If something is wet, it is covered in water or another liquid. **2** If the weather is wet, it is raining. **3** If something such as paint, ink, or cement is wet, it is not yet dry or solid. **4** *INFORMAL* If you say someone is wet, you mean they are weak and lacking confidence *E.G. Don't be so wet!* ▶ NOUN **5** In northern and central Australia, the wet is the rainy season.
▶ VERB **6** To wet something is to put water or some other liquid over it. **7** If people wet themselves or wet their beds, they urinate in their clothes or bed because they cannot control their bladder.

**wetness** NOUN

**wet suit** wet suits

NOUN a close-fitting rubber suit which a diver wears to keep his or her body warm.

**whack** whacks whacking whacked

VERB If you whack someone or something, you hit them hard.

**whale** whales

NOUN a very large sea mammal which breathes out water through a hole on the top of its head.

**whaling**
NOUN Whaling is the work of hunting and killing whales for oil or food.

**wharf** wharves
*Said* "**worf**" NOUN a platform beside a

river or the sea, where ships load or unload.

**what**

PRONOUN **1** 'What' is used in questions *E.G. What time is it?* **2** 'What' is used in indirect questions and statements *E.G. I don't know what you mean.* **3** 'What' can be used at the beginning of a clause to refer to something with a particular quality *E.G. It is impossible to decide what is real and what is invented.* ▶ ADJECTIVE **4** 'What' can be used at the beginning of a clause to show that you are talking about the whole amount that is available to you *E.G. Their spouses try to earn what money they can.* **5** You say 'what' to emphasize an opinion or reaction *E.G. What nonsense!* ▶ PHRASE **6** You say **what about** at the beginning of a question when you are making a suggestion or offer *E.G. What about a drink?*

**whatever**

PRONOUN **1** You use 'whatever' to refer to anything or everything of a particular type *E.G. He said he would do whatever he could.* **2** You use 'whatever' when you do not know the precise nature of something *E.G. Whatever it is, I don't like it.* ▶ CONJUNCTION **3** You use 'whatever' to mean no matter what *E.G. Whatever happens, you have to behave decently.* ▶ ADVERB **4** You use 'whatever' to emphasize a negative statement or a question *E.G. You have no proof whatever… Whatever is wrong with you?*

**whatsoever**

ADVERB You use 'whatsoever' to emphasize a negative statement *E.G. I have no memory of it whatsoever.*

**wheat**

NOUN Wheat is a cereal plant grown for its grain which is used to make flour.

**wheel** wheels wheeling wheeled

NOUN **1** a circular object which turns on a rod attached to its centre. Wheels are fixed underneath vehicles so that they can move along. **2** The wheel of a car is its steering wheel. ▶ VERB **3** If you wheel something such as a bicycle, you push it. **4** If someone or something wheels, they move round in the shape of a circle *E.G. Cameron wheeled around and hit him.*

**wheelbarrow** wheelbarrows

NOUN a small cart with a single wheel at the front, used for carrying things in the garden.

**wheelchair** wheelchairs

NOUN a chair with wheels in which sick, injured, or disabled people can move around.

**wheeze** wheezes wheezing wheezed

VERB If someone wheezes, they breathe with difficulty, making a whistling sound, usually because they have a chest complaint such as asthma.

**wheezy** ADJECTIVE

**whelk** whelks

NOUN a snail-like shellfish with a strong shell and a soft edible body.

**when**

ADVERB **1** You use 'when' to ask what time something happened or will happen *E.G. When are you leaving?* ▶ CONJUNCTION **2** You use 'when' to refer to a time in the past *E.G. I met him when I was sixteen.* **3** You use 'when' to introduce the reason for an

the QUeen stood on the QUay (quay) ▶ SPELLING NOTE

opinion, comment, or question *E.G. How did you pass the exam when you hadn't studied for it?* 4 'When' is used to mean although *E.G. He drives when he could walk.*

## whence
ADVERB or CONJUNCTION; *OLD-FASHIONED* Whence means from where ☑ You should not write *from whence* because *whence* already means 'from where'.

## whenever
CONJUNCTION Whenever means at any time, or every time that something happens *E.G. I still go on courses whenever I can.*

## where
ADVERB 1 You use 'where' to ask which place something is in, is coming from, or is going to *E.G. Where is Philip?* ▶ CONJUNCTION, PRONOUN, or ADVERB 2 You use 'where' when asking about or referring to something *E.G. I hardly know where to begin.* ▶ CONJUNCTION 3 You use 'where' to refer to the place in which something is situated or happening *E.G. I don't know where we are.* 4 'Where' can introduce a clause that contrasts with the other part of the sentence *E.G. A teacher will be listened to, where a parent might not.*

## whereabouts
NOUN 1 The whereabouts of a person or thing is the place where they are. ▶ ADVERB 2 You use 'whereabouts' when you are asking more precisely where something is *E.G. Whereabouts in Canada are you from?* ·

## whereas
CONJUNCTION Whereas introduces a comment that contrasts with the other part of the sentence *E.G. Her*

eyes were blue, whereas mine were brown.

## whereby
PRONOUN; *FORMAL* Whereby means by which *E.G. a new system whereby you pay the bill quarterly.*

## whereupon
CONJUNCTION; *FORMAL* Whereupon means at which point *E.G. His enemies rejected his message, whereupon he tried again.*

## wherever
CONJUNCTION 1 'Wherever' means in every place or situation *E.G. Alex heard the same thing wherever he went.* 2 You use 'wherever' to show that you do not know where a place or person is *E.G. the nearest police station, wherever that is.*

## wherewithal
NOUN If you have the wherewithal to do something, you have enough money to do it.

## whet whets whetting whetted
PHRASE To **whet someone's appetite** for something, means to increase their desire for it.

## whether
CONJUNCTION You use 'whether' when you are talking about two or more alternatives *E.G. I don't know whether that's true or false.*

## whey
*Rhymes with "**day**"* NOUN Whey is the watery liquid that is separated from the curds in sour milk when cheese is made.

## which
ADJECTIVE or PRONOUN 1 You use 'which' to ask about alternatives or to refer to a choice between alternatives *E.G. Which room are you in?* ▶ PRONOUN 2 'Which' at the beginning of a clause

identifies the thing you are talking about or gives more information about it E.G. *certain wrongs which exist in our society*.

☑ See the usage note at *that*.

**whichever**

ADJECTIVE or PRONOUN You use 'whichever' when you are talking about different alternatives or possibilities E.G. *Make your pizzas round or square, whichever you prefer*.

**whiff** whiffs

NOUN **1** a slight smell of something. **2** a slight sign or trace of something E.G. *a whiff of criticism*.

**while** whiles whiling whiled

CONJUNCTION **1** If something happens while something else is happening, the two things happen at the same time. **2** While also means but E.G. *Men tend to gaze more, while women dart quick glances*. ► NOUN **3** a period of time E.G. *a little while earlier*. ► PHRASE **4** If an action or activity is **worth your while**, it will be helpful or useful to you if you do it.

**while away** VERB If you while away the time in a particular way, you pass the time that way because you have nothing else to do.

**whilst**

CONJUNCTION Whilst means the same as while.

**whim** whims

NOUN a sudden desire or fancy.

▪ fancy, impulse

**whimper** whimpers whimpering whimpered

VERB **1** When children or animals whimper, they make soft, low, unhappy sounds. **2** If you whimper something, you say it in an unhappy or frightened way, as if you are about to cry.

**whimsical**

ADJECTIVE unusual and slightly playful E.G. *an endearing, whimsical charm*.

**whine** whines whining whined

VERB **1** To whine is to make a long, high-pitched noise, especially one which sounds sad or unpleasant. **2** If someone whines about something, they complain about it in an annoying way. ► NOUN **3** A whine is the noise made by something or someone whining.

**whinge** whinges whinging or whingeing whinged

VERB If someone whinges about something, they complain about it in an annoying way.

**whinny** whinnies whinnying whinnied

VERB When a horse whinnies, it neighs softly.

**whip** whips whipping whipped

NOUN **1** a thin piece of leather or rope attached to a handle, which is used for hitting people or animals. ► VERB **2** If you whip a person or animal, you hit them with a whip. **3** When the wind whips something, it strikes it. **4** If you whip something out or off, you take it out or off very quickly E.G. *She had whipped off her glasses.* **5** If you whip cream or eggs, you beat them until they are thick and frothy or stiff.

**whip up** VERB If you whip up a strong emotion, you make people feel it E.G. *The thought whipped up his temper*.

**whip bird** whip birds

NOUN an Australian bird whose cry ends with a sound like the crack of a whip.

there's SAND in my SANDwich (<u>sand</u>wich)    ▸ **SPELLING NOTE**

**whiplash injury** whiplash injuries

NOUN a neck injury caused by your head suddenly jerking forwards and then back again, for example in a car accident.

**whippet** whippets

NOUN a small, thin dog used for racing.

**whirl** whirls whirling whirled

VERB 1 When something whirls, or when you whirl it round, it turns round very fast. ▶ NOUN 2 You can refer to a lot of intense activity as a whirl of activity.

📖 from Old Norse *hvirfla* meaning 'to turn about'

**whirlpool** whirlpools

NOUN a small circular area in a river or the sea where the water is moving quickly round and round so that objects floating near it are pulled into its centre.

**whirlwind** whirlwinds

NOUN 1 a tall column of air which spins round and round very fast. ▶ ADJECTIVE 2 more rapid than usual *E.G. a whirlwind tour*.

**whirr** whirrs whirring whirred; also spelt **whir**

VERB 1 When something such as a machine whirrs, it makes a series of low sounds so fast that it sounds like one continuous sound. ▶ NOUN 2 the noise made by something whirring.

**whisk** whisks whisking whisked

VERB 1 If you whisk someone or something somewhere, you take them there quickly *E.G. We were whisked away into a private room*. 2 If you whisk eggs or cream, you stir air into them quickly. ▶ NOUN 3 a kitchen tool used for quickly stirring air into eggs or cream.

**whisker** whiskers

NOUN The whiskers of an animal such as a cat or mouse are the long, stiff hairs near its mouth.

**whisky** whiskies

NOUN Whisky is a strong alcoholic drink made from grain such as barley.

📖 from Scottish Gaelic *uisge beatha* meaning 'water of life'

**whisper** whispers whispering whispered

VERB 1 When you whisper, you talk to someone very quietly, using your breath and not your throat. ▶ NOUN 2 If you talk in a whisper, you whisper.

**whist**

NOUN Whist is a card game for four players in which one pair of players tries to win more tricks than the other pair.

**whistle** whistles whistling whistled

VERB 1 When you whistle a tune or whistle, you produce a clear musical sound by forcing your breath out between your lips. 2 If something whistles, it makes a loud, high sound *E.G. The kettle whistled*. ▶ NOUN 3 A whistle is the sound something or someone makes when they whistle. 4 a small metal tube that you blow into to produce a whistling sound.

**whit**

NOUN FORMAL You say 'not a whit' or 'no whit' to emphasize that something is not the case at all *E.G. It does not matter one whit to the customer*.

**white** whiter whitest; whites

NOUN OR ADJECTIVE 1 White is the lightest

possible colour. **2** Someone who is white has a pale skin and is of European origin. ▶ ADJECTIVE **3** If someone goes white, their face becomes very pale because they are afraid, shocked, or ill. **4** White coffee contains milk or cream. ▶ NOUN **5** The white of an egg is the transparent liquid surrounding the yolk, which turns white when it is cooked.
**whiteness** NOUN

**white-collar**
ADJECTIVE White-collar workers work in offices rather than doing manual work E.G. *a white-collar union.*

**white lie white lies**
NOUN a harmless lie, especially one told to prevent someone's feelings from being hurt.

**whitewash**
NOUN **1** Whitewash is a mixture of lime and water used for painting walls white. **2** an attempt to hide unpleasant facts E.G. *the refusal to accept official whitewash in the enquiry.*

**whither**
ADVERB or CONJUNCTION; OLD-FASHIONED Whither means to what place E.G. *Whither shall I wander?*

**whiting**
NOUN a sea fish related to the cod.

**whittle whittles whittling whittled**
VERB If you whittle a piece of wood, you shape it by shaving or cutting small pieces off it.

**whittle away** or **whittle down**
VERB To whittle away at something or to whittle it down means to make it smaller or less effective E.G. *The 250 entrants had been whittled down to 34.*

**whizz whizzes whizzing whizzed;** also spelt **whiz**
VERB; INFORMAL If you whizz somewhere, you move there quickly.

**who**
PRONOUN **1** You use 'who' when you are asking about someone's identity E.G. *Who gave you that black eye?* **2** 'Who' at the beginning of a clause refers to the person or people you are talking about E.G. *a shipyard worker who wants to be a postman.*

**whoa**
Said "woh" INTERJECTION Whoa is a command used to slow down or stop a horse.

**whoever**
PRONOUN **1** 'Whoever' means the person who E.G. *Whoever bought it for you has to make the claim.* **2** 'Whoever' also means no matter who E.G. *I pity him, whoever he is.* **3** 'Whoever' is used in questions give emphasis to who E.G. *Whoever thought of such a thing?*

**whole wholes**
NOUN or ADJECTIVE **1** The whole of something is all of it E.G. *the whole of Africa... Have the whole cake.* ▶ ADVERB **2** in one piece E.G. *He swallowed it whole.* ▶ PHRASE **3** You use **as a whole** to emphasize that you are talking about all of something E.G. *The country as a whole is in a very odd mood.* **4** You say **on the whole** to mean that something is generally true E.G. *On the whole, we should be glad they are gone.*
**wholeness** NOUN

**wholehearted**
ADJECTIVE enthusiastic and totally sincere E.G. *wholehearted approval.*
**wholeheartedly** ADVERB

a b c d e f g h i j k l m n o p q r s t u v w x y z

**wholemeal**
ADJECTIVE Wholemeal flour is made from the complete grain of the wheat plant, including the husk.

**wholesale**
ADJECTIVE or ADVERB 1 Wholesale refers to the activity of buying goods cheaply in large quantities and selling them again, especially to shopkeepers E.G. *We buy fruit and vegetables wholesale.* ▸ ADJECTIVE 2 Wholesale also means done to an excessive extent E.G. *the wholesale destruction of wild plant species.*
**wholesaler** NOUN

**wholesome**
ADJECTIVE good and likely to improve your life, behaviour, or health E.G. *good wholesome entertainment.*

**wholly**
*Said "hoe-lee"* ADVERB completely.

**whom**
PRONOUN Whom is the object form of 'who' E.G. *the girl whom Albert would marry.*

**whoop** whoops whooping whooped
VERB 1 If you whoop, you shout loudly in a happy or excited way. ▸ NOUN 2 a loud cry of happiness or excitement E.G. *whoops of delight.*

**whooping cough**
*Said "hoop-ing"* NOUN Whooping cough is an acute infectious disease which makes people cough violently and produce a loud sound when they breathe.

**whore** whores
*Said "hore"* NOUN; OFFENSIVE a prostitute, or a woman believed to act like a prostitute.

**whose**
PRONOUN 1 You use 'whose' to ask who

something belongs to E.G. *Whose gun is this?* 2 You use 'whose' at the beginning of a clause which gives information about something relating or belonging to the thing or person you have just mentioned E.G. *a wealthy gentleman whose marriage is breaking up.*

✔ Many people are confused about the difference between *whose* and *who's*. *Whose* is used to show possession in a question or when something is being described: *whose bag is this?... The person whose car is blocking the exit.* *Who's*, with the apostrophe, is a short form of *who is* or *who has*: *who's that girl?... Who's got my ruler?*

**why**
ADVERB or PRONOUN You use 'why' when you are asking about the reason for something, or talking about it E.G. *Why did you do it?... He wondered why she suddenly looked happier.*

**wick** wicks
NOUN the cord in the middle of a candle, which you set alight.

**wicked**
ADJECTIVE 1 very bad E.G. *a wicked thing to do.* 2 mischievous in an amusing or attractive way E.G. *a wicked sense of humour.*
**wickedly** ADVERB **wickedness** NOUN
🏛 from Old English *wicce* meaning 'witch'
▤ (sense 1) bad, evil, sinful

**wicker**
ADJECTIVE A wicker basket or chair is made from twigs, canes, or reeds that have been woven together.

**wicket** wickets
NOUN 1 In cricket, the wicket is one of the two sets of stumps and bails at

which the bowler aims the ball. **2** The grass between the wickets on a cricket pitch is also called the wicket.

**wide** wider widest

ADJECTIVE **1** measuring a large distance from one side to the other. **2** If there is a wide variety, range, or selection of something, there are many different kinds of it E.G. *a wide range of colours*. ► ADVERB **3** If you open or spread something wide, you open it to its fullest extent.

**widely** ADVERB

■ (sense 2) broad, extensive, large

**wide-awake**

ADJECTIVE completely awake.

**widen** widens widening widened

VERB **1** If something widens or if you widen it, it becomes bigger from one side to the other. **2** You can say that something widens when it becomes greater in size or scope E.G. *the opportunity to widen your outlook*.

**wide-ranging**

ADJECTIVE extending over a variety of different things or over a large area E.G. *a wide-ranging survey*.

**widespread**

ADJECTIVE existing or happening over a large area or to a great extent E.G. *the widespread use of chemicals*.

■ common, general, universal

**widow** widows

NOUN a woman whose husband has died.

**widowed**

ADJECTIVE If someone is widowed, their husband or wife has died.

**widower** widowers

NOUN a man whose wife has died.

**width** widths

NOUN The width of something is the distance from one side or edge to the other.

**wield** wields wielding wielded

*Said "weeld"* VERB **1** If you wield a weapon or tool, you carry it and use it. **2** If someone wields power, they have it and are able to use it.

**wife** wives

NOUN A man's wife is the woman he is married to.

**Wi-Fi**

NOUN a system of accessing the Internet from machines such as laptop computers that aren't physically connected to a network.

**wig** wigs

NOUN a false head of hair worn to cover someone's own hair or to hide their baldness.

🏛 short for *periwig* from Italian *perrucca* meaning 'wig'

**wiggle** wiggles wiggling wiggled

VERB **1** If you wiggle something, you move it up and down or from side to side with small jerky movements. ► NOUN **2** a small jerky movement or line.

**wigwam** wigwams

NOUN a kind of tent used by North American Indians.

🏛 from American Indian *wikwam* meaning 'their house'

**wiki** wikis

NOUN a website (or page within one) that can be edited by anyone who looks it up on the Internet.

**wild** wilder wildest; wilds

ADJECTIVE **1** Wild animals, birds, and plants live and grow in natural surroundings and are not looked after by people. **2** Wild land is natural and has not been cultivated E.G. *wild areas of countryside*. **3** Wild weather or sea is stormy and rough. **4** Wild behaviour is excited and

a
b
c
d
e
f
g
h
i
j
k
l
m
n
o
p
q
r
s
t
u
v
w
x
y
z

A B C D E F G H I J K L M N O P Q R S T U V W X Y Z

uncontrolled E.G. *wild with excitement.*
**5** A wild idea or scheme is original and crazy. ➤ NOUN **6** The wild is a free and natural state of living E.G. *There are about 200 left in the wild.* **7** The wilds are remote areas where few people live, far away from towns.
**wildly** ADVERB

**wilderness** wildernesses
NOUN an area of natural land which is not cultivated.

**wildfire**
NOUN If something spreads like wildfire, it spreads very quickly.

**wild-goose chase** wild-goose chases
NOUN a hopeless or useless search.

**wildlife**
NOUN Wildlife means wild animals and plants.

**Wild West**
NOUN The Wild West was the western part of the United States when it was first being settled by Europeans.

**wiles**
PLURAL NOUN Wiles are clever or crafty tricks used to persuade people to do something.

**wilful**
ADJECTIVE **1** Wilful actions or attitudes are deliberate and often intended to hurt someone E.G. *wilful damage.*
**2** Someone who is wilful is obstinate and determined to get their own way E.G. *a wilful little boy.*
**wilfully** ADVERB
■ (sense 2) headstrong, stubborn

**will**
VERB **1** You use 'will' to form the future tense E.G. *Robin will be quite annoyed.* **2** You use 'will' to say that you intend to do something E.G. *I will not deceive you.* **3** You use 'will' when inviting

someone to do or have something E.G. *Will you have another coffee?* **4** You use 'will' when asking or telling someone to do something E.G. *Will you do me a favour?… You will do as I say.* **5** You use 'will' to say that you are assuming something to be the case E.G. *As you will have gathered, I was surprised.*

**will** wills willing willed
VERB **1** If you will something to happen, you try to make it happen by mental effort E.G. *I willed my eyes to open.* **2** If you will something to someone, you leave it to them when you die E.G. *Penbrook Farm is willed to her.* ➤ NOUN **3** Will is the determination to do something E.G. *the will to win.*
**4** If something is the will of a person or group, they want it to happen E.G. *the will of the people.* **5** a legal document in which you say what you want to happen to your money and property when you die. ➤ PHRASE **6** If you can do something **at will**, you can do it whenever you want.

**willing**
ADJECTIVE **1** If you are willing to do something, you will do it if someone wants you to. **2** Someone who is willing is eager and enthusiastic E.G. *a willing helper.*
**willingly** ADVERB **willingness** NOUN
■ (sense 1) game, prepared, ready

**willow** willows
NOUN A willow or willow tree is a tree with long, thin branches and narrow leaves that often grows near water.

**wilt** wilts wilting wilted
VERB **1** If a plant wilts, it droops because it needs more water or is dying. **2** If someone wilts, they gradually lose strength or

confidence *E.G. James visibly wilted under pressure.*

**wily wilier wiliest**
*Said "wie-lee"* ADJECTIVE clever and cunning.

**wimp wimps**
NOUN; *INFORMAL* someone who is feeble and timid.

**win wins winning won**
VERB 1 If you win a fight, game, or argument, you defeat your opponent. 2 If you win a prize, you get it as a reward for succeeding in something. 3 If you win something you want, such as approval or support, you succeed in getting it.
▶ NOUN 4 a victory in a game or contest.

**win over** VERB If you win someone over, you persuade them to support you.

**wince winces wincing winced**
VERB When you wince, the muscles of your face tighten suddenly because of pain, fear, or distress.

**winch winches winching winched**
NOUN 1 a machine used to lift heavy objects. It consists of a cylinder around which a rope or chain is wound. ▶ VERB 2 If you winch an object or person somewhere, you lift, lower, or pull them using a winch.

**wind winds**
*Rhymes with "tinned"* NOUN 1 a current of air moving across the earth's surface. 2 Your wind is the ability to breathe easily *E.G. Brown had recovered her wind.* 3 Wind is air swallowed with food or drink, or gas produced in your stomach, which causes discomfort. 4 The wind section of an orchestra is the group of musicians who play wind instruments.

**wind winds winding wound**
*Rhymes with "mind"* VERB 1 If a road or river winds in a particular direction, it twists and turns in that direction. 2 When you wind something round something else, you wrap it round it several times. 3 When you wind a clock or machine or wind it up, you turn a key or handle several times to make it work.

**wind up** VERB 1 When you wind up something such as an activity or a business, you finish it or close it. 2 If you wind up in a particular place, you end up there.

**windfall windfalls**
NOUN a sum of money that you receive unexpectedly.

**wind instrument wind instruments**
NOUN an instrument you play by using your breath, for example a flute, an oboe, or a trumpet.

**windmill windmills**
NOUN a machine for grinding grain or pumping water. It is driven by vanes or sails turned by the wind.

**window windows**
NOUN a space in a wall or roof or in the side of a vehicle, usually with glass in it so that light can pass through and people can see in or out.

**window box window boxes**
NOUN a long, narrow container on a windowsill in which plants are grown.

**windowsill windowsills**
NOUN a ledge along the bottom of a window, either on the inside or outside of a building.

**windpipe windpipes**
NOUN the tube which carries air into

a
b
c
d
e
f
g
h
i
j
k
l
m
n
o
p
q
r
s
t
u
v
**w**
x
y
z

A
B
C
D
E
F
G
H
I
J
K
L
M
N
O
P
Q
R
S
T
U
V
W
X
Y
Z

your lungs when you breathe.

**windscreen** windscreens
NOUN the glass at the front of a
vehicle through which the driver looks.

**windsurfing**
NOUN Windsurfing is the sport of
moving along the surface of the sea
or a lake standing on a board with a
sail on it.

**windswept**
ADJECTIVE A windswept place is
exposed to strong winds E.G. a
windswept beach.

**windy** windier windiest
ADJECTIVE If it is windy, there is a lot of
wind.

**wine** wines
NOUN Wine is the red or white
alcoholic drink which is normally
made from grapes.
📖 from Latin vinum meaning 'wine'

**wing** wings
NOUN 1 A bird's or insect's wings are
the parts of its body that it uses for
flying. 2 An aeroplane's wings are the
long, flat parts on each side that
support it while it is in the air. 3 A
wing of a building is a part which
sticks out from the main part or
which has been added later. 4 A
wing of an organization, especially a
political party, is a group within it
with a particular role or particular
beliefs E.G. the left wing of the party.
▶ PLURAL NOUN 5 The wings in a theatre
are the sides of the stage which are
hidden from the audience.
**winged** ADJECTIVE

**wink** winks winking winked
VERB 1 When you wink, you close one
eye briefly, often as a signal that
something is a joke or a secret.
▶ NOUN 2 the closing of your eye

when you wink.

**winkle** winkles
NOUN a small sea-snail with a hard
shell and a soft edible body.

**winner** winners
NOUN The winner of a prize, race, or
competition is the person or thing
that wins it.
🔲 champion, victor

**winning** winnings
ADJECTIVE 1 The winning team or entry
in a competition is the one that has
won. 2 attractive and charming E.G. a
winning smile. ▶ PLURAL NOUN 3 Your
winnings are the money you have
won in a competition or by
gambling.

**winter** winters
NOUN Winter is the season between
autumn and spring.

**wintry**
ADJECTIVE Something wintry has
features that are typical of winter E.G.
the wintry dawn.

**wipe** wipes wiping wiped
VERB 1 If you wipe something, you rub
its surface lightly to remove dirt or
liquid. 2 If you wipe dirt or liquid off
something, you remove it using a
cloth or your hands E.G. Anne wiped
the tears from her eyes.

**wipe out** VERB To wipe out people
or places is to destroy them
completely.

**wire** wires wiring wired
NOUN 1 Wire is metal in the form of a
long, thin, flexible thread which can
be used to make or fasten things or
to conduct an electric current. ▶ VERB
2 If you wire one thing to another,
you fasten them together using wire.
3 If you wire something or wire it up,
you connect it so that electricity can

pass through it.
**wired** ADJECTIVE

**wireless** wirelesses

NOUN; *OLD-FASHIONED* a radio.

**wiring**

NOUN The wiring in a building is the system of wires that supply electricity to the rooms.

**wiry** wirier wiriest

ADJECTIVE **1** Wiry people are thin but with strong muscles. **2** Wiry things are stiff and rough to the touch E.G. *wiry hair.*

**wisdom**

NOUN **1** Wisdom is the ability to use experience and knowledge in order to make sensible decisions or judgments. **2** If you talk about the wisdom of an action or a decision, you are talking about how sensible it is.

**wisdom tooth** wisdom teeth

NOUN Your wisdom teeth are the four molar teeth at the back of your mouth which grow much later than other teeth.

**wise** wiser wisest

ADJECTIVE **1** Someone who is wise can use their experience and knowledge to make sensible decisions and judgments. ▶ PHRASE **2** If you say that someone is **none the wiser** or **no wiser**, you mean that they know no more about something than they did before E.G. *I left the conference none the wiser.*

■ (sense 1) judicious, prudent, sensible

**wisecrack** wisecracks

NOUN a clever remark, intended to be amusing but often unkind.

**wish** wishes wishing wished

NOUN **1** a longing or desire for

something, often something difficult to achieve or obtain. **2** something desired or wanted E.G. *That wish came true two years later.* ▶ PLURAL NOUN **3** Good wishes are expressions of hope that someone will be happy or successful E.G. *best wishes on your birthday.* ▶ VERB **4** If you wish to do something, you want to do it E.G. *We wished to return.* **5** If you wish something were the case, you would like it to be the case, but know it is not very likely E.G. *I wish I were tall.*

**wishbone** wishbones

NOUN a V-shaped bone in the breast of most birds.

**wishful thinking**

NOUN If someone's hope or wish is wishful thinking, it is unlikely to come true.

**wishy-washy**

ADJECTIVE; *INFORMAL* If a person or their ideas are wishy-washy, then their ideas are not firm or clear E.G. *wishy-washy reasons.*

**wisp** wisps

NOUN **1** A wisp of grass or hair is a small, thin, untidy bunch of it. **2** A wisp of smoke is a long, thin streak of it.

**wispy** ADJECTIVE

**wistful**

ADJECTIVE sadly thinking about something, especially something you want but cannot have E.G. *A wistful look came into her eyes.*

**wistfully** ADVERB

**wit** wits

NOUN **1** Wit is the ability to use words or ideas in an amusing and clever way. **2** Wit means sense E.G. *They haven't got the wit to realize what they're doing.* ▶ PLURAL NOUN **3** Your wits

a
b
c
d
e
f
g
h
i
j
k
l
m
n
o
p
q
r
s
t
u
v
**w**
x
y
z

are the ability to think and act quickly in a difficult situation E.G. *the man who lived by his wits.* ▶ PHRASE 4 If someone is **at their wits' end**, they are so worried and exhausted by problems or difficulties that they do not know what to do.

**witch** witches
NOUN a woman claimed to have magic powers and to be able to use them for good or evil.

**witchcraft**
NOUN Witchcraft is the skill or art of using magic powers, especially evil ones.

■ black magic, sorcery, wizardry

**witch doctor** witch doctors
NOUN a man in some societies, especially in Africa, who appears to have magic powers.

**witchetty grub** witchetty grubs
NOUN a large Australian caterpillar that is eaten by Aborigines as food.

**with**
PREPOSITION 1 'With' someone means in their company E.G. *He was at home with me.* 2 'With' is used to show who your opponent is in a fight or competition E.G. *next week's game with Brazil.* 3 'With' can mean using or having E.G. *Apply the colour with a brush… a bloke with a moustache.* 4 'With' is used to show how someone does something or how they feel E.G. *She looked at him with hatred.* 5 'With' can mean concerning E.G. *a problem with her telephone bill.* 6 'With' is used to show support E.G. *Are you with us or against us?*

**withdraw** withdraws withdrawing withdrew withdrawn
VERB 1 If you withdraw something,

you remove it or take it out E.G. *He withdrew the money from his bank.* 2 If you withdraw to another place, you leave where you are and go there E.G. *He withdrew to his study.* 3 If you withdraw from an activity, you back out of it E.G. *They withdrew from the conference.*

**withdrawal** withdrawals
NOUN 1 The withdrawal of something is the act of taking it away E.G. *the withdrawal of Russian troops.* 2 The withdrawal of a statement is the act of saying formally that you wish to change or deny it. 3 an amount of money you take from your bank or building society account.

**withdrawal symptoms**
PLURAL NOUN Withdrawal symptoms are the unpleasant effects suffered by someone who has suddenly stopped taking a drug to which they are addicted.

**withdrawn** 1 Withdrawn is the past participle of **withdraw**. ▶ ADJECTIVE 2 unusually shy or quiet.

**wither** withers withering withered
VERB 1 When something withers or withers away, it becomes weaker until it no longer exists. 2 If a plant withers, it wilts or shrivels up and dies.

**withering**
ADJECTIVE A withering look or remark makes you feel ashamed, stupid, or inferior.

**withhold** withholds withholding withheld
VERB; FORMAL If you withhold something that someone wants, you do not let them have it.

**within**
PREPOSITION OR ADVERB 1 'Within' means in

or inside. ► PREPOSITION **2** 'Within' can mean not going beyond certain limits E.G. *Stay within the budget.*
**3** 'Within' can mean before a period of time has passed E.G. *You must write back within fourteen days.*

**without**
PREPOSITION **1** 'Without' means not having, feeling, or showing E.G. *Didier looked on without emotion.*
**2** 'Without' can mean not using E.G. *You can't get in without a key.*
**3** 'Without' can mean not in someone's company E.G. *He went without me.* **4** 'Without' can indicate that something does not happen when something else happens E.G. *Stone signalled the ship, again without response.*

**withstand withstands withstanding withstood**
VERB When something or someone withstands a force or action, they survive it or do not give in to it E.G. *ships designed to withstand the North Atlantic winter.*

**witness witnesses witnessing witnessed**
NOUN **1** someone who has seen an event such as an accident and can describe what happened. **2** someone who appears in a court of law to say what they know about a crime or other event. **3** someone who writes their name on a document that someone else has signed, to confirm that it is really that person's signature. ► VERB **4** FORMAL If you witness an event, you see it.
■ (sense 1) bystander, observer, onlooker

**witticism witticisms**
*Said "wit-tiss-izm"* NOUN a clever and amusing remark or joke.

**witty wittier wittiest**
ADJECTIVE amusing in a clever way E.G. *this witty novel.*
**wittily** ADVERB

**wives**
the plural of **wife**.

**wizard wizards**
NOUN a man in a fairy story who has magic powers.

**wizened**
*Said "wiz-nd"* ADJECTIVE having a wrinkled skin, especially with age E.G. *a wizened old man.*

**WMD**
NOUN an abbreviation for 'weapon(s) of mass destruction'

**wobbegong wobbegongs**
*Said "wob-bi-gong"* NOUN an Australian shark with a richly patterned brown-and-white skin.

**wobble wobbles wobbling wobbled**
VERB If something wobbles, it shakes or moves from side to side because it is loose or unsteady E.G. *a cyclist who wobbled into my path.*
🏛 from German *wabbeln* meaning 'waver'

**wobbly**
ADJECTIVE unsteady E.G. *a wobbly table.*

**woe woes** LITERARY
NOUN **1** Woe is great unhappiness or sorrow. ► PLURAL NOUN **2** Someone's woes are their problems or misfortunes.

**wok woks**
NOUN a large bowl-shaped metal pan used for Chinese-style cooking.

**woke**
the past tense of **wake**.

**woken**
the past participle of **wake**.

A
B
C
D
E
F
G
H
I
J
K
L
M
N
O
P
Q
R
S
T
U
V
W
X
Y
Z

**wolf** wolves; wolfs wolfing
wolfed
NOUN **1** a wild animal related to the
dog. Wolves hunt in packs and kill
other animals for food. ▶ VERB
**2** INFORMAL If you wolf food or wolf it
down, you eat it up quickly and greedily.

**woman** women
NOUN **1** an adult female human being.
**2** Woman can refer to women in
general E.G. *man's inhumanity to
woman*.

**womanhood**
NOUN Womanhood is the state of
being a woman rather than a girl E.G.
*on the verge of womanhood*.

**womb** wombs
*Said* "**woom**" NOUN A woman's womb
is the part inside her body where her
unborn baby grows.

**wombat** wombats
*Said* "**wom**-bat" NOUN a short-legged
furry Australian animal which eats
plants.

**wonder** wonders wondering
wondered
VERB **1** If you wonder about
something, you think about it with
curiosity or doubt. **2** If you wonder at
something, you are surprised and
amazed at it E.G. *He wondered at her
anger.* ▶ NOUN **3** Wonder is a feeling of
surprise and amazement.
**4** something or someone that
surprises and amazes people E.G. *the
wonders of science.*
■ (sense 4) marvel, miracle,
phenomenon

**wonderful**
ADJECTIVE **1** making you feel happy and
pleased E.G. *It was wonderful to be
together.* **2** very impressive E.G. *Nature
is a wonderful thing.*

**wonderfully** ADVERB
■ (sense 2) amazing, magnificent,
remarkable

**wondrous**
ADJECTIVE; LITERARY amazing and
impressive.

**wont**
*Rhymes with "don't"* ADJECTIVE; OLD-
FASHIONED If someone is wont to do
something, they do it often E.G. *a
gesture he was wont to use.*

**woo** woos wooing wooed
VERB **1** If you woo people, you try to
get them to help or support you E.G.
*attempts to woo the women's vote.*
**2** OLD-FASHIONED When a man woos a
woman, he tries to get her to marry
him.

**wood** woods
NOUN **1** Wood is the substance which
forms the trunks and branches of
trees. **2** a large area of trees growing
near each other.

**wooded**
ADJECTIVE covered in trees E.G. *a
wooded area nearby.*

**wooden**
ADJECTIVE made of wood E.G. *a wooden
box.*

**woodland** woodlands
NOUN Woodland is land that is mostly
covered with trees.

**woodpecker** woodpeckers
NOUN a climbing bird with a long,
sharp beak that it uses to drill holes
into trees to find insects.

**woodwind**
ADJECTIVE Woodwind instruments are
musical instruments such as flutes,
oboes, clarinets, and bassoons,
that are played by being blown into.

**woodwork**
NOUN **1** Woodwork refers to the parts

of a house, such as stairs, doors or window-frames, that are made of wood. **2** Woodwork is the craft or skill of making things out of wood.

**woodworm** woodworm or woodworms

NOUN **1** Woodworm are the larvae of a kind of beetle. They make holes in wood by feeding on it. **2** Woodworm is damage caused to wood by woodworm making holes in it.

**woody** woodier woodiest

ADJECTIVE **1** Woody plants have hard tough stems. **2** A woody area has a lot of trees in it.

**woof** woofs

NOUN the sound that a dog makes when it barks.

**wool** wools

NOUN **1** Wool is the hair that grows on sheep and some other animals. **2** Wool is also yarn spun from the wool of animals which is used to knit, weave, and make such things as clothes, blankets, and carpets.

**woollen** woollens

ADJECTIVE **1** made from wool. ▶ NOUN **2** Woollens are clothes made of wool.

**woolly** woollier woolliest

ADJECTIVE **1** made of wool or looking like wool E.G. *a woolly hat.* **2** If you describe people or their thoughts as woolly, you mean that they seem confused and unclear.

**woolshed** woolsheds

NOUN In Australian and New Zealand English, a large building in which sheep are sheared.

**woomera** woomeras

NOUN a stick with a notch at one end used by Australian Aborigines to help fire a dart or spear.

**word** words wording worded

NOUN **1** a single unit of language in speech or writing which has a meaning. **2** A word can mean something brief said, such as a remark, statement, or conversation E.G. *a word of praise… Could I have a word?* **3** A word can also be a message E.G. *The word is that Sharon is exhausted.* **4** Your word is a promise E.G. *He gave me his word.* **5** The word can be a command E.G. *I gave the word to start.* ▶ PLURAL NOUN **6** The words of a play or song are the spoken or sung text. ▶ VERB **7** When you word something, you choose your words in order to express your ideas accurately or acceptably E.G. *the best way to word our invitations.*

**wording**

NOUN The wording of a piece of writing or a speech is the words used in it, especially when these words have been carefully chosen to have a certain effect.

**word processor** word processors

NOUN an electronic machine which has a keyboard and a visual display unit and which is used to produce, store, and organize printed material.

**work** works working worked

VERB **1** People who work have a job which they are paid to do E.G. *My husband works for a national newspaper.* **2** When you work, you do the tasks that your job involves. **3** To work the land is to cultivate it. **4** If someone works a machine, they control or operate it. **5** If a machine works, it operates properly and effectively E.G. *The radio doesn't work.* **6** If something such as an idea or a system works, it is successful E.G. *The*

a b c d e f g h i j k l m n o p q r s t u v **w** x y z

*housing benefit system is not working.*
**7** If something works its way into a particular position, it gradually moves there *E.G. The cable had worked loose.* ▸ NOUN **8** People who have work or who are in work have a job which they are paid to do *E.G. She's trying to find work.* **9** Work is the tasks that have to be done. **10** something done or made *E.G. a work of art.* **11** In physics, work is transfer of energy. It is calculated by multiplying a force by the distance moved by the point to which the force has been applied. Work is measured in joules. ▸ PLURAL NOUN **12** A works is a place where something is made by an industrial process *E.G. the old steel works.* **13** Works are large scale building, digging, or general construction activities *E.G. building works.*
■ (sense 4) control, handle, operate
■ (sense 5) function, go, run

**work out** VERB **1** If you work out a solution to a problem, you find the solution. **2** If a situation works out in a particular way, it happens in that way.

**work up** VERB **1** If you work up to something, you gradually progress towards it. **2** If you work yourself up or work someone else up, you make yourself or the other person very upset or angry about something.
**worked up** ADJECTIVE

**workable**
ADJECTIVE Something workable can operate successfully or can be used for a particular purpose *E.G. a workable solution… This plan simply isn't workable.*

**workaholic workaholics**
NOUN a person who finds it difficult to stop working and do other things.

**worker workers**
NOUN a person employed in a particular industry or business *E.G. a defence worker.*

**workforce workforces**
NOUN The workforce is all the people who work in a particular place.

**workhouse workhouses**
NOUN In the past a workhouse was a building to which very poor people were sent and made to work in return for food and shelter.

**working workings**
ADJECTIVE **1** Working people have jobs which they are paid to do. **2** Working can mean related to, used for, or suitable for work *E.G. the working week… working conditions.* **3** Working can mean sufficient to be useful or to achieve what is required *E.G. a working knowledge of Hebrew.* ▸ PLURAL NOUN **4** The workings of a piece of equipment, an organization, or a system are the ways in which it operates *E.G. the workings of the European Union.*

**working class working classes**
NOUN The working class or working classes are the group of people in society who do not own much property and who do jobs which involve physical rather than intellectual skills.

**workload workloads**
NOUN the amount of work that a person or a machine has to do.

**workman workmen**
NOUN a man whose job involves using physical rather than intellectual skills.

**workmanship**
NOUN Workmanship is the skill with

which something is made or a job is completed.

**workmate** workmates
NOUN Someone's workmate is the fellow worker with whom they do their job.

**workout** workouts
NOUN a session of physical exercise or training.

**workplace**
NOUN Your workplace is the building or company where you work.

**workshop** workshops
NOUN 1 a room or building that contains tools or machinery used for making or repairing things E.G. *an engineering workshop*. 2 a period of discussion or practical work in which a group of people learn about a particular subject E.G. *a theatre workshop*.

**world** worlds
NOUN 1 The world is the earth, the planet we live on. 2 You can use 'world' to refer to people generally E.G. *The eyes of the world are upon me.* 3 Someone's world is the life they lead and the things they experience E.G. *We come from different worlds.* 4 A world is a division or section of the earth, its history, or its people, such as the Arab World, or the Ancient World. 5 A particular world is a field of activity and the people involved in it E.G. *the world of football.*
▶ ADJECTIVE 6 'World' is used to describe someone or something that is one of the best or most important of its kind E.G. *a world leader.* ▶ PHRASE 7 If you **think the world** of someone, you like or admire them very much.
🏛 from Old English *weorold* from *wer* meaning 'man' and *ald* meaning 'age'

**worldly** worldlier worldliest
ADJECTIVE 1 relating to the ordinary activities of life rather than spiritual things E.G. *opportunities for worldly pleasures.* 2 experienced and knowledgeable about life.

**world war** world wars
NOUN a war that involves countries all over the world.

**worldwide**
ADJECTIVE throughout the world E.G. *a worldwide increase in skin cancers.*

**World Wide Web**
NOUN The World Wide Web is another name for the Internet, the worldwide communication system which people use through computers.

**worm** worms worming wormed
NOUN 1 a small thin animal without bones or legs, which lives in the soil or off other creatures. 2 an insect such as a beetle or moth at a very early stage in its life. 3 a computer program that makes many copies of itself within a network, usually harming the system. ▶ VERB 4 If you worm an animal, you give it medicine in order to kill the worms that are living as parasites in its intestines.

**worm out** VERB If you worm information out of someone, you gradually persuade them to give you it.

**worn**
1 Worn is the past participle of **wear**. ▶ ADJECTIVE 2 damaged or thin because of long use. 3 looking old or exhausted E.G. *Her husband looks frail and worn.*

**worn-out**
ADJECTIVE 1 used until it is too thin or too damaged to be of further use E.G.

a
b
c
d
e
f
g
h
i
j
k
l
m
n
o
p
q
r
s
t
u
v
**w**
x
y
z

A B C D E F G H I J K L M N O P Q R S T U V W X Y Z

*a worn-out cardigan.* **2** extremely tired *E.G. You must be worn-out after the drive.*

**worried**
ADJECTIVE unhappy and anxious about a problem or about something unpleasant that might happen.
■ anxious, concerned, troubled

**worry** worries worrying worried
VERB **1** If you worry, you feel anxious and fearful about a problem or about something unpleasant that might happen. **2** If something worries you, it causes you to feel uneasy or fearful *E.G. a puzzle which had worried her all her life.* **3** If you worry someone with a problem, you disturb or bother them by telling them about it *E.G. I didn't want to worry the boys with this.* **4** If a dog worries sheep or other animals, it frightens or harms them by chasing them or biting them. ▶ NOUN **5** Worry is a feeling of unhappiness and unease caused by a problem or by thinking of something unpleasant that might happen *E.G. the major source of worry.* **6** a person or thing that causes you to feel anxious or uneasy *E.G. Inflation is the least of our worries.*
**worrying** ADJECTIVE
🏛 from Old English *wyrgan* meaning 'strangle'
■ (sense 1) be anxious, fret
■ (sense 2) bother, perturb, trouble
■ (sense 5) anxiety, concern

**worse**
ADJECTIVE or ADVERB **1** Worse is the comparative form of **bad** and **badly**. **2** If someone who is ill gets worse, they become more ill than before. ▶ PHRASE **3** If someone or something is **none the worse** for something, they

have not been harmed by it *E.G. He appeared none the worse for the accident.*

**worsen** worsens worsening worsened
VERB If a situation worsens, it becomes more difficult or unpleasant *E.G. My relationship with my mother worsened.*
■ decline, deteriorate, get worse

**worse off**
ADJECTIVE If you are worse off, you have less money or are in a more unpleasant situation than before *E.G. There are people much worse off than me.*

**worship** worships worshipping worshipped
VERB **1** ⟨RE⟩ If you worship a god, you show your love and respect by praying or singing hymns. **2** If you worship someone or something, you love them or admire them very much. ▶ NOUN **3** Worship is the feeling of respect, love, or admiration you feel for something or someone.
**worshipper** NOUN
■ (sense 2) adore, idolize, love
■ (sense 3) adoration, devotion

**worst**
ADJECTIVE or ADVERB Worst is the superlative of **bad** and **badly**.

**worth**
PREPOSITION **1** If something is worth a sum of money, it has that value *E.G. a house worth 85,000 dollars.* **2** If something is worth doing, it deserves to be done. ▶ NOUN **3** A particular amount of money's worth of something is the quantity of it that you can buy for that money *E.G. five pound's worth of petrol.* **4** Someone's worth is the value or

usefulness they are considered to have.

**worthless**

ADJECTIVE having no real value or use *E.G. a worthless piece of junk.*

**worthwhile**

ADJECTIVE important enough to justify the time, money, or effort spent on it *E.G. a worthwhile career.*

**worthy worthier worthiest**

ADJECTIVE If someone or something is worthy of something, they deserve it *E.G. a worthy champion.*

**would**

VERB 1 You use 'would' to say what someone thought was going to happen *E.G. We were sure it would be a success.* 2 You use 'would' when you are referring to the result or effect of a possible situation *E.G. If readers can help I would be most grateful.* 3 You use 'would' when referring to someone's willingness to do something *E.G. I wouldn't change places with him if you paid me.* 4 You use 'would' in polite questions *E.G. Would you like some lunch?*

**would-be**

ADJECTIVE wanting to be or claiming to be *E.G. a would-be pop singer.*

**wound wounds wounding wounded**

NOUN 1 an injury to part of your body, especially a cut in your skin and flesh. ▶ VERB 2 If someone wounds you, they damage your body using a gun, knife, or other weapon. 3 If you are wounded by what someone says or does, your feelings are hurt.
**wounded** ADJECTIVE

**wow**

INTERJECTION Wow is an expression of admiration or surprise.

**WPC WPCs**

NOUN In Britain, a female member of the police force. WPC is an abbreviation for 'woman police constable'.

**wrangle wrangles wrangling wrangled**

VERB 1 If you wrangle with someone, you argue noisily or angrily, often about something unimportant. ▶ NOUN 2 an argument that is difficult to settle.
**wrangling** NOUN

**wrap wraps wrapping wrapped**

VERB 1 If you wrap something or wrap something up, you fold a piece of paper or cloth tightly around it to cover or enclose it. 2 If you wrap paper or cloth round something, you put or fold the paper round it. 3 If you wrap your arms, fingers, or legs round something, you coil them round it.

**wrap up** VERB If you wrap up, you put warm clothes on.

**wrapped up**

ADJECTIVE; *INFORMAL* If you are wrapped up in a person or thing, you give that person or thing all your attention.

**wrapper wrappers**

NOUN a piece of paper, plastic, or foil which covers and protects something that you buy *E.G. sweet wrappers.*

**wrapping wrappings**

NOUN Wrapping is the material used to cover and protect something.

**wrath**

*Said* "**roth**" NOUN; *LITERARY* Wrath is great anger *E.G. the wrath of his father.*

**wreak wreaks wreaking wreaked**

*Said* "**reek**" VERB To wreak havoc or damage is to cause it.

a
b
c
d
e
f
g
h
i
j
k
l
m
n
o
p
q
r
s
t
u
v
w
x
y
z

**wreath** wreaths
*Said "reeth"* NOUN an arrangement of flowers and leaves, often in the shape of a circle, which is put on a grave as a sign of remembrance for the dead person.

**wreck** wrecks wrecking wrecked
VERB 1 If someone wrecks something, they break it, destroy it, or spoil it completely. 2 If a ship is wrecked, it has been so badly damaged that it can no longer sail. ▶ NOUN 3 a vehicle which has been badly damaged in an accident. 4 If you say someone is a wreck, you mean that they are in a very poor physical or mental state of health and cannot cope with life.
**wrecked** ADJECTIVE

**wreckage**
NOUN Wreckage is what remains after something has been badly damaged or destroyed.

**wren** wrens
NOUN a very small brown songbird.

**wrench** wrenches wrenching wrenched
VERB 1 If you wrench something, you give it a sudden and violent twist or pull E.G. *Nick wrenched open the door.* 2 If you wrench a limb or a joint, you twist and injure it. ▶ NOUN 3 a metal tool with parts which can be adjusted to fit around nuts or bolts to loosen or tighten them. 4 a painful parting from someone or something.

**wrest** wrests wresting wrested
*Said "rest"* VERB; FORMAL If you wrest something from someone else you take it from them violently or with effort E.G. *to try and wrest control of the island from the Mafia.*

**wrestle** wrestles wrestling wrestled
VERB 1 If you wrestle someone or wrestle with them, you fight them by holding or throwing them, but not hitting them. 2 When you wrestle with a problem, you try to deal with it.
**wrestler** NOUN

**wrestling**
NOUN Wrestling is a sport in which two people fight and try to win by throwing or holding their opponent on the ground.

**wretch** wretches
NOUN; OLD-FASHIONED someone who is thought to be wicked or very unfortunate. 🏛 from Old English *wrecca* meaning 'exile' or 'despised person'

**wretched**
*Said "ret-shid"* ADJECTIVE 1 very unhappy or unfortunate E.G. *a wretched childhood.* 2 INFORMAL You use wretched to describe something or someone you feel angry about or dislike E.G. *a wretched bully.*

**wriggle** wriggles wriggling wriggled
VERB 1 If someone wriggles, they twist and turn their body or a part of their body using quick movements E.G. *He wriggled his arms and legs.* 2 If you wriggle somewhere, you move there by twisting and turning E.G. *I wriggled out of the van.*
**wriggly** ADJECTIVE

**wring** wrings wringing wrung
VERB 1 When you wring a wet cloth or wring it out, you squeeze the water out of it by twisting it. 2 If you wring your hands, you hold them together and twist and turn them, usually because you are worried or upset. 3 If someone wrings a bird's neck, they kill the bird by twisting and breaking its neck.

**SPELLING NOTE**
Plaice the fish has a glittering 'EYE' (I) (plaice)

**wrinkle wrinkles wrinkling wrinkled**

NOUN **1** Wrinkles are lines in someone's skin, especially on the face, which form as they grow old. ► VERB **2** If something wrinkles, folds or lines develop on it *E.G. silk so rich it doesn't wrinkle.* **3** When you wrinkle your nose, forehead, or eyes, you tighten the muscles in your face so that the skin folds into lines.
**wrinkled** ADJECTIVE **wrinkly** ADJECTIVE
🎞 from Old English *wrinclian* meaning 'to wind around'
▤ (sense 1) crease, fold

**wrist wrists**

NOUN the part of your body between your hand and your arm which bends when you move your hand.

**writ writs**

NOUN a legal document that orders a person to do or not to do a particular thing.

**write writes writing wrote written**

VERB **1** When you write something, you use a pen or pencil to form letters, words, or numbers on a surface. **2** If you write something such as a poem, a book, or a piece of music, you create it. **3** When you write to someone or write them a letter, you express your feelings in a letter. **4** When someone writes something such as a cheque, they put the necessary information on it and sign it. **5** When you write data you transfer it to a computer's memory.

**write down** VERB If you write something down, you record it on a piece of paper.

**write up** VERB If you write up

something, you write a full account of it, often using notes that you have made.

**writer writers**

NOUN **1** a person who writes books, stories, or articles as a job. **2** The writer of something is the person who wrote it.

**writhe writhes writhing writhed**

*Said* "**rieth**" VERB If you writhe, you twist and turn your body, often because you are in pain.

**writing writings**

NOUN **1** Writing is something that has been written or printed *E.G. Apply in writing for the information.* **2** Your writing is the way you write with a pen or pencil. **3** Writing is also a piece of written work, especially the style of language used *E.G. witty writing.* **4** An author's writings are his or her written works.

**written**

**1** Written is the past participle of **write.** ► ADJECTIVE **2** taken down in writing *E.G. a written agreement.*

**wrong wrongs wronging wronged**

ADJECTIVE **1** not working properly or unsatisfactory *E.G. There was something wrong with the car.* **2** not correct or truthful *E.G. the wrong answer.* **3** bad or immoral *E.G. It is wrong to kill people.* ► NOUN **4** an unjust action or situation *E.G. the wrongs of our society.* ► VERB **5** If someone wrongs you, they treat you in an unfair or unjust way.
**wrongly** ADVERB
▤ (sense 2) erroneous, inaccurate, incorrect

**wrongful**

ADJECTIVE A wrongful act is regarded

I went to see (C) the doctor's new practiCe (practice)     **SPELLING NOTE**

a b c d e f g h i j k l m n o p q r s t u v **w** x y z

A
B
C
D
E
F
G
H
I
J
K
L
M
N
O
P
Q
R
S
T
U
V
**W**
X
Y
Z

as illegal, unfair, or immoral _E.G._
_wrongful imprisonment._

## wrought iron

NOUN Wrought iron is a pure type of
iron that is formed into decorative
shapes.

## wry

ADJECTIVE A wry expression shows that
you find a situation slightly amusing
because you know more about it
than other people.

**wryly** ADVERB

# Xx

## X or x

**1** 'X' is used to represent the name of an unknown or secret person or place *E.G. The victim was referred to as Mr X throughout Tuesday's court proceedings.* **2** People sometimes write 'X' on a map to mark a precise position. **3** 'X' is used to represent a kiss at the bottom of a letter, a vote on a ballot paper, or the signature of someone who cannot write.

## xenophobia

*Said* "zen-nof-**foe**-bee-a" NOUN a fear or strong dislike of people from other countries.

**xenophobic** ADJECTIVE

 from Greek *xenos* meaning 'stranger' and *phobos* meaning 'fear'

## Xerox Xeroxes

*Said* "**zeer**-roks" NOUN TRADEMARK **1** a machine that makes photographic copies of sheets of paper with writing or printing on them. **2** a copy made by a Xerox machine.

## Xmas

NOUN; INFORMAL Xmas means the same as Christmas.

## X-ray X-rays X-raying X-rayed

NOUN **1** a stream of radiation of very short wavelength that can pass through some solid materials. X-rays are used by doctors to examine the bones or organs inside a person's body. **2** a picture made by sending X-rays through someone's body in order to examine the inside of it.
▶ VERB **3** If you are X-rayed, a picture is made of the inside of your body by passing X-rays through it.

## xylem

*Said* "**zy**-lem" NOUN; TECHNICAL Xylem is a plant tissue that conducts water and mineral salts from the roots and carries them through the plant. It forms the wood in trees and shrubs.

## xylophone xylophones

*Said* "**zy**-lo-fone" NOUN a musical instrument made of a row of wooden bars of different lengths. It is played by hitting the bars with special hammers.

# Yy

**-y**
SUFFIX '-y' forms nouns E.G. *anarchy.*
from Old French *-ie*

**yabby** yabbies
NOUN a small edible Australian crayfish.

**yacht** yachts
*Said* "yot" NOUN a boat with sails or an engine, used for racing or for pleasure trips.

**yachting**
NOUN Yachting is the sport or activity of sailing a yacht.

**yachtsman** yachtsmen
NOUN a man who sails a yacht.

**yachtswoman** NOUN

**yak** yaks
NOUN a type of long-haired ox with long horns, found mainly in Tibet.

**yakka** or **yacker**
NOUN; INFORMAL In Australian and New Zealand English, yakka or yacker is work.

**yam** yams
NOUN a root vegetable which grows in tropical regions.

**yank** yanks yanking yanked
VERB 1 If you yank something, you pull or jerk it suddenly with a lot of force.
▶ NOUN 2 INFORMAL A Yank is an American
☑ When *Yank* means 'an American' it starts with a capital letter.

**Yankee** Yankees
NOUN the same as a Yank.

**yap** yaps yapping yapped
VERB If a dog yaps, it barks with a high-pitched sound.

**yard** yards
NOUN 1 a unit of length equal to 36 inches or about 91.4 centimetres.
2 an enclosed area that is usually next to a building and is often used for a particular purpose E.G. *a ship repair yard.*

**yardstick** yardsticks
NOUN someone or something you use as a standard against which to judge other people or things E.G. *He had no yardstick by which to judge university.*

**yarn** yarns
NOUN 1 Yarn is thread used for knitting or making cloth. 2 INFORMAL a yarn is a story that someone tells, often with invented details to make it more interesting or exciting E.G. *fishermen's yarns.*

**yashmak** yashmaks
NOUN a veil that some Muslim women wear over their faces when they are in public.

**yawn** yawns yawning yawned
VERB When you yawn, you open your mouth wide and take in more air than usual. You often yawn when you are tired or bored

**yawning**
ADJECTIVE A yawning gap or opening is very wide.

**ye**
AN OLD WORD; PRONOUN 1 Ye used to mean 'you'. ▶ ADJECTIVE 2 Ye also used to mean 'the'.

**yeah**
INTERJECTION; INFORMAL Yeah means 'yes'.

**year** years
NOUN 1 a period of twelve months or 365 days (366 days in a leap year), which is the time taken for the earth to travel once around the sun. 2 a period of twelve consecutive

995

months, not always January to December, on which administration or organization is based E.G. *the current financial year.* ▸ PHRASE **3** If something happens **year in, year out**, it happens every year E.G. *a tradition kept up year in, year out.*
**yearly** ADJECTIVE or ADVERB

**yearling** yearlings
NOUN an animal between one and two years old.

**yearn** yearns yearning yearned
*Rhymes with* "learn" VERB If you yearn for something, you want it very much indeed E.G. *He yearned to sleep.*
**yearning** NOUN

**yeast** yeasts
NOUN Yeast is a kind of fungus which is used to make bread rise, and to make liquids ferment in order to produce alcohol.

**yell** yells yelling yelled
VERB **1** If you yell, you shout loudly, usually because you are angry, excited, or in pain. ▸ NOUN **2** a loud shout.

**yellow** yellower yellowest; yellows yellowing yellowed
NOUN or ADJECTIVE **1** Yellow is the colour of buttercups, egg yolks, or lemons. ▸ VERB **2** When something yellows or is yellowed, it becomes yellow, often because it is old. ▸ ADJECTIVE **3** INFORMAL If you say someone is yellow, you mean they are cowardly.
**yellowish** ADJECTIVE

**yellow box** yellow boxes
NOUN a large spreading Australian tree which is a source of honey.

**yellow fever**
NOUN Yellow fever is a serious infectious disease that is found in tropical countries. It causes fever and jaundice.

**yelp** yelps yelping yelped
VERB **1** When people or animals yelp, they give a sudden, short cry. ▸ NOUN **2** a sudden, short cry.

**yen**
NOUN **1** The yen is the main unit of currency in Japan. **2** If you have a yen to do something, you have a strong desire to do it E.G. *Mike had a yen to try cycling.*

**yes**
INTERJECTION You use 'yes' to agree with someone, to say that something is true, or to accept something.

**yesterday**
NOUN or ADVERB **1** Yesterday is the day before today. **2** You also use 'yesterday' to refer to the past E.G. *Leave yesterday's sadness behind you.*

**yet**
ADVERB **1** If something has not happened yet, it has not happened up to the present time E.G. *It isn't quite dark yet.* **2** If something should not be done yet, it should not be done now, but later E.G. *Don't switch off yet.* **3** 'Yet' can mean there is still a possibility that something can happen E.G. *We'll make a soldier of you yet.* **4** You can use 'yet' when you want to say how much longer a situation will continue E.G. *The service doesn't start for an hour yet.* **5** 'Yet' can be used for emphasis E.G. *She'd changed her mind yet again.* ▸ CONJUNCTION **6** You can use 'yet' to introduce a fact which is rather surprising E.G. *He isn't a smoker yet he always carries a lighter.*

**yeti** yetis
*Said* "yet-tee" NOUN A yeti, or

abominable snowman, is a large hairy apelike animal which some people believe exists in the Himalayas.

**yew yews**

NOUN an evergreen tree with bright red berries.

**Yiddish**

NOUN Yiddish is a language derived mainly from German, which many Jewish people of European origin speak.

from German *jüdisch* meaning 'Jewish'

**yield yields yielding yielded**

VERB 1 If you yield to someone or something, you stop resisting and give in to them E.G. *Russia recently yielded to US pressure.* 2 If you yield something that you have control of or responsibility for, you surrender it E.G. *They refused to yield control of their weapons.* 3 If something yields, it breaks or gives way E.G. *The handle would yield to her grasp.* 4 To yield something is to produce it E.G. *One season's produce yields food for the following year.* ► NOUN 5 A yield is an amount of food, money, or profit produced from a given area of land or from an investment.

**yippee**

INTERJECTION 'Yippee!' is an exclamation of happiness or excitement.

**yob yobs**

NOUN; *INFORMAL* a noisy, badly behaved boy or young man.

**yodel yodels yodelling yodelled**

*Said "yoe-dl"* VERB When someone yodels, they sing normal notes with high quick notes in between. This style of singing is associated with the Swiss and Austrian Alps.

**yoga**

*Said "yoe-ga"* NOUN Yoga is a Hindu method of mental and physical exercise or discipline.

from Sanskrit *yoga* meaning 'union'

**yogurt yogurts;** also spelt **yoghurt**

*Said "yog-gurt or yoe-gurt"* NOUN Yogurt is a slightly sour thick liquid made from milk that has had bacteria added to it.

**yoke yokes**

NOUN 1 a wooden bar attached to two collars which is laid across the necks of animals such as oxen to hold them together, and to which a plough or other tool may be attached. 2 LITERARY If people are under a yoke of some kind, they are being oppressed E.G. *two women who escape the yoke of insensitive men.*

**yokel yokels**

*Said "yoe-kl"* NOUN someone who lives in the country and is regarded as being rather stupid and old-fashioned.

**yolk yolks**

*Rhymes with "joke"* NOUN the yellow part in the middle of an egg.

from Old English *geoloca*, from *geolu* meaning 'yellow'

**Yom Kippur**

*Said "yom kip-poor"* NOUN Yom Kippur is an annual Jewish religious holiday, which is a day of fasting and prayers. It is also called the Day of Atonement.

**yonder**

ADVERB or ADJECTIVE; AN OLD WORD over there E.G. *There's an island yonder.*

**yore**

AN OLD-FASHIONED PHRASE Of yore means existing a long time ago E.G. *nostalgia for the days of yore.*

**Yorkshire pudding** Yorkshire puddings
NOUN In Britain, Yorkshire pudding is a kind of baked batter made of flour, milk, and eggs, and usually eaten with roast beef.

**you**
PRONOUN 1 'You' refers to the person or group of people that a person is speaking or writing to. 2 'You' also refers to people in general *E.G. You can get a two-bedroom villa quite cheaply.*

**young** younger youngest
ADJECTIVE 1 A young person, animal, or plant has not lived very long and is not yet mature. ▶ NOUN 2 The young are young people in general. 3 The young of an animal are its babies.
■ (sense 1) immature, undeveloped
■ (sense 3) babies, offspring, progeny

**youngster** youngsters
NOUN a child or young person.

**your**
ADJECTIVE 1 'Your' means belonging or relating to the person or group of people that someone is speaking to *E.G. I do like your name.* 2 'Your' is used to show that something belongs or relates to people in general *E.G. Your driving ability is affected by just one or two drinks.*

**yours**
PRONOUN 'Yours' refers to something belonging or relating to the person or group of people that someone is speaking to *E.G. His hair is longer than yours.*

**yourself** yourselves
PRONOUN 1 'Yourself' is used when the person being spoken to does the action and is affected by it *E.G. Why can't you do it yourself?* 2 'Yourself' is used to emphasize 'you' *E.G. Do you yourself want a divorce?*

**youth** youths
NOUN 1 Someone's youth is the period of their life before they are a fully mature adult. 2 Youth is the quality or condition of being young and often inexperienced. 3 a boy or young man. 4 The youth are young people thought of as a group *E.G. the youth of today.*

**youthful** ADJECTIVE

**youth hostel** youth hostels
NOUN a place where young people can stay cheaply when they are on holiday.

**yo-yo** yo-yos
NOUN a round wooden or plastic toy attached to a piece of string. You play by making the yo-yo rise and fall on the string.

**Yugoslav** Yugoslavs
*Said "yoo-goe-slahv"* ADJECTIVE 1 belonging or relating to the country that used to be known as Yugoslavia. ▶ NOUN 2 someone who came from the country that used be known as Yugoslavia.

**Yule**
NOUN; OLD WORD Yule means Christmas. ▥ from Old English *geola* a pagan winter feast

**yuppie** yuppies
NOUN If you say people are yuppies, you think they are young, middle-class, and earn a lot of money which they spend on themselves

a
b
c
d
e
f
g
h
i
j
k
l
m
n
o
p
q
r
s
t
u
v
w
x
y
z

# Zz

A B C D E F G H I J K L M N O P Q R S T U V W X Y Z

**TIP** Many words which sound as if they begin with letter *z* actually begin with letter *x*, for example *Xerox*, *xylem* and *xylophone*.

**Zambian Zambians**
*Said* "**zam**-bee-an" ADJECTIVE
1 belonging or relating to Zambia.
▶ NOUN 2 someone who comes from Zambia.

**zany zanier zaniest**
ADJECTIVE odd and ridiculous E.G. *zany humour*.
▣ from Italian *zanni* meaning 'clown'

**zap zaps zapping zapped**
VERB INFORMAL 1 To zap someone is to kill them, usually by shooting. 2 To zap also is to move somewhere quickly E.G. *I zapped over to Paris*.

**zeal**
NOUN Zeal is very great enthusiasm.
**zealous** ADJECTIVE

**zealot zealots**
*Said* "**zel**-lot" NOUN a person who acts with very great enthusiasm, especially in following a political or religious cause.

**zebra zebras**
NOUN a type of African wild horse with black and white stripes over its body.

**zebra crossing zebra crossings**
NOUN a place where people can cross the road safely. The road is marked with black and white stripes.

**Zen** or **Zen Buddhism**
NOUN Zen is a form of Buddhism that concentrates on learning through meditation and intuition.

**zenith**
NOUN LITERARY The zenith of something is the time when it is at its most successful or powerful E.G. *the zenith of his military career*.

**zero zeros** or **zeroes zeroing zeroed** 1 Zero is the number 0. 2 Zero is freezing point, 0° Centigrade. ADJECTIVE 3 Zero means there is none at all of a particular thing E.G. *His chances are zero*. ▶ VERB 4 To zero in on a target is to aim at or to move towards it E.G. *The headlines zeroed in on the major news stories*.
▣ from Arabic *sifr* meaning 'cipher' or 'empty'

**zest**
NOUN 1 Zest is a feeling of pleasure and enthusiasm E.G. *zest for life*. 2 Zest is a quality which adds extra flavour or interest to something E.G. *brilliant ideas to add zest to your wedding list*. 3 The zest of an orange or lemon is the outside of the peel which is used to flavour food or drinks.

**zigzag zigzags zigzagging zigzagged**
NOUN 1 a line which has a series of sharp, angular turns to the right and left in it, like a continuous series of 'W's. ▶ VERB 2 To zigzag is to move forward by going at an angle first right and then left E.G. *He zigzagged his way across the racecourse*.

**Zimbabwean Zimbabweans**
*Said* "zim-**bahb**-wee-an" ADJECTIVE
1 belonging or relating to Zimbabwe. ▶ NOUN 2 someone who comes from Zimbabwe.

**zinc**

NOUN Zinc is a bluish-white metal used in alloys and to coat other metals to stop them rusting.

**zing**

NOUN; *INFORMAL* Zing is a quality in something that makes it lively or interesting *E.G. There's a real zing around the studio.*

**zip** zips zipping zipped

NOUN 1 a long narrow fastener with two rows of teeth that are closed or opened by a small clip pulled between them. ▶ VERB 2 When you zip something or zip it up, you fasten it using a zip.

**zipper** zippers

NOUN the same as a **zip**.

**zodiac**

*Said "zoe-dee-ak"* NOUN The zodiac is an imaginary strip in the sky which contains the planets and stars which astrologers think are important influences on people. It is divided into 12 sections, each with a special name and symbol.

📖 from Greek *zōdiakos kuklos* meaning 'circle of signs'

**zombie** zombies

NOUN 1 *INFORMAL* If you refer to someone as a zombie, you mean that they seem to be unaware of what is going on around them and to act without thinking about what they are doing. 2 In voodoo, a zombie is a dead person who has been brought back to life by witchcraft.

📖 from an African word *zumbi* meaning 'good-luck charm'

**zone** zones

NOUN an area that has particular features or properties *E.G. a war zone.*

**zoo** zoos

NOUN a place where live animals are kept so that people can look at them.

**zoology**

*Said "zoo-ol-loj-jee"* NOUN Zoology is the scientific study of animals.

**zoological** ADJECTIVE **zoologist** NOUN

**zoom** zooms zooming zoomed

VERB 1 To zoom is to move very quickly *E.G. They zoomed to safety.* 2 If a camera zooms in on something, it gives a close-up picture of it.

**zucchini**

*Said "zoo-keen-nee"* PLURAL NOUN Zucchini are small vegetable marrows with dark green skin. They are also called **courgettes**.

**Zulu** Zulus

*Said "zoo-loo"* NOUN 1 The Zulus are a group of Black people who live in southern Africa. 2 Zulu is the language spoken by the Zulus.